The Maastricht Collection

Europa Law Publishing, Amsterdam 2013

The Maastricht Collection (Sixth Edition)

Edited by Sascha Hardt & Nicole Kornet

Volume III: International and European Private Law

Europa Law Publishing is a publishing company specializing in European Union law, international trade law, public international law, environmental law and comparative national law.
For further information please contact Europa Law Publishing via email: info@europalawpublishing.com or visit our website at: www.europalawpublishing.com.

All rights reserved. No part of this publication may be reproduced or transmitted, in any form or by any means, or stored in any retrieval system of any nature, without the written permission of the publisher. Application for permission for use of copyright material shall be made to the publishers. Full acknowledgement of author, publisher and source must be given.

Voor zover het maken van kopieën uit deze uitgave is toegestaan op grond van artikel 16h t/m 16m Auteurswet 1912 *juncto* het Besluit van 27 november 2002, Stb. 575, dient men de daarvoor wettelijk verschuldigde vergoedingen te voldoen aan de Stichting Reprorecht (Postbus 3060, 2130 KB Hoofddorp).
Voor het overnemen van (een) gedeelte(n) uit deze uitgave in bloemlezingen, readers en andere compilatiewerken (artikel 16 Auteurswet 1912) dient men zich tot de uitgever te wenden.

© Europa Law Publishing, S. Hardt, N. Kornet, 2019

Typeset in Scala and Scala Sans, Graphic design by G2K Designers, Groningen/Amsterdam

NUR 828
ISBN 9789089522115 (volumes I-IV)
ISBN 9789089522153 (volume I)
ISBN 9789089522160 (volume II)
ISBN 9789089522177 (volume III)
ISBN 9789089522146 (volume IV)

Preface to the sixth edition

The Faculty of Law of Maastricht University attaches great importance to the study of European and comparative law. Its curriculum includes several internationally oriented Master programmes and the *European Law School* bachelor programme, in which law is taught from a European and comparative perspective from the very first day. These four volumes, *The Maastricht Collection*, are based on the Maastricht Law Faculty's expertise and experience in teaching European, international, and comparative law.

The Maastricht Collection comprises a selection of legal instruments and provisions which have proven to be particularly relevant and useful to students and practitioners of European and comparative law. It includes constitutions, codes and statutory legislation from France, Germany, the Netherlands, and the United Kingdom, international treaties, and instruments of international organisations, as well as legal instruments of the European Union.

The content of the present sixth edition of *The Maastricht Collection* is divided into four volumes, corresponding to different areas of the law. Volume I contains selected international treaties and protocols, important resolutions of international organisations, international and European fundamental rights instruments, as well as the Treaties and selected secondary legislation of the European Union; Volume II contains national instruments from France, Germany, the Netherlands, and the United Kingdom in the areas of constitutional law (where the US constitution is also included as one of the standard points of reference of comparative constitutional law), administrative law, as well as criminal law and procedure; Volume III contains instruments from international and European private law, including international treaties and secondary EU legislation on international business law, private international law, European company law, European private law and civil procedure, as well as tax law; Volume IV contains national legislation from France, Germany, the Netherlands, and the United Kingdom in the area of private law and civil procedure.

Next to a comprehensive update and revision of all the instruments in *The Maastricht Collection*, this sixth edition also contains a number of useful additions, such as legislation relating to Brexit and statutory legislation from France, Germany, the Netherlands, and the United Kingdom in the area of criminal procedure. With these updates and additions, *The Maastricht Collection* now presents itself as an even more comprehensive resource for students of European, international, and comparative law.

While many of the materials included in these four volumes are reproduced in the original English, *The Maastricht Collection* remains true to its original aim of facilitating the study of comparative law by offering fresh translations of legal instruments from different national legal traditions. Many existing translations of written law, including officious translations available on government websites, are significantly out of date and not sufficiently faithful to the original. They often seek to turn old-fashioned or ambiguous original texts into modern and elegant English. Or, instead of translating, they seek to *explain* how certain terms or formulations are interpreted in practice. The translations contained in *The Maastricht Collection* remain true to the content, style, and syntax of the original as far as possible, allowing the reader to appreciate not only the substance but also the authentic form of legal sources.

Formatting styles, such as the use of §§ ('Paragraphs') rather than 'Articles' in most German statutes, and 'Sections' in UK legislation, or the absence of paragraph numbering in French legislation, are preserved. In the interest of consistency of style, the headings of individual articles are suppressed in translated materials. Enactment formulas are omitted; preambles are retained unless indicated otherwise. For easy reference within translated texts, key legal terms and proper names are added in the original language as in-text citations between square brackets.

The idea to create *The Maastricht Collection* came about during a conversation between Philipp Kiiver and Nicole Kornet about the need for English language learning resources for students following a programme on European and comparative law taught entirely in English. Just like students who follow a curriculum oriented on national law, these students also need a compilation of legislation relevant to their studies. Since the publication of the second edition, the editorship of the Maastricht Collection has since been continued by Sascha Hardt and Nicole Kornet. We are more than grateful to Philipp for being such a driving force behind the idea of *The Maastricht Collection*.

We would in particular like to thank Sarah Sørensen, a student of the *European Law School* and assistant to the editors, without whose meticulous hard work and dedication this edition of *The Maastricht Collection* and its publication in keeping with the regular two-year interval would not have been possible.

We would further like to thank the following people for their contributions and input to this and the previous editions: Dr. Bram Akkermans, Prof. Chris Backes, Dr. Anna Berlee, Stephanie Blom, Claire Boost, Caroline Calomme, Sylvain Caris, Prof. Fons Coomans, Merel Dekker, Prof. Mariolina Eliantonio, Prof. Sjef van Erp, Dr. Catalina Goanta, Dr. Franziska Grashof, Dr. Nicola Gundt, Prof. René de Groot, Heike Hauröder, Prof. Aalt-Willem Heringa, Dr. Sander Jansen, Prof. Anselm Kamperman Sanders, Prof. André Klip, Maartje Krabbe, Giesela Kristoferitsch, Prof. Raymond Luja, Prof. Gerrit van Maanen, Prof. Mieke Olaerts, Dr. Christina Peristeridou, Dr. Eveline Ramaekers, Dr. Stephan Rammeloo, Prof. Remco van Rhee, Dr. David Roef, Gereon Foetering, Dr. Kees Saarloos, Dr. René Seerden, Prof. Jan Smits, Prof. Taru Spronken, Dr. Ilse van den Driessche, Dr. Jacob van der Velde, Prof. Luc Verhey, Dr. Remme Verkerk, Yvonne Walhof, Dr. Stefan Weishaar, Dr. Daniëlle Wenders, Rob van de Westelaken, Irene Wieczorek and Prof. Jan Willems.

Maastricht, June 2019,

Dr. Sascha Hardt, Assistant Professor of Comparative Constitutional Law
Dr. Nicole Kornet, Senior Lecturer in Commercial Law and programme coordinator of the *European Law School*

Preface to the sixth edition
Contents

VOLUME III: INTERNATIONAL AND EUROPEAN PRIVATE LAW

PART	I	International Business Law	
		United Nations Convention on Contracts for the International Sale of Goods (Vienna, 1980)	2
		Convention on the Contract for the International Carriage of Goods by Road (CMR)	16
		International Convention for the Unification of Certain Rules of Law relating to Bills of Lading ("Hague-Visby Rules")	26
		United Nations Convention on the Recognition and Enforcement of Foreign Arbitral Awards	30
PART	II	**Private International Law**	
		Regulation (EU) No 1215/2012 [Brussels I; recast]	34
		Council Regulation (EC) No 2201/2003 [Brussels II Bis]	52
		Regulation (EC) 593/2008 [Rome I]	67
		Regulation (EC) 864/2007 [Rome II]	77
		Council Regulation (EU) No 1259/2010 [Rome III]	85
		Council Regulation (EC) No 4/2009 [Maintenance Regulation]	91
		Hague Maintenance Protocol	110
		Regulation (EU) No 650/2012 (Succession)	114
		Hague Convention (1980)	138
		Hague Convention (1996)	144
		Hague Convention (2005)	153
PART	III	**European Company Law**	
		Council Directive 2001/86/EC (Involvement of Employees)	162
		Directive 2004/25/EC (Takeover Bids)	169
		Directive 2007/36/EC (Certain Rights of Shareholders)	180
		Directive 2009/102/EC ("Twelfth Company Law Directive")	187
		Directive 2013/34/EU (Consolidated Financial Statements)	190
		Directive 2014/95/EU (Disclosure of Non-Financial Information)	223
		Directive (EU) 2017/828 (Long-Term Shareholder Engagement)	229
		Directive (EU) 2017/1132 (Company Law; Codification)	247
		Council Regulation (EEC) No 2137/85 (European Economic Interest Grouping; EEIG)	294
		Council Regulation (EC) No 2157/2001 (Statute for a European Company)	302
		Proposal for a Regulation on a European Private Company	318

THE MAASTRICHT COLLECTION

		Proposal for a Directive on Single-Member Private Limited Liability Companies	331
PART	IV	**European Private Law**	
		Council Directive 85/374/EEC (Product Liability)	342
		Council Directive 86/653/EEC (Commercial Agency)	346
		Council Directive 87/102/EEC (Consumer Credit)	351
		Council Directive 93/7/EEC (Cultural Objects)	357
		Council Directive 93/13/EEC (Unfair Terms)	361
		Directive 1999/44/EC (Consumer Sales and Associated Guarantees)	366
		Directive 2000/31/EC (E-Commerce')	371
		Directive 2011/7/EU (Combating Late Payment; recast)	385
		Directive 2002/47/EC (Financial Collateral Arrangements)	393
		Directive 2009/44/EC (Financial Collateral Arrangements; amendments)	400
		Directive 2005/29/EC (Unfair Commercial Practices)	406
		Directive 2008/122/EC (Timeshare)	417
		Directive 2011/83/EU (Consumer Rights)	429
		Directive 2015/2302 (Package Travel)	448
		Council Regulation (EC) No 1346/2000 (Insolvency Proceedings)	469
		Directive 2014/17/EU (Consumers Mortgage Credit Agreements)	483
		The Principles of European Contract Law [PECL]	518
		The Principles of European Tort Law [PETL]	540
PART	V	**European Civil Procedure**	
		Council Regulation (EC) No 1206/2001 (Taking Evidence)	546
		Regulation (EC) No 805/2004 (European Enforcement Order)	551
		Regulation (EC) No 1896/2006 (European Order for Payment Procedure)	557
		Regulation (EC) No 861/2007 (European Small Claims Procedure)	563
		Regulation (EC) No 1393/2007 (Service of Documents)	568
		Directive 2008/52/EC (Mediation)	573
PART	VI	**Tax Law**	
		Council Directive (EU) 2016/1164 (Tax Avoidance)	576
		OECD Model Convention	586

VOL III PART I

International Business Law

PART I INTERNATIONAL BUSINESS LAW

United Nations Convention on Contracts for the International Sale of Goods (Vienna, 1980)

Preamble. *The States Parties to this Convention,*
Bearing in Mind the broad objectives in the resolutions adopted by the sixth special session of the General Assembly of the United Nations on the establishment of a New International Economic Order,
Considering that the development of international trade on the basis of equality and mutual benefit is an important element in promoting friendly relations among States,
Being of the Opinion that the adoption of uniform rules which govern contracts for the international sale of goods and take into account the different social, economic and legal systems would contribute to the removal of legal barriers in international trade and promote the development of international trade,
have decreed as follows:

Part I. Sphere of application and general provisions

Chapter I. Sphere of Application

Article 1. (1) This Convention applies to contracts of sale of goods between parties whose places of business are in different States:
(a) when the States are Contracting States; or
(b) when the rules of private international law lead to the application of the law of a Contracting State.
(2) The fact that the parties have their places of business in different States is to be disregarded whenever this fact does not appear either from the contract or from any dealings between, or from information disclosed by, the parties at any time before or at the conclusion of the contract.
(3) Neither the nationality of the parties nor the civil or commercial character of the parties or of the contract is to be taken into consideration in determining the application of this Convention.

Article 2. This Convention does not apply to sales:
(a) of goods bought for personal, family or household use, unless the seller, at any time before or at the conclusion of the contract, neither knew nor ought to have known that the goods were bought for any such use;
(b) by auction;
(c) on execution or otherwise by authority of law;
(d) of stocks, shares, investment securities, negotiable instruments or money;
(e) of ships, vessels, hovercraft or aircraft;
(f) of electricity.

Article 3. (1) Contracts for the supply of goods to be manufactured or produced are to be considered sales unless the party who orders the goods undertakes to supply a substantial part of the materials necessary for such manufacture or production.
(2) This Convention does not apply to contracts in which the preponderant part of the obligations of the party who furnishes the goods consists in the supply of labour or other services.

Article 4. This Convention governs only the formation of the contract of sale and the rights and obligations of the seller and the buyer arising from such a contract. In particular, except as otherwise expressly provided in this Convention, it is not concerned with:
(a) the validity of the contract or of any of its provisions or of any usage;
(b) the effect which the contract may have on the property in the goods sold.

Article 5. This Convention does not apply to the liability of the seller for death or personal injury caused by the goods to any person.

Article 6. The parties may exclude the application of this Convention or, subject to article 12, derogate from or vary the effect of any of its provisions.

Chapter II. General Provisions

Article 7. (1) In the interpretation of this Convention, regard is to be had to its international character and to the need to promote uniformity in its application and the observance of good faith in international trade.
(2) Questions concerning matters governed by this Convention which are not expressly settled in it

are to be settled in conformity with the general principles on which it is based or, in the absence of such principles, in conformity with the law applicable by virtue of the rules of private international law.

Article 8. (1) For the purposes of this Convention statements made by and other conduct of a party are to be interpreted according to his intent where the other party knew or could not have been unaware what that intent was.

(2) If the preceding paragraph is not applicable, statements made by and other conduct of a party are to be interpreted according to the understanding that a reasonable person of the same kind as the other party would have had in the same circumstances.

(3) In determining the intent of a party or the understanding a reasonable person would have had, due consideration is to be given to all relevant circumstances of the case including the negotiations, any practices which the parties have established between themselves, usages and any subsequent conduct of the parties.

Article 9. (1) The parties are bound by any usage to which they have agreed and by any practices which they have established between themselves.

(2) The parties are considered, unless otherwise agreed, to have impliedly made applicable to their contract or its formation a usage of which the parties knew or ought to have known and which in international trade is widely known to, and regularly observed by, parties to contracts of the type involved in the particular trade concerned.

Article 10. For the purposes of this Convention:
(a) if a party has more than one place of business, the place of business is that which has the closest relationship to the contract and its performance, having regard to the circumstances known to or contemplated by the parties at any time before or at the conclusion of the contract;
(b) if a party does not have a place of business, reference is to be made to his habitual residence.

Article 11. A contract of sale need not be concluded in or evidenced by writing and is not subject to any other requirement as to form. It may be proved by any means, including witnesses.

Article 12. Any provision of article 11, article 29 or Part II of this Convention that allows a contract of sale or its modification or termination by agreement or any offer, acceptance or other indication of intention to be made in any form other than in writing does not apply where any party has his place of business in a Contracting State which has made a declaration under article 96 of this Convention. The parties may not derogate from or vary the effect or this article.

Article 13. For the purposes of this Convention "writing" includes telegram and telex.

Part II: Formation of the Contract

Article 14. (1) A proposal for concluding a contract addressed to one or more specific persons constitutes an offer if it is sufficiently definite and indicates the intention of the offeror to be bound in case of acceptance. A proposal is sufficiently definite if it indicates the goods and expressly or implicitly fixes or makes provision for determining the quantity and the price.

(2) A proposal other than one addressed to one or more specific persons is to be considered merely as an invitation to make offers, unless the contrary is clearly indicated by the person making the proposal.

Article 15. (1) An offer becomes effective when it reaches the offeree.

(2) An offer, even if it is irrevocable, may be withdrawn if the withdrawal reaches the offeree before or at the same time as the offer.

Article 16. (1) Until a contract is concluded an offer may be revoked if the revocation reaches the offeree before he has dispatched an acceptance.

(2) However, an offer cannot be revoked:
(a) if it indicates, whether by stating a fixed time for acceptance or otherwise, that it is irrevocable; or
(b) if it was reasonable for the offeree to rely on the offer as being irrevocable and the offeree has acted in reliance on the offer.

Article 17. An offer, even if it is irrevocable, is terminated when a rejection reaches the offeror.

Article 18. (1) A statement made by or other conduct of the offeree indicating assent to an offer is an acceptance. Silence or inactivity does not in itself amount to acceptance.

(2) An acceptance of an offer becomes effective at the moment the indication of assent reaches the

PART I INTERNATIONAL BUSINESS LAW

offeror. An acceptance is not effective if the indication of assent does not reach the offeror within the time he has fixed or, if no time is fixed, within a reasonable time, due account being taken of the circumstances of the transaction, including the rapidity of the means of communication employed by the offeror. An oral offer must be accepted immediately unless the circumstances indicate otherwise.
(3) However, if, by virtue of the offer or as a result of practices which the parties have established between themselves or of usage, the offeree may indicate assent by performing an act, such as one relating to the dispatch of the goods or payment of the price, without notice to the offeror, the acceptance is effective at the moment the act is performed, provided that the act is performed within the period of time laid down in the preceding paragraph.

Article 19. (1) A reply to an offer which purports to be an acceptance but contains additions, limitations or other modifications is a rejection of the offer and constitutes a counter-offer.
(2) However, a reply to an offer which purports to be an acceptance but contains additional or different terms which do not materially alter the terms of the offer constitutes an acceptance, unless the offeror, without undue delay, objects orally to the discrepancy or dispatches a notice to that effect. If he does not so object, the terms of the contract are the terms of the offer with the modifications contained in the acceptance.
(3) Additional or different terms relating, among other things, to the price, payment, quality and quantity of the goods, place and time of delivery, extent of one party's liability to the other or the settlement of disputes are considered to alter the terms of the offer materially.

Article 20. (1) A period of time for acceptance fixed by the offeror in a telegram or a letter begins to run from the moment the telegram is handed in for dispatch or from the date shown on the letter or, if no such date is shown, from the date shown on the envelope. A period of time for acceptance fixed by the offeror by telephone, telex or other means of instantaneous communication, begins to run from the moment that the offer reaches the offeree.
(2) Official holidays or non-business days occurring during the period for acceptance are included in calculating the period. However, if a notice of acceptance cannot be delivered at the address of the offeror on the last day of the period because that day falls on an official holiday or a non-business day at the place of business of the offeror, the period is extended until the first business day which follows.

Article 21. (1) A late acceptance is nevertheless effective as an acceptance if without delay the offeror orally so informs the offeree or dispatches a notice to that effect.
(2) If a letter or other writing containing a late acceptance shows that it has been sent in such circumstances that if its transmission had been normal it would have reached the offeror in due time, the late acceptance is effective as an acceptance unless, without delay, the offeror orally informs the offeree that he considers his offer as having lapsed or dispatches a notice to that effect.

Article 22. An acceptance may be withdrawn if the withdrawal reaches the offeror before or at the same time as the acceptance would have become effective.

Article 23. A contract is concluded at the moment when an acceptance of an offer becomes effective in accordance with the provisions of this Convention.

Article 24. For the purposes of this Part of the Convention, an offer, declaration of acceptance or any other indication of intention "reaches" the addressee when it is made orally to him or delivered by any other means to him personally, to his place of business or mailing address or, if he does not have a place of business or mailing address, to his habitual residence.

Part III. Sale of Goods

Chapter I. General Provisions

Article 25. A breach of contract committed by one of the parties is fundamental if it results in such detriment to the other party as substantially to deprive him of what he is entitled to expect under the contract, unless the party in breach did not foresee and a reasonable person of the same kind in the same circumstances would not have foreseen such a result.

Article 26. A declaration of avoidance of the contract is effective only if made by notice to the other party.

Article 27. Unless otherwise expressly provided in this Part of the Convention, if any notice, request or other communication is given or made by a party in accordance with this Part and by means appropriate in the circumstances, a delay or error in the transmission of the communication or its failure to arrive does not deprive that party of the right to rely on the communication.

Article 28. If, in accordance with the provisions of this Convention, one party is entitled to require performance of any obligation by the other party, a court is not bound to enter a judgement for specific performance unless the court would do so under its own law in respect of similar contracts of sale not governed by this Convention.

Article 29. (1) A contract may be modified or terminated by the mere agreement of the parties.
(2) A contract in writing which contains a provision requiring any modification or termination by agreement to be in writing may not be otherwise modified or terminated by agreement. However, a party may be precluded by his conduct from asserting such a provision to the extent that the other party has relied on that conduct.

Chapter II. Obligations of the Seller

Article 30. The seller must deliver the goods, hand over any documents relating to them and transfer the property in the goods, as required by the contract and this Convention.

Section I. Delivery of the goods and handing over of documents

Article 31. If the seller is not bound to deliver the goods at any other particular place, his obligation to deliver consists:
(a) if the contract of sale involves carriage of the goods - in handing the goods over to the first carrier for transmission to the buyer;
(b) if, in cases not within the preceding subparagraph, the contract related to specific goods, or uni-dentified goods to be drawn from a specific stock or to be manufactured or produced, and at the time of the conclusion of the contract the parties knew that the goods were at, or were to be manufactured or produced at, a particular place - in placing the goods at the buyer's disposal at that place;
(c) in other cases - in placing the goods at the buyer's disposal at the place where the seller had his place of business at the time of the conclusion of the contract.

Article 32. (1) If the seller, in accordance with the contract or this Convention, hands the goods over to a carrier and if the goods are not clearly identified to the contract by markings on the goods, by shipping documents or otherwise, the seller must give the buyer notice of the consignment specifying the goods.
(2) If the seller is bound to arrange for carriage of the goods, he must make such contracts as are necessary for carriage to the place fixed by means of transportation appropriate in the circumstances and according to the usual terms for such transportation.
(3) If the seller is not bound to effect insurance in respect of the carriage of the goods, he must, at the buyer's request, provide him with all available information necessary to enable him to effect such insurance.

Article 33. The seller must deliver the goods:
(a) if a date is fixed by or determinable from the contract, on that date;
(b) if a period of time is fixed by or determinable from the contract, at any time within that period unless circumstances indicate that the buyer is to choose a date; or
(c) in any other case, within a reasonable time after the conclusion of the contract.

Article 34. If the seller is bound to hand over documents relating to the goods, he must hand them over at the time and place and in the form required by the contract. If the seller has handed over documents before that time, he may, up to that time, cure any lack of conformity in the documents, if the exercise of this right does not cause the buyer unreasonable inconvenience or unreasonable expense. However, the buyer retains any right to claim damages as provided for in this Convention.

Section II. Conformity of the goods and third party claims

Article 35. (1) The seller must deliver goods which are of the quantity, quality and description required by the contract and which are contained or packaged in the manner required by the contract.
(2) Except where the parties have agreed otherwise, the goods do not conform with the contract unless they:
(a) are fit for the purposes for which goods of the same description would ordinarily be used;
(b) are fit for any particular purpose expressly or impliedly made known to the seller at the time of the conclusion of the contract, except where the circumstances show that the buyer did not rely, or

PART I   INTERNATIONAL BUSINESS LAW

that it was unreasonable for him to rely, on the seller's skill and judgement;
(c) possess the qualities of goods which the seller has held out to the buyer as a sample or model;
(d) are contained or packaged in the manner usual for such goods or, where there is no such manner, in a manner adequate to preserve and protect the goods.
(3) The seller is not liable under subparagraphs (a) to (d) of the preceding paragraph for any lack of conformity of the goods if at the time of the conclusion of the contract the buyer knew or could not have been unaware of such lack of conformity.

Article 36. (1) The seller is liable in accordance with the contract and this Convention for any lack of conformity which exists at the time when the risk passes to the buyer, even though the lack of conformity becomes apparent only after that time.
(2) The seller is also liable for any lack of conformity which occurs after the time indicated in the preceding paragraph and which is due to a breach of any of his obligations, including a breach of any guarantee that for a period of time the goods will remain fit for their ordinary purpose or for some particular purpose or will retain specified qualities or characteristics.

Article 37. If the seller has delivered goods before the date for delivery, he may, up to that date, deliver any missing part or make up any deficiency in the quantity of the goods delivered, or deliver goods in replacement of any non-conforming goods delivered or remedy any lack of conformity in the goods delivered, provided that the exercise of this right does not cause the buyer unreasonable inconvenience or unreasonable expense. However, the buyer retains any right to claim damages as provided for in this Convention.

Article 38. (1) The buyer must examine the goods, or cause them to be examined, within as short a period as is practicable in the circumstances.
(2) If the contract involves carriage of the goods, examination may be deferred until after the goods have arrived at their destination.
(3) If the goods are redirected in transit or redispatched by the buyer without a reasonable opportunity for examination by him and at the time of the conclusion of the contract the seller knew or ought to have known of the possibility of such redirection or redispatch, examination may be deferred until after the goods have arrived at the new destination.

Article 39. (1) The buyer loses the right to rely on a lack of conformity of the goods if he does not give notice to the seller specifying the nature of the lack of conformity within a reasonable time after he has discovered it or ought to have discovered it.
(2) In any event, the buyer loses the right to rely on a lack of conformity of the goods if he does not give the seller notice thereof at the latest within a period of two years from the date on which the goods were actually handed over to the buyer, unless this time-limit is inconsistent with a contractual period of guarantee.

Article 40. The seller is not entitled to rely on the provisions of articles 38 and 39 if the lack of conformity relates to facts of which he knew or could not have been unaware and which he did not disclose to the buyer.

Article 41. The seller must deliver goods which are free from any right or claim of a third party, unless the buyer agreed to take the goods subject to that right or claim. However, if such right or claim is based on industrial property or other intellectual property, the seller's obligation is governed by article 42.

Article 42. (1) The seller must deliver goods which are free from any right or claim of a third party based on industrial property or other intellectual property, of which at the time of the conclusion of the contract the seller knew or could not have been unaware, provided that the right or claim is based on industrial property or other intellectual property:
(a) under the law of the State where the goods will be resold or otherwise used, if it was contemplated by the parties at the time of the conclusion of the contract that the goods would be resold or otherwise used in that State; or
(b) in any other case, under the law of the State where the buyer has his place of business.
(2) The obligation of the seller under the preceding paragraph does not extend to cases where:
(a) at the time of the conclusion of the contract the buyer knew or could not have been unaware of the right or claim; or
(b) the right or claim results from the seller's compliance with technical drawings, designs, formulae or other such specifications furnished by the buyer.

Article 43. (1) The buyer loses the right to rely on the provisions of article 41 or Article 42 if he does not give notice to the seller specifying the nature of the right or claim of the third party within a reasonable time after he has become aware or ought to have become aware of the right or claim.
(2) The seller is not entitled to rely on the provisions of the preceding paragraph if he knew of the right or claim of the third party and the nature of it.

Article 44. Notwithstanding the provisions of paragraph (1) of article 39 and paragraph (1) of article 43, the buyer may reduce the price in accordance with Article 50 or claim damages, except for loss of profit, if he has a reasonable excuse for his failure to give the required notice.

Section III. Remedies for breach of contract by the seller

Article 45. (1) If the seller fails to perform any of his obligations under the contract or this Convention, the buyer may:
(a) exercise the rights provided in articles 46 to 52;
(b) claim damages as provided in articles 74 to 77.
(2) The buyer is not deprived of any right he may have to claim damages by exercising his right to other remedies.
(3) No period of grace may be granted to the seller by a court or arbitral tribunal when the buyer resorts to a remedy for breach of contract.

Article 46. (1) The buyer may require performance by the seller of his obligations unless the buyer has resorted to a remedy which is inconsistent with this requirement.
(2) If the goods do not conform with the contract, the buyer may require delivery of substitute goods only if the lack of conformity constitutes a fundamental breach of contract and a request for substitute goods is made either in conjunction with notice given under article 39 or within a reasonable time thereafter.
(3) If the goods do not conform with the contract, the buyer may require the seller to remedy the lack of conformity by repair, unless this is unreasonable having regard to all the circumstances. A request for repair must be made either in conjunction with notice given under article 39 or within a reasonable time thereafter.

Article 47. (1) The buyer may fix an additional period of time of reasonable length for performance by the seller of his obligations.
(2) Unless the buyer has received notice from the seller that he will not
perform within the period so fixed, the buyer may not, during that period, resort to any remedy for breach of contract. However, the buyer is not deprived thereby of any right he may have to claim damages for delay in performance.

Article 48. (1) Subject to article 49, the seller may, even after the date for delivery, remedy at his own expense any failure to perform his obligations, if he can do so without unreasonable delay and without causing the buyer unreasonable inconvenience or uncertainty of reimbursement by the seller of expenses advanced by the buyer. However, the buyer retains any right to claim damages as provided for in this Convention.
(2) If the seller requests the buyer to make known whether he will accept performance and the buyer does not comply with the request within a reasonable time, the seller may perform within the time indicated in his request. The buyer may not, during that period of time, resort to any remedy which is inconsistent with performance by the seller.
(3) A notice by the seller that he will perform within a specified period of time is assumed to include a request, under the preceding paragraph, that the buyer make known his decision.
(4) A request or notice by the seller under paragraph (2) or (3) of this Article is not effective unless received by the buyer.

Article 49. (1) The buyer may declare the contract avoided:
(a) if the failure by the seller to perform any of his obligations under the contract or this Convention amounts to a fundamental breach of contract; or
(b) in case of non-delivery, if the seller does not deliver the goods within the additional period of time fixed by the buyer in accordance with paragraph (1) of article 47 or declares that he will not deliver within the period so fixed.
(2) However, in cases where the seller has delivered the goods, the buyer loses the right to declare the contract avoided unless he does so:
(a) in respect of late delivery, within a reasonable time after he has become aware that delivery has been made;

PART I   INTERNATIONAL BUSINESS LAW

(b) in respect of any breach other than late delivery, within a reasonable time:
(i) after he knew or ought to have known of the breach;
(ii) after the expiration of any additional period of time fixed by the buyer in accordance with paragraph (1) of article 47, or after the seller has declared that he will not perform his obligations within such an additional period; or
(iii) after the expiration of any additional period of time indicated by the seller in accordance with paragraph (2) of article 48, or after the buyer has declared that he will not accept performance.

Article 50. If the goods do not conform with the contract and whether or not the price has already been paid, the buyer may reduce the price in the same proportion as the value that the goods actually delivered had at the time of the delivery bears to the value that conforming goods would have had at that time. However, if the seller remedies any failure to perform his obligations in accordance with article 37 or article 48 or if the buyer refuses to accept performance by the seller in accordance with those Articles, the buyer may not reduce the price.

Article 51. (1) If the seller delivers only a part of the goods or if only a part of the goods delivered is in conformity with the contract, articles 46 to 50 apply in respect of the part which is missing or which does not conform.
(2) The buyer may declare the contract avoided in its entirety only if the failure to make delivery completely or in conformity with the contract amounts to a fundamental breach of the contract.

Article 52. (1) If the seller delivers the goods before the date fixed, the buyer may take delivery or refuse to take delivery.
(2) If the seller delivers a quantity of goods greater than that provided for in the contract, the buyer may take delivery or refuse to take delivery of the excess quantity. If the buyer takes delivery of all or part of the excess quantity, he must pay for it at the contract rate.

Chapter III. Obligations of the Buyer

Article 53. The buyer must pay the price for the goods and take delivery of them as required by the contract and this Convention.

Section I. Payment of the price

Article 54. The buyer's obligation to pay the price includes taking such steps and complying with such formalities as may be required under the contract or any laws and regulations to enable payment to be made.

Article 55. Where a contract has been validly concluded but does not expressly or implicitly fix or make provision for determining the price, the parties are considered, in the absence of any indication to the contrary, to have impliedly made reference to the price generally charged at the time of the conclusion of the contract for such goods sold under comparable circumstances in the trade concerned.

Article 56. If the price is fixed according to the weight of the goods, in case of doubt it is to be determined by the net weight.

Article 57. (1) If the buyer is not bound to pay the price at any other particular place, he must pay it to the seller:
(a) at the seller's place of business; or
(b) if the payment is to be made against the handing over of the goods or of documents, at the place where the handing over takes place.
(2) The seller must bear any increases in the expenses incidental to payment which is caused by a change in his place of business subsequent to the conclusion of the contract.

Article 58. (1) If the buyer is not bound to pay the price at any other specific time, he must pay it when the seller places either the goods or documents controlling their disposition at the buyer's disposal in accordance with the contract and this Convention. The seller may make such payment a condition for handing over the goods or documents.
(2) If the contract involves carriage of the goods, the seller may dispatch the goods on terms whereby the goods, or documents controlling their disposition, will not be handed over to the buyer except against payment of the price.
(3) The buyer is not bound to pay the price until he has had an opportunity to examine the goods, unless the procedures for delivery or payment agreed upon by the parties are inconsistent with his having such an opportunity.

Article 59. The buyer must pay the price on the date fixed by or determinable from the contract and this Convention without the need for any request or compliance with any formality on the part of the seller.

Section II. Taking delivery

Article 60. The buyer's obligation to take delivery consists:
(a) in doing all the acts which could reasonably be expected of him in order to enable the seller to make delivery; and
(b) in taking over the goods.

Section III. Remedies for breach of contract by the buyer

Article 61. (1) If the buyer fails to perform any of his obligations under the contract or this Convention, the seller may:
(a) exercise the rights provided in articles 62 to 65;
(b) claim damages as provided in articles 74 to 77.
(2) The seller is not deprived of any right he may have to claim damages by exercising his right to other remedies.
(3) No period of grace may be granted to the buyer by a court or arbitral tribunal when the seller resorts to a remedy for breach of contract.

Article 62. The seller may require the buyer to pay the price, take delivery or perform his other obligations, unless the seller has resorted to a remedy which is inconsistent with this requirement.

Article 63. (1) The seller may fix an additional period of time of reasonable length for performance by the buyer of his obligations.
(2) Unless the seller has received notice from the buyer that he will not perform within the period so fixed, the seller may not, during that period, resort to any remedy for breach of contract. However, the seller is not deprived thereby of any right he may have to claim damages for delay in performance.

Article 64. (1) The seller may declare the contract avoided:
(a) if the failure by the buyer to perform any of his obligations under the contract or this Convention amounts to a fundamental breach of contract; or
(b) if the buyer does not, within the additional period of time fixed by the seller in accordance with paragraph (1) of article 63, perform his obligation to pay the price or take delivery of the goods, or if he declares that he will not do so within the period so fixed.
(2) However, in cases where the buyer has paid the price, the seller loses the right to declare the contract avoided unless he does so:
(a) in respect of late performance by the buyer, before the seller has become aware that performance has been rendered; or
(b) in respect of any breach other than late performance by the buyer, within a reasonable time:
(i) after the seller knew or ought to have known of the breach; or
(ii) after the expiration of any additional period of time fixed by
the seller in accordance with paragraph (1) or article 63, or after the buyer has declared that he will not perform his obligations within such an additional period.

Article 65. (1) If under the contract the buyer is to specify the form, measurement or other features of the goods and he fails to make such specification either on the date agreed upon or within a reasonable time after receipt of a request from the seller, the seller may, without prejudice to any other rights he may have, make the specification himself in accordance with the requirements of the buyer that may be known to him.
(2) If the seller makes the specification himself, he must inform the buyer of the details thereof and must fix a reasonable time within which the buyer may make a different specification. If, after receipt of such a communication, the buyer fails to do so within the time so fixed, the specification made by the seller is binding.

Chapter IV: Passing of Risk

Article 66. Loss of or damage to the goods after the risk has passed to the buyer does not discharge him from his obligation to pay the price, unless the loss or damage is due to an act or omission of the seller.

Article 67. (1) If the contract of sale involves carriage of the goods and the seller is not bound to

hand them over at a particular place, the risk passes to the buyer when the goods are handed over to the first carrier for transmission to the buyer in accordance with the contract of sale. If the seller is bound to hand the goods over to a carrier at a particular place, the risk does not pass to the buyer until the goods are handed over to the carrier at that place. The fact that the seller is authorized to retain documents controlling the disposition of the goods does not affect the passage of the risk.
(2) Nevertheless, the risk does not pass to the buyer until the goods are clearly identified to the contract, whether by markings on the goods, by shipping documents, by notice given to the buyer or otherwise.

Article 68. The risk in respect of goods sold in transit passes to the buyer from the time of the conclusion of the contract. However, if the circumstances so indicate, the risk is assumed by the buyer from the time the goods were handed over to the carrier who issued the documents embodying the contract of carriage. Nevertheless, if at the time of the conclusion of the contract of sale the seller knew or ought to have known that the goods had been lost or damaged and did not disclose this to the buyer, the loss or damage is at the risk of the seller.

Article 69. (1) In cases not within articles 67 and 68, the risk passes to the buyer when he takes over the goods or, if he does not do so in due time, from the time when the goods are placed at his disposal and he commits a breach of contract by failing to take delivery.
(2) However, if the buyer is bound to take over the goods at a place other than a place of business of the seller, the risk passes when delivery is due and the buyer is aware of the fact that the goods are placed at his disposal at that place.
(3) If the contract relates to goods not then identified, the goods are considered not to be placed at the disposal of the buyer until they are clearly identified to the contract.

Article 70. If the seller has committed a fundamental breach of contract, articles 67, 68 and 69 do not impair the remedies available to the buyer on account of the breach.

Chapter V: Provisions Common to the Obligations of the Seller and of the Buyer

Section I. Anticipatory breach and instalment contracts

Article 71. (1) A party may suspend the performance of his obligations if, after the conclusion of the contract, it becomes apparent that the other party will not perform a substantial part of his obligations as a result of:
(a) a serious deficiency in his ability to perform or in his creditworthiness; or
(b) his conduct in preparing to perform or in performing the contract.
(2) If the seller has already dispatched the goods before the grounds described in the preceding paragraph become evident, he may prevent the handing over of the goods to the buyer even though the buyer holds a document which entitles him to obtain them. The present paragraph relates only to the rights in the goods as between the buyer and the seller.
(3) A party suspending performance, whether before or after dispatch of the goods, must immediately give notice of the suspension to the other party and must continue with performance if the other party provides adequate assurance of his performance.

Article 72. (1) If prior to the date for performance of the contract it is clear that one of the parties will commit a fundamental breach of contract, the other party may declare the contract avoided.
(2) If time allows, the party intending to declare the contract avoided must give reasonable notice to the other party in order to permit him to provide adequate assurance of his performance.
(3) The requirements of the preceding paragraph do not apply if the other party has declared that he will not perform his obligations.

Article 73. (1) In the case of a contract for delivery of goods by instalments, if the failure of one party to perform any of his obligations in respect of any instalment constitutes a fundamental breach of contract with respect to that instalment, the other party may declare the contract avoided with respect to that instalment.
(2) If one party's failure to perform any of his obligations in respect of any instalment gives the other party good grounds to conclude that a fundamental breach of contract will occur with respect to future instalments, he may declare the contract avoided for the future, provided that he does so within a reasonable time.
(3) A buyer who declares the contract avoided in respect of any delivery may, at the same time, declare it avoided in respect of deliveries already made or of future deliveries if, by reason of their interdependence, those deliveries could not be used for the purpose contemplated by the parties at the time of the conclusion of the contract.

Section II. Damages

Article 74. Damages for breach of contract by one party consist of a sum equal to the loss, including loss of profit, suffered by the other party as a consequence of the breach. Such damages may not exceed the loss which the party in breach foresaw or ought to have foreseen at the time of the conclusion of the contract, in the light of the facts and matters of which he then knew or ought to have known, as a possible consequence of the breach of contract.

Article 75. If the contract is avoided and if, in a reasonable manner and within a reasonable time after avoidance, the buyer has bought goods in replacement or the seller has resold the goods, the party claiming damages may recover the difference between the contract price and the price in the substitute transaction as well as any further damages recoverable under article 74.

Article 76. (1) If the contract is avoided and there is a current price for the goods, the party claiming damages may, if he has not made a purchase or resale under article 75, recover the difference between the price fixed by the contract and the current price at the time of avoidance as well as any further damages recoverable under article 74. If, however, the party claiming damages has avoided the contract after taking over the goods, the current price at the time of such taking over shall be applied instead of the current price at the time of avoidance.
(2) For the purposes of the preceding paragraph, the current price is the price prevailing at the place where delivery of the goods should have been made or, if there is no current price at that place, the price at such other place as serves as a reasonable substitute, making due allowance for differences in the cost of transporting the goods.

Article 77. A party who relies on a breach of contract must take such measures as are reasonable in the circumstances to mitigate the loss, including loss of profit, resulting from the breach. If he fails to take such measures, the party in breach may claim a reduction in the damages in the amount by which the loss should have been mitigated.

Section III. Interest

Article 78. If a party fails to pay the price or any other sum that is in arrears, the other party is entitled to interest on it, without prejudice to any claim for damages recoverable under article 74.

Section IV. Exemptions

Article 79. (1) A party is not liable for a failure to perform any of his obligations if he proves that the failure was due to an impediment beyond his control and that he could not reasonably be expected to have taken the impediment into account at the time of the conclusion of the contract or to have avoided or overcome it or its consequences.
(2) If the party's failure is due to the failure by a third person whom he has engaged to perform the whole or a part of the contract, that party is exempt from liability only if:
(a) he is exempt under the preceding paragraph; and
(b) the person whom he has so engaged would be so exempt if the provisions of that paragraph were applied to him.
(3) The exemption provided by this article has effect for the period during which the impediment exists.
(4) The party who fails to perform must give notice to the other party of the impediment and its effect on his ability to perform. If the notice is not received by the other party within a reasonable time after the party who fails to perform knew or ought to have known of the impediment, he is liable for damages resulting from such non-receipt.
(5) Nothing in this article prevents either party from exercising any right other than to claim damages under this Convention.

Article 80. A party may not rely on a failure of the other party to perform, to the extent that such failure was caused by the first party's act or omission.

Section V. Effects of avoidance

Article 81. (1) Avoidance of the contract releases both parties from their obligations under it, subject to any damages which may be due. Avoidance does not affect any provision of the contract for the settlement of disputes or any other provision of the contract governing the rights and obligations of the parties consequent upon the avoidance of the contract.
(2) A party who has performed the contract either wholly or in part may claim restitution from the

Article 82. (1) The buyer loses the right to declare the contract avoided or to require the seller to deliver substitute goods if it is impossible for him to make restitution of the goods substantially in the condition in which he received them.
(2) The preceding paragraph does not apply:
(a) if the impossibility of making restitution of the goods or of making restitution of the goods substantially in the condition in which the buyer received them is not due to his act or omission;
(b) if the goods or part of the goods have perished or deteriorated as a result of the examination provided for in article 38; or
(c) if the goods or part of the goods have been sold in the normal course of business or have been consumed or transformed by the buyer in the course normal use before he discovered or ought to have discovered the lack of conformity.

Article 83. A buyer who has lost the right to declare the contract avoided or to require the seller to deliver substitute goods in accordance with article 82 retains all other remedies under the contract and this Convention.

Article 84. (1) If the seller is bound to refund the price, he must also pay interest on it, from the date on which the price was paid.
(2) The buyer must account to the seller for all benefits which he has derived from the goods or part of them:
(a) if he must make restitution of the goods or part of them; or
(b) if it is impossible for him to make restitution of all or part of the goods or to make restitution of all or part of the goods substantially in the condition in which he received them, but he has nevertheless declared the contract avoided or required the seller to deliver substitute goods.

Section VI. Preservation of the goods

Article 85. If the buyer is in delay in taking delivery of the goods or, where payment of the price and delivery of the goods are to be made concurrently, if he fails to pay the price, and the seller is either in possession of the goods or otherwise able to control their disposition, the seller must take such steps as are reasonable in the circumstances to preserve them. He is entitled to retain them until he has been reimbursed his reasonable expenses by the buyer.

Article 86. (1) If the buyer has received the goods and intends to exercise any right under the contract or this Convention to reject them, he must take such steps to preserve them as are reasonable in the circumstances. He is entitled to retain them until he has been reimbursed his reasonable expenses by the seller.
(2) If goods dispatched to the buyer have been placed at his disposal at their destination and he exercises the right to reject them, he must take possession of them on behalf of the seller, provided that this can be done without payment of the price and without unreasonable inconvenience or unreasonable expense. This provision does not apply if the seller or a person authorized to take charge of the goods on his behalf is present at the destination. If the buyer takes possession of the goods under this paragraph, his rights and obligations are governed by the preceding paragraph.

Article 87. A party who is bound to take steps to preserve the goods may deposit them in a warehouse of a third person at the expense of the other party provided that the expense incurred is not unreasonable.

Article 88. (1) A party who is bound to preserve the goods in accordance with article 85 or 86 may sell them by any appropriate means if there has been an unreasonable delay by the other party in taking possession of the goods or in taking them back or in paying the price or the cost of preservation, provided that reasonable notice of the intention to sell has been given to the other party.
(2) If the goods are subject to rapid deterioration or their preservation would involve unreasonable expense, a party who is bound to preserve the goods in accordance with article 85 or 86 must take reasonable measures to sell them. To the extent possible he must give notice to the other party of his intention to sell.
(3) A party selling the goods has the right to retain out of the proceeds of sale an amount equal to the reasonable expenses of preserving the goods and of selling them. He must account to the other party for the balance.

UN CONVENTION ON CONTRACTS FOR THE INTERNATIONAL SALE OF GOODS (CISG)

Part IV: Final Provisions

Article 89. The Secretary-General of the United Nations is hereby designated as the depositary for this Convention.

Article 90. This Convention does not prevail over any international agreement which has already been or may be entered into and which contains provisions concerning the matters governed by this Convention, provided that the parties have their places of business in States parties to such agreement.

Article 91. (1) This Convention is open for signature at the concluding meeting of the United Nations Conference on Contracts for the International Sale of Goods and will remain open for signature by all States at the Headquarters of the United Nations, New York until 30 September 1981.
(2) This Convention is subject to ratification, acceptance or approval by the signatory States.
(3) This Convention is open for accession by all States which are not signatory States as from the date it is open for signature.
(4) Instruments of ratification, acceptance, approval and accession are to be deposited with the Secretary-General of the United Nations.

Article 92. (1) A Contracting State may declare at the time of signature, ratification, acceptance, approval or accession that it will not be bound by Part II of this Convention or that it will not be bound by Part III of this Convention.
(2) A Contracting State which makes a declaration in accordance with the preceding paragraph in respect of Part II or Part III of this Convention is not to be considered a Contracting State within paragraph (1) of article 1 of this Convention in respect of matters governed by the Part to which the declaration applies.

Article 93. (1) If a Contracting State has two or more territorial units in which, according to its constitution, different systems of law are applicable in relation to the matters dealt with in this Convention, it may, at the time of signature, ratification, acceptance, approval or accession, declare that this Convention is to extend to all its territorial units or only to one or more of them, and may amend its declaration by submitting another declaration at any time.
(2) These declarations are to be notified to the depositary and are to state expressly the territorial units to which the Convention extends.
(3) If, by virtue of a declaration under this article, this Convention extends to one or more but not all of the territorial units of a Contracting State, and if the place of business of a party is located in that State, this place of business, for the purposes of this Convention, is considered not to be in a Contracting State, unless it is in a territorial unit to which the Convention extends.
(4) If a Contracting State makes no declaration under paragraph (1) of this Article, the Convention is to extend to all territorial units of that State.

Article 94. (1) Two or more Contracting States which have the same or closely related legal rules on matters governed by this Convention may at any time declare that the Convention is not to apply to contracts of sale or to their formation where the parties have their places of business in those States. Such declarations may be made jointly or by reciprocal unilateral declarations.
(2) A Contracting State which has the same or closely related legal rules on matters governed by this Convention as one or more non-Contracting States may at any time declare that the Convention is not to apply to contracts of sale or to their formation where the parties have their places of business in those States.
(3) If a State which is the object of a declaration under the preceding paragraph subsequently becomes a Contracting State, the declaration made will, as from the date on which the Convention enters into force in respect of the new Contracting State, have the effect of a declaration made under paragraph (1), provided that the new Contracting State joins in such declaration or makes a reciprocal unilateral declaration.

Article 95. Any State may declare at the time of the deposit of its instrument of ratification, acceptance, approval or accession that it will not be bound by subparagraph (1)(b) of article 1 of this Convention.

Article 96. A Contracting State whose legislation requires contracts of sale to be concluded in or evidenced by writing may at any time make a declaration in accordance with article 12 that any provision of article 11, article 29, or Part II of this Convention, that allows a contract of sale or its modification or termination by agreement or any offer, acceptance, or other indication of intention to be made in any form other than in writing, does not apply where any party has his place of business in that State.

Article 97. (1) Declarations made under this Convention at the time of signature are subject to confirmation upon ratification, acceptance or approval.
(2) Declarations and confirmations of declarations are to be in writing and be formally notified to the depositary.
(3) A declaration takes effect simultaneously with the entry into force of this Convention in respect of the State concerned. However, a declaration of which the depositary receives formal notification after such entry into force takes effect on the first day of the month following the expiration of six months after the date of its receipt by the depositary. Reciprocal unilateral declarations under article 94 take effect on the first day of the month following the expiration of six months after the receipt of the latest declaration by the depositary.
(4) Any State which makes a declaration under this Convention may withdraw it at any time by a formal notification in writing addressed to the depositary. Such withdrawal is to take effect on the first day of the month following the expiration of six months after the date of the receipt of the notification by the depositary.
(5) A withdrawal of a declaration made under article 94 renders inoperative, as from the date on which the withdrawal takes effect, any reciprocal declaration made by another State under that article.

Article 98. No reservations are permitted except those expressly authorized in this Convention.

Article 99. (1) This Convention enters into force, subject to the provisions of paragraph (6) of this article, on the first day of the month following the expiration of twelve months after the date of deposit of the tenth instrument of ratification, acceptance, approval or accession, including an instrument which contains a declaration made under article 92.
(2) When a State ratifies, accepts, approves or accedes to this Convention after the deposit of the tenth instrument of ratification, acceptance, approval or accession, this Convention, with the exception of the Part excluded, enters into force in respect of that State, subject to the provisions of paragraph (6) of this article, on the first day of the month following the expiration of twelve months after the date of the deposit of its instrument of ratification, acceptance, approval or accession.
(3) A State which ratifies, accepts, approves or accedes to this Convention and is a party to either or both the Convention relating to a Uniform Law on the Formation of Contracts for the International Sale of Goods done at The Hague on 1 July 1964 (1964 Hague Formation Convention) and the Convention relating to a Uniform Law on the International Sale of Goods done at The Hague on 1 July 1964 (1964 Hague Sales Convention) shall at the same time denounce, as the case may be, either or both the 1964 Hague Sales Convention and the 1964 Hague Formation Convention by notifying the Government of the Netherlands to that effect.
(4) A State party to the 1964 Hague Sales Convention which ratifies, accepts, approves or accedes to the present Convention and declares or has declared under article 52 that it will not be bound by Part II of this Convention shall at the time of ratification, acceptance, approval or accession denounce the 1964 Hague Sales Convention by notifying the Government of the Netherlands to that effect.
(5) A State party to the 1964 Hague Formation Convention which ratifies, accepts, approves or accedes to the present Convention and declares or has declared under article 92 that it will not be bound by Part III of this Convention shall at the time of ratification, acceptance, approval or accession denounce the 1964 Hague Formation Convention by notifying the Government of the Netherlands to that effect.
(6) For the purpose of this article, ratifications, acceptances, approvals and accessions in respect of this Convention by States parties to the 1964 Hague Formation Convention or to the 1964 Hague Sales Convention shall not be effective until such denunciations as may be required on the part of those States in respect of the latter two Conventions have themselves become effective. The depositary of this Convention shall consult with the Government of the Netherlands, as the depositary of the 1964 Conventions, so as to ensure necessary co-ordination in this respect.

Article 100. (1) This Convention applies to the formation of a contract only when the proposal for concluding the contract is made on or after the date when the Convention enters into force in respect of the Contracting States referred to in subparagraph (1)(a) or the Contracting State referred to in subparagraph (1)(b) of article 1.
(2) This Convention applies only to contracts concluded on or after the date when the Convention enters into force in respect of the Contracting States referred to in subparagraph (1)(a) or the Contracting State referred to in subparagraph (1)(b) of article 1.

Article 101. (1) A Contracting State may denounce this Convention, or Part II or Part III of the Convention, by a formal notification in writing addressed to the depositary.

(2) The denunciation takes effect on the first day of the month following the expiration of twelve months after the notification is received by the depositary. Where a longer period for the denunciation to take effect is specified in the notification, the denunciation takes effect upon the expiration of such longer period after the notification is received by the depositary.

PART I   INTERNATIONAL BUSINESS LAW

Convention on the Contract for the International Carriage of Goods by Road (CMR) (Geneva, 1956) as amended by the Protocol amending the Convention for the International Carriage of Goods by Road (Geneva, 1978)

Preamble. *The Contracting Parties,*
Having recognized the desirability of standardizing the conditions governing the contract for the international carriage of goods by road, particularly with respect to the documents used for such carriage and to the carrier's liability,
Have agreed as follows:

Chapter I: Scope of Application

Article 1. (1) This Convention shall apply to every contract for the carriage of goods by road in vehicles for reward, when the place of taking over of the goods and the place designated for delivery, as specified in the contract, are situated in two different countries, of which at least one is a contracting country, irrespective of the place of residence and the nationality of the parties.
(2) For the purpose of this Convention, "vehicles" means motor vehicles, articulated vehicles, trailers and semi-trailers as defined in article 4 of the Convention on Road Traffic dated 19 September 1949.
(3) This Convention shall apply also where carriage coming within its scope is carried out by States or by governmental institutions or organizations.
(4) This Convention shall not apply:
(a) To carriage performed under the terms of any international postal convention;
(b) To funeral consignments;
(c) To furniture removal.
(5) The Contracting Parties agree not to vary any of the provisions of this Convention by special agreements between two or more of them, except to make it inapplicable to their frontier traffic or to authorize the use in transport operations entirely confined to their territory of consignment notes representing a title to the goods.

Article 2. (1) Where the vehicle containing the goods is carried over part of the journey by sea, rail, inland waterways or air, and, except where the provisions of article 14 are applicable, the goods are not unloaded from the vehicle, this Convention shall nevertheless apply to the whole of the carriage. Provided that to the extent it is proved that any loss, damage or delay in delivery of the goods which occurs during the carriage by the other means of transport was not caused by act or omission of the carrier by road, but by some event which could only occurred in the course of and by reason of the carriage by that other means of transport, the liability of the carrier by road shall be determined not by this convention but in the manner in which the liability of the carrier by the other means of transport would have been determined if a contract for the carriage the goods alone had been made by the sender with the carrier by the other means of transport in accordance with the conditions prescribed by law for the carriage of goods by that means of transport. If, however, there are no such prescribed conditions, the liability of the carrier by road shall be determined by this convention.
(2) If the carrier by road is also himself the carrier by the other means of transport, his liability shall also be determined in accordance with the provisions paragraph 1 of this article, but as if, in his capacities as carrier by road and carrier by the other means of transport, he were two separate persons.

Chapter II: Persons for Whom the Carrier is Responsible

Article 3. For the purposes of this Convention the carrier shall be responsible for the acts of omissions of his agents and servants and of any other persons of whose services he makes use for the performance of the carriage, when such agents, servants or other persons are acting within the scope of their employment, as if such acts or omissions were his own.

Chapter III: Conclusion and Performance of the Contract of Carriage

Article 4. The contract of carriage shall be confirmed by the making out of a consignment note. The absence, irregularity or loss of the consignment note shall not affect the existence or the validity of the contract of carriage which shall remain subject the provisions of this Convention.

Article 5. (1) The consignment note shall be made out in three original copies signed by the sender and by the carrier. These signatures may be printed or replaced by the stamps of the sender and the carrier if the law of the country in which the consignment note has been made out so permits.
The first copy shall be handed to the sender, the second shall accompany the goods and the third shall

be retained by the carrier.

(2) When the goods which are to be carried have to be loaded in different vehicles, or are of different kinds or are divided into different lots, the sender or the carrier shall have the right to require a separate consignment note to be made out for each vehicle used, or for each kind or lot of goods.

Article 6. (1). The consignment note shall contain the following particulars:
(a) The date of the consignment note and the place at which it is made out;
(b) The name and address of the sender;
(c) The name and address of the carrier;
(d) The place and the date of taking over of the goods and the place designated for delivery;
(e) The name and address of the consignee;
(f) The description in common use of the nature of the goods and the method of packing, and, in the case of dangerous goods, their generally recognized description;
(g) The number of packages and their special marks and numbers;
(h) The gross weight of the goods or their quantity otherwise expressed;
(i) Charges relating to the carriage (carriage charges, supplementary charges, customs duties and other charges incurred from the making of the contract to the time of delivery);
(j) The requisite instructions for Customs and other formalities;
(k) A statement that the carriage is subject, notwithstanding any clause to the contrary, to the provisions of this Convention.
(2) Where applicable the consignment note shall also contain the following particulars:
(a) A statement that trans-shipment is not allowed;
(b) Then charges which the sender undertakes to pay;
(c) The amount of "cash on delivery" charges;
(d) A declaration of the value of the goods and the amount representing special interest in delivery;
(e) The sender's instructions to the carrier regarding insurance of the goods;
(f) The agreed time limit within which the carriage is to be carried out;
(g) A list of the documents handed to the carrier.
(3) The parties may enter in the consignment note any other particulars which they may deem useful.

Article 7. (1). The sender shall be responsible for all expenses, loss and damage sustained by the carrier by reason of the inaccuracy or inadequacy of:
(a) The particulars specified in article 6, paragraph 1, (b), (d), (e), (f), (g), (h) and (j);
(b) The particular specified in article 6, paragraph 2;
(c) Any other particulars or instructions given by him to enable the consignment note to be made out or for the purpose of their being entered therein.
(2) If, at the request of the sender, the carrier enters in the consignment note the particulars referred to in paragraph 1 of this article, he shall be deemed, unless the contrary is proved, to have done so on behalf of the sender.
(3) If the consignment note does not contain the statement specified in article 6, paragraph 1 (k), the carrier shall be liable for all expenses, loss and damage sustained through such omission by the person entitled to dispose of the goods.

Article 8. (1) On taking over the goods, the carrier shall check:
(a) The accuracy of the statements in the consignment note as to the number of packages and their marks and numbers, and
(b) The apparent condition of the goods and their packaging.
(2). Where the carrier has no reasonable means of checking the accuracy of e statements referred to in paragraph 1 (a) of this article, he shall enter his reservations in the consignment note together with the grounds on which they are based. He shall likewise specify the grounds for any reservations which he makes with regard to the apparent condition of the goods and their packaging, such reservations shall not bind the sender unless he has expressly agreed to be bound by them in the consignment note.
(3) The sender shall be entitled to require the carrier to check the gross weight the goods or their quantity otherwise expressed. He may also require the contents of the packages to be checked. The carrier shall be entitled to claim the cost of such checking. The result of the checks shall be entered in the consignment note.

Article 9. (1) The consignment note shall be prima facie evidence of the making of the contract of carriage, the conditions of the contract and the receipt of the goods by the carrier.
(2) If the consignment note contains no specific reservations by the carrier, it shall be presumed, unless the contrary is proved, that the goods and their packaging appeared to be in good condition

when the carrier took them over and that the number of packages, their marks and numbers corresponded with the statements in the consignment note.

Article 10. The sender shall be liable to the carrier for damage to persons, equipment or other goods, and for any expenses due to defective packing of the goods, unless the defect was apparent or known to the carrier at the time when he took over the goods and he made no reservations concerning it.

Article 11. (1). For the purposes of the Customs or other formalities which have to be completed before delivery of the goods, the sender shall attach the necessary documents to the consignment note or place them at the disposal of the carrier and shall furnish him with all the information which he requires.
(2) The carrier shall not be under any duty to enquire into either the accuracy or the adequacy of such documents and information. The sender shall be liable to the carrier for any damage caused by the absence, inadequacy or irregularity of such documents and information, except in the case of some wrongful act or neglect on the part of the carrier.
(3) The liability of the carrier for the consequences arising from the loss or incorrect use of the documents specified in and accompanying the consignment note or deposited with the carrier shall be that of an agent, provided that the compensation payable by the carrier shall not exceed that payable in the event of loss of the goods.

Article 12. (1) The sender has the right to dispose of the goods, in particular by asking the carrier to stop the goods in transit, to change the place at which delivery is to take place or to deliver the goods to a consignee other than the consignee indicated in the consignment note.
(2) This right shall cease to exist when the second copy of the consignment note is handed to the consignee or when the consignee exercises his right under article 13, paragraph 1; from that time onwards the carrier shall obey the orders of the consignee.
(3) The consignee shall, however, have the right of disposal from the time when the consignment note is drawn up, if the sender makes an entry to that effect in the consignment note.
(4) If in exercising his right of disposal the consignee has ordered the delivery of the goods to another person, that other person shall not be entitled to name other consignees.
(5) The exercise of the right of disposal shall be subject to the following conditions:
(a) That the sender or, in the case referred to in paragraph 3 of this article, the consignee who wishes to exercise the right produces the first copy of the consignment note on which the new instructions to the carrier have been entered and indemnifies the carrier against all expenses, loss and damage involved in carrying out such instructions;
(b) That the carrying out of such instructions is possible at the time when the instructions reach the person who is to carry them out and does not either interfere with the normal working of the carriers' undertaking or prejudice the senders or consignees of other consignments;
(c) That the instructions do not result in a division of the consignment.
(6) When, by reason of the provisions of paragraph 5 (b) of this article, the carrier cannot carry out the instructions which he receives, he shall immediately notify the person who gave him such instructions.
(7) A carrier who has not carried out the instructions given under the conditions provided for in this article or who has carried them out without requiring the first copy of the consignment note to be produced, shall be liable to the person entitled to make a claim for any loss or damage caused thereby.

Article 13. (1) After arrival of the goods at the place designated for delivery, the consignee shall be entitled to require the carrier to deliver to him, against a receipt, the second copy of the consignment note and the goods. If the loss of the goods established or if the goods have not arrived after the expiry of the period provided for in article 19, the consignee shall be entitled to enforce in his own name against the carrier any rights arising from the contract of carriage.
(2) The consignee who avails himself of the rights granted to him under paragraph 1 of this article shall pay the charges shown to be due on the consignment note, but in the event of dispute on this matter the carrier shall not be required to deliver the goods unless security has been furnished by the consignee.

Article 14. (1) If for any reason it is or becomes impossible to carry out the contract in accordance with the terms laid down in the consignment note before the goods reach the place designated for delivery, the carrier shall ask for instructions from the person entitled to dispose of the goods in accordance with the provisions of article 12.
(2) Nevertheless, if circumstances are such as to allow the carriage to be carried out under conditions differing from those laid down in the consignment note and if the carrier has been unable to obtain

instructions in reasonable time the person entitled to dispose of the goods in accordance with the provisions of article 12, he shall take such steps as seem to him to be in the best interests the person entitled to dispose of the goods.

Article 15. (1) Where circumstances prevent delivery of the goods after their arrival at the place designated for delivery, the carrier shall ask the sender for his instructions. If the consignee refuses the goods the sender shall be entitled to dispose of them without being obliged to produce the first copy of the consignment note.
(2) Even if he has refused the goods, the consignee may nevertheless require delivery so long as the carrier has not received instructions to the contrary from the sender.
(3) When circumstances preventing delivery of the goods arise after the consignee, in exercise of his rights under article 12, paragraph 3, has given an order for the goods to be delivered to another person, paragraphs 1 and 2 of this article shall apply as if the consignee were the sender and that other person were the consignee.

Article 16. (1) The carrier shall be entitled to recover the cost of his request for instructions and any expenses entailed in carrying out such instructions, unless such expenses were caused by the wrongful act or neglect of the carrier.
(2) In the cases referred to in article 14, paragraph 1, and in article 15, the carrier may immediately unload the goods for account of the person entitled to dispose of them and thereupon the carriage shall be deemed to be at an end. The carrier shall then hold the goods on behalf of the person so entitled. He may, however, entrust them to a third party, and in that case he shall not be under any liability except for the exercise of reasonable care in the choice of such third party. The charges due under the consignment note and all other expenses shall remain chargeable against the goods.
(3) The carrier may sell the goods, without awaiting instructions from the person entitled to dispose of them, if the goods are perishable or their condition warrants such a course, or when the storage expenses would be out of proportion to the value of the goods. He may also proceed to the sale of the goods in other cases if after the expiry of a reasonable period he has not received from the person entitled to dispose of the goods instructions to the contrary which he may reasonably be required to carry out.
(4) If the goods have been sold pursuant to this article, the proceeds of sale, after deduction of the expenses chargeable against the goods, shall be placed at the disposal of the person entitled to dispose of the goods. If these charges exceed the proceeds of sale, the carrier shall be entitled to the difference.
(5) The procedure in the case of sale shall be determined by the law or custom of the place where the goods are situated.

Chapter IV: Liability of the Carrier

Article 17. (1) The carrier shall be liable for the total or partial loss of the goods and for damage thereto occurring between the time when he takes over the goods and the time of delivery, as well as for any delay in delivery.
(2) The carrier shall, however, be relieved of liability if the loss, damage or delay was caused by the wrongful act or neglect of the claimant, by the instructions of the claimant given otherwise than as the result of a wrongful act or neglect on the part of the carrier, by inherent vice of the goods or through circumstances which the carrier could not avoid and the consequences of which he was unable to prevent.
(3) The carrier shall not be relieved of liability by reason of the defective condition of the vehicle used by him in order to perform the carriage, or by reason of the wrongful act or neglect of the person from whom he may have hired the vehicle or of the agents or servants of the latter.
(4) Subject to article 18, paragraphs 2 to 5, the carrier shall be relieved of liability when the loss or damage arises from the special risks inherent in one more of the following circumstances:
(a) Use of open unsheeted vehicles, when their use has been expressly agreed and specified in the consignment note;
(b) The lack of, or defective condition of packing in the case of goods which, by their nature, are liable to wastage or to be damaged when not packed or when not properly packed;
(c) Handling, loading, stowage or unloading of the goods by the sender, the consignee or person acting on behalf of the sender or the consignee;
(d) The nature of certain kinds of goods which particularly exposes them to total or partial loss or to damage, especially through breakage, rust, decay, desiccation, leakage, normal wastage, or the action of moth or vermin;
(e) Insufficiency or inadequacy of marks or numbers on the packages;

(f) The carriage of livestock.
(5) Where under this article the carrier is not under any liability in respect some of the factors causing the loss, damage or delay, he shall only be liable the extent that those factors for which he is liable under this article have contributed to the loss, damage or delay.

Article 18. (1) The burden of proving that loss, damage or delay was due to one of the specified in article 17, paragraph 2, shall rest upon the carrier.
(2) When the carrier establishes that in the circumstances of the case, the loss damage could be attributed to one or more of the special risks referred to in article 17, paragraph 4, it shall be presumed that it was so caused. The claimant shall, however, be entitled to prove that the loss or damage was not, in fact, attributable either wholly or partly to one of these risks.
(3) This presumption shall not apply in the circumstances set out in article 17, paragraph 4 (a), if there has been an abnormal shortage, or a loss of any package.
(4) If the carriage is performed in vehicles specially equipped to protect the goods from the effects of heat, cold, variations in temperature or the humidity of the air, the carrier shall not be entitled to claim the benefit of article 17, paragraph 4 (d), unless he proves that all steps incumbent on him in the circumstances with respect to the choice, maintenance and use of such equipment were taken and that he complied with any special instructions issued to him.
(5) The carrier shall not be entitled to claim the benefit of article 17, paragraph 4 (f), unless he proves that all steps normally incumbent on him in the circumstances were taken and that he complied with any special instructions issued to him.

Article 19. Delay in delivery shall be said to occur when the goods have not been delivered within the agreed time-limit or when, failing an agreed time-limit, the actual duration of the carriage having regard to the circumstances of the case, and in particular, in the case of partial loads, the time required for making up a complete load in the normal way, exceeds the time it would be reasonable to allow a diligent carrier.

Article 20. (1) The fact that goods have not been delivered within thirty days following the expiry of the agreed time-limit, or, if there is no agreed time-limit, within sixty days from the time when the carrier took over the goods, shall be conclusive evidence of the loss of the goods, and the person entitled to make a claim may thereupon treat them as lost.
(2) The person so entitled may, on receipt of compensation for the missing goods, request in writing that he shall be notified immediately should the goods be recovered in the course of the year following the payment of compensation. He shall be given a written acknowledgement of such request.
(3) Within the thirty days following receipt of such notification, the person entitled as aforesaid may require the goods to be delivered to him against payment of the charges shown to be due on the consignment note and also against refund of the compensation he received less any charges included therein but without prejudice to any claims to compensation for delay in delivery under article 23 and where applicable, article 26.
(4) In the absence of the request mentioned in paragraph 2 or of any instructions given within the period of thirty days specified in paragraph 3, or if the goods are not recovered until more than one year after the payment of compensation, the carrier shall be entitled to deal with them in accordance with the law place where the goods are situated.

Article 21. Should the goods have been delivered to the consignee without collection of the "cash on delivery" charge which should have been collected by the carrier under terms of the contract of carriage, the carrier shall be liable to the sender for compensation not exceeding the amount of such charge without prejudice to his right of action against the consignee.

Article 22. (1) When the sender hands goods of a dangerous nature to the carrier, he shall inform the carrier of the exact nature of the danger and indicate if necessary, precautions to be taken. If this information has not been entered in the consignment note, the burden of proving, by some other means, that the carrier knew the exact nature of the danger constituted by the carriage of the said goods shall rest upon the sender or the consignee.
(2) Goods of a dangerous nature which, in the circumstance referred to in paragraph 1 of this article, the carrier did not know were dangerous, may, at any time or place, be unloaded, destroyed or rendered harmless by the carrier without compensation; further, the sender shall be liable for all expenses, loss or damage arising out of their handing over for carriage or of their carriage.

Article 23. (1) When, under the provisions of this Convention, a carrier is liable for compensation in respect of total or partial loss of goods, such compensation shall be calculated by reference to the

value of the goods at the place and time at which they were accepted for carriage.
(2) The value of the goods shall be fixed according to the commodity exchange price or, if there is no such price, according to the current market price or, if there is no commodity exchange price or current market price, by reference to normal value of goods of the same kind and quality.
(3) Compensation shall not, however, exceed 8.33 units of account per kilogram of gross weight short.
(4) In addition, the carriage charges, Customs duties and other charges incurred in respect of the carriage of the goods shall be refunded in full in case of total loss and in proportion to the loss sustained in case of partial loss, but no further damage shall be payable.
(5) In the case of delay if the claimant proves that damage has resulted therefrom the carrier shall pay compensation for such damage not exceeding the carriage charges.
(6) Higher compensation may only be claimed where the value of the goods or a special interest in delivery has been declared in accordance with articles 24 and 26.

Article 24. The sender may, against payment of a surcharge to be agreed upon, declare in the consignment note a value for the goods exceeding the limit laid down in article 23, paragraph 3, and in that case the amount of the declared value shall be substituted for that limit.

Article 25. (1) In case of damage, the carrier shall be liable for the amount by which the goods have diminished in value, calculated by reference to the value of the goods fixed in accordance with article 23, paragraphs 1, 2 and 4.
(2) The compensation may not, however, exceed:
(a) If the whole consignment has been damaged, the amount payable in the case of total loss;
(b) If part only of the consignment has been damaged, the amount payable in the case of loss of the part affected.

Article 26. (1) The sender may, against payment of a surcharge to be agreed upon, fix the amount of a special interest in delivery in the case of loss or damage or of the agreed time-limit being exceeded, by entering such amount in the consignment note.
(2) If a declaration of a special interest in delivery has been made, compensation for the additional loss or damage proved may be claimed, up to the total amount of the interest declared, independently of the compensation provided for in articles 23, 24 and 25.

Article 27. (1) The claimant shall be entitled to claim interest on compensation payable. Such interest, calculated at five per centum per annum, shall accrue from the date on which the claim was sent in writing to the carrier or, if no such claim has been made, from the date on which legal proceedings were instituted.
(2) When the amounts on which the calculation of the compensation is based are not expressed in the currency of the country in which payment is claimed, conversion shall be at the rate of exchange applicable on the day and at the place of payment of compensation.

Article 28. (1) In cases where, under the law applicable, loss, damage or delay arising out of carriage under this Convention gives rise to an extra-contractual claim, the carrier may avail himself of the provisions of this Convention which exclude his liability of which fix or limit the compensation due.
(2) In cases where the extra-contractual liability for loss, damage or delay of one of the persons for whom the carrier is responsible under the terms of article 3 is in issue, such person may also avail himself of the provisions of this Convention which exclude the liability of the carrier or which fix or limit the compensation due.

Article 29. (1) The carrier shall not be entitled to avail himself of the provisions of this chapter which exclude or limit his liability or which shift the burden of proof if the damage was caused by his willful misconduct or by such default on his part as, in accordance with the law of the court or tribunal seised of the case, is considered as equivalent to willful misconduct.
(2) The same provision shall apply if the willful misconduct or default is committed by the agents or servants of the carrier or by any other persons of whose services he makes use for the performance of the carriage, when such agents, servants or other persons are acting within the scope of their employment. Furthermore, in such a case such agents, servants or other persons shall not be entitled to avail themselves, with regard to their personal liability, of the provisions of this chapter referred to in paragraph (1).

Chapter V: Claims and Actions

Article 30. (1) If the consignee takes delivery of the goods without duly checking their condition

with the carrier or without sending him reservations giving a general indication of the loss or damage, not later than the time of delivery in the case of apparent loss or damage and within seven days of delivery, Sundays and public holidays excepted, in the case of loss or damage which is not apparent, the fact of this taking delivery shall be prima facie, evidence that he has received the goods in the condition described in the consignment note. In the case of loss or damage which is not apparent the reservations referred to shall be made in writing.
(2) When the condition of the goods has been duly checked by the consignee and the carrier, evidence contradicting the result of this checking shall only be admissible in the case of loss or damage which is not apparent and provided that the consignee has duly sent reservations in writing to the carrier within seven days, Sundays and public holidays excepted, from the date of checking.
(3) No compensation shall be payable for delay in delivery unless a reservation has been sent in writing to the carrier, within twenty-one days from the time that the goods were placed at the disposal of the consignee.
(4) In calculating the time-limits provided for in this article the date of delivery, or the date of checking, or the date when the goods were placed at the disposal of the consignee, as the case may be, shall not be included.
(5) The carrier and the consignee shall give each other every reasonable facility for making the requisite investigations and checks.

Article 31. (1) In legal proceedings arising out of carriage under this Convention, the plaintiff may bring an action in any court or tribunal of a contracting country designated by agreement between the parties and, in addition, in the courts or tribunals of a country within whose territory:
(a) The defendant is ordinarily resident, or has his principal place of business, or the branch or agency through which the contract of carriage was made, or (b) The place where the goods were taken over by the carrier or the place designated for delivery is situated.
(2) Where in respect of a claim referred to in paragraph 1 of this article an action is pending before a court or tribunal competent under that paragraph, or where in respect of such a claim a judgement has been entered by such a court or tribunal no new action shall be started between the same parties on the same grounds unless the judgement of the court or tribunal before which the first action was brought is not enforceable in the country in which the fresh proceedings are brought.
(3) When a judgement entered by a court or tribunal of a contracting country in any such action as is referred to in paragraph 1 of this article has become enforceable in that country, it shall also become enforceable in each of the other contracting States, as soon as the formalities required in the country concerned have been complied with. These formalities shall not permit the merits of the case to be re-opened.
(4) The provisions of paragraph 3 of this article shall apply to judgements after trial, judgements by default and settlements confirmed by an order of the court, but shall not apply to interim judgements or to awards of damages, in addition to costs against a plaintiff who wholly or partly fails in his action.
(5) Security for costs shall not be required in proceedings arising out of carriage under this Convention from nationals of contracting countries resident or having their place of business in one of those countries.

Article 32. (1) The period of limitation for an action arising out of carriage under this Convention shall be one year. Nevertheless, in the case of willful misconduct, or such default as in accordance with the law of the court or tribunal seised of the case, is considered as equivalent to willful misconduct, the period of limitation shall be three years. The period of limitation shall begin to run:
(a) In the case of partial loss, damage or delay in delivery, from the date of delivery;
(b) In the case of total loss, from the thirtieth day after the expiry of the agreed time-limit or where there is no agreed time-limit from the sixtieth day from the date on which the goods were taken over by the carrier;
(c) In all other cases, on the expiry of a period of three months after the making of the contract of carriage.
The day on which the period of limitation begins to run shall not be included in the period.
(2) A written claim shall suspend the period of limitation until such date as the carrier rejects the claim by notification in writing and returns the documents attached thereto. If a part of the claim is admitted the period of limitation shall start to run again only in respect of that part of the claim still in dispute. The burden of proof of the receipt of the claim, or of the reply and of the return of the documents, shall rest with the party relying upon these facts. The running of the period of limitation shall not be suspended by further claims having the same object.
(3) Subject to the provisions of paragraph 2 above, the extension of the period of limitation shall be

governed by the law of the court or tribunal seized of the case. That law shall also govern the fresh accrual of rights of action.

(4) A right of action which has become barred by lapse of time may not be exercised by way of counterclaim or set-off.

Article 33. The contract of carriage may contain a clause conferring competence on an arbitration tribunal if the clause conferring competence on the tribunal provides that the tribunal shall apply this Convention.

Chapter VI: Provisions Relating to Carriage Performed by Successive Carrier

Article 34. If carriage governed by a single contract is performed by successive road carriers, each of them shall be responsible for the performance of the whole operation, the second carrier and each succeeding carrier becoming a party to the contract of carriage, under the terms of the consignment note, by reason of his acceptance of the goods and the consignment note.

Article 35. (1) A carrier accepting the goods from a previous carrier shall give the latter a dated and signed receipt. He shall enter his name and address on the second copy of the consignment note. Where applicable, he shall enter on the second copy of the consignment note and on the receipt reservations of the kind provided for in article 8, paragraph (2).

(2) The provisions of article 9 shall apply to the relations between successive carriers.

Article 36. Except in the case of a counterclaim or a setoff raised in an action concerning a claim based on the same contract of carriage, legal proceedings in respect of liability for loss, damage or delay may only be brought against the first carrier, the last carrier or the carrier who was performing that portion of the carriage during which the event causing the loss, damage or delay occurred, an action may be brought at the same time against several of these carriers.

Article 37. A carrier who has paid compensation in compliance with the provisions of this Convention, shall be entitled to recover such compensation, together with interest thereon and all costs and expenses incurred by reason of the claim, from the other carriers who have taken part in the carriage, subject to the following provisions:

(a) The carrier responsible for the loss or damage shall be solely liable for the compensation whether paid by himself or by another carrier;

(b) When the loss or damage has been caused by the action of two or more carriers, each of them shall pay an amount proportionate to his share of liability; should it be impossible to apportion the liability, each carrier shall be liable in proportion to the share of the payment for the carriage which is due to him;

(c) If it cannot be ascertained to which carriers liability is attributable for the loss or damage, the amount of the compensation shall be apportioned between all the carriers as laid down in (b) above.

Article 38. If one of the carriers is insolvent, the share of the compensation due from him and unpaid by him shall be divided among the other carriers in proportion to the share of the payment for the carriage due to them.

Article 39. (1) No carrier against whom a claim is made under articles 37 and 38 shall be entitled to dispute the validity of the payment made by the carrier making the claim if the amount of the compensation was determined by judicial authority after the first mentioned carrier had been given due notice of the proceedings and afforded an opportunity of entering an appearance.

(2) A carrier wishing to take proceedings to enforce his right of recovery may make his claim before the competent court or tribunal of the country in which one of the carriers concerned is ordinarily resident, or has his principal place of business or the branch or agency through which the contract of carriage was made. All the carriers concerned may be made defendants in the same action.

(3) The provisions of article 31, paragraphs 3 and 4, shall apply to judgements entered in the proceedings referred to in articles 37 and 38.

(4) The provisions of article 32 shall apply to claims between carriers. The period of limitation shall, however, begin to run either on the date of the final judicial decision fixing the amount of compensation payable under the provisions of this Convention, or, if there is no such judicial decision, from the actual date of payment.

Article 40. Carriers shall be free to agree among themselves on provisions other than those laid down in articles 37 and 38.

PART I INTERNATIONAL BUSINESS LAW

Chapter VII: Nullity of Stipulation to the Convention

Article 41. (1) Subject to the provisions of article 40, any stipulation which would directly or indirectly derogate from the provisions of this Convention shall be null and void. The nullity of such a stipulation shall not involve the nullity of the other provisions of the contract.
(2) In particular, a benefit of insurance in favour of the carrier or any other similar clause, or any clause shifting the burden of proof shall be null and void.

Chapter VIII: Final Provisions

Article 42. (1) This Convention is open for signature or accession by countries members of the Economic Commission for Europe and countries admitted to the Commission in a consultative capacity under paragraph (8) of the Commission's terms of reference.
(2) Such countries as may participate in certain activities of the Economic Commission for Europe in accordance with paragraph (11) of the Commission's terms of reference may become Contracting Parties to this Convention by acceding thereto after its entry into force.
(3) The Convention shall be open for signature until 31 August 1956 inclusive. Thereafter, it shall be open for accession.
(4) This Convention shall be ratified.
(5) Ratification or accession shall be effected by the deposit of an instrument with the Secretary-General of the United Nations.

Article 43. (1) This Convention shall come into force on the ninetieth day after five of the countries referred to in article 42, paragraph (1), have deposited their instruments of ratification or accession.
(2) For any country ratifying or acceding to it after five countries have deposited their instruments of ratification of accession, this Convention shall enter into force on the ninetieth day after the said country has deposited its instrument of ratification or accession.

Article 44. (1) Any Contracting Party may denounce this Convention by so notifying the Secretary-General of the United Nations.
(2) Denunciation shall take effect twelve months after the date of receipt by the Secretary-General of the notification of denunciation.

Article 45. If, after the entry into force of this Convention, the number of Contracting Parties is reduced, as a result of denunciations, to less than five, the Convention shall cease to be in force from the date in which the last of such denunciations takes effect.

Article 46. (1) Any country may, at the time of depositing its instrument of ratification or accession or at any time thereafter, declare by notification addressed to the Secretary-General of the United Nations that this Convention shall extend to all or any of the territories for the international relations of which it is responsible. The Convention shall extend to the territory or territories named in the notification as from the ninetieth day after its receipt by the Secretary-General or, if on that day the Convention has not yet entered into force, at the time of its entry into force.
(2) Any country which has made a declaration under the preceding paragraph extending this Convention to any territory for whose international relations it is responsible may denounce the Convention separately in respect of that territory in accordance with the provisions of article 44.

Article 47. Any dispute between two or more Contracting Parties relating to the interpretation or application of this Convention, which the parties are unable to settle by negotiation or other means may, at the request of any one of the Contracting Parties concerned, be referred for settlement to the International Court of Justice.

Article 48. (1) Each Contracting Party may, at the time of signing, ratifying, or acceding to, this Convention, declare that it does not consider itself as bound by article 47 of the Convention. Other Contracting Parties shall not be bound by article 47 in respect of any Contracting Party which has entered such a reservation.
(2) Any Contracting Party having entered a reservation as provided for in paragraph 1 may at any time withdraw such reservation by notifying the Secretary-General of the United Nations.
(3) No other reservation to this Convention shall be permitted.

Article 49. (1) After this Convention has been in force for three years, any Contracting Party may, by notification to the Secretary-General of the United Nations, request that a conference be convened for the purpose of reviewing the Convention. The Secretary-General shall notify all Contracting Parties of the request and a review conference shall be convened by the Secretary-General if, within a period

PART I INTERNATIONAL BUSINESS LAW

International Convention for the Unification of Certain Rules of Law relating to Bills of Lading (Brussels, 1928) as modified by the Visby Amendments (Protocol to Amend the International Convention for the Unification of Certain Rules of Law relating to Bills of Lading (Brussels, 1968) and the SDR Protocol (Brussels, 1979), "The Hague-Visby Rules".

Article I. In these Rules the following words are employed, with the meanings set out below:
(a) 'Carrier' includes the owner or the charterer who enters into a contract of carriage with a shipper.
(b) 'Contract of carriage' applies only to contracts of carriage covered by a bill of lading or any similar document of title, in so far as such document relates to the carriage of goods by sea, including any bill of lading or any similar document as aforesaid issued under or pursuant to a charter party from the moment at which such bill of lading or similar document of title regulates the relations between a carrier and a holder of the same.
(c) 'Goods' includes goods, wares, merchandise, and articles of every kind whatsoever except live animals and cargo which by the contract of carriage is stated as being carried on deck and is so carried.
(d) 'Ship' means any vessel used for the carriage of goods by sea.
(e) 'Carriage of goods' covers the period from the time when the goods are loaded on to the time they are discharged from the ship.

Article II. Subject to the provisions of Article VI, under every contract of carriage of goods by sea the carrier, in relation to the loading, handling, stowage, carriage, custody, care and discharge of such goods, shall be subject to the responsibilities and liabilities and entitled to the rights and immunities hereinafter set forth.

Article III. (1) The carrier shall be bound before and at the beginning of the voyage to exercise due diligence to:
(a) Make the ship seaworthy;
(b) Properly man, equip and supply the ship;
(c) Make the holds, refrigerating and cool chambers, and all other parts of the ship in which goods are carried, fit and safe for their reception, carriage and preservation.
(2) Subject to the provisions of Article IV, the carrier shall properly and carefully load, handle, stow, carry, keep, care for, and discharge the goods carried.
(3) After receiving the goods into his charge the carrier or the master or agent of the carrier shall, on demand of the shipper, issue to the shipper a bill of lading showing among other things:
(a) The leading marks necessary for identification of the goods as the same are furnished in writing by the shipper before the loading of such goods starts, provided such marks are stamped or otherwise shown clearly upon the goods if uncovered, or on the cases or coverings in which such goods are contained, in such a manner as should ordinarily remain legible until the end of the voyage.
(b) Either the number of packages or pieces, or the quantity, or weight, as the case may be, as furnished in writing by the shipper.
(c) The apparent order and condition of the goods.
Provided that no carrier, master or agent of the carrier shall be bound to state or show in the bill of lading any marks, number, quantity or weight which he has reasonable ground for suspecting not accurately to represent the goods actually received, or which he has had no reasonable means of checking.
(4) Such a bill of lading shall be prima facie evidence of the receipt by the carrier of the goods as therein described in accordance with paragraph 3 (a), (b) and (c). However, proof to the contrary shall not be admissible when the bill of lading has been transferred to a third party acting in good faith.
(5) The shipper shall be deemed to have guaranteed to the carrier the accuracy at the time of shipment of the marks, number, quantity and weight, as furnished by him, and the shipper shall indemnify the carrier against all loss, damages and expenses arising or resulting from inaccuracies in such particulars. The right of the carrier to such indemnity shall in no way limit his responsibility and liability under the contract of carriage to any person other than the shipper.
(6) Unless notice of loss or damage and the general nature of such loss or damage be given in writing to the carrier or his agent at the port of discharge before or at the time of the removal of the goods into the custody of the person entitled to delivery thereof under the contract of carriage, or, if the loss or damage be not apparent, within three days, such removal shall be prima facie evidence of the delivery by the carrier of the goods as described in the bill of lading.
The notice in writing need not be given if the state of the goods has, at the time of their receipt, been the subject of joint survey or inspection.

of four months following the date of notification by the Secretary General, not less than one-fourth of the Contracting Parties notify him of their concurrence with the request.

(2) If a conference is convened in accordance with the preceding paragraph, the Secretary-General shall notify all the Contracting Parties and invite them to submit within a period of three months such proposals as they may wish the Conference to consider. The Secretary-General shall circulate to all Contracting Parties the provisional agenda for the conference together with the texts of such proposals at least three months before the date on which the conference is to meet.

(3) The Secretary-General shall invite to any conference convened in accordance with this article all countries referred to in article 42, paragraph (1), and countries which have become Contracting Parties under article 42, paragraph (2).

Article 50. In addition to the notifications provided for in article 49, the Secretary-General of the United Nations shall notify the countries referred to in article 42, paragraph 1, and the countries which have become Contracting Parties under article 42, paragraph (2), of:

(a) Ratification and accessions under article 42;
(b) The dates of entry into force of this Convention in accordance with article 43;
(c) Denunciations under article 44;
(d) The termination of this Convention in accordance with article 45;
(e) Notifications received in accordance with article 46;
(f) Declarations and notifications received in accordance with article 48, paragraphs 1 and 2.

Article 51. After 31 August 1956, the original of this Convention shall be deposited with the Secretary-General of the United Nations, who shall transmit certified true copies to each of the countries mentioned in article 42, paragraphs 1 and 2.

HAGUE VISBY RULES (HVR)

Subject to paragraph 6bis the carrier and the ship shall in any event be discharged from all liability whatsoever in respect of the goods, unless suit is brought within one year of their delivery or of the date when they should have been delivered. This period, may however, be extended if the parties so agree after the cause of action has arisen.

In the case of any actual or apprehended loss or damage the carrier and the receiver shall give all reasonable facilities to each other for inspecting and tallying the goods.

(6 bis) An action for indemnity against a third person may be brought even after the expiration of the year provided for in the preceding paragraph if brought within the time allowed by the law of the Court seized of the case. However, the time allowed shall be not less than three months, commencing from the day when the person bringing such action for indemnity has settled the claim or has been served with process in the action against himself.

(7) After the goods are loaded the bill of lading to be issued by the carrier, master, or agent of the carrier, to the shipper shall, if the shipper so demands be a 'shipped' bill of lading, provided that if the shipper shall have previously taken up any document of title to such goods, he shall surrender the same as against the issue of the 'shipped' bill of lading, but at the option of the carrier such document of title may be noted at the port of shipment by the carrier, master, or agent with the name or names of the ship or ships upon which the goods have been shipped and the date or dates of shipment, and when so noted, if it shows the particulars mentioned in paragraph 3 of Article III, shall for the purpose of this article be deemed to constitute a 'shipped' bill of lading.

(8) Any clause, covenant, or agreement in a contract of carriage relieving the carrier or the ship from liability for loss or damage to, or in connection with, goods arising from negligence, fault, or failure in the duties and obligations provided in this article or lessening such liability otherwise than as provided in these Rules, shall be null and void and of no effect. A benefit of insurance in favour of the carrier or similar clause shall be deemed to be a clause relieving the carrier from liability.

Article IV. (1) Neither the carrier nor the ship shall be liable for loss or damage arising or resulting from unseaworthiness unless caused by want of due diligence on the part of the carrier to make the ship seaworthy, and to secure that the ship is properly manned, equipped and supplied, and to make the holds, refrigerating and cool chambers and all other parts of the ship in which goods are carried fit and safe for their reception, carriage and preservation in accordance with the provisions of paragraph 1 of Article III. Whenever loss or damage has resulted from unseaworthiness the burden of proving the exercise of due diligence shall be on the carrier or other person claiming exemption under this article.

(2) Neither the carrier nor the ship shall be responsible for loss or damage arising or resulting from:

(a) Act, neglect, or default of the master, mariner, pilot, or the servants of the carrier in the navigation or in the management of the ship.
(b) Fire unless caused by the actual fault or privity of the carrier.
(c) Perils, dangers and accidents of the sea or other navigable waters.
(d) Act of God.
(e) Act of war.
(f) Act of public enemies.
(g) Arrest or restraint of princes, rulers or people, or seizure under legal process.
(h) Quarantine restrictions.
(i) Act or omission of the shipper or owner of the goods, his agent or representative.
(j) Strikes or lockouts or stoppage or restraint of labour from whatever cause, whether partial or general.
(k) Riots and civil commotions.
(l) Saving or attempting to save life or property at sea.
(m) Wastage in bulk of weight or any other loss or damage arising from inherent defect, quality or vice of the goods.
(n) Insufficiency of packing.
(o) Insufficiency or inadequacy of marks.
(p) Latent defects not discoverable by due diligence.
(q) Any other cause arising without the actual fault or privity of the carrier, or without the fault or neglect of the agents or servants of the carrier, but the burden of proof shall be on the person claiming the benefit of this exception to show that neither the actual fault or privity of the carrier nor the fault or neglect of the agents or servants of the carrier contributed to the loss or damage.

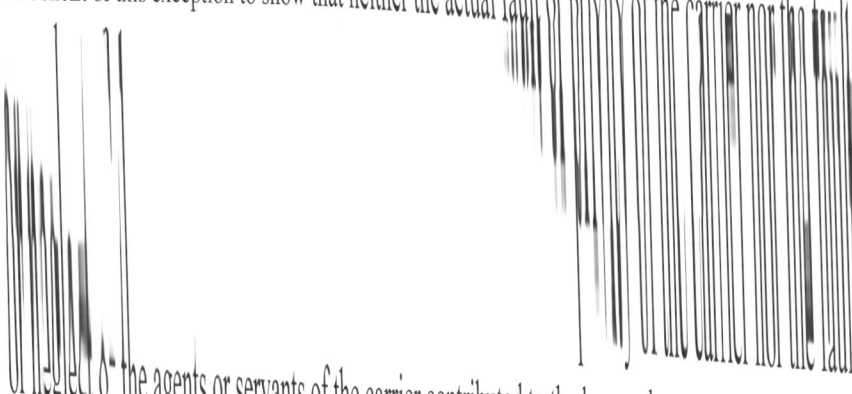

(3) The shipper shall not be responsible for loss or damage sustained by the carrier or the ship arising or resulting from any cause without the act, fault or neglect of the shipper, his agents or his servants.

(4) Any deviation in saving or attempting to save life or property at sea or any reasonable deviation

shall not be deemed to be an infringement or breach of these Rules or of the contract of carriage, and the carrier shall not be liable for any loss or damage resulting therefrom.

(5) (a) Unless the nature and value of such goods have been declared by the shipper before shipment and inserted in the bill of lading, neither the carrier nor the ship shall in any event be or become liable for any loss or damage to or in connection with the goods in an amount exceeding the equivalent of 666.67 units of account per package or unit or 2 units of account per kilo of gross weight of the goods lost or damaged, whichever is the higher.

(b) The total amount recoverable shall be calculated by reference to the value of such goods at the place and time at which the goods are discharged from the ship in accordance with the contract or should have been so discharged.

The value of the goods shall be fixed according to the commodity exchange price, or, if there be no such price, according to the current market price, or, if there be no commodity exchange price or current market price, by reference to the normal value of goods of the same kind and quality.

(c) Where a container, pallet or similar article of transport is used to consolidate goods, the number of packages or units enumerated in the bill of lading as packed in such article of transport shall be deemed the number of packages or units for the purpose of this paragraph as far as these packages or units are concerned. Except as aforesaid such article of transport shall be considered the package or unit.

(d) The unit of account mentioned in this Article is the special drawing right as defined by the International Monetary Fund. The amounts mentioned in sub-paragraph (a) of this paragraph shall be converted into national currency on the basis of the value of that currency on a date to be determined by the law of the Court seized of the case.

(e) Neither the carrier nor the ship shall be entitled to the benefit of the limitation of liability provided for in this paragraph if it is proved that the damage resulted from an act or omission of the carrier done with intent to cause damage, or recklessly and with knowledge that damage would probably result.

(f) The declaration mentioned in sub-paragraph (a) of this paragraph, if embodied in the bill of lading, shall be prima facie evidence, but shall not be binding or conclusive on the carrier.

(g) By agreement between the carrier, master or agent of the carrier and the shipper other maximum amounts than those mentioned in sub-paragraph (a) of this paragraph may be fixed, provided that no maximum amount so fixed shall be less than the appropriate maximum mentioned in that sub-paragraph.

(h) Neither the carrier nor the ship shall be responsible in any event for loss or damage to, or in connection with, goods if the nature or value thereof has been knowingly mis-stated by the shipper in the bill of lading.

(6) Goods of an inflammable, explosive or dangerous nature to the shipment whereof the carrier, master or agent of the carrier has not consented with knowledge of their nature and character, may at any time before discharge be landed at any place, or destroyed or rendered innocuous by the carrier without compensation and the shipper of such goods shall be liable for all damages and expenses directly or indirectly arising out of or resulting from such shipment. If any such goods shipped with such knowledge and consent shall become a danger to the ship or cargo, they may in like manner be landed at any place, or destroyed or rendered innocuous by the carrier without liability on the part of the carrier except to general average, if any.

Article IV *bis*. (1) The defences and limits of liability provided for in these Rules shall apply in any action against the carrier in respect of loss or damage to goods covered by a contract of carriage whether the action be founded in contract or in tort.

(2) If such an action is brought against a servant or agent of the carrier (such servant or agent not being an independent contractor), such servant or agent shall be entitled to avail himself of the defences and limits of liability which the carrier is entitled to invoke under these Rules.

(3) The aggregate of the amounts recoverable from the carrier, and such servants and agents, shall in no case exceed the limit provided for in these Rules.

(4) Nevertheless, a servant or agent of the carrier shall not be entitled to avail himself of the provisions of this article, if it is proved that the damage resulted from an act or omission of the servant or agent done with intent to cause damage or recklessly and with knowledge that damage would probably result.

Article V. A carrier shall be at liberty to surrender in whole or in part all or any of his rights and immunities or to increase any of his responsibilities and obligations under these Rules, provided such surrender or increase shall be embodied in the bill of lading issued to the shipper. The provisions of these Rules shall not be applicable to charter parties, but if bills of lading are issued in the case of a ship under a charter party they shall comply with the terms of these Rules. Nothing in these Rules shall be held to prevent the insertion in a bill of lading of any lawful provision regarding general average.

Article VI. Notwithstanding the provisions of the preceding articles, a carrier, master or agent of the carrier and a shipper shall in regard to any particular goods be at liberty to enter into any agreement in any terms as to the responsibility and liability of the carrier for such goods, and as to the rights and immunities of the carrier in respect of such goods, or his obligation as to seaworthiness, so far as this stipulation is not contrary to public policy, or the care or diligence of his servants or agents in regard to the loading, handling, stowage, carriage, custody, care and discharge of the goods carried by sea, provided that in this case no bill of lading has been or shall be issued and that the terms agreed shall be embodied in a receipt which shall be a non-negotiable document and shall be marked as such. An agreement so entered into shall have full legal effect.

Provided that this article shall not apply to ordinary commercial shipments made in the ordinary course of trade, but only to other shipments where the character or condition of the property to be carried or the circumstances, terms and conditions under which the carriage is to be performed are such as reasonably to justify a special agreement.

Article VII. Nothing herein contained shall prevent a carrier or a shipper from entering into any agreement, stipulation, condition, reservation or exemption as to the responsibility and liability of the carrier or the ship for the loss or damage to, or in connection with, the custody and care and handling of goods prior to the loading on, and subsequent to the discharge from, the ship on which the goods are carried by sea.

Article VIII. The provisions of these Rules shall not affect the rights and obligations of the carrier under any statute for the time being in force relating to the limitation of the liability of owners of sea-going vessels.

Article IX. These Rules shall not affect the provisions of any international Convention or national law governing liability for nuclear damage.

Article X. The provisions of these Rules shall apply to every bill of lading relating to the carriage of goods between ports in two different States if
(a) the bill of lading is issued in a contracting State, or
(b) the carriage is from a port in a contracting State, or
(c) the contract contained in or evidenced by the bill of lading provides that these Rules or legislation of any State giving effect to them are to govern the contract;
whatever may be the nationality of the ship, the carrier, the shipper, the consignee, or any other interested person.

(The last two paragraphs of this Article are not reproduced. They require contracting States to apply the Rules to bills of lading mentioned in the Article and authorise them to apply the Rules to other bills of lading). (Article 11 to 16 of the International Convention for the unification of certain rules of law relating to bills of lading signed at Brussels on August 25, 1974 are not reproduced. They deal with the coming into force of the Convention, procedure for ratification, accession and denunciation and the right to call for a fresh conference to consider amendments to the Rules contained in the Convention).

PART I INTERNATIONAL BUSINESS LAW

United Nations Convention on the Recognition and Enforcement of Foreign Arbitral Awards (New York, 1958)

Article I. (1) This Convention shall apply to the recognition and enforcement of arbitral awards made in the territory of a State other than the State where the recognition and enforcement of such awards are sought, and arising out of differences between persons, whether physical or legal. It shall also apply to arbitral awards not considered as domestic awards in the State where their recognition and enforcement are sought.
(2) The term "arbitral awards" shall include not only awards made by arbitrators appointed for each case but also those made by permanent arbitral bodies to which the parties have submitted.
(3) When signing, ratifying or acceding to this Convention, or notifying extension under article X hereof, any State may on the basis of reciprocity declare that it will apply the Convention to the recognition and enforcement of awards made only in the territory of another Contracting State. It may also declare that it will apply the Convention only to differences arising out of legal relationships, whether contractual or not, which are considered as commercial under the national law of the State making such declaration.

Article II. (1) Each Contracting State shall recognize an agreement in writing under which the parties undertake to submit to arbitration all or any differences which have arisen or which may arise between them in respect of a defined legal relationship, whether contractual or not, concerning a subject matter capable of settlement by arbitration.
(2) The term "agreement in writing" shall include an arbitral clause in a contract or an arbitration agreement, signed by the parties or contained in an exchange of letters or telegrams.
(3) The court of a Contracting State, when seized of an action in a matter in respect of which the parties have made an agreement within the meaning of this article, at the request of one of the parties, refer the parties to arbitration, unless it finds that the said agreement is null and void, inoperative or incapable of being performed.

Article III. Each Contracting State shall recognize arbitral awards as binding and enforce them in accordance with the rules of procedure of the territory where the award is relied upon, under the conditions laid down in the following articles. There shall not be imposed substantially more onerous conditions or higher fees or charges on the recognition or enforcement of arbitral awards to which this Convention applies than are imposed on the recognition or enforcement of domestic arbitral awards.

Article IV. (1) To obtain the recognition and enforcement mentioned in the preceding article, the party applying for recognition and enforcement shall, at the time of the application, supply:
(a) The duly authenticated original award or a duly certified copy thereof;
(b) The original agreement referred to in article II or a duly certified copy thereof.
(2) If the said award or agreement is not made in an official language of the country in which the award is relied upon, the party applying for recognition and enforcement of the award shall produce a translation of these documents into such language. The translation shall be certified by an official or sworn translator or by a diplomatic or consular agent.

Article V. (1) Recognition and enforcement of the award may be refused, at the request of the party against whom it is invoked, only if that party furnishes to the competent authority where the recognition and enforcement is sought, proof that:
(a) The parties to the agreement referred to in article II were, under the law applicable to them, under some incapacity, or the said agreement is not valid under the law to which the parties have subjected it or, failing any indication thereon, under the law of the country where the award was made; or
(b) The party against whom the award is invoked was not given proper notice of the appointment of the arbitrator or of the arbitration proceedings or was otherwise unable to present his case; or
(c) The award deals with a difference not contemplated by or not falling within the terms of the submission to arbitration, or it contains decisions on matters beyond the scope of the submission to arbitration, provided that, if the decisions on matters submitted to arbitration can be separated from those not so submitted, that part of the award which contains decisions on matters submitted to arbitration may be recognized and enforced; or
(d) The composition of the arbitral authority or the arbitral procedure was not in accordance with the agreement of the parties, or, failing such agreement, was not in accordance with the law of the country where the arbitration took place; or
(e) The award has not yet become binding on the parties, or has been set aside or suspended by a

competent authority of the country in which, or under the law of which, that award was made.
(2) Recognition and enforcement of an arbitral award may also be refused if the competent authority in the country where recognition and enforcement is sought finds that:
(a) The subject matter of the difference is not capable of settlement by arbitration under the law of that country; or
(b) The recognition or enforcement of the award would be contrary to the public policy of that country.

Article VI. If an application for the setting aside or suspension of the award has been made to a competent authority referred to in article V (1) (e), the authority before which the award is sought to be relied upon may, if it considers it proper, adjourn the decision on the enforcement of the award and may also, on the application of the party claiming enforcement of the award, order the other party to give suitable security.

Article VII. (1) The provisions of the present Convention shall not affect the validity of multilateral or bilateral agreements concerning the recognition and enforcement of arbitral awards entered into by the Contracting States nor deprive any interested party of any right he may have to avail himself of an arbitral award in the manner and to the extent allowed by the law or the treaties of the country where such award is sought to be relied upon.
(2) The Geneva Protocol on Arbitration Clauses of 1923 and the Geneva Convention on the Execution of Foreign Arbitral Awards of 1927 shall cease to have effect between Contracting States on their becoming bound and to the extent that they become bound, by this Convention.

Article VIII. (1) This Convention shall be open until 31 December 1958 for signature on behalf of any Member of the United Nations and also on behalf of any other State which is or hereafter becomes a member of any specialized agency of the United Nations, or which is or hereafter becomes a party to the Statute of the International Court of Justice, or any other State to which an invitation has been addressed by the General Assembly of the United Nations.
(2) This Convention shall be ratified and the instrument of ratification shall be deposited with the Secretary-General of the United Nations.

Article IX. (1) This Convention shall be open for accession to all States referred to in article VIII.
(2) Accession shall be effected by the deposit of an instrument of accession with the Secretary-General of the United Nations.

Article X. (1) Any State may, at the time of signature, ratification or accession, declare that this Convention shall extend to all or any of the territories for the international relations of which it is responsible. Such a declaration shall take effect when the Convention enters into force for the State concerned.
(2) At any time thereafter any such extension shall be made by notification addressed to the Secretary-General of the United Nations and shall take effect as from the ninetieth day after the day of receipt by the Secretary-General of the United Nations of this notification, or as from the date of entry into force of the Convention for the State concerned, whichever is the later.
(3) With respect to those territories to which this Convention is not extended at the time of signature, ratification or accession, each State concerned shall consider the possibility of taking the necessary steps in order to extend the application of this Convention to such territories, subject, where necessary for constitutional reasons, to the consent of the Governments of such territories.

Article XI. In the case of a federal or non-unitary State, the following provisions shall apply:
(a) With respect to those articles of this Convention that come within the legislative jurisdiction of the federal authority, the obligations of the federal Government shall to this extent be the same as those of Contracting States which are not federal States;
(b) With respect to those articles of this Convention that come within the legislative jurisdiction of constituent states or provinces which are not, under the constitutional system of the federation, bound to take legislative action, the federal Government shall bring such articles with a favourable recommendation to the notice of the appropriate authorities of constituent states or provinces at the earliest possible moment;
(c) A federal State Party to this Convention shall, at the request of any other Contracting State transmitted through the Secretary-General of the United Nations, supply a statement of the law and practice of the federation and its constituent units in regard to any particular provision of this Convention, showing the extent to which effect has been given to that provision by legislative or other action.

Article XII. (1) This Convention shall come into force on the ninetieth day following the date of deposit of the third instrument of ratification or accession.

(2) For each State ratifying or acceding to this Convention after the deposit of the third instrument of ratification or accession, this Convention shall enter into force on the ninetieth day after deposit by such State of its instrument of ratification or accession.

Article XIII. (1) Any Contracting State may denounce this Convention by a written notification to the Secretary-General of the United Nations. Denunciation shall take effect one year after the date of receipt of the notification by the Secretary-General.

(2) Any State which has made a declaration or notification under article X may, at any time thereafter, by notification to the Secretary-General of the United Nations, declare that this Convention shall cease to extend to the territory concerned one year after the date of the receipt of the notification by the Secretary-General.

(3) This Convention shall continue to be applicable to arbitral awards in respect of which recognition and enforcement proceedings have been instituted before the denunciation takes effect.

Article XIV. A Contracting State shall not be entitled to avail itself of the present Convention against other Contracting States except to the extent that it is itself bound to apply the Convention.

Article XV. The Secretary-General of the United Nations shall notify the States contemplated in article VIII of the following:

(a) Signatures and ratifications in accordance with article VIII;
(b) Accessions in accordance with article IX;
(c) Declarations and notifications under articles I, X and XI;
(d) The date upon which this Convention enters into force in accordance with article XII;
(e) Denunciations and notifications in accordance with article XIII.

Article XVI. (1) This Convention, of which the Chinese, English, French, Russian and Spanish texts shall be equally authentic, shall be deposited in the archives of the United Nations.

(2) The Secretary-General of the United Nations shall transmit a certified copy of this Convention to the States contemplated in article VIII.

VOL III PART II

Private International Law

PART II   PRIVATE INTERNATIONAL LAW

Regulation (EU) No 1215/2012 of the European Parliament and of the Council of 12 December 2012 on jurisdiction and the recognition and enforcement of judgments in civil and commercial matters (recast) (OJ L351, 20.12.2012, pp. 1–32) [footnotes omitted].

THE EUROPEAN PARLIAMENT AND THE COUNCIL OF THE EUROPEAN UNION,
Having regard to the Treaty on the Functioning of the European Union, and in particular Article 67(4) and points (a), (c) and (e) of Article 81(2) thereof,
Having regard to the proposal from the European Commission,
After transmission of the draft legislative act to the national parliaments,
Having regard to the opinion of the European Economic and Social Committee,
Acting in accordance with the ordinary legislative procedure,
Whereas:
(1) On 21 April 2009, the Commission adopted a report on the application of Council Regulation (EC) No 44/2001 of 22 December 2000 on jurisdiction and the recognition and enforcement of judgments in civil and commercial matters. The report concluded that, in general, the operation of that Regulation is satisfactory, but that it is desirable to improve the application of certain of its provisions, to further facilitate the free circulation of judgments and to further enhance access to justice. Since a number of amendments are to be made to that Regulation it should, in the interests of clarity, be recast.
(2) At its meeting in Brussels on 10 and 11 December 2009, the European Council adopted a new multiannual programme entitled "The Stockholm Programme – an open and secure Europe serving and protecting citizens". In the Stockholm Programme the European Council considered that the process of abolishing all intermediate measures (the exequatur) should be continued during the period covered by that Programme. At the same time the abolition of the exequatur should also be accompanied by a series of safeguards.
(3) The Union has set itself the objective of maintaining and developing an area of freedom, security and justice, inter alia, by facilitating access to justice, in particular through the principle of mutual recognition of judicial and extra-judicial decisions in civil matters. For the gradual establishment of such an area, the Union is to adopt measures relating to judicial cooperation in civil matters having cross-border implications, particularly when necessary for the proper functioning of the internal market.
(4) Certain differences between national rules governing jurisdiction and recognition of judgments hamper the sound operation of the internal market. Provisions to unify the rules of conflict of jurisdiction in civil and commercial matters, and to ensure rapid and simple recognition and enforcement of judgments given in a Member State, are essential.
(5) Such provisions fall within the area of judicial cooperation in civil matters within the meaning of Article 81 of the Treaty on the Functioning of the European Union (TFEU).
(6) In order to attain the objective of free circulation of judgments in civil and commercial matters, it is necessary and appropriate that the rules governing jurisdiction and the recognition and enforcement of judgments be governed by a legal instrument of the Union which is binding and directly applicable.
(7) On 27 September 1968, the then Member States of the European Communities, acting under Article 220, fourth indent, of the Treaty establishing the European Economic Community, concluded the Brussels Convention on Jurisdiction and the Enforcement of Judgments in Civil and Commercial Matters, subsequently amended by conventions on the accession to that Convention of new Member States ("the 1968 Brussels Convention"). On 16 September 1988, the then Member States of the European Communities and certain EFTA States concluded the Lugano Convention on Jurisdiction and the Enforcement of Judgments in Civil and Commercial Matters ("the 1988 Lugano Convention"), which is a parallel convention to the 1968 Brussels Convention. The 1988 Lugano Convention became applicable to Poland on 1 February 2000.
(8) On 22 December 2000, the Council adopted Regulation (EC) No 44/2001, which replaces the 1968 Brussels Convention with regard to the territories of the Member States covered by the TFEU, as between the Member States except Denmark. By Council Decision 2006/325/EC, the Community concluded an agreement with Denmark ensuring the application of the provisions of Regulation (EC) No 44/2001 in Denmark. The 1988 Lugano Convention was revised by the Convention on Jurisdiction and the Recognition and Enforcement of Judgments in Civil and Commercial Matters, signed at Lugano on 30 October 2007 by the Community, Denmark, Iceland, Norway and Switzerland ("the 2007 Lugano Convention").
(9) The 1968 Brussels Convention continues to apply to the territories of the Member States which fall within the territorial scope of that Convention and which are excluded from this Regulation

pursuant to Article 355 of the TFEU.

(10) The scope of this Regulation should cover all the main civil and commercial matters apart from certain well-defined matters, in particular maintenance obligations, which should be excluded from the scope of this Regulation following the adoption of Council Regulation (EC) No 4/2009 of 18 December 2008 on jurisdiction, applicable law, recognition and enforcement of decisions and cooperation in matters relating to maintenance obligations.

(11) For the purposes of this Regulation, courts or tribunals of the Member States should include courts or tribunals common to several Member States, such as the Benelux Court of Justice when it exercises jurisdiction on matters falling within the scope of this Regulation. Therefore, judgments given by such courts should be recognised and enforced in accordance with this Regulation.

(12) This Regulation should not apply to arbitration. Nothing in this Regulation should prevent the courts of a Member State, when seised of an action in a matter in respect of which the parties have entered into an arbitration agreement, from referring the parties to arbitration, from staying or dismissing the proceedings, or from examining whether the arbitration agreement is null and void, inoperative or incapable of being performed, in accordance with their national law.

A ruling given by a court of a Member State as to whether or not an arbitration agreement is null and void, inoperative or incapable of being performed should not be subject to the rules of recognition and enforcement laid down in this Regulation, regardless of whether the court decided on this as a principal issue or as an incidental question.

On the other hand, where a court of a Member State, exercising jurisdiction under this Regulation or under national law, has determined that an arbitration agreement is null and void, inoperative or incapable of being performed, this should not preclude that court's judgment on the substance of the matter from being recognised or, as the case may be, enforced in accordance with this Regulation. This should be without prejudice to the competence of the courts of the Member States to decide on the recognition and enforcement of arbitral awards in accordance with the Convention on the Recognition and Enforcement of Foreign Arbitral Awards, done at New York on 10 June 1958 ("the 1958 New York Convention"), which takes precedence over this Regulation.

This Regulation should not apply to any action or ancillary proceedings relating to, in particular, the establishment of an arbitral tribunal, the powers of arbitrators, the conduct of an arbitration procedure or any other aspects of such a procedure, nor to any action or judgment concerning the annulment, review, appeal, recognition or enforcement of an arbitral award.

(13) There must be a connection between proceedings to which this Regulation applies and the territory of the Member States. Accordingly, common rules of jurisdiction should, in principle, apply when the defendant is domiciled in a Member State.

(14) A defendant not domiciled in a Member State should in general be subject to the national rules of jurisdiction applicable in the territory of the Member State of the court seised.

However, in order to ensure the protection of consumers and employees, to safeguard the jurisdiction of the courts of the Member States in situations where they have exclusive jurisdiction and to respect the autonomy of the parties, certain rules of jurisdiction in this Regulation should apply regardless of the defendant's domicile.

(15) The rules of jurisdiction should be highly predictable and founded on the principle that jurisdiction is generally based on the defendant's domicile. Jurisdiction should always be available on this ground save in a few well-defined situations in which the subject-matter of the dispute or the autonomy of the parties warrants a different connecting factor. The domicile of a legal person must be defined autonomously so as to make the common rules more transparent and avoid conflicts of jurisdiction.

(16) In addition to the defendant's domicile, there should be alternative grounds of jurisdiction based on a close connection between the court and the action or in order to facilitate the sound administration of justice. The existence of a close connection should ensure legal certainty and avoid the possibility of the defendant being sued in a court of a Member State which he could not reasonably have foreseen. This is important, particularly in disputes concerning non-contractual obligations arising out of violations of privacy and rights relating to personality, including defamation.

(17) The owner of a cultural object as defined in Article 1(1) of Council Directive 93/7/EEC of 15 March 1993 on the return of cultural objects unlawfully removed from the territory of a Member State should be able under this Regulation to initiate proceedings as regards a civil claim for the recovery, based on ownership, of such a cultural object in the courts for the place where the cultural object is situated at the time the court is seised. Such proceedings should be without prejudice to proceedings initiated under Directive 93/7/EEC.

(18) In relation to insurance, consumer and employment contracts, the weaker party should be protected by rules of jurisdiction more favourable to his interests than the general rules.

PART II   PRIVATE INTERNATIONAL LAW

(19) The autonomy of the parties to a contract, other than an insurance, consumer or employment contract, where only limited autonomy to determine the courts having jurisdiction is allowed, should be respected subject to the exclusive grounds of jurisdiction laid down in this Regulation.

(20) Where a question arises as to whether a choice-of-court agreement in favour of a court or the courts of a Member State is null and void as to its substantive validity, that question should be decided in accordance with the law of the Member State of the court or courts designated in the agreement, including the conflict-of-laws rules of that Member State.

(21) In the interests of the harmonious administration of justice it is necessary to minimise the possibility of concurrent proceedings and to ensure that irreconcilable judgments will not be given in different Member States. There should be a clear and effective mechanism for resolving cases of lis pendens and related actions, and for obviating problems flowing from national differences as to the determination of the time when a case is regarded as pending. For the purposes of this Regulation, that time should be defined autonomously.

(22) However, in order to enhance the effectiveness of exclusive choice-of-court agreements and to avoid abusive litigation tactics, it is necessary to provide for an exception to the general lis pendens rule in order to deal satisfactorily with a particular situation in which concurrent proceedings may arise. This is the situation where a court not designated in an exclusive choice-of-court agreement has been seised of proceedings and the designated court is seised subsequently of proceedings involving the same cause of action and between the same parties. In such a case, the court first seised should be required to stay its proceedings as soon as the designated court has been seised and until such time as the latter court declares that it has no jurisdiction under the exclusive choice-of-court agreement. This is to ensure that, in such a situation, the designated court has priority to decide on the validity of the agreement and on the extent to which the agreement applies to the dispute pending before it. The designated court should be able to proceed irrespective of whether the non-designated court has already decided on the stay of proceedings.

This exception should not cover situations where the parties have entered into conflicting exclusive choice-of-court agreements or where a court designated in an exclusive choice-of-court agreement has been seised first. In such cases, the general lis pendens rule of this Regulation should apply.

(23) This Regulation should provide for a flexible mechanism allowing the courts of the Member States to take into account proceedings pending before the courts of third States, considering in particular whether a judgment of a third State will be capable of recognition and enforcement in the Member State concerned under the law of that Member State and the proper administration of justice.

(24) When taking into account the proper administration of justice, the court of the Member State concerned should assess all the circumstances of the case before it. Such circumstances may include connections between the facts of the case and the parties and the third State concerned, the stage to which the proceedings in the third State have progressed by the time proceedings are initiated in the court of the Member State and whether or not the court of the third State can be expected to give a judgment within a reasonable time.

That assessment may also include consideration of the question whether the court of the third State has exclusive jurisdiction in the particular case in circumstances where a court of a Member State would have exclusive jurisdiction.

(25) The notion of provisional, including protective, measures should include, for example, protective orders aimed at obtaining information or preserving evidence as referred to in Articles 6 and 7 of Directive 2004/48/EC of the European Parliament and of the Council of 29 April 2004 on the enforcement of intellectual property rights. It should not include measures which are not of a protective nature, such as measures ordering the hearing of a witness. This should be without prejudice to the application of Council Regulation (EC) No 1206/2001 of 28 May 2001 on cooperation between the courts of the Member States in the taking of evidence in civil or commercial matters.

(26) Mutual trust in the administration of justice in the Union justifies the principle that judgments given in a Member State should be recognised in all Member States without the need for any special procedure. In addition, the aim of making cross-border litigation less time-consuming and costly justifies the abolition of the declaration of enforceability prior to enforcement in the Member State addressed. As a result, a judgment given by the courts of a Member State should be treated as if it had been given in the Member State addressed.

(27) For the purposes of the free circulation of judgments, a judgment given in a Member State should be recognised and enforced in another Member State even if it is given against a person not domiciled in a Member State.

(28) Where a judgment contains a measure or order which is not known in the law of the Member State addressed, that measure or order, including any right indicated therein, should, to the extent

possible, be adapted to one which, under the law of that Member State, has equivalent effects attached to it and pursues similar aims. How, and by whom, the adaptation is to be carried out should be determined by each Member State.

(29) The direct enforcement in the Member State addressed of a judgment given in another Member State without a declaration of enforceability should not jeopardise respect for the rights of the defence. Therefore, the person against whom enforcement is sought should be able to apply for refusal of the recognition or enforcement of a judgment if he considers one of the grounds for refusal of recognition to be present. This should include the ground that he had not had the opportunity to arrange for his defence where the judgment was given in default of appearance in a civil action linked to criminal proceedings. It should also include the grounds which could be invoked on the basis of an agreement between the Member State addressed and a third State concluded pursuant to Article 59 of the 1968 Brussels Convention.

(30) A party challenging the enforcement of a judgment given in another Member State should, to the extent possible and in accordance with the legal system of the Member State addressed, be able to invoke, in the same procedure, in addition to the grounds for refusal provided for in this Regulation, the grounds for refusal available under national law and within the time-limits laid down in that law. The recognition of a judgment should, however, be refused only if one or more of the grounds for refusal provided for in this Regulation are present.

(31) Pending a challenge to the enforcement of a judgment, it should be possible for the courts in the Member State addressed, during the entire proceedings relating to such a challenge, including any appeal, to allow the enforcement to proceed subject to a limitation of the enforcement or to the provision of security.

(32) In order to inform the person against whom enforcement is sought of the enforcement of a judgment given in another Member State, the certificate established under this Regulation, if necessary accompanied by the judgment, should be served on that person in reasonable time before the first enforcement measure. In this context, the first enforcement measure should mean the first enforcement measure after such service.

(33) Where provisional, including protective, measures are ordered by a court having jurisdiction as to the substance of the matter, their free circulation should be ensured under this Regulation. However, provisional, including protective, measures which were ordered by such a court without the defendant being summoned to appear should not be recognised and enforced under this Regulation unless the judgment containing the measure is served on the defendant prior to enforcement. This should not preclude the recognition and enforcement of such measures under national law. Where provisional, including protective, measures are ordered by a court of a Member State not having jurisdiction as to the substance of the matter, the effect of such measures should be confined, under this Regulation, to the territory of that Member State.

(34) Continuity between the 1968 Brussels Convention, Regulation (EC) No 44/2001 and this Regulation should be ensured, and transitional provisions should be laid down to that end. The same need for continuity applies as regards the interpretation by the Court of Justice of the European Union of the 1968 Brussels Convention and of the Regulations replacing it.

(35) Respect for international commitments entered into by the Member States means that this Regulation should not affect conventions relating to specific matters to which the Member States are parties.

(36) Without prejudice to the obligations of the Member States under the Treaties, this Regulation should not affect the application of bilateral conventions and agreements between a third State and a Member State concluded before the date of entry into force of Regulation (EC) No 44/2001 which concern matters governed by this Regulation.

(37) In order to ensure that the certificates to be used in connection with the recognition or enforcement of judgments, authentic instruments and court settlements under this Regulation are kept up-to-date, the power to adopt acts in accordance with Article 290 of the TFEU should be delegated to the Commission in respect of amendments to Annexes I and II to this Regulation. It is of particular importance that the Commission carry out appropriate consultations during its preparatory work, including at expert level. The Commission, when preparing and drawing up delegated acts, should ensure a simultaneous, timely and appropriate transmission of relevant documents to the European Parliament and to the Council.

(38) This Regulation respects fundamental rights and observes the principles recognised in the Charter of Fundamental Rights of the European Union, in particular the right to an effective remedy and to a fair trial guaranteed in Article 47 of the Charter.

(39) Since the objective of this Regulation cannot be sufficiently achieved by the Member States and can be better achieved at Union level, the Union may adopt measures in accordance with the princi-

PART II   PRIVATE INTERNATIONAL LAW

ple of subsidiarity as set out in Article 5 of the Treaty on European Union (TEU). In accordance with the principle of proportionality, as set out in that Article, this Regulation does not go beyond what is necessary in order to achieve that objective.

(40) The United Kingdom and Ireland, in accordance with Article 3 of the Protocol on the position of the United Kingdom and Ireland, annexed to the TEU and to the then Treaty establishing the European Community, took part in the adoption and application of Regulation (EC) No 44/2001. In accordance with Article 3 of Protocol No 21 on the position of the United Kingdom and Ireland in respect of the area of freedom, security and justice, annexed to the TEU and to the TFEU, the United Kingdom and Ireland have notified their wish to take part in the adoption and application of this Regulation.

(41) In accordance with Articles 1 and 2 of Protocol No 22 on the position of Denmark annexed to the TEU and to the TFEU, Denmark is not taking part in the adoption of this Regulation and is not bound by it or subject to its application, without prejudice to the possibility for Denmark of applying the amendments to Regulation (EC) No 44/2001 pursuant to Article 3 of the Agreement of 19 October 2005 between the European Community and the Kingdom of Denmark on jurisdiction and the recognition and enforcement of judgments in civil and commercial matters,

HAVE ADOPTED THIS REGULATION:

Chapter I. Scope and Definitions

Article 1. (1) This Regulation shall apply in civil and commercial matters whatever the nature of the court or tribunal. It shall not extend, in particular, to revenue, customs or administrative matters or to the liability of the State for acts and omissions in the exercise of State authority (*acta iure imperii*).

(2) This Regulation shall not apply to:

(a) the status or legal capacity of natural persons, rights in property arising out of a matrimonial relationship or out of a relationship deemed by the law applicable to such relationship to have comparable effects to marriage;

(b) bankruptcy, proceedings relating to the winding-up of insolvent companies or other legal persons, judicial arrangements, compositions and analogous proceedings;

(c) social security;

(d) arbitration;

(e) maintenance obligations arising from a family relationship, parentage, marriage or affinity;

(f) wills and succession, including maintenance obligations arising by reason of death.

Article 2. For the purposes of this Regulation:

(a) "judgment" means any judgment given by a court or tribunal of a Member State, whatever the judgment may be called, including a decree, order, decision or writ of execution, as well as a decision on the determination of costs or expenses by an officer of the court.

For the purposes of Chapter III, "judgment" includes provisional, including protective, measures ordered by a court or tribunal which by virtue of this Regulation has jurisdiction as to the substance of the matter. It does not include a provisional, including protective, measure which is ordered by such a court or tribunal without the defendant being summoned to appear, unless the judgment containing the measure is served on the defendant prior to enforcement;

(b) "court settlement" means a settlement which has been approved by a court of a Member State or concluded before a court of a Member State in the course of proceedings;

(c) "authentic instrument" means a document which has been formally drawn up or registered as an authentic instrument in the Member State of origin and the authenticity of which:

(i) relates to the signature and the content of the instrument; and

(ii) has been established by a public authority or other authority empowered for that purpose;

(d) "Member State of origin" means the Member State in which, as the case may be, the judgment has been given, the court settlement has been approved or concluded, or the authentic instrument has been formally drawn up or registered;

(e) "Member State addressed" means the Member State in which the recognition of the judgment is invoked or in which the enforcement of the judgment, the court settlement or the authentic instrument is sought;

(f) "court of origin" means the court which has given the judgment the recognition of which is invoked or the enforcement of which is sought.

Article 3. For the purposes of this Regulation, "court" includes the following authorities to the extent that they have jurisdiction in matters falling within the scope of this Regulation:

(a) in Hungary, in summary proceedings concerning orders to pay (fizetési meghagyásos eljárás), the notary (közjegyz);

(b) in Sweden, in summary proceedings concerning orders to pay (betalningsföreläggande) and assistance (handräckning), the Enforcement Authority (Kronofogdemyndigheten).

Chapter II. Jurisdiction

Section 1. General provisions

Article 4. (1) Subject to this Regulation, persons domiciled in a Member State shall, whatever their nationality, be sued in the courts of that Member State.
(2) Persons who are not nationals of the Member State in which they are domiciled shall be governed by the rules of jurisdiction applicable to nationals of that Member State.

Article 5. (1) Persons domiciled in a Member State may be sued in the courts of another Member State only by virtue of the rules set out in Sections 2 to 7 of this Chapter.
(2) In particular, the rules of national jurisdiction of which the Member States are to notify the Commission pursuant to point (a) of Article 76(1) shall not be applicable as against the persons referred to in paragraph (1).

Article 6. (1) If the defendant is not domiciled in a Member State, the jurisdiction of the courts of each Member State shall, subject to Article 18(1), Article 21(2) and Articles 24 and 25, be determined by the law of that Member State.
(2) As against such a defendant, any person domiciled in a Member State may, whatever his nationality, avail himself in that Member State of the rules of jurisdiction there in force, and in particular those of which the Member States are to notify the Commission pursuant to point (a) of Article 76(1), in the same way as nationals of that Member State.

Section 2. Special jurisdiction

Article 7. A person domiciled in a Member State may be sued in another Member State:
(1) (a) in matters relating to a contract, in the courts for the place of performance of the obligation in question;
(b) for the purpose of this provision and unless otherwise agreed, the place of performance of the obligation in question shall be:
- in the case of the sale of goods, the place in a Member State where, under the contract, the goods were delivered or should have been delivered,
- in the case of the provision of services, the place in a Member State where, under the contract, the services were provided or should have been provided;
(c) if point (b) does not apply then point (a) applies;
(2) in matters relating to tort, delict or quasi-delict, in the courts for the place where the harmful event occurred or may occur;
(3) as regards a civil claim for damages or restitution which is based on an act giving rise to criminal proceedings, in the court seised of those proceedings, to the extent that that court has jurisdiction under its own law to entertain civil proceedings;
(4) as regards a civil claim for the recovery, based on ownership, of a cultural object as defined in point 1 of Article 1 of Directive 93/7/EEC initiated by the person claiming the right to recover such an object, in the courts for the place where the cultural object is situated at the time when the court is seised;
(5) as regards a dispute arising out of the operations of a branch, agency or other establishment, in the courts for the place where the branch, agency or other establishment is situated;
(6) as regards a dispute brought against a settlor, trustee or beneficiary of a trust created by the operation of a statute, or by a written instrument, or created orally and evidenced in writing, in the courts of the Member State in which the trust is domiciled;
(7) as regards a dispute concerning the payment of remuneration claimed in respect of the salvage of a cargo or freight, in the court under the authority of which the cargo or freight in question:
(a) has been arrested to secure such payment; or
(b) could have been so arrested, but bail or other security has been given;
provided that this provision shall apply only if it is claimed that the defendant has an interest in the cargo or freight or had such an interest at the time of salvage.

Article 8. A person domiciled in a Member State may also be sued:
(1) where he is one of a number of defendants, in the courts for the place where any one of them is domiciled, provided the claims are so closely connected that it is expedient to hear and determine them together to avoid the risk of irreconcilable judgments resulting from separate proceedings;

PART II   PRIVATE INTERNATIONAL LAW

(2) as a third party in an action on a warranty or guarantee or in any other third-party proceedings, in the court seised of the original proceedings, unless these were instituted solely with the object of removing him from the jurisdiction of the court which would be competent in his case;
(3) on a counter-claim arising from the same contract or facts on which the original claim was based, in the court in which the original claim is pending;
(4) in matters relating to a contract, if the action may be combined with an action against the same defendant in matters relating to rights in rem in immovable property, in the court of the Member State in which the property is situated.

Article 9. Where by virtue of this Regulation a court of a Member State has jurisdiction in actions relating to liability from the use or operation of a ship, that court, or any other court substituted for this purpose by the internal law of that Member State, shall also have jurisdiction over claims for limitation of such liability.

Section 3. Jurisdiction in matters relating to insurance

Article 10. In matters relating to insurance, jurisdiction shall be determined by this Section, without prejudice to Article 6 and point 5 of Article 7.

Article 11. (1) An insurer domiciled in a Member State may be sued:
(a) in the courts of the Member State in which he is domiciled;
(b) in another Member State, in the case of actions brought by the policyholder, the insured or a beneficiary, in the courts for the place where the claimant is domiciled; or
(c) if he is a co-insurer, in the courts of a Member State in which proceedings are brought against the leading insurer.
(2) An insurer who is not domiciled in a Member State but has a branch, agency or other establishment in one of the Member States shall, in disputes arising out of the operations of the branch, agency or establishment, be deemed to be domiciled in that Member State.

Article 12. In respect of liability insurance or insurance of immovable property, the insurer may in addition be sued in the courts for the place where the harmful event occurred. The same applies if movable and immovable property are covered by the same insurance policy and both are adversely affected by the same contingency.

Article 13. (1) In respect of liability insurance, the insurer may also, if the law of the court permits it, be joined in proceedings which the injured party has brought against the insured.
(2) Articles 10, 11 and 12 shall apply to actions brought by the injured party directly against the insurer, where such direct actions are permitted.
(3) If the law governing such direct actions provides that the policyholder or the insured may be joined as a party to the action, the same court shall have jurisdiction over them.

Article 14. (1) Without prejudice to Article 13(3), an insurer may bring proceedings only in the courts of the Member State in which the defendant is domiciled, irrespective of whether he is the policyholder, the insured or a beneficiary.
(2) The provisions of this Section shall not affect the right to bring a counter-claim in the court in which, in accordance with this Section, the original claim is pending.

Article 15. The provisions of this Section may be departed from only by an agreement:
(1) which is entered into after the dispute has arisen;
(2) which allows the policyholder, the insured or a beneficiary to bring proceedings in courts other than those indicated in this Section;
(3) which is concluded between a policyholder and an insurer, both of whom are at the time of conclusion of the contract domiciled or habitually resident in the same Member State, and which has the effect of conferring jurisdiction on the courts of that Member State even if the harmful event were to occur abroad, provided that such an agreement is not contrary to the law of that Member State;
(4) which is concluded with a policyholder who is not domiciled in a Member State, except in so far as the insurance is compulsory or relates to immovable property in a Member State; or
(5) which relates to a contract of insurance in so far as it covers one or more of the risks set out in Article 16.

Article 16. The following are the risks referred to in point 5 of Article 15:
(1) any loss of or damage to:
(a) seagoing ships, installations situated offshore or on the high seas, or aircraft, arising from perils which relate to their use for commercial purposes;

(b) goods in transit other than passengers' baggage where the transit consists of or includes carriage by such ships or aircraft;
(2) any liability, other than for bodily injury to passengers or loss of or damage to their baggage:
(a) arising out of the use or operation of ships, installations or aircraft as referred to in point 1(a) in so far as, in respect of the latter, the law of the Member State in which such aircraft are registered does not prohibit agreements on jurisdiction regarding insurance of such risks;
(b) for loss or damage caused by goods in transit as described in point 1(b);
(3) any financial loss connected with the use or operation of ships, installations or aircraft as referred to in point 1(a), in particular loss of freight or charter-hire;
(4) any risk or interest connected with any of those referred to in points 1 to 3;
(5) notwithstanding points 1 to 4, all "large risks" as defined in Directive 2009/138/EC of the European Parliament and of the Council of 25 November 2009 on the taking-up and pursuit of the business of Insurance and Reinsurance (Solvency II) [14].

Section 4. Jurisdiction over consumer contracts

Article 17. (1) In matters relating to a contract concluded by a person, the consumer, for a purpose which can be regarded as being outside his trade or profession, jurisdiction shall be determined by this Section, without prejudice to Article 6 and point 5 of Article 7, if:
(a) it is a contract for the sale of goods on instalment credit terms;
(b) it is a contract for a loan repayable by instalments, or for any other form of credit, made to finance the sale of goods; or
(c) in all other cases, the contract has been concluded with a person who pursues commercial or professional activities in the Member State of the consumer's domicile or, by any means, directs such activities to that Member State or to several States including that Member State, and the contract falls within the scope of such activities.
(2) Where a consumer enters into a contract with a party who is not domiciled in a Member State but has a branch, agency or other establishment in one of the Member States, that party shall, in disputes arising out of the operations of the branch, agency or establishment, be deemed to be domiciled in that Member State.
(3) This Section shall not apply to a contract of transport other than a contract which, for an inclusive price, provides for a combination of travel and accommodation.

Article 18. (1) A consumer may bring proceedings against the other party to a contract either in the courts of the Member State in which that party is domiciled or, regardless of the domicile of the other party, in the courts for the place where the consumer is domiciled.
(2) Proceedings may be brought against a consumer by the other party to the contract only in the courts of the Member State in which the consumer is domiciled.
(3) This Article shall not affect the right to bring a counter-claim in the court in which, in accordance with this Section, the original claim is pending.

Article 19. The provisions of this Section may be departed from only by an agreement:
(1) which is entered into after the dispute has arisen;
(2) which allows the consumer to bring proceedings in courts other than those indicated in this Section; or
(3) which is entered into by the consumer and the other party to the contract, both of whom are at the time of conclusion of the contract domiciled or habitually resident in the same Member State, and which confers jurisdiction on the courts of that Member State, provided that such an agreement is not contrary to the law of that Member State.

Section 5. Jurisdiction over individual contracts of employment

Article 20. (1) In matters relating to individual contracts of employment, jurisdiction shall be determined by this Section, without prejudice to Article 6, point 5 of Article 7 and, in the case of proceedings brought against an employer, point 1 of Article 8.
(2) Where an employee enters into an individual contract of employment with an employer who is not domiciled in a Member State but has a branch, agency or other establishment in one of the Member States, the employer shall, in disputes arising out of the operations of the branch, agency or establishment, be deemed to be domiciled in that Member State.

Article 21. (1) An employer domiciled in a Member State may be sued:
(a) in the courts of the Member State in which he is domiciled; or
(b) in another Member State:

(i) in the courts for the place where or from where the employee habitually carries out his work or in the courts for the last place where he did so; or
(ii) if the employee does not or did not habitually carry out his work in any one country, in the courts for the place where the business which engaged the employee is or was situated.
(2) An employer not domiciled in a Member State may be sued in a court of a Member State in accordance with point (b) of paragraph (1).

Article 22. (1) An employer may bring proceedings only in the courts of the Member State in which the employee is domiciled.
(2) The provisions of this Section shall not affect the right to bring a counter-claim in the court in which, in accordance with this Section, the original claim is pending.

Article 23. The provisions of this Section may be departed from only by an agreement:
(1) which is entered into after the dispute has arisen; or
(2) which allows the employee to bring proceedings in courts other than those indicated in this Section.

Section 6. Exclusive jurisdiction

Article 24. The following courts of a Member State shall have exclusive jurisdiction, regardless of the domicile of the parties:
(1) in proceedings which have as their object rights in rem in immovable property or tenancies of immovable property, the courts of the Member State in which the property is situated.
However, in proceedings which have as their object tenancies of immovable property concluded for temporary private use for a maximum period of six consecutive months, the courts of the Member State in which the defendant is domiciled shall also have jurisdiction, provided that the tenant is a natural person and that the landlord and the tenant are domiciled in the same Member State;
(2) in proceedings which have as their object the validity of the constitution, the nullity or the dissolution of companies or other legal persons or associations of natural or legal persons, or the validity of the decisions of their organs, the courts of the Member State in which the company, legal person or association has its seat. In order to determine that seat, the court shall apply its rules of private international law;
(3) in proceedings which have as their object the validity of entries in public registers, the courts of the Member State in which the register is kept;
(4) in proceedings concerned with the registration or validity of patents, trade marks, designs, or other similar rights required to be deposited or registered, irrespective of whether the issue is raised by way of an action or as a defence, the courts of the Member State in which the deposit or registration has been applied for, has taken place or is under the terms of an instrument of the Union or an international convention deemed to have taken place.
Without prejudice to the jurisdiction of the European Patent Office under the Convention on the Grant of European Patents, signed at Munich on 5 October 1973, the courts of each Member State shall have exclusive jurisdiction in proceedings concerned with the registration or validity of any European patent granted for that Member State;
(5) in proceedings concerned with the enforcement of judgments, the courts of the Member State in which the judgment has been or is to be enforced.

Section 7. Prorogation of jurisdiction

Article 25. (1) If the parties, regardless of their domicile, have agreed that a court or the courts of a Member State are to have jurisdiction to settle any disputes which have arisen or which may arise in connection with a particular legal relationship, that court or those courts shall have jurisdiction, unless the agreement is null and void as to its substantive validity under the law of that Member State. Such jurisdiction shall be exclusive unless the parties have agreed otherwise. The agreement conferring jurisdiction shall be either:
(a) in writing or evidenced in writing;
(b) in a form which accords with practices which the parties have established between themselves; or
(c) in international trade or commerce, in a form which accords with a usage of which the parties are or ought to have been aware and which in such trade or commerce is widely known to, and regularly observed by, parties to contracts of the type involved in the particular trade or commerce concerned.
(2) Any communication by electronic means which provides a durable record of the agreement shall be equivalent to "writing".
(3) The court or courts of a Member State on which a trust instrument has conferred jurisdiction shall

have exclusive jurisdiction in any proceedings brought against a settlor, trustee or beneficiary, if relations between those persons or their rights or obligations under the trust are involved.
(4) Agreements or provisions of a trust instrument conferring jurisdiction shall have no legal force if they are contrary to Articles 15, 19 or 23, or if the courts whose jurisdiction they purport to exclude have exclusive jurisdiction by virtue of Article 24.
(5) An agreement conferring jurisdiction which forms part of a contract shall be treated as an agreement independent of the other terms of the contract.
The validity of the agreement conferring jurisdiction cannot be contested solely on the ground that the contract is not valid.

Article 26. (1) Apart from jurisdiction derived from other provisions of this Regulation, a court of a Member State before which a defendant enters an appearance shall have jurisdiction. This rule shall not apply where appearance was entered to contest the jurisdiction, or where another court has exclusive jurisdiction by virtue of Article 24.
(2) In matters referred to in Sections 3, 4 or 5 where the policyholder, the insured, a beneficiary of the insurance contract, the injured party, the consumer or the employee is the defendant, the court shall, before assuming jurisdiction under paragraph (1), ensure that the defendant is informed of his right to contest the jurisdiction of the court and of the consequences of entering or not entering an appearance.

Section 8. Examination as to jurisdiction and admissibility

Article 27. Where a court of a Member State is seised of a claim which is principally concerned with a matter over which the courts of another Member State have exclusive jurisdiction by virtue of Article 24, it shall declare of its own motion that it has no jurisdiction.

Article 28. (1) Where a defendant domiciled in one Member State is sued in a court of another Member State and does not enter an appearance, the court shall declare of its own motion that it has no jurisdiction unless its jurisdiction is derived from the provisions of this Regulation.
(2) The court shall stay the proceedings so long as it is not shown that the defendant has been able to receive the document instituting the proceedings or an equivalent document in sufficient time to enable him to arrange for his defence, or that all necessary steps have been taken to this end.
(3) Article 19 of Regulation (EC) No 1393/2007 of the European Parliament and of the Council of 13 November 2007 on the service in the Member States of judicial and extrajudicial documents in civil or commercial matters (service of documents) [15] shall apply instead of paragraph (2) of this Article if the document instituting the proceedings or an equivalent document had to be transmitted from one Member State to another pursuant to that Regulation.
(4) Where Regulation (EC) No 1393/2007 is not applicable, Article 15 of the Hague Convention of 15 November 1965 on the Service Abroad of Judicial and Extrajudicial Documents in Civil or Commercial Matters shall apply if the document instituting the proceedings or an equivalent document had to be transmitted abroad pursuant to that Convention.

Section 9. Lis pendens — **related actions**

Article 29. (1) Without prejudice to Article 31(2), where proceedings involving the same cause of action and between the same parties are brought in the courts of different Member States, any court other than the court first seised shall of its own motion stay its proceedings until such time as the jurisdiction of the court first seised is established.
(2) In cases referred to in paragraph (1), upon request by a court seised of the dispute, any other court seised shall without delay inform the former court of the date when it was seised in accordance with Article 32.
(3) Where the jurisdiction of the court first seised is established, any court other than the court first seised shall decline jurisdiction in favour of that court.

Article 30. (1) Where related actions are pending in the courts of different Member States, any court other than the court first seised may stay its proceedings.
(2) Where the action in the court first seised is pending at first instance, any other court may also, on the application of one of the parties, decline jurisdiction if the court first seised has jurisdiction over the actions in question and its law permits the consolidation thereof.
(3) For the purposes of this Article, actions are deemed to be related where they are so closely connected that it is expedient to hear and determine them together to avoid the risk of irreconcilable judgments resulting from separate proceedings.

PART II   PRIVATE INTERNATIONAL LAW

Article 31. (1) Where actions come within the exclusive jurisdiction of several courts, any court other than the court first seised shall decline jurisdiction in favour of that court.
(2) Without prejudice to Article 26, where a court of a Member State on which an agreement as referred to in Article 25 confers exclusive jurisdiction is seised, any court of another Member State shall stay the proceedings until such time as the court seised on the basis of the agreement declares that it has no jurisdiction under the agreement.
(3) Where the court designated in the agreement has established jurisdiction in accordance with the agreement, any court of another Member State shall decline jurisdiction in favour of that court.
(4) Paragraphs 2 and 3 shall not apply to matters referred to in Sections 3, 4 or 5 where the policyholder, the insured, a beneficiary of the insurance contract, the injured party, the consumer or the employee is the claimant and the agreement is not valid under a provision contained within those Sections.

Article 32. (1) For the purposes of this Section, a court shall be deemed to be seised:
(a) at the time when the document instituting the proceedings or an equivalent document is lodged with the court, provided that the claimant has not subsequently failed to take the steps he was required to take to have service effected on the defendant; or
(b) if the document has to be served before being lodged with the court, at the time when it is received by the authority responsible for service, provided that the claimant has not subsequently failed to take the steps he was required to take to have the document lodged with the court.
The authority responsible for service referred to in point (b) shall be the first authority receiving the documents to be served.
(2) The court, or the authority responsible for service, referred to in paragraph (1), shall note, respectively, the date of the lodging of the document instituting the proceedings or the equivalent document, or the date of receipt of the documents to be served.

Article 33. (1) Where jurisdiction is based on Article 4 or on Articles 7, 8 or 9 and proceedings are pending before a court of a third State at the time when a court in a Member State is seised of an action involving the same cause of action and between the same parties as the proceedings in the court of the third State, the court of the Member State may stay the proceedings if:
(a) it is expected that the court of the third State will give a judgment capable of recognition and, where applicable, of enforcement in that Member State; and
(b) the court of the Member State is satisfied that a stay is necessary for the proper administration of justice.
(2) The court of the Member State may continue the proceedings at any time if:
(a) the proceedings in the court of the third State are themselves stayed or discontinued;
(b) it appears to the court of the Member State that the proceedings in the court of the third State are unlikely to be concluded within a reasonable time; or
(c) the continuation of the proceedings is required for the proper administration of justice.
(3) The court of the Member State shall dismiss the proceedings if the proceedings in the court of the third State are concluded and have resulted in a judgment capable of recognition and, where applicable, of enforcement in that Member State.
(4) The court of the Member State shall apply this Article on the application of one of the parties or, where possible under national law, of its own motion.

Article 34. (1) Where jurisdiction is based on Article 4 or on Articles 7, 8 or 9 and an action is pending before a court of a third State at the time when a court in a Member State is seised of an action which is related to the action in the court of the third State, the court of the Member State may stay the proceedings if:
(a) it is expedient to hear and determine the related actions together to avoid the risk of irreconcilable judgments resulting from separate proceedings;
(b) it is expected that the court of the third State will give a judgment capable of recognition and, where applicable, of enforcement in that Member State; and
(c) the court of the Member State is satisfied that a stay is necessary for the proper administration of justice.
(2) The court of the Member State may continue the proceedings at any time if:
(a) it appears to the court of the Member State that there is no longer a risk of irreconcilable judgments;
(b) the proceedings in the court of the third State are themselves stayed or discontinued;
(c) it appears to the court of the Member State that the proceedings in the court of the third State are unlikely to be concluded within a reasonable time; or

(d) the continuation of the proceedings is required for the proper administration of justice.
(3) The court of the Member State may dismiss the proceedings if the proceedings in the court of the third State are concluded and have resulted in a judgment capable of recognition and, where applicable, of enforcement in that Member State.
(4) The court of the Member State shall apply this Article on the application of one of the parties or, where possible under national law, of its own motion.

Section 10. Provisional, including protective, measures

Article 35. Application may be made to the courts of a Member State for such provisional, including protective, measures as may be available under the law of that Member State, even if the courts of another Member State have jurisdiction as to the substance of the matter.

Chapter III. Recognition and Enforcement

Section 1. Recognition

Article 36. (1) A judgment given in a Member State shall be recognised in the other Member States without any special procedure being required.
(2) Any interested party may, in accordance with the procedure provided for in Subsection 2 of Section 3, apply for a decision that there are no grounds for refusal of recognition as referred to in Article 45.
(3) If the outcome of proceedings in a court of a Member State depends on the determination of an incidental question of refusal of recognition, that court shall have jurisdiction over that question.

Article 37. (1) A party who wishes to invoke in a Member State a judgment given in another Member State shall produce:
(a) a copy of the judgment which satisfies the conditions necessary to establish its authenticity; and
(b) the certificate issued pursuant to Article 53.
(2) The court or authority before which a judgment given in another Member State is invoked may, where necessary, require the party invoking it to provide, in accordance with Article 57, a translation or a transliteration of the contents of the certificate referred to in point (b) of paragraph (1). The court or authority may require the party to provide a translation of the judgment instead of a translation of the contents of the certificate if it is unable to proceed without such a translation.

Article 38. The court or authority before which a judgment given in another Member State is invoked may suspend the proceedings, in whole or in part, if:
(a) the judgment is challenged in the Member State of origin; or
(b) an application has been submitted for a decision that there are no grounds for refusal of recognition as referred to in Article 45 or for a decision that the recognition is to be refused on the basis of one of those grounds.

Section 2. Enforcement

Article 39. A judgment given in a Member State which is enforceable in that Member State shall be enforceable in the other Member States without any declaration of enforceability being required.

Article 40. An enforceable judgment shall carry with it by operation of law the power to proceed to any protective measures which exist under the law of the Member State addressed.

Article 41. (1) Subject to the provisions of this Section, the procedure for the enforcement of judgments given in another Member State shall be governed by the law of the Member State addressed. A judgment given in a Member State which is enforceable in the Member State addressed shall be enforced there under the same conditions as a judgment given in the Member State addressed.
(2) Notwithstanding paragraph (1), the grounds for refusal or of suspension of enforcement under the law of the Member State addressed shall apply in so far as they are not incompatible with the grounds referred to in Article 45.
(3) The party seeking the enforcement of a judgment given in another Member State shall not be required to have a postal address in the Member State addressed. Nor shall that party be required to have an authorised representative in the Member State addressed unless such a representative is mandatory irrespective of the nationality or the domicile of the parties.

Article 42. (1) For the purposes of enforcement in a Member State of a judgment given in another Member State, the applicant shall provide the competent enforcement authority with:
(a) a copy of the judgment which satisfies the conditions necessary to establish its authenticity; and

PART II   PRIVATE INTERNATIONAL LAW

(b) the certificate issued pursuant to Article 53, certifying that the judgment is enforceable and containing an extract of the judgment as well as, where appropriate, relevant information on the recoverable costs of the proceedings and the calculation of interest.
(2) For the purposes of enforcement in a Member State of a judgment given in another Member State ordering a provisional, including a protective, measure, the applicant shall provide the competent enforcement authority with:
(a) a copy of the judgment which satisfies the conditions necessary to establish its authenticity;
(b) the certificate issued pursuant to Article 53, containing a description of the measure and certifying that:
(i) the court has jurisdiction as to the substance of the matter;
(ii) the judgment is enforceable in the Member State of origin; and
(c) where the measure was ordered without the defendant being summoned to appear, proof of service of the judgment.
(3) The competent enforcement authority may, where necessary, require the applicant to provide, in accordance with Article 57, a translation or a transliteration of the contents of the certificate.
(4) The competent enforcement authority may require the applicant to provide a translation of the judgment only if it is unable to proceed without such a translation.

Article 43. (1) Where enforcement is sought of a judgment given in another Member State, the certificate issued pursuant to Article 53 shall be served on the person against whom the enforcement is sought prior to the first enforcement measure. The certificate shall be accompanied by the judgment, if not already served on that person.
(2) Where the person against whom enforcement is sought is domiciled in a Member State other than the Member State of origin, he may request a translation of the judgment in order to contest the enforcement if the judgment is not written in or accompanied by a translation into either of the following languages:
(a) a language which he understands; or
(b) the official language of the Member State in which he is domiciled or, where there are several official languages in that Member State, the official language or one of the official languages of the place where he is domiciled.
Where a translation of the judgment is requested under the first subparagraph, no measures of enforcement may be taken other than protective measures until that translation has been provided to the person against whom enforcement is sought.
This paragraph shall not apply if the judgment has already been served on the person against whom enforcement is sought in one of the languages referred to in the first subparagraph or is accompanied by a translation into one of those languages.
(3) This Article shall not apply to the enforcement of a protective measure in a judgment or where the person seeking enforcement proceeds to protective measures in accordance with Article 40.

Article 44. (1) In the event of an application for refusal of enforcement of a judgment pursuant to Subsection 2 of Section 3, the court in the Member State addressed may, on the application of the person against whom enforcement is sought:
(a) limit the enforcement proceedings to protective measures;
(b) make enforcement conditional on the provision of such security as it shall determine; or
(c) suspend, either wholly or in part, the enforcement proceedings.
(2) The competent authority in the Member State addressed shall, on the application of the person against whom enforcement is sought, suspend the enforcement proceedings where the enforceability of the judgment is suspended in the Member State of origin.

Section 3. Refusal of recognition and enforcement

Subsection 1. Refusal of recognition

Article 45. (1) On the application of any interested party, the recognition of a judgment shall be refused:
(a) if such recognition is manifestly contrary to public policy (*ordre public*) in the Member State addressed;
(b) where the judgment was given in default of appearance, if the defendant was not served with the document which instituted the proceedings or with an equivalent document in sufficient time and in such a way as to enable him to arrange for his defence, unless the defendant failed to commence proceedings to challenge the judgment when it was possible for him to do so;
(c) if the judgment is irreconcilable with a judgment given between the same parties in the Member

State addressed;
(d) if the judgment is irreconcilable with an earlier judgment given in another Member State or in a third State involving the same cause of action and between the same parties, provided that the earlier judgment fulfils the conditions necessary for its recognition in the Member State addressed; or
(e) if the judgment conflicts with:
(i) Sections 3, 4 or 5 of Chapter II where the policyholder, the insured, a beneficiary of the insurance contract, the injured party, the consumer or the employee was the defendant; or
(ii) Section 6 of Chapter II.
(2) In its examination of the grounds of jurisdiction referred to in point (e) of paragraph (1), the court to which the application was submitted shall be bound by the findings of fact on which the court of origin based its jurisdiction.
(3) Without prejudice to point (e) of paragraph (1), the jurisdiction of the court of origin may not be reviewed. The test of public policy referred to in point (a) of paragraph (1) may not be applied to the rules relating to jurisdiction.
(4) The application for refusal of recognition shall be made in accordance with the procedures provided for in Subsection 2 and, where appropriate, Section 4.

Subsection 2. Refusal of enforcement

Article 46. On the application of the person against whom enforcement is sought, the enforcement of a judgment shall be refused where one of the grounds referred to in Article 45 is found to exist.

Article 47. (1) The application for refusal of enforcement shall be submitted to the court which the Member State concerned has communicated to the Commission pursuant to point (a) of Article 75 as the court to which the application is to be submitted.
(2) The procedure for refusal of enforcement shall, in so far as it is not covered by this Regulation, be governed by the law of the Member State addressed.
(3) The applicant shall provide the court with a copy of the judgment and, where necessary, a translation or transliteration of it.
The court may dispense with the production of the documents referred to in the first subparagraph if it already possesses them or if it considers it unreasonable to require the applicant to provide them. In the latter case, the court may require the other party to provide those documents.
(4) The party seeking the refusal of enforcement of a judgment given in another Member State shall not be required to have a postal address in the Member State addressed. Nor shall that party be required to have an authorised representative in the Member State addressed unless such a representative is mandatory irrespective of the nationality or the domicile of the parties.

Article 48. The court shall decide on the application for refusal of enforcement without delay.

Article 49. (1) The decision on the application for refusal of enforcement may be appealed against by either party.
(2) The appeal is to be lodged with the court which the Member State concerned has communicated to the Commission pursuant to point (b) of Article 75 as the court with which such an appeal is to be lodged.

Article 50. The decision given on the appeal may only be contested by an appeal where the courts with which any further appeal is to be lodged have been communicated by the Member State concerned to the Commission pursuant to point (c) of Article 75.

Article 51. (1) The court to which an application for refusal of enforcement is submitted or the court which hears an appeal lodged under Article 49 or Article 50 may stay the proceedings if an ordinary appeal has been lodged against the judgment in the Member State of origin or if the time for such an appeal has not yet expired. In the latter case, the court may specify the time within which such an appeal is to be lodged.
(2) Where the judgment was given in Ireland, Cyprus or the United Kingdom, any form of appeal available in the Member State of origin shall be treated as an ordinary appeal for the purposes of paragraph (1).

Section 4. Common provisions

Article 52. Under no circumstances may a judgment given in a Member State be reviewed as to its substance in the Member State addressed.

Article 53. The court of origin shall, at the request of any interested party, issue the certificate using the form set out in Annex I.

PART II PRIVATE INTERNATIONAL LAW

Article 54. (1) If a judgment contains a measure or an order which is not known in the law of the Member State addressed, that measure or order shall, to the extent possible, be adapted to a measure or an order known in the law of that Member State which has equivalent effects attached to it and which pursues similar aims and interests.
Such adaptation shall not result in effects going beyond those provided for in the law of the Member State of origin.
(2) Any party may challenge the adaptation of the measure or order before a court.
(3) If necessary, the party invoking the judgment or seeking its enforcement may be required to provide a translation or a transliteration of the judgment.

Article 55. A judgment given in a Member State which orders a payment by way of a penalty shall be enforceable in the Member State addressed only if the amount of the payment has been finally determined by the court of origin.

Article 56. No security, bond or deposit, however described, shall be required of a party who in one Member State applies for the enforcement of a judgment given in another Member State on the ground that he is a foreign national or that he is not domiciled or resident in the Member State addressed.

Article 57. (1) When a translation or a transliteration is required under this Regulation, such translation or transliteration shall be into the official language of the Member State concerned or, where there are several official languages in that Member State, into the official language or one of the official languages of court proceedings of the place where a judgment given in another Member State is invoked or an application is made, in accordance with the law of that Member State.
(2) For the purposes of the forms referred to in Articles 53 and 60, translations or transliterations may also be into any other official language or languages of the institutions of the Union that the Member State concerned has indicated it can accept.
(3) Any translation made under this Regulation shall be done by a person qualified to do translations in one of the Member States.

Chapter IV. Authentic Instruments and Court Settlements

Article 58. (1) An authentic instrument which is enforceable in the Member State of origin shall be enforceable in the other Member States without any declaration of enforceability being required. Enforcement of the authentic instrument may be refused only if such enforcement is manifestly contrary to public policy (*ordre public*) in the Member State addressed.
The provisions of Section 2, Subsection 2 of Section 3, and Section 4 of Chapter III shall apply as appropriate to authentic instruments.
(2) The authentic instrument produced must satisfy the conditions necessary to establish its authenticity in the Member State of origin.

Article 59. A court settlement which is enforceable in the Member State of origin shall be enforced in the other Member States under the same conditions as authentic instruments.

Article 60. The competent authority or court of the Member State of origin shall, at the request of any interested party, issue the certificate using the form set out in Annex II containing a summary of the enforceable obligation recorded in the authentic instrument or of the agreement between the parties recorded in the court settlement.

Chapter V. General Provisions

Article 61. No legalisation or other similar formality shall be required for documents issued in a Member State in the context of this Regulation.

Article 62. (1) In order to determine whether a party is domiciled in the Member State whose courts are seised of a matter, the court shall apply its internal law.
(2) If a party is not domiciled in the Member State whose courts are seised of the matter, then, in order to determine whether the party is domiciled in another Member State, the court shall apply the law of that Member State.

Article 63. (1) For the purposes of this Regulation, a company or other legal person or association of natural or legal persons is domiciled at the place where it has its:
(a) statutory seat;
(b) central administration; or

(c) principal place of business.
(2) For the purposes of Ireland, Cyprus and the United Kingdom, "statutory seat" means the registered office or, where there is no such office anywhere, the place of incorporation or, where there is no such place anywhere, the place under the law of which the formation took place.
(3) In order to determine whether a trust is domiciled in the Member State whose courts are seised of the matter, the court shall apply its rules of private international law.

Article 64. Without prejudice to any more favourable provisions of national laws, persons domiciled in a Member State who are being prosecuted in the criminal courts of another Member State of which they are not nationals for an offence which was not intentionally committed may be defended by persons qualified to do so, even if they do not appear in person. However, the court seised of the matter may order appearance in person; in the case of failure to appear, a judgment given in the civil action without the person concerned having had the opportunity to arrange for his defence need not be recognised or enforced in the other Member States.

Article 65. (1) The jurisdiction specified in point 2 of Article 8 and Article 13 in actions on a warranty or guarantee or in any other third-party proceedings may be resorted to in the Member States included in the list established by the Commission pursuant to point (b) of Article 76(1) and Article 76(2) only in so far as permitted under national law. A person domiciled in another Member State may be invited to join the proceedings before the courts of those Member States pursuant to the rules on third-party notice referred to in that list.
(2) Judgments given in a Member State by virtue of point 2 of Article 8 or Article 13 shall be recognised and enforced in accordance with Chapter III in any other Member State. Any effects which judgments given in the Member States included in the list referred to in paragraph (1) may have, in accordance with the law of those Member States, on third parties by application of paragraph (1) shall be recognised in all Member States.
(3) The Member States included in the list referred to in paragraph (1) shall, within the framework of the European Judicial Network in civil and commercial matters established by Council Decision 2001/470/EC [16] ("the European Judicial Network") provide information on how to determine, in accordance with their national law, the effects of the judgments referred to in the second sentence of paragraph (2).

Chapter VI. Transitional Provisions

Article 66. (1) This Regulation shall apply only to legal proceedings instituted, to authentic instruments formally drawn up or registered and to court settlements approved or concluded on or after 10 January 2015.
(2) Notwithstanding Article 80, Regulation (EC) No 44/2001 shall continue to apply to judgments given in legal proceedings instituted, to authentic instruments formally drawn up or registered and to court settlements approved or concluded before 10 January 2015 which fall within the scope of that Regulation.

Chapter VII. Relationship with other Instruments

Article 67. This Regulation shall not prejudice the application of provisions governing jurisdiction and the recognition and enforcement of judgments in specific matters which are contained in instruments of the Union or in national legislation harmonised pursuant to such instruments.

Article 68 (1) This Regulation shall, as between the Member States, supersede the 1968 Brussels Convention, except as regards the territories of the Member States which fall within the territorial scope of that Convention and which are excluded from this Regulation pursuant to Article 355 of the TFEU.
(2) In so far as this Regulation replaces the provisions of the 1968 Brussels Convention between the Member States, any reference to that Convention shall be understood as a reference to this Regulation.

Article 69. Subject to Articles 70 and 71, this Regulation shall, as between the Member States, supersede the conventions that cover the same matters as those to which this Regulation applies. In particular, the conventions included in the list established by the Commission pursuant to point (c) of Article 76(1) and Article 76(2) shall be superseded.

Article 70. (1) The conventions referred to in Article 69 shall continue to have effect in relation to matters to which this Regulation does not apply.
(2) They shall continue to have effect in respect of judgments given, authentic instruments formally

drawn up or registered and court settlements approved or concluded before the date of entry into force of Regulation (EC) No 44/2001.

Article 71. (1) This Regulation shall not affect any conventions to which the Member States are parties and which, in relation to particular matters, govern jurisdiction or the recognition or enforcement of judgments.
(2) With a view to its uniform interpretation, paragraph (1) shall be applied in the following manner:
(a) this Regulation shall not prevent a court of a Member State which is party to a convention on a particular matter from assuming jurisdiction in accordance with that convention, even where the defendant is domiciled in another Member State which is not party to that convention. The court hearing the action shall, in any event, apply Article 28 of this Regulation;
(b) judgments given in a Member State by a court in the exercise of jurisdiction provided for in a convention on a particular matter shall be recognised and enforced in the other Member States in accordance with this Regulation.
Where a convention on a particular matter to which both the Member State of origin and the Member State addressed are parties lays down conditions for the recognition or enforcement of judgments, those conditions shall apply. In any event, the provisions of this Regulation on recognition and enforcement of judgments may be applied.

Article 72. This Regulation shall not affect agreements by which Member States, prior to the entry into force of Regulation (EC) No 44/2001, undertook pursuant to Article 59 of the 1968 Brussels Convention not to recognise judgments given, in particular in other Contracting States to that Convention, against defendants domiciled or habitually resident in a third State where, in cases provided for in Article 4 of that Convention, the judgment could only be founded on a ground of jurisdiction specified in the second paragraph of Article 3 of that Convention.

Article 73. (1) This Regulation shall not affect the application of the 2007 Lugano Convention.
(2) This Regulation shall not affect the application of the 1958 New York Convention.
(3) This Regulation shall not affect the application of bilateral conventions and agreements between a third State and a Member State concluded before the date of entry into force of Regulation (EC) No 44/2001 which concern matters governed by this Regulation.

Chapter VIII. Final Provisions

Article 74. The Member States shall provide, within the framework of the European Judicial Network and with a view to making the information available to the public, a description of national rules and procedures concerning enforcement, including authorities competent for enforcement, and information on any limitations on enforcement, in particular debtor protection rules and limitation or prescription periods.
The Member States shall keep this information permanently updated.

Article 75. By 10 January 2014, the Member States shall communicate to the Commission:
(a) the courts to which the application for refusal of enforcement is to be submitted pursuant to Article 47(1);
(b) the courts with which an appeal against the decision on the application for refusal of enforcement is to be lodged pursuant to Article 49(2);
(c) the courts with which any further appeal is to be lodged pursuant to Article 50; and
(d) the languages accepted for translations of the forms as referred to in Article 57(2).
The Commission shall make the information publicly available through any appropriate means, in particular through the European Judicial Network.

Article 76. (1) The Member States shall notify the Commission of:
(a) the rules of jurisdiction referred to in Articles 5(2) and 6(2);
(b) the rules on third-party notice referred to in Article 65; and
(c) the conventions referred to in Article 69.
(2) The Commission shall, on the basis of the notifications by the Member States referred to in paragraph (1), establish the corresponding lists.
(3) The Member States shall notify the Commission of any subsequent amendments required to be made to those lists. The Commission shall amend those lists accordingly.
(4) The Commission shall publish the lists and any subsequent amendments made to them in the *Official Journal of the European Union*.
(5) The Commission shall make all information notified pursuant to paragraphs 1 and 3 publicly available through any other appropriate means, in particular through the European Judicial Network.

Article 77. The Commission shall be empowered to adopt delegated acts in accordance with Article 78 concerning the amendment of Annexes I and II.

Article 78. (1) The power to adopt delegated acts is conferred on the Commission subject to the conditions laid down in this Article.

(2) The power to adopt delegated acts referred to in Article 77 shall be conferred on the Commission for an indeterminate period of time from 9 January 2013.

(3) The delegation of power referred to in Article 77 may be revoked at any time by the European Parliament or by the Council. A decision to revoke shall put an end to the delegation of the power specified in that decision. It shall take effect the day following the publication of the decision in the *Official Journal of the European Union* or at a later date specified therein. It shall not affect the validity of any delegated acts already in force.

(4) As soon as it adopts a delegated act, the Commission shall notify it simultaneously to the European Parliament and to the Council.

(5) A delegated act adopted pursuant to Article 77 shall enter into force only if no objection has been expressed either by the European Parliament or the Council within a period of two months of notification of that act to the European Parliament and the Council or if, before the expiry of that period, the European Parliament and the Council have both informed the Commission that they will not object. That period shall be extended by two months at the initiative of the European Parliament or of the Council.

Article 79. By 11 January 2022 the Commission shall present a report to the European Parliament, to the Council and to the European Economic and Social Committee on the application of this Regulation. That report shall include an evaluation of the possible need for a further extension of the rules on jurisdiction to defendants not domiciled in a Member State, taking into account the operation of this Regulation and possible developments at international level. Where appropriate, the report shall be accompanied by a proposal for amendment of this Regulation.

Article 80. This Regulation shall repeal Regulation (EC) No 44/2001. References to the repealed Regulation shall be construed as references to this Regulation and shall be read in accordance with the correlation table set out in Annex III.

Article 81. This Regulation shall enter into force on the twentieth day following that of its publication in the *Official Journal of the European Union*. It shall apply from 10 January 2015, with the exception of Articles 75 and 76, which shall apply from 10 January 2014.

This Regulation shall be binding in its entirety and directly applicable in the Member States in accordance with the Treaties.

[The annex is omitted.]

PART II   PRIVATE INTERNATIONAL LAW

Council Regulation (EC) No 2201/2003 of 27 November 2003 concerning jurisdiction and the recognition and enforcement of judgments in matrimonial matters and the matters of parental responsibility, repealing Regulation (EC) No 1347/2000 [Brussels II bis] (OJ L 338, 23.12.2003, p. 1–29) [footnotes omitted].

THE COUNCIL OF THE EUROPEAN UNION,
Having regard to the Treaty establishing the European Community, and in particular Article 61(c) and Article 67(1) thereof,
Having regard to the proposal from the Commission,
Having regard to the opinion of the European Parliament,
Having regard to the opinion of the European Economic and Social Committee,
Whereas:
(1) The European Community has set the objective of creating an area of freedom, security and justice, in which the free movement of persons is ensured. To this end, the Community is to adopt, among others, measures in the field of judicial cooperation in civil matters that are necessary for the proper functioning of the internal market.
(2) The Tampere European Council endorsed the principle of mutual recognition of judicial decisions as the cornerstone for the creation of a genuine judicial area, and identified visiting rights as a priority.
(3) Council Regulation (EC) No 1347/2000 sets out rules on jurisdiction, recognition and enforcement of judgments in matrimonial matters and matters of parental responsibility for the children of both spouses rendered on the occasion of the matrimonial proceedings. The content of this Regulation was substantially taken over from the Convention of 28 May 1998 on the same subject matter.
(4) On 3 July 2000 France presented an initiative for a Council Regulation on the mutual enforcement of judgments on rights of access to children.
(5) In order to ensure equality for all children, this Regulation covers all decisions on parental responsibility, including measures for the protection of the child, independently of any link with a matrimonial proceeding.
(6) Since the application of the rules on parental responsibility often arises in the context of matrimonial proceedings, it is more appropriate to have a single instrument for matters of divorce and parental responsibility.
(7) The scope of this Regulation covers civil matters, whatever the nature of the court or tribunal
(8) As regards judgments on divorce, legal separation or marriage annulment, this Regulation should apply only to the dissolution of matrimonial ties and should not deal with issues such as the grounds for divorce, property consequences of the marriage or any other ancillary measures.
(9) As regards the property of the child, this Regulation should apply only to measures for the protection of the child, i.e. (i) the designation and functions of a person or body having charge of the child's property, representing or assisting the child, and (ii) the administration, conservation or disposal of the child's property. In this context, this Regulation should, for instance, apply in cases where the parents are in dispute as regards the administration of the child's property. Measures relating to the child's property which do not concern the protection of the child should continue to be governed by Council Regulation (EC) No 44/2001 of 22 December 2000 on jurisdiction and the recognition and enforcement of judgments in civil and commercial matters.
(10) This Regulation is not intended to apply to matters relating to social security, public measures of a general nature in matters of education or health or to decisions on the right of asylum and on immigration. In addition it does not apply to the establishment of parenthood, since this is a different matter from the attribution of parental responsibility, nor to other questions linked to the status of persons. Moreover, it does not apply to measures taken as a result of criminal offences committed by children.
(11) Maintenance obligations are excluded from the scope of this Regulation as these are already covered by Council Regulation No 44/2001. The courts having jurisdiction under this Regulation will generally have jurisdiction to rule on maintenance obligations by application of Article 5(2) of Council Regulation No 44/2001.
(12) The grounds of jurisdiction in matters of parental responsibility established in the present Regulation are shaped in the light of the best interests of the child, in particular on the criterion of proximity. This means that jurisdiction should lie in the first place with the Member State of the child's habitual residence, except for certain cases of a change in the child's residence or pursuant to an agreement between the holders of parental responsibility.
(13) In the interest of the child, this Regulation allows, by way of exception and under certain conditions, that the court having jurisdiction may transfer a case to a court of another Member State if this

court is better placed to hear the case. However, in this case the second court should not be allowed to transfer the case to a third court.

(14) This Regulation should have effect without prejudice to the application of public international law concerning diplomatic immunities. Where jurisdiction under this Regulation cannot be exercised by reason of the existence of diplomatic immunity in accordance with international law, jurisdiction should be exercised in accordance with national law in a Member State in which the person concerned does not enjoy such immunity.

(15) Council Regulation (EC) No 1348/2000 of 29 May 2000 on the service in the Member States of judicial and extrajudicial documents in civil or commercial matters should apply to the service of documents in proceedings instituted pursuant to this Regulation.

(16) This Regulation should not prevent the courts of a Member State from taking provisional, including protective measures, in urgent cases, with regard to persons or property situated in that State.

(17) In cases of wrongful removal or retention of a child, the return of the child should be obtained without delay, and to this end the Hague Convention of 25 October 1980 would continue to apply as complemented by the provisions of this Regulation, in particular Article 11. The courts of the Member State to or in which the child has been wrongfully removed or retained should be able to oppose his or her return in specific, duly justified cases. However, such a decision could be replaced by a subsequent decision by the court of the Member State of habitual residence of the child prior to the wrongful removal or retention. Should that judgment entail the return of the child, the return should take place without any special procedure being required for recognition and enforcement of that judgment in the Member State to or in which the child has been removed or retained.

(18) Where a court has decided not to return a child on the basis of Article 13 of the 1980 Hague Convention, it should inform the court having jurisdiction or central authority in the Member State where the child was habitually resident prior to the wrongful removal or retention. Unless the court in the latter Member State has been seised, this court or the central authority should notify the parties. This obligation should not prevent the central authority from also notifying the relevant public authorities in accordance with national law.

(19) The hearing of the child plays an important role in the application of this Regulation, although this instrument is not intended to modify national procedures applicable.

(20) The hearing of a child in another Member State may take place under the arrangements laid down in Council Regulation (EC) No 1206/2001 of 28 May 2001 on cooperation between the courts of the Member States in the taking of evidence in civil or commercial matters.

(21) The recognition and enforcement of judgments given in a Member State should be based on the principle of mutual trust and the grounds for non-recognition should be kept to the minimum required.

(22) Authentic instruments and agreements between parties that are enforceable in one Member State should be treated as equivalent to "judgments" for the purpose of the application of the rules on recognition and enforcement.

(23) The Tampere European Council considered in its conclusions (point 34) that judgments in the field of family litigation should be "automatically recognised throughout the Union without any intermediate proceedings or grounds for refusal of enforcement". This is why judgments on rights of access and judgments on return that have been certified in the Member State of origin in accordance with the provisions of this Regulation should be recognised and enforceable in all other Member States without any further procedure being required. Arrangements for the enforcement of such judgments continue to be governed by national law.

(24) The certificate issued to facilitate enforcement of the judgment should not be subject to appeal. It should be rectified only where there is a material error, i.e. where it does not correctly reflect the judgment.

(25) Central authorities should cooperate both in general matter and in specific cases, including for purposes of promoting the amicable resolution of family disputes, in matters of parental responsibility. To this end central authorities shall participate in the European Judicial Network in civil and commercial matters created by Council Decision 2001/470/EC of 28 May 2001 establishing a European Judicial Network in civil and commercial matters.

(26) The Commission should make publicly available and update the lists of courts and redress procedures communicated by the Member States.

(27) The measures necessary for the implementation of this Regulation should be adopted in accordance with Council Decision 1999/468/EC of 28 June 1999 laying down the procedures for the exercise of implementing powers conferred on the Commission.

(28) This Regulation replaces Regulation (EC) No 1347/2000 which is consequently repealed.

(29) For the proper functioning of this Regulation, the Commission should review its application and propose such amendments as may appear necessary.

PART II   PRIVATE INTERNATIONAL LAW

(30) The United Kingdom and Ireland, in accordance with Article 3 of the Protocol on the position of the United Kingdom and Ireland annexed to the Treaty on European Union and the Treaty establishing the European Community, have given notice of their wish to take part in the adoption and application of this Regulation.

(31) Denmark, in accordance with Articles 1 and 2 of the Protocol on the position of Denmark annexed to the Treaty on European Union and the Treaty establishing the European Community, is not participating in the adoption of this Regulation and is therefore not bound by it nor subject to its application.

(32) Since the objectives of this Regulation cannot be sufficiently achieved by the Member States and can therefore be better achieved at Community level, the Community may adopt measures, in accordance with the principle of subsidiarity as set out in Article 5 of the Treaty. In accordance with the principle of proportionality, as set out in that Article, this Regulation does not go beyond what is necessary in order to achieve those objectives.

(33) This Regulation recognises the fundamental rights and observes the principles of the Charter of Fundamental Rights of the European Union. In particular, it seeks to ensure respect for the fundamental rights of the child as set out in Article 24 of the Charter of Fundamental Rights of the European Union,

HAS ADOPTED THE PRESENT REGULATION:

Chapter 1. Scope and Definitions

Article 1. (1) This Regulation shall apply, whatever the nature of the court or tribunal, in civil matters relating to:
(a) divorce, legal separation or marriage annulment;
(b) the attribution, exercise, delegation, restriction or termination of parental responsibility.
(2) The matters referred to in paragraph (1)(b) may, in particular, deal with:
(a) rights of custody and rights of access;
(b) guardianship, curatorship and similar institutions;
(c) the designation and functions of any person or body having charge of the child's person or property, representing or assisting the child;
(d) the placement of the child in a foster family or in institutional care;
(e) measures for the protection of the child relating to the administration, conservation or disposal of the child's property.
(3) This Regulation shall not apply to:
(a) the establishment or contesting of a parent-child relationship;
(b) decisions on adoption, measures preparatory to adoption, or the annulment or revocation of adoption;
(c) the name and forenames of the child;
(d) emancipation;
(e) maintenance obligations;
(f) trusts or succession;
(g) measures taken as a result of criminal offences committed by children.

Article 2. For the purposes of this Regulation:
(1) the term "court" shall cover all the authorities in the Member States with jurisdiction in the matters falling within the scope of this Regulation pursuant to Article 1;
(2) the term "judge" shall mean the judge or an official having powers equivalent to those of a judge in the matters falling within the scope of the Regulation;
(3) the term "Member State" shall mean all Member States with the exception of Denmark;
(4) the term "judgment" shall mean a divorce, legal separation or marriage annulment, as well as a judgment relating to parental responsibility, pronounced by a court of a Member State, whatever the judgment may be called, including a decree, order or decision;
(5) the term "Member State of origin" shall mean the Member State where the judgment to be enforced was issued;
(6) the term "Member State of enforcement" shall mean the Member State where enforcement of the judgment is sought;
(7) the term "parental responsibility" shall mean all rights and duties relating to the person or the property of a child which are given to a natural or legal person by judgment, by operation of law or by an agreement having legal effect. The term shall include rights of custody and rights of access;
(8) the term "holder of parental responsibility" shall mean any person having parental responsibility over a child;

(9) the term "rights of custody" shall include rights and duties relating to the care of the person of a child, and in particular the right to determine the child's place of residence;
(10) the term "rights of access" shall include in particular the right to take a child to a place other than his or her habitual residence for a limited period of time;
(11) the term "wrongful removal or retention" shall mean a child's removal or retention where:
(a) it is in breach of rights of custody acquired by judgment or by operation of law or by an agreement having legal effect under the law of the Member State where the child was habitually resident immediately before the removal or retention;
and
(b) provided that, at the time of removal or retention, the rights of custody were actually exercised, either jointly or alone, or would have been so exercised but for the removal or retention. Custody shall be considered to be exercised jointly when, pursuant to a judgment or by operation of law, one holder of parental responsibility cannot decide on the child's place of residence without the consent of another holder of parental responsibility.

Chapter II. Jurisdiction

Section 1. Divorce, legal separation and marriage annulment

Article 3. (1) In matters relating to divorce, legal separation or marriage annulment, jurisdiction shall lie with the courts of the Member State
(a) in whose territory:
- the spouses are habitually resident, or
- the spouses were last habitually resident, insofar as one of them still resides there, or
- the respondent is habitually resident, or
- in the event of a joint application, either of the spouses is habitually resident, or
- the applicant is habitually resident if he or she resided there for at least a year immediately before the application was made, or
- the applicant is habitually resident if he or she resided there for at least six months immediately before the application was made and is either a national of the Member State in question or, in the case of the United Kingdom and Ireland, has his or her "domicile" there;
(b) of the nationality of both spouses or, in the case of the United Kingdom and Ireland, of the "domicile" of both spouses.
(2) For the purpose of this Regulation, "domicile" shall have the same meaning as it has under the legal systems of the United Kingdom and Ireland.

Article 4. The court in which proceedings are pending on the basis of Article 3 shall also have jurisdiction to examine a counterclaim, insofar as the latter comes within the scope of this Regulation.

Article 5. Without prejudice to Article 3, a court of a Member State that has given a judgment on a legal separation shall also have jurisdiction for converting that judgment into a divorce, if the law of that Member State so provides.

Article 6. A spouse who:
(a) is habitually resident in the territory of a Member State; or
(b) is a national of a Member State, or, in the case of the United Kingdom and Ireland, has his or her "domicile" in the territory of one of the latter Member States,
may be sued in another Member State only in accordance with Articles 3, 4 and 5.

Article 7. (1) Where no court of a Member State has jurisdiction pursuant to Articles 3, 4 and 5, jurisdiction shall be determined, in each Member State, by the laws of that State.
(2) As against a respondent who is not habitually resident and is not either a national of a Member State or, in the case of the United Kingdom and Ireland, does not have his "domicile" within the territory of one of the latter Member States, any national of a Member State who is habitually resident within the territory of another Member State may, like the nationals of that State, avail himself of the rules of jurisdiction applicable in that State.

Section 2. Parental responsibility

Article 8. (1) The courts of a Member State shall have jurisdiction in matters of parental responsibility over a child who is habitually resident in that Member State at the time the court is seised.
(2) Paragraph 1 shall be subject to the provisions of Articles 9, 10 and 12.

Article 9. Continuing jurisdiction of the child's former habitual residence

PART II   PRIVATE INTERNATIONAL LAW

(1) Where a child moves lawfully from one Member State to another and acquires a new habitual residence there, the courts of the Member State of the child's former habitual residence shall, by way of exception to Article 8, retain jurisdiction during a three-month period following the move for the purpose of modifying a judgment on access rights issued in that Member State before the child moved, where the holder of access rights pursuant to the judgment on access rights continues to have his or her habitual residence in the Member State of the child's former habitual residence.
(2) Paragraph 1 shall not apply if the holder of access rights referred to in paragraph (1) has accepted the jurisdiction of the courts of the Member State of the child's new habitual residence by participating in proceedings before those courts without contesting their jurisdiction.

Article 10. In case of wrongful removal or retention of the child, the courts of the Member State where the child was habitually resident immediately before the wrongful removal or retention shall retain their jurisdiction until the child has acquired a habitual residence in another Member State and:
(a) each person, institution or other body having rights of custody has acquiesced in the removal or retention;
or
(b) the child has resided in that other Member State for a period of at least one year after the person, institution or other body having rights of custody has had or should have had knowledge of the whereabouts of the child and the child is settled in his or her new environment and at least one of the following conditions is met:
(i) within one year after the holder of rights of custody has had or should have had knowledge of the whereabouts of the child, no request for return has been lodged before the competent authorities of the Member State where the child has been removed or is being retained;
(ii) a request for return lodged by the holder of rights of custody has been withdrawn and no new request has been lodged within the time limit set in paragraph (i);
(iii) a case before the court in the Member State where the child was habitually resident immediately before the wrongful removal or retention has been closed pursuant to Article 11(7);
(iv) a judgment on custody that does not entail the return of the child has been issued by the courts of the Member State where the child was habitually resident immediately before the wrongful removal or retention.

Article 11. (1) Where a person, institution or other body having rights of custody applies to the competent authorities in a Member State to deliver a judgment on the basis of the Hague Convention of 25 October 1980 on the Civil Aspects of International Child Abduction (hereinafter "the 1980 Hague Convention"), in order to obtain the return of a child that has been wrongfully removed or retained in a Member State other than the Member State where the child was habitually resident immediately before the wrongful removal or retention, paragraphs 2 to 8 shall apply.
(2) When applying Articles 12 and 13 of the 1980 Hague Convention, it shall be ensured that the child is given the opportunity to be heard during the proceedings unless this appears inappropriate having regard to his or her age or degree of maturity.
(3) A court to which an application for return of a child is made as mentioned in paragraph (1) shall act expeditiously in proceedings on the application, using the most expeditious procedures available in national law.
Without prejudice to the first subparagraph, the court shall, except where exceptional circumstances make this impossible, issue its judgment no later than six weeks after the application is lodged.
(4) A court cannot refuse to return a child on the basis of Article 13b of the 1980 Hague Convention if it is established that adequate arrangements have been made to secure the protection of the child after his or her return.
(5) A court cannot refuse to return a child unless the person who requested the return of the child has been given an opportunity to be heard.
(6) If a court has issued an order on non-return pursuant to Article 13 of the 1980 Hague Convention, the court must immediately either directly or through its central authority, transmit a copy of the court order on non-return and of the relevant documents, in particular a transcript of the hearings before the court, to the court with jurisdiction or central authority in the Member State where the child was habitually resident immediately before the wrongful removal or retention, as determined by national law. The court shall receive all the mentioned documents within one month of the date of the non-return order.
(7) Unless the courts in the Member State where the child was habitually resident immediately before the wrongful removal or retention have already been seised by one of the parties, the court or central authority that receives the information mentioned in paragraph (6) must notify it to the parties and invite them to make submissions to the court, in accordance with national law, within three months of

the date of notification so that the court can examine the question of custody of the child. Without prejudice to the rules on jurisdiction contained in this Regulation, the court shall close the case if no submissions have been received by the court within the time limit.
(8) Notwithstanding a judgment of non-return pursuant to Article 13 of the 1980 Hague Convention, any subsequent judgment which requires the return of the child issued by a court having jurisdiction under this Regulation shall be enforceable in accordance with Section 4 of Chapter III below in order to secure the return of the child.

Article 12. (1) The courts of a Member State exercising jurisdiction by virtue of Article 3 on an application for divorce, legal separation or marriage annulment shall have jurisdiction in any matter relating to parental responsibility connected with that application where:
(a) at least one of the spouses has parental responsibility in relation to the child; and
(b) the jurisdiction of the courts has been accepted expressly or otherwise in an unequivocal manner by the spouses and by the holders of parental responsibility, at the time the court is seised, and is in the superior interests of the child.
(2) The jurisdiction conferred in paragraph (1) shall cease as soon as:
(a) the judgment allowing or refusing the application for divorce, legal separation or marriage annulment has become final;
(b) in those cases where proceedings in relation to parental responsibility are still pending on the date referred to in (a), a judgment in these proceedings has become final;
(c) the proceedings referred to in (a) and (b) have come to an end for another reason.
(3) The courts of a Member State shall also have jurisdiction in relation to parental responsibility in proceedings other than those referred to in paragraph (1) where:
(a) the child has a substantial connection with that Member State, in particular by virtue of the fact that one of the holders of parental responsibility is habitually resident in that Member State or that the child is a national of that Member State; and
(b) the jurisdiction of the courts has been accepted expressly or otherwise in an unequivocal manner by all the parties to the proceedings at the time the court is seised and is in the best interests of the child.
(4) Where the child has his or her habitual residence in the territory of a third State which is not a contracting party to the Hague Convention of 19 October 1996 on jurisdiction, applicable law, recognition, enforcement and cooperation in respect of parental responsibility and measures for the protection of children, jurisdiction under this Article shall be deemed to be in the child's interest, in particular if it is found impossible to hold proceedings in the third State in question.

Article 13. (1) Where a child's habitual residence cannot be established and jurisdiction cannot be determined on the basis of Article 12, the courts of the Member State where the child is present shall have jurisdiction.
(2) Paragraph 1 shall also apply to refugee children or children internationally displaced because of disturbances occurring in their country.

Article 14. Where no court of a Member State has jurisdiction pursuant to Articles 8 to 13, jurisdiction shall be determined, in each Member State, by the laws of that State.

Article 15. (1) By way of exception, the courts of a Member State having jurisdiction as to the substance of the matter may, if they consider that a court of another Member State, with which the child has a particular connection, would be better placed to hear the case, or a specific part thereof, and where this is in the best interests of the child:
(a) stay the case or the part thereof in question and invite the parties to introduce a request before the court of that other Member State in accordance with paragraph (4); or
(b) request a court of another Member State to assume jurisdiction in accordance with paragraph (5).
(2) Paragraph 1 shall apply:
(a) upon application from a party; or
(b) of the court's own motion; or
(c) upon application from a court of another Member State with which the child has a particular connection, in accordance with paragraph (3).
A transfer made of the court's own motion or by application of a court of another Member State must be accepted by at least one of the parties.
(3) The child shall be considered to have a particular connection to a Member State as mentioned in paragraph (1), if that Member State:
(a) has become the habitual residence of the child after the court referred to in paragraph (1) was seised; or

PART II   PRIVATE INTERNATIONAL LAW

(b) is the former habitual residence of the child; or
(c) is the place of the child's nationality; or
(d) is the habitual residence of a holder of parental responsibility; or
(e) is the place where property of the child is located and the case concerns measures for the protection of the child relating to the administration, conservation or disposal of this property.
(4) The court of the Member State having jurisdiction as to the substance of the matter shall set a time limit by which the courts of that other Member State shall be seised in accordance with paragraph (1). If the courts are not seised by that time, the court which has been seised shall continue to exercise jurisdiction in accordance with Articles 8 to 14.
(5) The courts of that other Member State may, where due to the specific circumstances of the case, this is in the best interests of the child, accept jurisdiction within six weeks of their seisure in accordance with paragraph (1)(a) or 1(b). In this case, the court first seised shall decline jurisdiction. Otherwise, the court first seised shall continue to exercise jurisdiction in accordance with Articles 8 to 14.
(6) The courts shall cooperate for the purposes of this Article, either directly or through the central authorities designated pursuant to Article 53.

Section 3. Common provisions

Article 16. (1) A court shall be deemed to be seised:
(a) at the time when the document instituting the proceedings or an equivalent document is lodged with the court, provided that the applicant has not subsequently failed to take the steps he was required to take to have service effected on the respondent; or
(b) if the document has to be served before being lodged with the court, at the time when it is received by the authority responsible for service, provided that the applicant has not subsequently failed to take the steps he was required to take to have the document lodged with the court.

Article 17. Where a court of a Member State is seised of a case over which it has no jurisdiction under this Regulation and over which a court of another Member State has jurisdiction by virtue of this Regulation, it shall declare of its own motion that it has no jurisdiction.

Article 18. (1) Where a respondent habitually resident in a State other than the Member State where the action was brought does not enter an appearance, the court with jurisdiction shall stay the proceedings so long as it is not shown that the respondent has been able to receive the document instituting the proceedings or an equivalent document in sufficient time to enable him to arrange for his defence, or that all necessary steps have been taken to this end.
(2) Article 19 of Regulation (EC) No 1348/2000 shall apply instead of the provisions of paragraph (1) of this Article if the document instituting the proceedings or an equivalent document had to be transmitted from one Member State to another pursuant to that Regulation.
(3) Where the provisions of Regulation (EC) No 1348/2000 are not applicable, Article 15 of the Hague Convention of 15 November 1965 on the service abroad of judicial and extrajudicial documents in civil or commercial matters shall apply if the document instituting the proceedings or an equivalent document had to be transmitted abroad pursuant to that Convention.

Article 19. (1) Where proceedings relating to divorce, legal separation or marriage annulment between the same parties are brought before courts of different Member States, the court second seised shall of its own motion stay its proceedings until such time as the jurisdiction of the court first seised is established.
(2) Where proceedings relating to parental responsibility relating to the same child and involving the same cause of action are brought before courts of different Member States, the court second seised shall of its own motion stay its proceedings until such time as the jurisdiction of the court first seised is established.
(3) Where the jurisdiction of the court first seised is established, the court second seised shall decline jurisdiction in favour of that court.
In that case, the party who brought the relevant action before the court second seised may bring that action before the court first seised.

Article 20. (1) In urgent cases, the provisions of this Regulation shall not prevent the courts of a Member State from taking such provisional, including protective, measures in respect of persons or assets in that State as may be available under the law of that Member State, even if, under this Regulation, the court of another Member State has jurisdiction as to the substance of the matter.
(2) The measures referred to in paragraph (1) shall cease to apply when the court of the Member State having jurisdiction under this Regulation as to the substance of the matter has taken the measures it considers appropriate.

Chapter III. Recognition and Enforcement

Section 1. Recognition

Article 21. (1) A judgment given in a Member State shall be recognised in the other Member States without any special procedure being required.
(2) In particular, and without prejudice to paragraph (3), no special procedure shall be required for updating the civil-status records of a Member State on the basis of a judgment relating to divorce, legal separation or marriage annulment given in another Member State, and against which no further appeal lies under the law of that Member State.
(3) Without prejudice to Section 4 of this Chapter, any interested party may, in accordance with the procedures provided for in Section 2 of this Chapter, apply for a decision that the judgment be or not be recognised.
The local jurisdiction of the court appearing in the list notified by each Member State to the Commission pursuant to Article 68 shall be determined by the internal law of the Member State in which proceedings for recognition or non-recognition are brought.
(4) Where the recognition of a judgment is raised as an incidental question in a court of a Member State, that court may determine that issue.

Article 22. A judgment relating to a divorce, legal separation or marriage annulment shall not be recognised:
(a) if such recognition is manifestly contrary to the public policy of the Member State in which recognition is sought;
(b) where it was given in default of appearance, if the respondent was not served with the document which instituted the proceedings or with an equivalent document in sufficient time and in such a way as to enable the respondent to arrange for his or her defence unless it is determined that the respondent has accepted the judgment unequivocally;
(c) if it is irreconcilable with a judgment given in proceedings between the same parties in the Member State in which recognition is sought; or
(d) if it is irreconcilable with an earlier judgment given in another Member State or in a non-Member State between the same parties, provided that the earlier judgment fulfils the conditions necessary for its recognition in the Member State in which recognition is sought.

Article 23. A judgment relating to parental responsibility shall not be recognised:
(a) if such recognition is manifestly contrary to the public policy of the Member State in which recognition is sought taking into account the best interests of the child;
(b) if it was given, except in case of urgency, without the child having been given an opportunity to be heard, in violation of fundamental principles of procedure of the Member State in which recognition is sought;
(c) where it was given in default of appearance if the person in default was not served with the document which instituted the proceedings or with an equivalent document in sufficient time and in such a way as to enable that person to arrange for his or her defence unless it is determined that such person has accepted the judgment unequivocally;
(d) on the request of any person claiming that the judgment infringes his or her parental responsibility, if it was given without such person having been given an opportunity to be heard;
(e) if it is irreconcilable with a later judgment relating to parental responsibility given in the Member State in which recognition is sought;
(f) if it is irreconcilable with a later judgment relating to parental responsibility given in another Member State or in the non-Member State of the habitual residence of the child provided that the later judgment fulfils the conditions necessary for its recognition in the Member State in which recognition is sought. or
(g) if the procedure laid down in Article 56 has not been complied with.

Article 24. The jurisdiction of the court of the Member State of origin may not be reviewed. The test of public policy referred to in Articles 22(a) and 23(a) may not be applied to the rules relating to jurisdiction set out in Articles 3 to 14.

Article 25. The recognition of a judgment may not be refused because the law of the Member State in which such recognition is sought would not allow divorce, legal separation or marriage annulment on the same facts.

Article 26. Under no circumstances may a judgment be reviewed as to its substance.

PART II   PRIVATE INTERNATIONAL LAW

Article 27. (1) A court of a Member State in which recognition is sought of a judgment given in another Member State may stay the proceedings if an ordinary appeal against the judgment has been lodged.
(2) A court of a Member State in which recognition is sought of a judgment given in Ireland or the United Kingdom may stay the proceedings if enforcement is suspended in the Member State of origin by reason of an appeal.

Section 2. Application for a declaration of enforceability

Article 28. (1) A judgment on the exercise of parental responsibility in respect of a child given in a Member State which is enforceable in that Member State and has been served shall be enforced in another Member State when, on the application of any interested party, it has been declared enforceable there.
(2) However, in the United Kingdom, such a judgment shall be enforced in England and Wales, in Scotland or in Northern Ireland only when, on the application of any interested party, it has been registered for enforcement in that part of the United Kingdom.

Article 29. (1) An application for a declaration of enforceability shall be submitted to the court appearing in the list notified by each Member State to the Commission pursuant to Article 68.
(2) The local jurisdiction shall be determined by reference to the place of habitual residence of the person against whom enforcement is sought or by reference to the habitual residence of any child to whom the application relates.
Where neither of the places referred to in the first subparagraph can be found in the Member State of enforcement, the local jurisdiction shall be determined by reference to the place of enforcement.

Article 30. (1) The procedure for making the application shall be governed by the law of the Member State of enforcement.
(2) The applicant must give an address for service within the area of jurisdiction of the court applied to. However, if the law of the Member State of enforcement does not provide for the furnishing of such an address, the applicant shall appoint a representative ad litem.
(3) The documents referred to in Articles 37 and 39 shall be attached to the application.

Article 31. (1) The court applied to shall give its decision without delay. Neither the person against whom enforcement is sought, nor the child shall, at this stage of the proceedings, be entitled to make any submissions on the application.
(2) The application may be refused only for one of the reasons specified in Articles 22, 23 and 24.
(3) Under no circumstances may a judgment be reviewed as to its substance.

Article 32. The appropriate officer of the court shall without delay bring to the notice of the applicant the decision given on the application in accordance with the procedure laid down by the law of the Member State of enforcement.

Article 33. Appeal against the decision
(1) The decision on the application for a declaration of enforceability may be appealed against by either party.
(2) The appeal shall be lodged with the court appearing in the list notified by each Member State to the Commission pursuant to Article 68.
(3) The appeal shall be dealt with in accordance with the rules governing procedure in contradictory matters.
(4) If the appeal is brought by the applicant for a declaration of enforceability, the party against whom enforcement is sought shall be summoned to appear before the appellate court. If such person fails to appear, the provisions of Article 18 shall apply.
(5) An appeal against a declaration of enforceability must be lodged within one month of service thereof. If the party against whom enforcement is sought is habitually resident in a Member State other than that in which the declaration of enforceability was given, the time for appealing shall be two months and shall run from the date of service, either on him or at his residence. No extension of time may be granted on account of distance.

Article 34. The judgment given on appeal may be contested only by the proceedings referred to in the list notified by each Member State to the Commission pursuant to Article 68.

Article 35. (1) The court with which the appeal is lodged under Articles 33 or 34 may, on the application of the party against whom enforcement is sought, stay the proceedings if an ordinary appeal has been lodged in the Member State of origin, or if the time for such appeal has not yet expired. In the

latter case, the court may specify the time within which an appeal is to be lodged.
(2) Where the judgment was given in Ireland or the United Kingdom, any form of appeal available in the Member State of origin shall be treated as an ordinary appeal for the purposes of paragraph (1).

Article 36. (1) Where a judgment has been given in respect of several matters and enforcement cannot be authorised for all of them, the court shall authorise enforcement for one or more of them.
(2) An applicant may request partial enforcement of a judgment.

Section 3. Provisions common to Sections 1 and 2

Article 37. (1) A party seeking or contesting recognition or applying for a declaration of enforceability shall produce:
(a) a copy of the judgment which satisfies the conditions necessary to establish its authenticity; and
(b) the certificate referred to in Article 39.
(2) In addition, in the case of a judgment given in default, the party seeking recognition or applying for a declaration of enforceability shall produce:
(a) the original or certified true copy of the document which establishes that the defaulting party was served with the document instituting the proceedings or with an equivalent document; or
(b) any document indicating that the defendant has accepted the judgment unequivocally.

Article 38. (1) If the documents specified in Article 37(1)(b) or (2) are not produced, the court may specify a time for their production, accept equivalent documents or, if it considers that it has sufficient information before it, dispense with their production.
(2) If the court so requires, a translation of such documents shall be furnished. The translation shall be certified by a person qualified to do so in one of the Member States.

Article 39. The competent court or authority of a Member State of origin shall, at the request of any interested party, issue a certificate using the standard form set out in Annex I (judgments in matrimonial matters) or in Annex II (judgments on parental responsibility).

Section 4. Enforceability of certain judgments concerning rights of access and of certain judgments which require the return of the child

Article 40. (1) This Section shall apply to:
(a) rights of access; and
(b) the return of a child entailed by a judgment given pursuant to Article 11(8).
(2) The provisions of this Section shall not prevent a holder of parental responsibility from seeking recognition and enforcement of a judgment in accordance with the provisions in Sections 1 and 2 of this Chapter.

Article 41. (1) The rights of access referred to in Article 40(1)(a) granted in an enforceable judgment given in a Member State shall be recognised and enforceable in another Member State without the need for a declaration of enforceability and without any possibility of opposing its recognition if the judgment has been certified in the Member State of origin in accordance with paragraph (2).
Even if national law does not provide for enforceability by operation of law of a judgment granting access rights, the court of origin may declare that the judgment shall be enforceable, notwithstanding any appeal.
(2) The judge of origin shall issue the certificate referred to in paragraph (1) using the standard form in Annex III (certificate concerning rights of access) only if:
(a) where the judgment was given in default, the person defaulting was served with the document which instituted the proceedings or with an equivalent document in sufficient time and in such a way as to enable that person to arrange for his or her defense, or, the person has been served with the document but not in compliance with these conditions, it is nevertheless established that he or she accepted the decision unequivocally;
(b) all parties concerned were given an opportunity to be heard; and
(c) the child was given an opportunity to be heard, unless a hearing was considered inappropriate having regard to his or her age or degree of maturity.
The certificate shall be completed in the language of the judgment.
(3) Where the rights of access involve a cross-border situation at the time of the delivery of the judgment, the certificate shall be issued ex officio when the judgment becomes enforceable, even if only provisionally. If the situation subsequently acquires a cross-border character, the certificate shall be issued at the request of one of the parties.

Article 42. (1) The return of a child referred to in Article 40(1)(b) entailed by an enforceable judg-

PART II PRIVATE INTERNATIONAL LAW

ment given in a Member State shall be recognised and enforceable in another Member State without the need for a declaration of enforceability and without any possibility of opposing its recognition if the judgment has been certified in the Member State of origin in accordance with paragraph (2). Even if national law does not provide for enforceability by operation of law, notwithstanding any appeal, of a judgment requiring the return of the child mentioned in Article 11(b)(8), the court of origin may declare the judgment enforceable.

(2) The judge of origin who delivered the judgment referred to in Article 40(1)(b) shall issue the certificate referred to in paragraph (1) only if:

(a) the child was given an opportunity to be heard, unless a hearing was considered inappropriate having regard to his or her age or degree of maturity;

(b) the parties were given an opportunity to be heard; and

(c) the court has taken into account in issuing its judgment the reasons for and evidence underlying the order issued pursuant to Article 13 of the 1980 Hague Convention.

In the event that the court or any other authority takes measures to ensure the protection of the child after its return to the State of habitual residence, the certificate shall contain details of such measures. The judge of origin shall of his or her own motion issue that certificate using the standard form in Annex IV (certificate concerning return of the child(ren)).

The certificate shall be completed in the language of the judgment.

Article 43. (1) The law of the Member State of origin shall be applicable to any rectification of the certificate.

(2) No appeal shall lie against the issuing of a certificate pursuant to Articles 41(1) or 42(1).

Article 44. The certificate shall take effect only within the limits of the enforceability of the judgment.

Article 45. (1) A party seeking enforcement of a judgment shall produce:

(a) a copy of the judgment which satisfies the conditions necessary to establish its authenticity; and

(b) the certificate referred to in Article 41(1) or Article 42(1).

(2) For the purposes of this Article,

- the certificate referred to in Article 41(1) shall be accompanied by a translation of point 12 relating to the arrangements for exercising right of access,

- the certificate referred to in Article 42(1) shall be accompanied by a translation of its point 14 relating to the arrangements for implementing the measures taken to ensure the child's return.

The translation shall be into the official language or one of the official languages of the Member State of enforcement or any other language that the Member State of enforcement expressly accepts. The translation shall be certified by a person qualified to do so in one of the Member States.

Section 5. Authentic instruments and agreements

Article 46. Documents which have been formally drawn up or registered as authentic instruments and are enforceable in one Member State and also agreements between the parties that are enforceable in the Member State in which they were concluded shall be recognised and declared enforceable under the same conditions as judgments.

Section 6. Other Provisions

Article 47. (1) The enforcement procedure is governed by the law of the Member State of enforcement.

(2) Any judgment delivered by a court of another Member State and declared to be enforceable in accordance with Section 2 or certified in accordance with Article 41(1) or Article 42(1) shall be enforced in the Member State of enforcement in the same conditions as if it had been delivered in that Member State.

In particular, a judgment which has been certified according to Article 41(1) or Article 42(1) cannot be enforced if it is irreconcilable with a subsequent enforceable judgment.

Article 48. (1) The courts of the Member State of enforcement may make practical arrangements for organising the exercise of rights of access, if the necessary arrangements have not or have not sufficiently been made in the judgment delivered by the courts of the Member State having jurisdiction as to the substance of the matter and provided the essential elements of this judgment are respected.

(2) The practical arrangements made pursuant to paragraph (1) shall cease to apply pursuant to a later judgment by the courts of the Member State having jurisdiction as to the substance of the matter.

Article 49. The provisions of this Chapter, with the exception of Section 4, shall also apply to the determination of the amount of costs and expenses of proceedings under this Regulation and to the enforcement of any order concerning such costs and expenses.

Article 50. An applicant who, in the Member State of origin, has benefited from complete or partial legal aid or exemption from costs or expenses shall be entitled, in the procedures provided for in Articles 21, 28, 41, 42 and 48 to benefit from the most favourable legal aid or the most extensive exemption from costs and expenses provided for by the law of the Member State of enforcement.

Article 51. No security, bond or deposit, however described, shall be required of a party who in one Member State applies for enforcement of a judgment given in another Member State on the following grounds:
(a) that he or she is not habitually resident in the Member State in which enforcement is sought; or
(b) that he or she is either a foreign national or, where enforcement is sought in either the United Kingdom or Ireland, does not have his or her "domicile" in either of those Member States.

Article 52. No legalisation or other similar formality shall be required in respect of the documents referred to in Articles 37, 38 and 45 or in respect of a document appointing a representative ad litem.

Chapter IV. Cooperation between Central Authorities in Matters of Parental Responsibility

Article 53. Each Member State shall designate one or more central authorities to assist with the application of this Regulation and shall specify the geographical or functional jurisdiction of each. Where a Member State has designated more than one central authority, communications shall normally be sent direct to the relevant central authority with jurisdiction. Where a communication is sent to a central authority without jurisdiction, the latter shall be responsible for forwarding it to the central authority with jurisdiction and informing the sender accordingly.

Article 54. The central authorities shall communicate information on national laws and procedures and take measures to improve the application of this Regulation and strengthening their cooperation. For this purpose the European Judicial Network in civil and commercial matters created by Decision No 2001/470/EC shall be used.

Article 55. The central authorities shall, upon request from a central authority of another Member State or from a holder of parental responsibility, cooperate on specific cases to achieve the purposes of this Regulation. To this end, they shall, acting directly or through public authorities or other bodies, take all appropriate steps in accordance with the law of that Member State in matters of personal data protection to:
(a) collect and exchange information:
(i) on the situation of the child;
(ii) on any procedures under way; or
(iii) on decisions taken concerning the child;
(b) provide information and assistance to holders of parental responsibility seeking the recognition and enforcement of decisions on their territory, in particular concerning rights of access and the return of the child;
(c) facilitate communications between courts, in particular for the application of Article 11(6) and (7) and Article 15;
(d) provide such information and assistance as is needed by courts to apply Article 56; and
(e) facilitate agreement between holders of parental responsibility through mediation or other means, and facilitate cross-border cooperation to this end.

Article 56. (1) Where a court having jurisdiction under Articles 8 to 15 contemplates the placement of a child in institutional care or with a foster family and where such placement is to take place in another Member State, it shall first consult the central authority or other authority having jurisdiction in the latter State where public authority intervention in that Member State is required for domestic cases of child placement.
(2) The judgment on placement referred to in paragraph (1) may be made in the requesting State only if the competent authority of the requested State has consented to the placement.
(3) The procedures for consultation or consent referred to in paragraphs 1 and 2 shall be governed by the national law of the requested State.
(4) Where the authority having jurisdiction under Articles 8 to 15 decides to place the child in a foster family, and where such placement is to take place in another Member State and where no public authority intervention is required in the latter Member State for domestic cases of child placement, it shall so inform the central authority or other authority having jurisdiction in the latter State.

PART II   PRIVATE INTERNATIONAL LAW

Article 57. (1) Any holder of parental responsibility may submit, to the central authority of the Member State of his or her habitual residence or to the central authority of the Member State where the child is habitually resident or present, a request for assistance as mentioned in Article 55. In general, the request shall include all available information of relevance to its enforcement. Where the request for assistance concerns the recognition or enforcement of a judgment on parental responsibility that falls within the scope of this Regulation, the holder of parental responsibility shall attach the relevant certificates provided for in Articles 39, 41(1) or 42(1).
(2) Member States shall communicate to the Commission the official language or languages of the Community institutions other than their own in which communications to the central authorities can be accepted.
(3) The assistance provided by the central authorities pursuant to Article 55 shall be free of charge.
(4) Each central authority shall bear its own costs.

Article 58. (1) In order to facilitate the application of this Regulation, central authorities shall meet regularly.
(2) These meetings shall be convened in compliance with Decision No 2001/470/EC establishing a European Judicial Network in civil and commercial matters.

Chapter V. Relations with other Instruments

Article 59. (1) Subject to the provisions of Articles 60, 63, 64 and paragraph (2) of this Article, this Regulation shall, for the Member States, supersede conventions existing at the time of entry into force of this Regulation which have been concluded between two or more Member States and relate to matters governed by this Regulation.
(2) (a) Finland and Sweden shall have the option of declaring that the Convention of 6 February 1931 between Denmark, Finland, Iceland, Norway and Sweden comprising international private law provisions on marriage, adoption and guardianship, together with the Final Protocol thereto, will apply, in whole or in part, in their mutual relations, in place of the rules of this Regulation. Such declarations shall be annexed to this Regulation and published in the *Official Journal of the European Union*. They may be withdrawn, in whole or in part, at any moment by the said Member States.
(b) The principle of non-discrimination on the grounds of nationality between citizens of the Union shall be respected.
(c) The rules of jurisdiction in any future agreement to be concluded between the Member States referred to in subparagraph (a) which relate to matters governed by this Regulation shall be in line with those laid down in this Regulation.
(d) Judgments handed down in any of the Nordic States which have made the declaration provided for in subparagraph (a) under a forum of jurisdiction corresponding to one of those laid down in Chapter II of this Regulation, shall be recognised and enforced in the other Member States under the rules laid down in Chapter III of this Regulation.
(3) Member States shall send to the Commission:
(a) a copy of the agreements and uniform laws implementing these agreements referred to in paragraph (2)(a) and (c);
(b) any denunciations of, or amendments to, those agreements or uniform laws.

Article 60. In relations between Member States, this Regulation shall take precedence over the following Conventions in so far as they concern matters governed by this Regulation:
(a) the Hague Convention of 5 October 1961 concerning the Powers of Authorities and the Law Applicable in respect of the Protection of Minors;
(b) the Luxembourg Convention of 8 September 1967 on the Recognition of Decisions Relating to the Validity of Marriages;
(c) the Hague Convention of 1 June 1970 on the Recognition of Divorces and Legal Separations;
(d) the European Convention of 20 May 1980 on Recognition and Enforcement of Decisions concerning Custody of Children and on Restoration of Custody of Children; and
(e) the Hague Convention of 25 October 1980 on the Civil Aspects of International Child Abduction.

Article 61. Relation with the Hague Convention of 19 October 1996 on Jurisdiction, Applicable law, Recognition, Enforcement and Cooperation in Respect of Parental Responsibility and Measures for the Protection of Children
As concerns the relation with the Hague Convention of 19 October 1996 on Jurisdiction, Applicable law, Recognition, Enforcement and Cooperation in Respect of Parental Responsibility and Measures for the Protection of Children, this Regulation shall apply:
(a) where the child concerned has his or her habitual residence on the territory of a Member State;

(b) as concerns the recognition and enforcement of a judgment given in a court of a Member State on the territory of another Member State, even if the child concerned has his or her habitual residence on the territory of a third State which is a contracting Party to the said Convention.

Article 62. (1) The agreements and conventions referred to in Articles 59(1), 60 and 61 shall continue to have effect in relation to matters not governed by this Regulation.
(2) The conventions mentioned in Article 60, in particular the 1980 Hague Convention, continue to produce effects between the Member States which are party thereto, in compliance with Article 60.

Article 63. (1) This Regulation shall apply without prejudice to the International Treaty (Concordat) between the Holy See and Portugal, signed at the Vatican City on 7 May 1940.
(2) Any decision as to the invalidity of a marriage taken under the Treaty referred to in paragraph (1) shall be recognised in the Member States on the conditions laid down in Chapter III, Section 1.
(3) The provisions laid down in paragraphs 1 and 2 shall also apply to the following international treaties (Concordats) with the Holy See:
(a) "Concordato lateranense" of 11 February 1929 between Italy and the Holy See, modified by the agreement, with additional Protocol signed in Rome on 18 February 1984;
(b) Agreement between the Holy See and Spain on legal affairs of 3 January 1979.
(4) Recognition of the decisions provided for in paragraph (2) may, in Italy or in Spain, be subject to the same procedures and the same checks as are applicable to decisions of the ecclesiastical courts handed down in accordance with the international treaties concluded with the Holy See referred to in paragraph (3).
(5) Member States shall send to the Commission:
(a) a copy of the Treaties referred to in paragraphs 1 and 3;
(b) any denunciations of or amendments to those Treaties.

Chapter VI Transitional Provisions

Article 64. (1) The provisions of this Regulation shall apply only to legal proceedings instituted, to documents formally drawn up or registered as authentic instruments and to agreements concluded between the parties after its date of application in accordance with Article 72.
(2) Judgments given after the date of application of this Regulation in proceedings instituted before that date but after the date of entry into force of Regulation (EC) No 1347/2000 shall be recognised and enforced in accordance with the provisions of Chapter III of this Regulation if jurisdiction was founded on rules which accorded with those provided for either in Chapter II or in Regulation (EC) No 1347/2000 or in a convention concluded between the Member State of origin and the Member State addressed which was in force when the proceedings were instituted.
(3) Judgments given before the date of application of this Regulation in proceedings instituted after the entry into force of Regulation (EC) No 1347/2000 shall be recognised and enforced in accordance with the provisions of Chapter III of this Regulation provided they relate to divorce, legal separation or marriage annulment or parental responsibility for the children of both spouses on the occasion of these matrimonial proceedings.
(4) Judgments given before the date of application of this Regulation but after the date of entry into force of Regulation (EC) No 1347/2000 in proceedings instituted before the date of entry into force of Regulation (EC) No 1347/2000 shall be recognised and enforced in accordance with the provisions of Chapter III of this Regulation provided they relate to divorce, legal separation or marriage annulment or parental responsibility for the children of both spouses on the occasion of these matrimonial proceedings and that jurisdiction was founded on rules which accorded with those provided for either in Chapter II of this Regulation or in Regulation (EC) No 1347/2000 or in a convention concluded between the Member State of origin and the Member State addressed which was in force when the proceedings were instituted.

Chapter VII. Final Provisions

Article 65. No later than 1 January 2012, and every five years thereafter, the Commission shall present to the European Parliament, to the Council and to the European Economic and Social Committee a report on the application of this Regulation on the basis of information supplied by the Member States. The report shall be accompanied if need be by proposals for adaptations.

Article 66. With regard to a Member State in which two or more systems of law or sets of rules concerning matters governed by this Regulation apply in different territorial units:
(a) any reference to habitual residence in that Member State shall refer to habitual residence in a territorial unit;

PART II PRIVATE INTERNATIONAL LAW

(b) any reference to nationality, or in the case of the United Kingdom "domicile", shall refer to the territorial unit designated by the law of that State;
(c) any reference to the authority of a Member State shall refer to the authority of a territorial unit within that State which is concerned;
(d) any reference to the rules of the requested Member State shall refer to the rules of the territorial unit in which jurisdiction, recognition or enforcement is invoked.

Article 67. The Member States shall communicate to the Commission within three months following the entry into force of this Regulation:
(a) the names, addresses and means of communication for the central authorities designated pursuant to Article 53;
(b) the languages accepted for communications to central authorities pursuant to Article 57(2); and
(c) the languages accepted for the certificate concerning rights of access pursuant to Article 45(2).
The Member States shall communicate to the Commission any changes to this information.
The Commission shall make this information publicly available.

Article 68. The Member States shall notify to the Commission the lists of courts and redress procedures referred to in Articles 21, 29, 33 and 34 and any amendments thereto.
The Commission shall update this information and make it publicly available through the publication in the *Official Journal of the European Union* and any other appropriate means.

Article 69. Any amendments to the standard forms in Annexes I to IV shall be adopted in accordance with the consultative procedure set out in Article 70(2).

Article 70. (1) The Commission shall be assisted by a committee (committee).
(2) Where reference is made to this paragraph, Articles 3 and 7 of Decision 1999/468/EC shall apply.
(3) The committee shall adopt its rules of procedure.

Article 71. (1) Regulation (EC) No 1347/2000 shall be repealed as from the date of application of this Regulation.
(2) Any reference to Regulation (EC) No 1347/2000 shall be construed as a reference to this Regulation according to the comparative table in Annex V.

Article 72. This Regulation shall enter into force on 1 August 2004.
The Regulation shall apply from 1 March 2005, with the exception of Articles 67, 68, 69 and 70, which shall apply from 1 August 2004.
This Regulation shall be binding in its entirety and directly applicable in the Member States in accordance with the Treaty establishing the European Community.

[The annexes are omitted.]

EU: ROME I REGULATION

Regulation (EC) 593/2008 of 17 June 2008 of the European Parliament and the Council on the law applicable to contractual obligations [Rome I] (OJ L177, 4.7.2008, pp. 6 – 16) [footnotes omitted].

THE EUROPEAN PARLIAMENT AND THE COUNCIL OF THE EUROPEAN UNION,
Having regard to the Treaty establishing the European Community, and in particular Article 61(c) and the second indent of Article 67(5) thereof,
Having regard to the proposal from the Commission,
Having regard to the opinion of the European Economic and Social Committee,
Acting in accordance with the procedure laid down in Article 251 of the Treaty,
Whereas:
(1) The Community has set itself the objective of maintaining and developing an area of freedom, security and justice. For the progressive establishment of such an area, the Community is to adopt measures relating to judicial cooperation in civil matters with a cross-border impact to the extent necessary for the proper functioning of the internal market.
(2) According to Article 65, point (b) of the Treaty, these measures are to include those promoting the compatibility of the rules applicable in the Member States concerning the conflict of laws and of jurisdiction
(3) The European Council meeting in Tampere on 15 and 16 October 1999 endorsed the principle of mutual recognition of judgments and other decisions of judicial authorities as the cornerstone of judicial cooperation in civil matters and invited the Council and the Commission to adopt a programme of measures to implement that principle.
(4) On 30 November 2000 the Council adopted a joint Commission and Council programme of measures for implementation of the principle of mutual recognition of decisions in civil and commercial matters. The programme identifies measures relating to the harmonisation of conflict-of-law rules as those facilitating the mutual recognition of judgments.
(5) The Hague Programme, adopted by the European Council on 5 November 2004, called for work to be pursued actively on the conflict-of-law rules regarding contractual obligations (Rome I).
(6) The proper functioning of the internal market creates a need, in order to improve the predictability of the outcome of litigation, certainty as to the law applicable and the free movement of judgments, for the conflict-of-law rules in the Member States to designate the same national law irrespective of the country of the court in which an action is brought.
(7) The substantive scope and the provisions of this Regulation should be consistent with Council Regulation (EC) No 44/2001 of 22 December 2000 on jurisdiction and the recognition and enforcement of judgments in civil and commercial matters (Brussels I) and Regulation (EC) No 864/2007 of the European Parliament and of the Council of 11 July 2007 on the law applicable to non-contractual obligations (Rome II).
(8) Family relationships should cover parentage, marriage, affinity and collateral relatives. The reference in Article 1(2) to relationships having comparable effects to marriage and other family relationships should be interpreted in accordance with the law of the Member State in which the court is seized.
(9) Obligations under bills of exchange, cheques and promissory notes and other negotiable instruments should also cover bills of lading to the extent that the obligations under the bill of lading arise out of its negotiable character.
(10) Obligations arising out of dealings prior to the conclusion of the contract are covered by Article 12 of Regulation (EC) No 864/2007. Such obligations should therefore be excluded from the scope of this Regulation.
(11) The parties' freedom to choose the applicable law should be one of the cornerstones of the system of conflict-of-law rules in matters of contractual obligations.
(12) An agreement between the parties to confer on one or more courts or tribunals of a Member State exclusive jurisdiction to determine disputes under the contract should be one of the factors to be taken into account in determining whether a choice of law has been clearly demonstrated.
(13) This Regulation does not preclude parties from incorporating by reference into their contract a non-State body of law or an international convention.
(14) Should the Community adopt, in an appropriate legal instrument, rules of substantive contract law, including standard terms and conditions, such instrument may provide that the parties may choose to apply those rules.
(15) Where a choice of law is made and all other elements relevant to the situation are located in a country other than the country whose law has been chosen, the choice of law should not prejudice the application of provisions of the law of that country which cannot be derogated from by agree-

PART II   PRIVATE INTERNATIONAL LAW

ment. This rule should apply whether or not the choice of law was accompanied by a choice of court or tribunal. Whereas no substantial change is intended as compared with Article 3(3) of the 1980 Convention on the Law Applicable to Contractual Obligations (the Rome Convention), the wording of this Regulation is aligned as far as possible with Article 14 of Regulation (EC) No 864/2007.

(16) To contribute to the general objective of this Regulation, legal certainty in the European judicial area, the conflict-of-law rules should be highly foreseeable. The courts should, however, retain a degree of discretion to determine the law that is most closely connected to the situation.

(17) As far as the applicable law in the absence of choice is concerned, the concept of "provision of services" and "sale of goods" should be interpreted in the same way as when applying Article 5 of Regulation (EC) No 44/2001 in so far as sale of goods and provision of services are covered by that Regulation. Although franchise and distribution contracts are contracts for services, they are the subject of specific rules.

(18) As far as the applicable law in the absence of choice is concerned, multilateral systems should be those in which trading is conducted, such as regulated markets and multilateral trading facilities as referred to in Article 4 of Directive 2004/39/EC of the European Parliament and of the Council of 21 April 2004 on markets in financial instruments, regardless of whether or not they rely on a central counterparty.

(19) Where there has been no choice of law, the applicable law should be determined in accordance with the rule specified for the particular type of contract. Where the contract cannot be categorised as being one of the specified types or where its elements fall within more than one of the specified types, it should be governed by the law of the country where the party required to effect the characteristic performance of the contract has his habitual residence. In the case of a contract consisting of a bundle of rights and obligations capable of being categorised as falling within more than one of the specified types of contract, the characteristic performance of the contract should be determined having regard to its centre of gravity.

(20) Where the contract is manifestly more closely connected with a country other than that indicated in Article 4(1) or (2), an escape clause should provide that the law of that other country is to apply. In order to determine that country, account should be taken, inter alia, of whether the contract in question has a very close relationship with another contract or contracts.

(21) In the absence of choice, where the applicable law cannot be determined either on the basis of the fact that the contract can be categorised as one of the specified types or as being the law of the country of habitual residence of the party required to effect the characteristic performance of the contract, the contract should be governed by the law of the country with which it is most closely connected. In order to determine that country, account should be taken, inter alia, of whether the contract in question has a very close relationship with another contract or contracts.

(22) As regards the interpretation of contracts for the carriage of goods, no change in substance is intended with respect to Article 4(4), third sentence, of the Rome Convention. Consequently, single-voyage charter parties and other contracts the main purpose of which is the carriage of goods should be treated as contracts for the carriage of goods. For the purposes of this Regulation, the term "consignor" should refer to any person who enters into a contract of carriage with the carrier and the term "the carrier" should refer to the party to the contract who undertakes to carry the goods, whether or not he performs the carriage himself.

(23) As regards contracts concluded with parties regarded as being weaker, those parties should be protected by conflict-of-law rules that are more favourable to their interests than the general rules.

(24) With more specific reference to consumer contracts, the conflict-of-law rule should make it possible to cut the cost of settling disputes concerning what are commonly relatively small claims and to take account of the development of distance-selling techniques. Consistency with Regulation (EC) No 44/2001 requires both that there be a reference to the concept of directed activity as a condition for applying the consumer protection rule and that the concept be interpreted harmoniously in Regulation (EC) No 44/2001 and this Regulation, bearing in mind that a joint declaration by the Council and the Commission on Article 15 of Regulation (EC) No 44/2001 states that "for Article 15(1)(c) to be applicable it is not sufficient for an undertaking to target its activities at the Member State of the consumer's residence, or at a number of Member States including that Member State; a contract must also be concluded within the framework of its activities". The declaration also states that "the mere fact that an Internet site is accessible is not sufficient for Article 15 to be applicable, although a factor will be that this Internet site solicits the conclusion of distance contracts and that a contract has actually been concluded at a distance, by whatever means. In this respect, the language or currency which a website uses does not constitute a relevant factor.".

(25) Consumers should be protected by such rules of the country of their habitual residence that cannot be derogated from by agreement, provided that the consumer contract has been concluded

as a result of the professional pursuing his commercial or professional activities in that particular country. The same protection should be guaranteed if the professional, while not pursuing his commercial or professional activities in the country where the consumer has his habitual residence, directs his activities by any means to that country or to several countries, including that country, and the contract is concluded as a result of such activities.

(26) For the purposes of this Regulation, financial services such as investment services and activities and ancillary services provided by a professional to a consumer, as referred to in sections A and B of Annex I to Directive 2004/39/EC, and contracts for the sale of units in collective investment undertakings, whether or not covered by Council Directive 85/611/EEC of 20 December 1985 on the coordination of laws, regulations and administrative provisions relating to undertakings for collective investment in transferable securities (UCITS), should be subject to Article 6 of this Regulation. Consequently, when a reference is made to terms and conditions governing the issuance or offer to the public of transferable securities or to the subscription and redemption of units in collective investment undertakings, that reference should include all aspects binding the issuer or the offeror to the consumer, but should not include those aspects involving the provision of financial services.

(27) Various exceptions should be made to the general conflict-of-law rule for consumer contracts. Under one such exception the general rule should not apply to contracts relating to rights in rem in immovable property or tenancies of such property unless the contract relates to the right to use immovable property on a timeshare basis within the meaning of Directive 94/47/EC of the European Parliament and of the Council of 26 October 1994 on the protection of purchasers in respect of certain aspects of contracts relating to the purchase of the right to use immovable properties on a timeshare basis.

(28) It is important to ensure that rights and obligations which constitute a financial instrument are not covered by the general rule applicable to consumer contracts, as that could lead to different laws being applicable to each of the instruments issued, therefore changing their nature and preventing their fungible trading and offering. Likewise, whenever such instruments are issued or offered, the contractual relationship established between the issuer or the offeror and the consumer should not necessarily be subject to the mandatory application of the law of the country of habitual residence of the consumer, as there is a need to ensure uniformity in the terms and conditions of an issuance or an offer. The same rationale should apply with regard to the multilateral systems covered by Article 4(1)(h), in respect of which it should be ensured that the law of the country of habitual residence of the consumer will not interfere with the rules applicable to contracts concluded within those systems or with the operator of such systems.

(29) For the purposes of this Regulation, references to rights and obligations constituting the terms and conditions governing the issuance, offers to the public or public take-over bids of transferable securities and references to the subscription and redemption of units in collective investment undertakings should include the terms governing, inter alia, the allocation of securities or units, rights in the event of over-subscription, withdrawal rights and similar matters in the context of the offer as well as those matters referred to in Articles 10, 11, 12 and 13, thus ensuring that all relevant contractual aspects of an offer binding the issuer or the offeror to the consumer are governed by a single law.

(30) For the purposes of this Regulation, financial instruments and transferable securities are those instruments referred to in Article 4 of Directive 2004/39/EC.

(31) Nothing in this Regulation should prejudice the operation of a formal arrangement designated as a system under Article 2(a) of Directive 98/26/EC of the European Parliament and of the Council of 19 May 1998 on settlement finality in payment and securities settlement systems.

(32) Owing to the particular nature of contracts of carriage and insurance contracts, specific provisions should ensure an adequate level of protection of passengers and policy holders. Therefore, Article 6 should not apply in the context of those particular contracts.

(33) Where an insurance contract not covering a large risk covers more than one risk, at least one of which is situated in a Member State and at least one of which is situated in a third country, the special rules on insurance contracts in this Regulation should apply only to the risk or risks situated in the relevant Member State or Member States.

(34) The rule on individual employment contracts should not prejudice the application of the overriding mandatory provisions of the country to which a worker is posted in accordance with Directive 96/71/EC of the European Parliament and of the Council of 16 December 1996 concerning the posting of workers in the framework of the provision of services.

(35) Employees should not be deprived of the protection afforded to them by provisions which cannot be derogated from by agreement or which can only be derogated from to their benefit.

(36) As regards individual employment contracts, work carried out in another country should be

PART II   PRIVATE INTERNATIONAL LAW

regarded as temporary if the employee is expected to resume working in the country of origin after carrying out his tasks abroad. The conclusion of a new contract of employment with the original employer or an employer belonging to the same group of companies as the original employer should not preclude the employee from being regarded as carrying out his work in another country temporarily.

(37) Considerations of public interest justify giving the courts of the Member States the possibility, in exceptional circumstances, of applying exceptions based on public policy and overriding mandatory provisions. The concept of "overriding mandatory provisions" should be distinguished from the expression "provisions which cannot be derogated from by agreement" and should be construed more restrictively.

(38) In the context of voluntary assignment, the term "relationship" should make it clear that Article 14(1) also applies to the property aspects of an assignment, as between assignor and assignee, in legal orders where such aspects are treated separately from the aspects under the law of obligations. However, the term "relationship" should not be understood as relating to any relationship that may exist between assignor and assignee. In particular, it should not cover preliminary questions as regards a voluntary assignment or a contractual subrogation. The term should be strictly limited to the aspects which are directly relevant to the voluntary assignment or contractual subrogation in question.

(39) For the sake of legal certainty there should be a clear definition of habitual residence, in particular for companies and other bodies, corporate or unincorporated. Unlike Article 60(1) of Regulation (EC) No 44/2001, which establishes three criteria, the conflict-of-law rule should proceed on the basis of a single criterion; otherwise, the parties would be unable to foresee the law applicable to their situation.

(40) A situation where conflict-of-law rules are dispersed among several instruments and where there are differences between those rules should be avoided. This Regulation, however, should not exclude the possibility of inclusion of conflict-of-law rules relating to contractual obligations in provisions of Community law with regard to particular matters.

This Regulation should not prejudice the application of other instruments laying down provisions designed to contribute to the proper functioning of the internal market in so far as they cannot be applied in conjunction with the law designated by the rules of this Regulation. The application of provisions of the applicable law designated by the rules of this Regulation should not restrict the free movement of goods and services as regulated by Community instruments, such as Directive 2000/31/EC of the European Parliament and of the Council of 8 June 2000 on certain legal aspects of information society services, in particular electronic commerce, in the Internal Market (Directive on electronic commerce).

(41) Respect for international commitments entered into by the Member States means that this Regulation should not affect international conventions to which one or more Member States are parties at the time when this Regulation is adopted. To make the rules more accessible, the Commission should publish the list of the relevant conventions in the Official Journal of the European Union on the basis of information supplied by the Member States

(42) The Commission will make a proposal to the European Parliament and to the Council concerning the procedures and conditions according to which Member States would be entitled to negotiate and conclude, on their own behalf, agreements with third countries in individual and exceptional cases, concerning sectoral matters and containing provisions on the law applicable to contractual obligations.

(43) Since the objective of this Regulation cannot be sufficiently achieved by the Member States and can therefore, by reason of the scale and effects of this Regulation, be better achieved at Community level, the Community may adopt measures, in accordance with the principle of subsidiarity as set out in Article 5 of the Treaty. In accordance with the principle of proportionality, as set out in that Article, this Regulation does not go beyond what is necessary to attain its objective.

(44) In accordance with Article 3 of the Protocol on the position of the United Kingdom and Ireland, annexed to the Treaty on European Union and to the Treaty establishing the European Community, Ireland has notified its wish to take part in the adoption and application of the present Regulation.

(45) In accordance with Articles 1 and 2 of the Protocol on the position of the United Kingdom and Ireland, annexed to the Treaty on European Union and to the Treaty establishing the European Community, and without prejudice to Article 4 of the said Protocol, the United Kingdom is not taking part in the adoption of this Regulation and is not bound by it or subject to its application.

(46) In accordance with Articles 1 and 2 of the Protocol on the position of Denmark, annexed to the Treaty on European Union and to the Treaty establishing the European Community, Denmark is not taking part in the adoption of this Regulation and is not bound by it or subject to its application,

HAVE ADOPTED THIS REGULATION:

Chapter I. Scope

Article 1. (1) This Regulation shall apply, in situations involving a conflict of laws, to contractual obligations in civil and commercial matters.
It shall not apply, in particular, to revenue, customs or administrative matters.
(2) The following shall be excluded from the scope of this Regulation:
(a) questions involving the status or legal capacity of natural persons, without prejudice to Article 13;
(b) obligations arising out of family relationships and relationships deemed by the law applicable to such relationships to have comparable effects, including maintenance obligations;
(c) obligations arising out of matrimonial property regimes, property regimes of relationships deemed by the law applicable to such relationships to have comparable effects to marriage, and wills and succession;
(d) obligations arising under bills of exchange, cheques and promissory notes and other negotiable instruments to the extent that the obligations under such other negotiable instruments arise out of their negotiable character;
(e) arbitration agreements and agreements on the choice of court;
(f) questions governed by the law of companies and other bodies, corporate or unincorporated, such as the creation, by registration or otherwise, legal capacity, internal organisation or winding-up of companies and other bodies, corporate or unincorporated, and the personal liability of officers and members as such for the obligations of the company or body;
(g) the question whether an agent is able to bind a principal, or an organ to bind a company or other body corporate or unincorporated, in relation to a third party;
(h) the constitution of trusts and the relationship between settlors, trustees and beneficiaries;
(i) obligations arising out of dealings prior to the conclusion of a contract;
(j) insurance contracts arising out of operations carried out by organisations other than undertakings referred to in Article 2 of Directive 2002/83/EC of the European Parliament and of the Council of 5 November 2002 concerning life assurance the object of which is to provide benefits for employed or self-employed persons belonging to an undertaking or group of undertakings, or to a trade or group of trades, in the event of death or survival or of discontinuance or curtailment of activity, or of sickness related to work or accidents at work.
(3) This Regulation shall not apply to evidence and procedure, without prejudice to Article 18.
(4) In this Regulation, the term "Member State" shall mean Member States to which this Regulation applies. However, in Article 3(4) and Article 7 the term shall mean all the Member States.

Article 2. Any law specified by this Regulation shall be applied whether or not it is the law of a Member State.

Chapter II. Uniform Rules

Article 3. (1) A contract shall be governed by the law chosen by the parties. The choice shall be made expressly or clearly demonstrated by the terms of the contract or the circumstances of the case. By their choice the parties can select the law applicable to the whole or to part only of the contract.
(2) The parties may at any time agree to subject the contract to a law other than that which previously governed it, whether as a result of an earlier choice made under this Article or of other provisions of this Regulation. Any change in the law to be applied that is made after the conclusion of the contract shall not prejudice its formal validity under Article 11 or adversely affect the rights of third parties.
(3) Where all other elements relevant to the situation at the time of the choice are located in a country other than the country whose law has been chosen, the choice of the parties shall not prejudice the application of provisions of the law of that other country which cannot be derogated from by agreement.
(4) Where all other elements relevant to the situation at the time of the choice are located in one or more Member States, the parties' choice of applicable law other than that of a Member State shall not prejudice the application of provisions of Community law, where appropriate as implemented in the Member State of the forum, which cannot be derogated from by agreement.
(5) The existence and validity of the consent of the parties as to the choice of the applicable law shall be determined in accordance with the provisions of Articles 10, 11 and 13.

Article 4. (1) To the extent that the law applicable to the contract has not been chosen in accordance with Article 3 and without prejudice to Articles 5 to 8, the law governing the contract shall be determined as follows:

(a) a contract for the sale of goods shall be governed by the law of the country where the seller has his habitual residence;
(b) a contract for the provision of services shall be governed by the law of the country where the service provider has his habitual residence;
(c) a contract relating to a right in rem in immovable property or to a tenancy of immovable property shall be governed by the law of the country where the property is situated;
(d) notwithstanding point (c), a tenancy of immovable property concluded for temporary private use for a period of no more than six consecutive months shall be governed by the law of the country where the landlord has his habitual residence, provided that the tenant is a natural person and has his habitual residence in the same country;
(e) a franchise contract shall be governed by the law of the country where the franchisee has his habitual residence;
(f) a distribution contract shall be governed by the law of the country where the distributor has his habitual residence;
(g) a contract for the sale of goods by auction shall be governed by the law of the country where the auction takes place, if such a place can be determined;
(h) a contract concluded within a multilateral system which brings together or facilitates the bringing together of multiple third-party buying and selling interests in financial instruments, as defined by Article 4(1), point (17) of Directive 2004/39/EC, in accordance with non-discretionary rules and governed by a single law, shall be governed by that law.
(2) Where the contract is not covered by paragraph (1) or where the elements of the contract would be covered by more than one of points (a) to (h) of paragraph (1), the contract shall be governed by the law of the country where the party required to effect the characteristic performance of the contract has his habitual residence.
(3) Where it is clear from all the circumstances of the case that the contract is manifestly more closely connected with a country other than that indicated in paragraphs 1 or 2, the law of that other country shall apply.
(4) Where the law applicable cannot be determined pursuant to paragraphs 1 or 2, the contract shall be governed by the law of the country with which it is most closely connected.

Article 5. (1) To the extent that the law applicable to a contract for the carriage of goods has not been chosen in accordance with Article 3, the law applicable shall be the law of the country of habitual residence of the carrier, provided that the place of receipt or the place of delivery or the habitual residence of the consignor is also situated in that country. If those requirements are not met, the law of the country where the place of delivery as agreed by the parties is situated shall apply.
(2) To the extent that the law applicable to a contract for the carriage of passengers has not been chosen by the parties in accordance with the second subparagraph, the law applicable shall be the law of the country where the passenger has his habitual residence, provided that either the place of departure or the place of destination is situated in that country. If these requirements are not met, the law of the country where the carrier has his habitual residence shall apply.
The parties may choose as the law applicable to a contract for the carriage of passengers in accordance with Article 3 only the law of the country where:
(a) the passenger has his habitual residence; or
(b) the carrier has his habitual residence; or
(c) the carrier has his place of central administration; or
(d) the place of departure is situated; or
(e) the place of destination is situated.
(3) Where it is clear from all the circumstances of the case that the contract, in the absence of a choice of law, is manifestly more closely connected with a country other than that indicated in paragraphs 1 or 2, the law of that other country shall apply.

Article 6. (1) Without prejudice to Articles 5 and 7, a contract concluded by a natural person for a purpose which can be regarded as being outside his trade or profession ("the consumer") with another person acting in the exercise of his trade or profession ("the professional") shall be governed by the law of the country where the consumer has his habitual residence, provided that the professional:
(a) pursues his commercial or professional activities in the country where the consumer has his habitual residence, or
(b) by any means, directs such activities to that country or to several countries including that country, and the contract falls within the scope of such activities.
(2) Notwithstanding paragraph (1), the parties may choose the law applicable to a contract which fulfils the requirements of paragraph (1), in accordance with Article 3. Such a choice

may not, however, have the result of depriving the consumer of the protection afforded to him by provisions that cannot be derogated from by agreement by virtue of the law which, in the absence of choice, would have been applicable on the basis of paragraph (1).
(3) If the requirements in points (a) or (b) of paragraph (1) are not fulfilled, the law applicable to a contract between a consumer and a professional shall be determined pursuant to Articles 3 and 4.
(4) Paragraphs 1 and 2 shall not apply to:
(a) a contract for the supply of services where the services are to be supplied to the consumer exclusively in a country other than that in which he has his habitual residence;
(b) a contract of carriage other than a contract relating to package travel within the meaning of Council Directive 90/314/EEC of 13 June 1990 on package travel,
package holidays and package tours;
(c) a contract relating to a right in rem in immovable property or a tenancy of immovable property other than a contract relating to the right to use immovable properties on a timeshare basis within the meaning of Directive 94/47/EC;
(d) rights and obligations which constitute a financial instrument and rights and obligations constituting the terms and conditions governing the issuance or offer to the public and public take-over bids of transferable securities, and the subscription and redemption of units in collective investment undertakings in so far as these activities do not constitute provision of a financial service;
(e) a contract concluded within the type of system falling within the scope of Article 4(1), point (h).

Article 7. ( ) This Article shall apply to contracts referred to in paragraph (2), whether or not the risk covered is situated in a Member State, and to all other insurance contracts covering risks situated inside the territory of the Member States. It shall not apply to reinsurance contracts.
(2) An insurance contract covering a large risk as defined in Article 5(d) of the First Council Directive 73/239/EEC of 24 July 1973 on the coordination of laws, regulations and administrative provisions relating to the taking-up and pursuit of the business of direct insurance other than life assurance1 shall be governed by the law chosen by the parties in accordance with Article 3 of this Regulation. To the extent that the applicable law has not been chosen by the parties, the insurance contract shall be governed by the law of the country where the insurer has his habitual residence. Where it is clear from all the circumstances of the case that the contract is manifestly more closely connected with another country, the law of that other country shall apply.
(3) In the case of an insurance contract other than a contract falling within paragraph (2), only the following laws may be chosen by the parties in accordance with Article 3:
(a) the law of any Member State where the risk is situated at the time of conclusion of the contract;
(b) the law of the country where the policy holder has his habitual residence;
(c) in the case of life assurance, the law of the Member State of which the policy holder is a national;
(d) for insurance contracts covering risks limited to events occurring in one Member State other than the Member State where the risk is situated, the law of that Member State;
(e) where the policy holder of a contract falling under this paragraph pursues a commercial or industrial activity or a liberal profession and the insurance contract covers two or more risks which relate to those activities and are situated in different Member States, the law of any of the Member States concerned or the law of the country of habitual residence of the policy holder.
Where, in the cases set out in points (a), (b) or (e), the Member States referred to grant greater freedom of choice of the law applicable to the insurance contract, the parties may take advantage of that freedom.
To the extent that the law applicable has not been chosen by the parties in accordance with this paragraph, such a contract shall be governed by the law of the Member State in which the risk is situated at the time of conclusion of the contract.
(4) The following additional rules shall apply to insurance contracts covering risks for which a Member State imposes an obligation to take out insurance:
(a) the insurance contract shall not satisfy the obligation to take out insurance unless it complies with the specific provisions relating to that insurance laid down by the Member State that imposes the obligation. Where the law of the Member State in which the risk is situated and the law of the Member State imposing the obligation to take out insurance contradict each other, the latter shall prevail;
(b) by way of derogation from paragraphs 2 and 3, a Member State may lay down that the insurance contract shall be governed by the law of the Member State that imposes the obligation to take out insurance.
(5) For the purposes of paragraph (3), third subparagraph, and paragraph (4), where the contract covers risks situated in more than one Member State, the contract shall be considered as constituting

several contracts each relating to only one Member State.

(6) For the purposes of this Article, the country in which the risk is situated shall be determined in accordance with Article 2(d) of the Second Council Directive 88/357/EEC of 22 June 1988 on the coordination of laws, regulations and administrative provisions relating to direct insurance other than life assurance and laying down provisions to facilitate the effective exercise of freedom to provide services1 and, in the case of life assurance, the country in which the risk is situated shall be the country of the commitment within the meaning of Article 1(1)(g) of Directive 2002/83/EC.

Article 8. (1) An individual employment contract shall be governed by the law chosen by the parties in accordance with Article 3. Such a choice of law may not, however, have the result of depriving the employee of the protection afforded to him by provisions that cannot be derogated from by agreement under the law that, in the absence of choice, would have been applicable pursuant to paragraphs 2, 3 and 4 of this Article.

(2) To the extent that the law applicable to the individual employment contract has not been chosen by the parties, the contract shall be governed by the law of the country in which or, failing that, from which the employee habitually carries out his work in performance of the contract. The country where the work is habitually carried out shall not be deemed to have changed if he is temporarily employed in another country.

(3) Where the law applicable cannot be determined pursuant to paragraph (2), the contract shall be governed by the law of the country where the place of business through which the employee was engaged is situated.

(4) Where it appears from the circumstances as a whole that the contract is more closely connected with a country other than that indicated in paragraphs 2 or 3, the law of that other country shall apply.

Article 9. (1) Overriding mandatory provisions are provisions the respect for which is regarded as crucial by a country for safeguarding its public interests, such as its political, social or economic organisation, to such an extent that they are applicable to any situation falling within their scope, irrespective of the law otherwise applicable to the contract under this Regulation.

(2) Nothing in this Regulation shall restrict the application of the overriding mandatory provisions of the law of the forum.

(3) Effect may be given to the overriding mandatory provisions of the law of the country where the obligations arising out of the contract have to be or have been performed, in so far as those overriding mandatory provisions render the performance of the contract unlawful. In considering whether to give effect to those provisions, regard shall be had to their nature and purpose and to the consequences of their application or non-application.

Article 10. (1) The existence and validity of a contract, or of any term of a contract, shall be determined by the law which would govern it under this Regulation if the contract or term were valid.

(2) Nevertheless, a party, in order to establish that he did not consent, may rely upon the law of the country in which he has his habitual residence if it appears from the circumstances that it would not be reasonable to determine the effect of his conduct in accordance with the law specified in paragraph (1).

Article 11. (1) A contract concluded between persons who, or whose agents, are in the same country at the time of its conclusion is formally valid if it satisfies the formal requirements of the law which governs it in substance under this Regulation or of the law of the country where it is concluded.

(2) A contract concluded between persons who, or whose agents, are in different countries at the time of its conclusion is formally valid if it satisfies the formal requirements of the law which governs it in substance under this Regulation, or of the law of either of the countries where either of the parties or their agent is present at the time of conclusion, or of the law of the country where either of the parties had his habitual residence at that time.

(3) A unilateral act intended to have legal effect relating to an existing or contemplated contract is formally valid if it satisfies the formal requirements of the law which governs or would govern the contract in substance under this Regulation, or of the law of the country where the act was done, or of the law of the country where the person by whom it was done had his habitual residence at that time.

(4) Paragraphs 1, 2 and 3 of this Article shall not apply to contracts that fall within the scope of Article 6. The form of such contracts shall be governed by the law of the country where the consumer has his habitual residence.

(5) Notwithstanding paragraphs 1 to 4, a contract the subject matter of which is a right in rem in immovable property or a tenancy of immovable property shall be subject to the requirements of form of the law of the country where the property is situated if by that law:

(a) those requirements are imposed irrespective of the country where the contract is concluded and

irrespective of the law governing the contract, and
(b) those requirements cannot be derogated from by agreement.

Article 12. (1) The law applicable to a contract by virtue of this Regulation shall govern in particular:
(a) interpretation;
(b) performance;
(c) within the limits of the powers conferred on the court by its procedural law, the consequences of a total or partial breach of obligations, including the assessment of damages in so far as it is governed by rules of law;
(d) the various ways of extinguishing obligations, and prescription and limitation of actions;
(e) the consequences of nullity of the contract.
(2) In relation to the manner of performance and the steps to be taken in the event of defective performance, regard shall be had to the law of the country in which performance takes place.

Article 13. In a contract concluded between persons who are in the same country, a natural person who would have capacity under the law of that country may invoke his incapacity resulting from the law of another country, only if the other party to the contract was aware of that incapacity at the time of the conclusion of the contract or was not aware thereof as a result of negligence.

Article 14. (1) The relationship between assignor and assignee under a voluntary assignment or contractual subrogation of a claim against another person ("the debtor") shall be governed by the law that applies to the contract between the assignor and assignee under this Regulation.
(2) The law governing the assigned or subrogated claim shall determine its assignability, the relationship between the assignee and the debtor, the conditions under which the assignment or subrogation can be invoked against the debtor and whether the debtor's obligations have been discharged.
(3) The concept of assignment in this Article includes outright transfers of claims, transfers of claims by way of security and pledges or other security rights over claims.

Article 15. Where a person ("the creditor") has a contractual claim against another ("the debtor") and a third person has a duty to satisfy the creditor, or has in fact satisfied the creditor in discharge of that duty, the law which governs the third person's duty to satisfy the creditor shall determine whether and to what extent the third person is entitled to exercise against the debtor the rights which the creditor had against the debtor under the law governing their relationship.

Article 16. If a creditor has a claim against several debtors who are liable for the same claim, and one of the debtors has already satisfied the claim in whole or in part, the law governing the debtor's obligation towards the creditor also governs the debtor's right to claim recourse from the other debtors. The other debtors may rely on the defences they had against the creditor to the extent allowed by the law governing their obligations towards the creditor.

Article 17. Where the right to set-off is not agreed by the parties, set-off shall be governed by the law applicable to the claim against which the right to set-off is asserted.

Article 18. (1) The law governing a contractual obligation under this Regulation shall apply to the extent that, in matters of contractual obligations, it contains rules which raise presumptions of law or determine the burden of proof.
(2) A contract or an act intended to have legal effect may be proved by any mode of proof recognised by the law of the forum or by any of the laws referred to in Article 11 under which that contract or act is formally valid, provided that such mode of proof can be administered by the forum.

Chapter III. Other Provisions

Article 19. (1) For the purposes of this Regulation, the habitual residence of companies and other bodies, corporate or unincorporated, shall be the place of central administration.
The habitual residence of a natural person acting in the course of his business activity shall be his principal place of business.
(2) Where the contract is concluded in the course of the operations of a branch, agency or any other establishment, or if, under the contract, performance is the responsibility of such a branch, agency or establishment, the place where the branch, agency or any other establishment is located shall be treated as the place of habitual residence.
(3) For the purposes of determining the habitual residence, the relevant point in time shall be the time of the conclusion of the contract.

Article 20. The application of the law of any country specified by this Regulation means the applica-

PART II PRIVATE INTERNATIONAL LAW

tion of the rules of law in force in that country other than its rules of private international law, unless provided otherwise in this Regulation.

Article 21. The application of a provision of the law of any country specified by this Regulation may be refused only if such application is manifestly incompatible with the public policy (*ordre public*) of the forum.

Article 22. (1) Where a State comprises several territorial units, each of which has its own rules of law in respect of contractual obligations, each territorial unit shall be considered as a country for the purposes of identifying the law applicable under this Regulation.
(2) A Member State where different territorial units have their own rules of law in respect of contractual obligations shall not be required to apply this Regulation to conflicts solely between the laws of such units.

Article 23. With the exception of Article 7, this Regulation shall not prejudice the application of provisions of Community law which, in relation to particular matters, lay down conflict-of-law rules relating to contractual obligations.

Article 24. (1) This Regulation shall replace the Rome Convention in the Member States, except as regards the territories of the Member States which fall within the territorial scope of that Convention and to which this Regulation does not apply pursuant to Article 299 of the Treaty.
(2) In so far as this Regulation replaces the provisions of the Rome Convention, any reference to that Convention shall be understood as a reference to this Regulation.

Article 25. (1) This Regulation shall not prejudice the application of international conventions to which one or more Member States are parties at the time when this Regulation is adopted and which lay down conflict-of-law rules relating to contractual obligations.
(2) However, this Regulation shall, as between Member States, take precedence over conventions concluded exclusively between two or more of them in so far as such conventions concern matters governed by this Regulation.

Article 26. (1) By 17 June 2009, Member States shall notify the Commission of the conventions referred to in Article 25(1). After that date, Member States shall notify the Commission of all denunciations of such conventions.
(2) Within six months of receipt of the notifications referred to in paragraph (1), the Commission shall publish in the *Official Journal of the European Union*:
(a) a list of the conventions referred to in paragraph (1);
(b) the denunciations referred to in paragraph (1).

Article 27. (1) By 17 June 2013, the Commission shall submit to the European Parliament, the Council and the European Economic and Social Committee a report on the application of this Regulation. If appropriate, the report shall be accompanied by proposals to amend this Regulation. The report shall include:
(a) a study on the law applicable to insurance contracts and an assessment of the impact of the provisions to be introduced, if any; and
(b) an evaluation on the application of Article 6, in particular as regards the coherence of Community law in the field of consumer protection.
(2) By 17 June 2010, the Commission shall submit to the European Parliament, the Council and the European Economic and Social Committee a report on the question of the effectiveness of an assignment or subrogation of a claim against third parties and the priority of the assigned or subrogated claim over a right of another person. The report shall be accompanied, if appropriate, by a proposal to amend this Regulation and an assessment of the impact of the provisions to be introduced.

Article 28. This Regulation shall apply to contracts concluded after 17 December 2009.

Chapter IV. Final Provisions

Article 29. This Regulation shall enter into force on the twentieth day following its publication in the *Official Journal of the European Union*.
It shall apply from 17 December 2009 except for Article 26 which shall apply from 17 June 2009.
This Regulation shall be binding in its entirety and directly applicable in the Member States in accordance with the Treaty establishing the European Community.

EU: ROME II REGULATION

Regulation (EC) 864/2007 of the European Parliament and of the Council of 11 July 2007 on the law applicable to non-contractual obligations [Rome II] (OJ L199, 31.7.2007, pp. 40 – 49) [footnotes omitted].

THE EUROPEAN PARLIAMENT AND THE COUNCIL OF THE EUROPEAN UNION,
Having regard to the Treaty establishing the European Community, and in particular Articles 61(c) and 67 thereof,
Having regard to the proposal from the Commission,
Having regard to the opinion of the European Economic and Social Committee,
Acting in accordance with the procedure laid down in Article 251 of the Treaty in the light of the joint text approved by the Conciliation Committee on 25 June 2007,
Whereas:
(1) The Community has set itself the objective of maintaining and developing an area of freedom, security and justice. For the progressive establishment of such an area, the Community is to adopt measures relating to judicial cooperation in civil matters with a cross-border impact to the extent necessary for the proper functioning of the internal market.
(2) According to Article 65(b) of the Treaty, these measures are to include those promoting the compatibility of the rules applicable in the Member States concerning the conflict of laws and of jurisdiction.
(3) The European Council meeting in Tampere on 15 and 16 October 1999 endorsed the principle of mutual recognition of judgments and other decisions of judicial authorities as the cornerstone of judicial cooperation in civil matters and invited the Council and the Commission to adopt a programme of measures to implement the principle of mutual recognition.
(4) On 30 November 2000, the Council adopted a joint Commission and Council programme of measures for implementation of the principle of mutual recognition of decisions in civil and commercial matters. The programme identifies measures relating to the harmonisation of conflict-of-law rules as those facilitating the mutual recognition of judgments.
(5) The Hague Programme, adopted by the European Council on 5 November 2004, called for work to be pursued actively on the rules of conflict of laws regarding non-contractual obligations (Rome II).
(6) The proper functioning of the internal market creates a need, in order to improve the predictability of the outcome of litigation, certainty as to the law applicable and the free movement of judgments, for the conflict-of-law rules in the Member States to designate the same national law irrespective of the country of the court in which an action is brought.
(7) The substantive scope and the provisions of this Regulation should be consistent with Council Regulation (EC) No 44/2001 of 22 December 2000 on jurisdiction and the recognition and enforcement of judgments in civil and commercial matters (Brussels I) and the instruments dealing with the law applicable to contractual obligations.
(8) This Regulation should apply irrespective of the nature of the court or tribunal seised.
(9) Claims arising out of acta iure imperii should include claims against officials who act on behalf of the State and liability for acts of public authorities, including liability of publicly appointed officeholders. Therefore, these matters should be excluded from the scope of this Regulation.
(10) Family relationships should cover parentage, marriage, affinity and collateral relatives. The reference in Article 1(2) to relationships having comparable effects to marriage and other family relationships should be interpreted in accordance with the law of the Member State in which the court is seised.
(11) The concept of a non-contractual obligation varies from one Member State to another. Therefore for the purposes of this Regulation non-contractual obligation should be understood as an autonomous concept. The conflict-of-law rules set out in this Regulation should also cover non-contractual obligations arising out of strict liability.
(12) The law applicable should also govern the question of the capacity to incur liability in tort/delict.
(13) Uniform rules applied irrespective of the law they designate may avert the risk of distortions of competition between Community litigants.
(14) The requirement of legal certainty and the need to do justice in individual cases are essential elements of an area of justice. This Regulation provides for the connecting factors which are the most appropriate to achieve these objectives. Therefore, this Regulation provides for a general rule but also for specific rules and, in certain provisions, for an "escape clause" which allows a departure from these rules where it is clear from all the circumstances of the case that the tort/delict is manifestly more closely connected with another country. This set of rules thus creates a flexible framework

PART II   PRIVATE INTERNATIONAL LAW

of conflict-of-law rules. Equally, it enables the court seised to treat individual cases in an appropriate manner.

(15) The principle of the lex loci delicti commissi is the basic solution for non-contractual obligations in virtually all the Member States, but the practical application of the principle where the component factors of the case are spread over several countries varies. This situation engenders uncertainty as to the law applicable.

(16) Uniform rules should enhance the foreseeability of court decisions and ensure a reasonable balance between the interests of the person claimed to be liable and the person who has sustained damage. A connection with the country where the direct damage occurred (lex loci damni) strikes a fair balance between the interests of the person claimed to be liable and the person sustaining the damage, and also reflects the modern approach to civil liability and the development of systems of strict liability.

(17) The law applicable should be determined on the basis of where the damage occurs, regardless of the country or countries in which the indirect consequences could occur. Accordingly, in cases of personal injury or damage to property, the country in which the damage occurs should be the country where the injury was sustained or the property was damaged respectively.

(18) The general rule in this Regulation should be the lex loci damni provided for in Article 4(1). Article 4(2) should be seen as an exception to this general principle, creating a special connection where the parties have their habitual residence in the same country. Article 4(3) should be understood as an 'escape clause' from Article 4(1) and (2), where it is clear from all the circumstances of the case that the tort/delict is manifestly more closely connected with another country.

(19) Specific rules should be laid down for special torts/delicts where the general rule does not allow a reasonable balance to be struck between the interests at stake.

(20) The conflict-of-law rule in matters of product liability should meet the objectives of fairly spreading the risks inherent in a modern high-technology society, protecting consumers' health, stimulating innovation, securing undistorted competition and facilitating trade. Creation of a cascade system of connecting factors, together with a foreseeability clause, is a balanced solution in regard to these objectives. The first element to be taken into account is the law of the country in which the person sustaining the damage had his or her habitual residence when the damage occurred, if the product was marketed in that country. The other elements of the cascade are triggered if the product was not marketed in that country, without prejudice to Article 4(2) and to the possibility of a manifestly closer connection to another country.

(21) The special rule in Article 6 is not an exception to the general rule in Article 4(1) but rather a clarification of it. In matters of unfair competition, the conflict-of-law rule should protect competitors, consumers and the general public and ensure that the market economy functions properly. The connection to the law of the country where competitive relations or the collective interests of consumers are, or are likely to be, affected generally satisfies these objectives.

(22) The non-contractual obligations arising out of restrictions of competition in Article 6(3) should cover infringements of both national and Community competition law. The law applicable to such non-contractual obligations should be the law of the country where the market is, or is likely to be, affected. In cases where the market is, or is likely to be, affected in more than one country, the claimant should be able in certain circumstances to choose to base his or her claim on the law of the court seised.

(23) For the purposes of this Regulation, the concept of restriction of competition should cover prohibitions on agreements between undertakings, decisions by associations of undertakings and concerted practices which have as their object or effect the prevention, restriction or distortion of competition within a Member State or within the internal market, as well as prohibitions on the abuse of a dominant position within a Member State or within the internal market, where such agreements, decisions, concerted practices or abuses are prohibited by Articles 81 and 82 of the Treaty or by the law of a Member State.

(24) "Environmental damage" should be understood as meaning adverse change in a natural resource, such as water, land or air, impairment of a function performed by that resource for the benefit of another natural resource or the public, or impairment of the variability among living organisms.

(25) Regarding environmental damage, Article 174 of the Treaty, which provides that there should be a high level of protection based on the precautionary principle and the principle that preventive action should be taken, the principle of priority for corrective action at source and the principle that the polluter pays, fully justifies the use of the principle of discriminating in favour of the person sustaining the damage. The question of when the person seeking compensation can make the choice of the law applicable should be determined in accordance with the law of the Member State in which

the court is seised.

(26) Regarding infringements of intellectual property rights, the universally acknowledged principle of the lex loci protectionis should be preserved. For the purposes of this Regulation, the term 'intellectual property rights' should be interpreted as meaning, for instance, copyright, related rights, the sui generis right for the protection of databases and industrial property rights.

(27) The exact concept of industrial action, such as strike action or lock-out, varies from one Member State to another and is governed by each Member State's internal rules. Therefore, this Regulation assumes as a general principle that the law of the country where the industrial action was taken should apply, with the aim of protecting the rights and obligations of workers and employers.

(28) The special rule on industrial action in Article 9 is without prejudice to the conditions relating to the exercise of such action in accordance with national law and without prejudice to the legal status of trade unions or of the representative organisations of workers as provided for in the law of the Member States.

(29) Provision should be made for special rules where damage is caused by an act other than a tort/delict, such as unjust enrichment, negotiorum gestio and culpa in contrahendo.

(30) Culpa in contrahendo for the purposes of this Regulation is an autonomous concept and should not necessarily be interpreted within the meaning of national law. It should include the violation of the duty of disclosure and the breakdown of contractual negotiations. Article 12 covers only non-contractual obligations presenting a direct link with the dealings prior to the conclusion of a contract. This means that if, while a contract is being negotiated, a person suffers personal injury, Article 4 or other relevant provisions of this Regulation should apply.

(31) To respect the principle of party autonomy and to enhance legal certainty, the parties should be allowed to make a choice as to the law applicable to a non-contractual obligation. This choice should be expressed or demonstrated with reasonable certainty by the circumstances of the case. Where establishing the existence of the agreement, the court has to respect the intentions of the parties. Protection should be given to weaker parties by imposing certain conditions on the choice.

(32) Considerations of public interest justify giving the courts of the Member States the possibility, in exceptional circumstances, of applying exceptions based on public policy and overriding mandatory provisions. In particular, the application of a provision of the law designated by this Regulation which would have the effect of causing non-compensatory exemplary or punitive damages of an excessive nature to be awarded may, depending on the circumstances of the case and the legal order of the Member State of the court seised, be regarded as being contrary to the public policy (ordre public) of the forum.

(33) According to the current national rules on compensation awarded to victims of road traffic accidents, when quantifying damages for personal injury in cases in which the accident takes place in a State other than that of the habitual residence of the victim, the court seised should take into account all the relevant actual circumstances of the specific victim, including in particular the actual losses and costs of after-care and medical attention.

(34) In order to strike a reasonable balance between the parties, account must be taken, in so far as appropriate, of the rules of safety and conduct in operation in the country in which the harmful act was committed, even where the non-contractual obligation is governed by the law of another country. The term "rules of safety and conduct" should be interpreted as referring to all regulations having any relation to safety and conduct, including, for example, road safety rules in the case of an accident.

(35) A situation where conflict-of-law rules are dispersed among several instruments and where there are differences between those rules should be avoided. This Regulation, however, does not exclude the possibility of inclusion of conflict-of-law rules relating to non-contractual obligations in provisions of Community law with regard to particular matters.

This Regulation should not prejudice the application of other instruments laying down provisions designed to contribute to the proper functioning of the internal market in so far as they cannot be applied in conjunction with the law designated by the rules of this Regulation. The application of provisions of the applicable law designated by the rules of this Regulation should not restrict the free movement of goods and services as regulated by Community instruments, such as Directive 2000/31/EC of the European Parliament and of the Council of 8 June 2000 on certain legal aspects of information society services, in particular electronic commerce, in the Internal Market (Directive on electronic commerce).

(36) Respect for international commitments entered into by the Member States means that this Regulation should not affect international conventions to which one or more Member States are parties at the time this Regulation is adopted. To make the rules more accessible, the Commission should publish the list of the relevant conventions in the Official Journal of the European Union on the basis

of information supplied by the Member States.

(37) The Commission will make a proposal to the European Parliament and the Council concerning the procedures and conditions according to which Member States would be entitled to negotiate and conclude on their own behalf agreements with third countries in individual and exceptional cases, concerning sectoral matters, containing provisions on the law applicable to non-contractual obligations.

(38) Since the objective of this Regulation cannot be sufficiently achieved by the Member States, and can therefore, by reason of the scale and effects of this Regulation, be better achieved at Community level, the Community may adopt measures, in accordance with the principle of subsidiarity set out in Article 5 of the Treaty. In accordance with the principle of proportionality set out in that Article, this Regulation does not go beyond what is necessary to attain that objective.

(39) In accordance with Article 3 of the Protocol on the position of the United Kingdom and Ireland annexed to the Treaty on European Union and to the Treaty establishing the European Community, the United Kingdom and Ireland are taking part in the adoption and application of this Regulation.

(40) In accordance with Articles 1 and 2 of the Protocol on the position of Denmark, annexed to the Treaty on European Union and to the Treaty establishing the European Community, Denmark does not take part in the adoption of this Regulation, and is not bound by it or subject to its application,

HAVE ADOPTED THIS REGULATION:

Chapter 1. Scope

Article 1. (1) This Regulation shall apply, in situations involving a conflict of laws, to non-contractual obligations in civil and commercial matters. It shall not apply, in particular, to revenue, customs or administrative matters or to the liability of the State for acts and omissions in the exercise of State authority (*acta iure imperii*).

(2) The following shall be excluded from the scope of this Regulation:

(a) non-contractual obligations arising out of family relationships and relationships deemed by the law applicable to such relationships to have comparable effects including maintenance obligations;

(b) non-contractual obligations arising out of matrimonial property regimes, property regimes of relationships deemed by the law applicable to such relationships to have comparable effects to marriage, and wills and succession;

(c) non-contractual obligations arising under bills of exchange, cheques and promissory notes and other negotiable instruments to the extent that the obligations under such other negotiable instruments arise out of their negotiable character;

(d) non-contractual obligations arising out of the law of companies and other bodies corporate or unincorporated regarding matters such as the creation, by registration or otherwise, legal capacity, internal organisation or winding-up of companies and other bodies corporate or unincorporated, the personal liability of officers and members as such for the obligations of the company or body and the personal liability of auditors to a company or to its members in the statutory audits of accounting documents;

(e) non-contractual obligations arising out of the relations between the settlors, trustees and beneficiaries of a trust created voluntarily;

(f) non-contractual obligations arising out of nuclear damage;

(g) non-contractual obligations arising out of violations of privacy and rights relating to personality, including defamation.

(3) This Regulation shall not apply to evidence and procedure, without prejudice to Articles 21 and 22.

(4) For the purposes of this Regulation, "Member State" shall mean any Member State other than Denmark.

Article 2. (1) For the purposes of this Regulation, damage shall cover any consequence arising out of tort/delict, unjust enrichment, *negotiorum gestio* or *culpa in contrahendo*.

(2) This Regulation shall apply also to non-contractual obligations that are likely to arise.

(3) Any reference in this Regulation to:

(a) an event giving rise to damage shall include events giving rise to damage that are likely to occur; and

(b) damage shall include damage that is likely to occur.

Article 3. Any law specified by this Regulation shall be applied whether or not it is the law of a Member State.

Chapter II. Torts/Delicts

Article 4. (1) Unless otherwise provided for in this Regulation, the law applicable to a non-contractual obligation arising out of a tort/delict shall be the law of the country in which the damage occurs irrespective of the country in which the event giving rise to the damage occurred and irrespective of the country or countries in which the indirect consequences of that event occur.
(2) However, where the person claimed to be liable and the person sustaining damage both have their habitual residence in the same country at the time when the damage occurs, the law of that country shall apply.
(3) Where it is clear from all the circumstances of the case that the tort/delict is manifestly more closely connected with a country other than that indicated in paragraphs 1 or 2, the law of that other country shall apply. A manifestly closer connection with another country might be based in particular on a pre-existing relationship between the parties, such as a contract, that is closely connected with the tort/delict in question.

Article 5. (1) Without prejudice to Article 4(2), the law applicable to a non-contractual obligation arising out of damage caused by a product shall be:
(a) the law of the country in which the person sustaining the damage had his or her habitual residence when the damage occurred, if the product was marketed in that country; or, failing that,
(b) the law of the country in which the product was acquired, if the product was marketed in that country; or failing that,
(c) the law of the country in which the damage occurred, if the product was marketed in that country. However, the law applicable shall be the law of the country in which the person claimed to be liable is habitually resident if he or she could not reasonably foresee the marketing of the product, or a product of the same type, in the country the law of which is applicable under (a), (b) or (c).
(2) Where it is clear from all the circumstances of the case that the tort/delict is manifestly more closely connected with a country other than that indicated in paragraph (1), the law of that other country shall apply. A manifestly closer connection with another country might be based in particular on a pre-existing relationship between the parties, such as a contract, that is closely connected with the tort/delict in question.

Article 6. (1) The law applicable to a non-contractual obligation arising out of an act of unfair competition shall be the law of the country where competitive relations or the collective interests of consumers are, or are likely to be, affected.
(2) Where an act of unfair competition affects exclusively the interests of a specific competitor, Article 4 shall apply.
(3) (a) The law applicable to a non-contractual obligation arising out of a restriction of competition shall be the law of the country where the market is, or is likely to be, affected.
(b) When the market is, or is likely to be, affected in more than one country, the person seeking compensation for damage who sues in the court of the domicile of the defendant, may instead choose to base his or her claim on the law of the court seised, provided that the market in that Member State is amongst those directly and substantially affected by the restriction of competition out of which the non-contractual obligation on which the claim is based arises; where the claimant sues, in accordance with the applicable rules on jurisdiction, more than one defendant in that court, he or she can only choose to base his or her claim on the law of that court if the restriction of competition on which the claim against each of these defendants relies directly and substantially affects also the market in the Member State of that court.
(4) The law applicable under this Article may not be derogated from by an agreement pursuant to Article 14.

Article 7. The law applicable to a non-contractual obligation arising out of environmental damage or damage sustained by persons or property as a result of such damage shall be the law determined pursuant to Article 4(1), unless the person seeking compensation for damage chooses to base his or her claim on the law of the country in which the event giving rise to the damage occurred.

Article 8. (1) The law applicable to a non-contractual obligation arising from an infringement of an intellectual property right shall be the law of the country for which protection is claimed.
(2) In the case of a non-contractual obligation arising from an infringement of a unitary Community intellectual property right, the law applicable shall, for any question that is not governed by the relevant Community instrument, be the law of the country in which the act of infringement was committed.
(3) The law applicable under this Article may not be derogated from by an agreement pursuant to Article 14.

PART II PRIVATE INTERNATIONAL LAW

Article 9. Without prejudice to Article 4(2), the law applicable to a non-contractual obligation in respect of the liability of a person in the capacity of a worker or an employer or the organisations representing their professional interests for damages caused by an industrial action, pending or carried out, shall be the law of the country where the action is to be, or has been, taken.

Chapter III. Unjust Enrichment, Negotiorum Gestio and Culpa in Contrahendo

Article 10. (1) If a non-contractual obligation arising out of unjust enrichment, including payment of amounts wrongly received, concerns a relationship existing between the parties, such as one arising out of a contract or a tort/delict, that is closely connected with that unjust enrichment, it shall be governed by the law that governs that relationship.
(2) Where the law applicable cannot be determined on the basis of paragraph (1) and the parties have their habitual residence in the same country when the event giving rise to unjust enrichment occurs, the law of that country shall apply.
(3) Where the law applicable cannot be determined on the basis of paragraphs 1 or 2, it shall be the law of the country in which the unjust enrichment took place.
(4) Where it is clear from all the circumstances of the case that the non-contractual obligation arising out of unjust enrichment is manifestly more closely connected with a country other than that indicated in paragraphs 1, 2 and 3, the law of that other country shall apply.

Article 11. (1) If a non-contractual obligation arising out of an act performed without due authority in connection with the affairs of another person concerns a relationship existing between the parties, such as one arising out of a contract or a tort/delict, that is closely connected with that non-contractual obligation, it shall be governed by the law that governs that relationship.
(2) Where the law applicable cannot be determined on the basis of paragraph (1), and the parties have their habitual residence in the same country when the event giving rise to the damage occurs, the law of that country shall apply.
(3) Where the law applicable cannot be determined on the basis of paragraphs 1 or 2, it shall be the law of the country in which the act was performed.
(4) Where it is clear from all the circumstances of the case that the non-contractual obligation arising out of an act performed without due authority in connection with the affairs of another person is manifestly more closely connected with a country other than that indicated in paragraphs 1, 2 and 3, the law of that other country shall apply.

Article 12. (1) The law applicable to a non-contractual obligation arising out of dealings prior to the conclusion of a contract, regardless of whether the contract was actually concluded or not, shall be the law that applies to the contract or that would have been applicable to it had it been entered into.
(2) Where the law applicable cannot be determined on the basis of paragraph (1), it shall be:
(a) the law of the country in which the damage occurs, irrespective of the country in which the event giving rise to the damage occurred and irrespective of the country or countries in which the indirect consequences of that event occurred; or
(b) where the parties have their habitual residence in the same country at the time when the event giving rise to the damage occurs, the law of that country; or
(c) where it is clear from all the circumstances of the case that the non-contractual obligation arising out of dealings prior to the conclusion of a contract is manifestly more closely connected with a country other than that indicated in points (a) and (b), the law of that other country.

Article 13. For the purposes of this Chapter, Article 8 shall apply to non-contractual obligations arising from an infringement of an intellectual property right.

Chapter IV. Freedom of Choice

Article 14. (1) The parties may agree to submit non-contractual obligations to the law of their choice:
(a) by an agreement entered into after the event giving rise to the damage occurred; or
(b) where all the parties are pursuing a commercial activity, also by an agreement freely negotiated before the event giving rise to the damage occurred.
The choice shall be expressed or demonstrated with reasonable certainty by the circumstances of the case and shall not prejudice the rights of third parties.
(2) Where all the elements relevant to the situation at the time when the event giving rise to the damage occurs are located in a country other than the country whose law has been chosen, the choice of the parties shall not prejudice the application of provisions of the law of that other country which cannot be derogated from by agreement.
(3) Where all the elements relevant to the situation at the time when the event giving rise to the damage occurs are located in one or more of the Member States, the parties' choice of the law

applicable other than that of a Member State shall not prejudice the application of provisions of Community law, where appropriate as implemented in the Member State of the forum, which cannot be derogated from by agreement.

Chapter V. Common Rules

Article 15. The law applicable to non-contractual obligations under this Regulation shall govern in particular:
(a) the basis and extent of liability, including the determination of persons who may be held liable for acts performed by them;
(b) the grounds for exemption from liability, any limitation of liability and any division of liability;
(c) the existence, the nature and the assessment of damage or the remedy claimed;
(d) within the limits of powers conferred on the court by its procedural law, the measures which a court may take to prevent or terminate injury or damage or to ensure the provision of compensation;
(e) the question whether a right to claim damages or a remedy may be transferred, including by inheritance;
(f) persons entitled to compensation for damage sustained personally;
(g) liability for the acts of another person;
(h) the manner in which an obligation may be extinguished and rules of prescription and limitation, including rules relating to the commencement, interruption and suspension of a period of prescription or limitation.

Article 16. Nothing in this Regulation shall restrict the application of the provisions of the law of the forum in a situation where they are mandatory irrespective of the law otherwise applicable to the non-contractual obligation.

Article 17. In assessing the conduct of the person claimed to be liable, account shall be taken, as a matter of fact and in so far as is appropriate, of the rules of safety and conduct which were in force at the place and time of the event giving rise to the liability.

Article 18. The person having suffered damage may bring his or her claim directly against the insurer of the person liable to provide compensation if the law applicable to the non-contractual obligation or the law applicable to the insurance contract so provides.

Article 19. Where a person (the creditor) has a non-contractual claim upon another (the debtor), and a third person has a duty to satisfy the creditor, or has in fact satisfied the creditor in discharge of that duty, the law which governs the third person's duty to satisfy the creditor shall determine whether, and the extent to which, the third person is entitled to exercise against the debtor the rights which the creditor had against the debtor under the law governing their relationship.

Article 20 If a creditor has a claim against several debtors who are liable for the same claim, and one of the debtors has already satisfied the claim in whole or in part, the question of that debtor's right to demand compensation from the other debtors shall be governed by the law applicable to that debtor's non-contractual obligation towards the creditor.

Article 21 A unilateral act intended to have legal effect and relating to a non-contractual obligation shall be formally valid if it satisfies the formal requirements of the law governing the non-contractual obligation in question or the law of the country in which the act is performed.

Article 22. (1) The law governing a non-contractual obligation under this Regulation shall apply to the extent that, in matters of non-contractual obligations, it contains rules which raise presumptions of law or determine the burden of proof.
(2) Acts intended to have legal effect may be proved by any mode of proof recognised by the law of the forum or by any of the laws referred to in Article 21 under which that act is formally valid, provided that such mode of proof can be administered by the forum.

Chapter VI. Other Provisions

Article 23. (1) For the purposes of this Regulation, the habitual residence of companies and other bodies, corporate or unincorporated, shall be the place of central administration.
Where the event giving rise to the damage occurs, or the damage arises, in the course of operation of a branch, agency or any other establishment, the place where the branch, agency or any other establishment is located shall be treated as the place of habitual residence.
(2) For the purposes of this Regulation, the habitual residence of a natural person acting in the course of his or her business activity shall be his or her principal place of business.

PART II PRIVATE INTERNATIONAL LAW

Article 24. The application of the law of any country specified by this Regulation means the application of the rules of law in force in that country other than its rules of private international law.

Article 25. (1) Where a State comprises several territorial units, each of which has its own rules of law in respect of non-contractual obligations, each territorial unit shall be considered as a country for the purposes of identifying the law applicable under this Regulation.
(2) A Member State within which different territorial units have their own rules of law in respect of non-contractual obligations shall not be required to apply this Regulation to conflicts solely between the laws of such units.

Article 26. The application of a provision of the law of any country specified by this Regulation may be refused only if such application is manifestly incompatible with the public policy (*ordre public*) of the forum.

Article 27. This Regulation shall not prejudice the application of provisions of Community law which, in relation to particular matters, lay down conflict-of-law rules relating to non-contractual obligations.

Article 28. (1) This Regulation shall not prejudice the application of international conventions to which one or more Member States are parties at the time when this Regulation is adopted and which lay down conflict-of-law rules relating to non-contractual obligations.
(2) However, this Regulation shall, as between Member States, take precedence over conventions concluded exclusively between two or more of them in so far as such conventions concern matters governed by this Regulation.

Chapter VII. Final Provisions

Article 29. (1) By 11 July 2008, Member States shall notify the Commission of the conventions referred to in Article 28(1). After that date, Member States shall notify the Commission of all denunciations of such conventions.
(2) The Commission shall publish in the *Official Journal of the European Union* within six months of receipt:
(i) a list of the conventions referred to in paragraph (1);
(ii) the denunciations referred to in paragraph (1).

Article 30. (1) Not later than 20 August 2011, the Commission shall submit to the European Parliament, the Council and the European Economic and Social Committee a report on the application of this Regulation. If necessary, the report shall be accompanied by proposals to adapt this Regulation. The report shall include:
(i) a study on the effects of the way in which foreign law is treated in the different jurisdictions and on the extent to which courts in the Member States apply foreign law in practice pursuant to this Regulation;
(ii) a study on the effects of Article 28 of this Regulation with respect to the Hague Convention of 4 May 1971 on the law applicable to traffic accidents.
(2) Not later than 31 December 2008, the Commission shall submit to the European Parliament, the Council and the European Economic and Social Committee a study on the situation in the field of the law applicable to non-contractual obligations arising out of violations of privacy and rights relating to personality, taking into account rules relating to freedom of the press and freedom of expression in the media, and conflict-of-law issues related to Directive 95/46/EC of the European Parliament and of the Council of 24 October 1995 on the protection of individuals with regard to the processing of personal data and on the free movement of such data [7].

Article 31. This Regulation shall apply to events giving rise to damage which occur after its entry into force.

Article 32. This Regulation shall apply from 11 January 2009, except for Article 29, which shall apply from 11 July 2008.
This Regulation shall be binding in its entirety and directly applicable in the Member States in accordance with the Treaty establishing the European Community.

Council Regulation (EU) No 1259/2010 of 20 December 2010 implementing enhanced cooperation in the area of the law applicable to divorce and legal separation [Rome III] (O.J. L323, 22.11.2012, pp. 18-19) [footnotes omitted].

THE COUNCIL OF THE EUROPEAN UNION,
Having regard to the Treaty on the Functioning of the European Union, and in particular Article 81(3) thereof,
Having regard to Council Decision 2010/405/EU of 12 July 2010 authorising enhanced cooperation in the area of the law applicable to divorce and legal separation,
Having regard to the proposal from the European Commission,
After transmission of the draft legislative act to the national parliaments,
Having regard to the opinion of the European Parliament,
Having regard to the opinion of the European Economic and Social Committee,
Acting in accordance with a special legislative procedure,
Whereas:
(1) The Union has set itself the objective of maintaining and developing an area of freedom, security and justice, in which the free movement of persons is assured. For the gradual establishment of such an area, the Union must adopt measures relating to judicial cooperation in civil matters having cross-border implications, particularly when necessary for the proper functioning of the internal market.
(2) Pursuant to Article 81 of the Treaty on the Functioning of the European Union, those measures are to include measures aimed at ensuring the compatibility of the rules applicable in the Member States concerning conflict of laws.
(3) On 14 March 2005 the Commission adopted a Green Paper on applicable law and jurisdiction in divorce matters. The Green Paper launched a wide-ranging public consultation on possible solutions to the problems that may arise under the current situation.
(4) On 17 July 2006 the Commission proposed a Regulation amending Council Regulation (EC) No 2201/2003 as regards jurisdiction and introducing rules concerning applicable law in matrimonial matters.
(5) At its meeting in Luxembourg on 5 and 6 June 2008, the Council concluded that there was a lack of unanimity on the proposal and that there were insurmountable difficulties that made unanimity impossible both then and in the near future. It established that the proposal's objectives could not be attained within a reasonable period by applying the relevant provisions of the Treaties.
(6) Belgium, Bulgaria, Germany, Greece, Spain, France, Italy, Latvia, Luxembourg, Hungary, Malta, Austria, Portugal, Romania and Slovenia subsequently addressed a request to the Commission indicating that they intended to establish enhanced cooperation between themselves in the area of applicable law in matrimonial matters. On 3 March 2010, Greece withdrew its request.
(7) On 12 July 2010 the Council adopted Decision 2010/405/EU authorising enhanced cooperation in the area of the law applicable to divorce and legal separation.
(8) According to Article 328(1) of the Treaty on the Functioning of the European Union, when enhanced cooperation is being established, it is to be open to all Member States, subject to compliance with any conditions of participation laid down by the authorising decision. It is also to be open to them at any other time, subject to compliance with the acts already adopted within that framework, in addition to those conditions. The Commission and the Member States participating in enhanced cooperation shall ensure that they promote participation by as many Member States as possible. This Regulation should be binding in its entirety and directly applicable only in the participating Member States in accordance with the Treaties.
(9) This Regulation should create a clear, comprehensive legal framework in the area of the law applicable to divorce and legal separation in the participating Member States, provide citizens with appropriate outcomes in terms of legal certainty, predictability and flexibility, and prevent a situation from arising where one of the spouses applies for divorce before the other one does in order to ensure that the proceeding is governed by a given law which he or she considers more favourable to his or her own interests.
(10) The substantive scope and enacting terms of this Regulation should be consistent with Regulation (EC) No 2201/2003. However, it should not apply to marriage annulment.
This Regulation should apply only to the dissolution or loosening of marriage ties. The law determined by the conflict-of-laws rules of this Regulation should apply to the grounds for divorce and legal separation.
Preliminary questions such as legal capacity and the validity of the marriage, and matters such as the effects of divorce or legal separation on property, name, parental responsibility, maintenance

PART II   PRIVATE INTERNATIONAL LAW

obligations or any other ancillary measures should be determined by the conflict-of-laws rules applicable in the participating Member State concerned.

(11) In order to clearly delimit the territorial scope of this Regulation, the Member States participating in the enhanced cooperation should be specified.

(12) This Regulation should be universal, i.e. it should be possible for its uniform conflict-of-laws rules to designate the law of a participating Member State, the law of a non-participating Member State or the law of a State which is not a member of the European Union.

(13) This Regulation should apply irrespective of the nature of the court or tribunal seized. Where applicable, a court should be deemed to be seized in accordance with Regulation (EC) No 2201/2003.

(14) In order to allow the spouses to choose an applicable law with which they have a close connection or, in the absence of such choice, in order that that law might apply to their divorce or legal separation, the law in question should apply even if it is not that of a participating Member State. Where the law of another Member State is designated, the network created by Council Decision 2001/470/EC of 28 May 2001 establishing a European Judicial Network in civil and commercial matters, could play a part in assisting the courts with regard to the content of foreign law.

(15) Increasing the mobility of citizens calls for more flexibility and greater legal certainty. In order to achieve that objective, this Regulation should enhance the parties' autonomy in the areas of divorce and legal separation by giving them a limited possibility to choose the law applicable to their divorce or legal separation.

(16) Spouses should be able to choose the law of a country with which they have a special connection or the law of the forum as the law applicable to divorce and legal separation. The law chosen by the spouses must be consonant with the fundamental rights recognised by the Treaties and the Charter of Fundamental Rights of the European Union.

(17) Before designating the applicable law, it is important for spouses to have access to up-to-date information concerning the essential aspects of national and Union law and of the procedures governing divorce and legal separation. To guarantee such access to appropriate, good-quality information, the Commission regularly updates it in the Internet-based public information system set up by Council Decision 2001/470/EC.

(18) The informed choice of both spouses is a basic principle of this Regulation. Each spouse should know exactly what are the legal and social implications of the choice of applicable law. The possibility of choosing the applicable law by common agreement should be without prejudice to the rights of, and equal opportunities for, the two spouses. Hence judges in the participating Member States should be aware of the importance of an informed choice on the part of the two spouses concerning the legal implications of the choice-of-law agreement concluded.

(19) Rules on material and formal validity should be defined so that the informed choice of the spouses is facilitated and that their consent is respected with a view to ensuring legal certainty as well as better access to justice. As far as formal validity is concerned, certain safeguards should be introduced to ensure that spouses are aware of the implications of their choice. The agreement on the choice of applicable law should at least be expressed in writing, dated and signed by both parties. However, if the law of the participating Member State in which the two spouses have their habitual residence at the time the agreement is concluded lays down additional formal rules, those rules should be complied with. For example, such additional formal rules may exist in a participating Member State where the agreement is inserted in a marriage contract. If, at the time the agreement is concluded, the spouses are habitually resident in different participating Member States which lay down different formal rules, compliance with the formal rules of one of these States would suffice. If, at the time the agreement is concluded, only one of the spouses is habitually resident in a participating Member State which lays down additional formal rules, these rules should be complied with.

(20) An agreement designating the applicable law should be able to be concluded and modified at the latest at the time the court is seized, and even during the course of the proceeding if the law of the forum so provides. In that event, it should be sufficient for such designation to be recorded in court in accordance with the law of the forum.

(21) Where no applicable law is chosen, and with a view to guaranteeing legal certainty and predictability and preventing a situation from arising in which one of the spouses applies for divorce before the other one does in order to ensure that the proceeding is governed by a given law which he considers more favourable to his own interests, this Regulation should introduce harmonised conflict-of-laws rules on the basis of a scale of successive connecting factors based on the existence of a close connection between the spouses and the law concerned. Such connecting factors should be chosen so as to ensure that proceedings relating to divorce or legal separation are governed by a law with which the spouses have a close connection.

(22) Where this Regulation refers to nationality as a connecting factor for the application of the law of a State, the question of how to deal with cases of multiple nationality should be left to national law, in full observance of the general principles of the European Union.

(23) If the court is seized in order to convert a legal separation into divorce, and where the parties have not made any choice as to the law applicable, the law which applied to the legal separation should also apply to the divorce. Such continuity would promote predictability for the parties and increase legal certainty. If the law applied to the legal separation does not provide for the conversion of legal separation into divorce, the divorce should be governed by the conflict-of-laws rules which apply in the absence of a choice by the parties. This should not prevent the spouses from seeking divorce on the basis of other rules in this Regulation.

(24) In certain situations, such as where the applicable law makes no provision for divorce or where it does not grant one of the spouses equal access to divorce or legal separation on grounds of their sex, the law of the court seized should nevertheless apply. This, however, should be without prejudice to the public policy clause.

(25) Considerations of public interest should allow courts in the Member States the opportunity in exceptional circumstances to disregard the application of a provision of foreign law in a given case where it would be manifestly contrary to the public policy of the forum. However, the courts should not be able to apply the public policy exception in order to disregard a provision of the law of another State when to do so would be contrary to the Charter of Fundamental Rights of the European Union, and in particular Article 21 thereof, which prohibits all forms of discrimination.

(26) Where this Regulation refers to the fact that the law of the participating Member State whose court is seized does not provide for divorce, this should be interpreted to mean that the law of this Member State does not have the institute of divorce. In such a case, the court should not be obliged to pronounce a divorce by virtue of this Regulation.

Where this Regulation refers to the fact that the law of the participating Member State whose court is seized does not deem the marriage in question valid for the purposes of divorce proceedings, this should be interpreted to mean, inter alia, that such a marriage does not exist in the law of that Member State. In such a case, the court should not be obliged to pronounce a divorce or a legal separation by virtue of this Regulation.

(27) Since there are States and participating Member States in which two or more systems of law or sets of rules concerning matters governed by this Regulation coexist, there should be a provision governing the extent to which this Regulation applies in the different territorial units of those States and participating Member States or to different categories of persons of those States and participating Member States.

(28) In the absence of rules designating the applicable law, parties choosing the law of the State of the nationality of one of them should at the same time indicate which territorial unit's law they have agreed upon in case the State whose law is chosen comprises several territorial units each of which has its own system of law or a set of rules in respect of divorce.

(29) Since the objectives of this Regulation, namely the enhancement of legal certainty, predictability and flexibility in international matrimonial proceedings and hence the facilitation of the free movement of persons within the Union, cannot be sufficiently achieved by the Member States and can therefore, by reasons of the scale and effects of this Regulation be better achieved at Union level, the Union may adopt measures, by means of enhanced cooperation where appropriate, in accordance with the principle of subsidiarity as set out in Article 5 of the Treaty on European Union. In accordance with the principle of proportionality, as set out in that Article, this Regulation does not go beyond what is necessary in order to achieve those objectives.

(30) This Regulation respects fundamental rights and observes the principles recognised by the Charter of Fundamental Rights of the European Union, and in particular by Article 21 thereof, which states that any discrimination based on any ground such as sex, race, colour, ethnic or social origin, genetic features, language, religion or belief, political or any other opinion, membership of a national minority, property, birth, disability, age or sexual orientation shall be prohibited. This Regulation should be applied by the courts of the participating Member States in observance of those rights and principles,

HAS ADOPTED THIS REGULATION:

Chapter I. Scope, Relation with Regulation (EC) No 2201/2003, Definitions and Universal Application

Article 1. (1) This Regulation shall apply, in situations involving a conflict of laws, to divorce and legal separation.

(2) This Regulation shall not apply to the following matters, even if they arise merely as a prelimi-

PART II   PRIVATE INTERNATIONAL LAW

nary question within the context of divorce or legal separation proceedings:
(a) the legal capacity of natural persons;
(b) the existence, validity or recognition of a marriage;
(c) the annulment of a marriage;
(d) the name of the spouses;
(e) the property consequences of the marriage;
(f) parental responsibility;
(g) maintenance obligations;
(h) trusts or successions.

Article 2. This Regulation shall not affect the application of Regulation (EC) No 2201/2003.

Article 3. For the purposes of this Regulation:
(1) 'participating Member State' means a Member State which participates in enhanced cooperation on the law applicable to divorce and legal separation by virtue of Decision 2010/405/EU, or by virtue of a decision adopted in accordance with the second or third subparagraph of Article 331(1) of the Treaty on the Functioning of the European Union;
(2) the term 'court' shall cover all the authorities in the participating Member States with jurisdiction in the matters falling within the scope of this Regulation.

Article 4. The law designated by this Regulation shall apply whether or not it is the law of a participating Member State.

Chapter II. Uniform Rules on the Law Applicable to Divorce and Legal Separation

Article 5. (1) The spouses may agree to designate the law applicable to divorce and legal separation provided that it is one of the following laws:
(a) the law of the State where the spouses are habitually resident at the time the agreement is concluded; or
(b) the law of the State where the spouses were last habitually resident, in so far as one of them still resides there at the time the agreement is concluded; or
(c) the law of the State of nationality of either spouse at the time the agreement is concluded; or
(d) the law of the forum.
(2) Without prejudice to paragraph (3), an agreement designating the applicable law may be concluded and modified at any time, but at the latest at the time the court is seized.
(3) If the law of the forum so provides, the spouses may also designate the law applicable before the court during the course of the proceeding. In that event, such designation shall be recorded in court in accordance with the law of the forum.

Article 6. (1) The existence and validity of an agreement on choice of law or of any term thereof, shall be determined by the law which would govern it under this Regulation if the agreement or term were valid.
(2) Nevertheless, a spouse, in order to establish that he did not consent, may rely upon the law of the country in which he has his habitual residence at the time the court is seized if it appears from the circumstances that it would not be reasonable to determine the effect of his conduct in accordance with the law specified in paragraph (1).

Article 7. (1) The agreement referred to in Article 5(1) and (2), shall be expressed in writing, dated and signed by both spouses. Any communication by electronic means which provides a durable record of the agreement shall be deemed equivalent to writing.
(2) However, if the law of the participating Member State in which the two spouses have their habitual residence at the time the agreement is concluded lays down additional formal requirements for this type of agreement, those requirements shall apply.
(3) If the spouses are habitually resident in different participating Member States at the time the agreement is concluded and the laws of those States provide for different formal requirements, the agreement shall be formally valid if it satisfies the requirements of either of those laws.
(4) If only one of the spouses is habitually resident in a participating Member State at the time the agreement is concluded and that State lays down additional formal requirements for this type of agreement, those requirements shall apply.

Article 8. In the absence of a choice pursuant to Article 5, divorce and legal separation shall be subject to the law of the State:
(a) where the spouses are habitually resident at the time the court is seized; or, failing that

(b) where the spouses were last habitually resident, provided that the period of residence did not end more than 1 year before the court was seized, in so far as one of the spouses still resides in that State at the time the court is seized; or, failing that
(c) of which both spouses are nationals at the time the court is seized; or, failing that
(d) where the court is seized.

Article 9. (1) Where legal separation is converted into divorce, the law applicable to divorce shall be the law applied to the legal separation, unless the parties have agreed otherwise in accordance with Article 5.
(2) However, if the law applied to the legal separation does not provide for the conversion of legal separation into divorce, Article 8 shall apply, unless the parties have agreed otherwise in accordance with Article 5.

Article 10. Where the law applicable pursuant to Article 5 or Article 8 makes no provision for divorce or does not grant one of the spouses equal access to divorce or legal separation on grounds of their sex, the law of the forum shall apply.

Article 11. Where this Regulation provides for the application of the law of a State, it refers to the rules of law in force in that State other than its rules of private international law.

Article 12. Application of a provision of the law designated by virtue of this Regulation may be refused only if such application is manifestly incompatible with the public policy of the forum.

Article 13. Nothing in this Regulation shall oblige the courts of a participating Member State whose law does not provide for divorce or does not deem the marriage in question valid for the purposes of divorce proceedings to pronounce a divorce by virtue of the application of this Regulation.

Article 14. Where a State comprises several territorial units each of which has its own system of law or a set of rules concerning matters governed by this Regulation:
(a) any reference to the law of such State shall be construed, for the purposes of determining the law applicable under this Regulation, as referring to the law in force in the relevant territorial unit;
(b) any reference to habitual residence in that State shall be construed as referring to habitual residence in a territorial unit;
(c) any reference to nationality shall refer to the territorial unit designated by the law of that State, or, in the absence of relevant rules, to the territorial unit chosen by the parties or, in absence of choice, to the territorial unit with which the spouse or spouses has or have the closest connection.

Article 15. In relation to a State which has two or more systems of law or sets of rules applicable to different categories of persons concerning matters governed by this Regulation, any reference to the law of such a State shall be construed as referring to the legal system determined by the rules in force in that State. In the absence of such rules, the system of law or the set of rules with which the spouse or spouses has or have the closest connection applies.

Article 16 A participating Member State in which different systems of law or sets of rules apply to matters governed by this Regulation shall not be required to apply this Regulation to conflicts of laws arising solely between such different systems of law or sets of rules.

Chapter III. Other Provisions

Article 17 (1) By 21 September 2011 the participating Member States shall communicate to the Commission their national provisions, if any, concerning:
(a) the formal requirements applicable to agreements on the choice of applicable law pursuant to Article 7(2) to (4); and
(b) the possibility of designating the applicable law in accordance with Article 5(3).
The participating Member States shall inform the Commission of any subsequent changes to these provisions
(2) The Commission shall make all information communicated in accordance with paragraph (1) publicly available through appropriate means, in particular through the website of the European Judicial Network in civil and commercial matters.

Article 18. (1) This Regulation shall apply only to legal proceedings instituted and to agreements of the kind referred to in Article 5 concluded as from 21 June 2012.
However, effect shall also be given to an agreement on the choice of the applicable law concluded before 21 June 2012, provided that it complies with Articles 6 and 7.

PART II PRIVATE INTERNATIONAL LAW

(2) This Regulation shall be without prejudice to agreements on the choice of applicable law concluded in accordance with the law of a participating Member State whose court is seized before 21 June 2012.

Article 19. (1) Without prejudice to the obligations of the participating Member States pursuant to Article 351 of the Treaty on the Functioning of the European Union, this Regulation shall not affect the application of international conventions to which one or more participating Member States are party at the time when this Regulation is adopted or when the decision pursuant to the second or third subparagraph of Article 331(1) of the Treaty on the Functioning of the European Union is adopted and which lay down conflict-of-laws rules relating to divorce or separation.
(2) However, this Regulation shall, as between participating Member States, take precedence over conventions concluded exclusively between two or more of them in so far as such conventions concern matters governed by this Regulation.

Article 20. (1) By 31 December 2015, and every 5 years thereafter, the Commission shall present to the European Parliament, the Council and the European Economic and Social Committee a report on the application of this Regulation. The report shall be accompanied, where appropriate, by proposals to adapt this Regulation.
(2) To that end, the participating Member States shall communicate to the Commission the relevant information on the application of this Regulation by their courts.

Chapter IV. Final Provisions

Article 21. This Regulation shall enter into force on the day following its publication in the *Official Journal of the European Union*.
It shall apply from 21 June 2012, with the exception of Article 17, which shall apply from 21 June 2011.
For those participating Member States which participate in enhanced cooperation by virtue of a decision adopted in accordance with the second or third subparagraph of Article 331(1) of the Treaty on the Functioning of the European Union, this Regulation shall apply as from the date indicated in the decision concerned.
This Regulation shall be binding in its entirety and directly applicable in the participating Member States in accordance with the Treaties.

Council Regulation (EC) No 4/2009 of 18 December 2008 on jurisdiction, applicable law, recognition and enforcement of decisions and cooperation in matters relating to maintenance obligations [Maintenance Regulation] (OJ L007, 10.01.2009, pp. 1-79) [footnotes omitted].

THE COUNCIL OF THE EUROPEAN UNION,
Having regard to the Treaty establishing the European Community, and in particular Article 61(c) and Article 67(2) thereof,
Having regard to the proposal from the Commission,
Having regard to the opinion of the European Parliament,
Having regard to the opinion of the European Economic and Social Committee,
Whereas:
(1) The Community has set itself the objective of maintaining and developing an area of freedom, security and justice, in which the free movement of persons is ensured. For the gradual establishment of such an area, the Community is to adopt, among others, measures relating to judicial cooperation in civil matters having cross-border implications, in so far as necessary for the proper functioning of the internal market.
(2) In accordance with Article 65(b) of the Treaty, these measures must aim, inter alia, to promote the compatibility of the rules applicable in the Member States concerning the conflict of laws and of jurisdiction.
(3) In this respect, the Community has among other measures already adopted Council Regulation (EC) No 44/2001 of 22 December 2000 on jurisdiction and the recognition and enforcement of judgments in civil and commercial matters, Council Decision 2001/470/EC of 28 May 2001 establishing a European Judicial Network in civil and commercial matters, Council Regulation (EC) No 1206/2001 of 28 May 2001 on cooperation between the courts of the Member States in the taking of evidence in civil or commercial matters, Council Directive 2003/8/EC of 27 January 2003 to improve access to justice in cross-border disputes by establishing minimum common rules relating to legal aid for such disputes, Council Regulation (EC) No 2201/2003 of 27 November 2003 on jurisdiction and the recognition and enforcement of judgments in matrimonial matters and in matters of parental responsibility, Regulation (EC) No 805/2004 of the European Parliament and of the Council of 21 April 2004 creating a European Enforcement Order for uncontested claims, and Regulation (EC) No 1393/2007 of the European Parliament and of the Council of 13 November 2007 on the service in the Member States of judicial and extrajudicial documents in civil or commercial matters (service of documents).
(4) The European Council in Tampere on 15 and 16 October 1999 invited the Council and the Commission to establish special common procedural rules to simplify and accelerate the settlement of cross-border disputes concerning, inter alia, maintenance claims. It also called for the abolition of intermediate measures required for the recognition and enforcement in the requested State of a decision given in another Member State, particularly a decision relating to a maintenance claim.
(5) A programme of measures for the enforcement of the principle of mutual recognition of decisions in civil and commercial matters, common to the Commission and to the Council, was adopted on 30 November 2000. That programme provides for the abolition of the exequatur procedure for maintenance claims in order to boost the effectiveness of the means by which maintenance creditors safeguard their rights.
(6) The European Council meeting in Brussels on 4 and 5 November 2004 adopted a new programme called "The Hague Programme: strengthening freedom, security and justice in the European Union" (hereinafter referred to as The Hague Programme).
(7) At its meeting on 2 and 3 June 2005, the Council adopted a Council and Commission Action Plan which implements The Hague Programme in concrete actions and which mentions the necessity of adopting proposals on maintenance obligations.
(8) In the framework of The Hague Conference on Private International Law, the Community and its Member States took part in negotiations which led to the adoption on 23 November 2007 of the Convention on the International Recovery of Child Support and other Forms of Family Maintenance (hereinafter referred to as the 2007 Hague Convention) and the Protocol on the Law Applicable to Maintenance Obligations (hereinafter referred to as the 2007 Hague Protocol). Both those instruments should therefore be taken into account in this Regulation.
(9) A maintenance creditor should be able to obtain easily, in a Member State, a decision which will be automatically enforceable in another Member State without further formalities.
(10) In order to achieve this goal, it is advisable to create a Community instrument in matters relating to maintenance obligations bringing together provisions on jurisdiction, conflict of laws, recognition and enforceability, enforcement, legal aid and cooperation between Central Authorities.
(11) The scope of this Regulation should cover all maintenance obligations arising from a family

PART II PRIVATE INTERNATIONAL LAW

relationship, parentage, marriage or affinity, in order to guarantee equal treatment of all maintenance creditors. For the purposes of this Regulation, the term "maintenance obligation" should be interpreted autonomously.

(12) In order to take account of the various ways of resolving maintenance obligation issues in the Member States, this Regulation should apply both to court decisions and to decisions given by administrative authorities, provided that the latter offer guarantees with regard to, in particular, their impartiality and the right of all parties to be heard. Those authorities should therefore apply all the rules of this Regulation.

(13) For the reasons set out above, this Regulation should also ensure the recognition and enforcement of court settlements and authentic instruments without affecting the right of either party to such a settlement or instrument to challenge the settlement or instrument before the courts of the Member State of origin.

(14) It should be provided in this Regulation that for the purposes of an application for the recognition and enforcement of a decision relating to maintenance obligations the term "creditor" includes public bodies which are entitled to act in place of a person to whom maintenance is owed or to claim reimbursement of benefits provided to the creditor in place of maintenance. Where a public body acts in this capacity, it should be entitled to the same services and the same legal aid as a creditor.

(15) In order to preserve the interests of maintenance creditors and to promote the proper administration of justice within the European Union, the rules on jurisdiction as they result from Regulation (EC) No 44/2001 should be adapted. The circumstance that the defendant is habitually resident in a third State should no longer entail the non-application of Community rules on jurisdiction, and there should no longer be any referral to national law. This Regulation should therefore determine the cases in which a court in a Member State may exercise subsidiary jurisdiction.

(16) In order to remedy, in particular, situations of denial of justice this Regulation should provide a forum necessitatis allowing a court of a Member State, on an exceptional basis, to hear a case which is closely connected with a third State. Such an exceptional basis may be deemed to exist when proceedings prove impossible in the third State in question, for example because of civil war, or when an applicant cannot reasonably be expected to initiate or conduct proceedings in that State. Jurisdiction based on the forum necessitatis should, however, be exercised only if the dispute has a sufficient connection with the Member State of the court seised, for instance the nationality of one of the parties.

(17) An additional rule of jurisdiction should provide that, except under specific conditions, proceedings to modify an existing maintenance decision or to have a new decision given can be brought by the debtor only in the State in which the creditor was habitually resident at the time the decision was given and in which he remains habitually resident. To ensure proper symmetry between the 2007 Hague Convention and this Regulation, this rule should also apply as regards decisions given in a third State which is party to the said Convention in so far as that Convention is in force between that State and the Community and covers the same maintenance obligations in that State and in the Community.

(18) For the purposes of this Regulation, it should be provided that in Ireland the concept of "domicile" replaces the concept of "nationality" which is also the case in the United Kingdom, subject to this Regulation being applicable in the latter Member State in accordance with Article 4 of the Protocol on the position of the United Kingdom and Ireland annexed to the Treaty on European Union and the Treaty establishing the European Community.

(19) In order to increase legal certainty, predictability and the autonomy of the parties, this Regulation should enable the parties to choose the competent court by agreement on the basis of specific connecting factors. To protect the weaker party, such a choice of court should not be allowed in the case of maintenance obligations towards a child under the age of 18.

(20) It should be provided in this Regulation that, for Member States bound by the 2007 Hague Protocol, the rules on conflict of laws in respect of maintenance obligations will be those set out in that Protocol. To that end, a provision referring to the said Protocol should be inserted. The 2007 Hague Protocol will be concluded by the Community in time to enable this Regulation to apply. To take account of a scenario in which the 2007 Hague Protocol does not apply to all the Member States a distinction for the purposes of recognition, enforceability and enforcement of decisions needs to be made in this Regulation between the Member States bound by the 2007 Hague Protocol and those not bound by it.

(21) It needs to be made clear in this Regulation that these rules on conflict of laws determine only the law applicable to maintenance obligations and do not determine the law applicable to the establishment of the family relationships on which the maintenance obligations are based. The establishment of family relationships continues to be covered by the national law of the Member States, including their rules of private international law.

(22) In order to ensure swift and efficient recovery of a maintenance obligation and to prevent delaying actions, decisions in matters relating to maintenance obligations given in a Member State should in principle be provisionally enforceable. This Regulation should therefore provide that the court of origin should be able to declare the decision provisionally enforceable even if the national law does not provide for enforceability by operation of law and even if an appeal has been or could still be lodged against the decision under national law.
(23) To limit the costs of proceedings subject to this Regulation, the greatest possible use of modern communications technologies, particularly for hearing parties, would be helpful.
(24) The guarantees provided by the application of rules on conflict of laws should provide the justification for having decisions relating to maintenance obligations given in a Member State bound by the 2007 Hague Protocol recognised and regarded as enforceable in all the other Member States without any procedure being necessary and without any form of control on the substance in the Member State of enforcement.
(25) Recognition in a Member State of a decision relating to maintenance obligations has as its only object to allow the recovery of the maintenance claim determined in the decision. It does not imply the recognition by that Member State of the family relationship, parentage, marriage or affinity underlying the maintenance obligations which gave rise to the decision.
(26) For decisions on maintenance obligations given in a Member State not bound by the 2007 Hague Protocol, there should be provision in this Regulation for a procedure for recognition and declaration of enforceability. That procedure should be modelled on the procedure and the grounds for refusing recognition set out in Regulation (EC) No 44/2001. To accelerate proceedings and enable the creditor to recover his claim quickly, the court seised should be required to give its decision within a set time, unless there are exceptional circumstances.
(27) It would also be appropriate to limit as far as possible the formal enforcement requirements likely to increase the costs to be borne by the maintenance creditor. To that end, this Regulation should provide that a maintenance creditor ought not to be required to have a postal address or an authorised representative in the Member State of enforcement, without this otherwise affecting the internal organisation of the Member States in matters relating to enforcement proceedings.
(28) In order to limit the costs of enforcement proceedings, no translation should be required unless enforcement is contested, and without prejudice to the rules applicable to service of documents.
(29) In order to guarantee compliance with the requirements of a fair trial, this Regulation should provide for the right of a defendant who did not enter an appearance in the court of origin of a Member State bound by the 2007 Hague Protocol to apply for a review of the decision given against him at the stage of enforcement. However, the defendant must apply for this review within a set period which should start no later than the day on which, in the enforcement proceedings, his property was first made non-disposable in whole or in part. That right to apply for a review should be an extraordinary remedy granted to the defendant in default and not affecting the application of any extraordinary remedies laid down in the law of the Member State of origin provided that those remedies are not incompatible with the right to a review under this Regulation.
(30) In order to speed up the enforcement in another Member State of a decision given in a Member State bound by the 2007 Hague Protocol it is necessary to limit the grounds of refusal or of suspension of enforcement which may be invoked by the debtor on account of the cross-border nature of the maintenance claim. This limitation should not affect the grounds of refusal or of suspension laid down in national law which are not incompatible with those listed in this Regulation, such as the debtor's discharge of his debt at the time of enforcement or the unattachable nature of certain assets.
(31) To facilitate cross-border recovery of maintenance claims, provision should be made for a system of cooperation between Central Authorities designated by the Member States. These Authorities should assist maintenance creditors and debtors in asserting their rights in another Member State by submitting applications for recognition, enforceability and enforcement of existing decisions, for the modification of such decisions or for the establishment of a decision. They should also exchange information in order to locate debtors and creditors, and identify their income and assets, as necessary. Lastly, they should cooperate with each other by exchanging general information and promoting cooperation amongst the competent authorities in their Member States.
(32) A Central Authority designated under this Regulation should bear its own costs, except in specifically determined cases, and should provide assistance for all applicants residing in its Member State. The criterion for determining a person's right to request assistance from a Central Authority should be less strict than the connecting factor of "habitual residence" used elsewhere in this Regulation. However, the "residence" criterion should exclude mere presence.
(33) In order to provide full assistance to maintenance creditors and debtors and to facilitate as much as possible cross-border recovery of maintenance, the Central Authorities should be able to obtain a

certain amount of personal information. This Regulation should therefore oblige the Member States to ensure that their Central Authorities have access to such information through the public authorities or administrations which hold the information concerned in the course of their ordinary activities. It should however be left to each Member State to decide on the arrangements for such access. Accordingly, a Member State should be able to designate the public authorities or administrations which will be required to supply the information to the Central Authority in accordance with this Regulation, including, if appropriate, public authorities or administrations already designated in the context of other systems for access to information. Where a Member State designates public authorities or administrations, it should ensure that its Central Authority is able to access the requisite information held by those bodies as provided for in this Regulation. A Member State should also be able to allow its Central Authority to access requisite information from any other legal person which holds it and controls its processing.

(34) In the context of access to personal data and the use and transmission thereof, the requirements of Directive 95/46/EC of the European Parliament and of the Council of 24 October 1995 on the protection of individuals with regard to the processing of personal data and on the free movement of such data, as transposed into the national law of the Member States, should be complied with.

(35) For the purposes of the application of this Regulation it is however necessary to define the specific conditions of access to personal data and of the use and transmission of such data. In this context, the opinion of the European Data Protection Supervisor has been taken into consideration. Notification of the data subject should take place in accordance with national law. It should however be possible to defer the notification to prevent the debtor from transferring his assets and thus jeopardising the recovery of the maintenance claim.

(36) On account of the costs of proceedings it is appropriate to provide for a very favourable legal aid scheme, that is, full coverage of the costs relating to proceedings concerning maintenance obligations in respect of children under the age of 21 initiated via the Central Authorities. Specific rules should therefore be added to the current rules on legal aid in the European Union which exist by virtue of Directive 2003/8/EC thus setting up a special legal aid scheme for maintenance obligations. In this context, the competent authority of the requested Member State should be able, exceptionally, to recover costs from an applicant having received free legal aid and lost the case, provided that the person's financial situation so permits. This would apply, in particular, where someone well-off had acted in bad faith.

(37) In addition, for maintenance obligations other than those referred to in the preceding recital, all parties should be guaranteed the same treatment in terms of legal aid at the time of enforcement of a decision in another Member State. Accordingly, the provisions of this Regulation on continuity of legal aid should be understood as also granting such aid to a party who, while not having received legal aid in the proceedings to obtain or amend a decision in the Member State of origin, did then benefit from such aid in that State in the context of an application for enforcement of the decision. Similarly, a party who benefited from free proceedings before an administrative authority listed in Annex X should, in the Member State of enforcement, benefit from the most favourable legal aid or the most extensive exemption from costs or expenses, provided that he shows that he would have so benefited in the Member State of origin.

(38) In order to minimise the costs of translating supporting documents the court seised should only require a translation of such documents when this is necessary, without prejudice to the rights of the defence and the rules applicable concerning service of documents.

(39) To facilitate the application of this Regulation, Member States should be obliged to provide the Commission with the names and contact details of their Central Authorities and with other information. That information should be made available to practitioners and to the public through publication in the Official Journal of the European Union or through electronic access to the European Judicial Network in civil and commercial matters established by Decision 2001/470/EC. Furthermore, the use of forms provided for in this Regulation should facilitate and speed up communication between the Central Authorities and make it possible to submit applications electronically.

(40) The relationship between this Regulation and the bilateral or multilateral conventions and agreements on maintenance obligations to which the Member States are party should be specified. In this context it should be stipulated that Member States which are party to the Convention of 23 March 1962 between Sweden, Denmark, Finland, Iceland and Norway on the recovery of maintenance by the Member States may continue to apply that Convention since it contains more favourable rules on recognition and enforcement than those in this Regulation. As regards the conclusion of future bilateral agreements on maintenance obligations with third States, the procedures and conditions under which Member States would be authorised to negotiate and conclude such agreements on their own behalf should be determined in the course of discussions relating to a Commission proposal on

the subject.

(41) In calculating the periods and time limits provided for in this Regulation, Regulation (EEC, Euratom) No 1182/71 of the Council of 3 June 1971 determining the rules applicable to periods, dates and time limits should apply.

(42) The measures necessary for the implementation of this Regulation should be adopted in accordance with Council Decision 1999/468/EC of 28 June 1999 laying down the procedures for the exercise of implementing powers conferred on the Commission.

(43) In particular, the Commission should be empowered to adopt any amendments to the forms provided for in this Regulation in accordance with the advisory procedure provided for in Article 3 of Decision 1999/468/EC. For the establishment of the list of the administrative authorities falling within the scope of this Regulation, and the list of authorities competent to certify the right to legal aid, the Commission should be empowered to act in accordance with the management procedure provided for in Article 4 of that Decision.

(44) This Regulation should amend Regulation (EC) No 44/2001 by replacing the provisions of that Regulation applicable to maintenance obligations. Subject to the transitional provisions of this Regulation, Member States should, in matters relating to maintenance obligations, apply the provisions of this Regulation on jurisdiction, recognition, enforceability and enforcement of decisions and on legal aid instead of those of Regulation (EC) No 44/2001 as from the date on which this Regulation becomes applicable.

(45) Since the objectives of this Regulation, namely the introduction of a series of measures to ensure the effective recovery of maintenance claims in cross-border situations and thus to facilitate the free movement of persons within the European Union, cannot be sufficiently achieved by the Member States and can therefore, by reason of the scale and effects of this Regulation, be better achieved at Community level, the Community may adopt measures in accordance with the principle of subsidiarity as set out in Article 5 of the Treaty. In accordance with the principle of proportionality as set out in that Article this Regulation does not go beyond what is necessary to achieve those objectives.

(46) In accordance with Article 3 of the Protocol on the position of the United Kingdom and Ireland, annexed to the Treaty on European Union and to the Treaty establishing the European Community, Ireland has given notice of its wish to take part in the adoption and application of this Regulation.

(47) In accordance with Articles 1 and 2 of the Protocol on the position of the United Kingdom and Ireland, annexed to the Treaty on European Union and to the Treaty establishing the European Community, the United Kingdom is not taking part in the adoption of this Regulation and is not bound by it or subject to its application. This is, however, without prejudice to the possibility for the United Kingdom of notifying its intention of accepting this Regulation after its adoption in accordance with Article 4 of the said Protocol.

(48) In accordance with Articles 1 and 2 of the Protocol on the position of Denmark annexed to the Treaty on European Union and the Treaty establishing the European Community, Denmark is not taking part in the adoption of this Regulation and is not bound by it or subject to its application, without prejudice to the possibility for Denmark of applying the amendments made here to Regulation (EC) No 44/2001 pursuant to Article 3 of the Agreement of 19 October 2005 between the European Community and the Kingdom of Denmark on jurisdiction and the recognition and enforcement of judgments in civil and commercial matters,

HAS ADOPTED THIS REGULATION:

Chapter I. Scope and Definitions

Article 1. (1) This Regulation shall apply to maintenance obligations arising from a family relationship, parentage, marriage or affinity.

(2) In this Regulation, the term "Member State" shall mean Member States to which this Regulation applies.

Article 2. (1) For the purposes of this Regulation:

(1) the term "decision" shall mean a decision in matters relating to maintenance obligations given by a court of a Member State, whatever the decision may be called, including a decree, order, judgment or writ of execution, as well as a decision by an officer of the court determining the costs or expenses. For the purposes of Chapters VII and VIII, the term "decision" shall also mean a decision in matters relating to maintenance obligations given in a third State;

(2) the term "court settlement" shall mean a settlement in matters relating to maintenance obligations which has been approved by a court or concluded before a court in the course of proceedings;

(3) the term "authentic instrument" shall mean:

(a) a document in matters relating to maintenance obligations which has been formally drawn up or registered as an authentic instrument in the Member State of origin and the authenticity of which:

PART II   PRIVATE INTERNATIONAL LAW

(i) relates to the signature and the content of the instrument, and
(ii) has been established by a public authority or other authority empowered for that purpose; or,
(b) an arrangement relating to maintenance obligations concluded with administrative authorities of the Member State of origin or authenticated by them;
(4) the term "Member State of origin" shall mean the Member State in which, as the case may be, the decision has been given, the court settlement has been approved or concluded, or the authentic instrument has been established;
(5) the term "Member State of enforcement" shall mean the Member State in which the enforcement of the decision, the court settlement or the authentic instrument is sought;
(6) the term "requesting Member State" shall mean the Member State whose Central Authority transmits an application pursuant to Chapter VII;
(7) the term "requested Member State" shall mean the Member State whose Central Authority receives an application pursuant to Chapter VII;
(8) the term "2007 Hague Convention Contracting State" shall mean a State which is a contracting party to the Hague Convention of 23 November 2007 on the International Recovery of Child Support and other Forms of Family Maintenance (hereinafter referred to as the 2007 Hague Convention) to the extent that the said Convention applies between the Community and that State;
(9) the term "court of origin" shall mean the court which has given the decision to be enforced;
(10) the term "creditor" shall mean any individual to whom maintenance is owed or is alleged to be owed;
(11) the term "debtor" shall mean any individual who owes or who is alleged to owe maintenance.
(2) For the purposes of this Regulation, the term "court" shall include administrative authorities of the Member States with competence in matters relating to maintenance obligations provided that such authorities offer guarantees with regard to impartiality and the right of all parties to be heard and provided that their decisions under the law of the Member State where they are established:
(i) may be made the subject of an appeal to or review by a judicial authority; and
(ii) have a similar force and effect as a decision of a judicial authority on the same matter.
These administrative authorities shall be listed in Annex X. That Annex shall be established and amended in accordance with the management procedure referred to in Article 73(2) at the request of the Member State in which the administrative authority concerned is established.
(3) For the purposes of Articles 3, 4 and 6, the concept of "domicile" shall replace that of "nationality" in those Member States which use this concept as a connecting factor in family matters.
For the purposes of Article 6, parties which have their "domicile" in different territorial units of the same Member State shall be deemed to have their common "domicile" in that Member State.

Chapter II. Jurisdiction

Article 3. In matters relating to maintenance obligations in Member States, jurisdiction shall lie with:
(a) the court for the place where the defendant is habitually resident, or
(b) the court for the place where the creditor is habitually resident, or
(c) the court which, according to its own law, has jurisdiction to entertain proceedings concerning the status of a person if the matter relating to maintenance is ancillary to those proceedings, unless that jurisdiction is based solely on the nationality of one of the parties, or
(d) the court which, according to its own law, has jurisdiction to entertain proceedings concerning parental responsibility if the matter relating to maintenance is ancillary to those proceedings, unless that jurisdiction is based solely on the nationality of one of the parties.

Article 4. (1) The parties may agree that the following court or courts of a Member State shall have jurisdiction to settle any disputes in matters relating to a maintenance obligation which have arisen or may arise between them:
(a) a court or the courts of a Member State in which one of the parties is habitually resident;
(b) a court or the courts of a Member State of which one of the parties has the nationality;
(c) in the case of maintenance obligations between spouses or former spouses:
(i) the court which has jurisdiction to settle their dispute in matrimonial matters; or
(ii) a court or the courts of the Member State which was the Member State of the spouses' last common habitual residence for a period of at least one year.
The conditions referred to in points (a), (b) or (c) have to be met at the time the choice of court agreement is concluded or at the time the court is seised.
The jurisdiction conferred by agreement shall be exclusive unless the parties have agreed otherwise.
(2) A choice of court agreement shall be in writing. Any communication by electronic means which provides a durable record of the agreement shall be equivalent to "writing".

(3) This Article shall not apply to a dispute relating to a maintenance obligation towards a child under the age of 18.
(4) If the parties have agreed to attribute exclusive jurisdiction to a court or courts of a State party to the Convention on jurisdiction and the recognition and enforcement of judgments in civil and commercial matters, signed on 30 October 2007 in Lugano (hereinafter referred to as the Lugano Convention), where that State is not a Member State, the said Convention shall apply except in the case of the disputes referred to in paragraph (3).

Article 5. Apart from jurisdiction derived from other provisions of this Regulation, a court of a Member State before which a defendant enters an appearance shall have jurisdiction. This rule shall not apply where appearance was entered to contest the jurisdiction.

Article 6. Where no court of a Member State has jurisdiction pursuant to Articles 3, 4 and 5 and no court of a State party to the Lugano Convention which is not a Member State has jurisdiction pursuant to the provisions of that Convention, the courts of the Member State of the common nationality of the parties shall have jurisdiction.

Article 7 Where no court of a Member State has jurisdiction pursuant to Articles 3, 4, 5 and 6, the courts of a Member State may, on an exceptional basis, hear the case if proceedings cannot reasonably be brought or conducted or would be impossible in a third State with which the dispute is closely connected.
The dispute must have a sufficient connection with the Member State of the court seised.

Article 8. (1) Where a decision is given in a Member State or a 2007 Hague Convention Contracting State where the creditor is habitually resident, proceedings to modify the decision or to have a new decision given cannot be brought by the debtor in any other Member State as long as the creditor remains habitually resident in the State in which the decision was given.
(2) Paragraph 1 shall not apply:
(a) where the parties have agreed in accordance with Article 4 to the jurisdiction of the courts of that other Member State;
(b) where the creditor submits to the jurisdiction of the courts of that other Member State pursuant to Article 5;
(c) where the competent authority in the 2007 Hague Convention Contracting State of origin cannot, or refuses to, exercise jurisdiction to modify the decision or give a new decision; or
(d) where the decision given in the 2007 Hague Convention Contracting State of origin cannot be recognised or declared enforceable in the Member State where proceedings to modify the decision or to have a new decision given are contemplated.

Article 9. For the purposes of this Chapter, a court shall be deemed to be seised:
(a) at the time when the document instituting the proceedings or an equivalent document is lodged with the court, provided that the claimant has not subsequently failed to take the steps he was required to take to have service effected on the defendant; or
(b) if the document has to be served before being lodged with the court, at the time when it is received by the authority responsible for service, provided that the claimant has not subsequently failed to take the steps he was required to take to have the document lodged with the court.

Article 10. Where a court of a Member State is seised of a case over which it has no jurisdiction under this Regulation it shall declare of its own motion that it has no jurisdiction.

Article 11. (1) Where a defendant habitually resident in a State other than the Member State where the action was brought does not enter an appearance, the court with jurisdiction shall stay the proceedings so long as it is not shown that the defendant has been able to receive the document instituting the proceedings or an equivalent document in sufficient time to enable him to arrange for his defence, or that all necessary steps have been taken to this end.
(2) Article 19 of Regulation (EC) No 1393/2007 shall apply instead of the provisions of paragraph (1) of this Article if the document instituting the proceedings or an equivalent document had to be transmitted from one Member State to another pursuant to that Regulation.
(3) Where the provisions of Regulation (EC) No 1393/2007 are not applicable, Article 15 of the Hague Convention of 15 November 1965 on the service abroad of judicial and extrajudicial documents in civil or commercial matters shall apply if the document instituting the proceedings or an equivalent document had to be transmitted abroad pursuant to that Convention.

Article 12. (1) Where proceedings involving the same cause of action and between the same parties

are brought in the courts of different Member States, any court other than the court first seised shall of its own motion stay its proceedings until such time as the jurisdiction of the court first seised is established.
(2) Where the jurisdiction of the court first seised is established, any court other than the court first seised shall decline jurisdiction in favour of that court.

Article 13. (1) Where related actions are pending in the courts of different Member States, any court other than the court first seised may stay its proceedings.
(2) Where these actions are pending at first instance, any court other than the court first seised may also, on the application of one of the parties, decline jurisdiction if the court first seised has jurisdiction over the actions in question and its law permits the consolidation thereof.
(3) For the purposes of this Article, actions are deemed to be related where they are so closely connected that it is expedient to hear and determine them together to avoid the risk of irreconcilable judgments resulting from separate proceedings.

Article 14. Application may be made to the courts of a Member State for such provisional, including protective, measures as may be available under the law of that State, even if, under this Regulation, the courts of another Member State have jurisdiction as to the substance of the matter.

Chapter III. Applicable Law

Article 15. The law applicable to maintenance obligations shall be determined in accordance with the Hague Protocol of 23 November 2007 on the law applicable to maintenance obligations (hereinafter referred to as the 2007 Hague Protocol) in the Member States bound by that instrument.

Chapter IV. Recognition, Enforceability and Enforcement of Decisions

Article 16. (1) This Chapter shall govern the recognition, enforceability and enforcement of decisions falling within the scope of this Regulation.
(2) Section 1 shall apply to decisions given in a Member State bound by the 2007 Hague Protocol.
(3) Section 2 shall apply to decisions given in a Member State not bound by the 2007 Hague Protocol.
(4) Section 3 shall apply to all decisions.

Section 1. Decisions given in a Member State bound by the 2007 Hague Protocol

Article 17. (1) A decision given in a Member State bound by the 2007 Hague Protocol shall be recognised in another Member State without any special procedure being required and without any possibility of opposing its recognition.
(2) A decision given in a Member State bound by the 2007 Hague Protocol which is enforceable in that State shall be enforceable in another Member State without the need for a declaration of enforceability.

Article 18. An enforceable decision shall carry with it by operation of law the power to proceed to any protective measures which exist under the law of the Member State of enforcement.

Article 19. (1) A defendant who did not enter an appearance in the Member State of origin shall have the right to apply for a review of the decision before the competent court of that Member State where:
(a) he was not served with the document instituting the proceedings or an equivalent document in sufficient time and in such a way as to enable him to arrange for his defence; or
(b) he was prevented from contesting the maintenance claim by reason of force majeure or due to extraordinary circumstances without any fault on his part;
unless he failed to challenge the decision when it was possible for him to do so.
(2) The time limit for applying for a review shall run from the day the defendant was effectively acquainted with the contents of the decision and was able to react, at the latest from the date of the first enforcement measure having the effect of making his property non-disposable in whole or in part. The defendant shall react promptly, in any event within 45 days. No extension may be granted on account of distance.
(3) If the court rejects the application for a review referred to in paragraph (1) on the basis that none of the grounds for a review set out in that paragraph apply, the decision shall remain in force.
If the court decides that a review is justified for one of the reasons laid down in paragraph (1), the decision shall be null and void. However, the creditor shall not lose the benefits of the interruption of prescription or limitation periods, or the right to claim retroactive maintenance acquired in the initial proceedings.

Article 20. (1) For the purposes of enforcement of a decision in another Member State, the claimant shall provide the competent enforcement authorities with:
(a) a copy of the decision which satisfies the conditions necessary to establish its authenticity;
(b) the extract from the decision issued by the court of origin using the form set out in Annex I;
(c) where appropriate, a document showing the amount of any arrears and the date such amount was calculated;
(d) where necessary, a transliteration or a translation of the content of the form referred to in point (b) into the official language of the Member State of enforcement or, where there are several official languages in that Member State, into the official language or one of the official languages of court proceedings of the place where the application is made, in accordance with the law of that Member State, or into another language that the Member State concerned has indicated it can accept. Each Member State may indicate the official language or languages of the institutions of the European Union other than its own which it can accept for the completion of the form.
(2) The competent authorities of the Member State of enforcement may not require the claimant to provide a translation of the decision. However, a translation may be required if the enforcement of the decision is challenged.
(3) Any translation under this Article must be done by a person qualified to do translations in one of the Member States.

Article 21. (1) The grounds of refusal or suspension of enforcement under the law of the Member State of enforcement shall apply in so far as they are not incompatible with the application of paragraphs 2 and 3.
(2) The competent authority in the Member State of enforcement shall, on application by the debtor, refuse, either wholly or in part, the enforcement of the decision of the court of origin if the right to enforce the decision of the court of origin is extinguished by the effect of prescription or the limitation of action, either under the law of the Member State of origin or under the law of the Member State of enforcement, whichever provides for the longer limitation period.
Furthermore, the competent authority in the Member State of enforcement may, on application by the debtor, refuse, either wholly or in part, the enforcement of the decision of the court of origin if it is irreconcilable with a decision given in the Member State of enforcement or with a decision given in another Member State or in a third State which fulfils the conditions necessary for its recognition in the Member State of enforcement.
A decision which has the effect of modifying an earlier decision on maintenance on the basis of changed circumstances shall not be considered an irreconcilable decision within the meaning of the second subparagraph.
(3) The competent authority in the Member State of enforcement may, on application by the debtor, suspend, either wholly or in part, the enforcement of the decision of the court of origin if the competent court of the Member State of origin has been seised of an application for a review of the decision of the court of origin pursuant to Article 19.
Furthermore, the competent authority of the Member State of enforcement shall, on application by the debtor, suspend the enforcement of the decision of the court of origin where the enforceability of that decision is suspended in the Member State of origin.

Article 22. The recognition and enforcement of a decision on maintenance under this Regulation shall not in any way imply the recognition of the family relationship, parentage, marriage or affinity underlying the maintenance obligation which gave rise to the decision.

Section 2. Decisions given in a Member State not bound by the 2007 Hague Protocol

Article 23. (1) A decision given in a Member State not bound by the 2007 Hague Protocol shall be recognised in the other Member States without any special procedure being required.
(2) Any interested party who raises the recognition of a decision as the principal issue in a dispute may, in accordance with the procedures provided for in this Section, apply for a decision that the decision be recognised.
(3) If the outcome of proceedings in a court of a Member State depends on the determination of an incidental question of recognition, that court shall have jurisdiction over that question.

Article 24. A decision shall not be recognised:
(a) if such recognition is manifestly contrary to public policy in the Member State in which recognition is sought. The test of public policy may not be applied to the rules relating to jurisdiction;
(b) where it was given in default of appearance, if the defendant was not served with the document which instituted the proceedings or with an equivalent document in sufficient time and in such a way

as to enable him to arrange for his defence, unless the defendant failed to commence proceedings to challenge the decision when it was possible for him to do so;

(c) if it is irreconcilable with a decision given in a dispute between the same parties in the Member State in which recognition is sought;

(d) if it is irreconcilable with an earlier decision given in another Member State or in a third State in a dispute involving the same cause of action and between the same parties, provided that the earlier decision fulfils the conditions necessary for its recognition in the Member State in which recognition is sought.

A decision which has the effect of modifying an earlier decision on maintenance on the basis of changed circumstances shall not be considered an irreconcilable decision within the meaning of points (c) or (d).

Article 25. A court of a Member State in which recognition is sought of a decision given in a Member State not bound by the 2007 Hague Protocol shall stay the proceedings if the enforceability of the decision is suspended in the Member State of origin by reason of an appeal.

Article 26. A decision given in a Member State not bound by the 2007 Hague Protocol and enforceable in that State shall be enforceable in another Member State when, on the application of any interested party, it has been declared enforceable there.

Article 27. (1) The application for a declaration of enforceability shall be submitted to the court or competent authority of the Member State of enforcement notified by that Member State to the Commission in accordance with Article 71.

(2) The local jurisdiction shall be determined by reference to the place of habitual residence of the party against whom enforcement is sought, or to the place of enforcement.

Article 28. (1) The application for a declaration of enforceability shall be accompanied by the following documents:

(a) a copy of the decision which satisfies the conditions necessary to establish its authenticity;

(b) an extract from the decision issued by the court of origin using the form set out in Annex II, without prejudice to Article 29;

(c) where necessary, a transliteration or a translation of the content of the form referred to in point (b) into the official language of the Member State of enforcement or, where there are several official languages in that Member State, into the official language or one of the official languages of court proceedings of the place where the application is made, in accordance with the law of that Member State, or into another language that the Member State concerned has indicated it can accept. Each Member State may indicate the official language or languages of the institutions of the European Union other than its own which it can accept for the completion of the form.

(2) The court or competent authority seised of the application may not require the claimant to provide a translation of the decision. However, a translation may be required in connection with an appeal under Articles 32 or 33.

(3) Any translation under this Article must be done by a person qualified to do translations in one of the Member States.

Article 29. (1) If the extract referred to in Article 28(1)(b) is not produced, the competent court or authority may specify a time for its production or accept an equivalent document or, if it considers that it has sufficient information before it, dispense with its production.

(2) In the situation referred to in paragraph (1), if the competent court or authority so requires, a translation of the documents shall be produced. The translation shall be done by a person qualified to do translations in one of the Member States.

Article 30. The decision shall be declared enforceable without any review under Article 24 immediately on completion of the formalities in Article 28 and at the latest within 30 days of the completion of those formalities, except where exceptional circumstances make this impossible. The party against whom enforcement is sought shall not at this stage of the proceedings be entitled to make any submissions on the application.

Article 31. (1) The decision on the application for a declaration of enforceability shall forthwith be brought to the notice of the applicant in accordance with the procedure laid down by the law of the Member State of enforcement.

(2) The declaration of enforceability shall be served on the party against whom enforcement is sought, accompanied by the decision, if not already served on that party.

EU: MAINTENANCE REGULATION

Article 32. (1) The decision on the application for a declaration of enforceability may be appealed against by either party.
(2) The appeal shall be lodged with the court notified by the Member State concerned to the Commission in accordance with Article 71.
(3) The appeal shall be dealt with in accordance with the rules governing procedure in contradictory matters.
(4) If the party against whom enforcement is sought fails to appear before the appellate court in proceedings concerning an appeal brought by the applicant, Article 11 shall apply even where the party against whom enforcement is sought is not habitually resident in any of the Member States.
(5) An appeal against the declaration of enforceability shall be lodged within 30 days of service thereof. If the party against whom enforcement is sought has his habitual residence in a Member State other than that in which the declaration of enforceability was given, the time for appealing shall be 45 days and shall run from the date of service, either on him in person or at his residence. No extension may be granted on account of distance.

Article 33. The decision given on appeal may be contested only by the procedure notified by the Member State concerned to the Commission in accordance with Article 71.

Article 34. (1) The court with which an appeal is lodged under Articles 32 or 33 shall refuse or revoke a declaration of enforceability only on one of the grounds specified in Article 24.
(2) Subject to Article 32(4), the court seised of an appeal under Article 32 shall give its decision within 90 days from the date it was seised, except where exceptional circumstances make this impossible.
(3) The court seised of an appeal under Article 33 shall give its decision without delay.

Article 35. The court with which an appeal is lodged under Articles 32 or 33 shall, on the application of the party against whom enforcement is sought, stay the proceedings if the enforceability of the decision is suspended in the Member State of origin by reason of an appeal.

Article 36. (1) When a decision must be recognised in accordance with this Section, nothing shall prevent the applicant from availing himself of provisional, including protective, measures in accordance with the law of the Member State of enforcement without a declaration of enforceability under Article 30 being required.
(2) The declaration of enforceability shall carry with it by operation of law the power to proceed to any protective measures.
(3) During the time specified for an appeal pursuant to Article 32(5) against the declaration of enforceability and until any such appeal has been determined, no measures of enforcement may be taken other than protective measures against the property of the party against whom enforcement is sought.

Article 37. (1) Where a decision has been given in respect of several matters and the declaration of enforceability cannot be given for all of them, the competent court or authority shall give it for one or more of them.
(2) An applicant may request a declaration of enforceability limited to parts of a decision.

Article 38. In proceedings for the issue of a declaration of enforceability, no charge, duty or fee calculated by reference to the value of the matter at issue may be levied in the Member State of enforcement.

Section 3. Common provisions

Article 39. The court of origin may declare the decision provisionally enforceable, notwithstanding any appeal, even if national law does not provide for enforceability by operation of law.

Article 40. (1) A party who wishes to invoke in another Member State a decision recognised within the meaning of Article 17(1) or recognised pursuant to Section 2 shall produce a copy of the decision which satisfies the conditions necessary to establish its authenticity.
(2) If necessary, the court before which the recognised decision is invoked may ask the party invoking the recognised decision to produce an extract issued by the court of origin using the form set out in Annex I or in Annex II, as the case may be.
The court of origin shall also issue such an extract at the request of any interested party.
(3) Where necessary, the party invoking the recognised decision shall provide a transliteration or a translation of the content of the form referred to in paragraph (2) into the official language of the Member State concerned or, where there are several official languages in that Member State, into the

official language or one of the official languages of court proceedings of the place where the recognised decision is invoked, in accordance with the law of that Member State, or into another language that the Member State concerned has indicated it can accept. Each Member State may indicate the official language or languages of the institutions of the European Union other than its own which it can accept for the completion of the form.

(4) Any translation under this Article must be done by a person qualified to do translations in one of the Member States.

Article 41. (1) Subject to the provisions of this Regulation, the procedure for the enforcement of decisions given in another Member State shall be governed by the law of the Member State of enforcement. A decision given in a Member State which is enforceable in the Member State of enforcement shall be enforced there under the same conditions as a decision given in that Member State of enforcement.

(2) The party seeking the enforcement of a decision given in another Member State shall not be required to have a postal address or an authorised representative in the Member State of enforcement, without prejudice to persons with competence in matters relating to enforcement proceedings.

Article 42. Under no circumstances may a decision given in a Member State be reviewed as to its substance in the Member State in which recognition, enforceability or enforcement is sought.

Article 43. Recovery of any costs incurred in the application of this Regulation shall not take precedence over the recovery of maintenance.

Chapter V. Access to Justice

Article 44. (1) Parties who are involved in a dispute covered by this Regulation shall have effective access to justice in another Member State, including enforcement and appeal or review procedures, in accordance with the conditions laid down in this Chapter.

In cases covered by Chapter VII, effective access to justice shall be provided by the requested Member State to any applicant who is resident in the requesting Member State.

(2) To ensure such effective access, Member States shall provide legal aid in accordance with this Chapter, unless paragraph (3) applies.

(3) In cases covered by Chapter VII, a Member State shall not be obliged to provide legal aid if and to the extent that the procedures of that Member State enable the parties to make the case without the need for legal aid, and the Central Authority provides such services as are necessary free of charge.

(4) Entitlements to legal aid shall not be less than those available in equivalent domestic cases.

(5) No security, bond or deposit, however described, shall be required to guarantee the payment of costs and expenses in proceedings concerning maintenance obligations.

Article 45. Legal aid granted under this Chapter shall mean the assistance necessary to enable parties to know and assert their rights and to ensure that their applications, lodged through the Central Authorities or directly with the competent authorities, are fully and effectively dealt with. It shall cover as necessary the following:

(a) pre-litigation advice with a view to reaching a settlement prior to bringing judicial proceedings;
(b) legal assistance in bringing a case before an authority or a court and representation in court;
(c) exemption from or assistance with the costs of proceedings and the fees to persons mandated to perform acts during the proceedings;
(d) in Member States in which an unsuccessful party is liable for the costs of the opposing party, if the recipient of legal aid loses the case, the costs incurred by the opposing party, if such costs would have been covered had the recipient been habitually resident in the Member State of the court seised;
(e) interpretation;
(f) translation of the documents required by the court or by the competent authority and presented by the recipient of legal aid which are necessary for the resolution of the case;
(g) travel costs to be borne by the recipient of legal aid where the physical presence of the persons concerned with the presentation of the recipient's case is required in court by the law or by the court of the Member State concerned and the court decides that the persons concerned cannot be heard to the satisfaction of the court by any other means.

Article 46. (1) The requested Member State shall provide free legal aid in respect of all applications by a creditor under Article 56 concerning maintenance obligations arising from a parent-child relationship towards a person under the age of 21.

(2) Notwithstanding paragraph (1), the competent authority of the requested Member State may, in relation to applications other than those under Article 56(1)(a) and (b), refuse free legal aid if it con-

siders that, on the merits, the application or any appeal or review is manifestly unfounded.

Article 47. (1) Subject to Articles 44 and 45, in cases not covered by Article 46, legal aid may be granted in accordance with national law, particularly as regards the conditions for the means test or the merits test.
(2) Notwithstanding paragraph (1), a party who, in the Member State of origin, has benefited from complete or partial legal aid or exemption from costs or expenses, shall be entitled, in any proceedings for recognition, enforceability or enforcement, to benefit from the most favourable legal aid or the most extensive exemption from costs or expenses provided for by the law of the Member State of enforcement.
(3) Notwithstanding paragraph (1), a party who, in the Member State of origin, has benefited from free proceedings before an administrative authority listed in Annex X, shall be entitled, in any proceedings for recognition, enforceability or enforcement, to benefit from legal aid in accordance with paragraph (2). To that end, he shall present a statement from the competent authority in the Member State of origin to the effect that he fulfils the financial requirements to qualify for the grant of complete or partial legal aid or exemption from costs or expenses.
Competent authorities for the purposes of this paragraph shall be listed in Annex XI. That Annex shall be established and amended in accordance with the management procedure referred to in Article 73(2).

Chapter VI. Court Settlements and Authentic Instruments

Article 48. (1) Court settlements and authentic instruments which are enforceable in the Member State of origin shall be recognised in another Member State and be enforceable there in the same way as decisions, in accordance with Chapter IV.
(2) The provisions of this Regulation shall apply as necessary to court settlements and authentic instruments.
(3) The competent authority of the Member State of origin shall issue, at the request of any interested party, an extract from the court settlement or the authentic instrument using the forms set out in Annexes I and II or in Annexes III and IV as the case may be.

Chapter VII. Cooperation between Central Authorities

Article 49. (1) Each Member State shall designate a Central Authority to discharge the duties which are imposed by this Regulation on such an authority.
(2) Federal Member States, Member States with more than one system of law or Member States having autonomous territorial units shall be free to appoint more than one Central Authority and shall specify the territorial or personal extent of their functions. Where a Member State has appointed more than one Central Authority, it shall designate the Central Authority to which any communication may be addressed for transmission to the appropriate Central Authority within that Member State. If a communication is sent to a Central Authority which is not competent, the latter shall be responsible for forwarding it to the competent Central Authority and for informing the sender accordingly.
(3) The designation of the Central Authority or Central Authorities, their contact details, and where appropriate the extent of their functions as specified in paragraph (2), shall be communicated by each Member State to the Commission in accordance with Article 71.

Article 50. (1) Central Authorities shall:
(a) cooperate with each other, including by exchanging information, and promote cooperation amongst the competent authorities in their Member States to achieve the purposes of this Regulation;
(b) seek as far as possible solutions to difficulties which arise in the application of this Regulation.
(2) Central authorities shall take measures to facilitate the application of this Regulation and to strengthen their cooperation. For this purpose the European Judicial Network in civil and commercial matters established by Decision 2001/470/EC shall be used.

Article 51. (1) Central Authorities shall provide assistance in relation to applications under Article 56 and shall in particular:
(a) transmit and receive such applications;
(b) initiate or facilitate the institution of proceedings in respect of such applications.
(2) In relation to such applications Central Authorities shall take all appropriate measures:
(a) where the circumstances require, to provide or facilitate the provision of legal aid;
(b) to help locate the debtor or the creditor, in particular pursuant to Articles 61, 62 and 63;
(c) to help obtain relevant information concerning the income and, if necessary, other financial circumstances of the debtor or creditor, including the location of assets, in particular pursuant to Articles 61, 62 and 63;

(d) to encourage amicable solutions with a view to obtaining voluntary payment of maintenance, where suitable by use of mediation, conciliation or similar processes;
(e) to facilitate the ongoing enforcement of maintenance decisions, including any arrears;
(f) to facilitate the collection and expeditious transfer of maintenance payments;
(g) to facilitate the obtaining of documentary or other evidence, without prejudice to Regulation (EC) No 1206/2001;
(h) to provide assistance in establishing parentage where necessary for the recovery of maintenance;
(i) to initiate or facilitate the institution of proceedings to obtain any necessary provisional measures which are territorial in nature and the purpose of which is to secure the outcome of a pending maintenance application;
(j) to facilitate the service of documents, without prejudice to Regulation (EC) No 1393/2007.
(3) The functions of the Central Authority under this Article may, to the extent permitted under the law of the Member State concerned, be performed by public bodies, or other bodies subject to the supervision of the competent authorities of that Member State. The designation of any such public bodies or other bodies, as well as their contact details and the extent of their functions, shall be communicated by each Member State to the Commission in accordance with Article 71.
(4) Nothing in this Article or in Article 53 shall impose an obligation on a Central Authority to exercise powers that can be exercised only by judicial authorities under the law of the requested Member State.

Article 52. The Central Authority of the requested Member State may require a power of attorney from the applicant only if it acts on his behalf in judicial proceedings or before other authorities, or in order to designate a representative so to act.

Article 53. (1) A Central Authority may make a request, supported by reasons, to another Central Authority to take appropriate specific measures under points (b), (c), (g), (h), (i) and (j) of Article 51(2) when no application under Article 56 is pending. The requested Central Authority shall take such measures as are appropriate if satisfied that they are necessary to assist a potential applicant in making an application under Article 56 or in determining whether such an application should be initiated.
(2) Where a request for measures under Article 51(2)(b) and (c) is made, the requested Central Authority shall seek the information requested, if necessary pursuant to Article 61. However, the information referred to in points (b), (c) and (d) of Article 61(2) may be sought only when the creditor produces a copy of the decision, court settlement or authentic instrument to be enforced, accompanied by the extract provided for in Articles 20, 28 or 48, as appropriate.
The requested Central Authority shall communicate the information obtained to the requesting Central Authority. Where that information was obtained pursuant to Article 61, this communication shall specify only the address of the potential defendant in the requested Member State. In the case of a request with a view to recognition, declaration of enforceability or enforcement, the communication shall, in addition, specify merely whether the debtor has income or assets in that State.
If the requested Central Authority is not able to provide the information requested it shall inform the requesting Central Authority without delay and specify the grounds for this impossibility.
(3) A Central Authority may also take specific measures at the request of another Central Authority in relation to a case having an international element concerning the recovery of maintenance pending in the requesting Member State.
(4) For requests under this Article, the Central Authorities shall use the form set out in Annex V.

Article 54. (1) Each Central Authority shall bear its own costs in applying this Regulation.
(2) Central Authorities may not impose any charge on an applicant for the provision of their services under this Regulation save for exceptional costs arising from a request for a specific measure under Article 53.
For the purposes of this paragraph, costs relating to locating the debtor shall not be regarded as exceptional.
(3) The requested Central Authority may not recover the costs of the services referred to in paragraph (2) without the prior consent of the applicant to the provision of those services at such cost.

Article 55. An application under this Chapter shall be made through the Central Authority of the Member State in which the applicant resides to the Central Authority of the requested Member State.

Article 56. (1) A creditor seeking to recover maintenance under this Regulation may make applications for the following:
(a) recognition or recognition and declaration of enforceability of a decision;

(b) enforcement of a decision given or recognised in the requested Member State;
(c) establishment of a decision in the requested Member State where there is no existing decision, including where necessary the establishment of parentage;
(d) establishment of a decision in the requested Member State where the recognition and declaration of enforceability of a decision given in a State other than the requested Member State is not possible;
(e) modification of a decision given in the requested Member State;
(f) modification of a decision given in a State other than the requested Member State.
(2) A debtor against whom there is an existing maintenance decision may make applications for the following:
(a) recognition of a decision leading to the suspension, or limiting the enforcement, of a previous decision in the requested Member State;
(b) modification of a decision given in the requested Member State;
(c) modification of a decision given in a State other than the requested Member State.
(3) For applications under this Article, the assistance and representation referred to in Article 45(b) shall be provided by the Central Authority of the requested Member State directly or through public authorities or other bodies or persons.
(4) Save as otherwise provided in this Regulation, the applications referred to in paragraphs 1 and 2 shall be determined under the law of the requested Member State and shall be subject to the rules of jurisdiction applicable in that Member State.

Article 57. (1) An application under Article 56 shall be made using the form set out in Annex VI or in Annex VII.
(2) An application under Article 56 shall as a minimum include:
(a) a statement of the nature of the application or applications;
(b) the name and contact details, including the address, and date of birth of the applicant;
(c) the name and, if known, address and date of birth of the defendant;
(d) the name and the date of birth of any person for whom maintenance is sought;
(e) the grounds upon which the application is based;
(f) in an application by a creditor, information concerning where the maintenance payment should be sent or electronically transmitted;
(g) the name and contact details of the person or unit from the Central Authority of the requesting Member State responsible for processing the application.
(3) For the purposes of paragraph (2)(b), the applicant's personal address may be replaced by another address in cases of family violence, if the national law of the requested Member State does not require the applicant to supply his or her personal address for the purposes of proceedings to be brought.
(4) As appropriate, and to the extent known, the application shall in addition in particular include:
(a) the financial circumstances of the creditor;
(b) the financial circumstances of the debtor, including the name and address of the employer of the debtor and the nature and location of the assets of the debtor;
(c) any other information that may assist with the location of the defendant.
(5) The application shall be accompanied by any necessary supporting information or documentation including, where appropriate, documentation concerning the entitlement of the applicant to legal aid. Applications under Article 56(1)(a) and (b) and under Article 56(2)(a) shall be accompanied, as appropriate, only by the documents listed in Articles 20, 28 and 48, or in Article 25 of the 2007 Hague Convention.

Article 58. (1) The Central Authority of the requesting Member State shall assist the applicant in ensuring that the application is accompanied by all the information and documents known by it to be necessary for consideration of the application.
(2) The Central Authority of the requesting Member State shall, when satisfied that the application complies with the requirements of this Regulation, transmit the application to the Central Authority of the requested Member State.
(3) The requested Central Authority shall, within 30 days from the date of receipt of the application, acknowledge receipt using the form set out in Annex VIII, and inform the Central Authority of the requesting Member State what initial steps have been or will be taken to deal with the application, and may request any further necessary documents and information. Within the same 30-day period, the requested Central Authority shall provide to the requesting Central Authority the name and contact details of the person or unit responsible for responding to inquiries regarding the progress of the application.
(4) Within 60 days from the date of acknowledgement, the requested Central Authority shall inform

the requesting Central Authority of the status of the application.
(5) Requesting and requested Central Authorities shall keep each other informed of:
(a) the person or unit responsible for a particular case;
(b) the progress of the case;
and shall provide timely responses to enquiries.
(6) Central Authorities shall process a case as quickly as a proper consideration of the issues will allow.
(7) Central Authorities shall employ the most rapid and efficient means of communication at their disposal.
(8) A requested Central Authority may refuse to process an application only if it is manifest that the requirements of this Regulation are not fulfilled. In such a case, that Central Authority shall promptly inform the requesting Central Authority of its reasons for refusal using the form set out in Annex IX.
(9) The requested Central Authority may not reject an application solely on the basis that additional documents or information are needed. However, the requested Central Authority may ask the requesting Central Authority to provide these additional documents or this information. If the requesting Central Authority does not do so within 90 days or a longer period specified by the requested Central Authority, the requested Central Authority may decide that it will no longer process the application. In this case, it shall promptly notify the requesting Central Authority using the form set out in Annex IX.

Article 59. (1) The request or application form shall be completed in the official language of the requested Member State or, if there are several official languages in that Member State, in the official language or one of the official languages of the place of the Central Authority concerned, or in any other official language of the institutions of the European Union which that Member State has indicated it can accept, unless the Central Authority of that Member State dispenses with translation.
(2) The documents accompanying the request or application form shall not be translated into the language determined in accordance with paragraph (1) unless a translation is necessary in order to provide the assistance requested, without prejudice to Articles 20, 28, 40 and 66.
(3) Any other communication between Central Authorities shall be in the language determined in accordance with paragraph (1) unless the Central Authorities agree otherwise.

Article 60. (1) In order to facilitate the application of this Regulation, Central Authorities shall meet regularly.
(2) These meetings shall be convened in compliance with Decision 2001/470/EC.

Article 61. (1) Under the conditions laid down in this Chapter and by way of exception to Article 51(4), the requested Central Authority shall use all appropriate and reasonable means to obtain the information referred to in paragraph (2) necessary to facilitate, in a given case, the establishment, the modification, the recognition, the declaration of enforceability or the enforcement of a decision.
The public authorities or administrations which, in the course of their ordinary activities, hold, within the requested State, the information referred to in paragraph (2) and which control the processing thereof within the meaning of Directive 95/46/EC shall, subject to limitations justified on grounds of national security or public safety, provide the information to the requested Central Authority at its request in cases where the requested Central Authority does not have direct access to it.
Member States may designate the public authorities or administrations able to provide the requested Central Authority with the information referred to in paragraph (2). Where a Member State makes such a designation, it shall ensure that its choice of authorities and administrations permits its Central Authority to have access, in accordance with this Article, to the information requested.
Any other legal person which holds within the requested Member State the information referred to in paragraph (2) and controls the processing thereof within the meaning of Directive 95/46/EC shall provide the information to the requested Central Authority at the latter's request if it is authorised to do so by the law of the requested Member State.
The requested Central Authority shall, as necessary, transmit the information thus obtained to the requesting Central Authority.
(2) The information referred to in this Article shall be the information already held by the authorities, administrations or persons referred to in paragraph (1). It shall be adequate, relevant and not excessive and shall relate to:
(a) the address of the debtor or of the creditor;
(b) the debtor's income;
(c) the identification of the debtor's employer and/or of the debtor's bank account(s);
(d) the debtor's assets.

For the purpose of obtaining or modifying a decision, only the information listed in point (a) may be requested by the requested Central Authority.

For the purpose of having a decision recognised, declared enforceable or enforced, all the information listed in the first subparagraph may be requested by the requested Central Authority. However, the information listed in point (d) may be requested only if the information listed in points (b) and (c) is insufficient to allow enforcement of the decision.

Article 62. (1) The Central Authorities shall, within their Member State, transmit the information referred to in Article 61(2) to the competent courts, the competent authorities responsible for service of documents and the competent authorities responsible for enforcement of a decision, as the case may be.
(2) Any authority or court to which information has been transmitted pursuant to Article 61 may use this only to facilitate the recovery of maintenance claims.
Except for information merely indicating the existence of an address, income or assets in the requested Member State, the information referred to in Article 61(2) may not be disclosed to the person having applied to the requesting Central Authority, subject to the application of procedural rules before a court.
(3) Any authority processing information transmitted to it pursuant to Article 61 may not store such information beyond the period necessary for the purposes for which it was transmitted.
(4) Any authority processing information communicated to it pursuant to Article 61 shall ensure the confidentiality of such information, in accordance with its national law.

Article 63. (1) Notification of the data subject of the communication of all or part of the information collected on him shall take place in accordance with the national law of the requested Member State.
(2) Where there is a risk that it may prejudice the effective recovery of the maintenance claim, such notification may be deferred for a period which shall not exceed 90 days from the date on which the information was provided to the requested Central Authority.

Chapter VIII. Public Bodies

Article 64. (1) For the purposes of an application for recognition and declaration of enforceability of decisions or for the purposes of enforcement of decisions, the term "creditor" shall include a public body acting in place of an individual to whom maintenance is owed or one to which reimbursement is owed for benefits provided in place of maintenance.
(2) The right of a public body to act in place of an individual to whom maintenance is owed or to seek reimbursement of benefits provided to the creditor in place of maintenance shall be governed by the law to which the body is subject.
(3) A public body may seek recognition and a declaration of enforceability or claim enforcement of:
(a) a decision given against a debtor on the application of a public body which claims payment of benefits provided in place of maintenance;
(b) a decision given between a creditor and a debtor to the extent of the benefits provided to the creditor in place of maintenance.
(4) The public body seeking recognition and a declaration of enforceability or claiming enforcement of a decision shall upon request provide any document necessary to establish its right under paragraph (2) and to establish that benefits have been provided to the creditor.

Chapter IX. General and Final Provisions

Article 65. No legalisation or other similar formality shall be required in the context of this Regulation.

Article 66. Without prejudice to Articles 20, 28 and 40, the court seised may require the parties to provide a translation of supporting documents which are not in the language of proceedings only if it deems a translation necessary in order to give a decision or to respect the rights of the defence.

Article 67. Without prejudice to Article 54, the competent authority of the requested Member State may recover costs from an unsuccessful party having received free legal aid pursuant to Article 46, on an exceptional basis and if his financial circumstances so allow.

Article 68. (1) Subject to Article 75(2), this Regulation shall modify Regulation (EC) No 44/2001 by replacing the provisions of that Regulation applicable to matters relating to maintenance obligations.
(2) This Regulation shall replace, in matters relating to maintenance obligations, Regulation (EC) No 805/2004, except with regard to European Enforcement Orders on maintenance obligations issued in a Member State not bound by the 2007 Hague Protocol.

PART II   PRIVATE INTERNATIONAL LAW

(3) In matters relating to maintenance obligations, this Regulation shall be without prejudice to the application of Directive 2003/8/EC, subject to Chapter V.
(4) This Regulation shall be without prejudice to the application of Directive 95/46/EC.

Article 69. (1) This Regulation shall not affect the application of bilateral or multilateral conventions and agreements to which one or more Member States are party at the time of adoption of this Regulation and which concern matters governed by this Regulation, without prejudice to the obligations of Member States under Article 307 of the Treaty.
(2) Notwithstanding paragraph (1), and without prejudice to paragraph (3), this Regulation shall, in relations between Member States, take precedence over the conventions and agreements which concern matters governed by this Regulation and to which Member States are party.
(3) This Regulation shall not preclude the application of the Convention of 23 March 1962 between Sweden, Denmark, Finland, Iceland and Norway on the recovery of maintenance by the Member States which are party thereto, since, with regard to the recognition, enforceability and enforcement of decisions, that Convention provides for:
(a) simplified and more expeditious procedures for the enforcement of decisions relating to maintenance obligations, and
(b) legal aid which is more favourable than that provided for in Chapter V of this Regulation.
However, the application of the said Convention may not have the effect of depriving the defendant of his protection under Articles 19 and 21 of this Regulation.

Article 70. The Member States shall provide within the framework of the European Judicial Network in civil and commercial matters established by Decision 2001/470/EC the following information with a view to making it available to the public:
(a) a description of the national laws and procedures concerning maintenance obligations;
(b) a description of the measures taken to meet the obligations under Article 51;
(c) a description of how effective access to justice is guaranteed, as required under Article 44, and
(d) a description of national enforcement rules and procedures, including information on any limitations on enforcement, in particular debtor protection rules and limitation or prescription periods.
Member States shall keep this information permanently updated.

Article 71. (1) By 18 September 2010, the Member States shall communicate to the Commission:
(a) the names and contact details of the courts or authorities with competence to deal with applications for a declaration of enforceability in accordance with Article 27(1) and with appeals against decisions on such applications in accordance with Article 32(2);
(b) the redress procedures referred to in Article 33;
(c) the review procedure for the purposes of Article 19 and the names and contact details of the courts having jurisdiction;
(d) the names and contact details of their Central Authorities and, where appropriate, the extent of their functions, in accordance with Article 49(3);
(e) the names and contact details of the public bodies or other bodies and, where appropriate, the extent of their functions, in accordance with Article 51(3);
(f) the names and contact details of the authorities with competence in matters of enforcement for the purposes of Article 21;
(g) the languages accepted for translations of the documents referred to in Articles 20, 28 and 40;
(h) the languages accepted by their Central Authorities for communication with other Central Authorities referred to in Article 59.
The Member States shall apprise the Commission of any subsequent changes to this information.
(2) The Commission shall publish the information communicated in accordance with paragraph (1) in the *Official Journal of the European Union*, with the exception of the addresses and other contact details of the courts and authorities referred to in points (a), (c) and (f).
(3) The Commission shall make all information communicated in accordance with paragraph (1) publicly available through any other appropriate means, in particular through the European Judicial Network in civil and commercial matters established by Decision 2001/470/EC.

Article 72. Any amendment to the forms provided for in this Regulation shall be adopted in accordance with the advisory procedure referred to in Article 73(3).

Article 73. (1) The Commission shall be assisted by the committee established by Article 70 of Regulation (EC) No 2201/2003.
(2) Where reference is made to this paragraph, Articles 4 and 7 of Decision 1999/468/EC shall apply. The period laid down in Article 4(3) of Decision 1999/468/EC shall be set at three months.
(3) Where reference is made to this paragraph, Articles 3 and 7 of Decision 1999/468/EC shall apply.

Article 74. By five years from the date of application determined in the third subparagraph of Article 76 at the latest, the Commission shall submit to the European Parliament, the Council and the European Economic and Social Committee a report on the application of this Regulation, including an evaluation of the practical experiences relating to the cooperation between Central Authorities, in particular regarding those Authorities' access to the information held by public authorities and administrations, and an evaluation of the functioning of the procedure for recognition, declaration of enforceability and enforcement applicable to decisions given in a Member State not bound by the 2007 Hague Protocol. If necessary the report shall be accompanied by proposals for adaptation.

Article 75. (1) This Regulation shall apply only to proceedings instituted, to court settlements approved or concluded, and to authentic instruments established after its date of application, subject to paragraphs 2 and 3.
(2) Sections 2 and 3 of Chapter IV shall apply:
(a) to decisions given in the Member States before the date of application of this Regulation for which recognition and the declaration of enforceability are requested after that date;
(b) to decisions given after the date of application of this Regulation following proceedings begun before that date, in so far as those decisions fall with the scope of Regulation (EC) No 44/2001 for the purposes of recognition and enforcement.
Regulation (EC) No 44/2001 shall continue to apply to procedures for recognition and enforcement under way on the date of application of this Regulation.
The first and second subparagraphs shall apply mutatis mutandis to court settlements approved or concluded and to authentic instruments established in the Member States.
(3) Chapter VII on cooperation between Central Authorities shall apply to requests and applications received by the Central Authority as from the date of application of this Regulation.

Article 76. This Regulation shall enter into force on the 20th day following its publication in the *Official Journal of the European Union*.
Articles 2(2), 47(3), 71, 72 and 73 shall apply from 18 September 2010.
Except for the provisions referred to in the second paragraph, this Regulation shall apply from 18 June 2011, subject to the 2007 Hague Protocol being applicable in the Community by that date. Failing that, this Regulation shall apply from the date of application of that Protocol in the Community.
This Regulation shall be binding in its entirety and directly applicable in the Member States in accordance with the Treaty establishing the European Community.

PART II   PRIVATE INTERNATIONAL LAW

Hague Protocol on the Law Applicable to Maintenance Obligations, of 23 November 2007.

The States signatory to this Protocol,
Desiring to establish common provisions concerning the law applicable to maintenance obligations,
Wishing to modernise the Hague Convention of 24 October 1956 on the law applicable to maintenance obligations towards children and the Hague Convention of 2 October 1973 on the Law Applicable to Maintenance Obligations,
Wishing to develop general rules on applicable law that may supplement the Hague Convention of 23 November 2007 on the International Recovery of Child Support and Other Forms of Family Maintenance,
Have resolved to conclude a Protocol for this purpose and have agreed upon the following provisions:

Article 1. (1) This Protocol shall determine the law applicable to maintenance obligations arising from a family relationship, parentage, marriage or affinity, including a maintenance obligation in respect of a child regardless of the marital status of the parents.
(2) Decisions rendered in application of this Protocol shall be without prejudice to the existence of any of the relationships referred to in paragraph (1).

Article 2. This Protocol applies even if the applicable law is that of a non-Contracting State.

Article 3. (1) Maintenance obligations shall be governed by the law of the State of the habitual residence of the creditor, save where this Protocol provides otherwise.
(2) In the case of a change in the habitual residence of the creditor, the law of the State of the new habitual residence shall apply as from the moment when the change occurs.

Article 4. (1) The following provisions shall apply in the case of maintenance obligations of -
(a) parents towards their children;
(b) persons, other than parents, towards persons who have not attained the age of 21 years, except for obligations arising out of the relationships referred to in Article 5; and
(c) children towards their parents.
(2) If the creditor is unable, by virtue of the law referred to in Article 3, to obtain maintenance from the debtor, the law of the forum shall apply.
(3) Notwithstanding Article 3, if the creditor has seised the competent authority of the State where the debtor has his habitual residence, the law of the forum shall apply. However, if the creditor is unable, by virtue of this law, to obtain maintenance from the debtor, the law of the State of the habitual residence of the creditor shall apply.
(4) If the creditor is unable, by virtue of the laws referred to in Article 3 and paragraphs 2 and 3 of this Article, to obtain maintenance from the debtor, the law of the State of their common nationality, if there is one, shall apply.

Article 5. In the case of a maintenance obligation between spouses, ex-spouses or parties to a marriage which has been annulled, Article 3 shall not apply if one of the parties objects and the law of another State, in particular the State of their last common habitual residence, has a closer connection with the marriage. In such a case the law of that other State shall apply.

Article 6. In the case of maintenance obligations other than those arising from a parent-child relationship towards a child and those referred to in Article 5, the debtor may contest a claim from the creditor on the ground that there is no such obligation under both the law of the State of the habitual residence of the debtor and the law of the State of the common nationality of the parties, if there is one.

Article 7. (1) Notwithstanding Articles 3 to 6, the maintenance creditor and debtor for the purpose only of a particular proceeding in a given State may expressly designate the law of that State as applicable to a maintenance obligation.
(2) A designation made before the institution of such proceedings shall be in an agreement, signed by both parties, in writing or recorded in any medium, the information contained in which is accessible so as to be usable for subsequent reference.

Article 8. (1) Notwithstanding Articles 3 to 6, the maintenance creditor and debtor may at any time designate one of the following laws as applicable to a maintenance obligation -
(a) the law of any State of which either party is a national at the time of the designation;
(b) the law of the State of the habitual residence of either party at the time of designation;

(c) the law designated by the parties as applicable, or the law in fact applied, to their property regime;
(d) the law designated by the parties as applicable, or the law in fact applied, to their divorce or legal separation.
(2) Such agreement shall be in writing or recorded in any medium, the information contained in which is accessible so as to be usable for subsequent reference, and shall be signed by both parties.
(3) Paragraph 1 shall not apply to maintenance obligations in respect of a person under the age of 18 years or of an adult who, by reason of an impairment or insufficiency of his or her personal faculties, is not in a position to protect his or her interest.
(4) Notwithstanding the law designated by the parties in accordance with paragraph (1), the question of whether the creditor can renounce his or her right to maintenance shall be determined by the law of the State of the habitual residence of the creditor at the time of the designation.
(5) Unless at the time of the designation the parties were fully informed and aware of the consequences of their designation, the law designated by the parties shall not apply where the application of that law would lead to manifestly unfair or unreasonable consequences for any of the parties.

Article 9. A State which has the concept of "domicile" as a connecting factor in family matters may inform the Permanent Bureau of the Hague Conference on Private International Law that, for the purpose of cases which come before its authorities, the word "nationality" in Articles 4 and 6 is replaced by "domicile" as defined in that State.

Article 10. The right of a public body to seek reimbursement of a benefit provided to the creditor in place of maintenance shall be governed by the law to which that body is subject.

Article 11. The law applicable to the maintenance obligation shall determine inter alia -
(a) whether, to what extent and from whom the creditor may claim maintenance;
(b) the extent to which the creditor may claim retroactive maintenance;
(c) the basis for calculation of the amount of maintenance, and indexation;
(d) who is entitled to institute maintenance proceedings, except for issues relating to procedural capacity and representation in the proceedings;
(e) prescription or limitation periods;
(f) the extent of the obligation of a maintenance debtor, where a public body seeks reimbursement of benefits provided for a creditor in place of maintenance.

Article 12. In the Protocol, the term "law" means the law in force in a State other than its choice of law rules.

Article 13. The application of the law determined under the Protocol may be refused only to the extent that its effects would be manifestly contrary to the public policy of the forum.

Article 14. Even if the applicable law provides otherwise, the needs of the creditor and the resources of the debtor as well as any compensation which the creditor was awarded in place of periodical maintenance payments shall be taken into account in determining the amount of maintenance.

Article 15. 1) A Contracting State in which different systems of law or sets of rules of law apply to maintenance obligations shall not be bound to apply the rules of the Protocol to conflicts solely between such different systems or sets of rules of law.
(2) This Article shall not apply to a Regional Economic Integration Organisation.

Article 16. (1) In relation to a State in which two or more systems of law or sets of rules of law with regard to any matter dealt with in this Protocol apply in different territorial units -
(a) any reference to the law of a State shall be construed as referring, where appropriate, to the law in force in the relevant territorial unit;
(b) any reference to competent authorities or public bodies of that State shall be construed as referring, where appropriate, to those authorised to act in the relevant territorial unit;
(c) any reference to habitual residence in that State shall be construed as referring, where appropriate, to habitual residence in the relevant territorial unit;
(d) any reference to the State of which two persons have a common nationality shall be construed as referring to the territorial unit designated by the law of that State or, in the absence of relevant rules, to the territorial unit with which the maintenance obligation is most closely connected;
(e) any reference to the State of which a person is a national shall be construed as referring to the territorial unit designated by the law of that State or, in the absence of relevant rules, to the territorial unit with which the person has the closest connection.
(2) For the purpose of identifying the applicable law under the Protocol in relation to a State which

PART II   PRIVATE INTERNATIONAL LAW

comprises two or more territorial units each of which has its own system of law or set of rules of law in respect of matters covered by this Protocol, the following rules apply -
(a) if there are rules in force in such a State identifying which territorial unit's law is applicable, the law of that unit applies;
(b) in the absence of such rules, the law of the relevant territorial unit as defined in paragraph 1 applies.
(3) This Article shall not apply to a Regional Economic Integration Organisation.

Article 17. For the purpose of identifying the applicable law under the Protocol in relation to a State which has two or more systems of law or sets of rules of law applicable to different categories of persons in respect of matters covered by this Protocol, any reference to the law of such State shall be construed as referring to the legal system determined by the rules in force in that State.

Article 18. As between the Contracting States, this Protocol replaces the Hague Convention of 2 October 1973 on the Law Applicable to Maintenance Obligations and the Hague Convention of 24 October 1956 on the law applicable to maintenance obligations towards children.

Article 19. (1) This Protocol does not affect any other international instrument to which Contracting States are or become Parties and which contains provisions on matters governed by the Protocol, unless a contrary declaration is made by the States Parties to such instrument.
(2) Paragraph 1 also applies to uniform laws based on special ties of a regional or other nature between the States concerned.

Article 20. In the interpretation of this Protocol, regard shall be had to its international character and to the need to promote uniformity in its application.

Article 21. (1) The Secretary General of the Hague Conference on Private International Law shall as necessary convene a Special Commission in order to review the practical operation of the Protocol.
(2) For the purpose of such review Contracting States shall co-operate with the Permanent Bureau of the Hague Conference on Private International Law in the gathering of case law concerning the application of the Protocol.

Article 22. This Protocol shall not apply to maintenance claimed in a Contracting State relating to a period prior to its entry into force in that State.

Article 23. (1) This Protocol is open for signature by all States.
(2) This Protocol is subject to ratification, acceptance or approval by the signatory States.
(3) This Protocol is open for accession by all States.
(4) Instruments of ratification, acceptance, approval or accession shall be deposited with the Ministry of Foreign Affairs of the Kingdom of the Netherlands, depositary of the Protocol.

Article 24. (1) A Regional Economic Integration Organisation which is constituted solely by sovereign States and has competence over some or all of the matters governed by the Protocol may equally sign, accept, approve or accede to the Protocol. The Regional Economic Integration Organisation shall in that case have the rights and obligations of a Contracting State, to the extent that the Organisation has competence over matters governed by the Protocol.
(2) The Regional Economic Integration Organisation shall, at the time of signature, acceptance, approval or accession, notify the depositary in writing of the matters governed by the Protocol in respect of which competence has been transferred to that Organisation by its Member States. The Organisation shall promptly notify the depositary in writing of any changes to its competence as specified in the most recent notice given under this paragraph.
(3) At the time of signature, acceptance, approval or accession, a Regional Economic Integration Organisation may declare, in accordance with Article 28, that it exercises competence over all the matters governed by the Protocol and that the Member States which have transferred competence to the Regional Economic Integration Organisation in respect of the matter in question shall be bound by the Protocol by virtue of the signature, acceptance, approval or accession of the Organisation.
(4) For the purposes of the entry into force of the Protocol, any instrument deposited by a Regional Economic Integration Organisation shall not be counted unless the Regional Economic Integration Organisation makes a declaration under paragraph (3).
(5) Any reference to a "Contracting State" or "State" in the Protocol applies equally to a Regional Economic Integration Organisation that is a Party to it, where appropriate. In the event that a declaration is made by a Regional Economic Integration Organisation under paragraph 3, any reference to a "Contracting State" or "State" in the Protocol applies equally to the relevant Member States of the Organisation, where appropriate.

Article 25. (1) The Protocol shall enter into force on the first day of the month following the expiration of three months after the deposit of the second instrument of ratification, acceptance, approval or accession referred to in Article 23.
(2) Thereafter the Protocol shall enter into force -
(a) for each State or each Regional Economic Integration Organisation referred to in Article 24 subsequently ratifying, accepting or approving the Protocol or acceding to it, on the first day of the month following the expiration of three months after the deposit of its instrument of ratification, acceptance, approval or accession;
(b) for a territorial unit to which the Protocol has been extended in accordance with Article 26, on the first day of the month following the expiration of three months after notification of the declaration referred to in that Article.

Article 26. (1) If a State has two or more territorial units in which different systems of law are applicable in relation to matters dealt with in this Protocol, it may at the time of signature, ratification, acceptance, approval or accession declare in accordance with Article 28 that the Protocol shall extend to all its territorial units or only to one or more of them and may modify this declaration by submitting another declaration at any time.
(2) Any such declaration shall be notified to the depositary and shall state expressly the territorial units to which the Protocol applies.
(3) If a State makes no declaration under this Article, the Protocol is to extend to all territorial units of that State.
(4) This Article shall not apply to a Regional Economic Integration Organisation.

Article 27. No reservations may be made to this Protocol.

Article 28. (1) Declarations referred to in Articles 24(3) and 26(1) may be made upon signature, ratification acceptance, approval or accession or at any time thereafter, and may be modified or withdrawn at any time.
(2) Declarations, modifications and withdrawals shall be notified to the depositary.
(3) A declaration made at the time of signature, ratification, acceptance, approval or accession shall take effect simultaneously with the entry into force of this Protocol for the State concerned.
(4) A declaration made at a subsequent time, and any modification or withdrawal of a declaration, shall take effect on the first day of the month following the expiration of three months after the date on which the notification is received by the depositary.

Article 29. (1) A Contracting State to this Protocol may denounce it by a notification in writing addressed to the depositary. The denunciation may be limited to certain territorial units of a State with a non-unified legal system to which the Protocol applies.
(2) The denunciation shall take effect on the first day of the month following the expiration of 12 months after the date on which the notification is received by the depositary. Where a longer period for the denunciation to take effect is specified in the notification, the denunciation shall take effect upon the expiration of such longer period after the date on which the notification is received by the depositary.

Article 30. The depositary shall notify the Members of the Hague Conference on Private International Law, and other States and Regional Economic Integration Organisations which have signed, ratified, accepted, approved or acceded in accordance with Articles 23 and 24 of the following -
(a) the signatures and ratifications, acceptances, approvals and accessions referred to in Articles 23 and 24;
(b) the date on which this Protocol enters into force in accordance with Article 25;
(c) the declarations referred to in Articles 24(3) and 26(1);
(d) the denunciations referred to in Article 29.

PART II   PRIVATE INTERNATIONAL LAW

Regulation (EU) No 650/2012 of the European Parliament and of the Council of 4 July 2012 on jurisdiction, applicable law, recognition and enforcement of decisions and acceptance and enforcement of authentic instruments in matters of succession and on the creation of a European Certificate of Succession (OJ L 201, 27.07.2012, pp. 107 – 134) [footnotes omitted]

THE EUROPEAN PARLIAMENT AND THE COUNCIL OF THE EUROPEAN UNION,
Having regard to the Treaty on the Functioning of the European Union, and in particular Article 81(2) thereof,
Having regard to the proposal from the European Commission,
Having regard to the opinion of the European Economic and Social Committee,
Acting in accordance with the ordinary legislative procedure,
Whereas:
(1) The Union has set itself the objective of maintaining and developing an area of freedom, security and justice in which the free movement of persons is ensured. For the gradual establishment of such an area, the Union is to adopt measures relating to judicial cooperation in civil matters having cross-border implications, particularly when necessary for the proper functioning of the internal market.
(2) In accordance with point (c) of Article 81(2) of the Treaty on the Functioning of the European Union, such measures may include measures aimed at ensuring the compatibility of the rules applicable in the Member States concerning conflict of laws and of jurisdiction.
(3) The European Council meeting in Tampere on 15 and 16 October 1999 endorsed the principle of mutual recognition of judgments and other decisions of judicial authorities as the cornerstone of judicial cooperation in civil matters and invited the Council and the Commission to adopt a programme of measures to implement that principle.
(4) A programme of measures for implementation of the principle of mutual recognition of decisions in civil and commercial matters, common to the Commission and to the Council, was adopted on 30 November 2000. That programme identifies measures relating to the harmonisation of conflict-of-laws rules as measures facilitating the mutual recognition of decisions, and provides for the drawing-up of an instrument relating to wills and succession.
(5) The European Council meeting in Brussels on 4 and 5 November 2004 adopted a new programme called "The Hague Programme: strengthening freedom, security and justice in the European Union". That programme underlines the need to adopt an instrument in matters of succession dealing, in particular, with the questions of conflict of laws, jurisdiction, mutual recognition and enforcement of decisions in the area of succession and a European Certificate of Succession.
(6) At its meeting in Brussels on 10 and 11 December 2009 the European Council adopted a new multiannual programme called "The Stockholm Programme – An open and secure Europe serving and protecting citizens". In that programme the European Council considered that mutual recognition should be extended to fields that are not yet covered but are essential to everyday life, for example succession and wills, while taking into consideration Member States' legal systems, including public policy (ordre public), and national traditions in this area.
(7) The proper functioning of the internal market should be facilitated by removing the obstacles to the free movement of persons who currently face difficulties in asserting their rights in the context of a succession having cross-border implications. In the European area of justice, citizens must be able to organise their succession in advance. The rights of heirs and legatees, of other persons close to the deceased and of creditors of the succession must be effectively guaranteed.
(8) In order to achieve those objectives, this Regulation should bring together provisions on jurisdiction, on applicable law, on recognition or, as the case may be, acceptance, enforceability and enforcement of decisions, authentic instruments and court settlements and on the creation of a European Certificate of Succession.
(9) The scope of this Regulation should include all civil-law aspects of succession to the estate of a deceased person, namely all forms of transfer of assets, rights and obligations by reason of death, whether by way of a voluntary transfer under a disposition of property upon death or a transfer through intestate succession.
(10) This Regulation should not apply to revenue matters or to administrative matters of a public-law nature. It should therefore be for national law to determine, for instance, how taxes and other liabilities of a public-law nature are calculated and paid, whether these be taxes payable by the deceased at the time of death or any type of succession-related tax to be paid by the estate or the beneficiaries. It should also be for national law to determine whether the release of succession property to beneficiaries under this Regulation or the recording of succession property in a register may be made subject to the payment of taxes.
(11) This Regulation should not apply to areas of civil law other than succession. For reasons of clar-

ity, a number of questions which could be seen as having a link with matters of succession should be explicitly excluded from the scope of this Regulation.

(12) Accordingly, this Regulation should not apply to questions relating to matrimonial property regimes, including marriage settlements as known in some legal systems to the extent that such settlements do not deal with succession matters, and property regimes of relationships deemed to have comparable effects to marriage. The authorities dealing with a given succession under this Regulation should nevertheless, depending on the situation, take into account the winding-up of the matrimonial property regime or similar property regime of the deceased when determining the estate of the deceased and the respective shares of the beneficiaries.

(13) Questions relating to the creation, administration and dissolution of trusts should also be excluded from the scope of this Regulation. This should not be understood as a general exclusion of trusts. Where a trust is created under a will or under statute in connection with intestate succession the law applicable to the succession under this Regulation should apply with respect to the devolution of the assets and the determination of the beneficiaries.

(14) Property rights, interests and assets created or transferred otherwise than by succession, for instance by way of gifts, should also be excluded from the scope of this Regulation. However, it should be the law specified by this Regulation as the law applicable to the succession which determines whether gifts or other forms of dispositions inter vivos giving rise to a right in rem prior to death should be restored or accounted for for the purposes of determining the shares of the beneficiaries in accordance with the law applicable to the succession.

(15) This Regulation should allow for the creation or the transfer by succession of a right in immovable or movable property as provided for in the law applicable to the succession. It should, however, not affect the limited number ("numerus clausus") of rights in rem known in the national law of some Member States. A Member State should not be required to recognise a right in rem relating to property located in that Member State if the right in rem in question is not known in its law.

(16) However, in order to allow the beneficiaries to enjoy in another Member State the rights which have been created or transferred to them by succession, this Regulation should provide for the adaptation of an unknown right in rem to the closest equivalent right in rem under the law of that other Member State. In the context of such an adaptation, account should be taken of the aims and the interests pursued by the specific right in rem and the effects attached to it. For the purposes of determining the closest equivalent national right in rem, the authorities or competent persons of the State whose law applied to the succession may be contacted for further information on the nature and the effects of the right. To that end, the existing networks in the area of judicial cooperation in civil and commercial matters could be used, as well as any other available means facilitating the understanding of foreign law.

(17) The adaptation of unknown rights in rem as explicitly provided for by this Regulation should not preclude other forms of adaptation in the context of the application of this Regulation.

(18) The requirements for the recording in a register of a right in immovable or movable property should be excluded from the scope of this Regulation. It should therefore be the law of the Member State in which the register is kept (for immovable property, the lex rei sitae) which determines under what legal conditions and how the recording must be carried out and which authorities, such as land registers or notaries, are in charge of checking that all requirements are met and that the documentation presented or established is sufficient or contains the necessary information. In particular, the authorities may check that the right of the deceased to the succession property mentioned in the document presented for registration is a right which is recorded as such in the register or which is otherwise demonstrated in accordance with the law of the Member State in which the register is kept. In order to avoid duplication of documents, the registration authorities should accept such documents drawn up in another Member State by the competent authorities whose circulation is provided for by this Regulation. In particular, the European Certificate of Succession issued under this Regulation should constitute a valid document for the recording of succession property in a register of a Member State. This should not preclude the authorities involved in the registration from asking the person applying for registration to provide such additional information, or to present such additional documents, as are required under the law of the Member State in which the register is kept, for instance information or documents relating to the payment of revenue. The competent authority may indicate to the person applying for registration how the missing information or documents can be provided.

(19) The effects of the recording of a right in a register should also be excluded from the scope of this Regulation. It should therefore be the law of the Member State in which the register is kept which determines whether the recording is, for instance, declaratory or constitutive in effect. Thus, where, for example, the acquisition of a right in immovable property requires a recording in a register under the law of the Member State in which the register is kept in order to ensure the erga omnes effect of

registers or to protect legal transactions, the moment of such acquisition should be governed by the law of that Member State.

(20) This Regulation should respect the different systems for dealing with matters of succession applied in the Member States. For the purposes of this Regulation, the term "court" should therefore be given a broad meaning so as to cover not only courts in the true sense of the word, exercising judicial functions, but also the notaries or registry offices in some Member States who or which, in certain matters of succession, exercise judicial functions like courts, and the notaries and legal professionals who, in some Member States, exercise judicial functions in a given succession by delegation of power by a court. All courts as defined in this Regulation should be bound by the rules of jurisdiction set out in this Regulation. Conversely, the term "court" should not cover non-judicial authorities of a Member State empowered under national law to deal with matters of succession, such as the notaries in most Member States where, as is usually the case, they are not exercising judicial functions.

(21) This Regulation should allow all notaries who have competence in matters of succession in the Member States to exercise such competence. Whether or not the notaries in a given Member State are bound by the rules of jurisdiction set out in this Regulation should depend on whether or not they are covered by the term "court" for the purposes of this Regulation.

(22) Acts issued by notaries in matters of succession in the Member States should circulate under this Regulation. When notaries exercise judicial functions they are bound by the rules of jurisdiction, and the decisions they give should circulate in accordance with the provisions on recognition, enforceability and enforcement of decisions. When notaries do not exercise judicial functions they are not bound by the rules of jurisdiction, and the authentic instruments they issue should circulate in accordance with the provisions on authentic instruments.

(23) In view of the increasing mobility of citizens and in order to ensure the proper administration of justice within the Union and to ensure that a genuine connecting factor exists between the succession and the Member State in which jurisdiction is exercised, this Regulation should provide that the general connecting factor for the purposes of determining both jurisdiction and the applicable law should be the habitual residence of the deceased at the time of death. In order to determine the habitual residence, the authority dealing with the succession should make an overall assessment of the circumstances of the life of the deceased during the years preceding his death and at the time of his death, taking account of all relevant factual elements, in particular the duration and regularity of the deceased's presence in the State concerned and the conditions and reasons for that presence. The habitual residence thus determined should reveal a close and stable connection with the State concerned taking into account the specific aims of this Regulation.

(24) In certain cases, determining the deceased's habitual residence may prove complex. Such a case may arise, in particular, where the deceased for professional or economic reasons had gone to live abroad to work there, sometimes for a long time, but had maintained a close and stable connection with his State of origin. In such a case, the deceased could, depending on the circumstances of the case, be considered still to have his habitual residence in his State of origin in which the centre of interests of his family and his social life was located. Other complex cases may arise where the deceased lived in several States alternately or travelled from one State to another without settling permanently in any of them. If the deceased was a national of one of those States or had all his main assets in one of those States, his nationality or the location of those assets could be a special factor in the overall assessment of all the factual circumstances.

(25) With regard to the determination of the law applicable to the succession the authority dealing with the succession may in exceptional cases – where, for instance, the deceased had moved to the State of his habitual residence fairly recently before his death and all the circumstances of the case indicate that he was manifestly more closely connected with another State – arrive at the conclusion that the law applicable to the succession should not be the law of the State of the habitual residence of the deceased but rather the law of the State with which the deceased was manifestly more closely connected. That manifestly closest connection should, however, not be resorted to as a subsidiary connecting factor whenever the determination of the habitual residence of the deceased at the time of death proves complex.

(26) Nothing in this Regulation should prevent a court from applying mechanisms designed to tackle the evasion of the law, such as fraude à la loi in the context of private international law.

(27) The rules of this Regulation are devised so as to ensure that the authority dealing with the succession will, in most situations, be applying its own law. This Regulation therefore provides for a series of mechanisms which would come into play where the deceased had chosen as the law to govern his succession the law of a Member State of which he was a national.

(28) One such mechanism should be to allow the parties concerned to conclude a choice-of-court

agreement in favour of the courts of the Member State of the chosen law. It would have to be determined on a case-by-case basis, depending in particular on the issue covered by the choice-of-court agreement, whether the agreement would have to be concluded between all parties concerned by the succession or whether some of them could agree to bring a specific issue before the chosen court in a situation where the decision by that court on that issue would not affect the rights of the other parties to the succession.

(29) If succession proceedings are opened by a court of its own motion, as is the case in certain Member States, that court should close the proceedings if the parties agree to settle the succession amicably out of court in the Member State of the chosen law. Where succession proceedings are not opened by a court of its own motion, this Regulation should not prevent the parties from settling the succession amicably out of court, for instance before a notary, in a Member State of their choice where this is possible under the law of that Member State. This should be the case even if the law applicable to the succession is not the law of that Member State.

(30) In order to ensure that the courts of all Member States may, on the same grounds, exercise jurisdiction in relation to the succession of persons not habitually resident in a Member State at the time of death, this Regulation should list exhaustively, in a hierarchical order, the grounds on which such subsidiary jurisdiction may be exercised.

(31) In order to remedy, in particular, situations of denial of justice, this Regulation should provide a forum necessitatis allowing a court of a Member State, on an exceptional basis, to rule on a succession which is closely connected with a third State. Such an exceptional basis may be deemed to exist when proceedings prove impossible in the third State in question, for example because of civil war, or when a beneficiary cannot reasonably be expected to initiate or conduct proceedings in that State. Jurisdiction based on forum necessitatis should, however, be exercised only if the case has a sufficient connection with the Member State of the court seised.

(32) In order to simplify the lives of heirs and legatees habitually resident in a Member State other than that in which the succession is being or will be dealt with, this Regulation should allow any person entitled under the law applicable to the succession to make declarations concerning the acceptance or waiver of the succession, of a legacy or of a reserved share, or concerning the limitation of his liability for the debts under the succession, to make such declarations in the form provided for by the law of the Member State of his habitual residence before the courts of that Member State. This should not preclude such declarations being made before other authorities in that Member State which are competent to receive declarations under national law. Persons choosing to avail themselves of the possibility to make declarations in the Member State of their habitual residence should themselves inform the court or authority which is or will be dealing with the succession of the existence of such declarations within any time limit set by the law applicable to the succession.

(33) It should not be possible for a person who wishes to limit his liability for the debts under the succession to do so by a mere declaration to that effect before the courts or other competent authorities of the Member State of his habitual residence where the law applicable to the succession requires him to initiate specific legal proceedings, for instance inventory proceedings, before the competent court. A declaration made in such circumstances by a person in the Member State of his habitual residence in the form provided for by the law of that Member State should therefore not be formally valid for the purposes of this Regulation. Nor should the documents instituting the legal proceedings be regarded as declarations for the purposes of this Regulation.

(34) In the interests of the harmonious functioning of justice, the giving of irreconcilable decisions in different Member States should be avoided. To that end, this Regulation should provide for general procedural rules similar to those of other Union instruments in the area of judicial cooperation in civil matters.

(35) One such procedural rule is a lis pendens rule which will come into play if the same succession case is brought before different courts in different Member States. That rule will then determine which court should proceed to deal with the succession case.

(36) Given that succession matters in some Member States may be dealt with by non-judicial authorities, such as notaries, who are not bound by the rules of jurisdiction under this Regulation, it cannot be excluded that an amicable out-of-court settlement and court proceedings relating to the same succession, or two amicable out-of-court settlements relating to the same succession, may be initiated in parallel in different Member States. In such a situation, it should be for the parties involved, once they become aware of the parallel proceedings, to agree among themselves how to proceed. If they cannot agree, the succession would have to be dealt with and decided upon by the courts having jurisdiction under this Regulation.

(37) In order to allow citizens to avail themselves, with all legal certainty, of the benefits offered by the internal market, this Regulation should enable them to know in advance which law will apply to

their succession. Harmonised conflict-of-laws rules should be introduced in order to avoid contradictory results. The main rule should ensure that the succession is governed by a predictable law with which it is closely connected. For reasons of legal certainty and in order to avoid the fragmentation of the succession, that law should govern the succession as a whole, that is to say, all of the property forming part of the estate, irrespective of the nature of the assets and regardless of whether the assets are located in another Member State or in a third State.

(38) This Regulation should enable citizens to organise their succession in advance by choosing the law applicable to their succession. That choice should be limited to the law of a State of their nationality in order to ensure a connection between the deceased and the law chosen and to avoid a law being chosen with the intention of frustrating the legitimate expectations of persons entitled to a reserved share.

(39) A choice of law should be made expressly in a declaration in the form of a disposition of property upon death or be demonstrated by the terms of such a disposition. A choice of law could be regarded as demonstrated by a disposition of property upon death where, for instance, the deceased had referred in his disposition to specific provisions of the law of the State of his nationality or where he had otherwise mentioned that law.

(40) A choice of law under this Regulation should be valid even if the chosen law does not provide for a choice of law in matters of succession. It should however be for the chosen law to determine the substantive validity of the act of making the choice, that is to say, whether the person making the choice may be considered to have understood and consented to what he was doing. The same should apply to the act of modifying or revoking a choice of law.

(41) For the purposes of the application of this Regulation, the determination of the nationality or the multiple nationalities of a person should be resolved as a preliminary question. The issue of considering a person as a national of a State falls outside the scope of this Regulation and is subject to national law, including, where applicable, international Conventions, in full observance of the general principles of the European Union.

(42) The law determined as the law applicable to the succession should govern the succession from the opening of the succession to the transfer of ownership of the assets forming part of the estate to the beneficiaries as determined by that law. It should include questions relating to the administration of the estate and to liability for the debts under the succession. The payment of the debts under the succession may, depending, in particular, on the law applicable to the succession, include the taking into account of a specific ranking of the creditors.

(43) The rules of jurisdiction laid down by this Regulation may, in certain cases, lead to a situation where the court having jurisdiction to rule on the succession will not be applying its own law. When that situation occurs in a Member State whose law provides for the mandatory appointment of an administrator of the estate, this Regulation should allow the courts of that Member State, when seised, to appoint one or more such administrators under their own law. This should be without prejudice to any choice made by the parties to settle the succession amicably out of court in another Member State where this is possible under the law of that Member State. In order to ensure a smooth coordination between the law applicable to the succession and the law of the Member State of the appointing court, the court should appoint the person(s) who would be entitled to administer the estate under the law applicable to the succession, such as for instance the executor of the will of the deceased or the heirs themselves or, if the law applicable to the succession so requires, a third-party administrator. The courts may, however, in specific cases where their law so requires, appoint a third party as administrator even if this is not provided for in the law applicable to the succession. If the deceased had appointed an executor of the will, that person may not be deprived of his powers unless the law applicable to the succession allows for the termination of his mandate.

(44) The powers exercised by the administrators appointed in the Member State of the court seised should be the powers of administration which they may exercise under the law applicable to the succession. Thus, if, for instance, the heir is appointed as administrator he should have the powers to administer the estate which an heir would have under that law. Where the powers of administration which may be exercised under the law applicable to the succession are not sufficient to preserve the assets of the estate or to protect the rights of the creditors or of other persons having guaranteed the debts of the deceased, the administrator(s) appointed in the Member State of the court seised may, on a residual basis, exercise powers of administration to that end provided for by the law of that Member State. Such residual powers could include, for instance, establishing a list of the assets of the estate and the debts under the succession, informing creditors of the opening of the succession and inviting them to make their claims known, and taking any provisional, including protective, measures intended to preserve the assets of the estate. The acts performed by an administrator in exercise of the residual powers should respect the law applicable to the succession as regards the transfer of

ownership of succession property, including any transaction entered into by the beneficiaries prior to the appointment of the administrator, liability for the debts under the succession and the rights of the beneficiaries, including, where applicable, the right to accept or to waive the succession. Such acts could, for instance, only entail the alienation of assets or the payment of debts where this would be allowed under the law applicable to the succession. Where under the law applicable to the succession the appointment of a third-party administrator changes the liability of the heirs, such a change of liability should be respected.

(45) This Regulation should not preclude creditors, for instance through a representative, from taking such further steps as may be available under national law, where applicable, in accordance with the relevant Union instruments, in order to safeguard their rights.

(46) This Regulation should allow for potential creditors in other Member States where assets are located to be informed of the opening of the succession. In the context of the application of this Regulation, consideration should therefore be given to the possibility of establishing a mechanism, if appropriate by way of the e-Justice portal, to enable potential creditors in other Member States to access the relevant information so that they can make their claims known.

(47) The law applicable to the succession should determine who the beneficiaries are in any given succession. Under most laws, the term "beneficiaries" would cover heirs and legatees and persons entitled to a reserved share although, for instance, the legal position of legatees is not the same under all laws. Under some laws, the legatee may receive a direct share in the estate whereas under other laws the legatee may acquire only a claim against the heirs.

(48) In order to ensure legal certainty for persons wishing to plan their succession in advance, this Regulation should lay down a specific conflict-of-laws rule concerning the admissibility and substantive validity of dispositions of property upon death. To ensure the uniform application of that rule, this Regulation should list which elements should be considered as elements pertaining to substantive validity. The examination of the substantive validity of a disposition of property upon death may lead to the conclusion that that disposition is without legal existence.

(49) An agreement as to succession is a type of disposition of property upon death the admissibility and acceptance of which vary among the Member States. In order to make it easier for succession rights acquired as a result of an agreement as to succession to be accepted in the Member States, this Regulation should determine which law is to govern the admissibility of such agreements, their substantive validity and their binding effects between the parties, including the conditions for their dissolution.

(50) The law which, under this Regulation, will govern the admissibility and substantive validity of a disposition of property upon death and, as regards agreements as to succession, the binding effects of such an agreement as between the parties, should be without prejudice to the rights of any person who, under the law applicable to the succession, has a right to a reserved share or another right of which he cannot be deprived by the person whose estate is involved.

(51) Where reference is made in this Regulation to the law which would have been applicable to the succession of the person making a disposition of property upon death if he had died on the day on which the disposition was, as the case may be, made, modified or revoked, such reference should be understood as a reference to either the law of the State of the habitual residence of the person concerned on that day or, if he had made a choice of law under this Regulation, the law of the State of his nationality on that day.

(52) This Regulation should regulate the validity as to form of all dispositions of property upon death made in writing by way of rules which are consistent with those of the Hague Convention of 5 October 1961 on the Conflicts of Laws Relating to the Form of Testamentary Dispositions. When determining whether a given disposition of property upon death is formally valid under this Regulation, the competent authority should disregard the fraudulent creation of an international element to circumvent the rules on formal validity.

(53) For the purposes of this Regulation, any provision of law limiting the permitted forms of dispositions of property upon death by reference to certain personal qualifications of the person making the disposition, such as, for instance, his age, should be deemed to pertain to matters of form. This should not be interpreted as meaning that the law applicable to the formal validity of a disposition of property upon death under this Regulation should determine whether or not a minor has the capacity to make a disposition of property upon death. That law should only determine whether a personal qualification such as, for instance, minority should bar a person from making a disposition of property upon death in a certain form.

(54) For economic, family or social considerations, certain immovable property, certain enterprises and other special categories of assets are subject to special rules in the Member State in which they are located imposing restrictions concerning or affecting the succession in respect of those assets.

PART II PRIVATE INTERNATIONAL LAW

This Regulation should ensure the application of such special rules. However, this exception to the application of the law applicable to the succession requires a strict interpretation in order to remain compatible with the general objective of this Regulation. Therefore, neither conflict-of-laws rules subjecting immovable property to a law different from that applicable to movable property nor provisions providing for a reserved share of the estate greater than that provided for in the law applicable to the succession under this Regulation may be regarded as constituting special rules imposing restrictions concerning or affecting the succession in respect of certain assets.

(55) To ensure uniform handling of a situation in which it is uncertain in what order two or more persons whose succession would be governed by different laws died, this Regulation should lay down a rule providing that none of the deceased persons is to have any rights in the succession of the other or others.

(56) In some situations an estate may be left without a claimant. Different laws provide differently for such situations. Under some laws, the State will be able to claim the vacant estate as an heir irrespective of where the assets are located. Under some other laws, the State will be able to appropriate only the assets located on its territory. This Regulation should therefore lay down a rule providing that the application of the law applicable to the succession should not preclude a Member State from appropriating under its own law the assets located on its territory. However, to ensure that this rule is not detrimental to the creditors of the estate, a proviso should be added enabling the creditors to seek satisfaction of their claims out of all the assets of the estate, irrespective of their location.

(57) The conflict-of-laws rules laid down in this Regulation may lead to the application of the law of a third State. In such cases regard should be had to the private international law rules of that State. If those rules provide for renvoi either to the law of a Member State or to the law of a third State which would apply its own law to the succession, such renvoi should be accepted in order to ensure international consistency. Renvoi should, however, be excluded in situations where the deceased had made a choice of law in favour of the law of a third State.

(58) Considerations of public interest should allow courts and other competent authorities dealing with matters of succession in the Member States to disregard, in exceptional circumstances certain provisions of a foreign law where, in a given case, applying such provisions would be manifestly incompatible with the public policy (ordre public) of the Member State concerned. However, the courts or other competent authorities should not be able to apply the public-policy exception in order to set aside the law of another State or to refuse to recognise or, as the case may be, accept or enforce a decision, an authentic instrument or a court settlement from another Member State when doing so would be contrary to the Charter of Fundamental Rights of the European Union, and in particular Article 21 thereof, which prohibits all forms of discrimination.

(59) In the light of its general objective, which is the mutual recognition of decisions given in the Member States in matters of succession, irrespective of whether such decisions were given in contentious or non-contentious proceedings, this Regulation should lay down rules relating to the recognition, enforceability and enforcement of decisions similar to those of other Union instruments in the area of judicial cooperation in civil matters.

(60) In order to take into account the different systems for dealing with matters of succession in the Member States, this Regulation should guarantee the acceptance and enforceability in all Member States of authentic instruments in matters of succession.

(61) Authentic instruments should have the same evidentiary effects in another Member State as they have in the Member State of origin, or the most comparable effects. When determining the evidentiary effects of a given authentic instrument in another Member State or the most comparable effects, reference should be made to the nature and the scope of the evidentiary effects of the authentic instrument in the Member State of origin. The evidentiary effects which a given authentic instrument should have in another Member State will therefore depend on the law of the Member State of origin.

(62) The "authenticity" of an authentic instrument should be an autonomous concept covering elements such as the genuineness of the instrument, the formal prerequisites of the instrument, the powers of the authority drawing up the instrument and the procedure under which the instrument is drawn up. It should also cover the factual elements recorded in the authentic instrument by the authority concerned, such as the fact that the parties indicated appeared before that authority on the date indicated and that they made the declarations indicated. A party wishing to challenge the authenticity of an authentic instrument should do so before the competent court in the Member State of origin of the authentic instrument under the law of that Member State.

(63) The term "the legal acts or legal relationships recorded in an authentic instrument" should be interpreted as referring to the contents as to substance recorded in the authentic instrument. The legal acts recorded in an authentic instrument could be, for instance, the agreement between the parties on the sharing-out or the distribution of the estate, or a will or an agreement as to succession,

or another declaration of intent. The legal relationships could be, for instance, the determination of the heirs and other beneficiaries as established under the law applicable to the succession, their respective shares and the existence of a reserved share, or any other element established under the law applicable to the succession. A party wishing to challenge the legal acts or legal relationships recorded in an authentic instrument should do so before the courts having jurisdiction under this Regulation, which should decide on the challenge in accordance with the law applicable to the succession.

(64) If a question relating to the legal acts or legal relationships recorded in an authentic instrument is raised as an incidental question in proceedings before a court of a Member State, that court should have jurisdiction over that question.

(65) An authentic instrument which is being challenged should not produce any evidentiary effects in a Member State other than the Member State of origin as long as the challenge is pending. If the challenge concerns only a specific matter relating to the legal acts or legal relationships recorded in the authentic instrument, the authentic instrument in question should not produce any evidentiary effects in a Member State other than the Member State of origin with regard to the matter being challenged as long as the challenge is pending. An authentic instrument which has been declared invalid as a result of a challenge should cease to produce any evidentiary effects.

(66) Should an authority, in the application of this Regulation, be presented with two incompatible authentic instruments, it should assess the question as to which authentic instrument, if any, should be given priority, taking into account the circumstances of the particular case. Where it is not clear from those circumstances which authentic instrument, if any, should be given priority, the question should be determined by the courts having jurisdiction under this Regulation, or, where the question is raised as an incidental question in the course of proceedings, by the court seised of those proceedings. In the event of incompatibility between an authentic instrument and a decision, regard should be had to the grounds of non-recognition of decisions under this Regulation.

(67) In order for a succession with cross-border implications within the Union to be settled speedily, smoothly and efficiently, the heirs, legatees, executors of the will or administrators of the estate should be able to demonstrate easily their status and/or rights and powers in another Member State, for instance in a Member State in which succession property is located. To enable them to do so, this Regulation should provide for the creation of a uniform certificate, the European Certificate of Succession (hereinafter referred to as "the Certificate"), to be issued for use in another Member State. In order to respect the principle of subsidiarity, the Certificate should not take the place of internal documents which may exist for similar purposes in the Member States.

(68) The authority which issues the Certificate should have regard to the formalities required for the registration of immovable property in the Member State in which the register is kept. For that purpose, this Regulation should provide for an exchange of information on such formalities between the Member States.

(69) The use of the Certificate should not be mandatory. This means that persons entitled to apply for a Certificate should be under no obligation to do so but should be free to use the other instruments available under this Regulation (decisions, authentic instruments and court settlements). However, no authority or person presented with a Certificate issued in another Member State should be entitled to request that a decision, authentic instrument or court settlement be presented instead of the Certificate.

(70) The Certificate should be issued in the Member State whose courts have jurisdiction under this Regulation. It should be for each Member State to determine in its internal legislation which authorities are to have competence to issue the Certificate, whether they be courts as defined for the purposes of this Regulation or other authorities with competence in matters of succession, such as, for instance, notaries. It should also be for each Member State to determine in its internal legislation whether the issuing authority may involve other competent bodies in the issuing process, for instance bodies competent to receive statutory declarations in lieu of an oath. The Member States should communicate to the Commission the relevant information concerning their issuing authorities in order for that information to be made publicly available.

(71) The Certificate should produce the same effects in all Member States. It should not be an enforceable title in its own right but should have an evidentiary effect and should be presumed to demonstrate accurately elements which have been established under the law applicable to the succession or under any other law applicable to specific elements, such as the substantive validity of dispositions of property upon death. The evidentiary effect of the Certificate should not extend to elements which are not governed by this Regulation, such as questions of affiliation or the question whether or not a particular asset belonged to the deceased. Any person who makes payments or passes on succession property to a person indicated in the Certificate as being entitled to accept such payment

or property as an heir or legatee should be afforded appropriate protection if he acted in good faith relying on the accuracy of the information certified in the Certificate. The same protection should be afforded to any person who, relying on the accuracy of the information certified in the Certificate, buys or receives succession property from a person indicated in the Certificate as being entitled to dispose of such property. The protection should be ensured if certified copies which are still valid are presented. Whether or not such an acquisition of property by a third person is effective should not be determined by this Regulation.

(72) The competent authority should issue the Certificate upon request. The original of the Certificate should remain with the issuing authority, which should issue one or more certified copies of the Certificate to the applicant and to any other person demonstrating a legitimate interest. This should not preclude a Member State, in accordance with its national rules on public access to documents, from allowing copies of the Certificate to be disclosed to members of the public. This Regulation should provide for redress against decisions of the issuing authority, including decisions to refuse the issue of a Certificate. Where the Certificate is rectified, modified or withdrawn, the issuing authority should inform the persons to whom certified copies have been issued so as to avoid wrongful use of such copies.

(73) Respect for international commitments entered into by the Member States means that this Regulation should not affect the application of international conventions to which one or more Member States are party at the time when this Regulation is adopted. In particular, the Member States which are Contracting Parties to the Hague Convention of 5 October 1961 on the Conflicts of Laws Relating to the Form of Testamentary Dispositions should be able to continue to apply the provisions of that Convention instead of the provisions of this Regulation with regard to the formal validity of wills and joint wills. Consistency with the general objectives of this Regulation requires, however, that this Regulation take precedence, as between Member States, over conventions concluded exclusively between two or more Member States in so far as such conventions concern matters governed by this Regulation.

(74) This Regulation should not preclude Member States which are parties to the Convention of 19 November 1934 between Denmark, Finland, Iceland, Norway and Sweden comprising private international law provisions on succession, wills and estate administration from continuing to apply certain provisions of that Convention, as revised by the intergovernmental agreement between the States parties thereto.

(75) In order to facilitate the application of this Regulation, provision should be made for an obligation requiring the Member States to communicate certain information regarding their legislation and procedures relating to succession within the framework of the European Judicial Network in civil and commercial matters established by Council Decision 2001/470/EC. In order to allow for the timely publication in the Official Journal of the European Union of all information of relevance for the practical application of this Regulation, the Member States should also communicate such information to the Commission before this Regulation starts to apply.

(76) Equally, to facilitate the application of this Regulation and to allow for the use of modern communication technologies, standard forms should be prescribed for the attestations to be provided in connection with the application for a declaration of enforceability of a decision, authentic instrument or court settlement and for the application for a European Certificate of Succession, as well as for the Certificate itself.

(77) In calculating the periods and time limits provided for in this Regulation, Regulation (EEC, Euratom) No 1182/71 of the Council of 3 June 1971 determining the rules applicable to periods, dates and time limits should apply.

(78) In order to ensure uniform conditions for the implementation of this Regulation, implementing powers should be conferred on the Commission with regard to the establishment and subsequent amendment of the attestations and forms pertaining to the declaration of enforceability of decisions, court settlements and authentic instruments and to the European Certificate of Succession. Those powers should be exercised in accordance with Regulation (EU) No 182/2011 of the European Parliament and of the Council of 16 February 2011 laying down the rules and general principles concerning mechanisms for control by Member States of the Commission's exercise of implementing powers.

(79) The advisory procedure should be used for the adoption of implementing acts establishing and subsequently amending the attestations and forms provided for in this Regulation in accordance with the procedure laid down in Article 4 of Regulation (EU) No 182/2011.

(80) Since the objectives of this Regulation, namely the free movement of persons, the organisation in advance by citizens of their succession in a Union context and the protection of the rights of heirs and legatees and of persons close to the deceased, as well as of the creditors of the succes-

sion, cannot be sufficiently achieved by the Member States and can therefore, by reason of the scale and effects of this Regulation, be better achieved at Union level, the Union may adopt measures in accordance with the principle of subsidiarity as set out in Article 5 of the Treaty on European Union. In accordance with the principle of proportionality, as set out in that Article, this Regulation does not go beyond what is necessary in order to achieve those objectives.

(81) This Regulation respects the fundamental rights and observes the principles recognised in the Charter of Fundamental Rights of the European Union. This Regulation must be applied by the courts and other competent authorities of the Member States in observance of those rights and principles.

(82) In accordance with Articles 1 and 2 of Protocol No 21 on the position of the United Kingdom and Ireland in respect of the area of freedom, security and justice, annexed to the Treaty on European Union and to the Treaty on the Functioning of the European Union, those Member States are not taking part in the adoption of this Regulation and are not bound by it or subject to its application. This is, however, without prejudice to the possibility for the United Kingdom and Ireland of notifying their intention of accepting this Regulation after its adoption in accordance with Article 4 of the said Protocol.

(83) In accordance with Articles 1 and 2 of Protocol No 22 on the position of Denmark, annexed to the Treaty on European Union and to the Treaty on the Functioning of the European Union, Denmark is not taking part in the adoption of this Regulation and is not bound by it or subject to its application,

HAVE ADOPTED THIS REGULATION:

Chapter I. Scope and Definitions

Article 1. (1) This Regulation shall apply to succession to the estates of deceased persons. It shall not apply to revenue, customs or administrative matters.

(2) The following shall be excluded from the scope of this Regulation:

(a) the status of natural persons, as well as family relationships and relationships deemed by the law applicable to such relationships to have comparable effects;

(b) the legal capacity of natural persons, without prejudice to point (c) of Article 23(2) and to Article 26;

(c) questions relating to the disappearance, absence or presumed death of a natural person;

(d) questions relating to matrimonial property regimes and property regimes of relationships deemed by the law applicable to such relationships to have comparable effects to marriage;

(e) maintenance obligations other than those arising by reason of death;

(f) the formal validity of dispositions of property upon death made orally;

(g) property rights, interests and assets created or transferred otherwise than by succession, for instance by way of gifts, joint ownership with a right of survivorship, pension plans, insurance contracts and arrangements of a similar nature, without prejudice to point (i) of Article 23(2);

(h) questions governed by the law of companies and other bodies, corporate or unincorporated, such as clauses in the memoranda of association and articles of association of companies and other bodies, corporate or unincorporated, which determine what will happen to the shares upon the death of the members;

(i) the dissolution, extinction and merger of companies and other bodies, corporate or unincorporated;

(j) the creation, administration and dissolution of trusts;

(k) the nature of rights in rem; and

(l) any recording in a register of rights in immovable or movable property, including the legal requirements for such recording, and the effects of recording or failing to record such rights in a register.

Article 2. This Regulation shall not affect the competence of the authorities of the Member States to deal with matters of succession.

Article 3. (1) For the purposes of this Regulation:

(a) "succession" means succession to the estate of a deceased person and covers all forms of transfer of assets, rights and obligations by reason of death, whether by way of a voluntary transfer under a disposition of property upon death or a transfer through intestate succession;

(b) "agreement as to succession" means an agreement, including an agreement resulting from mutual wills, which, with or without consideration, creates, modifies or terminates rights to the future estate or estates of one or more persons party to the agreement;

(c) "joint will" means a will drawn up in one instrument by two or more persons;

(d) "disposition of property upon death" means a will, a joint will or an agreement as to succession;

(e) "Member State of origin" means the Member State in which the decision has been given, the court settlement approved or concluded, the authentic instrument established or the European Certificate of Succession issued;

(f) "Member State of enforcement" means the Member State in which the declaration of enforceability or the enforcement of the decision, court settlement or authentic instrument is sought;

(g) "decision" means any decision in a matter of succession given by a court of a Member State, whatever the decision may be called, including a decision on the determination of costs or expenses by an officer of the court;

(h) "court settlement" means a settlement in a matter of succession which has been approved by a court or concluded before a court in the course of proceedings;

(i) "authentic instrument" means a document in a matter of succession which has been formally drawn up or registered as an authentic instrument in a Member State and the authenticity of which:

(i) relates to the signature and the content of the authentic instrument; and

(ii) has been established by a public authority or other authority empowered for that purpose by the Member State of origin.

(2) For the purposes of this Regulation, the term "court" means any judicial authority and all other authorities and legal professionals with competence in matters of succession which exercise judicial functions or act pursuant to a delegation of power by a judicial authority or act under the control of a judicial authority, provided that such other authorities and legal professionals offer guarantees with regard to impartiality and the right of all parties to be heard and provided that their decisions under the law of the Member State in which they operate:

(a) may be made the subject of an appeal to or review by a judicial authority; and

(b) have a similar force and effect as a decision of a judicial authority on the same matter.

The Member States shall notify the Commission of the other authorities and legal professionals referred to in the first subparagraph in accordance with Article 79.

Chapter II. Jurisdiction

Article 4. The courts of the Member State in which the deceased had his habitual residence at the time of death shall have jurisdiction to rule on the succession as a whole.

Article 5. (1) Where the law chosen by the deceased to govern his succession pursuant to Article 22 is the law of a Member State, the parties concerned may agree that a court or the courts of that Member State are to have exclusive jurisdiction to rule on any succession matter.

(2) Such a choice-of-court agreement shall be expressed in writing, dated and signed by the parties concerned. Any communication by electronic means which provides a durable record of the agreement shall be deemed equivalent to writing.

Article 6. Where the law chosen by the deceased to govern his succession pursuant to Article 22 is the law of a Member State, the court seised pursuant to Article 4 or Article 10:

(a) may, at the request of one of the parties to the proceedings, decline jurisdiction if it considers that the courts of the Member State of the chosen law are better placed to rule on the succession, taking into account the practical circumstances of the succession, such as the habitual residence of the parties and the location of the assets; or

(b) shall decline jurisdiction if the parties to the proceedings have agreed, in accordance with Article 5, to confer jurisdiction on a court or the courts of the Member State of the chosen law.

Article 7. The courts of a Member State whose law had been chosen by the deceased pursuant to Article 22 shall have jurisdiction to rule on the succession if:

(a) a court previously seised has declined jurisdiction in the same case pursuant to Article 6;

(b) the parties to the proceedings have agreed, in accordance with Article 5, to confer jurisdiction on a court or the courts of that Member State; or

(c) the parties to the proceedings have expressly accepted the jurisdiction of the court seised.

Article 8. A court which has opened succession proceedings of its own motion under Article 4 or Article 10 shall close the proceedings if the parties to the proceedings have agreed to settle the succession amicably out of court in the Member State whose law had been chosen by the deceased pursuant to Article 22.

Article 9. (1) Where, in the course of proceedings before a court of a Member State exercising jurisdiction pursuant to Article 7, it appears that not all the parties to those proceedings were party to the choice-of-court agreement, the court shall continue to exercise jurisdiction if the parties to the proceedings who were not party to the agreement enter an appearance without contesting the jurisdiction of the court.

(2) If the jurisdiction of the court referred to in paragraph (1) is contested by parties to the proceedings who were not party to the agreement, the court shall decline jurisdiction.
In that event, jurisdiction to rule on the succession shall lie with the courts having jurisdiction pursuant to Article 4 or Article 10.

Article 10. (1) Where the habitual residence of the deceased at the time of death is not located in a Member State, the courts of a Member State in which assets of the estate are located shall nevertheless have jurisdiction to rule on the succession as a whole in so far as:
(a) the deceased had the nationality of that Member State at the time of death; or, failing that,
(b) the deceased had his previous habitual residence in that Member State, provided that, at the time the court is seised, a period of not more than five years has elapsed since that habitual residence changed.
(2) Where no court in a Member State has jurisdiction pursuant to paragraph (1), the courts of the Member State in which assets of the estate are located shall nevertheless have jurisdiction to rule on those assets.

Article 11. Where no court of a Member State has jurisdiction pursuant to other provisions of this Regulation, the courts of a Member State may, on an exceptional basis, rule on the succession if proceedings cannot reasonably be brought or conducted or would be impossible in a third State with which the case is closely connected.
The case must have a sufficient connection with the Member State of the court seised.

Article 12. (1) Where the estate of the deceased comprises assets located in a third State, the court seised to rule on the succession may, at the request of one of the parties, decide not to rule on one or more of such assets if it may be expected that its decision in respect of those assets will not be recognised and, where applicable, declared enforceable in that third State.
(2) Paragraph 1 shall not affect the right of the parties to limit the scope of the proceedings under the law of the Member State of the court seised.

Article 13. In addition to the court having jurisdiction to rule on the succession pursuant to this Regulation, the courts of the Member State of the habitual residence of any person who, under the law applicable to the succession, may make, before a court, a declaration concerning the acceptance or waiver of the succession, of a legacy or of a reserved share, or a declaration designed to limit the liability of the person concerned in respect of the liabilities under the succession, shall have jurisdiction to receive such declarations where, under the law of that Member State, such declarations may be made before a court.

Article 14. For the purposes of this Chapter, a court shall be deemed to be seised:
(a) at the time when the document instituting the proceedings or an equivalent document is lodged with the court, provided that the applicant has not subsequently failed to take the steps he was required to take to have service effected on the defendant;
(b) if the document has to be served before being lodged with the court, at the time when it is received by the authority responsible for service, provided that the applicant has not subsequently failed to take the steps he was required to take to have the document lodged with the court; or
(c) if the proceedings are opened of the court's own motion, at the time when the decision to open the proceedings is taken by the court, or, where such a decision is not required, at the time when the case is registered by the court.

Article 15. Where a court of a Member State is seised of a succession matter over which it has no jurisdiction under this Regulation, it shall declare of its own motion that it has no jurisdiction.

Article 16. (1) Where a defendant habitually resident in a State other than the Member State where the action was brought does not enter an appearance, the court having jurisdiction shall stay the proceedings so long as it is not shown that the defendant has been able to receive the document instituting the proceedings or an equivalent document in time to arrange for his defence, or that all necessary steps have been taken to that end.
(2) Article 19 of Regulation (EC) No 1393/2007 of the European Parliament and of the Council of 13 November 2007 on the service in the Member States of judicial and extrajudicial documents in civil or commercial matters (service of documents) [9] shall apply instead of paragraph (1) of this Article if the document instituting the proceedings or an equivalent document had to be transmitted from one Member State to another pursuant to that Regulation.
(3) Where Regulation (EC) No 1393/2007 is not applicable, Article 15 of the Hague Convention of 15 November 1965 on the Service Abroad of Judicial and Extrajudicial Documents in Civil or Com-

mercial Matters shall apply if the document instituting the proceedings or an equivalent document had to be transmitted abroad pursuant to that Convention.

Article 17. (1) Where proceedings involving the same cause of action and between the same parties are brought in the courts of different Member States, any court other than the court first seised shall of its own motion stay its proceedings until such time as the jurisdiction of the court first seised is established.
(2) Where the jurisdiction of the court first seised is established, any court other than the court first seised shall decline jurisdiction in favour of that court.

Article 18. (1) Where related actions are pending in the courts of different Member States, any court other than the court first seised may stay its proceedings.
(2) Where those actions are pending at first instance, any court other than the court first seised may also, on the application of one of the parties, decline jurisdiction if the court first seised has jurisdiction over the actions in question and its law permits the consolidation thereof.
(3) For the purposes of this Article, actions are deemed to be related where they are so closely connected that it is expedient to hear and determine them together to avoid the risk of irreconcilable decisions resulting from separate proceedings.

Article 19. Application may be made to the courts of a Member State for such provisional, including protective, measures as may be available under the law of that State, even if, under this Regulation, the courts of another Member State have jurisdiction as to the substance of the matter.

Chapter III. Applicable Law

Article 20. Any law specified by this Regulation shall be applied whether or not it is the law of a Member State.

Article 21. (1) Unless otherwise provided for in this Regulation, the law applicable to the succession as a whole shall be the law of the State in which the deceased had his habitual residence at the time of death.
(2) Where, by way of exception, it is clear from all the circumstances of the case that, at the time of death, the deceased was manifestly more closely connected with a State other than the State whose law would be applicable under paragraph (1), the law applicable to the succession shall be the law of that other State.

Article 22. (1) A person may choose as the law to govern his succession as a whole the law of the State whose nationality he possesses at the time of making the choice or at the time of death.
A person possessing multiple nationalities may choose the law of any of the States whose nationality he possesses at the time of making the choice or at the time of death.
(2) The choice shall be made expressly in a declaration in the form of a disposition of property upon death or shall be demonstrated by the terms of such a disposition.
(3) The substantive validity of the act whereby the choice of law was made shall be governed by the chosen law.
(4) Any modification or revocation of the choice of law shall meet the requirements as to form for the modification or revocation of a disposition of property upon death.

Article 23. (1) The law determined pursuant to Article 21 or Article 22 shall govern the succession as a whole.
(2) That law shall govern in particular:
(a) the causes, time and place of the opening of the succession;
(b) the determination of the beneficiaries, of their respective shares and of the obligations which may be imposed on them by the deceased, and the determination of other succession rights, including the succession rights of the surviving spouse or partner;
(c) the capacity to inherit;
(d) disinheritance and disqualification by conduct;
(e) the transfer to the heirs and, as the case may be, to the legatees of the assets, rights and obligations forming part of the estate, including the conditions and effects of the acceptance or waiver of the succession or of a legacy;
(f) the powers of the heirs, the executors of the wills and other administrators of the estate, in particular as regards the sale of property and the payment of creditors, without prejudice to the powers referred to in Article 29(2) and (3);
(g) liability for the debts under the succession;

(h) the disposable part of the estate, the reserved shares and other restrictions on the disposal of property upon death as well as claims which persons close to the deceased may have against the estate or the heirs;
(i) any obligation to restore or account for gifts, advancements or legacies when determining the shares of the different beneficiaries; and
(j) the sharing-out of the estate.

Article 24. (1) A disposition of property upon death other than an agreement as to succession shall be governed, as regards its admissibility and substantive validity, by the law which, under this Regulation, would have been applicable to the succession of the person who made the disposition if he had died on the day on which the disposition was made.
(2) Notwithstanding paragraph (1), a person may choose as the law to govern his disposition of property upon death, as regards its admissibility and substantive validity, the law which that person could have chosen in accordance with Article 22 on the conditions set out therein.
(3) Paragraph 1 shall apply, as appropriate, to the modification or revocation of a disposition of property upon death other than an agreement as to succession. In the event of a choice of law in accordance with paragraph (2), the modification or revocation shall be governed by the chosen law.

Article 25. (1) An agreement as to succession regarding the succession of one person shall be governed, as regards its admissibility, its substantive validity and its binding effects between the parties, including the conditions for its dissolution, by the law which, under this Regulation, would have been applicable to the succession of that person if he had died on the day on which the agreement was concluded.
(2) An agreement as to succession regarding the succession of several persons shall be admissible only if it is admissible under all the laws which, under this Regulation, would have governed the succession of all the persons involved if they had died on the day on which the agreement was concluded.
An agreement as to succession which is admissible pursuant to the first subparagraph shall be governed, as regards its substantive validity and its binding effects between the parties, including the conditions for its dissolution, by the law, from among those referred to in the first subparagraph, with which it has the closest connection.
(3) Notwithstanding paragraphs 1 and 2, the parties may choose as the law to govern their agreement as to succession, as regards its admissibility, its substantive validity and its binding effects between the parties, including the conditions for its dissolution, the law which the person or one of the persons whose estate is involved could have chosen in accordance with Article 22 on the conditions set out therein.

Article 26. (1) For the purposes of Articles 24 and 25 the following elements shall pertain to substantive validity:
(a) the capacity of the person making the disposition of property upon death to make such a disposition;
(b) the particular causes which bar the person making the disposition from disposing in favour of certain persons or which bar a person from receiving succession property from the person making the disposition;
(c) the admissibility of representation for the purposes of making a disposition of property upon death;
(d) the interpretation of the disposition;
(e) fraud, duress, mistake and any other questions relating to the consent or intention of the person making the disposition.
(2) Where a person has the capacity to make a disposition of property upon death under the law applicable pursuant to Article 24 or Article 25, a subsequent change of the law applicable shall not affect his capacity to modify or revoke such a disposition.

Article 27. (1) A disposition of property upon death made in writing shall be valid as regards form if its form complies with the law:
(a) of the State in which the disposition was made or the agreement as to succession concluded;
(b) of a State whose nationality the testator or at least one of the persons whose succession is concerned by an agreement as to succession possessed, either at the time when the disposition was made or the agreement concluded, or at the time of death;
(c) of a State in which the testator or at least one of the persons whose succession is concerned by an agreement as to succession had his domicile, either at the time when the disposition was made or the agreement concluded, or at the time of death;

(d) of the State in which the testator or at least one of the persons whose succession is concerned by an agreement as to succession had his habitual residence, either at the time when the disposition was made or the agreement concluded, or at the time of death; or

(e) in so far as immovable property is concerned, of the State in which that property is located.

The determination of the question whether or not the testator or any person whose succession is concerned by the agreement as to succession had his domicile in a particular State shall be governed by the law of that State.

(2) Paragraph 1 shall also apply to dispositions of property upon death modifying or revoking an earlier disposition. The modification or revocation shall also be valid as regards form if it complies with any one of the laws according to the terms of which, under paragraph (1), the disposition of property upon death which has been modified or revoked was valid.

(3) For the purposes of this Article, any provision of law which limits the permitted forms of dispositions of property upon death by reference to the age, nationality or other personal conditions of the testator or of the persons whose succession is concerned by an agreement as to succession shall be deemed to pertain to matters of form. The same rule shall apply to the qualifications to be possessed by any witnesses required for the validity of a disposition of property upon death.

Article 28. A declaration concerning the acceptance or waiver of the succession, of a legacy or of a reserved share, or a declaration designed to limit the liability of the person making the declaration, shall be valid as to form where it meets the requirements of:

(a) the law applicable to the succession pursuant to Article 21 or Article 22; or

(b) the law of the State in which the person making the declaration has his habitual residence.

Article 29. (1) Where the appointment of an administrator is mandatory or mandatory upon request under the law of the Member State whose courts have jurisdiction to rule on the succession pursuant to this Regulation and the law applicable to the succession is a foreign law, the courts of that Member State may, when seised, appoint one or more administrators of the estate under their own law, subject to the conditions laid down in this Article.

The administrator(s) appointed pursuant to this paragraph shall be the person(s) entitled to execute the will of the deceased and/or to administer the estate under the law applicable to the succession. Where that law does not provide for the administration of the estate by a person who is not a beneficiary, the courts of the Member State in which the administrator is to be appointed may appoint a third-party administrator under their own law if that law so requires and there is a serious conflict of interests between the beneficiaries or between the beneficiaries and the creditors or other persons having guaranteed the debts of the deceased, a disagreement amongst the beneficiaries on the administration of the estate or a complex estate to administer due to the nature of the assets.

The administrator(s) appointed pursuant to this paragraph shall be the only person(s) entitled to exercise the powers referred to in paragraph (2) or 3.

(2) The person(s) appointed as administrator(s) pursuant to paragraph (1) shall exercise the powers to administer the estate which he or they may exercise under the law applicable to the succession. The appointing court may, in its decision, lay down specific conditions for the exercise of such powers in accordance with the law applicable to the succession.

Where the law applicable to the succession does not provide for sufficient powers to preserve the assets of the estate or to protect the rights of the creditors or of other persons having guaranteed the debts of the deceased, the appointing court may decide to allow the administrator(s) to exercise, on a residual basis, the powers provided for to that end by its own law and may, in its decision, lay down specific conditions for the exercise of such powers in accordance with that law.

When exercising such residual powers, however, the administrator(s) shall respect the law applicable to the succession as regards the transfer of ownership of succession property, liability for the debts under the succession, the rights of the beneficiaries, including, where applicable, the right to accept or to waive the succession, and, where applicable, the powers of the executor of the will of the deceased.

(3) Notwithstanding paragraph (2), the court appointing one or more administrators pursuant to paragraph (1) may, by way of exception, where the law applicable to the succession is the law of a third State, decide to vest in those administrators all the powers of administration provided for by the law of the Member State in which they are appointed.

When exercising such powers, however, the administrators shall respect, in particular, the determination of the beneficiaries and their succession rights, including their rights to a reserved share or claim against the estate or the heirs under the law applicable to the succession.

Article 30. Where the law of the State in which certain immovable property, certain enterprises or other special categories of assets are located contains special rules which, for economic, family or social considerations, impose restrictions concerning or affecting the succession in respect of those assets, those special rules shall apply to the succession in so far as, under the law of that State, they are applicable irrespective of the law applicable to the succession.

Article 31. Where a person invokes a right in rem to which he is entitled under the law applicable to the succession and the law of the Member State in which the right is invoked does not know the right in rem in question, that right shall, if necessary and to the extent possible, be adapted to the closest equivalent right in rem under the law of that State, taking into account the aims and the interests pursued by the specific right in rem and the effects attached to it.

Article 32. Where two or more persons whose successions are governed by different laws die in circumstances in which it is uncertain in what order their deaths occurred, and where those laws provide differently for that situation or make no provision for it at all, none of the deceased persons shall have any rights to the succession of the other or others.

Article 33. To the extent that, under the law applicable to the succession pursuant to this Regulation, there is no heir or legatee for any assets under a disposition of property upon death and no natural person is an heir by operation of law, the application of the law so determined shall not preclude the right of a Member State or of an entity appointed for that purpose by that Member State to appropriate under its own law the assets of the estate located on its territory, provided that the creditors are entitled to seek satisfaction of their claims out of the assets of the estate as a whole.

Article 34. (1) The application of the law of any third State specified by this Regulation shall mean the application of the rules of law in force in that State, including its rules of private international law in so far as those rules make a renvoi:
(a) to the law of a Member State; or
(b) to the law of another third State which would apply its own law.
(2) No renvoi shall apply with respect to the laws referred to in Article 21(2), Article 22, Article 27, point (b) of Article 28 and Article 30.

Article 35. The application of a provision of the law of any State specified by this Regulation may be refused only if such application is manifestly incompatible with the public policy (*ordre public*) of the forum.

Article 36. (1) Where the law specified by this Regulation is that of a State which comprises several territorial units each of which has its own rules of law in respect of succession, the internal conflict-of-laws rules of that State shall determine the relevant territorial unit whose rules of law are to apply.
(2) In the absence of such internal conflict-of-laws rules:
(a) any reference to the law of the State referred to in paragraph (1) shall, for the purposes of determining the law applicable pursuant to provisions referring to the habitual residence of the deceased, be construed as referring to the law of the territorial unit in which the deceased had his habitual residence at the time of death;
(b) any reference to the law of the State referred to in paragraph (1) shall, for the purposes of determining the law applicable pursuant to provisions referring to the nationality of the deceased, be construed as referring to the law of the territorial unit with which the deceased had the closest connection;
(c) any reference to the law of the State referred to in paragraph (1) shall, for the purposes of determining the law applicable pursuant to any other provisions referring to other elements as connecting factors, be construed as referring to the law of the territorial unit in which the relevant element is located.
(3) Notwithstanding paragraph (2), any reference to the law of the State referred to in paragraph (1) shall, for the purposes of determining the relevant law pursuant to Article 27, in the absence of internal conflict-of-laws rules in that State, be construed as referring to the law of the territorial unit with which the testator or the persons whose succession is concerned by the agreement as to succession had the closest connection.

Article 37. In relation to a State which has two or more systems of law or sets of rules applicable to different categories of persons in respect of succession, any reference to the law of that State shall be construed as referring to the system of law or set of rules determined by the rules in force in that State. In the absence of such rules, the system of law or the set of rules with which the deceased had the closest connection shall apply.

Article 38 A Member State which comprises several territorial units each of which has its own rules of law in respect of succession shall not be required to apply this Regulation to conflicts of laws arising between such units only.

Chapter IV. Recognition, Enforceability and Enforcement of Decisions

Article 39. (1) A decision given in a Member State shall be recognised in the other Member States without any special procedure being required.
(2) Any interested party who raises the recognition of a decision as the principal issue in a dispute may, in accordance with the procedure provided for in Articles 45 to 58, apply for that decision to be recognised.
(3) If the outcome of the proceedings in a court of a Member State depends on the determination of an incidental question of recognition, that court shall have jurisdiction over that question.

Article 40. A decision shall not be recognised:
(a) if such recognition is manifestly contrary to public policy (*ordre public*) in the Member State in which recognition is sought;
(b) where it was given in default of appearance, if the defendant was not served with the document which instituted the proceedings or with an equivalent document in sufficient time and in such a way as to enable him to arrange for his defence, unless the defendant failed to commence proceedings to challenge the decision when it was possible for him to do so;
(c) if it is irreconcilable with a decision given in proceedings between the same parties in the Member State in which recognition is sought;
(d) if it is irreconcilable with an earlier decision given in another Member State or in a third State in proceedings involving the same cause of action and between the same parties, provided that the earlier decision fulfils the conditions necessary for its recognition in the Member State in which recognition is sought.

Article 41. Under no circumstances may a decision given in a Member State be reviewed as to its substance.

Article 42. A court of a Member State in which recognition is sought of a decision given in another Member State may stay the proceedings if an ordinary appeal against the decision has been lodged in the Member State of origin.

Article 43. Decisions given in a Member State and enforceable in that State shall be enforceable in another Member State when, on the application of any interested party, they have been declared enforceable there in accordance with the procedure provided for in Articles 45 to 58.

Article 44. To determine whether, for the purposes of the procedure provided for in Articles 45 to 58, a party is domiciled in the Member State of enforcement, the court seised shall apply the internal law of that Member State.

Article 45. (1) The application for a declaration of enforceability shall be submitted to the court or competent authority of the Member State of enforcement communicated by that Member State to the Commission in accordance with Article 78.
(2) The local jurisdiction shall be determined by reference to the place of domicile of the party against whom enforcement is sought, or to the place of enforcement.

Article 46. (1) The application procedure shall be governed by the law of the Member State of enforcement.
(2) The applicant shall not be required to have a postal address or an authorised representative in the Member State of enforcement.
(3) The application shall be accompanied by the following documents:
(a) a copy of the decision which satisfies the conditions necessary to establish its authenticity;
(b) the attestation issued by the court or competent authority of the Member State of origin using the form established in accordance with the advisory procedure referred to in Article 81(2), without prejudice to Article 47.

Article 47. (1) If the attestation referred to in point (b) of Article 46(3) is not produced, the court or competent authority may specify a time for its production or accept an equivalent document or, if it considers that it has sufficient information before it, dispense with its production.
(2) If the court or competent authority so requires, a translation of the documents shall be produced. The translation shall be done by a person qualified to do translations in one of the Member States.

Article 48. The decision shall be declared enforceable immediately on completion of the formalities in Article 46 without any review under Article 40. The party against whom enforcement is sought shall not at this stage of the proceedings be entitled to make any submissions on the application.

Article 49. Notice of the decision on the application for a declaration of enforceability
(1) The decision on the application for a declaration of enforceability shall forthwith be brought to the notice of the applicant in accordance with the procedure laid down by the law of the Member State of enforcement.
(2) The declaration of enforceability shall be served on the party against whom enforcement is sought, accompanied by the decision, if not already served on that party.

Article 50. Appeal against the decision on the application for a declaration of enforceability
(1) The decision on the application for a declaration of enforceability may be appealed against by either party.
(2) The appeal shall be lodged with the court communicated by the Member State concerned to the Commission in accordance with Article 78.
(3) The appeal shall be dealt with in accordance with the rules governing procedure in contradictory matters.
(4) If the party against whom enforcement is sought fails to appear before the appellate court in proceedings concerning an appeal brought by the applicant, Article 16 shall apply even where the party against whom enforcement is sought is not domiciled in any of the Member States.
(5) An appeal against the declaration of enforceability shall be lodged within 30 days of service thereof. If the party against whom enforcement is sought is domiciled in a Member State other than that in which the declaration of enforceability was given, the time for appealing shall be 60 days and shall run from the date of service, either on him in person or at his residence. No extension may be granted on account of distance.

Article 51. The decision given on the appeal may be contested only by the procedure communicated by the Member State concerned to the Commission in accordance with Article 78.

Article 52. The court with which an appeal is lodged under Article 50 or Article 51 shall refuse or revoke a declaration of enforceability only on one of the grounds specified in Article 40. It shall give its decision without delay.

Article 53. The court with which an appeal is lodged under Article 50 or Article 51 shall, on the application of the party against whom enforcement is sought, stay the proceedings if the enforceability of the decision is suspended in the Member State of origin by reason of an appeal.

Article 54. (1) When a decision must be recognised in accordance with this Chapter, nothing shall prevent the applicant from availing himself of provisional, including protective, measures in accordance with the law of the Member State of enforcement without a declaration of enforceability under Article 48 being required.
(2) The declaration of enforceability shall carry with it by operation of law the power to proceed to any protective measures.
(3) During the time specified for an appeal pursuant to Article 50(5) against the declaration of enforceability and until any such appeal has been determined, no measures of enforcement may be taken other than protective measures against the property of the party against whom enforcement is sought.

Article 55. (1) Where a decision has been given in respect of several matters and the declaration of enforceability cannot be given for all of them, the court or competent authority shall give it for one or more of them.
(2) An applicant may request a declaration of enforceability limited to parts of a decision.

Article 56. An applicant who, in the Member State of origin, has benefited from complete or partial legal aid or exemption from costs or expenses shall be entitled, in any proceedings for a declaration of enforceability, to benefit from the most favourable legal aid or the most extensive exemption from costs or expenses provided for by the law of the Member State of enforcement.

Article 57. No security, bond or deposit, however described, shall be required of a party who in one Member State applies for recognition, enforceability or enforcement of a decision given in another Member State on the ground that he is a foreign national or that he is not domiciled or resident in the Member State of enforcement.

PART II PRIVATE INTERNATIONAL LAW

Article 58. In proceedings for the issue of a declaration of enforceability, no charge, duty or fee calculated by reference to the value of the matter at issue may be levied in the Member State of enforcement.

Chapter V. Authentic Instruments and Court Settlements

Article 59. (1) An authentic instrument established in a Member State shall have the same evidentiary effects in another Member State as it has in the Member State of origin, or the most comparable effects, provided that this is not manifestly contrary to public policy (*ordre public*) in the Member State concerned.
A person wishing to use an authentic instrument in another Member State may ask the authority establishing the authentic instrument in the Member State of origin to fill in the form established in accordance with the advisory procedure referred to in Article 81(2) describing the evidentiary effects which the authentic instrument produces in the Member State of origin.
(2) Any challenge relating to the authenticity of an authentic instrument shall be made before the courts of the Member State of origin and shall be decided upon under the law of that State. The authentic instrument challenged shall not produce any evidentiary effect in another Member State as long as the challenge is pending before the competent court.
(3) Any challenge relating to the legal acts or legal relationships recorded in an authentic instrument shall be made before the courts having jurisdiction under this Regulation and shall be decided upon under the law applicable pursuant to Chapter III. The authentic instrument challenged shall not produce any evidentiary effect in a Member State other than the Member State of origin as regards the matter being challenged as long as the challenge is pending before the competent court.
(4) If the outcome of proceedings in a court of a Member State depends on the determination of an incidental question relating to the legal acts or legal relationships recorded in an authentic instrument in matters of succession, that court shall have jurisdiction over that question.

Article 60. (1) An authentic instrument which is enforceable in the Member State of origin shall be declared enforceable in another Member State on the application of any interested party in accordance with the procedure provided for in Articles 45 to 58.
(2) For the purposes of point (b) of Article 46(3), the authority which established the authentic instrument shall, on the application of any interested party, issue an attestation using the form established in accordance with the advisory procedure referred to in Article 81(2).
(3) The court with which an appeal is lodged under Article 50 or Article 51 shall refuse or revoke a declaration of enforceability only if enforcement of the authentic instrument is manifestly contrary to public policy (*ordre public*) in the Member State of enforcement.

Article 61. (1) Court settlements which are enforceable in the Member State of origin shall be declared enforceable in another Member State on the application of any interested party in accordance with the procedure provided for in Articles 45 to 58.
(2) For the purposes of point (b) of Article 46(3), the court which approved the settlement or before which it was concluded shall, on the application of any interested party, issue an attestation using the form established in accordance with the advisory procedure referred to in Article 81(2).
(3) The court with which an appeal is lodged under Article 50 or Article 51 shall refuse or revoke a declaration of enforceability only if enforcement of the court settlement is manifestly contrary to public policy (*ordre public*) in the Member State of enforcement.

Chapter VI. European Certificate of Succession

Article 62. (1) This Regulation creates a European Certificate of Succession (hereinafter referred to as "the Certificate") which shall be issued for use in another Member State and shall produce the effects listed in Article 69.
(2) The use of the Certificate shall not be mandatory.
(3) The Certificate shall not take the place of internal documents used for similar purposes in the Member States. However, once issued for use in another Member State, the Certificate shall also produce the effects listed in Article 69 in the Member State whose authorities issued it in accordance with this Chapter.

Article 63. (1) The Certificate is for use by heirs, legatees having direct rights in the succession and executors of wills or administrators of the estate who, in another Member State, need to invoke their status or to exercise respectively their rights as heirs or legatees and/or their powers as executors of wills or administrators of the estate.
(2) The Certificate may be used, in particular, to demonstrate one or more of the following:

(a) the status and/or the rights of each heir or, as the case may be, each legatee mentioned in the Certificate and their respective shares of the estate;
(b) the attribution of a specific asset or specific assets forming part of the estate to the heir(s) or, as the case may be, the legatee(s) mentioned in the Certificate;
(c) the powers of the person mentioned in the Certificate to execute the will or administer the estate.

Article 64. The Certificate shall be issued in the Member State whose courts have jurisdiction under Article 4, Article 7, Article 10 or Article 11. The issuing authority shall be:
(a) a court as defined in Article 3(2); or
(b) another authority which, under national law, has competence to deal with matters of succession.

Article 65. (1) The Certificate shall be issued upon application by any person referred to in Article 63(1) (hereinafter referred to as "the applicant").
(2) For the purposes of submitting an application, the applicant may use the form established in accordance with the advisory procedure referred to in Article 81(2).
(3) The application shall contain the information listed below, to the extent that such information is within the applicant's knowledge and is necessary in order to enable the issuing authority to certify the elements which the applicant wants certified, and shall be accompanied by all relevant documents either in the original or by way of copies which satisfy the conditions necessary to establish their authenticity, without prejudice to Article 66(2):
(a) details concerning the deceased: surname (if applicable, surname at birth), given name(s), sex, date and place of birth, civil status, nationality, identification number (if applicable), address at the time of death, date and place of death;
(b) details concerning the applicant: surname (if applicable, surname at birth), given name(s), sex, date and place of birth, civil status, nationality, identification number (if applicable), address and relationship to the deceased, if any;
(c) details concerning the representative of the applicant, if any: surname (if applicable, surname at birth), given name(s), address and representative capacity;
(d) details of the spouse or partner of the deceased and, if applicable, ex-spouse(s) or ex-partner(s): surname (if applicable, surname at birth), given name(s), sex, date and place of birth, civil status, nationality, identification number (if applicable) and address;
(e) details of other possible beneficiaries under a disposition of property upon death and/or by operation of law: surname and given name(s) or organisation name, identification number (if applicable) and address;
(f) the intended purpose of the Certificate in accordance with Article 63;
(g) the contact details of the court or other competent authority which is dealing with or has dealt with the succession as such, if applicable;
(h) the elements on which the applicant founds, as appropriate, his claimed right to succession property as a beneficiary and/or his right to execute the will of the deceased and/or to administer the estate of the deceased;
(i) an indication of whether the deceased had made a disposition of property upon death; if neither the original nor a copy is appended, an indication regarding the location of the original;
(j) an indication of whether the deceased had entered into a marriage contract or into a contract regarding a relationship which may have comparable effects to marriage; if neither the original nor a copy of the contract is appended, an indication regarding the location of the original;
(k) an indication of whether any of the beneficiaries has made a declaration concerning acceptance or waiver of the succession;
(l) a declaration stating that, to the applicant's best knowledge, no dispute is pending relating to the elements to be certified;
(m) any other information which the applicant deems useful for the purposes of the issue of the Certificate.

Article 66. (1) Upon receipt of the application the issuing authority shall verify the information and declarations and the documents and other evidence provided by the applicant. It shall carry out the enquiries necessary for that verification of its own motion where this is provided for or authorised by its own law, or shall invite the applicant to provide any further evidence which it deems necessary.
(2) Where the applicant has been unable to produce copies of the relevant documents which satisfy the conditions necessary to establish their authenticity, the issuing authority may decide to accept other forms of evidence.
(3) Where this is provided for by its own law and subject to the conditions laid down therein, the issuing authority may require that declarations be made on oath or by a statutory declaration in lieu of an oath.

PART II PRIVATE INTERNATIONAL LAW

(4) The issuing authority shall take all necessary steps to inform the beneficiaries of the application for a Certificate. It shall, if necessary for the establishment of the elements to be certified, hear any person involved and any executor or administrator and make public announcements aimed at giving other possible beneficiaries the opportunity to invoke their rights.

(5) For the purposes of this Article, the competent authority of a Member State shall, upon request, provide the issuing authority of another Member State with information held, in particular, in the land registers, the civil status registers and registers recording documents and facts of relevance for the succession or for the matrimonial property regime or an equivalent property regime of the deceased, where that competent authority would be authorised, under national law, to provide another national authority with such information.

Article 67. (1) The issuing authority shall issue the Certificate without delay in accordance with the procedure laid down in this Chapter when the elements to be certified have been established under the law applicable to the succession or under any other law applicable to specific elements. It shall use the form established in accordance with the advisory procedure referred to in Article 81(2).

The issuing authority shall not issue the Certificate in particular if:

(a) the elements to be certified are being challenged; or

(b) the Certificate would not be in conformity with a decision covering the same elements.

(2) The issuing authority shall take all necessary steps to inform the beneficiaries of the issue of the Certificate.

Article 68. The Certificate shall contain the following information, to the extent required for the purpose for which it is issued:

(a) the name and address of the issuing authority;

(b) the reference number of the file;

(c) the elements on the basis of which the issuing authority considers itself competent to issue the Certificate;

(d) the date of issue;

(e) details concerning the applicant: surname (if applicable, surname at birth), given name(s), sex, date and place of birth, civil status, nationality, identification number (if applicable), address and relationship to the deceased, if any;

(f) details concerning the deceased: surname (if applicable, surname at birth), given name(s), sex, date and place of birth, civil status, nationality, identification number (if applicable), address at the time of death, date and place of death;

(g) details concerning the beneficiaries: surname (if applicable, surname at birth), given name(s) and identification number (if applicable);

(h) information concerning a marriage contract entered into by the deceased or, if applicable, a contract entered into by the deceased in the context of a relationship deemed by the law applicable to such a relationship to have comparable effects to marriage, and information concerning the matrimonial property regime or equivalent property regime;

(i) the law applicable to the succession and the elements on the basis of which that law has been determined;

(j) information as to whether the succession is testate or intestate, including information concerning the elements giving rise to the rights and/or powers of the heirs, legatees, executors of wills or administrators of the estate;

(k) if applicable, information in respect of each beneficiary concerning the nature of the acceptance or waiver of the succession;

(l) the share for each heir and, if applicable, the list of rights and/or assets for any given heir;

(m) the list of rights and/or assets for any given legatee;

(n) the restrictions on the rights of the heir(s) and, as appropriate, legatee(s) under the law applicable to the succession and/or under the disposition of property upon death;

(o) the powers of the executor of the will and/or the administrator of the estate and the restrictions on those powers under the law applicable to the succession and/or under the disposition of property upon death.

Article 69. (1) The Certificate shall produce its effects in all Member States, without any special procedure being required.

(2) The Certificate shall be presumed to accurately demonstrate elements which have been established under the law applicable to the succession or under any other law applicable to specific elements. The person mentioned in the Certificate as the heir, legatee, executor of the will or administrator of the estate shall be presumed to have the status mentioned in the Certificate and/or to hold the rights or the powers stated in the Certificate, with no conditions and/or restrictions being attached to

those rights or powers other than those stated in the Certificate.

(3) Any person who, acting on the basis of the information certified in a Certificate, makes payments or passes on property to a person mentioned in the Certificate as authorised to accept payment or property, shall be considered to have transacted with a person with authority to accept payment or property, unless he knows that the contents of the Certificate are not accurate or is unaware of such inaccuracy due to gross negligence.

(4) Where a person mentioned in the Certificate as authorised to dispose of succession property disposes of such property in favour of another person, that other person shall, if acting on the basis of the information certified in the Certificate, be considered to have transacted with a person with authority to dispose of the property concerned, unless he knows that the contents of the Certificate are not accurate or is unaware of such inaccuracy due to gross negligence.

(5) The Certificate shall constitute a valid document for the recording of succession property in the relevant register of a Member State, without prejudice to points (k) and (l) of Article 1(2).

Article 70. (1) The issuing authority shall keep the original of the Certificate and shall issue one or more certified copies to the applicant and to any person demonstrating a legitimate interest.

(2) The issuing authority shall, for the purposes of Articles 71(3) and 73(2), keep a list of persons to whom certified copies have been issued pursuant to paragraph (1).

(3) The certified copies issued shall be valid for a limited period of six months, to be indicated in the certified copy by way of an expiry date. In exceptional, duly justified cases, the issuing authority may, by way of derogation, decide that the period of validity is to be longer. Once this period has elapsed, any person in possession of a certified copy must, in order to be able to use the Certificate for the purposes indicated in Article 63, apply for an extension of the period of validity of the certified copy or request a new certified copy from the issuing authority.

Article 71. (1) The issuing authority shall, at the request of any person demonstrating a legitimate interest or of its own motion, rectify the Certificate in the event of a clerical error.

(2) The issuing authority shall, at the request of any person demonstrating a legitimate interest or, where this is possible under national law, of its own motion, modify or withdraw the Certificate where it has been established that the Certificate or individual elements thereof are not accurate.

(3) The issuing authority shall without delay inform all persons to whom certified copies of the Certificate have been issued pursuant to Article 70(1) of any rectification, modification or withdrawal thereof.

Article 72 (1) Decisions taken by the issuing authority pursuant to Article 67 may be challenged by any person entitled to apply for a Certificate.

Decisions taken by the issuing authority pursuant to Article 71 and point (a) of Article 73(1) may be challenged by any person demonstrating a legitimate interest.

The challenge shall be lodged before a judicial authority in the Member State of the issuing authority in accordance with the law of that State.

(2) If, as a result of a challenge as referred to in paragraph (1), it is established that the Certificate issued is not accurate, the competent judicial authority shall rectify, modify or withdraw the Certificate or ensure that it is rectified, modified or withdrawn by the issuing authority.

If, as a result of a challenge as referred to in paragraph (1), it is established that the refusal to issue the Certificate was unjustified, the competent judicial authority shall issue the Certificate or ensure that the issuing authority re-assesses the case and makes a fresh decision.

Article 73. (1) The effects of the Certificate may be suspended by:

(a) the issuing authority, at the request of any person demonstrating a legitimate interest, pending a modification or withdrawal of the Certificate pursuant to Article 71; or

(b) the judicial authority, at the request of any person entitled to challenge a decision taken by the issuing authority pursuant to Article 72, pending such a challenge.

(2) The issuing authority or, as the case may be, the judicial authority shall without delay inform all persons to whom certified copies of the Certificate have been issued pursuant to Article 70(1) of any suspension of the effects of the Certificate.

During the suspension of the effects of the Certificate no further certified copies of the Certificate may be issued.

Chapter VII. General and Final Provisions

Article 74. No legalisation or other similar formality shall be required in respect of documents issued in a Member State in the context of this Regulation.

PART II   PRIVATE INTERNATIONAL LAW

Article 75. (1) This Regulation shall not affect the application of international conventions to which one or more Member States are party at the time of adoption of this Regulation and which concern matters covered by this Regulation.

In particular, Member States which are Contracting Parties to the Hague Convention of 5 October 1961 on the Conflicts of Laws Relating to the Form of Testamentary Dispositions shall continue to apply the provisions of that Convention instead of Article 27 of this Regulation with regard to the formal validity of wills and joint wills.

(2) Notwithstanding paragraph (1), this Regulation shall, as between Member States, take precedence over conventions concluded exclusively between two or more of them in so far as such conventions concern matters governed by this Regulation.

(3) This Regulation shall not preclude the application of the Convention of 19 November 1934 between Denmark, Finland, Iceland, Norway and Sweden comprising private international law provisions on succession, wills and estate administration, as revised by the intergovernmental agreement between those States of 1 June 2012, by the Member States which are parties thereto, in so far as it provides for:

(a) rules on the procedural aspects of estate administration as defined by the Convention and assistance in that regard by the authorities of the States Contracting Parties to the Convention; and

(b) simplified and more expeditious procedures for the recognition and enforcement of decisions in matters of succession.

Article 76. This Regulation shall not affect the application of Council Regulation (EC) No 1346/2000 of 29 May 2000 on insolvency proceedings.

Article 77. The Member States shall, with a view to making the information available to the public within the framework of the European Judicial Network in civil and commercial matters, provide the Commission with a short summary of their national legislation and procedures relating to succession, including information on the type of authority which has competence in matters of succession and information on the type of authority competent to receive declarations of acceptance or waiver of the succession, of a legacy or of a reserved share.

The Member States shall also provide fact sheets listing all the documents and/or information usually required for the purposes of registration of immovable property located on their territory.

The Member States shall keep the information permanently updated.

Article 78. (1) By 16 November 2014, the Member States shall communicate to the Commission:

(a) the names and contact details of the courts or authorities with competence to deal with applications for a declaration of enforceability in accordance with Article 45(1) and with appeals against decisions on such applications in accordance with Article 50(2);

(b) the procedures to contest the decision given on appeal referred to in Article 51;

(c) the relevant information regarding the authorities competent to issue the Certificate pursuant to Article 64; and

(d) the redress procedures referred to in Article 72.

The Member States shall apprise the Commission of any subsequent changes to that information.

(2) The Commission shall publish the information communicated in accordance with paragraph (1) in the *Official Journal of the European Union*, with the exception of the addresses and other contact details of the courts and authorities referred to in point (a) of paragraph (1).

(3) The Commission shall make all information communicated in accordance with paragraph (1) publicly available through any other appropriate means, in particular through the European Judicial Network in civil and commercial matters.

Article 79. (1) The Commission shall, on the basis of the notifications by the Member States, establish the list of the other authorities and legal professionals referred to in Article 3(2).

(2) The Member States shall notify the Commission of any subsequent changes to the information contained in that list. The Commission shall amend the list accordingly.

(3) The Commission shall publish the list and any subsequent amendments in the *Official Journal of the European Union*.

(4) The Commission shall make all information notified in accordance with paragraphs 1 and 2 publicly available through any other appropriate means, in particular through the European Judicial Network in civil and commercial matters.

Article 80. The Commission shall adopt implementing acts establishing and subsequently amending the attestations and forms referred to in Articles 46, 59, 60, 61, 65 and 67. Those implementing acts shall be adopted in accordance with the advisory procedure referred to in Article 81(2).

Article 81. (1) The Commission shall be assisted by a committee. That committee shall be a committee within the meaning of Regulation (EU) No 182/2011.
(2) Where reference is made to this paragraph, Article 4 of Regulation (EU) No 182/2011 shall apply.

Article 82. By 18 August 2025 the Commission shall submit to the European Parliament, the Council and the European Economic and Social Committee a report on the application of this Regulation, including an evaluation of any practical problems encountered in relation to parallel out-of-court settlements of succession cases in different Member States or an out-of-court settlement in one Member State effected in parallel with a settlement before a court in another Member State. The report shall be accompanied, where appropriate, by proposals for amendments.

Article 83. (1) This Regulation shall apply to the succession of persons who die on or after 17 August 2015.
(2) Where the deceased had chosen the law applicable to his succession prior to 17 August 2015, that choice shall be valid if it meets the conditions laid down in Chapter III or if it is valid in application of the rules of private international law which were in force, at the time the choice was made, in the State in which the deceased had his habitual residence or in any of the States whose nationality he possessed.
(3) A disposition of property upon death made prior to 17 August 2015 shall be admissible and valid in substantive terms and as regards form if it meets the conditions laid down in Chapter III or if it is admissible and valid in substantive terms and as regards form in application of the rules of private international law which were in force, at the time the disposition was made, in the State in which the deceased had his habitual residence or in any of the States whose nationality he possessed or in the Member State of the authority dealing with the succession.
(4) If a disposition of property upon death was made prior to 17 August 2015 in accordance with the law which the deceased could have chosen in accordance with this Regulation, that law shall be deemed to have been chosen as the law applicable to the succession.

Article 84. This Regulation shall enter into force on the twentieth day following that of its publication in the *Official Journal of the European Union*. It shall apply from 17 August 2015, except for Articles 77 and 78, which shall apply from 16 January 2014, and Articles 79, 80 and 81, which shall apply from 5 July 2012.
This Regulation shall be binding in its entirety and directly applicable in the Member States in accordance with the Treaties.

PART II   PRIVATE INTERNATIONAL LAW

Hague Convention on the Civil Aspects of International Child Abduction (1980)

The States signatory to the present Convention,
Firmly convinced that the interests of children are of paramount importance in matters relating to their custody,
Desiring to protect children internationally from the harmful effects of their wrongful removal or retention and to establish procedures to ensure their prompt return to the State of their habitual residence, as well as to secure protection for rights of access,
Have resolved to conclude a Convention to this effect, and have agreed upon the following provisions -

Chapter I. Scope of the Convention

Article 1. The objects of the present Convention are -
(a) to secure the prompt return of children wrongfully removed to or retained in any Contracting State; and
(b) to ensure that rights of custody and of access under the law of one Contracting State are effectively respected in the other Contracting States.

Article 2. Contracting States shall take all appropriate measures to secure within their territories the implementation of the objects of the Convention. For this purpose they shall use the most expeditious procedures available.

Article 3. The removal or the retention of a child is to be considered wrongful where -
(a) it is in breach of rights of custody attributed to a person, an institution or any other body, either jointly or alone, under the law of the State in which the child was habitually resident immediately before the removal or retention; and
(b) at the time of removal or retention those rights were actually exercised, either jointly or alone, or would have been so exercised but for the removal or retention.
The rights of custody mentioned in sub-paragraph *(a)* above, may arise in particular by operation of law or by reason of a judicial or administrative decision, or by reason of an agreement having legal effect under the law of that State.

Article 4. The Convention shall apply to any child who was habitually resident in a Contracting State immediately before any breach of custody or access rights. The Convention shall cease to apply when the child attains the age of 16 years.

Article 5. For the purposes of this Convention –
(a) "rights of custody" shall include rights relating to the care of the person of the child and, in particular, the right to determine the child's place of residence;
(b) "rights of access" shall include the right to take a child for a limited period of time to a place other than the child's habitual residence.

Chapter II. Central Authorities

Article 6. A Contracting State shall designate a Central Authority to discharge the duties which are imposed by the Convention upon such authorities.
Federal States, States with more than one system of law or States having autonomous territorial organisations shall be free to appoint more than one Central Authority and to specify the territorial extent of their powers. Where a State has appointed more than one Central Authority, it shall designate the Central Authority to which applications may be addressed for transmission to the appropriate Central Authority within that State.

Article 7. Central Authorities shall co-operate with each other and promote co-operation amongst the competent authorities in their respective States to secure the prompt return of children and to achieve the other objects of this Convention.
In particular, either directly or through any intermediary, they shall take all appropriate measures -
(a) to discover the whereabouts of a child who has been wrongfully removed or retained;
(b) to prevent further harm to the child or prejudice to interested parties by taking or causing to be taken provisional measures;
(c) to secure the voluntary return of the child or to bring about an amicable resolution of the issues;
(d) to exchange, where desirable, information relating to the social background of the child;
(e) to provide information of a general character as to the law of their State in connection with the application of the Convention;

(f) to initiate or facilitate the institution of judicial or administrative proceedings with a view to obtaining the return of the child and, in a proper case, to make arrangements for organising or securing the effective exercise of rights of access;
(g) where the circumstances so require, to provide or facilitate the provision of legal aid and advice, including the participation of legal counsel and advisers;
(h) to provide such administrative arrangements as may be necessary and appropriate to secure the safe return of the child;
(i) to keep each other informed with respect to the operation of this Convention and, as far as possible, to eliminate any obstacles to its application.

Chapter III. Return of Children

Article 8. Any person, institution or other body claiming that a child has been removed or retained in breach of custody rights may apply either to the Central Authority of the child's habitual residence or to the Central Authority of any other Contracting State for assistance in securing the return of the child.
The application shall contain -
(a) information concerning the identity of the applicant, of the child and of the person alleged to have removed or retained the child;
(b) where available, the date of birth of the child;
(c) the grounds on which the applicant's claim for return of the child is based;
(d) all available information relating to the whereabouts of the child and the identity of the person with whom the child is presumed to be.
The application may be accompanied or supplemented by -
(e) an authenticated copy of any relevant decision or agreement;
(f) a certificate or an affidavit emanating from a Central Authority, or other competent authority of the State of the child's habitual residence, or from a qualified person, concerning the relevant law of that State;
(g) any other relevant document.

Article 9. If the Central Authority which receives an application referred to in Article 8 has reason to believe that the child is in another Contracting State, it shall directly and without delay transmit the application to the Central Authority of that Contracting State and inform the requesting Central Authority, or the applicant, as the case may be.

Article 10. The Central Authority of the State where the child is shall take or cause to be taken all appropriate measures in order to obtain the voluntary return of the child.

Article 11. The judicial or administrative authorities of Contracting States shall act expeditiously in proceedings for the return of children.
If the judicial or administrative authority concerned has not reached a decision within six weeks from the date of commencement of the proceedings, the applicant or the Central Authority of the requested State, on its own initiative or if asked by the Central Authority of the requesting State, shall have the right to request a statement of the reasons for the delay. If a reply is received by the Central Authority of the requested State, that Authority shall transmit the reply to the Central Authority of the requesting State, or to the applicant, as the case may be.

Article 12. Where a child has been wrongfully removed or retained in terms of Article 3 and, at the date of the commencement of the proceedings before the judicial or administrative authority of the Contracting State where the child is, a period of less than one year has elapsed from the date of the wrongful removal or retention, the authority concerned shall order the return of the child forthwith.
The judicial or administrative authority, even where the proceedings have been commenced after the expiration of the period of one year referred to in the preceding paragraph, shall also order the return of the child, unless it is demonstrated that the child is now settled in its new environment.
Where the judicial or administrative authority in the requested State has reason to believe that the child has been taken to another State, it may stay the proceedings or dismiss the application for the return of the child.

Article 13. Notwithstanding the provisions of the preceding Article, the judicial or administrative authority of the requested State is not bound to order the return of the child if the person, institution or other body which opposes its return establishes that -
(a) the person, institution or other body having the care of the person of the child was not actually exercising the custody rights at the time of removal or retention, or had consented to or subsequently

PART II PRIVATE INTERNATIONAL LAW

acquiesced in the removal or retention; or

(b) there is a grave risk that his or her return would expose the child to physical or psychological harm or otherwise place the child in an intolerable situation.

The judicial or administrative authority may also refuse to order the return of the child if it finds that the child objects to being returned and has attained an age and degree of maturity at which it is appropriate to take account of its views.

In considering the circumstances referred to in this Article, the judicial and administrative authorities shall take into account the information relating to the social background of the child provided by the Central Authority or other competent authority of the child's habitual residence.

Article 14. In ascertaining whether there has been a wrongful removal or retention within the meaning of Article 3, the judicial or administrative authorities of the requested State may take notice directly of the law of, and of judicial or administrative decisions, formally recognised or not in the State of the habitual residence of the child, without recourse to the specific procedures for the proof of that law or for the recognition of foreign decisions which would otherwise be applicable.

Article 15. The judicial or administrative authorities of a Contracting State may, prior to the making of an order for the return of the child, request that the applicant obtain from the authorities of the State of the habitual residence of the child a decision or other determination that the removal or retention was wrongful within the meaning of Article 3 of the Convention, where such a decision or determination may be obtained in that State. The Central Authorities of the Contracting States shall so far as practicable assist applicants to obtain such a decision or determination.

Article 16. After receiving notice of a wrongful removal or retention of a child in the sense of Article 3, the judicial or administrative authorities of the Contracting State to which the child has been removed or in which it has been retained shall not decide on the merits of rights of custody until it has been determined that the child is not to be returned under this Convention or unless an application under this Convention is not lodged within a reasonable time following receipt of the notice.

Article 17. The sole fact that a decision relating to custody has been given in or is entitled to recognition in the requested State shall not be a ground for refusing to return a child under this Convention, but the judicial or administrative authorities of the requested State may take account of the reasons for that decision in applying this Convention.

Article 18. The provisions of this Chapter do not limit the power of a judicial or administrative authority to order the return of the child at any time.

Article 19. A decision under this Convention concerning the return of the child shall not be taken to be a determination on the merits of any custody issue.

Article 20. The return of the child under the provisions of Article 12 may be refused if this would not be permitted by the fundamental principles of the requested State relating to the protection of human rights and fundamental freedoms.

Chapter IV. Rights of Access

Article 21. An application to make arrangements for organising or securing the effective exercise of rights of access may be presented to the Central Authorities of the Contracting States in the same way as an application for the return of a child.

The Central Authorities are bound by the obligations of co-operation which are set forth in Article 7 to promote the peaceful enjoyment of access rights and the fulfilment of any conditions to which the exercise of those rights may be subject. The Central Authorities shall take steps to remove, as far as possible, all obstacles to the exercise of such rights.

The Central Authorities, either directly or through intermediaries, may initiate or assist in the institution of proceedings with a view to organising or protecting these rights and securing respect for the conditions to which the exercise of these rights may be subject.

Chapter V. General Provisions

Article 22. No security, bond or deposit, however described, shall be required to guarantee the payment of costs and expenses in the judicial or administrative proceedings falling within the scope of this Convention.

Article 23. No legalisation or similar formality may be required in the context of this Convention.

Article 24. Any application, communication or other document sent to the Central Authority of the requested State shall be in the original language, and shall be accompanied by a translation into the official language or one of the official languages of the requested State or, where that is not feasible, a translation into French or English.

However, a Contracting State may, by making a reservation in accordance with Article 42, object to the use of either French or English, but not both, in any application, communication or other document sent to its Central Authority.

Article 25. Nationals of the Contracting States and persons who are habitually resident within those States shall be entitled in matters concerned with the application of this Convention to legal aid and advice in any other Contracting State on the same conditions as if they themselves were nationals of and habitually resident in that State.

Article 26. Each Central Authority shall bear its own costs in applying this Convention.

Central Authorities and other public services of Contracting States shall not impose any charges in relation to applications submitted under this Convention. In particular, they may not require any payment from the applicant towards the costs and expenses of the proceedings or, where applicable, those arising from the participation of legal counsel or advisers. However, they may require the payment of the expenses incurred or to be incurred in implementing the return of the child.

However, a Contracting State may, by making a reservation in accordance with Article 42, declare that it shall not be bound to assume any costs referred to in the preceding paragraph resulting from the participation of legal counsel or advisers or from court proceedings, except insofar as those costs may be covered by its system of legal aid and advice.

Upon ordering the return of a child or issuing an order concerning rights of access under this Convention, the judicial or administrative authorities may, where appropriate, direct the person who removed or retained the child, or who prevented the exercise of rights of access, to pay necessary expenses incurred by or on behalf of the applicant, including travel expenses, any costs incurred or payments made for locating the child, the costs of legal representation of the applicant, and those of returning the child.

Article 27. When it is manifest that the requirements of this Convention are not fulfilled or that the application is otherwise not well founded, a Central Authority is not bound to accept the application. In that case, the Central Authority shall forthwith inform the applicant or the Central Authority through which the application was submitted, as the case may be, of its reasons.

Article 28. A Central Authority may require that the application be accompanied by a written authorisation empowering it to act on behalf of the applicant, or to designate a representative so to act.

Article 29. This Convention shall not preclude any person, institution or body who claims that there has been a breach of custody or access rights within the meaning of Article 3 or 21 from applying directly to the judicial or administrative authorities of a Contracting State, whether or not under the provisions of this Convention.

Article 30. Any application submitted to the Central Authorities or directly to the judicial or administrative authorities of a Contracting State in accordance with the terms of this Convention, together with documents and any other information appended thereto or provided by a Central Authority, shall be admissible in the courts or administrative authorities of the Contracting States.

Article 31. In relation to a State which in matters of custody of children has two or more systems of law applicable in different territorial units -
(a) any reference to habitual residence in that State shall be construed as referring to habitual residence in a territorial unit of that State;
(b) any reference to the law of the State of habitual residence shall be construed as referring to the law of the territorial unit in that State where the child habitually resides.

Article 32. In relation to a State which in matters of custody of children has two or more systems of law applicable to different categories of persons, any reference to the law of that State shall be construed as referring to the legal system specified by the law of that State.

Article 33. A State within which different territorial units have their own rules of law in respect of custody of children shall not be bound to apply this Convention where a State with a unified system of law would not be bound to do so.

Article 34. This Convention shall take priority in matters within its scope over the *Convention of 5*

PART II PRIVATE INTERNATIONAL LAW

October 1961 concerning the powers of authorities and the law applicable in respect of the protection of minors, as between Parties to both Conventions. Otherwise the present Convention shall not restrict the application of an international instrument in force between the State of origin and the State addressed or other law of the State addressed for the purposes of obtaining the return of a child who has been wrongfully removed or retained or of organising access rights.

Article 35. This Convention shall apply as between Contracting States only to wrongful removals or retentions occurring after its entry into force in those States.

Where a declaration has been made under Article 39 or 40, the reference in the preceding paragraph to a Contracting State shall be taken to refer to the territorial unit or units in relation to which this Convention applies.

Article 36. Nothing in this Convention shall prevent two or more Contracting States, in order to limit the restrictions to which the return of the child may be subject, from agreeing among themselves to derogate from any provisions of this Convention which may imply such a restriction.

Chapter VI. Final Clauses

Article 37. The Convention shall be open for signature by the States which were Members of the Hague Conference on Private International Law at the time of its Fourteenth Session.

It shall be ratified, accepted or approved and the instruments of ratification, acceptance or approval shall be deposited with the Ministry of Foreign Affairs of the Kingdom of the Netherlands.

Article 38. Any other State may accede to the Convention.

The instrument of accession shall be deposited with the Ministry of Foreign Affairs of the Kingdom of the Netherlands.

The Convention shall enter into force for a State acceding to it on the first day of the third calendar month after the deposit of its instrument of accession.

The accession will have effect only as regards the relations between the acceding State and such Contracting States as will have declared their acceptance of the accession. Such a declaration will also have to be made by any Member State ratifying, accepting or approving the Convention after an accession. Such declaration shall be deposited at the Ministry of Foreign Affairs of the Kingdom of the Netherlands; this Ministry shall forward, through diplomatic channels, a certified copy to each of the Contracting States.

The Convention will enter into force as between the acceding State and the State that has declared its acceptance of the accession on the first day of the third calendar month after the deposit of the declaration of acceptance.

Article 39. Any State may, at the time of signature, ratification, acceptance, approval or accession, declare that the Convention shall extend to all the territories for the international relations of which it is responsible, or to one or more of them. Such a declaration shall take effect at the time the Convention enters into force for that State.

Such declaration, as well as any subsequent extension, shall be notified to the Ministry of Foreign Affairs of the Kingdom of the Netherlands.

Article 40. If a Contracting State has two or more territorial units in which different systems of law are applicable in relation to matters dealt with in this Convention, it may at the time of signature, ratification, acceptance, approval or accession declare that this Convention shall extend to all its territorial units or only to one or more of them and may modify this declaration by submitting another declaration at any time.

Any such declaration shall be notified to the Ministry of Foreign Affairs of the Kingdom of the Netherlands and shall state expressly the territorial units to which the Convention applies.

Article 41. Where a Contracting State has a system of government under which executive, judicial and legislative powers are distributed between central and other authorities within that State, its signature or ratification, acceptance or approval of, or accession to this Convention, or its making of any declaration in terms of Article 40 shall carry no implication as to the internal distribution of powers within that State.

Article 42. Any State may, not later than the time of ratification, acceptance, approval or accession, or at the time of making a declaration in terms of Article 39 or 40, make one or both of the reservations provided for in Article 24 and Article 26, third paragraph. No other reservation shall be permitted.

Any State may at any time withdraw a reservation it has made. The withdrawal shall be notified to

the Ministry of Foreign Affairs of the Kingdom of the Netherlands.
The reservation shall cease to have effect on the first day of the third calendar month after the notification referred to in the preceding paragraph.

Article 43. The Convention shall enter into force on the first day of the third calendar month after the deposit of the third instrument of ratification, acceptance, approval or accession referred to in Articles 37 and 38.
Thereafter the Convention shall enter into force -
(1) for each State ratifying, accepting, approving or acceding to it subsequently, on the first day of the third calendar month after the deposit of its instrument of ratification, acceptance, approval or accession;
(2) for any territory or territorial unit to which the Convention has been extended in conformity with Article 39 or 40, on the first day of the third calendar month after the notification referred to in that Article.

Article 44. The Convention shall remain in force for five years from the date of its entry into force in accordance with the first paragraph of Article 43 even for States which subsequently have ratified, accepted, approved it or acceded to it.
If there has been no denunciation, it shall be renewed tacitly every five years.
Any denunciation shall be notified to the Ministry of Foreign Affairs of the Kingdom of the Netherlands at least six months before the expiry of the five year period. It may be limited to certain of the territories or territorial units to which the Convention applies.
The denunciation shall have effect only as regards the State which has notified it. The Convention shall remain in force for the other Contracting States.

Article 45. The Ministry of Foreign Affairs of the Kingdom of the Netherlands shall notify the States Members of the Conference, and the States which have acceded in accordance with Article 38, of the following -
(1) the signatures and ratifications, acceptances and approvals referred to in Article 37;
(2) the accessions referred to in Article 38;
(3) the date on which the Convention enters into force in accordance with Article 43;
(4) the extensions referred to in Article 39;
(5) the declarations referred to in Articles 38 and 40;
(6) the reservations referred to in Article 24 and Article 26, third paragraph, and the withdrawals referred to in Article 42;
(7) the denunciations referred to in Article 44.

In witness whereof the undersigned, being duly authorised thereto, have signed this Convention.
Done at The Hague, on the 25th day of October, 1980, in the English and French languages, both texts being equally authentic, in a single copy which shall be deposited in the archives of the Government of the Kingdom of the Netherlands, and of which a certified copy shall be sent, through diplomatic channels, to each of the States Members of the Hague Conference on Private International Law at the date of its Fourteenth Session.

PART II   PRIVATE INTERNATIONAL LAW

Hague Convention on Jurisdiction, Applicable Law, Recognition, Enforcement and Co-Operation in respect of Parental Responsibility and Measures for the Protection of Children (1996)

The States signatory to the present Convention,
Considering the need to improve the protection of children in international situations,
Wishing to avoid conflicts between their legal systems in respect of jurisdiction, applicable law, recognition and enforcement of measures for the protection of children,
Recalling the importance of international co-operation for the protection of children,
Confirming that the best interests of the child are to be a primary consideration,
Noting that the Convention of 5 October 1961 concerning the powers of authorities and the law applicable in respect of the protection of minors is in need of revision,
Desiring to establish common provisions to this effect, taking into account the United Nations Convention on the Rights of the Child of 20 November 1989,
Have agreed on the following provisions -

Chapter I. Scope of the Convention

Article 1. (1) The objects of the present Convention are -
(a) to determine the State whose authorities have jurisdiction to take measures directed to the protection of the person or property of the child;
(b) to determine which law is to be applied by such authorities in exercising their jurisdiction;
(c) to determine the law applicable to parental responsibility;
(d) to provide for the recognition and enforcement of such measures of protection in all Contracting States;
(e) to establish such co-operation between the authorities of the Contracting States as may be necessary in order to achieve the purposes of this Convention.
(2) For the purposes of this Convention, the term 'parental responsibility' includes parental authority, or any analogous relationship of authority determining the rights, powers and responsibilities of parents, guardians or other legal representatives in relation to the person or the property of the child.

Article 2. The Convention applies to children from the moment of their birth until they reach the age of 18 years.

Article 3. The measures referred to in Article 1 may deal in particular with -
(a) the attribution, exercise, termination or restriction of parental responsibility, as well as its delegation;
(b) rights of custody, including rights relating to the care of the person of the child and, in particular, the right to determine the child's place of residence, as well as rights of access including the right to take a child for a limited period of time to a place other than the child's habitual residence;
(c) guardianship, curatorship and analogous institutions;
(d) the designation and functions of any person or body having charge of the child's person or property, representing or assisting the child;
(e) the placement of the child in a foster family or in institutional care, or the provision of care by *kafala* or an analogous institution;
(f) the supervision by a public authority of the care of a child by any person having charge of the child;
(g) the administration, conservation or disposal of the child's property.

Article 4. The Convention does not apply to -
(a) the establishment or contesting of a parent-child relationship;
(b) decisions on adoption, measures preparatory to adoption, or the annulment or revocation of adoption;
(c) the name and forenames of the child;
(d) emancipation;
(e) maintenance obligations;
(f) trusts or succession;
(g) social security;
(h) public measures of a general nature in matters of education or health;
(i) measures taken as a result of penal offences committed by children;
(j) decisions on the right of asylum and on immigration.

Chapter II. Jurisdiction

Article 5. (1) The judicial or administrative authorities of the Contracting State of the habitual residence of the child have jurisdiction to take measures directed to the protection of the child's person or property.
(2) Subject to Article 7, in case of a change of the child's habitual residence to another Contracting State, the authorities of the State of the new habitual residence have jurisdiction.

Article 6. (1) For refugee children and children who, due to disturbances occurring in their country, are internationally displaced, the authorities of the Contracting State on the territory of which these children are present as a result of their displacement have the jurisdiction provided for in paragraph 1 of Article 5.
(2) The provisions of the preceding paragraph also apply to children whose habitual residence cannot be established.

Article 7. (1) In case of wrongful removal or retention of the child, the authorities of the Contracting State in which the child was habitually resident immediately before the removal or retention keep their jurisdiction until the child has acquired a habitual residence in another State, and
(a) each person, institution or other body having rights of custody has acquiesced in the removal or retention; or
(b) the child has resided in that other State for a period of at least one year after the person, institution or other body having rights of custody has or should have had knowledge of the whereabouts of the child, no request for return lodged within that period is still pending, and the child is settled in his or her new environment.
(2) The removal or the retention of a child is to be considered wrongful where -
(a) it is in breach of rights of custody attributed to a person, an institution or any other body, either jointly or alone, under the law of the State in which the child was habitually resident immediately before the removal or retention; and
(b) at the time of removal or retention those rights were actually exercised, either jointly or alone, or would have been so exercised but for the removal or retention.
The rights of custody mentioned in sub-paragraph *a* above, may arise in particular by operation of law or by reason of a judicial or administrative decision, or by reason of an agreement having legal effect under the law of that State.
(3) So long as the authorities first mentioned in paragraph 1 keep their jurisdiction, the authorities of the Contracting State to which the child has been removed or in which he or she has been retained can take only such urgent measures under Article 11 as are necessary for the protection of the person or property of the child.

Article 8. (1) By way of exception, the authority of a Contracting State having jurisdiction under Article 5 or 6, if it considers that the authority of another Contracting State would be better placed in the particular case to assess the best interests of the child, may either
- request that other authority, directly or with the assistance of the Central Authority of its State, to assume jurisdiction to take such measures of protection as it considers to be necessary, or
- suspend consideration of the case and invite the parties to introduce such a request before the authority of that other State.
(2) The Contracting States whose authorities may be addressed as provided in the preceding paragraph are
(a) a State of which the child is a national,
(b) a State in which property of the child is located,
(c) a State whose authorities are seised of an application for divorce or legal separation of the child's parents, or for annulment of their marriage,
(d) a State with which the child has a substantial connection.
(3) The authorities concerned may proceed to an exchange of views.
(4) The authority addressed as provided in paragraph 1 may assume jurisdiction, in place of the authority having jurisdiction under Article 5 or 6, if it considers that this is in the child's best interests.

Article 9. (1) If the authorities of a Contracting State referred to in Article 8, paragraph 2, consider that they are better placed in the particular case to assess the child's best interests, they may either
- request the competent authority of the Contracting State of the habitual residence of the child, directly or with the assistance of the Central Authority of that State, that they be authorised to exercise jurisdiction to take the measures of protection which they consider to be necessary, or

PART II   PRIVATE INTERNATIONAL LAW

- invite the parties to introduce such a request before the authority of the Contracting State of the habitual residence of the child.
(2) The authorities concerned may proceed to an exchange of views.
(3) The authority initiating the request may exercise jurisdiction in place of the authority of the Contracting State of the habitual residence of the child only if the latter authority has accepted the request.

Article 10. (1) Without prejudice to Articles 5 to 9, the authorities of a Contracting State exercising jurisdiction to decide upon an application for divorce or legal separation of the parents of a child habitually resident in another Contracting State, or for annulment of their marriage, may, if the law of their State so provides, take measures directed to the protection of the person or property of such child if
(a) at the time of commencement of the proceedings, one of his or her parents habitually resides in that State and one of them has parental responsibility in relation to the child, and
(b) the jurisdiction of these authorities to take such measures has been accepted by the parents, as well as by any other person who has parental responsibility in relation to the child, and is in the best interests of the child.
(2) The jurisdiction provided for by paragraph 1 to take measures for the protection of the child ceases as soon as the decision allowing or refusing the application for divorce, legal separation or annulment of the marriage has become final, or the proceedings have come to an end for another reason.

Article 11. (1) In all cases of urgency, the authorities of any Contracting State in whose territory the child or property belonging to the child is present have jurisdiction to take any necessary measures of protection.
(2) The measures taken under the preceding paragraph with regard to a child habitually resident in a Contracting State shall lapse as soon as the authorities which have jurisdiction under Articles 5 to 10 have taken the measures required by the situation.
(3) The measures taken under paragraph 1 with regard to a child who is habitually resident in a non-Contracting State shall lapse in each Contracting State as soon as measures required by the situation and taken by the authorities of another State are recognised in the Contracting State in question.

Article 12. (1) Subject to Article 7, the authorities of a Contracting State in whose territory the child or property belonging to the child is present have jurisdiction to take measures of a provisional character for the protection of the person or property of the child which have a territorial effect limited to the State in question, in so far as such measures are not incompatible with measures already taken by authorities which have jurisdiction under Articles 5 to 10.
(2) The measures taken under the preceding paragraph with regard to a child habitually resident in a Contracting State shall lapse as soon as the authorities which have jurisdiction under Articles 5 to 10 have taken a decision in respect of the measures of protection which may be required by the situation.
(3) The measures taken under paragraph 1 with regard to a child who is habitually resident in a non-Contracting State shall lapse in the Contracting State where the measures were taken as soon as measures required by the situation and taken by the authorities of another State are recognised in the Contracting State in question.

Article 13. (1) The authorities of a Contracting State which have jurisdiction under Articles 5 to 10 to take measures for the protection of the person or property of the child must abstain from exercising this jurisdiction if, at the time of the commencement of the proceedings, corresponding measures have been requested from the authorities of another Contracting State having jurisdiction under Articles 5 to 10 at the time of the request and are still under consideration.
(2) The provisions of the preceding paragraph shall not apply if the authorities before whom the request for measures was initially introduced have declined jurisdiction.

Article 14. The measures taken in application of Articles 5 to 10 remain in force according to their terms, even if a change of circumstances has eliminated the basis upon which jurisdiction was founded, so long as the authorities which have jurisdiction under the Convention have not modified, replaced or terminated such measures.

Chapter III. Applicable Law

Article 15. (1) In exercising their jurisdiction under the provisions of Chapter II, the authorities of the Contracting States shall apply their own law.
(2) However, in so far as the protection of the person or the property of the child requires, they may

exceptionally apply or take into consideration the law of another State with which the situation has a substantial connection.
(3) If the child's habitual residence changes to another Contracting State, the law of that other State governs, from the time of the change, the conditions of application of the measures taken in the State of the former habitual residence.

Article 16. (1) The attribution or extinction of parental responsibility by operation of law, without the intervention of a judicial or administrative authority, is governed by the law of the State of the habitual residence of the child.
(2) The attribution or extinction of parental responsibility by an agreement or a unilateral act, without intervention of a judicial or administrative authority, is governed by the law of the State of the child's habitual residence at the time when the agreement or unilateral act takes effect.
(3) Parental responsibility which exists under the law of the State of the child's habitual residence subsists after a change of that habitual residence to another State.
(4) If the child's habitual residence changes, the attribution of parental responsibility by operation of law to a person who does not already have such responsibility is governed by the law of the State of the new habitual residence.

Article 17. The exercise of parental responsibility is governed by the law of the State of the child's habitual residence. If the child's habitual residence changes, it is governed by the law of the State of the new habitual residence.

Article 18. The parental responsibility referred to in Article 16 may be terminated, or the conditions of its exercise modified, by measures taken under this Convention.

Article 19. (1) The validity of a transaction entered into between a third party and another person who would be entitled to act as the child's legal representative under the law of the State where the transaction was concluded cannot be contested, and the third party cannot be held liable, on the sole ground that the other person was not entitled to act as the child's legal representative under the law designated by the provisions of this Chapter, unless the third party knew or should have known that the parental responsibility was governed by the latter law.
(2) The preceding paragraph applies only if the transaction was entered into between persons present on the territory of the same State.

Article 20. The provisions of this Chapter apply even if the law designated by them is the law of a non-Contracting State.

Article 21. (1) In this Chapter the term "law" means the law in force in a State other than its choice of law rules.
(2) However, if the law applicable according to Article 16 is that of a non-Contracting State and if the choice of law rules of that State designate the law of another non-Contracting State which would apply its own law, the law of the latter State applies. If that other non-Contracting State would not apply its own law, the applicable law is that designated by Article 16.

Article 22. The application of the law designated by the provisions of this Chapter can be refused only if this application would be manifestly contrary to public policy, taking into account the best interests of the child.

Chapter IV Recognition and Enforcement

Article 23. (1) The measures taken by the authorities of a Contracting State shall be recognised by operation of law in all other Contracting States.
(2) Recognition may however be refused -
(a) if the measure was taken by an authority whose jurisdiction was not based on one of the grounds provided for in Chapter II;
(b) if the measure was taken, except in a case of urgency, in the context of a judicial or administrative proceeding, without the child having been provided the opportunity to be heard, in violation of fundamental principles of procedure of the requested State;
(c) on the request of any person claiming that the measure infringes his or her parental responsibility, if such measure was taken, except in a case of urgency, without such person having been given an opportunity to be heard;
(d) if such recognition is manifestly contrary to public policy of the requested State, taking into account the best interests of the child;
(e) if the measure is incompatible with a later measure taken in the non-Contracting State of the

habitual residence of the child, where this later measure fulfils the requirements for recognition in the requested State;
(f) if the procedure provided in Article 33 has not been complied with.

Article 24. Without prejudice to Article 23, paragraph 1, any interested person may request from the competent authorities of a Contracting State that they decide on the recognition or non-recognition of a measure taken in another Contracting State. The procedure is governed by the law of the requested State.

Article 25. The authority of the requested State is bound by the findings of fact on which the authority of the State where the measure was taken based its jurisdiction.

Article 26. (1) If measures taken in one Contracting State and enforceable there require enforcement in another Contracting State, they shall, upon request by an interested party, be declared enforceable or registered for the purpose of enforcement in that other State according to the procedure provided in the law of the latter State.
(2) Each Contracting State shall apply to the declaration of enforceability or registration a simple and rapid procedure.
(3) The declaration of enforceability or registration may be refused only for one of the reasons set out in Article 23, paragraph 2.

Article 27. Without prejudice to such review as is necessary in the application of the preceding Articles, there shall be no review of the merits of the measure taken.

Article 28. Measures taken in one Contracting State and declared enforceable, or registered for the purpose of enforcement, in another Contracting State shall be enforced in the latter State as if they had been taken by the authorities of that State. Enforcement takes place in accordance with the law of the requested State to the extent provided by such law, taking into consideration the best interests of the child.

Chapter V. Co-operation

Article 29. (1) A Contracting State shall designate a Central Authority to discharge the duties which are imposed by the Convention on such authorities.
(2) Federal States, States with more than one system of law or States having autonomous territorial units shall be free to appoint more than one Central Authority and to specify the territorial or personal extent of their functions. Where a State has appointed more than one Central Authority, it shall designate the Central Authority to which any communication may be addressed for transmission to the appropriate Central Authority within that State.

Article 30. (1) Central Authorities shall co-operate with each other and promote co-operation amongst the competent authorities in their States to achieve the purposes of the Convention.
(2) They shall, in connection with the application of the Convention, take appropriate steps to provide information as to the laws of, and services available in, their States relating to the protection of children.

Article 31. The Central Authority of a Contracting State, either directly or through public authorities or other bodies, shall take all appropriate steps to -
(a) facilitate the communications and offer the assistance provided for in Articles 8 and 9 and in this Chapter;
(b) facilitate, by mediation, conciliation or similar means, agreed solutions for the protection of the person or property of the child in situations to which the Convention applies;
(c) provide, on the request of a competent authority of another Contracting State, assistance in discovering the whereabouts of a child where it appears that the child may be present and in need of protection within the territory of the requested State.

Article 32. On a request made with supporting reasons by the Central Authority or other competent authority of any Contracting State with which the child has a substantial connection, the Central Authority of the Contracting State in which the child is habitually resident and present may, directly or through public authorities or other bodies,
(a) provide a report on the situation of the child;
(b) request the competent authority of its State to consider the need to take measures for the protection of the person or property of the child.

Article 33. (1) If an authority having jurisdiction under Articles 5 to 10 contemplates the placement of the child in a foster family or institutional care, or the provision of care by *kafala* or an analogous institution, and if such placement or such provision of care is to take place in another Contracting State, it shall first consult with the Central Authority or other competent authority of the latter State. To that effect it shall transmit a report on the child together with the reasons for the proposed placement or provision of care.
(2) The decision on the placement or provision of care may be made in the requesting State only if the Central Authority or other competent authority of the requested State has consented to the placement or provision of care, taking into account the child's best interests.

Article 34. (1) Where a measure of protection is contemplated, the competent authorities under the Convention, if the situation of the child so requires, may request any authority of another Contracting State which has information relevant to the protection of the child to communicate such information.
(2) A Contracting State may declare that requests under paragraph 1 shall be communicated to its authorities only through its Central Authority.

Article 35. (1) The competent authorities of a Contracting State may request the authorities of another Contracting State to assist in the implementation of measures of protection taken under this Convention, especially in securing the effective exercise of rights of access as well as of the right to maintain direct contacts on a regular basis.
(2) The authorities of a Contracting State in which the child does not habitually reside may, on the request of a parent residing in that State who is seeking to obtain or to maintain access to the child, gather information or evidence and may make a finding on the suitability of that parent to exercise access and on the conditions under which access is to be exercised. An authority exercising jurisdiction under Articles 5 to 10 to determine an application concerning access to the child, shall admit and consider such information, evidence and finding before reaching its decision.
(3) An authority having jurisdiction under Articles 5 to 10 to decide on access may adjourn a proceeding pending the outcome of a request made under paragraph 2, in particular, when it is considering an application to restrict or terminate access rights granted in the State of the child's former habitual residence.
(4) Nothing in this Article shall prevent an authority having jurisdiction under Articles 5 to 10 from taking provisional measures pending the outcome of the request made under paragraph 2.

Article 36. In any case where the child is exposed to a serious danger, the competent authorities of the Contracting State where measures for the protection of the child have been taken or are under consideration, if they are informed that the child's residence has changed to, or that the child is present in another State, shall inform the authorities of that other State about the danger involved and the measures taken or under consideration.

Article 37. An authority shall not request or transmit any information under this Chapter if to do so would, in its opinion, be likely to place the child's person or property in danger, or constitute a serious threat to the liberty or life of a member of the child's family.

Article 38. (1) Without prejudice to the possibility of imposing reasonable charges for the provision of services, Central Authorities and other public authorities of Contracting States shall bear their own costs in applying the provisions of this Chapter.
(2) Any Contracting State may enter into agreements with one or more other Contracting States concerning the allocation of charges.

Article 39. Any Contracting State may enter into agreements with one or more other Contracting States with a view to improving the application of this Chapter in their mutual relations. The States which have concluded such an agreement shall transmit a copy to the depositary of the Convention.

Chapter VI. General Provisions

Article 40. (1) The authorities of the Contracting State of the child's habitual residence, or of the Contracting State where a measure of protection has been taken, may deliver to the person having parental responsibility or to the person entrusted with protection of the child's person or property, at his or her request, a certificate indicating the capacity in which that person is entitled to act and the powers conferred upon him or her.
(2) The capacity and powers indicated in the certificate are presumed to be vested in that person, in the absence of proof to the contrary.
(3) Each Contracting State shall designate the authorities competent to draw up the certificate.

PART II PRIVATE INTERNATIONAL LAW

Article 41. Personal data gathered or transmitted under the Convention shall be used only for the purposes for which they were gathered or transmitted.

Article 42. The authorities to whom information is transmitted shall ensure its confidentiality, in accordance with the law of their State.

Article 43. All documents forwarded or delivered under this Convention shall be exempt from legalisation or any analogous formality.

Article 44. Each Contracting State may designate the authorities to which requests under Articles 8, 9 and 33 are to be addressed.

Article 45. (1) The designations referred to in Articles 29 and 44 shall be communicated to the Permanent Bureau of the Hague Conference on Private International Law.
(2) The declaration referred to in Article 34, paragraph 2, shall be made to the depositary of the Convention.

Article 46. A Contracting State in which different systems of law or sets of rules of law apply to the protection of the child and his or her property shall not be bound to apply the rules of the Convention to conflicts solely between such different systems or sets of rules of law.

Article 47. In relation to a State in which two or more systems of law or sets of rules of law with regard to any matter dealt with in this Convention apply in different territorial units -
(1) any reference to habitual residence in that State shall be construed as referring to habitual residence in a territorial unit;
(2) any reference to the presence of the child in that State shall be construed as referring to presence in a territorial unit;
(3) any reference to the location of property of the child in that State shall be construed as referring to location of property of the child in a territorial unit;
(4) any reference to the State of which the child is a national shall be construed as referring to the territorial unit designated by the law of that State or, in the absence of relevant rules, to the territorial unit with which the child has the closest connection;
(5) any reference to the State whose authorities are seised of an application for divorce or legal separation of the child's parents, or for annulment of their marriage, shall be construed as referring to the territorial unit whose authorities are seised of such application;
(6) any reference to the State with which the child has a substantial connection shall be construed as referring to the territorial unit with which the child has such connection;
(7) any reference to the State to which the child has been removed or in which he or she has been retained shall be construed as referring to the relevant territorial unit to which the child has been removed or in which he or she has been retained;
(8) any reference to bodies or authorities of that State, other than Central Authorities, shall be construed as referring to those authorised to act in the relevant territorial unit;
(9) any reference to the law or procedure or authority of the State in which a measure has been taken shall be construed as referring to the law or procedure or authority of the territorial unit in which such measure was taken;
(10) any reference to the law or procedure or authority of the requested State shall be construed as referring to the law or procedure or authority of the territorial unit in which recognition or enforcement is sought.

Article 48. For the purpose of identifying the applicable law under Chapter III, in relation to a State which comprises two or more territorial units each of which has its own system of law or set of rules of law in respect of matters covered by this Convention, the following rules apply -
(a) if there are rules in force in such a State identifying which territorial unit's law is applicable, the law of that unit applies;
(b) in the absence of such rules, the law of the relevant territorial unit as defined in Article 47 applies.

Article 49. For the purpose of identifying the applicable law under Chapter III, in relation to a State which has two or more systems of law or sets of rules of law applicable to different categories of persons in respect of matters covered by this Convention, the following rules apply -
(a) if there are rules in force in such a State identifying which among such laws applies, that law applies;
(b) in the absence of such rules, the law of the system or the set of rules of law with which the child has the closest connection applies.

Article 50. This Convention shall not affect the application of the *Convention of 25 October 1980 on the Civil Aspects of International Child Abduction*, as between Parties to both Conventions. Nothing, however, precludes provisions of this Convention from being invoked for the purposes of obtaining the return of a child who has been wrongfully removed or retained or of organising access rights.

Article 51. In relations between the Contracting States this Convention replaces the *Convention of 5 October 1961 concerning the powers of authorities and the law applicable in respect of the protection of minors*, and the *Convention governing the guardianship of minors*, signed at The Hague 12 June 1902, without prejudice to the recognition of measures taken under the Convention of 5 October 1961 mentioned above.

Article 52. (1) This Convention does not affect any international instrument to which Contracting States are Parties and which contains provisions on matters governed by the Convention, unless a contrary declaration is made by the States Parties to such instrument.
(2) This Convention does not affect the possibility for one or more Contracting States to conclude agreements which contain, in respect of children habitually resident in any of the States Parties to such agreements, provisions on matters governed by this Convention.
(3) Agreements to be concluded by one or more Contracting States on matters within the scope of this Convention do not affect, in the relationship of such States with other Contracting States, the application of the provisions of this Convention.
(4) The preceding paragraphs also apply to uniform laws based on special ties of a regional or other nature between the States concerned.

Article 53. (1) The Convention shall apply to measures only if they are taken in a State after the Convention has entered into force for that State.
(2) The Convention shall apply to the recognition and enforcement of measures taken after its entry into force as between the State where the measures have been taken and the requested State.
Article 54
(1) Any communication sent to the Central Authority or to another authority of a Contracting State shall be in the original language, and shall be accompanied by a translation into the official language or one of the official languages of the other State or, where that is not feasible, a translation into French or English.
(2) However, a Contracting State may, by making a reservation in accordance with Article 60, object to the use of either French or English, but not both.
Article 55
(1) A Contracting State may, in accordance with Article 60,
(a) reserve the jurisdiction of its authorities to take measures directed to the protection of property of a child situated on its territory;
(b) reserve the right not to recognise any parental responsibility or measure in so far as it is incompatible with any measure taken by its authorities in relation to that property.
(2) The reservation may be restricted to certain categories of property.
Article 56
The Secretary General of the Hague Conference on Private International Law shall at regular intervals convoke a Special Commission in order to review the practical operation of the Convention.

Chapter VII. Final Clauses

Article 57. (1) The Convention shall be open for signature by the States which were Members of the Hague Conference on Private International Law at the time of its Eighteenth Session.
(2) It shall be ratified, accepted or approved and the instruments of ratification, acceptance or approval shall be deposited with the Ministry of Foreign Affairs of the Kingdom of the Netherlands, depositary of the Convention.

Article 58. (1) Any other State may accede to the Convention after it has entered into force in accordance with Article 61, paragraph 1.
(2) The instrument of accession shall be deposited with the depositary.
(3) Such accession shall have effect only as regards the relations between the acceding State and those Contracting States which have not raised an objection to its accession in the six months after the receipt of the notification referred to in sub-paragraph *b* of Article 63. Such an objection may also be raised by States at the time when they ratify, accept or approve the Convention after an accession. Any such objection shall be notified to the depositary.

PART II PRIVATE INTERNATIONAL LAW

Article 59. (1) If a State has two or more territorial units in which different systems of law are applicable in relation to matters dealt with in this Convention, it may at the time of signature, ratification, acceptance, approval or accession declare that the Convention shall extend to all its territorial units or only to one or more of them and may modify this declaration by submitting another declaration at any time.
(2) Any such declaration shall be notified to the depositary and shall state expressly the territorial units to which the Convention applies.
(3) If a State makes no declaration under this Article, the Convention is to extend to all territorial units of that State.

Article 60. (1) Any State may, not later than the time of ratification, acceptance, approval or accession, or at the time of making a declaration in terms of Article 59, make one or both of the reservations provided for in Articles 54, paragraph 2, and 55. No other reservation shall be permitted.
(2) Any State may at any time withdraw a reservation it has made. The withdrawal shall be notified to the depositary.
(3) The reservation shall cease to have effect on the first day of the third calendar month after the notification referred to in the preceding paragraph.

Article 61. (1) The Convention shall enter into force on the first day of the month following the expiration of three months after the deposit of the third instrument of ratification, acceptance or approval referred to in Article 57.
(2) Thereafter the Convention shall enter into force -
(a) for each State ratifying, accepting or approving it subsequently, on the first day of the month following the expiration of three months after the deposit of its instrument of ratification, acceptance, approval or accession;
(b) for each State acceding, on the first day of the month following the expiration of three months after the expiration of the period of six months provided in Article 58, paragraph 3;
(c) for a territorial unit to which the Convention has been extended in conformity with Article 59, on the first day of the month following the expiration of three months after the notification referred to in that Article.

Article 62. (1) A State Party to the Convention may denounce it by a notification in writing addressed to the depositary. The denunciation may be limited to certain territorial units to which the Convention applies.
(2) The denunciation takes effect on the first day of the month following the expiration of twelve months after the notification is received by the depositary. Where a longer period for the denunciation to take effect is specified in the notification, the denunciation takes effect upon the expiration of such longer period.

Article 63. The depositary shall notify the States Members of the Hague Conference on Private International Law and the States which have acceded in accordance with Article 58 of the following -
(a) the signatures, ratifications, acceptances and approvals referred to in Article 57;
(b) the accessions and objections raised to accessions referred to in Article 58;
(c) the date on which the Convention enters into force in accordance with Article 61;
(d) the declarations referred to in Articles 34, paragraph 2, and 59;
(e) the agreements referred to in Article 39;
(f) the reservations referred to in Articles 54, paragraph 2, and 55 and the withdrawals referred to in Article 60, paragraph 2;
(g) the denunciations referred to in Article 62.

In witness whereof the undersigned, being duly authorised thereto, have signed this Convention.
Done at The Hague, on the 19th day of October 1996, in the English and French languages, both texts being equally authentic, in a single copy which shall be deposited in the archives of the Government of the Kingdom of the Netherlands, and of which a certified copy shall be sent, through diplomatic channels, to each of the States Members of the Hague Conference on Private International Law at the date of its Eighteenth Session.

Hague Convention on Choice of Court Agreements (2005)

The States Parties to the present Convention,
Desiring to promote international trade and investment through enhanced judicial co-operation,
Believing that such co-operation can be enhanced by uniform rules on jurisdiction and on recognition and enforcement of foreign judgments in civil or commercial matters,
Believing that such enhanced co-operation requires in particular an international legal regime that provides certainty and ensures the effectiveness of exclusive choice of court agreements between parties to commercial transactions and that governs the recognition and enforcement of judgments resulting from proceedings based on such agreements,
Have resolved to conclude this Convention and have agreed upon the following provisions -

Chapter I. Scope and Definitions

Article 1. Scope. (1) This Convention shall apply in international cases to exclusive choice of court agreements concluded in civil or commercial matters.
(2) For the purposes of Chapter II, a case is international unless the parties are resident in the same Contracting State and the relationship of the parties and all other elements relevant to the dispute, regardless of the location of the chosen court, are connected only with that State.
(3) For the purposes of Chapter III, a case is international where recognition or enforcement of a foreign judgment is sought.

Article 2. Exclusions from scope. (1) This Convention shall not apply to exclusive choice of court agreements -
(a) to which a natural person acting primarily for personal, family or household purposes (a consumer) is a party;
(b) relating to contracts of employment, including collective agreements.
(2) This Convention shall not apply to the following matters -
(a) the status and legal capacity of natural persons;
(b) maintenance obligations;
(c) other family law matters, including matrimonial property regimes and other rights or obligations arising out of marriage or similar relationships;
(d) wills and succession;
(e) insolvency, composition and analogous matters;
((f) the carriage of passengers and goods;
(g) marine pollution, limitation of liability for maritime claims, general average, and emergency towage and salvage;
(h) anti-trust (competition) matters;
(i) liability for nuclear damage;
(j) claims for personal injury brought by or on behalf of natural persons;
(k) tort or delict claims for damage to tangible property that do not arise from a contractual relationship;
(l) rights in rem in immovable property, and tenancies of immovable property;
(m) the validity, nullity, or dissolution of legal persons, and the validity of decisions of their organs;
(n) the validity of intellectual property rights other than copyright and related rights;
(o) infringement of intellectual property rights other than copyright and related rights, except where infringement proceedings are brought for breach of a contract between the parties relating to such rights, or could have been brought for breach of that contract;
(p) the validity of entries in public registers.
(3) Notwithstanding paragraph 2, proceedings are not excluded from the scope of this Convention where a matter excluded under that paragraph arises merely as a preliminary question and not as an object of the proceedings. In particular, the mere fact that a matter excluded under paragraph 2 arises by way of defence does not exclude proceedings from the Convention, if that matter is not an object of the proceedings.
(4) This Convention shall not apply to arbitration and related proceedings.
(5) Proceedings are not excluded from the scope of this Convention by the mere fact that a State, including a government, a governmental agency or any person acting for a State, is a party thereto.
(6) Nothing in this Convention shall affect privileges and immunities of States or of international organisations, in respect of themselves and of their property.

Article 3. Exclusive choice of court agreements. For the purposes of this Convention -
(a) "exclusive choice of court agreement" means an agreement concluded by two or more parties that

PART II PRIVATE INTERNATIONAL LAW

meets the requirements of paragraph (c) and designates, for the purpose of deciding disputes which have arisen or may arise in connection with a particular legal relationship, the courts of one Contracting State or one or more specific courts of one Contracting State to the exclusion of the jurisdiction of any other courts;
(b) a choice of court agreement which designates the courts of one Contracting State or one or more specific courts of one Contracting State shall be deemed to be exclusive unless the parties have expressly provided otherwise;
(c) an exclusive choice of court agreement must be concluded or documented -
(i) in writing; or
(ii) by any other means of communication which renders information accessible so as to be usable for subsequent reference;
(d) an exclusive choice of court agreement that forms part of a contract shall be treated as an agreement independent of the other terms of the contract. The validity of the exclusive choice of court agreement cannot be contested solely on the ground that the contract is not valid.

Article 4. Other definitions. (1) In this Convention, "judgment" means any decision on the merits given by a court, whatever it may be called, including a decree or order, and a determination of costs or expenses by the court (including an officer of the court), provided that the determination relates to a decision on the merits which may be recognised or enforced under this Convention. An interim measure of protection is not a judgment.
(2) For the purposes of this Convention, an entity or person other than a natural person shall be considered to be resident in the State -
(a) where it has its statutory seat;
(b) under whose law it was incorporated or formed;
(c) where it has its central administration; or
(d) where it has its principal place of business.

Chapter II. Jurisdiction

Article 5. Jurisdiction of the chosen court. (1) The court or courts of a Contracting State designated in an exclusive choice of court agreement shall have jurisdiction to decide a dispute to which the agreement applies, unless the agreement is null and void under the law of that State.
(2) A court that has jurisdiction under paragraph 1 shall not decline to exercise jurisdiction on the ground that the dispute should be decided in a court of another State.
(3) The preceding paragraphs shall not affect rules -
(a) on jurisdiction related to subject matter or to the value of the claim;
(b) on the internal allocation of jurisdiction among the courts of a Contracting State. However, where the chosen court has discretion as to whether to transfer a case, due consideration should be given to the choice of the parties.

Article 6. Obligations of a court not chosen. A court of a Contracting State other than that of the chosen court shall suspend or dismiss proceedings to which an exclusive choice of court agreement applies unless -
(a) the agreement is null and void under the law of the State of the chosen court;
(b) a party lacked the capacity to conclude the agreement under the law of the State of the court seised;
(c) giving effect to the agreement would lead to a manifest injustice or would be manifestly contrary to the public policy of the State of the court seised;
(d) for exceptional reasons beyond the control of the parties, the agreement cannot reasonably be performed; or
(e) the chosen court has decided not to hear the case.

Article 7. Interim measures of protection. Interim measures of protection are not governed by this Convention. This Convention neither requires nor precludes the grant, refusal or termination of interim measures of protection by a court of a Contracting State and does not affect whether or not a party may request or a court should grant, refuse or terminate such measures.

Chapter III. Recognition and Enforcement

Article 8. Recognition and enforcement. (1) A judgment given by a court of a Contracting State designated in an exclusive choice of court agreement shall be recognised and enforced in other Contracting States in accordance with this Chapter. Recognition or enforcement may be refused only on the grounds specified in this Convention.

(2) Without prejudice to such review as is necessary for the application of the provisions of this Chapter, there shall be no review of the merits of the judgment given by the court of origin. The court addressed shall be bound by the findings of fact on which the court of origin based its jurisdiction, unless the judgment was given by default.
(3) A judgment shall be recognised only if it has effect in the State of origin, and shall be enforced only if it is enforceable in the State of origin.
(4) Recognition or enforcement may be postponed or refused if the judgment is the subject of review in the State of origin or if the time limit for seeking ordinary review has not expired. A refusal does not prevent a subsequent application for recognition or enforcement of the judgment.
(5) This Article shall also apply to a judgment given by a court of a Contracting State pursuant to a transfer of the case from the chosen court in that Contracting State as permitted by Article 5, paragraph 3. However, where the chosen court had discretion as to whether to transfer the case to another court, recognition or enforcement of the judgment may be refused against a party who objected to the transfer in a timely manner in the State of origin.

Article 9. Refusal of recognition or enforcement. Recognition or enforcement may be refused if -
(a) the agreement was null and void under the law of the State of the chosen court, unless the chosen court has determined that the agreement is valid;
(b) a party lacked the capacity to conclude the agreement under the law of the requested State;
(c) the document which instituted the proceedings or an equivalent document, including the essential elements of the claim,
(i) was not notified to the defendant in sufficient time and in such a way as to enable him to arrange for his defence, unless the defendant entered an appearance and presented his case without contesting notification in the court of origin, provided that the law of the State of origin permitted notification to be contested; or
(ii) was notified to the defendant in the requested State in a manner that is incompatible with fundamental principles of the requested State concerning service of documents;
(d) the judgment was obtained by fraud in connection with a matter of procedure;
(e) recognition or enforcement would be manifestly incompatible with the public policy of the requested State, including situations where the specific proceedings leading to the judgment were incompatible with fundamental principles of procedural fairness of that State;
(f) the judgment is inconsistent with a judgment given in the requested State in a dispute between the same parties; or
(g) the judgment is inconsistent with an earlier judgment given in another State between the same parties on the same cause of action, provided that the earlier judgment fulfils the conditions necessary for its recognition in the requested State.

Article 10. Preliminary questions. (1) Where a matter excluded under Article 2, paragraph 2, or under Article 21, arose as a preliminary question, the ruling on that question shall not be recognised or enforced under this Convention.
(2) Recognition or enforcement of a judgment may be refused if, and to the extent that, the judgment was based on a ruling on a matter excluded under Article 2, paragraph 2.
(3) However, in the case of a ruling on the validity of an intellectual property right other than copyright or a related right, recognition or enforcement of a judgment may be refused or postponed under the preceding paragraph only where -
(a) that ruling is inconsistent with a judgment or a decision of a competent authority on that matter given in the State under the law of which the intellectual property right arose; or
(b) proceedings concerning the validity of the intellectual property right are pending in that State.
(4) Recognition or enforcement of a judgment may be refused if, and to the extent that, the judgment was based on a ruling on a matter excluded pursuant to a declaration made by the requested State under Article 21.

Article 11. Damages. (1) Recognition or enforcement of a judgment may be refused if, and to the extent that, the judgment awards damages, including exemplary or punitive damages, that do not compensate a party for actual loss or harm suffered.
(2) The court addressed shall take into account whether and to what extent the damages awarded by the court of origin serve to cover costs and expenses relating to the proceedings.

Article 12. Judicial settlements (transactions judiciaires). Judicial settlements (transactions judiciaires) which a court of a Contracting State designated in an exclusive choice of court agreement has approved, or which have been concluded before that court in the course of proceedings, and which are enforceable in the same manner as a judgment in the State of origin, shall be enforced under this Convention in the same manner as a judgment.

PART II   PRIVATE INTERNATIONAL LAW

Article 13. Documents to be produced. (1) The party seeking recognition or applying for enforcement shall produce -
(a) a complete and certified copy of the judgment;
(b) the exclusive choice of court agreement, a certified copy thereof, or other evidence of its existence;
(c) if the judgment was given by default, the original or a certified copy of a document establishing that the document which instituted the proceedings or an equivalent document was notified to the defaulting party;
(d) any documents necessary to establish that the judgment has effect or, where applicable, is enforceable in the State of origin;
(e) in the case referred to in Article 12, a certificate of a court of the State of origin that the judicial settlement or a part of it is enforceable in the same manner as a judgment in the State of origin.
(2) If the terms of the judgment do not permit the court addressed to verify whether the conditions of this Chapter have been complied with, that court may require any necessary documents.
(3) An application for recognition or enforcement may be accompanied by a document, issued by a court (including an officer of the court) of the State of origin, in the form recommended and published by the Hague Conference on Private International Law.
(4) If the documents referred to in this Article are not in an official language of the requested State, they shall be accompanied by a certified translation into an official language, unless the law of the requested State provides otherwise.

Article 14. Procedure. The procedure for recognition, declaration of enforceability or registration for enforcement, and the enforcement of the judgment, are governed by the law of the requested State unless this Convention provides otherwise. The court addressed shall act expeditiously.

Article 15. Severability. Recognition or enforcement of a severable part of a judgment shall be granted where recognition or enforcement of that part is applied for, or only part of the judgment is capable of being recognised or enforced under this Convention.

Chapter IV. General Clauses

Article 16. Transitional provisions. (1) This Convention shall apply to exclusive choice of court agreements concluded after its entry into force for the State of the chosen court.
(2) This Convention shall not apply to proceedings instituted before its entry into force for the State of the court seised.

Article 17. Contracts of insurance and reinsurance. (1) Proceedings under a contract of insurance or reinsurance are not excluded from the scope of this Convention on the ground that the contract of insurance or reinsurance relates to a matter to which this Convention does not apply.
(2) Recognition and enforcement of a judgment in respect of liability under the terms of a contract of insurance or reinsurance may not be limited or refused on the ground that the liability under that contract includes liability to indemnify the insured or reinsured in respect of -
(a) a matter to which this Convention does not apply; or
(b) an award of damages to which Article 11 might apply.

Article 18. No legalization. All documents forwarded or delivered under this Convention shall be exempt from legalisation or any analogous formality, including an Apostille.

Article 19. Declarations limiting jurisdiction. A State may declare that its courts may refuse to determine disputes to which an exclusive choice of court agreement applies if, except for the location of the chosen court, there is no connection between that State and the parties or the dispute.

Article 20. Declarations limiting recognition and enforcement
A State may declare that its courts may refuse to recognise or enforce a judgment given by a court of another Contracting State if the parties were resident in the requested State, and the relationship of the parties and all other elements relevant to the dispute, other than the location of the chosen court, were connected only with the requested State.

Article 21. Declarations with respect to specific matters. (1) Where a State has a strong interest in not applying this Convention to a specific matter, that State may declare that it will not apply the Convention to that matter. The State making such a declaration shall ensure that the declaration is no broader than necessary and that the specific matter excluded is clearly and precisely defined.
(2) With regard to that matter, the Convention shall not apply -
(a) in the Contracting State that made the declaration;

(b) in other Contracting States, where an exclusive choice of court agreement designates the courts, or one or more specific courts, of the State that made the declaration.

Article 22. Reciprocal declarations on non-exclusive choice of court agreements. (1) A Contracting State may declare that its courts will recognise and enforce judgments given by courts of other Contracting States designated in a choice of court agreement concluded by two or more parties that meets the requirements of Article 3, paragraph (c), and designates, for the purpose of deciding disputes which have arisen or may arise in connection with a particular legal relationship, a court or courts of one or more Contracting States (a non-exclusive choice of court agreement).
(2) Where recognition or enforcement of a judgment given in a Contracting State that has made such a declaration is sought in another Contracting State that has made such a declaration, the judgment shall be recognised and enforced under this Convention, if -
(a) the court of origin was designated in a non-exclusive choice of court agreement;
(b) there exists neither a judgment given by any other court before which proceedings could be brought in accordance with the non-exclusive choice of court agreement, nor a proceeding pending between the same parties in any other such court on the same cause of action; and
(c) the court of origin was the court first seised.

Article 23. Uniform interpretation. In the interpretation of this Convention, regard shall be had to its international character and to the need to promote uniformity in its application.

Article 24. Review of operation of the Convention. The Secretary General of the Hague Conference on Private International Law shall at regular intervals make arrangements for -
(a) review of the operation of this Convention, including any declarations; and
(b) consideration of whether any amendments to this Convention are desirable.

Article 25. Non-unified legal systems. (1) In relation to a Contracting State in which two or more systems of law apply in different territorial units with regard to any matter dealt with in this Convention -
(a) any reference to the law or procedure of a State shall be construed as referring, where appropriate, to the law or procedure in force in the relevant territorial unit;
(b) any reference to residence in a State shall be construed as referring, where appropriate, to residence in the relevant territorial unit;
(c) any reference to the court or courts of a State shall be construed as referring, where appropriate, to the court or courts in the relevant territorial unit;
(d) any reference to a connection with a State shall be construed as referring, where appropriate, to a connection with the relevant territorial unit.
(2) Notwithstanding the preceding paragraph, a Contracting State with two or more territorial units in which different systems of law apply shall not be bound to apply this Convention to situations which involve solely such different territorial units.
(3) A court in a territorial unit of a Contracting State with two or more territorial units in which different systems of law apply shall not be bound to recognise or enforce a judgment from another Contracting State solely because the judgment has been recognised or enforced in another territorial unit of the same Contracting State under this Convention.
(4) This Article shall not apply to a Regional Economic Integration Organisation.

Article 26. Relationship with other international instruments. (1) This Convention shall be interpreted so far as possible to be compatible with other treaties in force for Contracting States, whether concluded before or after this Convention.
(2) This Convention shall not affect the application by a Contracting State of a treaty, whether concluded before or after this Convention, in cases where none of the parties is resident in a Contracting State that is not a Party to the treaty.
(3) This Convention shall not affect the application by a Contracting State of a treaty that was concluded before this Convention entered into force for that Contracting State, if applying this Convention would be inconsistent with the obligations of that Contracting State to any non-Contracting State. This paragraph shall also apply to treaties that revise or replace a treaty concluded before this Convention entered into force for that Contracting State, except to the extent that the revision or replacement creates new inconsistencies with this Convention.
(4) This Convention shall not affect the application by a Contracting State of a treaty, whether concluded before or after this Convention, for the purposes of obtaining recognition or enforcement of a judgment given by a court of a Contracting State that is also a Party to that treaty. However, the judgment shall not be recognised or enforced to a lesser extent than under this Convention.

PART II PRIVATE INTERNATIONAL LAW

(5) This Convention shall not affect the application by a Contracting State of a treaty which, in relation to a specific matter, governs jurisdiction or the recognition or enforcement of judgments, even if concluded after this Convention and even if all States concerned are Parties to this Convention. This paragraph shall apply only if the Contracting State has made a declaration in respect of the treaty under this paragraph. In the case of such a declaration, other Contracting States shall not be obliged to apply this Convention to that specific matter to the extent of any inconsistency, where an exclusive choice of court agreement designates the courts, or one or more specific courts, of the Contracting State that made the declaration.

(6) This Convention shall not affect the application of the rules of a Regional Economic Integration Organisation that is a Party to this Convention, whether adopted before or after this Convention -
(a) where none of the parties is resident in a Contracting State that is not a Member State of the Regional Economic Integration Organisation;
(b) as concerns the recognition or enforcement of judgments as between Member States of the Regional Economic Integration Organisation.

Chapter V. Final Clauses

Article 27. Signature, ratification, acceptance, approval or accession. (1) This Convention is open for signature by all States.
(2) This Convention is subject to ratification, acceptance or approval by the signatory States.
(3) This Convention is open for accession by all States.
(4) Instruments of ratification, acceptance, approval or accession shall be deposited with the Ministry of Foreign Affairs of the Kingdom of the Netherlands, depositary of the Convention.

Article 28. Declarations with respect to non-unified legal systems. (1) If a State has two or more territorial units in which different systems of law apply in relation to matters dealt with in this Convention, it may at the time of signature, ratification, acceptance, approval or accession declare that the Convention shall extend to all its territorial units or only to one or more of them and may modify this declaration by submitting another declaration at any time.
(2) A declaration shall be notified to the depositary and shall state expressly the territorial units to which the Convention applies.
(3) If a State makes no declaration under this Article, the Convention shall extend to all territorial units of that State.
(4) This Article shall not apply to a Regional Economic Integration Organisation.

Article 29. Regional Economic Integration Organisations. (1) A Regional Economic Integration Organisation which is constituted solely by sovereign States and has competence over some or all of the matters governed by this Convention may similarly sign, accept, approve or accede to this Convention. The Regional Economic Integration Organisation shall in that case have the rights and obligations of a Contracting State, to the extent that the Organisation has competence over matters governed by this Convention.
(2) The Regional Economic Integration Organisation shall, at the time of signature, acceptance, approval or accession, notify the depositary in writing of the matters governed by this Convention in respect of which competence has been transferred to that Organisation by its Member States. The Organisation shall promptly notify the depositary in writing of any changes to its competence as specified in the most recent notice given under this paragraph.
(3) For the purposes of the entry into force of this Convention, any instrument deposited by a Regional Economic Integration Organisation shall not be counted unless the Regional Economic Integration Organisation declares in accordance with Article 30 that its Member States will not be Parties to this Convention.
(4) Any reference to a "Contracting State" or "State" in this Convention shall apply equally, where appropriate, to a Regional Economic Integration Organisation that is a Party to it.

Article 30. Accession by a Regional Economic Integration Organisation without its Member States. (1) At the time of signature, acceptance, approval or accession, a Regional Economic Integration Organisation may declare that it exercises competence over all the matters governed by this Convention and that its Member States will not be Parties to this Convention but shall be bound by virtue of the signature, acceptance, approval or accession of the Organisation.
(2) In the event that a declaration is made by a Regional Economic Integration Organisation in accordance with paragraph 1, any reference to a "Contracting State" or "State" in this Convention shall apply equally, where appropriate, to the Member States of the Organisation.

Article 31. Entry into force. (1) This Convention shall enter into force on the first day of the month following the expiration of three months after the deposit of the second instrument of ratification, acceptance, approval or accession referred to in Article 27.
(2) Thereafter this Convention shall enter into force -
(a) for each State or Regional Economic Integration Organisation subsequently ratifying, accepting, approving or acceding to it, on the first day of the month following the expiration of three months after the deposit of its instrument of ratification, acceptance, approval or accession;
(b) for a territorial unit to which this Convention has been extended in accordance with Article 28, paragraph 1, on the first day of the month following the expiration of three months after the notification of the declaration referred to in that Article.

Article 32. Declarations. (1) Declarations referred to in Articles 19, 20, 21, 22 and 26 may be made upon signature, ratification, acceptance, approval or accession or at any time thereafter, and may be modified or withdrawn at any time.
(2) Declarations, modifications and withdrawals shall be notified to the depositary.
(3) A declaration made at the time of signature, ratification, acceptance, approval or accession shall take effect simultaneously with the entry into force of this Convention for the State concerned.
(4) A declaration made at a subsequent time, and any modification or withdrawal of a declaration, shall take effect on the first day of the month following the expiration of three months after the date on which the notification is received by the depositary.
(5) A declaration under Articles 19, 20, 21 and 26 shall not apply to exclusive choice of court agreements concluded before it takes effect.

Article 33. Denunciation. (1) This Convention may be denounced by notification in writing to the depositary. The denunciation may be limited to certain territorial units of a non-unified legal system to which this Convention applies.
(2) The denunciation shall take effect on the first day of the month following the expiration of twelve months after the date on which the notification is received by the depositary. Where a longer period for the denunciation to take effect is specified in the notification, the denunciation shall take effect upon the expiration of such longer period after the date on which the notification is received by the depositary.

Article 34. Notifications by the depositary. The depositary shall notify the Members of the Hague Conference on Private International Law, and other States and Regional Economic Integration Organisations which have signed, ratified, accepted, approved or acceded in accordance with Articles 27, 29 and 30 of the following -
(a) the signatures, ratifications, acceptances, approvals and accessions referred to in Articles 27, 29 and 30;
(b) the date on which this Convention enters into force in accordance with Article 31;
(c) the notifications, declarations, modifications and withdrawals of declarations referred to in Articles 19, 20, 21, 22, 26, 28, 29 and 30;
(d) the denunciations referred to in Article 33.

In witness whereof the undersigned, being duly authorised thereto, have signed this Convention.
Done at The Hague, on 30 June 2005, in the English and French languages, both texts being equally authentic, in a single copy which shall be deposited in the archives of the Government of the Kingdom of the Netherlands, and of which a certified copy shall be sent, through diplomatic channels, to each of the Member States of the Hague Conference on Private International Law as of the date of its Twentieth Session and to each State which participated in that Session.

European Company Law

PART III   EUROPEAN COMPANY LAW

Council Directive 2001/86/EC of 8 October 2001 supplementing the Statute for a European company with regard to the involvement of employees (OJ L 294, 10.11.2001, pp. 22 – 32) [footnotes omitted].

THE COUNCIL OF THE EUROPEAN UNION,
Having regard to the Treaty establishing the European Community, and in particular Article 308 thereof,
Having regard to the amended proposal from the Commission,
Having regard to the opinion of the European Parliament,
Having regard to the opinion of the Economic and Social Committee,
Whereas:
(1) In order to attain the objectives of the Treaty, Council Regulation (EC) No 2157/2001 establishes a Statute for a European company (SE).
(2) That Regulation aims at creating a uniform legal framework within which companies from different Member States should be able to plan and carry out the reorganisation of their business on a Community scale.
(3) In order to promote the social objectives of the Community, special provisions have to be set, notably in the field of employee involvement, aimed at ensuring that the establishment of an SE does not entail the disappearance or reduction of practices of employee involvement existing within the companies participating in the establishment of an SE. This objective should be pursued through the establishment of a set of rules in this field, supplementing the provisions of the Regulation.
(4) Since the objectives of the proposed action, as outlined above, cannot be sufficiently achieved by the Member States, in that the object is to establish a set of rules on employee involvement applicable to the SE, and can therefore, by reason of the scale and impact of the proposed action, be better achieved at Community level, the Community may adopt measures, in accordance with the principle of subsidiarity as set out in Article 5 of the Treaty. In accordance with the principle of proportionality, as set out in that Article, this Directive does not go beyond what is necessary to achieve these objectives.
(5) The great diversity of rules and practices existing in the Member States as regards the manner in which employees' representatives are involved in decision-making within companies makes it inadvisable to set up a single European model of employee involvement applicable to the SE.
(6) Information and consultation procedures at transnational level should nevertheless be ensured in all cases of creation of an SE.
(7) If and when participation rights exist within one or more companies establishing an SE, they should be preserved through their transfer to the SE, once established, unless the parties decide otherwise.
(8) The concrete procedures of employee transnational information and consultation, as well as, if applicable, participation, to apply to each SE should be defined primarily by means of an agreement between the parties concerned or, in the absence thereof, through the application of a set of subsidiary rules.
(9) Member States should still have the option of not applying the standard rules relating to participation in the case of a merger, given the diversity of national systems for employee involvement. Existing systems and practices of participation where appropriate at the level of participating companies must in that case be maintained by adapting registration rules.
(10) The voting rules within the special body representing the employees for negotiation purposes, in particular when concluding agreements providing for a level of participation lower than the one existing within one or more of the participating companies, should be proportionate to the risk of disappearance or reduction of existing systems and practices of participation. That risk is greater in the case of an SE established by way of transformation or merger than by way of creating a holding company or a common subsidiary.
(11) In the absence of an agreement subsequent to the negotiation between employees' representatives and the competent organs of the participating companies, provision should be made for certain standard requirements to apply to the SE, once it is established. These standard requirements should ensure effective practices of transnational information and consultation of employees, as well as their participation in the relevant organs of the SE if and when such participation existed before its establishment within the participating companies.
(12) Provision should be made for the employees' representatives acting within the framework of the Directive to enjoy, when exercising their functions, protection and guarantees which are similar to those provided to employees' representatives by the legislation and/or practice of the country of employment. They should not be subject to any discrimination as a result of the lawful exercise of

their activities and should enjoy adequate protection as regards dismissal and other sanctions.
(13) The confidentiality of sensitive information should be preserved even after the expiry of the employees' representatives terms of office and provision should be made to allow the competent organ of the SE to withhold information which would seriously harm, if subject to public disclosure, the functioning of the SE.
(14) Where an SE and its subsidiaries and establishments are subject to Council Directive 94/45/EC of 22 September 1994 on the establishment of a European Works Council or a procedure in Community-scale undertakings and Community-scale groups of undertakings for the purposes of informing and consulting employees, the provisions of that Directive and the provision transposing it into national legislation should not apply to it nor to its subsidiaries and establishments, unless the special negotiating body decides not to open negotiations or to terminate negotiations already opened.
(15) This Directive should not affect other existing rights regarding involvement and need not affect other existing representation structures, provided for by Community and national laws and practices.
(16) Member States should take appropriate measures in the event of failure to comply with the obligations laid down in this Directive.
(17) The Treaty has not provided the necessary powers for the Community to adopt the proposed Directive, other than those provided for in Article 308.
(18) It is a fundamental principle and stated aim of this Directive to secure employees' acquired rights as regards involvement in company decisions. Employee rights in force before the establishment of SEs should provide the basis for employee rights of involvement in the SE (the "before and after" principle). Consequently, that approach should apply not only to the initial establishment of an SE but also to structural changes in an existing SE and to the companies affected by structural change processes.
(19) Member States should be able to provide that representatives of trade unions may be members of a special negotiating body regardless of whether they are employees of a company participating in the establishment of an SE. Member States should in this context in particular be able to introduce this right in cases where trade union representatives have the right to be members of, and to vote in, supervisory or administrative company organs in accordance with national legislation.
(20) In several Member States, employee involvement and other areas of industrial relations are based on both national legislation and practice which in this context is understood also to cover collective agreements at various national, sectoral and/or company levels,
HAS ADOPTED THIS DIRECTIVE:

Section I. General

Article 1. (1) This Directive governs the involvement of employees in the affairs of European public limited-liability companies (Societas Europaea, hereinafter referred to as "SE"), as referred to in Regulation (EC) No 2157/2001.
(2) To this end, arrangements for the involvement of employees shall be established in every SE in accordance with the negotiating procedure referred to in Articles 3 to 6 or, under the circumstances specified in Article 7, in accordance with the Annex.

Article 2. For the purposes of this Directive:
(a) "SE" means any company established in accordance with Regulation (EC) No 2157/2001;
(b) "participating companies" means the companies directly participating in the establishing of an SE;
(c) "subsidiary" of a company means an undertaking over which that company exercises a dominant influence defined in accordance with Article 3(2) to (7) of Directive 94/45/EC;
(d) "concerned subsidiary or establishment" means a subsidiary or establishment of a participating company which is proposed to become a subsidiary or establishment of the SE upon its formation;
(e) "employees' representatives" means the employees' representatives provided for by national law and/or practice;
(f) "representative body" means the body representative of the employees set up by the agreements referred to in Article 4 or in accordance with the provisions of the Annex, with the purpose of informing and consulting the employees of an SE and its subsidiaries and establishments situated in the Community and, where applicable, of exercising participation rights in relation to the SE;
(g) "special negotiating body" means the body established in accordance with Article 3 to negotiate with the competent body of the participating companies regarding the establishment of arrangements for the involvement of employees within the SE;
(h) "involvement of employees" means any mechanism, including information, consultation and

participation, through which employees' representatives may exercise an influence on decisions to be taken within the company;

(i) "information" means the informing of the body representative of the employees and/or employees' representatives by the competent organ of the SE on questions which concern the SE itself and any of its subsidiaries or establishments situated in another Member State or which exceed the powers of the decision-making organs in a single Member State at a time, in a manner and with a content which allows the employees' representatives to undertake an in-depth assessment of the possible impact and, where appropriate, prepare consultations with the competent organ of the SE;

(j) "consultation" means the establishment of dialogue and exchange of views between the body representative of the employees and/or the employees' representatives and the competent organ of the SE, at a time, in a manner and with a content which allows the employees' representatives, on the basis of information provided, to express an opinion on measures envisaged by the competent organ which may be taken into account in the decision-making process within the SE;

(k) "participation" means the influence of the body representative of the employees and/or the employees' representatives in the affairs of a company by way of:

- the right to elect or appoint some of the members of the company's supervisory or administrative organ, or
- the right to recommend and/or oppose the appointment of some or all of the members of the company's supervisory or administrative organ.

Section II. Negotiating procedure

Article 3. (1) Where the management or administrative organs of the participating companies draw up a plan for the establishment of an SE, they shall as soon as possible after publishing the draft terms of merger or creating a holding company or after agreeing a plan to form a subsidiary or to transform into an SE, take the necessary steps, including providing information about the identity of the participating companies, concerned subsidiaries or establishments, and the number of their employees, to start negotiations with the representatives of the companies' employees on arrangements for the involvement of employees in the SE.

(2) For this purpose, a special negotiating body representative of the employees of the participating companies and concerned subsidiaries or establishments shall be created in accordance with the following provisions:

(a) in electing or appointing members of the special negotiating body, it must be ensured:

(i) that these members are elected or appointed in proportion to the number of employees employed in each Member State by the participating companies and concerned subsidiaries or establishments, by allocating in respect of a Member State one seat per portion of employees employed in that Member State which equals 10 %, or a fraction thereof, of the number of employees employed by the participating companies and concerned subsidiaries or establishments in all the Member States taken together;

(ii) that in the case of an SE formed by way of merger, there are such further additional members from each Member State as may be necessary in order to ensure that the special negotiating body includes at least one member representing each participating company which is registered and has employees in that Member State and which it is proposed will cease to exist as a separate legal entity following the registration of the SE, in so far as:

- the number of such additional members does not exceed 20 % of the number of members designated by virtue of point (i), and
- the composition of the special negotiating body does not entail a double representation of the employees concerned.

If the number of such companies is higher than the number of additional seats available pursuant to the first subparagraph, these additional seats shall be allocated to companies in different Member States by decreasing order of the number of employees they employ;

(b) Member States shall determine the method to be used for the election or appointment of the members of the special negotiating body who are to be elected or appointed in their territories. They shall take the necessary measures to ensure that, as far as possible, such members shall include at least one member representing each participating company which has employees in the Member State concerned. Such measures must not increase the overall number of members.

Member States may provide that such members may include representatives of trade unions whether or not they are employees of a participating company or concerned subsidiary or establishment. Without prejudice to national legislation and/or practice laying down thresholds for the establishing of a representative body, Member States shall provide that employees in undertakings or establishments in which there are no employees' representatives through no fault of their own have the right to elect or appoint members of the special negotiating body.

(3) The special negotiating body and the competent organs of the participating companies shall determine, by written agreement, arrangements for the involvement of employees within the SE.

To this end, the competent organs of the participating companies shall inform the special negotiating body of the plan and the actual process of establishing the SE, up to its registration.

(4) Subject to paragraph (6), the special negotiating body shall take decisions by an absolute majority of its members, provided that such a majority also represents an absolute majority of the employees. Each member shall have one vote. However, should the result of the negotiations lead to a reduction of participation rights, the majority required for a decision to approve such an agreement shall be the votes of two thirds of the members of the special negotiating body representing at least two thirds of the employees, including the votes of members representing employees employed in at least two Member States,

- in the case of an SE to be established by way of merger, if participation covers at least 25 % of the overall number of employees of the participating companies, or

- in the case of an SE to be established by way of creating a holding company or forming a subsidiary, if participation covers at least 50 % of the overall number of employees of the participating companies.

Reduction of participation rights means a proportion of members of the organs of the SE within the meaning of Article 2(k), which is lower than the highest proportion existing within the participating companies.

(5) For the purpose of the negotiations, the special negotiating body may request experts of its choice, for example representatives of appropriate Community level trade union organisations, to assist it with its work. Such experts may be present at negotiation meetings in an advisory capacity at the request of the special negotiating body, where appropriate to promote coherence and consistency at Community level. The special negotiating body may decide to inform the representatives of appropriate external organisations, including trade unions, of the start of the negotiations.

(6) The special negotiating body may decide by the majority set out below not to open negotiations or to terminate negotiations already opened, and to rely on the rules on information and consultation of employees in force in the Member States where the SE has employees. Such a decision shall stop the procedure to conclude the agreement referred to in Article 4. Where such a decision has been taken, none of the provisions of the Annex shall apply.

The majority required to decide not to open or to terminate negotiations shall be the votes of two thirds of the members representing at least two thirds of the employees, including the votes of members representing employees employed in at least two Member States.

In the case of an SE established by way of transformation, this paragraph shall not apply if there is participation in the company to be transformed.

The special negotiating body shall be reconvened on the written request of at least 10 % of the employees of the SE, its subsidiaries and establishments, or their representatives, at the earliest two years after the abovementioned decision, unless the parties agree to negotiations being reopened sooner. If the special negotiating body decides to reopen negotiations with the management but no agreement is reached as a result of those negotiations, none of the provisions of the Annex shall apply.

(7) Any expenses relating to the functioning of the special negotiating body and, in general, to negotiations shall be borne by the participating companies so as to enable the special negotiating body to carry out its task in an appropriate manner.

In compliance with this principle, Member States may lay down budgetary rules regarding the operation of the special negotiating body. They may in particular limit the funding to cover one expert only.

Article 4. (1) The competent organs of the participating companies and the special negotiating body shall negotiate in a spirit of cooperation with a view to reaching an agreement on arrangements for the involvement of the employees within the SE.

(2) Without prejudice to the autonomy of the parties, and subject to paragraph (4), the agreement referred to in paragraph (1) between the competent organs of the participating companies and the special negotiating body shall specify:

(a) the scope of the agreement;

(b) the composition, number of members and allocation of seats on the representative body which will be the discussion partner of the competent organ of the SE in connection with arrangements for the information and consultation of the employees of the SE and its subsidiaries and establishments;

(c) the functions and the procedure for the information and consultation of the representative body;

PART III   EUROPEAN COMPANY LAW

(d) the frequency of meetings of the representative body;

(e) the financial and material resources to be allocated to the representative body;

(f) if, during negotiations, the parties decide to establish one or more information and consultation procedures instead of a representative body, the arrangements for implementing those procedures;

(g) if, during negotiations, the parties decide to establish arrangements for participation, the substance of those arrangements including (if applicable) the number of members in the SE's administrative or supervisory body which the employees will be entitled to elect, appoint, recommend or oppose, the procedures as to how these members may be elected, appointed, recommended or opposed by the employees, and their rights;

(h) the date of entry into force of the agreement and its duration, cases where the agreement should be renegotiated and the procedure for its renegotiation.

(3) The agreement shall not, unless provision is made otherwise therein, be subject to the standard rules referred to in the Annex.

(4) Without prejudice to Article 13(3)(a), in the case of an SE established by means of transformation, the agreement shall provide for at least the same level of all elements of employee involvement as the ones existing within the company to be transformed into an SE.

Article 5. (1) Negotiations shall commence as soon as the special negotiating body is established and may continue for six months thereafter.

(2) The parties may decide, by joint agreement, to extend negotiations beyond the period referred to in paragraph (1), up to a total of one year from the establishment of the special negotiating body.

Article 6. Except where otherwise provided in this Directive, the legislation applicable to the negotiation procedure provided for in Articles 3 to 5 shall be the legislation of the Member State in which the registered office of the SE is to be situated.

Article 7. (1) In order to achieve the objective described in Article 1, Member States shall, without prejudice to paragraph (3) below, lay down standard rules on employee involvement which must satisfy the provisions set out in the Annex.

The standard rules as laid down by the legislation of the Member State in which the registered office of the SE is to be situated shall apply from the date of the registration of the SE where either:

(a) the parties so agree; or

(b) by the deadline laid down in Article 5, no agreement has been concluded, and:

- the competent organ of each of the participating companies decides to accept the application of the standard rules in relation to the SE and so to continue with its registration of the SE, and

- the special negotiating body has not taken the decision provided in Article 3(6).

(2) Moreover, the standard rules fixed by the national legislation of the Member State of registration in accordance with part 3 of the Annex shall apply only:

(a) in the case of an SE established by transformation, if the rules of a Member State relating to employee participation in the administrative or supervisory body applied to a company transformed into an SE;

(b) in the case of an SE established by merger:

- if, before registration of the SE, one or more forms of participation applied in one or more of the participating companies covering at least 25 % of the total number of employees in all the participating companies, or

- if, before registration of the SE, one or more forms of participation applied in one or more of the participating companies covering less than 25 % of the total number of employees in all the participating companies and if the special negotiating body so decides,

(c) in the case of an SE established by setting up a holding company or establishing a subsidiary:

- if, before registration of the SE, one or more forms of participation applied in one or more of the participating companies covering at least 50 % of the total number of employees in all the participating companies; or

- if, before registration of the SE, one or more forms of participation applied in one or more of the participating companies covering less than 50 % of the total number of employees in all the participating companies and if the special negotiating body so decides.

If there was more than one form of participation within the various participating companies, the special negotiating body shall decide which of those forms must be established in the SE. Member States may fix the rules which are applicable in the absence of any decision on the matter for an SE registered in their territory. The special negotiating body shall inform the competent organs of the participating companies of any decisions taken pursuant to this paragraph.

(3) Member States may provide that the reference provisions in part 3 of the Annex shall not apply in the case provided for in point (b) of paragraph (2).

Section III. Miscellaneous provisions

Article 8. (1) Member States shall provide that members of the special negotiating body or the representative body, and experts who assist them, are not authorised to reveal any information which has been given to them in confidence.

The same shall apply to employees' representatives in the context of an information and consultation procedure.

This obligation shall continue to apply, wherever the persons referred to may be, even after the expiry of their terms of office.

(2) Each Member State shall provide, in specific cases and under the conditions and limits laid down by national legislation, that the supervisory or administrative organ of an SE or of a participating company established in its territory is not obliged to transmit information where its nature is such that, according to objective criteria, to do so would seriously harm the functioning of the SE (or, as the case may be, the participating company) or its subsidiaries and establishments or would be prejudicial to them.

A Member State may make such dispensation subject to prior administrative or judicial authorisation.

(3) Each Member State may lay down particular provisions for SEs in its territory which pursue directly and essentially the aim of ideological guidance with respect to information and the expression of opinions, on condition that, on the date of adoption of this Directive, such provisions already exist in the national legislation.

(4) In applying paragraphs 1, 2 and 3, Member States shall make provision for administrative or judicial appeal procedures which the employees' representatives may initiate when the supervisory or administrative organ of an SE or participating company demands confidentiality or does not give information.

Such procedures may include arrangements designed to protect the confidentiality of the information in question.

Article 9. The competent organ of the SE and the representative body shall work together in a spirit of cooperation with due regard for their reciprocal rights and obligations.

The same shall apply to cooperation between the supervisory or administrative organ of the SE and the employees' representatives in conjunction with a procedure for the information and consultation of employees.

Article 10. The members of the special negotiating body, the members of the representative body, any employees' representatives exercising functions under the information and consultation procedure and any employees' representatives in the supervisory or administrative organ of an SE who are employees of the SE, its subsidiaries or establishments or of a participating company shall, in the exercise of their functions, enjoy the same protection and guarantees provided for employees' representatives by the national legislation and/or practice in force in their country of employment.

This shall apply in particular to attendance at meetings of the special negotiating body or representative body, any other meeting under the agreement referred to in Article 4(2)(f) or any meeting of the administrative or supervisory organ, and to the payment of wages for members employed by a participating company or the SE or its subsidiaries or establishments during a period of absence necessary for the performance of their duties.

Article 11. Member States shall take appropriate measures in conformity with Community law with a view to preventing the misuse of an SE for the purpose of depriving employees of rights to employee involvement or withholding such rights.

Article 12. (1) Each Member State shall ensure that the management of establishments of an SE and the supervisory or administrative organs of subsidiaries and of participating companies which are situated within its territory and the employees' representatives or, as the case may be, the employees themselves abide by the obligations laid down by this Directive, regardless of whether or not the SE has its registered office within its territory.

(2) Member States shall provide for appropriate measures in the event of failure to comply with this Directive; in particular they shall ensure that administrative or legal procedures are available to enable the obligations deriving from this Directive to be enforced.

Article 13. (1) Where an SE is a Community-scale undertaking or a controlling undertaking of a Community-scale group of undertakings within the meaning of Directive 94/45/EC or of Directive 97/74/EC extending the said Directive to the United Kingdom, the provisions of these Directives and the provisions transposing them into national legislation shall not apply to them or to their subsidiaries.

However, where the special negotiating body decides in accordance with Article 3(6) not to open negotiations or to terminate negotiations already opened, Directive 94/45/EC or Directive 97/74/EC and the provisions transposing them into national legislation shall apply.

(2) Provisions on the participation of employees in company bodies provided for by national legislation and/or practice, other than those implementing this Directive, shall not apply to companies established in accordance with Regulation (EC) No 2157/2001 and covered by this Directive.

(3) This Directive shall not prejudice:

(a) the existing rights to involvement of employees provided for by national legislation and/or practice in the Member States as enjoyed by employees of the SE and its subsidiaries and establishments, other than participation in the bodies of the SE;

(b) the provisions on participation in the bodies laid down by national legislation and/or practice applicable to the subsidiaries of the SE.

(4) In order to preserve the rights referred to in paragraph (3), Member States may take the necessary measures to guarantee that the structures of employee representation in participating companies which will cease to exist as separate legal entities are maintained after the registration of the SE.

Article 14. (1) Member States shall adopt the laws, regulations and administrative provisions necessary to comply with this Directive no later than 8 October 2004, or shall ensure by that date at the latest that management and labour introduce the required provisions by way of agreement, the Member States being obliged to take all necessary steps enabling them at all times to guarantee the results imposed by this Directive. They shall forthwith inform the Commission thereof.

(2) When Member States adopt these measures, they shall contain a reference to this Directive or shall be accompanied by such reference on the occasion of their official publication. The methods of making such reference shall be laid down by the Member States.

Article 15. No later than 8 October 2007, the Commission shall, in consultation with the Member States and with management and labour at Community level, review the procedures for applying this Directive, with a view to proposing suitable amendments to the Council where necessary.

Article 16. This Directive shall enter into force on the day of its publication in the Official Journal of the European Communities.

Article 17. This Directive is addressed to the Member States.

Directive 2004/25/EC of the European Parliament and the Council of 21 April 2004 on takeover bids (Text with EEA relevance) ("Thirteenth Company Law Directive") (O J L 142, 30.04.2004, pp. 12 – 23) [footnotes omitted].

THE EUROPEAN PARLIAMENT AND THE COUNCIL OF THE EUROPEAN UNION,
Having regard to the Treaty establishing the European Community, and in particular Article 44(1) thereof, Having regard to the proposal from the Commission,
Having regard to the opinion of the European Economic and Social Committee,
Acting in accordance with the procedure laid down in Article 251 of the Treaty,
Whereas:
(1) In accordance with Article 44(2)(g) of the Treaty, it is necessary to coordinate certain safeguards which, for the protection of the interests of members and others, Member States require of companies governed by the law of a Member State the securities of which are admitted to trading on a regulated market in a Member State, with a view to making such safeguards equivalent throughout the Community.
(2) It is necessary to protect the interests of holders of the securities of companies governed by the law of a Member State when those companies are the subject of takeover bids or of changes of control and at least some of their securities are admitted to trading on a regulated market in a Member State.
(3) It is necessary to create Community-wide clarity and transparency in respect of legal issues to be settled in the event of takeover bids and to prevent patterns of corporate restructuring within the Community from being distorted by arbitrary differences in governance and management cultures.
(4) In view of the public-interest purposes served by the central banks of the Member States, it seems inconceivable that they should be the targets of takeover bids. Since, for historical reasons, the securities of some of those central banks are listed on regulated markets in Member States, it is necessary to exclude them explicitly from the scope of this Directive.
(5) Each Member State should designate an authority or authorities to supervise those aspects of bids that are governed by this Directive and to ensure that parties to takeover bids comply with the rules made pursuant to this Directive. All those authorities should cooperate with one another.
(6) In order to be effective, takeover regulation should be flexible and capable of dealing with new circumstances as they arise and should accordingly provide for the possibility of exceptions and derogations. However, in applying any rules or exceptions laid down or in granting any derogations, supervisory authorities should respect certain general principles.
(7) Self-regulatory bodies should be able to exercise supervision.
(8) In accordance with general principles of Community law, and in particular the right to a fair hearing, decisions of a supervisory authority should in appropriate circumstances be susceptible to review by an independent court or tribunal. However, Member States should be left to determine whether rights are to be made available which may be asserted in administrative or judicial proceedings, either in proceedings against a supervisory authority or in proceedings between parties to a bid.
(9) Member States should take the necessary steps to protect the holders of securities, in particular those with minority holdings, when control of their companies has been acquired. The Member States should ensure such protection by obliging the person who has acquired control of a company to make an offer to all the holders of that company's securities for all of their holdings at an equitable price in accordance with a common definition. Member States should be free to establish further instruments for the protection of the interests of the holders of securities, such as the obligation to make a partial bid where the offeror does not acquire control of the company or the obligation to announce a bid at the same time as control of the company is acquired.
(10) The obligation to make a bid to all the holders of securities should not apply to those controlling holdings already in existence on the date on which the national legislation transposing this Directive enters into force.
(11) The obligation to launch a bid should not apply in the case of the acquisition of securities which do not carry the right to vote at ordinary general meetings of shareholders. Member States should, however, be able to provide that the obligation to make a bid to all the holders of securities relates not only to securities carrying voting rights but also to securities which carry voting rights only in specific circumstances or which do not carry voting rights. (12) To reduce the scope for insider dealing, an offeror should be required to announce his/her decision to launch a bid as soon as possible and to inform the supervisory authority of the bid.
(13) The holders of securities should be properly informed of the terms of a bid by means of an offer document. Appropriate information should also be given to the representatives of the company's employees or, failing that, to the employees directly.

PART III EUROPEAN COMPANY LAW

(14) The time allowed for the acceptance of a bid should be regulated.

(15) To be able to perform their functions satisfactorily, supervisory authorities should at all times be able to require the parties to a bid to provide information concerning themselves and should cooperate and supply information in an efficient and effective manner, without delay, to other authorities supervising capital markets. (16) In order to prevent operations which could frustrate a bid, the powers of the board of an offeree company to engage in operations of an exceptional nature should be limited, without unduly hindering the offeree company in carrying on its normal business activities.

(17) The board of an offeree company should be required to make public a document setting out its opinion of the bid and the reasons on which that opinion is based, including its views on the effects of implementation on all the company's interests, and specifically on employment.

(18) In order to reinforce the effectiveness of existing provisions concerning the freedom to deal in the securities of companies covered by this Directive and the freedom to exercise voting rights, it is essential that the defensive structures and mechanisms envisaged by such companies be transparent and that they be regularly presented in reports to general meetings of shareholders.

(19) Member States should take the necessary measures to afford any offeror the possibility of acquiring majority interests in other companies and of fully exercising control of them. To that end, restrictions on the transfer of securities, restrictions on voting rights, extraordinary appointment rights and multiple voting rights should be removed or suspended during the time allowed for the acceptance of a bid and when the general meeting of shareholders decides on defensive measures, on amendments to the articles of association or on the removal or appointment of board members at the first general meeting of shareholders following closure of the bid. Where the holders of securities have suffered losses as a result of the removal of rights, equitable compensation should be provided for in accordance with the technical arrangements laid down by Member States.

(20) All special rights held by Member States in companies should be viewed in the framework of the free movement of capital and the relevant provisions of the Treaty. Special rights held by Member States in companies which are provided for in private or public national law should be exempted from the 'breakthrough' rule if they are compatible with the Treaty.

(21) Taking into account existing differences in Member States' company law mechanisms and structures, Member States should be allowed not to require companies established within their territories to apply the provisions of this Directive limiting the powers of the board of an offeree company during the time allowed for the acceptance of a bid and those rendering ineffective barriers, provided for in the articles of association or in specific agreements. In that event Member States should at least allow companies established within their territories to make the choice, which must be reversible, to apply those provisions. Without prejudice to international agreements to which the European Community is a party, Member States should be allowed not to require companies which apply those provisions in accordance with the optional arrangements to apply them when they become the subject of offers launched by companies which do not apply the same provisions, as a consequence of the use of those optional arrangements.

(22) Member States should lay down rules to cover the possibility of a bid's lapsing, the offeror's right to revise his/her bid, the possibility of competing bids for a company's securities, the disclosure of the result of a bid, the irrevocability of a bid and the conditions permitted.

(23) The disclosure of information to and the consultation of representatives of the employees of the offeror and the offeree company should be governed by the relevant national provisions, in particular those adopted pursuant to Council Directive 94/45/EC of 22 September 1994 on the establishment of a European Works Council or a procedure in Community-scale undertakings and Community-scale groups of undertakings for the purposes of informing and consulting employees, Council Directive 98/59/EC of 20 July 1998 on the approximation of the laws of the Member States relating to collective redundancies, Council Directive 2001/86/EC of 8 October 2001 supplementing the statute for a European Company with regard to the involvement of employees and Directive 2002/14/EC of the European Parliament and of the Council of 11 March 2002 establishing a general framework for informing and consulting employees in the European Community — Joint declaration of the European Parliament, the Council and the Commission on employee representation. The employees of the companies concerned, or their representatives, should nevertheless be given an opportunity to state their views on the foreseeable effects of the bid on employment. Without prejudice to the rules of Directive 2003/6/EC of the European Parliament and of the Council of 28 January 2003 on insider dealing and market manipulation (market abuse) Member States may always apply or introduce national provisions concerning the disclosure of information to and the consultation of representatives of the employees of the offeror before an offer is launched.

(24) Member States should take the necessary measures to enable an offeror who, following a takeo-

ver bid, has acquired a certain percentage of a company's capital carrying voting rights to require the holders of the remaining securities to sell him/her their securities. Likewise, where, following a takeover bid, an offeror has acquired a certain percentage of a company's capital carrying voting rights, the holders of the remaining securities should be able to require him/her to buy their securities. These squeeze-out and sell-out procedures should apply only under specific conditions linked to takeover bids. Member States may continue to apply national rules to squeeze-out and sell-out procedures in other circumstances.

(25) Since the objectives of the action envisaged, namely to establish minimum guidelines for the conduct of takeover bids and ensure an adequate level of protection for holders of securities throughout the Community, cannot be sufficiently achieved by the Member States because of the need for transparency and legal certainty in the case of cross-border takeovers and acquisitions of control, and can therefore, by reason of the scale and effects of the action, be better achieved at Community level, the Community may adopt measures, in accordance with the principle of subsidiarity as set out in Article 5 of the Treaty. In accordance with the principle of proportionality as set out in that Article, this Directive does not go beyond what is necessary to achieve those objectives.

(26) The adoption of a Directive is the appropriate procedure for the establishment of a framework consisting of certain common principles and a limited number of general requirements which Member States are to implement through more detailed rules in accordance with their national systems and their cultural contexts.

(27) Member States should, however, provide for sanctions for any infringement of the national measures transposing this Directive.

(28) Technical guidance and implementing measures for the rules laid down in this Directive may from time to time be necessary, to take account of new developments on financial markets. For certain provisions, the Commission should accordingly be empowered to adopt implementing measures, provided that these do not modify the essential elements of this Directive and the Commission acts in accordance with the principles set out in this Directive, after consulting the European Securities Committee established by Commission Decision 2001/528/EC. The measures necessary for the implementation of this Directive should be adopted in accordance with Council Decision 1999/468/EC of 28 June 1999 laying down the procedures for the exercise of implementing powers conferred on the Commission and with due regard to the declaration made by the Commission in the European Parliament on 5 February 2002 concerning the implementation of financial services legislation. For the other provisions, it is important to entrust a contact committee with the task of assisting Member States and the supervisory authorities in the implementation of this Directive and of advising the Commission, if necessary, on additions or amendments to this Directive. In so doing, the contact committee may make use of the information which Member States are to provide on the basis of this Directive concerning takeover bids that have taken place on their regulated markets.

(29) The Commission should facilitate movement towards the fair and balanced harmonisation of rules on takeovers in the European Union. To that end, the Commission should be able to submit proposals for the timely revision of this Directive,

HAVE ADOPTED THIS DIRECTIVE:

Article 1. (1) This Directive lays down measures coordinating the laws, regulations, administrative provisions, codes of practice and other arrangements of the Member States, including arrangements established by organisations officially authorised to regulate the markets (hereinafter referred to as 'rules'), relating to takeover bids for the securities of companies governed by the laws of Member States, where all or some of those securities are admitted to trading on a regulated market within the meaning of Directive 93/22/EEC (2) in one or more Member States (hereinafter referred to as a 'regulated market').

(2) This Directive shall not apply to takeover bids for securities issued by companies, the object of which is the collective investment of capital provided by the public, which operate on the principle of risk-spreading and the units of which are, at the holders' request, repurchased or redeemed, directly or indirectly, out of the assets of those companies. Action taken by such companies to ensure that the stock exchange value of their units does not vary significantly from their net asset value shall be regarded as equivalent to such repurchase or redemption.

(3) This Directive shall not apply to takeover bids for securities issued by the Member States' central banks.

Article 2. (1) For the purposes of this Directive:
(a) 'takeover bid' or 'bid' shall mean a public offer (other than by the offeree company itself) made to the holders of the securities of a
company to acquire all or some of those securities, whether mandatory or voluntary, which follows or

has as its objective the acquisition of control of the offeree company in accordance with national law;
(b) 'offeree company' shall mean a company, the securities of which are the subject of a bid;
(c) 'offeror' shall mean any natural or legal person governed by public or private law making a bid;
(d) 'persons acting in concert' shall mean natural or legal persons who cooperate with the offeror or the offeree company on the basis of an agreement, either express or tacit, either oral or written, aimed either at acquiring control of the offeree company or at frustrating the successful outcome of a bid;
(e) 'securities' shall mean transferable securities carrying voting rights in a company;
(f) 'parties to the bid' shall mean the offeror, the members of the offeror's board if the offeror is a company, the offeree company, holders of securities of the offeree company and the members of the board of the offeree company, and persons acting in concert with such parties;
(g) 'multiple-vote securities' shall mean securities included in a distinct and separate class and carrying more than one vote each.
(2) For the purposes of paragraph (1)(d), persons controlled by another person within the meaning of Article 87 of Directive 2001/34/EC shall be deemed to be persons acting in concert with that other person and with each other.

Article 3. (1) For the purpose of implementing this Directive, Member States shall ensure that the following principles are complied with:
(a) all holders of the securities of an offeree company of the same class must be afforded equivalent treatment; moreover, if a person acquires control of a company, the other holders of securities must be protected;
(b) the holders of the securities of an offeree company must have sufficient time and information to enable them to reach a properly informed decision on the bid; where it advises the holders of securities, the board of the offeree company must give its views on the effects of implementation of the bid on employment, conditions of employment and the locations of the company's places of business;
(c) the board of an offeree company must act in the interests of the company as a whole and must not deny the holders of securities the opportunity to decide on the merits of the bid;
(d) false markets must not be created in the securities of the offeree company, of the offeror company or of any other company concerned by the bid in such a way that the rise or fall of the prices of the securities becomes artificial and the normal functioning of the markets is distorted;
(e) an offeror must announce a bid only after ensuring that he/she can fulfil in full any cash consideration, if such is offered, and after taking all reasonable measures to secure the implementation of any other type of consideration;
(f) an offeree company must not be hindered in the conduct of its affairs for longer than is reasonable by a bid for its securities.
(2) With a view to ensuring compliance with the principles laid down in paragraph (1), Member States:
(a) shall ensure that the minimum requirements set out in this Directive are observed;
(b) may lay down additional conditions and provisions more stringent than those of this Directive for the regulation of bids.

Article 4. (1) Member States shall designate the authority or authorities competent to supervise bids for the purposes of the rules which they make or introduce pursuant to this Directive. The authorities thus designated shall be either public authorities, associations or private bodies recognised by national law or by public authorities expressly empowered for that purpose by national law. Member States shall inform the Commission of those designations, specifying any divisions of functions that may be made. They shall ensure that those authorities exercise their functions impartially and independently of all parties to a bid.
(2) (a) The authority competent to supervise a bid shall be that of the Member State in which the offeree company has its registered
office if that company's securities are admitted to trading on a regulated market in that Member State.
(b) If the offeree company's securities are not admitted to trading on a regulated market in the Member State in which the company has its registered office, the authority competent to supervise the bid shall be that of the Member State on the regulated market of which the company's securities are admitted to trading. If the offeree company's securities are admitted to trading on regulated markets in more than one Member State, the authority competent to supervise the bid shall be that of the Member State on the regulated market of which the securities were first admitted to trading.
(c) If the offeree company's securities were first admitted to trading on regulated markets in more than one Member State simultaneously, the offeree company shall determine which of the supervisory authorities of those Member States shall be the authority competent to supervise the bid by notifying those regulated markets and their supervisory authorities on the first day of trading. If the

offeree company's securities have already been admitted to trading on regulated markets in more than one Member
State on the date laid down in Article 21(1) and were admitted simultaneously, the supervisory authorities of those Member States shall agree which one of them shall be the authority competent to supervise the bid within four weeks of the date laid down in Article 21(1). Otherwise, the offeree company shall determine which of those authorities shall be the competent authority on the first day of trading following that four-week period.

(d) Member States shall ensure that the decisions referred to in (c) are made public.

(e) In the cases referred to in (b) and (c), matters relating to the consideration offered in the case of a bid, in particular the price, and matters relating to the bid procedure, in particular the information on the offeror's decision to make a bid, the contents of the offer document and the disclosure of the bid, shall be dealt with in accordance with the rules of the Member State of the competent authority. In matters relating to the information to be provided to the employees of the offeree company and in matters relating to company law, in particular the percentage of voting rights which confers control and any derogation from the obligation to launch a bid, as well as the conditions under which the board of the offeree company may undertake any action which might result in the frustration of the bid, the applicable rules and the competent authority shall be those of the Member State in which the offeree company has its registered office.

(3) Member States shall ensure that all persons employed or formerly employed by their supervisory authorities are bound by professional secrecy. No information covered by professional secrecy may be divulged to any person or authority except under provisions laid down by law.

(4) The supervisory authorities of the Member States for the purposes of this Directive and other authorities supervising capital markets, in particular in accordance with Directive 93/22/EEC, Directive 2001/34/EC, Directive 2003/6/EC and Directive 2003/71/EC of the European Parliament and of the Council of 4 November 2003 on the prospectus to be published when securities are offered to the public or admitted to trading shall cooperate and supply each other with information wherever necessary for the application of the rules drawn up in accordance with this Directive and in particular in cases covered by paragraph (2)(b), (c) and (e). Information thus exchanged shall be covered by the obligation of professional secrecy to which persons employed or formerly employed by the supervisory authorities receiving the information are subject. Cooperation shall include the ability to serve the legal documents necessary to enforce measures taken by the competent authorities in connection with bids, as well as such other assistance as may reasonably be requested by the supervisory authorities concerned for the purpose of investigating any actual or alleged breaches of the rules made or introduced pursuant to this Directive.

(5) The supervisory authorities shall be vested with all the powers necessary for the purpose of carrying out their duties, including that of ensuring that the parties to a bid comply with the rules made or introduced pursuant to this Directive. Provided that the general principles laid down in Article 3(1) are respected, Member States may provide in the rules that they make or introduce pursuant to this Directive for derogations from those rules:

(i) by including such derogations in their national rules, in order to take account of circumstances determined at national level and/or

(ii) by granting their supervisory authorities, where they are competent, powers to waive such national rules, to take account of the circumstances referred to in (i) or in other specific circumstances, in which case a reasoned decision must be required.

(6) This Directive shall not affect the power of the Member States to designate judicial or other authorities responsible for dealing with disputes and for deciding on irregularities committed in the course of bids or the power of Member States to regulate whether and under which circumstances parties to a bid are entitled to bring administrative or judicial proceedings. In particular, this Directive shall not affect the power which courts may have in a Member State to decline to hear legal proceedings and to decide whether or not such proceedings affect the outcome of a bid. This Directive shall not affect the power of the Member States to determine the legal position concerning the liability of supervisory authorities or concerning litigation between the parties to a bid.

Article 5. (1) Where a natural or legal person, as a result of his/her own acquisition or the acquisition by persons acting in concert with him/her, holds securities of a company as referred to in Article 1(1) which, added to any existing holdings of those securities of his/hers and the holdings of those securities of persons acting in concert with him/her, directly or indirectly give him/her a specified percentage of voting rights in that company, giving him/her control of that company, Member States shall ensure that such a person is required to make a bid as a means of protecting the minority shareholders of that company. Such a bid shall be addressed at the earliest opportunity to all the holders of those securities for all their holdings at the equitable price as defined in paragraph (4).

(2) Where control has been acquired following a voluntary bid made in accordance with this Directive to all the holders of securities for all their holdings, the obligation laid down in paragraph (1) to launch a bid shall no longer apply.

(3) The percentage of voting rights which confers control for the purposes of paragraph (1) and the method of its calculation shall be determined by the rules of the Member State in which the company has its registered office.

(4) The highest price paid for the same securities by the offeror, or by persons acting in concert with him/her, over a period, to be determined by Member States, of not less than six months and not more than 12 before the bid referred to in paragraph (1) shall be regarded as the equitable price. If, after the bid has been made public and before the offer closes for acceptance, the offeror or any person acting in concert with him/her purchases securities at a price higher than the offer price, the offeror shall increase his/her offer so that it is not less than the highest price paid for the securities so acquired. Provided that the general principles laid down in Article 3(1) are respected, Member States may authorise their supervisory authorities to adjust the price referred to in the first subparagraph in circumstances and in accordance with criteria that are clearly determined. To that end, they may draw up a list of circumstances in which the highest price may be adjusted either upwards or downwards, for example where the highest price was set by agreement between the purchaser and a seller, where the market prices of the securities in question have been manipulated, where market prices in general or certain market prices in particular have been affected by exceptional occurrences, or in order to enable a firm in difficulty to be rescued. They may also determine the criteria to be applied in such cases, for example the average market value over a particular period, the break-up value of the company or other objective valuation criteria generally used in financial analysis. Any decision by a supervisory authority to adjust the equitable price shall be substantiated and made public.

(5) By way of consideration the offeror may offer securities, cash or a combination of both. However, where the consideration offered by the offeror does not consist of liquid securities admitted to trading on a regulated market, it shall include a cash alternative.

In any event, the offeror shall offer a cash consideration at least as an alternative where he/she or persons acting in concert with him/her, over a period beginning at the same time as the period determined by the Member State in accordance with paragraph (4) and ending when the offer closes for acceptance, has purchased for cash securities carrying 5 % or more of the voting rights in the offeree company. Member States may provide that a cash consideration must be offered, at least as an alternative, in all cases.

(6) In addition to the protection provided for in paragraph (1), Member States may provide for further instruments intended to protect the interests of the holders of securities in so far as those instruments do not hinder the normal course of a bid.

Article 6. (1) Member States shall ensure that a decision to make a bid is made public without delay and that the supervisory authority is informed of the bid. They may require that the supervisory authority must be informed before such a decision is made public. As soon as the bid has been made public, the boards of the offeree company and of the offeror shall inform the representatives of their respective employees or, where there are no such representatives, the employees themselves.

(2) Member States shall ensure that an offeror is required to draw up and make public in good time an offer document containing the information necessary to enable the holders of the offeree company's securities to reach a properly informed decision on the bid. Before the offer document is made public, the offeror shall communicate it to the supervisory authority. When it is made public, the boards of the offeree company and of the offeror shall communicate it to the representatives of their respective employees or, where there are no such representatives, to the employees themselves. Where the offer document referred to in the first subparagraph is subject to the prior approval of the supervisory authority and has been approved, it shall be recognised, subject to any translation required, in any other Member State on the market of which the offeree company's securities are admitted to trading, without its being necessary to obtain the approval of the supervisory authorities of that Member State. Those authorities may require the inclusion of additional information in the offer document only if such information is specific to the market of a Member State or Member States on which the offeree company's securities are admitted to trading and relates to the formalities to be complied with to accept the bid and to receive the consideration due at the close of the bid as well as to the tax arrangements to which the consideration offered to the holders of the securities will be subject.

(3) The offer document referred to in paragraph (2) shall state at least:
(a) the terms of the bid;
(b) the identity of the offeror and, where the offeror is a company, the type, name and registered office of that company;

(c) the securities or, where appropriate, the class or classes of securities for which the bid is made;
(d) the consideration offered for each security or class of securities and, in the case of a mandatory bid, the method employed in determining it, with particulars of the way in which that consideration is to be paid;
(e) the compensation offered for the rights which might be removed as a result of the breakthrough rule laid down in Article 11(4), with particulars of the way in which that compensation is to be paid and the method employed in determining it;
(f) the maximum and minimum percentages or quantities of securities which the offeror undertakes to acquire;
(g) details of any existing holdings of the offeror, and of persons acting in concert with him/her, in the offeree company;
(h) all the conditions to which the bid is subject; 2004L0025 — EN— 20.04.2009 —001.001 —11
(i) the offeror's intentions with regard to the future business of the offeree company and, in so far as it is affected by the bid, the offeror company and with regard to the safeguarding of the jobs of their employees and management, including any material change in
the conditions of employment, and in particular the offeror's strategic plans for the two companies and the likely repercussions on employment and the locations of the companies' places of business;
(j) the time allowed for acceptance of the bid;
(k) where the consideration offered by the offeror includes securities of any kind, information concerning those securities;
(l) information concerning the financing for the bid;
(m) the identity of persons acting in concert with the offeror or with the offeree company and, in the case of companies, their types, names, registered offices and relationships with the offeror and, where possible, with the offeree company;
(n) the national law which will govern contracts concluded between the offeror and the holders of the offeree company's securities as a result of the bid and the competent courts.
(4) The Commission may adopt rules modifying the list in paragraph
(3) Those measures, designed to amend non-essential elements of this Directive, shall be adopted in accordance with the regulatory procedure with scrutiny referred to in Article 18(2).
(5) Member States shall ensure that the parties to a bid are required to provide the supervisory authorities of their Member State at any time on request with all the information in their possession concerning the bid that is necessary for the supervisory authority to discharge its functions.

Article 7. (1) Member States shall provide that the time allowed for the acceptance of a bid may not be less than two weeks nor more than 10 weeks from the date of publication of the offer document. Provided that the general principle laid down in Article 3(1)(f) is respected, Member States may provide that the period of 10 weeks may be extended on condition that the offeror gives at least two weeks' notice of his/her intention of closing the bid.
(2) Member States may provide for rules changing the period referred to in paragraph (1) in specific cases. A Member State may authorise a supervisory authority to grant a derogation from the period referred to in paragraph (1) in order to allow the offeree company to call a general meeting of shareholders to consider the bid.

Article 8. (1) Member States shall ensure that a bid is made public in such a way as to ensure market transparency and integrity for the securities of the offeree company, of the offeror or of any other company affected by the bid, in particular in order to prevent the publication or dissemination of false or misleading information.
(2) Member States shall provide for the disclosure of all information and documents required by Article 6 in such a manner as to ensure that they are both readily and promptly available to the holders of securities at least in those Member States on the regulated markets of which the offeree company's securities are admitted to trading and to the representatives of the employees of the offeree company and the offeror or, where there are no such representatives, to the employees themselves.

Article 9. (1) Member States shall ensure that the rules laid down in paragraphs 2 to 5 are complied with.
(2) During the period referred to in the second subparagraph, the board of the offeree company shall obtain the prior authorisation of the general meeting of shareholders given for this purpose before taking any action, other than seeking alternative bids, which may result in the frustration of the bid and in particular before issuing any shares which may result in a lasting impediment to the offeror's acquiring control of the offeree company. Such authorisation shall be mandatory at least from the time the board of the offeree company receives the information referred to in the first sentence

of Article 6(1) concerning the bid and until the result of the bid is made public or the bid lapses. Member States may require that such authorisation be obtained at an earlier stage, for example as soon as the board of the offeree company becomes aware that the bid is imminent.

(3) As regards decisions taken before the beginning of the period referred to in the second subparagraph of paragraph (2) and not yet partly or fully implemented, the general meeting of shareholders shall approve or confirm any decision which does not form part of the normal course of the company's business and the implementation of which may result in the frustration of the bid.

(4) For the purpose of obtaining the prior authorisation, approval or confirmation of the holders of securities referred to in paragraphs 2 and 3, Member States may adopt rules allowing a general meeting of shareholders to be called at short notice, provided that the meeting does not take place within two weeks of notification's being given.

(5) The board of the offeree company shall draw up and make public a document setting out its opinion of the bid and the reasons on which it is based, including its views on the effects of implementation of the bid on all the company's interests and specifically employment, and on the offeror's strategic plans for the offeree company and their likely repercussions on employment and the locations of the company's places of business as set out in the offer document in accordance with Article 6(3)(i). The board of the offeree company shall at the same time communicate that opinion to the representatives of its employees or, where there are no such representatives, to the employees themselves. Where the board of the offeree company receives in good time a separate opinion from the representatives of its employees on the effects of the bid on employment, that opinion shall be appended to the document.

(6) For the purposes of paragraph (2), where a company has a two-tier board structure 'board' shall mean both the management board and the supervisory board.

Article 10. (1) Member States shall ensure that companies as referred to in Article 1(1) publish detailed information on the following:

(a) the structure of their capital, including securities which are not admitted to trading on a regulated market in a Member State, where appropriate with an indication of the different classes of shares and, for each class of shares, the rights and obligations attaching to it and the percentage of total share capital that it represents;

(b) any restrictions on the transfer of securities, such as limitations on the holding of securities or the need to obtain the approval of the company or other holders of securities, without prejudice to Article 46 of Directive 2001/34/EC;

(c) significant direct and indirect shareholdings (including indirect shareholdings through pyramid structures and cross-shareholdings) within the meaning of Article 85 of Directive 2001/34/EC;

(d) the holders of any securities with special control rights and a description of those rights;

(e) the system of control of any employee share scheme where the control rights are not exercised directly by the employees;

(f) any restrictions on voting rights, such as limitations of the voting rights of holders of a given percentage or number of votes, deadlines for exercising voting rights, or systems whereby, with the company's cooperation, the financial rights attaching to securities are separated from the holding of securities;

(g) any agreements between shareholders which are known to the company and may result in restrictions on the transfer of securities and/or voting rights within the meaning of Directive 2001/34/EC;

(h) the rules governing the appointment and replacement of board members and the amendment of the articles of association;

(i) the powers of board members, and in particular the power to issue or buy back shares;

(j) any significant agreements to which the company is a party and which take effect, alter or terminate upon a change of control of the company following a takeover bid, and the effects thereof, except where their nature is such that their disclosure would be seriously prejudicial to the company; this exception shall not apply where the company is specifically obliged to disclose such information on the basis of other legal requirements;

(k) any agreements between the company and its board members or employees providing for compensation if they resign or are made redundant without valid reason or if their employment ceases because of a takeover bid.

(2) The information referred to in paragraph (1) shall be published in the company's annual report as provided for in Article 46 of Directive 78/660/EEC (1) and Article 36 of Directive 83/349/EEC.

(3) Member States shall ensure, in the case of companies the securities of which are admitted to trading on a regulated market in a Member State, that the board presents an explanatory report to the annual general meeting of shareholders on the matters referred to in paragraph (1).

Article 11. (1) Without prejudice to other rights and obligations provided for in Community law for the companies referred to in Article 1(1), Member States shall ensure that the provisions laid down in paragraphs 2 to 7 apply when a bid has been made public.
(2) Any restrictions on the transfer of securities provided for in the articles of association of the offeree company shall not apply vis-à-vis the offeror during the time allowed for acceptance of the bid laid down in Article 7(1). Any restrictions on the transfer of securities provided for in contractual agreements between the offeree company and holders of its securities, or in contractual agreements between holders of the offeree company's securities entered into after the adoption of this Directive, shall not apply vis-à-vis the offeror during the time allowed for acceptance of the bid laid down in Article 7( ).
(3) Restrictions on voting rights provided for in the articles of association of the offeree company shall not have effect at the general meeting of shareholders which decides on any defensive measures in accordance with Article 9. Restrictions on voting rights provided for in contractual agreements between the offeree company and holders of its securities, or in contractual agreements between holders of the offeree company's securities entered into after the adoption of this Directive, shall not have effect at the general meeting of shareholders which decides on any defensive measures in accordance with Article 9. Multiple-vote securities shall carry only one vote each at the general meeting of shareholders which decides on any defensive measures in accordance with Article 9.
(4) Where, following a bid, the offeror holds 75 % or more of the capital carrying voting rights, no restrictions on the transfer of securities or on voting rights referred to in paragraphs 2 and 3 nor any extraordinary rights of shareholders concerning the appointment or removal of board members provided for in the articles of association of the offeree company shall apply; multiple-vote securities shall carry only one vote each at the first general meeting of shareholders following closure of the bid, called by the offeror in order to amend the articles of association or to remove or appoint board members. To that end, the offeror shall have the right to convene a general meeting of shareholders at short notice, provided that the meeting does not take place within two weeks of notification.
(5) Where rights are removed on the basis of paragraphs 2, 3, or 4 and/or Article 12, equitable compensation shall be provided for any loss suffered by the holders of those rights. The terms for determining such compensation and the arrangements for its payment shall be set by Member States.
(6) Paragraphs 3 and 4 shall not apply to securities where the restrictions on voting rights are compensated for by specific pecuniary advantages.
(7) This Article shall not apply either where Member States hold securities in the offeree company which confer special rights on the Member States which are compatible with the Treaty, or to special rights provided for in national law which are compatible with the Treaty or to cooperatives.

Article 12. (1) Member States may reserve the right not to require companies as referred to in Article 1(1) which have their registered offices within their territories to apply Article 9(2) and (3) and/or Article 11.
(2) Where Member States make use of the option provided for in paragraph (1), they shall nevertheless grant companies which have their registered offices within their territories the option, which shall be reversible, of applying Article 9(2) and (3) and/or Article 11, without prejudice to Article 11(7). The decision of the company shall be taken by the general meeting of shareholders, in accordance with the law of the Member State in which the company has its registered office in accordance with the rules applicable to amendment of the articles of association. The decision shall be communicated to the supervisory authority of the Member State in which the company has its registered office and to all the supervisory authorities of Member States in which its securities are admitted to trading on regulated markets or where such admission has been requested.
(3) Member States may, under the conditions determined by national law, exempt companies which apply Article 9(2) and (3) and/or Article 11 from applying Article 9(2) and (3) and/or Article 11 if they become the subject of an offer launched by a company which does not apply the same Articles as they do, or by a company controlled, directly or indirectly, by the latter, pursuant to Article 1 of Directive 83/349/EEC.
(4) Member States shall ensure that the provisions applicable to the respective companies are disclosed without delay.
(5) Any measure applied in accordance with paragraph (3) shall be subject to the authorisation of the general meeting of shareholders of the offeree company, which must be granted no earlier than 18 months before the bid was made public in accordance with Article 6(1).

Article 13. Other rules applicable to the conduct of bids. Member States shall also lay down rules which govern the conduct of bids, at least as regards the following:
(a) the lapsing of bids;

(b) the revision of bids;
(c) competing bids;
(d) the disclosure of the results of bids;
(e) the irrevocability of bids and the conditions permitted.

Article 14. Information for and consultation of employees' representatives. This Directive shall be without prejudice to the rules relating to information and to consultation of representatives of and, if Member States so provide, co-determination with the employees of the offeror and the offeree company governed by the relevant national provisions, and in particular those adopted pursuant to Directives 94/45/EC, 98/59/EC, 2001/86/EC and 2002/14/EC.

Article 15. (1) Member States shall ensure that, following a bid made to all the holders of the offeree company's securities for all of their securities, paragraphs 2 to 5 apply.
(2) Member States shall ensure that an offeror is able to require all the holders of the remaining securities to sell him/her those securities at a fair price. Member States shall introduce that right in one of the following situations:
(a) where the offeror holds securities representing not less than 90 % of the capital carrying voting rights and 90 % of the voting rights in the offeree company, or
(b) where, following acceptance of the bid, he/she has acquired or has firmly contracted to acquire securities representing not less than 90 % of the offeree company's capital carrying voting rights and 90 % of the voting rights comprised in the bid. In the case referred to in (a), Member States may set a higher threshold that may not, however, be higher than 95 % of the capital carrying voting rights and 95 % of the voting rights.
(3) Member States shall ensure that rules are in force that make it possible to calculate when the threshold is reached. Where the offeree company has issued more than one class of securities, Member States may provide that the right of squeeze-out can be exercised only in the class in which the threshold laid down in paragraph (2) has been reached.
(4) If the offeror wishes to exercise the right of squeeze-out he/she shall do so within three months of the end of the time allowed for acceptance of the bid referred to in Article 7.
(5) Member States shall ensure that a fair price is guaranteed. That price shall take the same form as the consideration offered in the bid or shall be in cash. Member States may provide that cash shall be offered at least as an alternative. Following a voluntary bid, in both of the cases referred to in paragraph (2)(a) and (b), the consideration offered in the bid shall be presumed to be fair where, through acceptance of the bid, the offeror has acquired securities representing not less than 90 % of the capital carrying voting rights comprised in the bid. Following a mandatory bid, the consideration offered in the bid shall be presumed to be fair.

Article 16. (1) Member States shall ensure that, following a bid made to all the holders of the offeree company's securities for all of their securities, paragraphs 2 and 3 apply.
(2) Member States shall ensure that a holder of remaining securities is able to require the offeror to buy his/her securities from him/her at a fair price under the same circumstances as provided for in Article 15(2).
(3) Article 15(3) to (5) shall apply mutatis mutandis.

Article 17. Member States shall determine the sanctions to be imposed for infringement of the national measures adopted pursuant to this Directive and shall take all necessary steps to ensure that they are put into effect. The sanctions thus provided for shall be effective, proportionate and dissuasive. Member States shall notify the Commission of those measures no later than the date laid down in Article 21(1) and of any subsequent change thereto at the earliest opportunity.

Article 18. (1) The Commission shall be assisted by the European Securities Committee established by Decision 2001/528/EC (hereinafter referred to as 'the Committee').
(2) Where reference is made to this paragraph, Article 5a(1) to (4) and Article 7 of Decision 1999/468/EC shall apply, having regard to the provisions of Article 8 thereof.

Article 19. (1) A contact committee shall be set up which has as its functions:
(a) to facilitate, without prejudice to Articles 226 and 227 of the Treaty, the harmonised application of this Directive through regular meetings dealing with practical problems arising in connection with its application;
(b) to advise the Commission, if necessary, on additions or amendments to this Directive.
(2) It shall not be the function of the contact committee to appraise the merits of decisions taken by the supervisory authorities in individual cases.

Article 20. Five years after the date laid down in Article 21(1), the Commission shall examine this Directive in the light of the experience acquired in applying it and, if necessary, propose its revision. That examination shall include a survey of the control structures and barriers to takeover bids that are not covered by this Directive. To that end, Member States shall provide the Commission annually with information on the takeover bids which have been launched against companies the securities of which are admitted to trading on their regulated markets. That information shall include the nationalities of the companies involved, the results of the offers and any other information relevant to the understanding of how takeover bids operate in practice.

Article 21. (1) Member States shall bring into force the laws, regulations and administrative provisions necessary to comply with this Directive no later than 20 May 2006. They shall forthwith inform the Commission thereof. When Member States adopt those provisions, they shall contain a reference to this Directive or shall be accompanied by such reference on the occasion of their official publication. The methods of making such reference shall be laid down by the Member States.
(2) Member States shall communicate to the Commission the text of the main provisions of national law that they adopt in the fields covered by this Directive.

Article 22. This Directive shall enter into force on the 20th day after that of its publication in the *Official Journal of the European Union*.

Article 23. This Directive is addressed to the Member States.

PART III   EUROPEAN COMPANY LAW

Directive 2007/36/EC of the European Parliament and of the Council of 11 July 2007 on the exercise of certain rights of shareholders in listed companies (OJ L 184, 14.07.2007, pp. 17 – 24) [footnotes omitted].

THE EUROPEAN PARLIAMENT AND THE COUNCIL OF THE EUROPEAN UNION,
Having regard to the Treaty establishing the European Community, and in particular Articles 44 and 95 thereof,
Having regard to the proposal from the Commission, Having regard to the opinion of the European Economic and Social Committee,
Acting in accordance with the procedure laid down in Article 251 of the Treaty,
Whereas:
(1) In its Communication to the Council and the European Parliament of 21 May 2003, entitled "Modernising Company Law and enhancing Corporate Governance in the European Union — A Plan to Move Forward", the Commission indicated that new tailored initiatives should be taken with a view to enhancing shareholders' rights in listed companies and that problems relating to cross-border voting should be solved as a matter of urgency.
(2) In its Resolution of 21 April 2004, the European Parliament expressed its support for the Commission's intention to strengthen shareholders' rights, in particular through the extension of the rules on transparency, proxy voting rights, the possibility of participating in general meetings via electronic means and ensuring that cross-border voting rights are able to be exercised.
(3) Holders of shares carrying voting rights should be able to exercise those rights given that they are reflected in the price that has to be paid at the acquisition of the shares. Furthermore, effective shareholder control is a pre-requisite to sound corporate governance and should, therefore, be facilitated and encouraged. It is therefore necessary to adopt measures to approximate the laws of the Member States to this end. Obstacles which deter shareholders from voting, such as making the exercise of voting rights subject to the blocking of shares during a certain period before the general meeting, should be removed. However, this Directive does not affect existing Community legislation on units issued by collective investment undertakings or on units acquired or disposed of in such undertakings.
(4) The existing Community legislation is not sufficient to achieve this objective. Directive 2001/34/EC of the European Parliament and of the Council of 28 May 2001 on the admission of securities to official stock exchange listing and on information to be published on those securities focuses on the information issuers have to disclose to the market and accordingly does not deal with the shareholder voting process itself. Moreover, Directive 2004/109/EC of the European Parliament and of the Council of 15 December 2004 on the harmonisation of transparency requirements in relation to information about issuers whose securities are admitted to trading on a regulated market imposes on issuers an obligation to make available certain information and documents relevant to general meetings, but such information and documents are to be made available in the issuer's home Member State. Therefore, certain minimum standards should be introduced with a view to protecting investors and promoting the smooth and effective exercise of shareholder rights attaching to voting shares. As regards rights other than the right to vote, Member States are free to extend the application of these minimum standards also to non-voting shares, to the extent that those shares do not enjoy such standards already.
(5) Significant proportions of shares in listed companies are held by shareholders who do not reside in the Member State in which the company has its registered office. Non-resident shareholders should be able to exercise their rights in relation to the general meeting as easily as shareholders who reside in the Member State in which the company has its registered office. This requires that existing obstacles which hinder the access of non-resident shareholders to the information relevant to the general meeting and the exercise of voting rights without physically attending the general meeting be removed. The removal of these obstacles should also benefit resident shareholders who do not or cannot attend the general meeting.
(6) Shareholders should be able to cast informed votes at, or in advance of, the general meeting, no matter where they reside. All shareholders should have sufficient time to consider the documents intended to be submitted to the general meeting and determine how they will vote their shares. To this end, timely notice should be given of the general meeting, and shareholders should be provided with the complete information intended to be submitted to the general meeting. The possibilities which modern technologies offer to make information instantly accessible should be exploited. This Directive presupposes that all listed companies already have an Internet site.
(7) Shareholders should, in principle, have the possibility to put items on the agenda of the general meeting and to table draft resolutions for items on the agenda. Without prejudice to different time-

EU: DIRECTIVE 2007/36 ON CERTAIN RIGHTS OF SHAREHOLDERS

frames and modalities which are currently in use across the Community, the exercise of those rights should be made subject to two basic rules, namely that any threshold required for the exercise of those rights should not exceed 5 % of the company's share capital and that all shareholders should in every case receive the final version of the agenda in sufficient time to prepare for the discussion and voting on each item on the agenda.

(8) Every shareholder should, in principle, have the possibility to ask questions related to items on the agenda of the general meeting and to have them answered, while the rules on how and when questions are to be asked and answered should be left to be determined by Member States.

(9) Companies should face no legal obstacles in offering to their shareholders any means of electronic participation in the general meeting. Voting without attending the general meeting in person, whether by correspondence or by electronic means, should not be subject to constraints other than those necessary for the verification of identity and the security of electronic communications. However, this should not prevent Member States from adopting rules aimed at ensuring that the results of the voting reflect the intentions of the shareholders in all circumstances, including rules aimed at addressing situations where new circumstances occur or are revealed after a shareholder has cast his vote by correspondence or by electronic means.

(10) Good corporate governance requires a smooth and effective process of proxy voting. Existing limitations and constraints which make proxy voting cumbersome and costly should therefore be removed. But good corporate governance also requires adequate safeguards against a possible abuse of proxy voting. The proxy holder should therefore be bound to observe any instructions he may have received from the shareholder and Member States should be able to introduce appropriate measures ensuring that the proxy holder does not pursue any interest other than that of the shareholder, irrespective of the reason that has given rise to the conflict of interests. Measures against possible abuse may, in particular, consist of regimes which Member States may adopt in order to regulate the activity of persons who actively engage in the collection of proxies or who have in fact collected more than a certain significant number of proxies, notably to ensure an adequate degree of reliability and transparency. Shareholders have an unfettered right under this Directive to appoint such persons as proxy holders to attend and vote at general meetings in their name. This Directive does not, however, affect any rules or sanctions that Member States may impose on such persons where votes have been cast by making fraudulent use of proxies collected. Moreover, this Directive does not impose any obligation on companies to verify that proxy holders cast votes in accordance with the voting instructions of the appointing shareholders.

(11) Where financial intermediaries are involved, the effectiveness of voting upon instructions relies, to a great extent, on the efficiency of the chain of intermediaries, given that investors are frequently unable to exercise the voting rights attached to their shares without the cooperation of every intermediary in the chain, who may not have an economic stake in the shares. In order to enable the investor to exercise his voting rights in cross-border situations, it is therefore important that intermediaries facilitate the exercise of voting rights. Further consideration should be given to this issue by the Commission in the context of a Recommendation, with a view to ensuring that investors have access to effective voting services and that voting rights are exercised in accordance with the instructions given by those investors.

(12) While the timing of disclosure to the administrative, management or supervisory body as well as to the public of votes cast in advance of the general meeting electronically or by correspondence is an important matter of corporate governance, it can be determined by Member States.

(13) Voting results should be established through methods that reflect the voting intentions expressed by shareholders, and they should be made transparent after the general meeting at least through the company's internet site.

(14) Since the objective of this Directive, namely to allow shareholders effectively to make use of their rights throughout the Community, cannot be sufficiently achieved by the Member States on the basis of the existing Community legislation and can therefore, by reason of the scale and effects of the measures, be better achieved at Community level, the Community may adopt measures, in accordance with the principle of subsidiarity as set out in Article 5 of the Treaty. In accordance with the principle of proportionality, as set out in that Article, this Directive does not go beyond what is necessary in order to achieve that objective.

(15) In accordance with paragraph (3)4 of the Interinstitutional Agreement on better law-making, Member States are encouraged to draw up, for themselves and in the interests of the Community, their own tables illustrating, as far as possible, the correlation between this Directive and the transposition measures, and to make them public,

HAVE ADOPTED THIS DIRECTIVE:

PART III EUROPEAN COMPANY LAW

Chapter I. General Provisions

Article 1. (1) This Directive establishes requirements in relation to the exercise of certain shareholder rights attaching to voting shares in relation to general meetings of companies which have their registered office in a Member State and whose shares are admitted to trading on a regulated market situated or operating within a Member State.
(2) The Member State competent to regulate matters covered in this Directive shall be the Member State in which the company has its registered office, and references to the "applicable law" are references to the law of that Member State.
(3) Member States may exempt from this Directive the following types of companies:
(a) collective investment undertakings within the meaning of Article 1(2) of Council Directive 85/611/EEC of 20 December 1985 on the coordination of laws, regulations and administrative provisions relating to undertakings for collective investment in transferable securities (UCITS);
(b) undertakings the sole object of which is the collective investment of capital provided by the public, which operate on the principle of risk spreading and which do not seek to take legal or management control over any of the issuers of their underlying investments, provided that these collective investment undertakings are authorised and subject to the supervision of competent authorities and that they have a depositary exercising functions equivalent to those under Directive 85/611/EEC;
(c) cooperative societies.

Article 2. For the purposes of this Directive the following definitions shall apply:
(a) "regulated market" means a market as defined in Article 4(1), point 14, of Directive 2004/39/EC of the European Parliament and of the Council of 21 April 2004 on markets in financial instruments;
(b) "shareholder" means the natural or legal person that is recognised as a shareholder under the applicable law;
(c) "proxy" means the empowerment of a natural or legal person by a shareholder to exercise some or all rights of that shareholder in the general meeting in his name.

Article 3. This Directive shall not prevent Member States from imposing further obligations on companies or from otherwise taking further measures to facilitate the exercise by shareholders of the rights referred to in this Directive.

Chapter II. General Meetings of Shareholders

Article 4. The company shall ensure equal treatment for all shareholders who are in the same position with regard to participation and the exercise of voting rights in the general meeting.

Article 5. (1) Without prejudice to Articles 9(4) and 11(4) of Directive 2004/25/EC of the European Parliament and of the Council of 21 April 2004 on takeover bids, Member States shall ensure that the company issues the convocation of the general meeting in one of the manners specified in paragraph (2) of this Article not later than on the 21st day before the day of the meeting. Member States may provide that, where the company offers the facility for shareholders to vote by electronic means accessible to all shareholders, the general meeting of shareholders may decide that it shall issue the convocation of a general meeting which is not an annual general meeting in one of the manners specified in paragraph (2) of this Article not later than on the 14th day before the day of the meeting. This decision is to be taken by a majority of not less than two thirds of the votes attaching to the shares or the subscribed capital represented and for a duration not later than the next annual general meeting. Member States need not apply the minimum periods referred to in the first and second subparagraphs for the second or subsequent convocation of a general meeting issued for lack of a quorum required for the meeting convened by the first convocation, provided that this Article has been complied with for the first convocation and no new item is put on the agenda, and that at least 10 days elapse between the final convocation and the date of the general meeting.
(2) Without prejudice to further requirements for notification or publication laid down by the competent Member State as defined in Article 1(2), the company shall be required to issue the convocation referred to in paragraph (1) of this Article in a manner ensuring fast access to it on a non-discriminatory basis. The Member State shall require the company to use such media as may reasonably be relied upon for the effective dissemination of information to the public throughout the Community. The Member State may not impose an obligation to use only media whose operators are established on its territory. The Member State need not apply the first subparagraph to companies that are able to identify the names and addresses of their shareholders from a current register of shareholders, provided that the company is under an obligation to send the convocation to each of its registered shareholders. In either case the company may not charge any specific cost for issuing the convocation in the prescribed manner.

EU: DIRECTIVE 2007/36 ON CERTAIN RIGHTS OF SHAREHOLDERS

(3) The convocation referred to in paragraph (1) shall at least:
(a) indicate precisely when and where the general meeting is to take place, and the proposed agenda for the general meeting;
(b) contain a clear and precise description of the procedures that shareholders must comply with in order to be able to participate and to cast their vote in the general meeting. This includes information concerning:
(i) the rights available to shareholders under Article 6, to the extent that those rights can be exercised after the issuing of the convocation, and under Article 9, and the deadlines by which those rights may be exercised; the convocation may confine itself to stating only the deadlines by which those rights may be exercised, provided it contains a reference to more detailed information concerning those rights being made available on the Internet site of the company;
(ii) the procedure for voting by proxy, notably the forms to be used to vote by proxy and the means by which the company is prepared to accept electronic notifications of the appointment of proxy holders; and
(iii) where applicable, the procedures for casting votes by correspondence or by electronic means;
(c) where applicable, state the record date as defined in Article 7(2) and explain that only those who are shareholders on that date shall have the right to participate and vote in the general meeting;
(d) indicate where and how the full, unabridged text of the documents and draft resolutions referred to in points (c) and (d) of paragraph (4) may be obtained;
(e) indicate the address of the Internet site on which the information referred to in paragraph (4) will be made available.
(4) Member States shall ensure that, for a continuous period beginning not later than on the 21 day before the day of the general meeting and including the day of the meeting, the company shall make available to its shareholders on its Internet site at least the following information:
(a) the convocation referred to in paragraph (1);
(b) the total number of shares and voting rights at the date of the convocation (including separate totals for each class of shares where the company's capital is divided into two or more classes of shares);
(c) the documents to be submitted to the general meeting;
(d) a draft resolution or, where no resolution is proposed to be adopted, a comment from a competent body within the company, to be designated by the applicable law, for each item on the proposed agenda of the general meeting; moreover, draft resolutions tabled by shareholders shall be added to the Internet site as soon as practicable after the company has received them;
(e) where applicable, the forms to be used to vote by proxy and to vote by correspondence, unless those forms are sent directly to each shareholder.
Where the forms referred to in point (e) cannot be made available on the Internet for technical reasons, the company shall indicate on its Internet site how the forms can be obtained on paper. In this case the company shall be required to send the forms by postal services and free of charge to every shareholder who so requests.
Where, pursuant to Articles 9(4) or 11(4) of Directive 2004/25/EC, or to the second subparagraph of paragraph (1) of this Article, the convocation of the general meeting is issued later than on the 21st day before the meeting, the period specified in this paragraph shall be shortened accordingly.

Article 6. (1) Member States shall ensure that shareholders, acting individually or collectively:
(a) have the right to put items on the agenda of the general meeting, provided that each such item is accompanied by a justification or a draft resolution to be adopted in the general meeting; and
(b) have the right to table draft resolutions for items included or to be included on the agenda of a general meeting.
Member States may provide that the right referred to in point (a) may be exercised only in relation to the annual general meeting, provided that shareholders, acting individually or collectively, have the right to call, or to require the company to call, a general meeting which is not an annual general meeting with an agenda including at least all the items requested by those shareholders.
Member States may provide that those rights shall be exercised in writing (submitted by postal services or electronic means).
(2) Where any of the rights specified in paragraph (1) is subject to the condition that the relevant shareholder or shareholders hold a minimum stake in the company, such minimum stake shall not exceed 5 % of the share capital.
(3) Each Member State shall set a single deadline, with reference to a specified number of days prior to the general meeting or the convocation, by which shareholders may exercise the right referred to in paragraph (1), point (a). In the same manner each Member State may set a deadline for the exercise

of the right referred to in paragraph (1), point (b).
(4) Member States shall ensure that, where the exercise of the right referred to in paragraph (1), point (a) entails a modification of the agenda for the general meeting already communicated to shareholders, the company shall make available a revised agenda in the same manner as the previous agenda in advance of the applicable record date as defined in Article 7(2) or, if no record date applies, sufficiently in advance of the date of the general meeting so as to enable other shareholders to appoint a proxy or, where applicable, to vote by correspondence.

Article 7. (1) Member States shall ensure:
(a) that the rights of a shareholder to participate in a general meeting and to vote in respect of any of his shares are not subject to any requirement that his shares be deposited with, or transferred to, or registered in the name of, another natural or legal person before the general meeting; and
(b) that the rights of a shareholder to sell or otherwise transfer his shares during the period between the record date, as defined in paragraph (2), and the general meeting to which it applies are not subject to any restriction to which they are not subject at other times.
(2) Member States shall provide that the rights of a shareholder to participate in a general meeting and to vote in respect of his shares shall be determined with respect to the shares held by that shareholder on a specified date prior to the general meeting (the record date).
Member States need not apply the first subparagraph to companies that are able to identify the names and addresses of their shareholders from a current register of shareholders on the day of the general meeting.
(3) Each Member State shall ensure that a single record date applies to all companies. However, a Member State may set one record date for companies which have issued bearer shares and another record date for companies which have issued registered shares, provided that a single record date applies to each company which has issued both types of shares. The record date shall not lie more than 30 days before the date of the general meeting to which it applies. In implementing this provision and Article 5(1), each Member State shall ensure that at least eight days elapse between the latest permissible date for the convocation of the general meeting and the record date. In calculating that number of days those two dates shall not be included. In the circumstances described in Article 5(1), third subparagraph, however, a Member State may require that at least six days elapse between the latest permissible date for the second or subsequent convocation of the general meeting and the record date. In calculating that number of days those two dates shall not be included.
(4) Proof of qualification as a shareholder may be made subject only to such requirements as are necessary to ensure the identification of shareholders and only to the extent that they are proportionate to achieving that objective.

Article 8. (1) Member States shall permit companies to offer to their shareholders any form of participation in the general meeting by electronic means, notably any or all of the following forms of participation:
(a) real-time transmission of the general meeting;
(b) real-time two-way communication enabling shareholders to address the general meeting from a remote location;
(c) a mechanism for casting votes, whether before or during the general meeting, without the need to appoint a proxy holder who is physically present at the meeting.
(2) The use of electronic means for the purpose of enabling shareholders to participate in the general meeting may be made subject only to such requirements and constraints as are necessary to ensure the identification of shareholders and the security of the electronic communication, and only to the extent that they are proportionate to achieving those objectives.
This is without prejudice to any legal rules which Member States have adopted or may adopt concerning the decision-making process within the company for the introduction or implementation of any form of participation by electronic means.

Article 9. (1) Every shareholder shall have the right to ask questions related to items on the agenda of the general meeting. The company shall answer the questions put to it by shareholders.
(2) The right to ask questions and the obligation to answer are subject to the measures which Member States may take, or allow companies to take, to ensure the identification of shareholders, the good order of general meetings and their preparation and the protection of confidentiality and business interests of companies. Member States may allow companies to provide one overall answer to questions having the same content.
Member States may provide that an answer shall be deemed to be given if the relevant information is available on the company's Internet site in a question and answer format.

EU: DIRECTIVE 2007/36 ON CERTAIN RIGHTS OF SHAREHOLDERS

Article 10. (1) Every shareholder shall have the right to appoint any other natural or legal person as a proxy holder to attend and vote at a general meeting in his name. The proxy holder shall enjoy the same rights to speak and ask questions in the general meeting as those to which the shareholder thus represented would be entitled.

Apart from the requirement that the proxy holder possess legal capacity, Member States shall abolish any legal rule which restricts, or allows companies to restrict, the eligibility of persons to be appointed as proxy holders.

(2) Member States may limit the appointment of a proxy holder to a single meeting, or to such meetings as may be held during a specified period.

Without prejudice to Article 13(5), Member States may limit the number of persons whom a shareholder may appoint as proxy holders in relation to any one general meeting. However, if a shareholder has shares of a company held in more than one securities account, such limitation shall not prevent the shareholder from appointing a separate proxy holder as regards shares held in each securities account in relation to any one general meeting. This does not affect rules prescribed by the applicable law that prohibit the casting of votes differently in respect of shares held by one and the same shareholder.

(3) Apart from the limitations expressly permitted in paragraphs 1 and 2, Member States shall not restrict or allow companies to restrict the exercise of shareholder rights through proxy holders for any purpose other than to address potential conflicts of interest between the proxy holder and the shareholder, in whose interest the proxy holder is bound to act, and in doing so Member States shall not impose any requirements other than the following:

(a) Member States may prescribe that the proxy holder disclose certain specified facts which may be relevant for the shareholders in assessing any risk that the proxy holder might pursue any interest other than the interest of the shareholder;

(b) Member States may restrict or exclude the exercise of shareholder rights through proxy holders without specific voting instructions for each resolution in respect of which the proxy holder is to vote on behalf of the shareholder;

(c) Member States may restrict or exclude the transfer of the proxy to another person, but this shall not prevent a proxy holder who is a legal person from exercising the powers conferred upon it through any member of its administrative or management body or any of its employees.

A conflict of interest within the meaning of this paragraph may in particular arise where the proxy holder:

(i) is a controlling shareholder of the company, or is another entity controlled by such shareholder;

(ii) is a member of the administrative, management or supervisory body of the company, or of a controlling shareholder or controlled entity referred to in point (i);

(iii) is an employee or an auditor of the company, or of a controlling shareholder or controlled entity referred to in ( );

(iv) has a family relationship with a natural person referred to in points (i) to (iii).

(4) The proxy holder shall cast votes in accordance with the instructions issued by the appointing shareholder.

Member States may require proxy holders to keep a record of the voting instructions for a defined minimum period and to confirm on request that the voting instructions have been carried out.

(5) A person acting as a proxy holder may hold a proxy from more than one shareholder without limitation as to the number of shareholders so represented. Where a proxy holder holds proxies from several shareholders, the applicable law shall enable him to cast votes for a certain shareholder differently from votes cast for another shareholder.

Article 11. (1) Member States shall permit shareholders to appoint a proxy holder by electronic means. Moreover, Member States shall permit companies to accept the notification of the appointment by electronic means, and shall ensure that every company offers to its shareholders at least one effective method of notification by electronic means.

(2) Member States shall ensure that proxy holders may be appointed, and that such appointment be notified to the company, only in writing. Beyond this basic formal requirement, the appointment of a proxy holder, the notification of the appointment to the company and the issuance of voting instructions, if any, to the proxy holder may be made subject only to such formal requirements as are necessary to ensure the identification of the shareholder and of the proxy holder, or to ensure the possibility of verifying the content of voting instructions, respectively, and only to the extent that they are proportionate to achieving those objectives.

(3) The provisions of this Article shall apply mutatis mutandis for the revocation of the appointment of a proxy holder.

PART III EUROPEAN COMPANY LAW

Article 12. Member States shall permit companies to offer their shareholders the possibility to vote by correspondence in advance of the general meeting. Voting by correspondence may be made subject only to such requirements and constraints as are necessary to ensure the identification of shareholders and only to the extent that they are proportionate to achieving that objective.

Article 13. (1) This Article applies where a natural or legal person who is recognised as a shareholder by the applicable law acts in the course of a business on behalf of another natural or legal person (the client).
(2) Where the applicable law imposes disclosure requirements as a prerequisite for the exercise of voting rights by a shareholder referred to in paragraph (1), such requirements shall not go beyond a list disclosing to the company the identity of each client and the number of shares voted on his behalf.
(3) Where the applicable law imposes formal requirements on the authorisation of a shareholder referred to in paragraph (1) to exercise voting rights, or on voting instructions, such formal requirements shall not go beyond what is necessary to ensure the identification of the client, or the possibility of verifying the content of voting instructions, respectively, and is proportionate to achieving those objectives.
(4) A shareholder referred to in paragraph (1) shall be permitted to cast votes attaching to some of the shares differently from votes attaching to the other shares.
(5) Where the applicable law limits the number of persons whom a shareholder may appoint as proxy holders in accordance with Article 10(2), such limitation shall not prevent a shareholder referred to in paragraph (1) of this Article from granting a proxy to each of his clients or to any third party designated by a client.

Article 14. (1) The company shall establish for each resolution at least the number of shares for which votes have been validly cast, the proportion of the share capital represented by those votes, the total number of votes validly cast as well as the number of votes cast in favour of and against each resolution and, where applicable, the number of abstentions.
However, Member States may provide or allow companies to provide that if no shareholder requests a full account of the voting, it shall be sufficient to establish the voting results only to the extent needed to ensure that the required majority is reached for each resolution.
(2) Within a period of time to be determined by the applicable law, which shall not exceed 15 days after the general meeting, the company shall publish on its Internet site the voting results established in accordance with paragraph (1).
(3) This Article is without prejudice to any legal rules that Member States have adopted or may adopt concerning the formalities required in order for a resolution to become valid or the possibility of a subsequent legal challenge to the voting result.

Chapter III. Final Provisions

Article 15. Member States shall bring into force the laws, regulations and administrative provisions necessary to comply with this Directive by 3 August 2009 at the latest. They shall forthwith communicate to the Commission the text of those measures.
Notwithstanding the first paragraph, Member States which on 1 July 2006 had in force national measures restricting or prohibiting the appointment of a proxy holder in the case of Article 10(3), second subparagraph, point (ii), shall bring into force the laws, regulations and administrative provisions necessary in order to comply with Article 10(3) as concerns such restriction or prohibition by 3 August 2012 at the latest. Member States shall forthwith communicate the number of days specified under Articles 6(3) and 7(3), and any subsequent changes thereof, to the Commission, which shall publish this information in the *Official Journal of the European Union*. When Member States adopt the measures referred to in the first paragraph, they shall contain a reference to this Directive or shall be accompanied by such reference on the occasion of their official publication. The methods of making such reference shall be laid down by the Member States.

Article 16. This Directive shall enter into force on the 20th day following its publication in the *Official Journal of the European Union*.

Article 17. This Directive is addressed to the Member States.

EU: DIRECTIVE 2009/102 ON SINGLE-MEMBER PRIVATE LIMITED LIABILITY COMPANIES

Directive 2009/102/EC of the European Parliament and of the Council of 16 September 2009 in the area of company law on single-member private limited liability companies ("Twelfth Company Law Directive") (Text with EEA relevance) (OJ L 258, 01.10.2009 pp. 20 –25) [footnotes omitted].

THE EUROPEAN PARLIAMENT AND THE COUNCIL OF THE EUROPEAN UNION,
Having regard to the Treaty establishing the European Community, and in particular Article 44 thereof,
Having regard to the proposal from the Commission,
Having regard to the opinion of the European Economic and Social Committee,
Acting in accordance with the procedure laid down in Article 251 of the Treaty, Whereas:
(1) Twelfth Council Company Law Directive 89/667/EEC of 21 December 1989 on single-member private limited liability companies has been substantially amended several times. In the interests of clarity and rationality the said Directive should be codified.
(2) Certain safeguards which, for the protection of the interests of members and others, are required by Member States of companies and firms within the meaning of the second paragraph of Article 48 of the Treaty should be coordinated with a view to making such safeguards equivalent throughout the Community.
(3) In this field, First Council Directive 68/151/EEC of 9 March 1968 on coordination of safeguards which, for the protection of the interests of members and others, are required by Member States of companies within the meaning of the second paragraph of Article 58 of the Treaty, with a view to making such safeguards equivalent throughout the Community, Fourth Council Directive 78/660/EEC of 25 July 1978 based on Article 54(3)(g) of the Treaty on the annual accounts of certain types of companies and Seventh Council Directive 83/349/EEC of 13 June 1983 based on Article 54(3)(g) of the Treaty on consolidated accounts, respectively concerning disclosure, the validity of commitments, nullity, annual accounts and consolidated accounts, apply to all share-capital companies. However, Second Council Directive 77/91/EEC of 13 December 1976 on coordination of safeguards which, for the protection of the interests of members and others, are required by Member States of companies within the meaning of the second paragraph of Article 58 of the Treaty, in respect of the formation of public limited liability companies and the maintenance and alteration of their capital, with a view to making such safeguards equivalent, Third Council Directive 78/855/EEC of 9 October 1978 based on Article 54(3)(g) of the Treaty concerning mergers of public limited liability companies, and Sixth Council Directive 82/891/EEC of 17 December 1982 based on Article 54(3)(g) of the Treaty, concerning the division of public limited liability companies, relating respectively to formation and capital, mergers and divisions, apply only to public limited liability companies.
(4) A legal instrument is required allowing the limitation of liability of the individual entrepreneur throughout the Community, without prejudice to the laws of the Member States, which, in exceptional circumstances, require that entrepreneur to be liable for the obligations of his undertaking.
(5) A private limited liability company may be a single-member company from the time of its formation, or may become one because its shares have come to be held by a single shareholder. Pending the coordination of national provisions on the laws relating to groups, Member States may lay down certain special provisions and penalties for cases where a natural person is the sole member of several companies or where a single-member company or any other legal person is the sole member of a company. The sole aim of this power is to take account of the differences which exist in certain national laws. For that purpose, Member States may in specific cases lay down restrictions on the use of single-member companies or remove the limits on the liabilities of sole members. Member States are free to lay down rules to cover the risks that single-member companies may present as a consequence of having single members, particularly in order to ensure that the subscribed capital is paid.
(6) The fact that all the shares have come to be held by a single shareholder and the identity of the sole member should be disclosed by an entry in a register accessible to the public.
(7) Decisions taken by the sole member exercising the powers of the general meeting should be recorded in writing.
(8) Contracts between a sole member and his company as represented by him should likewise be recorded in writing, in so far as such contracts do not relate to current operations concluded under normal conditions.
(9) This Directive should be without prejudice to the obligations of the Member States relating to the time limits for transposition into national law and application of the Directives set out in Annex II, Part B,
HAVE ADOPTED THIS DIRECTIVE:

PART III   EUROPEAN COMPANY LAW

Article 1. The coordination measures prescribed by this Directive shall apply to the laws, regulations and administrative provisions of the Member States relating to the types of company listed in Annex I.

Article 2. (1) A company may have a sole member when it is formed and also when all its shares come to be held by a single person (single-member company).
(2) Member States may, pending coordination of national laws relating to groups, lay down special provisions or penalties for cases where:
(a) a natural person is the sole member of several companies; or
(b) a single-member company or any other legal person is the sole member of a company.

Article 3. Where a company becomes a single-member company because all its shares come to be held by a single person, that fact, together with the identity of the sole member, must either be recorded in the file or entered in the register as referred to in Article 3(1) and (2) of Directive 68/151/EEC or be entered in a register kept by the company and accessible to the public.

Article 4. (1) The sole member shall exercise the powers of the general meeting of the company.
(2) Decisions taken by the sole member in the field referred to in paragraph (1) shall be recorded in minutes or drawn up in writing.

Article 5. (1) Contracts between the sole member and his company as represented by him shall be recorded in minutes or drawn up in writing.
(2) Member States need not apply paragraph (1) to current operations concluded under normal conditions.

Article 6. Where a Member State allows single-member companies as defined by Article 2(1) in the case of public limited companies as well, this Directive shall apply.

Article 7. A Member State need not allow the formation of single-member companies where its legislation provides that an individual entrepreneur may set up an undertaking the liability of which is limited to a sum dedicated to a stated activity, on condition that safeguards are laid down for such undertakings which are equivalent to those imposed by this Directive or by any other Community provisions applicable to the companies referred to in Article 1.

Article 8. Member States shall communicate to the Commission the texts of the main provisions of national law which they adopt in the field covered by this Directive.

Article 9. Directive 89/667/EEC, as amended by the acts listed in Annex II, Part A, is repealed, without prejudice to the obligations of the Member States relating to the time limits for transposition into national law and application of the Directives set out in Annex II, Part B. References to the repealed Directive shall be construed as references to this Directive and shall be read in accordance with the correlation table in Annex III.

Article 10. This Directive shall enter into force on the 20th day following its publication in the *Official Journal of the European Union*.

Article 11. This Directive is addressed to the Member States.

Annex I. Types of companies referred to in Article 1
— Belgium: 'société privée à responsabilité limitée/besloten vennootschap met beperkte aansprakelijkheid',
— Bulgaria: 'дружество с ограничена отговорност, акционерно дружество',
— Czech Republic: 'společnost s ručením omezeným',
— Denmark: 'anpartsselskaber',
— Germany: 'Gesellschaft mit beschränkter Haftung',
— Estonia: 'aktsiaselts, osaühing',
— Ireland: 'private company limited by shares or by guarantee',
— Greece: 'εταιρεία περιορισμένης ευθύνης',
— Spain: 'sociedad de responsabilidad limitada',
— France: 'société à responsabilité limitée',
— Italy: 'società a responsabilità limitata',
— Cyprus: 'ιδιωτική εταιρεία περιορισμένης ευθύνης με μετοχές ή με εγγύηση',
— Latvia: 'sabiedrība ar ierobežotu atbildību',
— Lithuania: 'uždaroji akcinė bendrovė',

EU: DIRECTIVE 2009/102 ON SINGLE-MEMBER PRIVATE LIMITED LIABILITY COMPANIES

— Luxembourg: 'société à responsabilité limitée',
— Hungary: 'korlátolt felelősségű társaság, részvénytársaság',
— Malta: 'kumpannija privata/Private limited liability company',
— The Netherlands: 'besloten vennootschap met beperkte aansprakelijkheid',
— Austria: 'Aktiengesellschaft, Gesellschaft mit beschränkter Haftung',
— Poland: 'spółka z ograniczoną odpowiedzialnością',
— Portugal: 'sociedade por quotas',
— Romania: 'societate cu răspundere limitată',
— Slovenia: 'družba z omejeno odgovornostjo',
— Slovakia: 'spoločnosť s ručením obmedzeným',
— Finland: 'osakeyhtiö/aktiebolag',
— Sweden: 'aktiebolag',
— United Kingdom: 'private company limited by shares or by guarantee'

PART III   EUROPEAN COMPANY LAW

Directive 2013/34/EU of the European Parliament and of the Council of 26 June 2013 on the annual financial statements, consolidated financial statements and related reports of certain types of undertakings, amending Directive 2006/43/EC of the European Parliament and of the Council and repealing Council Directives 78/660/EEC and 83/349/EEC (Text with EEA relevance) [footnotes omitted[.

THE EUROPEAN PARLIAMENT AND THE COUNCIL OF THE EUROPEAN UNION,
Having regard to the Treaty on the Functioning of the European Union, and in particular Article 50(1) thereof,
Having regard to the proposal from the European Commission,
After transmission of the draft legislative act to the national parliaments,
Having regard to the opinion of the European Economic and Social Committee,
Acting in accordance with the ordinary legislative procedure,
Whereas:
(1) This Directive takes into account the Commission's better regulation programme, and, in particular, the Commission Communication entitled "Smart Regulation in the European Union", which aims at designing and delivering regulation of the highest quality whilst respecting the principles of subsidiarity and proportionality and ensuring that the administrative burdens are proportionate to the benefits they bring. The Commission Communication entitled "Think Small First – Small Business Act for Europe", adopted in June 2008 and revised in February 2011, recognises the central role played by small and medium-sized enterprises (SMEs) in the Union economy and aims to improve the overall approach to entrepreneurship and to anchor the "think small first" principle in policy-making from regulation to public service. The European Council of 24 and 25 March 2011 welcomed the Commission's intention to present the "Single Market Act" with measures creating growth and jobs, bringing tangible results to citizens and businesses.
The Commission Communication entitled "Single Market Act", adopted in April 2011, proposes to simplify the Fourth Council Directive 78/660/EEC of 25 July 1978 based on Article 54(3)(g) of the Treaty on the annual accounts of certain types of companies and the Seventh Council Directive 83/349/EEC of 13 June 1983 based on the Article 54(3)(g) of the Treaty on consolidated accounts (the Accounting Directives) as regards financial information obligations and to reduce administrative burdens, in particular for SMEs. "The Europe 2020 Strategy" for smart, sustainable and inclusive growth aims to reduce administrative burdens and improve the business environment, in particular for SMEs, and to promote the internationalisation of SMEs. The European Council of 24 and 25 March 2011 also called for the overall regulatory burden, in particular for SMEs, to be reduced at both Union and national level and suggested measures to increase productivity, such as the removal of red tape and the improvement of the regulatory framework for SMEs.
(2) On 18 December 2008 the European Parliament adopted a non-legislative resolution on accounting requirements as regards small and medium-sized companies, particularly micro-entities, stating that the Accounting Directives are often very burdensome for small and medium-sized companies, and in particular for micro-entities, and asking the Commission to continue its efforts to review those Directives.
(3) The coordination of national provisions concerning the presentation and content of annual financial statements and management reports, the measurement bases used therein and their publication in respect of certain types of undertakings with limited liability is of special importance for the protection of shareholders, members and third parties. Simultaneous coordination is necessary in those fields for such types of undertakings because, on the one hand, some undertakings operate in more than one Member State and, on the other hand, such undertakings offer no safeguards to third parties beyond the amounts of their net assets.
(4) Annual financial statements pursue various objectives and do not merely provide information for investors in capital markets but also give an account of past transactions and enhance corporate governance. Union accounting legislation needs to strike an appropriate balance between the interests of the addressees of financial statements and the interest of undertakings in not being unduly burdened with reporting requirements.
(5) The scope of this Directive should include certain undertakings with limited liability such as public and private limited liability companies. Additionally, there is a substantial number of partnerships and limited partnerships all the fully liable members of which are constituted either as public or as private limited liability companies, and such partnerships should therefore be subject to the coordination measures of this Directive. This Directive should also ensure that partnerships fall within its scope where members of a partnership which are not constituted as private or public limited companies in fact have limited liability for the partnership's obligations because that liability

is limited by other undertakings within the scope of this Directive. The exclusion of not-for-profit undertakings from the scope of this Directive is consistent with its purpose, in line with point (g) of Article 50(2) of the Treaty on the Functioning of the European Union (TFEU).

(6) The scope of this Directive should be principles-based and should ensure that it is not possible for an undertaking to exclude itself from that scope by creating a group structure containing multiple layers of undertakings established inside or outside the Union.

(7) The provisions of this Directive should apply only to the extent that they are not inconsistent with, or contradicted by, provisions on the financial reporting of certain types of undertakings or provisions regarding the distribution of an undertaking's capital which are laid down in other legislative acts in force accepted by one or more Union institutions.

(8) It is necessary, moreover, to establish minimum equivalent legal requirements at Union level as regards the extent of the financial information that should be made available to the public by undertakings that are in competition with one another.

(9) Annual financial statements should be prepared on a prudent basis and should give a true and fair view of an undertaking's assets and liabilities, financial position and profit or loss. It is possible that, in exceptional cases, a financial statement does not give such a true and fair view where provisions of this Directive are applied. In such cases, the undertaking should depart from such provisions in order to give a true and fair view. The Member States should be allowed to define such exceptional cases and to lay down the relevant special rules which are to apply in those cases. Those exceptional cases should be understood to be only very unusual transactions and unusual situations and should, for instance, not be related to entire specific sectors.

(10) This Directive should ensure that the requirements for small undertakings are to a large extent harmonised throughout the Union. This Directive is based on the "think small first" principle. In order to avoid disproportionate administrative burdens on those undertakings, Member States should only be allowed to require a few disclosures by way of notes that are additional to the mandatory notes. In the case of a single filing system, however, Member States may in certain cases require a limited number of additional disclosures where these are explicitly required by their national tax legislation and are strictly necessary for the purposes of tax collection. It should be possible for Member States to impose requirements on medium-sized and large undertakings that go further than the minimum requirements prescribed by this Directive.

(11) Where this Directive allows Member States to impose additional requirements on, for instance, small undertakings, this means that Member States can make use of this option in full or in part by requiring less than the option allows for. In the same way, where this Directive allows Member States to make use of an exemption in relation to, for instance, small undertakings, this means that Member States can exempt such undertakings wholly or in part.

(12) Small, medium-sized and large undertakings should be defined and distinguished by reference to balance sheet total, net turnover and the average number of employees during the financial year, as those criteria typically provide objective evidence as to the size of an undertaking. However, where a parent undertaking is not preparing consolidated financial statements for the group, Member States should be allowed to take steps they deem necessary to require that such an undertaking be classified as a larger undertaking by determining its size and resulting category on a consolidated or aggregated basis. Where a Member State applies one or more of the optional exemptions for micro-undertakings, micro-undertakings should also be defined by reference to balance sheet total, net turnover and the average number of employees during the financial year. Member States should not be obliged to define separate categories for medium-sized and large undertakings in their national legislation if medium-sized undertakings are subject to the same requirements as large undertakings.

(13) Micro-undertakings have limited resources with which to comply with demanding regulatory requirements. Where no specific rules are in place for micro-undertakings, the rules applying to small undertakings apply to them. Those rules place on them administrative burdens which are disproportionate to their size and are, therefore, relatively more onerous for micro-undertakings as compared to other small undertakings. Therefore, it should be possible for Member States to exempt micro-undertakings from certain obligations applying to small undertakings that would impose excessive administrative burdens on them. However, micro-undertakings should still be subject to any national obligation to keep records showing their business transactions and financial position. Moreover, investment undertakings and financial holding undertakings should be excluded from the benefits of simplifications applicable to micro-undertakings.

(14) Member States should take into account the specific conditions and needs of their own markets when making a decision about whether or how to implement a distinct regime for micro-undertakings within the context of this Directive.

(15) Publication of financial statements can be burdensome for micro-undertakings. At the same time,

Member States need to ensure compliance with this Directive. Accordingly, Member States making use of the exemptions for micro-undertakings provided for in this Directive should be allowed to exempt micro-undertakings from a general publication requirement, provided that balance sheet information is duly filed, in accordance with national law, with at least one designated competent authority and that the information is forwarded to the business register, so that a copy should be obtainable upon application. In such cases, the obligation laid down in this Directive to publish any accounting document in accordance with Article 3(5) of Directive 2009/101/EC of the European Parliament and of the Council of 16 September 2009 on coordination of safeguards which, for the protection of the interests of members and third parties, are required by Member States of companies within the meaning of the second paragraph of Article 48 of the Treaty, with a view to making such safeguards equivalent, should not apply.

(16) To ensure the disclosure of comparable and equivalent information, recognition and measurement principles should include the going concern, the prudence, and the accrual basis. Set-offs between asset and liability items and income and expense items should not be allowed and components of assets and liabilities should be valued separately. In specific cases, however, Member States should be allowed to permit or require undertakings to perform set-offs between asset and liability items and income and expense items. The presentation of items in financial statements should have regard to the economic reality or commercial substance of the underlying transaction or arrangement. Member States should, however, be allowed to exempt undertakings from applying that principle.

(17) The principle of materiality should govern recognition, measurement, presentation, disclosure and consolidation in financial statements. According to the principle of materiality, information that is considered immaterial may, for instance, be aggregated in the financial statements. However, while a single item might be considered to be immaterial, immaterial items of a similar nature might be considered material when taken as a whole. Member States should be allowed to limit the mandatory application of the principle of materiality to presentation and disclosure. The principle of materiality should not affect any national obligation to keep complete records showing business transactions and financial position.

(18) Items recognised in annual financial statements should be measured on the basis of the principle of purchase price or production cost to ensure the reliability of information contained in financial statements. However, Member States should be allowed to permit or require undertakings to revalue fixed assets in order that more relevant information may be provided to the users of financial statements.

(19) The need for comparability of financial information throughout the Union makes it necessary to require Member States to allow a system of fair value accounting for certain financial instruments. Furthermore, systems of fair value accounting provide information that can be of more relevance to the users of financial statements than purchase price or production cost-based information. Accordingly, Member States should permit the adoption of a fair value system of accounting by all undertakings or classes of undertaking, other than micro-undertakings making use of the exemptions provided for in this Directive, in respect of both annual and consolidated financial statements or, if a Member State so chooses, in respect of consolidated financial statements only. Furthermore, Member States should be allowed to permit or require fair value accounting for assets other than financial instruments.

(20) A limited number of layouts for the balance sheet is necessary to allow users of financial statements to better compare the financial position of undertakings within the Union. Member States should require the use of one layout for the balance sheet and should be allowed to offer a choice from amongst permitted layouts. However, Member States should be able to permit or require undertakings to modify the layout and present a balance sheet distinguishing between current and non-current items. A profit and loss account layout showing the nature of expenses and a profit and loss account layout showing the function of expenses should be permitted. Member States should require the use of one layout for the profit and loss account and should be allowed to offer a choice from amongst permitted layouts. Member States should also be able to allow undertakings to present a statement of performance instead of a profit and loss account prepared in accordance with one of the permitted layouts. Simplifications of the required layouts may be made available for small and medium-sized undertakings. However, Member States should be allowed to restrict layouts of the balance sheet and profit and loss account if necessary for the electronic filing of financial statements.

(21) For comparability reasons, a common framework for recognition, measurement and presentation of, inter alia, value adjustments, goodwill, provisions, stocks of goods and fungible assets, and income and expenditure of exceptional size or incidence should be provided.

(22) The recognition and measurement of some items in financial statements are based on estimates,

judgements and models rather than exact depictions. As a result of the uncertainties inherent in business activities, certain items in financial statements cannot be measured precisely but can only be estimated. Estimation involves judgements based on the latest available reliable information. The use of estimates is an essential part of the preparation of financial statements. This is especially true in the case of provisions, which by their nature are more uncertain than most other items in the balance sheet. Estimates should be based on a prudent judgement of the management of the undertaking and calculated on an objective basis, supplemented by experience of similar transactions and, in some cases, even reports from independent experts. The evidence considered should include any additional evidence provided by events after the balance-sheet date.

(23) The information presented in the balance sheet and in the profit and loss account should be supplemented by disclosures by way of notes to the financial statements. Users of financial statements typically have a limited need for supplementary information from small undertakings, and it can be costly for small undertakings to collate that supplementary information. A limited disclosure regime for small undertakings is, therefore, justified. However, where a micro- or small undertaking considers that it is beneficial to provide additional disclosures of the types required of medium-sized and large undertakings, or other disclosures not provided for in this Directive, it should not be prevented from doing so

(24) Disclosure in respect of accounting policies is one of the key elements of the notes to the financial statements. Such disclosure should include, in particular, the measurement bases applied to various items, a statement on the conformity of those accounting policies with the going concern concept and any significant changes to the accounting policies adopted.

(25) Users of financial statements prepared by medium-sized and large undertakings typically have more sophisticated needs. Therefore, further disclosures should be provided in certain areas. Exemption from certain disclosure obligations is justified where such disclosure would be prejudicial to certain persons or to the undertaking.

(26) The management report and the consolidated management report are important elements of financial reporting. A fair review of the development of the business and of its position should be provided, in a manner consistent with the size and complexity of the business. The information should not be restricted to the financial aspects of the undertaking's business, and there should be an analysis of environmental and social aspects of the business necessary for an understanding of the undertaking's development, performance or position. In cases where the consolidated management report and the parent undertaking management report are presented in a single report, it may be appropriate to give greater emphasis to those matters which are significant to the undertakings included in the consolidation taken as a whole. However, having regard to the potential burden placed on small and medium-sized undertakings, it is appropriate to provide that Member States may choose to waive the obligation to provide non-financial information in the management report of such undertakings.

(27) Member States should have the possibility of exempting small undertakings from the obligation to draw up a management report provided that such undertakings include, in the notes to the financial statements, the data concerning the acquisition of own shares referred to in Article 24(2) of Directive 2012/30/EU of the European Parliament and of the Council of 25 October 2012 on coordination of safeguards which, for the protection of the interests of members and others, are required by Member States of companies within the meaning of the second paragraph of Article 54 of the Treaty on the Functioning of the European Union, in respect of the formation of public limited liability companies and the maintenance and alteration of their capital, with a view to making such safeguards equivalent.

(28) Given that listed undertakings can have a prominent role in the economies in which they operate, the provisions of this Directive concerning the corporate governance statement should apply to undertakings whose transferable securities are admitted to trading on a regulated market.

(29) Many undertakings own other undertakings and the aim of coordinating the legislation governing consolidated financial statements is to protect the interests subsisting in companies with share capital. Consolidated financial statements should be drawn up so that financial information concerning such undertakings may be conveyed to members and third parties. National law governing consolidated financial statements should therefore be coordinated in order to achieve the objectives of comparability and equivalence in the information which undertakings should publish within the Union. However, given the lack of an arm's-length transaction price, Member States should be allowed to permit intra-group transfers of participating interests, so-called common control transactions, to be accounted for using the pooling of interests method of accounting, in which the book value of shares held in an undertaking included in a consolidation is set off against the corresponding percentage of capital only.

(30) In Directive 83/349/EEC there was a requirement to prepare consolidated financial statements

for groups in cases where either the parent undertaking or one or more of the subsidiary undertakings was established as one of the types of undertakings listed in Annex I or Annex II to this Directive. Member States had the option of exempting parent undertakings from the requirement to draw up consolidated accounts in cases where the parent undertaking was not of the type listed in Annex I or Annex II. This Directive requires only parent undertakings of the types listed in Annex I or, in certain circumstances, Annex II to draw up consolidated financial statements, but does not preclude Member States from extending the scope of this Directive to cover other situations as well. In substance there is therefore no change, as it remains up to the Member States to decide whether to require undertakings which do not fall within the scope of this Directive to prepare consolidated financial statements.

(31) Consolidated financial statements should present the activities of a parent undertaking and its subsidiaries as a single economic entity (a group). Undertakings controlled by the parent undertaking should be considered as subsidiary undertakings. Control should be based on holding a majority of voting rights, but control may also exist where there are agreements with fellow shareholders or members. In certain circumstances control may be effectively exercised where the parent holds a minority or none of the shares in the subsidiary. Member States should be entitled to require that undertakings not subject to control, but which are managed on a unified basis or have a common administrative, managerial or supervisory body, be included in consolidated financial statements.

(32) A subsidiary undertaking which is itself a parent undertaking should draw up consolidated financial statements. Nevertheless, Member States should be entitled to exempt such a parent undertaking from the obligation to draw up such consolidated financial statements in certain circumstances, provided that its members and third parties are sufficiently protected.

(33) Small groups should be exempt from the obligation to prepare consolidated financial statements as the users of small undertakings' financial statements do not have sophisticated information needs and it can be costly to prepare consolidated financial statements in addition to the annual financial statements of the parent and subsidiary undertakings. Member States should be able to exempt medium-sized groups from the obligation to prepare consolidated financial statements on the same cost/benefit grounds unless any of the affiliated undertakings is a public-interest entity.

(34) Consolidation requires the full incorporation of the assets and liabilities and of the income and expenditure of group undertakings, the separate disclosure of non-controlling interests in the consolidated balance sheet within capital and reserves and the separate disclosure of non-controlling interests in the profit and loss of the group in the consolidated profit and loss accounts. However, the necessary corrections should be made to eliminate the effects of the financial relations between the undertakings consolidated.

(35) Recognition and measurement principles applicable to the preparation of annual financial statements should also apply to the preparation of consolidated financial statements. However, Member States should be allowed to permit the general provisions and principles stated in this Directive to be applied differently in annual financial statements than in consolidated financial statements.

(36) Associated undertakings should be included in consolidated financial statements by means of the equity method. The provisions on measurement of associated undertakings should in substance remain unchanged from Directive 83/349/EEC, and the methods allowed under that Directive can still be applied. Member States should also be able to permit or require that a jointly managed undertaking be proportionately consolidated within consolidated financial statements.

(37) Consolidated financial statements should include all disclosures by way of notes to the financial statements for the undertakings included in the consolidation taken as a whole. The names, registered offices and group interest in the undertakings' capital should also be disclosed in respect of subsidiaries, associated undertakings, jointly managed undertakings and participating interests.

(38) The annual financial statements of all undertakings to which this Directive applies should be published in accordance with Directive 2009/101/EC. It is, however, appropriate to provide that certain derogations may be granted in this area for small and medium-sized undertakings.

(39) The Member States are strongly encouraged to develop electronic publication systems that allow undertakings to file accounting data, including statutory financial statements, only once and in a form that allows multiple users to access and use the data easily. With regard to the reporting of financial statements, the Commission is encouraged to explore means for a harmonised electronic format. Such systems should, however, not be burdensome to small and medium-sized undertakings.

(40) The Members of the administrative, management and supervisory bodies of an undertaking should, as a minimum requirement, be collectively responsible to the undertaking for drawing up and publishing annual financial statements and management reports. The same approach should also apply to members of the administrative, management and supervisory bodies of undertakings drawing up consolidated financial statements. Those bodies act within the competences assigned to them

by national law. This should not prevent Member States from going further and providing for direct responsibility to shareholders or even other stakeholders.

(41) Liability for drawing up and publishing annual financial statements and consolidated financial statements, as well as management reports and consolidated management reports, is based on national law. Appropriate liability rules, as laid down by each Member State under its national law, should be applicable to members of the administrative, management and supervisory bodies of an undertaking. Member States should be allowed to determine the extent of the liability.

(42) In order to promote credible financial reporting processes across the Union, members of the body within an undertaking that is responsible for the preparation of the undertaking's financial statements should ensure that the financial information included in the undertaking's annual financial statement and the group's consolidated financial statement gives a true and fair view.

(43) Annual financial statements and consolidated financial statements should be audited. The requirement that an audit opinion should state whether annual or consolidated financial statements give a true and fair view in accordance with the relevant financial reporting framework should not be understood as restricting the scope of that opinion but as clarifying the context in which it is expressed. The annual financial statements of small undertakings should not be covered by this audit obligation, as audit can be a significant administrative burden for that category of undertaking, while for many small undertakings the same persons are both shareholders and managers and, therefore, have limited need for third-party assurance on financial statements. However, this Directive should not prevent Member States from imposing an audit on their small undertakings, taking into account the specific conditions and needs of small undertakings and the users of their financial statements. Furthermore, it is more appropriate to define the content of the audit report in Directive 2006/43/EC of the European Parliament and of the Council of 17 May 2006 on statutory audits of annual accounts and consolidated accounts. Therefore that directive should be amended accordingly.

(44) In order to provide for enhanced transparency of payments made to governments, large undertakings and public-interest entities which are active in the extractive industry or logging of primary forests should disclose material payments made to governments in the countries in which they operate in a separate report, on an annual basis. Such undertakings are active in countries rich in natural resources, in particular minerals, oil, natural gas and primary forests. The report should include types of payments comparable to those disclosed by an undertaking participating in the Extractive Industries Transparency Initiative (EITI). The initiative is also complementary to the Forest Law Enforcement, Governance and Trade Action Plan of the European Union (EU FLEGT) and the provisions of Regulation (EU) No 995/2010 of the European Parliament and of the Council of 20 October 2010 laying down the obligations of operators who place timber and timber products on the market, which require traders of timber products to exercise due diligence in order to prevent illegal wood from entering the Union market.

(45) The report should serve to help governments of resource-rich countries to implement the EITI principles and criteria and account to their citizens for payments such governments receive from undertakings active in the extractive industry or loggers of primary forests operating within their jurisdiction. The report should incorporate disclosures on a country and project basis. A project should be defined as the operational activities that are governed by a single contract, license, lease, concession or similar legal agreements and form the basis for payment liabilities to a government. Nonetheless, if multiple such agreements are substantially interconnected, this should be considered a project. Substantially interconnected legal agreements should be understood as a set of operationally and geographically integrated contracts, licenses, leases or concessions or related agreements with substantially similar terms that are signed with a government, giving rise to payment liabilities. Such agreements can be governed by a single contract, joint venture, production sharing agreement, or other overarching legal agreement.

(46) Any payment, whether made as a single payment or as a series of related payments, need not be taken into account in the report if it is below EUR 100 000 within a financial year. This means that, in the case of any arrangement providing for periodic payments or instalments (e.g. rental fees), the undertaking must consider the aggregate amount of the related periodic payments or instalments of the related payments in determining whether the threshold has been met for that series of payments, and accordingly, whether disclosure is required.

(47) Undertakings active in the extractive industry or the logging of primary forests should not be required to disaggregate and allocate payments on a project basis where payments are made in respect of obligations imposed on the undertakings at the entity level rather than the project level. For instance, if an undertaking has more than one project in a host country, and that country's government levies corporate income taxes on the undertaking with respect to the undertaking's income in the country as a whole, and not with respect to a particular project or operation within the country,

the undertaking would be permitted to disclose the resulting income tax payment or payments without specifying a particular project associated with the payment.

(48) An undertaking active in the extractive industry or in the logging of primary forests generally does not need to disclose dividends paid to a government as a common or ordinary shareholder of that undertaking as long as the dividend is paid to the government on the same terms as to other shareholders. However, the undertaking will be required to disclose any dividends paid in lieu of production entitlements or royalties.

(49) In order to address the potential for circumvention of disclosure requirements, this Directive should specify that payments are to be disclosed with respect to the substance of the activity or payment concerned. Therefore, the undertaking should not be able to avoid disclosure by, for example, re-characterising an activity that would otherwise be covered by this Directive. In addition, payments or activities should not be artificially split or aggregated with a view to evading such disclosure requirements.

(50) In order to ascertain the circumstances in which undertakings should be exempted from the reporting requirements provided for in Chapter 10, the power to adopt delegated acts in accordance with Article 290 of the TFEU should be delegated to the Commission in respect of determining the criteria to be applied when assessing whether third country reporting requirements are equivalent to the requirements of that Chapter. It is of particular importance that the Commission carry out appropriate consultations during its preparatory work, including at expert level. The Commission, when preparing and drawing up delegated acts, should ensure a simultaneous, timely and appropriate transmission of relevant documents to the European Parliament and to the Council.

(51) In order to ensure uniform conditions for the implementation of Article 46(1), implementing powers should be conferred upon the Commission. Those powers should be exercised in accordance with Regulation (EU) No 182/2011 of the European Parliament and of the Council of 16 February 2011 laying down the rules and general principles concerning mechanisms for the control by Member States of the Commission's exercise of implementing powers.

(52) The reporting regime should be subject to a review and a report by the Commission within three years of the expiry of the deadline for transposition of this Directive by the Member States. That review should consider the effectiveness of the regime and take into account international developments, including issues of competitiveness and energy security. The review should also consider the extension of reporting requirements to additional industry sectors and whether the report should be audited. In addition, the review should take into account the experience of preparers and users of the payments information and consider whether it would be appropriate to include additional payment information such as effective tax rates and recipient details such as bank account information.

(53) In line with the conclusions of the G8 Summit in Deauville in May 2011 and in order to promote a level international playing field, the Commission should continue to encourage all the international partners to introduce similar requirements concerning reporting on payments to governments. Continued work on the relevant international accounting standard is particularly important in this context.

(54) In order to take account of future changes to the laws of the Member States and to Union legislation concerning company types, the Commission should be empowered to adopt delegated acts in accordance with Article 290 of the TFEU in order to update the lists of undertakings contained in Annexes I and II. The use of delegated acts is also necessary in order to adapt the undertaking size criteria, as with the passage of time inflation will erode their real value. It is of particular importance that the Commission carry out appropriate consultations during its preparatory work, including at expert level. The Commission, when preparing and drawing up delegated acts, should ensure a simultaneous, timely and appropriate transmission of relevant documents to the European Parliament and to the Council.

(55) Since the objectives of this Directive, namely facilitating cross-border investment and improving Union-wide comparability and public confidence in financial statements and reports through enhanced and consistent specific disclosures, cannot be sufficiently achieved by the Member States and can therefore, by reason of the scale and the effects of this Directive, be better achieved at Union level, the Union may adopt measures, in accordance with the principle of subsidiarity as set out in Article 5 of the Treaty on European Union. In accordance with the principle of proportionality, as set out in that Article, this Directive does not go beyond what is necessary in order to achieve those objectives.

(56) This Directive replaces Directives 78/660/EEC and 83/349/EEC. Therefore, those Directives should be repealed.

(57) This Directive respects fundamental rights and observes the principles recognised, in particular, by the Charter of Fundamental Rights of the European Union.

(58) In accordance with the Joint Political Declaration of Member States and the Commission on explanatory documents of 28 September 2011, Member States have undertaken to accompany, in justified cases, the notification of their transposition measures with one or more documents explaining the relationship between the components of a directive and the corresponding parts of national transposition instruments. With regard to this Directive, the legislator considers the transmission of correlation tables to be justified,
HAVE ADOPTED THIS DIRECTIVE:

Chapter 1. Scope, Definitions and Categories of Undertakings and Groups

Article 1. (1) The coordination measures prescribed by this Directive shall apply to the laws, regulations and administrative provisions of the Member States relating to the types of undertakings listed:
(a) in Annex I;
(b) in Annex II, where all of the direct or indirect members of the undertaking having otherwise unlimited liability in fact have limited liability by reason of those members being undertakings which are:
(i) of the types listed in Annex I; or
(ii) not governed by the law of a Member State but which have a legal form comparable to those listed in Annex I.
(2) Member States shall inform the Commission within a reasonable period of time of changes in the types of undertakings in their national law that may affect the accuracy of Annex I or Annex II. In such a case, the Commission shall be empowered to adapt, by means of delegated acts in accordance with Article 49, the lists of undertakings contained in Annexes I and II.

Article 2. For the purposes of this Directive, the following definitions shall apply:
(1) 'public-interest entities' means undertakings within the scope of Article 1 which are:
(a) governed by the law of a Member State and whose transferable securities are admitted to trading on a regulated market of any Member State within the meaning of point (14) of Article 4(1) of Directive 2004/39/EC of the European Parliament and of the Council of 21 April 2004 on markets in financial instruments;
(b) credit institutions as defined in point (1) of Article 4 of Directive 2006/48/EC of the European Parliament and of the Council of 14 June 2006 relating to the taking up and pursuit of the business of credit institutions, other than those referred to in Article 2 of that Directive;
(c) insurance undertakings within the meaning of Article 2(1) of Council Directive 91/674/EEC of 19 December 1991 on the annual accounts of insurance undertakings; or
(d) designated by Member States as public-interest entities, for instance undertakings that are of significant public relevance because of the nature of their business, their size or the number of their employees;
(2) 'participating interest' means rights in the capital of other undertakings, whether or not represented by certificates, which, by creating a durable link with those undertakings, are intended to contribute to the activities of the undertaking which holds those rights. The holding of part of the capital of another undertaking is presumed to constitute a participating interest where it exceeds a percentage threshold fixed by the Member States which is lower than or equal to 20 %;
(3) 'related party' has the same meaning as in the international accounting standards adopted in accordance with Regulation (EC) No 1606/2002 of the European Parliament and of the Council of 19 July 2002 on the application of international accounting standards;
(4) 'fixed assets' means those assets which are intended for use on a continuing basis for the undertaking's activities;
(5) 'net turnover' means the amounts derived from the sale of products and the provision of services after deducting sales rebates and value added tax and other taxes directly linked to turnover;
(6) 'purchase price' means the price payable and any incidental expenses minus any incidental reductions in the cost of acquisition;
(7) 'production cost' means the purchase price of raw materials, consumables and other costs directly attributable to the item in question. Member States shall permit or require the inclusion of a reasonable proportion of fixed or variable overhead costs indirectly attributable to the item in question, to the extent that they relate to the period of production. Distribution costs shall not be included;
(8) 'value adjustment' means the adjustments intended to take account of changes in the values of individual assets established at the balance sheet date, whether the change is final or not;
(9) 'parent undertaking' means an undertaking which controls one or more subsidiary undertakings;
(10) 'subsidiary undertaking' means an undertaking controlled by a parent undertaking, including any subsidiary undertaking of an ultimate parent undertaking;

PART III   EUROPEAN COMPANY LAW

(11) 'group' means a parent undertaking and all its subsidiary undertakings;
(12) 'affiliated undertakings' means any two or more undertakings within a group;
(13) 'associated undertaking' means an undertaking in which another undertaking has a participating interest, and over whose operating and financial policies that other undertaking exercises significant influence. An undertaking is presumed to exercise a significant influence over another undertaking where it has 20 % or more of the shareholders' or members' voting rights in that other undertaking;
(14) 'investment undertakings' means:
(a) undertakings the sole object of which is to invest their funds in various securities, real property and other assets, with the sole aim of spreading investment risks and giving their shareholders the benefit of the results of the management of their assets,
(b) undertakings associated with investment undertakings with fixed capital, if the sole object of those associated undertakings is to acquire fully paid shares issued by those investment undertakings without prejudice to point (h) of Article 22(1) of Directive 2012/30/EU;
(15) 'financial holding undertakings' means undertakings the sole object of which is to acquire holdings in other undertakings and to manage such holdings and turn them to profit, without involving themselves directly or indirectly in the management of those undertakings, without prejudice to their rights as shareholders;
(16) 'material' means the status of information where its omission or misstatement could reasonably be expected to influence decisions that users make on the basis of the financial statements of the undertaking. The materiality of individual items shall be assessed in the context of other similar items.

Article 3. (1) In applying one or more of the options in Article 36, Member States shall define micro-undertakings as undertakings which on their balance sheet dates do not exceed the limits of at least two of the three following criteria:
(a) balance sheet total: EUR 350 000;
(b) net turnover: EUR 700 000;
(c) average number of employees during the financial year: 10.
(2) Small undertakings shall be undertakings which on their balance sheet dates do not exceed the limits of at least two of the three following criteria:
(a) balance sheet total: EUR 4 000 000;
(b) net turnover: EUR 8 000 000;
(c) average number of employees during the financial year: 50.
Member States may define thresholds exceeding the thresholds in points (a) and (b) of the first subparagraph. However, the thresholds shall not exceed EUR 6 000 000 for the balance sheet total and EUR 12 000 000 for the net turnover.
(3) Medium-sized undertakings shall be undertakings which are not micro-undertakings or small undertakings and which on their balance sheet dates do not exceed the limits of at least two of the three following criteria:
(a) balance sheet total: EUR 20 000 000;
(b) net turnover: EUR 40 000 000;
(c) average number of employees during the financial year: 250.
(4) Large undertakings shall be undertakings which on their balance sheet dates exceed at least two of the three following criteria:
(a) balance sheet total: EUR 20 000 000;
(b) net turnover: EUR 40 000 000;
(c) average number of employees during the financial year: 250.
(5) Small groups shall be groups consisting of parent and subsidiary undertakings to be included in a consolidation and which, on a consolidated basis, do not exceed the limits of at least two of the three following criteria on the balance sheet date of the parent undertaking:
(a) balance sheet total: EUR 4 000 000;
(b) net turnover: EUR 8 000 000;
(c) average number of employees during the financial year: 50.
Member States may define thresholds exceeding the thresholds in points (a) and (b) of the first subparagraph. However, the thresholds shall not exceed EUR 6 000 000 for the balance sheet total and EUR 12 000 000 for the net turnover.
(6) Medium-sized groups shall be groups which are not small groups, which consist of parent and subsidiary undertakings to be included in a consolidation and which, on a consolidated basis, do not exceed the limits of at least two of the three following criteria on the balance sheet date of the parent undertaking:

(a) balance sheet total: EUR 20 000 000;
(b) net turnover: EUR 40 000 000;
(c) average number of employees during the financial year: 250.
(7) Large groups shall be groups consisting of parent and subsidiary undertakings to be included in a consolidation and which, on a consolidated basis, exceed the limits of at least two of the three following criteria on the balance sheet date of the parent undertaking:
(a) balance sheet total: EUR 20 000 000;
(b) net turnover: EUR 40 000 000;
(c) average number of employees during the financial year: 250.
(8) Member States shall permit the set-off referred to in Article 24(3) and any elimination as a consequence of Article 24(7) not to be effected when the limits in paragraphs 5 to 7 of this Article are calculated. In such cases, the limits for the balance sheet total and net turnover criteria shall be increased by 20 %.
(9) In the case of those Member States which have not adopted the euro, the amount in national currency equivalent to the amounts set out in paragraphs 1 to 7 shall be that obtained by applying the exchange rate published in the *Official Journal of the European Union* as at the date of the entry into force of any Directive setting those amounts.
For the purposes of conversion into the national currencies of those Member States which have not adopted the euro, the amounts in euro specified in paragraphs 1, 3, 4, 6 and 7 may be increased or decreased by not more than 5 % in order to produce round sum amounts in the national currencies.
(10) Where, on its balance sheet date, an undertaking or a group exceeds or ceases to exceed the limits of two of the three criteria set out in paragraphs 1 to 7, that fact shall affect the application of the derogations provided for in this Directive only if it occurs in two consecutive financial years.
(11) The balance sheet total referred to in paragraphs 1 to 7 of this Article shall consist of the total value of the assets in A to E under 'Assets' in the layout set out in Annex III or of the assets in A to E in the layout set out in Annex IV.
(12) When calculating the thresholds in paragraphs 1 to 7, Member States may require the inclusion of income from other sources for undertakings for which "net turnover" is not relevant. Member States may require parent undertakings to calculate their thresholds on a consolidated basis rather than on an individual basis. Member States may also require affiliated undertakings to calculate their thresholds on a consolidated or aggregated basis where such undertakings have been established for the sole purpose of avoiding the reporting of certain information.
(13) In order to adjust for the effects of inflation, the Commission shall at least every five years review and, where appropriate, amend, by means of delegated acts in accordance with Article 49, the thresholds referred to in paragraphs 1 to 7 of this Article, taking into account measures of inflation as published in the *Official Journal of the European Union*.

Chapter 2. General Provisions and Principles

Article 4. (1) The annual financial statements shall constitute a composite whole and shall for all undertakings comprise, as a minimum, the balance sheet, the profit and loss account and the notes to the financial statements.
Member States may require undertakings other than small undertakings to include other statements in the annual financial statements in addition to the documents referred to in the first subparagraph.
(2) The annual financial statements shall be drawn up clearly and in accordance with the provisions of this Directive.
(3) The annual financial statements shall give a true and fair view of the undertaking's assets, liabilities, financial position and profit or loss. Where the application of this Directive would not be sufficient to give a true and fair view of the undertaking's assets, liabilities, financial position and profit or loss, such additional information as is necessary to comply with that requirement shall be given in the notes to the financial statements.
(4) Where in exceptional cases the application of a provision of this Directive is incompatible with the obligation laid down in paragraph (3), that provision shall be disapplied in order to give a true and fair view of the undertaking's assets, liabilities, financial position and profit or loss. The disapplication of any such provision shall be disclosed in the notes to the financial statements together with an explanation of the reasons for it and of its effect on the undertaking's assets, liabilities, financial position and profit or loss.
The Member States may define the exceptional cases in question and lay down the relevant special rules which are to apply in those cases.
(5) Member States may require undertakings other than small undertakings to disclose information in their annual financial statements which is additional to that required pursuant to this Directive.

PART III   EUROPEAN COMPANY LAW

(6) By way of derogation from paragraph (5), Member States may require small undertakings to prepare, disclose and publish information in the financial statements which goes beyond the requirements of this Directive, provided that any such information is gathered under a single filing system and the disclosure requirement is contained in the national tax legislation for the strict purposes of tax collection. The information required in accordance with this paragraph shall be included in the relevant part of the financial statements.

(7) Member States shall communicate to the Commission any additional information they require in accordance with paragraph (6) upon the transposition of this Directive and when they introduce new requirements in accordance with paragraph (6) in national law.

(8) Member States using electronic solutions for filing and publishing annual financial statements shall ensure that small undertakings are not required to publish, in accordance with Chapter 7, the additional disclosures required by national tax legislation, as referred to in paragraph (6).

Article 5. The document containing the financial statements shall state the name of the undertaking and the information prescribed by points (a) and (b) of Article 5 of Directive 2009/101/EC.

Article 6. (1) Items presented in the annual and consolidated financial statements shall be recognised and measured in accordance with the following general principles:
(a) the undertaking shall be presumed to be carrying on its business as a going concern;
(b) accounting policies and measurement bases shall be applied consistently from one financial year to the next;
(c) recognition and measurement shall be on a prudent basis, and in particular:
(i) only profits made at the balance sheet date may be recognised,
(ii) all liabilities arising in the course of the financial year concerned or in the course of a previous financial year shall be recognised, even if such liabilities become apparent only between the balance sheet date and the date on which the balance sheet is drawn up, and
(iii) all negative value adjustments shall be recognised, whether the result of the financial year is a profit or a loss;
(d) amounts recognised in the balance sheet and profit and loss account shall be computed on the accrual basis;
(e) the opening balance sheet for each financial year shall correspond to the closing balance sheet for the preceding financial year;
(f) the components of asset and liability items shall be valued separately;
(g) any set-off between asset and liability items, or between income and expenditure items, shall be prohibited;
(h) items in the profit and loss account and balance sheet shall be accounted for and presented having regard to the substance of the transaction or arrangement concerned;
(i) items recognised in the financial statements shall be measured in accordance with the principle of purchase price or production cost; and
(j) the requirements set out in this Directive regarding recognition, measurement, presentation, disclosure and consolidation need not be complied with when the effect of complying with them is immaterial.

(2) Notwithstanding point (g) of paragraph (1), Member States may in specific cases permit or require undertakings to perform a set-off between asset and liability items, or between income and expenditure items, provided that the amounts which are set off are specified as gross amounts in the notes to the financial statements.

(3) Member States may exempt undertakings from the requirements of point (h) of paragraph (1).

(4) Member States may limit the scope of point (j) of paragraph (1) to presentation and disclosures.

(5) In addition to those amounts recognised in accordance with point (c)(ii) of paragraph (1), Member States may permit or require the recognition of all foreseeable liabilities and potential losses arising in the course of the financial year concerned or in the course of a previous financial year, even if such liabilities or losses become apparent only between the balance sheet date and the date on which the balance sheet is drawn up.

Article 7. (1) By way of derogation from point (i) of Article 6(1), Member States may permit or require, in respect of all undertakings or any classes of undertaking, the measurement of fixed assets at revalued amounts. Where national law provides for the revaluation basis of measurement, it shall define its content and limits and the rules for its application.

(2) Where paragraph (1) is applied, the amount of the difference between measurement on a purchase price or production cost basis and measurement on a revaluation basis shall be entered in the balance sheet in the revaluation reserve under 'Capital and reserves'.

The revaluation reserve may be capitalised in whole or in part at any time.

The revaluation reserve shall be reduced where the amounts transferred to that reserve are no longer necessary for the implementation of the revaluation basis of accounting. The Member States may lay down rules governing the application of the revaluation reserve, provided that transfers to the profit and loss account from the revaluation reserve may be made only where the amounts transferred have been entered as an expense in the profit and loss account or reflect increases in value which have actually been realised. No part of the revaluation reserve may be distributed, either directly or indirectly, unless it represents a gain actually realised.

Save as provided under the second and third subparagraphs of this paragraph, the revaluation reserve may not be reduced.

(3) Value adjustments shall be calculated each year on the basis of the revalued amount. However, by way of derogation from Articles 9 and 13, Member States may permit or require that only the amount of the value adjustments arising as a result of the purchase price or production cost measurement basis be shown under the relevant items in the layouts set out in Annexes V and VI and that the difference arising as a result of the measurement on a revaluation basis under this Article be shown separately in the layouts.

Article 8. (1) By way of derogation from point (i) of Article 6(1) and subject to the conditions set out in this Article:
(a) Member States shall permit or require, in respect of all undertakings or any classes of undertaking, the measurement of financial instruments, including derivative financial instruments, at fair value; and
(b) Member States may permit or require, in respect of all undertakings or any classes of undertaking, the measurement of specified categories of assets other than financial instruments at amounts determined by reference to fair value.

Such permission or requirement may be restricted to consolidated financial statements.

(2) For the purpose of this Directive, commodity-based contracts that give either contracting party the right to settle in cash or some other financial instrument shall be considered to be derivative financial instruments except where such contracts:
(a) were entered into and continue to meet the undertaking's expected purchase, sale or usage requirements at the time they were entered into and subsequently;
(b) were designated as commodity-based contracts at their inception; and
(c) are expected to be settled by delivery of the commodity.

(3) Point (a) of paragraph (1) shall apply only to the following liabilities:
(a) liabilities held as part of a trading portfolio; and
(b) derivative financial instruments.

(4) Measurement according to point (a) of paragraph (1) shall not apply to the following:
(a) non-derivative financial instruments held to maturity;
(b) loans and receivables originated by the undertaking and not held for trading purposes; and
(c) interests in subsidiaries, associated undertakings and joint ventures, equity instruments issued by the undertaking, contracts for contingent consideration in a business combination, and other financial instruments with such special characteristics that the instruments, according to what is generally accepted, are accounted for differently from other financial instruments.

(5) By way of derogation from point (i) of Article 6(1), Member States may, in respect of any assets and liabilities which qualify as hedged items under a fair value hedge accounting system, or identified portions of such assets or liabilities, permit measurement at the specific amount required under that system.

(6) By way of derogation from paragraphs 3 and 4, Member States may permit or require the recognition, measurement and disclosure of financial instruments in conformity with international accounting standards adopted in accordance with Regulation (EC) No 1606/2002.

(7) The fair value within the meaning of this Article shall be determined by reference to one of the following values:
(a) in the case of financial instruments for which a reliable market can readily be identified, the market value. Where the market value is not readily identifiable for an instrument but can be identified for its components or for a similar instrument, the market value may be derived from that of its components or of the similar instrument;
(b) in the case of financial instruments for which a reliable market cannot be readily identified, a value resulting from generally accepted valuation models and techniques, provided that such valuation models and techniques ensure a reasonable approximation of the market value.

Financial instruments that cannot be measured reliably by any of the methods described in points (a) and (b) of the first subparagraph shall be measured in accordance with the principle of purchase price or production cost in so far as measurement on that basis is possible.

(8) Notwithstanding point (c) of Article 6(1), where a financial instrument is measured at fair value, a change in value shall be included in the profit and loss account, except in the following cases, where such a change shall be included directly in a fair value reserve:

(a) the instrument accounted for is a hedging instrument under a system of hedge accounting that allows some or all of the change in value not to be shown in the profit and loss account; or

(b) the change in value relates to an exchange difference arising on a monetary item that forms part of an undertaking's net investment in a foreign entity.

Member States may permit or require a change in the value of an available for sale financial asset, other than a derivative financial instrument, to be included directly in a fair value reserve. That fair value reserve shall be adjusted when amounts shown therein are no longer necessary for the implementation of points (a) and (b) of the first subparagraph.

(9) Notwithstanding point (c) of Article 6(1), Member States may permit or require, in respect of all undertakings or any classes of undertaking, that, where assets other than financial instruments are measured at fair value, a change in the value be included in the profit and loss account.

Chapter 3. Balance Sheet and Profit and Loss Account

Article 9. (1) The layout of the balance sheet and of the profit and loss account shall not be changed from one financial year to the next. Departures from that principle shall, however, be permitted in exceptional cases in order to give a true and fair view of the undertaking's assets, liabilities, financial position and profit or loss. Any such departure and the reasons therefor shall be disclosed in the notes to the financial statements.

(2) In the balance sheet and in the profit and loss account the items set out in Annexes III to VI shall be shown separately in the order indicated. Member States shall permit a more detailed subdivision of those items, subject to adherence to the prescribed layouts. Member States shall permit the addition of subtotals and of new items, provided that the contents of such new items are not covered by any of the items in the prescribed layouts. Member States may require such subdivision or subtotals or new items.

(3) The layout, nomenclature and terminology of items in the balance sheet and profit and loss account that are preceded by arabic numerals shall be adapted where the special nature of an undertaking so requires. Member States may require such adaptations for undertakings which form part of a particular economic sector.

Member States may permit or require balance sheet and profit and loss account items that are preceded by arabic numerals to be combined where they are immaterial in amount for the purposes of giving a true and fair view of the undertaking's assets, liabilities, financial position and profit or loss or where such combination makes for greater clarity, provided that the items so combined are dealt with separately in the notes to the financial statements.

(4) By way of derogation from paragraphs 2 and 3 of this Article, Member States may limit the undertaking's ability to depart from the layouts set out in Annexes III to VI to the extent that this is necessary in order for the financial statements to be filed electronically.

(5) In respect of each balance sheet and profit and loss account item, the figure for the financial year to which the balance sheet and the profit and loss account relate and the figure relating to the corresponding item for the preceding financial year shall be shown. Where those figures are not comparable, Member States may require the figure for the preceding financial year to be adjusted. Any case of non-comparability or any adjustment of the figures shall be disclosed, with explanations, in the notes to the financial statements.

(6) Member States may permit or require adaptation of the layout of the balance sheet and profit and loss account in order to include the appropriation of profit or the treatment of loss.

(7) In respect of the treatment of participating interests in annual financial statements:

(a) Member States may permit or require participating interests to be accounted for using the equity method as provided for in Article 27, taking account of the essential adjustments resulting from the particular characteristics of annual financial statements as compared to consolidated financial statements;

(b) Member States may permit or require that the proportion of the profit or loss attributable to the participating interest be recognised in the profit and loss account only to the extent of the amount corresponding to dividends already received or the payment of which can be claimed; and

(c) where the profit attributable to the participating interest and recognised in the profit and loss account exceeds the amount of dividends already received or the payment of which can be claimed, the amount of the difference shall be placed in a reserve which cannot be distributed to shareholders.

EU: DIRECTIVE 2013/34 ON CONSOLIDATED FINANCIAL STATEMENTS

Article 10. For the presentation of the balance sheet, Member States shall prescribe one or both of the layouts set out in Annexes III and IV. If a Member State prescribes both layouts, it shall permit undertakings to choose which of the prescribed layouts to adopt.

Article 11. Member States may permit or require undertakings, or certain classes of undertaking, to present items on the basis of a distinction between current and non-current items in a different layout from that set out in Annexes III and IV, provided that the information given is at least equivalent to that otherwise to be provided in accordance with Annexes III and IV.

Article 12. (1) Where an asset or liability relates to more than one layout item, its relationship to other items shall be disclosed either under the item where it appears or in the notes to the financial statements.
(2) Own shares and shares in affiliated undertakings shall be shown only under the items prescribed for that purpose.
(3) Whether particular assets are to be shown as fixed assets or current assets shall depend upon the purpose for which they are intended.
(4) Rights to immovables and other similar rights as defined by national law shall be shown under 'Land and buildings'.
(5) The purchase price or production cost or revalued amount, where Article 7(1) applies, of fixed assets with limited useful economic lives shall be reduced by value adjustments calculated to write off the value of such assets systematically over their useful economic lives.
(6) Value adjustments to fixed assets shall be subject to the following:
(a) Member States may permit or require value adjustments to be made in respect of financial fixed assets, so that they are valued at the lower figure to be attributed to them at the balance sheet date;
(b) value adjustments shall be made in respect of fixed assets, whether their useful economic lives are limited or not, so that they are valued at the lower figure to be attributed to them at the balance sheet date if it is expected that the reduction in their value will be permanent;
(c) the value adjustments referred to in points (a) and (b) shall be charged to the profit and loss account and disclosed separately in the notes to the financial statements if they have not been shown separately in the profit and loss account;
(d) measurement at the lower of the values provided for in points (a) and (b) may not continue if the reasons for which the value adjustments were made have ceased to apply; this provision shall not apply to value adjustments made in respect of goodwill.
(7) Value adjustments shall be made in respect of current assets with a view to showing them at the lower market value or, in particular circumstances, another lower value to be attributed to them at the balance sheet date.
Measurement at the lower value provided for in the first subparagraph may not continue if the reasons for which the value adjustments were made no longer apply.
(8) Member States may permit or require that interest on capital borrowed to finance the production of fixed or current assets be included within production costs, to the extent that it relates to the period of production. Any application of this provision shall be disclosed in the notes to the financial statements.
(9) Member States may permit the purchase price or production cost of stocks of goods of the same category and all fungible items including investments to be calculated either on the basis of weighted average prices, on the basis of the 'first in, first out' (FIFO) method, the 'last in, first out' (LIFO) method, or a method reflecting generally accepted best practice.
(10) Where the amount repayable on account of any debt is greater than the amount received, Member States may permit or require that the difference be shown as an asset. It shall be shown separately in the balance sheet or in the notes to the financial statements. The amount of that difference shall be written off by a reasonable amount each year and completely written off no later than at the time of repayment of the debt.
(11) Intangible assets shall be written off over the useful economic life of the intangible asset.
In exceptional cases where the useful life of goodwill and development costs cannot be reliably estimated, such assets shall be written off within a maximum period set by the Member State. That maximum period shall not be shorter than five years and shall not exceed 10 years. An explanation of the period over which goodwill is written off shall be provided within the notes to the financial statements.
Where national law authorises the inclusion of costs of development under 'Assets' and the costs of development have not been completely written off, Member States shall require that no distribution of profits take place unless the amount of the reserves available for distribution and profits brought forward is at least equal to that of the costs not written off.

Where national law authorises the inclusion of formation expenses under 'Assets', they shall be written off within a period of maximum five years. In that case, Member States shall require that the third subparagraph apply mutatis mutandis to formation expenses.

In exceptional cases, the Member States may permit derogations from the third and fourth subparagraphs. Such derogations and the reasons therefor shall be disclosed in the notes to the financial statements.

(12) Provisions shall cover liabilities the nature of which is clearly defined and which at the balance sheet date are either likely to be incurred or certain to be incurred, but uncertain as to their amount or as to the date on which they will arise.

The Member States may also authorise the creation of provisions intended to cover expenses the nature of which is clearly defined and which at the balance sheet date are either likely to be incurred or certain to be incurred, but uncertain as to their amount or as to the date on which they will arise. At the balance sheet date, a provision shall represent the best estimate of the expenses likely to be incurred or, in the case of a liability, of the amount required to meet that liability. Provisions shall not be used to adjust the values of assets.

Article 13. (1) For the presentation of the profit and loss account, Member States shall prescribe one or both of the layouts set out in Annexes V and VI. If a Member State prescribes both layouts, it may permit undertakings to choose which of the prescribed layouts to adopt.

(2) By way of derogation from Article 4(1), Member States may permit or require all undertakings, or any classes of undertaking, to present a statement of their performance instead of the presentation of profit and loss items in accordance with Annexes V and VI, provided that the information given is at least equivalent to that otherwise required by Annexes V and VI.

Article 14. (1) Member States may permit small undertakings to draw up abridged balance sheets showing only those items in Annexes III and IV preceded by letters and roman numerals, disclosing separately:

(a) the information required in brackets in D (II) under 'Assets' and C under 'Capital, reserves and liabilities' of Annex III, but in the aggregate for each; or

(b) the information required in brackets in D (II) of Annex IV.

(2) Member States may permit small and medium-sized undertakings to draw up abridged profit and loss accounts within the following limits:

(a) in Annex V, items 1 to 5 may be combined under one item called 'Gross profit or loss';

(b) in Annex VI, items 1, 2, 3 and 6 may be combined under one item called 'Gross profit or loss'.

Chapter 4. Notes to the Financial Statements

Article 15. Where notes to the balance sheet and profit and loss account are presented in accordance with this Chapter, the notes shall be presented in the order in which items are presented in the balance sheet and in the profit and loss account.

Article 16. (1) In the notes to the financial statements all undertakings shall, in addition to the information required under other provisions of this Directive, disclose information in respect of the following:

(a) accounting policies adopted;

(b) where fixed assets are measured at revalued amounts, a table showing:

(i) movements in the revaluation reserve in the financial year, with an explanation of the tax treatment of items therein, and

(ii) the carrying amount in the balance sheet that would have been recognised had the fixed assets not been revalued;

(c) where financial instruments and/or assets other than financial instruments are measured at fair value:

(i) the significant assumptions underlying the valuation models and techniques where fair values have been determined in accordance with point (b) of Article 8(7),

(ii) for each category of financial instrument or asset other than financial instruments, the fair value, the changes in value included directly in the profit and loss account and changes included in fair value reserves,

(iii) for each class of derivative financial instrument, information about the extent and the nature of the instruments, including significant terms and conditions that may affect the amount, timing and certainty of future cash flows, and

(iv) a table showing movements in fair value reserves during the financial year;

(d) the total amount of any financial commitments, guarantees or contingencies that are not included

in the balance sheet, and an indication of the nature and form of any valuable security which has been provided; any commitments concerning pensions and affiliated or associated undertakings shall be disclosed separately;
(e) the amount of advances and credits granted to members of the administrative, managerial and supervisory bodies, with indications of the interest rates, main conditions and any amounts repaid or written off or waived, as well as commitments entered into on their behalf by way of guarantees of any kind, with an indication of the total for each category;
(f) the amount and nature of individual items of income or expenditure which are of exceptional size or incidence;
(g) amounts owed by the undertaking becoming due and payable after more than five years, as well as the undertaking's entire debts covered by valuable security furnished by the undertaking, with an indication of the nature and form of the security; and
(h) the average number of employees during the financial year.
(2) Member States may require mutatis mutandis that small undertakings are to disclose information as required in points (a), (m), (p), (q) and (r) of Article 17(1).
For the purposes of applying the first subparagraph, the information required in point (p) of Article 17(1) shall be limited to the nature and business purpose of the arrangements referred to in that point.
For the purposes of applying the first subparagraph, the disclosure of the information required in point (r) of Article 17(1) shall be limited to transactions entered into with the parties listed in the fourth subparagraph of that point.
(3) Member States shall not require disclosure for small undertakings beyond what is required or permitted by this Article.

Article 17. (1) In the notes to the financial statements, medium-sized and large undertakings and public-interest entities shall, in addition to the information required under Article 16 and any other provisions of this Directive, disclose information in respect of the following matters:
(a) for the various fixed asset items:
(i) the purchase price or production cost or, where an alternative basis of measurement has been followed, the fair value or revalued amount at the beginning and end of the financial year,
(ii) additions, disposals and transfers during the financial year,
(iii) the accumulated value adjustments at the beginning and end of the financial year,
(iv) value adjustments charged during the financial year,
(v) movements in accumulated value adjustments in respect of additions, disposals and transfers during the financial year, and
(vi) where interest is capitalised in accordance with Article 12(8), the amount capitalised during the financial year.
(b) if fixed or current assets are the subject of value adjustments for taxation purposes alone, the amount of the adjustments and the reasons for making them;
(c) where financial instruments are measured at purchase price or production cost:
(i) for each class of derivative financial instrument:
— the fair value of the instruments, if such a value can be determined by any of the methods prescribed in point (a) of Article 8(7), and
— information about the extent and nature of the instruments,
(ii) for financial fixed assets carried at an amount in excess of their fair value:
— the book value and the fair value of either the individual assets or appropriate groupings of those individual assets, and
— the reasons for not reducing the book value, including the nature of the evidence underlying the assumption that the book value will be recovered;
(d) the amount of the emoluments granted in respect of, the financial year to the members of administrative, managerial and supervisory bodies by reason of their responsibilities and any commitments arising or entered into in respect of retirement pensions of former members of those bodies, with an indication of the total for each category of body.
Member States may waive the requirement to disclose such information where its disclosure would make it possible to identify the financial position of a specific member of such a body;
(e) the average number of employees during the financial year, broken down by categories and, if they are not disclosed separately in the profit and loss account, the staff costs relating to the financial year, broken down between wages and salaries, social security costs and pension costs;
(f) where a provision for deferred tax is recognised in the balance sheet, the deferred tax balances at the end of the financial year, and the movement in those balances during the financial year;
(g) the name and registered office of each of the undertakings in which the undertaking, either itself

or through a person acting in his own name but on the undertaking's behalf, holds a participating interest, showing the proportion of the capital held, the amount of capital and reserves, and the profit or loss for the latest financial year of the undertaking concerned for which financial statements have been adopted; the information concerning capital and reserves and the profit or loss may be omitted where the undertaking concerned does not publish its balance sheet and is not controlled by the undertaking.

Member States may allow the information required to be disclosed by the first subparagraph of this point to take the form of a statement filed in accordance with Article 3(1) and (3) of Directive 2009/101/EC; the filing of such a statement shall be disclosed in the notes to the financial statements. Member States may also allow that information to be omitted when its nature is such that it would be seriously prejudicial to any of the undertakings to which it relates. Member States may make such omissions subject to prior administrative or judicial authorisation. Any such omission shall be disclosed in the notes to the financial statements;

(h) the number and the nominal value or, in the absence of a nominal value, the accounting par value of the shares subscribed during the financial year within the limits of the authorised capital, without prejudice as far as the amount of that capital is concerned to point (e) of Article 2 of Directive 2009/101/EC or to points (c) and (d) of Article 2 of Directive 2012/30/EU;

(i) where there is more than one class of shares, the number and the nominal value or, in the absence of a nominal value, the accounting par value for each class;

(j) the existence of any participation certificates, convertible debentures, warrants, options or similar securities or rights, with an indication of their number and the rights they confer;

(k) the name, the head or registered office and the legal form of each of the undertakings of which the undertaking is a member having unlimited liability;

(l) the name and registered office of the undertaking which draws up the consolidated financial statements of the largest body of undertakings of which the undertaking forms part as a subsidiary undertaking;

(m) the name and registered office of the undertaking which draws up the consolidated financial statements of the smallest body of undertakings of which the undertaking forms part as a subsidiary undertaking and which is also included in the body of undertakings referred to in point (l);

(n) the place where copies of the consolidated financial statements referred to in points (l) and (m) may be obtained, provided that they are available;

(o) the proposed appropriation of profit or treatment of loss, or where applicable, the appropriation of the profit or treatment of the loss;

(p) the nature and business purpose of the undertaking's arrangements that are not included in the balance sheet and the financial impact on the undertaking of those arrangements, provided that the risks or benefits arising from such arrangements are material and in so far as the disclosure of such risks or benefits is necessary for the purposes of assessing the financial position of the undertaking;

(q) the nature and the financial effect of material events arising after the balance sheet date which are not reflected in the profit and loss account or balance sheet; and

(r) transactions which have been entered into with related parties by the undertaking, including the amount of such transactions, the nature of the related party relationship and other information about the transactions necessary for an understanding of the financial position of the undertaking. Information about individual transactions may be aggregated according to their nature except where separate information is necessary for an understanding of the effects of related party transactions on the financial position of the undertaking.

Member States may permit or require that only transactions with related parties that have not been concluded under normal market conditions be disclosed.

Member States may permit that transactions entered into between one or more members of a group be not disclosed, provided that subsidiaries which are party to the transaction are wholly owned by such a member.

Member States may permit that a medium-sized undertaking limit the disclosure of transactions with related parties to transactions entered into with:

(i) owners holding a participating interest in the undertaking;

(ii) undertakings in which the undertaking itself has a participating interest; and

(iii) members of the administrative, management or supervisory bodies of the undertaking.

(2) Member States shall not be required to apply point (g) of paragraph (1) to an undertaking which is a parent undertaking governed by their national laws in the following cases:

(a) where the undertaking in which that parent undertaking holds a participating interest for the purposes of point (g) of paragraph (1) is included in consolidated financial statements drawn up by that parent undertaking, or in the consolidated financial statements of a larger body of undertakings as

referred to in Article 23(4);
(b) where that participating interest has been dealt with by that parent undertaking in its annual financial statements in accordance with Article 9(7), or in the consolidated financial statements drawn up by that parent undertaking in accordance with Article 27(1) to (8).

Article 18. (1) In the notes to the financial statements, large undertakings and public-interest entities shall, in addition to the information required under Articles 16 and 17 and any other provisions of this Directive, disclose information in respect of the following matters:
(a) the net turnover broken down by categories of activity and into geographical markets, in so far as those categories and markets differ substantially from one another, taking account of the manner in which the sale of products and the provision of services are organised; and
(b) the total fees for the financial year charged by each statutory auditor or audit firm for the statutory audit of the annual financial statements, and the total fees charged by each statutory auditor or audit firm for other assurance services, for tax advisory services and for other non-audit services.
(2) Member States may allow the information referred to in point (a) of paragraph (1) to be omitted where the disclosure of that information would be seriously prejudicial to the undertaking. Member States may make such omissions subject to prior administrative or judicial authorisation. Any such omission shall be disclosed in the notes to the financial statements.
(3) Member States may provide that point (b) of paragraph (1) is not to apply to the annual financial statements of an undertaking where that undertaking is included within the consolidated financial statements required to be drawn up under Article 22, provided that such information is given in the notes to the consolidated financial statements.

Chapter 5. Management Report

Article 19. (1) The management report shall include a fair review of the development and performance of the undertaking's business and of its position, together with a description of the principal risks and uncertainties that it faces.
The review shall be a balanced and comprehensive analysis of the development and performance of the undertaking's business and of its position, consistent with the size and complexity of the business.
To the extent necessary for an understanding of the undertaking's development, performance or position, the analysis shall include both financial and, where appropriate, non-financial key performance indicators relevant to the particular business, including information relating to environmental and employee matters. In providing the analysis, the management report shall, where appropriate, include references to, and additional explanations of, amounts reported in the annual financial statements.
(2) The management report shall also give an indication of:
(a) the undertaking's likely future development;
(b) activities in the field of research and development;
(c) the information concerning acquisitions of own shares prescribed by Article 24(2) of Directive 2012/30/EU;
(d) the existence of branches of the undertaking; and
(e) in relation to the undertaking's use of financial instruments and where material for the assessment of its assets, liabilities, financial position and profit or loss:
(i) the undertaking's financial risk management objectives and policies, including its policy for hedging each major type of forecasted transaction for which hedge accounting is used; and
(ii) the undertaking's exposure to price risk, credit risk, liquidity risk and cash flow risk.
(3) Member States may exempt small undertakings from the obligation to prepare management reports, provided that they require the information referred to in Article 24(2) of Directive 2012/30/EU concerning the acquisition by an undertaking of its own shares to be given in the notes to the financial statements.
(4) Member States may exempt small and medium-sized undertakings from the obligation set out in the third subparagraph of paragraph (1) in so far as it relates to non-financial information.

Article 20 (1) Undertakings referred to in point (1)(a) of Article 2 shall include a corporate governance statement in their management report. That statement shall be included as a specific section of the management report and shall contain at least the following information:
(a) a reference to the following, where applicable:
(i) the corporate governance code to which the undertaking is subject,
(ii) the corporate governance code which the undertaking may have voluntarily decided to apply,
(iii) all relevant information about the corporate governance practices applied over and above the requirements of national law.
Where reference is made to a corporate governance code referred to in points (i) or (ii), the undertak-

ing shall also indicate where the relevant texts are publicly available. Where reference is made to the information referred to in point (iii), the undertaking shall make details of its corporate governance practices publicly available;
(b) where an undertaking, in accordance with national law, departs from a corporate governance code referred to in points (a)(i) or (ii), an explanation by the undertaking as to which parts of the corporate governance code it departs from and the reasons for doing so; where the undertaking has decided not to refer to any provisions of a corporate governance code referred to in points (a)(i) or (ii) it shall explain its reasons for not doing so;
(c) a description of the main features of the undertaking's internal control and risk management systems in relation to the financial reporting process;
(d) the information required by points (c), (d), (f), (h) and (i) of Article 10(1) of Directive 2004/25/EC of the European Parliament and of the Council of 21 April 2004 on takeover bids, where the undertaking is subject to that Directive;
(e) unless the information is already fully provided for in national law, a description of the operation of the shareholder meeting and its key powers and a description of shareholders' rights and how they can be exercised; and
(f) the composition and operation of the administrative, management and supervisory bodies and their committees.
(2) Member States may permit the information required by paragraph (1) of this Article to be set out in:
(a) a separate report published together with the management report in the manner set out in Article 30; or
(b) a document publicly available on the undertaking's website, to which reference is made in the management report.
That separate report or that document referred to in points (a) and (b), respectively, may cross-refer to the management report, where the information required by point (d) of paragraph (1) of this Article is made available in that management report.
(3) The statutory auditor or audit firm shall express an opinion in accordance with the second subparagraph of Article 34(1) regarding information prepared under points (c) and (d) of paragraph (1) of this Article and shall check that the information referred to in points (a), (b), (e) and (f) of paragraph (1) of this Article has been provided.
(4) Member States may exempt undertakings referred to in paragraph (1) which have only issued securities other than shares admitted to trading on a regulated market, within the meaning of point (14) of Article 4(1) of Directive 2004/39/EC, from the application of points (a), (b), (e) and (f) of paragraph (1) of this Article, unless such undertakings have issued shares which are traded in a multilateral trading facility, within the meaning of point (15) of Article 4(1) of Directive 2004/39/EC.

Chapter 6. Consolidated Financial Statements and Reports

Article 21. For the purposes of this Chapter, a parent undertaking and all of its subsidiary undertakings shall be undertakings to be consolidated where the parent undertaking is an undertaking to which the coordination measures prescribed by this Directive apply by virtue of Article 1(1).

Article 22. (1) A Member State shall require any undertaking governed by its national law to draw up consolidated financial statements and a consolidated management report if that undertaking (a parent undertaking):
(a) has a majority of the shareholders' or members' voting rights in another undertaking (a subsidiary undertaking);
(b) has the right to appoint or remove a majority of the members of the administrative, management or supervisory body of another undertaking (a subsidiary undertaking) and is at the same time a shareholder in or member of that undertaking;
(c) has the right to exercise a dominant influence over an undertaking (a subsidiary undertaking) of which it is a shareholder or member, pursuant to a contract entered into with that undertaking or to a provision in its memorandum or articles of association, where the law governing that subsidiary undertaking permits its being subject to such contracts or provisions.
A Member State need not prescribe that a parent undertaking must be a shareholder in or member of its subsidiary undertaking. Those Member States the laws of which do not provide for such contracts or clauses shall not be required to apply this provision; or
(d) is a shareholder in or member of an undertaking, and:
(i) a majority of the members of the administrative, management or supervisory bodies of that undertaking (a subsidiary undertaking) who have held office during the financial year, during the preceding

financial year and up to the time when the consolidated financial statements are drawn up, have been appointed solely as a result of the exercise of its voting rights; or

(ii) controls alone, pursuant to an agreement with other shareholders in or members of that undertaking (a subsidiary undertaking), a majority of shareholders' or members' voting rights in that undertaking. The Member States may introduce more detailed provisions concerning the form and contents of such agreements.

Member States shall prescribe at least the arrangements referred to in point (ii). They may subject the application of point (i) to the requirement that the voting rights represent at least 20 % of the total. However, point (i) shall not apply where a third party has the rights referred to in points (a), (b) or (c) with regard to that undertaking.

(2) In addition to the cases mentioned in paragraph (1), Member States may require any undertaking governed by their national law to draw up consolidated financial statements and a consolidated management report if:

(a) that undertaking (a parent undertaking) has the power to exercise, or actually exercises, dominant influence or control over another undertaking (the subsidiary undertaking); or

(b) that undertaking (a parent undertaking) and another undertaking (the subsidiary undertaking) are managed on a unified basis by the parent undertaking.

(3) For the purposes of points (a), (b) and (d) of paragraph (1), the voting rights and the rights of appointment and removal of any other subsidiary undertaking as well as those of any person acting in his own name but on behalf of the parent undertaking or of another subsidiary undertaking shall be added to those of the parent undertaking.

(4) For the purposes of points (a), (b) and (d) of paragraph (1), the rights mentioned in paragraph (3) shall be reduced by the rights:

(a) attaching to shares held on behalf of a person who is neither the parent undertaking nor a subsidiary of that parent undertaking; or

(b) attaching to shares:

(i) held by way of security, provided that the rights in question are exercised in accordance with the instructions received, or

(ii) held in connection with the granting of loans as part of normal business activities, provided that the voting rights are exercised in the interests of the person providing the security.

(5) For the purposes of points (a) and (d) of paragraph (1), the total of the shareholders' or members' voting rights in the subsidiary undertaking shall be reduced by the voting rights attaching to the shares held by that undertaking itself, by a subsidiary undertaking of that undertaking or by a person acting in his own name but on behalf of those undertakings.

(6) Without prejudice to Article 23(9), a parent undertaking and all of its subsidiary undertakings shall be undertakings to be consolidated regardless of where the registered offices of such subsidiary undertakings are situated.

(7) Without prejudice to this Article and Articles 21 and 23, a Member State may require any undertaking governed by its national law to draw up consolidated financial statements and a consolidated management report if:

(a) that undertaking and one or more other undertakings to which it is not related as described in paragraphs 1 or 2, are managed on a unified basis in accordance with:

(i) a contract concluded with that undertaking, or

(ii) the memorandum or articles of association of those other undertakings; or

(b) the administrative, management or supervisory bodies of that undertaking and of one or more other undertakings to which it is not related, as described in paragraphs 1 or 2, consist in the majority of the same persons in office during the financial year and until the consolidated financial statements are drawn up.

(8) Where the Member State option referred to in paragraph (7) is exercised, the undertakings described in that paragraph and all of their subsidiary undertakings shall be consolidated, where one or more of those undertakings is established as one of the types of undertaking listed in Annex I or Annex II.

(9) Paragraph 6 of this Article, Article 23(1), (2), (9) and (10) and Articles 24 to 29 shall apply to the consolidated financial statements and the consolidated management report referred to in paragraph (7) of this Article, subject to the following modifications:

(a) references to parent undertakings shall be understood to refer to all of the undertakings specified in paragraph (7) of this Article; and

(b) without prejudice to Article 24(3), the items 'capital', 'share premium account', 'revaluation reserve', 'reserves', 'profit or loss brought forward', and 'profit or loss for the financial year' to be included in the consolidated financial statements shall be the aggregate amounts attributable to each of the undertakings specified in paragraph (7) of this Article.

Article 23. (1) Small groups shall be exempted from the obligation to draw up consolidated financial statements and a consolidated management report, except where any affiliated undertaking is a public-interest entity.
(2) Member States may exempt medium-sized groups from the obligation to draw up consolidated financial statements and a consolidated management report, except where any affiliated undertaking is a public-interest entity.
(3) Notwithstanding paragraphs 1 and 2 of this Article, a Member State shall, in the following cases, exempt from the obligation to draw up consolidated financial statements and a consolidated management report any parent undertaking (the exempted undertaking) governed by its national law which is also a subsidiary undertaking, including a public-interest entity unless that public-interest entity falls under point (1)(a) of Article 2, the own parent undertaking of which is governed by the law of a Member State and:
(a) the parent undertaking of the exempted undertaking holds all of the shares in the exempted undertaking. The shares in the exempted undertaking held by members of its administrative, management or supervisory bodies pursuant to a legal obligation or an obligation in its memorandum or articles of association shall be ignored for this purpose; or
(b) the parent undertaking of the exempted undertaking holds 90 % or more of the shares in the exempted undertaking and the remaining shareholders in or members of the exempted undertaking have approved the exemption.
(4) The exemptions referred to in paragraph (3) shall fulfil all of the following conditions:
(a) the exempted undertaking and, without prejudice to paragraph (9), all of its subsidiary undertakings are consolidated in the financial statements of a larger body of undertakings, the parent undertaking of which is governed by the law of a Member State;
(b) the consolidated financial statements referred to in point (a) and the consolidated management report of the larger body of undertakings are drawn up by the parent undertaking of that body, in accordance with the law of the Member State by which that parent undertaking is governed, in accordance with this Directive or international accounting standards adopted in accordance with Regulation (EC) No 1606/2002;
(c) in relation to the exempted undertaking the following documents are published in the manner prescribed by the law of the Member State by which that exempted undertaking is governed, in accordance with Article 30:
(i) the consolidated financial statements referred to in point (a) and the consolidated management report referred to in point (b),
(ii) the audit report, and
(iii) where appropriate, the appendix referred to in paragraph (6).
That Member State may require that the documents referred to in points (i), (ii) and (iii) be published in its official language and that the translation be certified;
(d) the notes to the annual financial statements of the exempted undertaking disclose the following:
(i) the name and registered office of the parent undertaking that draws up the consolidated financial statements referred to in point (a), and
(ii) the exemption from the obligation to draw up consolidated financial statements and a consolidated management report.
(5) In cases not covered by paragraph (3), a Member State may, without prejudice to paragraphs 1, 2 and 3 of this Article, exempt from the obligation to draw up consolidated financial statements and a consolidated management report any parent undertaking (the exempted undertaking) governed by its national law which is also a subsidiary undertaking, including a public-interest entity unless that public-interest entity falls under point (1)(a) of Article 2, the parent undertaking of which is governed by the law of a Member State, provided that all the conditions set out in paragraph (4) are fulfilled and provided further:
(a) that the shareholders in or members of the exempted undertaking who own a minimum proportion of the subscribed capital of that undertaking have not requested the preparation of consolidated financial statements at least six months before the end of the financial year;
(b) that the minimum proportion referred to in point (a) does not exceed the following limits:
(i) 10 % of the subscribed capital in the case of public limited liability companies and limited partnerships with share capital; and
(ii) 20 % of the subscribed capital in the case of undertakings of other types;
(c) that the Member State does not make the exemption subject to:
(i) the condition that the parent undertaking, which prepared the consolidated financial statements

referred to in point (a) of paragraph (4), is governed by the national law of the Member State granting the exemption, or

(ii) conditions relating to the preparation and auditing of those financial statements.

(6) A Member State may make the exemptions provided for in paragraphs 3 and 5 subject to the disclosure of additional information, in accordance with this Directive, in the consolidated financial statements referred to in point (a) of paragraph (4), or in an appendix thereto, if that information is required of undertakings governed by the national law of that Member State which are obliged to prepare consolidated financial statements and are in the same circumstances.

(7) Paragraphs 3 to 6 shall apply without prejudice to Member State legislation on the drawing-up of consolidated financial statements or consolidated management reports in so far as those documents are required:

(a) for the information of employees or their representatives; or

(b) by an administrative or judicial authority for its own purposes.

(8) Without prejudice to paragraphs 1, 2, 3 and 5 of this Article, a Member State which provides for exemptions under paragraphs 3 and 5 of this Article may also exempt from the obligation to draw up consolidated financial statements and a consolidated management report any parent undertaking (the exempted undertaking) governed by its national law which is also a subsidiary undertaking, including a public-interest entity unless that public-interest entity falls under point (1)(a) of Article 2, the parent undertaking of which is not governed by the law of a Member State, if all of the following conditions are fulfilled:

(a) the exempted undertaking and, without prejudice to paragraph (9), all of its subsidiary undertakings are consolidated in the financial statements of a larger body of undertakings;

(b) the consolidated financial statements referred to in point (a) and, where appropriate, the consolidated management report are drawn up:

(i) in accordance with this Directive,

(ii) in accordance with international accounting standards adopted pursuant to Regulation (EC) No 1606/2002,

(iii) in a manner equivalent to consolidated financial statements and consolidated management reports drawn up in accordance with this Directive, or

(iv) in a manner equivalent to international accounting standards as determined in accordance with Commission Regulation (EC) No 1569/2007 of 21 December 2007 establishing a mechanism for the determination of equivalence of accounting standards applied by third country issuers of securities pursuant to Directives 2003/71/EC and 2004/109/EC of the European Parliament and of the Council;

(c) the consolidated financial statements referred to in point (a) have been audited by one or more statutory auditor(s) or audit firm(s) authorised to audit financial statements under the national law governing the undertaking which drew up those statements.

Points (c) and (d) of paragraph (4) and paragraphs 5, 6 and 7 shall apply.

(9) An undertaking, including a public-interest entity, need not be included in consolidated financial statements where at least one of the following conditions is fulfilled:

(a) in extremely rare cases where the information necessary for the preparation of consolidated financial statements in accordance with this Directive cannot be obtained without disproportionate expense or undue delay;

(b) the shares of that undertaking are held exclusively with a view to their subsequent resale; or

(c) severe long-term restrictions substantially hinder:

(i) the parent undertaking in the exercise of its rights over the assets or management of that undertaking; or

(ii) the exercise of unified management of that undertaking where it is in one of the relationships defined in Article 22(7).

(10) Without prejudice to point (b) of Article 6(1), Article 21 and paragraphs 1 and 2 of this Article, any parent undertaking, including a public-interest entity, shall be exempted from the obligation imposed in Article 22 if:

(a) it only has subsidiary undertakings which are immaterial, both individually and collectively; or

(b) all its subsidiary undertakings can be excluded from consolidation by virtue of paragraph (9) of this Article

Article 24. (1) Chapters 2 and 3 shall apply in respect of consolidated financial statements, taking into account the essential adjustments resulting from the particular characteristics of consolidated financial statements as compared to annual financial statements.

(2) The assets and liabilities of undertakings included in a consolidation shall be incorporated in full in the consolidated balance sheet.

(3) The book values of shares in the capital of undertakings included in a consolidation shall be set off against the proportion which they represent of the capital and reserves of those undertakings in accordance with the following:
(a) except in the case of shares in the capital of the parent undertaking held either by that undertaking itself or by another undertaking included in the consolidation, which shall be treated as own shares in accordance with Chapter 3, that set-off shall be effected on the basis of book values as they stand on the date on which those undertakings are included in a consolidation for the first time. Differences arising from that set-off shall, as far as possible, be entered directly against those items in the consolidated balance sheet which have values above or below their book values;
(b) a Member State may permit or require set-offs on the basis of the values of identifiable assets and liabilities as at the date of acquisition of the shares or, in the event of acquisition in two or more stages, as at the date on which the undertaking became a subsidiary;
(c) any difference remaining after the application of point (a) or resulting from the application of point (b) shall be shown as goodwill in the consolidated balance sheet;
(d) the methods used to calculate the value of goodwill and any significant changes in value in relation to the preceding financial year shall be explained in the notes to the financial statements;
(e) where the offsetting of positive and negative goodwill is authorised by a Member State, the notes to the financial statements shall include an analysis of the goodwill;
(f) negative goodwill may be transferred to the consolidated profit and loss account where such a treatment is in accordance with the principles set out in Chapter 2.
(4) Where shares in subsidiary undertakings included in the consolidation are held by persons other than those undertakings, the amount attributable to those shares shall be shown separately in the consolidated balance sheet as non-controlling interests.
(5) The income and expenditure of undertakings included in a consolidation shall be incorporated in full in the consolidated profit and loss account.
(6) The amount of any profit or loss attributable to the shares referred to in paragraph (4) shall be shown separately in the consolidated profit and loss account as the profit or loss attributable to non-controlling interests.
(7) Consolidated financial statements shall show the assets, liabilities, financial positions, profits or losses of the undertakings included in a consolidation as if they were a single undertaking. In particular, the following shall be eliminated from the consolidated financial statements:
(a) debts and claims between the undertakings;
(b) income and expenditure relating to transactions between the undertakings; and
(c) profits and losses resulting from transactions between the undertakings, where they are included in the book values of assets.
(8) Consolidated financial statements shall be drawn up as at the same date as the annual financial statements of the parent undertaking.
A Member State may, however, permit or require consolidated financial statements to be drawn up as at another date in order to take account of the balance sheet dates of the largest number or the most important of the undertakings included in the consolidation, provided that:
(a) that fact shall be disclosed in the notes to the consolidated financial statements and reasons given;
(b) account shall be taken, or disclosure made, of important events concerning the assets and liabilities, the financial position and the profit or loss of an undertaking included in a consolidation which have occurred between that undertaking's balance sheet date and the consolidated balance sheet date; and
(c) where an undertaking's balance sheet date precedes or follows the consolidated balance sheet date by more than three months, that undertaking shall be consolidated on the basis of interim financial statements drawn up as at the consolidated balance sheet date.
(9) If the composition of the undertakings included in a consolidation has changed significantly in the course of a financial year, the consolidated financial statements shall include information which makes the comparison of successive sets of consolidated financial statements meaningful. This obligation may be fulfilled by the preparation of an adjusted comparative balance sheet and an adjusted comparative profit and loss account.
(10) Assets and liabilities included in consolidated financial statements shall be measured on a uniform basis and in accordance with Chapter 2.
(11) An undertaking which draws up consolidated financial statements shall apply the same measurement bases as are applied in its annual financial statements. However, Member States may permit or require that other measurement bases in accordance with Chapter 2 be used in consolidated financial statements. Where use is made of this derogation, that fact shall be disclosed in the notes to the consolidated financial statements and reasons given.

(12) Where assets and liabilities included in consolidated financial statements have been measured by undertakings included in the consolidation using bases differing from those used for the purposes of the consolidation, those assets and liabilities shall be re-measured in accordance with the bases used for the consolidation. Departures from this requirement shall be permitted in exceptional cases. Any such departures shall be disclosed in the notes to the consolidated financial statements and reasons given.

(13) Deferred tax balances shall be recognised on consolidation provided that it is probable that a charge to tax will arise within the foreseeable future for one of the undertakings included in the consolidation.

(14) Where assets included in consolidated financial statements have been the subject of value adjustments solely for tax purposes, they shall be incorporated in the consolidated financial statements only after those adjustments have been eliminated.

Article 25. (1) A Member State may permit or require the book values of shares held in the capital of an undertaking included in the consolidation to be set off against the corresponding percentage of capital only, provided that the undertakings in the business combination are ultimately controlled by the same party both before and after the business combination, and that control is not transitory.

(2) Any difference arising under paragraph (1) shall be added to or deducted from consolidated reserves, as appropriate.

(3) The application of the method described in paragraph (1), the resulting movement in reserves and the names and registered offices of the undertakings concerned shall be disclosed in the notes to the consolidated financial statements.

Article 26. (1) Where an undertaking included in a consolidation manages another undertaking jointly with one or more undertakings not included in that consolidation, Member States may permit or require the inclusion of that other undertaking in the consolidated financial statements in proportion to the rights in its capital held by the undertaking included in the consolidation.

(2) Article 23(9) and (10) and Article 24 shall apply mutatis mutandis to the proportional consolidation referred to in paragraph (1) of this Article.

Article 27. (1) Where an undertaking included in a consolidation has an associated undertaking, that associated undertaking shall be shown in the consolidated balance sheet as a separate item with an appropriate heading.

(2) When this Article is applied for the first time to an associated undertaking, that associated undertaking shall be shown in the consolidated balance sheet either:

(a) at its book value calculated in accordance with the measurement rules laid down in Chapters 2 and 3. The difference between that value and the amount corresponding to the proportion of capital and reserves represented by the participating interest in that associated undertaking shall be disclosed separately in the consolidated balance sheet or in the notes to the consolidated financial statements. That difference shall be calculated as at the date on which that method is used for the first time; or

(b) at an amount corresponding to the proportion of the associated undertaking's capital and reserves represented by the participating interest in that associated undertaking. The difference between that amount and the book value calculated in accordance with the measurement rules laid down in Chapters 2 and 3 shall be disclosed separately in the consolidated balance sheet or in the notes to the consolidated financial statements. That difference shall be calculated as at the date on which that method is used for the first time.

A Member State may prescribe the application of one or other of the options provided for in points (a) and (b). In such cases, the consolidated balance sheet or the notes to the consolidated financial statements shall indicate which of those options has been used.

In addition, for the purposes of points (a) and (b), a Member State may permit or require the calculation of the difference as at the date of acquisition of the shares or, where they were acquired in two or more stages, as at the date on which the undertaking became an associated undertaking.

(3) Where an associated undertaking's assets or liabilities have been valued by methods other than those used for consolidation in accordance with Article 24(11), they may, for the purpose of calculating the difference referred to in points (a) and (b) of paragraph (2), be revalued by the methods used for consolidation. Where such revaluation has not been carried out, that fact shall be disclosed in the notes to the consolidated financial statements. A Member State may require such revaluation.

(4) The book value referred to in point (a) of paragraph (2), or the amount corresponding to the proportion of the associated undertaking's capital and reserves referred to in point (b) of paragraph (2), shall be increased or reduced by the amount of any variation which has taken place during the financial year in the proportion of the associated undertaking's capital and reserves represented by

that participating interest; it shall be reduced by the amount of the dividends relating to that participating interest.
(5) In so far as the positive difference referred to in points (a) and (b) of paragraph (2) cannot be related to any category of assets or liabilities, it shall be treated in accordance with the rules applicable to the item 'goodwill' as set out in point (d) of Article 12(6), the first subparagraph of Article 12(11), point (c) of Article 24(3), and Annex III and Annex IV.
(6) The proportion of the profit or loss of the associated undertakings attributable to the participating interests in such associated undertakings shall be shown in the consolidated profit and loss account as a separate item under an appropriate heading.
(7) The eliminations referred to in Article 24(7) shall be effected in so far as the facts are known or can be ascertained.
(8) Where an associated undertaking draws up consolidated financial statements, paragraphs 1 to 7 shall apply to the capital and reserves shown in such consolidated financial statements.
(9) This Article need not be applied where the participating interest in the capital of the associated undertaking is not material.

Article 28. (1) The notes to the consolidated financial statements shall set out the information required by Articles 16, 17 and 18, in addition to any other information required under other provisions of this Directive, in a way which facilitates the assessment of the financial position of the undertakings included in the consolidation taken as a whole, taking account of the essential adjustments resulting from the particular characteristics of consolidated financial statements as compared to annual financial statements, including the following:
(a) in disclosing transactions between related parties, transactions between related parties included in a consolidation that are eliminated on consolidation shall not be included;
(b) in disclosing the average number of employees employed during the financial year, there shall be separate disclosure of the average number of employees employed by undertakings that are proportionately consolidated; and
(c) in disclosing the amounts of emoluments and advances and credits granted to members of the administrative, managerial and supervisory bodies, only amounts granted by the parent undertaking and its subsidiary undertakings to members of the administrative, managerial and supervisory bodies of the parent undertaking shall be disclosed.
(2) The notes to the consolidated financial statements shall, in addition to the information required under paragraph (1), set out the following information:
(a) in relation to undertakings included in the consolidation:
(i) the names and registered offices of those undertakings,
(ii) the proportion of the capital held in those undertakings, other than the parent undertaking, by the undertakings included in the consolidation or by persons acting in their own names but on behalf of those undertakings, and
(iii) information as to which of the conditions referred to in Article 22(1), (2) and (7) following the application of Article 22(3), (4) and (5) has formed the basis on which the consolidation has been carried out. That disclosure may, however, be omitted where consolidation has been carried out on the basis of point (a) of Article 22(1) and where the proportion of the capital and the proportion of the voting rights held are the same.
The same information shall be given in respect of undertakings excluded from a consolidation on the grounds of immateriality pursuant to point (j) of Article 6(1) and Article 23(10), and an explanation shall be given for the exclusion of the undertakings referred to in Article 23(9);
(b) the names and registered offices of associated undertakings included in the consolidation as described in Article 27(1) and the proportion of their capital held by undertakings included in the consolidation or by persons acting in their own names but on behalf of those undertakings;
(c) the names and registered offices of undertakings proportionally consolidated under Article 26, the factors on which joint management of those undertakings is based, and the proportion of their capital held by the undertakings included in the consolidation or by persons acting in their own names but on behalf of those undertakings; and
(d) in relation to each of the undertakings, other than those referred to in points (a), (b) and (c), in which undertakings included in the consolidation, either themselves or through persons acting in their own names but on behalf of those undertakings, hold a participating interest:
(i) the name and registered office of those undertakings,
(ii) the proportion of the capital held,
(iii) the amount of the capital and reserves, and the profit or loss for the latest financial year of the undertaking concerned for which financial statements have been adopted.

The information concerning capital and reserves and the profit or loss may also be omitted where the undertaking concerned does not publish its balance sheet.

(3) Member States may allow the information required by points (a) to (d) of paragraph (2) to take the form of a statement filed in accordance with Article 3(3) of Directive 2009/101/EC. The filing of such a statement shall be disclosed in the notes to the consolidated financial statements. Member States may also allow that information to be omitted when its nature is such that its disclosure would be seriously prejudicial to any of the undertakings to which it relates. Member States may make such omissions subject to prior administrative or judicial authorisation. Any such omission shall be disclosed in the notes to the consolidated financial statements.

Article 29. (1) The consolidated management report shall, as a minimum, in addition to any other information required under other provisions of this Directive, set out the information required by Articles 19 and 20, taking account of the essential adjustments resulting from the particular characteristics of a consolidated management report as compared to a management report in a way which facilitates the assessment of the position of the undertakings included in the consolidation taken as a whole.

(2) The following adjustments to the information required by Articles 19 and 20 shall apply:
(a) in reporting details of own shares acquired, the consolidated management report shall indicate the number and nominal value or, in the absence of a nominal value, the accounting par value of all of the parent undertaking's shares held by that parent undertaking, by subsidiary undertakings of that parent undertaking or by a person acting in his own name but on behalf of any of those undertakings. A Member State may permit or require the disclosure of those particulars in the notes to the consolidated financial statements;
(b) in reporting on internal control and risk management systems, the corporate governance statement shall refer to the main features of the internal controls and risk management systems for the undertakings included in the consolidation, taken as a whole.

(3) Where a consolidated management report is required in addition to the management report, the two reports may be presented as a single report.

Chapter 7. Publication

Article 30. (1) Member States shall ensure that undertakings publish within a reasonable period of time, which shall not exceed 12 months after the balance sheet date, the duly approved annual financial statements and the management report, together with the opinion submitted by the statutory auditor or audit firm referred to in Article 34 of this Directive, as laid down by the laws of each Member State in accordance with Chapter 2 of Directive 2009/101/EC.

Member States may, however, exempt undertakings from the obligation to publish the management report where a copy of all or part of any such report can be easily obtained upon request at a price not exceeding its administrative cost.

(2) Member States may exempt an undertaking referred to in Annex II to which the coordination measures prescribed by this Directive apply by virtue of point (b) of Article 1(1) from publishing its financial statements in accordance with Article 3 of Directive 2009/101/EC, provided that those financial statements are available to the public at its head office, in the following cases:
(a) all the members of the undertaking concerned that have unlimited liability are undertakings referred to in Annex I governed by the laws of Member States other than the Member State whose law governs that undertaking, and none of those undertakings publishes the financial statements of the undertaking concerned with its own financial statements;
(b) all the members of the undertaking concerned that have unlimited liability are undertakings which are not governed by the laws of a Member State but which have a legal form comparable to those referred to in Directive 2009/101/EC.

Copies of the financial statements shall be obtainable upon request. The price of such a copy may not exceed its administrative cost.

(3) Paragraph 1 shall apply with respect to consolidated financial statements and consolidated management reports.

Where the undertaking drawing up the consolidated financial statements is established as one of the types of undertaking listed in Annex II and is not required by the national law of its Member State to publish the documents referred to in paragraph (1) in the same manner as prescribed in Article 3 of Directive 2009/101/EC, it shall, as a minimum, make those documents available to the public at its head office and a copy shall be provided upon request, the price of which shall not exceed its administrative cost.

Article 31. (1) Member States may exempt small undertakings from the obligation to publish their

profit and loss accounts and management reports.
(2) Member States may permit medium-sized undertakings to publish:
(a) abridged balance sheets showing only those items preceded by letters and roman numerals in Annexes III and IV and disclosing separately, either in the balance sheet or in the notes to the financial statements:
(i) C (I) (3), C (II) (1), (2), (3) and (4), C (III) (1), (2), (3) and (4), D (II) (2), (3) and (6) and D (III) (1) and (2) under 'Assets' and C, (1), (2), (6), (7) and (9) under 'Capital, reserves and liabilities' in Annex III,
(ii) C (I) (3), C (II) (1), (2), (3) and (4), C (III) (1), (2), (3) and (4), D (II) (2), (3) and (6), D (III) (1) and (2), F (1), (2), (6), (7) and (9) and (I) (1), (2), (6), (7) and (9) in Annex IV,
(iii) the information required as indicated in brackets in D (II) under 'Assets' and C under 'Capital, reserves and liabilities' in Annex III, in total for all the items concerned and separately for D (II) (2) and (3) under 'Assets' and C (1), (2), (6), (7) and (9) under 'Capital, reserves and liabilities',
(iv) the information required as indicated in brackets in D (II) in Annex IV, in total for all the items concerned, and separately for D (II) (2) and (3);
(b) abridged notes to their financial statements without the information required in points (f) and (j) of Article 17(1).
This paragraph shall be without prejudice to Article 30(1), in so far as that Article relates to the profit and loss account, the management report and the opinion of the statutory auditor or audit firm.

Article 32. (1) Where the annual financial statements and the management report are published in full, they shall be reproduced in the form and text on the basis of which the statutory auditor or audit firm has drawn up his/her/its opinion. They shall be accompanied by the full text of the audit report.
(2) If the annual financial statements are not published in full, the abridged version of those financial statements, which shall not be accompanied by the audit report, shall:
(a) indicate that the version published is abridged;
(b) refer to the register in which the financial statements have been filed in accordance with Article 3 of Directive 2009/101/EC or, where the financial statements have not yet been filed, disclose that fact;
(c) disclose whether an unqualified, qualified or adverse audit opinion was expressed by the statutory auditor or audit firm, or whether the statutory auditor or audit firm was unable to express an audit opinion;
(d) disclose whether the audit report included a reference to any matters to which the statutory auditor or audit firm drew attention by way of emphasis without qualifying the audit opinion.

Article 33. (1) Member States shall ensure that the members of the administrative, management and supervisory bodies of an undertaking, acting within the competences assigned to them by national law, have collective responsibility for ensuring that:
(a) the annual financial statements, the management report and, when provided separately, the corporate governance statement; and
(b) the consolidated financial statements, consolidated management reports and, when provided separately, the consolidated corporate governance statement,
are drawn up and published in accordance with the requirements of this Directive and, where applicable, with the international accounting standards adopted in accordance with Regulation (EC) No 1606/2002.
(2) Member States shall ensure that their laws, regulations and administrative provisions on liability, at least towards the undertaking, apply to the members of the administrative, management and supervisory bodies of the undertakings for breach of the duties referred to in paragraph (1).

Chapter 8. Auditing

Article 34. (1) Member States shall ensure that the financial statements of public-interest entities, medium-sized and large undertakings are audited by one or more statutory auditors or audit firms approved by Member States to carry out statutory audits on the basis of Directive 2006/43/EC.
The statutory auditor(s) or audit firm(s) shall also:
(a) express an opinion on:
(i) whether the management report is consistent with the financial statements for the same financial year, and
(ii) whether the management report has been prepared in accordance with the applicable legal requirements;
(b) state whether, in the light of the knowledge and understanding of the undertaking and its environment obtained in the course of the audit, he, she or it has identified material misstatements in the

management report, and shall give an indication of the nature of any such misstatements.
(2) The first subparagraph of paragraph (1) shall apply mutatis mutandis with respect to consolidated financial statements. The second subparagraph of paragraph (1) shall apply mutatis mutandis with respect to consolidated financial statements and consolidated management reports.

Article 35. Article 28 of Directive 2006/43/EC is replaced by the following:
"Article 28.
1. The audit report shall include:
(a) an introduction which shall, as a minimum, identify the financial statements that are the subject of the statutory audit, together with the financial reporting framework that has been applied in their preparation
(b) a description of the scope of the statutory audit which shall, as a minimum, identify the auditing standards in accordance with which the statutory audit was conducted;
(c) an audit opinion, which shall be either unqualified, qualified or an adverse opinion and shall state clearly the opinion of the statutory auditor as to:
(i) whether the annual financial statements give a true and fair view in accordance with the relevant financial reporting framework, and,
(ii) where appropriate, whether the annual financial statements comply with statutory requirements. If the statutory auditor is unable to express an audit opinion, the report shall contain a disclaimer of opinion;
(d) a reference to any matters to which the statutory auditor draws attention by way of emphasis without qualifying the audit opinion;
(e) the opinion and statement referred to in the second subparagraph of Article 34(1) of Directive 2013/34/EU of the European Parliament and of the Council of 26 June 2013 on the annual financial statements, consolidated financial statements and related reports of certain types of undertakings, amending Directive 2006/43/EC of the European Parliament and of the Council and repealing Council Directives 78/660/EEC and 83/349/EEC.
(2) The audit report shall be signed and dated by the statutory auditor. Where an audit firm carries out the statutory audit, the audit report shall bear the signature of at least the statutory auditor(s) carrying out the statutory audit on behalf of the audit firm. In exceptional circumstances Member States may provide that such signature(s) need not be disclosed to the public if such disclosure could lead to an imminent and significant threat to the personal security of any person. In any case the name(s) of the person(s) involved shall be known to the relevant competent authorities.
(3) The audit report on the consolidated financial statements shall comply with the requirements set out in of paragraphs 1 and 2. In reporting on the consistency of the management report and the financial statements as required by point (e) of paragraph (1), the statutory auditor or audit firm shall consider the consolidated financial statements and the consolidated management report. Where the annual financial statements of the parent undertaking are attached to the consolidated financial statements, the audit reports required by this Article may be combined.

Chapter 9. Provisions Concerning Exemptions and Restrictions on Exemptions

Article 36. (1) Member States may exempt micro-undertakings from any or all of the following obligations
(a) the obligation to present 'Prepayments and accrued income' and 'Accruals and deferred income'. Where a Member State makes use of that option, it may permit those undertakings, only in respect of other charges as referred to in point (b)(vi) of paragraph (2) of this Article, to depart from point (d) of Article 6(1) with regard to the recognition of 'Prepayments and accrued income' and 'Accruals and deferred income', provided that this fact is disclosed in the notes to the financial statements or, in accordance with point (b) of this paragraph, at the foot of the balance sheet;
(b) the obligation to draw up notes to the financial statements in accordance with Article 16, provided that the information required by points (d) and (e) of Article 16(1) of this Directive and by Article 24(2) of Directive 2012/30/EU is disclosed at the foot of the balance sheet;
(c) the obligation to prepare a management report in accordance with Chapter 5, provided that the information required by Article 24(2) of Directive 2012/30/EU is disclosed in the notes to the financial statements or, in accordance with point (b) of this paragraph, at the foot of the balance sheet;
(d) the obligation to publish annual financial statements in accordance with Chapter 7 of this Directive, provided that the balance sheet information contained therein is duly filed, in accordance with national law, with at least one competent authority designated by the Member State concerned. Whenever the competent authority is not the central register, commercial register or companies register, as referred to in Article 3(1) of Directive 2009/101/EC, the competent authority is required

to provide the register with the information filed.

(2) Member States may permit micro-undertakings:

(a) to draw up only an abridged balance sheet showing separately at least those items preceded by letters in Annexes III or IV, where applicable. In cases where point (a) of paragraph (1) of this Article applies, items E under 'Assets' and D under 'Liabilities' in Annex III or items E and K in Annex IV shall be excluded from the balance sheet;

(b) to draw up only an abridged profit and loss account showing separately at least the following items, where applicable:

(i) net turnover,

(ii) other income,

(iii) cost of raw materials and consumables,

(iv) staff costs,

(v) value adjustments,

(vi) other charges,

(vii) tax,

(viii) profit or loss.

(3) Member States shall not permit or require the application of Article 8 to any micro-undertaking making use of any of the exemptions provided for in paragraphs 1 and 2 of this Article.

(4) In respect of micro-undertakings, annual financial statements drawn up in accordance with paragraphs 1, 2 and 3 of this Article shall be regarded as giving the true and fair view required by Article 4(3), and consequently Article 4(4) shall not apply to such financial statements.

(5) If point (a) of paragraph (1) of this Article applies, the balance sheet total referred to in point (a) of Article 3(1) shall consist of the assets referred to in items A to D under 'Assets' in Annex III or items A to D in Annex IV.

(6) Without prejudice to this Article, Member States shall ensure that micro-undertakings are otherwise regarded as small undertakings.

(7) Member States shall not make available the derogations provided for in paragraphs 1, 2 and 3 in respect of investment undertakings or financial holding undertakings.

(8) Member States which at 19 July 2013 have brought into force laws, regulations or administrative provisions in compliance with Directive 2012/6/EU of the European Parliament and of the Council of 14 March 2012 amending Council Directive 78/660/EEC on the annual accounts of certain types of companies as regards micro-entities, may be exempted from the requirements set out in Article 3(9) with regard to the conversion into national currencies of thresholds set out in Article 3(1) when applying the first sentence of Article 53(1).

(9) By 20 July 2018 the Commission shall submit to the European Parliament, to the Council and to the European Economic and Social Committee a report on the situation of micro-undertakings taking account, in particular, of the situation at national level regarding the number of undertakings covered by the size criteria and the reduction of administrative burdens resulting from the exemption from the publication requirement.

Article 37. Notwithstanding the provisions of Directives 2009/101/EC and 2012/30/EU, a Member State shall not be required to apply the provisions of this Directive concerning the content, auditing and publication of the annual financial statements and the management report to undertakings governed by their national laws which are subsidiary undertakings, where the following conditions are fulfilled:

(1) the parent undertaking is subject to the laws of a Member State;

(2) all shareholders or members of the subsidiary undertaking have, in respect of each financial year in which the exemption is applied, declared their agreement to the exemption from such obligation;

(3) the parent undertaking has declared that it guarantees the commitments entered into by the subsidiary undertaking;

(4) the declarations referred to in points (2) and (3) of this Article are published by the subsidiary undertaking as laid down by the laws of the Member State in accordance with Chapter 2 of Directive 2009/101/EC;

(5) the subsidiary undertaking is included in the consolidated financial statements drawn up by the parent undertaking in accordance with this Directive;

(6) the exemption is disclosed in the notes to the consolidated financial statements drawn up by the parent undertaking; and

(7) the consolidated financial statements referred to in point (5) of this Article, the consolidated management report, and the audit report are published for the subsidiary undertaking as laid down by the laws of the Member State in accordance with Chapter 2 of Directive 2009/101/EC.

Article 38. (1) Member States may require undertakings referred to in point (a) of Article 1(1) which are governed by their laws and which are members having unlimited liability of any undertaking referred to in point (b) of Article 1(1) ('the undertaking concerned'), to draw up, have audited and publish, with their own financial statements, the financial statements of the undertaking concerned in accordance with this Directive; in such case the requirements of this Directive shall not apply to the undertaking concerned.
(2) Member States shall not be required to apply the requirements of this Directive to the undertaking concerned where:
(a) the financial statements of the undertaking concerned are drawn up, audited and published in accordance with the provisions of this Directive by an undertaking which:
(i) is a member having unlimited liability of that undertaking concerned, and
(ii) is governed by the laws of another Member State;
(b) the undertaking concerned is included in consolidated financial statements drawn up, audited and published in accordance with this Directive by:
(i) a member having unlimited liability, or
(ii) where the undertaking concerned is included in the consolidated financial statements of a larger body of undertakings drawn up, audited and published in conformity with this Directive, a parent undertaking governed by the laws of a Member State. This exemption shall be disclosed in the notes to the consolidated financial statements.
(3) In the cases referred to in paragraph (2), the undertaking concerned shall, upon request, reveal the name of the undertaking publishing the financial statements.

Article 39. A Member State shall not be required to apply the provisions of this Directive concerning the auditing and publication of the profit and loss account to undertakings governed by its national laws which are parent undertakings, provided that the following conditions are fulfilled:
(1) the parent undertaking draws up consolidated financial statements in accordance with this Directive and is included in those consolidated financial statements;
(2) the exemption is disclosed in the notes to the annual financial statements of the parent undertaking;
(3) the exemption is disclosed in the notes to the consolidated financial statements drawn up by the parent undertaking; and
(4) the profit or loss of the parent undertaking, determined in accordance with this Directive, is shown in its balance sheet.

Article 40. Unless expressly provided for in this Directive, Member States shall not make the simplifications and exemptions set out in this Directive available to public-interest entities. A public-interest entity shall be treated as a large undertaking regardless of its net turnover, balance sheet total or average number of employees during the financial year.

Chapter 10 Report on payments to governments

Article 41. For the purpose of this Chapter, the following definitions shall apply:
(1) 'undertaking active in the extractive industry' means an undertaking with any activity involving the exploration, prospection, discovery, development, and extraction of minerals, oil, natural gas deposits or other materials, within the economic activities listed in Section B, Divisions 05 to 08 of Annex I to Regulation (EC) No 1893/2006 of the European Parliament and of the Council of 20 December 2006 establishing the statistical classification of economic activities NACE Revision 2;
(2) 'undertaking active in the logging of primary forests' means an undertaking with activities as referred to in Section A, Division 02, Group 02.2 of Annex I to Regulation (EC) No 1893/2006, in primary forests;
(3) 'government' means any national, regional or local authority of a Member State or of a third country. It includes a department, agency or undertaking controlled by that authority as laid down in Article 22(1) to (6) of this Directive;
(4) 'project' means the operational activities that are governed by a single contract, license, lease, concession or similar legal agreements and form the basis for payment liabilities with a government. Nonetheless, if multiple such agreements are substantially interconnected, this shall be considered a project;
(5) 'payment' means an amount paid, whether in money or in kind, for activities, as described in points 1 and 2, of the following types:
(a) production entitlements;
(b) taxes levied on the income, production or profits of companies, excluding taxes levied on consumption such as value added taxes, personal income taxes or sales taxes;

(c) royalties;
(d) dividends;
(e) signature, discovery and production bonuses;
(f) licence fees, rental fees, entry fees and other considerations for licences and/or concessions; and
(g) payments for infrastructure improvements.

Article 42. (1) Member States shall require large undertakings and all public-interest entities active in the extractive industry or the logging of primary forests to prepare and make public a report on payments made to governments on an annual basis.
(2) That obligation shall not apply to any undertaking governed by the law of a Member State which is a subsidiary or parent undertaking, where both of the following conditions are fulfilled:
(a) the parent undertaking is subject to the laws of a Member State; and
(b) the payments to governments made by the undertaking are included in the consolidated report on payments to governments drawn up by that parent undertaking in accordance with Article 44.

Article 43. (1) Any payment, whether made as a single payment or as a series of related payments, need not be taken into account in the report if it is below EUR 100 000 within a financial year.
(2) The report shall disclose the following information in relation to activities as described in points (1) and (2) of Article 41 in respect of the relevant financial year:
(a) the total amount of payments made to each government;
(b) the total amount per type of payment as specified in points (5)(a) to (g) of Article 41 made to each government;
(c) where those payments have been attributed to a specific project, the total amount per type of payment as specified in point (5)(a) to (g) of Article 41, made for each such project and the total amount of payments for each such project.
Payments made by the undertaking in respect of obligations imposed at entity level may be disclosed at the entity level rather than at project level.
(3) Where payments in kind are made to a government, they shall be reported in value and, where applicable, in volume. Supporting notes shall be provided to explain how their value has been determined.
(4) The disclosure of the payments referred to in this Article shall reflect the substance, rather than the form, of the payment or activity concerned. Payments and activities may not be artificially split or aggregated to avoid the application of this Directive.
(5) In the case of those Member States which have not adopted the euro, the euro threshold identified in paragraph (1) shall be converted into national currency by:
(a) applying the exchange rate published in the *Official Journal of the European Union* as at the date of the entry into force of any Directive fixing that threshold, and
(b) rounding to the nearest hundred.

Article 44. (1) A Member State shall require any large undertaking or any public-interest entity active in the extractive industry or the logging of primary forests and governed by its national law to draw up a consolidated report on payments to governments in accordance with Articles 42 and 43 if that parent undertaking is under the obligation to prepare consolidated financial statements as laid down in Article 22(1) to (6).
A parent undertaking is considered to be active in the extractive industry or the logging of primary forests if any of its subsidiary undertakings are active in the extractive industry or the logging of primary forests.
The consolidated report shall only include payments resulting from extractive operations and/or operations relating to the logging of primary forests.
(2) The obligation to draw up the consolidated report referred to in paragraph (1) shall not apply to:
(a) a parent undertaking of a small group, as defined in Article 3(5), except where any affiliated undertaking is a public-interest entity;
(b) a parent undertaking of a medium-sized group, as defined in Article 3(6), except where any affiliated undertaking is a public-interest entity; and
(c) a parent undertaking governed by the law of a Member State which is also a subsidiary undertaking, if its own parent undertaking is governed by the law of a Member State.
(3) An undertaking, including a public-interest entity, need not be included in a consolidated report on payments to governments where at least one of the following conditions is fulfilled:
(a) severe long-term restrictions substantially hinder the parent undertaking in the exercise of its rights over the assets or management of that undertaking;
(b) extremely rare cases where the information necessary for the preparation of the consolidated

report on payments to governments in accordance with this Directive cannot be obtained without disproportionate expense or undue delay;
(c) the shares of that undertaking are held exclusively with a view to their subsequent resale.
The above exemptions shall apply only if they are also used for the purposes of the consolidated financial statements.

Article 45. (1) The report referred to in Article 42 and the consolidated report referred to in Article 44 on payments to governments shall be published as laid down by the laws of each Member State in accordance with Chapter 2 of Directive 2009/101/EC.
(2) Member States shall ensure that the members of the responsible bodies of an undertaking, acting within the competences assigned to them by national law, have responsibility for ensuring that, to the best of their knowledge and ability, the report on payments to governments is drawn up and published in accordance with the requirements of this Directive.

Article 46. (1) Undertakings referred to in Articles 42 and 44 that prepare and make public a report complying with third-country reporting requirements assessed, in accordance with Article 47, as equivalent to the requirements of this Chapter are exempt from the requirements of this Chapter except for the obligation to publish this report as laid down by the laws of each Member State in accordance with Chapter 2 of Directive 2009/101/EC.
(2) The Commission shall be empowered to adopt delegated acts in accordance with Article 49 identifying the criteria to be applied when assessing, for the purposes of paragraph (1) of this Article, the equivalence of third-country reporting requirements and the requirements of this Chapter.
(3) The criteria identified by the Commission in accordance with paragraph (2) shall:
(a) include the following:
(i) target undertakings,
(ii) target recipients of payments,
(iii) payments captured,
(iv) attribution of payments captured,
(v) breakdown of payments captured,
(vi) triggers for reporting on a consolidated basis,
(vii) reporting medium,
(viii) frequency of reporting, and
(ix) anti-evasion measures;
(b) otherwise be limited to criteria which facilitate a direct comparison of third-country reporting requirements with the requirements of this Chapter.

Article 47. The Commission shall be empowered to adopt implementing acts identifying those third-country reporting requirements which, after applying the equivalence criteria identified in accordance with Article 46, it considers equivalent to the requirements of this Chapter. Those implementing acts shall be adopted in accordance with the examination procedure referred to in Article 50(2).

Article 48. The Commission shall review and report on the implementation and effectiveness of this Chapter, in particular as regards the scope of, and compliance with, the reporting obligations and the modalities of the reporting on a project basis.
The review shall take into account international developments, in particular with regard to enhancing transparency of payments to governments, assess the impacts of other international regimes and consider the effects on competitiveness and security of energy supply. It shall be completed by 21 July 2018.
The report shall be submitted to the European Parliament and to the Council, together with a legislative proposal, if appropriate. That report shall consider the extension of the reporting requirements to additional industry sectors and whether the report on payments to governments should be audited. The report shall also consider the disclosure of additional information on the average number of employees, the use of subcontractors and any pecuniary penalties administered by a country.
In addition, the report shall analyse the feasibility of the introduction of an obligation for all Union issuers to carry out due diligence when sourcing minerals to ensure that supply chains have no connection to conflict parties and respect the EITI and OECD recommendations on responsible supply chain management.

Chapter 11. Final Provisions

Article 49. (1) The power to adopt delegated acts is conferred on the Commission subject to the conditions laid down in this Article.

(2) The power to adopt delegated acts referred to in Article 1(2), Article 3(13) and Article 46(2) shall be conferred on the Commission for an indeterminate period of time from the date referred to in Article 54.
(3) The delegation of power referred to in Article 1(2), Article 3(13) and Article 46(2) may be revoked at any time by the European Parliament or by the Council. A decision to revoke shall put an end to the delegation of the power specified in that decision. It shall take effect the day following the publication of that decision in the *Official Journal of the European Union* or at a later date specified therein. It shall not affect the validity of any delegated acts already in force.
(4) As soon as it adopts a delegated act, the Commission shall notify it simultaneously to the European Parliament and to the Council.
(5) A delegated act adopted pursuant to Article 1(2), Article 3(13) or Article 46(2) shall enter into force only if no objection has been expressed either by the European Parliament or the Council within a period of two months of notification of that act to the European Parliament and the Council or if, before the expiry of that period, the European Parliament and the Council have both informed the Commission that they will not object. That period shall be extended by two months at the initiative of the European Parliament or the Council.

Article 50. (1) The Commission shall be assisted by a committee. That committee shall be a committee within the meaning of Regulation (EU) No 182/2011.
(2) Where reference is made to this paragraph, Article 5 of Regulation (EU) No 182/2011 shall apply.

Article 51. Member States shall provide for penalties applicable to infringements of the national provisions adopted in accordance with this Directive and shall take all the measures necessary to ensure that those penalties are enforced. The penalties provided for shall be effective, proportionate and dissuasive.

Article 52. Directives 78/660/EEC and 83/349/EEC are repealed.
References to the repealed Directives shall be construed as references to this Directive and shall be read in accordance with the correlation table in Annex VII.

Article 53. (1) Member States shall bring into force the laws, regulations and administrative provisions necessary to comply with this Directive by 20 July 2015. They shall immediately inform the Commission thereof.
Member States may provide that the provisions referred to in the first subparagraph are first to apply to financial statements for financial years beginning on 1 January 2016 or during the calendar year 2016.
When Member States adopt those provisions, they shall contain a reference to this Directive or be accompanied by such a reference on the occasion of their official publication. The methods of making such reference shall be laid down by Member States.
(2) Member States shall communicate to the Commission the text of the main provisions of national law which they adopt in the field covered by this Directive.

Article 54. This Directive shall enter into force on the twentieth day following that of its publication in the *Official Journal of the European Union*.

Article 55. This Directive is addressed to the Member States.

EU: DIRECTIVE 2014/95 ON DISCLOSURE OF NON-FINANCIAL INFORMATION

Directive 2014/95/EU of the European Parliament and of the Council of 22 October 2014 amending Directive 2013/34/EU as regards disclosure of non-financial and diversity information by certain large undertakings and groups (Text with EEA relevance) [footnotes omitted].

THE EUROPEAN PARLIAMENT AND THE COUNCIL OF THE EUROPEAN UNION,
Having regard to the Treaty on the Functioning of the European Union, and in particular Article 50(1) thereof,
Having regard to the proposal from the European Commission,
After transmission of the draft legislative act to the national parliaments,
Having regard to the opinion of the European Economic and Social Committee,
Acting in accordance with the ordinary legislative procedure,
Whereas:
(1) In its communication entitled 'Single Market Act — Twelve levers to boost growth and strengthen confidence — "Working together to create new growth"', adopted on 13 April 2011, the Commission identified the need to raise to a similarly high level across all Member States the transparency of the social and environmental information provided by undertakings in all sectors. This is fully consistent with the possibility for Member States to require, as appropriate, further improvements to the transparency of undertakings' non-financial information, which is by its nature a continuous endeavour.
(2) The need to improve undertakings' disclosure of social and environmental information, by presenting a legislative proposal in this field, was reiterated in the Commission communication entitled 'A renewed EU strategy 2011-14 for Corporate Social Responsibility', adopted on 25 October 2011.
(3) In its resolutions of 6 February 2013 on, respectively, 'Corporate Social Responsibility: accountable, transparent and responsible business behaviour and sustainable growth' and 'Corporate Social Responsibility: promoting society's interests and a route to sustainable and inclusive recovery', the European Parliament acknowledged the importance of businesses divulging information on sustainability such as social and environmental factors, with a view to identifying sustainability risks and increasing investor and consumer trust. Indeed, disclosure of non-financial information is vital for managing change towards a sustainable global economy by combining long-term profitability with social justice and environmental protection. In this context, disclosure of non-financial information helps the measuring, monitoring and managing of undertakings' performance and their impact on society. Thus, the European Parliament called on the Commission to bring forward a legislative proposal on the disclosure of non-financial information by undertakings allowing for high flexibility of action, in order to take account of the multidimensional nature of corporate social responsibility (CSR) and the diversity of the CSR policies implemented by businesses matched by a sufficient level of comparability to meet the needs of investors and other stakeholders as well as the need to provide consumers with easy access to information on the impact of businesses on society.
(4) The coordination of national provisions concerning the disclosure of non-financial information in respect of certain large undertakings is of importance for the interests of undertakings, shareholders and other stakeholders alike. Coordination is necessary in those fields because most of those undertakings operate in more than one Member State.
(5) It is also necessary to establish a certain minimum legal requirement as regards the extent of the information that should be made available to the public and authorities by undertakings across the Union. The undertakings subject to this Directive should give a fair and comprehensive view of their policies, outcomes, and risks.
(6) In order to enhance the consistency and comparability of non-financial information disclosed throughout the Union, certain large undertakings should prepare a non-financial statement containing information relating to at least environmental matters, social and employee-related matters, respect for human rights, anti-corruption and bribery matters. Such statement should include a description of the policies, outcomes and risks related to those matters and should be included in the management report of the undertaking concerned. The non-financial statement should also include information on the due diligence processes implemented by the undertaking, also regarding, where relevant and proportionate, its supply and subcontracting chains, in order to identify, prevent and mitigate existing and potential adverse impacts. It should be possible for Member States to exempt undertakings which are subject to this Directive from the obligation to prepare a non-financial statement when a separate report corresponding to the same financial year and covering the same content is provided.
(7) Where undertakings are required to prepare a non-financial statement, that statement should contain, as regards environmental matters, details of the current and foreseeable impacts of the undertaking's operations on the environment, and, as appropriate, on health and safety, the use of

renewable and/or non-renewable energy, greenhouse gas emissions, water use and air pollution. As regards social and employee-related matters, the information provided in the statement may concern the actions taken to ensure gender equality, implementation of fundamental conventions of the International Labour Organisation, working conditions, social dialogue, respect for the right of workers to be informed and consulted, respect for trade union rights, health and safety at work and the dialogue with local communities, and/or the actions taken to ensure the protection and the development of those communities. With regard to human rights, anti-corruption and bribery, the non-financial statement could include information on the prevention of human rights abuses and/or on instruments in place to fight corruption and bribery.

(8) The undertakings which are subject to this Directive should provide adequate information in relation to matters that stand out as being most likely to bring about the materialisation of principal risks of severe impacts, along with those that have already materialised. The severity of such impacts should be judged by their scale and gravity. The risks of adverse impact may stem from the undertaking's own activities or may be linked to its operations, and, where relevant and proportionate, its products, services and business relationships, including its supply and subcontracting chains. This should not lead to undue additional administrative burdens for small and medium-sized undertakings.

(9) In providing this information, undertakings which are subject to this Directive may rely on national frameworks, Union-based frameworks such as the Eco-Management and Audit Scheme (EMAS), or international frameworks such as the United Nations (UN) Global Compact, the Guiding Principles on Business and Human Rights implementing the UN 'Protect, Respect and Remedy' Framework, the Organisation for Economic Co-operation and Development (OECD) Guidelines for Multinational Enterprises, the International Organisation for Standardisation's ISO 26000, the International Labour Organisation's Tripartite Declaration of principles concerning multinational enterprises and social policy, the Global Reporting Initiative, or other recognised international frameworks.

(10) Member States should ensure that adequate and effective means exist to guarantee disclosure of non-financial information by undertakings in compliance with this Directive. To that end, Member States should ensure that effective national procedures are in place to enforce compliance with the obligations laid down by this Directive, and that those procedures are available to all persons and legal entities having a legitimate interest, in accordance with national law, in ensuring that the provisions of this Directive are respected.

(11) Paragraph 47 of the outcome document of the United Nations Rio+20 conference, entitled 'The Future We Want', recognises the importance of corporate sustainability reporting and encourages undertakings, where appropriate, to consider integrating sustainability information into their reporting cycle. It also encourages industry, interested governments and relevant stakeholders with the support of the United Nations system, as appropriate, to develop models for best practice, and facilitate action for the integration of financial and non-financial information, taking into account experiences from already existing frameworks.

(12) Investors' access to non-financial information is a step towards reaching the milestone of having in place by 2020 market and policy incentives rewarding business investments in efficiency under the roadmap to a resource-efficient Europe.

(13) The European Council, in its conclusions of 24 and 25 March 2011, called for the overall regulatory burden, in particular for small and medium-sized enterprises ('SMEs'), to be reduced at both European and national levels, and suggested measures to increase productivity, while the Europe 2020 Strategy for smart, sustainable and inclusive growth aims to improve the business environment for SMEs and to promote their internationalisation. Thus, in accordance with the 'think small first' principle, the new disclosure requirements should apply only to certain large undertakings and groups.

(14) The scope of those non-financial disclosure requirements should be defined by reference to the average number of employees, balance sheet total and net turnover. SMEs should be exempted from additional requirements, and the obligation to disclose a non-financial statement should apply only to those large undertakings which are public-interest entities and to those public-interest entities which are parent undertakings of a large group, in each case having an average number of employees in excess of 500, in the case of a group on a consolidated basis. This should not prevent Member States from requiring disclosure of non-financial information from undertakings and groups other than undertakings which are subject to this Directive.

(15) Many of the undertakings which fall within the scope of Directive 2013/34/EU of the European Parliament and of the Council (3) are members of groups of undertakings. Consolidated management reports should be drawn up so that the information concerning such groups of undertakings may be conveyed to members and third parties. National law governing consolidated management reports

should therefore be coordinated in order to achieve the objectives of comparability and consistency of the information which undertakings should publish within the Union.

(16) Statutory auditors and audit firms should only check that the non-financial statement or the separate report has been provided. In addition, it should be possible for Member States to require that the information included in the non-financial statement or in the separate report be verified by an independent assurance services provider.

(17) With a view to facilitating the disclosure of non-financial information by undertakings, the Commission should prepare non-binding guidelines, including general and sectoral non-financial key performance indicators. The Commission should take into account current best practices, international developments and the results of related Union initiatives. The Commission should carry out appropriate consultations, including with relevant stakeholders. When referring to environmental aspects, the Commission should cover at least land use, water use, greenhouse gas emissions and the use of materials.

(18) Diversity of competences and views of the members of administrative, management and supervisory bodies of undertakings facilitates a good understanding of the business organisation and affairs of the undertaking concerned. It enables members of those bodies to constructively challenge the management decisions and to be more open to innovative ideas, addressing the similarity of views of members, also known as the 'group-think' phenomenon. It contributes thus to effective oversight of the management and to successful governance of the undertaking. It is therefore important to enhance transparency regarding the diversity policy applied. This would inform the market of corporate governance practices and thus put indirect pressure on undertakings to have more diversified boards.

(19) The obligation to disclose diversity policies in relation to the administrative, management and supervisory bodies with regard to aspects such as, for instance, age, gender or educational and professional backgrounds should apply only to certain large undertakings. Disclosure of the diversity policy should be part of the corporate governance statement, as laid down by Article 20 of Directive 2013/34/EU. If no diversity policy is applied there should not be any obligation to put one in place, but the corporate governance statement should include a clear explanation as to why this is the case.

(20) Initiatives at Union level, including country-by-country reporting for several sectors, as well as the references made by the European Council, in its conclusions of 22 May 2013 and of 19 and 20 December 2013, to country-by-country reporting by large companies and groups, similar provisions in Directive 2013/36/EU of the European Parliament and of the Council (4), and international efforts to improve transparency in financial reporting have been noted. Within the context of the G8 and the G20, the OECD has been asked to draw up a standardised reporting template for multinational undertakings to report to tax authorities where they make their profits and pay taxes around the world. Such developments complement the proposals contained in this Directive, as appropriate measures for their respective purposes.

(21) Since the objective of this Directive, namely to increase the relevance, consistency and comparability of information disclosed by certain large undertakings and groups across the Union, cannot be sufficiently achieved by the Member States but can rather, by reason of its effect, be better achieved at Union level, the Union may adopt measures, in accordance with the principle of subsidiarity as set out in Article 5 of the Treaty on European Union. In accordance with the principle of proportionality as set out in that Article, this Directive does not go beyond what is necessary in order to achieve that objective.

(22) This Directive respects the fundamental rights and observes the principles recognised in particular by the Charter of Fundamental Rights of the European Union, including freedom to conduct a business, respect for private life and the protection of personal data. This Directive has to be implemented in accordance with those rights and principles.

(23) Directive 2013/34/EU should therefore be amended accordingly,

HAVE ADOPTED THIS DIRECTIVE:

Article 1. Directive 2013/34/EU is amended as follows:

(1) The following Article is inserted:

'Article 19a

Non-financial statement

1. Large undertakings which are public-interest entities exceeding on their balance sheet dates the criterion of the average number of 500 employees during the financial year shall include in the management report a non-financial statement containing information to the extent necessary for an understanding of the undertaking's development, performance, position and impact of its activity,

relating to, as a minimum, environmental, social and employee matters, respect for human rights, anti-corruption and bribery matters, including:

(a) a brief description of the undertaking's business model;

(b) a description of the policies pursued by the undertaking in relation to those matters, including due diligence processes implemented;

(c) the outcome of those policies;

(d) the principal risks related to those matters linked to the undertaking's operations including, where relevant and proportionate, its business relationships, products or services which are likely to cause adverse impacts in those areas, and how the undertaking manages those risks;

(e) non-financial key performance indicators relevant to the particular business.

Where the undertaking does not pursue policies in relation to one or more of those matters, the non-financial statement shall provide a clear and reasoned explanation for not doing so.

The non-financial statement referred to in the first subparagraph shall also, where appropriate, include references to, and additional explanations of, amounts reported in the annual financial statements.

Member States may allow information relating to impending developments or matters in the course of negotiation to be omitted in exceptional cases where, in the duly justified opinion of the members of the administrative, management and supervisory bodies, acting within the competences assigned to them by national law and having collective responsibility for that opinion, the disclosure of such information would be seriously prejudicial to the commercial position of the undertaking, provided that such omission does not prevent a fair and balanced understanding of the undertaking's development, performance, position and impact of its activity.

In requiring the disclosure of the information referred to in the first subparagraph, Member States shall provide that undertakings may rely on national, Union-based or international frameworks, and if they do so, undertakings shall specify which frameworks they have relied upon.

2. Undertakings fulfilling the obligation set out in paragraph 1 shall be deemed to have fulfilled the obligation relating to the analysis of non-financial information set out in the third subparagraph of Article 19(1).

3. An undertaking which is a subsidiary undertaking shall be exempted from the obligation set out in paragraph 1 if that undertaking and its subsidiary undertakings are included in the consolidated management report or the separate report of another undertaking, drawn up in accordance with Article 29 and this Article.

4. Where an undertaking prepares a separate report corresponding to the same financial year whether or not relying on national, Union-based or international frameworks and covering the information required for the non-financial statement as provided for in paragraph 1, Member States may exempt that undertaking from the obligation to prepare the non-financial statement laid down in paragraph 1, provided that such separate report:

(a) is published together with the management report in accordance with Article 30; or

(b) is made publicly available within a reasonable period of time, not exceeding six months after the balance sheet date, on the undertaking's website, and is referred to in the management report.

Paragraph 2 shall apply mutatis mutandis to undertakings preparing a separate report as referred to in the first subparagraph of this paragraph.

5. Member States shall ensure that the statutory auditor or audit firm checks whether the non-financial statement referred to in paragraph 1 or the separate report referred to in paragraph 4 has been provided.

6. Member States may require that the information in the non-financial statement referred to in paragraph 1 or in the separate report referred to in paragraph 4 be verified by an independent assurance services provider.'.

(2) Article 20 is amended as follows:

(a) in paragraph 1, the following point is added:

'(g) a description of the diversity policy applied in relation to the undertaking's administrative, management and supervisory bodies with regard to aspects such as, for instance, age, gender, or educational and professional backgrounds, the objectives of that diversity policy, how it has been implemented and the results in the reporting period. If no such policy is applied, the statement shall contain an explanation as to why this is the case.';

(b) paragraph 3 is replaced by the following:

'3. The statutory auditor or audit firm shall express an opinion in accordance with the second subparagraph of Article 34(1) regarding information prepared under points (c) and (d) of paragraph 1 of this Article and shall check that the information referred to in points (a), (b), (e), (f) and (g) of paragraph 1 of this Article has been provided.';

(c) paragraph 4 is replaced by the following:

'4. Member States may exempt undertakings referred to in paragraph 1 which have only issued securities other than shares admitted to trading on a regulated market within the meaning of point (14) of Article 4(1) of Directive 2004/39/EC from the application of points (a), (b), (e), (f) and (g) of paragraph 1 of this Article, unless such undertakings have issued shares which are traded in a multilateral trading facility within the meaning of point 15 of Article 4(1) of Directive 2004/39/EC.';
(d) the following paragraph is added:
'5. Notwithstanding Article 40, point (g) of paragraph 1 shall not apply to small and medium-sized undertakings.'.
(3) The following Article is inserted:
'Article 29a
Consolidated non-financial statement
1. Public-interest entities which are parent undertakings of a large group exceeding on its balance sheet dates, on a consolidated basis, the criterion of the average number of 500 employees during the financial year shall include in the consolidated management report a consolidated non-financial statement containing information to the extent necessary for an understanding of the group's development, performance, position and impact of its activity, relating to, as a minimum, environmental, social and employee matters, respect for human rights, anti-corruption and bribery matters, including:
(a) a brief description of the group's business model;
(b) a description of the policies pursued by the group in relation to those matters, including due diligence processes implemented;
(c) the outcome of those policies;
(d) the principal risks related to those matters linked to the group's operations including, where relevant and proportionate, its business relationships, products or services which are likely to cause adverse impacts in those areas, and how the group manages those risks;
(e) non-financial key performance indicators relevant to the particular business.
Where the group does not pursue policies in relation to one or more of those matters, the consolidated non-financial statement shall provide a clear and reasoned explanation for not doing so.
The consolidated non-financial statement referred to in the first subparagraph shall also, where appropriate, include references to, and additional explanations of, amounts reported in the consolidated financial statements.
Member States may allow information relating to impending developments or matters in the course of negotiation to be omitted in exceptional cases where, in the duly justified opinion of the members of the administrative, management and supervisory bodies, acting within the competences assigned to them by national law and having collective responsibility for that opinion, the disclosure of such information would be seriously prejudicial to the commercial position of the group, provided that such omission does not prevent a fair and balanced understanding of the group's development, performance, position and impact of its activity.
In requiring the disclosure of the information referred to in the first subparagraph, Member States shall provide that the parent undertaking may rely on national, Union-based or international frameworks, and if it does so, the parent undertaking shall specify which frameworks it has relied upon.
2. A parent undertaking fulfilling the obligation set out in paragraph 1 shall be deemed to have fulfilled the obligation relating to the analysis of non-financial information set out in the third subparagraph of Article 19(1) and in Article 29.
3. A parent undertaking which is also a subsidiary undertaking shall be exempted from the obligation set out in paragraph 1 if that exempted parent undertaking and its subsidiaries are included in the consolidated management report or the separate report of another undertaking, drawn up in accordance with Article 29 and this Article.
4. Where a parent undertaking prepares a separate report corresponding to the same financial year, referring to the whole group, whether or not relying on national, Union-based or international frameworks and covering the information required for the consolidated non-financial statement as provided for in paragraph 1, Member States may exempt that parent undertaking from the obligation to prepare the consolidated non-financial statement laid down in paragraph 1, provided that such separate report:
(a) is published together with the consolidated management report in accordance with Article 30; or
(b) is made publicly available within a reasonable period of time, not exceeding six months after the balance sheet date, on the parent undertaking's website, and is referred to in the consolidated management report.
Paragraph 2 shall apply mutatis mutandis to parent undertakings preparing a separate report as referred to in the first subparagraph of this paragraph.
5. Member States shall ensure that the statutory auditor or audit firm checks whether the consolidated non-financial statement referred to in paragraph 1 or the separate report referred to in paragraph 4 has been provided.

6. Member States may require that the information in the consolidated non-financial statement referred to in paragraph 1 or in the separate report referred to in paragraph 4 be verified by an independent assurance services provider.'.

(4) In Article 33, paragraph 1 is replaced by the following:

'1. Member States shall ensure that the members of the administrative, management and supervisory bodies of an undertaking, acting within the competences assigned to them by national law, have collective responsibility for ensuring that:

(a) the annual financial statements, the management report, the corporate governance statement when provided separately and the report referred to in Article 19a(4); and

(b) the consolidated financial statements, the consolidated management reports, the consolidated corporate governance statement when provided separately and the report referred to in Article 29a(4), are drawn up and published in accordance with the requirements of this Directive and, where applicable, with the international accounting standards adopted in accordance with Regulation (EC) No 1606/2002.'.

(5) In Article 34, the following paragraph is added:

'3. This Article shall not apply to the non-financial statement referred to in Article 19a(1) and the consolidated non-financial statement referred to in Article 29a(1) or to the separate reports referred to in Articles 19a(4) and 29a(4).'.

(6) In Article 48, the following paragraph is inserted before the last paragraph:

'The report shall also consider, taking into account developments in the OECD and the results of related European initiatives, the possibility of introducing an obligation requiring large undertakings to produce on an annual basis a country-by-country report for each Member State and third country in which they operate, containing information on, as a minimum, profits made, taxes paid on profits and public subsidies received.'.

Article 2. The Commission shall prepare non-binding guidelines on methodology for reporting non-financial information, including non-financial key performance indicators, general and sectoral, with a view to facilitating relevant, useful and comparable disclosure of non-financial information by undertakings. In doing so, the Commission shall consult relevant stakeholders.

The Commission shall publish the guidelines by 6 December 2016.

Article 3. The Commission shall submit a report to the European Parliament and to the Council on the implementation of this Directive, including, among other aspects, its scope, particularly as regards large non-listed undertakings, its effectiveness and the level of guidance and methods provided. The report shall be published by 6 December 2018 and shall be accompanied, if appropriate, by legislative proposals.

Article 4. (1) Member States shall bring into force the laws, regulations and administrative provisions necessary to comply with this Directive by 6 December 2016. They shall immediately inform the Commission thereof.

Member States shall provide that the provisions referred to in the first subparagraph are to apply to all undertakings within the scope of Article 1 for the financial year starting on 1 January 2017 or during the calendar year 2017.

When Member States adopt those provisions, they shall contain a reference to this Directive or shall be accompanied by such reference on the occasion of their official publication. The methods of making such reference shall be laid down by Member States.

(2) Member States shall communicate to the Commission the text of the main provisions of national law which they adopt in the field covered by this Directive.

Article 5. This Directive shall enter into force on the twentieth day following that of its publication in the *Official Journal of the European Union*.

Article 6. This Directive is addressed to the Member States.

EU: DIRECTIVE 2017/828 ON LONG-TERM SHAREHOLDER ENGAGEMENT

Directive (EU) 2017/828 of the European Parliament and of the Council of 17 May 2017 amending Directive 2007/36/EC as regards the encouragement of long-term shareholder engagement [footnotes omitted].

THE EUROPEAN PARLIAMENT AND THE COUNCIL OF THE EUROPEAN UNION,
Having regard to the Treaty on the Functioning of the European Union, and in particular Articles 50 and 114 thereof, Having regard to the proposal from the European Commission,
After transmission of the draft legislative act to the national parliaments,
Having regard to the opinion of the European Economic and Social Committee, Acting in accordance with the ordinary legislative procedure,
Whereas:
(1) Directive 2007/36/EC of the European Parliament and of the Council establishes requirements in relation to the exercise of certain shareholder rights attached to voting shares in relation to general meetings of companies which have their registered office in a Member State and the shares of which are admitted to trading on a regulated market situated or operating within a Member State.
(2) The financial crisis has revealed that shareholders in many cases supported managers' excessive short-term risk taking. Moreover, there is clear evidence that the current level of 'monitoring' of investee companies and engagement by institutional investors and asset managers is often inadequate and focuses too much on short- term returns, which may lead to suboptimal corporate governance and performance.
(3) In its communication of 12 December 2012 entitled 'Action Plan: European company law and corporate governance — a modern legal framework for more engaged shareholders and sustainable companies', the Commission announced a number of actions in the area of corporate governance, in particular to encourage long-term shareholder engagement and to enhance transparency between companies and investors.
(4) Shares of listed companies are often held through complex chains of intermediaries which render the exercise of shareholder rights more difficult and may act as an obstacle to shareholder engagement. Companies are often unable to identify their shareholders. The identification of shareholders is a prerequisite to direct communication between the shareholders and the company and therefore essential to facilitating the exercise of shareholder rights
and shareholder engagement. This is particularly relevant in cross-border situations and when using electronic means. Listed companies should therefore have the right to identify their shareholders in order to be able to communicate with them directly. Intermediaries should be required, upon the request of the company, to communicate to the company the information regarding shareholder identity. However, Member States should be allowed to exclude from the identification requirement shareholders holding only a small number of shares.
(5) In order to achieve that objective, a certain level of information on shareholder identity needs to be transmitted to the company. That information should include at least the name and contact details of the shareholder and, where the shareholder is a legal person, its registration number or, if no registration number is available, a unique identifier, such as the Legal Entity Identifier (LEI code), and the number of shares held by the shareholder as well as, if requested by the company, the categories or classes of shares held and the date of their acquisition. The transmission of less information would be insufficient to allow the company to identify its shareholders in order to communicate with them.
(6) Under this Directive, the personal data of shareholders should be processed to enable the company to identify its existing shareholders in order to communicate directly with them, with a view to facilitating the exercise of shareholder rights and shareholder engagement with the company. This is without prejudice to Member State law providing for processing of the personal data of shareholders for other purposes, such as to enable shareholders to cooperate with each other.
(7) In order to enable the company to communicate directly with its existing shareholders with a view to facilitating the exercise of shareholder rights and shareholder engagement, the company and the intermediaries should be allowed to store personal data relating to the shareholders for as long as they remain shareholders. However, companies and intermediaries are often not aware that a person has ceased to be a shareholder unless they have been informed by the person or have obtained that information through a new shareholder identification exercise, which often takes place only once a year in relation to the annual general meeting or other important events such as takeover bids or mergers. Companies and intermediaries should therefore be allowed to store personal data until the date on which they have become aware of the fact that a person has ceased to be a shareholder and for a maximum period of 12 months after becoming aware of that fact. This is without prejudice to the fact that the company or intermediary may need to store the personal data of persons who have ceased to be shareholders for other purposes, such as ensuring adequate records for the purposes

of keeping track of succession in title of the shares of a company, maintaining necessary records in respect of general meetings, including in relation to the validity of its resolutions, fulfilling by the company of its obligations in respect of the payment of dividends or interest relating to shares or any other sums to be paid to former shareholders.

(8) The effective exercise of shareholder rights depends to a large extent on the efficiency of the chain of inter mediaries maintaining securities accounts on behalf of shareholders or of other persons, especially in a cross- border context. In the chain of intermediaries, especially when the chain involves many intermediaries, information is not always passed from the company to its shareholders and shareholders' votes are not always correctly transmitted to the company. This Directive aims to improve the transmission of information along the chain of intermediaries to facilitate the exercise of shareholder rights.

(9) In view of their important role, intermediaries should be obliged to facilitate the exercise of rights by shareholders, whether shareholders exercise those rights themselves or nominate a third person to do so. When shareholders do not want to exercise the rights themselves and have nominated the intermediary to do so, the latter should exercise those rights upon the explicit authorisation and instruction of the shareholders and for their benefit.

(10) It is important to ensure that shareholders who engage with an investee company by voting know whether their votes have been correctly taken into account. Confirmation of receipt of votes should be provided in the case of electronic voting. In addition, each shareholder who casts a vote in a general meeting should at least have the possibility to verify after the general meeting whether the vote has been validly recorded and counted by the company.

(11) In order to promote equity investment throughout the Union and to facilitate the exercise of rights related to shares, this Directive should establish a high degree of transparency with regard to charges, including prices and fees, for the services provided by intermediaries. Discrimination between the charges levied for the exercise of shareholder rights domestically and on a cross-border basis is a deterrent to cross-border investment and the efficient functioning of the internal market and should be prohibited. Any differences between the charges levied for the domestic and the cross-border exercise of shareholder rights should be allowed only if they are duly justified and reflect the variation in actual costs incurred for delivering the services by intermediaries.

(12) The chain of intermediaries may include intermediaries that have neither their registered office nor their head office in the Union. Nevertheless, the activities carried out by third-country intermediaries could have effects on the long- term sustainability of Union companies and on corporate governance in the Union. Moreover, in order to achieve the objectives pursued by this Directive, it is necessary to ensure that information is transmitted throughout the chain of intermediaries. If third-country intermediaries were not subject to this Directive and did not have the same obligations relating to the transmission of information as Union intermediaries, the flow of information would risk being interrupted. Third-country intermediaries which provide services with respect to shares of companies that have their registered office in the Union and the shares of which are admitted to trading on a regulated market situated or operating within the Union should therefore be subject to the rules on shareholder identification, transmission of information, facilitation of shareholder rights, and transparency and non-discrimination of costs to ensure the effective application of the provisions on shares held via such intermediaries.

(13) This Directive is without prejudice to national law regulating the holding and ownership of securities and arrangements maintaining the integrity of securities and does not affect the beneficial owners or other persons who are not shareholders under the applicable national law.

(14) Effective and sustainable shareholder engagement is one of the cornerstones of the corporate governance model of listed companies, which depends on checks and balances between the different organs and different stakeholders. Greater involvement of shareholders in corporate governance is one of the levers that can help improve the financial and non-financial performance of companies, including as regards environmental, social and governance factors, in particular as referred to in the Principles for Responsible Investment, supported by the United Nations. In addition, greater involvement of all stakeholders, in particular employees, in corporate governance is an important factor in ensuring a more long-term approach by listed companies that needs to be encouraged and taken into consideration.

(15) Institutional investors and asset managers are often important shareholders of listed companies in the Union and can therefore play an important role in the corporate governance of those companies, but also more generally with regard to their strategy and long-term performance. However, the experience of the last years has shown that institutional investors and asset managers often do not engage with companies in which they hold shares and evidence shows that capital markets often exert pressure on companies to perform in the short term, which may jeopardise the long-term financial

and non-financial performance of companies and may, among other negative consequences, lead to a suboptimal level of investments, for example in research and development, to the detriment of the long-term performance of both the companies and the investors.

(16) Institutional investors and asset managers are often not transparent about their investment strategies, their engagement policy and the implementation thereof. Public disclosure of such information could have a positive impact on investor awareness, enable ultimate beneficiaries such as future pensioners optimise investment decisions, facilitate the dialogue between companies and their shareholders, encourage shareholder engagement and strengthen their accountability to stakeholders and to civil society.

(17) Institutional investors and asset managers should therefore be more transparent as regards their approach to shareholder engagement. They should either develop and publicly disclose a policy on shareholder engagement or explain why they have chosen not to do so. The policy on shareholder engagement should describe how institutional investors and asset managers integrate shareholder engagement in their investment strategy, which different engagement activities they choose to carry out and how they do so. The engagement policy should also include policies to manage actual or potential conflicts of interests, in particular situations in which the institutional investors or asset managers or their affiliated undertakings have significant business relationships with the investee company. The engagement policy or the explanation should be publicly available online.

(18) Institutional investors and asset managers should publicly disclose information about the implementation of their engagement policy and in particular how they have exercised their voting rights. However, with a view to reducing the possible administrative burden, investors should be able to decide not to publish every vote cast if the vote is considered to be insignificant due to the subject matter of the vote or to the size of the holding in the company. Such insignificant votes may include votes cast on purely procedural matters or votes cast in companies where the investor has a very minor stake compared to the investor's holdings in other investee companies. Investors should set their own criteria regarding which votes are insignificant on the basis of the subject matter of the vote or the size of the holding in the company, and apply them consistently.

(19) A medium to long-term approach is a key enabler of responsible stewardship of assets. The institutional investors should therefore disclose to the public, annually, information explaining how the main elements of their equity investment strategy are consistent with the profile and duration of their liabilities and how those elements contribute to the medium to long-term performance of their assets. Where they make use of an asset manager, either through discretionary mandates involving the management of assets on an individual basis or through pooled funds, institutional investors should disclose to the public certain key elements of the arrangement with the asset manager, in particular how it incentivises the asset manager to align its investment strategy and decisions with the profile and duration of the liabilities of the institutional investor, in particular long-term liabilities, how it evaluates the asset manager's performance, including its remuneration, how it monitors portfolio turnover costs incurred by the asset manager and how it incentivises the asset manager to engage in the best medium to long-term interest of the institutional investor. This would contribute to a proper alignment of interests between the final beneficiaries of institutional investors, the asset managers and the investee companies and potentially to the development of longer-term investment strategies and longer-term relationships with investee companies involving shareholder engagement.

(20) Asset managers should give information to the institutional investor that is sufficient to allow the latter to assess whether and how the manager acts in the best long-term interests of the investor and whether the asset manager pursues a strategy that provides for efficient shareholder engagement. In principle, the relationship between the asset manager and the institutional investor is a matter for bilateral contractual arrangements. However, although big institutional investors may be able to request detailed reporting from the asset manager, especially if the assets are managed on the basis of a discretionary mandate, for smaller and less sophisticated institutional investors it is crucial to set a minimum set of legal requirements, so that they can properly assess, and hold to account, the asset manager. Therefore, asset managers should be required to disclose to institutional investors how their investment strategy and the implementation thereof contribute to the medium to long-term performance of the assets of the institutional investor or of the fund. That disclosure should cover reporting on the key material medium to long-term risks associated with the portfolio investments, including corporate governance matters and other medium to long-term risks. That information is key to allowing the institutional investor to assess whether the asset manager carries out a medium to long-term analysis of the equity and the portfolio which is a key enabler of efficient shareholder engagement. As those medium to long-term risks will impact the returns of the investors, more effective integration of those matters into investment processes may be crucial for institutional investors.

PART III   EUROPEAN COMPANY LAW

(21) Moreover, asset managers should disclose to institutional investors the composition, turnover and turnover costs of their portfolio as well as their policy on securities lending. The level of portfolio turnover is a significant indicator of whether an asset manager's processes are fully aligned with the identified strategy and interests of the institutional investor and indicates whether the asset manager holds equities for a period of time that enables it to engage with the company in an effective way. High portfolio turnover may be an indicator of a lack of conviction in investment decisions and momentum-following behaviour, neither of which is likely to be in the institutional investor's best interests in the long term, especially as an increase in turnover raises the costs faced by the investor and can influence systemic risk. On the other hand, unexpectedly low turnover may signal inattention to risk management or a drift towards a more passive investment approach. Securities lending can cause controversy in the area of shareholder engagement under which the investors' shares are in effect sold, subject to a buyback right. Sold shares have to be recalled for engagement purposes, including voting at the general meeting. It is therefore important that the asset manager reports on its policy on securities lending and how it is applied to fulfil its engagement activities, particularly at the time of the general meeting of the investee company.

(22) The asset manager should also inform the institutional investor whether and, if so, how the asset manager makes investment decisions on the basis of an evaluation of the medium to long-term performance of the investee company, including its non-financial performance. Such information is particularly useful to indicate whether the asset manager adopts a long-term oriented and active approach to asset management and takes social, environmental and governance matters into account.

(23) The asset manager should provide proper information to the institutional investor on whether and, if so, which conflicts of interests have arisen in connection with engagement activities and how the asset manager has dealt with them. For example, conflicts of interests may prevent the asset manager from voting or from engaging at all. All such situations should be disclosed to the institutional investor.

(24) Member States should be allowed to provide that where the assets of an institutional investor are not managed on an individual basis but are pooled together with assets of other investors and managed via a fund, information should also be provided to other investors, at least upon request, in order to allow all the other investors of the same fund to be able to receive that information if they so wish.

(25) Many institutional investors and asset managers use the services of proxy advisors who provide research, advice and recommendations on how to vote in general meetings of listed companies. While proxy advisors play an important role in corporate governance by contributing to reducing the costs of the analysis related to company information, they may also have an important influence on the voting behaviour of investors. In particular, investors with highly diversified portfolios and many foreign shareholdings rely more on proxy recommendations.

(26) In view of their importance, proxy advisors should be subject to transparency requirements. Member States should ensure that proxy advisors that are subject to a code of conduct effectively report on their application of that code. They should also disclose certain key information relating to the preparation of their research, advice and voting recommendations and any actual or potential conflicts of interests or business relationships that may influence the preparation of the research, advice and voting recommendations. That information should remain publicly available for a period of at least three years in order to allow institutional investors to choose the services of proxy advisors taking into account their performance in the past.

(27) Third-country proxy advisors which have neither their registered office nor their head office in the Union may provide analysis with respect to Union companies. In order to ensure a level playing field between Union and third-country proxy advisors, this Directive should also apply to third-country proxy advisors which carry out their activities through an establishment in the Union, regardless of the form of that establishment.

(28) Directors contribute to the long-term success of the company. The form and structure of directors' remuneration are matters primarily falling within the competence of the company, its relevant boards, shareholders and, where applicable, employee representatives. It is therefore important to respect the diversity of corporate governance systems within the Union, which reflect different Member States' views about the roles of companies and of bodies responsible for the determination of the remuneration policy and of the remuneration of individual directors. Since remuneration is one of the key instruments for companies to align their interests and those of their directors and in view of the crucial role of directors in companies, it is important that the remuneration policy of companies is determined in an appropriate manner by competent bodies within the company and that shareholders have the possibility to express their views regarding the remuneration policy of the company.

(29) In order to ensure that shareholders have an effective say on remuneration policy, they should be granted the right to hold a binding or advisory vote on the remuneration policy, on the basis of a clear, understandable and comprehensive overview of the company's remuneration policy. The remuneration policy should contribute to the business strategy, long-term interests and sustainability of the company and should not be linked entirely or mainly to short-term objectives. Directors' performance should be assessed using both financial and non-financial performance criteria, including, where appropriate, environmental, social and governance factors. The remuneration policy should describe the different components of directors' pay and the range of their relative proportions. It can be designed as a frame within which the pay of directors is to be held. The remuneration policy should be publicly disclosed, without delay, after the vote by the shareholders at the general meeting.

(30) In exceptional circumstances, companies may need to derogate from certain rules in the remuneration policy such as criteria for fixed or variable remuneration. Therefore, Member States should be able to allow companies to apply such temporary derogation to the applicable remuneration policy if they specify in their remuneration policy how it would be applied in certain exceptional circumstances. Exceptional circumstances should only cover situations where the derogation from the remuneration policy is necessary to serve the long-term interests and sustainability of the company as a whole or assure its viability. The remuneration report should include information on remuneration awarded under such exceptional circumstances.

(31) To ensure that the implementation of the remuneration policy is in line with that policy, shareholders should be granted the right to vote on the company's remuneration report. In order to ensure corporate transparency, and accountability of the directors, the remuneration report should be clear and understandable and should provide a comprehensive overview of the remuneration of individual directors during the most recent financial year. Where the shareholders vote against the remuneration report, the company should explain, in the following remuneration report, how the vote of the shareholders was taken into account. However, for small and medium-sized companies, Member States should be able to provide, as an alternative to the vote on the remuneration report, for the remuneration report to be submitted to shareholders only for discussion in the annual general meeting as a separate item of the agenda. If a Member State uses this possibility, the company should explain, in the following remuneration report, in what manner the discussion at the general meeting was taken into account.

(32) In order to provide shareholders with easy access to the remuneration report, and to enable potential investors and stakeholders to be informed of directors' remuneration, the remuneration report should be published on the company's website. This should be without prejudice to the possibility of Member States also to require the publication of the report by other means, for example as part of the corporate governance statement or management report.

(33) The disclosure of individual directors' remuneration and the publication of the remuneration report are intended to provide increased corporate transparency and increased accountability of directors, as well as better shareholder oversight over directors' remuneration. This creates a necessary prerequisite for the exercise of shareholder rights and shareholder engagement in relation to remuneration. In particular, the disclosure of such information to shareholders is necessary to enable them to assess directors' remuneration and to express their views on the modalities and level of directors' pay as well as on the link between pay and performance of each individual director, in order to remedy potential situations in which the amount of remuneration of a director is not justified on the basis of his or her individual performance and the performance of the company. Publication of the remuneration report is necessary in order to enable not only shareholders, but also potential investors and stakeholders to assess directors' remuneration, to what extent that remuneration is linked to the performance of the company and how the company implements its remuneration policy in practice. The disclosure and publication of anonymised remuneration reports would not allow the achievement of those objectives.

(34) In order to increase corporate transparency, and the accountability of directors, and to enable shareholders, potential investors and stakeholders to obtain a full and reliable picture of the remuneration of each director, it is of particular importance that every element and total amount of remuneration are disclosed.

(35) In particular, in order to prevent the circumvention of the requirements laid down by this Directive by the company, to avoid any conflicts of interests and to ensure loyalty of the directors to the company, it is necessary to provide for the disclosure and the publication of the remuneration awarded or due to individual directors not only from the company itself, but also from any undertaking belonging to the same group. If remuneration awarded or due to individual directors by undertakings belonging to the same group as the company were excluded from the remuneration report, there would be a risk that companies try to circumvent the requirements laid down by this Directive by

providing directors with hidden remuneration via a controlled undertaking. In such a case, shareholders would not have a full and reliable picture of the remuneration granted to the directors by the company and the objectives pursued by this Directive would not be achieved.

(36) In order to provide a complete overview of directors' remuneration, the remuneration report should also disclose, where applicable, the amount of remuneration granted on the basis of the family situation of individual directors. The remuneration report should therefore also cover, where applicable, remuneration components such as family or child allowance. However, because personal data which refer to the family situation of individual directors or special categories of personal data within the meaning of Regulation (EU) 2016/679 of the European Parliament and of the Council (1) are particularly sensitive and require specific protection, the report should disclose only the amount of the remuneration and not the ground on which it was granted.

(37) Under this Directive, personal data included in the remuneration report should be processed for the purposes of increasing corporate transparency as regards directors' remuneration with the view to enhancing directors' account ability and shareholder oversight of directors' remuneration. This is without prejudice to Member State law providing for the processing of the personal data of directors for other purposes.

(38) It is essential to assess the remuneration and the performance of directors not only annually but also over an appropriate time period to enable shareholders, potential investors and stakeholders to assess properly whether the remuneration rewards long-term performance and to measure the middle-to-long-term evolution in directors' performance and remuneration, in particular in relation to company performance. In many cases, it is possible only after several years to evaluate whether the remuneration granted was in line with the long-term interests of the company. In particular the granting of long-term incentives may cover periods of up to seven to ten years and may be combined with deferral periods of several years.

(39) It is also important to be able to assess the remuneration of a director over the entire period of his or her directorship on a particular company's board. In the Union, directors remain on a company board for a period of six years on average, although in some Member States that period exceeds eight years.

(40) In order to limit interference with the directors' rights to privacy and to the protection of their personal data, public disclosure by companies of directors' personal data included in the remuneration report should be limited to 10 years. That period is consistent with other periods laid down by Union law related to the public disclosure of corporate governance documents. For example, under Article 4 of Directive 2004/109/EC of the European Parliament and the Council , the management report and the corporate governance statements must remain publicly available as part of the annual financial report for at least 10 years. There is a clear interest in having various types of corporate governance reports, including the remuneration report, available for 10 years, so as to provide the overall state of a company to shareholders and stakeholders.

(41) At the end of the 10-year period, the company should remove any personal data from the remuneration report or cease to disclose the remuneration report publicly as a whole. Following that period access to such personal data could be necessary for other purposes, such as in order to exercise legal actions. The provisions on remuneration should be without prejudice to the full exercise of fundamental rights guaranteed by the Treaties, in particular Article 153(5) of the Treaty on the Functioning of the European Union, general principles of national contract and labour law, Union and national law regarding involvement and the general responsibilities of the administrative, management and supervisory bodies of the company concerned, and the rights, where applicable, of the social partners to conclude and enforce collective agreements, in accordance with national law and customs. The provisions on remuneration should also, where applicable, be without prejudice to national law on the representation of employees in the administrative, management or supervisory body.

(42) Transactions with related parties may cause prejudice to companies and their shareholders, as they may give the related party the opportunity to appropriate value belonging to the company. Thus, adequate safeguards for the protection of companies' and shareholders' interests are of importance. For this reason Member States should ensure that material related party transactions are submitted to approval by the shareholders or by the administrative or supervisory body according to procedures that prevent the related party from taking advantage of its position and provide adequate protection for the interests of the company and of the shareholders who are not a related party, including minority shareholders.

(43) Where the related party transaction involves a director or a shareholder, that director or shareholder should not take part in the approval or vote. However, Member States should have the possibility to allow the shareholder who is a related party to take part in the vote provided that

national law foresees appropriate safeguards in relation to the voting process to protect the interests of companies and of the shareholders who are not a related party, including minority shareholders, such as for example a higher majority threshold for the approval of transactions.

(44) Companies should publicly announce material transactions no later than at the time of the conclusion of the transaction, identifying the related party, the date and the value of the transaction and any other information that is necessary to assess the fairness of the transaction. Public disclosure of such transaction, for example on a company's website or by other easily available means, is needed in order to allow shareholders, creditors, employees and other interested parties to be informed of potential impacts that such transactions may have on the value of the company. The precise identification of the related party is necessary to better assess the risks implied by the transaction and to enable challenges to the transaction, including by means of legal action.

(45) This Directive sets up transparency requirements for companies, institutional investors, asset managers and proxy advisors. Those transparency requirements are not intended to require companies, institutional investors, asset managers or proxy advisors to disclose to the public certain specific pieces of information the disclosure of which would be seriously prejudicial to their business position or, where they are not undertakings with a commercial purpose, to the interest of their members or beneficiaries. Such non-disclosure should not undermine the objectives of the disclosure requirements laid down in this Directive.

(46) In order to ensure uniform conditions for the implementation of the provisions on shareholder identification, transmission of information and facilitation of the exercise of shareholder rights, implementing powers should be conferred on the Commission. Those powers should be exercised in accordance with Regulation (EU) No 182/2011 of the European Parliament and of the Council.

(47) In particular, the Commission implementing acts should specify the minimum standardisation requirements as regards formats to be used and deadlines to be complied with. Empowering the Commission to adopt implementing acts allows those requirements to be kept up to date with market and supervisory developments and to prevent diverging implementation of the provisions across Member States. Such diverging implementation could result in the adoption of incompatible national standards, increasing the risks and costs of cross-border operations and thus jeopardising their effectiveness and efficiency and resulting in additional burdens for intermediaries.

(48) In exercising its implementing powers in accordance with this Directive, the Commission should take into account the relevant market developments and, in particular, existing self-regulatory initiatives such as, for example, Market Standards for Corporate Actions Processing and Market Standards for General Meetings, and should encourage the use of modern technologies in communication between companies and their shareholders, including through intermediaries and, where appropriate, other market participants.

(49) In order to ensure a more comparable and consistent presentation of the remuneration report, the Commission should adopt guidelines to specify its standardised presentation. Existing Member State practices as regards the presentation of the information included in the remuneration report are very different and, as a result, they provide an uneven level of transparency and protection for shareholders and investors. The result of the divergence of practices is that shareholders and investors are, in particular in the case of cross-border investments, subject to difficulties and costs when they want to understand and monitor the implementation of the remuneration policy and engage with the company on that specific issue. The Commission should consult Member States, as appropriate, before adopting its guidelines.

(50) In order to ensure that the requirements set out in this Directive or the measures implementing this Directive are applied in practice, any infringement of those requirements should be subject to penalties. To that end, penalties should be sufficiently dissuasive and proportionate.

(51) Since the objectives of this Directive cannot be sufficiently achieved by the Member States in view of the international nature of the Union equity market and action by Member States alone is likely to result in different sets of rules, which may undermine or create new obstacles to the functioning of the internal market, but can rather, by reason of their scale and effects, be better achieved at Union level, the Union may adopt measures, in accordance with the principle of subsidiarity as set out in Article 5 of the Treaty on European Union. In accordance with the principle of proportionality, as set out in that Article, this Directive does not go beyond what is necessary in order to achieve those objectives.

(52) This Directive should be applied in compliance with Union data protection law and the protection of privacy as enshrined in the Charter of Fundamental Rights of the European Union. Any processing of the personal data of natural persons under this Directive should be undertaken in accordance with Regulation (EU) 2016/679. In particular, data should be kept accurate and up to date, the data subject should be duly informed about the processing of personal data in accordance

with this Directive and should have the right of rectification of incomplete or inaccurate data as well as right to erasure of personal data. Moreover, any transmission of information regarding shareholder identity to third-country intermediaries should comply with the requirements laid down in Regulation (EU) 2016/679.

(53) Personal data under this Directive should be processed for the specific purposes set out in this Directive. The processing of those personal data for purposes other than the purposes for which they were initially collected should be carried out in accordance with Regulation (EU) 2016/679.

(54) This Directive is without prejudice to the provisions laid down in any sector-specific Union legislative act regulating specific types of company or specific types of entity, such as credit institutions, investments firms, asset managers, insurance companies and pension funds. The provisions of any sector-specific Union legislative act should be considered to be lex specialis in relation to this Directive and should prevail over this Directive to the extent that the requirements provided by this Directive contradict the requirements laid down in any sector-specific Union legislative act. However, the specific provisions of a sector-specific Union legislative act should not be interpreted in a way that undermines the effective application of this Directive or the achievement of its general aim. The mere existence of specific Union rules in a particular sector should not exclude the application of this Directive. Where this Directive provides for more specific provisions or adds requirements to the provisions laid down in any sector-specific Union legislative act, the provisions laid down by any sector-specific Union legislative act should be applied in conjunction with those of this Directive.

(55) This Directive does not prevent Member States from adopting or maintaining in force more stringent provisions in the field covered by this Directive to further facilitate the exercise of shareholder rights, to encourage shareholder engagement and to protect the interests of minority shareholders, as well as to fulfil other purposes such as the safety and soundness of credit and financial institutions. Such provisions should not, however, hamper the effective application of this Directive or the achievement of its objectives, and should, in any event, comply with the rules laid down in the Treaties.

(56) In accordance with the Joint Political Declaration of 28 September 2011 of Member States and the Commission on explanatory documents , Member States have undertaken to accompany, in justified cases, the notification of their transposition measures with one or more documents explaining the relationship between the components of a directive and the corresponding parts of national transposition instruments. With regard to this Directive, the legislator considers the transmission of such documents to be justified.

(57) The European Data Protection Supervisor was consulted in accordance with Article 28(2) of Regulation (EC) No 45/2001 of the European Parliament and of the Council and delivered an opinion on 28 October 2014,

HAVE ADOPTED THIS DIRECTIVE:

Article 1. Directive 2007/36/EC is amended as follows:

(1) Article 1 is amended as follows:

(a) paragraphs 1 and 2 are replaced by the following:

'1. This Directive establishes requirements in relation to the exercise of certain shareholder rights attached to voting shares in relation to general meetings of companies which have their registered office in a Member State and the shares of which are admitted to trading on a regulated market situated or operating within a Member State. It also establishes specific requirements in order to encourage shareholder engagement, in particular in the long term. Those specific requirements apply in relation to identification of shareholders, transmission of information, facilitation of exercise of shareholders rights, transparency of institutional investors, asset managers and proxy advisors, remuneration of directors and related party transactions.

2. The Member State competent to regulate matters covered in this Directive shall be the Member State in which the company has its registered office, and references to the "applicable law" are references to the law of that Member State.

For the purpose of application of Chapter Ib, the competent Member State shall be defined as follows:

(a) for institutional investors and asset managers, the home Member State as defined in any applicable sector- specific Union legislative act;

(b) for proxy advisors, the Member State in which the proxy advisor has its registered office, or, where the proxy advisor does not have its registered office in a Member State, the Member State in which the proxy advisor has its head office, or, where the proxy advisor has neither its registered office nor its head office in a Member State, the Member State in which the proxy advisor has an establishment.';

(b) in paragraph 3, points (a) and (b) are replaced by the following:
'(a) undertakings for collective investment in transferable securities (UCITS) within the meaning of Article 1(2) of Directive 2009/65/EC of the European Parliament and of the Council;
(b) collective investment undertakings within the meaning of point (a) of Article 4(1) of Directive 2011/61/EU of the European Parliament and of the Council';
(c) the following paragraph is inserted:
'3a. The companies referred to in paragraph 3 shall not be exempted from the provisions laid down in Chapter Ib.';
the following paragraphs are added:
'5. Chapter Ia shall apply to intermediaries in so far they provide services to shareholders or other inter mediaries with respect to shares of companies which have their registered office in a Member State and the shares of which are admitted to trading on a regulated market situated or operating within a Member State.
6. Chapter Ib shall apply to:
(a) institutional investors, to the extent that they invest directly or through an asset manager in shares traded on a regulated market;
(b) asset managers, to the extent that they invest in such shares on behalf of investors; and
(c) proxy advisors, to the extent that they provide services to shareholders with respect to shares of companies which have their registered office in a Member State and the shares of which are admitted to trading on a regulated market situated or operating within a Member State.
7. The provisions of this Directive are without prejudice to the provisions laid down in any sector-specific Union legislative act regulating specific types of company or specific types of entity. Where this Directive provides for more specific rules or adds requirements compared to the provisions laid down by any sector-specific Union legislative act, those provisions shall be applied in conjunction with the provisions of this Directive.'.
(2) Article 2 is amended as follows:
(a) point (a) is replaced by the following:
'(a) "regulated market" means a regulated market as defined in point (21) of Article 4(1) of Directive 2014/65/EU of the European Parliament and of the Council';
(b) the following points are added:
'(d) "intermediary" means a person, such as an investment firm as defined in point (1) of Article 4(1) of Directive 2014/65/EU, a credit institution as defined in point (1) of Article 4(1) of Regulation (EU) No 575/2013 of the European Parliament and of the Council (*) and a central securities depository as defined in point (1) of Article 2(1) of Regulation (EU) No 909/2014 of the European Parliament and of the Council, which provides services of safekeeping of shares, administration of shares or maintenance of securities accounts on behalf of shareholders or other persons;
(e) "institutional investor" means:
(i) an undertaking carrying out activities of life assurance within the meaning of points (a), (b) and (c) of Article 2(3) of Directive 2009/138/EC of the European Parliament and of the Council, and of reinsurance as defined in point (7) of Article 13 of that Directive provided that those activities cover life-insurance obligations, and which is not excluded pursuant to that Directive;
(ii) an institution for occupational retirement provision falling within the scope of Directive (EU) 2016/2341 of the European Parliament and of the Council in accordance with Article 2 thereof, unless a Member State has chosen not to apply that Directive in whole or in parts to that institution in accordance with Article 5 of that Directive;
(f) "asset manager" means an investment firm as defined in point (1) of Article 4(1) of Directive 2014/65/EU that provides portfolio management services to investors, an AIFM (alternative investment fund manager) as defined in point (b) of Article 4(1) of Directive 2011/61/EU that does not fulfil the conditions for an exemption in accordance with Article 3 of that Directive or a management company as defined in point (b) of Article 2(1) of Directive 2009/65/EC, or an investment company that is authorised in accordance with Directive 2009/65/EC provided that it has not designated a management company authorised under that Directive for its management;
(g) "proxy advisor" means a legal person that analyses, on a professional and commercial basis, the corporate disclosure and, where relevant, other information of listed companies with a view to informing investors' voting decisions by providing research, advice or voting recommendations that relate to the exercise of voting rights;
(h) "related party" has the same meaning as in the international accounting standards adopted in accordance with Regulation (EC) No 1606/2002 of the European Parliament and of the Council;
(i) "director" means:
(i) any member of the administrative, management or supervisory bodies of a company;

(ii) where they are not members of the administrative, management or supervisory bodies of a company, the chief executive officer and, if such function exists in a company, the deputy chief executive officer;

(iii) where so determined by a Member State, other persons who perform functions similar to those performed under point (i) or (ii);

(j) "information regarding shareholder identity" means information allowing the identity of a shareholder to be established, including at least the following information:

(i) name and contact details (including full address and, where available, email address) of the shareholder, and, where it is a legal person, its registration number, or, if no registration number is available, its unique identifier, such as legal entity identifier;

(ii) the number of shares held; and

(iii) only insofar they are requested by the company, one or more of the following details: the categories or classes of the shares held or the date from which the shares have been held.

(3) The following Chapters are inserted:

'CHAPTER Ia. Identification Of Shareholders, Transmission of Information and Facilitation of Exercise of ShareHolder Rights

Article 3a. Identification of shareholders. (1) Member States shall ensure that companies have the right to identify their shareholders. Member States may provide for companies having a registered office on their territory to be only allowed to request the identification of shareholders holding more than a certain percentage of shares or voting rights. Such a percentage shall not exceed 0,5 %.

(2) Member States shall ensure that, on the request of the company or of a third party nominated by the company, the intermediaries communicate without delay to the company the information regarding shareholder identity.

(3) Where there is more than one intermediary in a chain of intermediaries, Member States shall ensure that the request of the company, or of a third party nominated by the company, is transmitted between intermediaries without delay and that the information regarding shareholder identity is transmitted directly to the company or to a third party nominated by the company without delay by the intermediary who holds the requested information. Member States shall ensure that the company is able to obtain information regarding shareholder identity from any intermediary in the chain that holds the information.

Member States may provide for the company to be allowed to request the central securities depository or another intermediary or service provider to collect the information regarding shareholder identity, including from the intermediaries in the chain of intermediaries and to transmit the information to the company.

Member States may additionally provide that, at the request of the company, or of a third party nominated by the company, the intermediary is to communicate to the company without delay the details of the next intermediary in the chain of intermediaries.

(4) The personal data of shareholders shall be processed pursuant to this Article in order to enable the company to identify its existing shareholders in order to communicate with them directly with the view to facilitating the exercise of shareholder rights and shareholder engagement with the company. Without prejudice to any longer storage period laid down by any sector-specific Union legislative act, Member States shall ensure that companies and intermediaries do not store the personal data of shareholders transmitted to them in accordance with this Article for the purpose specified in this Article for longer than 12 months after they have become aware that the person concerned has ceased to be a shareholder.

Member States may provide by law for processing of the personal data of shareholders for other purposes.

(5) Member States shall ensure that legal persons have the right of rectification of incomplete or inaccurate information regarding their shareholder identity.

(6) Member States shall ensure that an intermediary that discloses information regarding shareholder identity in accordance with the rules laid down in this Article is not considered to be in breach of any restriction on disclosure of information imposed by contract or by any legislative, regulatory or administrative provision.

(7) By 10 June 2019, Member States shall provide the European Supervisory Authority (European Securities and Markets Authority) (ESMA), established by Regulation (EU) No 1095/2010 of the European Parliament and of the Council with information on whether they have limited shareholder identification to shareholders holding more than a certain percentage of the shares or voting rights in accordance with paragraph 1 and, if so, the applicable percentage. ESMA shall publish that information on its website.

(8) The Commission shall be empowered to adopt implementing acts to specify the minimum

requirements to transmit the information laid down in paragraph 2 as regards the format of information to be transmitted, the format of the request, including their security and interoperability, and the deadlines to be complied with. Those implementing acts shall be adopted by 10 September 2018 in accordance with the examination procedure referred to in Article 14a(2).

Article 3b. Transmission of information. (1) Member States shall ensure that the intermediaries are required to transmit the following information, without delay, from the company to the shareholder or to a third party nominated by the shareholder:

(a) the information which the company is required to provide to the shareholder, to enable the shareholder to exercise rights flowing from its shares, and which is directed to all shareholders in shares of that class; or

(b) where the information referred to in point (a) is available to shareholders on the website of the company, a notice indicating where on the website that information can be found.

(2) Member States shall require companies to provide intermediaries in a standardised and timely manner with the information referred to in point (a) of paragraph 1 or the notice referred to in point (b) of that paragraph.

(3) However, Member States shall not require that the information referred to in point (a) of paragraph 1 or the notice referred to in point (b) of that paragraph be transmitted or provided in accordance with paragraphs 1 and 2 where companies send that information or that notice directly to all their shareholders or to a third party nominated by the shareholder.

(4) Member States shall oblige intermediaries to transmit, without delay, to the company, in accordance with the instructions received from the shareholders, the information received from the shareholders related to the exercise of the rights flowing from their shares.

(5) Where there is more than one intermediary in a chain of intermediaries, information referred to in paragraphs 1 and 4 shall be transmitted between intermediaries without delay, unless the information can be directly transmitted by the intermediary to the company or to the shareholder or to a third party nominated by the shareholder.

(6) The Commission shall be empowered to adopt implementing acts to specify the minimum requirements to transmit information laid down in paragraphs 1 to 5 of this Article as regards the types and format of information to be transmitted, including their security and interoperability, and the deadlines to be complied with. Those implementing acts shall be adopted by 10 September 2018 in accordance with the examination procedure referred to in Article 14a(2).

Article 3c. Facilitation of the exercise of shareholder rights. (1) Member States shall ensure that the intermediaries facilitate the exercise of the rights by the shareholder, including the right to participate and vote in general meetings, which shall comprise at least one of the following:

(a) the intermediary makes the necessary arrangements for the shareholder or a third party nominated by the shareholder to be able to exercise themselves the rights;

(b) the intermediary exercises the rights flowing from the shares upon the explicit authorisation and instruction of the shareholder and for the shareholder's benefit.

(2) Member States shall ensure that when votes are cast electronically an electronic confirmation of receipt of the votes is sent to the person that casts the vote.

Member States shall ensure that after the general meeting the shareholder or a third party nominated by the shareholder can obtain, at least upon request, confirmation that their votes have been validly recorded and counted by the company, unless that information is already available to them. Member States may establish a deadline for requesting such confirmation. Such a deadline shall not be longer than three months from the date of the vote.

Where the intermediary receives confirmation as referred to in the first or second subparagraph, it shall transmit it without delay to the shareholder or a third party nominated by the shareholder. Where there is more than one intermediary in the chain of intermediaries the confirmation shall be transmitted between intermediaries without delay, unless the confirmation can be directly transmitted to the shareholder or a third party nominated by the shareholder.

(3) The Commission shall be empowered to adopt implementing acts to specify the minimum requirements to facilitate the exercise of shareholder rights laid down in paragraphs 1 and 2 of this Article as regards the types of the facilitation, the format of the electronic confirmation of receipt of the votes, the format for the transmission of the confirmation that the votes have been validly recorded and counted through the chain of intermediaries, including their security and interoperability, and the deadlines to be complied with. Those implementing acts shall be adopted by 10 September 2018 in accordance with the examination procedure referred to in Article 14a(2).

Article 3d. Non-discrimination, proportionality and transparency of costs. (1) Member States shall require intermediaries to disclose publicly any applicable charges for services provided for under this Chapter separately for each service.

(2) Member States shall ensure that any charges levied by an intermediary on shareholders, companies and other intermediaries shall be non-discriminatory and proportionate in relation to the actual costs incurred for delivering the services. Any differences between the charges levied between domestic and cross-border exercise of rights shall be permitted only where duly justified and where they reflect the variation in actual costs incurred for delivering the services.

(3) Member States may prohibit intermediaries from charging fees for the services provided for under this Chapter.

Article 3e. Third-country intermediaries. This Chapter also applies to intermediaries which have neither their registered office nor their head office in the Union when they provide services referred to in Article 1(5).

Article 3f. Information on implementation. (1) Competent authorities shall inform the Commission of substantial practical difficulties in enforcement of the provisions of this Chapter or non-compliance with the provisions of this Chapter by Union or third-country intermediaries.

(2) The Commission shall, in close cooperation with ESMA and the European Supervisory Authority (European Banking Authority), established by Regulation (EU) No 1093/2010 of the European Parliament and of the Council, submit a report to the European Parliament and to the Council on the implementation of this Chapter, including its effectiveness, difficulties in practical application and enforcement, while taking into account relevant market developments at the Union and international level. The report shall also address the appropriateness of the scope of application of this Chapter in relation to third-country intermediaries. The Commission shall publish the report by 10 June 2023.

Chapter Ib. Transparency of Institutional Investors, Asset Managers and Proxy Advisors

Article 3g. Engagement policy

(1) Member States shall ensure that institutional investors and asset managers either comply with the requirements set out in points (a) and (b) or publicly disclose a clear and reasoned explanation why they have chosen not to comply with one or more of those requirements.

(a) Institutional investors and asset managers shall develop and publicly disclose an engagement policy that describes how they integrate shareholder engagement in their investment strategy. The policy shall describe how they monitor investee companies on relevant matters, including strategy, financial and non-financial performance and risk, capital structure, social and environmental impact and corporate governance, conduct dialogues with investee companies, exercise voting rights and other rights attached to shares, cooperate with other shareholders, communicate with relevant stakeholders of the investee companies and manage actual and potential conflicts of interests in relation to their engagement.

(b) Institutional investors and asset managers shall, on an annual basis, publicly disclose how their engagement policy has been implemented, including a general description of voting behaviour, an explanation of the most significant votes and the use of the services of proxy advisors. They shall publicly disclose how they have cast votes in the general meetings of companies in which they hold shares. Such disclosure may exclude votes that are insignificant due to the subject matter of the vote or the size of the holding in the company.

(2) The information referred to in paragraph 1 shall be available free of charge on the institutional investor's or asset manager's website. Member States may provide for the information to be published, free of charge, by other means that are easily accessible online.

Where an asset manager implements the engagement policy, including voting, on behalf of an institutional investor, the institutional investor shall make a reference as to where such voting information has been published by the asset manager.

(3) Conflicts of interests rules applicable to institutional investors and asset managers, including Article 14 of Directive 2011/61/EU, point (b) of Article 12(1) and point (d) of 14(1) of Directive 2009/65/EC and the relevant implementing rules, and Article 23 of Directive 2014/65/EU shall also apply with regard to engagement activities.

Article 3h. Investment strategy of institutional investors and arrangements with asset managers.

(1) Member States shall ensure that institutional investors publicly disclose how the main elements of their equity investment strategy are consistent with the profile and duration of their liabilities, in particular long-term liabilities, and how they contribute to the medium to long-term performance of their assets.

(2) Member States shall ensure that where an asset manager invests on behalf of an institutional investor, whether on a discretionary client-by-client basis or through a collective investment undertaking, the institutional investor publicly discloses the following information regarding its arrangement with the asset manager:

(a) how the arrangement with the asset manager incentivises the asset manager to align its investment strategy and decisions with the profile and duration of the liabilities of the institutional investor, in particular long-term liabilities;

(b) how that arrangement incentivises the asset manager to make investment decisions based on assessments about medium to long-term financial and non-financial performance of the investee company and to engage with investee companies in order to improve their performance in the medium to long-term;
(c) how the method and time horizon of the evaluation of the asset manager's performance and the remuneration for asset management services are in line with the profile and duration of the liabilities of the institutional investor, in particular long-term liabilities, and take absolute long-term performance into account;
(d) how the institutional investor monitors portfolio turnover costs incurred by the asset manager and how it defines and monitors a targeted portfolio turnover or turnover range;
(e) the duration of the arrangement with the asset manager.
Where the arrangement with the asset manager does not contain one or more of such elements, the institutional investor shall give a clear and reasoned explanation why this is the case.
(3) The information referred to in paragraphs 1 and 2 of this Article shall be available, free of charge, on the institutional investor's website and shall be updated annually unless there is no material change. Member States may provide for that information to be available, free of charge, through other means that are easily accessible online.
Member States shall ensure that institutional investors regulated by Directive 2009/138/EC are allowed to include this information in their report on solvency and financial condition referred to in Article 51 of that Directive.
Article 3i. Transparency of asset managers. (1) Member States shall ensure that asset managers disclose, on an annual basis, to the institutional investor with which they have entered into the arrangements referred to in Article 3h how their investment strategy and implementation thereof complies with that arrangement and contributes to the medium to long-term performance of the assets of the institutional investor or of the fund. Such disclosure shall include reporting on the key material medium to long-term risks associated with the investments, on portfolio composition, turnover and turnover costs, on the use of proxy advisors for the purpose of engagement activities and their policy on securities lending and how it is applied to fulfil its engagement activities if applicable, particularly at the time of the general meeting of the investee companies. Such disclosure shall also include information on whether and, if so, how, they make investment decisions based on evaluation of medium to long-term performance of the investee company, including non- financial performance, and on whether and, if so, which conflicts of interests have arisen in connection with engagements activities and how the asset managers have dealt with them.
(2) Member States may provide for the information in paragraph 1 to be disclosed together with the annual report referred to in Article 68 of Directive 2009/65/EC or in Article 22 of Directive 2011/61/EU, or periodic communications referred to in Article 25(6) of Directive 2014/65/EU.
Where the information disclosed pursuant to paragraph 1 is already publicly available, the asset manager is not required to provide the information to the institutional investor directly.
(3) Member States may where the asset manager does not manage the assets on a discretionary client-by-client basis, require that the information disclosed pursuant to paragraph 1 also be provided to other investors of the same fund at least upon request.
Article 3j. Transparency of proxy advisors. (1) Member States shall ensure that proxy advisors publicly disclose reference to a code of conduct which they apply and report on the application of that code of conduct.
Where proxy advisors do not apply a code of conduct, they shall provide a clear and reasoned explanation why this is the case. Where proxy advisors apply a code of conduct but depart from any of its recommendations, they shall declare from which parts they depart, provide explanations for doing so and indicate, where appropriate, any alternative measures adopted.
Information referred to in this paragraph shall be made publicly available, free of charge, on the websites of proxy advisors and shall be updated on an annual basis.
(2) Member States shall ensure that, in order to adequately inform their clients about the accuracy and reliability of their activities, proxy advisors publicly disclose on an annual basis at least all of the following information in relation to the preparation of their research, advice and voting recommendations:
(a) the essential features of the methodologies and models they apply;
(b) the main information sources they use;
(c) the procedures put in place to ensure quality of the research, advice and voting recommendations and qualifications of the staff involved;
(d) whether and, if so, how they take national market, legal, regulatory and company-specific conditions into account

(e) the essential features of the voting policies they apply for each market;
(f) whether they have dialogues with the companies which are the object of their research, advice or voting recommendations and with the stakeholders of the company, and, if so, the extent and nature thereof;
(g) the policy regarding the prevention and management of potential conflicts of interests.
The information referred to in this paragraph shall be made publicly available on the websites of proxy advisors and shall remain available free of charge for at least three years from the date of publication. The information does not need to be disclosed separately where it is available as part of the disclosure under paragraph 1.
(3) Member States shall ensure that proxy advisors identify and disclose without delay to their clients any actual or potential conflicts of interests or business relationships that may influence the preparation of their research, advice or voting recommendations and the actions they have undertaken to eliminate, mitigate or manage the actual or potential conflicts of interests.
(4) This Article also applies to proxy advisors that have neither their registered office nor their head office in the Union which carry out their activities through an establishment located in the Union.
Article 3k. Review. (1) The Commission shall submit a report to the European Parliament and to the Council on the implementation of Articles 3g, 3h and 3i, including the assessment of the need to require asset managers to publicly disclose certain information under Article 3i, taking into account relevant Union and international market developments. The report shall be published by 10 June 2022 and shall be accompanied, if appropriate, by legislative proposals.
(2) The Commission shall, in close cooperation with ESMA, submit a report to the European Parliament and to the Council on the implementation of Article 3j, including the appropriateness of its scope of application and its effectiveness and the assessment of the need for establishing regulatory requirements for proxy advisors, taking into account relevant Union and international market developments. The report shall be published by 10 June 2023 and shall be accompanied, if appropriate, by legislative proposals.'
(4) The following Articles are inserted:
'Article 9a. Right to vote on the remuneration policy. (1) Member States shall ensure that companies establish a remuneration policy as regards directors and that shareholders have the right to vote on the remuneration policy at the general meeting.
(2) Member States shall ensure that the vote by the shareholders at the general meeting on the remuneration policy is binding. Companies shall pay remuneration to their directors only in accordance with a remuneration policy that has been approved by the general meeting.
Where no remuneration policy has been approved and the general meeting does not approve the proposed policy, the company may continue to pay remuneration to its directors in accordance with its existing practices and shall submit a revised policy for approval at the following general meeting. Where an approved remuneration policy exists and the general meeting does not approve the proposed new policy, the company shall continue to pay remuneration to its directors in accordance with the existing approved policy and shall submit a revised policy for approval at the following general meeting.
(3) However, Member States may provide for the vote at the general meeting on the remuneration policy to be advisory. In that case, companies shall pay remuneration to their directors only in accordance with a remuneration policy that has been submitted to such a vote at the general meeting. Where the general meeting rejects the proposed remuneration policy, the company shall submit a revised policy to a vote at the following general meeting.
(4) Member States may allow companies, in exceptional circumstances, to temporarily derogate from the remuneration policy, provided that the policy includes the procedural conditions under which the derogation can be applied and specifies the elements of the policy from which a derogation is possible.
Exceptional circumstances as referred to in the first subparagraph shall cover only situations in which the derogation from the remuneration policy is necessary to serve the long-term interests and sustainability of the company as a whole or to assure its viability.
(5) Member States shall ensure that companies submit the remuneration policy to a vote by the general meeting at every material change and in any case at least every four years.
(6) The remuneration policy shall contribute to the company's business strategy and long-term interests and sustainability and shall explain how it does so. It shall be clear and understandable and describe the different components of fixed and variable remuneration, including all bonuses and other benefits in whatever form, which can be awarded to directors and indicate their relative proportion.
The remuneration policy shall explain how the pay and employment conditions of employees of the company were taken into account when establishing the remuneration policy.

Where a company awards variable remuneration, the remuneration policy shall set clear, comprehensive and varied criteria for the award of the variable remuneration. It shall indicate the financial and non-financial performance criteria, including, where appropriate, criteria relating to corporate social responsibility, and explain how they contribute to the objectives set out in the first subparagraph, and the methods to be applied to determine to which extent the performance criteria have been fulfilled. It shall specify information on any deferral periods and on the possibility for the company to reclaim variable remuneration.

Where the company awards share-based remuneration, the policy shall specify vesting periods and where applicable retention of shares after vesting and explain how the share based remuneration contributes to the objectives set out in the first subparagraph.

The remuneration policy shall indicate the duration of the contracts or arrangements with directors and the applicable notice periods, the main characteristics of supplementary pension or early retirement schemes and the terms of the termination and payments linked to termination.

The remuneration policy shall explain the decision-making process followed for its determination, review and implementation, including, measures to avoid or manage conflicts of interests and, where applicable, the role of the remuneration committee or other committees concerned. Where the policy is revised, it shall describe and explain all significant changes and how it takes into account the votes and views of shareholders on the policy and reports since the most recent vote on the remuneration policy by the general meeting of shareholders.

(7) Member States shall ensure that after the vote on the remuneration policy at the general meeting the policy together with the date and the results of the vote is made public without delay on the website of the company and remains publicly available, free of charge, at least as long as it is applicable.

Article 9b. Information to be provided in and right to vote on the remuneration report.

(1) Member States shall ensure that the company draws up a clear and understandable remuneration report, providing a comprehensive overview of the remuneration, including all benefits in whatever form, awarded or due during the most recent financial year to individual directors, including to newly recruited and to former directors, in accordance with the remuneration policy referred to in Article 9a. Where applicable, the remuneration report shall contain the following information regarding each individual director's remuneration:

(a) the total remuneration split out by component, the relative proportion of fixed and variable remuneration, an explanation how the total remuneration complies with the adopted remuneration policy, including how it contributes to the long-term performance of the company, and information on how the performance criteria were applied;

(b) the annual change of remuneration, of the performance of the company, and of average remuneration on a full- time equivalent basis of employees of the company other than directors over at least the five most recent financial years, presented together in a manner which permits comparison;

(c) any remuneration from any undertaking belonging to the same group as defined in point (11) of Article 2 of Directive 2013/34/EU of the European Parliament and of the Council;

(d) the number of shares and share options granted or offered, and the main conditions for the exercise of the rights including the exercise price and date and any change thereof;

(e) information on the use of the possibility to reclaim variable remuneration;

(f) information on any deviations from the procedure for the implementation of the remuneration policy referred to in Article 9a(6) and on any derogations applied in accordance with Article 9a(4), including the explanation of the nature of the exceptional circumstances and the indication of the specific elements derogated from.

(2) Member States shall ensure that companies do not include in the remuneration report special categories of personal data of individual directors within the meaning of Article 9(1) of Regulation (EU) 2016/679 of the European Parliament and of the Councilor personal data which refer to the family situation of individual directors.

(3) Companies shall process the personal data of directors included in the remuneration report pursuant to this Article for the purpose of increasing corporate transparency as regards directors' remuneration with the view to enhancing directors' accountability and shareholder oversight over directors' remuneration.

Without prejudice to any longer period laid down by any sector-specific Union legislative act, Member States shall ensure that companies no longer make publicly available pursuant to paragraph 5 of this Article the personal data of directors included in the remuneration report in accordance with this Article after 10 years from the publication of the remuneration report.

Member States may provide by law for processing of the personal data of directors for other purposes.

(4) Member States shall ensure that the annual general meeting has the right to hold an advisory vote

on the remuneration report of the most recent financial year. The company shall explain in the following remuneration report how the vote by the general meeting has been taken into account.

However, for small and medium-sized companies as defined, respectively, in Article 3(2) and (3) of Directive 2013/34/EU, Member States may provide, as an alternative to a vote, for the remuneration report of the most recent financial year to be submitted for discussion in the annual general meeting as a separate item of the agenda. The company shall explain in the following remuneration report how the discussion in the general meeting has been taken into account.

(5) Without prejudice to Article 5(4), after the general meeting the companies shall make the remuneration report publicly available on their website, free of charge, for a period of 10 years, and may choose to keep it available for a longer period provided it no longer contains the personal data of directors. The statutory auditor or audit firm shall check that the information required by this Article has been provided.

Member States shall ensure that the directors of the company, acting within its field of competence assigned to them by national law, have collective responsibility for ensuring that the remuneration report is drawn up and published in accordance with the requirements of this Directive. Member States shall ensure that their laws, regulations and administrative provisions on liability, at least towards the company, apply to the directors of the company for breach of the duties referred to in this paragraph.

(6) The Commission shall, with a view to ensuring harmonisation in relation to this Article, adopt guidelines to specify the standardised presentation of the information laid down in paragraph 1.

Article 9c. Transparency and approval of related party transactions.

(1) Member States shall define material transactions for the purposes of this Article, taking into account:

(a) the influence that the information about the transaction may have on the economic decisions of shareholders of the company;

(b) the risk that the transaction creates for the company and its shareholders who are not a related party, including minority shareholders.

When defining material transactions Member States shall set one or more quantitative ratios based on the impact of the transaction on the financial position, revenues, assets, capitalisation, including equity, or turnover of the company or take into account the nature of transaction and the position of the related party.

Member States may adopt different materiality definitions for the application of paragraph 4 than those for the application of paragraphs 2 and 3 and may differentiate the definitions according to the company size.

(2) Member States shall ensure that companies publicly announce material transactions with related parties at the latest at the time of the conclusion of the transaction. The announcement shall contain at least information on the nature of the related party relationship, the name of the related party, the date and the value of the transaction and other information necessary to assess whether or not the transaction is fair and reasonable from the perspective of the company and of the shareholders who are not a related party, including minority shareholders.

(3) Member States may provide for the public announcement referred to in paragraph 2 to be accompanied by a report assessing whether or not the transaction is fair and reasonable from the perspective of the company and of the shareholders who are not a related party, including minority shareholders, and explaining the assumptions it is based upon together with the methods used.

The report shall be produced by one of the following:

(a) an independent third party;

(b) the administrative or supervisory body of the company;

(c) the audit committee or any committee the majority of which is composed of independent directors.

Member States shall ensure that the related parties do not take part in the preparation of the report.

(4) Member States shall ensure that material transactions with related parties are approved by the general meeting or by the administrative or supervisory body of the company according to procedures which prevent the related party from taking advantage of its position and provide adequate protection for the interests of the company and of the shareholders who are not a related party, including minority shareholders.

Member States may provide for shareholders in the general meeting to have the right to vote on material transactions with related parties which have been approved by the administrative or supervisory body of the company.

Where the related party transaction involves a director or a shareholder, the director or shareholder shall not take part in the approval or the vote.

EU: DIRECTIVE 2017/828 ON LONG-TERM SHAREHOLDER ENGAGEMENT

Member States may allow the shareholder who is a related party to take part in the vote provided that national law ensures appropriate safeguards which apply before or during the voting process to protect the interests of the company and of the shareholders who are not a related party, including minority shareholders, by preventing the related party from approving the transaction despite the opposing opinion of the majority of the shareholders who are not a related party or despite the opposing opinion of the majority of the independent directors.

(5) Paragraphs 2, 3 and 4 shall not apply to transactions entered into in the ordinary course of business and concluded on normal market terms. For such transactions the administrative or supervisory body of the company shall establish an internal procedure to periodically assess whether these conditions are fulfilled. The related parties shall not take part in that assessment.

However, Member States may provide for companies to apply the requirements in paragraph 2, 3 or 4 to transactions entered into in the ordinary course of business and concluded on normal market terms.

(6) Member States may exclude, or may allow companies to exclude, from the requirements in paragraphs 2, 3 and 4:

(a) transactions entered into between the company and its subsidiaries provided that they are wholly owned or that no other related party of the company has an interest in the subsidiary undertaking or that national law provides for adequate protection of interests of the company, of the subsidiary and of their shareholders who are not a related party, including minority shareholders in such transactions;

(b) clearly defined types of transactions for which national law requires approval by the general meeting, provided that fair treatment of all shareholders and the interests of the company and of the shareholders who are not a related party, including minority shareholders, are specifically addressed and adequately protected in such provisions of law;

(c) transactions regarding remuneration of directors, or certain elements of remuneration of directors, awarded or due in accordance with Article 9a;

(d) transactions entered into by credit institutions on the basis of measures, aiming at safeguarding their stability, adopted by the competent authority in charge of the prudential supervision within the meaning of Union law;

(e) transactions offered to all shareholders on the same terms where equal treatment of all shareholders and protection of the interests of the company is ensured.

(7) Member States shall ensure that companies publicly announce material transactions concluded between the related party of the company and that company's subsidiary. Member States may also provide that the announcement is accompanied by a report assessing whether or not the transaction is fair and reasonable from the perspective of the company and of the shareholders who are not a related party, including minority shareholders and explaining the assumptions it is based upon together with the methods used. The exemptions provided in paragraph 5 and 6 shall also apply to the transactions specified in this paragraph.

(8) Member States shall ensure that transactions with the same related party that have been concluded in any 12-month period or in the same financial year and have not been subject to the obligations listed in paragraph 2, 3 or 4 are aggregated for the purposes of those paragraphs.

(9) This Article is without prejudice to the rules on public disclosure of inside information as referred to in Article 17 of Regulation (EU) No 596/2014 of the European Parliament and of the Council'.

(5) The following Chapter is inserted:

'Chapter IIa. Implementing Acts and Penalties

Article 14a. Committee procedure. (1) The Commission shall be assisted by the European Securities Committee established by Commission Decision 2001/528/EC. That committee shall be a committee within the meaning of Regulation (EU) No 182/2011 of the European Parliament and of the Council.

(2) Where reference is made to this paragraph, Article 5 of Regulation (EU) No 182/2011 shall apply.

Article 14b. Measures and penalties. Member States shall lay down the rules on measures and penalties applicable to infringements of national provisions adopted pursuant to this Directive and shall take all measures necessary to ensure that they are implemented.

The measures and penalties provided for shall be effective, proportionate and dissuasive. Member States shall by 10 June 2019, notify the Commission of those rules and of those implementing measures and shall notify it, without delay, of any subsequent amendments affecting them.'

Article 2. (1) Member States shall bring into force the laws, regulations and administrative provisions necessary to comply with this Directive by 10 June 2019. They shall immediately inform the Commission thereof.

When Member States adopt those measures, they shall contain a reference to this Directive or shall be accompanied by such reference on the occasion of their official publication. The methods of making such reference shall be laid down by Member States.

Notwithstanding the first subparagraph, Member States shall, not later than 24 months after the adoption of the implementing acts referred to in Articles 3a(8), 3b(6) and 3c(3) of Directive 2007/36/EC, bring into force the laws, regulations and administrative provisions necessary to comply with Articles 3a, 3b and 3c of that Directive.

(2) Member States shall communicate to the Commission the text of the main measures of national law which they adopt in the field covered by this Directive.

Article 3. This Directive shall enter into force on the twentieth day following that of its publication in the Official Journal of the European Union.

Article 4. This Directives is addressed to the Member States.

EU: DIRECTIVE 2017/1132 ON COMPANY LAW (CODIFICATION)

Directive (EU) 2017/1132 of the European Parliament and of the Council of 14 June 2017 relating to certain aspects of company law (Codification) [footnotes omitted].

THE EUROPEAN PARLIAMENT AND THE COUNCIL OF THE EUROPEAN UNION,
Having regard to the Treaty on the Functioning of the European Union, and in particular Article 50(1) and (2)(g) thereof,
Having regard to the proposal from the European Commission,
After transmission of the draft legislative act to the national parliaments,
Having regard to the opinion of the European Economic and Social Committee,
Acting in accordance with the ordinary legislative procedure,
Whereas:
(1) Council Directives 82/891/EEC and 89/666/EEC and Directives 2005/56/EC, 2009/101/EC, 2011/35/EU and 2012/30/EU of the European Parliament and of the Council have been substantially amended several times. In the interests of clarity and rationality those Directives should be codified.
(2) The coordination provided for in Article 50(2)(g) of the Treaty and in the General Programme for the abolition of restrictions on freedom of establishment, which was begun by the First Council Directive 68/151/EEC, is especially important in relation to public limited liability companies because their activities predominate in the economy of the Member States and frequently extend beyond their national boundaries.
(3) In order to ensure minimum equivalent protection for both shareholders and creditors of public limited liability companies, the coordination of national provisions relating to the formation of such companies and to the maintenance, increase or reduction of their capital is particularly important.
(4) In the Union, the statutes or instrument of incorporation of a public limited liability company must make it possible for any interested person to acquaint oneself with the basic particulars of the company, including the exact composition of its capital.
(5) The protection of third parties should be ensured by provisions which restrict to the greatest possible extent the grounds on which obligations entered into in the name of companies limited by shares or otherwise having limited liability are not valid.
(6) It is necessary, in order to ensure certainty in the law as regards relations between companies and third parties, and also between members, to limit the cases in which nullity can arise and the retroactive effect of a declaration of nullity, and to fix a short time limit within which third parties may enter an objection to any such declaration.
(7) The coordination of national provisions concerning disclosure, the validity of obligations entered into by, and the nullity of, companies limited by shares or otherwise having limited liability, is of special importance, particularly for the purpose of protecting the interests of third parties.
(8) The basic documents of a company should be disclosed in order for third parties to be able to ascertain their contents and other information concerning the company, especially particulars of the persons who are authorised to bind the company.
(9) Without prejudice to substantive requirements and formalities established by the national law of the Member States, companies should be able to choose to file their compulsory documents and particulars by paper means or by electronic means.
(10) Interested parties should be able to obtain from the register a copy of such documents and particulars by paper means as well as by electronic means.
(11) Member States should be allowed to decide to keep the national gazette, designated for publication of compulsory documents and particulars, in paper form or electronic form, or to provide for disclosure by equally effective means.
(12) Cross-border access to company information should be facilitated by allowing, in addition to the compulsory disclosure made in one of the languages permitted in the company's Member State, the voluntary registration in additional languages of the required documents and particulars. Third parties acting in good faith should be able to rely on the translations thereof.
(13) It is appropriate to clarify that the statement of the compulsory particulars set out in this Directive should be included in all company letters and order forms, whether they are in paper form or use any other medium. In the light of technological developments, it is also appropriate to provide that that statement of compulsory particulars be placed on any company website.
(14) The opening of a branch, like the creation of a subsidiary, is one of the possibilities currently open to companies in the exercise of their right of establishment in another Member State.
(15) In respect of branches, the lack of coordination, in particular concerning disclosure, gives rise to some disparities, in the protection of shareholders and third parties, between companies which operate in other Member States by opening branches and those which operate there by creating subsidiaries.

PART III EUROPEAN COMPANY LAW

(16) To ensure the protection of persons who deal with companies through the intermediary of branches, measures in respect of disclosure are required in the Member State in which a branch is situated. In certain respects, the economic and social influence of a branch can be comparable to that of a subsidiary company, so that there is public interest in disclosure of the company at the branch. To effect such disclosure, it is necessary to make use of the procedure already instituted for companies with share capital within the Union.

(17) Such disclosure relates to a range of important documents and particulars and amendments thereto.

(18) Such disclosure, with the exception of the powers of representation, the name and legal form, and the winding-up of the company and the insolvency proceedings to which it is subject, can be confined to information concerning a branch itself together with a reference to the register of the company of which that branch is part, since under existing Union rules, all information covering the company as such is available in that register.

(19) National provisions in respect of the disclosure of accounting documents relating to a branch can no longer be justified following the coordination of national law in respect of the drawing up, audit and disclosure of companies' accounting documents. It is accordingly sufficient to disclose, in the register of the branch, the accounting documents as audited and disclosed by the company.

(20) Letters and order forms used by a branch should give at least the same information as letters and order forms used by the company, and state the register in which the branch is entered.

(21) To ensure that the purposes of this Directive are fully realised and to avoid any discrimination on the basis of a company's country of origin, this Directive should also cover branches opened by companies governed by the law of third countries and set up in legal forms comparable to companies to which this Directive applies. For such branches it is necessary to apply specific provisions that are different from those that apply to the branches of companies governed by the law of other Member States since this Directive does not apply to companies from third countries.

(22) This Directive in no way affects the disclosure requirements for branches under other provisions of, for example, employment law on workers' rights to information and tax law, or for statistical purposes.

(23) The interconnection of central, commercial and companies registers is a measure required to create a more business-friendly legal and fiscal environment. It should contribute to fostering the competitiveness of European business by reducing administrative burdens and increasing legal certainty and thus contributing to an exit from the global economic and financial crisis, which is one of the priorities of the agenda of Europe 2020. It should also improve cross-border communication between registers by using innovations in information and communication technology.

(24) The Multiannual European e-Justice action plan 2009–2013 provided for the development of a European e-Justice portal ('the portal') as the single European electronic access point for legal information, judicial and administrative institutions, registers, databases and other services and considers the interconnection of central, commercial and companies registers to be important.

(25) Cross-border access to business information on companies and their branches opened in other Member States can only be improved if all Member States engage in enabling electronic communication to take place between registers and transmitting information to individual users in a standardised way, by means of identical content and interoperable technologies, throughout the Union. This interoperability of registers should be ensured by the registers of Member States ('domestic registers') providing services, which should constitute interfaces with the European central platform ('the platform'). The platform should be a centralised set of information technology tools integrating services and should form a common interface. That interface should be used by all domestic registers. The platform should also provide services constituting an interface with the portal serving as the European electronic access point, and to the optional access points established by Member States. The platform should be conceived only as an instrument for the interconnection of registers and not as a distinct entity possessing legal personality. On the basis of unique identifiers, the platform should be capable of distributing information from each of the Member States' registers to the competent registers of other Member States in a standard message format (an electronic form of messages exchanged between information technology systems, such as, for example, xml) and in the relevant language version.

(26) This Directive is not aimed at establishing any centralised registers database storing substantive information about companies. At the stage of implementation of the system of interconnection of central, commercial and companies registers ('the system of interconnection of registers'), only the set of data necessary for the correct functioning of the platform should be defined. The scope of those data should include, in particular, operational data, dictionaries and glossaries. It should be determined taking also into account the need to ensure the efficient operation of the system of

interconnection of registers. Those data should be used for the purpose of enabling the platform to perform its functions and should never be made publicly available in a direct form. Moreover, the platform should modify neither the content of the data on companies stored in domestic registers nor the information about companies transmitted through the system of interconnection of registers.

(27) Since the objective of Directive 2012/17/EU of the European Parliament and of the Council was not to harmonise national systems of central, commercial and companies registers, that Directive did not impose any obligation on Member States to change their internal systems of registers, in particular as regards the management and storage of data, fees, and the use and disclosure of information for national purposes.

(28) The portal should deal, through the use of the platform, with queries submitted by individual users concerning the information on companies and their branches opened in other Member States which is stored in the domestic registers. That should enable the search results to be presented on the portal, including the explanatory labels in all the official languages of the Union, listing the information provided. In addition, in order to improve the protection of third parties in other Member States, basic information on the legal value of documents and particulars disclosed pursuant to the laws of Member States adopted in accordance with this Directive should be available on the portal.

(29) Member States should be able to establish one or more optional access points, which may have an impact on the use and operation of the platform. Therefore, the Commission should be notified of their establishment and of any significant changes to their operation, in particular of their closure. Such notification should not in any way restrict the powers of Member States as to the establishment and operation of the optional access points.

(30) Companies and their branches opened in other Member States should have a unique identifier allowing them to be unequivocally identified within the Union. The identifier is intended to be used for communication between registers through the system of interconnection of registers. Therefore, companies and branches should not be obliged to include the unique identifier in the company letters or order forms mentioned in this Directive. They should continue to use their domestic registration number for their own communication purposes.

(31) It should be made possible to establish a clear connection between the register of a company and the registers of its branches opened in other Member States, consisting of the exchange of information on the opening and termination of any winding-up or insolvency proceedings of the company and on the striking-off of the company from the register, if this entails legal consequences in the Member State of the register of the company. While Member States should be able to decide on the procedures they follow with respect to the branches registered in their territory, they should ensure, at least, that the branches of a dissolved company are struck off the register without undue delay and, if applicable, after liquidation proceedings of the branch concerned. This obligation should not apply to branches of companies that have been struck off the register but which have a legal successor, such as in the case of any change in the legal form of the company, a merger or division, or a cross-border transfer of its registered office.

(32) The provisions of this Directive relating to the interconnection of registers should not apply to a branch opened in a Member State by a company which is not governed by the law of a Member State.

(33) Member States should ensure that, in the event of any changes to information entered in the registers concerning companies, the information is updated without undue delay. The update should be disclosed, normally, within 21 days of receipt of the complete documentation regarding those changes, including the legality check in accordance with national law. That time limit should be interpreted as requiring Member States to make reasonable efforts to meet the deadline laid down in this Directive. It should not be applicable as regards the accounting documents which companies are obliged to submit for each financial year. That exclusion is justified by the overload of work on domestic registers during reporting periods. In accordance with general legal principles common to all Member States, the time limit of 21 days should be suspended in cases of force majeure.

(34) If the Commission decides to develop and/or operate the platform through a third party, this should be done in accordance with Regulation (EU, Euratom) No 966/2012 of the European Parliament and of the Council. An appropriate degree of Member States' involvement in this process should be ensured by establishing the technical specifications for the purpose of the public procurement procedure by means of implementing acts adopted in accordance with the examination procedure referred to in Article 5 of Regulation (EU) No 182/2011 of the European Parliament and of the Council.

(35) If the Commission decides to operate the platform through a third party, the continuity of the provision of services by the system of interconnection of registers and a proper public supervision of the functioning of the platform should be ensured. Detailed rules on the operational management of the platform should be adopted by means of implementing acts adopted in accordance with the

examination procedure referred to in Article 5 of Regulation (EU) No 182/2011. In any case, the involvement of Member States in the functioning of the whole system should be ensured by means of a regular dialogue between the Commission and the representatives of Member States on the issues concerning the operation of the system of interconnection of registers and its future development.

(36) The interconnection of central, commercial and companies registers necessitates the coordination of national systems having varying technical characteristics. This entails the adoption of technical measures and specifications which need to take account of differences between registers. In order to ensure uniform conditions for the implementation of this Directive, implementing powers should be conferred on the Commission to tackle those technical and operational issues. Those powers should be exercised in accordance with the examination procedure referred to in Article 5 of Regulation (EU) No 182/2011.

(37) This Directive should not limit the right of Member States to charge fees for obtaining information on companies through the system of interconnection of registers, if such fees are required under national law. Therefore, technical measures and specifications for the system of interconnection of registers should allow for the establishment of payment modalities. In this respect, this Directive should not prejudice any specific technical solution as the payment modalities should be determined at the stage of adoption of the implementing acts, taking into account widely available online payment facilities.

(38) It could be desirable for third countries to be able, in the future, to participate in the system of interconnection of registers.

(39) An equitable solution regarding the funding of the system of interconnection of registers entails participation both by the Union and by its Member States in the financing of that system. Member States should bear the financial burden of adjusting their domestic registers to that system, while the central elements, namely the platform and the portal serving as the European electronic access point, should be funded from an appropriate budget line in the general budget of the Union. In order to supplement non-essential elements of this Directive, the power to adopt acts in accordance with Article 290 of the Treaty should be delegated to the Commission in respect of the charging of fees for obtaining company information. This does not affect the possibility for the domestic registers to charge fees, but it could involve an additional fee in order to co-finance the maintenance and functioning of the platform. It is of particular importance that the Commission carry out appropriate consultations during its preparatory work, including at expert level. The Commission, when preparing and drawing up delegated acts, should ensure a simultaneous, timely and appropriate transmission of relevant documents to the European Parliament and to the Council.

(40) Union provisions are necessary for maintaining the capital, which constitutes the creditors' security, in particular by prohibiting any reduction thereof by distribution to shareholders where the latter are not entitled to it and by imposing limits on the right of public limited liability companies to acquire their own shares.

(41) The restrictions on a public limited liability company's acquisition of its own shares apply not only to acquisitions made by a company itself but also to those made by any person acting in his own name but on the company's behalf.

(42) In order to prevent a public limited liability company from using another company in which it holds a majority of the voting rights or on which it can exercise a dominant influence to make such acquisitions without complying with the restrictions imposed in that respect, the arrangements governing a company's acquisition of its own shares should cover the most important and most frequent cases of the acquisition of shares by such other companies. Those arrangements should cover subscription for shares in the public limited liability company.

(43) In order to prevent the circumvention of this Directive, companies limited by shares or otherwise having limited liability governed by this Directive and companies governed by the laws of third countries, and having comparable legal forms, should also be covered by the arrangements referred to in recital 42.

(44) Where the relationship between a public limited liability company and another company such as referred to in recital 42 is only indirect, it would appear to be justified to relax the provisions applicable when that relationship is direct, by providing for the suspension of voting rights as a minimum measure, for the purpose of achieving the aims of this Directive.

(45) Furthermore, it is justifiable to exempt cases in which the specific nature of a professional activity rules out the possibility of the attainment of the objectives of this Directive being endangered.

(46) It is necessary, having regard to the objectives of Article 50(2)(g) of the Treaty, that the Member States' laws relating to the increase or reduction of capital ensure that the principles of equal treatment of shareholders in the same position and of protection of creditors whose claims exist prior to the decision on reduction are observed and harmonised.

(47) In order to enhance standardised creditor protection in all Member States, creditors should be able to resort, under certain conditions, to judicial or administrative proceedings where their claims are at stake, as a consequence of a reduction in the capital of a public limited liability company.
(48) In order to ensure that market abuse is prevented, Member States should take into account, for the purpose of the implementation of this Directive, the provisions of Regulation (EU) No 596/2014 of the European Parliament and of the Council.
(49) The protection of the interests of members and third parties requires that the laws of the Member States relating to mergers of public limited liability companies be coordinated, and that provision for mergers be made in the laws of all the Member States.
(50) In the context of such coordination, it is particularly important that the shareholders of merging companies be kept adequately informed in as objective a manner as possible, and that their rights be suitably protected. However, there is no reason to require an examination of the draft terms of a merger by an independent expert for the shareholders if all the shareholders agree that it can be dispensed with.
(51) Creditors, including debenture holders, and persons having other claims on the merging companies should be protected so that the merger does not adversely affect their interests.
(52) The disclosure requirements for the protection of the interests of members and third parties should include mergers so that third parties are kept adequately informed.
(53) The safeguards afforded to members and third parties in connection with mergers of public limited liability companies should cover certain legal practices which in important respects are similar to merger, so that the obligation to provide such protection cannot be evaded.
(54) To ensure certainty in the law as regards relations between the companies concerned, between them and third parties, and between the members, it is necessary to limit the cases in which nullity can arise by providing that defects be remedied wherever that is possible, and by restricting the period within which nullification proceedings can be commenced.
(55) This Directive also facilitates the cross-border merger of limited liability companies. The laws of the Member States should allow the cross-border merger of a national limited liability company with a limited liability company from another Member State if the national law of the relevant Member States permits mergers between such types of company.
(56) In order to facilitate cross-border merger operations, it should be specified that, unless this Directive provides otherwise, each company taking part in a cross-border merger, and each third party concerned, remains subject to the provisions and formalities of the national law which would be applicable in the case of a national merger. None of the provisions and formalities of national law, to which reference is made in this Directive, should introduce restrictions on freedom of establishment or on the free movement of capital, save where these can be justified in accordance with the case-law of the Court of Justice of the European Union and in particular, by requirements of the general interest and are both necessary for, and proportionate to, the attainment of such overriding requirements
(57) The common draft terms of a cross-border merger should be drawn up in the same terms for each of the companies concerned in the various Member States. The minimum content of such common draft terms should therefore be specified, while leaving the companies free to agree on other terms.
(58) In order to protect the interests of members and others, both the common draft terms of the cross-border merger and the completion of the cross-border merger should be publicised for each merging company via an entry in the appropriate public register.
(59) The laws of all the Member States should provide for the drawing-up at national level of a report on the common draft terms of the cross-border merger by one or more experts on behalf of each of the companies that are merging. In order to limit experts' costs connected with cross-border mergers, provision should be made for the possibility of drawing up a single report intended for all members of companies taking part in a cross-border merger operation. The common draft terms of the cross-border merger should be approved by the general meeting of each of those companies.
(60) In order to facilitate cross-border merger operations, it should be provided that monitoring of the completion and legality of the decision-making process in each merging company should be carried out by the national authority having jurisdiction over each of those companies, whereas monitoring of the completion and legality of the cross-border merger should be carried out by the national authority having jurisdiction over the company resulting from the cross-border merger. The national authority in question could be a court, a notary or any other competent authority appointed by the Member State concerned. The national law determining the date on which the cross-border merger takes effect, this being the law to which the company resulting from the cross-border merger is subject, should also be specified.

PART III   EUROPEAN COMPANY LAW

(61) In order to protect the interests of members and others, the legal effects of the cross-border merger, distinguishing as to whether the company resulting from the cross-border merger is an acquiring company or a new company, should be specified. In the interests of legal certainty, it should no longer be possible, after the date on which a cross-border merger takes effect, to declare the merger null and void.

(62) This Directive is without prejudice to the application of the legislation on the control of concentrations between undertakings, both at Union level, by Council Regulation (EC) No 139/2004, and at Member State level.

(63) This Directive does not affect Union legislation regulating credit intermediaries and other financial undertakings and national rules made or introduced pursuant to such Union legislation.

(64) This Directive is without prejudice to Member State legislation demanding information on the place of central administration or the principal place of business proposed for the company resulting from the cross-border merger.

(65) Employees' rights, other than rights of participation, should remain subject to the national provisions referred to in Council Directives 98/59/EC and 2001/23/EC, and in Directives 2002/14/EC and 2009/38/EC of the European Parliament and of the Council.

(66) If employees have participation rights in one of the merging companies under the circumstances set out in this Directive and, if the national law of the Member State in which the company resulting from the cross-border merger has its registered office does not provide for the same level of participation as operated in the relevant merging companies, including in committees of the supervisory board that have decision-making powers, or does not provide for the same entitlement to exercise rights for employees of establishments resulting from the cross-border merger, the participation of employees in the company resulting from the cross-border merger and their involvement in the definition of such rights should be regulated. To that end, the principles and procedures provided for in Council Regulation (EC) No 2157/2001 and in Council Directive 2001/86/EC, should be taken as a basis, subject, however, to modifications that are deemed necessary because the resulting company will be subject to the national laws of the Member State where it has its registered office. A prompt start to negotiations under Article 133 of this Directive, with a view to not unnecessarily delaying mergers, may be ensured by Member States in accordance with Article 3(2)(b) of Directive 2001/86/EC.

(67) For the purpose of determining the level of employee participation operated in the relevant merging companies, account should also be taken of the proportion of employee representatives amongst the members of the management group, which covers the profit units of the companies, subject to employee participation.

(68) The protection of the interests of members and third parties requires that the laws of the Member States relating to divisions of public limited liability companies be coordinated where Member States permit such operations.

(69) In the context of such coordination, it is particularly important that the shareholders of the companies involved in a division be kept adequately informed in as objective a manner as possible, and that their rights be suitably protected.

(70) Creditors, including debenture holders, and persons having other claims on the companies involved in a division of public limited liability companies, should be protected so that the division does not adversely affect their interests.

(71) Disclosure requirements under Section 1 of Chapter III of Title I of this Directive should include divisions so that third parties are kept adequately informed.

(72) The safeguards afforded to members and third parties in connection with divisions should cover certain legal practices which in important respects are similar to division, so that the obligation to provide such protection cannot be evaded.

(73) To ensure certainty in the law as regards relations between the public limited liability companies involved in the division, between them and third parties, and between the members, the cases in which nullity can arise should be limited by providing that defects should be remedied wherever that is possible and by restricting the period within which nullification proceedings can be commenced.

(74) Company websites or other websites offer, in certain cases, an alternative to publication via the companies registers. Member States should be able to designate those other websites which companies can use free of charge for such publication, such as websites of business associations or chambers of commerce or the central electronic platform referred to in this Directive. Where the possibility exists of using company or other websites for publication of draft terms of merger and/or division and of other documents that have to be made available to shareholders and creditors in the process, guarantees relating to the security of the website and the authenticity of the documents should be met.

(75) Member States should be able to provide that the extensive reporting or information requirements relating to the merger or division of companies, laid down in Chapter I and Chapter III of Title

II, need not be complied with where all the shareholders of the companies involved in the merger or division agree that such compliance can be dispensed with.

(76) Any modification of Chapter I and Chapter III of Title II allowing such agreement by shareholders, should be without prejudice to the systems of protection of the interests of creditors of the companies involved, and to rules aimed at ensuring the provision of necessary information to the employees of those companies and to public authorities, such as tax authorities, controlling the merger or division in accordance with existing Union law.

(77) It is not necessary to impose the requirement to draw up an accounting statement where an issuer whose securities are admitted to trading on a regulated market publishes half-yearly financial reports in accordance with Directive 2004/109/EC of the European Parliament and of the Council.

(78) An independent expert's report on consideration other than in cash is often not needed where an independent expert's report protecting the interests of shareholders or creditors also has to be drawn up in the context of the merger or the division. Member States should therefore have the possibility in such cases of dispensing companies from the reporting requirement regarding consideration other than in cash or of providing that both reports can be drawn up by the same expert.

(79) Directive 95/46/EC of the European Parliament and of the Council and Regulation (EC) No 45/2001 of the European Parliament and of the Council govern the processing of personal data, including the electronic transmission of personal data within the Member States. Any processing of personal data by the registers of Member States, by the Commission and, if applicable, by any third party involved in operating the platform should take place in compliance with those acts. The implementing acts to be adopted in relation to the system of interconnection of registers should, where appropriate, ensure such compliance, in particular by establishing the relevant tasks and responsibilities of all the participants concerned and the organisational and technical rules applicable to them.

(80) This Directive respects fundamental rights and observes the principles enshrined in the Charter of Fundamental Rights of the European Union, in particular Article 8 thereof, which states that everyone has the right to the protection of personal data concerning him or her.

(81) This Directive should be without prejudice to the obligations of the Member States relating to the time limits for the transposition into national law and the dates of application of the directives set out in Annex III, Part B,

HAVE ADOPTED THIS DIRECTIVE:

Title I. General Provisions and the Establishment and Functioning of Limited Liability Companies

Chapter I. Subject Matter

Article 1. This Directive lays down measures concerning the following:

— the coordination of safeguards which, for the protection of the interests of members and others, are required by Member States of companies within the meaning of the second paragraph of Article 54 of the Treaty, in respect of the formation of public limited liability companies and the maintenance and alteration of their capital, with a view to making such safeguards equivalent,

— the coordination of safeguards which, for the protection of the interests of members and third parties, are required by Member States of companies within the meaning of the second paragraph of Article 54 of the Treaty, in respect of disclosure, the validity of obligations entered into by, and the nullity of, companies limited by shares or otherwise having limited liability, with a view to making such safeguards equivalent,

— the disclosure requirements in respect of branches opened in a Member State by certain types of company governed by the law of another State,

— mergers of public limited liability companies,

— cross-border mergers of limited liability companies,

— the division of public limited liability companies.

Chapter II. Incorporation and nullity of the company and validity of its obligations

Section 1. Incorporation of the public liability company

Article 2. 1. The coordination measures prescribed by this Section shall apply to the provisions laid down by law, regulation or administrative action in Member States relating to the types of company listed in Annex I. The name for any company of the types listed in Annex I shall comprise or be accompanied by a description which is distinct from the description required of other types of companies.

2. Member States may decide not to apply this Section to investment companies with variable

capital and to cooperatives incorporated as one of the types of company listed in Annex I. In so far as the laws of the Member States make use of this option, they shall require such companies to include the words 'investment company with variable capital', or 'cooperative' in all documents indicated in Article 26.

The term 'investment company with variable capital', within the meaning of this Directive, means only those companies:

— the exclusive object of which is to invest their funds in various stocks and shares, land or other assets with the sole aim of spreading investment risks and giving their shareholders the benefit of the results of the management of their assets, which offer their own shares for subscription by the public, and

— the statutes of which provide that, within the limits of a minimum and maximum capital, they may at any time issue, redeem or resell their shares.

Article 3. The statutes or the instrument of incorporation of a company shall always give at least the following information:

(a) the type and name of the company;
(b) the objects of the company;
(c) where the company has no authorised capital, the amount of the subscribed capital;
(d) where the company has an authorised capital, the amount thereof and also the amount of the capital subscribed at the time the company is incorporated or is authorised to commence business, and at the time of any change in the authorised capital, without prejudice to Article 14(e);
(e) in so far as they are not legally determined, the rules governing the number of, and the procedure for, appointing members of the bodies responsible for representing the company vis-à-vis third parties, administration, management, supervision or control of the company and the allocation of powers among those bodies;
(f) the duration of the company, except where this is indefinite.

Article 4. The following information at least shall appear in either the statutes or the instrument of incorporation or a separate document published in accordance with the procedure laid down in the laws of each Member State in accordance with Article 16:

(a) the registered office;
(b) the nominal value of the shares subscribed and, at least once a year, the number thereof;
(c) the number of shares subscribed without stating the nominal value, where such shares may be issued under national law;
(d) the special conditions, if any, limiting the transfer of shares;
(e) where there are several classes of shares, the information referred to in points (b), (c) and (d) for each class and the rights attaching to the shares of each class;
(f) whether the shares are registered or bearer, where national law provides for both types, and any provisions relating to the conversion of such shares unless the procedure is laid down by law;
(g) the amount of the subscribed capital paid up at the time the company is incorporated or is authorised to commence business;
(h) the nominal value of the shares or, where there is no nominal value, the number of shares issued for a consideration other than in cash, together with the nature of the consideration and the name of the person providing the consideration;
(i) the identity of the natural or legal persons or companies or firms by which or in whose name the statutes or the instrument of incorporation, or where the company was not formed at the same time, the drafts of those documents, have been signed;
(j) the total amount, or at least an estimate, of all the costs payable by the company or chargeable to it by reason of its formation and, where appropriate, before the company is authorised to commence business;
(k) any special advantage granted, at the time the company is formed or up to the time it receives authorisation to commence business, to anyone who has taken part in the formation of the company or in transactions leading to the grant of such authorisation.

Article 5. 1. Where the laws of a Member State prescribe that a company may not commence business without authorisation, they shall also make provision for responsibility for liabilities incurred by or on behalf of the company during the period before such authorisation is granted or refused.
2. Paragraph 1 shall not apply to liabilities under contracts concluded by the company conditionally upon its being granted authorisation to commence business.

Article 6. 1. Where the laws of a Member State require a company to be formed by more than one member, the fact that all the shares are held by one person or that the number of members has fallen

below the legal minimum after incorporation of the company shall not lead to the automatic dissolution of the company.
2. If, in the cases referred to in paragraph 1, the laws of a Member State permit the company to be wound up by order of the court, the judge having jurisdiction shall be able to give the company sufficient time to regularise its position.
3. Where a winding-up order as referred to in paragraph 2 is made, the company shall enter into liquidation.

Section 2. Nullity of the limited liability company and validity of its obligations

Article 7. 1. The coordination measures prescribed by this Section shall apply to the laws, regulations and administrative provisions of the Member States relating to the types of company listed in Annex II.
2. If, before a company being formed has acquired legal personality, action has been carried out in its name and the company does not assume the obligations arising from such action, the persons who acted shall without limit, be jointly and severally liable therefor, unless otherwise agreed.

Article 8. Completion of the formalities of disclosure of the particulars concerning the persons who, as an organ of the company, are authorised to represent it, shall constitute a bar to any irregularity in their appointment being relied upon as against third parties, unless the company proves that such third parties had knowledge thereof.

Article 9. . Acts done by the organs of the company shall be binding upon it even if those acts are not within the objects of the company, unless such acts exceed the powers that the law confers or allows to be conferred on those organs.
However, Member States may provide that the company shall not be bound where such acts are outside the objects of the company, if it proves that the third party knew that the act was outside those objects or could not in view of the circumstances have been unaware of it. Disclosure of the statutes shall not of itself be sufficient proof thereof.
2. The limits on the powers of the organs of the company, arising under the statutes or from a decision of the competent organs, may not be relied on as against third parties, even if they have been disclosed.
3. If national law provides that authority to represent a company may, in derogation from the legal rules governing the subject, be conferred by the statutes on a single person or on several persons acting jointly, that law may provide that such a provision in the statutes may be relied on as against third parties on condition that it relates to the general power of representation; the question whether such a provision in the statutes can be relied on as against third parties shall be governed by Article 16.

Article 10. In all Member States whose laws do not provide for preventive administrative or judicial control, at the time of formation of a company, the instrument of constitution, the company statutes and any amendments to those documents shall be drawn up and certified in due legal form.

Article 11. The laws of the Member States may not provide for the nullity of companies otherwise than in accordance with the following provisions:
(a) nullity must be ordered by decision of a court of law;
(b) nullity may be ordered only on the grounds:
(i) that no instrument of constitution was executed or that the rules of preventive control or the requisite legal formalities were not complied with;
(ii) that the objects of the company are unlawful or contrary to public policy;
(iii) that the instrument of constitution or the statutes do not state the name of the company, the amount of the individual subscriptions of capital, the total amount of the capital subscribed or the objects of the company;
(iv) of failure to comply with provisions of national law concerning the minimum amount of capital to be paid up;
(v) of the incapacity of all the founder members;
(vi) that, contrary to the national law governing the company, the number of founder members is less than two.
Apart from the grounds of nullity referred to in the first paragraph, a company shall not be subject to any cause of non-existence, absolute nullity, relative nullity or declaration of nullity.

Article 12. 1. The question whether a decision of nullity pronounced by a court of law may be relied on as against third parties shall be governed by Article 16. Where the national law entitles a third

party to challenge the decision, he may do so only within six months of public notice of the decision of the court being given.
2. Nullity shall entail the winding-up of the company, as may dissolution.
3. Nullity shall not of itself affect the validity of any commitments entered into by or with the company, without prejudice to the consequences of the company's being wound up.
4. The laws of each Member State may make provision for the consequences of nullity as between members of the company.
5. Holders of shares in the capital of a company shall remain obliged to pay up the capital agreed to be subscribed by them but which has not been paid up, to the extent that commitments entered into with creditors so require.

Chapter III. Disclosure and interconnection of central, commercial and companies registers

Section 1. General provisions

Article 13. The coordination measures prescribed by this Section shall apply to the laws, regulations and administrative provisions of the Member States relating to the types of company listed in Annex II.

Article 14. Member States shall take the measures required to ensure compulsory disclosure by companies of at least the following documents and particulars:
(a) the instrument of constitution, and the statutes if they are contained in a separate instrument;
(b) any amendments to the instruments referred to in point (a), including any extension of the duration of the company;
(c) after every amendment of the instrument of constitution or of the statutes, the complete text of the instrument or statutes as amended to date;
(d) the appointment, termination of office and particulars of the persons who either as a body constituted pursuant to law or as members of any such body:
(i) are authorised to represent the company in dealings with third parties and in legal proceedings; it shall be apparent from the disclosure whether the persons authorised to represent the company may do so alone or are required to act jointly;
(ii) take part in the administration, supervision or control of the company;
(e) at least once a year, the amount of the capital subscribed, where the instrument of constitution or the statutes mention an authorised capital, unless any increase in the capital subscribed necessitates an amendment of the statutes;
(f) the accounting documents for each financial year which are required to be published in accordance with Council Directives 86/635/EEC and 91/674/EEC and Directive 2013/34/EU of the European Parliament and of the Council;
(g) any change of the registered office of the company;
(h) the winding-up of the company;
(i) any declaration of nullity of the company by the courts;
(j) the appointment of liquidators, particulars concerning them, and their respective powers, unless such powers are expressly and exclusively derived from law or from the statutes of the company;
(k) any termination of a liquidation and, in Member States where striking off the register entails legal consequences, the fact of any such striking off.

Article 15. 1. Member States shall take the measures required to ensure that any changes in the documents and particulars referred to in Article 14 are entered in the competent register referred to in the first subparagraph of Article 16(1) and are disclosed, in accordance with Article 16(3) and (5), normally within 21 days of receipt of the complete documentation regarding those changes including, if applicable, the legality check as required under national law for entry in the file.
2. Paragraph 1 shall not apply to the accounting documents referred to in Article 14(f).

Article 16. 1. In each Member State, a file shall be opened in a central, commercial or companies register ('the register'), for each of the companies registered therein.
Member States shall ensure that companies have a unique identifier allowing them to be unequivocally identified in communications between registers through the system of interconnection of central, commercial and companies registers established in accordance with Article 22(2) ('the system of interconnection of registers'). That unique identifier shall comprise, at least, elements making it possible to identify the Member State of the register, the domestic register of origin and the company number in that register and, where appropriate, features to avoid identification errors.
2. For the purposes of this Article, 'by electronic means' shall mean that the information is sent ini-

tially and received at its destination by means of electronic equipment for the processing (including digital compression) and storage of data, and entirely transmitted, conveyed and received in a manner to be determined by Member States by wire, by radio, by optical means or by other electromagnetic means.

3. All documents and particulars which are required to be disclosed pursuant to Article 14 shall be kept in the file, or entered in the register; the subject matter of the entries in the register shall in every case appear in the file.

Member States shall ensure that the filing by companies, as well as by other persons and bodies required to make or assist in making notifications, of all documents and particulars which are required to be disclosed pursuant to Article 14 is possible by electronic means. In addition, Member States may require all, or certain categories of, companies to file all, or certain types of, such documents and particulars by electronic means.

All documents and particulars referred to in Article 14 which are filed, whether by paper means or by electronic means, shall be kept in the file, or entered in the register, in electronic form. To this end, Member States shall ensure that all such documents and particulars which are filed by paper means are converted by the register to electronic form.

The documents and particulars referred to in Article 14 that have been filed by paper means up to 31 December 2006, shall not be required to be converted automatically into electronic form by the register. Member States shall nevertheless ensure that they are converted into electronic form by the register upon receipt of an application for disclosure by electronic means submitted in accordance with the measures adopted to give effect to paragraph 4 of this Article.

4. A copy of all or any part of the documents or particulars referred to in Article 14 shall be obtainable on application. Applications may be submitted to the register by paper means or by electronic means as the applicant chooses.

Copies as referred to in the first subparagraph shall be obtainable from the register by paper means or by electronic means as the applicant chooses. This shall apply in the case of all documents and particulars already filed. However, Member States may decide that all, or certain types of, documents and particulars filed by paper means on or before a date which may not be later than 31 December 2006 shall not be obtainable from the register by electronic means if a specified period has elapsed between the date of filing and the date of the application submitted to the register. Such specified period may not be less than 10 years.

The price of obtaining a copy of the whole or any part of the documents or particulars referred to in Article 14, whether by paper means or by electronic means, shall not exceed the administrative cost thereof.

Paper copies supplied to an applicant shall be certified as 'true copies', unless the applicant dispenses with such certification. Electronic copies supplied shall not be certified as 'true copies', unless the applicant explicitly requests such a certification.

Member States shall take the necessary measures to ensure that certification of electronic copies guarantees both the authenticity of their origin and the integrity of their contents, by means at least of an advanced electronic signature within the meaning of Article 2(2) of Directive 1999/93/EC of the European Parliament and of the Council.

5. Disclosure of the documents and particulars referred to in paragraph 3 shall be effected by publication in the national gazette designated for that purpose by the Member State, either of the full text or of a partial text, or by means of a reference to the document which has been deposited in the file or entered in the register. The national gazette designated for that purpose may be kept in electronic form.

Member States may decide to replace publication in the national gazette with equally effective means, which shall entail at least the use of a system whereby the information disclosed can be accessed in chronological order through a central electronic platform.

6. The documents and particulars may be relied on by the company as against third parties only after they have been disclosed in accordance with paragraph 5, unless the company proves that the third parties had knowledge thereof.

However, with regard to transactions taking place before the sixteenth day following the disclosure, the documents and particulars shall not be relied on as against third parties who prove that it was impossible for them to have had knowledge thereof.

7. Member States shall take the necessary measures to avoid any discrepancy between what is disclosed in accordance with paragraph 5 and what appears in the register or file.

However, in cases of discrepancy, the text disclosed in accordance with paragraph 5 may not be relied on as against third parties; such third parties may nevertheless rely thereon, unless the company proves that they had knowledge of the texts deposited in the file or entered in the register.

Third parties may, moreover, always rely on any documents and particulars in respect of which the disclosure formalities have not yet been completed, save where non-disclosure causes them not to have effect.

Article 17. 1. Member States shall ensure that up-to-date information is made available explaining the provisions of national law pursuant to which third parties may rely on particulars and each type of document referred to in Article 14, in accordance with Article 16(5), (6) and (7).
2. Member States shall provide the information required for publication on the European e-Justice portal ('the portal') in accordance with the portal's rules and technical requirements.
3. The Commission shall publish that information on the portal in all the official languages of the Union.

Article 18. 1. Electronic copies of the documents and particulars referred to in Article 14 shall also be made publicly available through the system of interconnection of registers.
2. Member States shall ensure that the documents and particulars referred to in Article 14 are available through the system of interconnection of registers in a standard message format and accessible by electronic means. Member States shall also ensure that minimum standards for the security of data transmission are respected.
3. The Commission shall provide a search service in all the official languages of the Union in respect of companies registered in the Member States, in order to make available through the portal:
(a) the documents and particulars referred to in Article 14;
(b) the explanatory labels, available in all the official languages of the Union, listing those particulars and the types of those documents.

Article 19. 1. The fees charged for obtaining the documents and particulars referred to in Article 14 through the system of interconnection of registers shall not exceed the administrative costs thereof.
2. Member States shall ensure that the following particulars are available free of charge through the system of interconnection of registers:
(a) the name and legal form of the company;
(b) the registered office of the company and the Member State where it is registered; and
(c) the registration number of the company.
In addition to those particulars, Member States may choose to make further documents and particulars available free of charge.

Article 20. 1. The register of a company shall, through the system of interconnection of registers, make available, without delay, the information on the opening and termination of any winding-up or insolvency proceedings of the company and on the striking-off of the company from the register, if this entails legal consequences in the Member State of the register of the company.
2. The register of the branch shall, through the system of interconnection of registers, ensure receipt, without delay, of the information referred to in paragraph 1.
3. The exchange of information referred to in paragraphs 1 and 2 shall be free of charge for the registers.

Article 21. 1. Documents and particulars to be disclosed pursuant to Article 14 shall be drawn up and filed in one of the languages permitted by the language rules applicable in the Member State in which the file referred to in Article 16(1) is opened.
2. In addition to the compulsory disclosure referred to in Article 16, Member States shall allow translations of documents and particulars referred to in Article 14 to be disclosed voluntarily in accordance with Article 16 in any official language(s) of the Union.
Member States may prescribe that the translation of such documents and particulars be certified.
Member States shall take the necessary measures to facilitate access by third parties to the translations voluntarily disclosed.
3. In addition to the compulsory disclosure referred to in Article 16, and to the voluntary disclosure provided for under paragraph 2 of this Article, Member States may allow the documents and particulars concerned to be disclosed, in accordance with Article 16, in any other language(s).
Member States may prescribe that the translation of such documents and particulars be certified.
4. In cases of discrepancy between the documents and particulars disclosed in the official languages of the register and the translation voluntarily disclosed, the latter may not be relied upon as against third parties. Third parties may nevertheless rely on the translations voluntarily disclosed, unless the company proves that the third parties had knowledge of the version which was the subject of the compulsory disclosure.

Article 22. 1. A European central platform ('the platform') shall be established.
2. The system of interconnection of registers shall be composed of:
— the registers of Member States,
— the platform,
— the portal serving as the European electronic access point.
3. Member States shall ensure the interoperability of their registers within the system of interconnection of registers via the platform.
4. Member States may establish optional access points to the system of interconnection of registers. They shall notify the Commission without undue delay of the establishment of such access points and of any significant changes to their operation.
5. Access to information from the system of interconnection of registers shall be ensured through the portal and through the optional access points established by the Member States.
6. The establishment of the system of interconnection of registers shall not affect existing bilateral agreements concluded between Member States concerning the exchange of information on companies.

Article 23. 1. The Commission shall decide to develop and/or operate the platform either by its own means or through a third party.
If the Commission decides to develop and/or operate the platform through a third party, the choice of the third party and the enforcement by the Commission of the agreement concluded with that third party shall be done in accordance with Regulation (EU, Euratom) No 966/2012.
2. If the Commission decides to develop the platform through a third party, it shall, by means of implementing acts, establish the technical specifications for the purpose of the public procurement procedure and the duration of the agreement to be concluded with that third party.
3. If the Commission decides to operate the platform through a third party, it shall, by means of implementing acts, adopt detailed rules on the operational management of the platform.
The operational management of the platform shall include, in particular:
— the supervision of the functioning of the platform,
— the security and protection of data distributed and exchanged using the platform,
— the coordination of relations between Member States' registers and the third party.
The supervision of the functioning of the platform shall be carried out by the Commission.
4. The implementing acts referred to in paragraphs 2 and 3 shall be adopted in accordance with the examination procedure referred to in Article 164(2).

Article 24. By means of implementing acts, the Commission shall adopt the following:
(a) the technical specification defining the methods of communication by electronic means for the purpose of the system of interconnection of registers;
(b) the technical specification of the communication protocols;
(c) the technical measures ensuring the minimum information technology security standards for communication and distribution of information within the system of interconnection of registers;
(d) the technical specification defining the methods of exchange of information between the register of the company and the register of the branch as referred to in Articles 20 and 34;
(e) the detailed list of data to be transmitted for the purpose of exchange of information between registers, as referred to in Articles 20, 34 and 130;
(f) the technical specification defining the structure of the standard message format for the purpose of the exchange of information between the registers, the platform and the portal;
(g) the technical specification defining the set of the data necessary for the platform to perform its functions as well as the method of storage, use and protection of such data;
(h) the technical specification defining the structure and use of the unique identifier for communication between registers;
(i) the specification defining the technical methods of operation of the system of interconnection of registers as regards the distribution and exchange of information, and the specification defining the information technology services, provided by the platform, ensuring the delivery of messages in the relevant language version;
(j) the harmonised criteria for the search service provided by the portal;
(k) the payment modalities, taking into account available payment facilities such as online payment;
(l) the details of the explanatory labels listing the particulars and the types of documents referred to in Article 14;
(m) the technical conditions of availability of services provided by the system of interconnection of registers;
(n) the procedure and technical requirements for the connection of the optional access points to the platform.

Those implementing acts shall be adopted in accordance with the examination procedure referred to in Article 164(2).

Article 25. 1. The establishment and future development of the platform and the adjustments to the portal resulting from this Directive shall be financed from the general budget of the Union.
2. The maintenance and functioning of the platform shall be financed from the general budget of the Union and may be co-financed by fees for access to the system of interconnection of registers charged to its individual users. Nothing in this paragraph shall affect fees at the national level.
3. By means of delegated acts and in accordance with Article 163, the Commission may adopt rules on whether to co-finance the platform by charging fees, and, in that case, the amount of the fees charged to individual users in accordance with paragraph 2 of this Article.
4. Any fees imposed in accordance with paragraph 2 of this Article shall be without prejudice to the fees, if any, charged by Member States for obtaining documents and particulars as referred to in Article 19(1).
5. Any fees imposed in accordance with paragraph 2 of this Article shall not be charged for obtaining the particulars referred to in Article 19(2)(a), (b) and (c).
6. Each Member State shall bear the costs of adjusting its domestic registers, as well as their maintenance and functioning costs resulting from this Directive.

Article 26. Member States shall prescribe that letters and order forms, whether they are in paper form or use any other medium, are to state the following particulars:
(a) the information necessary in order to identify the register in which the file referred to in Article 16 is kept, together with the number of the company in that register;
(b) the legal form of the company, the location of its registered office and, where appropriate, the fact that the company is being wound up.
Where, in those documents, mention is made of the capital of the company, the reference shall be to the capital subscribed and paid up.
Member States shall prescribe that company websites are to contain at least the particulars referred to in the first paragraph and, if applicable, a reference to the capital subscribed and paid up.

Article 27. Each Member State shall determine by which persons the disclosure formalities are to be carried out.

Article 28. Member States shall provide for appropriate penalties at least in the case of:
(a) failure to disclose accounting documents as required by Article 14(f);
(b) omission from commercial documents or from any company website of the compulsory particulars provided for in Article 26.

Section 2. Disclosure rules applicable to branches of companies from other Member States

Article 29. 1. Documents and particulars relating to a branch opened in a Member State by a company of a type listed in Annex II, which is governed by the law of another Member State, shall be disclosed pursuant to the law of the Member State of the branch, in accordance with Article 16.
2. Where disclosure requirements in respect of the branch differ from those in respect of the company, the branch's disclosure requirements shall take precedence with regard to transactions carried out with the branch.
3. The documents and particulars referred to in Article 30(1) shall be made publicly available through the system of interconnection of registers. Article 18 and Article 19(1) shall apply mutatis mutandis.
4. Member States shall ensure that branches have a unique identifier allowing them to be unequivocally identified in communications between registers through the system of interconnection of registers. That unique identifier shall comprise, at least, elements making it possible to identify the Member State of the register, the domestic register of origin and the branch number in that register, and, where appropriate, features to avoid identification errors.

Article 30. 1. The compulsory disclosure provided for in Article 29 shall cover the following documents and particulars only:
(a) the address of the branch;
(b) the activities of the branch;
(c) the register in which the company file referred to in Article 16 is kept, together with the registration number in that register;
(d) the name and legal form of the company and the name of the branch, if that is different from the name of the company;

(e) the appointment, termination of office and particulars of the persons who are authorised to represent the company in dealings with third parties and in legal proceedings:
— as a company organ constituted pursuant to law or as members of any such organ, in accordance with the disclosure by the company as provided for in Article 14(d),
— as permanent representatives of the company for the activities of the branch, with an indication of the extent of their powers;
(f) — the winding-up of the company, the appointment of liquidators, particulars concerning them and their powers and the termination of the liquidation in accordance with disclosure by the company as provided for in Article 14(h), (j) and (k),
— insolvency proceedings, arrangements, compositions, or any analogous proceedings to which the company is subject;
(g) the accounting documents in accordance with Article 31;
(h) the closure of the branch.
2. The Member State in which the branch has been opened may provide for the disclosure, as referred to in Article 29, of
(a) the signature of the persons referred to in points (e) and (f) of paragraph 1 of this Article;
(b) the instruments of constitution and the memorandum and articles of association if they are contained in a separate instrument, in accordance with points (a), (b) and (c) of Article 14, together with amendments to those documents;
(c) an attestation from the register referred to in point (c) of paragraph 1 of this Article relating to the existence of the company;
(d) an indication of the securities on the company's property situated in that Member State, provided such disclosure relates to the validity of those securities.

Article 31. The compulsory disclosure provided for by Article 30(1)(g) shall be limited to the accounting documents of the company as drawn up, audited and disclosed pursuant to the law of the Member State by which the company is governed in accordance with Directive 2006/43/EC of the European Parliament and of the Council and Directive 2013/34/EU.

Article 32. The Member State in which the branch has been opened may stipulate that the documents referred to in Article 30(2)(b) and Article 31 are to be published in another official language of the Union and that the translations of such documents are to be certified.

Article 33. Where a company has opened more than one branch in a Member State, the disclosure referred to in Article 30(2)(b) and Article 31 may be made in the register of the branch of the company's choice.
In the case referred to in the first paragraph, compulsory disclosure by the other branches shall cover the particulars of the branch register of which disclosure was made, together with the number of that branch in that register.

Article 34. 1. Article 20 shall apply to the register of the company and to the register of the branch respectively.
2. Member States shall determine the procedure to be followed upon receipt of the information referred to in Article 20(1) and (2). Such procedure shall ensure that, where a company has been dissolved or otherwise struck off the register, its branches are likewise struck off the register without undue delay.
3. The second sentence of paragraph 2 shall not apply to branches of companies that have been struck off the register as a consequence of any change in the legal form of the company concerned, a merger or division, or a cross-border transfer of its registered office.

Article 35. Member States shall prescribe that letters and order forms used by a branch shall state, in addition to the information prescribed by Article 26, the register in which the file in respect of the branch is kept together with the number of the branch in that register.

Section 3. Disclosure rules applicable to branches of companies from third countries

Article 36. . Documents and particulars concerning a branch opened in a Member State by a company which is not governed by the law of a Member State but which is of a legal form comparable with the types of company listed in Annex II, shall be disclosed in accordance with the law of the Member State of the branch as laid down in Article 16.
2. Article 29(2) shall apply.

Article 37. The compulsory disclosure provided for in Article 36 shall cover at least the following documents and particulars:

(a) the address of the branch;
(b) the activities of the branch;
(c) the law of the State by which the company is governed;
(d) where that law so provides, the register in which the company is entered and the registration number of the company in that register;
(e) the instruments of constitution, and memorandum and articles of association if they are contained in a separate instrument, with all amendments to those documents;
(f) the legal form of the company, its principal place of business and its object and, at least annually, the amount of subscribed capital if those particulars are not given in the documents referred to in point (e);
(g) the name of the company and the name of the branch if that is different from the name of the company;
(h) the appointment, termination of office and particulars of the persons who are authorised to represent the company in dealings with third parties and in legal proceedings:
— as a company organ constituted pursuant to law or as members of any such organ,
as permanent representatives of the company for the activities of the branch.
The extent of the powers of the persons authorised to represent the company shall be stated, as well as whether those persons may represent the company alone or are required to act jointly;
(i)
— the winding-up of the company and the appointment of liquidators, particulars concerning them and their powers and the termination of the liquidation,
— insolvency proceedings, arrangements, compositions or any analogous proceedings to which the company is subject;
(j) the accounting documents in accordance with Article 38;
(k) the closure of the branch.

Article 38. 1. The compulsory disclosure provided for by Article 37(j) shall apply to the accounting documents of the company as drawn up, audited and disclosed pursuant to the law of the State which governs the company. Where they are not drawn up in accordance with or in a manner equivalent to Directive 2013/34/EU, Member States may require that accounting documents relating to the activities of the branch be drawn up and disclosed.
2. Articles 32 and 33 shall apply.

Article 39. Member States shall prescribe that letters and order forms used by a branch state the register in which the file in respect of the branch is kept together with the number of the branch in that register. Where the law of the State by which the company is governed requires entry in a register, the register in which the company is entered, and the registration number of the company in that register shall also be stated.

Section 4. Application and implementing arrangements

Article 40. Member States shall provide for appropriate penalties in the event of failure to disclose the matters set out in Articles 29, 30, 31, 36, 37 and 38 and of omission from letters and order forms of the compulsory particulars provided for in Articles 35 and 39.

Article 41. Each Member State shall determine who shall carry out the disclosure formalities provided for in Sections 2 and 3.

Article 42. 1. Articles 31 and 38 shall not apply to branches opened by credit institutions and financial institutions covered by Council Directive 89/117/EEC.
2. Pending subsequent coordination, the Member States need not apply Articles 31 and 38 to branches opened by insurance companies.

Article 43. The Contact Committee set up pursuant to Article 52 of Council Directive 78/660/EEC shall also:
(a) facilitate, without prejudice to Articles 258 and 259 of the Treaty, the harmonised application of the provisions of Sections 2, 3 and this Section, through regular meetings dealing, in particular, with practical problems arising in connection with their application;
(b) advise the Commission, if necessary, on any additions or amendments to the provisions of Sections 2, 3 and this Section.

Chapter IV. Capital maintenance and alteration

Section 1. Capital requirements

Article 44. 1. The coordination measures prescribed by this Chapter shall apply to the provisions laid down by law, regulation or administrative action in Member States relating to the types of company listed in Annex I.
2. The Member States may decide not to apply the provisions of this Chapter to investment companies with variable capital and to cooperatives incorporated as one of the types of company listed in Annex I. In so far as the laws of the Member States make use of this option, they shall require such companies to include the words 'investment company with variable capital', or 'cooperative' in all documents indicated in Article 26.

Article 45. 1. The laws of the Member States shall require that, in order for a company to be incorporated or obtain authorisation to commence business, a minimum capital shall be subscribed the amount of which shall be not less than EUR 25 000.
2. Every five years the European Parliament and the Council, acting on a proposal from the Commission in accordance with Article 50(1) and Article 50(2)(g) of the Treaty, shall examine and, if need be, revise the amount expressed in paragraph 1 in euro in the light of economic and monetary trends in the Union and of the tendency to allow only large and medium-sized undertakings to opt for the types of company listed in Annex I.

Article 46. Subscribed capital may be formed only of assets capable of economic assessment. However, an undertaking to perform work or supply services may not form part of those assets.

Article 47. Shares may not be issued at a price lower than their nominal value, or, where there is no nominal value, their accountable par.
However, Member States may allow those who undertake to place shares in the exercise of their profession to pay less than the total price of the shares for which they subscribe in the course of this transaction.

Article 48 Shares issued for consideration shall be paid up at the time the company is incorporated or is authorised to commence business at not less than 25 % of their nominal value or, in the absence of a nominal value, their accountable par.
However, where shares are issued for consideration other than in cash at the time the company is incorporated or is authorised to commence business, the consideration shall be transferred in full within five years of that time.

Section 2. Safeguards as regards statutory capital

Article 49. 1. A report on any consideration other than in cash shall be drawn up before the company is incorporated or is authorised to commence business, by one or more independent experts appointed or approved by an administrative or judicial authority. Such experts may be natural persons as well as legal persons and companies or firms under the laws of each Member State.
2. The experts' report referred to in paragraph 1 shall contain at least a description of each of the assets comprising the consideration as well as of the methods of valuation used and shall state whether the values arrived at by the application of those methods correspond at least to the number and nominal value or, where there is no nominal value, to the accountable par and, where appropriate, to the premium on the shares to be issued for them.
3. The experts' report shall be published in the manner laid down by the laws of each Member State, in accordance with Article 16.
4. Member States may decide not to apply this Article where 90 % of the nominal value, or where there is no nominal value, of the accountable par, of all the shares is issued to one or more companies for a consideration other than in cash, and where the following requirements are met:
(a) with regard to the company in receipt of such consideration, the persons referred to in point (i) of Article 4 have agreed to dispense with the experts' report;
(b) such agreement has been published as provided for in paragraph 3;
(c) the companies furnishing such consideration have reserves which may not be distributed under the law or the statutes and which are at least equal to the nominal value or, where there is no nominal value, the accountable par of the shares issued for consideration other than in cash;
(d) the companies furnishing such consideration guarantee, up to an amount equal to that indicated in point (c), the debts of the recipient company arising between the time the shares are issued for a consideration other than in cash and one year after the publication of that company's annual accounts for the financial year during which such consideration was furnished. Any transfer of such shares shall be prohibited during that period;
(e) the guarantee referred to in point (d) has been published as provided for in paragraph 3; and

(f) the companies furnishing such consideration shall place a sum equal to that indicated in point (c) into a reserve which may not be distributed until three years after publication of the annual accounts of the recipient company for the financial year during which such consideration was furnished or, if necessary, until such later date as all claims relating to the guarantee referred to in point (d) which are submitted during this period have been settled.

5.   Member States may decide not to apply this Article to the formation of a new company by way of merger or division where a report by one or more independent experts on the draft terms of merger or division is drawn up.

Where Member States decide to apply this Article in the cases referred to in the first subparagraph, they may provide that the report drawn up under paragraph 1 of this Article and the report by one or more independent experts on the draft terms of merger or division may be drawn up by the same expert or experts.

Article 50. 1.   Member States may decide not to apply Article 49(1), (2) and (3) where, upon a decision of the administrative or management body, transferable securities as defined in point 44 of Article 4(1) of Directive 2014/65/EU of the European Parliament and of the Council or money-market instruments as defined in point 17 of Article 4(1) of that Directive are contributed as consideration other than in cash, and those securities or money-market instruments are valued at the weighted average price at which they have been traded on one or more regulated markets as defined in point 21 of Article 4(1) of that Directive during a sufficient period, to be determined by national law, preceding the effective date of the contribution of the respective consideration other than in cash.

However, where that price has been affected by exceptional circumstances that would significantly change the value of the asset at the effective date of its contribution, including situations where the market for such transferable securities or money-market instruments has become illiquid, a revaluation shall be carried out on the initiative and under the responsibility of the administrative or management body.

For the purposes of such revaluation, Article 49(1), (2) and (3) shall apply.

2.   Member States may decide not to apply Article 49(1), (2) and (3) where, upon a decision of the administrative or management body, assets, other than the transferable securities and money-market instruments referred to in paragraph 1 of this Article, are contributed as consideration other than in cash which have already been subject to a fair value opinion by a recognised independent expert and where the following conditions are fulfilled:

(a) the fair value is determined for a date not more than six months before the effective date of the asset contribution; and

(b) the valuation has been performed in accordance with generally accepted valuation standards and principles in the Member State which are applicable to the kind of assets to be contributed.

In the case of new qualifying circumstances that would significantly change the fair value of the asset at the effective date of its contribution, a revaluation shall be carried out on the initiative and under the responsibility of the administrative or management body.

For the purposes of the revaluation referred to in the second subparagraph, Article 49(1), (2) and (3) shall apply.

In the absence of such a revaluation, one or more shareholders holding an aggregate percentage of at least 5 % of the company's subscribed capital on the date the decision on the increase in the capital is taken, may demand a valuation by an independent expert, in which case Article 49(1), (2) and (3) shall apply.

Such shareholder(s) may submit a demand up until the effective date of the asset contribution, provided that, at the date of the demand, the shareholder(s) in question still hold(s) an aggregate percentage of at least 5 % of the company's subscribed capital, as it was on the date the decision on the increase in the capital was taken.

3.   Member States may decide not to apply Article 49(1), (2) and (3) where, upon a decision of the administrative or management body, assets, other than the transferable securities and money-market instruments referred to in paragraph 1 of this Article, are contributed as consideration other than in cash the fair value of which is derived from the value of an individual asset from the statutory accounts of the previous financial year provided that the statutory accounts have been subject to an audit in accordance with Directive 2006/43/EC.

The second to fifth subparagraphs of paragraph 2 of this Article shall apply mutatis mutandis.

Article 51. 1.   Where consideration other than in cash as referred to in Article 50 is provided without an experts' report as referred to in Article 49(1), (2) and (3), in addition to the requirements set out in point (h) of Article 4 and within one month of the effective date of the asset contribution, a declaration containing the following shall be published:

(a) a description of the consideration other than in cash at issue;
(b) its value, the source of this valuation and, where appropriate, the method of valuation;
(c) a statement whether the value arrived at corresponds at least to the number, to the nominal value or, where there is no nominal value, the accountable par and, where appropriate, to the premium on the shares to be issued for such consideration; and
(d) a statement that no new qualifying circumstances with regard to the original valuation have occurred.

The publication of the declaration shall be effected in the manner laid down by the laws of each Member State in accordance with Article 16.

2. Where consideration other than in cash is proposed to be provided without an experts' report, as referred to in Article 49(1), (2) and (3), in relation to an increase in the capital proposed to be made under Article 68(2), an announcement containing the date when the decision on the increase was taken and the information listed in paragraph 1 of this Article shall be published, in the manner laid down by the laws of each Member State in accordance with Article 16, before the contribution of the asset as consideration other than in cash is to become effective. In that event, the declaration pursuant to paragraph 1 of this Article shall be limited to the statement that no new qualifying circumstances have occurred since the aforementioned announcement was published.

3. Each Member State shall provide for adequate safeguards ensuring compliance with the procedure set out in Article 50 and in this Article where a contribution for a consideration other than in cash is provided without an experts' report as referred to in Article 49(1), (2) and (3).

Article 52 1. If, before the expiry of a time limit laid down by national law of at least two years from the time the company is incorporated or is authorised to commence business, the company acquires any asset belonging to a person or company or firm referred to in point (i) of Article 4 for a consideration of not less than one-tenth of the subscribed capital, the acquisition shall be examined and details of it published in the manner provided for in Article 49(1), (2) and (3), and it shall be submitted for the approval of a general meeting.

Articles 50 and 51 shall apply mutatis mutandis.

Member States may also require these provisions to be applied when the assets belong to a shareholder or to any other person.

2. Paragraph 1 shall not apply to acquisitions effected in the normal course of the company's business, to acquisitions effected at the instance or under the supervision of an administrative or judicial authority, or to stock exchange acquisitions.

Article 53. Subject to the provisions relating to the reduction of subscribed capital, the shareholders may not be released from the obligation to pay up their contributions.

Article 54. Pending coordination of national laws at a subsequent date, Member States shall adopt the measures necessary to require provision of at least the same safeguards as are laid down in Articles 3 to 6 and Articles 45 to 53 in the event of the conversion of another type of company into a public limited liability company.

Article 55. Articles 3 to 6 and Articles 45 to 54 shall be without prejudice to the provisions of Member States on competence and procedure relating to the modification of the statutes or of the instrument of incorporation.

Section 3. Rules on distribution

Article 56. 1. Except for cases of reductions of subscribed capital, no distribution to shareholders may be made when on the closing date of the last financial year the net assets as set out in the company's annual accounts are or, following such a distribution, would become, lower than the amount of the subscribed capital plus those reserves which may not be distributed under the law or the statutes of the company.

2. Where the uncalled part of the subscribed capital is not included in the assets shown in the balance sheet, that amount shall be deducted from the amount of subscribed capital referred to in paragraph 1

3. The amount of a distribution to shareholders may not exceed the amount of the profits at the end of the last financial year plus any profits brought forward and sums drawn from reserves available for this purpose, less any losses brought forward and sums placed to reserve in accordance with the law or the statutes.

4. The term 'distribution' used in paragraphs 1 and 3 includes, in particular, the payment of divi-

dends and of interest relating to shares.

5. When the laws of a Member State allow the payment of interim dividends, at least the following conditions shall apply:

(a) interim accounts shall be drawn up showing that the funds available for distribution are sufficient;

(b) the amount to be distributed may not exceed the total profits made since the end of the last financial year for which the annual accounts have been drawn up, plus any profits brought forward and sums drawn from reserves available for this purpose, less losses brought forward and sums to be placed to reserve pursuant to the requirements of the law or the statutes.

6. Paragraphs 1 to 5 shall not affect the provisions of the Member States as regards increases in subscribed capital by capitalisation of reserves.

7. The laws of a Member State may provide for derogation from paragraph 1 in the case of investment companies with fixed capital.

For the purposes of this paragraph, the term 'investment company with fixed capital' means only companies:

(a) the exclusive object of which is to invest their funds in various stocks and shares, land or other assets with the sole aim of spreading investment risks and giving their shareholders the benefit of the results of the management of their assets; and

(b) which offer their own shares for subscription by the public.

In so far as the laws of Member States make use of the option they shall:

(a) require such companies to include the term 'investment company' in all documents indicated in Article 26;

(b) not permit any such company whose net assets fall below the amount specified in paragraph 1 to make a distribution to shareholders when on the closing date of the last financial year the company's total assets as set out in the annual accounts are, or following such distribution would become, less than one-and-a-half times the amount of the company's total liabilities to creditors as set out in the annual accounts; and

(c) require any such company which makes a distribution when its net assets fall below the amount specified in paragraph 1 to include in its annual accounts a note to that effect.

Article 57. Any distribution made contrary to Article 56 shall be returned by shareholders who have received it if the company proves that those shareholders knew of the irregularity of the distributions made to them, or could not in view of the circumstances have been unaware of it.

Article 58. 1. In the case of a serious loss of the subscribed capital, a general meeting of shareholders shall be called within the period laid down by the laws of the Member States, to consider whether the company should be wound up or any other measures taken.

2. The amount of a loss deemed to be serious within the meaning of paragraph 1 shall not be set by the laws of Member States at a figure higher than half the subscribed capital.

Section 4. Rules on companies' aquisitions of their own shares

Article 59. 1. The shares of a company may not be subscribed for by the company itself.

2. If the shares of a company have been subscribed for by a person acting in his or her own name, but on behalf of the company, the subscriber shall be deemed to have subscribed for them for his or her own account.

3. The persons or companies or firms referred to in point (i) of Article 4 or, in cases of an increase in subscribed capital, the members of the administrative or management body shall be liable to pay for shares subscribed in contravention of this Article.

However, the laws of a Member State may provide that any such person may be released from his or her obligation if they prove that no fault is attributable to them personally.

Article 60. 1. Without prejudice to the principle of equal treatment of all shareholders who are in the same position, and to Regulation (EU) No 596/2014, Member States may permit a company to acquire its own shares, either itself or through a person acting in his or her own name but on the company's behalf. To the extent that the acquisitions are permitted, Member States shall make such acquisitions subject to the following conditions:

(a) authorisation is given by the general meeting, which shall determine the terms and conditions of such acquisitions, and, in particular, the maximum number of shares to be acquired, the duration of the period for which the authorisation is given, the maximum length of which shall be determined by national law without, however, exceeding five years, and, in the case of acquisition for value, the maximum and minimum consideration. Members of the administrative or management body shall satisfy themselves that, at the time when each authorised acquisition is effected, the conditions

referred to in points (b) and (c) are respected;
(b) the acquisitions, including shares previously acquired by the company and held by it, and shares acquired by a person acting in his or her own name but on the company's behalf, cannot have the effect of reducing the net assets below the amount referrred to in Article 56(1) and (2); and
(c) only fully paid-up shares can be included in the transaction.
Furthermore, Member States may subject acquisitions within the meaning of the first subparagraph to any of the following conditions:
(a) the nominal value or, in the absence thereof, the accountable par of the acquired shares, including shares previously acquired by the company and held by it, and shares acquired by a person acting in his own name but on the company's behalf, does not exceed a limit to be determined by Member States; this limit may not be lower than 10 % of the subscribed capital;
(b) the power of the company to acquire its own shares within the meaning of the first subparagraph, the maximum number of shares to be acquired, the duration of the period for which the power is given and the maximum or minimum consideration are laid down in the statutes or in the instrument of incorporation of the company;
(c) the company complies with appropriate reporting and notification requirements;
(d) certain companies, as determined by Member States, can be required to cancel the acquired shares provided that an amount equal to the nominal value of the shares cancelled is included in a reserve which cannot be distributed to the shareholders, except in the event of a reduction in the subscribed capital; this reserve may be used only for the purposes of increasing the subscribed capital by the capitalisation of reserves;
(e) the acquisition does not prejudice the satisfaction of creditors' claims.
2. The laws of a Member State may provide for derogations from the first sentence of point (a) of the first subparagraph of paragraph 1 where the acquisition of a company's own shares is necessary to prevent serious and imminent harm to the company. In such a case, the next general meeting shall be informed by the administrative or management body of the reasons for and nature of the acquisitions effected, of the number and nominal value or, in the absence of a nominal value, the accountable par, of the shares acquired, of the proportion of the subscribed capital which they represent, and of the consideration for those shares.
3. Member States may decide not to apply the first sentence of point (a) of the first subparagraph of paragraph 1 to shares acquired by either the company itself or by a person acting in his or her own name but on the company's behalf, for distribution to that company's employees or to the employees of an associate company. Such shares shall be distributed within 12 months of their acquisition.

Article 61 1. Member States may decide not to apply Article 60 to:
(a) shares acquired in carrying out a decision to reduce capital, or in the circumstances referred to in Article 82;
(b) shares acquired as a result of a universal transfer of assets;
(c) fully paid-up shares acquired free of charge or by banks and other financial institutions as purchasing commission;
(d) shares acquired by virtue of a legal obligation or resulting from a court ruling for the protection of minority shareholders in the event, particularly, of a merger, a change in the company's object or form, transfer abroad of the registered office, or the introduction of restrictions on the transfer of shares;
(e) shares acquired from a shareholder in the event of failure to pay them up;
(f) shares acquired in order to indemnify minority shareholders in associated companies;
(g) fully paid-up shares acquired under a sale enforced by a court order for the payment of a debt owed to the company by the owner of the shares; and
(h) fully paid-up shares issued by an investment company with fixed capital, as defined in the second subparagraph of Article 56(7), and acquired at the investor's request by that company or by an associate company. Point (a) of the third subparagraph of Article 56(7) shall apply. Such acquisitions may not have the effect of reducing the net assets below the amount of the subscribed capital plus any reserves the distribution of which is forbidden by law.
2. Shares acquired in the cases listed in points (b) to (g) of paragraph 1 shall, however, be disposed of within not more than three years of their acquisition unless the nominal value or, in the absence of a nominal value, the accountable par of the shares acquired, including shares which the company may have acquired through a person acting in his own name but on the company's behalf, does not exceed 10 % of the subscribed capital.
3. If the shares are not disposed of within the period laid down in paragraph 2, they shall be cancelled. The laws of a Member State may make this cancellation subject to a corresponding reduction

PART III EUROPEAN COMPANY LAW

in the subscribed capital. Such a reduction shall be prescribed where the acquisition of shares to be cancelled results in the net assets having fallen below the amount specified in Article 56(1) and (2).

Article 62. Shares acquired in contravention of Articles 60 and 61 shall be disposed of within one year of their acquisition. If they are not disposed of within that period, Article 61(3) shall apply.

Article 63. 1. Where the laws of a Member State permit a company to acquire its own shares, either itself or through a person acting in his or her own name but on the company's behalf, they shall make the holding of these shares at all times subject to at least the following conditions:
(a) among the rights attaching to the shares, the right to vote attaching to the company's own shares must in any event be suspended;
(b) if the shares are included among the assets shown in the balance sheet, a reserve of the same amount, unavailable for distribution, shall be included among the liabilities.
2. Where the laws of a Member State permit a company to acquire its own shares, either itself or through a person acting in his or her own name but on the company's behalf, they shall require the annual report to state at least:
(a) the reasons for acquisitions made during the financial year;
(b) the number and nominal value or, in the absence of a nominal value, the accountable par of the shares acquired and disposed of during the financial year and the proportion of the subscribed capital which they represent;
(c) in the case of acquisition or disposal for a value, the consideration for the shares;
(d) the number and nominal value or, in the absence of a nominal value, the accountable par of all the shares acquired and held by the company and the proportion of the subscribed capital which they represent.

Article 64. 1. Where Member States permit a company to, either directly or indirectly, advance funds or make loans or provide security, with a view to the acquisition of its shares by a third party, they shall make such transactions subject to the conditions set out in paragraphs 2 to 5.
2. The transactions shall take place under the responsibility of the administrative or management body at fair market conditions, especially with regard to interest received by the company and with regard to security provided to the company for the loans and advances referred to in paragraph 1. The credit standing of the third party or, in the case of multiparty transactions, of each counterparty thereto shall have been duly investigated.
3. The transactions shall be submitted by the administrative or management body to the general meeting for prior approval, whereby the general meeting shall act in accordance with the rules for a quorum and a majority laid down in Article 83.
The administrative or management body shall present a written report to the general meeting, indicating:
(a) the reasons for the transaction;
(b) the interest of the company in entering into such a transaction;
(c) the conditions on which the transaction is entered into;
(d) the risks involved in the transaction for the liquidity and solvency of the company; and
(e)the price at which the third party is to acquire the shares.
This report shall be submitted to the register for publication in accordance with Article 16.
4. The aggregate financial assistance granted to third parties shall at no time result in the reduction of the net assets below the amount specified in Article 56(1) and (2), taking into account also any reduction of the net assets that may have occurred through the acquisition, by the company or on behalf of the company, of its own shares in accordance with Article 60(1).
The company shall include, among the liabilities in the balance sheet, a reserve, unavailable for distribution, of the amount of the aggregate financial assistance.
5. Where a third party by means of financial assistance from a company acquires that company's own shares within the meaning of Article 60(1) or subscribes for shares issued in the course of an increase in the subscribed capital, such acquisition or subscription shall be made at a fair price.
6. Paragraphs 1 to 5 shall not apply to transactions concluded by banks and other financial institutions in the normal course of business, nor to transactions effected with a view to the acquisition of shares by or for the company's employees or the employees of an associate company.
However, these transactions may not have the effect of reducing the net assets below the amount specified in Article 56(1).
7. Paragraphs 1 to 5 shall not apply to transactions effected with a view to acquisition of shares as described in of Article 61(1)(h).

Article 65. In cases where individual members of the administrative or management body of the company being party to a transaction referred to in Article 64(1) of this Directive, or of the administrative or management body of a parent undertaking within the meaning of Article 22 of Directive 2013/34/EU or such parent undertaking itself, or individuals acting in their own name, but on behalf of the members of such bodies or on behalf of such undertaking, are counterparties to such a transaction, Member States shall ensure through adequate safeguards that such transaction does not conflict with the company's best interests.

Article 66. 1. The acceptance of the company's own shares as security, either by the company itself or through a person acting in his own name but on the company's behalf, shall be treated as an acquisition for the purposes of Article 60, Article 61(1), and Articles 63 and 64.
2. The Member States may decide not to apply paragraph 1 to transactions concluded by banks and other financial institutions in the normal course of business.

Article 67 1. The subscription, acquisition or holding of shares in a public limited liability company by another company of a type listed in Annex II in which the public limited liability company directly or indirectly holds a majority of the voting rights or on which it can directly or indirectly exercise a dominant influence shall be regarded as having been effected by the public limited liability company itself.
The first subparagraph shall also apply where the other company is governed by the law of a third country and has a legal form comparable to those listed in Annex II.
However, where the public limited liability company holds a majority of the voting rights indirectly or can exercise a dominant influence indirectly, Member States need not apply the first and the second subparagraphs if they provide for the suspension of the voting rights attached to the shares in the public limited liability company held by the other company.
2. In the absence of coordination of national legislation on groups of companies, Member States may:
(a) define the cases in which a public limited liability company shall be regarded as being able to exercise a dominant influence on another company; if a Member State exercises this option, its national law shall in any event provide that a dominant influence can be exercised if a public limited liability company:
(i) has the right to appoint or dismiss a majority of the members of the administrative organ, of the management organ or of the supervisory organ, and is at the same time a shareholder or member of the other company; or
(ii) is a shareholder or member of the other company and has sole control of a majority of the voting rights of its shareholders or members under an agreement concluded with other shareholders or members of that company.
Member States shall not be obliged to make provision for any cases other than those referred to in points (i) and (ii) of the first subparagraph;
(b) define the cases in which a public limited liability company shall be regarded as indirectly holding voting rights or as able indirectly to exercise a dominant influence;
(c) specify the circumstances in which a public limited liability company shall be regarded as holding voting rights.
3. Member States need not apply the first and second subparagraphs of paragraph 1 where the subscription, acquisition or holding is effected on behalf of a person other than the person subscribing, acquiring or holding the shares, who is neither the public limited liability company referred to in paragraph 1 nor another company in which the public limited liability company directly or indirectly holds a majority of the voting rights or on which it can directly or indirectly exercise a dominant influence.
4. Member States need not apply the first and second subparagraphs of paragraph 1 where the subscription, acquisition or holding is effected by the other company in its capacity and in the context of its activities as a professional dealer in securities, provided that it is a member of a stock exchange situated or operating within a Member State, or is approved or supervised by an authority of a Member State competent to supervise professional dealers in securities which, within the meaning of this Directive, may include credit institutions.
5. Member States need not apply the first and second subparagraphs of paragraph 1 where shares in a public limited liability company held by another company were acquired before the relationship between the two companies corresponded to the criteria laid down in paragraph 1.
However, the voting rights attached to those shares shall be suspended and the shares shall be taken into account when it is determined whether the condition laid down in Article 60(1)(b) is fulfilled.
6. Member States need not apply Article 61(2) or (3) or Article 62 where shares in a public limited liability company are acquired by another company on condition that they provide for:

(a) the suspension of the voting rights attached to the shares in the public limited liability company held by the other company; and

(b) the members of the administrative or the management organ of the public limited liability company to be obliged to buy back from the other company the shares referred to in Article 61(2) and (3) and Article 62 at the price at which the other company acquired them; this sanction shall be inapplicable only where the members of the administrative or the management organ of the public limited liability company prove that that company played no part whatsoever in the subscription for or acquisition of the shares in question.

Section 5. Rules for the increase and reduction of capital

Article 68. 1. Any increase in capital shall be decided upon by the general meeting. Both that decision and the increase in the subscribed capital shall be published in the manner laid down by the laws of each Member State, in accordance with Article 16.

2. Nevertheless, the statutes or instrument of incorporation or the general meeting, the decision of which is to be published in accordance with the rules referred to in paragraph 1, may authorise an increase in the subscribed capital up to a maximum amount which they shall fix with due regard for any maximum amount provided for by law. Where appropriate, the increase in the subscribed capital shall be decided on within the limits of the amount fixed by the company body empowered to do so. The power of such body in this respect shall be for a maximum period of five years and may be renewed one or more times by the general meeting, each time for a period not exceeding five years.

3. Where there are several classes of shares, the decision by the general meeting concerning the increase in capital referred to in paragraph 1 or the authorisation to increase the capital referred to in paragraph 2, shall be subject to a separate vote at least for each class of shareholder whose rights are affected by the transaction.

4. This Article shall apply to the issue of all securities which are convertible into shares or which carry the right to subscribe for shares, but not to the conversion of such securities, nor to the exercise of the right to subscribe.

Article 69. Shares issued for consideration, in the course of an increase in subscribed capital, shall be paid up to at least 25 % of their nominal value or, in the absence of a nominal value, of their accountable par. Where provision is made for an issue premium, it shall be paid in full.

Article 70. 1. Where shares are issued for consideration other than in cash in the course of an increase in the subscribed capital, the consideration shall be transferred in full within a period of five years from the decision to increase the subscribed capital.

2. The consideration referred to in paragraph 1 shall be the subject of a report drawn up before the increase in capital is made by one or more experts who are independent of the company and appointed or approved by an administrative or judicial authority. Such experts may be natural persons as well as legal persons and companies and firms under the laws of each Member State.
Article 49(2) and (3) and Articles 50 and 51 shall apply.

3. Member States may decide not to apply paragraph 2 in the event of an increase in subscribed capital made in order to give effect to a merger, a division or a public offer for the purchase or exchange of shares and to pay the shareholders of the company which is being absorbed or divided, or which is the object of the public offer for the purchase or exchange of shares.
In the case of a merger or a division, however, Member States shall apply the first subparagraph only where a report by one or more independent experts on the draft terms of merger or division is drawn up.
Where Member States decide to apply paragraph 2 in the case of a merger or a division, they may provide that the report under this Article and the report by one or more independent experts on the draft terms of merger or division may be drawn up by the same expert or experts.

4. Member States may decide not to apply paragraph 2 if all the shares issued in the course of an increase in subscribed capital are issued for a consideration other than in cash to one or more companies, on condition that all the shareholders in the company which receive the consideration have agreed not to have an experts' report drawn up and that the requirements of points (b) to (f) of Article 49(4) are met.

Article 71. Where an increase in capital is not fully subscribed, the capital will be increased by the amount of the subscriptions received only if the conditions of the issue so provide.

Article 72. 1. Whenever the capital is increased by consideration in cash, the shares shall be offered on a pre-emptive basis to shareholders in proportion to the capital represented by their shares.

2. The laws of a Member State:
(a) need not apply paragraph 1 to shares which carry a limited right to participate in distributions within the meaning of Article 56 and/or in the company's assets in the event of liquidation; or
(b) may permit, where the subscribed capital of a company having several classes of shares carrying different rights with regard to voting, or participation in distributions within the meaning of Article 56 or in assets in the event of liquidation, is increased by issuing new shares in only one of these classes, the right of pre-emption of shareholders of the other classes to be exercised only after the exercise of this right by the shareholders of the class in which the new shares are being issued.
3. Any offer of subscription on a pre-emptive basis and the period within which this right shall be exercised shall be published in the national gazette appointed in accordance with Article 16. However, the laws of a Member State need not provide for such publication where all of a company's shares are registered. In such case, all the company's shareholders shall be informed in writing. The right of pre-emption shall be exercised within a period which shall not be less than 14 days from the date of publication of the offer or from the date of dispatch of the letters to the shareholders.
4. The right of pre-emption may not be restricted or withdrawn by the statutes or instrument of incorporation. This may, however, be done by decision of the general meeting. The administrative or management body shall be required to present to such a meeting a written report indicating the reasons for restriction or withdrawal of the right of pre-emption, and justifying the proposed issue price. The general meeting shall act in accordance with the rules for a quorum and a majority laid down in Article 83. Its decision shall be published in the manner laid down by the laws of each Member State, in accordance with Article 16.
5. The laws of a Member State may provide that the statutes, the instrument of incorporation or the general meeting, acting in accordance with the rules for a quorum, a majority and publication set out in paragraph 4 of this Article, may give the power to restrict or withdraw the right of pre-emption to the company body which is empowered to decide on an increase in subscribed capital within the limit of the authorised capital. This power may not be granted for a longer period than the power for which provision is made in Article 68(2).
6. Paragraphs 1 to 5 shall apply to the issue of all securities which are convertible into shares or which carry the right to subscribe for shares, but not to the conversion of such securities, nor to the exercise of the right to subscribe.
7. The right of pre-emption is not excluded for the purposes of paragraphs 4 and 5 where, in accordance with the decision to increase the subscribed capital, shares are issued to banks or other financial institutions with a view to their being offered to shareholders of the company in accordance with paragraphs 1 and 3.

Article 73. Any reduction in the subscribed capital, except under a court order, shall be subject at least to a decision of the general meeting acting in accordance with the rules for a quorum and a majority laid down in Article 83 without prejudice to Articles 79 and 80. Such decision shall be published in the manner laid down by the laws of each Member State in accordance with Article 16. The notice convening the meeting shall specify at least the purpose of the reduction and the way in which it is to be carried out.

Article 74. Where there are several classes of shares, the decision by the general meeting concerning a reduction in the subscribed capital shall be subject to a separate vote, at least for each class of shareholders whose rights are affected by the transaction.

Article 75. 1. In the event of a reduction in the subscribed capital, at least the creditors whose claims antedate the publication of the decision on the reduction shall at least have the right to obtain security for claims which have not fallen due by the date of that publication. Member States may not set aside such a right unless the creditor has adequate safeguards, or unless such safeguards are not necessary having regard to the assets of the company.
Member States shall lay down the conditions for the exercise of the right provided for in the first subparagraph. In any event, Member States shall ensure that the creditors are authorised to apply to the appropriate administrative or judicial authority for adequate safeguards provided that they can credibly demonstrate that due to the reduction in the subscribed capital the satisfaction of their claims is at stake, and that no adequate safeguards have been obtained from the company.
2. The laws of the Member States shall also stipulate at least that the reduction shall be void, or that no payment may be made for the benefit of the shareholders, until the creditors have obtained satisfaction or a court has decided that their application should not be acceded to.
3. This Article shall apply where the reduction in the subscribed capital is brought about by the total or partial waiving of the payment of the balance of the shareholders' contributions.

Article 76. 1. Member States need not apply Article 75 to a reduction in the subscribed capital the purpose of which is to offset losses incurred or to include sums of money in a reserve provided that, following this operation, the amount of such reserve is not more than 10 % of the reduced subscribed capital. Except in the event of a reduction in the subscribed capital, this reserve may not be distributed to shareholders; it may be used only for offsetting losses incurred or for increasing the subscribed capital by the capitalisation of such reserve, in so far as the Member States permit such an operation.

2. In the cases referred to in paragraph 1, the laws of the Member States shall at least provide for the measures necessary to ensure that the amounts deriving from the reduction of subscribed capital may not be used for making payments or distributions to shareholders, or discharging shareholders from the obligation to make their contributions.

Article 77. The subscribed capital may not be reduced to an amount less than the minimum capital laid down in accordance with Article 45.

However, Member States may permit such a reduction if they also provide that the decision to reduce the subscribed capital may take effect only when the subscribed capital is increased to an amount at least equal to the prescribed minimum.

Article 78. Where the laws of a Member State authorise total or partial redemption of the subscribed capital without reduction of the latter, they shall at least require that the following conditions are observed:

(a) where the statutes or instrument of incorporation provide for redemption, the latter shall be decided on by the general meeting voting at least under the usual conditions of quorum and majority; where the statutes or instrument of incorporation do not provide for redemption, the latter shall be decided upon by the general meeting acting at least under the conditions of quorum and majority laid down in Article 83; the decision shall be published in the manner prescribed by the laws of Member States, in accordance with Article 16;

(b) only sums which are available for distribution within the meaning of Article 56(1) to (4) may be used for redemption purposes;

(c) shareholders whose shares are redeemed shall retain their rights in the company, with the exception of their rights to the repayment of their investment and participation in the distribution of an initial dividend on unredeemed shares.

Article 79. 1. Where the laws of a Member State allow companies to reduce their subscribed capital by compulsory withdrawal of shares, they shall require that at least the following conditions are observed:

(a) compulsory withdrawal must be prescribed or authorised by the statutes or instrument of incorporation before the shares which are to be withdrawn are subscribed for;

(b) where the compulsory withdrawal is authorised merely by the statutes or instrument of incorporation, it shall be decided upon by the general meeting unless it has been unanimously approved by the shareholders concerned;

(c) the company body deciding on the compulsory withdrawal shall fix the terms and manner thereof, where they have not already been fixed by the statutes or instrument of incorporation;

(d) Article 75 shall apply except in the case of fully paid-up shares which are made available to the company free of charge or are withdrawn using sums available for distribution in accordance with Article 56(1) to (4); in these cases, an amount equal to the nominal value or, in the absence thereof, to the accountable par of all the withdrawn shares must be included in a reserve; except in the event of a reduction in the subscribed capital, this reserve may not be distributed to shareholders; it can be used only for offsetting losses incurred or for increasing the subscribed capital by the capitalisation of such reserve, in so far as Member States permit such an operation; and

(e) the decision on compulsory withdrawal shall be published in the manner laid down by the laws of each Member State in accordance with Article 16.

2. The first paragraph of Article 73 and Articles 74, 76 and 83 shall not apply to the cases to which paragraph 1 of this Article refers.

Article 80. 1. In the case of a reduction in the subscribed capital by the withdrawal of shares acquired by the company itself or by a person acting in his own name but on behalf of the company, the withdrawal shall always be decided on by the general meeting.

2. Article 75 shall apply unless the shares are fully paid up and are acquired free of charge or using sums available for distribution in accordance with Article 56(1) to (4); in these cases an amount equal to the nominal value or, in the absence thereof, to the accountable par of all the shares withdrawn shall be included in a reserve. Except in the event of a reduction in the subscribed capital, this reserve

may not be distributed to shareholders. It may be used only for offsetting losses incurred or for increasing the subscribed capital by the capitalisation of such reserve, in so far as the Member States permit such an operation.

3. Articles 74, 76 and 83 shall not apply to the cases to which paragraph 1 of this Article refers.

Article 81 In the cases covered by Article 78, Article 79(1)(b) and Article 80(1), when there are several classes of shares, the decision by the general meeting concerning redemption of the subscribed capital or its reduction by withdrawal of shares shall be subject to a separate vote, at least for each class of shareholders whose rights are affected by the transaction.

Article 82 Where the laws of a Member State authorise companies to issue redeemable shares, they shall require that the following conditions, at least, are complied with for the redemption of such shares:

(a) redemption must be authorised by the company's statutes or instrument of incorporation before the redeemable shares are subscribed for;
(b) the shares must be fully paid up;
(c) the terms and the manner of redemption must be laid down in the company's statutes or instrument of incorporation;
(d) redemption can be only effected by using sums available for distribution in accordance with Article 56(1) to (4) or the proceeds of a new issue made with a view to effecting such redemption;
(e) an amount equal to the nominal value or, in the absence thereof, to the accountable par of all the redeemed shares must be included in a reserve which cannot be distributed to the shareholders, except in the event of a reduction in the subscribed capital; it may be used only for the purpose of increasing the subscribed capital by the capitalisation of reserves;
(f) point (e) shall not apply to redemption using the proceeds of a new issue made with a view to effecting such redemption;
(g) where provision is made for the payment of a premium to shareholders in consequence of a redemption, the premium may be paid only from sums available for distribution in accordance with Article 56(1) to (4), or from a reserve other than that referred to in point (e) of this Article which may not be distributed to shareholders except in the event of a reduction in the subscribed capital; this reserve may be used only for the purposes of increasing the subscribed capital by the capitalisation of reserves or for covering the costs referred to in point (j) of Article 4 or the cost of issuing shares or debentures or for the payment of a premium to holders of redeemable shares or debentures;
(h) notification of redemption shall be published in the manner laid down by the laws of each Member State in accordance with Article 16.

Article 83. The laws of the Member States shall provide that the decisions referred to in Article 72(4) and (5) and Articles 73, 74, 78 and 81 are to be taken at least by a majority of not less than two thirds of the votes attaching to the securities or the subscribed capital represented.

The laws of the Member States may, however, lay down that a simple majority of the votes specified in the first paragraph is sufficient when at least half the subscribed capital is represented.

Section 6. Application and implementing arrangements

Article 84. 1. Member States may derogate from the first paragraph of Article 48, the first sentence of Article 60(1)(a) and Articles 68, 69 and 72 to the extent that such derogations are necessary for the adoption or application of provisions designed to encourage the participation of employees, or other groups of persons defined by national law, in the capital of undertakings.

2. Member States may decide not to apply the first sentence of Article 60(1)(a) and Articles 73, 74 and 79 to 82 to companies incorporated under a special law which issue both capital shares and workers' shares, the latter being issued to the company's employees as a body, who are represented at general meetings of shareholders by delegates having the right to vote.

3. Member States shall ensure that Article 49, Articles 58(1) and 68(1), (2) and (3), the first subparagraph of Article 70(2), Articles 72 to 75, 79, 80 and 81 do not apply in the case of use of the resolution tools, powers and mechanisms provided for in Title IV of Directive 2014/59/EU of the European Parliament and of the Council.

Article 85. For the purposes of the implementation of this Chapter, the laws of the Member States shall ensure equal treatment to all shareholders who are in the same position.

Article 86. Member States may decide not to apply points (g), (i), (j) and (k) of Article 4 to companies already in existence at the date of entry into force of the laws, regulations and administrative provisions adopted in order to comply with Council Directive 77/91/EEC (35).

PART III   EUROPEAN COMPANY LAW

Title II. Mergers and Divisions of Limited Liability Companies

Chapter I. Mergers of Public Limited Liability Companies

Section 1. General Provisions on Mergers

Article 87. 1. The coordination measures laid down by this Chapter shall apply to the laws, regulations and administrative provisions of the Member States relating to the types of company listed in Annex I.
2. Member States need not apply this Chapter to cooperatives incorporated as one of the types of company listed in Annex I. In so far as the laws of the Member States make use of this option, they shall require such companies to include the word 'cooperative' in all the documents referred to in Article 26.
3. Member States need not apply this Chapter in cases where the company or companies which are being acquired or will cease to exist are the subject of bankruptcy proceedings, proceedings relating to the winding-up of insolvent companies, judicial arrangements, compositions and analogous proceedings.
4. Member States shall ensure that this Chapter does not apply to the company or companies which are the subject of the use of resolution tools, powers and mechanisms provided for in Title IV of Directive 2014/59/EU.

Article 88. Member States shall, as regards companies governed by their national laws, make provision for rules governing mergers by the acquisition of one or more companies by another company and merger by the formation of a new company.

Article 89. 1. For the purposes of this Chapter, 'merger by acquisition' shall mean the operation whereby one or more companies are wound up without going into liquidation and transfer to another all their assets and liabilities in exchange for the issue to the shareholders of the company or companies being acquired of shares in the acquiring company and a cash payment, if any, not exceeding 10 % of the nominal value of the shares so issued or, where they have no nominal value, of their accounting par value.
2. A Member State's laws may provide that merger by acquisition may also be effected where one or more of the companies being acquired is in liquidation, provided that this option is restricted to companies which have not yet begun to distribute their assets to their shareholders.

Article 90. 1. For the purposes of this Chapter, 'merger by the formation of a new company' shall mean the operation whereby several companies are wound up without going into liquidation and transfer to a company that they set up all their assets and liabilities in exchange for the issue to their shareholders of shares in the new company and a cash payment, if any, not exceeding 10 % of the nominal value of the shares so issued or, where they have no nominal value, of their accounting par value.
2. A Member State's laws may provide that merger by the formation of a new company may also be effected where one or more of the companies which are ceasing to exist is in liquidation, provided that this option is restricted to companies which have not yet begun to distribute their assets to their shareholders.

Section 2. Merger by acquisition

Article 91. 1. The administrative or management bodies of the merging companies shall draw up draft terms of merger in writing.
2. Draft terms of merger shall specify at least:
(a) the type, name and registered office of each of the merging companies;
(b) the share exchange ratio and the amount of any cash payment;
(c) the terms relating to the allotment of shares in the acquiring company;
(d) the date from which the holding of such shares entitles the holders to participate in profits and any special conditions affecting that entitlement;
(e) the date from which the transactions of the company being acquired shall be treated for accounting purposes as being those of the acquiring company;
(f) the rights conferred by the acquiring company on the holders of shares to which special rights are attached and the holders of securities other than shares, or the measures proposed concerning them;
(g) any special advantage granted to the experts referred to in Article 96(1) and members of the merging companies' administrative, management, supervisory or controlling bodies.

Article 92. Draft terms of merger shall be published in the manner prescribed by the laws of the

Member States in accordance with Article 16, for each of the merging companies, at least one month before the date fixed for the general meeting which is to decide thereon.

Any of the merging companies shall be exempt from the publication requirement laid down in Article 16 if, for a continuous period beginning at least one month before the date fixed for the general meeting which is to decide on the draft terms of merger and ending not earlier than the conclusion of that meeting, it makes the draft terms of such merger available on its website free of charge for the public. Member States shall not subject that exemption to any requirements or constraints other than those which are necessary in order to ensure the security of the website and the authenticity of the documents, and may impose such requirements or constraints only to the extent that they are proportionate in order to achieve those objectives.

By way of derogation from the second paragraph of this Article, Member States may require that publication be effected via the central electronic platform referred to in Article 16(5). Member States may alternatively require that such publication be made on any other website designated by them for that purpose. Where Member States avail themselves of one of those possibilities, they shall ensure that companies are not charged a specific fee for such publication.

Where a website other than the central electronic platform is used, a reference giving access to that website shall be published on the central electronic platform at least one month before the date fixed for the general meeting. That reference shall include the date of publication of the draft terms of merger on the website and shall be accessible to the public free of charge. Companies shall not be charged a specific fee for such publication.

The prohibition precluding the charging of companies of a specific fee for publication, laid down in the third and fourth paragraphs, shall not affect the ability of Member States to pass on to companies the costs in respect of the central electronic platform.

Member States may require companies to maintain the information for a specific period after the general meeting on their website or, where applicable, on the central electronic platform or the other website designated by the Member State concerned. Member States may determine the consequences of temporary disruption of access to the website or to the central electronic platform, caused by technical or other factors.

Article 93. 1. A merger shall require at least the approval of the general meeting of each of the merging companies. The laws of the Member States shall provide that this approval decision shall require a majority of not less than two thirds of the votes attached either to the shares or to the subscribed capital represented.

The laws of a Member State may, however, provide that a simple majority of the votes specified in the first subparagraph shall be sufficient when at least half of the subscribed capital is represented. Moreover, where appropriate, the rules governing alterations to the memorandum and articles of association shall apply.

2. Where there is more than one class of shares, the decision concerning a merger shall be subject to a separate vote by at least each class of shareholders whose rights are affected by the transaction.

3. The decision shall cover both the approval of the draft terms of merger and any alterations to the memorandum and articles of association necessitated by the merger.

Article 94. The laws of a Member State need not require approval of the merger by the general meeting of the acquiring company where the following conditions are fulfilled:

(a) the publication provided for in Article 92 is effected, for the acquiring company, at least one month before the date fixed for the general meeting of the company or companies being acquired which is to decide on the draft terms of merger;

(b) at least one month before the date specified in point (a), all shareholders of the acquiring company are entitled to inspect the documents specified in Article 97(1) at the registered office of the acquiring company;

(c) one or more shareholders of the acquiring company holding a minimum percentage of the subscribed capital is entitled to require that a general meeting of the acquiring company be called to decide whether to approve the merger; this minimum percentage may not be fixed at more than 5 %. Member States may, however, provide for the exclusion of non-voting shares from this calculation.

For the purposes of point (b) of the first paragraph, Article 97(2), (3) and (4) shall apply.

Article 95. 1. The administrative or management bodies of each of the merging companies shall draw up a detailed written report explaining the draft terms of merger and setting out the legal and economic grounds for them, in particular the share exchange ratio.

That report shall also describe any special valuation difficulties which have arisen.

2. The administrative or management bodies of each of the companies involved shall inform the

general meeting of their company, and the administrative or management bodies of the other companies involved, so that the latter may inform their respective general meetings of any material change in the assets and liabilities between the date of preparation of the draft terms of merger and the date of the general meetings which are to decide on the draft terms of merger.

3. Member States may provide that the report referred to in paragraph 1 and/or the information referred to in paragraph 2 shall not be required if all the shareholders and the holders of other securities conferring the right to vote of each of the companies involved in the merger have so agreed.

Article 96. 1. One or more experts, acting on behalf of each of the merging companies but independent of them, appointed or approved by a judicial or administrative authority, shall examine the draft terms of merger and draw up a written report to the shareholders. However, the laws of the Member States may provide for the appointment of one or more independent experts for all the merging companies, if such appointment is made by a judicial or administrative authority at the joint request of those companies. Such experts may, depending on the laws of each Member State, be natural or legal persons or companies or firms.

2. In the report referred to in paragraph 1, the experts shall in any case state whether in their opinion the share exchange ratio is fair and reasonable. Their statement shall at least:
(a) indicate the method or methods used to arrive at the share exchange ratio proposed;
(b) state whether such method or methods are adequate in the case in question, indicate the values arrived at using each such methods and give an opinion on the relative importance attributed to such methods in arriving at the value decided on.
The report shall also describe any special valuation difficulties which have arisen.

3. Each expert shall be entitled to obtain from the merging companies all relevant information and documents and to carry out all necessary investigations.

4. Neither an examination of the draft terms of merger nor an expert report shall be required if all the shareholders and the holders of other securities conferring the right to vote of each of the companies involved in the merger have so agreed.

Article 97. 1. All shareholders shall be entitled to inspect at least the following documents at the registered office at least one month before the date fixed for the general meeting which is to decide on the draft terms of merger:
(a) the draft terms of merger;
(b) the annual accounts and annual reports of the merging companies for the preceding three financial years;
(c) where applicable, an accounting statement drawn up on a date which shall not be earlier than the first day of the third month preceding the date of the draft terms of merger, if the latest annual accounts relate to a financial year which ended more than six months before that date;
(d) where applicable, the reports of the administrative or management bodies of the merging companies provided for in Article 95;
(e) where applicable, the report referred to in Article 96(1).
For the purposes of point (c) of the first subparagraph, an accounting statement shall not be required if the company publishes a half-yearly financial report in accordance with Article 5 of Directive 2004/109/EC and makes it available to shareholders in accordance with this paragraph. Furthermore, Member States may provide that an accounting statement shall not be required if all the shareholders and the holders of other securities conferring the right to vote of each of the companies involved in the merger have so agreed.

2. The accounting statement provided for in point (c) of the first subparagraph of paragraph 1 shall be drawn up using the same methods and the same layout as the last annual balance sheet.
However, the laws of a Member State may provide that:
(a) it is not necessary to take a fresh physical inventory;
(b) the valuations shown in the last balance sheet are to be altered only to reflect entries in the books of account; the following shall nevertheless be taken into account:
— interim depreciation and provisions,
— material changes in actual value not shown in the books.

3. Every shareholder shall be entitled to obtain, on request and free of charge, full or, if so desired, partial copies of the documents referred to in paragraph 1.
Where a shareholder has consented to the use by the company of electronic means for conveying information, such copies may be provided by electronic mail.

4. A company shall be exempt from the requirement to make the documents referred to in paragraph 1 available at its registered office if, for a continuous period beginning at least one month before the date fixed for the general meeting which is to decide on the draft terms of merger and ending not ear-

lier than the conclusion of that meeting, it makes them available on its website. Member States shall not subject that exemption to any requirements or constraints other than those which are necessary in order to ensure the security of the website and the authenticity of the documents and may impose such requirements or constraints only to the extent that they are proportionate in order to achieve those objectives.

Paragraph 3 shall not apply if the website gives shareholders the possibility, throughout the period referred to in the first subparagraph of this paragraph, of downloading and printing the documents referred to in paragraph 1. However, in that case Member States may provide that the company is to make those documents available at its registered office for consultation by the shareholders.

Member States may require companies to maintain the information on their website for a specific period after the general meeting. Member States may determine the consequences of temporary disruption of access to the website caused by technical or other factors.

Article 98. Protection of the rights of the employees of each of the merging companies shall be regulated in accordance with Directive 2001/23/EC.

Article 99. 1. The laws of the Member States shall provide for an adequate system of protection of the interests of creditors of the merging companies whose claims antedate the publication of the draft terms of merger and have not fallen due at the time of such publication.

2. For the purposes of paragraph 1, the laws of the Member States shall at least provide that such creditors shall be entitled to obtain adequate safeguards where the financial situation of the merging companies makes such protection necessary and where those creditors do not already have such safeguards.

Member States shall lay down the conditions for the protection provided for in paragraph 1 and in the first subparagraph of this paragraph. In any event, Member States shall ensure that the creditors are authorised to apply to the appropriate administrative or judicial authority for adequate safeguards provided that they can credibly demonstrate that due to the merger the satisfaction of their claims is at stake and that no adequate safeguards have been obtained from the company.

3. Such protection may be different for the creditors of the acquiring company and for those of the company being acquired.

Article 100. Without prejudice to the rules governing the collective exercise of their rights, Article 99 shall apply to the debenture holders of the merging companies, except where the merger has been approved by a meeting of the debenture holders, if such a meeting is provided for under national laws, or by the debenture holders individually.

Article 101. Holders of securities, other than shares, to which special rights are attached shall be given rights in the acquiring company at least equivalent to those they possessed in the company being acquired, unless the alteration of those rights has been approved by a meeting of the holders of such securities, if such a meeting is provided for under national laws, or by the holders of those securities individually, or unless the holders are entitled to have their securities repurchased by the acquiring company.

Article 102. 1. Where the laws of a Member State do not provide for judicial or administrative preventive supervision of the legality of mergers, or where such supervision does not extend to all the legal acts required for a merger, the minutes of the general meetings which decide on the merger and, where appropriate, the merger contract subsequent to such general meetings shall be drawn up and certified in due legal form. In cases where the merger need not be approved by the general meetings of all the merging companies, the draft terms of merger shall be drawn up and certified in due legal form.

2. The notary or the authority competent to draw up and certify the document in due legal form shall check and certify the existence and validity of the legal acts and formalities required of the company for which that notary or authority is acting and of the draft terms of merger.

Article 103. The laws of the Member States shall determine the date on which a merger takes effect.

Article 104. 1. A merger shall be publicised in the manner prescribed by the laws of each Member State, in accordance with Article 16, in respect of each of the merging companies.

2. The acquiring company may itself carry out the publication formalities relating to the company or companies being acquired.

Article 105. 1. A merger shall have the following consequences ipso jure and simultaneously:
(a) the transfer, both as between the company being acquired and the acquiring company and, as

regards third parties, to the acquiring company of all the assets and liabilities of the company being acquired;
(b) the shareholders of the company being acquired become shareholders of the acquiring company; and
(c) the company being acquired ceases to exist.
2. No shares in the acquiring company shall be exchanged for shares in the company being acquired held either:
(a) by the acquiring company itself or through a person acting in his own name but on its behalf; or
(b) by the company being acquired itself or through a person acting in his own name but on its behalf.
3. The foregoing shall not affect the laws of Member States which require the completion of special formalities for the transfer of certain assets, rights and obligations by the acquired company to be effective as against third parties. The acquiring company may carry out such formalities itself; however, the laws of the Member States may permit the company being acquired to continue to carry out such formalities for a limited period which may not, save in exceptional cases, be fixed at more than six months from the date on which the merger takes effect.

Article 106. The laws of the Member States shall at least lay down rules governing the civil liability, towards the shareholders of the company being acquired, of the members of the administrative or management bodies of that company in respect of misconduct on the part of members of those bodies in preparing and implementing the merger.

Article 107. The laws of the Member States shall at least lay down rules governing the civil liability, towards the shareholders of the company being acquired, of the experts responsible for drawing up on behalf of that company the report referred to in Article 96(1), in respect of misconduct on the part of those experts in the performance of their duties.

Article 108. 1. The laws of the Member States may lay down nullity rules for mergers in accordance with the following conditions only:
(a) nullity is to be ordered in a court judgment;
(b) mergers which have taken effect pursuant to Article 103 may be declared void only if there has been no judicial or administrative preventive supervision of their legality, or if they have not been drawn up and certified in due legal form, or if it is shown that the decision of the general meeting is void or voidable under national law;
(c) nullification proceedings may not be initiated more than six months after the date on which the merger becomes effective as against the person alleging nullity or where the situation has been rectified;
(d) where it is possible to remedy a defect liable to render a merger void, the competent court is to grant the companies involved a period of time within which to rectify the situation;
(e) a judgment declaring a merger void is to be published in the manner prescribed by the laws of each Member State in accordance with Article 16;
(f) where the laws of a Member State permit a third party to challenge such a judgment, that party may only do so within six months of publication of the judgment in the manner prescribed by Section 1 of Chapter III of Title I;
(g) a judgment declaring a merger void does not of itself affect the validity of obligations owed by or in relation to the acquiring company which arose before the judgment was published and after the date on which the merger takes effect; and
(h) companies which have been parties to a merger are jointly and severally liable in respect of the obligations of the acquiring company referred to in point (g).
2. By way of derogation from point (a) of paragraph 1, the laws of a Member State may also provide for the nullity of a merger to be ordered by an administrative authority if an appeal against such a decision lies to a court. Point (b) and points (d) to (h) of paragraph 1shall apply by analogy to the administrative authority. Such nullification proceedings may not be initiated more than six months after the date on which the merger takes effect.
3. The laws of the Member States on the nullity of a merger pronounced following any supervision other than judicial or administrative preventive supervision of legality shall not be affected.

Section 3. Merger by formation of a new company

Article 109. 1. Articles 91, 92, 93 and 95 to 108 shall apply, without prejudice to Articles 11 and 12, to merger by formation of a new company. For this purpose, 'merging companies' and 'company being acquired' shall mean the companies which will cease to exist, and 'acquiring company' shall mean the new company.

Article 91(2)(a) shall also apply to the new company.

2. The draft terms of merger and, if they are contained in a separate document, the memorandum or draft memorandum of association and the articles or draft articles of association of the new company shall be approved at a general meeting of each of the companies that will cease to exist.

Section 4. Acquisition of one company by another which holds 90 % or more of its shares

Article 110. Member States shall make provision, in respect of companies governed by their laws, for the operation whereby one or more companies are wound up without going into liquidation and transfer all their assets and liabilities to another company which is the holder of all their shares and other securities conferring the right to vote at general meetings. Such operations shall be regulated by the provisions of Section 2 of this Chapter. However, Member States shall not impose the requirements set out in points (b), (c) and (d) of Article 91(2), Articles 95 and 96, points (d) and (e) of Article 97(1), point (b) of Article 105(1) and Articles 106 and 107.

Article 111. Member States shall not apply Article 93 to the operations referred to in Article 110 if the following conditions are fulfilled:
(a) the publication provided for in Article 92 is effected, as regards each company involved in the operation, at least one month before the operation takes effect;
(b) at least one month before the operation takes effect, all shareholders of the acquiring company are entitled to inspect the documents referred to in points (a), (b) and (c) of Article 97(1) at the company's registered office;
(c) point (c) of the first paragraph of Article 94 applies.
For the purposes of point (b) of the first paragraph of this Article, Article 97(2), (3) and (4) shall apply.

Article 112. The Member States may apply Articles 110 and 111 to operations whereby one or more companies are wound up without going into liquidation and transfer all their assets and liabilities to another company, if all the shares and other securities specified in Article 110 of the company or companies being acquired are held by the acquiring company and/or by persons holding those shares and securities in their own names but on behalf of that company.

Article 113. Where a merger by acquisition is carried out by a company which holds 90 % or more, but not all, of the shares and other securities conferring the right to vote at general meetings of the company or companies being acquired, Member States shall not require approval of the merger by the general meeting of the acquiring company if the following conditions are fulfilled:
(a) the publication provided for in Article 92 is effected, as regards the acquiring company, at least one month before the date fixed for the general meeting of the company or companies being acquired which is to decide on the draft terms of merger;
(b) at least one month before the date specified in point (a), all shareholders of the acquiring company are entitled to inspect the documents specified in points (a) and (b) and, where applicable, points (c), (d) and (e) of Article 97(1) at the company's registered office;
(c) point (c) of the first paragraph of Article 94 applies.
For the purposes of point (b) of the first paragraph of this Article, Article 97(2), (3) and (4) shall apply.

Article 114. Member States shall not impose the requirements set out in Articles 95, 96 and 97 in the case of a merger within the meaning of Article 113 if the following conditions are fulfilled:
(a) the minority shareholders of the company being acquired are entitled to have their shares acquired by the acquiring company;
(b) if they exercise that right, they are entitled to receive consideration corresponding to the value of their shares;
(c) in the event of disagreement regarding such consideration, it is possible for the value of the consideration to be determined by a court or by an administrative authority designated by the Member State for that purpose.
A Member State need not apply the first paragraph if the laws of that Member State entitle the acquiring company, without a previous public takeover offer, to require all the holders of the remaining securities of the company or companies to be acquired, to sell those securities to it prior to the merger at a fair price.

Article 115. The Member States may apply Articles 113 and 114 to operations whereby one or more companies are wound up without going into liquidation and transfer all their assets and liabilities to another company, if 90 % or more, but not all, of the shares and other securities referred to in Article

113 of the company or companies being acquired are held by that acquiring company and/or by persons holding those shares and securities in their own names but on behalf of that company.

Section 5. Other operations treated as mergers

Article 116. Where in the case of one of the operations referred to in Article 88 the laws of a Member State permit a cash payment to exceed 10 %, Sections 2 and 3 of this Chapter and Articles 113, 114 and 115 shall apply.

Article 117. Where the laws of a Member State permit one of the operations referred to in Articles 88, 110 and 116, without all of the transferring companies thereby ceasing to exist, Section 2, except for point (c) of Article 105(1), and Section 3 or 4 of this Chapter shall apply as appropriate.

Chapter II. Cross-border mergers of limited liability companies

Article 118. This Chapter shall apply to mergers of limited liability companies formed in accordance with the law of a Member State and having their registered office, central administration or principal place of business within the Union, provided at least two of them are governed by the laws of different Member States (hereinafter referred to as 'cross-border mergers').

Article 119. For the purposes of this Chapter:
(1) 'limited liability company', hereinafter referred to as 'company', means:
(a) a company of a type listed in Annex II; or
(b) a company with share capital and having legal personality, possessing separate assets which alone serve to cover its debts and that is subject, under the national law governing it, to conditions concerning guarantees such as are provided for by Section 2 of Chapter II of Title I and Section 1 of Chapter III of Title I for the protection of the interests of members and others;
(2) 'merger' means an operation whereby:
(a) one or more companies, on being dissolved without going into liquidation, transfer all their assets and liabilities to another existing company, the acquiring company, in exchange for the issue to their members of securities or shares representing the capital of that other company and, if applicable, a cash payment not exceeding 10 % of the nominal value, or, in the absence of a nominal value, of the accounting par value of those securities or shares; or
(b) two or more companies, on being dissolved without going into liquidation, transfer all their assets and liabilities to a company that they form, the new company, in exchange for the issue to their members of securities or shares representing the capital of that new company and, if applicable, a cash payment not exceeding 10 % of the nominal value, or in the absence of a nominal value, of the accounting par value of those securities or shares; or
(c) a company, on being dissolved without going into liquidation, transfers all its assets and liabilities to the company holding all the securities or shares representing its capital.

Article 120. 1. Notwithstanding Article 119(2), this Chapter shall also apply to cross-border mergers where the law of at least one of the Member States concerned allows the cash payment referred to in Article 119(2)(a) and (b) to exceed 10 % of the nominal value, or, in the absence of a nominal value, of the accounting par value of the securities or shares representing the capital of the company resulting from the cross-border merger.
2. Member States may decide not to apply this Chapter to cross-border mergers involving a cooperative society even in the cases where the latter would fall within the definition of a limited liability company as laid down in Article 119(1).
3. This Chapter shall not apply to cross-border mergers involving a company the object of which is the collective investment of capital provided by the public, which operates on the principle of risk-spreading and the units of which are, at the holders' request, repurchased or redeemed, directly or indirectly, out of the assets of that company. Action taken by such a company to ensure that the stock exchange value of its units does not vary significantly from its net asset value shall be regarded as equivalent to such repurchase or redemption.
4. Member States shall ensure that this Chapter does not apply to the company or companies that are the subject of the use of resolution tools, powers and mechanisms provided for in Title IV of Directive 2014/59/EU.

Article 121. 1. Save as otherwise provided in this Chapter,
(a) cross-border mergers shall only be possible between types of companies which may merge under the national law of the relevant Member States;
(b) a company taking part in a cross-border merger shall comply with the provisions and formalities

of the national law to which it is subject. The laws of a Member State enabling its national authorities to oppose a given internal merger on grounds of public interest shall also be applicable to a cross-border merger where at least one of the merging companies is subject to the law of that Member State. This provision shall not apply to the extent that Article 21 of Regulation (EC) No 139/2004 is applicable.

2. The provisions and formalities referred to in point (b) of paragraph 1 shall, in particular, include those concerning the decision-making process relating to the merger and, taking into account the cross-border nature of the merger, the protection of creditors of the merging companies, debenture holders and the holders of securities or shares, as well as of employees as regards rights other than those governed by Article 133. A Member State may, in the case of companies participating in a cross-border merger and governed by its law, adopt provisions designed to ensure appropriate protection for minority members who have opposed the cross-border merger.

Article 122. The management or administrative organ of each of the merging companies shall draw up the common draft terms of a cross-border merger. The common draft terms of a cross-border merger shall include at least the following particulars:

(a) the form, name and registered office of the merging companies and those proposed for the company resulting from the cross-border merger;
(b) the ratio applicable to the exchange of securities or shares representing the company capital and the amount of any cash payment;
(c) the terms for the allotment of securities or shares representing the capital of the company resulting from the cross-border merger;
(d) the likely repercussions of the cross-border merger on employment;
(e) the date from which the holding of such securities or shares representing the company capital will entitle the holders to share in profits and any special conditions affecting that entitlement;
(f) the date from which the transactions of the merging companies will be treated for accounting purposes as being those of the company resulting from the cross-border merger;
(g) the rights conferred by the company resulting from the cross-border merger on members enjoying special rights or on holders of securities other than shares representing the company capital, or the measures proposed concerning them;
(h) any special advantages granted to the experts who examine the draft terms of the cross-border merger or to members of the administrative, management, supervisory or controlling organs of the merging companies;
(i) the statutes of the company resulting from the cross-border merger;
(j) where appropriate, information on the procedures by which arrangements for the involvement of employees in the definition of their rights to participation in the company resulting from the cross-border merger are determined pursuant to Article 133;
(k) information on the evaluation of the assets and liabilities which are transferred to the company resulting from the cross-border merger;
(l) dates of the merging companies' accounts used to establish the conditions of the cross-border merger.

Article 123. 1. The common draft terms of the cross-border merger shall be published in the manner prescribed by the laws of each Member State in accordance with Article 16 for each of the merging companies at least one month before the date of the general meeting which is to decide thereon.

Any of the merging companies shall be exempt from the publication requirement laid down in Article 16 if, for a continuous period beginning at least one month before the date fixed for the general meeting which is to decide on the common draft terms of the cross-border merger and ending not earlier than the conclusion of that meeting, it makes the common draft terms of such merger available on its website free of charge for the public. Member States shall not subject that exemption to any requirements or constraints other than those which are necessary in order to ensure the security of the website and the authenticity of the documents and may impose such requirements or constraints only to the extent that they are proportionate in order to achieve those objectives.

By way of derogation from the second subparagraph, Member States may require that publication be effected via the central electronic platform referred to in Article 16(5). Member States may alternatively require that such publication be made on any other website designated by them for that purpose. Where Member States avail themselves of one of those possibilities, they shall ensure that companies are not charged a specific fee for such publication.

Where a website other than the central electronic platform is used, a reference giving access to that website shall be published on the central electronic platform at least one month before the date fixed for the general meeting. That reference shall include the date of publication of the common draft terms of cross-border merger on the website and shall be accessible to the public free of charge. Companies shall not be charged a specific fee for such publication.

The prohibition precluding the charging of companies of a specific fee for publication, laid down in the third and fourth subparagraphs, shall not affect the ability of Member States to pass on to companies the costs in respect of the central electronic platform.

Member States may require companies to maintain the information for a specific period after the general meeting on their website or, where applicable, on the central electronic platform or the other website designated by the Member State concerned. Member States may determine the consequences of temporary disruption of access to the website or to the central electronic platform, caused by technical or other factors.

2. For each of the merging companies and subject to the additional requirements imposed by the Member State to which the company concerned is subject, the following particulars shall be published in the national gazette of that Member State:

(a) the type, name and registered office of every merging company;

(b) the register in which the documents referred to in Article 16(3) are filed in respect of each merging company, and the number of the entry in that register;

(c) an indication, for each of the merging companies, of the arrangements made for the exercise of the rights of creditors and of any minority members of the merging companies and the address at which complete information on those arrangements may be obtained free of charge.

Article 124. The management or administrative organ of each of the merging companies shall draw up a report intended for the members explaining and justifying the legal and economic aspects of the cross-border merger and explaining the implications of the cross-border merger for members, creditors and employees.

The report shall be made available to the members and to the representatives of the employees or, where there are no such representatives, to the employees themselves, not less than one month before the date of the general meeting referred to in Article 126.

Where the management or administrative organ of any of the merging companies receives, in good time, an opinion from the representatives of their employees, as provided for under national law, that opinion shall be appended to the report.

Article 125. 1. An independent expert report intended for members and made available not less than one month before the date of the general meeting referred to in Article 126 shall be drawn up for each merging company. Depending on the law of each Member State, such experts may be natural persons or legal persons.

2. As an alternative to experts operating on behalf of each of the merging companies, one or more independent experts, appointed for that purpose at the joint request of the companies by a judicial or administrative authority in the Member State of one of the merging companies or of the company resulting from the cross-border merger or approved by such an authority, may examine the common draft terms of cross-border merger and draw up a single written report to all the members.

3. The expert report shall include at least the particulars provided for in Article 96(2). The experts shall be entitled to secure from each of the merging companies all information they consider necessary for the discharge of their duties.

4. Neither an examination of the common draft terms of cross-border merger by independent experts nor an expert report shall be required if all the members of each of the companies involved in the cross-border merger have so agreed.

Article 126. 1. After taking note of the reports referred to in Articles 124 and 125, the general meeting of each of the merging companies shall decide on the approval of the common draft terms of cross-border merger.

2. The general meeting of each of the merging companies may reserve the right to make implementation of the cross-border merger conditional on express ratification by it of the arrangements decided on with respect to the participation of employees in the company resulting from the cross-border merger.

3. The laws of a Member State need not require approval of the merger by the general meeting of the acquiring company if the conditions laid down in Article 94 are fulfilled.

Article 127. 1. Each Member State shall designate the court, notary or other authority competent to scrutinise the legality of the cross-border merger as regards that part of the procedure which concerns each merging company subject to its national law.

2. In each Member State concerned the authority referred to in paragraph 1 shall issue, without delay to each merging company subject to that State's national law, a certificate conclusively attesting

to the proper completion of the pre-merger acts and formalities.

3. If the law of a Member State to which a merging company is subject provides for a procedure to scrutinise and amend the ratio applicable to the exchange of securities or shares, or a procedure to compensate minority members, without preventing the registration of the cross-border merger, such procedure shall only apply if the other merging companies situated in Member States which do not provide for such procedure explicitly accept, when approving the draft terms of the cross-border merger in accordance with Article 126(1), the possibility for the members of that merging company to have recourse to such procedure, to be initiated before the court having jurisdiction over that merging company. In such cases, the authority referred to in paragraph 1 may issue the certificate referred to in paragraph 2 even if such procedure has commenced. The certificate shall, however, indicate that the procedure is pending. The decision in the procedure shall be binding on the company resulting from the cross-border merger and all its members.

Article 128. 1. Each Member State shall designate the court, notary or other authority competent to scrutinise the legality of the cross-border merger as regards that part of the procedure which concerns the completion of the cross-border merger and, where appropriate, the formation of a new company resulting from the cross-border merger where the company created by the cross-border merger is subject to its national law. The said authority shall in particular ensure that the merging companies have approved the common draft terms of cross-border merger in the same terms and, where appropriate, that arrangements for employee participation have been determined in accordance with Article 133.
2. For the purpose of paragraph 1, each merging company shall submit to the authority referred to in paragraph 1 the certificate referred to in Article 127(2) within six months of its issue together with the common draft terms of cross-border merger approved by the general meeting referred to in Article 126.

Article 129. The law of the Member State to whose jurisdiction the company resulting from the cross-border merger is subject shall determine the date on which the cross-border merger takes effect. That date shall be after the scrutiny referred to in Article 128 has been carried out.

Article 130. The law of each of the Member States to whose jurisdiction the merging companies were subject shall determine, with respect to the territory of that State, the arrangements, in accordance with Article 16, for publicising the completion of the cross-border merger in the public register in which each of the companies is required to file documents.
The registry for the registration of the company resulting from the cross-border merger shall notify, through the system of interconnection of registers established in accordance with Article 22(2) and without delay, the registry in which each of the companies was required to file documents that the cross-border merger has taken effect. Deletion of the old registration, if applicable, shall be effected on receipt of that notification, and not before.

Article 131. 1. A cross-border merger carried out as laid down in subpoints (a) and (c) of point (2) of Article 119 shall, from the date referred to in Article 129, have the following consequences:
(a) all the assets and liabilities of the company being acquired shall be transferred to the acquiring company;
(b) the members of the company being acquired shall become members of the acquiring company;
(c) the company being acquired shall cease to exist.
2. A cross-border merger carried out as laid down in subpoint (b) of point 2 Article 119 shall, from the date referred to in Article 129, have the following consequences:
(a) all the assets and liabilities of the merging companies shall be transferred to the new company;
(b) the members of the merging companies shall become members of the new company;
(c) the merging companies shall cease to exist.
3. Where, in the case of a cross-border merger of companies covered by this Chapter, the laws of the Member States require the completion of special formalities before the transfer of certain assets, rights and obligations by the merging companies becomes effective against third parties, those formalities shall be carried out by the company resulting from the cross-border merger.
4. The rights and obligations of the merging companies arising from contracts of employment or from employment relationships and existing at the date on which the cross-border merger takes effect shall, by reason of that cross-border merger taking effect, be transferred to the company resulting from the cross-border merger on the date on which the cross-border merger takes effect.
5. No shares in the acquiring company shall be exchanged for shares in the company being acquired held either:
(a) by the acquiring company itself or through a person acting in his or her own name but on its behalf;

(b) by the company being acquired itself or through a person acting in his or her own name but on its behalf.

Article 132. 1. Where a cross-border merger by acquisition is carried out by a company which holds all the shares and other securities conferring the right to vote at general meetings of the company or companies being acquired:
— Article 122(b), (c) and (e), Article 125 and Article 131(1)(b) shall not apply,
— Article 126(1) shall not apply to the company or companies being acquired.
2. Where a cross-border merger by acquisition is carried out by a company which holds 90 % or more, but not all, of the shares and other securities conferring the right to vote at general meetings of the company or companies being acquired, reports by an independent expert or experts and the documents necessary for scrutiny shall be required only to the extent that the national law governing either the acquiring company or the company or companies being acquired so requires, in accordance with Chapter I of Title II.

Article 133. 1. Without prejudice to paragraph 2, the company resulting from the cross-border merger shall be subject to the rules in force concerning employee participation, if any, in the Member State where it has its registered office.
2. However, the rules in force concerning employee participation, if any, in the Member State where the company resulting from the cross-border merger has its registered office shall not apply, where at least one of the merging companies has, in the six months prior to the publication of the draft terms of the cross-border merger as referred to in Article 123, an average number of employees that exceeds 500 and is operating under an employee participation system within the meaning of point (k) of Article 2 of Directive 2001/86/EC, or where the national law applicable to the company resulting from the cross-border merger does not:
(a) provide for at least the same level of employee participation as operated in the relevant merging companies, measured by reference to the proportion of employee representatives amongst the members of the administrative or supervisory organ or their committees or of the management group which covers the profit units of the company, subject to employee representation; or
(b) provide for employees of establishments of the company resulting from the cross-border merger that are situated in other Member States the same entitlement to exercise participation rights as is enjoyed by those employees employed in the Member State where the company resulting from the cross-border merger has its registered office.
3. In the cases referred to in paragraph 2, the participation of employees in the company resulting from the cross-border merger and their involvement in the definition of such rights shall be regulated by the Member States, mutatis mutandis and subject to paragraphs 4 to 7, in accordance with the principles and procedures laid down in Article 12(2), (3) and (4) of Regulation (EC) No 2157/2001 and the following provisions of Directive 2001/86/EC:
(a) Article 3(1), (2) and (3), the first indent of the first subparagraph of Article 3(4), the second subparagraph of Article 3(4) and Article 3(5) and (7);
(b) Article 4(1), Article 4(2)(a), (g) and (h) and Article 4(3);
(c) Article 5;
(d) Article 6;
(e) Article 7(1), point (b) of the first subparagraph of Article 7(2), the second subparagraph of Article 7(2) and Article 7(3). However, for the purposes of this Chapter, the percentages required by point (b) of the first subparagraph of Article 7(2) of Directive 2001/86/EC for the application of the standard rules contained in Part 3 of the Annex to that Directive shall be raised from 25 to 33 1/3 %;
(f) Articles 8, 10 and 12;
(g) Article 13(4);
(h) point (b) of Part 3 of the Annex.
4. When regulating the principles and procedures referred to in paragraph 3, Member States:
(a) shall confer on the relevant organs of the merging companies the right to choose without any prior negotiation to be directly subject to the standard rules for participation referred to in point (h) of paragraph 3, as laid down by the legislation of the Member State in which the company resulting from the cross-border merger is to have its registered office, and to abide by those rules from the date of registration;
(b) shall confer on the special negotiating body the right to decide, by a majority of two thirds of its members representing at least two thirds of the employees, including the votes of members representing employees in at least two different Member States, not to open negotiations or to terminate negotiations already opened and to rely on the rules on participation in force in the Member State where the registered office of the company resulting from the cross-border merger will be situated;

(c) may, in the case where, following prior negotiations, standard rules for participation apply and notwithstanding such rules, decide to limit the proportion of employee representatives in the administrative organ of the company resulting from the cross-border merger. However, if in one of the merging companies employee representatives constituted at least one third of the administrative or supervisory board, the limitation may never result in a lower proportion of employee representatives in the administrative organ than one third.

5. The extension of participation rights to employees of the company resulting from the cross-border merger employed in other Member States, referred to in point (b) of paragraph 2, shall not entail any obligation for Member States which choose to do so to take those employees into account when calculating the size of workforce thresholds giving rise to participation rights under national law.

6. Where at least one of the merging companies is operating under an employee participation system and the company resulting from the cross-border merger is to be governed by such a system in accordance with the rules referred to in paragraph 2, that company shall be obliged to take a legal form allowing for the exercise of participation rights.

7. Where the company resulting from the cross-border merger is operating under an employee participation system, that company shall be obliged to take measures to ensure that employees' participation rights are protected in the event of subsequent domestic mergers for a period of three years after the cross-border merger has taken effect, by applying mutatis mutandis the rules laid down in this Article.

Article 134. A cross-border merger which has taken effect as provided for in Article 129 may not be declared null and void.

Chapter III. Divisions of public limited liability companies

Section 1. General provisions

Article 135. 1. Where Member States permit the types of companies listed in Annex I coming under their laws to carry out division operations by acquisition as defined in Article 136, they shall make those operations subject to Section 2 of this Chapter.

2. Where Member States permit the types of companies referred to in paragraph 1 to carry out division operations by the formation of new companies as defined in Article 155, they shall make those operations subject to Section 3 of this Chapter.

3. Where Member States permit the types of companies referred to in paragraph 1 to carry out operations whereby a division by acquisition as defined in Article 136(1) is combined with a division by the formation of one or more new companies as defined in Article 155(1), they shall make those operations subject to Section 2 of this Chapter and Article 156.

4. Article 87(2), (3) and (4) shall apply.

Section 2. Division by acquisition

Article 136. 1. For the purposes of this Chapter, 'division by acquisition' shall mean the operation whereby, after being wound up without going into liquidation, a company transfers to more than one company all its assets and liabilities in exchange for the allocation to the shareholders of the company being divided of shares in the companies receiving contributions as a result of the division (hereinafter referred to as 'recipient companies') and possibly a cash payment not exceeding 10 % of the nominal value of the shares allocated or, where they have no nominal value, of their accounting par value.

2. Article 89(2) shall apply.

3. In so far as this Chapter refers to provisions of Chapter I of Title II, the term 'merging companies' shall mean 'the companies involved in a division', the term 'company being acquired' shall mean 'the company being divided', the term 'acquiring company' shall mean 'each of the recipient companies' and the term 'draft terms of merger' shall mean 'draft terms of division'.

Article 137. 1. The administrative or management bodies of the companies involved in a division shall draw up draft terms of division in writing.

2. Draft terms of division shall specify at least:

(a) the type, name and registered office of each of the companies involved in the division;
(b) the share exchange ratio and the amount of any cash payment;
(c) the terms relating to the allotment of shares in the recipient companies;
(d) the date from which the holding of such shares entitles the holders to participate in profits and any special conditions affecting that entitlement;
(e) the date from which the transactions of the company being divided shall be treated for accounting

purposes as being those of one or other of the recipient companies;
(f) the rights conferred by the recipient companies on the holders of shares to which special rights are attached and the holders of securities other than shares, or the measures proposed concerning them;
(g) any special advantage granted to the experts referred to in Article 142(1) and members of the administrative, management, supervisory or controlling bodies of the companies involved in the division;
(h) the precise description and allocation of the assets and liabilities to be transferred to each of the recipient companies;
(i) the allocation to the shareholders of the company being divided of shares in the recipient companies and the criterion upon which such allocation is based.
3. Where an asset is not allocated by the draft terms of division and where the interpretation of those terms does not make a decision on its allocation possible, the asset or the consideration therefor shall be allocated to all the recipient companies in proportion to the share of the net assets allocated to each of those companies under the draft terms of division.
Where a liability is not allocated by the draft terms of division and where the interpretation of those terms does not make a decision on its allocation possible, each of the recipient companies shall be jointly and severally liable for it. Member States may provide that such joint and several liability be limited to the net assets allocated to each company.

Article 138. Draft terms of division shall be published in the manner prescribed by the laws of each Member State in accordance with Article 16 for each of the companies involved in a division, at least one month before the date of the general meeting which is to decide thereon.
Any of the companies involved in the division shall be exempt from the publication requirement laid down in Article 16 if, for a continuous period beginning at least one month before the date fixed for the general meeting which is to decide on the draft terms of division and ending not earlier than the conclusion of that meeting, it makes the draft terms of division available on its website free of charge for the public. Member States shall not subject that exemption to any requirements or constraints other than those which are necessary in order to ensure the security of the website and the authenticity of the documents and may impose such requirements or constraints only to the extent that they are proportionate in order to achieve those objectives.
By way of derogation from the second paragraph, Member States may require that publication be effected via the central electronic platform referred to in Article 16(5). Member States may alternatively require that such publication be made on any other website designated by them for that purpose. Where Member States avail themselves of one of those possibilities, they shall ensure that companies are not charged a specific fee for such publication.
Where a website other than the central electronic platform is used, a reference giving access to that website shall be published on that central electronic platform at least one month before the date fixed for the general meeting. That reference shall include the date of publication of the draft terms of division on the website and shall be accessible to the public free of charge. Companies shall not be charged a specific fee for such publication.
The prohibition precluding the charging to companies of a specific fee for publication, laid down in the third and fourth paragraphs, shall not affect the ability of Member States to pass on to companies the costs in respect of the central electronic platform.
Member States may require companies to maintain the information for a specific period after the general meeting on their website or, where applicable, on the central electronic platform or the other website designated by the Member State concerned. Member States may determine the consequences of temporary disruption of access to the website or to the central electronic platform, caused by technical or other factors.

Article 139. 1. A division shall require at least the approval of a general meeting of each company involved in the division. Article 93 shall apply with regard to the majority required for such decisions, their scope and the need for separate votes.
2. Where shares in the recipient companies are allocated to the shareholders of the company being divided otherwise than in proportion to their rights in the capital of that company, Member States may provide that the minority shareholders of that company may exercise the right to have their shares purchased. In such case, they shall be entitled to receive consideration corresponding to the value of their shares. In the event of a dispute concerning such consideration, it shall be possible for the consideration to be determined by a court.

Article 140. The laws of a Member State need not require approval of a division by a general meeting of a recipient company if the following conditions are fulfilled:

(a) the publication provided for in Article 138 is effected, for each recipient company, at least one month before the date fixed for the general meeting of the company being divided which is to decide on the draft terms of division;
(b) at least one month before the date specified in point (a), all shareholders of each recipient company are entitled to inspect the documents specified in Article 143(1) at the registered office of that company;
(c) one or more shareholders of any recipient company holding a minimum percentage of the subscribed capital is entitled to require that a general meeting of such recipient company be called to decide whether to approve the division. Such minimum percentage may not be fixed at more than 5 %. Member States may, however, provide for the exclusion of non-voting shares from this calculation.
For the purposes of point (b) of the first paragraph, Article 143(2), (3) and (4) shall apply.

Article 141. 1. The administration or management bodies of each of the companies involved in the division shall draw up a detailed written report explaining the draft terms of division and setting out the legal and economic grounds for them, in particular the share exchange ratio and the criterion determining the allocation of shares.
2. The report shall also describe any special valuation difficulties which have arisen.
Where applicable, it shall disclose the preparation of the report on the consideration other than in cash referred to in Article 70(2) for recipient companies and the register where that report must be lodged.
3. The administrative or management bodies of a company being divided shall inform the general meeting of that company and the administrative or management bodies of the recipient companies so that they can inform their respective general meetings of any material change in the assets and liabilities between the date of preparation of the draft terms of division and the date of the general meeting of the company being divided which is to decide on the draft terms of division.

Article 142. 1. One or more experts acting on behalf of each of the companies involved in the division but independent of them, appointed or approved by a judicial or administrative authority, shall examine the draft terms of division and draw up a written report to the shareholders. However, the laws of a Member State may provide for the appointment of one or more independent experts for all of the companies involved in a division if such appointment is made by a judicial or administrative authority at the joint request of those companies. Such experts may, depending on the laws of each Member State, be natural or legal persons or companies or firms.
2. Article 96(2) and (3) shall apply.

Article 143. 1. All shareholders shall be entitled to inspect at least the following documents at the registered office at least one month before the date of the general meeting which is to decide on the draft terms of division:
(a) the draft terms of division;
(b) the annual accounts and annual reports of the companies involved in the division for the preceding three financial years;
(c) where applicable, an accounting statement drawn up as at a date which shall not be earlier than the first day of the third month preceding the date of the draft terms of division, if the latest annual accounts relate to a financial year which ended more than six months before that date;
(d) where applicable, the reports of the administrative or management bodies of the companies involved in the division provided for in Article 141(1);
(e) where applicable, the reports provided for in Article 142.
For the purposes of point (c) of the first subparagraph, an accounting statement shall not be required if the company publishes a half-yearly financial report in accordance with Article 5 of Directive 2004/109/EC and makes it available to shareholders in accordance with this paragraph.
2. The accounting statement provided for in point (c) of paragraph 1 shall be drawn up using the same methods and the same layout as the last annual balance sheet.
However, the laws of a Member State may provide that:
(a) it shall not be necessary to take a fresh physical inventory;
(b) the valuations shown in the last balance sheet shall be altered only to reflect entries in the books of account; the following shall nevertheless be taken into account:
(i) interim depreciation and provisions,
(ii) material changes in actual value not shown in the books.
3. Every shareholder shall be entitled to obtain, on request and free of charge, full or, if so desired, partial copies of the documents referred to in paragraph 1.

Where a shareholder has consented to the use by the company of electronic means for conveying information, such copies may be provided by electronic mail.

4. A company shall be exempt from the requirement to make the documents referred to in paragraph 1 available at its registered office if, for a continuous period beginning at least one month before the date fixed for the general meeting which is to decide on the draft terms of division and ending not earlier than the conclusion of that meeting, it makes them available on its website. Member States shall not subject that exemption to requirements or constraints other than those which are necessary in order to ensure the security of the website and the authenticity of the documents, and may impose such requirements or constraints only to the extent that they are proportionate in order to achieve those objectives.

Paragraph 3 shall not apply if the website gives shareholders the possibility, throughout the period referred to in the first subparagraph of this paragraph, of downloading and printing the documents referred to in paragraph 1. However, in that case Member States may provide that the company is to make those documents available at its registered office for consultation by the shareholders.

Member States may require companies to maintain the information on their website for a specific period after the general meeting. Member States may determine the consequences of temporary disruption of access to the website caused by technical or other factors.

Article 144. 1. Neither an examination of the draft terms of division nor an expert report as provided for in Article 142(1) shall be required if all the shareholders and the holders of other securities conferring the right to vote of each of the companies involved in the division have so agreed.

2. Member States may permit the non-application of Article 141 and points (c) and (d) of Article 143(1) if all the shareholders and the holders of other securities conferring the right to vote of each of the companies involved in the division have so agreed.

Article 145. Protection of the rights of the employees of each of the companies involved in a division shall be regulated in accordance with Directive 2001/23/EC.

Article 146. 1. The laws of Member States shall provide for an adequate system of protection for the interests of the creditors of the companies involved in a division whose claims antedate publication of the draft terms of division and have not yet fallen due at the time of such publication.

2. For the purpose of paragraph 1, the laws of the Member States shall at least provide that such creditors shall be entitled to obtain adequate safeguards where the financial situation of the company being divided, and that of the company to which the obligation is to be transferred in accordance with the draft terms of division, make such protection necessary, and where those creditors do not already have such safeguards.

Member States shall lay down the conditions for the protection provided for in paragraph 1 and in the first subparagraph of this paragraph. In any event, Member States shall ensure that the creditors are authorised to apply to the appropriate administrative or judicial authority for adequate safeguards provided that they can credibly demonstrate that due to the division the satisfaction of their claims is at stake and that no adequate safeguards have been obtained from the company.

3. In so far as a creditor of the company to which the obligation has been transferred in accordance with the draft terms of division has not obtained satisfaction, the recipient companies shall be jointly and severally liable for that obligation. Member States may limit that liability to the net assets allocated to each of those companies other than the one to which the obligation has been transferred. However, they need not apply this paragraph where the division operation is subject to the supervision of a judicial authority in accordance with Article 157 and a majority in number representing three-quarters in value of the creditors or any class of creditors of the company being divided have agreed to forego such joint and several liability at a meeting held pursuant to point (c) of Article 157(l).

4. Article 99(3) shall apply.

5. Without prejudice to the rules governing the collective exercise of their rights, paragraphs 1 to 4 shall apply to the debenture holders of the companies involved in the division except where the division has been approved by a meeting of the debenture holders, if such a meeting is provided for under national laws, or by the debenture holders individually.

6. Member States may provide that the recipient companies shall be jointly and severally liable for the obligations of the company being divided. In such case they need not apply paragraphs 1 to 5.

7. Where a Member State combines the system of creditor protection set out in paragraphs 1 to 5 with the joint and several liability of the recipient companies as referred to in paragraph 6, it may limit such joint and several liability to the net assets allocated to each of those companies.

Article 147. Holders of securities, other than shares, to which special rights are attached, shall be given rights in the recipient companies against which such securities may be invoked in accordance with the draft terms of division, at least equivalent to the rights they possessed in the company being divided, unless the alteration of those rights has been approved by a meeting of the holders of such securities, if such a meeting is provided for under national laws, or by the holders of those securities individually, or unless the holders are entitled to have their securities repurchased.

Article 148. Where the laws of a Member State do not provide for judicial or administrative preventive supervision of the legality of divisions or where such supervision does not extend to all the legal acts required for a division, Article 102 shall apply.

Article 149. The laws of Member States shall determine the date on which a division takes effect.

Article 150. 1. A division shall be published in the manner prescribed by the laws of each Member State in accordance with Article 16 in respect of each of the companies involved in a division.
2. Any recipient company may itself carry out the publication formalities relating to the company being divided.

Article 151. 1. A division shall have the following consequences ipso jure and simultaneously:
(a) the transfer, both as between the company being divided and the recipient companies and as regards third parties, to each of the recipient companies of all the assets and liabilities of the company being divided; such transfer shall take effect with the assets and liabilities being divided in accordance with the allocation laid down in the draft terms of division or in Article 137(3);
(b) the shareholders of the company being divided become shareholders of one or more of the recipient companies in accordance with the allocation laid down in the draft terms of division;
(c) the company being divided ceases to exist.
2. No shares in a recipient company shall be exchanged for shares held in the company being divided either:
(a) by that recipient company itself or by a person acting in his own name but on its behalf; or
(b) by the company being divided itself or by a person acting in his own name but on its behalf.
3. The foregoing shall not affect the laws of Member States which require the completion of special formalities for the transfer of certain assets, rights and obligations by a company being divided to be effective as against third parties. The recipient company or companies to which such assets, rights or obligations are transferred in accordance with the draft terms of division or with Article 137(3) may carry out those formalities themselves; however, the laws of Member States may permit a company being divided to continue to carry out those formalities for a limited period which may not, save in exceptional circumstances, be fixed at more than six months from the date on which the division takes effect.

Article 152. The laws of Member States shall at least lay down rules governing the civil liability of members of the administrative or management bodies of a company being divided towards the shareholders of that company in respect of misconduct on the part of members of those bodies in preparing and implementing the division and the civil liability of the experts responsible for drawing up for that company the report provided for in Article 142 in respect of misconduct on the part of those experts in the performance of their duties.

Article 153. 1. The laws of Member States may lay down nullity rules for divisions in accordance with the following conditions only:
(a) nullity must be ordered in a court judgment;
(b) divisions which have taken effect pursuant to Article 149 are declared void only if there has been no judicial or administrative preventive supervision of their legality, or if they have not been drawn up and certified in due legal form, or if it is shown that the decision of the general meeting is void or voidable under national law;
(c) nullification proceedings are not initiated more than six months after the date on which the division becomes effective as against the person alleging nullity or if the situation has been rectified;
(d) where it is possible to remedy a defect liable to render a division void, the competent court grants the companies involved a period of time within which to rectify the situation;
(e) a judgment declaring a division void is published in the manner prescribed by the laws of each Member State in accordance with Article 16;
(f) where the laws of a Member State permit a third party to challenge such a judgment, he does so only within six months of publication of the judgment in the manner prescribed by Chapter III of Title I;
(g) a judgment declaring a division void does not of itself affect the validity of obligations owed by

or in relation to the recipient companies which arose before the judgment was published and after the date referred to in Article 149;

(h) each of the recipient companies is liable for its obligations arising after the date on which the division took effect and before the date on which the decision pronouncing the nullity of the division was published. The company being divided shall also be liable for such obligations; Member States may provide that this liability be limited to the share of net assets transferred to the recipient company on whose account such obligations arose.

2. By way of derogation from point (a) of paragraph 1 of this Article, the laws of a Member State may also provide for the nullity of a division to be ordered by an administrative authority if an appeal against such a decision lies to a court. Point (b) and points (d) to (h) of paragraph 1 of this Article shall apply by analogy to the administrative authority. Such nullification proceedings may not be initiated more than six months after the date referred to in Article 149.

3. The foregoing shall not affect the laws of the Member States on the nullity of a division pronounced following any supervision of legality.

Article 154. Without prejudice to Article 140, Member States shall not require approval of the division by the general meeting of the company being divided if the recipient companies together hold all the shares of the company being divided and all other securities conferring the right to vote at general meetings of the company being divided, and the following conditions are fulfilled:

(a) each of the companies involved in the operation carries out the publication provided for in Article 138 at least one month before the operation takes effect;

(b) at least one month before the operation takes effect, all shareholders of companies involved in the operation are entitled to inspect the documents specified in Article 143(1), at their company's registered office;

(c) where a general meeting of the company being divided, required for the approval of the division, is not summoned, the information provided for in Article 141(3) covers any material change in the asset and liabilities after the date of preparation of the draft terms of division.

For the purposes of point (b) of the first paragraph, Article 143(2), (3) and (4) and Article 144 shall apply.

Section 3. Division by the formation of new companies

Article 155. 1. For the purposes of this Chapter, 'division by the formation of new companies' means the operation whereby, after being wound up without going into liquidation, a company transfers to more than one newly-formed company all its assets and liabilities in exchange for the allocation to the shareholders of the company being divided of shares in the recipient companies, and possibly a cash payment not exceeding 10 % of the nominal value of the shares allocated or, where they have no nominal value, of their accounting par value.

2. Article 90(2) shall apply.

Article 156. 1. Articles 137, 138, 139, and 141, Article 142(1) and (2) and Articles 143 to 153 shall apply, without prejudice to Articles 11 and 12, to division by the formation of new companies. For this purpose, the term 'companies involved in a division' shall refer to the company being divided and the term 'recipient companies' shall refer to each of the new companies.

2. In addition to the information specified in Article 137(2), the draft terms of division shall indicate the form, name and registered office of each of the new companies.

3. The draft terms of division and, if they are contained in a separate document, the memorandum or draft memorandum of association and the articles or draft articles of association of each of the new companies shall be approved at a general meeting of the company being divided.

4. Member States shall not impose the requirements set out in Articles 141 and 142 and in points (c), (d) and (e) of Article 143(1) where the shares in each of the new companies are allocated to the shareholders of the company being divided in proportion to their rights in the capital of that company.

Section 4. Divisions under the supervision of a judicial authority

Article 157. 1. Member States may apply paragraph 2 where division operations are subject to the supervision of a judicial authority having the power:

(a) to call a general meeting of the shareholders of the company being divided in order to decide upon the division;

(b) to ensure that the shareholders of each of the companies involved in a division have received or can obtain at least the documents referred to in Article 143 in time to examine them before the date of the general meeting of their company called to decide upon the division. Where a Member State makes use of the option provided for in Article 140, the period shall be long enough for the shareholders of the recipient companies to be able to exercise the rights conferred on them by that Article;

(c) to call any meeting of creditors of each of the companies involved in a division in order to decide upon the division;

(d) to ensure that the creditors of each of the companies involved in a division have received or can obtain at least the draft terms of division in time to examine them before the date referred to in point (b);

(e) to approve the draft terms of division.

2. Where the judicial authority establishes that the conditions referred to in points (b) and (d) of paragraph 1 have been fulfilled and that no prejudice would be caused to shareholders or creditors, it may relieve the companies involved in the division from applying:

(a) Article 138, on condition that the adequate system of protection of the interest of the creditors referred to in Article 146(1) covers all claims regardless of their date;

(b) the conditions referred to in points (a) and (b) of Article 140 where a Member State makes use of the option provided for in Article 140;

(c) Article 143, as regards the period and the manner prescribed for the inspection of the documents referred to therein.

Section 5. Other operations treated as divisions

Article 158. Where, in the case of one of the operations specified in Article 135, the laws of a Member State permit the cash payment to exceed 10 %, Sections 2, 3 and 4 of this Chapter shall apply.

Article 159. Where the laws of a Member State permit one of the operations specified in Article 135 without the company being divided ceasing to exist, Sections 2, 3 and 4 of this Chapter shall apply, except for point (c) of Article 151(1).

Section 6. Application arrangements

Article 160. Member States need not apply Articles 146 and 147 as regards the holders of convertible debentures and other securities convertible into shares if, at the time when the provisions referred to in Article 26(1) or (2) of Directive 82/891/EEC came into force, the position of those holders in the event of a division had previously been determined by the conditions of issue.

Title III. Final Provisions

Article 161. The processing of personal data carried out in the context of this Directive shall be subject to Directive 95/46/EC.

Article 162. 1. The Commission shall, not later than 8 June 2022, publish a report concerning the functioning of the system of interconnection of registers, in particular examining its technical operation and its financial aspects.

2. That report shall be accompanied, if appropriate, by proposals for amending provisions of this Directive relating to the system of interconnection of registers.

3. The Commission and the representatives of the Member States shall regularly convene to discuss matters covered by this Directive relating to the system of interconnection of registers in any appropriate forum.

4. By 30 June 2016, the Commission shall review the functioning of those provisions which concern the reporting and documentation requirements in the case of mergers and divisions and which have been amended or added by Directive 2009/109/EC of the European Parliament and of the Council, and in particular their effects on the reduction of administrative burdens on companies, in the light of experience acquired in their application, and shall present a report to the European Parliament and the Council, accompanied if necessary by proposals to amend those provisions.

Article 163. 1. The power to adopt delegated acts is conferred on the Commission subject to the conditions laid down in this Article.

2. The power to adopt delegated acts referred to in Article 25(3) shall be conferred on the Commission for an indeterminate period of time.

3. The delegation of power referred to in Article 25(3) may be revoked at any time by the European Parliament or by the Council. A decision to revoke shall put an end to the delegation of the power specified in that decision. It shall take effect the day following the publication of the decision in the Official Journal of the European Union or at a later date specified therein. It shall not affect the validity of any delegated acts already in force.

4. As soon as it adopts a delegated act, the Commission shall notify it simultaneously to the European Parliament and to the Council.

5. A delegated act adopted pursuant to Article 25(3) shall enter into force only if no objection has been expressed either by the European Parliament or the Council within a period of three months of notification of that act to the European Parliament and the Council or if, before the expiry of that period, the European Parliament and the Council have both informed the Commission that they will not object. That period shall be extended by three months at the initiative of the European Parliament or of the Council.

Article 164. 1. The Commission shall be assisted by a committee. That committee shall be a committee within the meaning of Regulation (EU) No 182/2011.
2. Where reference is made to this paragraph, Article 5 of Regulation (EU) No 182/2011 shall apply.

Article 165. Member States shall communicate to the Commission the text of the main provisions of national law which they adopt in the fields covered by this Directive.

Article 166. Directives 82/891/EEC, 89/666/EEC, 2005/56/EC, 2009/101/EC, 2011/35/EU and 2012/30/EU, as amended by the Directives listed in Part A of Annex III, are repealed, without prejudice to the obligations of the Member States relating to the time limits for the transposition into national law and the dates of application of the Directives set out in Part B of Annex III. References to the repealed Directives shall be construed as references to this Directive and shall be read in accordance with the correlation table in Annex IV.

Article 167. This Directive shall enter into force on the twentieth day following that of its publication in the Official Journal of the European Union.

Article 168. This Directive is addressed to the Member States.

Annex I. Types of Companies Referred to in Article 2(1) and (2), Article 44(1) and (2), Article 45(2), Article 87(1) and (2) and Article 135(1)
— Belgium: société anonyme/naamloze vennootschap;
— Bulgaria: акционерно дружество;
— the Czech Republic: akciová společnost;
— Denmark: aktieselskab;
— Germany: Aktiengesellschaft;
— Estonia: aktsiaselts;
— Ireland: cuideachta phoiblí faoi theorainn scaireanna/public company limited by shares, cuideachta phoiblí faoi theorainn ráthaíochta agus a bhfuil scairchaipiteal aici/public company limited by guarantee and having a share capital;
— Greece: ανώνυμη εταιρεία;
— Spain: sociedad anónima;
— France: société anonyme;
— Croatia: dioničko društvo;
— Italy: società per azioni;
— Cyprus: δημόσιες εταιρείες περιορισμένης ευθύνης με μετοχές, δημόσιες εταιρείες περιορισμένης ευθύνης με εγγύηση που διαθέτουν μετοχικό κεφάλαιο;
— Latvia: akciju sabiedrība;
— Lithuania: akcinė bendrovė;
— Luxembourg: société anonyme;
— Hungary: nyilvánosan működő részvénytársaság;
— Malta: kumpanija pubblika ta' responsabbiltà limitata/public limited liability company;
— the Netherlands: naamloze vennootschap;
— Austria: Aktiengesellschaft;
— Poland: spółka akcyjna;
— Portugal: sociedade anónima;
— Romania: societate pe acțiuni;
— Slovenia: delniška družba;
— Slovakia: akciová spoločnosť;
— Finland: julkinen osakeyhtiö/publikt aktiebolag;
— Sweden: aktiebolag;
— the United Kingdom: public company limited by shares, public company limited by guarantee and having a share capital.

EU: DIRECTIVE 2017/1132 ON COMPANY LAW (CODIFICATION)

Annex II. Types of Companies Referred to in Articles 7(1) and 13, Articles 29(1), 36(1) and 67(1) and Pont (A) of Article 119(1)

— Belgium naamloze vennootschap/société anonyme, commanditaire vennootschap op aandelen/société en commandite par actions, personenvennootschap met beperkte aansprakelijkheid/société de personnes à responsabilité limitée;

— Bulgaria: акционерно дружество, дружество с ограничена отговорност, командитно дружество с акции;

— Czech Republic: společnost s ručením omezeným, akciová společnost;

— Denmark: aktieselskab, kommanditaktieselskab, anpartsselskab;

— Germany: die Aktiengesellschaft, die Kommanditgesellschaft auf Aktien, die Gesellschaft mit beschränkter Haftung;

— Estonia: aktsiaselts, osaühing;

— Ireland: cuideachtaí atá corpraithe faoi dhliteanas teoranta/companies incorporated with limited liability;

— Greece: ανώνυμη εταιρεία, εταιρεία περιορισμένης ευθύνης, ετερόρρυθμη κατά μετοχές εταιρεία;

— Spain: la sociedad anónima, la sociedad comanditaria por acciones, la sociedad de responsabilidad limitada;

— France: société anonyme, société en commandite par actions, société à responsabilité limitée, société par actions simplifiée;

— Croatia: dioničko društvo, društvo s ograničenom odgovornošću;

— Italy: società per azioni, società in accomandita per azioni, società a responsabilità limitata;

— Cyprus: δημόσιες εταιρείες περιορισμένης ευθύνης με μετοχές ή με εγγύηση, ιδιωτικές εταιρείες περιορισμένης ευθύνης με μετοχές ή με εγγύηση;

— Latvia akciju sabiedrība, sabiedrība ar ierobežotu atbildību, komandītsabiedrība;

— Lithuania: akcinė bendrovė, uždaroji akcinė bendrovė;

— Luxembourg: société anonyme, société en commandite par actions, société à responsabilité limitée;

— Hungary: részvénytársaság, korlátolt felelősségű társaság;

— Malta kumpannija pubblika/public limited liability company, kumpannija privata/private limited liability company;

— the Netherlands: naamloze vennootschap, besloten vennootschap met beperkte aansprakelijkheid;

— Austria: die Aktiengesellschaft, die Gesellschaft mit beschränkter Haftung;

— Poland: spółka z ograniczoną odpowiedzialnością, spółka komandytowo-akcyjna, spółka akcyjna;

— Portugal: sociedade anónima de responsabilidade limitada, sociedade em comandita por ações, sociedade por quotas de responsabilidade limitada;

— Romania: societate pe acțiuni, societate cu răspundere limitată, societate în comandită pe acțiuni;

— Slovenia: delniška družba, družba z omejeno odgovornostjo, komaditna delniška družba;

— Slovakia: akciová spoločnosť, spoločnosť s ručením obmedzeným;

— Finland: yksityinen osakeyhtiö/privat aktiebolag, julkinen osakeyhtiö/publikt aktiebolag;

— Sweden: aktiebolag;

— United Kingdom: companies incorporated with limited liability.

PART III EUROPEAN COMPANY LAW

Council Regulation (EEC) No 2137/85 of 25 July 1985 on the European Economic Interest Grouping (EEIG) (OJ L 199, 31.07.1985, pp. 1 – 9) [footnotes omitted].

THE COUNCIL OF THE EUROPEAN COMMUNITIES,
Having regard to the Treaty establishing the European Economic Community, and in particular Article 235 thereof,
Having regard to the proposal from the Commission,
Having regard to the opinion of the European Parliament,
Having regard to the opinion of the Economic and Social Committee,
Whereas a harmonious development of economic activities and a continuous and balanced expansion throughout the Community depend on the establishmend and smooth functioning of a common market offering conditions analogous to those of a national market; whereas to bring about this single market and to increase its unity a legal framework which facilitates the adaptation of their activities to the economic conditions of the Community should be created for natural persons, companies, firms and other legal bodies in particular; whereas to that end it is necessary that those natural persons, companies, firms and other legal bodies should be able to cooperate effectively across frontiers;
Whereas cooperation of this nature can encounter legal, fiscal or psychological difficulties; whereas the creation of an appropriate Community legal instrument in the form of a European Economic Interest Grouping would contribute to the achievement of the abovementioned objectives and therefore proves necessary; Whereas the Treaty does not provide the necessary powers for the creation of such a legal instrument;
Whereas a grouping's ability to adapt to economic conditions must be guaranteed by the considerable freedom for its members in their contractual relations and the internal organization of the grouping;
Whereas a grouping differs from a firm or company principally in its purpose, which is only to facilitate or develop the economic activities of its members to enable them to improve their own results; whereas, by reason of that ancillary nature, a grouping's activities must be related to the economic activities of its members but not replace them so that, to that extent, for example, a grouping may not itself, with regard to third parties, practise a profession, the concept of economic activities being interpreted in the widest sense;
Whereas access to grouping form must be made as widely available as possible to natural persons, companies, firms and other legal bodies, in keeping with the aims of this Regulation; whereas this Regulation shall not, however, prejudice the application at national level of legal rules and/or ethical codes concerning the conditions for the pursuit of business and professional activities;
Whereas this Regulation does not itself confer on any person the right to participate in a grouping, even where the conditions it lays down are fulfilled; Whereas the power provided by this Regulation to prohibit or restrict participation in grouping on grounds of public interest is without prejudice to the laws of Member States which govern the pursuit of activities and which may provide further prohibitions or restrictions or otherwise control or supervise participation in a grouping by any natural person, company, firm or other legal body or any class of them;
Whereas, to enable a grouping to achieve its purpose, it should be endowed with legal capacity and provision should be made for it to be represented vis-à-vis third parties by an organ legally separate from its membership;
Whereas the protection of third parties requires widespread publicity; whereas the members of a grouping have unlimited joint and several liability for the grouping's debts and other liabilities, including those relating to tax or social security, without, however, that principle's affecting the freedom to exclude or restrict the liability of one or more of its members in respect of a particular debt or other liability by means of a specific contract between the grouping and a third party;
Whereas matters relating to the status or capacity of natural persons and to the capacity of legal persons are governed by national law; Whereas the grounds for winding up which are peculiar to the grouping should be specific while referring to national law for its liquidation and the conclusion thereof;
Whereas groupings are subject to national laws relating to insolvency and cessation of payments; whereas such laws may provide other grounds for the winding up of groupings;
Whereas this Regulation provides that the profits or losses resulting from the activities of a grouping shall be taxable only in the hands of its members; whereas it is understood that otherwise national tax laws apply, particularly as regards the apportionment of profits, tax procedures and any obligations imposed by national tax law;
Whereas in matters not covered by this Regulation the laws of the Member States and Community law are applicable, for example with regard to:

EU: REGULATION 2137/85 ON EUROPEAN ECONOMICS INTEREST GROUPING

- social and labour laws,
- competition law,
- intellectual property law;

Whereas the activities of groupings are subject to the provisions of Member States' laws on the pursuit and supervision of activities; whereas in the event of abuse or circumvention of the laws of a Member State by a grouping or its members that Member State may impose appropriate sanctions;

Whereas the Member States are free to apply or to adopt any laws, regulations or administrative measures which do not conflict with the scope or objectives of this Regulation;

Whereas this Regulation must enter into force immediately in its entirety; whereas the implementation of some provisions must nevertheless be deferred in order to allow the Member States first to set up the necessary machinery for the registration of groupings in their territories and the disclosure of certain matters relating to groupings; whereas, with effect from the date of implementation of this Regulation, groupings set up may operate without territorial restrictions,

HAS ADOPTED THIS REGULATION:

Article 1. (1) European Economic Interest Groupings shall be formed upon the terms, in the manner and with the effects laid down in this Regulation. Accordingly, parties intending to form a grouping must conclude a contract and have the registration provided for in Article 6 carried out.

(2) A grouping so formed shall, from the date of its registration as provided for in Article 6, have the capacity, in its own name, to have rights and obligations of all kinds, to make contracts or accomplish other legal acts, and to sue and be sued.

(3) The Member States shall determine whether or not groupings registered at their registries, pursuant to Article 6, have legal personality.

Article 2. (1) Subject to the provisions of this Regulation, the law applicable, on the one hand, to the contract for the formation of a grouping, except as regards matters relating to the status or capacity of natural persons and to the capacity of legal persons and, on the other hand, to the internal organization of a grouping shall be the internal law of the State in which the official address is situated, as laid down in the contract for the formation of the grouping.

(2) Where a State comprises several territorial units, each of which has its own rules of law applicable to the matters referred to in paragraph (1), each territorial unit shall be considered as a State for the purposes of identifying the law applicable under this Article.

Article 3. (1) The purpose of a grouping shall be to facilitate or develop the economic activities of its members and to improve or increase the results of those activities; its purpose is not to make profits for itself. Its activity shall be related to the economic activities of its members and must not be more than ancillary to those activities.

(2) Consequently, a grouping may not:

(a) exercise, directly or indirectly, a power of management or supervision over its members' own activities or over the activities of another undertaking, in particular in the fields of personnel, finance and investment;

(b) directly or indirectly, on any basis whatsoever, hold shares of any kind in a member undertaking; the holding of shares in another undertaking shall be possible only in so far as it is necessary for the achievement of the grouping's objects and if it is done on its members' behalf;

(c) employ more than 500 persons;

(d) be used by a company to make a loan to a director of a company, or any person connected with him, when the making of such loans is restricted or controlled under the Member States' laws governing companies. Nor must a grouping be used for the transfer of any property between a company and a director, or any person connected with him, except to the extent allowed by the Member States' laws governing companies. For the purposes of this provision the making of a loan includes entering into any transaction or arrangement of similar effect, and property includes moveable and immoveable property;

(e) be a member of another European Economic Interest Grouping.

Article 4. (1) Only the following may be members of a grouping:

(a) companies or firms within the meaning of the second paragraph of Article 58 of the Treaty and other legal bodies governed by public or private law, which have been formed in accordance with the law of a Member State and which have their registered or statutory office and central adminsitration in the Community; where, under the law of a Member State, a company, firm or other legal body is not obliged to have a registered or statutory office, it shall be sufficient for such a company, firm or other legal body to have its central administration in the Community;

(b) natural persons who carry on any industrial, commercial, craft or agricultural activity or who provide professional or other services in the Community.

(2) A grouping must comprise at least:

(a) two companies, firms or other legal bodies, within the meaning of paragraph (1), which have their central administrations in different Member States, or

(b) two natural persons, within the meaning of paragraph (1), who carry on their principal activities in different Member States, or

(c) a company, firm or other legal body within the meaning of paragraph (1) and a natural person, of which the first has its central administration in one Member State and the second carries on his principal activity in another Member State.

(3) A Member State may provide that groupings registered at its registries in accordance with Article 6 may have no more than 20 members. For this purpose, that Member State may provide that, in accordance with its laws, each member of a legal body formed under its laws, other than a registered company, shall be treated as a separate member of a grouping.

(4) Any Member State may, on grounds of that State's public interest, prohibit or restrict participation in groupings by certain classes of natural persons, companies, firms, or other legal bodies.

Article 5. A contract for the formation of a grouping shall include at least:
(a) the name of the grouping preceded or followed either by the words 'European Economic Interest Grouping' or by the initials 'EEIG', unless those words or initials already form part of the name;
(b) the official address of the grouping;
(c) the objects for which the grouping is formed;
(d) the name, business name, legal form, permanent address or registered office, and the number and place of registration, if any, of each member of the grouping;
(e) the duration of the grouping, except where this is indefinite.

Article 6. A grouping shall be registered in the State in which it has its official address, at the registry designated pursuant to Article 39 (1).

Article 7. A contract for the formation of a grouping shall be filed at the registry referred to in Article 6.

The following documents and particulars must also be filed at that registry: (a) any amendment to the contract for the formation of a grouping, including any change in the composition of a grouping;
(b) notice of the setting up or closure of any establishment of the grouping;
(c) any judicial decision establishing or declaring the nullity of a grouping, in accordance with Article 15;
(d) notice of the appointment of the manager or managers of a grouping, their names and any other identification particulars required by the law of the Member State in which the register is kept, notification that they may act alone or must act jointly, and the termination of any manager's appointment;
(e) notice of a member's assignment of his participation in a grouping or a proportion thereof, in accordance with Article 22 (1);
(f) any decision by members ordering or establishing the winding up of a grouping, in accordance with Article 31, or any judicial decision ordering such winding up, in accordance with Articles 31 or 32;
(g) notice of the appointment of the liquidator or liquidators of a grouping, as referred to in Article 35, their names and any other identification particulars required by the law of the Member State in which the register is kept, and the termination of any liquidator's appointment;
(h) notice of the conclusion of a grouping's liquidation, as referred to in Article 35 (2);
(i) any proposal to transfer the official address, as referred to in Article 14 (1);
(j) any clause exempting a new member from the payment of debts and other liabilities which originated prior to his admission, in accordance with Article 26 (2).

Article 8. The following must be published, as laid down in Article 39, in the gazette referred to in paragraph (1) of that Article:
(a) the particulars which must be included in the contract for the formation of a grouping, pursuant to Article 5, and any amendments thereto;
(b) the number, date and place of registration as well as notice of the termination of that registration;
(c) the documents and particulars referred to in Article 7 (b) to (j).
The particulars referred to in (a) and (b) must be published in full. The documents and particulars referred to in (c) may be published either in full or in extract form or by means of a reference to their filing at the registry, in accordance with the national legislation applicable.

Article 9. (1) The documents and particulars which must be published pursuant to this Regulation

may be relied on by a grouping as against third parties under the conditions laid down by the national law applicable pursuant to Article 3 (5) and (7) of Council Directive 68/151/EEC of 9 March 1968 on coordination of safeguards which, for the protection of the interests of members and others, are required by Member States of companies within the meaning of the second paragraph of Article 58 of the Treaty, with a view to making such safeguards equivalent throughout the Community (1).
(2) If activities have been carried on on behalf of a grouping before its registration in accordance with Article 6 and if the grouping does not, after its registration, assume the obligations arising out of such activities, the natural persons, companies, firms or other legal bodies which carried on those activities shall bear unlimited joint and several liability for them.

Article 10. Any grouping establishment situated in a Member State other than that in which the official address is situated shall be registered in that State. For the purpose of such registration, a grouping shall file, at the appropriate registry in that Member State, copies of the documents which must be filed at the registry of the Member State in which the official address is situated, together, if necessary, with a translation which conforms with the practice of the registry where the establishment is registered.

Article 11. Notice that a grouping has been formed or that the liquidation of a grouping has been concluded stating the number, date and place of registration and the date, place and title of publication, shall be given in the Official Journal of the European Communities after it has been published in the gazette referred to in Article 39 (1).

Article 12. The official address referred to in the contract for the formation of a grouping must be situated in the Community.
The official address must be fixed either:
(a) where the grouping has its central administration, or
(b) where one of the members of the grouping has its central administration or, in the case of a natural person, has principal activity, provided that the grouping carries on an activity there.

Article 13. The official address of a grouping may be transferred within the Community.
When such a transfer does not result in a change in the law applicable pursuant to Article 2, the decision to transfer shall be taken in accordance with the conditions laid down in the contract for the formation of the grouping.

Article 14. (1) When the transfer of the official address results in a change in the law applicable pursuant to Article 2, a transfer proposal must be drawn up, filed and published in accordance with the conditions laid down in Articles 7 and 8.
No decision to transfer may be taken for two months after publication of the proposal. Any such decision must be taken by the members of the grouping unanimously. The transfer shall take effect on the date on which the grouping is registered, in accordance with Article 6, at the registry for the new official address. That registration may not be effected until evidence has been produced that the proposal to transfer the official address has been published.
(2) The termination of a grouping's registration at the registry for its old official address may not be effected until evidence has been produced that the grouping has been registered at the registry for its new official address.
(3) Upon publication of a grouping's new registration the new official address may be relied on as against third parties in accordance with the conditions referred to in Article 9 (1); however, as long as the termination of the grouping's registration at the registry for the old official address has not been published, third parties may continue to rely on the old official address unless the grouping proves that such third parties were aware of the new official address.
(4) The laws of a Member State may provide that, as regards groupings registered under Article 6 in that Member State, the transfer of an official address which would result in a change of the law applicable shall not take effect if, within the two-month period referred to in paragraph (1), a competent authority in that Member State opposes it. Such opposition may be based only on grounds of public interest. Review by a judicial authority must be possible.

Article 15. (1) Where the law applicable to a grouping by virtue of Article 2 provides for the nullity of that grouping, such nullity must be established or declared by judicial decision. However, the court to which the matter is referred must, where it is possible for the affairs of the grouping to be put in order, allow time to permit that to be done.
(2) The nullity of a grouping shall entail its liquidation in accordance with the conditions laid down in Article 35.

PART III   EUROPEAN COMPANY LAW

(3) A decision establishing or declaring the nullity of a grouping may be relied on as against third parties in accordance with the conditions laid down in Article 9 (1).
Such a decision shall not of itself affect the validity of liabilities, owed by or to a grouping, which originated before it could be relied on as against third parties in accordance with the conditions laid down in the previous subparagraph.

Article 16. (1) The organs of a grouping shall be the members acting collectively and the manager or managers.
A contract for the formation of a grouping may provide for other organs; if it does it shall determine their powers.
(2) The members of a grouping, acting as a body, may take any decision for the purpose of achieving the objects of the grouping.

Article 17. (1) Each member shall have one vote. The contract for the formation of a grouping may, however, give more than one vote to certain members, provided that no one member holds a majority of the votes.
(2) A unanimous decision by the members shall be required to:
(a) alter the objects of a grouping;
(b) alter the number of votes allotted to each member;
(c) alter the conditions for the taking of decisions;
(d) extend the duration of a grouping beyond any period fixed in the contract for the formation of the grouping;
(e) alter the contribution by every member or by some members to the grouping's financing;
(f) alter any other obligation of a member, unless otherwise provided by the contract for the formation of the grouping;
(g) make any alteration to the contract for the formation of the grouping not covered by this paragraph, unless otherwise provided by that contract.
(3) Except where this Regulation provides that decisions must be taken unanimously, the contract for the formation of a grouping may prescribe the conditions for a quorum and for a majority, in accordance with which the decisions, or some of them, shall be taken. Unless otherwise provided for by the contract, decisions shall be taken unanimously.
(4) On the initiative of a manager or at the request of a member, the manager or managers must arrange for the members to be consulted so that the latter can take a decision.

Article 18. Each member shall be entitled to obtain information from the manager or managers concerning the grouping's business and to inspect the grouping's books and business records.

Article 19. (1) A grouping shall be managed by one or more natural persons appointed in the contract for the formation of the grouping or by decision of the members. No person may be a manager of a grouping if:
- by virtue of the law applicable to him, or
- by virtue of the internal law of the State in which the grouping has its official address, or
- following a judicial or administrative decision made or recognized in a Member State
he may not belong to the administrative or management body of a company, may not manage an undertaking or may not act as manager of a European Economic Interest Grouping.
(2) A Member State may, in the case of groupings registered at their registries pursuant to Article 6, provide that legal persons may be managers on condition that such legal persons designate one or more natural persons, whose particulars shall be the subject of the filing provisions of Article 7 (d) to represent them.
If a Member State exercises this option, it must provide that the representative or representatives shall be liable as if they were themselves managers of the groupings concerned. The restrictions imposed in paragraph (1) shall also apply to those representatives.
(3) The contract for the formation of a grouping or, failing that, a unanimous decision by the members shall determine the conditions for the appointment and removal of the manager or managers and shall lay down their powers.

Article 20. (1) Only the manager or, where there are two or more, each of the managers shall represent a grouping in respect of dealings with third parties. Each of the managers shall bind the grouping as regards third parties when he acts on behalf of the grouping, even where his acts do not fall within the objects of the grouping, unless the grouping proves that the third party knew or could not, under the circumstances, have been unaware that the act fell outside the objects of the grouping; publication of the particulars referred to in Article 5 (c) shall not of itself be proof thereof. No limitation on the powers of the manager or managers, whether deriving from the contract for the formation of the grouping or from a decision by the members, may be relied on as against thrid parties even if it is published.

(2) The contract for the formation of the grouping may provide that the grouping shall be validly bound only by two or more managers acting jointly. Such a clause may be relied on as against third parties in accordance with the conditions referred to in Article 9 (1) only if it is published in accordance with Article 8.

Article 21 (1) The profits resulting from a grouping's activities shall be deemed to be the profits of the members and shall be apportioned among them in the proportions laid down in the contract for the formation of the grouping or, in the absence of any such provision, in equal shares.

(2) The members of a grouping shall contribute to the payment of the amount by which expenditure exceeds income in the proportions laid down in the contract for the formation of the grouping or, in the absence of any such provision, in equal shares.

Article 22. (1) Any member of a grouping may assign his participation in the grouping, or a proportion thereof, either to another member or to a third party; the assignment shall not take effect without the unanimous authorization of the other members.

(2) A member of a grouping may use his participation in the grouping as security only after the other members have given their unanimous authorization, unless otherwise laid down in the contract for the formation of the grouping. The holder of the security may not at any time become a member of the grouping by virtue of that security.

Article 23. No grouping may invite investment by the public.

Article 24. (1) The members of a grouping shall have unlimited joint and several liability for its debts and other liabilities of whatever nature. National law shall determine the consequences of such liability.

(2) Creditors may not proceed against a member for payment in respect of debts and other liabilities, in accordance with the conditions laid down in paragraph (1), before the liquidation of a grouping is concluded, unless they have first requested the grouping to pay and payment has not been made within an appropriate period.

Article 25. Letters, order forms and similar documents must indicate legibly:

(a) the name of the grouping preceded or followed either by the words 'European Economic Interest Grouping' or by the initials 'EEIG', unless those words or initials already occur in the name;

(b) the location of the registry referred to in Article 6, in which the grouping is registered, together with the number of the grouping's entry at the registry;

(c) the grouping's official address;

(d) where applicable, that the managers must act jointly;

(e) where applicable, that the grouping is in liquidation, pursuant to Articles 15, 31, 32 or 36.

Every establishment of a grouping, when registered in accordance with Article 10, must give the above particulars, together with those relating to its own registration, on the documents referred to in the first paragraph of this Article uttered by it.

Article 26. (1) A decision to admit new members shall be taken unanimously by the members of the grouping.

(2) Every new member shall be liable, in accordance with the conditions laid down in Article 24, for the grouping's debts and other liabilities, including those arising out of the grouping's activities before his admission. He may, however, be exempted by a clause in the contract for the formation of the grouping or in the instrument of admission from the payment of debts and other liabilities which originated before his admission. Such a clause may be relied on as against third parties, under the conditions referred to in Article 9 (1), only if it is published in accordance with Article 8.

Article 27. (1) A member of a grouping may withdraw in accordance with the conditions laid down in the contract for the formation of a grouping or, in the absence of such conditions, with the unanimous agreement of the other members.

Any member of a grouping may, in addition, withdraw on just and proper grounds.

(2) Any member of a grouping may be expelled for the reasons listed in the contract for the formation of the grouping and, in any case, if he seriously fails in his obligations or if he causes or threatens to cause serious disruption in the operation of the grouping. Such expulsion may occur only by the decision of a court to which joint application has been made by a majority of the other members, unless otherwise provided by the contract for the formation of a grouping.

PART III   EUROPEAN COMPANY LAW

Article 28. (1) A member of a grouping shall cease to belong to it on death or when he no longer complies with the conditions laid down in Article 4 (1). In addition, a Member State may provide, for the purposes of its liquidation, winding up, insolvency or cessation of payments laws, that a member shall cease to be a member of any grouping at the moment determined by those laws.
(2) In the event of the death of a natural person who is a member of a grouping, no person may become a member in his place except under the conditions laid down in the contract for the formation of the grouping or, failing that, with the unanimous agreement of the remaining members.

Article 29. As soon as a member ceases to belong to a grouping, the manager or managers must inform the other members of that fact; they must also take the steps required as listed in Articles 7 and 8. In addition, any person concerned may take those steps.

Article 30. Except where the contract for the formation of a grouping provides otherwise and without prejudice to the rights acquired by a person under Articles 22 (1) or 28 (2), a grouping shall continue to exist for the remaining members after a member has ceased to belong to it, in accordance with the conditions laid down in the contract for the formation of the grouping or determined by unanimous decision of the members in question.

Article 31. (1) A grouping may be wound up by a decision of its members ordering its winding up. Such a decision shall be taken unanimously, unless otherwise laid down in the contract for the formation of the grouping.
(2) A grouping must be wound up by a decision of its members:
(a) noting the expiry of the period fixed in the contract for the formation of the grouping or the existence of any other cause for winding up provided for in the contract, or
(b) noting the accomplishment of the grouping's purpose or the impossibility of pursuing it further. Where, three months after one of the situation referred to in the first subparagraph has occurred, a members' decision establishing the winding up of the grouping has not been taken, any member may petition the court to order winding up.
(3) A grouping must also be wound up by a decision of its members or of the remaining member when the conditions laid down in Article 4 (2) are no longer fulfilled.
(4) After a grouping has been wound up by decision of its members, the manager or managers must take the steps required as listed in Articles 7 and 8. In addition, any person concerned may take those steps.

Article 32. (1) On application by any person concerned or by a competent authority, in the event of the infringement of Articles 3, 12 or 31 (3), the court must order a grouping to be wound up, unless its affairs can be and are put in order before the court has delivered a substantive ruling.
(2) On applications by a member, the court may order a grouping to be wound up on just and proper grounds.
(3) A Member State may provide that the court may, on application by a competent authority, order the winding up of a grouping which has its official address in the State to which that authority belongs, wherever the grouping acts in contravention of that State's public interest, if the law of that State provides for such a possibility in respect of registered companies or other legal bodies subject to it.

Article 33. When a member ceases to belong to a grouping for any reason other than the assignment of his rights in accordance with the conditions laid down in Article 22 (1), the value of his rights and obligations shall be determined taking into account the assets and liabilities of the grouping as they stand when he ceases to belong to it. The value of the rights and obligations of a departing member may not be fixed in advance.

Article 34. Without prejudice to Article 37 (1), any member who ceases to belong to a grouping shall remain answerable, in accordance with the conditions laid down in Article 24, for the debts and other liabilities arising out of the grouping's activities before he ceased to be a member.

Article 35. (1) The winding up of a grouping shall entail its liquidation.
(2) The liquidation of a grouping and the conclusion of its liquidation shall be governed by national law.
(3) A grouping shall retain its capacity, within the meaning of Article 1 (2), until its liquidation is concluded.
(4) The liquidator or liquidators shall take the steps required as listed in Articles 7 and 8.

Article 36. Groupings shall be subject to national laws governing insolvency and cessation of payments. The commencement of proceedings against a grouping on grounds of its insolvency or cessation of payments shall not by itself cause the commencement of such proceedings against its members.

Article 37. (1) A period of limitation of five years after the publication, pursuant to Article 8, of notice of a member's ceasing to belong to a grouping shall be substituted for any longer period which may be laid down by the relevant national law for actions against that member in connection with debts and other liabilities arising out of the grouping's activities before he ceased to be a member.
(2) A period of limitation of five years after the publication, pursuant to Article 8, of notice of the conclusion of the liquidation of a grouping shall be substituted for any longer period which may be laid down by the relevant national law for actions against a member of the grouping in connection with debts and other liabilities arising out of the grouping's activities.

Article 38. Where a grouping carries on any activity in a Member State in contravention of that State's public interest, a competent authority of that State may prohibit that activity. Review of that competent authority's decision by a judicial authority shall be possible. Article 39
(1) The Member States shall designate the registry or registries responsible for effecting the registration referred to in Articles 6 and 10 and shall lay down the rules governing registration. They shall prescribe the conditions under which the documents referred to in Articles 7 and 10 shall be filed. They shall ensure that the documents and particulars referred to in Article 8 are published in the appropriate official gazette of the Member State in which the grouping has its official address, and may prescribe the manner of publication of the documents and particulars referred to in Article 8 (c). The Member States shall also ensure that anyone may, at the appropriate registry pursuant to Article 6 or, where appropriate, Article 10, inspect the documents referred to in Article 7 and obtain, even by post, full or partial copies thereof.
The Member States may provide for the payment of fees in connection with the operations referred to in the preceding subparagraphs; those fees may not, however, exceed the administrative cost thereof.
(2) The Member States shall ensure that the information to be published in the Official Journal of the European Communities pursuant to Article 11 is forwarded to the Office for Official Publications of the European Communities within one month of its publication in the official gazette referred to in paragraph (1).
(3) The Member States shall provide for appropriate penalties in the event of failure to comply with the provisions of Articles 7, 8 and 10 on disclosure and in the event of failure to comply with Article 25.

Article 40. The profits or losses resulting from the activities of a grouping shall be taxable only in the hands of its members.

Article 41. (1) The Member States shall take the measures requried by virtue of Article 39 before 1 July 1989. They shall immediately communicate them to the Commission.
(2) For information purposes, the Member States shall inform the Commission of the classes of natural persons, companies, firms and other legal bodies which they prohibit from participating in groupings pursuant to Article 4 (4). The Commission shall inform the other Member States.

Article 42. (1) Upon the adoption of this Regulation, a Contact Committee shall be set up under the auspices of the Commission. Its function shall be:
(a) to facilitate, without prejudice to Articles 169 and 170 of the Treaty, application of this Regulation through regular consultation dealing in particular with practical problems arising in connection with its application;
(b) to advise the Commission, if necessary, on additions or amendments to this Regulation.
(2) The Contact Committee shall be composed of representatives of the Member States and representatives of the Commission. The chairman shall be a representative of the Commission. The Commission shall provide the secretariat.
(3) The Contact Committee shall be convened by its chairman either on his own initiative or at the request of one of its members.

Article 43. This Regulation shall enter into force on the third day following its publication in the Official Journal of the European Communities. It shall apply from 1 July 1989, with the exception of Articles 39, 41 and 42 which shall apply as from the entry into force of the Regulation. This Regulation shall be binding in its entirety and directly applicable in all Member States.

PART III   EUROPEAN COMPANY LAW

Council Regulation (EC) No 2157/2001 of 8 October 2001 on the Statute for a European company (SE) (O J L 294, 10.11.2001, pp. 1 – 21). Consolidated version as last amended by Council Regulation (EC) 1791/2006 of 20 November 2006 [footnotes omitted].

THE COUNCIL OF THE EUROPEAN UNION,
Having regard to the Treaty establishing the European Community, and in particular Article 308 thereof,
Having regard to the proposal from the Commission,
Having regard to the opinion of the European Parliament,
Having regard to the opinion of the Economic and Social Committee,
Whereas:
(1) The completion of the internal market and the improvement it brings about in the economic and social situation throughout the Community mean not only that barriers to trade must be removed, but also that the structures of production must be adapted to the Community dimension. For that purpose it is essential that companies the business of which is not limited to satisfying purely local needs should be able to plan and carry out the reorganisation of their business on a Community scale.
(2) Such reorganisation presupposes that existing companies from different Member States are given the option of combining their potential by means of mergers. Such operations can be carried out only with due regard to the rules of competition laid down in the Treaty.
(3) Restructuring and cooperation operations involving companies from different Member States give rise to legal and psychological difficulties and tax problems. The approximation of Member States' company law by means of Directives based on Article 44 of the Treaty can overcome some of those difficulties. Such approximation does not, however, release companies governed by different legal systems from the obligation to choose a form of company governed by a particular national law.
(4) The legal framework within which business must be carried on in the Community is still based largely on national laws and therefore no longer corresponds to the economic framework within which it must develop if the objectives set out in Article 18 of the Treaty are to be achieved. That situation forms a considerable obstacle to the creation of groups of companies from different Member States.
(5) Member States are obliged to ensure that the provisions applicable to European companies under this Regulation do not result either in discrimination arising out of unjustified different treatment of European companies compared with public limitedliability companies or in disproportionate restrictions on the formation of a European company or on the transfer of its registered office.
(6) It is essential to ensure as far as possible that the economic unit and the legal unit of business in the Community coincide. For that purpose, provision should be made for the creation, side by side with companies governed by a particular national law, of companies formed and carrying on business under the law created by a Community Regulation directly applicable in all Member States.
(7) The provisions of such a Regulation will permit the creation and management of companies with a European dimension, free from the obstacles arising from the disparity and the limited territorial application of national company law.
(8) The Statute for a European public limited-liability company (hereafter referred to as 'SE') is among the measures to be adopted by the Council before 1992 listed in the Commission's White Paper on completing the internal market, approved by the European Council that met in Milan in June 1985. The European Council that met in Brussels in 1987 expressed the wish to see such a Statute created swiftly.
(9) Since the Commission's submission in 1970 of a proposal for a Regulation on the Statute for a European public limited-liability company, amended in 1975, work on the approximation of national company law has made substantial progress, so that on those points where the functioning of an SE does not need uniform Community rules reference may be made to the law governing public limited-liability companies in the Member State where it has its registered office.
(10) Without prejudice to any economic needs that may arise in the future, if the essential objective of legal rules governing SEs is to be attained, it must be possible at least to create such a company as a means both of enabling companies from different Member States to merge or to create a holding company and of enabling companies and other legal persons carrying on economic activities and governed by the laws of different Member States to form joint subsidiaries.
(11) In the same context it should be possible for a public limitedliability company with a registered office and head office within the Community to transform itself into an SE without going into liquidation, provided it has a subsidiary in a Member State other than that of its registered office.
(12) National provisions applying to public limited-liability companies that offer their securities to the public and to securities transactions should also apply where an SE is formed by means of an

offer of securities to the public and to SEs wishing to utilize such financial instruments.
(13) The SE itself must take the form of a company with share capital, that being the form most suited, in terms of both financing and management, to the needs of a company carrying on business on a European scale. In order to ensure that such companies are of reasonable size, a minimum amount of capital should be set so that they have sufficient assets without making it difficult for small and medium-sized undertakings to form SEs.
(14) An SE must be efficiently managed and properly supervised. It must be borne in mind that there are at present in the Community two different systems for the administration of public limitedliability companies. Although an SE should be allowed to choose between the two systems, the respective responsibilities of those responsible for management and those responsible for supervision should be clearly defined.
(15) Under the rules and general principles of private international law, where one undertaking controls another governed by a different legal system, its ensuing rights and obligations as regards the protection of minority shareholders and third parties are governed by the law governing the controlled undertaking, without prejudice to the obligations imposed on the controlling undertaking by its own law, for example the requirement to prepare consolidated accounts.
(16) Without prejudice to the consequences of any subsequent coordination of the laws of the Member States, specific rules for SEs are not at present required in this field. The rules and general principles of private international law should therefore be applied both where an SE exercises control and where it is the controlled company.
(17) The rule thus applicable where an SE is controlled by another undertaking should be specified, and for this purpose reference should be made to the law governing public limited-liability companies in the Member State in which the SE has its registered office.
(18) Each Member State must be required to apply the sanctions applicable to public limited-liability companies governed by its law in respect of infringements of this Regulation.
(19) The rules on the involvement of employees in the European company are laid down in Directive 2001/86/EC, and those provisions thus form an indissociable complement to this Regulation and must be applied concomitantly.
(20) This Regulation does not cover other areas of law such as taxation, competition, intellectual property or insolvency. The provisions of the Member States' law and of Community law are therefore applicable in the above areas and in other areas not covered by this Regulation.
(21) Directive 2001/86/EC is designed to ensure that employees have a right of involvement in issues and decisions affecting the life of their SE. Other social and labour legislation questions, in particular the right of employees to information and consultation as regulated in the Member States, are governed by the national provisions applicable, under the same conditions, to public limited-liability companies.
(22) The entry into force of this Regulation must be deferred so that each Member State may incorporate into its national law the provisions of Directive 2001/86/EC and set up in advance the necessary machinery for the formation and operation of SEs with registered offices within its territory, so that the Regulation and the Directive may be applied concomitantly.
(23) A company the head office of which is not in the Community should be allowed to participate in the formation of an SE provided that company is formed under the law of a Member State, has its registered office in that Member State and has a real and continuous link with a Member State's economy according to the principles established in the 1962 General Programme for the abolition of restrictions on freedom of establishment. Such a link exists in particular if a company has an establishment in that Member State and conducts operations therefrom.
(24) The SE should be enabled to transfer its registered office to another Member State. Adequate protection of the interests of minority shareholders who oppose the transfer, of creditors and of holders of other rights should be proportionate. Such transfer should not affect the rights originating before the transfer.
(25) This Regulation is without prejudice to any provision which may be inserted in the 1968 Brussels Convention or in any text adopted by Member States or by the Council to replace such Convention, relating to the rules of jurisdiction applicable in the case of transfer of the registered offices of a public limitedliability company from one Member State to another.
(26) Activities by financial institutions are regulated by specific directives and the national law implementing those directives and additional national rules regulating those activities apply in full to an SE.
(27) In view of the specific Community character of an SE, the 'real seat' arrangement adopted by this Regulation in respect of SEs is without prejudice to Member States' laws and does not pre-empt any choices to be made for other Community texts on company law.

(28) The Treaty does not provide, for the adoption of this Regulation, powers of action other than those of Article 308 thereof.
(29) Since the objectives of the intended action, as outlined above, cannot be adequately attained by the Member States in as much as a European public limited-liability company is being established at European level and can therefore, because of the scale and impact of such company, be better attained at Community level, the Community may take measures in accordance with the principle of subsidiarity enshrined in Article 5 of the Treaty. In accordance with the principle of proportionality as set out in the said Article, this Regulation does not go beyond what is necessary to attain these objectives,
HAS ADOPTED THIS REGULATION:

Title I. General Provisions

Article 1. (1) A company may be set up within the territory of the Community in the form of a European public limited-liability company (SocietasEuropaea or SE) on the conditions and in the manner laid down in this Regulation.
(2) The capital of an SE shall be divided into shares. No shareholder shall be liable for more than the amount he has subscribed.
(3) An SE shall have legal personality.
(4) Employee involvement in an SE shall be governed by the provisions of Directive 2001/86/EC.

Article 2. (1) Public limited-liability companies such as referred to in Annex I, formed under the law of a Member State, with registered offices and head offices within the Community may form an SE by means of a merger provided that at least two of them are governed by the law of different Member States.
(2) Public and private limited-liability companies such as referred to in Annex II, formed under the law of a Member State, with registered offices and head offices within the Community may promote the formation of a holding SE provided that each of at least two of them:
(a) is governed by the law of a different Member State, or
(b) has for at least two years had a subsidiary company governed by the law of another Member State or a branch situated in another Member State.
(3) Companies and firms within the meaning of the second paragraph of Article 48 of the Treaty and other legal bodies governed by public or private law, formed under the law of a Member State, with registered offices and head offices within the Community may form a subsidiary SE by subscribing for its shares, provided that each of at least two of them:
(a) is governed by the law of a different Member State, or
(b) has for at least two years had a subsidiary company governed by the law of another Member State or a branch situated in another Member State.
(4) A public limited-liability company, formed under the law of a Member State, which has its registered office and head office within the Community may be transformed into an SE if for at least two years it has had a subsidiary company governed by the law of another Member State.
(5) A Member State may provide that a company the head office of which is not in the Community may participate in the formation of an SE provided that company is formed under the law of a Member State, has its registered office in that Member State and has a real and continuous link with a Member State's economy.

Article 3. (1) For the purposes of Article 2(1), (2) and (3), an SE shall be regarded as a public limited-liability company governed by the law of the Member State in which it has its registered office.
(2) An SE may itself set up one or more subsidiaries in the form of SEs. The provisions of the law of the Member State in which a subsidiary SE has its registered office that require a public limitedliability company to have more than one shareholder shall not apply in the case of the subsidiary SE. The provisions of national law implementing the twelfth Council Company Law Directive (89/667/EEC) of 21 December 1989 on single-member private limited-liability companies shall apply to SEs mutatis mutandis.

Article 4. (1) The capital of an SE shall be expressed in euro.
(2) The subscribed capital shall not be less than EUR 120 000.
(3) The laws of a Member State requiring a greater subscribed capital for companies carrying on certain types of activity shall apply to SEs with registered offices in that Member State.

Article 5. Subject to Article 4(1) and (2), the capital of an SE, its maintenance and changes thereto, together with its shares, bonds and other similar securities shall be governed by the provisions which would apply to a public limited-liability company with a registered office in the Member State in which the SE is registered.

Article 6. For the purposes of this Regulation, 'the statutes of the SE' shall mean both the instrument of incorporation and, where they are the subject of a separate document, the statutes of the SE.

Article 7. The registered office of an SE shall be located within the Community, in the same Member State as its head office. A Member State may in addition impose on SEs registered in its territory the obligation of locating their head office and their registered office in the same place.

Article 8. (1) The registered office of an SE may be transferred to another Member State in accordance with paragraphs 2 to 13. Such a transfer shall not result in the winding up of the SE or in the creation of a new legal person.
(2) The management or administrative organ shall draw up a transfer proposal and publicise it in accordance with Article 13, without prejudice to any additional forms of publication provided for by the Member State of the registered office. That proposal shall state the current name, registered office and number of the SE and shall cover:
(a) the proposed registered office of the SE;
(b) the proposed statutes of the SE including, where appropriate, its new name;
(c) any implication the transfer may have on employees' involvement;
(d) the proposed transfer timetable;
(e) any rights provided for the protection of shareholders and/or creditors.
(3) The management or administrative organ shall draw up a report explaining and justifying the legal and economic aspects of the transfer and explaining the implications of the transfer for shareholders, creditors and employees.
(4) An SE's shareholders and creditors shall be entitled, at least one month before the general meeting called upon to decide on the transfer, to examine at the SE's registered office the transfer proposal and the report drawn up pursuant to paragraph (3) and, on request, to obtain copies of those documents free of charge.
(5) A Member State may, in the case of SEs registered within its territory, adopt provisions designed to ensure appropriate protection for minority shareholders who oppose a transfer.
(6) No decision to transfer may be taken for two months after publication of the proposal. Such a decision shall be taken as laid down in Article 59.
(7) Before the competent authority issues the certificate mentioned in paragraph (8), the SE shall satisfy it that, in respect of any liabilities arising prior to the publication of the transfer proposal, the interests of creditors and holders of other rights in respect of the SE (including those of public bodies) have been adequately protected in accordance with requirements laid down by the Member State where the SE has its registered office prior to the transfer. A Member State may extend the application of the first subparagraph to liabilities that arise (or may arise) prior to the transfer. The first and second subparagraphs shall be without prejudice to the application to SEs of the national legislation of Member States concerning the satisfaction or securing of payments to public bodies.
(8) In the Member State in which an SE has its registered office the court, notary or other competent authority shall issue a certificate attesting to the completion of the acts and formalities to be accomplished before the transfer.
(9) The new registration may not be effected until the certificate referred to in paragraph (8) has been submitted, and evidence produced that the formalities required for registration in the country of the new registered office have been completed.
(10) The transfer of an SE's registered office and the consequent amendment of its statutes shall take effect on the date on which the SE is registered, in accordance with Article 12, in the register for its new registered office.
(11) When the SE's new registration has been effected, the registry for its new registration shall notify the registry for its old registration. Deletion of the old registration shall be effected on receipt of that notification, but not before.
(12) The new registration and the deletion of the old registration shall be publicised in the Member States concerned in accordance with Article 13.
(13) On publication of an SE's new registration, the new registered office may be relied on as against third parties. However, as long as the deletion of the SE's registration from the register for its previous registered office has not been publicised, third parties may continue to rely on the previous registered office unless the SE proves that such third parties were aware of the new registered office.
(14) The laws of a Member State may provide that, as regards SEs registered in that Member State, the transfer of a registered office which would result in a change of the law applicable shall not take

effect if any of that Member State's competent authorities opposes it within the two-month period referred to in paragraph (6). Such opposition may be based only on grounds of public interest. Where an SE is supervised by a national financial supervisory authority according to Community directives the right to oppose the change of registered office applies to this authority as well. Review by a judicial authority shall be possible.

(15) An SE may not transfer its registered office if proceedings for winding up, liquidation, insolvency or suspension of payments or other similar proceedings have been brought against it.

(16) An SE which has transferred its registered office to another Member State shall be considered, in respect of any cause of action arising prior to the transfer as determined in paragraph (1)0, as having its registered office in the Member States where the SE was registered prior to the transfer, even if the SE is sued after the transfer.

Article 9. (1) An SE shall be governed:
(a) by this Regulation,
(b) where expressly authorised by this Regulation, by the provisions of its statutes or
(c) in the case of matters not regulated by this Regulation or, where matters are partly regulated by it, of those aspects not covered by it, by:
(i) the provisions of laws adopted by Member States in implementation of Community measures relating specifically to SEs;
(ii) the provisions of Member States' laws which would apply to a public limited-liability company formed in accordance with the law of the Member State in which the SE has its registered office;
(iii) the provisions of its statutes, in the same way as for a public limited-liability company formed in accordance with the law of the Member State in which the SE has its registered office.
(2) The provisions of laws adopted by Member States specifically for the SE must be in accordance with Directives applicable to public limited-liability companies referred to in Annex I.
(3) If the nature of the business carried out by an SE is regulated by specific provisions of national laws, those laws shall apply in full to the SE.

Article 10. Subject to this Regulation, an SE shall be treated in every Member State as if it were a public limited-liability company formed in accordance with the law of the Member State in which it has its registered office.

Article 11. (1) The name of an SE shall be preceded or followed by the abbreviation SE.
(2) Only SEs may include the abbreviation SE in their name.
(3) Nevertheless, companies, firms and other legal entities registered in a Member State before the date of entry into force of this Regulation in the names of which the abbreviation SE appears shall not be required to alter their names.

Article 12. (1) Every SE shall be registered in the Member State in which it has its registered office in a register designated by the law of that Member State in accordance with Article 3 of the first Council Directive (68/151/ EEC) of 9 March 1968 on coordination of safeguards which, for the protection of the interests of members and others, are required by Member States of companies within the meaning of the second paragraph of Article 58 of the Treaty, with a view to making such safeguards equivalent throughout the Community (1).
(2) An SE may not be registered unless an agreement on arrangements for employee involvement pursuant to Article 4 of Directive 2001/86/ EC has been concluded, or a decision pursuant to Article 3(6) of the Directive has been taken, or the period for negotiations pursuant to Article 5 of the Directive has expired without an agreement having been concluded.
(3) In order for an SE to be registered in a Member State which has made use of the option referred to in Article 7(3) of Directive 2001/86/ EC, either an agreement pursuant to Article 4 of the Directive must have been concluded on the arrangements for employee involvement, including participation, or none of the participating companies must have been governed by participation rules prior to the registration of the SE.
(4) The statutes of the SE must not conflict at any time with the arrangements for employee involvement which have been so determined. Where new such arrangements determined pursuant to the Directive conflict with the existing statutes, the statutes shall to the extent necessary be amended. In this case, a Member State may provide that the management organ or the administrative organ of the SE shall be entitled to proceed to amend the statutes without any further decision from the general shareholders meeting.

Article 13. Publication of the documents and particulars concerning an SE which must be publicised under this Regulation shall be effected in the manner laid down in the laws of the Member State in which the SE has its registered office in accordance with Directive 68/151/EEC.

Article 14. (1) Notice of an SE's registration and of the deletion of such a registration shall be published for information purposes in the Official Journal of the European Communities after publication in accordance with Article 13. That notice shall state the name, number, date and place of registration of the SE, the date and place of publication and the title of publication, the registered office of the SE and its sector of activity.
(2) Where the registered office of an SE is transferred in accordance with Article 8, notice shall be published giving the information provided for in paragraph (1), together with that relating to the new registration.
(3) The particulars referred to in paragraph (1) shall be forwarded to the Office for Official Publications of the European Communities within one month of the publication referred to in Article 13.

Title II. Formation

Section I. General

Article 15. (1) Subject to this Regulation, the formation of an SE shall be governed by the law applicable to public limited-liability companies in the Member State in which the SE establishes its registered office.
(2) The registration of an SE shall be publicised in accordance with Article 13.

Article 16. (1) An SE shall acquire legal personality on the date on which it is registered in the register referred to in Article 12.
(2) If acts have been performed in an SE's name before its registration in accordance with Article 12 and the SE does not assume the obligations arising out of such acts after its registration, the natural persons, companies, firms or other legal entities which performed those acts shall be jointly and severally liable therefor, without limit, in the absence of agreement to the contrary.

Section II. Formation by merger

Article 17. (1) An SE may be formed by means of a merger in accordance with Article 2(1).
(2) Such a merger may be carried out in accordance with:
(a) the procedure for merger by acquisition laid down in Article 3(1) of the third Council Directive (78/855/EEC) of 9 October 1978 based on Article 54(3)(g) of the Treaty concerning mergers of public limited-liability companies or
(b) the procedure for merger by the formation of a new company laid down in Article 4(1) of the said Directive. In the case of a merger by acquisition, the acquiring company shall take the form of an SE when the merger takes place. In the case of a merger by the formation of a new company, the SE shall be the newly formed company.

Article 18. For matters not covered by this section or, where a matter is partly covered by it, for aspects not covered by it, each company involved in the formation of an SE by merger shall be governed by the provisions of the law of the Member State to which it is subject that apply to mergers of public limited-liability companies in accordance with Directive 78/855/EEC.

Article 19. The laws of a Member State may provide that a company governed by the law of that Member State may not take part in the formation of an SE by merger if any of that Member State's competent authorities opposes it before the issue of the certificate referred to in Article 25(2). Such opposition may be based only on grounds of public interest. Review by a judicial authority shall be possible.

Article 20. (1) The management or administrative organs of merging companies shall draw up draft terms of merger. The draft terms of merger shall include the following particulars:
(a) the name and registered office of each of the merging companies together with those proposed for the SE;
(b) the share-exchange ratio and the amount of any compensation;
(c) the terms for the allotment of shares in the SE;
(d) the date from which the holding of shares in the SE will entitle the holders to share in profits and any special conditions affecting that entitlement;
(e) the date from which the transactions of the merging companies will be treated for accounting purposes as being those of the SE;
(f) the rights conferred by the SE on the holders of shares to which special rights are attached and on the holders of securities other than shares, or the measures proposed concerning them;

(g) any special advantage granted to the experts who examine the draft terms of merger or to members of the administrative, management, supervisory or controlling organs of the merging companies;
(h) the statutes of the SE;
(i) information on the procedures by which arrangements for employee involvement are determined pursuant to Directive 2001/86/EC.
(2) The merging companies may include further items in the draft terms of merger.

Article 21. For each of the merging companies and subject to the additional requirements imposed by the Member State to which the company concerned is subject, the following particulars shall be published in the national gazette of that Member State:
(a) the type, name and registered office of every merging company;
(b) the register in which the documents referred to in Article 3(2) of Directive 68/151/EEC are filed in respect of each merging company, and the number of the entry in that register;
(c) an indication of the arrangements made in accordance with Article 24 for the exercise of the rights of the creditors of the company in question and the address at which complete information on those arrangements may be obtained free of charge;
(d) an indication of the arrangements made in accordance with Article 24 for the exercise of the rights of minority shareholders of the company in question and the address at which complete information on those arrangements may be obtained free of charge;
(e) the name and registered office proposed for the SE.

Article 22. As an alternative to experts operating on behalf of each of the merging companies, one or more independent experts as defined in Article 10 of Directive 78/855/EEC, appointed for those purposes at the joint request of the companies by a judicial or administrative authority in the Member State of one of the merging companies or of the proposed SE, may examine the draft terms of merger and draw up a single report to all the shareholders. The experts shall have the right to request from each of the merging companies any information they consider necessary to enable them to complete their function.

Article 23. (1) The general meeting of each of the merging companies shall approve the draft terms of merger.
(2) Employee involvement in the SE shall be decided pursuant to Directive 2001/86/EC. The general meetings of each of the merging companies may reserve the right to make registration of the SE conditional upon its express ratification of the arrangements so decided.

Article 24. (1) The law of the Member State governing each merging company shall apply as in the case of a merger of public limited-liability companies, taking into account the cross-border nature of the merger, with regard to the protection of the interests of:
(a) creditors of the merging companies;
(b) holders of bonds of the merging companies;
(c) holders of securities, other than shares, which carry special rights in the merging companies.
(2) A Member State may, in the case of the merging companies governed by its law, adopt provisions designed to ensure appropriate protection for minority shareholders who have opposed the merger.

Article 25. (1) The legality of a merger shall be scrutinised, as regards the part of the procedure concerning each merging company, in accordance with the law on mergers of public limited-liability companies of the Member State to which the merging company is subject.
(2) In each Member State concerned the court, notary or other competent authority shall issue a certificate conclusively attesting to the completion of the pre-merger acts and formalities.
(3) If the law of a Member State to which a merging company is subject provides for a procedure to scrutinise and amend the share exchange ratio, or a procedure to compensate minority shareholders, without preventing the registration of the merger, such procedures shall only apply if the other merging companies situated in Member States which do not provide for such procedure explicitly accept, when approving the draft terms of the merger in accordance with Article 23 (1), the possibility for the shareholders of that merging company to have recourse to such procedure. In such cases, the court, notary or other competent authorities may issue the certificate referred to in paragraph (2) even if such a procedure has been commenced. The certificate must, however, indicate that the procedure is pending. The decision in the procedure shall be binding on the acquiring company and all its shareholders.

Article 26. (1) The legality of a merger shall be scrutinised, as regards the part of the procedure concerning the completion of the merger and the formation of the SE, by the court, notary or other

authority competent in the Member State of the proposed registered office of the SE to scrutinise that aspect of the legality of mergers of public limitedliability companies.
(2) To that end each merging company shall submit to the competent authority the certificate referred to in Article 25(2) within six months of its issue together with a copy of the draft terms of merger approved by that company.
(3) The authority referred to in paragraph (1) shall in particular ensure that the merging companies have approved draft terms of merger in the same terms and that arrangements for employee involvement have been determined pursuant to Directive 2001/86/EC.
(4) That authority shall also satisfy itself that the SE has been formed in accordance with the requirements of the law of the Member State in which it has its registered office in accordance with Article 15.

Article 27. (1) A merger and the simultaneous formation of an SE shall take effect on the date on which the SE is registered in accordance with Article 12.
(2) The SE may not be registered until the formalities provided for in Articles 25 and 26 have been completed.

Article 28. For each of the merging companies the completion of the merger shall be publicised as laid down by the law of each Member State in accordance with Article 3 of Directive 68/151/EEC.

Article 29. (1) A merger carried out as laid down in Article 17(2)(a) shall have the following consequences ipso jure and simultaneously:
(a) all the assets and liabilities of each company being acquired are transferred to the acquiring company;
(b) the shareholders of the company being acquired become shareholders of the acquiring company;
(c) the company being acquired ceases to exist;
(d) the acquiring company adopts the form of an SE.
(2) A merger carried out as laid down in Article 17(2)(b) shall have the following consequences ipso jure and simultaneously:
(a) all the assets and liabilities of the merging companies are transferred to the SE;
(b) the shareholders of the merging companies become shareholders of the SE;
(c) the merging companies cease to exist.
(3) Where, in the case of a merger of public limited-liability companies, the law of a Member State requires the completion of any special formalities before the transfer of certain assets, rights and obligations by the merging companies becomes effective against third parties, those formalities shall apply and shall be carried out either by the merging companies or by the SE following its registration.
(4) The rights and obligations of the participating companies on terms and conditions of employment arising from national law, practice and individual employment contracts or employment relationships and existing at the date of the registration shall, by reason of such registration be transferred to the SE upon its registration.

Article 30. A merger as provided for in Article 2(1) may not be declared null and void once the SE has been registered.
The absence of scrutiny of the legality of the merger pursuant to Articles 25 and 26 may be included among the grounds for the winding-up of the SE.

Article 31. (1) Where a merger within the meaning of Article 17(2)(a) is carried out by a company which holds all the shares and other securities conferring the right to vote at general meetings of another company, neither Article 20(1)(b), (c) and (d), Article 29(1)(b) nor Article 22 shall apply. National law governing each merging company and mergers of public limited-liability companies in accordance with Article 24 of Directive 78/855/EEC shall nevertheless apply.
(2) Where a merger by acquisition is carried out by a company which holds 90 % or more but not all of the shares and other securities conferring the right to vote at general meetings of another company, reports by the management or administrative body, reports by an independent expert or experts and the documents necessary for scrutiny shall be required only to the extent that the national law governing either the acquiring company or the company being acquired so requires. Member States may, however, provide that this paragraph may apply where a company holds shares conferring 90 % or more but not all of the voting rights.

Section III. Formation of a holding SE

Article 32. (1) A holding SE may be formed in accordance with Article 2(2). A company promoting the formation of a holding SE in accordance with Article 2(2) shall continue to exist.

(2) The management or administrative organs of the companies which promote such an operation shall draw up, in the same terms, draft terms for the formation of the holding SE. The draft terms shall include a report explaining and justifying the legal and economic aspects of the formation and indicating the implications for the shareholders and for the employees of the adoption of the form of a holding SE. The draft terms shall also set out the particulars provided for in Article 20(1)(a), (b), (c), (f), (g), (h) and (i) and shall fix the minimum proportion of the shares in each of the companies promoting the operation which the shareholders must contribute to the formation of the holding SE. That proportion shall be shares conferring more than 50 % of the permanent voting rights.

(3) For each of the companies promoting the operation, the draft terms for the formation of the holding SE shall be publicised in the manner laid down in each Member State's national law in accordance with Article 3 of Directive 68/151/EEC at least one month before the date of the general meeting called to decide thereon.

(4) One or more experts independent of the companies promoting the operation, appointed or approved by a judicial or administrative authority in the Member State to which each company is subject in accordance with national provisions adopted in implementation of Directive 78/855/EEC, shall examine the draft terms of formation drawn up in accordance with paragraph (2) and draw up a written report for the shareholders of each company. By agreement between the companies promoting the operation, a single written report may be drawn up for the shareholders of all the companies by one or more independent experts, appointed or approved by a judicial or
administrative authority in the Member State to which one of the companies promoting the operation or the proposed SE is subject in accordance with national provisions adopted in implementation of Directive 78/855/EEC.

(5) The report shall indicate any particular difficulties of valuation and state whether the proposed share-exchange ratio is fair and reasonable, indicating the methods used to arrive at it and whether such methods are adequate in the case in question.

(6) The general meeting of each company promoting the operation shall approve the draft terms of formation of the holding SE.
Employee involvement in the holding SE shall be decided pursuant to Directive 2001/86/EC. The general meetings of each company promoting the operation may reserve the right to make registration of the holding SE conditional upon its express ratification of the arrangements so decided.

(7) These provisions shall apply mutatis mutandis to private limited liability companies.

Article 33. (1) The shareholders of the companies promoting such an operation shall have a period of three months in which to inform the promoting companies whether they intend to contribute their shares to the formation of the holding SE. That period shall begin on the date upon which the terms for the formation of the holding SE have been finally determined in accordance with Article 32.

(2) The holding SE shall be formed only if, within the period referred to in paragraph (1), the shareholders of the companies promoting the operation have assigned the minimum proportion of shares in each company in accordance with the draft terms of formation and if all the other conditions are fulfilled.

(3) If the conditions for the formation of the holding SE are all fulfilled in accordance with paragraph (2), that fact shall, in respect of each of the promoting companies, be publicised in the manner laid down in the national law governing each of those companies adopted in implementation of Article 3 of Directive 68/151/EEC. Shareholders of the companies promoting the operation who have not indicated whether they intend to make their shares available to the promoting companies for the purpose of forming the holding SE within the period referred to in paragraph (1) shall have a further month in which to do so.

(4) Shareholders who have contributed their securities to the formation of the SE shall receive shares in the holding SE.

(5) The holding SE may not be registered until it is shown that the formalities referred to in Article 32 have been completed and that the conditions referred to in paragraph (2) have been fulfilled.

Article 34. A Member State may, in the case of companies promoting such an operation, adopt provisions designed to ensure protection for minority shareholders who oppose the operation, creditors and employees.

Section IV. Formation of a subsidiary SE

Article 35. An SE may be formed in accordance with Article 2(3).

Article 36. Companies, firms and other legal entities participating in such an operation shall be subject to the provisions governing their participation in the formation of a subsidiary in the form of a public limited-liability company under national law.

EU: REGULATION 2157/2001 ON STATUTE FOR A EUROPEAN COMPANY (SE)

Section V. Conversion of an existing public limited-liability company into an SE

Article 37. (1) An SE may be formed in accordance with Article 2(4).
(2) Without prejudice to Article 12 the conversion of a public limitedliability company into an SE shall not result in the winding up of the company or in the creation of a new legal person.
(3) The registered office may not be transferred from one Member State to another pursuant to Article 8 at the same time as the conversion is effected.
(4) The management or administrative organ of the company in question shall draw up draft terms of conversion and a report explaining and justifying the legal and economic aspects of the conversion and indicating the implications for the shareholders and for the employees of the adoption of the form of an SE.
(5) The draft terms of conversion shall be publicised in the manner laid down in each Member State's law in accordance with Article 3 of Directive 68/151/EEC at least one month before the general meeting called upon to decide thereon.
(6) Before the general meeting referred to in paragraph (7) one or more independent experts appointed or approved, in accordance with the national provisions adopted in implementation of Article 10 of Directive 78/855/EEC, by a judicial or administrative authority in the Member State to which the company being converted into an SE is subject shall certify in compliance with Directive 77/91/EEC mutatis mutandis that the company has net assets at least equivalent to its capital plus those reserves which must not be distributed under the law or the Statutes.
(7) The general meeting of the company in question shall approve the draft terms of conversion together with the statutes of the SE. The decision of the general meeting shall be passed as laid down in the provisions of national law adopted in implementation of Article 7 of Directive 78/855/EEC.
(8) Member States may condition a conversion to a favourable vote of a qualified majority or unanimity in the organ of the company to be converted within which employee participation is organised.
(9) The rights and obligations of the company to be converted on terms and conditions of employment arising from national law, practice and individual employment contracts or employment relationships and existing at the date of the registration shall, by reason of such registration be transferred to the SE.

Title III. Structure of the SE

Article 38. Under the conditions laid down by this Regulation an SE shall comprise:
(a) a general meeting of shareholders and
(b) either a supervisory organ and a management organ (two-tier system) or an administrative organ (one-tier system) depending on the form adopted in the statutes.

Section I. Two-tier system

Article 39. (1) The management organ shall be responsible for managing the SE. A Member State may provide that a managing director or managing directors shall be responsible for the current management under the same conditions as for public limited-liability companies that have registered offices within that Member State's territory.
(2) The member or members of the management organ shall be appointed and removed by the supervisory organ.
A Member State may, however, require or permit the statutes to provide that the member or members of the management organ shall be appointed and removed by the general meeting under the same conditions as for public limited-liability companies that have registered offices within its territory.
(3) No person may at the same time be a member of both the management organ and the supervisory organ of the same SE. The supervisory organ may, however, nominate one of its members to act as a member of the management organ in the event of a vacancy.
During such a period the functions of the person concerned as a member of the supervisory organ shall be suspended. A Member State may impose a time limit on such a period.
(4) The number of members of the management organ or the rules for determining it shall be laid down in the SE's statutes. A Member State may, however, fix a minimum and/or a maximum number.
(5) Where no provision is made for a two-tier system in relation to public limited-liability companies with registered offices within its territory, a Member State may adopt the appropriate measures in relation to SEs.

Article 40. (1) The supervisory organ shall supervise the work of the management organ. It may not itself exercise the power to manage the SE.
(2) The members of the supervisory organ shall be appointed by the general meeting. The members

of the first supervisory organ may, however, be appointed by the statutes. This shall apply without prejudice to Article 47(4) or to any employee participation arrangements determined pursuant to Directive 2001/86/EC.
(3) The number of members of the supervisory organ or the rules for determining it shall be laid down in the statutes. A Member State may, however, stipulate the number of members of the supervisory organ for SEs registered within its territory or a minimum and/or a maximum number.

Article 41. (1) The management organ shall report to the supervisory organ at least once every three months on the progress and foreseeable development of the SE's business.
(2) In addition to the regular information referred to in paragraph (1), the management organ shall promptly pass the supervisory organ any information on events likely to have an appreciable effect on the SE.
(3) The supervisory organ may require the management organ to provide information of any kind which it needs to exercise supervision in accordance with Article 40(1). A Member State may provide that each member of the supervisory organ also be entitled to this facility.
(4) The supervisory organ may undertake or arrange for any investigations necessary for the performance of its duties.
(5) Each member of the supervisory organ shall be entitled to examine all information submitted to it.

Article 42. The supervisory organ shall elect a chairman from among its members. If half of the members are appointed by employees, only a member appointed by the general meeting of shareholders may be elected chairman.

Section II. The one-tier system

Article 43. (1) The administrative organ shall manage the SE. A Member State may provide that a managing director or managing directors shall be responsible for the day-to-day management under the same conditions as for public limited-liability companies that have registered offices within that Member State's territory.
(2) The number of members of the administrative organ or the rules for determining it shall be laid down in the SE's statutes. A Member State may, however, set a minimum and, where necessary, a maximum number of members.
The administrative organ shall, however, consist of at least three members where employee participation is regulated in accordance with Directive 2001/86/EC.
(3) The member or members of the administrative organ shall be appointed by the general meeting. The members of the first administrative organ may, however, be appointed by the statutes. This shall apply without prejudice to Article 47(4) or to any employee participation arrangements determined pursuant to Directive 2001/86/EC.
(4) Where no provision is made for a one-tier system in relation to public limited-liability companies with registered offices within its territory, a Member State may adopt the appropriate measures in relation to SEs.

Article 44. (1) The administrative organ shall meet at least once every three months at intervals laid down by the statutes to discuss the progress and foreseeable development of the SE's business.
(2) Each member of the administrative organ shall be entitled to examine all information submitted to it.

Article 45. The administrative organ shall elect a chairman from among its members. If half of the members are appointed by employees, only a member appointed by the general meeting of shareholders may be elected chairman.

Section III. Rules common to the one-tier and two-tier systems

Article 46. (1) Members of company organs shall be appointed for a period laid down in the statutes not exceeding six years.
(2) Subject to any restrictions laid down in the statutes, members may be reappointed once or more than once for the period determined in accordance with paragraph (1).

Article 47. (1) An SE's statutes may permit a company or other legal entity to be a member of one of its organs, provided that the law applicable to public limited-liability companies in the Member State in which the SE's registered office is situated does not provide otherwise. That company or other legal entity shall designate a natural person to exercise its functions on the organ in question.
(2) No person may be a member of any SE organ or a representative of a member within the meaning of paragraph (1) who:

(a) is disqualified, under the law of the Member State in which the SE's registered office is situated, from serving on the corresponding organ of a public limited-liability company governed by the law of that Member State, or
(b) is disqualified from serving on the corresponding organ of a public limited-liability company governed by the law of a Member State owing to a judicial or administrative decision delivered in a Member State.
(3) An SE's statutes may, in accordance with the law applicable to public limited-liability companies in the Member State in which the SE's registered office is situated, lay down special conditions of eligibility for members representing the shareholders.
(4) This Regulation shall not affect national law permitting a minority of shareholders or other persons or authorities to appoint some of the members of a company organ.

Article 48. (1) An SE's statutes shall list the categories of transactions which require authorisation of the management organ by the supervisory organ in the two-tier system or an express decision by the administrative organ in the one-tier system.
A Member State may, however, provide that in the two-tier system the supervisory organ may itself make certain categories of transactions subject to authorisation.
(2) A Member State may determine the categories of transactions which must at least be indicated in the statutes of SEs registered within its territory.

Article 49. The members of an SE's organs shall be under a duty, even after they have ceased to hold office, not to divulge any information which they have concerning the SE the disclosure of which might be prejudicial to the company's interests, except where such disclosure is required or permitted under national law provisions applicable to public limitedliability companies or is in the public interest.

Article 50. (1) Unless otherwise provided by this Regulation or the statutes, the internal rules relating to quorums and decision-taking in SE organs shall be as follows:
(a) quorum: at least half of the members must be present or represented;
(b) decision-taking: a majority of the members present or represented.
(2) Where there is no relevant provision in the statutes, the chairman of each organ shall have a casting vote in the event of a tie. There shall be no provision to the contrary in the statutes, however, where half of the supervisory organ consists of employees' representatives.
(3) Where employee participation is provided for in accordance with Directive 2001/86/EC, a Member State may provide that the supervisory organ's quorum and decision-making shall, by way of derogation from the provisions referred to in paragraphs 1 and 2, be subject to the rules applicable, under the same conditions, to public limited-liability companies governed by the law of the Member State concerned.

Article 51. Members of an SE's management, supervisory and administrative organs shall be liable, in accordance with the provisions applicable to public limited-liability companies in the Member State in which the SE's registered office is situated, for loss or damage sustained by the SE following any breach on their part of the legal, statutory or other obligations inherent in their duties.

Section IV. General meeting

Article 52. The general meeting shall decide on matters for which it is given sole responsibility by:
(a) this Regulation or
(b) the legislation of the Member State in which the SE's registered office is situated adopted in implementation of Directive 2001/86/ EC. Furthermore, the general meeting shall decide on matters for which responsibility is given to the general meeting of a public limitedliability company governed by the law of the Member State in which the SE's registered office is situated, either by the law of that Member State or by the SE's statutes in accordance with that law.

Article 53. Without prejudice to the rules laid down in this section, the organisation and conduct of general meetings together with voting procedures shall be governed by the law applicable to public limited-liability companies in the Member State in which the SE's registered office is situated.

Article 54. (1) An SE shall hold a general meeting at least once each calendar year, within six months of the end of its financial year, unless the law of the Member State in which the SE's registered office is situated applicable to public limited-liability companies carrying on the same type of activity as the SE provides for more frequent meetings. A Member State may, however, provide that the first general meeting may be held at any time in the 18 months following an SE's incorporation.

(2) General meetings may be convened at any time by the management organ, the administrative organ, the supervisory organ or any other organ or competent authority in accordance with the national law applicable to public limited-liability companies in the Member State in which the SE's registered office is situated.

Article 55. (1) One or more shareholders who together hold at least 10 % of an SE's subscribed capital may request the SE to convene a general meeting and draw up the agenda therefor; the SE's statutes or national legislation may provide for a smaller proportion under the same conditions as those applicable to public limited-liability companies.
(2) The request that a general meeting be convened shall state the items to be put on the agenda.
(3) If, following a request made under paragraph (1), a general meeting is not held in due time and, in any event, within two months, the competent judicial or administrative authority within the jurisdiction of which the SE's registered office is situated may order that a general meeting be convened within a given period or authorise either the shareholders who have requested it or their representatives to convene a general meeting. This shall be without prejudice to any national provisions which allow the shareholders themselves to convene general meetings.

Article 56. One or more shareholders who together hold at least 10 % of an SE's subscribed capital may request that one or more additional items be put on the agenda of any general meeting. The procedures and time limits applicable to such requests shall be laid down by the national law of the Member State in which the SE's registered office is situated or, failing that, by the SE's statutes. The above proportion may be reduced by the statutes or by the law of the Member State in which the SE's registered office is situated under the same conditions as are applicable to public limited-liability companies.

Article 57. Save where this Regulation or, failing that, the law applicable to public limited-liability companies in the Member State in which an SE's registered office is situated requires a larger majority, the general meeting's decisions shall be taken by a majority of the votes validly cast.

Article 58. The votes cast shall not include votes attaching to shares in respect of which the shareholder has not taken part in the vote or has abstained or has returned a blank or spoilt ballot paper.

Article 59. (1) Amendment of an SE's statutes shall require a decision by the general meeting taken by a majority which may not be less than two thirds of the votes cast, unless the law applicable to public limitedliability companies in the Member State in which an SE's registered office is situated requires or permits a larger majority.
(2) A Member State may, however, provide that where at least half of an SE's subscribed capital is represented, a simple majority of the votes referred to in paragraph (1) shall suffice.
(3) Amendments to an SE's statutes shall be publicised in accordance with Article 13.

Article 60. (1) Where an SE has two or more classes of shares, every decision by the general meeting shall be subject to a separate vote by each class of shareholders whose class rights are affected thereby.
(2) Where a decision by the general meeting requires the majority of votes specified in Article 59(1) or (2), that majority shall also be required for the separate vote by each class of shareholders whose class rights are affected by the decision.

Title IV. Annual Accounts and Consolidated Accounts

Article 61. Subject to Article 62 an SE shall be governed by the rules applicable to public limited-liability companies under the law of the Member State in which its registered office is situated as regards the preparation of its annual and, where appropriate, consolidated accounts including the accompanying annual report and the auditing and publication of those accounts.

Article 62. (1) An SE which is a credit or financial institution shall be governed by the rules laid down in the national law of the Member State in which its registered office is situated in implementation of Directive 2000/12/ EC of the European Parliament and of the Council of 20 March 2000 relating to the taking up and pursuit of the business of credit institutions as regards the preparation of its annual and, where appropriate, consolidated accounts, including the accompanying annual report and the auditing and publication of those accounts.
(2) An SE which is an insurance undertaking shall be governed by the rules laid down in the national law of the Member State in which its registered office is situated in implementation of Council Directive 91/674/EEC of 19 December 1991 on the annual accounts and consolidated accounts of insurance undertakings (2) as regards the preparation of its annual and, where appropriate, consoli-

dated accounts including the accompanying annual report and the auditing and publication of those accounts.

Title V. Winding Up, Liquidation, Insolvency and, Cessation of Payments

Article 63. As regards winding up, liquidation, insolvency, cessation of payments and similar procedures, an SE shall be governed by the legal provisions which would apply to a public limited-liability company formed in accordance with the law of the Member State in which its registered office is situated, including provisions relating to decision-making by the general meeting.

Article 64. (1) When an SE no longer complies with the requirement laid down in Article 7, the Member State in which the SE's registered office is situated shall take appropriate measures to oblige the SE to regularise its position within a specified period either:
(a) by re-establishing its head office in the Member State in which its registered office is situated or
(b) by transferring the registered office by means of the procedure laid down in Article 8.
(2) The Member State in which the SE's registered office is situated shall put in place the measures necessary to ensure that an SE which fails to regularise its position in accordance with paragraph (1) is liquidated.
(3) The Member State in which the SE's registered office is situated shall set up a judicial remedy with regard to any established infringement of Article 7. That remedy shall have a suspensory effect on the procedures laid down in paragraphs 1 and 2.
(4) Where it is established on the initiative of either the authorities or any interested party that an SE has its head office within the territory of a Member State in breach of Article 7, the authorities of that Member State shall immediately inform the Member State in which the SE's registered office is situated.

Article 65. Without prejudice to provisions of national law requiring additional publication, the initiation and termination of winding up, liquidation, insolvency or cessation of payment procedures and any decision to continue operating shall be publicised in accordance with Article 13.

Article 66. (1) An SE may be converted into a public limited-liability company governed by the law of the Member State in which its registered office is situated. No decision on conversion may be taken before two years have elapsed since its registration or before the first two sets of annual accounts have been approved.
(2) The conversion of an SE into a public limited-liability company shall not result in the winding up of the company or in the creation of a new legal person.
(3) The management or administrative organ of the SE shall draw up draft terms of conversion and a report explaining and justifying the legal and economic aspects of the conversion and indicating the implications of the adoption of the public limited-liability company for the shareholders and for the employees.
(4) The draft terms of conversion shall be publicised in the manner laid down in each Member State's law in accordance with Article 3 of Directive 68/151/EEC at least one month before the general meeting called to decide thereon.
(5) Before the general meeting referred to in paragraph (6), one or more independent experts appointed or approved, in accordance with the national provisions adopted in implementation of Article 10 of Directive 78/855/EEC, by a judicial or administrative authority in the Member State to which the SE being converted into a public limitedliability company is subject shall certify that the company has assets at least equivalent to its capital.
(6) The general meeting of the SE shall approve the draft terms of conversion together with the statutes of the public limited-liability company. The decision of the general meeting shall be passed as laid down in the provisions of national law adopted in implementation of Article 7 of Directive 78/855/EEC.

Title VI. Additional and Transitional Provisions

Article 67. (1) If and so long as the third phase of economic and monetary union (EMU) does not apply to it each Member State may make SEs with registered offices within its territory subject to the same provisions as apply to public limited-liability companies covered by its legislation as regards the expression of their capital. An SE may, in any case, express its capital in euro as well. In that event the national currency/euro conversion rate shall be that for the last day of the month preceding that of the formation of the SE.
(2) If and so long as the third phase of EMU does not apply to the Member State in which an SE has its registered office, the SE may, however, prepare and publish its annual and, where appropri-

ate, consolidated accounts in euro. The Member State may require that the SE's annual and, where appropriate, consolidated accounts be prepared and published in the national currency under the same conditions as those laid down for public limited-liability companies governed by the law of that Member State. This shall not prejudice the additional possibility for an SE of publishing its annual and, where appropriate, consolidated accounts in euro in accordance with Council Directive 90/604/EEC of 8 November 1990 amending Directive 78/60/EEC on annual accounts and Directive 83/349/EEC on consolidated accounts as concerns the exemptions for small and medium-sized companies and the publication of accounts in ecu.

Title VII. Final Provisions

Article 68. (1) The Member States shall make such provision as is appropriate to ensure the effective application of this Regulation.
(2) Each Member State shall designate the competent authorities within the meaning of Articles 8, 25, 26, 54, 55 and 64. It shall inform the Commission and the other Member States accordingly.

Article 69. Five years at the latest after the entry into force of this Regulation, the Commission shall forward to the Council and the European Parliament a report on the application of the Regulation and proposals for amendments, where appropriate. The report shall, in particular, analyse the appropriateness of:
(a) allowing the location of an SE's head office and registered office in different Member States;
(b) broadening the concept of merger in Article 17(2) in order to admit also other types of merger than those defined in Articles 3(1) and 4 (1) of Directive 78/855/EEC;
(c) revising the jurisdiction clause in Article 8(16) in the light of any provision which may have been inserted in the 1968 Brussels Convention or in any text adopted by Member States or by the Council to replace such Convention;
(d) allowing provisions in the statutes of an SE adopted by a Member State in execution of authorisations given to the Member States by this Regulation or laws adopted to ensure the effective application of this Regulation in respect to the SE which deviate from or are complementary to these laws, even when such provisions would not be authorised in the statutes of a public limited-liability company having its registered office in the Member State.

Article 70. This Regulation shall enter into force on 8 October 2004. This Regulation shall be binding in its entirety and directly applicable in all Member States.

Annex I. Public Limited-Liability Companies Referred to in Article 2(1)
BELGIUM: la société anonyme/de naamloze vennootschap
DENMARK: aktieselskaber
GERMANY: die Aktiengesellschaft
GREECE: ανω΄νυμη εταιρι΄α
SPAIN: la sociedad ano΄ nima
FRANCE: la société anonyme
IRELAND: public companies limited by shares
public companies limited by guarantee having a share capital
ITALY: società per azioni
LUXEMBOURG: la société anonyme
NETHERLANDS: de naamloze vennootschap
AUSTRIA: die Aktiengesellschaft
PORTUGAL: a sociedade ano΄ nima de responsabilidade limitada
FINLAND: julkinen osakeyhtiö/publikt aktiebolag
SWEDEN: publikt aktiebolag
UNITED KINGDOM: public companies limited by shares
public companies limited by guarantee having a share capital

Annex II. Public and Private Limited-Liability Companies Referred to in Article 2(2)
BELGIUM: la société anonyme/de naamloze vennootschap,
la société privée à responsabilité limitée/besloten vennootschap met beperkte aansprakelijkheid
DENMARK: aktieselskaber,
anpartselskaber
GERMANY: die Aktiengesellschaft,
die Gesellschaft mit beschränkter Haftung
GREECE: ανω΄νυμη εταιρι΄α

EU: REGULATION 2157/2001 ON STATUTE FOR A EUROPEAN COMPANY (SE)

εταιρι΄α περιορισμε΄νης ευθυ΄νης
SPAIN: la sociedad anó nima,
la sociedad de responsabilidad limitada
FRANCE: la société anonyme,
la société à responsabilité limitée
IRELAND: public companies limited by shares,
public companies limited by guarantee having a share capital,
private companies limited by shares,
private companies limited by guarantee having a share capital
ITALY: società per azioni,
società a responsabilità limitata
LUXEMBOURG: la société anonyme,
la société à responsabilité limitée
NETHERLANDS: de naamloze vennootschap,
de besloten vennootschap met beperkte aansprakelijkheid
AUSTRIA: die Aktiengesellschaft,
die Gesellschaft mit beschränkter Haftung
PORTUGAL: a sociedade anó nima de responsabilidade limitada,
a sociedade por quotas de responsabilidade limitada
FINLAND: osakeyhtiö
aktiebolag
SWEDEN: aktiebolag
UNITED KINGDOM: public companies limited by shares,
public companies limited by guarantee having a share capital,
private companies limited by shares,
private companies limited by guarantee having a share capital

PART III EUROPEAN COMPANY LAW

Proposal for a Council Regulation on the Statute for a European private company (Text with EEA relevance) Brussels, COM (2008) 396/3 [footnotes omitted].

THE COUNCIL OF THE EUROPEAN UNION,
Having regard to the Treaty establishing the European Community, and in particular Article 308 thereof,
Having regard to the proposal from the Commission,
Having regard to the opinion of the European Parliament,
Having regard to the opinion of the European Economic and Social Committee,
Whereas:
(1) The legal framework in which business is carried out in the Community remains largely national. This exposes companies to a wide diversity of national laws, company forms and company regimes. The approximation of national laws by means of directives based on Article 44 of the Treaty can overcome some of these difficulties. Such approximation, however, does not release persons seeking to create companies from the obligation to adopt in each Member State a company form governed by the national law of that Member State.
(2) Existing Community forms of company, notably the European Company (SE), whose legal form was established by Council Regulation (EC) No 2157/2001 of 8 October 2001 on the Statute for a European Company18 are designed for large companies. The minimum capital requirement for an SE and the restrictions on its formation make that form of company unsuitable for many businesses, in particular of a smaller size. In view of the problems faced by such businesses as a result of the diversity of company law regimes and the unsuitability of the SE for small businesses, it is appropriate to provide for a European company form specifically designed for small businesses, which it is possible to create throughout the Community.
(3) Since a private company (hereinafter "SPE") which may be created throughout the Community is intended for small businesses, a legal form should be provided which is as uniform as possible throughout the Community and as many matters as possible should be left to the contractual freedom of shareholders, while a high level of legal certainty is ensured for shareholders, creditors, employees and third parties in general. Given that a high degree of flexibility and freedom is to be left to the shareholders to organise the internal affairs of the SPE, the private nature of the company should also be reflected by the fact that its shares may not be offered to the public or negotiated on the capital markets, including being admitted to trading or listed on regulated markets.
(4) In order to enable businesses to reap the full benefits of the internal market, the SPE should be able to have its registered office and principal place of business in different Member States and to transfer its registered office from one Member State to another, with or without also transferring its central administration or principal place of business.
(5) To enable businesses to gain efficiencies and save costs, the SPE should be available in every Member State, with as few variations as possible as regards the company form.
(6) To ensure a high degree of uniformity of the SPE, as many matters pertaining to the company form as possible should be governed by this Regulation, either through substantive rules or by reserving matters to the articles of association of the SPE. It is therefore appropriate to provide for a list of matters, to be set out in an Annex, in respect of which the shareholders of the SPE are obliged to lay down rules in the articles of association. In relation to those matters only Community law should apply, and consequently shareholders should be able to set out rules to regulate those matters, which are different from the rules prescribed by the law of the Member State where the SPE is registered, in relation to national forms of private limited-liability companies. National law should apply to matters where this is provided for by this Regulation and to all other matters that are not covered by the articles of this Regulation, such as insolvency, employment and tax, or are not reserved by it to the articles of association.
(7) In order to make the SPE an accessible company form for individuals and small businesses, it should be capable of being created ex nihilo or of resulting from the transformation, the merger or the division of existing national companies. The creation of an SPE by way of transformation, merger or division of companies should be governed by the applicable national law.
(8) In order to reduce the costs and administrative burdens associated with company registration, the formalities for the registration of the SPE should be limited to those requirements which are necessary to ensure legal certainty and the validity of the documents filed upon the creation of a SPE should be subject to a single verification, which may take place either before or after registration. For the purposes of registration, it is appropriate to use the registries designated by First Council Directive 68/151/EEC of 9 March 1968 on the co-ordination of safeguards which, for the protection of the interests of members and others, are required by Member States of companies within the

meaning of the second paragraph of Article 58 of the Treaty, with a view to making such safeguards equivalent throughout the Community19. (9) Since small businesses often require long term financial and personal commitment, they should be able to adapt the structure of their share capital and the rights attached to shares to their specific circumstances. SPE shareholders should therefore be free to determine the rights attached to their shares, the procedure for the variation of those rights, the procedure to be followed if shares are transferred and any restriction on such transfer. (10) In order to preserve both the operation of the SPE and the freedom of shareholders, the SPE should have the possibility of applying to court to expel shareholders who seriously harm its interests and shareholders of the SPE whose interest suffered serious harm as a result of specific events should have the right to withdraw from the SPE.

(11) The SPE should not be subject to a high mandatory capital requirement since this would be a barrier to the creation of SPEs. Creditors, however, should be protected from excessive distributions to shareholders which could affect the ability of the SPE to pay its debts. To this end, distributions that leave the SPE with liabilities exceeding the value of the assets of the SPE should be prohibited. Shareholders, however, should also be free to require the management body of the SPE to sign a solvency certificate.

(12) Since creditors should be granted protection in the event of a reduction of the capital of the SPE, certain rules should be laid down concerning when such reductions are to take effect.

(13) Since small businesses need legal structures that can be adapted to their needs and size and are able to evolve as activity develops, shareholders of the SPE should be free to determine in their articles of association the internal organisation which is best suited to their needs. An SPE may opt for one or more individual managing directors, a unitary or a dual board structure. However, mandatory rules ensuring the protection of minority shareholders should be introduced in order to avoid any unfair treatment of shareholders, in particular certain key resolutions should be adopted by a majority of no less than two-thirds of the total voting rights attached to the shares issued by the SPE. While a limit may be introduced on the right to request a resolution or to request an independent expert to investigate abuses, such right may not be made conditional on the ownership of more than 5% of the voting rights of the SPE, although the articles of association of the SPE may provide for a lower threshold.

(14) Competent national authorities should monitor the completion and legality of the transfer of the registered office of an SPE to another Member State. The timely access of shareholders, creditors and employees to the transfer proposal and to the report of the management body should be ensured.

(15) Employees' rights of participation should be governed by the legislation of the Member State in which the SPE has its registered office (the "home Member State"). The SPE should not be used for the purpose of circumventing such rights. Where the national legislation of the Member State to which the SPE transfers its registered office does not provide for at least the same level of employee participation as the home Member State, the participation of employees in the company following the transfer should in certain circumstances be negotiated. Should such negotiations fail, the provisions applying in the company before the transfer should continue to apply after the transfer.

(16) Employees' rights other than rights of participation should remain subject to Council Directive 94/45/EC of 22 September 1994 on the establishment of a European Works Council or a procedure in Community-scale undertakings and Community-scale groups of undertakings for the purposes of informing and consulting employees, Council Directive 98/59/EC of 20 July 1998 on the approximation of the laws of the Member States relating to collective redundancies, Council Directive 2001/23/EC of 12 March 2001 on the approximation of the law of the Member States relating to the safeguarding of employees' rights in the event of transfers of undertakings, businesses or parts of undertakings or businesses and Directive 2002/14/EC of the European Parliament and of the Council of 11 March 2002 establishing a general framework for informing and consulting employees in the European Community.

(17) The Member States should lay down rules on penalties applicable to infringements of the provisions of this Regulation, including infringements of the obligation to regulate in the articles of association of the SPE the matters prescribed by this Regulation, and should ensure that they are implemented. Those penalties must be effective, proportionate and dissuasive.

(18) The Treaty does not provide, for the adoption of this Regulation, powers other than those under Article 308. (19) Since the objectives of the proposed action cannot be sufficiently achieved by the Member States in so far as they involve the creation of a company form with common features throughout the Community and can therefore, by reason of the scale of the action, be better achieved at Community level, the Community may adopt measures, in accordance with the principle of subsidiarity laid down in Article 5 of the Treaty. In accordance with the principle of proportionality as set out in that Article, this Regulation does not go beyond what is necessary to achieve those objectives

HAS ADOPTED THIS REGULATION:

Chapter I. General Provisions

Article 1. This Regulation lays down the conditions governing the establishment and operation within the Community of companies in the form of a European private company with limited liability (Societas Privata Europaea, hereinafter "SPE").

Article 2. (1) For the purposes of this Regulation, the following definitions shall apply:
(a) 'shareholder' means the founding shareholder and any other person whose name is entered in the list of shareholders in accordance with Articles 15-16;
(b) 'distribution' means any financial benefit derived directly or indirectly from the SPE by a shareholder, in relation to the shares held by him, including any transfer of money or property, as well as the incurring of a debt;
(c) 'director' means any individual managing director, any member of the management, administrative board or supervisory body of an SPE;
(d) 'management body' means one or more individual managing directors, the management board (dual board) or the administrative board (unitary board), designated in the articles of association of the SPE as being responsible for the management of the SPE;
(e) 'supervisory body' means the supervisory board (dual board), designated in the articles of association of the SPE as being responsible for the supervision of the management body;
(f) 'home Member State' means the Member State in which the SPE has its registered office immediately before any transfer of its registered office to another Member State;
(g) 'host Member State' means the Member State to which the registered office of the SPE is transferred.
(2) For the purposes of point (b) of paragraph (1), distributions may be made through a purchase of property, the redemption or other kind of acquisition of shares or by any other means.

Article 3. (1) An SPE shall comply with the following requirements:
(a) its capital shall be divided into shares,
(b) a shareholder shall not be liable for more than the amount he has subscribed or agreed to subscribe,
(c) it shall have legal personality,
(d) its shares shall not be offered to the public and shall not be publicly traded,
(e) it may be formed by one or more natural persons and/or legal entities, hereinafter "founding shareholders".
(2) For the purposes of point (d) of paragraph (1), shares shall be regarded as 'offered to the public' where a communication is addressed to persons in any form and by any means, and it presents sufficient information on the terms of the offer and the shares to be offered so as to enable an investor to decide to purchase or subscribe to these shares, including when shares are placed through financial intermediaries.
(3) For the purposes of point (e) of paragraph (1), 'legal entities' shall mean any company or firm within the meaning of the second paragraph of Article 48 of the Treaty, a European public limited-liability company as provided for in Regulation (EC) No 2001/2157, hereinafter "European Company", a European Co-operative Society as provided for in Council Regulation (EC) No 1435/2003, a European Economic Interest Grouping as provided for in Council Regulation (EEC) No 2137/85 and an SPE.

Article 4. (1) An SPE shall be governed by this Regulation and also, as regards the matters listed in Annex I, by its articles of association. However, where a matter is not covered by the articles of this Regulation or by Annex I, an SPE shall be governed by the law, including the provisions implementing Community law, which applies to private limited-liability companies in the Member State in which the SPE has its registered office, hereinafter "applicable national law".

Chapter II. Formation

Article 5. (1) Member States shall allow the formation of an SPE by any of the following methods:
(a) the creation of a SPE in accordance with this Regulation;
(b) the transformation of an existing company;
(c) the merger of existing companies;
(d) the division of an existing company.
(2) Formation of the SPE by the transformation, merger or division of existing companies shall be governed by the national law applicable to the transforming company, to each of the merging compa-

nies or to the dividing company. Formation by transformation shall not give rise to the winding up of the company or any loss or interruption of its legal personality.
(3) For the purposes of paragraphs 1 and 2, 'company' shall mean any form of company that may be set up under the law of the Member States, a European Company and, where applicable, an SPE.

Article 6. The name of an SPE shall be followed by the abbreviation "SPE". Only an SPE may add the abbreviation "SPE" to its name.

Article 7. An SPE shall have its registered office and its central administration or principal place of business in the Community. An SPE shall not be under any obligation to have its central administration or principal place of business in the Member State in which it has its registered office.

Article 8. (1) An SPE shall have articles of association that cover at least the matters set out in this Regulation, as provided for in Annex I.
(2) The articles of association of a SPE shall be in writing and signed by every founding shareholder.
(3) The articles of association and any amendments thereto may be relied upon as
follows:
(a) in relation to the shareholders and the management body of the SPE and its supervisory body, if any, from the date on which they are signed or, in the case
of amendments, adopted;
(b) in relation to third parties, in accordance with the provisions of the applicable national law implementing paragraphs 5, 6 and 7 of Article 3 of Directive
68/151/EEC.

Article 9. (1) Each SPE shall be registered in the Member State in which it has its registered office in a register designated by the applicable national law in accordance with Article 3 of
Directive 68/151/EEC24.
(2) The SPE shall acquire legal personality on the date on which it is entered in the register.
(3) In the case of a merger by acquisition, the acquiring company shall adopt the form of an SPE on the day the merger is registered.
In the case of a division by acquisition, the recipient company shall adopt the form of an SPE on the day the division is registered.

Article 10. (1) Application for registration shall be made by the founding shareholders of the SPE or by any person authorised by them. Such application may be made by electronic means.
(2) Member States shall not require any particulars and documents to be supplied upon application for the registration of a SPE other than the following:
(a) the name of the SPE and the address of its registered office;
(b) the names, addresses and any other information necessary to identify the persons who are authorised to represent the SPE in dealings with third parties and in legal proceedings, or take part in the administration, supervision or control of the SPE;
(c) the share capital of the SPE;
(d) the share classes and the number of shares in each share class;
(e) the total number of shares;
(f) the nominal value or accountable par of the shares;
(g) the articles of association of the SPE;
(h) where the SPE was formed as a result of a transformation, merger or division of companies, the resolution on the transformation, merger or division that led to the creation of the SPE.
(3) The documents and particulars referred to in paragraph (2) shall be provided in the language required by the applicable national law.
(4) Registration of the SPE may be subject to only one of the following requirements:
(a) a control by an administrative or judicial body of the legality of the documents and particulars of the SPE;
(b) the certification of the documents and particulars of the SPE.
(5) The SPE shall submit any change in the particulars or documents referred to in points
(a) to (g) of paragraph (2) to the register within 14 calendar days of the day on which the change takes place. After every amendment to the articles of association, the SPE shall submit its complete text to the register as amended to date.
(6) The registration of an SPE shall be disclosed.

Article 11. (1) The disclosure of the documents and particulars concerning an SPE which must be disclosed under this Regulation shall be effected in accordance with the applicable national law

implementing Article 3 of Directive 68/151/EEC.
(2) The letters and order forms of an SPE, whether they are in paper or electronic form, as well as its website, if any, shall state the following particulars:
(a) the information necessary to identify the register referred to in Article 9, with the number of entry of the SPE in that register;
(b) the name of the SPE, the address of its registered office and, where appropriate, the fact that the company is being wound up.

Article 12. Where acts were performed on behalf of an SPE before its registration, the SPE may assume the obligations arising out of such acts after its registration. Where the SPE does not assume those obligations, the persons who performed those acts shall be jointly and severally liable, without limit.

Article 13. Branches of an SPE shall be governed by the law of the Member State in which the branch is located, including the relevant provisions implementing Council Directive 89/666/EEC25.

Chapter III. Shares

Article 14. (1) The shares of the SPE shall be entered in the list of shareholders.
(2) Shares carrying the same rights and obligations shall constitute one class.
(3) Subject to Article 27, the adoption of an amendment to the articles of association of the SPE which varies the rights attached to a class of shares (including any change to the procedure for varying the rights attached to a class of share) shall require the consent of a majority of not less than two-thirds of the voting rights attached to the shares issued in that class.
(4) Where a share is owned by more than one person, those persons shall be regarded as one shareholder in relation to the SPE. They shall exercise their rights through a common representative, who in the absence of any notification to the SPE shall be the person whose name appears first in the list of shareholders for that share. They shall be jointly and severally liable for the commitments attached to the share.

Article 15. (1) The management body of the SPE shall draw up a list of shareholders. The list shall contain at least the following:
(a) the name and address of each shareholder;
(b) the number of shares held by the shareholder concerned, their nominal value or accountable par;
(c) where a share is owned by more than one person, the names and addresses of the co-owners and of the common representative;
(d) the date of acquisition of the shares;
(e) the amount of each consideration in cash, if any, paid or to be paid by the shareholder concerned;
(f) the value and nature of each consideration in kind, if any, provided or to be provided by the shareholder concerned;
(g) the date on which a shareholder ceases to be a member of the SPE.
(2) The list of shareholders shall, unless proven otherwise, constitute evidence of the authenticity of the matters listed in points (a) to (g) of paragraph (1).
(3) The list of shareholders and any amendments thereto shall be kept by the management body and may be inspected by the shareholders or third parties on request.

Article 16. (1) Subject to Article 27, a decision introducing or amending a restriction on or prohibition of the transfer of shares may be adopted only with the consent of all shareholders affected by the restriction or prohibition in question.
(2) All agreements on the transfer of shares shall be in written form.
(3) On notification of a transfer, the management body shall, without undue delay, enter the shareholder in the list referred to in Article 15, provided that the transfer has been executed in accordance with this Regulation and the articles of association of the SPE and the shareholder submits reasonable evidence as to his lawful ownership of the share.
(4) Subject to paragraph (3), any transfer of shares shall become effective as follows:
(a) in relation to the SPE, on the day the shareholder notifies the SPE of the transfer;
(b) in relation to third parties, on the day the shareholder is entered in the list referred to in Article 15.
(5) A transfer of shares shall be valid only if it complies with this Regulation and the articles of association. The provisions of the applicable national law concerning the protection of persons who acquire shares in good faith shall apply.

Article 17. (1) On the basis of a resolution of the shareholders and on an application by the SPE, the

competent court may order the expulsion of a shareholder if he has caused serious harm to the SPE's interest or the continuation of the shareholder as a member of the SPE is detrimental to its proper operation. An application to the court shall be made within 60 calendar days of the resolution of the shareholders.
(2) The court shall decide whether, as an interim measure, the voting and other nonpecuniary rights of such shareholder should be suspended until a final decision is taken.
(3) If the court orders the expulsion of a shareholder, it shall decide whether his shares are to be acquired by the other shareholders and/or by the SPE itself and on payment of the price of the shares.

Article 18. (1) A shareholder shall have the right to withdraw from the SPE if the activities of the SPE are being or have been conducted in a manner which causes serious harm to the interests of the shareholder as a result of one or more of the following events:
(a) the SPE has been deprived of a significant part of its assets;
(b) the registered office of the SPE has been transferred to another Member State;
(c) the activities of the SPE have changed substantially;
(d) no dividend has been distributed for at least 3 years even though the SPE's financial position would have permitted such distribution.
(2) The shareholder shall submit his withdrawal in writing to the SPE stating his reasons for the withdrawal.
(3) The management body of the SPE shall, on receipt of the notice referred to in paragraph (2), without undue delay, request a resolution of the shareholders on the purchase of the shareholder's shares by the other shareholders or by the SPE itself.
(4) Where the shareholders of the SPE fail to adopt a resolution referred to in paragraph (3) or do not accept the shareholder's reasons for withdrawal within 30 calendar days of the submission of the notice referred to in paragraph (2), the management body shall notify the shareholder of that fact without undue delay.
(5) In the case of a dispute regarding the price of the shares, their value shall be determined by an independent expert appointed by the parties or, failing an agreement between them, by the competent court or administrative authority.
(6) On an application of the shareholder, the competent court may, if satisfied that the interests of the shareholder have suffered serious harm, order the acquisition of his shares by the other shareholders or by the SPE itself and the payment of the price of the shares.
An application to the court shall be made either within 60 calendar days of the resolution of the shareholders referred to in paragraph (3) or, where no resolution is adopted within 30 calendar days of the shareholder submitting his notice of withdrawal to the SPE, within 60 calendar days of the expiry of that period.

Chapter IV. Capital

Article 19. (1) Without prejudice to Article 42, the capital of the SPE shall be expressed in euro.
(2) The capital of the SPE shall be fully subscribed.
(3) The shares of the SPE do not need to be fully paid on issue.
(4) The capital of the SPE shall be at least EUR 1.

Article 20. (1) Shareholders must pay the agreed consideration in cash or provide the agreed consideration in kind in accordance with the articles of association of the SPE.
(2) Except in the case of a reduction of the share capital, shareholders may not be released from the obligation to pay or provide the agreed consideration.
(3) Without prejudice to paragraphs 1 and 2, the liability of shareholders for the consideration paid or provided shall be governed by the applicable national law.

Article 21. (1) Without prejudice to Article 24, the SPE may, on the basis of a proposal of the management body, make a distribution to shareholders provided that, after the distribution, the assets of the SPE fully cover its liabilities. The SPE may not distribute those reserves that may not be distributed under its articles of association.
(2) If the articles of association so require, the management body of the SPE, in addition to complying with paragraph (1), shall sign a statement, hereinafter a 'solvency certificate', before a distribution is made, certifying that the SPE will be able to pay its debts as they become due in the normal course of business within one year of the date of the distribution. Shareholders shall be provided with the solvency certificate before the resolution on the distribution referred to in Article 27 is taken. The solvency certificate shall be disclosed.

Article 22. Any shareholder who has received distributions made contrary to Article 21 must return those distributions to the SPE, provided that the SPE proves that the shareholder knew or in view of the circumstances should have been aware of the irregularities.

Article 23. (1) The SPE shall not, directly or indirectly, subscribe for its own shares.
(2) In the case of acquisition by the SPE of its own shares, Articles 21 and 22 shall apply mutatis mutandis. Shares may not be purchased by the SPE unless they are fully paid. The SPE shall always have at least one issued share.
(3) The right to vote and other non-pecuniary rights attached to the SPE's own shares shall be suspended, while the SPE is the registered owner of its own shares.
(4) Where the SPE cancels its own shares, its share capital shall be reduced accordingly.
(5) Shares acquired by the SPE in contravention of this Regulation or the articles of association shall be sold or cancelled within one year of their acquisition.
(6) Subject to paragraph (5) and to the articles of association of the SPE, the cancellation of shares shall be governed by the applicable national law.
(7) This Article shall apply mutatis mutandis to any shares acquired by a person acting in his own name but on behalf of the SPE.

Article 24. (1) In the case of a reduction of the share capital of the SPE, Articles 21 and 22 shall apply mutatis mutandis.
(2) Following the disclosure of the resolution of the shareholders to reduce the capital of the SPE, those creditors whose claims antedate the disclosure of the resolution shall have the right to apply to the competent court for an order that the SPE provide them
with adequate safeguards. An application shall be made within 30 calendar days of the disclosure of the resolution.
(3) The court may order the SPE to provide safeguards only if the creditor credibly demonstrates that due to the reduction in the capital the satisfaction of his claims is at stake, and that no adequate safeguards have been obtained from the SPE.
(4) A capital reduction shall take effect as follows:
(a) where the SPE has no creditors at the time when the resolution is adopted, on its adoption;
(b) where the SPE has creditors at the time when the resolution is adopted and no creditor has made an application within 30 calendar days of the disclosure of the resolution of the shareholders, on the thirty-first calendar day following that disclosure;
(c) where the SPE has creditors at the time when the resolution is adopted and an application is made by a creditor within 30 calendar days of the disclosure of the resolution of shareholders, on the first date on which the SPE has complied with all orders by the competent court to provide adequate safeguards or, if earlier, the first date on which the court has determined, in relation to all applications that the SPE need not provide any safeguards.
(5) If the purpose of a reduction of the capital is to offset losses incurred by the SPE, the reduced amount may be used only for this purpose and shall not be distributed to the shareholders.
(6) A capital reduction shall be disclosed.
(7) In the case of a capital reduction, the equal treatment of shareholders in the same position shall be ensured.

Article 25. (1) An SPE shall be subject to the requirements of the applicable national law as regards preparation, filing, auditing and publication of accounts.
(2) The management body shall keep the books of the SPE. The bookkeeping of the SPE shall be governed by the applicable national law.

Chapter V. Organisation of the SPE

Article 26. (1) The SPE shall have a management body, which shall be responsible for the management of the SPE. The management body may exercise all the powers of the SPE not required by this Regulation or the articles of association to be exercised by the shareholders.
(2) The shareholders shall determine the organisation of the SPE, subject to this
Regulation.

Article 27. (1) Without prejudice to paragraph (2), at least the following matters shall be decided by a resolution of the shareholders by a majority as defined in the articles of association of the SPE:
(a) variation of rights attaching to shares;
(b) expulsion of a shareholder;
(c) withdrawal of a shareholder;

(d) approval of the annual accounts;
(e) distribution to the shareholders;
(f) acquisition of own shares;
(g) redemption of shares;
(h) increase of share capital;
(i) reduction of share capital;
(j) appointment and removal of directors and their terms of office;
(k) where the SPE has an auditor, appointment and removal of the auditor;
(l) transfer of the registered office of the SPE to another Member State;
(m) transformation of the SPE;
(n) mergers and divisions;
(o) winding up;
(p) amendments to the articles of association, not covering matters mentioned in points (a) to (o).
(2) Resolutions on the matters indicated in points (a), (b), (c), (i), (l), (m) (n), (o) and (p) of paragraph (1) shall be taken by a qualified majority. For the purposes of the first subparagraph, the qualified majority may not be less
than two-thirds of the total voting rights attached to the shares issued by the SPE.
(3) The adoption of resolutions shall not require the organisation of a general meeting. The management body shall provide all shareholders with the proposals for resolutions together with sufficient information to enable them to take an informed decision. Resolutions shall be recorded in writing. Copies of the decisions taken shall be sent to every shareholder.
(4) Resolutions of the shareholders shall comply with this Regulation and the articles of association of the SPE. The right of shareholders to challenge resolutions shall be governed by the applicable national law.
(5) If the SPE has only one shareholder, he shall exercise the rights and fulfill the obligations of the shareholders of the SPE set out in this Regulation and the articles of association of the SPE.
(6) Resolutions on matters indicated in paragraph (1) shall be disclosed.
(7) Resolutions may be relied on as follows:
(a) in relation to the shareholders, the management body of the SPE and its supervisory body, if any, on the date they are adopted,
(b) in relation to third parties, in accordance with the provisions of the applicable national law implementing paragraphs 5, 6 and 7 of Article 3 of Directive 68/151/EEC.

Article 28. (1) Shareholders shall have the right to be duly informed and to ask questions to the management body about resolutions, annual accounts and all other matters relating to the activities of the SPE.
(2) The management body may refuse to give access to the information only if doing so could cause serious harm to the business interests of the SPE.

Article 29. (1) Shareholders holding 5% of the voting rights attached to the shares of the SPE shall have the right to request the management body to submit a proposal for a resolution to the shareholders. The request must state the reasons and indicate the matters that should be subject to such resolution. If the request is refused or if the management body does not submit a proposal within 14 calendar days of receiving the request, the shareholders concerned may then submit a proposal for a resolution to the shareholders regarding the matters in question.
(2) In the case of suspicion of serious breach of law or of the articles of association of the SPE, shareholders holding 5% of the voting rights attached to the shares of the SPE shall have the right to request the competent court or administrative authority to appoint an independent expert to investigate and report on the findings of the investigation to shareholders.
The expert shall be allowed access to the documents and records of the SPE and to require information from the management body.
(3) The articles of association may grant the rights set out in paragraphs 1 and 2 to individual shareholders or to shareholders holding less than 5% of the voting rights attached to the shares of the SPE.

Article 30. (1) Only a natural person may be a director of an SPE.
(2) A person who acts as a director without having been formally appointed shall be considered a director as regards all duties and liabilities to which the latter are subject.
(3) A person who is disqualified under national law from serving as a director of a company by a judicial or administrative decision of a Member State may not become or serve as a director of an SPE.
(4) Disqualification of a person serving as a director of the SPE shall be governed by the applicable national law.

PART III   EUROPEAN COMPANY LAW

Article 31. (1) A director shall have a duty to act in the best interests of the SPE. He shall act with the care and skill that can reasonably be required in the conduct of the business.
(2) The duties of directors shall be owed to the SPE.
(3) Subject to the articles of association of the SPE, a director shall avoid any situation that can be reasonably regarded as likely to give rise to an actual or potential conflict between his personal interests and those of the SPE or between his obligations towards the SPE and his duty to any other legal or natural person.
(4) A director of the SPE shall be liable to the company for any act or omission in breach of his duties deriving from this Regulation, the articles of association of the SPE or a resolution of shareholders which causes loss or damage to the SPE. Where such breach has been committed by more than one director, all directors concerned shall be jointly and severally liable.
(5) Without prejudice to the provisions of this Regulation, the liability of directors shall be governed by the applicable national law.

Article 32. Related party transactions shall be governed by the provisions of the applicable national law implementing Council Directives 78/660/EEC26 and 83/349/EEC27.

Article 33. (1) The SPE shall be represented in relation to third parties by one or more directors. Acts undertaken by the directors shall be binding on the SPE even if they are not within the objects of the SPE.
(2) The articles of association of the SPE may provide that directors are to exercise jointly the general power of representation. Any other limitation of the powers of the directors, following from the articles of association, a resolution of shareholders or a decision of the management or supervisory body, if any, may not be relied on against third parties even if they have been disclosed.
(3) Directors may delegate the right to represent the SPE in accordance with the articles of association.

Chapter VI. Employee Participation

Article 34. (1) The SPE shall be subject to the rules on employee participation, if any, applicable in the Member State in which it has its registered office, subject to the provisions of this Article.
(2) In the case of the transfer of the registered office of an SPE Article 38 shall apply.
(3) In the case of a cross-border merger of an SPE with an SPE or other company registered in another Member State, the provisions of the laws of the Member States implementing Directive 2005/56/EC of the European Parliament and of the Council28 shall apply.

Chapter VII. Transfer of the Registered Office of the SPE

Article 35. (1) The registered office of an SPE may be transferred to another Member State in accordance with this Chapter. The transfer of the registered office of an SPE shall not result in the winding-up of the SPE or in any interruption or loss of the SPE's legal personality or affect any right or obligation under any contract entered into by the SPE existing before the transfer.
(2) Paragraph 1 shall not apply to SPEs against which proceedings for winding-up, liquidation, insolvency or suspension of payments have been brought, or in respect of which preventive measures have been taken by the competent authorities to avoid the opening of such proceedings.
(3) A transfer shall take effect on the date of registration of the SPE in the host Member State. From that date, for matters covered by the second paragraph of Article 4, the SPE shall be regulated by the law of the host Member State.
(4) For the purpose of judicial or administrative proceedings commenced before the transfer of the registered office, the SPE shall be considered, following the registration referred to in paragraph (3), as having its registered office in the home Member State.

Article 36. (1) The management body of an SPE planning a transfer shall draw up a transfer proposal, which shall include at least the following particulars:
(a) the name of the SPE and the address of its registered office in the home Member State;
(b) the name of the SPE and the address of its proposed registered office in the host Member State;
(c) the proposed articles of association for the SPE in the host Member State;
(d) the proposed timetable for the transfer;
(e) the date from which it is proposed that the transactions of the SPE are to be regarded for accounting purposes as having been carried out in the host Member State;
(f) the consequences of the transfer for employees, and the proposed measures concerning them;
(g) where appropriate, detailed information on the transfer of the central administration or principal place of business of the SPE.

(2) At least one month before the resolution of the shareholders referred to in paragraph (4) is taken, the management body of the SPE shall:
(a) submit the transfer proposal to the shareholders and employee representatives, or where there are no such representatives, to the employees of the SPE for examination and make it available to the creditors for inspection;
(b) disclose the transfer proposal.
(3) The management body of the SPE shall draw up a report to the shareholders explaining and justifying the legal and economic aspects of the proposed transfer and setting out the implications of the transfer for shareholders, creditors and employees. The report shall be submitted to the shareholders and the employee representatives, or where there are no such representatives, to the employees themselves together with the transfer proposal. Where the management body receives in time the opinion of the employee representatives on the transfer, that opinion shall be submitted to the shareholders.
(4) The transfer proposal shall be submitted to the shareholders for approval in accordance with the rules of the articles of association of the SPE relating to the amendment of the articles of association.
(5) Where the SPE is subject to an employee participation regime, shareholders may reserve the right to make the implementation of the transfer conditional on their express ratification of the arrangements with respect to the participation of employees in the host Member State.
(6) The protection of any minority shareholders who oppose the transfer and of the creditors of the SPE shall be governed by the law of the home Member State.

Article 37. (1) Each Member State shall designate a competent authority to scrutinise the legality of the transfer by verifying compliance with the transfer procedure laid down in Article 36.
(2) The competent authority of the home Member State shall verify, without undue delay, that the requirements of Article 36 have been met and, if that is found to be the case, shall issue a certificate confirming that all the formalities required under the transfer procedure have been completed in the home Member State.
(3) Within one month of the receipt of the certificate referred to in paragraph (2), the SPE shall present the following documents to the competent authority in the host Member State:
(a) the certificate provided for in paragraph (2);
(b) the proposed articles of association for the SPE in the host Member State, as approved by the shareholders;
(c) the transfer proposal, as approved by the shareholders. Those documents shall be deemed to be sufficient to enable the registration of the SPE in the host Member State.
(4) The competent authority in the host Member State shall, within 14 calendar days of receipt of the documents referred to in paragraph (3), verify that the substantive and formal conditions required for the transfer of the registered office are met and if that
is found to be the case, take the measures necessary for the registration of the SPE.
(5) The competent authority of the host Member State may refuse to register an SPE only on the grounds that the SPE does not meet all the substantive or formal requirements under this Chapter. The SPE shall be registered when it has fulfilled all requirements under this Chapter.
(6) Using the notification form set out in Annex II, the competent authority of the host Member State shall, without undue delay, notify the competent authority responsible for removing the SPE from the register in the home Member State of the registration of the SPE in the host Member State. Removal from the register shall be effected as soon as, but not before, a notification has been received.
(7) Registrations in the host Member State and removals from the register in the home Member State shall be disclosed.

Article 38. (1) The SPE shall be subject, as from the date of registration, to the rules in force in the host Member State, if any, concerning arrangements for the participation of employees.
(2) Paragraph 1 shall not apply where the employees of the SPE in the home Member State account for at least one third of the total number of employees of the SPE including subsidiaries or branches of the SPE in any Member State, and where one of the following conditions is met:
(a) the legislation of the host Member State does not provide for at least the same level of participation as that operated in the SPE in the home Member State prior to its registration in the host Member State. The level of employee participation shall be measured by reference to the proportion of employee representatives amongst the members of the administrative or supervisory body or their committees or of the management group which covers the profit units
of the SPE, subject to employee representation;
(b) the legislation of the host Member State does not confer on the employees of establishments of the SPE that are situated in other Member States the same entitlement to exercise participation rights as such employees enjoyed before the transfer.

(3) Where one of the conditions set out in points a) or b) of paragraph (2) is met, the management body of the SPE shall take the necessary steps, as soon as possible, after disclosure of the transfer proposal, to start negotiations with the representatives of the SPE's employees with a view to reaching an agreement on arrangements for the participation of the employees.
(4) The agreement between the management body of the SPE and the representatives of the employees shall specify:
(a) the scope of the agreement;
(b) where, during the negotiations, the parties decide to establish arrangements for participation in the SPE following the transfer, the substance of those arrangements including, where applicable, the number of members in the company's administrative or supervisory body employees will be entitled to elect, appoint, recommend or oppose, the procedures as to how these members may be elected, appointed, recommended or opposed by employees, and their rights;
(c) the date of entry into force of the agreement and its duration, and any cases in which the agreement should be renegotiated and the procedure for its renegotiation.
(5) Negotiations shall be limited to a period of six months. The parties may agree to extend negotiations beyond this period for an additional six-month period. The negotiations shall otherwise be governed by the law of the home Member State.
(6) In the absence of an agreement, the participation arrangements existing in the home Member State shall be maintained.

Chapter VIII. Restructuring, Dissolution, and Nullity

Article 39. The transformation, merger and division of the SPE shall be governed by the applicable national law.

Article 40. (1) The SPE shall be dissolved in the following circumstances:
(a) by expiry of the period for which it was established;
(b) by the resolution of the shareholders;
(c) in cases set out in the applicable national law.
(2) Winding-up shall be governed by the applicable national law.
(3) Liquidation, insolvency, suspension of payments and similar procedures shall be governed by the applicable national law and by Council Regulation (EC) No 1346/200029.
(4) Dissolution of the SPE shall be disclosed.

Article 41. The nullity of the SPE shall be governed by the provisions of the applicable national law implementing Article 11(1) of Directive 68/151/EEC, points (a), (b), (c) and (e), except for the reference in point (c) to the objects of the company, of Article 11(2) and Article 12 of that Directive.

Chapter IX. Additional and Transitional Provisions

Article 42. (1) Member States in which the third phase of the economic and monetary union (EMU) does not apply may require SPEs having their registered office in their territory to express their capital in the national currency. An SPE may also express its capital in euro. The national currency/euro conversion rate shall be as on the last day of the month preceding the registration of the SPE.
(2) An SPE may prepare and publish its annual and, where applicable, consolidated accounts in euro in Member States where the third phase of the economic and monetary union (EMU) does not apply. However such Member States may also require SPEs to prepare and publish their annual and, where applicable, consolidated accounts in the national currency in accordance with the applicable national law.

Chapter X. Final Provisions

Article 43. Member States shall make such provision as is appropriate to ensure the effective application of this Regulation.

Article 44. The Member States shall lay down the rules on penalties applicable to infringements of the provisions of this Regulation and shall take all measures necessary to ensure that they are implemented. The penalties provided for must be effective, proportionate and dissuasive. The Member States shall notify those provisions to the Commission by 1 July 2010 at the latest and shall notify it without delay of any subsequent amendment affecting them.

Article 45. Member States shall notify the form of private limited-liability company referred to in the second paragraph of Article 4 to the Commission by 1 July 2010 at the latest. The Commission shall publish this information in the *Official Journal of the European Union*.

Article 46. (1) The authorities responsible for the register referred to in Article 9(1) shall notify the Commission before 31 March each year, of the name, registered office and registration number of the SPEs registered in and removed from the register in the preceding year as well as the total number of registered SPEs.

(2) The authorities referred to in paragraph (1) shall cooperate with each other to ensure that the documents and particulars of the SPEs listed in Article 10(2) are also accessible through the registers of all other Member States.

Article 47. The Commission shall, no later than 30 June 2015, review the application of this Regulation.

Article 48. This Regulation shall enter into force on the twentieth day following that of its publication in the *Official Journal of the European Union*.

It shall apply from 1 July 2010. This Regulation shall be binding in its entirety and directly applicable in all Member States.

Annex I. The articles of association of an SPE shall regulate at least the following:

Chapter II – Formation
– the name of the SPE,
– the names and addresses of the founding shareholders of the SPE and the nominal value or accountable par of the shares held by them,
– the initial capital of the SPE,

Chapter III. Shares
– whether sub-division, consolidation or redenomination of the shares is permitted and any applicable requirements,
– the pecuniary and non-pecuniary rights and the obligations attached to the shares (share classes), in particular
– (a) the participation in the assets and profits of the company, if any,
– (b) the votes attached to the shares, if any,
– the procedure for agreeing on any variation of the rights and obligations attached to the shares (share classes), and, subject to Article 14(3), the required majority of voting rights,
– any pre-emption rights either on issue or on transfer of shares, if any, and any applicable requirements,
– where the transfer of shares is restricted or prohibited, the details of the restriction or prohibition, in particular the form, time limit, the applicable procedure, and the rules applicable in the event of the death or dissolution of a shareholder, – where the approval of the share transfer by the SPE or by the shareholders is required or other rights are provided for shareholders or for the SPE on the transfer of shares (for example, right of first refusal), a deadline by which the transferor is to be notified of the decision,
– whether, in addition to Article 17, shareholders have any rights to require other shareholders to sell their shares, and any applicable requirements,
– whether, in addition to Article 18, shareholders have the right to sell their shares to other shareholders or to the SPE, who are obliged to buy those shares, and the applicable requirements,

Chapter IV. Capital
– the financial year of the SPE and how it may be changed,
– whether the SPE is required to establish reserves and if so, the type of reserve, the circumstances in which it is to be established and whether it is distributable,
– whether consideration in kind are to be evaluated by an independent expert and any formalities that must be complied with,
– the time when the payment or provision of the consideration is to be made and any conditions relating to such payment or provision,
– whether or not the SPE can provide financial assistance, in particular advance funds, make loans or provide security, with a view to the acquisition of its shares by a third party,
– whether interim dividends can be paid and any applicable requirements,
– whether the management body is required to sign a solvency certificate before a distribution is made, and the applicable requirements,
– the procedure the SPE must follow to recover any unlawful distribution,
– whether the acquisition of own shares is permitted and, if permitted, the procedure to be followed, including the conditions under which the shares may be held, transferred or cancelled,
– the procedure for increasing, reducing or otherwise changing the share capital, and any applicable requirements, Chapter V – Organisation of the SPE

– the method of adopting shareholder resolutions,
– subject to the provisions of this Regulation, the majority required to adopt shareholder resolution,
– the resolutions to be adopted by the shareholders, in addition to those listed in Article 27(1), the quorum and the required majority of voting rights,
– subject to Articles 21, 27 and 29, the rules on proposing resolutions,
– the period of time and the manner in which the shareholders are to be informed of proposals for shareholder resolutions and, if the articles of association provide for general meetings, general meetings,
– the way in which the shareholders obtain the text of any proposed shareholder resolution and any other preparatory documents in relation to the adoption of a resolution,
– the manner in which copies of an adopted resolution are made available to the shareholders,
– where the articles of association provide for the adoption of some or all resolutions at a general meeting, the manner of convening the general meeting, the working methods and the rules on voting by proxy,
– the procedure and time limits for the SPE to respond to requests from shareholders for information, to grant access to the documents of the SPE, and to notify resolutions that have been adopted by shareholders,
– whether the SPE's management body is composed of one or more managing directors, a management board (dual board) or an administrative board (unitary board),
– where there is an administrative board (unitary board), its composition and organisation,
– where there is a management board (dual board), its composition and organisation,
– where there is a management board (dual board) or one or more managing directors, whether the SPE has a supervisory body, and if so, its composition and organisation and its relationship with the management body,
– any eligibility criterion of directors,
– the procedure for appointing and removing directors,
– whether the SPE has an auditor and where the articles of association provide that the SPE should have an auditor, the procedure for his appointment, removal and resignation,
– any specific duties of directors other than those mentioned in this Regulation,
– whether situations involving an actual or potential conflict of interest by a director may be authorised and, if so, an indication of who may authorise such a conflict and the applicable requirements and procedures for the
authorisation of such a conflict,
– whether related party transactions as referred to in Article 32 need to be authorised and the applicable requirements,
– the rules on representation of the SPE by the management body, in particular if the directors have the right to represent the SPE jointly or separately and any delegation of this right,
– the rules on delegation of any management power to another person.

Annex II. Notification form concerning the registration of the transfer of the registered office of an SPE notification concerning the registration of the transfer of the registered office of an SPE.

EU: PROPOSAL FOR A DIRECTIVE ON SINGLE-MEMBER PRIVATE COMPANY

Proposal for a Directive of the European Parliament and of the Council on single-member private limited liability companies, COM (2014) 0212 [footnotes omitted].

THE EUROPEAN PARLIAMENT AND THE COUNCIL OF THE EUROPEAN UNION,
Having regard to the Treaty on the Functioning of the European Union, and in particular Article 50 thereof,
Having regard to the proposal from the European Commission,
After transmission of the draft legislative act to the national Parliaments,
Having regard to the opinion of the European Economic and Social Committee,
Acting in accordance with the ordinary legislative procedure,
Whereas:
(1) Directive 2009/102/EC of the European Parliament and of the Council of 16 September 2009 in the area of company law on single-member private limited-liability companies, has made it possible for individual entrepreneurs to operate under limited liability throughout the Union.
(2) Part I of this Directive takes over the provisions of Directive 2009/102/EC as regards all single-member limited liability companies. It requires that in case all shares come to be held by a single shareholder, its identity should be disclosed to the public by the entry in the register. This Directive also provides that decisions taken by the single shareholder exercising the power of the general meeting as well as the contracts between the shareholder and the company should be recorded in writing, unless they relate to contracts concluded under market conditions in the ordinary course of business.
(3) Establishing single-member limited liability companies as subsidiaries in other Member States entails costs due to the diverse legal and administrative requirements which must be met in the Member States concerned. Such divergent requirements continue to exist among Member States.
(4) The Commission Communication entitled "Integrated Industrial Policy for the Globalisation Era - Putting Competitiveness and Sustainability at Centre Stage" encourages the creation, growth and internationalisation of small and medium-sized enterprises (SMEs). This is important for the Union economy as SMEs account for two-thirds of employment in the Union and offer significant potential for growth and for the creation of jobs.
(5) The improvement of the business environment, especially for SMEs, by reducing transaction costs in Europe, promoting clusters and promoting the internationalisation of SMEs, were the key elements of the initiative "Industrial policy for the globalisation era" outlined in the Commission Communication on the Europe 2020 strategy.
(6) In line with the Europe 2020 strategy, the Review of the Small Business Act for Europe advocated further progress in making smart regulation a reality, enhancing market access and promoting entrepreneurship, job creation and inclusive growth.
(7) In order to facilitate the cross-border activities of SMEs and the establishment of single-member companies as subsidiaries in other Member States, the costs and administrative burdens involved in setting-up these companies should be reduced.
(8) The availability of a harmonised legal framework governing the formation of single-member companies, including the establishment of a uniform template for the articles of association should contribute to the progressive abolition of restrictions on freedom of establishment as regards the conditions for setting up subsidiaries in the territories of Member States and lead to a reduction in costs.
(9) Single-member private limited liability companies formed and operating in compliance with this Directive should add to their names a common, easily identifiable abbreviation – SUP (Societas Unius Personae).
(10) To respect Member States' existing traditions of company law, flexibility should be afforded to them as regards the manner and extent to which they wish to apply harmonised rules governing the formation and operation of SUPs. Member States may apply Part 2 of this Directive to all single-member private limited liability companies so that all such companies would operate and be known as SUPs. Alternatively, they should provide for the establishment of an SUP as a separate company law form which would exist in parallel with other forms of single-member private limited liability company provided for in national law.
(11) To ensure that the harmonised rules are applied as widely as possible, both natural and legal persons should be entitled to form SUPs. For the same reason private limited liability companies that were not formed as SUPs should be able to benefit from the SUP framework. They should be able to be transformed into SUPs in accordance with applicable national law.
(12) To enable business to enjoy the full benefits of the internal market, Member States should not require the registered office of an SUP and its central administration to be in the same Member State.
(13) In order to make it easier and less costly to establish subsidiaries in other Member States, the founders of SUPs should not be obliged to be physically present before any Member State's registra-

tion body. The register should be accessible from any Member State and a company founder should be able to make use of existing points of single contact created under Directive 2006/123/EC of the European Parliament and of the Council as a gateway to national on-line registration points. It should, therefore, be possible to establish SUPs from distance and fully by electronic means.

(14) In order to ensure a high level of transparency, all documents registered at the register of companies should be made publicly available via the system of interconnection of registers referred to in Article 4a(2) of Directive 2009/101/EC of the European Parliament and of the Council[20].

(15) To ensure a high level of uniformity and on-line accessibility, the documents used to register SUPs should follow a uniform format available in all official languages of the Union. Each Member State may require registration to be completed in an official language of the Member State concerned, but are also encouraged to allow for registration in other official languages of the Union.

(16) In line with the recommendations set out in the European Commission's 2011 Review of the Small Business Act to reduce the start-up time for new enterprises, SUPs should receive the certificate of registration in the relevant register of a Member State within three working days. This facility should only be available to the newly created companies and not to existing entities that wish to convert to SUPs as the registration of such entities by their very nature, may take more time.

(17) Each Member State should designate a competent electronic registration point. To support the designated bodies in exchanging information about the identity of the founder, Member States may use the means provided for under Regulation (EU) No 1024/2012 of the European Parliament and of the Council.

(18) Provisions concerning the establishment of single-member private limited companies should not affect the right of Member States to maintain existing rules concerning the verification of the registration process, provided that the whole registration procedure may be completed electronically and at a distance.

(19) The use of the template of articles of association should be required if the SUP is registered electronically. If another form of registration is allowed by national law, the template does not have to be used, but the articles of association need to comply with the requirements of the Directive. The minimum capital required for the formation of a single-member private limited liability company varies among the Member States. Most Member States have already taken steps towards abolishing the minimum capital requirement or keeping it at a nominal level. The SUPs should not be subject to a high mandatory capital requirement, since this would act as a barrier to their formation. Creditors, however, should be protected from excessive distributions to single-members, which could affect the capacity of an SUP to pay its debts. Such protection should be ensured by the imposition of minimum balance sheet requirements (liabilities not exceeding assets) and the solvency statement prepared and signed by the management body. There should be no further restrictions placed on the use of capital by the single-member.

(20) In order to prevent abuse and simplify control SUPs should neither issue any further shares nor should the single share be split. Nor should SUPs acquire or own their single share whether directly or indirectly. Rights attached to the single share should only be exercised by one person. Where Member States allow for co-ownership of a single share, only one representative should be entitled to act on behalf of the co-owners and be considered as a single-member for the purpose of this Directive.

(21) In order to ensure a high level of transparency, decisions taken by the single-member of an SUP exercising the powers of the general meeting should be recorded in writing. Such decisions should be disclosed to the company and their written record kept for at least five years.

(22) The management body of an SUP should be composed of one or more directors. Only natural persons should be appointed as directors, unless the Member State of registration allows legal persons to act as directors.

(23) In order to facilitate the operation of groups of companies, instructions issued by the single-member to the management body should be binding. Only where following such instructions would entail violating the national law of the Member State in which the company is registered, the management body should not follow them. With the exception of any provision in the articles of association which limit the company's representation to all directors jointly, any other limitation of powers of the directors, following from the articles of association, should not be binding insofar as it concerns third parties.

(24) The Member States should lay down rules on penalties applicable to the infringements of the provisions of this Directive and should ensure that they are implemented. Those penalties should be effective, proportionate and dissuasive.

(25) In order to reduce the administrative and legal costs associated with the formation of companies and to ensure a high level of consistency in the registration process across Member States,

EU: PROPOSAL FOR A DIRECTIVE ON SINGLE-MEMBER PRIVATE COMPANY

implementing powers to adopt the templates for registration and for the articles of association of an SUP should be conferred on the Commission. Those powers should be exercised in accordance with Regulation (EU) No 182/2011 of the European Parliament and of the Council.

(26) In order to accommodate future changes to the laws of Member States and to Union legislation concerning company types, the power to adopt acts in accordance with Article 290 of the Treaty on the Functioning of the European Union should be delegated to the Commission to update the list of undertakings contained in Annex I. It is of particular importance that the Commission carry out appropriate consultations during its preparatory work, including at experts' level. The Commission, when preparing and drawing-up delegated acts, should ensure a simultaneous, timely and appropriate transmission of relevant documents to the European Parliament and Council.

(27) In accordance with the Joint Political Declaration of Member States and the Commission of 28 September 2011 on explanatory documents[24], Member States have undertaken to accompany, in justified cases, the notification of their transposition measures with one or more documents explaining the relationship between the components of a directive and the corresponding parts of national transposition instruments. With regard to this Directive, the legislator considers the transmission of such documents to be justified.

(28) Since the objectives of this Directive, namely, to facilitate the establishment of single-member private limited liability companies, including SUPs cannot be sufficiently achieved by the Member States, but can rather, by reason of their scale and effects, be better achieved at Union level, the Union may adopt measures, in accordance with the principle of subsidiarity as set out in Article 5 of the Treaty on European Union. In accordance with the principle of proportionality, as set out in that Article, this Directive does not go beyond what is necessary to achieve those objectives.

(29) Since substantial amendments are being made to Directive 2009/102/EC, in the interests of clarity and legal certainty that Directive should be repealed.

HAVE ADOPTED THIS DIRECTIVE:

Part 1 General Provisions

Article 1. (1) The coordination measures provided for in this Directive shall apply to the laws, regulations and administrative provisions of the Member States relating to:
(a) the types of company listed in Annex I;
(b) Societas Unius Personae (SUP) referred to in Article 6.
(2) Member States shall inform the Commission within two months of any changes to the types of private limited companies provided for in their national law affecting the contents of Annex I. In such a case the Commission shall be empowered to adapt, by means of delegated acts in accordance with Article 26, the list of companies contained in Annex I.
(3) Where a Member State allows other companies than those listed in Annex I to be established as or become single-member companies, as defined in Article 2 (1), Part 1 of this Directive shall also apply to them.

Article 2. For the purposes of this Directive, the following definitions shall apply:
(1) "single-member company" means a company whose shares are held by a single person;
(2) "conversion" means any process by which an existing company becomes or ceases to be an SUP;
(3) "distribution" means any financial benefit derived directly or indirectly from the SUP by the single-member, in relation to the single share, including any transfer of money or property. Distributions may take the form of a dividend, and may be made through a purchase or sale of property or by any other means;
(4) "articles of association" means articles of association or statutes or any other rules or instruments of incorporation establishing a company;
(5) "director" means any member of the management body either formally appointed or who de facto acts as a director.

Article 3. Where a company becomes a single-member company because all its shares come to be held by a single person, that fact, together with the identity of the sole member, must either be recorded in the file or entered in the register as referred to in Article 3(1) and (3) of Directive 2009/101/EC or be entered in a register kept by the company and accessible to the public.

Article 4. (1) The single-member shall exercise the powers of the general meeting of the company.
(2) Decisions taken by the single-member exercising powers referred to in paragraph 1 shall be recorded in writing.

Article 5. (1) Contracts between the single-member and the company shall be recorded in writing.

(2) Member States may decide not to apply paragraph 1 to contracts concluded under market conditions in the ordinary course of business which are not detrimental to the single-member company.

Part 2. Societas Unius Personae

Chapter 1. Legal form and General Principles

Article 6. (1) Member States shall provide for the possibility of registering private single-member limited liability companies in accordance with the rules and procedures set out in this Part. Such companies shall be referred to as SUPs.
(2) Member States shall not hinder SUPs from being single-members in other companies.

Article 7. (1) Member States shall grant SUPs full legal personality.
(2) Member States shall provide that the single-member shall not be liable for any amount exceeding the subscribed share capital.
(3) The name of a company, which has the legal form of an SUP, shall be followed by the abbreviation 'SUP'. Only an SUP may use the abbreviation 'SUP'.
(4) The SUP, and its articles of association, shall be governed by the national law of the Member State where the SUP is registered (hereinafter 'applicable national law').
(5) Member States shall provide that the SUP is set up for an unlimited period of time, unless provided otherwise in the articles of association.

Chapter 2. Formation

Article 8. An SUP may be incorporated by a natural or legal person.

Article 9. (1) Member States shall ensure that an SUP may be formed by the conversion of the types of companies listed in Annex I.
(2) The formation of an SUP by conversion shall not result in any winding-up procedures, any loss or interruption of the legal personality or affect any rights or obligations existing prior to the conversion.
(3) Member States shall ensure that a company shall not become an SUP unless:
(a) a resolution of its shareholders is passed or a decision of its single-member is taken authorising the conversion of the company into an SUP;
(b) its articles of association comply with the applicable national law; and
(c) its net assets are at least equivalent to the amount of its subscribed share capital plus those reserves which may not be distributed according to its articles of association.

Article 10. An SUP shall have its registered office and either its central administration or its principal place of business in the Union.

Chapter 3. Articles of Association

Article 11. (1) Member States shall require that the articles of association of the SUP shall cover at least the subject matters provided for in paragraph (2)
(2) The uniform template of articles of association shall cover the questions of formation, shares, share capital, organisation, accounts and the dissolution of an SUP.
It shall be made available by electronic means.
(3) The Commission shall adopt the uniform template of articles of association by an implementing act. That implementing act shall be adopted in accordance with the examination procedure referred to in Article 27.

Article 12. (1) An SUP may, after registration, amend its articles of association by electronic or other means in accordance with applicable national law. This information shall be entered in the register of companies in the Member State of registration.
(2) The amended articles of association of the SUP shall cover at least the subject matters provided for in the uniform template referred to in Article 11(2).

Chapter 4. Registration

Article 13. (1) Member States may only require for the registration of an SUP the following information or documentation:
(a) the name of the SUP;
(b) the address of the registered office, the central administration and/or the principal place of business of the SUP;
(c) the business object of the SUP;

(d) the names, the addresses and any other information necessary to identify the founding member and, where applicable, the beneficial owner and a representative that registers the SUP on the member's behalf;
(e) the names, addresses and any other information necessary to identify the persons who are authorised to represent the SUP in dealings with third parties and in legal proceedings and whether they have not been disqualified by laws of Member States referred to in Article 22;
(f) the share capital of the SUP;
(g) the nominal value of the single-share, where relevant;
(h) the articles of association of the SUP;
(i) where applicable, the decision authorising the company's conversion into an SUP.
(2) The Commission shall establish, by means of an implementing act, a template to be used for the registration of SUPs in the registers of companies of the Member States in accordance with paragraph (1) That implementing act shall be adopted in accordance with the examination procedure referred to in Article 27.

Article 14. (1) An SUP shall be registered in the Member State in which it is to have its registered office.
(2) An SUP shall acquire legal personality on the date on which it is entered in the register of companies of the Member State of registration.
(3) Member States shall ensure that the registration procedure for newly incorporated SUPs may be completed electronically in its entirety without it being necessary for the founding member to appear before any authority in the Member State of registration (on-line registration).
(4) National on-line registration web-sites shall include links to the registration web-sites in other Member States. Member States shall ensure that the following templates are used for on-line registration:
(a) the uniform template of articles of association referred to in Article 11, and
(b) the registration template referred to in Article 13.
Member States shall issue a certificate of registration confirming that the registration procedure has been completed. The certificate of registration shall be issued no later than three working days from the receipt of all the necessary documentation by the competent authority.
(5) Member States may lay down rules for verifying the identity of the founding member, and any other person making the registration on the member's behalf, and the acceptability of the documents and other information submitted to the registration body. Any identification issued in another Member State by the authorities of that State or on their behalf, including identification issued electronically, shall be recognised and accepted for the purposes of the verification by the Member State of registration.
Where, for the purposes of the first subparagraph, it is necessary for Member States to have recourse to administrative cooperation between them, they shall apply Regulation (EU) No 1024/2012.
(6) Member States shall not make the registration of an SUP conditional on obtaining any licence or authorisation. The registration of the SUP, all documents provided during the process of registration and subsequent changes to them, shall be disclosed in the relevant register of companies immediately after registration.

Chapter 5. Single share

Article 15. (1) An SUP shall not issue more than one share. This single share shall not be split.
(2) An SUP shall not, directly or indirectly, acquire or own its single share.
(3) Where in accordance with the applicable national law, a single share of an SUP is owned by more than one person, those persons shall be regarded as one member in relation to the SUP. They shall exercise their rights through one representative and shall notify the management body of the SUP, without undue delay, of the name of that representative and any change thereto. Until such notification, the exercise of their rights in the SUP shall be suspended. The owners of the single share shall be jointly and severally liable for the commitments made by the representative.
The identity of the representative shall be recorded in the relevant register of companies.

Chapter 6. Share Capital

Article 16. (1) The share capital of an SUP shall be at least EUR 1. In Member States in which the euro is not the national currency, the share capital shall be at least equivalent to one unit of that Member States' currency.
(2) The capital of the SUP shall be fully subscribed.
(3) Member States shall not impose any maximum value on the single share.

(4) Member States shall ensure that the SUP is not subject to rules requiring the company to build up legal reserves. Member States shall allow companies to build reserves in accordance with their articles of association.
(5) Member States shall require letter and order forms whether in paper form or in any other medium, to state the capital subscribed and paid up. If the company has a website, that information shall also be made available on it.

Article 17. (1) The consideration for the share shall be fully paid up at the moment of registration of an SUP.
(2) In case of on-line registration, the consideration shall be paid into the bank account of the SUP. The subsequent increase or decrease of share capital shall be allowed at least in cash and in kind.
(3) In case of cash payment, the Member State of registration of an SUP shall accept payment into a bank account of a bank operating in the Union as evidence of payment or increase in the share capital.

Article 18. (1) An SUP may, on the basis of a recommendation from the management body, make a distribution to the single-member provided that it complies with paragraphs 2 and (3)
(2) An SUP shall not make a distribution to the single-member if on the closing date of the last financial year the net assets as set out in the SUP's annual accounts are, or following such a distribution would become, lower than the amount of the share capital plus those reserves which may not be distributed under the articles of association of the SUP. The calculation shall be based on the most recently adopted balance sheet. Any change in the share capital or in the part of the reserves which may not be distributed occurring subsequently to the closing date of the financial year shall also be taken into account.
(3) The SUP shall not make a distribution to the single-member if it results in the SUP being unable to pay its debts as they become due and payable after distribution. The management body must certify in writing that, having made full inquiry into the affairs and prospects of the SUP, it has formed a reasonable opinion that the SUP will be able to pay its debts as they fall due in the normal course of business in the year following the date of the proposed distribution (a "solvency statement"). The solvency statement must be signed by the management body and a copy of it must be provided to the single member 15 days before the resolution on the distribution is adopted.
(4) The solvency statement shall be disclosed. If the company has a website, this information shall also be made available on it.
(5) Any director shall be personally liable for recommending or ordering a distribution if that director knew, or, in view of the circumstances, ought to have known that the distribution would be contrary to paragraph 2 or 3. The same applies to the single-member with regard to any decision to make a distribution referred to in Article 21.

Article 19. Member States shall ensure that any distributions paid out contrary to Article 18(2) or (3) are refunded to the SUP, where it is established that the single-member knew, or, in view of the circumstances, ought to have known that the distribution would be contrary to Article 18(2) or (3).

Article 20. Member States shall ensure that reductions of the share capital of an SUP that lead de facto to a distribution to the single-member comply with Article 18(2) and (3).

Chapter 7. Organisation

Article 21. (1) Decisions taken by the single-member of an SUP shall be recorded in writing by the single-member. Records of decisions taken shall be kept for at least five years.
(2) A single member shall decide on the following:
(a) approval of the annual accounts;
(b) distribution to the member;
(c) increase of share capital;
(d) reduction of share capital;
(e) appointment and removal of directors;
(f) remuneration, if any, of directors, including when the single member is a director;
(g) change of the registered office;
(h) appointment and removal of the auditor, where applicable;
(i) conversion of the SUP into another company form;
(j) dissolution of the SUP;
(k) any amendments to the articles of association.
The single member may not delegate the decisions referred to in the first subparagraph to the management body.

(3) The single-member shall be allowed to take decisions without calling a general meeting. No formal restrictions shall be imposed by Member States on the power of the single member to take decisions, including as regards the place and the time at which such decisions may be taken.

Article 22. (1) An SUP shall be managed by a management body comprising one or more directors.
(2) The number of directors shall be specified in the articles of association.
(3) The management body may exercise all the powers of the SUP that are not exercised by the single member or, where applicable, by the supervisory board.
(4) The directors shall be natural persons, or legal persons, where allowed by applicable national law. They shall be appointed for an unlimited period of time, unless otherwise specified in the single-member's decision appointing them or in the articles of association. The single member may become a director.
(5) The single-member may remove a director, by means of a decision, at any time. Once removed from the office, a director shall be immediately deprived of the authority and power to act as a director on behalf of the SUP. Any other rights or obligations under the applicable national law shall not be affected.
(6) A natural person who is disqualified by either the law or a judicial or administrative decision of the Member State of registration cannot serve as a director. If the director has been disqualified by a judicial or administrative decision taken in another Member State and this decision remains in force, the decision must be disclosed upon registration in accordance with Article 13. A Member State may refuse, as a matter of public policy, the registration of a company if a director is the subject of an outstanding disqualification in another Member State.
Where, for the purposes of this paragraph, Member States need to have recourse to administrative cooperation between them, they shall apply Regulation (EU) No 1024/2012.
(7) Any person, whose directions or instructions the directors of the company are accustomed to follow, without having been formally appointed, shall be considered a director as regards all duties and liabilities to which directors are subject. A person shall not be considered a director solely on the grounds that the management body acts on advice given by him or her in a professional capacity.

Article 23. (1) The single-member shall have the right to give instructions to the management body.
(2) Instructions given by the single-member shall not be binding for any director insofar as they violate the articles of association or the applicable national law.

Article 24. (1) An SUP's management body, comprising one or more directors, shall have the authority to represent the SUP, including when entering into agreements with third parties and in legal proceedings.
(2) Directors may represent the SUP individually, including when entering into agreements with third parties and in legal proceedings, unless the articles of association provide for joint representation. Any other limitation of the powers of the directors, by the articles of association, by a decision of the single-member or by a decision of the management body, may not be relied upon in any dispute with third parties, even if that limitation has been disclosed. Acts undertaken by the management body shall be binding on the SUP, even if they are not within the object of the SUP.
(3) The management body may delegate the right to represent the SUP insofar as it is allowed by the articles of association. The duty of the management body to file for bankruptcy or to commence any similar insolvency procedure shall not be delegated.

Article 25. (1) Member States shall ensure that their national law requires SUPs to be dissolved or transformed into another form of company if SUPs cease to comply with the requirements laid down in this Directive. If an SUP fails to take appropriate steps to convert into another company law form, the competent authority shall be granted the powers necessary to dissolve the SUP.
(2) An SUP may, at any moment, decide to convert into another company law form following the procedure laid down by applicable national law.
(3) A SUP that has been converted into another company law form or dissolved in accordance with paragraphs 1 or 2, shall cease to use the abbreviation SUP.

Part 3. Final Provisions

Article 26. (1) The power to adopt delegated acts is conferred on the Commission subject to the conditions laid down in this Article.
(2) The delegation of power referred to in Article 1(2) shall be conferred on the Commission for an indeterminate period of time.
(3) The delegation of power referred to in Article 1(2) may be revoked at any time by the European

PART III EUROPEAN COMPANY LAW

Parliament or by the Council. A decision to revoke shall put an end to the delegation of the power specified in that decision. It shall take effect the day following the publication of the decision in the Official Journal of the European Union or at a later date specified therein. It shall not affect the validity of any delegated acts already in force.
(4) As soon as it adopts a delegated act, the Commission shall notify it simultaneously to the European Parliament and to the Council.
(5) A delegated act adopted pursuant to Article 1(2) shall enter into force only if no objection has been expressed either by the European Parliament or the Council within a period of two months of notification of that act to the European Parliament and the Council or if, before the expiry of that period, the European Parliament and the Council have both informed the Commission that they will not object. That period shall be extended by two months at the initiative of the European Parliament or the Council.

Article 27. (1) The European Commission shall be assisted by the Company Law Committee. That committee shall be a committee within the meaning of Regulation (EU) No 182/2011.
(2) Where reference is made to this paragraph, Article 5 of Regulation (EU) No 182/2011 shall apply.

Article 28. Member States shall provide for penalties applicable to infringements of the national provisions adopted to implement this Directive and shall take all the measures necessary to ensure that those penalties are enforced. The penalties provided for shall be effective, proportionate and dissuasive.

Article 29. (1) Directive 2009/102/EC is repealed 24 months after the date of adoption of this Directive plus one day.
(2) References to the repealed Directive shall be construed as references to this Directive and shall be read in accordance with the correlation table in Annex II.

Article 30. In the Annex to Regulation (EU) No 1024/2012, the following point 6 is added:
"6. Directive [.../.../EU] of the European Parliament and of the Council of [...] on Single-Member Private Limited Liability Companies: Articles 14 and 2(2)

Article 31. (1) Member States shall adopt and publish 24 months after the date of adoption of this Directive at the latest, the laws, regulations and administrative provisions necessary to comply with this Directive. They shall forthwith communicate to the Commission the text of those provisions.
(2) They shall apply those provisions from 24 months after the date of adoption of this Directive plus one day.
When Member States adopt those provisions, they shall contain a reference to this Directive or be accompanied by such a reference on the occasion of their official publication. Member States shall determine how such reference is to be made.
Member States shall communicate to the Commission the text of the main provisions of national law which they adopt in the field covered by this Directive.

Article 32. The Directive shall enter into force on the twentieth day following that of its publication in the Official Journal of the European Union.

Article 33. This Directive is addressed to the Member States.

Annex I. Types of companies referred to in Article 1(1)(a)
— Belgium: 'société privée à responsabilité limitée/besloten vennootschap met beperkte aansprakelijkheid',
— Bulgaria: 'дружество с ограничена отговорност',
— Czech Republic: 'společnost s ručením omezeným',
— Denmark: 'anpartsselskab',
— Germany: 'Gesellschaft mit beschränkter Haftung',
— Estonia: 'osaühing',
— Ireland: 'private company limited by shares or by guarantee/cuideachta phríobháideach faoi theorainn scaireanna nó ráthaíochta',
— Greece: 'εταιρεία περιορισμένης ευθύνης',
— Croatia: 'društvo s ograničenom odgovornošću'
— Spain: 'sociedad de responsabilidad limitada',
— France: 'société à responsabilité limitée',
— Italy: 'società a responsabilità limitata',
— Cyprus: 'ιδιωτική εταιρεία περιορισμένης ευθύνης με μετοχές ή με εγγύηση',

EU: PROPOSAL FOR A DIRECTIVE ON SINGLE-MEMBER PRIVATE COMPANY

— Latvia: 'sabiedrība ar ierobežotu atbildību',
— Lithuania: 'uždaroji akcinė bendrovė',
— Luxembourg: 'société à responsabilité limitée',
— Hungary: 'korlátolt felelősségű társaság',
— Malta: 'kumpannija privata/private limited liability company',
— The Netherlands: 'besloten vennootschap met beperkte aansprakelijkheid',
— Austria: 'Gesellschaft mit beschränkter Haftung',
— Poland: 'spółka z ograniczoną odpowiedzialnością',
— Portugal: 'sociedade por quotas',
— Romania: 'societate cu răspundere limitată',
— Slovenia: 'družba z omejeno odgovornostjo',
— Slovakia: 'spoločnosť s ručením obmedzeným',
— Finland: 'yksityinen osakeyhtiö/privat aktiebolag',
— Sweden: 'privat aktiebolag',
— United Kingdom: 'private company limited by shares or by guarantee'

Annex II. Correlation Table
Directive 2009/102/EC || This Directive
Article 1 || Article 1 (1)
Article 2 (1) || Article 2
Article 2 (2) || -
Article 3 || Article 3
Article 4 || Article 4
Article 5 || Article 5
Article 6 || Article 1 (3)
Article 7 || -
Article 8 || Article 31
Article 9 || Article 29
Article 10 || Article 32
Article 11 || Article 33

VOL III PART IV

European Private Law

PART IV   EUROPEAN PRIVATE LAW

Council Directive 85/374/EEC of 25 July 1985 on the approximation of the laws, regulations and administrative provisions of the Member States concerning liability for defective products (OJL 210, 07.08.1985, pp. 29 – 33) as amended by Directive 99/34/EC [footnotes omitted].

THE COUNCIL OF THE EUROPEAN COMMUNITIES,
Having regard to the Treaty establishing the European Economic Community, and in particular Article 100 thereof, Having regard to the proposal from the Commission,
Having regard to the opinion of the European Parliament,
Having regard to the opinion of the Economic and Social Committee,
Whereas approximation of the laws of the Member States concerning the liability of the producer for damage caused by the defectiveness of his products is necessary because the existing divergences may distort competition and affect the movement of goods within the common market and entail a differing degree of protection of the consumer against damage caused by a defective product to his health or property;
Whereas liability without fault on the part of the producer is the sole means of adequately solving the problem, peculiar to our age of increasing technicality, of a fair apportionment of the risks inherent in modern technological production;
Whereas liability without fault should apply only to movables which have been industrially produced, whereas, as a result, it is appropriate to exclude liability for agricultural products and game, except where they have undergone a processing of an industrial nature which could cause a defect in these products; whereas the liability provided for in this Directive should also apply to movables which are used in the construction of immovables or are installed in immovables;
Whereas protection of the consumer requires that all producers involved in the production process should be made liable, in so far as their finished product, component part or any raw material supplied by them was defective; Whereas, for the same reason, liability should extend to importers of products into the Community and to persons who present themselves as producers by affixing their name, trade mark or other distinguishing feature or who supply a product the producer of which cannot be identified;
Whereas, in situations where several persons are liable for the same damage, the protection of the consumer requires that the injured person should be able to claim full compensation for the damage from any one of them; whereas, to protect the physical well-being and property of the consumer, the defectiveness of the product should be determined by reference not to its fitness for use but to the lack of the safety which the public at large is entitled to expect; whereas the safety is assessed by excluding any misuse of the product not reasonable under the circumstances;
Whereas a fair apportionment of risk between the injured person and the producer implies that the producer should be able to free himself from liability if he furnishes proof as to the existence of certain exonerating circumstances; Whereas the protection of the consumer requires that the liability of the producer remains unaffected by acts or omissions of other persons having contributed to cause the damage; whereas, however, the contributory negligence of the injured person may be taken into account to reduce or disallow such liability;
Whereas the protection of the consumer requires compensation for death and personal injury as well as compensation for damage to property; whereas the latter should nevertheless be limited to goods for private use or consumption and be subject to a deduction of a lower threshold of a fixed amount in order to avoid litigation in an excessive number of cases; Whereas this Directive should not prejudice compensation for pain and suffering and other non-material damages payable, where appropriate, under the law applicable to the case;
Whereas a uniform period of limitation for the bringing of action for compensation is in the interests both of the injured person and of the producer;
Whereas products age in the course of time, higher safety standards are developed and the state of science and technology progresses; whereas, therefore, it would not be reasonable to make the producer liable for an unlimited period for the defectiveness of his product; whereas, therefore, liability should expire after a reasonable length of time, without prejudice to claims pending at law;
Whereas, to achieve effective protection of consumers, no contractual derogation should be permitted as regards the liability of the producer in relation to the injured person;
Whereas under the legal systems of the Member States an injured party may have a claim for damages based on grounds of contractual liability or on grounds of non-contractual liability other than that provided for in this Directive; in so far as these provisions also serve to attain the objective of effective protection of consumers, they should remain unaffected by this Directive; whereas, in so far as effective protection of consumers in the sector of pharmaceutical products is already also attained in a Member State under a special liability system, claims based on this system should similarly remain possible;

Whereas, to the extent that liability for nuclear injury or damage is already covered in all Member States by adequate special rules, it has been possible to exclude damage of this type from the scope of this Directive; Whereas, since the exclusion of primary agricultural products and game from the scope of this Directive may be felt, in certain Member States, in view of what is expected for the protection of consumers, to restrict unduly such protection, it should be possible for a Member State to extend liability to such products;

Whereas, for similar reasons, the possibility offered to a producer to free himself from liability if he proves that the state of scientific and technical knowledge at the time when he put the product into circulation was not such as to enable the existence of a defect to be discovered may be felt in certain Member States to restrict unduly the protection of the consumer; whereas it should therefore be possible for a Member State to maintain in its legislation or to provide by new legislation that this exonerating circumstance is not admitted; whereas, in the case of new legislation, making use of this derogation should, however, be subject to a Community stand-still procedure, in order to raise, if possible, the level of protection in a uniform manner throughout the Community;

Whereas, taking into account the legal traditions in most of the Member States, it is inappropriate to set any financial ceiling on the producer's liability without fault; whereas, in so far as there are, however, differing traditions, it seems possible to admit that a Member State may derogate from the principle of unlimited liability by providing a limit for the total liability of the producer for damage resulting from a death or personal injury and caused by identical items with the same defect, provided that this limit is established at a level sufficiently high to guarantee adequate protection of the consumer and the correct functioning of the common market;

Whereas the harmonization resulting from this cannot be total at the present stage, but opens the way towards greater harmonization; whereas it is therefore necessary that the Council receive at regular intervals, reports from the Commission on the application of this Directive, accompanied, as the case may be, by appropriate proposals;

Whereas it is particularly important in this respect that a re-examination be carried out of those parts of the Directive relating to the derogations open to the Member States, at the expiry of a period of sufficient length to gather practical experience on the effects of these derogations on the protection of consumers and on the functioning of the common market,

HAS ADOPTED THIS DIRECTIVE:

Article 1. The producer shall be liable for damage caused by a defect in his product.

Article 2. For the purpose of this Directive 'product' means all movables even if incorporated into another movable or into an immovable. 'Product' includes electricity.

Article 3. (1) 'Producer' means the manufacturer of a finished product, the producer of any raw material or the manufacturer of a component part and any person who, by putting his name, trade mark or other distinguishing feature on the product presents himself as its producer.
(2) Without prejudice to the liability of the producer, any person who imports into the Community a product for sale, hire, leasing or any form of distribution in the course of his business shall be deemed to be a producer within the meaning of this Directive and shall be responsible as a producer.
(3) Where the producer of the product cannot be identified, each supplier of the product shall be treated as its producer unless he informs the injured person, within a reasonable time, of the identity of the producer or of the person who supplied him with the product. The same shall apply, in the case of an imported product, if this product does not indicate the identity of the importer referred to in paragraph (2), even if the name of the producer is indicated.

Article 4. The injured person shall be required to prove the damage, the defect and the causal relationship between defect and damage.

Article 5. Where, as a result of the provisions of this Directive, two or more persons are liable for the same damage, they shall be liable jointly and severally, without prejudice to the provisions of national law concerning the rights of contribution or recourse.

Article 6. (1) A product is defective when it does not provide the safety which a person is entitled to expect, taking all circumstances into account, including:
(a) the presentation of the product;
(b) the use to which it could reasonably be expected that the product would be put;
(c) the time when the product was put into circulation.
(2) A product shall not be considered defective for the sole reason that a better product is subsequently put into circulation.

PART IV EUROPEAN PRIVATE LAW

Article 7. The producer shall not be liable as a result of this Directive if he proves:
(a) that he did not put the product into circulation; or
(b) that, having regard to the circumstances, it is probable that the defect which caused the damage did not exist at the time when the product was put into circulation by him or that this defect came into being afterwards; or
(c) that the product was neither manufactured by him for sale or any form of distribution for economic purpose nor manufactured or distributed by him in the course of his business; or
(d) that the defect is due to compliance of the product with mandatory regulations issued by the public authorities; or
(e) that the state of scientific and technical knowledge at the time when he put the product into circulation was not such as to enable the existence of the defect to be discovered; or
(f) in the case of a manufacturer of a component, that the defect is attributable to the design of the product in which the component has been fitted or to the instructions given by the manufacturer of the product.

Article 8. (1) Without prejudice to the provisions of national law concerning the right of contribution or recourse, the liability of the producer shall not be reduced when the damage is caused both by a defect in product and by the act or omission of a third party.
(2) The liability of the producer may be reduced or disallowed when, having regard to all the circumstances, the damage is caused both by a defect in the product and by the fault of the injured person or any person for whom the injured person is responsible.

Article 9. For the purpose of Article 1, 'damage' means:
(a) damage caused by death or by personal injuries;
(b) damage to, or destruction of, any item of property other than the defective product itself, with a lower threshold of 500 ECU, provided that the item of property:
(i) is of a type ordinarily intended for private use or consumption, and
(ii) was used by the injured person mainly for his own private use or consumption.
This Article shall be without prejudice to national provisions relating to non-material damage.

Article 10. (1) Member States shall provide in their legislation that a limitation period of three years shall apply to proceedings for the recovery of damages as provided for in this Directive. The limitation period shall begin to run from the day on which the plaintiff became aware, or should reasonably have become aware, of the damage, the defect and the identity of the producer.
(2) The laws of Member States regulating suspension or interruption of the limitation period shall not be affected by this Directive.

Article 11. Member States shall provide in their legislation that the rights conferred upon the injured person pursuant to this Directive shall be extinguished upon the expiry of a period of 10 years from the date on which the producer put into circulation the actual product which caused the damage, unless the injured person has in the meantime instituted proceedings against the producer.

Article 12. The liability of the producer arising from this Directive may not, in relation to the injured person, be limited or excluded by a provision limiting his liability or exempting him from liability.

Article 13. This Directive shall not affect any rights which an injured person may have according to the rules of the law of contractual or non-contractual liability or a special liability system existing at the moment when this Directive is notified.

Article 14. This Directive shall not apply to injury or damage arising from nuclear accidents and covered by international conventions ratified by the Member States.

Article 15. (1) Each Member State may:
by way of derogation from Article 7 (e), maintain or, subject to the procedure set out in paragraph (2) of this Article, provide in this legislation that the producer shall be liable even if he proves that the state of scientific and technical knowledge at the time when he put the product into circulation was not such as to enable the existence of a defect to be discovered.
(2) A Member State wishing to introduce the measure specified in paragraph (1) (b) shall communicate the text of the proposed measure to the Commission. The Commission shall inform the other Member States thereof.
The Member State concerned shall hold the proposed measure in abeyance for nine months after the Commission is informed and provided that in the meantime the Commission has not submitted to the Council a proposal amending this Directive on the relevant matter. However, if within three months

of receiving the said information, the Commission does not advise the Member State concerned that it intends submitting such a proposal to the Council, the Member State may take the proposed measure immediately.

If the Commission does submit to the Council such a proposal amending this Directive within the aforementioned nine months, the Member State concerned shall hold the proposed measure in abeyance for a further period of 18 months from the date on which the proposal is submitted.

(3) Ten years after the date of notification of this Directive, the Commission shall submit to the Council a report on the effect that rulings by the courts as to the application of Article 7 (e) and of paragraph (1) (b) of this Article have on consumer protection and the functioning of the common market. In the light of this report the Council, acting on a proposal from the Commission and pursuant to the terms of Article 100 of the Treaty, shall decide whether to repeal Article 7 (e).

Article 16. (1) Any Member State may provide that a producer's total liability for damage resulting from a death or personal injury and caused by identical items with the same defect shall be limited to an amount which may not be less than 70 million ECU.

(2) Ten years after the date of notification of this Directive, the Commission shall submit to the Council a report on the effect on consumer protection and the functioning of the common market of the implementation of the financial limit on liability by those Member States which have used the option provided for in paragraph (1). In the light of this report the Council, acting on a proposal from the Commission and pursuant to the terms of Article 100 of the Treaty, shall decide whether to repeal paragraph (1).

Article 17. This Directive shall not apply to products put into circulation before the date on which the provisions referred to in Article 19 enter into force.

Article 18. (1) For the purposes of this Directive, the ECU shall be that defined by Regulation (EEC) No 3180/78 (1), as amended by Regulation (EEC) No 2626/84 (2). The equivalent in national currency shall initially be calculated at the rate obtaining on the date of adoption of this Directive.

(2) Every five years the Council, acting on a proposal from the Commission, shall examine and, if need be, revise the amounts in this Directive, in the light of economic and monetary trends in the Community.

Article 19. (1) Member States shall bring into force, not later than three years from the date of notification of this Directive, the laws, regulations and administrative provisions necessary to comply with this Directive. They shall forthwith inform the Commission thereof (1).

(2) The procedure set out in Article 15 (2) shall apply from the date of notification of this Directive.

Article 20. Member States shall communicate to the Commission the texts of the main provisions of national law which they subsequently adopt in the field governed by this Directive.

Article 21. Every five years the Commission shall present a report to the Council on the application of this Directive and, if necessary, shall submit appropriate proposals to it.

Article 22. This Directive is addressed to the Member States.

PART IV   EUROPEAN PRIVATE LAW

Council Directive 86/653/EEC of 18 December 1986 on the coordination of the laws of the Member States relating to self-employed commercial agents (OJ L 382, 31/12/1986 P. 0017 – 0021) [footnotes omitted].

THE COUNCIL OF THE EUROPEAN COMMUNITIES,
Having regard to the Treaty establishing the European Economic Community, and in particular Articles 57(2) and 100 thereof,
Having regard to the proposal from the Commission,
Having regard to the opinion of the European Parliament,
Having regard to the opinion of the Economic and Social Committee,
Whereas the restrictions on the freedom of establishment and the freedom to provide services in respect of activities of intermediaries in commerce, industry and small craft industries were abolished by Directive 64/224/EEC;
Whereas the differences in national laws concerning commercial representation substantially affect the conditions of competition and the carrying-on of that activity within the Community and are detrimental both to the protection available to commercial agents vis-à-vis their principals and to the security of commercial transactions; whereas moreover those differences are such as to inhibit substantially the conclusion and operation of commerical representation contracts where principal and commercial agents are established in different Member States;
Whereas trade in goods between Member States should be carried on under conditions which are similar to those of a single market, and this necessitates approximation of the legal systems of the Member States to the extent required for the proper functioning of the common market; whereas in this regard the rules concerning conflict of laws do not, in the matter of commercial representation, remove the inconsistencies referred to above, nor would they even if they were made uniform, and accordingly the proposed harmonization is necessary notwithstanding the existence of those rules; Whereas in this regard the legal relationship between commercial agent and principal must be given priority;
Whereas it is appropriate to be guided by the principles of Article 117 of the Treaty and to maintain improvementsalready made, when harmonizing the laws of the Member States relating to commercial agents;
Whereas additional transitional periods should be allowed for certain Member States which have to make a particular effort to adapt their regulations, especially those concerning indemnity for termination of contract between the principal and the commercial agent, to the requirements of this Directive,
HAS ADOPTED THIS DIRECTIVE:

Chapter I. Scope

Article 1. (1) The harmonization measures prescribed by this Directive shall apply to the laws, regulations and administrative provisions of the Member States governing the relations between commercial agents and their principals.
(2) For the purposes of this Directive, 'commercial agent' shall mean a self-employed intermediary who has continuing authority to negotiate the sale or the purchase of goods on behalf of another person, hereinafter called the 'principal', or to negotiate and conclude such transactions on behalf of and in the name of that principal.
(3) A commercial agent shall be understood within the meaning of this Directive as not including in particular:
- a person who, in his capacity as an officer, is empowered to enter into commitments binding on a company or association,
- a partner who is lawfully authorized to enter into commitments binding on his partners,
- a receiver, a receiver and manager, a liquidator or a trustee in bankruptcy.

Article 2. (1) This Directive shall not apply to:
- commercial agents whose activities are unpaid,
- commercial agents when they operate on commodity exchanges or in the commodity market, or
- the body known is the Crown Agents for Overseas Governments and Administrations, as set up under the Crown Agents Act 1979 in the United Kingdom, or its subsidiaries.
(2) Each of the Member States shall have the right to provide that the Directive shall not apply to those persons whose activities as commercial agents are considered secondary by the law of that Member State.

Chapter II. Rights and Obligations

Article 3. (1) In performing has activities a commercial agent must look after his principal's interests and act dutifully and in good faith.
(2) In particular, a commercial agent must:
(a) make proper efforts to negotiate and, where appropriate, conclude the transactions he is instructed to take care of;
(b) communicate to his principal all the necessary information available to him;
(c) comply with reasonable instructions given by his principal.

Article 4. (1) In his relations with his commercial agent a principal must act dutifully and in good faith.
(2) A principal must in particular:
(a) provide his commercial agent with the necessary documentation relating to the goods concerned;
(b) obtain for his commercial agent the information necessary for the performance of the agency contract, and in particular notify the commercial agent within a reasonable period once he anticipates that the volume of commercial transactions will be significantly lower than that which the commercial agent could normally have expected.
(3) A principal must, in addition, inform the commercial agent within a reasonable period of his acceptance, refusal, and of any non-execution of a commercial transaction which the commercial agent has procured for the principal.

Article 5. The parties may not derogate from the provisions of Articles 3 and 4.

Chapter III. Remuneration

Article 6. (1) In the absence of any agreement on this matter between the parties, and without prejudice to the application of the compulsory provisions of the Member States concerning the level of remuneration, a commercial agent shall be entitled to the remuneration that commercial agents appointed for the goods forming the subject of his agency contract are customarily allowed in the place where he carries on his activities. If there is no such customary practice a commercial agent shall be entitled to reasonable remuneration taking into account all the aspects of the transaction.
(2) Any part of the remuneration which varies with the number or value of business transactions shall be deemed to be commission within the meaning of this Directive.
(3) Articles 7 to 12 shall not apply if the commercial agent is not remunerated wholly or in part by commission.

Article 7. (1) A commercial agent shall be entitled to commission on commercial transactions concluded during the period covered by the agency contract:
(a) where the transaction has been concluded as a result of his action; or
(b) where the transaction is concluded with a third party whom he has previously acquired as a customer for transactions of the same kind.
(2) A commercial agent shall also be entitled to commission on transactions concluded during the period covered by the agency contract:
- either where he is entrusted with a specific geographical area or group of customers,
- or where he has an exclusive right to a specific geographical area or group of customers,
and where the transaction has been entered into with a customer belonging to that area or group. Member State shall include in their legislation one of the possibilities referred to in the above two indents.

Article 8. A commercial agent shall be entitled to commission on commercial transactions concluded after the agency contract has terminated:
(a) if the transaction is mainly attributable to the commercial agent's efforts during the period covered by the agency contract and if the transaction was entered into within a reasonable period after that contract terminated; or
(b) if, in accordance with the conditions mentioned in Article 7, the order of the third party reached the principal or the commercial agent before the agency contract terminated.

Article 9. A commercial agent shall not be entitled to the commission referred to in Article 7, if that commission is payable, pursuant to Article 8, to the previous commercial agent, unless it is equitable because of the circumstances for the commission to be shared between the commercial agents.

Article 10. (1) The commission shall become due as soon as and to the extent that one of the following circumstances obtains:
(a) the principal has executed the transaction; or

(b) the principal should, according to his agreement with the third party, have executed the transaction; or
(c) the third party has executed the transaction.
(2) The commission shall become due at the latest when the third party has executed his part of the transaction or should have done so if the principal had executed his part of the transaction, as he should have.
(3) The commission shall be paid not later than on the last day of the month following the quarter in which it became due.
(4) Agreements to derogate from paragraphs 2 and 3 to the detriment of the commercial agent shall not be permitted.

Article 11. (1) The right to commission can be extinguished only if and to the extent that:
- it is established that the contract between the third party and the principal will not be executed, and
- that face is due to a reason for which the principal is not to blame.
(2) Any commission which the commercial agent has already received shall be refunded if the right to it is extinguished.
(3) Agreements to derogate from paragraph (1) to the detriment of the commercial agent shall not be permitted.

Article 12. (1). The principal shall supply his commercial agent with a statement of the commission due, not later than the last day of the month following the quarter in which the commission has become due. This statement shall set out the main components used in calculating the amount of commission.
(2) A commercial agent shall be entitled to demand that he be provided with all the information, and in particular an extract from the books, which is available to his principal and which he needs in order to check the amount of the commission due to him.
(3) Agreements to derogate from paragraphs 1 and 2 to the detriment of the commercial agent shall not be permitted.
(4) This Directive shall not conflict with the internal provisions of Member States which recognize the right of a commercial agent to inspect a principal's books.

Chapter IV. Conclusion and Termination of the Agency Contract

Article 13. (1) Each party shall be entitled to receive from the other on request a signed written document setting out the terms of the agency contract including any terms subsequently agreed. Waiver of this right shall not be permitted.
(2) Notwithstanding paragraph (1) a Member State may provide that an agency contract shall not be valid unless evidenced in writing.

Article 14. An agency contract for a fixed period which continues to be performed by both parties after that period has expired shall be deemed to be converted into an agency contract for an indefinite period.

Article 15. (1) Where an agency contract is concluded for an indefinite period either party may terminate it by notice.
(2) The period of notice shall be one month for the first year of the contract, two months for the second year commenced, and three months for the third year commenced and subsequent years. The parties may not agree on shorter periods of notice.
(3) Member States may fix the period of notice at four months for the fourth year of the contract, five months for the fifth year and six months for the sixth and subsequent years. They may decide that the parties may not agree to shorter periods.
(4) If the parties agree on longer periods than those laid down in paragraphs 2 and 3, the period of notice to be observed by the principal must not be shorter than that to be observed by the commercial agent.
(5) Unless otherwise agreed by the parties, the end of the period of notice must coincide with the end of a calendar month.
(6) The provision of this Article shall apply to an agency contract for a fixed period where it is converted under Article 14 into an agency contract for an indefinite period, subject to the proviso that the earlier fixed period must be taken into account in the calculation of the period of notice.

Article 16. Nothing in this Directive shall affect the application of the law of the Member States where the latter provides for the immediate termination of the agency contract:
(a) because of the failure of one party to carry out all or part of his obligations;
(b) where exceptional circumstances arise.

Article 17. (1) Member States shall take the measures necessary to ensure that the commercial agent is, after termination of the agency contract, indemnified in accordance with paragraph (2) or compensated for damage in accordance with paragraph (3).
(2) (a) The commercial agent shall be entitled to an indemnity if and to the extent that:
- he has brought the principal new customers or has significantly increased the volume of business with existing customers and the principal continues to derive substantial benefits from the business with such customers, and
- the payment of this indemnity is equitable having regard to all the circumstances and, in particular, the commission lost by the commercial agent on the business transacted with such customers. Member States may provide for such circumstances also to include the application or otherwise of a restraint of trade clause, within the meaning of Article 20;
(b) The amount of the indemnity may not exceed a figure equivalent to an indemnity for one year calculated from the commercial agent's average annual remuneration over the preceding five years and if the contract goes back less than five years the indemnity shall be calculated on the average for the period in question;
(c) The grant of such an indemnity shall not prevent the commercial agent from seeking damages.
(3) The commercial agent shall be entitled to compensation for the damage he suffers as a result of the termination of his relations with the principal.
Such damage shall be deemed to occur particularly when the termination takes place in circumstances:
- depriving the commercial agent of the commission which proper performance of the agency contract would have procured him whilst providing the principal with substantial benefits linked to the commercial agent's activities,
- and/or which have not enabled the commercial agent to amortize the costs and expenses that he had incurred for the performance of the agency contract on the principal's advice.
(4) Entitlement to the indemnity as provided for in paragraph (2) or to compensation for damage as provided for under paragraph (3), shall also arise where the agency contract is terminated as a result of the commercial agent's death.
(5) The commercial agent shall lose his entitlement to the indemnity in the instances provided for in paragraph (2) or to compensation for damage in the instances provided for in paragraph (3), if within one year following termination of the contract he has not notified the principal that he intends pursuing his entitlement.
(6) The Commission shall submit to the Council, within eight years following the date of notification of this Directive, a report on the implementation of this Article, and shall if necessary submit to it proposals for amendments.

Article 18. The indemnity or compensation referred to in Article 17 shall not be payable:
(a) where the principal has terminated the agency contract because of default attributable to the commercial agent which would justify immediate termination of the agency contract under national law;
(b) where the commercial agent has terminated the agency contract, unless such termination is justified by circumstances attributable to the principal or on grounds of age, infirmity or illness of the commercial agent in consequence of which he cannot reasonably be required to continue his activities;
(c) where, with the agreement of the principal, the commercial agent assigns his rights and duties under the agency contract to another person.

Article 19. The parties may not derogate from Articles 17 and 18 to the detriment of the commercial agent before the agency contract expires.

Article 20. (1) For the purposes of this Directive an agreement restricting the business activities of a commercial agent following termination of the agency contract is hereinafter referred to as a restraint of trade clause.
(2) A restraint of trade clause shall be valid only if and to the extent that:
(a) it is concluded in writing; and
(b) it relates to the geographical area or the group of customers and the geographical area entrusted to the commercial agent and to the kind of goods covered by his agency under the contract.
(3) A restraint of trade clause shall be valid for not more than two years after termination of the agency contract.
(4) This Article shall not affect provisions of national law which impose other restrictions on the validity or enforceability of restraint of trade clauses or which enable the courts to reduce the obligations on the parties resulting from such an agreement.

PART IV   EUROPEAN PRIVATE LAW

Chapter V. General and Final Provisions

Article 21. Nothing in this Directive shall require a Member State to provide for the disclosure of information where such disclosure would be contrary to public policy.

Article 22. (1) Member States shall bring into force the provisions necessary to comply with this Directive before 1 January 1990. They shall for with inform the Commission thereof. Such provisions shall apply at least to contracts concluded after their entry into force. They shall apply to contracts in operation by 1 January 1994 at the latest.
(2) As from the notification of this Directive, Member States shall communicate to the Commission the main laws, regulations and administrative provisions which they adopt in the field governed by this Directive.
(3) However, with regard to Ireland and the United Kingdom, 1 January 1990 referred to in paragraph (1) shall be replaced by 1 January 1994.
With regard to Italy, 1 January 1990 shall be replaced by 1 January 1993 in the case of the obligations deriving from Article 17.

Article 23. This Directive is addressed to the Member States.

EU: DIRECTIVE 87/102 ON CONSUMER CREDIT

Council Directive 87/102/EEC of 22 December 1986 for the approximation of the laws, regulations and administrative provisions of the Member States concerning consumer credit (OJ L 042, 12.02.1987 pp. 48 – 53) as amended by Directive 90/88 and Directive 98/7 [footnotes omitted].

THE COUNCIL OF THE EUROPEAN COMMUNITIES,
Having regard to the Treaty establishing the European Economic Community, and in particular Article 100 thereof,
Having regard to the proposal from the Commission,
Having regard to the opinion of the European Parliament,
Having regard to the opinion of the Economic and Social Committee,
Whereas wide differences exist in the laws of the Member States in the field of consumer credit;
Whereas these differences of law can lead to distortions of competition between grantors of credit in the common market;
Whereas these differences limit the opportunities the consumer has to obtain credit in other Member States; whereas they affect the volume and the nature of the credit sought, and also the purchase of goods and services;
Whereas, as a result, these differences have an influence on the free movement of goods and services obtainable by consumers on credit and thus directly affect the functioning of the common market;
Whereas, given the increasing volume of credit granted in the Community to consumers, the establishment of a common market in consumer credit would benefit alike consumers, grantors of credit, manufacturers, wholesalers and retailers of goods and providers of services;
Whereas the programmes of the European Economic Community for a consumer protection and information policy provide, inter alia, that the consumer should be protected against unfair credit terms and that a harmonization of the general conditions governing consumer credit should be undertaken as a priority;
Whereas differences of law and practice result in unequal consumer protection in the field of consumer credit from one Member State to another;
Whereas there has been much change in recent years in the types of credit available to and used by consumers; whereas new forms of consumer credit have emerged and continue to develop;
Whereas the consumer should receive adequate information on the conditions and cost of credit and on his obligations; whereas this information should include, inter alia, the annual percentage rate of charge for credit, or, failing that, the total amount that the consumer must pay for credit; whereas, pending a decision on a Community method or methods of calculating the annual percentage rate of charge, Member States should be able to retain existing methods or practices for calculating this rate, or failing that, should establish provisions for indicating the total cost of the credit to the consumer;
Whereas the terms of credit may be disadvantageous to the consumer; whereas better protection of consumers can be achieved by adopting certain requirements which are to apply to all forms of credit;
Whereas, having regard to the character of certain credit agreements or types of transaction, these agreements or transactions should be partially or entirely excluded from the field of application of this Directive;
Whereas it should be possible for Member States, in consultation with the Commission, to exempt from the Directive certain forms of credit of a non-commercial character granted under particular conditions;
Whereas the practices existing in some Member States in respect of authentic acts drawn up before a notary or judge are such as to render the application of certain provisions of this Directive unnecessary in the case of such acts; whereas it should therefore be possible for Member States to exempt such acts from those provisions;
Whereas credit agreements for very large financial amounts tend to differ from the usual consumer credit agreements; whereas the application of the provisions of this Directive to agreements for very small amounts could create unnecessary administrative burdens both for consumers and grantors of credit; whereas therefore, agreements above or below specified financial limits should be excluded from the Directive;
Whereas the provision of information on the cost of credit in advertising and at the business premises of the creditor or credit broker can make it easier for the consumer to compare different offers;
Whereas consumer protection is further improved if credit agreements are made in writing and contain certain minimum particulars concerning the contractual terms;
Whereas, in the case of credit granted for the acquisition of goods, Member States should lay down

the conditions in which goods may be repossessed, particularly if the consumer has not given his consent; whereas the account between the parties should upon repossession be made up in such manner as to ensure that the repossession does not entail any unjustified enrichment;

Whereas the consumer should be allowed to discharge his obligations before the due date; whereas the consumer should then be entitled to an equitable reduction in the total cost of the credit;

Whereas the assignment of the creditor's rights arising under a credit agreement should not be allowed to weaken the position of the consumer;

Whereas those Member States which permit consumers to use bills of exchange, promissory notes or cheques in connection with credit agreements should ensure that the consumer is suitably protected when so using such instruments;

Whereas, as regards goods or services which the consumer has contracted to acquire on credit, the consumer should, at least in the circumstances defined below, have rights vis-à-vis the grantor of credit which are in addition to his normal contractual rights against him and against the supplier of the goods or services; whereas the circumstances referred to above are those where the grantor of credit and the supplier of goods or services have a pre-existing agreement whereunder credit is made available exclusively by that grantor of credit to customers of that supplier for the purpose of enabling the consumer to acquire goods or services from the latter;

Whereas the ECU is as defined in Council Regulation (EEC) No 3180/78, as last amended by Regulation (EEC) No 2626/84; whereas Member States should to a limited extent be at liberty to round off the amounts in national currency resulting from the conversion of amounts of this Directive expressed in ECU; whereas the amounts in this Directive should be periodically re-examined in the light of economic and monetary trends in the Community, and, if need be, revised;

Whereas suitable measures should be adopted by Member States for authorizing persons offering credit or offering to arrange credit agreements or for inspecting or monitoring the activities of persons granting credit or arranging for credit to be granted or for enabling consumers to complain about credit agreements or credit conditions;

Whereas credit agreements should not derogate, to the detriment of the consumer, from the provisions adopted in implementation of this Directive or corresponding to its provisions; whereas those provisions should not be circumvented as a result of the way in which agreements are formulated;

Whereas, since this Directive provides for a certain degree of approximation of the laws, regulations and administrative provisions of the Member States concerning consumer credit and for a certain level of consumer protection, Member States should not be prevented from retaining or adopting more stringent measures to protect the consumer, with due regard for their obligations under the Treaty;

Whereas, not later than 1 January 1995, the Commission should present to the Council a report concerning the operation of this Directive,

HAS ADOPTED THIS DIRECTIVE:

Article 1. (1). This Directive applies to credit agreements.

(2). For the purpose of this Directive:

(a) 'consumer' means a natural person who, in transactions covered by this Directive, is acting for purposes which can be regarded as outside his trade or profession;

(b) 'creditor' means a natural or legal person who grants credit in the course of his trade, business or profession, or a group of such persons;

(c) 'credit agreement' means an agreement whereby a creditor grants or promises to grant to a consumer a credit in the form of a deferred payment, a loan or other similar financial accommodation. Agreements for the provision on a continuing basis of a service or a utility, where the consumer has the right to pay for them, for the duration of their provision, by means of instalments, are not deemed to be credit agreements for the purpose of this Directive;

'(d) "total cost of the credit to the consumer" means all the costs, including interest and other charges, which the consumer has to pay for the credit.';

'(e) "annual percentage rate of charge" means the total cost of the credit to theconsumer, expressed as an annual percentage of the amount of the credit granted and calculated in accordance with Article 1a'.

Article 1a. (1) The annual percentage rate of charge which shall be that rate, on an annual basis which equalizes the present value of all commitments (loans, repayments and charges), future or existing, agreed by the creditor and the borrower, shall be calculated in accordance with the mathematical formula set out in Annex II.

(b) Four examples of the method of calculation are given in Annex III, by way of illustration.

(2) For the purpose of calculating the annual percentage rate of charge, the "total cost of the credit to

EU: DIRECTIVE 87/102 ON CONSUMER CREDIT

the consumer" as defined in Article 1 (2) (d) shall be determined, with the exception of the following charges:
(i) charges payable by the borrower for non-compliance with any of his commitments laid down in the credit agreement;
(ii) charges other than the purchase price which, in purchases of goods or services, the consumer is obliged to pay whether the transaction is paid in cash or by credit;
(iii) charges for the transfer of funds and charges for keeping an account intended to receive payments towards the reimbursement of the credit the payment of interest and other charges except where the consumer doesn ot have reasonable freedom of choice in the matter and where such charges are abnormally high; this provision shall not, however, apply to charges for collection of such reimbursements or payments, whether made in cash or otherwise;
(iv) membership subscriptions to associations or groups and arising from agreements separate from the credit agreement, even though such subscriptions have an effect on the credit terms;
(v) charges for insurance or guarantees; included are, however, those designed to ensure payment to the creditor, in the event of the death, invalidity, illness or unemployment of the consumer, of a sum equal to or less than the total amount of the credit together with relevant interest and other charges which have to be imposed by the creditor as a condition for credit being granted.
(3) (repealed).
(4) (a) The annual percentage rate of charge shall be calculated at the time the credit contract is concluded, without prejudice to the provisions of Article 3 concerning advertisements and special offers.
(b) The calculation shall be made on the assumption that the credit contract is valid for the period agreed and that the creditor and the consumer fulfil their obligations under the terms and by the dates agreed.
(5) (repealed).
(6) In the case of credit contracts containing clauses allowing variations in the rate of interest and the amount or level of other charges contained in the annual percentage rate of charge but unquantifiable at the time when it is calculated, the annual percentage rate of charge shall be calculated on the assumption that interest and other charges remain fixed and will apply until the end of the credit contract. 7. Where necessary, the following assumptions may be made in calculating the annual percentage rate of charge:
- if the contract does not specify a credit limit, the amount of credit granted shall be equal to the amount fixed by the relevant Member State, without exceeding a figure equivalent to ECU 2 000;
- if there is no fixed timetable for repayment, and one cannot be deduced from the terms of the agreement and the means for repaying the credit granted, the duration of the credit shall be deemed to be one year;
- unless otherwise specified, where the contract provides for more than one repayment date, the credit will be made available and the repayments made at the earliest time provided for in the agreement.

Article 2. (1) This Directive shall not apply to:
(a) credit agreements or agreements promising to grant credit:
- intended primarily for the purpose of acquiring or retaining property rights in land or in an existing or projected building,
- intended for the purpose of renovating or improving a building as such;
(b) hiring agreements except where these provide that the title will pass ultimately to the hirer;
(c) credit granted or made available without payment of interest or any other charge;
(d) credit agreements under which no interest is charged provided the consumer agrees to repay the credit in a single payment;
(e) credit in the form of advances on a current account granted by a credit institution or financial institution other than on credit card accounts.
Nevertheless, the provisions of Article 6 shall apply to such credits;
(f) credit agreements involving amounts less than 200 ECU or more than 20 000 ECU;
(g) credit agreements under which the consumer is required to repay the credit:
- either, within a period not exceeding three months,
- or, by a maximum number of four payments within a period not exceeding 12 months.
(2) A Member State may, in consultation with the Commission, exempt from the application of this Directive certain types of credit which fulfil the following conditions:
- they are granted at rates of charge below those prevailing in the market, and
- they are not offered to the public generally.
(3) The provisions of Article 1a and of Articles 4 to 12 shall not apply to credit agreements or agreements promising to grant credit, secured by mortgage on immovable property, insofar as these are not

already excluded from the Directive under paragraph (1) (a).
(4) Member States may exempt from the provisions of Articles 6 to 12 credit agreements in the form of an authentic act signed before a notary or judge.

Article 3. Without prejudice to Council Directive 84/450/EEC of 10 September 1984 relating to the approximation of the laws, regulations and administrative provisions of the Member States concerning misleading advertising, and to the rules and principles applicable to unfair advertising, any advertisement, or any offer which is displayed at business premises, in which a person offers credit or offers to arrange a credit agreement and in which a rate of interest or any figures relating to the cost of the credit are indicated, shall also include a statement of the annual percentage rate of charge, by means of a representative example if no other means is practicable.

Article 4. (1). Credit agreements shall be made in writing. The consumer shall receive a copy of the written agreement.
(2) The written agreement shall include:
(a) a statement of the annual percentage rate of charge;
(b) a statement of the conditions under which the annual percentage rate of charge may be amended
(c) a statement of the amount, number and frequency or dates of the payments which the consumer must make to repay the credit, as well as of the payments for interest and other charges; the total amount of these payments should also be indicated where possible;
(d) a statement of the cost items referred to in Article 1a (2) with the exception of expenditure related to the breach of contractual obligations which were not included in the calculation of the annual percentage rate of charge but which have to be paid by the consumer in given circumstances, together with a statement indentifying such circumstances. Where the exact amount of those items is known, that sum is to be indicated; if that is not the case, either a method of calculation or as accurate an estimate as possible is to be provided where possible.
In cases where it is not possible to state the annual percentage rate of charge, the consumer shall be provided with adequate information in the written agreement. This information shall at least include the information provided for in the second indent of Article 6 (1).
(3) The written agreement shall further include the other essential terms of the contract.
By way of illustration, the Annex to this Directive contains a list of terms which Member States may require to be included in the written agreement as being essential.

Article 5. (repealed).

Article 6. (1) Notwithstanding the exclusion provided for in Article 2 (1) (e), where there is an agreement between a credit institution or financial institution and a consumer for the granting of credit in the form of an advance on a current account, other than on credit card accounts, the consumer shall be informed at the time or before the agreement is concluded:
- of the credit limit, if any,
- of the annual rate of interest and the charges applicable from the time the agreement is concluded and the conditions under which these may be amended,
- of the procedure for terminating the agreement.
This information shall be confirmed in writing.
(2) Furthermore, during the period of the agreement, the consumer shall be informed of any change in the annual rate of interest or in the relevant charges at the time it occurs. Such information may be given in a statement of account or in any other manner acceptable to Member States.
(3). In Member States where tacitly accepted overdrafts are permissible, the Member States concerned shall ensure that the consumer is informed of the annual rate of interest and the charges applicable, and of any amendment thereof, where the overdraft extends beyond a period of three months.

Article 7. In the case of credit granted for the acquisition of goods, Member States shall lay down the conditions under which goods may be repossessed, in particular if the consumer has not given his consent. They shall further ensure that where the creditor recovers possession of the goods the account between the parties shall be made up so as to ensure that the repossession does not entail any unjustified enrichment.

Article 8. The consumer shall be entitled to discharge his obligations under a credit agreement before the time fixed by the agreement. In this event, in accordance with the rules laid down by the Member States, the consumer shall be entitled to an equitable reduction in the total cost of the credit.

Article 9. Where the creditor's rights under a credit agreement are assigned to a third person, the consumer shall be entitled to plead against that third person any defence which was available to him against the original creditor, including set-off where the latter is permitted in the Member State concerned.

Article 10. The Member States which, in connection with credit agreements, permit the consumer:
(a) to make payment by means of bills of exchange including promissory notes;
(b) to give security by means of bills of exchange including promissory notes and cheques,
shall ensure that the consumer is suitably protected when using these instruments in those ways.

Article 11. (1) Member States shall ensure that the existence of a credit agreement shall not in any way affect the rights of the consumer against the supplier of goods or services purchased by means of such an agreement in cases where the goods or services are not supplied or are otherwise not in conformity with the contract for their supply.
(2) Where:
(a) in order to buy goods or obtain services the consumer enters into a credit agreement with a person other than the supplier of them; and
(b) the grantor of the credit and the supplier of the goods or services have a pre-existing agreement whereunder credit is made available exclusively by that grantor of credit to customers of that supplier for the acquisition of goods or services from that supplier; and
(c) the consumer referred to in subparagraph (a) obtains his credit pursuant to that pre-existing agreement; and
(d) the goods or services covered by the credit agreement are not supplied, or are supplied only in part, or are not in conformity with the contract for supply of them; and
(e) the consumer has pursued his remedies against the supplier but has failed to obtain the satisfaction to which he is entitled,
the consumer shall have the right to pursue remedies against the grantor of credit. Member States shall determine to what extent and under what conditions these remedies shall be exercisable.
(3) Paragraph 2 shall not apply where the individual transaction in question is for an amount less than the equivalent of 200 ECU.

Article 12. (1) Member States shall:
(a) ensure that persons offering credit or offering to arrange credit agreements shall obtain official authorization to do so, either specifically or as suppliers of goods and services; or
(b) ensure that persons granting credit or arranging for credit to be granted shall be subject to inspection or monitoring of their activities by an institution or official body; or
(c) promote the establishment of appropriate bodies to receive complaints concerning credit agreements or credit conditions and to provide relevant information or advice to consumers regarding them.
(2) Member States may provide that the authorization referred to in paragraph (1) (a) shall not be required where persons offering to conclude or arrange credit agreements satisfy the definition in Article 1 of the first Council Directive of 12 December 1977 on the coordination of laws, regulations and administrative provisions relating to the taking up and pursuit of the business of credit institutions and are authorized in accordance with the provisions of that Directive.
Where persons granting credit or arranging for credit to be granted have been authorized both specifically, under the provisions of paragraph (1) (a) and also under the provisions of the aforementioned Directive, but the latter authorization is subsequently withdrawn, the competent authority responsible for issuing the specific authorization to grant credit under paragraph (1) (a) shall be informed and shall decide whether the persons concerned may continue to grant credit, or arrange for credit to be granted, or whether the specific authorization granted under paragraph (1) (a) should be withdrawn.

Article 13. (1) For the purposes of this Directive, the ECU shall be that defined by Regulation (EEC) No 3180/78, as amended by Regulation (EEC) No 2626/84. The equivalent in national currency shall initially be calculated at the rate obtaining on the date of adoption of this Directive.
Member States may round off the amounts in national currency resulting from the conversion of the amounts in ECU provided such rounding off does not exceed 10 ECU.
(2) Every five years, and for the first time in 1995, the Council, acting on a proposal from the Commission, shall examine and, if need be, revise the amounts in this Directive, in the light of economic and monetary trends in the Community.

Article 14. (1) Member States shall ensure that credit agreements shall not derogate, to the detriment of the consumer, from the provisions of national law implementing or corresponding to this Directive.
(2). Member States shall further ensure that the provisions which they adopt in implementation of this directive are not circumvented as a result of the way in which agreements are formulated, in particular by the device of distributing the amount of credit over several agreements.

Article 15. This Directive shall not preclude Member States from retaining or adopting more stringent provisions to protect consumers consistent with their obligations under the Treaty.

Article 16. (1) Member States shall bring into force the measures necessary to comply with this Directive not later than 1 January 1990 and shall forthwith inform the Commission thereof.
(2) Member States shall communicate to the Commission the texts of the main provisions of national law which they adopt in the field covered by this Directive.

Article 17. Not later than 1 January 1995 the Commission shall present a report to the Council concerning the operation of this Directive.

Article 18. This Directive is addressed to the Member States.

Annex I. List of terms referred to in Article 4(3)
(1) Credit agreements for financing the supply of particular goods or services:
1.2 // (i) // a description of the goods or services covered by the agreement; // (ii) // the cash price and the price payable under the credit agreement; // (iii) // the amount of the deposit, if any, the number and amount of instalments and the dates on which they fall due, or the method of ascertaining any of the same if unknown at the time the agreement is concluded; // (iv) // an indication that the consumer will be entitled, as provided in Article 8, to a reduction if he repays early; // (v) // who owns the goods (if ownership does not pass immediately to the consumer) and the terms on which the consumer becomes the owner of them; // (vi) // a description of the security required, if any; // (vii) // the cooling-off period, if any; // (viii) // an indication of the insurance (s) required, if any, and, when the choice of insurer is not left to the consumer, an indication of the cost thereof //(ix) the obligation on the consumer to save a certain amount of money which must be placed in a special account'.
(2) Credit agreements operated by credit cards:
1.2 // (i) // the amount of the credit limit, if any; // (ii) // the terms of repayment or the means of determining them; // (iii) // the cooling-off period, if any.
(3) Credit agreements operated by running account which are not otherwise covered by the Directive:
1.2 // (i) // the amount of the credit limit, if any, or the method of determining it; // (ii) // the terms of use and repayment; // (iii) // the cooling-off period, if any.
4. Other credit agreements covered by the Directive:
1.2 // (i) // the amount of the credit limit, if any; // (ii) // an indication of the security required, if any; // (iii) // the terms of repayment; // (iv) // the cooling-off period, if any; // (v) // an indication that the consumer will be entitled, as provided in Article 8, to a reduction if he repays early.

[Annexes II and III are omitted.]

Council Directive 93/7/EEC of 15 March 1993 on the return of cultural objects unlawfully removed from the territory of a Member State (OJ L 07, 27.03.1993, pp. 74 – 79) as amended by Directive 96/100 [footnotes omitted].

THE COUNCIL OF THE EUROPEAN COMMUNITIES,
Having regard to the Treaty establishing the European Economic Community, and in particular Article 100a thereof,
Having regard to the proposal from the Commission, In cooperation with the European Parliament,
Having regard to the opinion of the Economic and Social Committee,
Whereas Article 8a of the Treaty provides for the establishment, not later than 1 January 1993, of the internal market, which is to comprise an area without internal frontiers in which the free movement of goods, persons, services and capital is ensured in accordance with the provisions of the Treaty;
Whereas, under the terms and within the limits of Article 36 of the Treaty, Member States will, after 1992, retain the right to define their national treasures and to take the necessary measures to protect them in this area without internal frontiers;
Whereas arrangements should therefore be introduced enabling Member States to secure the return to their territory of cultural objects which are classified as national treasures within the meaning of the said Article 36 and have been removed from their territory in breach of the abovementioned national measures or of Council Regulation (EEC) No 3911/92 of 9 December 1992 on the export of cultural goods; whereas the implementation of these arrangements should be as simple and efficient as possible; whereas, to facilitate cooperation with regard to return, the scope of the arrangements should be confined to items belonging to common categories of cultural object; whereas the Annex to this Directive is consequently not intended to define objects which rank as 'national treasures' within the meaning of the said Article 36, but merely categories of object which may be classified as such and may accordingly be covered by the return procedure introduced by this Directive;
Whereas cultural objects classified as national treasures and forming an integral part of public collections or inventories of ecclesiastical institutions but which do not fall within these common categories should also be covered by this Directive;
Whereas administrative cooperation should be established between Member States as regards their national treasures, in close liaison with their cooperation in the field of stolen works of art and involving in particular the recording, with Interpol and other qualified bodies issuing similar lists, of lost, stolen or illegally removed cultural objects forming part of their national treasures and their public collections;
Whereas the procedure introduced by this Directive is a first step in establishing cooperation between Member States in this field in the context of the internal market; whereas the aim is mutual recognition of the relevant national laws; whereas provision should therefore be made, in particular, for the Commission to be assisted by an advisory committee;
Whereas Regulation (EEC) No 3911/92 introduces, together with this Directive, a Community system to protect Member States' cultural goods; whereas the date by which Member States have to comply with this Directive has to be as close as possible to the date of entry into force of that Regulation; whereas, having regard to the nature of their legal systems and the scope of the changes to their legislation necessary to implement this Directive, some Member States will need a longer period,
HAS ADOPTED THIS DIRECTIVE:

Article 1. For the purposes of this Directive:
(1) 'Cultural object' shall mean an object which:
- is classified, before or after its unlawful removal from the territory of a Member State, among the 'national treasures possessing artistic, historic or archaeological value' under national legislation or administrative procedures within the meaning of Article 36 of the Treaty, and
- belongs to one of the categories listed in the Annex or does not belong to one of these categories but forms an integral part of:
- public collections listed in the inventories of museums, archives or libraries' conservation collection. For the purposes of this Directive, 'public collections' shall mean collections which are the property of a Member State, local or regional authority within a Member States or an institution situated in the territory of a Member State and defined as public in accordance with the legislation of that Member State, such institution being the property of, or significantly financed by, that Member State or a local or regional authority;
- the inventories of ecclesiastical institutions.
(2) 'Unlawfully removed from the territory of a Member State' shall mean:
- removed from the territory of a Member State in breach of its rules on the protection of national

treasures or in breach of Regulation (EEC) No 3911/92, or - not returned at the end of a period of lawful temporary removal or any breach of another condition governing such temporary removal.
(3) 'Requesting Member State' shall mean the Member State from whose territory the cultural object has been unlawfully removed.
(4) 'Requested Member State' shall mean the Member State in whose territory a cultural object unlawfully removed from the territory of another Member State is located.
(5) 'Return' shall mean the physical return of the cultural object to the territory of the requesting Member State.
(6) 'Possessor' shall mean the person physically holding the cultural object on his own account.
(7) 'Holder' shall mean the person physically holding the cultural object for third parties.

Article 2. Cultural objects which have been unlawfully removed from the territory of a Member State shall be returned in accordance with the procedure and in the circumstances provided for in this Directive.

Article 3. Each Member State shall appoint one or more central authorities to carry out the tasks provided for in this Directive.
Member States shall inform the Commission of all the central authorities they appoint pursuant to this Article.
The Commission shall publish a list of these central authorities and any changes concerning them in the C series of the Official Journal of the European Communities.

Article 4. Member States' central authorities shall cooperate and promote consultation between the Member States' competent national authorities. The latter shall in particular:
(1) upon application by the requesting Member State, seek a specified cultural object which as been unlawfully removed from its territory, identifying the possessor and/or holder. The application must include all information needed to facilitate this search, with particular reference to the actual or presumed location of the object;
(2) notify the Member States concerned, where a cultural object is found in their own territory and there are reasonable grounds for believing that it has been unlawfully removed from the territory of another Member State;
(3) enable the competent authorities of the requesting Member State to check that the object in question is a cultural object, provided that the check is made within 2 months of the notification provided for in paragraph (2). If it is not made within the stipulated period, paragraphs 4 and 5 shall cease to apply;
(4) take any necessary measures, in cooperation with the Member State concerned, for the physical preservation of the cultural object;
(5) prevent, by the necessary interim measures, any action to evade the return procedure;
(6) act as intermediary between the possessor and/or holder and the requesting Member State with regard to return. To this end, the competent authorities of the requested Member States may, without prejudice to Article 5, first facilitate the implementation of an arbitration procedure, in accordance with the national legislation of the requested State and provided that the requesting State and the possessor or holder give their formal approval.

Article 5. The requesting Member State may initiate, before the competent court in the requested Member State, proceedings against the possessor or, failing him, the holder, with the aim of securing the return of a cultural object which has been unlawfully removed from its territory.
Proceedings may be brought only where the document initiating them is accompanied by:
- a document describing the object covered by the request and stating that it is a cultural object,
- a declaration by the competent authorities of the requesting Member State that the cultural object has been unlawfully removed from its territory.

Article 6. The central authority of the requesting Member State shall forthwith inform the central authority of the requested Member State that proceedings have been initiated with the aim of securing the return of the object in question.
The central authority of the requested Member State shall forthwith inform the central authorities of the other Member States.

Article 7. (1) Member States shall lay down in their legislation that the return proceedings provided for in this Directive may not be brought more than one year after the requesting Member State became aware of the location of the cultural object and of the identity of its possessor or holder.
Such proceedings may, at all events, not be brought more than 30 years after the object was unlaw-

fully removed from the territory of the requesting Member State. However, in the case of objects forming part of public collections, referred to in Article 1 (1), and ecclesiastical goods in the Member States where they are subject to special protection arrangements under national law, return proceedings shall be subject to a time-limit of 75 years, except in Member States where proceedings are not subject to a time-limit or in the case of bilateral agreements between Member States laying down a period exceeding 75 years.

(2) Return proceedings may not be brought if removal from the national territory of the requesting Member State is no longer unlawful at the time when they are to be initiated.

Article 8. Save as otherwise provided in Articles 7 and 13, the competent court shall order the return of the cultural object in question where it is found to be a cultural object within the meaning of Article 1 (1) and to have been removed unlawfully from national territory.

Article 9. Where return of the object is ordered, the competent court in the requested States shall award the possessor such compensation as it deems fair according to the circumstances of the case, provided that it is satisfied that the possessor exercised due care and attention in acquiring the object. The burden of proof shall be governed by the legislation of the requested Member State.
In the case of a donation or succession, the possessor shall not be in a more favourable position than the person from whom he acquired the object by that means. The requesting Member State shall pay such compensation upon return of the object.

Article 10. Expenses incurred in implementing a decision ordering the return of a cultural object shall be borne by the requesting Member State. The same applies to the costs of the measures referred to in Article 4 (4).

Article 11. Payment of the fair compensation and of the expenses referred to in Articles 9 and 10 respectively shall be without prejudice to the requesting Member State's right to take action with a view to recovering those amounts from the persons responsible for the unlawful removal of the cultural object from its territory.

Article 12. Ownership of the cultural object after return shall be governed by that law of the requesting Member State.

Article 13. This Directive shall apply only to cultural objects unlawfully removed from the territory of a Member State on or after 1 January 1993.

Article 14. (1) Each Member State may extend its obligation to return cultural objects to cover categories of objects other than those listed in the Annex.
(2) Each Member State may apply the arrangements provided for by this Directive to requests for the return of cultural objects unlawfully removed from the territory of other Member States prior to 1 January 1993.

Article 15. This Directive shall be without prejudice to any civil or criminal proceedings that may be brought, under the national laws of the Member States, by the requesting Member State and/or the owner of a cultural object that has been stolen.

Article 16. (1) Member States shall send the Commission every three years, and for the first time in February 1996, a report on the application of this Directive.
(2) The Commission shall send the European Parliament, the Council and the Economic and Social Committee, every three years, a report reviewing the application of this Directive.
(3) The Council shall review the effectiveness of this Directive after a period of application of three years and, acting on a proposal from the Commission, make any necessary adaptations.
(4) In any event, the Council acting on a proposal from the Commission, shall examine every three years and, where appropriate, update the amounts indicated in the Annex, on the basis of economic and monetary indicators in the Community.

Article 17. The Commission shall be assisted by the Committee set up by Article 8 of Regulation (EEC) No 3911/92.
The Committee shall examine any question arising from the application of the Annex to this Directive which may be tabled by the chairman either on his own initiative or at the request of the representative of a Member State.

Article 18. Member States shall bring into force the laws, regulations and administrative provisions necessary to comply with this Directive within nine months of its adoption, except as far as the Kingdom of Belgium, the Federal Republic of Germany and the Kingdom of the Netherlands are concerned, which must conform to this Directive at the latest twelve months from the date of its adoption. They shall forthwith inform the Commission thereof. When Member States adopt these measures, they shall contain a reference to this Directive or shall be accompanied by such reference on the occasion of their official publication. The methods of making such a reference shall be laid down by the Member States.

Article 19. This Directive is addressed to the Member States.

Annex. Categories referred to in the second indent of Article 1 (1) to which objects classified as 'national treasures' within the meaning of Article 36 of the Treaty must belong in order to qualify for return under this Directive

A. (1) Archaeological objects more than 100 years old which are the products of:
- land or underwater excavations and finds,
- archaeological sites,
- archaeological collections.

(2) Elements forming an integral part of artistic, historical or religious monuments which have been dismembered, more than 100 years old.

(3) Pictures and paintings, other than those included in Category 3A or 4, executed entirely by hand on any material and in any medium.

(3A) Water-colours, gouaches and pastels executed entirely by hand on any material.

(4) Mosaics in any material executed entirely by hand, other than those falling in Categories 1 or 2, and drawings in any medium executed entirely by hand on any material.

(5) Original engravings, prints, serigraphs and lithographs with their respective plates and original posters.

(6) Original sculptures or statuary and copies produced by the same process as the original other than those in category 1.

(7) Photographs, films and negatives thereof.

(8) Incunabula and manuscripts, including maps and musical scores, singly or in collections.

(9) Books more than 100 years old, singly or in collections.

(10) Printed maps more than 200 years old.

(11) Archives and any elements thereof, of any kind, on any medium, comprising elements more than 50 years old.

(12) (a) Collections (2) and specimens from zoological, botanical, mineralogical or anatomical collections;

(b) Collections (2) of historical, palaeontological, ethnographic or numismatic interest.

(13) Means of transport more than 75 years old.

(14) Any other antique item not included in categories A 1 to A 13, more than 50 years old. The cultural objects in categories A 1 to A 14 are covered by this Directive only if their value corresponds to, or exceeds, the financial thresholds under B.

B. Financial thresholds applicable to certain categories under A (in ecus)
VALUE: 0 (Zero)
- 1 (Archaeological objects)
- 2 (Dismembered monuments)
- 8 (Incunabula and manuscripts)
- 11 (Archives)
15 000
- 4 (Mosaics and drawings)
- 5 (Engravings)
- 7 (Photographs)
- 10 (Printed maps)
30 000
- 3A. (Water colours, gouaches and pastels)`.
50 000
- 6 (Statuary)
- 9 (Books)
- 12 (Collections)
- 13 (Means of transport)
- 14 (Any other item)
150 000
- 3 (Pictures)

Council Directive 93/13/EEC of 5 April 1993 on unfair terms in consumer contracts (OJ L 095, 21.04.1993, pp. 29 – 34) [footnotes omitted].

THE COUNCIL OF THE ERUOPEAN COMMUNITIES, Having regard to the Treaty establishing the European Economic Community, and in particular Article 100 A thereof, Having regard to the proposal from the Commission,
In cooperation with the European Parliament,
Having regard to the opinion of the Economic and Social Committee,
Whereas it is necessary to adopt measures with the aim of progressively establishing the internal market before 31 December 1992; Whereas the internal market comprises an area without internal frontiers in which goods, persons, services and capital move freely;
Whereas the laws of Member States relating to the terms of contract between the seller of goods or supplier of services, on the one hand, and the consumer of them, on the other hand, show many disparities, with the result that the national markets for the sale of goods and services to consumers differ from each other and that distortions of competition may arise amongst the sellers and suppliers, notably when they sell and supply in other Member States;
Whereas, in particular, the laws of Member States relating to unfair terms in consumer contracts show marked divergences;
Whereas it is the responsibility of the Member States to ensure that contracts concluded with consumers do not contain unfair terms;
Whereas, generally speaking, consumers do not know the rules of law which, in Member States other than their own, govern contracts for the sale of goods or services; Whereas this lack of awareness may deter them from direct transactions for the purchase of goods or services in another Member State;
Whereas, in order to facilitate the establishment of the internal market and to safeguard the citizen in his role as consumer when acquiring goods and services under contracts which are governed by the laws of Member States other than his own, it is essential to remove unfair terms from those contracts;
Whereas sellers of goods and suppliers of services will thereby be helped in their task of selling goods and supplying services, both at home and throughout the internal market; whereas competition will thus be stimulated, so contributing to increased choice for Community citizens as consumers;
Whereas the two Community programmes for a consumer protection and information policy underlined the importance of safeguarding consumers in the matter of unfair terms of contract; Whereas this protection ought to be provided by laws and regulations which are either harmonized at Community level or adopted directly at that level;
Whereas in accordance with the principle laid down under the heading 'Protection of the economic interests of the consumers', as stated in those programmes: 'acquirers of goods and services should be protected against the abuse of power by the seller or supplier, in particular against one-sided standard contracts and the unfair exclusion of essential rights in contracts';
Whereas more effective protection of the consumer can be achieved by adopting uniform rules of law in the matter of unfair terms; whereas those rules should apply to all contracts concluded between sellers or suppliers and consumers; whereas as a result inter alia contracts relating to employment, contracts relating to succession rights, contracts relating to rights under family law and contracts relating to the incorporation and organization of companies or partnership agreements must be excluded from this Directive;
Whereas the consumer must receive equal protection under contracts concluded by word of mouth and written contracts regardless, in the latter case, of whether the terms of the contract are contained in one or more documents;
Whereas, however, as they now stand, national laws allow only partial harmonization to be envisaged; whereas, in particular, only contractual terms which have not been individually negotiated are covered by this Directive; whereas Member States should have the option, with due regard for the Treaty, to afford consumers a higher level of protection through national provisions that are more stringent than those of this Directive;
Whereas the statutory or regulatory provisions of the Member States which directly or indirectly determine the terms of consumer contracts are presumed not to contain unfair terms; whereas, therefore, it does not appear to be necessary to subject the terms which reflect mandatory statutory or regulatory provisions and the principles or provisions of international conventions to which the Member States or the Community are party; whereas in that respect the wording 'mandatory statutory or regulatory provisions' in Article 1 (2) also covers rules which, according to the law, shall apply between the contracting parties provided that no other arrangements have been established;
Whereas Member States must however ensure that unfair terms are not included, particularly

because this Directive also applies to trades, business or professions of a public nature;
Whereas it is necessary to fix in a general way the criteria for assessing the unfair character of contract terms; Whereas the assessment, according to the general criteria chosen, of the unfair character of terms, in particular in sale or supply activities of a public nature providing collective services which take account of solidarity among users, must be supplemented by a means of making an overall evaluation of the different interests involved; whereas this constitutes the requirement of good faith; whereas, in making an assessment of good faith, particular regard shall be had to the strength of the bargaining positions of the parties, whether the consumer had an inducement to agree to the term and whether the goods or services were sold or supplied to the special order of the consumer; whereas the requirement of good faith may be satisfied by the seller or supplier where he deals fairly and equitably with the other party whose legitimate interests he has to take into account;
Whereas, for the purposes of this Directive, the annexed list of terms can be of indicative value only and, because of the cause of the minimal character of the Directive, the scope of these terms may be the subject of amplification or more restrictive editing by the Member States in their national laws; Whereas the nature of goods or services should have an influence on assessing the unfairness of contractual terms; Whereas, for the purposes of this Directive, assessment of unfair character shall not be made of terms which describe the main subject matter of the contract nor the quality/price ratio of the goods or services supplied; whereas the main subject matter of the contract and the price/quality ratio may nevertheless be taken into account in assessing the fairness of other terms; whereas it follows, inter alia, that in insurance contracts, the terms which clearly define or circumscribe the insured risk and the insurer's liability shall not be subject to such assessment since these restrictions are taken into account in calculating the premium paid by the consumer;
Whereas contracts should be drafted in plain, intelligible language, the consumer should actually be given an opportunity to examine all the terms and, if in doubt, the interpretation most favourable to the consumer should prevail;
Whereas Member States should ensure that unfair terms are not used in contracts concluded with consumers by a seller or supplier and that if, nevertheless, such terms are so used, they will not bind the consumer, and the contract will continue to bind the parties upon those terms if it is capable of continuing in existence without the unfair provisions; whereas there is a risk that, in certain cases, the consumer may be deprived of protection under this Directive by designating the law of a non-Member country as the law applicable to the contract; whereas provisions should therefore be included in this Directive designed to avert this risk;
Whereas persons or organizations, if regarded under the law of a Member State as having a legitimate interest in the matter, must have facilities for initiating proceedings concerning terms of contract drawn up for general use in contracts concluded with consumers, and in particular unfair terms, either before a court or before an administrative authority competent to decide upon complaints or to initiate appropriate legal proceedings; whereas this possibility does not, however, entail prior verification of the general conditions obtaining in individual economic sectors;
Whereas the courts or administrative authorities of the Member States must have at their disposal adequate and effective means of preventing the continued application of unfair terms in consumer contracts,
HAS ADOPTED THIS DIRECTIVE:

Article 1. (1) The purpose of this Directive is to approximate the laws, regulations and administrative provisions of the Member States relating to unfair terms in contracts concluded between a seller or supplier and a consumer.
(2) The contractual terms which reflect mandatory statutory or regulatory provisions and the provisions or principles of international conventions to which the Member States or the Community are party, particularly in the transport area, shall not be subject to the provisions of this Directive.

Article 2. For the purposes of this Directive:
(a) 'unfair terms' means the contractual terms defined in Article 3;
(b) 'consumer' means any natural person who, in contracts covered by this Directive, is acting for purposes which are outside his trade, business or profession;
(c) 'seller or supplier' means any natural or legal person who, in contracts covered by this Directive, is acting for purposes relating to his trade, business or profession, whether publicly owned or privately owned.

Article 3. (1) A contractual term which has not been individually negotiated shall be regarded as unfair if, contrary to the requirement of good faith, it causes a significant imbalance in the parties' rights and obligations arising under the contract, to the detriment of the consumer.

(2) A term shall always be regarded as not individually negotiated where it has been drafted in advance and the consumer has therefore not been able to influence the substance of the term, particularly in the context of a pre-formulated standard contract. The fact that certain aspects of a term or one specific term have been individually negotiated shall not exclude the application of this Article to the rest of a contract if an overall assessment of the contract indicates that it is nevertheless a pre-formulated standard contract. Where any seller or supplier claims that a standard term has been individually negotiated, the burden of proof in this respect shall be incumbent on him.

(3) The Annex shall contain an indicative and non-exhaustive list of the terms which may be regarded as unfair.

Article 4. (1) Without prejudice to Article 7, the unfairness of a contractual term shall be assessed, taking into account the nature of the goods or services for which the contract was concluded and by referring, at the time of conclusion of the contract, to all the circumstances attending the conclusion of the contract and to all the other terms of the contract or of another contract on which it is dependent.

(2) Assessment of the unfair nature of the terms shall relate neither to the definition of the main subject matter of the contract nor to the adequacy of the price and remuneration, on the one hand, as against the services or goods supplies in exchange, on the other, in so far as these terms are in plain intelligible language.

Article 5. In the case of contracts where all or certain terms offered to the consumer are in writing, these terms must always be drafted in plain, intelligible language. Where there is doubt about the meaning of a term, the interpretation most favourable to the consumer shall prevail. This rule on interpretation shall not apply in the context of the procedures laid down in Article 7 (2).

Article 6. (1) Member States shall lay down that unfair terms used in a contract concluded with a consumer by a seller or supplier shall, as provided for under their national law, not be binding on the consumer and that the contract shall continue to bind the parties upon those terms if it is capable of continuing in existence without the unfair terms.

(2) Member States shall take the necessary measures to ensure that the consumer does not lose the protection granted by this Directive by virtue of the choice of the law of a non-Member country as the law applicable to the contract if the latter has a close connection with the territory of the Member States.

Article 7. (1) Member States shall ensure that, in the interests of consumers and of competitors, adequate and effective means exist to prevent the continued use of unfair terms in contracts concluded with consumers by sellers or suppliers.

(2) The means referred to in paragraph (1) shall include provisions whereby persons or organizations, having a legitimate interest under national law in protecting consumers, may take action according to the national law concerned before the courts or before competent administrative bodies for a decision as to whether contractual terms drawn up for general use are unfair, so that they can apply appropriate and effective means to prevent the continued use of such terms.

(3) With due regard for national laws, the legal remedies referred to in paragraph (2) may be directed separately or jointly against a number of sellers or suppliers from the same economic sector or their associations which use or recommend the use of the same general contractual terms or similar terms.

Article 8. Member States may adopt or retain the most stringent provisions compatible with the Treaty in the area covered by this Directive, to ensure a maximum degree of protection for the consumer.

Article 9. The Commission shall present a report to the European Parliament and to the Council concerning the application of this Directive five years at the latest after the date in Article 10 (1).

Article 10. (1) Member States shall bring into force the laws, regulations and administrative provisions necessary to comply with this Directive no later than 31 December 1994. They shall forthwith inform the Commission thereof.

These provisions shall be applicable to all contracts concluded after 31 December 1994.

(2) When Member States adopt these measures, they shall contain a reference to this Directive or shall be accompanied by such reference on the occasion of their official publication. The methods of making such a reference shall be laid down by the Member States.

(3) Member States shall communicate the main provisions of national law which they adopt in the field covered by this Directive to the Commission.

PART IV   EUROPEAN PRIVATE LAW

Article 11. This Directive is addressed to the Member States.

Annex. Terms referred to in Article 3 (1)

Terms which have the object or effect of:

(a) excluding or limiting the legal liability of a seller or supplier in the event of the death of a consumer or personal injury to the latter resulting from an act or omission of that seller or supplier;

(b) inappropriately excluding or limiting the legal rights of the consumer vis-à-vis the seller or supplier or another party in the event of total or partial non-performance or inadequate performance by the seller or supplier of any of the contractual obligations, including the option of offsetting a debt owed to the seller or supplier against any claim which the consumer may have against him;

(c) making an agreement binding on the consumer whereas provision of services by the seller or supplier is subject to a condition whose realization depends on his own will alone;

(d) permitting the seller or supplier to retain sums paid by the consumer where the latter decides not to conclude or perform the contract, without providing for the consumer to receive compensation of an equivalent amount from the seller or supplier where the latter is the party cancelling the contract;

(e) requiring any consumer who fails to fulfil his obligation to pay a disproportionately high sum in compensation;

(f) authorizing the seller or supplier to dissolve the contract on a discretionary basis where the same facility is not granted to the consumer, or permitting the seller or supplier to retain the sums paid for services not yet supplied by him where it is the seller or supplier himself who dissolves the contract;

(g) enabling the seller or supplier to terminate a contract of indeterminate duration without reasonable notice except where there are serious grounds for doing so;

(h) automatically extending a contract of fixed duration where the consumer does not indicate otherwise, when the deadline fixed for the consumer to express this desire not to extend the contract is unreasonably early;

(i) irrevocably binding the consumer to terms with which he had no real opportunity of becoming acquainted before the conclusion of the contract;

(j) enabling the seller or supplier to alter the terms of the contract unilaterally without a valid reason which is specified in the contract;

(k) enabling the seller or supplier to alter unilaterally without a valid reason any characteristics of the product or service to be provided;

(l) providing for the price of goods to be determined at the time of delivery or allowing a seller of goods or supplier of services to increase their price without in both cases giving the consumer the corresponding right to cancel the contract if the final price is too high in relation to the price agreed when the contract was concluded;

(m) giving the seller or supplier the right to determine whether the goods or services supplied are in conformity with the contract, or giving him the exclusive right to interpret any term of the contract;

(n) limiting the seller's or supplier's obligation to respect commitments undertaken by his agents or making his commitments subject to compliance with a particular formality;

(o) obliging the consumer to fulfil all his obligations where the seller or supplier does not perform his;

(p) giving the seller or supplier the possibility of transferring his rights and obligations under the contract, where this may serve to reduce the guarantees for the consumer, without the latter's agreement;

(q) excluding or hindering the consumer's right to take legal action or exercise any other legal remedy, particularly by requiring the consumer to take disputes exclusively to arbitration not covered by legal provisions, unduly restricting the evidence available to him or imposing on him a burden of proof which, according to the applicable law, should lie with another party to the contract.

(2) Scope of subparagraphs (g), (j) and (l)

(a) Subparagraph (g) is without hindrance to terms by which a supplier of financial services reserves the right to terminate unilaterally a contract of indeterminate duration without notice where there is a valid reason, provided that the supplier is required to inform the other contracting party or parties thereof immediately.

(b) Subparagraph (j) is without hindrance to terms under which a supplier of financial services reserves the right to alter the rate of interest payable by the consumer or due to the latter, or the amount of other charges for financial services without notice where there is a valid reason, provided that the supplier is required to inform the other contracting party or parties thereof at the earliest opportunity and that the latter are free to dissolve the contract immediately.

Subparagraph (j) is also without hindrance to terms under which a seller or supplier reserves the right to alter unilaterally the conditions of a contract of indeterminate duration, provided that he is required to inform the consumer with reasonable notice and that the consumer is free to dissolve the contract.

(c) Subparagraphs (g), (j) and (l) do not apply to:
- transactions in transferable securities, financial instruments and other products or services where the price is linked to fluctuations in a stock exchange quotation or index or a financial market rate that the seller or supplier does not control;
- contracts for the purchase or sale of foreign currency, traveller's cheques or international money orders denominated in foreign currency;
(d) Subparagraph (l) is without hindrance to price-indexation clauses, where lawful, provided that the method by which prices vary is explicitly described.

PART IV   EUROPEAN PRIVATE LAW

Directive 1999/44/EC of the European Parliament and of the Council of 25 May 1999 on certain aspects of the sale of consumer goods and associated guarantees (OJL 17, 07.07.1999, pp. 12 -16) [footnotes omitted].

THE EUROPEAN PARLIAMENT AND THE COUNCIL OF THE EUROPEAN UNION,
Having regard to the Treaty establishing the European Community, and in particular Article 95 thereof,
Having regard to the proposal from the Commission,
Having regard to the opinion of the Economic and Social Committee, Acting in accordance with the procedure laid down in Article 251 of the Treaty in the light of the joint text approved by the Conciliation Committee on 18 May 1999(3),
(1) Whereas Article 153(1) and (3) of the Treaty provides that the Community should contribute to the achievement of a high level of consumer protection by the measures it adopts pursuant to Article 95 thereof;
(2) Whereas the internal market comprises an area without internal frontiers in which the free movement of goods, persons, services and capital is guaranteed; whereas free movement of goods concerns not only transactions by persons acting in the course of a business but also transactions by private individuals; whereas it implies that consumers resident in one Member State should be free to purchase goods in the territory of another Member State on the basis of a uniform minimum set of fair rules governing the sale of consumer goods;
(3) Whereas the laws of the Member States concerning the sale of consumer goods are somewhat disparate, with the result that national consumer goods markets differ from one another and that competition between sellers may be distorted;
(4) Whereas consumers who are keen to benefit from the large market by purchasing goods in Member States other than their State of residence play a fundamental role in the completion of the internal market; whereas the artificial reconstruction of frontiers and the compartmentalisation of markets should be prevented; whereas the opportunities available to consumers have been greatly broadened by new communication technologies which allow ready access to distribution systems in other Member States or in third countries; whereas, in the absence of minimum harmonisation of the rules governing the sale of consumer goods, the development of the sale of goods through the medium of new distance communication technologies risks being impeded;
(5) Whereas the creation of a common set of minimum rules of consumer law, valid no matter where goods are purchased within the Community, will strengthen consumer confidence and enable consumers to make the most of the internal market;
(6) Whereas the main difficulties encountered by consumers and the main source of disputes with sellers concern the non-conformity of goods with the contract; whereas it is therefore appropriate to approximate national legislation governing the sale of consumer goods in this respect, without however impinging on provisions and principles of national law relating to contractual and non-contractual liability;
(7) Whereas the goods must, above all, conform with the contractual specifications; whereas the principle of conformity with the contract may be considered as common to the different national legal traditions; whereas in certain national legal traditions it may not be possible to rely solely on this principle to ensure a minimum level of protection for the consumer; whereas under such legal traditions, in particular, additional national provisions may be useful to ensure that the consumer is protected in cases where the parties have agreed no specific contractual terms or where the parties have concluded contractual terms or agreements which directly or indirectly waive or restrict the rights of the consumer and which, to the extent that these rights result from this Directive, are not binding on the consumer;
(8) Whereas, in order to facilitate the application of the principle of conformity with the contract, it is useful to introduce a rebuttable presumption of conformity with the contract covering the most common situations; whereas that presumption does not restrict the principle of freedom of contract; whereas, furthermore, in the absence of specific contractual terms, as well as where the minimum protection clause is applied, the elements mentioned in this presumption may be used to determine the lack of conformity of the goods with the contract; whereas the quality and performance which consumers can reasonably expect will depend inter alia on whether the goods are new or second-hand; whereas the elements mentioned in the presumption are cumulative; whereas, if the circumstances of the case render any particular element manifestly inappropriate, the remaining elements of the presumption nevertheless still apply;
(9) Whereas the seller should be directly liable to the consumer for the conformity of the goods with the contract; whereas this is the traditional solution enshrined in the legal orders of the Member

EU: DIRECTIVE 1999/44 ON CONSUMER SALES AND ASSOCIATED GUARANTEES

States; whereas nevertheless the seller should be free, as provided for by national law, to pursue remedies against the producer, a previous seller in the same chain of contracts or any other intermediary, unless he has renounced that entitlement; whereas this Directive does not affect the principle of freedom of contract between the seller, the producer, a previous seller or any other intermediary; whereas the rules governing against whom and how the seller may pursue such remedies are to be determined by national law;

(10) Whereas, in the case of non-conformity of the goods with the contract, consumers should be entitled to have the goods restored to conformity with the contract free of charge, choosing either repair or replacement, or, failing this, to have the price reduced or the contract rescinded;

(11) Whereas the consumer in the first place may require the seller to repair the goods or to replace them unless those remedies are impossible or disproportionate; whereas whether a remedy is disproportionate should be determined objectively; whereas a remedy would be disproportionate if it imposed, in comparison with the other remedy, unreasonable costs; whereas, in order to determine whether the costs are unreasonable, the costs of one remedy should be significantly higher than the costs of the other remedy;

(12) Whereas in cases of a lack of conformity, the seller may always offer the consumer, by way of settlement, any available remedy; whereas it is for the consumer to decide whether to accept or reject this proposal;

(13) Whereas, in order to enable consumers to take advantage of the internal market and to buy consumer goods in another Member State, it should be recommended that, in the interests of consumers, the producers of consumer goods that are marketed in several Member States attach to the product a list with at least one contact address in every Member State where the product is marketed;

(14) Whereas the references to the time of delivery do not imply that Member States have to change their rules on the passing of the risk;

(15) Whereas Member States may provide that any reimbursement to the consumer may be reduced to take account of the use the consumer has had of the goods since they were delivered to him; whereas the detailed arrangements whereby rescission of the contract is effected may be laid down in national law;

(16) Whereas the specific nature of second-hand goods makes it generally impossible to replace them; whereas therefore the consumer's right of replacement is generally not available for these goods; whereas for such goods, Member States may enable the parties to agree a shortened period of liability;

(17) Whereas it is appropriate to limit in time the period during which the seller is liable for any lack of conformity which exists at the time of delivery of the goods; whereas Member States may also provide for a limitation on the period during which consumers can exercise their rights, provided such a period does not expire within two years from the time of delivery; whereas where, under national legislation, the time when a limitation period starts is not the time of delivery of the goods, the total duration of the limitation period provided for by national law may not be shorter than two years from the time of delivery;

(18) Whereas Member States may provide for suspension or interruption of the period during which any lack of conformity must become apparent and of the limitation period, where applicable and in accordance with their national law, in the event of repair, replacement or negotiations between seller and consumer with a view to an amicable settlement;

(19) Whereas Member States should be allowed to set a period within which the consumer must inform the seller of any lack of conformity; whereas Member States may ensure a higher level of protection for the consumer by not introducing such an obligation; whereas in any case consumers throughout the Community should have at least two months in which to inform the seller that a lack of conformity exists;

(20) Whereas Member States should guard against such a period placing at a disadvantage consumers shopping across borders; whereas all Member States should inform the Commission of their use of this provision; whereas the Commission should monitor the effect of the varied application of this provision on consumers and on the internal market; whereas information on the use made of this provision by a Member State should be available to the other Member States and to consumers and consumer organisations throughout the Community; whereas a summary of the situation in all Member States should therefore be published in the Official Journal of the European Communities;

(21) Whereas, for certain categories of goods, it is current practice for sellers and producers to offer guarantees on goods against any defect which becomes apparent within a certain period; whereas this practice can stimulate competition; whereas, while such guarantees are legitimate marketing tools, they should not mislead the consumer; whereas, to ensure that consumers are not misled, guarantees should contain certain information, including a statement that the guarantee does not affect the consumer's legal rights;

(22) Whereas the parties may not, by common consent, restrict or waive the rights granted to consumers, since otherwise the legal protection afforded would be thwarted; whereas this principle should apply also to clauses which imply that the consumer was aware of any lack of conformity of the consumer goods existing at the time the contract was concluded; whereas the protection granted to consumers under this Directive should not be reduced on the grounds that the law of a non-member State has been chosen as being applicable to the contract;
(23) Whereas legislation and case-law in this area in the various Member States show that there is growing concern to ensure a high level of consumer protection; whereas, in the light of this trend and the experience acquired in implementing this Directive, it may be necessary to envisage more far-reaching harmonisation, notably by providing for the producer's direct liability for defects for which he is responsible;
(24) Whereas Member States should be allowed to adopt or maintain in force more stringent provisions in the field covered by this Directive to ensure an even higher level of consumer protection;
(25) Whereas, according to the Commission recommendation of 30 March 1998 on the principles applicable to the bodies responsible for out-of-court settlement of consumer disputes, Member States can create bodies that ensure impartial and efficient handling of complaints in a national and cross-border context and which consumers can use as mediators;
(26) Whereas it is appropriate, in order to protect the collective interests of consumers, to add this Directive to the list of Directives contained in the Annex to Directive 98/27/EC of the European Parliament and of the Council of 19 May 1998 on injunctions for the protection of consumers' interests,
HAVE ADOPTED THIS DIRECTIVE:

Article 1. (1) The purpose of this Directive is the approximation of the laws, regulations and administrative provisions of the Member States on certain aspects of the sale of consumer goods and associated guarantees in order to ensure a uniform minimum level of consumer protection in the context of the internal market.
(2) For the purposes of this Directive:
(a) consumer: shall mean any natural person who, in the contracts covered by this Directive, is acting for purposes which are not related to his trade, business or profession;
(b) consumer goods: shall mean any tangible movable item, with the exception of:
- goods sold by way of execution or otherwise by authority of law,
- water and gas where they are not put up for sale in a limited volume or set quantity,
- electricity;
(c) seller: shall mean any natural or legal person who, under a contract, sells consumer goods in the course of his trade, business or profession;
(d) producer: shall mean the manufacturer of consumer goods, the importer of consumer goods into the territory of the Community or any person purporting to be a producer by placing his name, trade mark or other distinctive sign on the consumer goods;
(e) guarantee: shall mean any undertaking by a seller or producer to the consumer, given without extra charge, to reimburse the price paid or to replace, repair or handle consumer goods in any way if they do not meet the specifications set out in the guarantee statement or in the relevant advertising;
(f) repair: shall mean, in the event of lack of conformity, bringing consumer goods into conformity with the contract of sale.
(3) Member States may provide that the expression "consumer goods" does not cover second-hand goods sold at public auction where consumers have the opportunity of attending the sale in person.
(4) Contracts for the supply of consumer goods to be manufactured or produced shall also be deemed contracts of sale for the purpose of this Directive.

Article 2. (1) The seller must deliver goods to the consumer which are in conformity with the contract of sale.
(2) Consumer goods are presumed to be in conformity with the contract if they:
(a) comply with the description given by the seller and possess the qualities of the goods which the seller has held out to the consumer as a sample or model;
(b) are fit for any particular purpose for which the consumer requires them and which he made known to the seller at the time of conclusion of the contract and which the seller has accepted;
(c) are fit for the purposes for which goods of the same type are normally used;
(d) show the quality and performance which are normal in goods of the same type and which the consumer can reasonably expect, given the nature of the goods and taking into account any public statements on the specific characteristics of the goods made about them by the seller, the producer or his representative, particularly in advertising or on labelling.
(3) There shall be deemed not to be a lack of conformity for the purposes of this Article if, at the time

the contract was concluded, the consumer was aware, or could not reasonably be unaware of, the lack of conformity, or if the lack of conformity has its origin in materials supplied by the consumer.
(4) The seller shall not be bound by public statements, as referred to in paragraph (2)(d) if he:
- shows that he was not, and could not reasonably have been, aware of the statement in question,
- shows that by the time of conclusion of the contract the statement had been corrected, or
- shows that the decision to buy the consumer goods could not have been influenced by the statement.
(5) Any lack of conformity resulting from incorrect installation of the consumer goods shall be deemed to be equivalent to lack of conformity of the goods if installation forms part of the contract of sale of the goods and the goods were installed by the seller or under his responsibility. This shall apply equally if the product, intended to be installed by the consumer, is installed by the consumer and the incorrect installation is due to a shortcoming in the installation instructions.

Article 3. (1) The seller shall be liable to the consumer for any lack of conformity which exists at the time the goods were delivered.
(2) In the case of a lack of conformity, the consumer shall be entitled to have the goods brought into conformity free of charge by repair or replacement, in accordance with paragraph (3), or to have an appropriate reduction made in the price or the contract rescinded with regard to those goods, in accordance with paragraphs 5 and 6.
(3) In the first place, the consumer may require the seller to repair the goods or he may require the seller to replace them, in either case free of charge, unless this is impossible or disproportionate.
A remedy shall be deemed to be disproportionate if it imposes costs on the seller which, in comparison with the alternative remedy, are unreasonable, taking into account:
- the value the goods would have if there were no lack of conformity,
- the significance of the lack of conformity, and
- whether the alternative remedy could be completed without significant inconvenience to the consumer
Any repair or replacement shall be completed within a reasonable time and without any significant inconvenience to the consumer, taking account of the nature of the goods and the purpose for which the consumer required the goods.
(4) The terms "free of charge" in paragraphs 2 and 3 refer to the necessary costs incurred to bring the goods into conformity, particularly the cost of postage, labour and materials.
(5) The consumer may require an appropriate reduction of the price or have the contract rescinded:
- if the consumer is entitled to neither repair nor replacement, or
- if the seller has not completed the remedy within a reasonable time, or
- if the seller has not completed the remedy without significant inconvenience to the consumer.
(6) The consumer is not entitled to have the contract rescinded if the lack of conformity is minor.

Article 4. Where the final seller is liable to the consumer because of a lack of conformity resulting from an act or omission by the producer, a previous seller in the same chain of contracts or any other intermediary, the final seller shall be entitled to pursue remedies against the person or persons liable in the contractual chain. the person or persons liable against whom the final seller may pursue remedies, together with the relevant actions and conditions of exercise, shall be determined by national law.

Article 5. (1) The seller shall be held liable under Article 3 where the lack of conformity becomes apparent within two years as from delivery of the goods. If, under national legislation, the rights laid down in Article 3(2) are subject to a limitation period, that period shall not expire within a period of two years from the time of delivery.
(2) Member States may provide that, in order to benefit from his rights, the consumer must inform the seller of the lack of conformity within a period of two months from the date on which he detected such lack of conformity. Member States shall inform the Commission of their use of this paragraph. The Commission shall monitor the effect of the existence of this option for the Member States on consumers and on the internal market. Not later than 7 January 2003, the Commission shall prepare a report on the use made by Member States of this paragraph. This report shall be published in the Official Journal of the European Communities.
(3) Unless proved otherwise, any lack of conformity which becomes apparent within six months of delivery of the goods shall be presumed to have existed at the time of delivery unless this presumption is incompatible with the nature of the goods or the nature of the lack of conformity.

Article 6. (1) A guarantee shall be legally binding on the offerer under the conditions laid down in the guarantee statement and the associated advertising.
(2) The guarantee shall:

- state that the consumer has legal rights under applicable national legislation governing the sale of consumer goods and make clear that those rights are not affected by the guarantee,
- set out in plain intelligible language the contents of the guarantee and the essential particulars necessary for making claims under the guarantee, notably the duration and territorial scope of the guarantee as well as the name and address of the guarantor.

(3) On request by the consumer, the guarantee shall be made available in writing or feature in another durable medium available and accessible to him.

(4) Within its own territory, the Member State in which the consumer goods are marketed may, in accordance with the rules of the Treaty, provide that the guarantee be drafted in one or more languages which it shall determine from among the official languages of the Community.

(5) Should a guarantee infringe the requirements of paragraphs 2, 3 or 4, the validity of this guarantee shall in no way be affected, and the consumer can still rely on the guarantee and require that it be honoured.

Article 7. (1) Any contractual terms or agreements concluded with the seller before the lack of conformity is brought to the seller's attention which directly or indirectly waive or restrict the rights resulting from this Directive shall, as provided for by national law, not be binding on the consumer. Member States may provide that, in the case of second-hand goods, the seller and consumer may agree contractual terms or agreements which have a shorter time period for the liability of the seller than that set down in Article 5(1). Such period may not be less than one year.

(2) Member States shall take the necessary measures to ensure that consumers are not deprived of the protection afforded by this Directive as a result of opting for the law of a non-member State as the law applicable to the contract where the contract has a close connection with the territory of the Member States.

Article 8. (1) The rights resulting from this Directive shall be exercised without prejudice to other rights which the consumer may invoke under the national rules governing contractual or non-contractual liability.

(2) Member States may adopt or maintain in force more stringent provisions, compatible with the Treaty in the field covered by this Directive, to ensure a higher level of consumer protection.

Article 9. Member States shall take appropriate measures to inform the consumer of the national law transposing this Directive and shall encourage, where appropriate, professional organisations to inform consumers of their rights.

Article 10. The Annex to Directive 98/27/EC shall be completed as follows: "10. Directive 1999/44/EC of the European Parliament and of the Council of 25 May 1999 on certain aspects of the sale of consumer goods and associated guarantees (OJ L 171, 7.7.1999, p. 12).".

Article 11. (1) Member States shall bring into force the laws, regulations and administrative provisions necessary to comply with this Directive not later than 1 January 2002. They shall forthwith inform the Commission thereof. When Member States adopt these measures, they shall contain a reference to this Directive, or shall be accompanied by such reference at the time of their official publication. The procedure for such reference shall be adopted by Member States.

(2) Member States shall communicate to the Commission the provisions of national law which they adopt in the field covered by this Directive.

Article 12. The Commission shall, not later than 7 July 2006, review the application of this Directive and submit to the European Parliament and the Council a report. The report shall examine, inter alia, the case for introducing the producer's direct liability and, if appropriate, shall be accompanied by proposals.

Article 13. This Directive shall enter into force on the day of its publication in the Official Journal of the European Communities.

Article 14. This Directive is addressed to the Member States.

EU: DIRECTIVE 2000/31 ON ELECTRONIC COMMERCE

Directive 2000/31/EC of the European Parliament and of the Council of 8 June 2000 on certain legal aspects of information society services, in particular electronic commerce, in the Internal Market ('Directive on electronic commerce') (OJL 178, 17.07.2000, pp. 1 – 16) [footnotes omitted].

THE EUROPEAN PARLIAMENT AND THE COUNCIL OF THE EUROPEAN UNION,
Having regard to the Treaty establishing the European Community, and in particular Articles 47(2), 55 and 95 thereof,
Having regard to the proposal from the Commission,
Having regard to the opinion of the Economic and Social Committee,
Acting in accordance with the procedure laid down in Article 251 of the Treaty,
Whereas:
(1) The European Union is seeking to forge ever closer links between the States and peoples of Europe, to ensure economic and social progress; in accordance with Article 14(2) of the Treaty, the internal market comprises an area without internal frontiers in which the free movements of goods, services and the freedom of establishment are ensured; the development of information society services within the area without internal frontiers is vital to eliminating the barriers which divide the European peoples.
(2) The development of electronic commerce within the information society offers significant employment opportunities in the Community, particularly in small and medium-sized enterprises, and will stimulate economic growth and investment in innovation by European companies, and can also enhance the competitiveness of European industry, provided that everyone has access to the Internet.
(3) Community law and the characteristics of the Community legal order are a vital asset to enable European citizens and operators to take full advantage, without consideration of borders, of the opportunities afforded by electronic commerce; this Directive therefore has the purpose of ensuring a high level of Community legal integration in order to establish a real area without internal borders for information society services.
(4) It is important to ensure that electronic commerce could fully benefit from the internal market and therefore that, as with Council Directive 89/552/EEC of 3 October 1989 on the coordination of certain provisions laid down by law, regulation or administrative action in Member States concerning the pursuit of television broadcasting activities, a high level of Community integration is achieved.
(5) The development of information society services within the Community is hampered by a number of legal obstacles to the proper functioning of the internal market which make less attractive the exercise of the freedom of establishment and the freedom to provide services; these obstacles arise from divergences in legislation and from the legal uncertainty as to which national rules apply to such services; in the absence of coordination and adjustment of legislation in the relevant areas, obstacles might be justified in the light of the case-law of the Court of Justice of the European Communities; legal uncertainty exists with regard to the extent to which Member States may control services originating from another Member State.
(6) In the light of Community objectives, of Articles 43 and 49 of the Treaty and of secondary Community law, these obstacles should be eliminated by coordinating certain national laws and by clarifying certain legal concepts at Community level to the extent necessary for the proper functioning of the internal market; by dealing only with certain specific matters which give rise to problems for the internal market, this Directive is fully consistent with the need to respect the principle of subsidiarity as set out in Article 5 of the Treaty.
(7) In order to ensure legal certainty and consumer confidence, this Directive must lay down a clear and general framework to cover certain legal aspects of electronic commerce in the internal market.
(8) The objective of this Directive is to create a legal framework to ensure the free movement of information society services between Member States and not to harmonise the field of criminal law as such.
(9) The free movement of information society services can in many cases be a specific reflection in Community law of a more general principle, namely freedom of expression as enshrined in Article 10(1) of the Convention for the Protection of Human Rights and Fundamental Freedoms, which has been ratified by all the Member States; for this reason, directives covering the supply of information society services must ensure that this activity may be engaged in freely in the light of that Article, subject only to the restrictions laid down in paragraph (2) of that Article and in Article 46(1) of the Treaty; this Directive is not intended to affect national fundamental rules and principles relating to freedom of expression.
(10) In accordance with the principle of proportionality, the measures provided for in this Directive are strictly limited to the minimum needed to achieve the objective of the proper functioning of the

PART IV   EUROPEAN PRIVATE LAW

internal market; where action at Community level is necessary, and in order to guarantee an area which is truly without internal frontiers as far as electronic commerce is concerned, the Directive must ensure a high level of protection of objectives of general interest, in particular the protection of minors and human dignity, consumer protection and the protection of public health; according to Article 152 of the Treaty, the protection of public health is an essential component of other Community policies.

(11) This Directive is without prejudice to the level of protection for, in particular, public health and consumer interests, as established by Community acts; amongst others, Council Directive 93/13/EEC of 5 April 1993 on unfair terms in consumer contracts and Directive 97/7/EC of the European Parliament and of the Council of 20 May 1997 on the protection of consumers in respect of distance contracts form a vital element for protecting consumers in contractual matters; those Directives also apply in their entirety to information society services; that same Community acquis, which is fully applicable to information society services, also embraces in particular Council Directive 84/450/EEC of 10 September 1984 concerning misleading and comparative advertising, Council Directive 87/102/EEC of 22 December 1986 for the approximation of the laws, regulations and administrative provisions of the Member States concerning consumer credit, Council Directive 93/22/EEC of 10 May 1993 on investment services in the securities field, Council Directive 90/314/EEC of 13 June 1990 on package travel, package holidays and package tours, Directive 98/6/EC of the European Parliament and of the Council of 16 February 1998 on consumer production in the indication of prices of products offered to consumers, Council Directive 92/59/EEC of 29 June 1992 on general product safety, Directive 94/47/EC of the European Parliament and of the Council of 26 October 1994 on the protection of purchasers in respect of certain aspects on contracts relating to the purchase of the right to use immovable properties on a timeshare basis, Directive 98/27/EC of the European Parliament and of the Council of 19 May 1998 on injunctions for the protection of consumers' interests, Council Directive 85/374/EEC of 25 July 1985 on the approximation of the laws, regulations and administrative provisions concerning liability for defective products, Directive 1999/44/EC of the European Parliament and of the Council of 25 May 1999 on certain aspects of the sale of consumer goods and associated guarantees, the future Directive of the European Parliament and of the Council concerning the distance marketing of consumer financial services and Council Directive 92/28/EEC of 31 March 1992 on the advertising of medicinal products; this Directive should be without prejudice to Directive 98/43/EC of the European Parliament and of the Council of 6 July 1998 on the approximation of the laws, regulations and administrative provisions of the Member States relating to the advertising and sponsorship of tobacco products adopted within the framework of the internal market, or to directives on the protection of public health; this Directive complements information requirements established by the abovementioned Directives and in particular Directive 97/7/EC.

(12) It is necessary to exclude certain activities from the scope of this Directive, on the grounds that the freedom to provide services in these fields cannot, at this stage, be guaranteed under the Treaty or existing secondary legislation; excluding these activities does not preclude any instruments which might prove necessary for the proper functioning of the internal market; taxation, particularly value added tax imposed on a large number of the services covered by this Directive, must be excluded form the scope of this Directive.

(13) This Directive does not aim to establish rules on fiscal obligations nor does it pre-empt the drawing up of Community instruments concerning fiscal aspects of electronic commerce.

(14) The protection of individuals with regard to the processing of personal data is solely governed by Directive 95/46/EC of the European Parliament and of the Council of 24 October 1995 on the protection of individuals with regard to the processing of personal data and on the free movement of such data and Directive 97/66/EC of the European Parliament and of the Council of 15 December 1997 concerning the processing of personal data and the protection of privacy in the telecommunications sector which are fully applicable to information society services; these Directives already establish a Community legal framework in the field of personal data and therefore it is not necessary to cover this issue in this Directive in order to ensure the smooth functioning of the internal market, in particular the free movement of personal data between Member States; the implementation and application of this Directive should be made in full compliance with the principles relating to the protection of personal data, in particular as regards unsolicited commercial communication and the liability of intermediaries; this Directive cannot prevent the anonymous use of open networks such as the Internet.

(15) The confidentiality of communications is guaranteed by Article 5 Directive 97/66/EC; in accordance with that Directive, Member States must prohibit any kind of interception or surveillance of such communications by others than the senders and receivers, except when legally authorised.

(16) The exclusion of gambling activities from the scope of application of this Directive covers only games of chance, lotteries and betting transactions, which involve wagering a stake with monetary value; this does not cover promotional competitions or games where the purpose is to encourage the sale of goods or services and where payments, if they arise, serve only to acquire the promoted goods or services.

(17) The definition of information society services already exists in Community law in Directive 98/34/EC of the European Parliament and of the Council of 22 June 1998 laying down a procedure for the provision of information in the field of technical standards and regulations and of rules on information society services and in Directive 98/84/EC of the European Parliament and of the Council of 20 November 1998 on the legal protection of services based on, or consisting of, conditional access; this definition covers any service normally provided for remuneration, at a distance, by means of electronic equipment for the processing (including digital compression) and storage of data, and at the individual request of a recipient of a service; those services referred to in the indicative list in Annex V to Directive 98/34/EC which do not imply data processing and storage are not covered by this definition.

(18) Information society services span a wide range of economic activities which take place on-line; these activities can, in particular, consist of selling goods on-line; activities such as the delivery of goods as such or the provision of services off-line are not covered; information society services are not solely restricted to services giving rise to on-line contracting but also, in so far as they represent an economic activity, extend to services which are not remunerated by those who receive them, such as those offering on-line information or commercial communications, or those providing tools allowing for search, access and retrieval of data; information society services also include services consisting of the transmission of information via a communication network, in providing access to a communication network or in hosting information provided by a recipient of the service; television broadcasting within the meaning of Directive EEC/89/552 and radio broadcasting are not information society services because they are not provided at individual request; by contrast, services which are transmitted point to point, such as video-on-demand or the provision of commercial communications by electronic mail are information society services; the use of electronic mail or equivalent individual communications for instance by natural persons acting outside their trade, business or profession including their use for the conclusion of contracts between such persons is not an information society service; the contractual relationship between an employee and his employer is not an information society service; activities which by their very nature cannot be carried out at a distance and by electronic means, such as the statutory auditing of company accounts or medical advice requiring the physical examination of a patient are not information society services.

(19) The place at which a service provider is established should be determined in conformity with the case-law of the Court of Justice according to which the concept of establishment involves the actual pursuit of an economic activity through a fixed establishment for an indefinite period; this requirement is also fulfilled where a company is constituted for a given period; the place of establishment of a company providing services via an Internet website is not the place at which the technology supporting its website is located or the place at which its website is accessible but the place where it pursues its economic activity; in cases where a provider has several places of establishment it is important to determine from which place of establishment the service concerned is provided; in cases where it is difficult to determine from which of several places of establishment a given service is provided, this is the place where the provider has the centre of his activities relating to this particular service.

(20) The definition of "recipient of a service" covers all types of usage of information society services, both by persons who provide information on open networks such as the Internet and by persons who seek information on the Internet for private or professional reasons.

(21) The scope of the coordinated field is without prejudice to future Community harmonisation relating to information society services and to future legislation adopted at national level in accordance with Community law; the coordinated field covers only requirements relating to on-line activities such as on-line information, on-line advertising, on-line shopping, on-line contracting and does not concern Member States' legal requirements relating to goods such as safety standards, labelling obligations, or liability for goods, or Member States' requirements relating to the delivery or the transport of goods, including the distribution of medicinal products; the coordinated field does not cover the exercise of rights of pre-emption by public authorities concerning certain goods such as works of art.

(22) Information society services should be supervised at the source of the activity, in order to ensure an effective protection of public interest objectives; to that end, it is necessary to ensure that the competent authority provides such protection not only for the citizens of its own country but for all

PART IV   EUROPEAN PRIVATE LAW

Community citizens; in order to improve mutual trust between Member States, it is essential to state clearly this responsibility on the part of the Member State where the services originate; moreover, in order to effectively guarantee freedom to provide services and legal certainty for suppliers and recipients of services, such information society services should in principle be subject to the law of the Member State in which the service provider is established.

(23) This Directive neither aims to establish additional rules on private international law relating to conflicts of law nor does it deal with the jurisdiction of Courts; provisions of the applicable law designated by rules of private international law must not restrict the freedom to provide information society services as established in this Directive.

(24) In the context of this Directive, notwithstanding the rule on the control at source of information society services, it is legitimate under the conditions established in this Directive for Member States to take measures to restrict the free movement of information society services.

(25) National courts, including civil courts, dealing with private law disputes can take measures to derogate from the freedom to provide information society services in conformity with conditions established in this Directive. (26) Member States, in conformity with conditions established in this Directive, may apply their national rules on criminal law and criminal proceedings with a view to taking all investigative and other measures necessary for the detection and prosecution of criminal offences, without there being a need to notify such measures to the Commission.

(27) This Directive, together with the future Directive of the European Parliament and of the Council concerning the distance marketing of consumer financial services, contributes to the creating of a legal framework for the on-line provision of financial services; this Directive does not pre-empt future initiatives in the area of financial services in particular with regard to the harmonisation of rules of conduct in this field; the possibility for Member States, established in this Directive, under certain circumstances of restricting the freedom to provide information society services in order to protect consumers also covers measures in the area of financial services in particular measures aiming at protecting investors.

(28) The Member States' obligation not to subject access to the activity of an information society service provider to prior authorisation does not concern postal services covered by Directive 97/67/EC of the European Parliament and of the Council of 15 December 1997 on common rules for the development of the internal market of Community postal services and the improvement of quality of service consisting of the physical delivery of a printed electronic mail message and does not affect voluntary accreditation systems, in particular for providers of electronic signature certification service.

(29) Commercial communications are essential for the financing of information society services and for developing a wide variety of new, charge-free services; in the interests of consumer protection and fair trading, commercial communications, including discounts, promotional offers and promotional competitions or games, must meet a number of transparency requirements; these requirements are without prejudice to Directive 97/7/EC; this Directive should not affect existing Directives on commercial communications, in particular Directive 98/43/EC.

(30) The sending of unsolicited commercial communications by electronic mail may be undesirable for consumers and information society service providers and may disrupt the smooth functioning of interactive networks; the question of consent by recipient of certain forms of unsolicited commercial communications is not addressed by this Directive, but has already been addressed, in particular, by Directive 97/7/EC and by Directive 97/66/EC; in Member States which authorise unsolicited commercial communications by electronic mail, the setting up of appropriate industry filtering initiatives should be encouraged and facilitated; in addition it is necessary that in any event unsolicited commercial communities are clearly identifiable as such in order to improve transparency and to facilitate the functioning of such industry initiatives; unsolicited commercial communications by electronic mail should not result in additional communication costs for the recipient.

(31) Member States which allow the sending of unsolicited commercial communications by electronic mail without prior consent of the recipient by service providers established in their territory have to ensure that the service providers consult regularly and respect the opt-out registers in which natural persons not wishing to receive such commercial communications can register themselves.

(32) In order to remove barriers to the development of cross-border services within the Community which members of the regulated professions might offer on the Internet, it is necessary that compliance be guaranteed at Community level with professional rules aiming, in particular, to protect consumers or public health; codes of conduct at Community level would be the best means of determining the rules on professional ethics applicable to commercial communication; the drawing-up or, where appropriate, the adaptation of such rules should be encouraged without prejudice to the autonomy of professional bodies and associations.

(33) This Directive complements Community law and national law relating to regulated professions

maintaining a coherent set of applicable rules in this field.

(34) Each Member State is to amend its legislation containing requirements, and in particular requirements as to form, which are likely to curb the use of contracts by electronic means; the examination of the legislation requiring such adjustment should be systematic and should cover all the necessary stages and acts of the contractual process, including the filing of the contract; the result of this amendment should be to make contracts concluded electronically workable; the legal effect of electronic signatures is dealt with by Directive 1999/93/EC of the European Parliament and of the Council of 13 December 1999 on a Community framework for electronic signatures; the acknowledgement of receipt by a service provider may take the form of the on-line provision of the service paid for.

(35) This Directive does not affect Member States' possibility of maintaining or establishing general or specific legal requirements for contracts which can be fulfilled by electronic means, in particular requirements concerning secure electronic signatures.

(36) Member States may maintain restrictions for the use of electronic contracts with regard to contracts requiring by law the involvement of courts, public authorities, or professions exercising public authority; this possibility also covers contracts which require the involvement of courts, public authorities, or professions exercising public authority in order to have an effect with regard to third parties as well as contracts requiring by law certification or attestation by a notary.

(37) Member States' obligation to remove obstacles to the use of electronic contracts concerns only obstacles resulting from legal requirements and not practical obstacles resulting from the impossibility of using electronic means in certain cases.

(38) Member States' obligation to remove obstacles to the use of electronic contracts is to be implemented in conformity with legal requirements for contracts enshrined in Community law.

(39) The exceptions to the provisions concerning the contracts concluded exclusively by electronic mail or by equivalent individual communications provided for by this Directive, in relation to information to be provided and the placing of orders, should not enable, as a result, the by-passing of those provisions by providers of information society services.

(40) Both existing and emerging disparities in Member States' legislation and case-law concerning liability of service providers acting as intermediaries prevent the smooth functioning of the internal market, in particular by impairing the development of cross-border services and producing distortions of competition; service providers have a duty to act, under certain circumstances, with a view to preventing or stopping illegal activities; this Directive should constitute the appropriate basis for the development of rapid and reliable procedures for removing and disabling access to illegal information; such mechanisms could be developed on the basis of voluntary agreements between all parties concerned and should be encouraged by Member States; it is in the interest of all parties involved in the provision of information society services to adopt and implement such procedures; the provisions of this Directive relating to liability should not preclude the development and effective operation, by the different interested parties, of technical systems of protection and identification and of technical surveillance instruments made possible by digital technology within the limits laid down by Directives 95/46/EC and 97/66/EC.

(41) This Directive strikes a balance between the different interests at stake and establishes principles upon which industry agreements and standards can be based.

(42) The exemptions from liability established in this Directive cover only cases where the activity of the information society service provider is limited to the technical process of operating and giving access to a communication network over which information made available by third parties is transmitted or temporarily stored, for the sole purpose of making the transmission more efficient; this activity is of a mere technical, automatic and passive nature, which implies that the information society service provider has neither knowledge of nor control over the information which is transmitted or stored.

(43) A service provider can benefit from the exemptions for "mere conduit" and for "caching" when he is in no way involved with the information transmitted; this requires among other things that he does not modify the information that he transmits; this requirement does not cover manipulations of a technical nature which take place in the course of the transmission as they do not alter the integrity of the information contained in the transmission. (44) A service provider who deliberately collaborates with one of the recipients of his service in order to undertake illegal acts goes beyond the activities of "mere conduit" or "caching" and as a result cannot benefit from the liability exemptions established for these activities.

(45) The limitations of the liability of intermediary service providers established in this Directive do not affect the possibility of injunctions of different kinds; such injunctions can in particular consist of orders by courts or administrative authorities requiring the termination or prevention of any infringe-

PART IV   EUROPEAN PRIVATE LAW

ment, including the removal of illegal information or the disabling of access to it.
(46) In order to benefit from a limitation of liability, the provider of an information society service, consisting of the storage of information, upon obtaining actual knowledge or awareness of illegal activities has to act expeditiously to remove or to disable access to the information concerned; the removal or disabling of access has to be undertaken in the observance of the principle of freedom of expression and of procedures established for this purpose at national level; this Directive does not affect Member States' possibility of establishing specific requirements which must be fulfilled expeditiously prior to the removal or disabling of information.
(47) Member States are prevented from imposing a monitoring obligation on service providers only with respect to obligations of a general nature; this does not concern monitoring obligations in a specific case and, in particular, does not affect orders by national authorities in accordance with national legislation.
(48) This Directive does not affect the possibility for Member States of requiring service providers, who host information provided by recipients of their service, to apply duties of care, which can reasonably be expected from them and which are specified by national law, in order to detect and prevent certain types of illegal activities.
(49) Member States and the Commission are to encourage the drawing-up of codes of conduct; this is not to impair the voluntary nature of such codes and the possibility for interested parties of deciding freely whether to adhere to such codes.
(50) It is important that the proposed directive on the harmonisation of certain aspects of copyright and related rights in the information society and this Directive come into force within a similar time scale with a view to establishing a clear framework of rules relevant to the issue of liability of intermediaries for copyright and relating rights infringements at Community level.
(51) Each Member State should be required, where necessary, to amend any legislation which is liable to hamper the use of schemes for the out-of-court settlement of disputes through electronic channels; the result of this amendment must be to make the functioning of such schemes genuinely and effectively possible in law and in practice, even across borders.
(52) The effective exercise of the freedoms of the internal market makes it necessary to guarantee victims effective access to means of settling disputes; damage which may arise in connection with information society services is characterised both by its rapidity and by its geographical extent; in view of this specific character and the need to ensure that national authorities do not endanger the mutual confidence which they should have in one another, this Directive requests Member States to ensure that appropriate court actions are available; Member States should examine the need to provide access to judicial procedures by appropriate electronic means.
(53) Directive 98/27/EC, which is applicable to information society services, provides a mechanism relating to actions for an injunction aimed at the protection of the collective interests of consumers; this mechanism will contribute to the free movement of information society services by ensuring a high level of consumer protection. (54) The sanctions provided for under this Directive are without prejudice to any other sanction or remedy provided under national law; Member States are not obliged to provide criminal sanctions for infringement of national provisions adopted pursuant to this Directive.
(55) This Directive does not affect the law applicable to contractual obligations relating to consumer contracts; accordingly, this Directive cannot have the result of depriving the consumer of the protection afforded to him by the mandatory rules relating to contractual obligations of the law of the Member State in which he has his habitual residence.
(56) As regards the derogation contained in this Directive regarding contractual obligations concerning contracts concluded by consumers, those obligations should be interpreted as including information on the essential elements of the content of the contract, including consumer rights, which have a determining influence on the decision to contract.
(57) The Court of Justice has consistently held that a Member State retains the right to take measures against a service provider that is established in another Member State but directs all or most of his activity to the territory of the first Member State if the choice of establishment was made with a view to evading the legislation that would have applied to the provider had he been established on the territory of the first Member State.
(58) This Directive should not apply to services supplied by service providers established in a third country; in view of the global dimension of electronic commerce, it is, however, appropriate to ensure that the Community rules are consistent with international rules; this Directive is without prejudice to the results of discussions within international organisations (amongst others WTO, OECD, Uncitral) on legal issues.
(59) Despite the global nature of electronic communications, coordination of national regulatory

measures at European Union level is necessary in order to avoid fragmentation of the internal market, and for the establishment of an appropriate European regulatory framework; such coordination should also contribute to the establishment of a common and strong negotiating position in international forums.

(60) In order to allow the unhampered development of electronic commerce, the legal framework must be clear and simple, predictable and consistent with the rules applicable at international level so that it does not adversely affect the competitiveness of European industry or impede innovation in that sector.

(61) If the market is actually to operate by electronic means in the context of globalisation, the European Union and the major non-European areas need to consult each other with a view to making laws and procedures compatible.

(62) Cooperation with third countries should be strengthened in the area of electronic commerce, in particular with applicant countries, the developing countries and the European Union's other trading partners

(63) The adoption of this Directive will not prevent the Member States from taking into account the various social, societal and cultural implications which are inherent in the advent of the information society; in particular it should not hinder measures which Member States might adopt in conformity with Community law to achieve social, cultural and democratic goals taking into account their linguistic diversity, national and regional specificities as well as their cultural heritage, and to ensure and maintain public access to the widest possible range of information society services; in any case, the development of the information society is to ensure that Community citizens can have access to the cultural European heritage provided in the digital environment.

(64) Electronic communication offers the Member States an excellent means of providing public services in the cultural, educational and linguistic fields.

(65) The Council, in its resolution of 19 January 1999 on the consumer dimension of the information society, stressed that the protection of consumers deserved special attention in this field; the Commission will examine the degree to which existing consumer protection rules provide insufficient protection in the context of the information society and will identify, where necessary, the deficiencies of this legislation and those issues which could require additional measures; if need be, the Commission should make specific additional proposals to resolve such deficiencies that will thereby have been identified,

HAVE ADOPTED THIS DIRECTIVE:

Chapter I. General Provisions

Article 1. (1) This Directive seeks to contribute to the proper functioning of the internal market by ensuring the free movement of information society services between the Member States.

(2) This Directive approximates, to the extent necessary for the achievement of the objective set out in paragraph (1), certain national provisions on information society services relating to the internal market, the establishment of service providers, commercial communications, electronic contracts, the liability of intermediaries, codes of conduct, out-of-court dispute settlements, court actions and cooperation between Member States.

(3) This Directive complements Community law applicable to information society services without prejudice to the level of protection for, in particular, public health and consumer interests, as established by Community acts and national legislation implementing them in so far as this does not restrict the freedom to provide information society services.

(4) This Directive does not establish additional rules on private international law nor does it deal with the jurisdiction of Courts.

(5) This Directive shall not apply to:
(a) the field of taxation;
(b) questions relating to information society services covered by Directives 95/46/EC and 97/66/EC;
(c) questions relating to agreements or practices governed by cartel law;
(d) the following activities of information society services:
- the activities of notaries or equivalent professions to the extent that they involve a direct and specific connection with the exercise of public authority,
- the representation of a client and defence of his interests before the courts,
- gambling activities which involve wagering a stake with monetary value in games of chance, including lotteries and betting transactions.

(6) This Directive does not affect measures taken at Community or national level, in the respect of Community law, in order to promote cultural and linguistic diversity and to ensure the defence of pluralism.

Article 2. For the purpose of this Directive, the following terms shall bear the following meanings:
(a) "information society services": services within the meaning of Article 1(2) of Directive 98/34/EC as amended by Directive 98/48/EC;
(b) "service provider": any natural or legal person providing an information society service;
(c) "established service provider": a service provider who effectively pursues an economic activity using a fixed establishment for an indefinite period. The presence and use of the technical means and technologies required to provide the service do not, in themselves, constitute an establishment of the provider;
(d) "recipient of the service": any natural or legal person who, for professional ends or otherwise, uses an information society service, in particular for the purposes of seeking information or making it accessible;
(e) "consumer": any natural person who is acting for purposes which are outside his or her trade, business or profession;
(f) "commercial communication": any form of communication designed to promote, directly or indirectly, the goods, services or image of a company, organisation or person pursuing a commercial, industrial or craft activity or exercising a regulated profession. The following do not in themselves constitute commercial communications:
- information allowing direct access to the activity of the company, organisation or person, in particular a domain name or an electronic-mail address,
- communications relating to the goods, services or image of the company, organisation or person compiled in an independent manner, particularly when this is without financial consideration;
(g) "regulated profession": any profession within the meaning of either Article 1(d) of Council Directive 89/48/EEC of 21 December 1988 on a general system for the recognition of higher-education diplomas awarded on completion of professional education and training of at least three-years' duration or of Article 1(f) of Council Directive 92/51/EEC of 18 June 1992 on a second general system for the recognition of professional education and training to supplement Directive 89/48/EEC;
(h) "coordinated field": requirements laid down in Member States' legal systems applicable to information society service providers or information society services, regardless of whether they are of a general nature or specifically designed for them.
(i) The coordinated field concerns requirements with which the service provider has to comply in respect of:
- the taking up of the activity of an information society service, such as requirements concerning qualifications, authorisation or notification,
- the pursuit of the activity of an information society service, such as requirements concerning the behaviour of the service provider, requirements regarding the quality or content of the service including those applicable to advertising and contracts, or requirements concerning the liability of the service provider;
(ii) The coordinated field does not cover requirements such as:
- requirements applicable to goods as such,
- requirements applicable to the delivery of goods,
- requirements applicable to services not provided by electronic means.

Article 3. (1) Each Member State shall ensure that the information society services provided by a service provider established on its territory comply with the national provisions applicable in the Member State in question which fall within the coordinated field.
(2) Member States may not, for reasons falling within the coordinated field, restrict the freedom to provide information society services from another Member State.
(3) Paragraphs 1 and 2 shall not apply to the fields referred to in the Annex.
(4) Member States may take measures to derogate from paragraph (2) in respect of a given information society service if the following conditions are fulfilled:
(a) the measures shall be:
(i) necessary for one of the following reasons:
- public policy, in particular the prevention, investigation, detection and prosecution of criminal offences, including the protection of minors and the fight against any incitement to hatred on grounds of race, sex, religion or nationality, and violations of human dignity concerning individual persons,
- the protection of public health,
- public security, including the safeguarding of national security and defence,
- the protection of consumers, including investors;
(ii) taken against a given information society service which prejudices the objectives referred to in point (i) or which presents a serious and grave risk of prejudice to those objectives;

(iii) proportionate to those objectives;
(b) before taking the measures in question and without prejudice to court proceedings, including preliminary proceedings and acts carried out in the framework of a criminal investigation, the Member State has:
- asked the Member State referred to in paragraph (1) to take measures and the latter did not take such measures, or they were inadequate,
- notified the Commission and the Member State referred to in paragraph (1) of its intention to take such measures.
(5) Member States may, in the case of urgency, derogate from the conditions stipulated in paragraph (4)(b). Where this is the case, the measures shall be notified in the shortest possible time to the Commission and to the Member State referred to in paragraph (1), indicating the reasons for which the Member State considers that there is urgency.
(6) Without prejudice to the Member State's possibility of proceeding with the measures in question, the Commission shall examine the compatibility of the notified measures with Community law in the shortest possible time; where it comes to the conclusion that the measure is incompatible with Community law, the Commission shall ask the Member State in question to refrain from taking any proposed measures or urgently to put an end to the measures in question.

Chapter II. Principles

Section I. Establishment and information requirements

Article 4. (1) Member States shall ensure that the taking up and pursuit of the activity of an information society service provider may not be made subject to prior authorisation or any other requirement having equivalent effect.
(2) Paragraph 1 shall be without prejudice to authorisation schemes which are not specifically and exclusively targeted at information society services, or which are covered by Directive 97/13/EC of the European Parliament and of the Council of 10 April 1997 on a common framework for general authorisations and individual licences in the field of telecommunications services.

Article 5. (1) In addition to other information requirements established by Community law, Member States shall ensure that the service provider shall render easily, directly and permanently accessible to the recipients of the service and competent authorities, at least the following information:
(a) the name of the service provider;
(b) the geographic address at which the service provider is established;
(c) the details of the service provider, including his electronic mail address, which allow him to be contacted rapidly and communicated with in a direct and effective manner;
(d) where the service provider is registered in a trade or similar public register, the trade register in which the service provider is entered and his registration number, or equivalent means of identification in that register;
(e) where the activity is subject to an authorisation scheme, the particulars of the relevant supervisory authority;
(f) as concerns the regulated professions:
- any professional body or similar institution with which the service provider is registered,
- the professional title and the Member State where it has been granted,
- a reference to the applicable professional rules in the Member State of establishment and the means to access them;
(g) where the service provider undertakes an activity that is subject to VAT, the identification number referred to in Article 22(1) of the sixth Council Directive 77/388/EEC of 17 May 1977 on the harmonisation of the laws of the Member States relating to turnover taxes - Common system of value added tax: uniform basis of assessment.
(2) In addition to other information requirements established by Community law, Member States shall at least ensure that, where information society services refer to prices, these are to be indicated clearly and unambiguously and, in particular, must indicate whether they are inclusive of tax and delivery costs.

Section II. Commercial communications

Article 6. In addition to other information requirements established by Community law, Member States shall ensure that commercial communications which are part of, or constitute, an information society service comply at least with the following conditions:
(a) the commercial communication shall be clearly identifiable as such;

(b) the natural or legal person on whose behalf the commercial communication is made shall be clearly identifiable;
(c) promotional offers, such as discounts, premiums and gifts, where permitted in the Member State where the service provider is established, shall be clearly identifiable as such, and the conditions which are to be met to qualify for them shall be easily accessible and be presented clearly and unambiguously;
(d) promotional competitions or games, where permitted in the Member State where the service provider is established, shall be clearly identifiable as such, and the conditions for participation shall be easily accessible and be presented clearly and unambiguously.

Article 7. (1) In addition to other requirements established by Community law, Member States which permit unsolicited commercial communication by electronic mail shall ensure that such commercial communication by a service provider established in their territory shall be identifiable clearly and unambiguously as such as soon as it is received by the recipient.
(2) Without prejudice to Directive 97/7/EC and Directive 97/66/EC, Member States shall take measures to ensure that service providers undertaking unsolicited commercial communications by electronic mail consult regularly and respect the opt-out registers in which natural persons not wishing to receive such commercial communications can register themselves.

Article 8. (1) Member States shall ensure that the use of commercial communications which are part of, or constitute, an information society service provided by a member of a regulated profession is permitted subject to compliance with the professional rules regarding, in particular, the independence, dignity and honour of the profession, professional secrecy and fairness towards clients and other members of the profession.
(2) Without prejudice to the autonomy of professional bodies and associations, Member States and the Commission shall encourage professional associations and bodies to establish codes of conduct at Community level in order to determine the types of information that can be given for the purposes of commercial communication in conformity with the rules referred to in paragraph (1)
(3) When drawing up proposals for Community initiatives which may become necessary to ensure the proper functioning of the Internal Market with regard to the information referred to in paragraph (2), the Commission shall take due account of codes of conduct applicable at Community level and shall act in close cooperation with the relevant professional associations and bodies.
(4) This Directive shall apply in addition to Community Directives concerning access to, and the exercise of, activities of the regulated professions.

Section III. Contracts concluded by electronic means

Article 9. (1) Member States shall ensure that their legal system allows contracts to be concluded by electronic means. Member States shall in particular ensure that the legal requirements applicable to the contractual process neither create obstacles for the use of electronic contracts nor result in such contracts being deprived of legal effectiveness and validity on account of their having been made by electronic means.
(2) Member States may lay down that paragraph (1) shall not apply to all or certain contracts falling into one of the following categories:
(a) contracts that create or transfer rights in real estate, except for rental rights;
(b) contracts requiring by law the involvement of courts, public authorities or professions exercising public authority;
(c) contracts of suretyship granted and on collateral securities furnished by persons acting for purposes outside their trade, business or profession;
(d) contracts governed by family law or by the law of succession.
(3) Member States shall indicate to the Commission the categories referred to in paragraph (2) to which they do not apply paragraph (1). Member States shall submit to the Commission every five years a report on the application of paragraph (2) explaining the reasons why they consider it necessary to maintain the category referred to in paragraph (2)(b) to which they do not apply paragraph (1).

Article 10. (1) In addition to other information requirements established by Community law, Member States shall ensure, except when otherwise agreed by parties who are not consumers, that at least the following information is given by the service provider clearly, comprehensibly and unambiguously and prior to the order being placed by the recipient of the service:
(a) the different technical steps to follow to conclude the contract;
(b) whether or not the concluded contract will be filed by the service provider and whether it will be accessible;

(c) the technical means for identifying and correcting input errors prior to the placing of the order;
(d) the languages offered for the conclusion of the contract.
(2) Member States shall ensure that, except when otherwise agreed by parties who are not consumers, the service provider indicates any relevant codes of conduct to which he subscribes and information on how those codes can be consulted electronically.
(3) Contract terms and general conditions provided to the recipient must be made available in a way that allows him to store and reproduce them.
(4) Paragraphs 1 and 2 shall not apply to contracts concluded exclusively by exchange of electronic mail or by equivalent individual communications.

Article 11. (1) Member States shall ensure, except when otherwise agreed by parties who are not consumers, that in cases where the recipient of the service places his order through technological means, the following principles apply:
- the service provider has to acknowledge the receipt of the recipient's order without undue delay and by electronic means,
- the order and the acknowledgment of receipt are deemed to be received when the parties to whom they are addressed are able to access them.
(2) Member States shall ensure that, except when otherwise agreed by parties who are not consumers, the service provider makes available to the recipient of the service appropriate, effective and accessible technical means allowing him to identify and correct input errors, prior to the placing of the order.
(3) Paragraph 1, first indent, and paragraph (2) shall not apply to contracts concluded exclusively by exchange of electronic mail or by equivalent individual communications.

Section IV. Liability of intermediary service providers

Article 12. "Mere conduit"
(1) Where an information society service is provided that consists of the transmission in a communication network of information provided by a recipient of the service, or the provision of access to a communication network, Member States shall ensure that the service provider is not liable for the information transmitted, on condition that the provider:
(a) does not initiate the transmission;
(b) does not select the receiver of the transmission; and
(c) does not select or modify the information contained in the transmission.
(2) The acts of transmission and of provision of access referred to in paragraph (1) include the automatic, intermediate and transient storage of the information transmitted in so far as this takes place for the sole purpose of carrying out the transmission in the communication network, and provided that the information is not stored for any period longer than is reasonably necessary for the transmission.
(3) This Article shall not affect the possibility for a court or administrative authority, in accordance with Member States' legal systems, of requiring the service provider to terminate or prevent an infringement.

Article 13. "Caching"
(1) Where an information society service is provided that consists of the transmission in a communication network of information provided by a recipient of the service, Member States shall ensure that the service provider is not liable for the automatic, intermediate and temporary storage of that information, performed for the sole purpose of making more efficient the information's onward transmission to other recipients of the service upon their request, on condition that:
(a) the provider does not modify the information;
(b) the provider complies with conditions on access to the information;
(c) the provider complies with rules regarding the updating of the information, specified in a manner widely recognised and used by industry;
(d) the provider does not interfere with the lawful use of technology, widely recognised and used by industry, to obtain data on the use of the information; and
(e) the provider acts expeditiously to remove or to disable access to the information it has stored upon obtaining actual knowledge of the fact that the information at the initial source of the transmission has been removed from the network, or access to it has been disabled, or that a court or an administrative authority has ordered such removal or disablement.
(2) This Article shall not affect the possibility for a court or administrative authority, in accordance with Member States' legal systems, of requiring the service provider to terminate or prevent an infringement.

Article 14. (1) Where an information society service is provided that consists of the storage of information provided by a recipient of the service, Member States shall ensure that the service provider is not liable for the information stored at the request of a recipient of the service, on condition that:
(a) the provider does not have actual knowledge of illegal activity or information and, as regards claims for damages, is not aware of facts or circumstances from which the illegal activity or information is apparent; or
(b) the provider, upon obtaining such knowledge or awareness, acts expeditiously to remove or to disable access to the information.
(2) Paragraph 1 shall not apply when the recipient of the service is acting under the authority or the control of the provider.
(3) This Article shall not affect the possibility for a court or administrative authority, in accordance with Member States' legal systems, of requiring the service provider to terminate or prevent an infringement, nor does it affect the possibility for Member States of establishing procedures governing the removal or disabling of access to information.

Article 15. (1) Member States shall not impose a general obligation on providers, when providing the services covered by Articles 12, 13 and 14, to monitor the information which they transmit or store, nor a general obligation actively to seek facts or circumstances indicating illegal activity.
(2) Member States may establish obligations for information society service providers promptly to inform the competent public authorities of alleged illegal activities undertaken or information provided by recipients of their service or obligations to communicate to the competent authorities, at their request, information enabling the identification of recipients of their service with whom they have storage agreements.

Chapter III. Implementation

Article 16. (1) Member States and the Commission shall encourage:
(a) the drawing up of codes of conduct at Community level, by trade, professional and consumer associations or organisations, designed to contribute to the proper implementation of Articles 5 to 15;
(b) the voluntary transmission of draft codes of conduct at national or Community level to the Commission;
(c) the accessibility of these codes of conduct in the Community languages by electronic means;
(d) the communication to the Member States and the Commission, by trade, professional and consumer associations or organisations, of their assessment of the application of their codes of conduct and their impact upon practices, habits or customs relating to electronic commerce;
(e) the drawing up of codes of conduct regarding the protection of minors and human dignity.
(2) Member States and the Commission shall encourage the involvement of associations or organisations representing consumers in the drafting and implementation of codes of conduct affecting their interests and drawn up in accordance with paragraph (1)(a). Where appropriate, to take account of their specific needs, associations representing the visually impaired and disabled should be consulted.

Article 17. (1) Member States shall ensure that, in the event of disagreement between an information society service provider and the recipient of the service, their legislation does not hamper the use of out-of-court schemes, available under national law, for dispute settlement, including appropriate electronic means.
(2) Member States shall encourage bodies responsible for the out-of-court settlement of, in particular, consumer disputes to operate in a way which provides adequate procedural guarantees for the parties concerned.
(3) Member States shall encourage bodies responsible for out-of-court dispute settlement to inform the Commission of the significant decisions they take regarding information society services and to transmit any other information on the practices, usages or customs relating to electronic commerce.

Article 18. (1) Member States shall ensure that court actions available under national law concerning information society services' activities allow for the rapid adoption of measures, including interim measures, designed to terminate any alleged infringement and to prevent any further impairment of the interests involved.
(2) The Annex to Directive 98/27/EC shall be supplemented as follows: "11. Directive 2000/31/EC of the European Parliament and of the Council of 8 June 2000 on certain legal aspects on information society services, in particular electronic commerce, in the internal market (Directive on electronic commerce) (OJ L 178, 17.7.2000, p. 1)."

Article 19. (1) Member States shall have adequate means of supervision and investigation necessary to implement this Directive effectively and shall ensure that service providers supply them with the requisite information.

(2) Member States shall cooperate with other Member States; they shall, to that end, appoint one or several contact points, whose details they shall communicate to the other Member States and to the Commission.

(3) Member States shall, as quickly as possible, and in conformity with national law, provide the assistance and information requested by other Member States or by the Commission, including by appropriate electronic means.

(4) Member States shall establish contact points which shall be accessible at least by electronic means and from which recipients and service providers may:

(a) obtain general information on contractual rights and obligations as well as on the complaint and redress mechanisms available in the event of disputes, including practical aspects involved in the use of such mechanisms;

(b) obtain the details of authorities, associations or organisations from which they may obtain further information or practical assistance.

(5) Member States shall encourage the communication to the Commission of any significant administrative or judicial decisions taken in their territory regarding disputes relating to information society services and practices, usages and customs relating to electronic commerce. The Commission shall communicate these decisions to the other Member States.

Article 20. Member States shall determine the sanctions applicable to infringements of national provisions adopted pursuant to this Directive and shall take all measures necessary to ensure that they are enforced. The sanctions they provide for shall be effective, proportionate and dissuasive.

Chapter IV. Final Provisions

Article 21. (1) Before 17 July 2003, and thereafter every two years, the Commission shall submit to the European Parliament, the Council and the Economic and Social Committee a report on the application of this Directive, accompanied, where necessary, by proposals for adapting it to legal, technical and economic developments in the field of information society services, in particular with respect to crime prevention, the protection of minors, consumer protection and to the proper functioning of the internal market.

(2) In examining the need for an adaptation of this Directive, the report shall in particular analyse the need for proposals concerning the liability of providers of hyperlinks and location tool services, "notice and take down" procedures and the attribution of liability following the taking down of content. The report shall also analyse the need for additional conditions for the exemption from liability, provided for in Articles 12 and 13, in the light of technical developments, and the possibility of applying the internal market principles to unsolicited commercial communications by electronic mail.

Article 22. (1) Member States shall bring into force the laws, regulations and administrative provisions necessary to comply with this Directive before 17 January 2002. They shall forthwith inform the Commission thereof.

(2) When Member States adopt the measures referred to in paragraph (1), these shall contain a reference to this Directive or shall be accompanied by such reference at the time of their official publication. The methods of making such reference shall be laid down by Member States.

Article 23. This Directive shall enter into force on the day of its publication in the Official Journal of the European Communities.

Article 24. This Directive is addressed to the Member States.

Annex. Derogations from Article 3

As provided for in Article 3(3), Article 3(1) and (2) do not apply to:

- copyright, neighbouring rights, rights referred to in Directive 87/54/EEC and Directive 96/9/EC as well as industrial property rights,
- the emission of electronic money by institutions in respect of which Member States have applied one of the derogations provided for in Article 8(1) of Directive 2000/46/EC,
- Article 44(2) of Directive 85/611/EEC,
- Article 30 and Title IV of Directive 92/49/EEC, Title IV of Directive 92/96/EEC, Articles 7 and 8 of Directive 88/357/EEC and Article 4 of Directive 90/619/EEC,
- the freedom of the parties to choose the law applicable to their contract,
- contractual obligations concerning consumer contacts,

PART IV   EUROPEAN PRIVATE LAW

- formal validity of contracts creating or transferring rights in real estate where such contracts are subject to mandatory formal requirements of the law of the Member State where the real estate is situated,
- the permissibility of unsolicited commercial communications by electronic mail.

EU: DIRECTIVE 2011/7 ON COMBATING LATE PAYMENTS (RECAST)

Directive 2011/7/EU of the European Parliament and of the Council of 16 February 2011 on combating late payment in commercial transactions (recast) (Text with EEA relevance) (OJ L048, 23.02.2011, pp.1 – 10) [footnotes omitted].

THE EUROPEAN PARLIAMENT AND THE COUNCIL OF THE EUROPEAN UNION,
Having regard to the Treaty on the Functioning of the European Union, and in particular Article 114 thereof,
Having regard to the proposal from the European Commission,
Having regard to the opinion of the European Economic and Social Committee,
Acting in accordance with the ordinary legislative procedure,
Whereas:

(1) A number of substantive changes are to be made to Directive 2000/35/EC of the European Parliament and of the Council of 29 June 2000 on combating late payment in commercial transactions. It is desirable, for reasons of clarity and rationalisation, that the provisions in question be recast.

(2) Most goods and services are supplied within the internal market by economic operators to other economic operators and to public authorities on a deferred payment basis whereby the supplier gives its client time to pay the invoice, as agreed between parties, as set out in the supplier's invoice or as laid down by law.

(3) Many payments in commercial transactions between economic operators or between economic operators and public authorities are made later than agreed in the contract or laid down in the general commercial conditions. Although the goods are delivered or the services performed, many corresponding invoices are paid well after the deadline. Such late payment negatively affects liquidity and complicates the financial management of undertakings. It also affects their competitiveness and profitability when the creditor needs to obtain external financing because of late payment. The risk of such negative effects strongly increases in periods of economic downturn when access to financing is more difficult.

(4) Judicial claims related to late payment are already facilitated by Council Regulation (EC) No 44/2001 of 22 December 2000 on jurisdiction and the recognition and enforcement of judgments in civil and commercial matters, Regulation (EC) No 805/2004 of the European Parliament and of the Council of 21 April 2004 creating a European Enforcement Order for uncontested claims, Regulation (EC) No 1896/2006 of the European Parliament and of the Council of 12 December 2006 creating a European order for payment procedure and Regulation (EC) No 861/2007 of the European Parliament and of the Council of 11 July 2007 establishing a European Small Claims Procedure. However, in order to discourage late payment in commercial transactions, it is necessary to lay down complementary provisions.

(5) Undertakings should be able to trade throughout the internal market under conditions which ensure that transborder operations do not entail greater risks than domestic sales. Distortions of competition would ensue if substantially different rules applied to domestic and transborder operations.

(6) In its Communication of 25 June 2008 entitled " "Think Small First" — A "Small Business Act" for Europe", the Commission emphasised that small and medium-sized enterprises' (SMEs) access to finance should be facilitated and that a legal and business environment supportive of timely payments in commercial transactions should be developed. It should be noted that public authorities have a special responsibility in this regard. The criteria for the definition of SMEs are set out in Commission Recommendation 2003/361/EC of 6 May 2003 concerning the definition of micro, small and medium-sized enterprises.

(7) One of the priority actions of the Commission Communication of 26 November 2008 entitled "European Economic Recovery Plan" is the reduction of administrative burdens and the promotion of entrepreneurship by, inter alia, ensuring that, as a matter of principle, invoices, including to SMEs, for supplies and services are paid within 1 month to ease liquidity constraints.

(8) The scope of this Directive should be limited to payments made as remuneration for commercial transactions. This Directive should not regulate transactions with consumers, interest in connection with other payments, for instance payments under the laws on cheques and bills of exchange, or payments made as compensation for damages including payments from insurance companies. Furthermore, Member States should be able to exclude debts that are subject to insolvency proceedings, including proceedings aimed at debt restructuring.

(9) This Directive should regulate all commercial transactions irrespective of whether they are carried out between private or public undertakings or between undertakings and public authorities, given that public authorities handle a considerable volume of payments to undertakings. It should therefore also regulate all commercial transactions between main contractors and their suppliers and subcontractors.

PART IV   EUROPEAN PRIVATE LAW

(10) The fact that the liberal professions are covered by this Directive should not oblige Member States to treat them as undertakings or merchants for purposes outside the scope of this Directive.
(11) The delivery of goods and the provision of services for remuneration to which this Directive applies should also include the design and execution of public works and building and civil engineering works.
(12) Late payment constitutes a breach of contract which has been made financially attractive to debtors in most Member States by low or no interest rates charged on late payments and/or slow procedures for redress. A decisive shift to a culture of prompt payment, including one in which the exclusion of the right to charge interest should always be considered to be a grossly unfair contractual term or practice, is necessary to reverse this trend and to discourage late payment. Such a shift should also include the introduction of specific provisions on payment periods and on the compensation of creditors for the costs incurred, and, inter alia, that the exclusion of the right to compensation for recovery costs should be presumed to be grossly unfair.
(13) Accordingly, provision should be made for business-to-business contractual payment periods to be limited, as a general rule, to 60 calendar days. However, there may be circumstances in which undertakings require more extensive payment periods, for example when undertakings wish to grant trade credit to their customers. It should therefore remain possible for the parties to expressly agree on payment periods longer than 60 calendar days, provided, however, that such extension is not grossly unfair to the creditor.
(14) In the interest of consistency of Union legislation, the definition of "contracting authorities" in Directive 2004/17/EC of the European Parliament and of the Council of 31 March 2004 coordinating the procurement procedures of entities operating in the water, energy, transport and postal services sectors and in Directive 2004/18/EC of the European Parliament and of the Council of 31 March 2004 on the coordination of procedures for the award of public works contracts, public supply contracts and public services contracts should apply for the purposes of this Directive.
(15) Statutory interest due for late payment should be calculated on a daily basis as simple interest, in accordance with Regulation (EEC, Euratom) No 1182/71 of the Council of 3 June 1971 determining the rules applicable to periods, dates and time limits.
(16) This Directive should not oblige a creditor to claim interest for late payment. In the event of late payment, this Directive should allow a creditor to resort to charging interest for late payment without giving any prior notice of non-performance or other similar notice reminding the debtor of his obligation to pay.
(17) A debtor's payment should be regarded as late, for the purposes of entitlement to interest for late payment, where the creditor does not have the sum owed at his disposal on the due date provided that he has fulfilled his legal and contractual obligations.
(18) Invoices trigger requests for payment and are important documents in the chain of transactions for the supply of goods and services, inter alia, for determining payment deadlines. For the purposes of this Directive, Member States should promote systems that give legal certainty as regards the exact date of receipt of invoices by the debtors, including in the field of e-invoicing where the receipt of invoices could generate electronic evidence and which is partly governed by the provisions on invoicing contained in Council Directive 2006/112/EC of 28 November 2006 on the common system of value added tax.
(19) Fair compensation of creditors for the recovery costs incurred due to late payment is necessary to discourage late payment. Recovery costs should also include the recovery of administrative costs and compensation for internal costs incurred due to late payment for which this Directive should determine a fixed minimum sum which may be cumulated with interest for late payment. Compensation in the form of a fixed sum should aim at limiting the administrative and internal costs linked to the recovery. Compensation for the recovery costs should be determined without prejudice to national provisions according to which a national court may award compensation to the creditor for any additional damage regarding the debtor's late payment.
(20) In addition to an entitlement to payment of a fixed sum to cover internal recovery costs, creditors should also be entitled to reimbursement of the other recovery costs they incur as a result of late payment by a debtor. Such costs should include, in particular, those incurred by creditors in instructing a lawyer or employing a debt collection agency.
(21) This Directive should be without prejudice to the right of Member States to provide for fixed sums for compensation of recovery costs which are higher and therefore more favourable to the creditor, or to increase those sums, inter alia, in order to keep pace with inflation.
(22) This Directive should not prevent payments by instalments or staggered payments. However, each instalment or payment should be paid on the agreed terms and should be subject to the rules for late payment set out in this Directive.

EU: DIRECTIVE 2011/7 ON COMBATING LATE PAYMENTS (RECAST)

(23) As a general rule, public authorities benefit from more secure, predictable and continuous revenue streams than undertakings. In addition, many public authorities can obtain financing at more attractive conditions than undertakings. At the same time, public authorities depend less than undertakings on building stable commercial relationships for the achievement of their aims. Long payment periods and late payment by public authorities for goods and services lead to unjustified costs for undertakings. It is therefore appropriate to introduce specific rules as regards commercial transactions for the supply of goods or services by undertakings to public authorities, which should provide in particular for payment periods normally not exceeding 30 calendar days, unless otherwise expressly agreed in the contract and provided it is objectively justified in the light of the particular nature or features of the contract, and in any event not exceeding 60 calendar days.

(24) However, account should be taken of the specific situation of public authorities carrying out economic activities of an industrial or commercial nature by offering goods or services on the market as a public undertaking. For that purpose, Member States should be allowed, under certain conditions, to extend the statutory payment period up to a maximum of 60 calendar days.

(25) A particular cause for concern in connection with late payment is the situation of health services in a large number of Member States. Healthcare systems, as a fundamental part of Europe's social infrastructure, are often obliged to reconcile individual needs with the available finances, as the population of Europe ages, as expectations rise, and as medicine advances. All systems have to deal with the challenge of prioritising healthcare in a way that balances the needs of individual patients with the financial resources available. Member States should therefore be able to grant public entities providing healthcare a certain amount of flexibility in meeting their commitments. For that purpose, Member States should be allowed, under certain conditions, to extend the statutory payment period up to a maximum of 60 calendar days. Member States should, nonetheless, make every effort to ensure that payments in the healthcare sector are made within the statutory payment periods.

(26) In order not to jeopardise the achievement of the objective of this Directive, Member States should ensure that in commercial transactions the maximum duration of a procedure of acceptance or verification does not exceed, as a general rule, 30 calendar days. Nevertheless, it should be possible for a verification procedure to exceed 30 calendar days, for example in the case of particularly complex contracts, when expressly agreed in the contract and in any tender documents and if it is not grossly unfair to the creditor.

(27) The Union institutions are in a situation comparable to that of the public authorities of Member States with regard to their financing and commercial relationships. Council Regulation (EC, Euratom) No 1605/2002 of 25 June 2002 on the Financial Regulation applicable to the general budget of the European Communities specifies that the validation, authorisation and payment of expenditure by Union institutions must be completed within the time limits laid down in its implementing rules. Those implementing rules are currently set out in Commission Regulation (EC, Euratom) No 2342/2002 of 23 December 2002 laying down detailed rules for the implementation of Council Regulation (EC, Euratom) No 1605/2002 on the Financial Regulation applicable to the general budget of the European Communities, and specify the circumstances in which creditors which are paid late are entitled to receive default interest. In the context of the ongoing review of those Regulations, it should be ensured that the maximum time limits for payment by the Union institutions are aligned with statutory periods applicable to public authorities in accordance with this Directive.

(28) This Directive should prohibit abuse of freedom of contract to the disadvantage of the creditor. As a result, where a term in a contract or a practice relating to the date or period for payment, the rate of interest for late payment or the compensation for recovery costs is not justified on the grounds of the terms granted to the debtor, or it mainly serves the purpose of procuring the debtor additional liquidity at the expense of the creditor, it may be regarded as constituting such an abuse. For that purpose, and in accordance with the academic "Draft Common Frame of Reference", any contractual term or practice which grossly deviates from good commercial practice and is contrary to good faith and fair dealing should be regarded as unfair to the creditor. In particular, the outright exclusion of the right to charge interest should always be considered as grossly unfair, whereas the exclusion of the right to compensation for recovery costs should be presumed to be grossly unfair. This Directive should not affect national provisions relating to the way contracts are concluded or regulating the validity of contractual terms which are unfair to the debtor.

(29) In the context of enhanced efforts to prevent the abuse of freedom of contract to the detriment of creditors, organisations officially recognised as representing undertakings and organisations with a legitimate interest in representing undertakings should be able to take action before national courts or administrative bodies in order to prevent the continued use of contract terms or practices which are grossly unfair to the creditor.

(30) In order to contribute to the achievement of the objective of this Directive, Member States should

foster the spread of good practices, including by encouraging the publication of a list of prompt payers.

(31) It is desirable to ensure that creditors are in a position to exercise a retention of title clause on a non-discriminatory basis throughout the Union, if the retention of title clause is valid under the applicable national provisions designated by private international law.

(32) This Directive only defines the term "enforceable title" but should not regulate the various procedures for forced execution of such a title or the conditions under which forced execution of such a title can be stopped or suspended.

(33) The consequences of late payment can be dissuasive only if they are accompanied by procedures for redress which are rapid and effective for the creditor. In accordance with the principle of non-discrimination set out in Article 18 of the Treaty on the Functioning of the European Union, those procedures should be available to all creditors who are established in the Union.

(34) In order to facilitate compliance with the provisions of this Directive, Member States should encourage recourse to mediation or other means of alternative dispute resolution. Directive 2008/52/EC of the European Parliament and of the Council of 21 May 2008 on certain aspects of mediation in civil and commercial matters already sets a framework for systems of mediation at Union level, especially for cross-border disputes, without preventing its application to internal mediation systems. Member States should also encourage interested parties to draw up voluntary codes of conduct aimed, in particular, at contributing to the implementation of this Directive.

(35) It is necessary to ensure that the recovery procedures for unchallenged claims related to late payment in commercial transactions be completed within a short period of time, including through an expedited procedure and irrespective of the amount of the debt.

(36) Since the objective of this Directive, namely combating late payment in the internal market, cannot be sufficiently achieved by the Member States and can, therefore, by reason of its scale and effect, be better achieved at the Union level, the Union may adopt measures, in accordance with the principle of subsidiarity as set out in Article 5 of the Treaty on European Union. In accordance with the principle of proportionality, as set out in that Article, this Directive does not go beyond what is necessary in order to achieve that objective.

(37) The obligation to transpose this Directive into national law should be confined to those provisions which represent a substantive change as compared with Directive 2000/35/EC. The obligation to transpose the provisions which are unchanged arises under that Directive.

(38) This Directive should be without prejudice to the obligations of the Member States relating to the time limits for transposition into national law and application of Directive 2000/35/EC.

(39) In accordance with point 34 of the Interinstitutional Agreement on better law-making, Member States are encouraged to draw up, for themselves and in the interest of the Union, their own tables which will, as far as possible, illustrate the correlation between this Directive and their transposition measures, and to make those tables public,

HAVE ADOPTED THIS DIRECTIVE:

Article 1. (1) The aim of this Directive is to combat late payment in commercial transactions, in order to ensure the proper functioning of the internal market, thereby fostering the competitiveness of undertakings and in particular of SMEs.

(2) This Directive shall apply to all payments made as remuneration for commercial transactions.

(3) Member States may exclude debts that are subject to insolvency proceedings instituted against the debtor, including proceedings aimed at debt restructuring.

Article 2. For the purposes of this Directive, the following definitions shall apply:

(1) "commercial transactions" means transactions between undertakings or between undertakings and public authorities which lead to the delivery of goods or the provision of services for remuneration;

(2) "public authority" means any contracting authority, as defined in point (a) of Article 2(1) of Directive 2004/17/EC and in Article 1(9) of Directive 2004/18/EC, regardless of the subject or value of the contract;

(3) "undertaking" means any organisation, other than a public authority, acting in the course of its independent economic or professional activity, even where that activity is carried out by a single person;

(4) "late payment" means payment not made within the contractual or statutory period of payment and where the conditions laid down in Article 3(1) or Article 4(1) are satisfied;

(5) "interest for late payment" means statutory interest for late payment or interest at a rate agreed upon between undertakings, subject to Article 7;

(6) "statutory interest for late payment" means simple interest for late payment at a rate which is equal to the sum of the reference rate and at least eight percentage points;

(7) "reference rate" means either of the following:
(a) for a Member State whose currency is the euro, either:
(i) the interest rate applied by the European Central Bank to its most recent main refinancing operations; or
(ii) the marginal interest rate resulting from variable-rate tender procedures for the most recent main refinancing operations of the European Central Bank;
(b) for a Member State whose currency is not the euro, the equivalent rate set by its national central bank;
(8) "amount due" means the principal sum which should have been paid within the contractual or statutory period of payment, including the applicable taxes, duties, levies or charges specified in the invoice or the equivalent request for payment;
(9) "retention of title" means the contractual agreement according to which the seller retains title to the goods in question until the price has been paid in full;
(10) "enforceable title" means any decision, judgment or order for payment issued by a court or other competent authority, including those that are provisionally enforceable, whether for immediate payment or payment by instalments, which permits the creditor to have his claim against the debtor collected by means of forced execution.

Article 3. (1) Member States shall ensure that, in commercial transactions between undertakings, the creditor is entitled to interest for late payment without the necessity of a reminder, where the following conditions are satisfied:
(a) the creditor has fulfilled its contractual and legal obligations; and
(b) the creditor has not received the amount due on time, unless the debtor is not responsible for the delay.
(2) Member States shall ensure that the applicable reference rate:
(a) for the first semester of the year concerned shall be the rate in force on 1 January of that year;
(b) for the second semester of the year concerned shall be the rate in force on 1 July of that year.
(3) Where the conditions set out in paragraph (1) are satisfied, Member States shall ensure the following:
(a) that the creditor is entitled to interest for late payment from the day following the date or the end of the period for payment fixed in the contract;
(b) where the date or period for payment is not fixed in the contract, that the creditor is entitled to interest for late payment upon the expiry of any of the following time limits:
(i) 30 calendar days following the date of receipt by the debtor of the invoice or an equivalent request for payment;
(ii) where the date of the receipt of the invoice or the equivalent request for payment is uncertain, 30 calendar days after the date of receipt of the goods or services;
(iii) where the debtor receives the invoice or the equivalent request for payment earlier than the goods or the services, 30 calendar days after the date of the receipt of the goods or services;
(iv) where a procedure of acceptance or verification, by which the conformity of the goods or services with the contract is to be ascertained, is provided for by statute or in the contract and if the debtor receives the invoice or the equivalent request for payment earlier or on the date on which such acceptance or verification takes place, 30 calendar days after that date.
(4) Where a procedure of acceptance or verification, by which the conformity of the goods or services with the contract is to be ascertained, is provided for, Member States shall ensure that the maximum duration of that procedure does not exceed 30 calendar days from the date of receipt of the goods or services, unless otherwise expressly agreed in the contract and provided it is not grossly unfair to the creditor within the meaning of Article 7.
(5) Member States shall ensure that the period for payment fixed in the contract does not exceed 60 calendar days, unless otherwise expressly agreed in the contract and provided it is not grossly unfair to the creditor within the meaning of Article 7.

Article 4. (1) Member States shall ensure that, in commercial transactions where the debtor is a public authority, the creditor is entitled upon expiry of the period defined in paragraphs 3, 4 or 6 to statutory interest for late payment, without the necessity of a reminder, where the following conditions are satisfied:
(a) the creditor has fulfilled its contractual and legal obligations; and
(b) the creditor has not received the amount due on time, unless the debtor is not responsible for the delay.
(2) Member States shall ensure that the applicable reference rate:
(a) for the first semester of the year concerned shall be the rate in force on 1 January of that year;

(b) for the second semester of the year concerned shall be the rate in force on 1 July of that year.
(3) Member States shall ensure that in commercial transactions where the debtor is a public authority:
(a) the period for payment does not exceed any of the following time limits:
(i) 30 calendar days following the date of receipt by the debtor of the invoice or an equivalent request for payment;
(ii) where the date of receipt of the invoice or the equivalent request for payment is uncertain, 30 calendar days after the date of the receipt of the goods or services;
(iii) where the debtor receives the invoice or the equivalent request for payment earlier than the goods or the services, 30 calendar days after the date of the receipt of the goods or services;
(iv) where a procedure of acceptance or verification, by which the conformity of the goods or services with the contract is to be ascertained, is provided for by statute or in the contract and if the debtor receives the invoice or the equivalent request for payment earlier or on the date on which such acceptance or verification takes place, 30 calendar days after that date;
(b) the date of receipt of the invoice is not subject to a contractual agreement between debtor and creditor.
(4) Member States may extend the time limits referred to in point (a) of paragraph (3) up to a maximum of 60 calendar days for:
(a) any public authority which carries out economic activities of an industrial or commercial nature by offering goods or services on the market and which is subject, as a public undertaking, to the transparency requirements laid down in Commission Directive 2006/111/EC of 16 November 2006 on the transparency of financial relations between Member States and public undertakings as well as on financial transparency within certain undertakings;
(b) public entities providing healthcare which are duly recognised for that purpose.
If a Member State decides to extend the time limits in accordance with this paragraph, it shall send a report on such extension to the Commission by 16 March 2018.
On that basis, the Commission shall submit a report to the European Parliament and the Council indicating which Member States have extended the time limits in accordance with this paragraph and taking into account the impact on the functioning of the internal market, in particular on SMEs. That report shall be accompanied by any appropriate proposals.
(5) Member States shall ensure that the maximum duration of a procedure of acceptance or verification referred to in point (iv) of point (a) of paragraph (3) does not exceed 30 calendar days from the date of receipt of the goods or services, unless otherwise expressly agreed in the contract and any tender documents and provided it is not grossly unfair to the creditor within the meaning of Article 7.
(6) Member States shall ensure that the period for payment fixed in the contract does not exceed the time limits provided for in paragraph (3), unless otherwise expressly agreed in the contract and provided it is objectively justified in the light of the particular nature or features of the contract, and that it in any event does not exceed 60 calendar days.

Article 5. This Directive shall be without prejudice to the ability of parties to agree, subject to the relevant provisions of applicable national law, on payment schedules providing for instalments. In such cases, where any of the instalments is not paid by the agreed date, interest and compensation provided for in this Directive shall be calculated solely on the basis of overdue amounts.

Article 6. (1) Member States shall ensure that, where interest for late payment becomes payable in commercial transactions in accordance with Article 3 or 4, the creditor is entitled to obtain from the debtor, as a minimum, a fixed sum of EUR 40.
(2) Member States shall ensure that the fixed sum referred to in paragraph (1) is payable without the necessity of a reminder and as compensation for the creditor's own recovery costs.
(3) The creditor shall, in addition to the fixed sum referred to in paragraph (1), be entitled to obtain reasonable compensation from the debtor for any recovery costs exceeding that fixed sum and incurred due to the debtor's late payment. This could include expenses incurred, inter alia, in instructing a lawyer or employing a debt collection agency.

Article 7. (1) Member States shall provide that a contractual term or a practice relating to the date or period for payment, the rate of interest for late payment or the compensation for recovery costs is either unenforceable or gives rise to a claim for damages if it is grossly unfair to the creditor.
In determining whether a contractual term or a practice is grossly unfair to the creditor, within the meaning of the first subparagraph, all circumstances of the case shall be considered, including:
(a) any gross deviation from good commercial practice, contrary to good faith and fair dealing;
(b) the nature of the product or the service; and
(c) whether the debtor has any objective reason to deviate from the statutory rate of interest for late

payment, from the payment period as referred to in Article 3(5), point (a) of Article 4(3), Article 4(4) and Article 4(6) or from the fixed sum as referred to in Article 6(1).
(2) For the purpose of paragraph (1), a contractual term or a practice which excludes interest for late payment shall be considered as grossly unfair.
(3) For the purpose of paragraph (1), a contractual term or a practice which excludes compensation for recovery costs as referred to in Article 6 shall be presumed to be grossly unfair.
(4) Member States shall ensure that, in the interests of creditors and competitors, adequate and effective means exist to prevent the continued use of contractual terms and practices which are grossly unfair within the meaning of paragraph (1).
(5) The means referred to in paragraph (4) shall include provisions whereby organisations officially recognised as representing undertakings, or organisations with a legitimate interest in representing undertakings may take action according to the applicable national law before the courts or before competent administrative bodies on the grounds that contractual terms or practices are grossly unfair within the meaning of paragraph (1), so that they can apply appropriate and effective means to prevent their continued use.

Article 8. (1) Member States shall ensure transparency regarding the rights and obligations stemming from this Directive, including by making publicly available the applicable rate of statutory interest for late payment.
(2) The Commission shall make publicly available on the Internet details of the current statutory rates of interest which apply in all the Member States in the event of late payment in commercial transactions.
(3) Member States shall, where appropriate, use professional publications, promotion campaigns or any other functional means to increase awareness of the remedies for late payment among undertakings.
(4) Member States may encourage the establishment of prompt payment codes which set out clearly defined payment time limits and a proper process for dealing with any payments that are in dispute, or any other initiatives that tackle the crucial issue of late payment and contribute to developing a culture of prompt payment which supports the objective of this Directive.

Article 9. (1) Member States shall provide in conformity with the applicable national provisions designated by private international law that the seller retains title to goods until they are fully paid for if a retention of title clause has been expressly agreed between the buyer and the seller before the delivery of the goods.
(2) Member States may adopt or retain provisions dealing with down payments already made by the debtor.

Article 10. (1) Member States shall ensure that an enforceable title can be obtained, including through an expedited procedure and irrespective of the amount of the debt, normally within 90 calendar days of the lodging of the creditor's action or application at the court or other competent authority, provided that the debt or aspects of the procedure are not disputed. Member States shall carry out this duty in accordance with their respective national laws, regulations and administrative provisions.
(2) National laws, regulations and administrative provisions shall apply the same conditions for all creditors who are established in the Union.
(3) When calculating the period referred to in paragraph (1), the following shall not be taken into account:
(a) periods for service of documents;
(b) any delays caused by the creditor, such as periods devoted to correcting applications.
(4) This Article shall be without prejudice to the provisions of Regulation (EC) No 1896/2006.

Article 11. By 16 March 2016, the Commission shall submit a report to the European Parliament and the Council on the implementation of this Directive. The report shall be accompanied by any appropriate proposals.

Article 12. (1) Member States shall bring into force the laws, regulations and administrative provisions necessary to comply with Articles 1 to 8 and 10 by 16 March 2013. They shall forthwith communicate to the Commission the text of those provisions.
When Member States adopt those measures, they shall contain a reference to this Directive or shall be accompanied by such reference on the occasion of their official publication. They shall also include a statement that references in existing laws, regulations and administrative provisions to the repealed Directive shall be construed as references to this Directive. The methods of making such reference and the formulation of such statement shall be laid down by Member States.

(2) Member States shall communicate to the Commission the text of the main provisions of national law which they adopt in the field covered by this Directive.

(3) Member States may maintain or bring into force provisions which are more favourable to the creditor than the provisions necessary to comply with this Directive.

(4) In transposing the Directive, Member States shall decide whether to exclude contracts concluded before 16 March 2013.

Article 13. Directive 2000/35/EC is repealed with effect from 16 March 2013, without prejudice to the obligations of the Member States relating to the time limit for its transposition into national law and its application. However, it shall remain applicable to contracts concluded before that date to which this Directive does not apply pursuant to Article 12(4).

References to the repealed Directive shall be construed as references to this Directive and be read in accordance with the correlation table set out in the Annex.

Article 14. This Directive shall enter into force on the 20th day following its publication in the Official Journal of the European Union.

Article 15. This Directive is addressed to the Member States.

[The annex is omitted.]

EU: DIRECTIVE 2002/47 ON FINANCIAL COLLATERAL ARRANGEMENTS

Directive 2002/47/EC of the European Parliament and of the Council of 6 June 2002 on financial collateral arrangements (OJL 168/43, 27.06.2002, pp.43-50) [footnotes omitted].

THE EUROPEAN PARLIAMENT AND THE COUNCIL OF THE EUROPEAN UNION,
Having regard to the Treaty establishing the European Community, and in particular Article 95 thereof,
Having regard to the proposal from the Commission,
Having regard to the opinion of the European Central Bank,
Having regard to the opinion of the Economic and Social Committee,
Acting in accordance with the procedure laid down in Article 251 of the Treaty,
Whereas: (1) Directive 98/26/EC of the European Parliament and of the Council of 19 May 1998 on settlement finality in payment and securities settlement systems constituted a milestone in establishing a sound legal framework for payment and securities settlement systems. Implementation of that Directive has demonstrated the importance of limiting systemic risk inherent in such systems stemming from the different influence of several jurisdictions, and the benefits of common rules in relation to collateral constituted to such systems.
(2) In its communication of 11 May 1999 to the European Parliament and to the Council on financial services:
implementing the framework for financial markets: action plan, the Commission undertook, after consultation with market experts and national authorities, to work on further proposals for legislative action on collateral urging further progress in the field of collateral, beyond Directive 98/26/EC.
(3) A Community regime should be created for the provision of securities and cash as collateral under both security interest and title transfer structures including repurchase agreements (repos). This will contribute to the integration and cost-efficiency of the financial market as well as to the stability of the financial system in the Community, thereby supporting the freedom to provide services and the free movement of capital in the single market in financial services. This Directive focuses on bilateral financial collateral arrangements.
(4) This Directive is adopted in a European legal context which consists in particular of the said Directive 98/26/EC as well as Directive 2001/24/EC of the European Parliament and of the Council of 4 April 2001 on the reorganisation and winding up of credit institutions, Directive 2001/17/EC of the European Parliament and of the Council of 19 March 2001 on the reorganisation and winding-up of insurance undertakings and Council Regulation (EC) No 1346/2000 of 29 May 2000 on insolvency proceedings. This Directive is in line with the general pattern of these previous legal acts and is not opposed to it. Indeed, this Directive complements these existing legal acts by dealing with further issues and going beyond them in connection with particular matters already dealt with by these legal acts.
(5) In order to improve the legal certainty of financial collateral arrangements, Member States should ensure that certain provisions of insolvency law do not apply to such arrangements, in particular, those that would inhibit the effective realisation of financial collateral or cast doubt on the validity of current techniques such as bilateral close-out netting, the provision of additional collateral in the form of top-up collateral and substitution of collateral.
(6) This Directive does not address rights which any person may have in respect of assets provided as financial collateral, and which arise otherwise than under the terms of the financial collateral arrangement and otherwise than on the basis of any legal provision or rule of law arising by reason of the commencement or continuation of winding-up proceedings or reorganisation measures, such as restitution arising from mistake, error or lack of capacity.
(7) The principle in Directive 98/26/EC, whereby the law applicable to book entry securities provided as collateral is the law of the jurisdiction where the relevant register, account or centralised deposit system is located, should be extended in order to create legal certainty regarding the use of such securities held in a cross-border context and used as financial collateral under the scope of this Directive.
(8) The lex rei sitae rule, according to which the applicable law for determining whether a financial collateral arrangement is properly perfected and therefore good against third parties is the law of the country where the financial collateral is located, is currently recognised by all Member States. Without affecting the application of this Directive to directly-held securities, the location of book entry securities provided as financial collateral and held through one or more intermediaries should be determined. If the collateral taker has a valid and effective collateral arrangement according to the governing law of the country in which the relevant account is maintained, then the validity against any competing title or interest and the enforceability of the collateral should be governed solely by the law of that country, thus preventing legal uncertainty as a result of other unforeseen legislation.

(9) In order to limit the administrative burdens for parties using financial collateral under the scope of this Directive, the only perfection requirement which national law may impose in respect of financial collateral should be that the financial collateral is delivered, transferred, held, registered or otherwise designated so as to be in the possession or under the control of the collateral taker or of a person acting on the collateral taker's behalf while not excluding collateral techniques where the collateral provider is allowed to substitute collateral or to withdraw excess collateral.

(10) For the same reasons, the creation, validity, perfection, enforceability or admissibility in evidence of a financial collateral arrangement, or the provision of financial collateral under a financial collateral arrangement, should not be made dependent on the performance of any formal act such as the execution of any document in a specific form or in a particular manner, the making of any filing with an official or public body or registration in a public register, advertisement in a newspaper or journal, in an official register or publication or in any other matter, notification to a public officer or the provision of evidence in a particular form as to the date of execution of a document or instrument, the amount of the relevant financial obligations or any other matter. This Directive must however provide a balance between market efficiency and the safety of the parties to the arrangement and third parties, thereby avoiding inter alia the risk of fraud. This balance should be achieved through the scope of this Directive covering only those financial collateral arrangements which provide for some form of dispossession, i.e. the provision of the financial collateral, and where the provision of the financial collateral can be evidenced in writing or in a durable medium, ensuring thereby the traceability of that collateral. For the purpose of this Directive, acts required under the law of a Member State as conditions for transferring or creating a security interest on financial instruments, other than book entry securities, such as endorsement in the case of instruments to order, or recording on the issuer's register in the case of registered instruments, should not be considered as formal acts.

(11) Moreover, this Directive should protect only financial collateral arrangements which can be evidenced. Such evidence can be given in writing or in any other legally enforceable manner provided by the law which is applicable to the financial collateral arrangement.

(12) The simplification of the use of financial collateral through the limitation of administrative burdens promotes the efficiency of the cross-border operations of the European Central Bank and the national central banks of Member States participating in the economic and monetary union, necessary for the implementation of the common monetary policy. Furthermore, the provision of limited protection of financial collateral arrangements from some rules of insolvency law in addition supports the wider aspect of the common monetary policy, where the participants in the money market balance the overall amount of liquidity in the market among themselves, by cross-border transactions backed by collateral.

(13) This Directive seeks to protect the validity of financial collateral arrangements which are based upon the transfer of the full ownership of the financial collateral, such as by eliminating the so-called re-characterisation of such financial collateral arrangements (including repurchase agreements) as security interests.

(14) The enforceability of bilateral close-out netting should be protected, not only as an enforcement mechanism for title transfer financial collateral arrangements including repurchase agreements but more widely, where close-out netting forms part of a financial collateral arrangement. Sound risk management practices commonly used in the financial market should be protected by enabling participants to manage and reduce their credit exposures arising from all kinds of financial transactions on a net basis, where the credit exposure is calculated by combining the estimated current exposures under all outstanding transactions with a counterparty, setting off reciprocal items to produce a single aggregated amount that is compared with the current value of the collateral.

(15) This Directive should be without prejudice to any restrictions or requirements under national law on bringing into account claims, on obligations to set-off, or on netting, for example relating to their reciprocity or the fact that they have been concluded prior to when the collateral taker knew or ought to have known of the commencement (or of any mandatory legal act leading to the commencement) of winding-up proceedings or reorganisation measures in respect of the collateral provider.

(16) The sound market practice favoured by regulators whereby participants in the financial market use top-up financial collateral arrangements to manage and limit their credit risk to each other by mark-to-market calculations of the current market value of the credit exposure and the value of the financial collateral and accordingly ask for top-up financial collateral or return the surplus of financial collateral should be protected against certain automatic avoidance rules. The same applies to the possibility of substituting for assets provided as financial collateral other assets of the same value. The intention is merely that the provision of top-up or substitution financial collateral cannot be questioned on the sole basis that the relevant financial obligations existed before that financial collateral was provided, or that the financial collateral was provided during a prescribed period.

EU: DIRECTIVE 2002/47 ON FINANCIAL COLLATERAL ARRANGEMENTS

However, this does not prejudice the possibility of questioning under national law the financial collateral arrangement and the provision of financial collateral as part of the initial provision, top-up or substitution of financial collateral, for example where this has been intentionally done to the detriment of the other creditors (this covers inter alia actions based on fraud or similar avoidance rules which may apply in a prescribed period).

(17) This Directive provides for rapid and non-formalistic enforcement procedures in order to safeguard financial stability and limit contagion effects in case of a default of a party to a financial collateral arrangement. However, this Directive balances the latter objectives with the protection of the collateral provider and third parties by explicitly confirming the possibility for Member States to keep or introduce in their national legislation an a posteriori control which the Courts can exercise in relation to the realisation or valuation of financial collateral and the calculation of the relevant financial obligations. Such control should allow for the judicial authorities to verify that the realisation or valuation has been conducted in a commercially reasonable manner.

(18) It should be possible to provide cash as collateral under both title transfer and secured structures respectively protected by the recognition of netting or by the pledge of cash collateral. Cash refers only to money which is represented by a credit to an account, or similar claims on repayment of money (such as money market deposits), thus explicitly excluding banknotes.

(19) This Directive provides for a right of use in case of security financial collateral arrangements, which increases liquidity in the financial market stemming from such reuse of 'pledged' securities. This reuse however should be without prejudice to national legislation about separation of assets and unfair treatment of creditors.

(20) This Directive does not prejudice the operation and effect of the contractual terms of financial instruments provided as financial collateral, such as rights and obligations and other conditions contained in the terms of issue and any other rights and obligations and other conditions which apply between the issuers and holders of such instruments.

(21) This Act complies with the fundamental rights and follows the principles laid down in particular in the Charter of Fundamental Rights of the European Union.

(22) Since the objective of the proposed action, namely to create a minimum regime relating to the use of financial collateral, cannot be sufficiently achieved by the Member States and can therefore, by reason of the scale and effects of the action, be better achieved at Community level, the Community may adopt measures, in accordance with the principle of subsidiarity as set out in Article 5 of the Treaty. In accordance with the principle of proportionality, as set out in that Article, this Directive does not go beyond what is necessary in order to achieve that objective,

HAVE ADOPTED THIS DIRECTIVE:

Article 1. (1) This Directive lays down a Community regime applicable to financial collateral arrangements which satisfy the requirements set out in paragraphs 2 and 5 and to financial collateral in accordance with the conditions set out in paragraphs 4 and 5.

(2) The collateral taker and the collateral provider must each belong to one of the following categories:

(a) a public authority (excluding publicly guaranteed undertakings unless they fall under points (b) to (e)) including:

(i) public sector bodies of Member States charged with or intervening in the management of public debt, and

(ii) public sector bodies of Member States authorised to hold accounts for customers;

(b) a central bank, the European Central Bank, the Bank for International Settlements, a multilateral development bank as defined in Article 1(19) of Directive 2000/12/EC of the European Parliament and of the Council of 20 March 2000 relating to the taking up and pursuit of the business of credit institutions (1), the International Monetary Fund and the European Investment Bank;

(c) a financial institution subject to prudential supervision including:

(i) a credit institution as defined in Article 1(1) of Directive 2000/12/EC, including the institutions listed in Article 2(3) of that Directive;

(ii) an investment firm as defined in Article 1(2) of Council Directive 93/22/EEC of 10 May 1993 on investment services in the securities field (1);

(iii) a financial institution as defined in Article 1(5) of Directive 2000/12/EC;

(iv) an insurance undertaking as defined in Article 1(a) of Council Directive 92/49/EEC of 18 June 1992 on the coordination of laws, regulations and administrative provisions relating to direct insurance other than life assurance (2) and a life assurance undertaking as defined in Article 1(a) of Council Directive 92/96/EEC of 10 November 1992 on the coordination of laws, regulations and administrative provisions relating to direct life assurance (3);

(v) an undertaking for collective investment in transferable securities (UCITS) as defined in Article 1(2) of Council Directive 85/611/EEC of 20 December 1985 on the coordination of laws, regulations and administrative provisions relating to undertakings for collective investment in transferable securities (UCITS) (4);

(vi) a management company as defined in Article 1a(2) of Directive 85/611/EEC;

(d) a central counterparty, settlement agent or clearing house, as defined respectively in Article 2(c), (d) and (e) of Directive 98/26/EC, including similar institutions regulated under national law acting in the futures, options and derivatives markets to the extent not covered by that Directive, and a person, other than a natural person, who acts in a trust or representative capacity on behalf of any one or more persons that includes any bondholders or holders of other forms of securitised debt or any institution as defined in points (a) to (d);

(e) a person other than a natural person, including unincorporated firms and partnerships, provided that the other party is an institution as defined in points (a) to (d).

(3) Member States may exclude from the scope of this Directive financial collateral arrangements where one of the parties is a person mentioned in paragraph (2)(e). If they make use of this option Member States shall inform the Commission which shall inform the other Member States thereof.

(4) (a) The financial collateral to be provided must consist of cash or financial instruments.

(b) Member States may exclude from the scope of this Directive financial collateral consisting of the collateral provider's own shares, shares in affiliated undertakings within the meaning of seventh Council Directive 83/349/EEC of 13 June 1983 on consolidated accounts (5), and shares in undertakings whose exclusive purpose is to own means of production that are essential for the collateral provider's business or to own real property.

(5) This Directive applies to financial collateral once it has been provided and if that provision can be evidenced in writing.

The evidencing of the provision of financial collateral must allow for the identification of the financial collateral to which it applies. For this purpose, it is sufficient to prove that the book entry securities collateral has been credited to, or forms a credit in, the relevant account and that the cash collateral has been credited to, or forms a credit in, a designated account. This Directive applies to financial collateral arrangements if that arrangement can be evidenced in writing or in a legally equivalent manner.

Article 2. (1) For the purpose of this Directive:

(a) 'financial collateral arrangement' means a title transfer financial collateral arrangement or a security financial collateral arrangement whether or not these are covered by a master agreement or general terms and conditions;

(b) 'title transfer financial collateral arrangement' means an arrangement, including repurchase agreements, under which a collateral provider transfers full ownership of financial collateral to a collateral taker for the purpose of securing or otherwise covering the performance of relevant financial obligations;

(c) 'security financial collateral arrangement' means an arrangement under which a collateral provider provides financial collateral by way of security in favour of, or to, a collateral taker, and where the full ownership of the financial collateral remains with the collateral provider when the security right is established;

(d) 'cash' means money credited to an account in any currency, or similar claims for the repayment of money, such as money market deposits;

(e) 'financial instruments' means shares in companies and other securities equivalent to shares in companies and bonds and other forms of debt instruments if these are negotiable on the capital market, and any other securities which are normally dealt in and which give the right to acquire any such shares, bonds or other securities by subscription, purchase or exchange or which give rise to a cash settlement (excluding instruments of payment), including units in collective investment undertakings, money market instruments and claims relating to or rights in or in respect of any of the foregoing;

(f) 'relevant financial obligations' means the obligations which are secured by a financial collateral arrangement and which give a right to cash settlement and/or delivery of financial instruments. Relevant financial obligations may consist of or include:

(i) present or future, actual or contingent or prospective obligations (including such obligations arising under a master agreement or similar arrangement);

(ii) obligations owed to the collateral taker by a person other than the collateral provider; or

(iii) obligations of a specified class or kind arising from time to time;

(g) 'book entry securities collateral' means financial collateral provided under a financial collateral

arrangement which consists of financial instruments, title to which is evidenced by entries in a register or account maintained by or on behalf of an intermediary;
(h) 'relevant account' means in relation to book entry securities collateral which is subject to a financial collateral arrangement, the register or account — which may be maintained by the collateral taker — in which the entries are made by which that book entry securities collateral is provided to the collateral taker;
(i) 'equivalent collateral':
(i) in relation to cash, means a payment of the same amount and in the same currency;
(ii) in relation to financial instruments, means financial instruments of the same issuer or debtor, forming part of the same issue or class and of the same nominal amount, currency and description or, where a financial collateral arrangement provides for the transfer of other assets following the occurrence of any event relating to or affecting any financial instruments provided as financial collateral, those other assets;
(j) 'winding-up proceedings' means collective proceedings involving realisation of the assets and distribution of the proceeds among the creditors, shareholders or members as appropriate, which involve any intervention by administrative or judicial authorities, including where the collective proceedings are terminated by a composition or other analogous measure, whether or not they are founded on insolvency or are voluntary or compulsory;
(k) 'reorganisation measures' means measures which involve any intervention by administrative or judicial authorities which are intended to preserve or restore the financial situation and which affect pre-existing rights of third parties, including but not limited to measures involving a suspension of payments, suspension of enforcement measures or reduction of claims;
(l) 'enforcement event' means an event of default or any similar event as agreed between the parties on the occurrence of which, under the terms of a financial collateral arrangement or by operation of law, the collateral taker is entitled to realise or appropriate financial collateral or a close-out netting provision comes into effect;
(m) 'right of use' means the right of the collateral taker to use and dispose of financial collateral provided under a security financial collateral arrangement as the owner of it in accordance with the terms of the security financial collateral arrangement;
(n) 'close-out netting provision' means a provision of a financial collateral arrangement, or of an arrangement of which a financial collateral arrangement forms part, or, in the absence of any such provision, any statutory rule by which, on the occurrence of an enforcement event, whether through the operation of netting or set-off or otherwise:
(i) the obligations of the parties are accelerated so as to be immediately due and expressed as an obligation to pay an amount representing their estimated current value, or are terminated and replaced by an obligation to pay such an amount; and/or
(ii) an account is taken of what is due from each party to the other in respect of such obligations, and a net sum equal to the balance of the account is payable by the party from whom the larger amount is due to the other party.
(2) References in this Directive to financial collateral being 'provided', or to the 'provision' of financial collateral, are to the financial collateral being delivered, transferred, held, registered or otherwise designated so as to be in the possession or under the control of the collateral taker or of a person acting on the collateral taker's behalf. Any right of substitution or to withdraw excess financial collateral in favour of the collateral provider shall not prejudice the financial collateral having been provided to the collateral taker as mentioned in this Directive.
(3) References in this Directive to 'writing' include recording by electronic means and any other durable medium.

Article 3. (1) Member States shall not require that the creation, validity, perfection, enforceability or admissibility in evidence of a financial collateral arrangement or the provision of financial collateral under a financial collateral arrangement be dependent on the performance of any formal act.
(2) Paragraph 1 is without prejudice to the application of this Directive to financial collateral only once it has been provided and if that provision can be evidenced in writing and where the financial collateral arrangement can be evidenced in writing or in a legally equivalent manner.

Article 4. (1) Member States shall ensure that on the occurrence of an enforcement event, the collateral taker shall be able to realise in the following manners, any financial collateral provided under, and subject to the terms agreed in, a security financial collateral arrangement:
(a) financial instruments by sale or appropriation and by setting off their value against, or applying their value in discharge of, the relevant financial obligations;
(b) cash by setting off the amount against or applying it in discharge of the relevant financial obligations.

PART IV   EUROPEAN PRIVATE LAW

(2) Appropriation is possible only if:
(a) this has been agreed by the parties in the security financial collateral arrangement; and
(b) the parties have agreed in the security financial collateral arrangement on the valuation of the financial instruments.
(3) Member States which do not allow appropriation on 27 June 2002 are not obliged to recognise it. If they make use of this option, Member States shall inform the Commission which in turn shall inform the other Member States thereof.
(4) The manners of realising the financial collateral referred to in paragraph (1) shall, subject to the terms agreed in the security financial collateral arrangement, be without any requirement to the effect that:
(a) prior notice of the intention to realise must have been given;
(b) the terms of the realisation be approved by any court, public officer or other person;
(c) the realisation be conducted by public auction or in any other prescribed manner; or
(d) any additional time period must have elapsed.
(5) Member States shall ensure that a financial collateral arrangement can take effect in accordance with its terms notwithstanding the commencement or continuation of winding-up proceedings or reorganisation measures in respect of the collateral provider or collateral taker.
(6) This Article and Articles 5, 6 and 7 shall be without prejudice to any requirements under national law to the effect that the realisation or valuation of financial collateral and the calculation of the relevant financial obligations must be conducted in a commercially reasonable manner.

Article 5. (1) If and to the extent that the terms of a security financial collateral arrangement so provide, Member States shall ensure that the collateral taker is entitled to exercise a right of use in relation to financial collateral provided under the security financial collateral arrangement.
(2) Where a collateral taker exercises a right of use, he thereby incurs an obligation to transfer equivalent collateral to replace the original financial collateral at the latest on the due date for the performance of the relevant financial obligations covered by the security financial collateral arrangement. Alternatively, the collateral taker shall, on the due date for the performance of the relevant financial obligations, either transfer equivalent collateral, or, if and to the extent that the terms of a security financial collateral arrangement so provide, set off the value of the equivalent collateral against or apply it in discharge of the relevant financial obligations.
(3) The equivalent collateral transferred in discharge of an obligation as described in paragraph (2), first subparagraph, shall be subject to the same security financial collateral agreement to which the original financial collateral was subject and shall be treated as having been provided under the security financial collateral arrangement at the same time as the original financial collateral was first provided.
(4) Member States shall ensure that the use of financial collateral by the collateral taker according to this Article does not render invalid or unenforceable the rights of the collateral taker under the security financial collateral arrangement in relation to the financial collateral transferred by the collateral taker in discharge of an obligation as described in paragraph (2), first subparagraph.
(5) If an enforcement event occurs while an obligation as described in paragraph (2) first subparagraph remains outstanding, the obligation may be the subject of a close-out netting provision.

Article 6. (1) Member States shall ensure that a title transfer financial collateral arrangement can take effect in accordance with its terms.
(2) If an enforcement event occurs while any obligation of the collateral taker to transfer equivalent collateral under a title transfer financial collateral arrangement remains outstanding, the obligation may be the subject of a close-out netting provision.

Article 7. (1) Member States shall ensure that a close-out netting provision can take effect in accordance with its terms:
(a) notwithstanding the commencement or continuation of winding-up proceedings or reorganisation measures in respect of the collateral provider and/or the collateral taker; and/or
(b) notwithstanding any purported assignment, judicial or other attachment or other disposition of or in respect of such rights.
(2) Member States shall ensure that the operation of a close-out netting provision may not be subject to any of the requirements that are mentioned in Article 4(4), unless otherwise agreed by the parties.

Article 8. (1) Member States shall ensure that a financial collateral arrangement, as well as the provision of financial collateral under such arrangement, may not be declared invalid or void or be reversed on the sole basis that the financial collateral arrangement has come into existence, or the financial collateral has been provided:

(a) on the day of the commencement of winding-up proceedings or reorganisation measures, but prior to the order or decree making that commencement; or

(b) in a prescribed period prior to, and defined by reference to, the commencement of such proceedings or measures or by reference to the making of any order or decree or the taking of any other action or occurrence of any other event in the course of such proceedings or measures.

(2) Member States shall ensure that where a financial collateral arrangement or a relevant financial obligation has come into existence, or financial collateral has been provided on the day of, but after the moment of the commencement of, winding-up proceedings or reorganisation measures, it shall be legally enforceable and binding on third parties if the collateral taker can prove that he was not aware, nor should have been aware, of the commencement of such proceedings or measures.

(3) Where a financial collateral arrangement contains:

(a) an obligation to provide financial collateral or additional financial collateral in order to take account of changes in the value of the financial collateral or in the amount of the relevant financial obligations, or

(b) a right to withdraw financial collateral on providing, by way of substitution or exchange, financial collateral of substantially the same value,

Member States shall ensure that the provision of financial collateral, additional financial collateral or substitute or replacement financial collateral under such an obligation or right shall not be treated as invalid or reversed or declared void on the sole basis that:

(i) such provision was made on the day of the commencement of winding-up proceedings or reorganisation measures, but prior to the order or decree making that commencement or in a prescribed period prior to, and defined by reference to, the commencement of winding-up proceedings or reorganisation measures or by reference to the making of any order or decree or the taking of any other action or occurrence of any other event in the course of such proceedings or measures; and/or

(ii) the relevant financial obligations were incurred prior to the date of the provision of the financial collateral, additional financial collateral or substitute or replacement financial collateral.

(4) Without prejudice to paragraphs 1, 2 and 3, this Directive leaves unaffected the general rules of national insolvency law in relation to the voidance of transactions entered into during the prescribed period referred to in paragraph (1)(b) and in paragraph (3)(i).

Article 9. (1) Any question with respect to any of the matters specified in paragraph (2) arising in relation to book entry securities collateral shall be governed by the law of the country in which the relevant account is maintained. The reference to the law of a country is a reference to its domestic law, disregarding any rule under which, in deciding the relevant question, reference should be made to the law of another country.

(2) The matters referred to in paragraph (1) are:

(a) the legal nature and proprietary effects of book entry securities collateral;

(b) the requirements for perfecting a financial collateral arrangement relating to book entry securities collateral and the provision of book entry securities collateral under such an arrangement, and more generally the completion of the steps necessary to render such an arrangement and provision effective against third parties;

(c) whether a person's title to or interest in such book entry securities collateral is overridden by or subordinated to a competing title or interest, or a good faith acquisition has occurred;

(d) the steps required for the realisation of book entry securities collateral following the occurrence of an enforcement event.

Article 10. Not later than 27 December 2006, the Commission shall present a report to the European Parliament and the Council on the application of this Directive, in particular on the application of Article 1(3), Article 4(3) and Article 5, accompanied where appropriate by proposals for its revision.

Article 11. Member States shall bring into force the laws, regulations and administrative provisions necessary to comply with this Directive by 27 December 2003 at the latest. They shall forthwith inform the Commission thereof. When Member States adopt those provisions, they shall contain a reference to this Directive or be accompanied by such reference on the occasion of their official publication. Member States shall determine how such reference is to be made.

Article 12. This Directive shall enter into force on the day of its publication in the Official Journal of the European Communities.

Article 13. This Directive is addressed to the Member States.

PART IV   EUROPEAN PRIVATE LAW

Directive 2009/44/EC of the European Parliament and of the Council of 6 May 2009 amending Directive 98/26/EC on settlement finality in payment and securities settlement systems and Directive 2002/47/EC on financial collateral arrangements as regards linked systems and credit claims (Text with EEA relevance) (OJ L146, 10.06.2009, pp. 37 – 43) [footnotes omitted].

THE EUROPEAN PARLIAMENT AND THE COUNCIL OF THE EUROPEAN UNION,
Having regard to the Treaty establishing the European Community, and in particular Article 95 thereof,
Having regard to the proposal from the Commission,
Having regard to the opinion of the European Central Bank,
Having regard to the opinion of the European Economic and Social Committee,
Acting in accordance with the procedure laid down in Article 251 of the Treaty,
Whereas:
(1) Directive 98/26/EC of the European Parliament and of the Council established a regime under which the finality of transfer orders and netting, as well as the enforceability of collateral security, are ensured in respect of both domestic and foreign participants in the payment and securities settlement systems.
(2) The Evaluation Report from the Commission of 7 April 2006 on the Settlement Finality Directive 98/26/EC concluded that Directive 98/26/EC is functioning well in general. The report highlighted that some important changes may be underway in the area of payment and securities settlement systems and also concluded that there is some need to clarify and simplify Directive 98/26/EC.
(3) The main change, however, is the increasing number of linkages between systems, which, at the time when Directive 98/26/EC was drafted, used to operate almost exclusively on a national and independent basis. This change is one of the results of Directive 2004/39/EC of the European Parliament and of the Council of 21 April 2004 on markets in financial instruments, and the European Code of conduct for clearing and settlement. In order to adapt to those developments, the concept of an interoperable system and the responsibility of system operators should be clarified.
(4) Directive 2002/47/EC of the European Parliament and of the Council created a uniform Community legal framework for the cross-border use of financial collateral and thus abolished most of the formal requirements traditionally imposed on collateral arrangements.
(5) The European Central Bank decided to introduce credit claims as an eligible type of collateral for Eurosystem credit operations from 1 January 2007. In order to maximise the economic impact of the use of credit claims, the European Central Bank recommended an extension of the scope of Directive 2002/47/EC. The Commission Evaluation Report of 20 December 2006 on the Financial Collateral Arrangements Directive (2002/47/EC) addressed this issue and subscribed to the opinion of the European Central Bank. The use of credit claims will increase the pool of available collateral. Moreover, further harmonisation in the area of payment and securities settlement systems would further contribute to a level playing field among credit institutions in all Member States. If the use of credit claims as collateral were to be facilitated further, consumers and debtors would also benefit as the use of credit claims as collateral could ultimately lead to more intense competition and better availability of credit.
(6) In order to facilitate the use of credit claims, it is important to abolish or prohibit any administrative rules, such as notification and registration obligations, that would make the assignments of credit claims impracticable. Similarly, in order not to compromise the position of collateral takers, debtors should be able validly to waive their set-off rights vis-à-vis creditors. The same rationale should also apply to the need to introduce the possibility for the debtor to waive bank secrecy rules, because otherwise the collateral taker may have insufficient information with which properly to assess the value of the underlying credit claims. Those provisions should be without prejudice to Directive 2008/48/EC of the European Parliament and of the Council of 23 April 2008 on credit agreements for consumers.
(7) Member States have made no use of the possibility under Article 4(3) of Directive 2002/47/EC to opt out of the right of appropriation of the collateral taker. That provision should therefore be deleted.
(8) Directives 98/26/EC and 2002/47/EC should therefore be amended accordingly.
(9) In accordance with point 34 of the Interinstitutional agreement on better law-making, Member States are encouraged to draw up, for themselves and in the interest of the Community, their own tables illustrating, as far as possible, the correlation between this Directive and the transposition measures, and to make them public,
HAVE ADOPTED THIS DIRECTIVE:

EU: DIRECTIVE 2009/44 ON FINANCIAL COLLATERAL ARRANGEMENTS (AMENDMENTS)

Article 1. Directive 98/26/EC is hereby amended as follows:
(1) Recital 8 shall be deleted.
(2) The following recital shall be inserted:
"(14a) Whereas national competent authorities or supervisors should ensure that the operators of the systems establishing the interoperable systems have agreed to the extent possible on common rules on the moment of entry into the interoperable systems. National competent authorities or supervisors should ensure that the rules on the moment of entry into an interoperable system are coordinated insofar as possible and necessary in order to avoid legal uncertainty in the event of default of a participating system.".
(3) The following recital shall be inserted:
"(22a) Whereas in the case of interoperable systems, a lack of coordination as to which rules apply on the moment of entry and irrevocability may expose participants in one system, or even the system operator itself, to the spill-over effects of a default in another system. In order to limit systemic risk, it is desirable to provide that system operators of interoperable systems coordinate the rules on the moment of entry and irrevocability in the systems they operate.".
(4) Article 1 shall be amended as follows:
(a) in point (a), the word "ecu" shall be replaced by the word "euro";
(b) in point (c), the second indent shall be replaced by the following:
"— operations of the central banks of the Member States or the European Central Bank in the context of their function as central banks.".
(5) Article 2 shall be amended as follows:
(a) point (a) shall be amended as follows:
(i) the first indent shall be replaced by the following:
"— between three or more participants, excluding the system operator of that system, a possible settlement agent, a possible central counterparty, a possible clearing house or a possible indirect participant, with common rules and standardised arrangements for the clearing, whether or not through a central counterparty, or execution of transfer orders between the participants,";
(ii) the following subparagraph is added:
"An arrangement entered into between interoperable systems shall not constitute a system.";
(b) in point (b), the first and second indents are replaced by the following:
"— a credit institution as defined in Article 4(1) of Directive 2006/48/EC of the European Parliament and of the Council of 14 June 2006 relating to the taking up and pursuit of the business of credit institutions (recast) including the institutions listed in Article 2 of that Directive,
— an investment firm as defined in Article 4(1)(1) of Directive 2004/39/EC of the European Parliament and of the Council of 21 April 2004 on markets in financial instruments, excluding the institutions set out in Article 2(1) thereof,
(c) point (f) shall be amended as follows:
(i) the first subparagraph shall be replaced by the following:
"(f) "participant" shall mean an institution, a central counterparty, a settlement agent, a clearing house or a system operator.";
(ii) the third subparagraph shall be replaced by the following:
"A Member State may decide that, for the purposes of this Directive, an indirect participant may be considered a participant if that is justified on the grounds of systemic risk. Where an indirect participant is considered to be a participant on grounds of systemic risk, this does not limit the responsibility of the participant through which the indirect participant passes transfer orders to the system.";
(d) point (g) shall be replaced by the following:
"(g) "indirect participant" shall mean an institution, a central counterparty, a settlement agent, a clearing house or a system operator with a contractual relationship with a participant in a system executing transfer orders which enables the indirect participant to pass transfer orders through the system, provided that the indirect participant is known to the system operator.";
(e) point (h) shall be replaced by the following:
"(h) "securities" shall mean all instruments referred to in section C of Annex I to Directive 2004/39/EC;";
(f) in point (i), the first indent shall be replaced by the following:
"— any instruction by a participant to place at the disposal of a recipient an amount of money by means of a book entry on the accounts of a credit institution, a central bank, a central counterparty or a settlement agent, or any instruction which results in the assumption or discharge of a payment obligation as defined by the rules of the system, or";
(g) point (l) shall be replaced by the following:
"(l) "settlement account" shall mean an account at a central bank, a settlement agent or a central

counterparty used to hold funds or securities and to settle transactions between participants in a system;";

(h) point (m) shall be replaced by the following:

"(m) "collateral security" shall mean all realisable assets, including, without limitations, financial collateral referred to in Article 1(4)(a) of Directive 2002/47/EC of the European Parliament and of the Council of 6 June 2002 on financial collateral arrangements, provided under a pledge (including money provided under a pledge), a repurchase or similar agreement, or otherwise, for the purpose of securing rights and obligations potentially arising in connection with a system, or provided to central banks of the Member States or to the European Central Bank;

(i) the following points shall be added:

"(n) "business day" shall cover both day and night-time settlements and shall encompass all events happening during the business cycle of a system;

(o) "interoperable systems" shall mean two or more systems whose system operators have entered into an arrangement with one another that involves cross-system execution of transfer orders;

(p) "system operator" shall mean the entity or entities legally responsible for the operation of a system. A system operator may also act as a settlement agent, central counterparty or clearing house.".

(6) Article 3 shall be amended as follows:

(a) paragraph (1) shall be replaced by the following:

"1. Transfer orders and netting shall be legally enforceable and binding on third parties even in the event of insolvency proceedings against a participant, provided that transfer orders were entered into the system before the moment of opening of such insolvency proceedings as defined in Article 6(1). This shall apply even in the event of insolvency proceedings against a participant (in the system concerned or in an interoperable system) or against the system operator of an interoperable system which is not a participant.

Where transfer orders are entered into a system after the moment of opening of insolvency proceedings and are carried out within the business day, as defined by the rules of the system, during which the opening of such proceedings occur, they shall be legally enforceable and binding on third parties only if the system operator can prove that, at the time that such transfer orders become irrevocable, it was neither aware, nor should have been aware, of the opening of such proceedings.";

(b) the following paragraph is added:

"4. In the case of interoperable systems, each system determines in its own rules the moment of entry into its system, in such a way as to ensure, to the extent possible, that the rules of all interoperable systems concerned are coordinated in this regard. Unless expressly provided for by the rules of all the systems that are party to the interoperable systems, one system's rules on the moment of entry shall not be affected by any rules of the other systems with which it is interoperable.".

(7) Article 4 shall be replaced by the following:

"Article 4

Member States may provide that the opening of insolvency proceedings against a participant or a system operator of an interoperable system shall not prevent funds or securities available on the settlement account of that participant from being used to fulfil that participant4s obligations in the system or in an interoperable system on the business day of the opening of the insolvency proceedings. Member States may also provide that such a participant's credit facility connected to the system be used against available, existing collateral security to fulfil that participant's obligations in the system or in an interoperable system.".

(8) In Article 5, the following paragraph shall be added:

"In the case of interoperable systems, each system determines in its own rules the moment of irrevocability, in such a way as to ensure, to the extent possible, that the rules of all interoperable systems concerned are coordinated in this regard. Unless expressly provided for by the rules of all the systems that are party to the interoperable systems, one system's rules on the moment of irrevocability shall not be affected by any rules of the other systems with which it is interoperable.".

(9) Article 7 shall be replaced by the following:

"Article 7

Insolvency proceedings shall not have retroactive effects on the rights and obligations of a participant arising from, or in connection with, its participation in a system before the moment of opening of such proceedings as defined in Article 6(1). This shall apply, inter alia, as regards the rights and obligations of a participant in an interoperable system, or of a system operator of an interoperable system which is not a participant.".

(10) Article 9 shall be replaced by the following:

"Article 9

EU: DIRECTIVE 2009/44 ON FINANCIAL COLLATERAL ARRANGEMENTS (AMENDMENTS)

1. The rights of a system operator or of a participant to collateral security provided to them in connection with a system or any interoperable system, and the rights of central banks of the Member States or the European Central Bank to collateral security provided to them, shall not be affected by insolvency proceedings against:
(a) the participant (in the system concerned or in an interoperable system);
(b) the system operator of an interoperable system which is not a participant;
(c) a counterparty to central banks of the Member States or the European Central Bank; or
(d) any third party which provided the collateral security.
Such collateral security may be realised for the satisfaction of those rights.
2. Where securities including rights in securities are provided as collateral security to participants, system operators or to central banks of the Member States or the European Central Bank as described in paragraph (1), and their right or that of any nominee, agent or third party acting on their behalf with respect to the securities is legally recorded on a register, account or centralised deposit system located in a Member State, the determination of the rights of such entities as holders of collateral security in relation to those securities shall be governed by the law of that Member State.".
(11) Article 10 shall be replaced by the following:
"Article 10
1. Member States shall specify the systems, and the respective system operators, which are to be included in the scope of this Directive and shall notify them to the Commission and inform the Commission of the authorities they have chosen in accordance with Article 6(2).
The system operator shall indicate to the Member State whose law is applicable the participants in the system, including any possible indirect participants, as well as any change in them.
In addition to the indication provided for in the second subparagraph, Member States may impose supervision or authorisation requirements on systems which fall under their jurisdiction.
An institution shall, on request, inform anyone with a legitimate interest of the systems in which it participates and provide information about the main rules governing the functioning of those systems.
2. A system designated prior to the entry into force of national provisions implementing Directive 2009/44/EC of the European Parliament and of the Council of 6 May 2009 amending Directive 98/26/EC on settlement finality in payment and securities settlement systems and Directive 2002/47/EC on financial collateral arrangements as regards linked systems and credit claims shall continue to be designated for the purposes of this Directive.
A transfer order which enters a system before the entry into force of national provisions implementing Directive 2009/44/EC, but is settled thereafter shall be deemed to be a transfer order for the purposes of this Directive.

Article 2. Directive 2002/47/EC is hereby amended as follows:
(1) Recital 9 shall be replaced by the following:
"(9) In order to limit the administrative burdens for parties using financial collateral under the scope of this Directive, the only perfection requirement regarding parties which national law may impose in respect of financial collateral should be that the financial collateral is under the control of the collateral taker or of a person acting on the collateral taker's behalf while not excluding collateral techniques where the collateral provider is allowed to substitute collateral or to withdraw excess collateral. This Directive should not prohibit Member States from requiring that a credit claim be delivered by means of inclusion in a list of claims.".
(2) Recital 20 shall be replaced by the following:
"(20) This Directive does not prejudice the operation or effect of the contractual terms of financial instruments or credit claims provided as financial collateral, such as rights, obligations or other conditions contained in the terms of issue of such instruments, or any other rights, obligations or other conditions which apply between the issuers and holders of such instruments or between the debtor and the creditor of such credit claims.".
(3) The following recital shall be added:
"(23) This Directive does not affect the rights of Member States to impose rules to ensure the effectiveness of financial collateral arrangements in relation to third parties as regards credit claims,".
(4) Article 1 shall be amended as follows:
(a) paragraph (2)(b) shall be replaced by the following:
"(b) a central bank, the European Central Bank, the Bank for International Settlements, a multilateral development bank as referred to in Annex VI, Part 1, Section 4 of Directive 2006/48/EC of the European Parliament and of the Council of 14 June 2006 relating to the taking up and pursuit of the business of credit institutions (recast), the International Monetary Fund and the European Investment Bank;

(b) in paragraph (2)(c), points (i) to (iv) shall be replaced by the following:
"(i) a credit institution as defined in Article 4(1) of Directive 2006/48/EC, including the institutions listed in Article 2 of that Directive;
(ii) an investment firm as defined in Article 4(1)(1) of Directive 2004/39/EC of the European Parliament and of the Council of 21 April 2004 on markets in financial instruments;
(iii) a financial institution as defined in Article 4(5) of Directive 2006/48/EC;
(iv) an insurance undertaking as defined in Article 1(a) of Council Directive 92/49/EEC of 18 June 1992 on the coordination of laws, regulations and administrative provisions relating to direct insurance other than life insurance (third non-life insurance Directive) and an assurance undertaking as defined in Article 1(1)(a) of Directive 2002/83/EC of the European Parliament and of the Council of 5 November 2002 concerning life assurance;
(c) paragraph (4)(a) shall be replaced by the following:
"(a) The financial collateral to be provided shall consist of cash, financial instruments or credit claims;";
(d) in paragraph (4), the following point shall be added:
"(c) Member States may exclude from the scope of this Directive credit claims where the debtor is a consumer as defined in Article 3(a) of Directive 2008/48/EC of the European Parliament and of the Council of 23 April 2008 on credit agreements for consumers or a micro or small enterprise as defined in Article 1 and Article 2(2) and (3) of the Annex to Commission Recommendation 2003/361/EC of 6 May 2003 concerning the definition of micro, small and medium-sized enterprises, save where the collateral taker or the collateral provider of such credit claims is one of the institutions referred under Article 1(2)(b) of this Directive.
(e) paragraph (5) shall be amended as follows:
(i) in the second subparagraph, the following sentence shall be added:
"For credit claims, the inclusion in a list of claims submitted in writing, or in a legally equivalent manner, to the collateral taker is sufficient to identify the credit claim and to evidence the provision of the claim provided as financial collateral between the parties.";
(ii) the following subparagraph shall be inserted after the second subparagraph:
"Without prejudice to the second subparagraph, Member States may provide that the inclusion in a list of claims submitted in writing, or in a legally equivalent manner, to the collateral taker is also sufficient to identify the credit claim and to evidence the provision of the claim provided as financial collateral against the debtor or third parties.".
(5) Article 2 shall be amended as follows:
(a) paragraph (1) is amended as follows:
(i) points (b) and (c) shall be replaced by the following:
"(b) "title transfer financial collateral arrangement" means an arrangement, including repurchase agreements, under which a collateral provider transfers full ownership of, or full entitlement to, financial collateral to a collateral taker for the purpose of securing or otherwise covering the performance of relevant financial obligations;
(c) "security financial collateral arrangement" means an arrangement under which a collateral provider provides financial collateral by way of security to or in favour of a collateral taker, and where the full or qualified ownership of, or full entitlement to, the financial collateral remains with the collateral provider when the security right is established;";
(ii) the following point shall be added:
"(o) "credit claims" means pecuniary claims arising out of an agreement whereby a credit institution, as defined in Article 4(1) of Directive 2006/48/EC, including the institutions listed in Article 2 of that Directive, grants credit in the form of a loan.";
(b) in paragraph (2), the second sentence shall be replaced by the following:
"Any right of substitution, right to withdraw excess financial collateral in favour of the collateral provider or, in the case of credit claims, right to collect the proceeds thereof until further notice, shall not prejudice the financial collateral having been provided to the collateral taker as mentioned in this Directive.".
(6) Article 3 shall be amended as follows:
(a) in paragraph (1), the following subparagraphs shall be added:
"Without prejudice to Article 1(5), when credit claims are provided as financial collateral, Member States shall not require that the creation, validity, perfection, priority, enforceability or admissibility in evidence of such financial collateral be dependent on the performance of any formal act such as the registration or the notification of the debtor of the credit claim provided as collateral. However, Member States may require the performance of a formal act, such as registration or notification, for purposes of perfection, priority, enforceability or admissibility in evidence against the debtor or third parties.

EU: DIRECTIVE 2009/44 ON FINANCIAL COLLATERAL ARRANGEMENTS (AMENDMENTS)

By 30 June 2014, the Commission shall report to the European Parliament and to the Council on whether this paragraph continues to be appropriate.";

(b) the following paragraph shall be added:

"3. Without prejudice to Council Directive 93/13/EEC of 5 April 1993 on unfair terms in consumer contracts and national provisions concerning unfair contract terms, Member States shall ensure that debtors of the credit claims may validly waive, in writing or in a legally equivalent manner:

(i) their rights of set-off vis-à-vis the creditors of the credit claim and vis-à-vis persons to whom the creditor assigned, pledged or otherwise mobilised the credit claim as collateral; and

(ii) their rights arising from banking secrecy rules that would otherwise prevent or restrict the ability of the creditor of the credit claim to provide information on the credit claim or the debtor for the purposes of using the credit claim as collateral.

(7) Article 4 shall be amended as follows:

(a) in paragraph (1), the following point shall be added:

"(c) credit claims, by sale or appropriation and by setting off their value against, or applying their value in discharge of, the relevant financial obligations.";

(b) in paragraph (2), point (b) shall be replaced by the following:

"(b) the parties have agreed in the security financial collateral arrangement on the valuation of the financial instruments and the credit claims.";

(c) paragraph (3) shall be deleted.

(8) In Article 5, the following paragraph shall be added:

"6. This Article shall not apply to credit claims.".

(9) The following Article shall be inserted after Article 9:

"Article 9a

Directive 2008/48/EC

The provisions of this Directive shall be without prejudice to Directive 2008/48/EC.".

Article 3. 1. Member States shall adopt and publish the laws, regulations and administrative provisions necessary to comply with this Directive by 30 December 2010. They shall forthwith inform the Commission thereof.

They shall apply those measures from 30 June 2011.

When Member States adopt those measures, they shall contain a reference to this Directive or shall be accompanied by such reference on the occasion of their official publication. The methods of making such reference shall be laid down by Member States.

2. Member States shall communicate to the Commission the text of the main provisions of national law which they adopt in the field covered by this Directive.

Article 4. This Directive shall enter into force on the 20th day following its publication in the Official Journal of the European Union.

Article 5. This Directive is addressed to the Member States.

PART IV   EUROPEAN PRIVATE LAW

Directive 2005/29/EC of the European Parliament and of the Council of 11 May 2005 concerning unfair business-to-consumer commercial practices in the internal market and amending Council Directive 84/450/EEC, Directives 97/7/EC, 98/27/EC and 2002/65/EC of the European Parliament and of the Council and Regulation (EC) No 2006/2004 of the European Parliament and of the Council ('Unfair Commercial Practices Directive') (OJL 149, 11.06.2000, pp. 22 -39) [footnotes omitted].

THE EUROPEAN PARLIAMENT AND THE COUNCIL OF THE EUROPEAN UNION,
Having regard to the Treaty establishing the European Community, and in particular Article 95 thereof,
Having regard to the proposal from the Commission,
Having regard to the opinion of the European Economic and Social Committee,
Acting in accordance with the procedure laid down in Article 251 of the Treaty,
Whereas:
(1) Article 153(1) and (3)(a) of the Treaty provides that the Community is to contribute to the attainment of a high level of consumer protection by the measures it adopts pursuant to Article 95 thereof.
(2) In accordance with Article 14(2) of the Treaty, the internal market comprises an area without internal frontiers in which the free movement of goods and services and freedom of establishment are ensured. The development of fair commercial practices within the area without internal frontiers is vital for the promotion of the development of cross-border activities.
(3) The laws of the Member States relating to unfair commercial practices show marked differences which can generate appreciable distortions of competition and obstacles to the smooth functioning of the internal market. In the field of advertising, Council Directive 84/450/EEC of 10 September 1984 concerning misleading and comparative advertising establishes minimum criteria for harmonising legislation on misleading advertising, but does not prevent the Member States from retaining or adopting measures which provide more extensive protection for consumers. As a result, Member States' provisions on misleading advertising diverge significantly.
(4) These disparities cause uncertainty as to which national rules apply to unfair commercial practices harming consumers' economic interests and create many barriers affecting business and consumers. These barriers increase the cost to business of exercising internal market freedoms, in particular when businesses wish to engage in cross border marketing, advertising campaigns and sales promotions. Such barriers also make consumers uncertain of their rights and undermine their confidence in the internal market.
(5) In the absence of uniform rules at Community level, obstacles to the free movement of services and goods across borders or the freedom of establishment could be justified in the light of the case-law of the Court of Justice of the European Communities as long as they seek to protect recognised public interest objectives and are proportionate to those objectives. In view of the Community's objectives, as set out in the provisions of the Treaty and in secondary Community law relating to freedom of movement, and in accordance with the Commission's policy on commercial communications as indicated in the Communication from the Commission entitled "The follow-up to the Green Paper on Commercial Communications in the Internal Market", such obstacles should be eliminated. These obstacles can only be eliminated by establishing uniform rules at Community level which establish a high level of consumer protection and by clarifying certain legal concepts at Community level to the extent necessary for the proper functioning of the internal market and to meet the requirement of legal certainty. (6) This Directive therefore approximates the laws of the Member States on unfair commercial practices, including unfair advertising, which directly harm consumers' economic interests and thereby indirectly harm the economic interests of legitimate competitors. In line with the principle of proportionality, this Directive protects consumers from the consequences of such unfair commercial practices where they are material but recognises that in some cases the impact on consumers may be negligible. It neither covers nor affects the national laws on unfair commercial practices which harm only competitors' economic interests or which relate to a transaction between traders; taking full account of the principle of subsidiarity, Member States will continue to be able to regulate such practices, in conformity with Community law, if they choose to do so. Nor does this Directive cover or affect the provisions of Directive 84/450/EEC on advertising which misleads business but which is not misleading for consumers and on comparative advertising. Further, this Directive does not affect accepted advertising and marketing practices, such as legitimate product placement, brand differentiation or the offering of incentives which may legitimately affect consumers' perceptions of products and influence their behaviour without impairing the consumer's ability to make an informed decision.
(7) This Directive addresses commercial practices directly related to influencing consumers'

transactional decisions in relation to products. It does not address commercial practices carried out primarily for other purposes, including for example commercial communication aimed at investors, such as annual reports and corporate promotional literature. It does not address legal requirements related to taste and decency which vary widely among the Member States. Commercial practices such as, for example, commercial solicitation in the streets, may be undesirable in Member States for cultural reasons. Member States should accordingly be able to continue to ban commercial practices in their territory, in conformity with Community law, for reasons of taste and decency even where such practices do not limit consumers' freedom of choice. Full account should be taken of the context of the individual case concerned in applying this Directive, in particular the general clauses thereof.

(8) This Directive directly protects consumer economic interests from unfair business-to-consumer commercial practices. Thereby, it also indirectly protects legitimate businesses from their competitors who do not play by the rules in this Directive and thus guarantees fair competition in fields coordinated by it. It is understood that there are other commercial practices which, although not harming consumers, may hurt competitors and business customers. The Commission should carefully examine the need for Community action in the field of unfair competition beyond the remit of this Directive and, if necessary, make a legislative proposal to cover these other aspects of unfair competition.

(9) This Directive is without prejudice to individual actions brought by those who have been harmed by an unfair commercial practice. It is also without prejudice to Community and national rules on contract law, on intellectual property rights, on the health and safety aspects of products, on conditions of establishment and authorisation regimes, including those rules which, in conformity with Community law, relate to gambling activities, and to Community competition rules and the national provisions implementing them. The Member States will thus be able to retain or introduce restrictions and prohibitions of commercial practices on grounds of the protection of the health and safety of consumers in their territory wherever the trader is based, for example in relation to alcohol, tobacco or pharmaceuticals. Financial services and immovable property, by reason of their complexity and inherent serious risks, necessitate detailed requirements, including positive obligations on traders. For this reason, in the field of financial services and immovable property, this Directive is without prejudice to the right of Member States to go beyond its provisions to protect the economic interests of consumers. It is not appropriate to regulate here the certification and indication of the standard of fineness of articles of precious metal.

(10) It is necessary to ensure that the relationship between this Directive and existing Community law is coherent, particularly where detailed provisions on unfair commercial practices apply to specific sectors. This Directive therefore amends Directive 84/450/EEC, Directive 97/7/EC of the European Parliament and of the Council of 20 May 1997 on the protection of consumers in respect of distance contracts, Directive 98/27/EC of the European Parliament and of the Council of 19 May 1998 on injunctions for the protection of consumers' interests and Directive 2002/65/EC of the European Parliament and of the Council of 23 September 2002 concerning the distance marketing of consumer financial services. This Directive accordingly applies only in so far as there are no specific Community law provisions regulating specific aspects of unfair commercial practices, such as information requirements and rules on the way the information is presented to the consumer. It provides protection for consumers where there is no specific sectoral legislation at Community level and prohibits traders from creating a false impression of the nature of products. This is particularly important for complex products with high levels of risk to consumers, such as certain financial services products. This Directive consequently complements the Community acquis, which is applicable to commercial practices harming consumers' economic interests.

(11) The high level of convergence achieved by the approximation of national provisions through this Directive creates a high common level of consumer protection. This Directive establishes a single general prohibition of those unfair commercial practices distorting consumers' economic behaviour. It also sets rules on aggressive commercial practices, which are currently not regulated at Community level.

(12) Harmonisation will considerably increase legal certainty for both consumers and business. Both consumers and business will be able to rely on a single regulatory framework based on clearly defined legal concepts regulating all aspects of unfair commercial practices across the EU. The effect will be to eliminate the barriers stemming from the fragmentation of the rules on unfair commercial practices harming consumer economic interests and to enable the internal market to be achieved in this area

(13) In order to achieve the Community's objectives through the removal of internal market barriers, it is necessary to replace Member States' existing, divergent general clauses and legal principles. The single, common general prohibition established by this Directive therefore covers unfair commercial practices distorting consumers' economic behaviour. In order to support consumer confidence the

PART IV   EUROPEAN PRIVATE LAW

general prohibition should apply equally to unfair commercial practices which occur outside any contractual relationship between a trader and a consumer or following the conclusion of a contract and during its execution. The general prohibition is elaborated by rules on the two types of commercial practices which are by far the most common, namely misleading commercial practices and aggressive commercial practices.

(14) It is desirable that misleading commercial practices cover those practices, including misleading advertising, which by deceiving the consumer prevent him from making an informed and thus efficient choice. In conformity with the laws and practices of Member States on misleading advertising, this Directive classifies misleading practices into misleading actions and misleading omissions. In respect of omissions, this Directive sets out a limited number of key items of information which the consumer needs to make an informed transactional decision. Such information will not have to be disclosed in all advertisements, but only where the trader makes an invitation to purchase, which is a concept clearly defined in this Directive. The full harmonisation approach adopted in this Directive does not preclude the Member States from specifying in national law the main characteristics of particular products such as, for example, collectors' items or electrical goods, the omission of which would be material when an invitation to purchase is made. It is not the intention of this Directive to reduce consumer choice by prohibiting the promotion of products which look similar to other products unless this similarity confuses consumers as to the commercial origin of the product and is therefore misleading. This Directive should be without prejudice to existing Community law which expressly affords Member States the choice between several regulatory options for the protection of consumers in the field of commercial practices. In particular, this Directive should be without prejudice to Article 13(3) of Directive 2002/58/EC of the European Parliament and of the Council of 12 July 2002 concerning the processing of personal data and the protection of privacy in the electronic communications sector.

(15) Where Community law sets out information requirements in relation to commercial communication, advertising and marketing that information is considered as material under this Directive. Member States will be able to retain or add information requirements relating to contract law and having contract law consequences where this is allowed by the minimum clauses in the existing Community law instruments. A non-exhaustive list of such information requirements in the acquis is contained in Annex II. Given the full harmonisation introduced by this Directive only the information required in Community law is considered as material for the purpose of Article 7(5) thereof. Where Member States have introduced information requirements over and above what is specified in Community law, on the basis of minimum clauses, the omission of that extra information will not constitute a misleading omission under this Directive. By contrast Member States will be able, when allowed by the minimum clauses in Community law, to maintain or introduce more stringent provisions in conformity with Community law so as to ensure a higher level of protection of consumers' individual contractual rights.

(16) The provisions on aggressive commercial practices should cover those practices which significantly impair the consumer's freedom of choice. Those are practices using harassment, coercion, including the use of physical force, and undue influence.

(17) It is desirable that those commercial practices which are in all circumstances unfair be identified to provide greater legal certainty. Annex I therefore contains the full list of all such practices. These are the only commercial practices which can be deemed to be unfair without a case-by-case assessment against the provisions of Articles 5 to 9. The list may only be modified by revision of the Directive.

(18) It is appropriate to protect all consumers from unfair commercial practices; however the Court of Justice has found it necessary in adjudicating on advertising cases since the enactment of Directive 84/450/EEC to examine the effect on a notional, typical consumer. In line with the principle of proportionality, and to permit the effective application of the protections contained in it, this Directive takes as a benchmark the average consumer, who is reasonably well-informed and reasonably observant and circumspect, taking into account social, cultural and linguistic factors, as interpreted by the Court of Justice, but also contains provisions aimed at preventing the exploitation of consumers whose characteristics make them particularly vulnerable to unfair commercial practices. Where a commercial practice is specifically aimed at a particular group of consumers, such as children, it is desirable that the impact of the commercial practice be assessed from the perspective of the average member of that group. It is therefore appropriate to include in the list of practices which are in all circumstances unfair a provision which, without imposing an outright ban on advertising directed at children, protects them from direct exhortations to purchase. The average consumer test is not a statistical test. National courts and authorities will have to exercise their own faculty of judgement, having regard to the case-law of the Court of Justice, to determine the typical reaction of the average consumer in a given case.

(19) Where certain characteristics such as age, physical or mental infirmity or credulity make consumers particularly susceptible to a commercial practice or to the underlying product and the economic behaviour only of such consumers is likely to be distorted by the practice in a way that the trader can reasonably foresee, it is appropriate to ensure that they are adequately protected by assessing the practice from the perspective of the average member of that group.

(20) It is appropriate to provide a role for codes of conduct, which enable traders to apply the principles of this Directive effectively in specific economic fields. In sectors where there are specific mandatory requirements regulating the behaviour of traders, it is appropriate that these will also provide evidence as to the requirements of professional diligence in that sector. The control exercised by code owners at national or Community level to eliminate unfair commercial practices may avoid the need for recourse to administrative or judicial action and should therefore be encouraged. With the aim of pursuing a high level of consumer protection, consumers' organisations could be informed and involved in the drafting of codes of conduct.

(21) Persons or organisations regarded under national law as having a legitimate interest in the matter must have legal remedies for initiating proceedings against unfair commercial practices, either before a court or before an administrative authority which is competent to decide upon complaints or to initiate appropriate legal proceedings. While it is for national law to determine the burden of proof, it is appropriate to enable courts and administrative authorities to require traders to produce evidence as to the accuracy of factual claims they have made.

(22) It is necessary that Member States lay down penalties for infringements of the provisions of this Directive and they must ensure that these are enforced. The penalties must be effective, proportionate and dissuasive.

(23) Since the objectives of this Directive, namely to eliminate the barriers to the functioning of the internal market represented by national laws on unfair commercial practices and to provide a high common level of consumer protection, by approximating the laws, regulations and administrative provisions of the Member States on unfair commercial practices, cannot be sufficiently achieved by the Member States and can therefore be better achieved at Community level, the Community may adopt measures, in accordance with the principle of subsidiarity as set out in Article 5 of the Treaty. In accordance with the principle of proportionality, as set out in that Article, this Directive does not go beyond what is necessary in order to eliminate the internal market barriers and achieve a high common level of consumer protection.

(24) It is appropriate to review this Directive to ensure that barriers to the internal market have been addressed and a high level of consumer protection achieved. The review could lead to a Commission proposal to amend this Directive, which may include a limited extension to the derogation in Article 3(5), and/or amendments to other consumer protection legislation reflecting the Commission's Consumer Policy Strategy commitment to review the existing acquis in order to achieve a high, common level of consumer protection.

(25) This Directive respects the fundamental rights and observes the principles recognised in particular by the Charter of Fundamental Rights of the European Union,

HAVE ADOPTED THIS DIRECTIVE:

Chapter I. General Provisions

Article 1. The purpose of this Directive is to contribute to the proper functioning of the internal market and achieve a high level of consumer protection by approximating the laws, regulations and administrative provisions of the Member States on unfair commercial practices harming consumers' economic interests.

Article 2. For the purposes of this Directive:
(a) "consumer" means any natural person who, in commercial practices covered by this Directive, is acting for purposes which are outside his trade, business, craft or profession;
(b) "trader" means any natural or legal person who, in commercial practices covered by this Directive, is acting for purposes relating to his trade, business, craft or profession and anyone acting in the name of or on behalf of a trader;
(c) "product" means any goods or service including immovable property, rights and obligations;
(d) "business-to-consumer commercial practices" (hereinafter also referred to as commercial practices) means any act, omission, course of conduct or representation, commercial communication including advertising and marketing, by a trader, directly connected with the promotion, sale or supply of a product to consumers;
(e) "to materially distort the economic behaviour of consumers" means using a commercial practice to appreciably impair the consumer's ability to make an informed decision, thereby causing the con-

sumer to take a transactional decision that he would not have taken otherwise;

(f) "code of conduct" means an agreement or set of rules not imposed by law, regulation or administrative provision of a Member State which defines the behaviour of traders who undertake to be bound by the code in relation to one or more particular commercial practices or business sectors;

(g) "code owner" means any entity, including a trader or group of traders, which is responsible for the formulation and revision of a code of conduct and/or for monitoring compliance with the code by those who have undertaken to be bound by it;

(h) "professional diligence" means the standard of special skill and care which a trader may reasonably be expected to exercise towards consumers, commensurate with honest market practice and/or the general principle of good faith in the trader's field of activity;

(i) "invitation to purchase" means a commercial communication which indicates characteristics of the product and the price in a way appropriate to the means of the commercial communication used and thereby enables the consumer to make a purchase;

(j) "undue influence" means exploiting a position of power in relation to the consumer so as to apply pressure, even without using or threatening to use physical force, in a way which significantly limits the consumer's ability to make an informed decision;

(k) "transactional decision" means any decision taken by a consumer concerning whether, how and on what terms to purchase, make payment in whole or in part for, retain or dispose of a product or to exercise a contractual right in relation to the product, whether the consumer decides to act or to refrain from acting;

(l) "regulated profession" means a professional activity or a group of professional activities, access to which or the pursuit of which, or one of the modes of pursuing which, is conditional, directly or indirectly, upon possession of specific professional qualifications, pursuant to laws, regulations or administrative provisions.

Article 3. (1) This Directive shall apply to unfair business-to-consumer commercial practices, as laid down in Article 5, before, during and after a commercial transaction in relation to a product.

(2) This Directive is without prejudice to contract law and, in particular, to the rules on the validity, formation or effect of a contract.

(3) This Directive is without prejudice to Community or national rules relating to the health and safety aspects of products.

(4) In the case of conflict between the provisions of this Directive and other Community rules regulating specific aspects of unfair commercial practices, the latter shall prevail and apply to those specific aspects.

(5) For a period of six years from 12 June 2007, Member States shall be able to continue to apply national provisions within the field approximated by this Directive which are more restrictive or prescriptive than this Directive and which implement directives containing minimum harmonisation clauses. These measures must be essential to ensure that consumers are adequately protected against unfair commercial practices and must be proportionate to the attainment of this objective. The review referred to in Article 18 may, if considered appropriate, include a proposal to prolong this derogation for a further limited period.

(6) Member States shall notify the Commission without delay of any national provisions applied on the basis of paragraph (5).

(7) This Directive is without prejudice to the rules determining the jurisdiction of the courts.

(8) This Directive is without prejudice to any conditions of establishment or of authorisation regimes, or to the deontological codes of conduct or other specific rules governing regulated professions in order to uphold high standards of integrity on the part of the professional, which Member States may, in conformity with Community law, impose on professionals.

(9) In relation to "financial services", as defined in Directive 2002/65/EC, and immovable property, Member States may impose requirements which are more restrictive or prescriptive than this Directive in the field which it approximates.

(10) This Directive shall not apply to the application of the laws, regulations and administrative provisions of Member States relating to the certification and indication of the standard of fineness of articles of precious metal.

Article 4. Member States shall neither restrict the freedom to provide services nor restrict the free movement of goods for reasons falling within the field approximated by this Directive.

Chapter II. Unfair Commercial Practices

Article 5. (1) Unfair commercial practices shall be prohibited.

(2) A commercial practice shall be unfair if:

(a) it is contrary to the requirements of professional diligence, and
(b) it materially distorts or is likely to materially distort the economic behaviour with regard to the product of the average consumer whom it reaches or to whom it is addressed, or of the average member of the group when a commercial practice is directed to a particular group of consumers.
(3) Commercial practices which are likely to materially distort the economic behaviour only of a clearly identifiable group of consumers who are particularly vulnerable to the practice or the underlying product because of their mental or physical infirmity, age or credulity in a way which the trader could reasonably be expected to foresee, shall be assessed from the perspective of the average member of that group. This is without prejudice to the common and legitimate advertising practice of making exaggerated statements or statements which are not meant to be taken literally.
(4) In particular, commercial practices shall be unfair which:
(a) are misleading as set out in Articles 6 and 7, or
(b) are aggressive as set out in Articles 8 and 9.
(5) Annex I contains the list of those commercial practices which shall in all circumstances be regarded as unfair. The same single list shall apply in all Member States and may only be modified by revision of this Directive.

Section I. Misleading commercial practices

Article 6. (1) A commercial practice shall be regarded as misleading if it contains false information and is therefore untruthful or in any way, including overall presentation, deceives or is likely to deceive the average consumer, even if the information is factually correct, in relation to one or more of the following elements, and in either case causes or is likely to cause him to take a transactional decision that he would not have taken otherwise:
(a) the existence or nature of the product;
(b) the main characteristics of the product, such as its availability, benefits, risks, execution, composition, accessories, after-sale customer assistance and complaint handling, method and date of manufacture or provision, delivery, fitness for purpose, usage, quantity, specification, geographical or commercial origin or the results to be expected from its use, or the results and material features of tests or checks carried out on the product;
(c) the extent of the trader's commitments, the motives for the commercial practice and the nature of the sales process, any statement or symbol in relation to direct or indirect sponsorship or approval of the trader or the product;
(d) the price or the manner in which the price is calculated, or the existence of a specific price advantage;
(e) the need for a service, part, replacement or repair;
(f) the nature, attributes and rights of the trader or his agent, such as his identity and assets, his qualifications, status, approval, affiliation or connection and ownership of industrial, commercial or intellectual property rights or his awards and distinctions;
(g) the consumer's rights, including the right to replacement or reimbursement under Directive 1999/44/EC of the European Parliament and of the Council of 25 May 1999 on certain aspects of the sale of consumer goods and associated guarantees, or the risks he may face.
(2) A commercial practice shall also be regarded as misleading if, in its factual context, taking account of all its features and circumstances, it causes or is likely to cause the average consumer to take a transactional decision that he would not have taken otherwise, and it involves:
(a) any marketing of a product, including comparative advertising, which creates confusion with any products, trade marks, trade names or other distinguishing marks of a competitor;
(b) non-compliance by the trader with commitments contained in codes of conduct by which the trader has undertaken to be bound, where:
(i) the commitment is not aspirational but is firm and is capable of being verified, and
(ii) the trader indicates in a commercial practice that he is bound by the code.

Article 7. (1) A commercial practice shall be regarded as misleading if, in its factual context, taking account of all its features and circumstances and the limitations of the communication medium, it omits material information that the average consumer needs, according to the context, to take an informed transactional decision and thereby causes or is likely to cause the average consumer to take a transactional decision that he would not have taken otherwise.
(2) It shall also be regarded as a misleading omission when, taking account of the matters described in paragraph (1), a trader hides or provides in an unclear, unintelligible, ambiguous or untimely manner such material information as referred to in that paragraph or fails to identify the commercial

intent of the commercial practice if not already apparent from the context, and where, in either case, this causes or is likely to cause the average consumer to take a transactional decision that he would not have taken otherwise.
(3) Where the medium used to communicate the commercial practice imposes limitations of space or time, these limitations and any measures taken by the trader to make the information available to consumers by other means shall be taken into account in deciding whether information has been omitted.
(4) In the case of an invitation to purchase, the following information shall be regarded as material, if not already apparent from the context:
(a) the main characteristics of the product, to an extent appropriate to the medium and the product;
(b) the geographical address and the identity of the trader, such as his trading name and, where applicable, the geographical address and the identity of the trader on whose behalf he is acting;
(c) the price inclusive of taxes, or where the nature of the product means that the price cannot reasonably be calculated in advance, the manner in which the price is calculated, as well as, where appropriate, all additional freight, delivery or postal charges or, where these charges cannot reasonably be calculated in advance, the fact that such additional charges may be payable;
(d) the arrangements for payment, delivery, performance and the complaint handling policy, if they depart from the requirements of professional diligence;
(e) for products and transactions involving a right of withdrawal or cancellation, the existence of such a right.
(5) Information requirements established by Community law in relation to commercial communication including advertising or marketing, a non-exhaustive list of which is contained in Annex II, shall be regarded as material.

Section II. Aggressive commercial practices

Article 8. A commercial practice shall be regarded as aggressive if, in its factual context, taking account of all its features and circumstances, by harassment, coercion, including the use of physical force, or undue influence, it significantly impairs or is likely to significantly impair the average consumer's freedom of choice or conduct with regard to the product and thereby causes him or is likely to cause him to take a transactional decision that he would not have taken otherwise.

Article 9. In determining whether a commercial practice uses harassment, coercion, including the use of physical force, or undue influence, account shall be taken of:
(a) its timing, location, nature or persistence;
(b) the use of threatening or abusive language or behaviour;
(c) the exploitation by the trader of any specific misfortune or circumstance of such gravity as to impair the consumer's judgement, of which the trader is aware, to influence the consumer's decision with regard to the product;
(d) any onerous or disproportionate non-contractual barriers imposed by the trader where a consumer wishes to exercise rights under the contract, including rights to terminate a contract or to switch to another product or another trader;
(e) any threat to take any action that cannot legally be taken.

Chapter III. Codes of Conduct

Article 10. This Directive does not exclude the control, which Member States may encourage, of unfair commercial practices by code owners and recourse to such bodies by the persons or organisations referred to in Article 11 if proceedings before such bodies are in addition to the court or administrative proceedings referred to in that Article. Recourse to such control bodies shall never be deemed the equivalent of foregoing a means of judicial or administrative recourse as provided for in Article 11.

Chapter 4. Final Provisions

Article 11. (1) Member States shall ensure that adequate and effective means exist to combat unfair commercial practices in order to enforce compliance with the provisions of this Directive in the interest of consumers. Such means shall include legal provisions under which persons or organisations regarded under national law as having a legitimate interest in combating unfair commercial practices, including competitors, may:
(a) take legal action against such unfair commercial practices; and/or
(b) bring such unfair commercial practices before an administrative authority competent either to decide on complaints or to initiate appropriate legal proceedings.
It shall be for each Member State to decide which of these facilities shall be available and whether to

enable the courts or administrative authorities to require prior recourse to other established means of dealing with complaints, including those referred to in Article 10. These facilities shall be available regardless of whether the consumers affected are in the territory of the Member State where the trader is located or in another Member State.

It shall be for each Member State to decide:

(a) whether these legal facilities may be directed separately or jointly against a number of traders from the same economic sector; and

(b) whether these legal facilities may be directed against a code owner where the relevant code promotes non-compliance with legal requirements.

(2) Under the legal provisions referred to in paragraph (1), Member States shall confer upon the courts or administrative authorities powers enabling them, in cases where they deem such measures to be necessary taking into account all the interests involved and in particular the public interest:

(a) to order the cessation of, or to institute appropriate legal proceedings for an order for the cessation of, unfair commercial practices; or

(b) if the unfair commercial practice has not yet been carried out but is imminent, to order the prohibition of the practice, or to institute appropriate legal proceedings for an order for the prohibition of the practice,

even without proof of actual loss or damage or of intention or negligence on the part of the trader. Member States shall also make provision for the measures referred to in the first subparagraph to be taken under an accelerated procedure:

- either with interim effect, or
- with definitive effect, on the understanding that it is for each Member State to decide which of the two options to select.

Furthermore, Member States may confer upon the courts or administrative authorities powers enabling them, with a view to eliminating the continuing effects of unfair commercial practices the cessation of which has been ordered by a final decision:

(a) to require publication of that decision in full or in part and in such form as they deem adequate;

(b) to require in addition the publication of a corrective statement.

(3) The administrative authorities referred to in paragraph (1) must:

(a) be composed so as not to cast doubt on their impartiality;

(b) have adequate powers, where they decide on complaints, to monitor and enforce the observance of their decisions effectively;

(c) normally give reasons for their decisions.

Where the powers referred to in paragraph (2) are exercised exclusively by an administrative authority, reasons for its decisions shall always be given. Furthermore, in this case, provision must be made for procedures whereby improper or unreasonable exercise of its powers by the administrative authority or improper or unreasonable failure to exercise the said powers can be the subject of judicial review.

Article 12. Member States shall confer upon the courts or administrative authorities powers enabling them in the civil or administrative proceedings provided for in Article 11:

(a) to require the trader to furnish evidence as to the accuracy of factual claims in relation to a commercial practice if, taking into account the legitimate interest of the trader and any other party to the proceedings, such a requirement appears appropriate on the basis of the circumstances of the particular case; and

(b) to consider factual claims as inaccurate if the evidence demanded in accordance with (a) is not furnished or is deemed insufficient by the court or administrative authority.

Article 13. Member States shall lay down penalties for infringements of national provisions adopted in application of this Directive and shall take all necessary measures to ensure that these are enforced. These penalties must be effective, proportionate and dissuasive.

Article 14. Directive 84/450/EEC is hereby amended as follows:

(1) Article 1 shall be replaced by the following: "Article 1 The purpose of this Directive is to protect traders against misleading advertising and the unfair consequences thereof and to lay down the conditions under which comparative advertising is permitted."

(2) in Article 2:

- point 3 shall be replaced by the following: "3. "trader" means any natural or legal person who is acting for purposes relating to his trade, craft, business or profession and any one acting in the name of or on behalf of a trader.",

- the following point shall be added: "4. "code owner" means any entity, including a trader or group

of traders, which is responsible for the formulation and revision of a code of conduct and/or for monitoring compliance with the code by those who have undertaken to be bound by it.";
(3) Article 3a shall be replaced by the following:"Article 3a. (1) Comparative advertising shall, as far as the comparison is concerned, be permitted when the following conditions are met:
(a) it is not misleading within the meaning of Articles 2(2), 3 and 7(1) of this Directive or Articles 6 and 7 of Directive 2005/29/EC of the European Parliament and of the Council of 11 May 2005 concerning unfair business-to-consumer commercial practices in the internal market;
(b) it compares goods or services meeting the same needs or intended for the same purpose;
(c) it objectively compares one or more material, relevant, verifiable and representative features of those goods and services, which may include price;
(d) it does not discredit or denigrate the trade marks, trade names, other distinguishing marks, goods, services, activities, or circumstances of a competitor;
(e) for products with designation of origin, it relates in each case to products with the same designation;
(f) it does not take unfair advantage of the reputation of a trade mark, trade name or other distinguishing marks of a competitor or of the designation of origin of competing products;
(g) it does not present goods or services as imitations or replicas of goods or services bearing a protected trade mark or trade name;
(h) it does not create confusion among traders, between the advertiser and a competitor or between the advertiser's trade marks, trade names, other distinguishing marks, goods or services and those of a competitor.
(4) Article 4 (1) shall be replaced by the following: "(1) Member States shall ensure that adequate and effective means exist to combat misleading advertising in order to enforce compliance with the provisions on comparative advertising in the interest of traders and competitors. Such means shall include legal provisions under which persons or organisations regarded under national law as having a legitimate interest in combating misleading advertising or regulating comparative advertising may:
(a) take legal action against such advertising; or
(b) bring such advertising before an administrative authority competent either to decide on complaints or to initiate appropriate legal proceedings.
It shall be for each Member State to decide which of these facilities shall be available and whether to enable the courts or administrative authorities to require prior recourse to other established means of dealing with complaints, including those referred to in Article 5.
It shall be for each Member State to decide:
(a) whether these legal facilities may be directed separately or jointly against a number of traders from the same economic sector; and
(b) whether these legal facilities may be directed against a code owner where the relevant code promotes non-compliance with legal requirements.";
(5) Article 7(1) shall be replaced by the following: "(1) This Directive shall not preclude Member States from retaining or adopting provisions with a view to ensuring more extensive protection, with regard to misleading advertising, for traders and competitors."

Article 15. (1) Article 9 of Directive 97/7/EC shall be replaced by the following: "Article 9. Given the prohibition of inertia selling practices laid down in Directive 2005/29/EC of 11 May 2005 of the European Parliament and of the Council concerning unfair business-to-consumer commercial practices in the internal market, Member States shall take the measures necessary to exempt the consumer from the provision of any consideration in cases of unsolicited supply, the absence of a response not constituting consent.
(2) Article 9 of Directive 2002/65/EC shall be replaced by the following: "Article 9. Given the prohibition of inertia selling practices laid down in Directive 2005/29/EC of 11 May 2005 of the European Parliament and of the Council concerning unfair business-to-consumer commercial practices in the internal market and without prejudice to the provisions of Member States' legislation on the tacit renewal of distance contracts, when such rules permit tacit renewal, Member States shall take measures to exempt the consumer from any obligation in the event of unsolicited supplies, the absence of a reply not constituting consent.

Article 16. (1) In the Annex to Directive 98/27/EC, point 1 shall be replaced by the following: "(1) Directive 2005/29/EC of the European Parliament and of the Council of 11 May 2005 concerning unfair business-to-consumer commercial practices in the internal market (OJ L 149, 11.6.2005, p. 22)."
(2) In the Annex to Regulation (EC) No 2006/2004 of the European Parliament and of the Council of 27 October 2004 on cooperation between national authorities responsible for the enforcement of

the consumer protection law (the Regulation on consumer protection cooperation) [12] the following point shall be added: "16. Directive 2005/29/EC of the European Parliament and of the Council of 11 May 2005 concerning unfair business-to-consumer commercial practices in the internal market (OJ L 149, 11.6.2005, p. 22)."

Article 17. Member States shall take appropriate measures to inform consumers of the national law transposing this Directive and shall, where appropriate, encourage traders and code owners to inform consumers of their codes of conduct.

Article 18. (1) By 12 June 2011 the Commission shall submit to the European Parliament and the Council a comprehensive report on the application of this Directive, in particular of Articles 3(9) and 4 and Annex I, on the scope for further harmonisation and simplification of Community law relating to consumer protection, and, having regard to Article 3(5), on any measures that need to be taken at Community level to ensure that appropriate levels of consumer protection are maintained. The report shall be accompanied, if necessary, by a proposal to revise this Directive or other relevant parts of Community law.
(2) The European Parliament and the Council shall endeavour to act, in accordance with the Treaty, within two years of the presentation by the Commission of any proposal submitted under paragraph (1).

Article 19. Member States shall adopt and publish the laws, regulations and administrative provisions necessary to comply with this Directive by 12 June 2007. They shall forthwith inform the Commission thereof and inform the Commission of any subsequent amendments without delay.
They shall apply those measures by 12 December 2007. When Member States adopt those measures, they shall contain a reference to this Directive or be accompanied by such a reference on the occasion of their official publication. Member States shall determine how such reference is to be made.

Article 20. This Directive shall enter into force on the day following its publication in the Official Journal of the European Union.

Article 21. This Directive is addressed to the Member States.

Annex I. Commercial practices which are in all circumstances considered unfair
(1) Claiming to be a signatory to a code of conduct when the trader is not.
(2) Displaying a trust mark, quality mark or equivalent without having obtained the necessary authorisation.
(3) Claiming that a code of conduct has an endorsement from a public or other body which it does not have.
(4) Claiming that a trader (including his commercial practices) or a product has been approved, endorsed or authorised by a public or private body when he/it has not or making such a claim without complying with the terms of the approval, endorsement or authorisation.
(5) Making an invitation to purchase products at a specified price without disclosing the existence of any reasonable grounds the trader may have for believing that he will not be able to offer for supply or to procure another trader to supply, those products or equivalent products at that price for a period that is, and in quantities that are, reasonable having regard to the product, the scale of advertising of the product and the price offered (bait advertising).
(6) Making an invitation to purchase products at a specified price and then:
(a) refusing to show the advertised item to consumers; or
(b) refusing to take orders for it or deliver it within a reasonable time; or
(c) demonstrating a defective sample of it,
with the intention of promoting a different product (bait and switch).
(7) Falsely stating that a product will only be available for a very limited time, or that it will only be available on particular terms for a very limited time, in order to elicit an immediate decision and deprive consumers of sufficient opportunity or time to make an informed choice.
(8) Undertaking to provide after-sales service to consumers with whom the trader has communicated prior to a transaction in a language which is not an official language of the Member State where the trader is located and then making such service available only in another language without clearly disclosing this to the consumer before the consumer is committed to the transaction.
(9) Stating or otherwise creating the impression that a product can legally be sold when it cannot.
(10). Presenting rights given to consumers in law as a distinctive feature of the trader's offer.
(11). Using editorial content in the media to promote a product where a trader has paid for the promotion without making that clear in the content or by images or sounds clearly identifiable by the

consumer (advertorial). This is without prejudice to Council Directive 89/552/EEC [1].

(12) Making a materially inaccurate claim concerning the nature and extent of the risk to the personal security of the consumer or his family if the consumer does not purchase the product.

(13) Promoting a product similar to a product made by a particular manufacturer in such a manner as deliberately to mislead the consumer into believing that the product is made by that same manufacturer when it is not.

(14) Establishing, operating or promoting a pyramid promotional scheme where a consumer gives consideration for the opportunity to receive compensation that is derived primarily from the introduction of other consumers into the scheme rather than from the sale or consumption of products.

(15) Claiming that the trader is about to cease trading or move premises when he is not.

(16) Claiming that products are able to facilitate winning in games of chance.

(17) Falsely claiming that a product is able to cure illnesses, dysfunction or malformations.

(18) Passing on materially inaccurate information on market conditions or on the possibility of finding the product with the intention of inducing the consumer to acquire the product at conditions less favourable than normal market conditions.

(19) Claiming in a commercial practice to offer a competition or prize promotion without awarding the prizes described or a reasonable equivalent.

(20) Describing a product as "gratis", "free", "without charge" or similar if the consumer has to pay anything other than the unavoidable cost of responding to the commercial practice and collecting or paying for delivery of the item.

(21) Including in marketing material an invoice or similar document seeking payment which gives the consumer the impression that he has already ordered the marketed product when he has not.

(22) Falsely claiming or creating the impression that the trader is not acting for purposes relating to his trade, business, craft or profession, or falsely representing oneself as a consumer.

(23) Creating the false impression that after-sales service in relation to a product is available in a Member State other than the one in which the product is sold.

Aggressive commercial practices

(24) Creating the impression that the consumer cannot leave the premises until a contract is formed.

(25) Conducting personal visits to the consumer's home ignoring the consumer's request to leave or not to return except in circumstances and to the extent justified, under national law, to enforce a contractual obligation.

(26) Making persistent and unwanted solicitations by telephone, fax, e-mail or other remote media except in circumstances and to the extent justified under national law to enforce a contractual obligation. This is without prejudice to Article 10 of Directive 97/7/EC and Directives 95/46/EC [2] and 2002/58/EC.

(27) Requiring a consumer who wishes to claim on an insurance policy to produce documents which could not reasonably be considered relevant as to whether the claim was valid, or failing systematically to respond to pertinent correspondence, in order to dissuade a consumer from exercising his contractual rights.

(28) Including in an advertisement a direct exhortation to children to buy advertised products or persuade their parents or other adults to buy advertised products for them. This provision is without prejudice to Article 16 of Directive 89/552/EEC on television broadcasting.

(29) Demanding immediate or deferred payment for or the return or safekeeping of products supplied by the trader, but not solicited by the consumer except where the product is a substitute supplied in conformity with Article 7(3) of Directive 97/7/EC (inertia selling).

(30) Explicitly informing a consumer that if he does not buy the product or service, the trader's job or livelihood will be in jeopardy.

(31) Creating the false impression that the consumer has already won, will win, or will on doing a particular act win, a prize or other equivalent benefit, when in fact either:
- there is no prize or other equivalent benefit, or
- taking any action in relation to claiming the prize or other equivalent benefit is subject to the consumer paying money or incurring a cost.

Directive 2008/122/EC of the European Parliament and of the Council of 14 January 2009 on the protection of consumers in respect of certain aspects of timeshare, long-term holiday product, resale and exchange contracts (Text with EEA relevance) (OJ L 33, 3.2.2009, pp. 10–30) [footnotes omitted].

THE EUROPEAN PARLIAMENT AND THE COUNCIL OF THE EUROPEAN UNION,
Having regard to the Treaty establishing the European Community, and in particular Article 95 thereof,
Having regard to the proposal from the Commission,
Having regard to the opinion of the European Economic and Social Committee,
Acting in accordance with the procedure laid down in Article 251 of the Treaty,
Whereas:

(1) Since the adoption of Directive 94/47/EC of the European Parliament and of the Council of 26 October 1994 on the protection of purchasers in respect of certain aspects of contracts relating to the purchase of the right to use immovable properties on a timeshare basis, timeshare has evolved and new holiday products similar to it have appeared on the market. These new holiday products and certain transactions related to timeshare, such as resale contracts and exchange contracts, are not covered by Directive 94/47/EC. In addition, experience with the application of Directive 94/47/EC has shown that some subjects already covered need to be updated or clarified, in order to prevent the development of products aiming at circumventing this Directive.

(2) The existing regulatory gaps create appreciable distortions of competition and cause serious problems for consumers, thus hindering the smooth functioning of the internal market. Directive 94/47/EC should therefore be replaced by a new up-to-date directive. Since tourism plays an increasingly important role in the economies of the Member States, greater growth and productivity in the timeshare and long-term holiday product industries should be encouraged by adopting certain common rules.

(3) In order to enhance legal certainty and fully achieve the benefits of the internal market for consumers and businesses, the relevant laws of the Member States need to be approximated further. Therefore, certain aspects of the marketing, sale and resale of timeshares and long-term holiday products as well as the exchange of rights deriving from timeshare contracts should be fully harmonised. Member States should not be allowed to maintain or introduce in their national legislation provisions diverging from those laid down in this Directive. Where no such harmonised provisions exist, Member States should remain free to maintain or introduce national legislation in conformity with Community law. Thus, Member States should, for instance, be able to maintain or introduce provisions on the effects of exercising the right of withdrawal in legal relationships falling outside the scope of this Directive or provisions according to which no commitment may be entered into between a consumer and a trader of a timeshare or long-term holiday product, nor any payment made between those persons, as long as the consumer has not signed a credit agreement to finance the purchase of those services.

(4) This Directive should be without prejudice to the application by Member States, in accordance with Community law, of the provisions of this Directive to areas not within its scope. Member States could therefore maintain or introduce national legislation corresponding to the provisions of this Directive or certain of its provisions in relation to transactions that fall outside the scope of this Directive.

(5) The different contracts covered by this Directive should be clearly defined in such a way as to preclude circumvention of its provisions.

(6) For the purposes of this Directive, timeshare contracts should not be understood as covering multiple reservations of accommodation, including hotel rooms, in so far as multiple reservations do not imply rights and obligations beyond those arising from separate reservations. Nor should timeshare contracts be understood as covering ordinary lease contracts since the latter refer to one single continuous period of occupation and not to multiple periods.

(7) For the purposes of this Directive, long-term holiday product contracts should not be understood as covering ordinary loyalty schemes which provide discounts on future stays in the hotels of a hotel chain, since membership in the scheme is not obtained for consideration nor is the consideration paid by the consumer primarily for the purpose of obtaining discounts or other benefits in respect of accommodation.

(8) This Directive should not affect the provisions of Council Directive 90/314/EEC of 13 June 1990 on package travel, package holidays and package tours.

(9) Directive 2005/29/EC of the European Parliament and of the Council of 11 May 2005 concerning unfair business-to-consumer commercial practices in the internal market (Unfair Commercial Practices Directive) prohibits misleading, aggressive and other unfair commercial business-to-consumer

PART IV   EUROPEAN PRIVATE LAW

practices. Given the nature of the products and the commercial practices related to timeshares, long-term holiday products, resale and exchange, it is appropriate to adopt more detailed and specific provisions regarding information requirements and sales events. The commercial purpose of invitations to sales events should be made clear to consumers. The provisions concerning pre-contractual information and the contract should be clarified and updated. In order to give consumers the possibility to acquaint themselves with the information before the conclusion of the contract, it should be provided by means which are easily accessible to them at that time.

(10) Consumers should have the right, which should not be refused by traders, to be provided with pre-contractual information and the contract in a language, of their choice, with which they are familiar. In addition, in order to facilitate the execution and the enforcement of the contract, Member States should be allowed to determine that further language versions of the contract should be provided to consumers.

(11) In order to provide consumers with the opportunity of fully understanding their rights and obligations under the contract, they should be allowed a period during which they may withdraw from the contract without having to justify the withdrawal and without bearing any cost. Currently the length of this period varies between Member States, and experience shows that the length prescribed in Directive 94/47/EC is not sufficiently long. The period should therefore be extended in order to achieve a high level of consumer protection and more clarity for consumers and traders. The length of the period, the modalities for and the effects of exercising the right of withdrawal should be harmonised.

(12) Consumers should have effective remedies in the event that traders do not comply with the provisions regarding pre-contractual information or the contract, in particular those laying down that the contract should include all the information required and that the consumer should receive a copy of the contract at the time of its conclusion. In addition to the remedies existing under national law, consumers should benefit from an extended withdrawal period where information has not been provided by traders. The exercise of the right of withdrawal should remain free of charge during that extended period regardless of what services consumers may have enjoyed. The expiration of the withdrawal period does not preclude consumers from seeking remedies in accordance with national law for breaches of the information requirements.

(13) Council Regulation (EEC, Euratom) No 1182/71 of 3 June 1971 determining the rules applicable to periods, dates and time limits should apply to the calculation of the periods set out in this Directive.

(14) The prohibition on advance payments to traders or any third party before the end of the withdrawal period should be clarified in order to improve consumer protection. For resale contracts, the prohibition of advance payment should apply until the actual sale takes place or the resale contract is terminated, but Member States should remain free to regulate the possibility and modalities of final payments to intermediaries where resale contracts are terminated.

(15) For long-term holiday product contracts, the price to be paid in the context of a staggered payment schedule could take into consideration the possibility that subsequent amounts could be adjusted after the first year in order to ensure that the real value of those instalments is maintained, for instance to take account of inflation.

(16) In the event of a consumer withdrawing from a contract where the price is entirely or partly covered by credit granted to the consumer by the trader or by a third party on the basis of an arrangement between that third party and the trader, the credit agreement should be terminated at no cost to the consumer. The same should apply to contracts for other related services provided by the trader or by a third party on the basis of an arrangement between that third party and the trader.

(17) Consumers should not be deprived of the protection granted by this Directive where the law applicable to the contract is that of a Member State. The law applicable to a contract should be determined in accordance with the Community rules on private international law, in particular Regulation (EC) No 593/2008 of the European Parliament and of the Council of 17 June 2008 on the law applicable to contractual obligations (Rome I).Under that Regulation, the law of a third country may be applicable, in particular where consumers are targeted by traders whilst on holiday in a country other than their country of residence. Given that such commercial practices are common in the area covered by this Directive and that the contracts involve considerable amounts of money, an additional safeguard should be provided in certain specific situations, in particular where the courts of any Member State have jurisdiction over the contract, to ensure that the consumer is not deprived of the protection granted by this Directive. This concept reflects the particular needs of consumer protection arising from the typical complexity, long-term nature and financial relevance of the contracts falling within the scope of this Directive.

(18) It should be determined in accordance with Council Regulation (EC) No 44/2001 of 22 December 2000 on jurisdiction and the recognition and enforcement of judgments in civil and commercial

matters which courts have jurisdiction in proceedings which have as their object matters covered by this Directive.

(19) In order to ensure that the protection afforded to consumers under this Directive is fully effective, in particular as regards compliance by traders with the information requirements both at the pre-contractual stage and in the contract, it is necessary that the Member States lay down effective, proportionate and dissuasive penalties for infringements of this Directive.

(20) It is necessary to ensure that persons or organisations having, under national law, a legitimate interest in the matter have legal remedies for initiating proceedings against infringements of this Directive.

(21) It is necessary to develop suitable and effective redress procedures in the Member States for settling disputes between consumers and traders. To this end, Member States should encourage the establishment of public or private bodies for settling disputes out of court.

(22) Member States should ensure that consumers are effectively informed of the national provisions transposing this Directive and encourage traders and code owners to inform consumers about their codes of conduct in this field. With the aim of pursuing a high level of consumer protection, consumer organisations could be informed of, and involved in, the drafting of codes of conduct.

(23) Since the objectives of this Directive cannot be sufficiently achieved by the Member States and can therefore be better achieved at Community level, the Community may adopt measures in accordance with the principle of subsidiarity as set out in Article 5 of the Treaty. In accordance with the principle of proportionality, as set out in that Article, this Directive does not go beyond what is necessary in order to eliminate the internal market barriers and achieve a high common level of consumer protection.

(24) This Directive respects the fundamental rights and observes the principles recognised in particular by the European Convention on Human Rights and Fundamental Freedoms and the Charter of Fundamental Rights of the European Union.

(25) In accordance with point 34 of the Interinstitutional agreement on better law-making [9], Member States are encouraged to draw up, for themselves and in the interests of the Community, their own tables, which will, as far as possible, illustrate the correlation between this Directive and the transposition measures, and to make them public,

HAVE ADOPTED THIS DIRECTIVE:

Article 1. (1). The purpose of this Directive is to contribute to the proper functioning of the internal market and to achieve a high level of consumer protection, by approximating the laws, regulations and administrative provisions of the Member States in respect of certain aspects of the marketing, sale and resale of timeshares and long-term holiday products as well as exchange contracts.

(2) This Directive applies to trader-to-consumer transactions.

This Directive is without prejudice to national legislation which:

(a) provides for general contract law remedies;

(b) relates to the registration of immovable or movable property and conveyance of immovable property;

(c) relates to conditions of establishment or authorisation regimes or licensing requirements; and

(d) relates to the determination of the legal nature of the rights which are the subject of the contracts covered by this Directive.

Article 2. (1) For the purposes of this Directive, the following definitions shall apply:

(a) "timeshare contract" means a contract of a duration of more than one year under which a consumer, for consideration, acquires the right to use one or more overnight accommodation for more than one period of occupation;

(b) "long-term holiday product contract" means a contract of a duration of more than one year under which a consumer, for consideration, acquires primarily the right to obtain discounts or other benefits in respect of accommodation, in isolation or together with travel or other services;

(c) "resale contract" means a contract under which a trader, for consideration, assists a consumer to sell or buy a timeshare or a long-term holiday product;

(d) "exchange contract" means a contract under which a consumer, for consideration, joins an exchange system which allows that consumer access to overnight accommodation or other services in exchange for granting to other persons temporary access to the benefits of the rights deriving from that consumer's timeshare contract;

(e) "trader" means a natural or legal person who is acting for purposes relating to that person's trade, business, craft or profession and anyone acting in the name of or on behalf of a trader;

(f) "consumer" means a natural person who is acting for purposes which are outside that person's trade, business, craft or profession;

(g) "ancillary contract" means a contract under which the consumer acquires services which are related to a timeshare contract or long-term holiday product contract and which are provided by the trader or a third party on the basis of an arrangement between that third party and the trader;
(h) "durable medium" means any instrument which enables the consumer or the trader to store information addressed personally to him in a way which is accessible for future reference for a period of time adequate for the purposes of the information and which allows the unchanged reproduction of the information stored;
(i) "code of conduct" means an agreement or set of rules not imposed by law, regulation or administrative provision of a Member State which defines the behaviour of traders who undertake to be bound by the code in relation to one or more particular commercial practices or business sectors;
(j) "code owner" means any entity, including a trader or group of traders, which is responsible for the formulation and revision of a code of conduct and/or for monitoring compliance with the code by those who have undertaken to be bound by it.
(2) In calculating the duration of a timeshare contract or a long-term holiday product contract, as defined in points (a) and (b) of paragraph (1) respectively, any provision in the contract allowing for tacit renewal or prolongation shall be taken into account.

Article 3. (1) Member States shall ensure that any advertising specifies the possibility of obtaining the information referred to in Article 4(1) and indicates where it can be obtained.
(2) Where a timeshare, long-term holiday product, resale or exchange contract is to be offered to a consumer in person at a promotion or sales event, the trader shall clearly indicate in the invitation the commercial purpose and the nature of the event.
(3) The information referred to in Article 4(1) shall be available to the consumer at any time during the event.
(4) A timeshare or a long-term holiday product shall not be marketed or sold as an investment.

Article 4. (1) In good time before the consumer is bound by any contract or offer, the trader shall provide the consumer, in a clear and comprehensible manner, with accurate and sufficient information, as follows:
(a) in the case of a timeshare contract: by means of the standard information form as set out in Annex I and information as listed in Part 3 of that form;
(b) in the case of a long-term holiday product contract: by means of the standard information form as set out in Annex II and information as listed in Part 3 of that form;
(c) in the case of a resale contract: by means of the standard information form as set out in Annex III and information as listed in Part 3 of that form;
(d) in the case of an exchange contract: by means of the standard information form as set out in Annex IV and information as listed in Part 3 of that form.
(2). The information referred to in paragraph (1) shall be provided, free of charge, by the trader on paper or on another durable medium which is easily accessible to the consumer.
(3). Member States shall ensure that the information referred to in paragraph (1) is drawn up in the language or one of the languages of the Member State in which the consumer is resident or a national, at the choice of the consumer, provided it is an official language of the Community.

Article 5. (1) Member States shall ensure that the contract is in writing, on paper or on another durable medium, and drawn up in the language or one of the languages of the Member State in which the consumer is resident or a national, at the choice of the consumer, provided it is an official language of the Community.
However, the Member State in which the consumer is resident may require that in addition:
(a) in every instance, the contract be provided to the consumer in the language or one of the languages of that Member State, provided it is an official language of the Community;
(b) in the case of a timeshare contract concerning one specific immovable property, the trader provide the consumer with a certified translation of the contract in the language or one of the languages of the Member State in which the property is situated, provided it is an official language of the Community.
The Member State on whose territory the trader carries out sale activities may require that, in every instance, the contract be provided to the consumer in the language or one of the languages of that Member State, provided it is an official language of the Community.
(2) The information referred to in Article 4(1) shall form an integral part of the contract and shall not be altered unless the parties expressly agree otherwise or the changes result from unusual and unforeseeable circumstances beyond the trader's control, the consequences of which could not have been avoided even if all due care had been exercised.
These changes shall be communicated to the consumer on paper or on another durable medium easily

accessible to him, before the contract is concluded.
The contract shall expressly mention any such changes.
(3) In addition to the information referred to in Article 4(1), the contract shall include:
(a) the identity, place of residence and signature of each of the parties; and
(b) the date and place of the conclusion of the contract.
(4) Before the conclusion of the contract, the trader shall explicitly draw the consumer's attention to the existence of the right of withdrawal, the length of the withdrawal period referred to in Article 6, and the ban on advance payments during the withdrawal period referred to in Article 9.
The corresponding contractual clauses shall be signed separately by the consumer.
The contract shall include a separate standard withdrawal form, as set out in Annex V, intended to facilitate the exercise of the right of withdrawal in accordance with Article 6.
(5) The consumer shall receive a copy or copies of the contract at the time of its conclusion.

Article 6. (1) In addition to the remedies available to the consumer under national law in the event of breach of the provisions of this Directive, Member States shall ensure that the consumer is given a period of 14 calendar days to withdraw from the timeshare, long-term holiday product, resale or exchange contract, without giving any reason.
(2) The withdrawal period shall be calculated:
(a) from the day of the conclusion of the contract or of any binding preliminary contract; or
(b) from the day when the consumer receives the contract or any binding preliminary contract if it is later than the date referred to in point (a).
(3) The withdrawal period shall expire:
(a) after one year and 14 calendar days from the day referred to in paragraph (2) of this Article, where a separate standard withdrawal form as required by Article 5(4) has not been filled in by the trader and provided to the consumer in writing, on paper or on another durable medium;
(b) after three months and 14 calendar days from the day referred to in paragraph (2) of this Article, where the information referred to in Article 4(1), including the applicable standard information form set out in Annexes I to IV, has not been provided to the consumer in writing, on paper or on another durable medium.
In addition, Member States shall provide for appropriate penalties in accordance with Article 15, in particular in the event that, on expiry of the withdrawal period, the trader has failed to comply with the information requirements set out in this Directive.
(4) Where a separate standard withdrawal form as required by Article 5(4) has been filled in by the trader and provided to the consumer in writing, on paper or on another durable medium, within one year from the day referred to in paragraph (2) of this Article, the withdrawal period shall start from the day the consumer receives that form. Similarly, where the information referred to in Article 4(1), including the applicable standard information form set out in Annexes I to IV, has been provided to the consumer in writing, on paper or on another durable medium, within three months from the day referred to in paragraph (2) of this Article, the withdrawal period shall start from the day the consumer receives such information.
(5) In the event that the exchange contract is offered to the consumer together with and at the same time as the timeshare contract, only a single withdrawal period in accordance with paragraph (1) shall apply to both contracts. The withdrawal period for both contracts shall be calculated according to the provisions of paragraph (2) as they apply to the timeshare contract.

Article 7. Where the consumer intends to exercise the right of withdrawal the consumer shall, before the expiry of the withdrawal period, notify the trader on paper or on another durable medium of the decision to withdraw. The consumer may use the standard withdrawal form set out in Annex V and provided by the trader in accordance with Article 5(4). The deadline is met if the notification is sent before the withdrawal period has expired.

Article 8. (1) The exercise of the right of withdrawal by the consumer terminates the obligation of the parties to perform the contract.
(2) Where the consumer exercises the right of withdrawal, the consumer shall neither bear any cost nor be liable for any value corresponding to the service which may have been performed before withdrawal.

Article 9. (1) Member States shall ensure that in relation to timeshare, long-term holiday product and exchange contracts any advance payment, provision of guarantees, reservation of money on accounts, explicit acknowledgement of debt or any other consideration to the trader or to any third party by the consumer before the end of the withdrawal period according to Article 6, is prohibited.
(2) Member States shall ensure that in relation to resale contracts any advance payment, provision

of guarantees, reservation of money on accounts, explicit acknowledgement of debt or any other consideration to the trader or to any third party by the consumer before the actual sale takes place or the resale contract is otherwise terminated, is prohibited.

Article 10. (1) For long-term holiday product contracts, payment shall be made according to a staggered payment schedule. Any payment of the price specified in the contract otherwise than in accordance with the staggered payment schedule shall be prohibited. The payments, including any membership fee, shall be divided into yearly instalments, each of which shall be of equal value. The trader shall send a written request for payment, on paper or on another durable medium, at least fourteen calendar days in advance of each due date.
(2). From the second instalment payment onwards, the consumer may terminate the contract without incurring any penalty by giving notice to the trader within fourteen calendar days of receiving the request for payment of each instalment. This right shall not affect rights to terminate the contract under existing national legislation.

Article 11. (1) Member States shall ensure that, where the consumer exercises the right to withdraw from the timeshare or long-term holiday product contract, any exchange contract ancillary to it or any other ancillary contract is automatically terminated, at no cost to the consumer.
(2) Without prejudice to Article 15 of Directive 2008/48/EC of the European Parliament and of the Council of 23 April 2008 on credit agreements for consumers [10], where the price is fully or partly covered by a credit granted to the consumer by the trader, or by a third party on the basis of an arrangement between the third party and the trader, the credit agreement shall be terminated, at no cost to the consumer, where the consumer exercises the right to withdraw from the timeshare, long-term holiday product, resale or exchange contract.
3. The Member States shall lay down detailed rules on the termination of such contracts.

Article 12. (1). Member States shall ensure that, where the law applicable to the contract is the law of a Member State, consumers may not waive the rights conferred on them by this Directive.
(2) Where the applicable law is that of a third country, consumers shall not be deprived of the protection granted by this Directive, as implemented in the Member State of the forum if:
- any of the immovable properties concerned is situated within the territory of a Member State, or,
- in the case of a contract not directly related to immovable property, the trader pursues commercial or professional activities in a Member State or, by any means, directs such activities to a Member State and the contract falls within the scope of such activities.

Article 13. (1) Member States shall ensure that, in the interests of consumers, adequate and effective means exist to ensure compliance by traders with this Directive.
(2) The means referred to in paragraph (1) shall include provisions whereby one or more of the following bodies, as determined by national law, shall be entitled to take action in accordance with national law before the courts or competent administrative bodies to ensure that the national provisions for implementing this Directive are applied:
(a) public bodies and authorities or their representatives;
(b) consumer organisations with a legitimate interest in protecting consumers;
(c) professional organisations with a legitimate interest in taking such action.

Article 14. (1). Member States shall take appropriate measures to inform consumers of the national law transposing this Directive and shall encourage, where appropriate, traders and code owners to inform consumers of their codes of conduct.
The Commission shall encourage the drawing up at Community level, particularly by professional bodies, organisations and associations, of codes of conduct aimed at facilitating the implementation of this Directive, in conformity with Community law. It shall also encourage traders and their branch organisations to inform consumers of any such codes, including, where appropriate, by means of a specific marking.
(2) Member States shall encourage the setting up or development of adequate and effective out-of-court complaints and redress procedures for the settlement of consumer disputes under this Directive and shall, where appropriate, encourage traders and their branch organisations to inform consumers of the availability of such procedures.

Article 15. (1). Member States shall provide for appropriate penalties in the event of a trader's failure to comply with the national provisions adopted pursuant to this Directive.
(2) Those penalties shall be effective, proportionate and dissuasive.

Article 16. (1) Member States shall adopt and publish, by 23 February 2011, the laws, regulations

and administrative provisions necessary to comply with this Directive. They shall forthwith communicate to the Commission the text of those provisions.
They shall apply those provisions from 23 February 2011.
When Member States adopt those provisions, they shall contain a reference to this Directive or be accompanied by such a reference on the occasion of their official publication. Member States shall determine how such reference is to be made.
(2) Member States shall communicate to the Commission the text of the main provisions of national law which they adopt in the field covered by this Directive.

Article 17. The Commission shall review this Directive and report to the European Parliament and the Council no later than 23 February 2014.
If necessary, it shall make further proposals to adapt it to developments in the area.
The Commission may request information from the Member States and the national regulatory authorities.

Article 18. Directive 94/47/EC shall be repealed.
References to the repealed Directive shall be construed as references to this Directive and shall be read in accordance with the correlation table in Annex VI.

Article 19. This Directive shall enter into force on the 20th day following its publication in the Official Journal of the European Union.

Article 20. This Directive is addressed to the Member States.

Annex I. Standard Information Form for Timeshare Contracts

Part 1:
Identity, place of residence and legal status of the trader(s) which will be party to the contract:
Short description of the product (e.g. description of the immovable property):
Exact nature and content of the right(s):
Exact period within which the right which is the subject of the contract may be exercised and, if necessary, its duration:
Date on which the consumer may start to exercise the contractual right:
If the contract concerns a specific property under construction, date when the accommodation and services/facilities will be completed/available:
Price to be paid by the consumer for acquiring the right(s):
Outline of additional obligatory costs imposed under the contract; type of costs and indication of amounts (e.g. annual fees, other recurrent fees, special levies, local taxes):
A summary of key services available to the consumer (e.g. electricity, water, maintenance, refuse collection) and an indication of the amount to be paid by the consumer for such services:
A summary of facilities available to the consumer (e.g. swimming pool or sauna):
Are these facilities included in the costs indicated above?
If not, specify what is included and what has to be paid for:
Is it possible to join an exchange scheme?
If yes, specify the name of the exchange scheme:
Indication of costs for membership/exchange:
Has the trader signed a code/codes of conduct and, if yes, where can it/they be found?

Part 2:
General information:
The consumer has the right to withdraw from this contract without giving any reason within 14 calendar days from the conclusion of the contract or any binding preliminary contract or receipt of those contracts if that takes place later.
During this withdrawal period, any advance payment by the consumer is prohibited. The prohibition concerns any consideration, including payment, provision of guarantees, reservation of money on accounts, explicit acknowledgement of debt etc. It includes not only payment to the trader, but also to third parties.
The consumer shall not bear any costs or obligations other than those specified in the contract.
In accordance with international private law, the contract may be governed by a law other than the law of the Member State in which the consumer is resident or is habitually domiciled and possible disputes may be referred to courts other than those of the Member State in which the consumer is resident or is habitually domiciled.
Signature of the consumer:

Part 3:
Additional information to which the consumer is entitled and where it can be obtained specifically (for instance, under which chapter of a general brochure) if not provided below:

1. INFORMATION ABOUT THE RIGHTS ACQUIRED

conditions governing the exercise of the right which is the subject of the contract within the territory of the Member States(s) in which the property or properties concerned are situated and information on whether those conditions have been fulfilled or, if they have not, what conditions remain to be fulfilled,

where the contract provides rights to occupy accommodation to be selected from a pool of accommodation, information on restrictions on the consumer's ability to use any accommodation in the pool at any time.

2. INFORMATION ON THE PROPERTIES

where the contract concerns a specific immovable property, an accurate and detailed description of that property and its location; where the contract concerns a number of properties (multi-resorts), an appropriate description of the properties and their location; where the contract concerns accommodation other than immovable property, an appropriate description of the accommodation and the facilities,

the services (e.g. electricity, water, maintenance, refuse collection) to which the consumer has or will have access to and under what conditions,

where applicable, the common facilities, such as swimming pool, sauna, etc., to which the consumer has or may have access and under what conditions.

3. ADDITIONAL REQUIREMENTS FOR ACCOMMODATION UNDER CONSTRUCTION (where applicable)

the state of completion of the accommodation and of the services rendering the accommodation fully operational (gas, electricity, water and telephone connections) and any facilities to which the consumer will have access,

the deadline for completion of the accommodation and of the services rendering it fully operational (gas, electricity, water and telephone connections) and a reasonable estimate of the deadline for the completion of any facilities to which the consumer will have access,

the number of the building permit and the name(s) and full address(es) of the competent authority or authorities,

a guarantee regarding completion of the accommodation or a guarantee regarding reimbursement of any payment made if the accommodation is not completed and, where appropriate, the conditions governing the operation of such guarantees.

4. INFORMATION ON THE COSTS

an accurate and appropriate description of all costs associated with the timeshare contract; how these costs will be allocated to the consumer and how and when such costs may be increased; the method for the calculation of the amount of charges relating to occupation of the property, the mandatory statutory charges (for example, taxes and fees) and the administrative overheads (for example, management, maintenance and repairs),

where applicable, information on whether there are any charges, mortgages, encumbrances or any other liens recorded against title to the accommodation.

5. INFORMATION ON TERMINATION OF THE CONTRACT

where appropriate, information on the arrangements for the termination of ancillary contracts and the consequences of such termination,

conditions for terminating the contract, the consequences of termination, and information on any liability of the consumer for any costs which might result from such termination.

6. ADDITIONAL INFORMATION

information on how maintenance and repairs of the property and its administration and management are arranged, including whether and how consumers may influence and participate in the decisions regarding these issues,

information on whether or not it is possible to join a system for the resale of the contractual rights, information about the relevant system and an indication of costs related to resale through this system,

indication of the language(s) available for communication with the trader in relation to the contract, for instance in relation to management decisions, increase of costs and the handling of queries and complaints,

where applicable, the possibility for out-of-court dispute resolution.

Acknowledgement of receipt of information:
Signature of the consumer:

Annex II. Standard Information Form for Long-Term Holiday Product Contracts

Part 1:

Identity, place of residence and legal status of the trader(s) which will be party to the contract:
Short description of the product:
Exact nature and content of the right(s):
Exact period within which the right which is the subject of the contract may be exercised and, if necessary, its duration:
Date on which the consumer may start to exercise the contractual right:
Price to be paid by the consumer for acquiring the right(s), including any recurring costs the consumer can expect to incur resulting from the right to obtain access to the accommodation, travel and any related products or services as specified:
The staggered payment schedule setting out equal amounts of instalments of this price for each year of the length of the contract and the dates on which they are due to be paid:
After year 1, subsequent amounts may be adjusted to ensure that the real value of those instalments is maintained, for instance to take account of inflation.
Outline of additional obligatory costs imposed under the contract; type of costs and indication of amounts (e.g. annual membership fees):
A summary of key services available to the consumer (e.g. discounted hotel stays and flights):
Are they included in the costs indicated above?
If not, specify what is included and what has to be paid for (e.g. three-night stay included in annual membership fee, all other accommodation must be paid for separately):
Has the trader signed a code/codes of conduct and, if yes, where can it/they be found?

Part 2:

General information:

The consumer has the right to withdraw from this contract without giving any reason within 14 calendar days from the conclusion of the contract or any binding preliminary contract or receipt of those contracts if that takes place later.
During this withdrawal period, any advance payment by the consumer is prohibited. The prohibition concerns any consideration, including payment, provision of guarantees, reservation of money on accounts, explicit acknowledgement of debt etc. It includes not only payment to the trader, but also to third parties.
The consumer has the right to terminate the contract without incurring any penalty by giving notice to the trader within 14 calendar days of receiving the request for payment for each annual instalment. The consumer shall not bear any costs or obligations other than those specified in the contract.
In accordance with international private law, the contract may be governed by a law other than the law of the Member State in which the consumer is resident or is habitually domiciled and possible disputes may be referred to courts other than those of the Member State in which the consumer is resident or is habitually domiciled.
Signature of the consumer:

Part 3:

Additional information to which the consumer is entitled and where it can be obtained specifically (for instance, under which chapter of a general brochure) if not provided below:

1. INFORMATION ABOUT THE RIGHTS ACQUIRED

an appropriate and correct description of discounts available for future bookings, illustrated by a set of examples of recent offers,
information on the restrictions on the consumer's ability to use the rights, such as limited availability or offers provided on a first-come-first-served basis, time limits on particular promotions and special discounts.

2. INFORMATION ON THE TERMINATION OF THE CONTRACT

where appropriate, information on the arrangements for the termination of ancillary contracts and the consequences of such termination,
conditions for terminating the contract, the consequences of termination, and information on any liability of the consumer for any costs which might result from such termination.

3. ADDITIONAL INFORMATION

indication of the language(s) available for communication with the trader in relation to the contract, for instance in relation to the handling of queries and complaints,
where applicable, the possibility for out-of-court dispute resolution.
Acknowledgement of receipt of information:
Signature of the consumer:

PART IV   EUROPEAN PRIVATE LAW

Annex III. Standard Information Form for Resale Contracts

Part 1:
Identity, place of residence and legal status of the trader(s) which will be party to the contract:
Short description of the services (e.g. marketing):
Duration of the contract:
Price to be paid by the consumer for acquiring the services:
Outline of additional obligatory costs imposed under the contract; type of costs and indication of amounts (e.g. local taxes, notary fees, cost of advertising):
Has the trader signed a code/codes of conduct and, if yes, where can it/they be found?

Part 2:
General information:
The consumer has the right to withdraw from this contract without giving any reason within 14 calendar days from the conclusion of the contract or any binding preliminary contract or receipt of those contracts if that takes place later.
Any advance payment by the consumer is prohibited until the actual sale has taken place or the resale contract otherwise is terminated. The prohibition concerns any consideration, including payment, provision of guarantees, reservation of money on accounts, explicit acknowledgement of debt etc. It includes not only payment to the trader, but also to third parties.
The consumer shall not bear any costs or obligations other than those specified in the contract.
In accordance with international private law, the contract may be governed by a law other than the law of the Member State in which the consumer is resident or is habitually domiciled and possible disputes may be referred to courts other than those of the Member State in which the consumer is resident or is habitually domiciled.
Signature of the consumer:

Part 3:
Additional information to which the consumer is entitled and where it can be obtained specifically (for instance, under which chapter of a general brochure) if not provided below:
conditions for terminating the contract, the consequences of termination, and information on any liability of the consumer for any costs which might result from such termination,
indication of the language(s) available for communication with the trader in relation to the contract, for instance in relation to the handling of queries and complaints,
where applicable, the possibility for out-of-court dispute resolution.
Acknowledgement of receipt of information:
Signature of the consumer:

Annex IV. Standard Information Form for Exchange Contracts

Part 1:
Identity, place of residence and legal status of the trader(s) which will be party to the contract:
Short description of the product:
Exact nature and content of the right(s):
Exact period within which the right which is the subject of the contract may be exercised and, if necessary, its duration:
Date on which the consumer may start to exercise the contractual right:
Price to be paid by the consumer for the exchange membership fees:
Outline of additional obligatory costs imposed under the contract; type of costs and indication of amounts (e.g. renewal fees, other recurrent fees, special levies, local taxes):
A summary of key services available to the consumer:
Are they included in the costs indicated above?
If not, specify what is included and what has to be paid for (type of costs and indication of amounts; e.g. an estimate of the price to be paid for individual exchange transactions, including any additional charges):
Has the trader signed a code/codes of conduct and, if yes, where can it/they be found?

Part 2:
General information:
The consumer has the right to withdraw from this contract without giving any reason within 14 calendar days from the conclusion of the contract or any binding preliminary contract or receipt of those contracts if that takes place later. In cases where the exchange contract is offered together with and at

the same time as the timeshare contract, only a single withdrawal period shall apply to both contracts. During this withdrawal period, any advance payment by the consumer is prohibited. The prohibition concerns any consideration, including payment, provision of guarantees, reservation of money on accounts, explicit acknowledgement of debt etc. It includes not only payment to the trader, but also to third parties.

The consumer shall not bear any costs or obligations other than those specified in the contract, In accordance with international private law, the contract may be governed by a law other than the law of the Member State in which the consumer is resident or is habitually domiciled and possible disputes may be referred to courts other than those of the Member State in which the consumer is resident or is habitually domiciled.

Signature of the consumer:

Part 3:

Additional information to which the consumer is entitled and where it can be obtained specifically (for instance, under which chapter of a general brochure) if not provided below:

1. INFORMATION ABOUT THE RIGHTS ACQUIRED

explanation of how the exchange system works; the possibilities and modalities for exchange; an indication of the value allotted to the consumer's timeshare in the exchange system and a set of examples of concrete exchange possibilities,

an indication of the number of resorts available and the number of members in the exchange system, including any limitations on the availability of particular accommodation selected by the consumer, for example, as the result of peak periods of demand, the potential need to book a long time in advance, and indications of any restrictions on the choice resulting from the timeshare rights deposited into the exchange system by the consumer.

2. INFORMATION ON THE PROPERTIES

a brief and appropriate description of the properties and their location; where the contract concerns accommodation other than immovable property, an appropriate description of the accommodation and the facilities; description of where the consumer can obtain further information.

3. INFORMATION ON THE COSTS

information on the obligation on the trader to provide details before an exchange is arranged, in respect of each proposed exchange, of any additional charges for which the consumer is liable in respect of the exchange.

4. INFORMATION ON THE TERMINATION OF THE CONTRACT

where appropriate, information on the arrangements for the termination of ancillary contracts and the consequences of such termination,

conditions for terminating the contract, the consequences of termination, and information on any liability of the consumer for any costs which might result from such termination.

5. ADDITIONAL INFORMATION

indication of the language(s) available for communication with the trader in relation to the contract, for instance in relation to the handling of queries and complaints,

where applicable, the possibility for out-of-court dispute resolution.

Acknowledgement of receipt of information:

Signature of the consumer:

Annex V. Separate Standard Withdrawal Form to Facilitate the Right of Withdrawal

Right of withdrawal

The consumer has the right to withdraw from this contract within 14 calendar days without giving any reason.

The right of withdrawal starts from … (to be filled in by the trader before providing the form to the consumer).

Where the consumer has not received this form, the withdrawal period starts when the consumer has received this form, but expires in any case after one year and 14 calendar days.

Where the consumer has not received all the required information, the withdrawal period starts when the consumer has received that information, but expires in any case after three months and 14 calendar days.

To exercise the right of withdrawal, the consumer shall notify the trader using the name and address indicated below by using a durable medium (e.g. written letter sent by post, e-mail). The consumer may use this form, but it is not obligatory.

Where the consumer exercises the right of withdrawal, the consumer shall not be liable for any costs. In addition to the right of withdrawal, national contract law rules may provide for consumer rights, e.g. to terminate the contract in case of omission of information.

PART IV   EUROPEAN PRIVATE LAW

Ban on advance payment

During the withdrawal period any advance payment by the consumer is prohibited. The prohibition concerns any consideration, including payment, provision of guarantees, reservation of money on accounts, explicit acknowledgement of debt, etc.

It includes not only payment to the trader, but also to third parties.

Notice of withdrawal

To (Name and address of the trader) (*):

I/We (**) hereby give notice that I/We (**) withdraw from the contract,

Date of conclusion of contract (*):

Name(s) of consumer(s) (***):

Address(es) of consumer(s) (***):

Signature(s) of consumer(s) (only if this form is notified on paper) (***):

Date (***):

(*) To be filled in by the trader before providing the form to the consumer.

(**) Delete as appropriate.

(***) To be filled in by the consumer(s) where this form is used to withdraw from the contract.

Acknowledgement of receipt of information:

Signature of the consumer:

EU: DIRECTIVE 2011/83 ON CONSUMER RIGHTS

Directive 2011/83/EU of the European Parliament and of the Council of 25 October 2011 on consumer rights, amending Council Directive 93/13/EEC and Directive 1999/44/EC of the European Parliament and of the Council and repealing Council Directive 85/577/EEC and Directive 97/7/EC of the European Parliament and of the Council (Text with EEA relevance) (OJ L 304, 22.11.2011, pp. 64–88) [footnotes omitted].

THE EUROPEAN PARLIAMENT AND THE COUNCIL OF THE EUROPEAN UNION,
Having regard to the Treaty on the Functioning of the European Union, and in particular Article 114 thereof,
Having regard to the proposal from the European Commission,
Having regard to the opinion of the European Economic and Social Committee,
Having regard to the opinion of the Committee of the Regions,
Acting in accordance with the ordinary legislative procedure,,
Whereas:
(1) Council Directive 85/577/EEC of 20 December 1985 to protect the consumer in respect of contracts negotiated away from business premises and Directive 97/7/EC of the European Parliament and of the Council of 20 May 1997 on the protection of consumers in respect of distance contracts lay down a number of contractual rights for consumers.
(2) Those Directives have been reviewed in the light of experience with a view to simplifying and updating the applicable rules, removing inconsistencies and closing unwanted gaps in the rules. That review has shown that it is appropriate to replace those two Directives by a single Directive. This Directive should therefore lay down standard rules for the common aspects of distance and off-premises contracts, moving away from the minimum harmonisation approach in the former Directives whilst allowing Member States to maintain or adopt national rules in relation to certain aspects.
(3) Article 169(1) and point (a) of Article 169(2) of the Treaty on the Functioning of the European Union (TFEU) provide that the Union is to contribute to the attainment of a high level of consumer protection through the measures adopted pursuant to Article 114 thereof.
(4) In accordance with Article 26(2) TFEU, the internal market is to comprise an area without internal frontiers in which the free movement of goods and services and freedom of establishment are ensured. The harmonisation of certain aspects of consumer distance and off-premises contracts is necessary for the promotion of a real consumer internal market striking the right balance between a high level of consumer protection and the competitiveness of enterprises, while ensuring respect for the principle of subsidiarity.
(5) The cross-border potential of distance selling, which should be one of the main tangible results of the internal market, is not fully exploited. Compared with the significant growth of domestic distance sales over the last few years, the growth in cross-border distance sales has been limited. This discrepancy is particularly significant for Internet sales for which the potential for further growth is high. The cross-border potential of contracts negotiated away from business premises (direct selling) is constrained by a number of factors including the different national consumer protection rules imposed upon the industry. Compared with the growth of domestic direct selling over the last few years, in particular in the services sector, for instance utilities, the number of consumers using this channel for cross-border purchases has remained flat. Responding to increased business opportunities in many Member States, small and medium-sized enterprises (including individual traders) or agents of direct selling companies should be more inclined to seek business opportunities in other Member States, in particular in border regions. Therefore the full harmonisation of consumer information and the right of withdrawal in distance and off-premises contracts will contribute to a high level of consumer protection and a better functioning of the business-to-consumer internal market.
(6) Certain disparities create significant internal market barriers affecting traders and consumers. Those disparities increase compliance costs to traders wishing to engage in the cross-border sale of goods or provision of services. Disproportionate fragmentation also undermines consumer confidence in the internal market.
(7) Full harmonisation of some key regulatory aspects should considerably increase legal certainty for both consumers and traders. Both consumers and traders should be able to rely on a single regulatory framework based on clearly defined legal concepts regulating certain aspects of business-to-consumer contracts across the Union. The effect of such harmonisation should be to eliminate the barriers stemming from the fragmentation of the rules and to complete the internal market in this area. Those barriers can only be eliminated by establishing uniform rules at Union level. Furthermore consumers should enjoy a high common level of protection across the Union.
(8) The regulatory aspects to be harmonised should only concern contracts concluded between traders and consumers. Therefore, this Directive should not affect national law in the area of contracts

PART IV   EUROPEAN PRIVATE LAW

relating to employment, contracts relating to succession rights, contracts relating to family law and contracts relating to the incorporation and organisation of companies or partnership agreements.

(9) This Directive establishes rules on information to be provided for distance contracts, off-premises contracts and contracts other than distance and off-premises contracts. This Directive also regulates the right of withdrawal for distance and off-premises contracts and harmonises certain provisions dealing with the performance and some other aspects of business-to-consumer contracts.

(10) This Directive should be without prejudice to Regulation (EC) No 593/2008 of the European Parliament and of the Council of 17 June 2008 on the law applicable to contractual obligations (Rome I).

(11) This Directive should be without prejudice to Union provisions relating to specific sectors, such as medicinal products for human use, medical devices, privacy and electronic communications, patients' rights in cross-border healthcare, food labelling and the internal market for electricity and natural gas.

(12) The information requirements provided for in this Directive should complete the information requirements of Directive 2006/123/EC of the European Parliament and of the Council of 12 December 2006 on services in the internal market and Directive 2000/31/EC of the European Parliament and of the Council of 8 June 2000 on certain legal aspects of information society services, in particular electronic commerce, in the Internal Market ('Directive on electronic commerce'). Member States should retain the possibility to impose additional information requirements applicable to service providers established in their territory.

(13) Member States should remain competent, in accordance with Union law, to apply the provisions of this Directive to areas not falling within its scope. Member States may therefore maintain or introduce national legislation corresponding to the provisions of this Directive, or certain of its provisions, in relation to contracts that fall outside the scope of this Directive. For instance, Member States may decide to extend the application of the rules of this Directive to legal persons or to natural persons who are not consumers within the meaning of this Directive, such as non-governmental organisations, start-ups or small and medium-sized enterprises. Similarly, Member States may apply the provisions of this Directive to contracts that are not distance contracts within the meaning of this Directive, for example because they are not concluded under an organised distance sales or service-provision scheme. Moreover, Member States may also maintain or introduce national provisions on issues not specifically addressed in this Directive, such as additional rules concerning sales contracts, including in relation to the delivery of goods, or requirements for the provision of information during the existence of a contract.

(14) This Directive should not affect national law in the area of contract law for contract law aspects that are not regulated by this Directive. Therefore, this Directive should be without prejudice to national law regulating for instance the conclusion or the validity of a contract (for instance in the case of lack of consent). Similarly, this Directive should not affect national law in relation to the general contractual legal remedies, the rules on public economic order, for instance rules on excessive or extortionate prices, and the rules on unethical legal transactions.

(15) This Directive should not harmonise language requirements applicable to consumer contracts. Therefore, Member States may maintain or introduce in their national law language requirements regarding contractual information and contractual terms.

(16) This Directive should not affect national laws on legal representation such as the rules relating to the person who is acting in the name of the trader or on his behalf (such as an agent or a trustee). Member States should remain competent in this area. This Directive should apply to all traders, whether public or private.

(17) The definition of consumer should cover natural persons who are acting outside their trade, business, craft or profession. However, in the case of dual purpose contracts, where the contract is concluded for purposes partly within and partly outside the person's trade and the trade purpose is so limited as not to be predominant in the overall context of the contract, that person should also be considered as a consumer.

(18) This Directive does not affect the freedom of Member States to define, in conformity with Union law, what they consider to be services of general economic interest, how those services should be organised and financed, in compliance with State aid rules, and which specific obligations they should be subject to.

(19) Digital content means data which are produced and supplied in digital form, such as computer programs, applications, games, music, videos or texts, irrespective of whether they are accessed through downloading or streaming, from a tangible medium or through any other means. Contracts for the supply of digital content should fall within the scope of this Directive. If digital content is supplied on a tangible medium, such as a CD or a DVD, it should be considered as goods within

the meaning of this Directive. Similarly to contracts for the supply of water, gas or electricity, where they are not put up for sale in a limited volume or set quantity, or of district heating, contracts for digital content which is not supplied on a tangible medium should be classified, for the purpose of this Directive, neither as sales contracts nor as service contracts. For such contracts, the consumer should have a right of withdrawal unless he has consented to the beginning of the performance of the contract during the withdrawal period and has acknowledged that he will consequently lose the right to withdraw from the contract. In addition to the general information requirements, the trader should inform the consumer about the functionality and the relevant interoperability of digital content. The notion of functionality should refer to the ways in which digital content can be used, for instance for the tracking of consumer behaviour; it should also refer to the absence or presence of any technical restrictions such as protection via Digital Rights Management or region coding. The notion of relevant interoperability is meant to describe the information regarding the standard hardware and software environment with which the digital content is compatible, for instance the operating system, the necessary version and certain hardware features. The Commission should examine the need for further harmonisation of provisions in respect of digital content and submit, if necessary, a legislative proposal for addressing this matter.

(20) The definition of distance contract should cover all cases where a contract is concluded between the trader and the consumer under an organised distance sales or service-provision scheme, with the exclusive use of one or more means of distance communication (such as mail order, Internet, telephone or fax) up to and including the time at which the contract is concluded. That definition should also cover situations where the consumer visits the business premises merely for the purpose of gathering information about the goods or services and subsequently negotiates and concludes the contract at a distance. By contrast, a contract which is negotiated at the business premises of the trader and finally concluded by means of distance communication should not be considered a distance contract. Neither should a contract initiated by means of distance communication, but finally concluded at the business premises of the trader be considered a distance contract. Similarly, the concept of distance contract should not include reservations made by a consumer through a means of distance communications to request the provision of a service from a professional, such as in the case of a consumer phoning to request an appointment with a hairdresser. The notion of an organised distance sales or service-provision scheme should include those schemes offered by a third party other than the trader but used by the trader, such as an online platform. It should not, however, cover cases where websites merely offer information on the trader, his goods and/or services and his contact details.

(21) An off-premises contract should be defined as a contract concluded with the simultaneous physical presence of the trader and the consumer, in a place which is not the business premises of the trader, for example at the consumer's home or workplace. In an off-premises context, the consumer may be under potential psychological pressure or may be confronted with an element of surprise, irrespective of whether or not the consumer has solicited the trader's visit. The definition of an off-premises contract should also include situations where the consumer is personally and individually addressed in an off-premises context but the contract is concluded immediately afterwards on the business premises of the trader or through a means of distance communication. The definition of an off-premises contract should not cover situations in which the trader first comes to the consumer's home strictly with a view to taking measurements or giving an estimate without any commitment of the consumer and where the contract is then concluded only at a later point in time on the business premises of the trader or via means of distance communication on the basis of the trader's estimate. In those cases, the contract is not to be considered as having been concluded immediately after the trader has addressed the consumer if the consumer has had time to reflect upon the estimate of the trader before concluding the contract. Purchases made during an excursion organised by the trader during which the products acquired are promoted and offered for sale should be considered as off-premises contracts.

(22) Business premises should include premises in whatever form (such as shops, stalls or lorries) which serve as a permanent or usual place of business for the trader. Market stalls and fair stands should be treated as business premises if they fulfil this condition. Retail premises where the trader carries out his activity on a seasonal basis, for instance during the tourist season at a ski or beach resort, should be considered as business premises as the trader carries out his activity in those premises on a usual basis. Spaces accessible to the public, such as streets, shopping malls, beaches, sports facilities and public transport, which the trader uses on an exceptional basis for his business activities as well as private homes or workplaces should not be regarded as business premises. The business premises of a person acting in the name or on behalf of the trader as defined in this Directive should be considered as business premises within the meaning of this Directive.

PART IV EUROPEAN PRIVATE LAW

(23) Durable media should enable the consumer to store the information for as long as it is necessary for him to protect his interests stemming from his relationship with the trader. Such media should include in particular paper, USB sticks, CD-ROMs, DVDs, memory cards or the hard disks of computers as well as e-mails.

(24) A public auction implies that traders and consumers attend or are given the possibility to attend the auction in person. The goods or services are offered by the trader to the consumer through a bidding procedure authorised by law in some Member States, to offer goods or services at public sale. The successful bidder is bound to purchase the goods or services. The use of online platforms for auction purposes which are at the disposal of consumers and traders should not be considered as a public auction within the meaning of this Directive.

(25) Contracts related to district heating should be covered by this Directive, similarly to the contracts for the supply of water, gas or electricity. District heating refers to the supply of heat, inter alia, in the form of steam or hot water, from a central source of production through a transmission and distribution system to multiple buildings, for the purpose of heating.

(26) Contracts related to the transfer of immovable property or of rights in immovable property or to the creation or acquisition of such immovable property or rights, contracts for the construction of new buildings or the substantial conversion of existing buildings as well as contracts for the rental of accommodation for residential purposes are already subject to a number of specific requirements in national legislation. Those contracts include for instance sales of immovable property still to be developed and hire-purchase. The provisions of this Directive are not appropriate to those contracts, which should be therefore excluded from its scope. A substantial conversion is a conversion comparable to the construction of a new building, for example where only the façade of an old building is retained. Service contracts in particular those related to the construction of annexes to buildings (for example a garage or a veranda) and those related to repair and renovation of buildings other than substantial conversion, should be included in the scope of this Directive, as well as contracts related to the services of a real estate agent and those related to the rental of accommodation for non-residential purposes.

(27) Transport services cover passenger transport and transport of goods. Passenger transport should be excluded from the scope of this Directive as it is already subject to other Union legislation or, in the case of public transport and taxis, to regulation at national level. However, the provisions of this Directive protecting consumers against excessive fees for the use of means of payment or against hidden costs should apply also to passenger transport contracts. In relation to transport of goods and car rental which are services, consumers should benefit from the protection afforded by this Directive, with the exception of the right of withdrawal.

(28) In order to avoid administrative burden being placed on traders, Member States may decide not to apply this Directive where goods or services of a minor value are sold off-premises. The monetary threshold should be established at a sufficiently low level as to exclude only purchases of small significance. Member States should be allowed to define this value in their national legislation provided that it does not exceed EUR 50. Where two or more contracts with related subjects are concluded at the same time by the consumer, the total cost thereof should be taken into account for the purpose of applying this threshold.

(29) Social services have fundamentally distinct features that are reflected in sector-specific legislation, partially at Union level and partially at national level. Social services include, on the one hand, services for particularly disadvantaged or low income persons as well as services for persons and families in need of assistance in carrying out routine, everyday tasks and, on the other hand, services for all people who have a special need for assistance, support, protection or encouragement in a specific life phase. Social services cover, inter alia, services for children and youth, assistance services for families, single parents and older persons, and services for migrants. Social services cover both short-term and long-term care services, for instance services provided by home care services or provided in assisted living facilities and residential homes or housing ('nursing homes'). Social services include not only those provided by the State at a national, regional or local level by providers mandated by the State or by charities recognised by the State but also those provided by private operators. The provisions of this Directive are not appropriate to social services which should be therefore excluded from its scope.

(30) Healthcare requires special regulations because of its technical complexity, its importance as a service of general interest as well as its extensive public funding. Healthcare is defined in Directive 2011/24/EU of the European Parliament and of the Council of 9 March 2011 on the application of patients' rights in cross-border healthcare as 'health services provided by health professionals to patients to assess, maintain or restore their state of health, including the prescription, dispensation and provision of medicinal products and medical devices'. Health professional is defined in

that Directive as a doctor of medicine, a nurse responsible for general care, a dental practitioner, a midwife or a pharmacist within the meaning of Directive 2005/36/EC of the European Parliament and of the Council of 7 September 2005 on the recognition of professional qualifications or another professional exercising activities in the healthcare sector which are restricted to a regulated profession as defined in point (a) of Article 3(1) of Directive 2005/36/EC, or a person considered to be a health professional according to the legislation of the Member State of treatment. The provisions of this Directive are not appropriate to healthcare which should be therefore excluded from its scope.

(31) Gambling should be excluded from the scope of this Directive. Gambling activities are those which involve wagering at stake with pecuniary value in games of chance, including lotteries, gambling in casinos and betting transactions. Member States should be able to adopt other, including more stringent, consumer protection measures in relation to such activities.

(32) The existing Union legislation, inter alia, relating to consumer financial services, package travel and timeshare contains numerous rules on consumer protection. For this reason, this Directive should not apply to contracts in those areas. With regard to financial services, Member States should be encouraged to draw inspiration from existing Union legislation in that area when legislating in areas not regulated at Union level, in such a way that a level playing field for all consumers and all contracts relating to financial services is ensured.

(33) The trader should be obliged to inform the consumer in advance of any arrangement resulting in the consumer paying a deposit to the trader, including an arrangement whereby an amount is blocked on the consumer's credit or debit card.

(34) The trader should give the consumer clear and comprehensible information before the consumer is bound by a distance or off-premises contract, a contract other than a distance or an off-premises contract, or any corresponding offer. In providing that information, the trader should take into account the specific needs of consumers who are particularly vulnerable because of their mental, physical or psychological infirmity, age or credulity in a way which the trader could reasonably be expected to foresee. However, taking into account such specific needs should not lead to different levels of consumer protection.

(35) The information to be provided by the trader to the consumer should be mandatory and should not be altered. Nevertheless, the contracting parties should be able to expressly agree to change the content of the contract subsequently concluded, for instance the arrangements for delivery.

(36) In the case of distance contracts, the information requirements should be adapted to take into account the technical constraints of certain media, such as the restrictions on the number of characters on certain mobile telephone screens or the time constraint on television sales spots. In such cases the trader should comply with a minimum set of information requirements and refer the consumer to another source of information, for instance by providing a toll free telephone number or a hypertext link to a webpage of the trader where the relevant information is directly available and easily accessible. As to the requirement to inform the consumer of the cost of returning goods which by their nature cannot normally be returned by post, it will be considered to have been met, for example, if the trader specifies one carrier (for instance the one he assigned for the delivery of the good) and one price concerning the cost of returning the goods. Where the cost of returning the goods cannot reasonably be calculated in advance by the trader, for example because the trader does not offer to arrange for the return of the goods himself, the trader should provide a statement that such a cost will be payable, and that this cost may be high, along with a reasonable estimation of the maximum cost, which could be based on the cost of delivery to the consumer.

(37) Since in the case of distance sales, the consumer is not able to see the goods before concluding the contract, he should have a right of withdrawal. For the same reason, the consumer should be allowed to test and inspect the goods he has bought to the extent necessary to establish the nature, characteristics and the functioning of the goods. Concerning off-premises contracts, the consumer should have the right of withdrawal because of the potential surprise element and/or psychological pressure. Withdrawal from the contract should terminate the obligation of the contracting parties to perform the contract.

(38) Trading websites should indicate clearly and legibly at the latest at the beginning of the ordering process whether any delivery restrictions apply and which means of payment are accepted.

(39) It is important to ensure for distance contracts concluded through websites that the consumer is able to fully read and understand the main elements of the contract before placing his order. To that end, provision should be made in this Directive for those elements to be displayed in the close vicinity of the confirmation requested for placing the order. It is also important to ensure that, in such situations, the consumer is able to determine the moment at which he assumes the obligation to pay the trader. Therefore, the consumer's attention should specifically be drawn, through an unambiguous formulation, to the fact that placing the order entails the obligation to pay the trader.

PART IV   EUROPEAN PRIVATE LAW

(40) The current varying lengths of the withdrawal periods both between the Member States and for distance and off-premises contracts cause legal uncertainty and compliance costs. The same withdrawal period should apply to all distance and off-premises contracts. In the case of service contracts, the withdrawal period should expire after 14 days from the conclusion of the contract. In the case of sales contracts, the withdrawal period should expire after 14 days from the day on which the consumer or a third party other than the carrier and indicated by the consumer, acquires physical possession of the goods. In addition the consumer should be able to exercise the right to withdraw before acquiring physical possession of the goods. Where multiple goods are ordered by the consumer in one order but are delivered separately, the withdrawal period should expire after 14 days from the day on which the consumer acquires physical possession of the last good. Where goods are delivered in multiple lots or pieces, the withdrawal period should expire after 14 days from the day on which the consumer acquires the physical possession of the last lot or piece.

(41) In order to ensure legal certainty, it is appropriate that Council Regulation (EEC, Euratom) No 1182/71 of 3 June 1971 determining the rules applicable to periods, dates and time limits should apply to the calculation of the periods contained in this Directive. Therefore, all periods contained in this Directive should be understood to be expressed in calendar days. Where a period expressed in days is to be calculated from the moment at which an event occurs or an action takes place, the day during which that event occurs or that action takes place should not be considered as falling within the period in question.

(42) The provisions relating to the right of withdrawal should be without prejudice to the Member States' laws and regulations governing the termination or unenforceability of a contract or the possibility for the consumer to fulfil his contractual obligations before the time determined in the contract.

(43) If the trader has not adequately informed the consumer prior to the conclusion of a distance or off-premises contract, the withdrawal period should be extended. However, in order to ensure legal certainty as regards the length of the withdrawal period, a 12-month limitation period should be introduced.

(44) Differences in the ways in which the right of withdrawal is exercised in the Member States have caused costs for traders selling cross-border. The introduction of a harmonised model withdrawal form that the consumer may use should simplify the withdrawal process and bring legal certainty. For these reasons, Member States should refrain from adding any presentational requirements to the Union-wide model form relating for example to the font size. However, the consumer should remain free to withdraw in his own words, provided that his statement setting out his decision to withdraw from the contract to the trader is unequivocal. A letter, a telephone call or returning the goods with a clear statement could meet this requirement, but the burden of proof of having withdrawn within the time limits fixed in the Directive should be on the consumer. For this reason, it is in the interest of the consumer to make use of a durable medium when communicating his withdrawal to the trader.

(45) As experience shows that many consumers and traders prefer to communicate via the trader's website, there should be a possibility for the trader to give the consumer the option of filling in a web-based withdrawal form. In this case the trader should provide an acknowledgement of receipt for instance by e-mail without delay.

(46) In the event that the consumer withdraws from the contract, the trader should reimburse all payments received from the consumer, including those covering the expenses borne by the trader to deliver goods to the consumer. The reimbursement should not be made by voucher unless the consumer has used vouchers for the initial transaction or has expressly accepted them. If the consumer expressly chooses a certain type of delivery (for instance 24-hour express delivery), although the trader had offered a common and generally acceptable type of delivery which would have incurred lower delivery costs, the consumer should bear the difference in costs between these two types of delivery.

(47) Some consumers exercise their right of withdrawal after having used the goods to an extent more than necessary to establish the nature, characteristics and the functioning of the goods. In this case the consumer should not lose the right to withdraw but should be liable for any diminished value of the goods. In order to establish the nature, characteristics and functioning of the goods, the consumer should only handle and inspect them in the same manner as he would be allowed to do in a shop. For example, the consumer should only try on a garment and should not be allowed to wear it. Consequently, the consumer should handle and inspect the goods with due care during the withdrawal period. The obligations of the consumer in the event of withdrawal should not discourage the consumer from exercising his right of withdrawal.

(48) The consumer should be required to send back the goods not later than 14 days after having informed the trader about his decision to withdraw from the contract. In situations where the trader or the consumer does not fulfil the obligations relating to the exercise of the right of withdrawal,

penalties provided for by national legislation in accordance with this Directive should apply as well as contract law provisions.

(49) Certain exceptions from the right of withdrawal should exist, both for distance and off-premises contracts. A right of withdrawal could be inappropriate for example given the nature of particular goods or services. That is the case for example with wine supplied a long time after the conclusion of a contract of a speculative nature where the value is dependent on fluctuations in the market ('vin en primeur'). The right of withdrawal should neither apply to goods made to the consumer's specifications or which are clearly personalised such as tailor-made curtains, nor to the supply of fuel, for example, which is a good, by nature inseparably mixed with other items after delivery. The granting of a right of withdrawal to the consumer could also be inappropriate in the case of certain services where the conclusion of the contract implies the setting aside of capacity which, if a right of withdrawal were exercised, the trader may find difficult to fill. This would for example be the case where reservations are made at hotels or concerning holiday cottages or cultural or sporting events.

(50) On the one hand, the consumer should benefit from his right of withdrawal even in case he has asked for the provision of services before the end of the withdrawal period. On the other hand, if the consumer exercises his right of withdrawal, the trader should be assured to be adequately paid for the service he has provided. The calculation of the proportionate amount should be based on the price agreed in the contract unless the consumer demonstrates that that total price is itself disproportionate, in which case the amount to be paid shall be calculated on the basis of the market value of the service provided. The market value should be defined by comparing the price of an equivalent service performed by other traders at the time of the conclusion of the contract. Therefore the consumer should request the performance of services before the end of the withdrawal period by making this request expressly and, in the case of off-premises contracts, on a durable medium. Similarly, the trader should inform the consumer on a durable medium of any obligation to pay the proportionate costs for the services already provided. For contracts having as their object both goods and services, the rules provided for in this Directive on the return of goods should apply to the goods aspects and the compensation regime for services should apply to the services aspects.

(51) The main difficulties encountered by consumers and one of the main sources of disputes with traders concern delivery of goods, including goods getting lost or damaged during transport and late or partial delivery. Therefore it is appropriate to clarify and harmonise the national rules as to when delivery should occur. The place and modalities of delivery and the rules concerning the determination of the conditions for the transfer of the ownership of the goods and the moment at which such transfer takes place, should remain subject to national law and therefore should not be affected by this Directive. The rules on delivery laid down in this Directive should include the possibility for the consumer to allow a third party to acquire on his behalf the physical possession or control of the goods. The consumer should be considered to have control of the goods where he or a third party indicated by the consumer has access to the goods to use them as an owner, or the ability to resell the goods (for example, when he has received the keys or possession of the ownership documents).

(52) In the context of sales contracts, the delivery of goods can take place in various ways, either immediately or at a later date. If the parties have not agreed on a specific delivery date, the trader should deliver the goods as soon as possible, but in any event not later than 30 days from the day of the conclusion of the contract. The rules regarding late delivery should also take into account goods to be manufactured or acquired specially for the consumer which cannot be reused by the trader without considerable loss. Therefore, a rule which grants an additional reasonable period of time to the trader in certain circumstances should be provided for in this Directive. When the trader has failed to deliver the goods within the period of time agreed with the consumer, before the consumer can terminate the contract, the consumer should call upon the trader to make the delivery within a reasonable additional period of time and be entitled to terminate the contract if the trader fails to deliver the goods even within that additional period of time. However, this rule should not apply when the trader has refused to deliver the goods in an unequivocal statement. Neither should it apply in certain circumstances where the delivery period is essential such as, for example, in the case of a wedding dress which should be delivered before the wedding. Nor should it apply in circumstances where the consumer informs the trader that delivery on a specified date is essential. For this purpose, the consumer may use the trader's contact details given in accordance with this Directive. In these specific cases, if the trader fails to deliver the goods on time, the consumer should be entitled to terminate the contract immediately after the expiry of the delivery period initially agreed. This Directive should be without prejudice to national provisions on the way the consumer should notify the trader of his will to terminate the contract.

(53) In addition to the consumer's right to terminate the contract where the trader has failed to fulfil his obligations to deliver the goods in accordance with this Directive, the consumer may, in accord-

ance with the applicable national law, have recourse to other remedies, such as granting the trader an additional period of time for delivery, enforcing the performance of the contract, withholding payment, and seeking damages.

(54) In accordance with Article 52(3) of Directive 2007/64/EC of the European Parliament and of the Council of 13 November 2007 on payment services in the internal market, Member States should be able to prohibit or limit traders' right to request charges from consumers taking into account the need to encourage competition and promote the use of efficient payment instruments. In any event, traders should be prohibited from charging consumers fees that exceed the cost borne by the trader for the use of a certain means of payment.

(55) Where the goods are dispatched by the trader to the consumer, disputes may arise, in the event of loss or damage, as to the moment at which the transfer of risk takes place. Therefore this Directive should provide that the consumer be protected against any risk of loss of or damage to the goods occurring before he has acquired the physical possession of the goods. The consumer should be protected during a transport arranged or carried out by the trader, even where the consumer has chosen a particular delivery method from a range of options offered by the trader. However, that provision should not apply to contracts where it is up to the consumer to take delivery of the goods himself or to ask a carrier to take delivery. Regarding the moment of the transfer of the risk, a consumer should be considered to have acquired the physical possession of the goods when he has received them.

(56) Persons or organisations regarded under national law as having a legitimate interest in protecting consumer contractual rights should be afforded the right to initiate proceedings, either before a court or before an administrative authority which is competent to decide upon complaints or to initiate appropriate legal proceedings.

(57) It is necessary that Member States lay down penalties for infringements of this Directive and ensure that they are enforced. The penalties should be effective, proportionate and dissuasive.

(58) The consumer should not be deprived of the protection granted by this Directive. Where the law applicable to the contract is that of a third country, Regulation (EC) No 593/2008 should apply, in order to determine whether the consumer retains the protection granted by this Directive.

(59) The Commission, following consultation with the Member States and stakeholders, should look into the most appropriate way to ensure that all consumers are made aware of their rights at the point of sale.

(60) Since inertia selling, which consists of unsolicited supply of goods or provision of services to consumers, is prohibited by Directive 2005/29/EC of the European Parliament and of the Council of 11 May 2005 concerning unfair business-to-consumer commercial practices in the internal market ('Unfair Commercial Practices Directive') but no contractual remedy is provided therein, it is necessary to introduce in this Directive the contractual remedy of exempting the consumer from the obligation to provide any consideration for such unsolicited supply or provision.

(61) Directive 2002/58/EC of the European Parliament and of the Council of 12 July 2002 concerning the processing of personal data and the protection of privacy in the electronic communications sector (Directive on privacy and electronic communications) already regulates unsolicited communications and provides for a high level of consumer protection. The corresponding provisions on the same issue contained in Directive 97/7/EC are therefore not needed.

(62) It is appropriate for the Commission to review this Directive if some barriers to the internal market are identified. In its review, the Commission should pay particular attention to the possibilities granted to Member States to maintain or introduce specific national provisions including in certain areas of Council Directive 93/13/EEC of 5 April 1993 on unfair terms in consumer contractsand Directive 1999/44/EC of the European Parliament and of the Council of 25 May 1999 on certain aspects of the sale of consumer goods and associated guarantees. That review could lead to a Commission proposal to amend this Directive; that proposal may include amendments to other consumer protection legislation reflecting the Commission's Consumer Policy Strategy commitment to review the Union acquis in order to achieve a high, common level of consumer protection.

(63) Directives 93/13/EEC and 1999/44/EC should be amended to require Member States to inform the Commission about the adoption of specific national provisions in certain areas.

(64) Directives 85/577/EEC and 97/7/EC should be repealed.

(65) Since the objective of this Directive, namely, through the achievement of a high level of consumer protection, to contribute to the proper functioning of the internal market, cannot be sufficiently achieved by the Member States and can therefore be better achieved at Union level, the Union may adopt measures, in accordance with the principle of subsidiarity as set out in Article 5 of the Treaty on European Union. In accordance with the principle of proportionality, as set out in that Article, this Directive does not go beyond what is necessary in order to achieve that objective.

(66) This Directive respects the fundamental rights and observes the principles recognised in particu-

lar by the Charter of Fundamental Rights of the European Union.
(67) In accordance with point 34 of the Interinstitutional agreement on better law-making, Member States are encouraged to draw up, for themselves and in the interests of the Union, their own tables, which will, as far as possible, illustrate the correlation between this Directive and the transposition measures, and to make them public,
HAVE ADOPTED THIS DIRECTIVE:

Article 1. The purpose of this Directive is, through the achievement of a high level of consumer protection, to contribute to the proper functioning of the internal market by approximating certain aspects of the laws, regulations and administrative provisions of the Member States concerning contracts concluded between consumers and traders.

Article 2. For the purpose of this Directive, the following definitions shall apply:
(1) 'consumer' means any natural person who, in contracts covered by this Directive, is acting for purposes which are outside his trade, business, craft or profession;
(2) 'trader' means any natural person or any legal person, irrespective of whether privately or publicly owned, who is acting, including through any other person acting in his name or on his behalf, for purposes relating to his trade, business, craft or profession in relation to contracts covered by this Directive;
(3) 'goods' means any tangible movable items, with the exception of items sold by way of execution or otherwise by authority of law; water, gas and electricity shall be considered as goods within the meaning of this Directive where they are put up for sale in a limited volume or a set quantity;
(4) 'goods made to the consumer's specifications' means non- prefabricated goods made on the basis of an individual choice of or decision by the consumer;
(5) 'sales contract' means any contract under which the trader transfers or undertakes to transfer the ownership of goods to the consumer and the consumer pays or undertakes to pay the price thereof, including any contract having as its object both goods and services;
(6) 'service contract' means any contract other than a sales contract under which the trader supplies or undertakes to supply a service to the consumer and the consumer pays or undertakes to pay the price thereof;
(7) 'distance contract' means any contract concluded between the trader and the consumer under an organised distance sales or service-provision scheme without the simultaneous physical presence of the trader and the consumer, with the exclusive use of one or more means of distance communication up to and including the time at which the contract is concluded;
(8) 'off-premises contract' means any contract between the trader and the consumer:
(a) concluded in the simultaneous physical presence of the trader and the consumer, in a place which is not the business premises of the trader;
(b) for which an offer was made by the consumer in the same circumstances as referred to in point (a);
(c) concluded on the business premises of the trader or through any means of distance communication immediately after the consumer was personally and individually addressed in a place which is not the business premises of the trader in the simultaneous physical presence of the trader and the consumer; or
(d) concluded during an excursion organised by the trader with the aim or effect of promoting and selling goods or services to the consumer;
(9) 'business premises' means:
(a) any immovable retail premises where the trader carries out his activity on a permanent basis; or
(b) any movable retail premises where the trader carries out his activity on a usual basis;
(10) 'durable medium' means any instrument which enables the consumer or the trader to store information addressed personally to him in a way accessible for future reference for a period of time adequate for the purposes of the information and which allows the unchanged reproduction of the information stored;
(11) 'digital content' means data which are produced and supplied in digital form;
(12) 'financial service' means any service of a banking, credit, insurance, personal pension, investment or payment nature;
(13) 'public auction' means a method of sale where goods or services are offered by the trader to consumers, who attend or are given the possibility to attend the auction in person, through a transparent, competitive bidding procedure run by an auctioneer and where the successful bidder is bound to purchase the goods or services;
(14) 'commercial guarantee' means any undertaking by the trader or a producer (the guarantor) to the consumer, in addition to his legal obligation relating to the guarantee of conformity, to reimburse the

price paid or to replace, repair or service goods in any way if they do not meet the specifications or any other requirements not related to conformity set out in the guarantee statement or in the relevant advertising available at the time of, or before the conclusion of the contract;

(15) 'ancillary contract' means a contract by which the consumer acquires goods or services related to a distance contract or an off-premises contract and where those goods are supplied or those services are provided by the trader or by a third party on the basis of an arrangement between that third party and the trader.

Article 3. (1) This Directive shall apply, under the conditions and to the extent set out in its provisions, to any contract concluded between a trader and a consumer. It shall also apply to contracts for the supply of water, gas, electricity or district heating, including by public providers, to the extent that these commodities are provided on a contractual basis.

(2) If any provision of this Directive conflicts with a provision of another Union act governing specific sectors, the provision of that other Union act shall prevail and shall apply to those specific sectors.

(3) This Directive shall not apply to contracts:

(a) for social services, including social housing, childcare and support of families and persons permanently or temporarily in need, including long-term care;

(b) for healthcare as defined in point (a) of Article 3 of Directive 2011/24/EU, whether or not they are provided via healthcare facilities;

(c) for gambling, which involves wagering a stake with pecuniary value in games of chance, including lotteries, casino games and betting transactions;

(d) for financial services;

(e) for the creation, acquisition or transfer of immovable property or of rights in immovable property;

(f) for the construction of new buildings, the substantial conversion of existing buildings and for rental of accommodation for residential purposes;

(g) which fall within the scope of Council Directive 90/314/EEC of 13 June 1990 on package travel, package holidays and package tours;

(h) which fall within the scope of Directive 2008/122/EC of the European Parliament and of the Council of 14 January 2009 on the protection of consumers in respect of certain aspects of timeshare, long-term holiday product, resale and exchange contracts;

(i) which, in accordance with the laws of Member States, are established by a public office-holder who has a statutory obligation to be independent and impartial and who must ensure, by providing comprehensive legal information, that the consumer only concludes the contract on the basis of careful legal consideration and with knowledge of its legal scope;

(j) for the supply of foodstuffs, beverages or other goods intended for current consumption in the household, and which are physically supplied by a trader on frequent and regular rounds to the consumer's home, residence or workplace;

(k) for passenger transport services, with the exception of Article 8(2) and Articles 19 and 22;

(l) concluded by means of automatic vending machines or automated commercial premises;

(m) concluded with telecommunications operators through public payphones for their use or concluded for the use of one single connection by telephone, Internet or fax established by a consumer.

(4) Member States may decide not to apply this Directive or not to maintain or introduce corresponding national provisions to off-premises contracts for which the payment to be made by the consumer does not exceed EUR 50. Member States may define a lower value in their national legislation.

(5) This Directive shall not affect national general contract law such as the rules on the validity, formation or effect of a contract, in so far as general contract law aspects are not regulated in this Directive.

(6) This Directive shall not prevent traders from offering consumers contractual arrangements which go beyond the protection provided for in this Directive.

Article 4. Member States shall not maintain or introduce, in their national law, provisions diverging from those laid down in this Directive, including more or less stringent provisions to ensure a different level of consumer protection, unless otherwise provided for in this Directive.

Article 5. (1) Before the consumer is bound by a contract other than a distance or an off-premises contract, or any corresponding offer, the trader shall provide the consumer with the following information in a clear and comprehensible manner, if that information is not already apparent from the context:

(a) the main characteristics of the goods or services, to the extent appropriate to the medium and to the goods or services;

(b) the identity of the trader, such as his trading name, the geographical address at which he is established and his telephone number;
(c) the total price of the goods or services inclusive of taxes, or where the nature of the goods or services is such that the price cannot reasonably be calculated in advance, the manner in which the price is to be calculated, as well as, where applicable, all additional freight, delivery or postal charges or, where those charges cannot reasonably be calculated in advance, the fact that such additional charges may be payable;
(d) where applicable, the arrangements for payment, delivery, performance, the time by which the trader undertakes to deliver the goods or to perform the service, and the trader's complaint handling policy;
(e) in addition to a reminder of the existence of a legal guarantee of conformity for goods, the existence and the conditions of after-sales services and commercial guarantees, where applicable;
(f) the duration of the contract, where applicable, or, if the contract is of indeterminate duration or is to be extended automatically, the conditions for terminating the contract;
(g) where applicable, the functionality, including applicable technical protection measures, of digital content;
(h) where applicable, any relevant interoperability of digital content with hardware and software that the trader is aware of or can reasonably be expected to have been aware of.
(2) Paragraph 1 shall also apply to contracts for the supply of water, gas or electricity, where they are not put up for sale in a limited volume or set quantity, of district heating or of digital content which is not supplied on a tangible medium.
(3) Member States shall not be required to apply paragraph (1) to contracts which involve day-to-day transactions and which are performed immediately at the time of their conclusion.
(4) Member States may adopt or maintain additional pre- contractual information requirements for contracts to which this Article applies.

Article 6. (1) Before the consumer is bound by a distance or off- premises contract, or any corresponding offer, the trader shall provide the consumer with the following information in a clear and comprehensible manner:
(a) the main characteristics of the goods or services, to the extent appropriate to the medium and to the goods or services;
(b) the identity of the trader, such as his trading name;
(c) the geographical address at which the trader is established and the trader's telephone number, fax number and e-mail address, where available, to enable the consumer to contact the trader quickly and communicate with him efficiently and, where applicable, the geographical address and identity of the trader on whose behalf he is acting;
(d) if different from the address provided in accordance with point (c), the geographical address of the place of business of the trader, and, where applicable, that of the trader on whose behalf he is acting, where the consumer can address any complaints;
(e) the total price of the goods or services inclusive of taxes, or where the nature of the goods or services is such that the price cannot reasonably be calculated in advance, the manner in which the price is to be calculated, as well as, where applicable, all additional freight, delivery or postal charges and any other costs or, where those charges cannot reasonably be calculated in advance, the fact that such additional charges may be payable. In the case of a contract of indeterminate duration or a contract containing a subscription, the total price shall include the total costs per billing period. Where such contracts are charged at a fixed rate, the total price shall also mean the total monthly costs. Where the total costs cannot be reasonably calculated in advance, the manner in which the price is to be calculated shall be provided;
(f) the cost of using the means of distance communication for the conclusion of the contract where that cost is calculated other than at the basic rate;
(g) the arrangements for payment, delivery, performance, the time by which the trader undertakes to deliver the goods or to perform the services and, where applicable, the trader's complaint handling policy;
(h) where a right of withdrawal exists, the conditions, time limit and procedures for exercising that right in accordance with Article 11(1), as well as the model withdrawal form set out in Annex I(B);
(i) where applicable, that the consumer will have to bear the cost of returning the goods in case of withdrawal and, for distance contracts, if the goods, by their nature, cannot normally be returned by post, the cost of returning the goods;
(j) that, if the consumer exercises the right of withdrawal after having made a request in accordance with Article 7(3) or Article 8(8), the consumer shall be liable to pay the trader reasonable costs in accordance with Article 14(3);

(k) where a right of withdrawal is not provided for in accordance with Article 16, the information that the consumer will not benefit from a right of withdrawal or, where applicable, the circumstances under which the consumer loses his right of withdrawal;
(l) a reminder of the existence of a legal guarantee of conformity for goods;
(m) where applicable, the existence and the conditions of after sale customer assistance, after-sales services and commercial guarantees;
(n) the existence of relevant codes of conduct, as defined in point (f) of Article 2 of Directive 2005/29/EC, and how copies of them can be obtained, where applicable;
(o) the duration of the contract, where applicable, or, if the contract is of indeterminate duration or is to be extended automatically, the conditions for terminating the contract;
(p) where applicable, the minimum duration of the consumer's obligations under the contract;
(q) where applicable, the existence and the conditions of deposits or other financial guarantees to be paid or provided by the consumer at the request of the trader;
(r) where applicable, the functionality, including applicable technical protection measures, of digital content;
(s) where applicable, any relevant interoperability of digital content with hardware and software that the trader is aware of or can reasonably be expected to have been aware of;
(t) where applicable, the possibility of having recourse to an out-of-court complaint and redress mechanism, to which the trader is subject, and the methods for having access to it.
(2) Paragraph 1 shall also apply to contracts for the supply of water, gas or electricity, where they are not put up for sale in a limited volume or set quantity, of district heating or of digital content which is not supplied on a tangible medium.
(3) In the case of a public auction, the information referred to in points (b), (c) and (d) of paragraph (1) may be replaced by the equivalent details for the auctioneer.
(4) The information referred to in points (h), (i) and (j) of paragraph (1) may be provided by means of the model instructions on withdrawal set out in Annex I(A). The trader shall have fulfilled the information requirements laid down in points (h), (i) and (j) of paragraph (1) if he has supplied these instructions to the consumer, correctly filled in.
(5) The information referred to in paragraph (1) shall form an integral part of the distance or off-premises contract and shall not be altered unless the contracting parties expressly agree otherwise.
(6) If the trader has not complied with the information requirements on additional charges or other costs as referred to in point (e) of paragraph (1), or on the costs of returning the goods as referred to in point (i) of paragraph (1), the consumer shall not bear those charges or costs.
(7) Member States may maintain or introduce in their national law language requirements regarding the contractual information, so as to ensure that such information is easily understood by the consumer.
(8) The information requirements laid down in this Directive are in addition to information requirements contained in Directive 2006/123/EC and Directive 2000/31/EC and do not prevent Member States from imposing additional information requirements in accordance with those Directives. Without prejudice to the first subparagraph, if a provision of Directive 2006/123/EC or Directive 2000/31/EC on the content and the manner in which the information is to be provided conflicts with a provision of this Directive, the provision of this Directive shall prevail.
(9) As regards compliance with the information requirements laid down in this Chapter, the burden of proof shall be on the trader.

Article 7. (1) With respect to off-premises contracts, the trader shall give the information provided for in Article 6(1) to the consumer on paper or, if the consumer agrees, on another durable medium. That information shall be legible and in plain, intelligible language.
(2) The trader shall provide the consumer with a copy of the signed contract or the confirmation of the contract on paper or, if the consumer agrees, on another durable medium, including, where applicable, the confirmation of the consumer's prior express consent and acknowledgement in accordance with point (m) of Article 16.
(3) Where a consumer wants the performance of services or the supply of water, gas or electricity, where they are not put up for sale in a limited volume or set quantity, or of district heating to begin during the withdrawal period provided for in Article 9(2), the trader shall require that the consumer makes such an express request on a durable medium.
(4) With respect to off-premises contracts where the consumer has explicitly requested the services of the trader for the purpose of carrying out repairs or maintenance for which the trader and the consumer immediately perform their contractual obligations and where the payment to be made by the consumer does not exceed EUR 200:

(a) the trader shall provide the consumer with the information referred to in points (b) and (c) of Article 6(1) and information about the price or the manner in which the price is to be calculated together with an estimate of the total price, on paper or, if the consumer agrees, on another durable medium. The trader shall provide the information referred to in points (a), (h) and (k) of Article 6(1), but may choose not to provide it on paper or another durable medium if the consumer expressly agrees;
(b) the confirmation of the contract provided in accordance with paragraph (2) of this Article shall contain the information provided for in Article 6(1).
Member States may decide not to apply this paragraph.
(5) Member States shall not impose any further formal pre- contractual information requirements for the fulfilment of the information obligations laid down in this Directive.

Article 8. (1) With respect to distance contracts, the trader shall give the information provided for in Article 6(1) or make that information available to the consumer in a way appropriate to the means of distance communication used in plain and intelligible language. In so far as that information is provided on a durable medium, it shall be legible.
(2) If a distance contract to be concluded by electronic means places the consumer under an obligation to pay, the trader shall make the consumer aware in a clear and prominent manner, and directly before the consumer places his order, of the information provided for in points (a), (e), (o) and (p) of Article 6(1).
The trader shall ensure that the consumer, when placing his order, explicitly acknowledges that the order implies an obligation to pay. If placing an order entails activating a button or a similar function, the button or similar function shall be labelled in an easily legible manner only with the words 'order with obligation to pay' or a corresponding unambiguous formulation indicating that placing the order entails an obligation to pay the trader. If the trader has not complied with this subparagraph, the consumer shall not be bound by the contract or order.
(3) Trading websites shall indicate clearly and legibly at the latest at the beginning of the ordering process whether any delivery restrictions apply and which means of payment are accepted.
(4) If the contract is concluded through a means of distance communication which allows limited space or time to display the information, the trader shall provide, on that particular means prior to the conclusion of such a contract, at least the pre-contractual information regarding the main characteristics of the goods or services, the identity of the trader, the total price, the right of withdrawal, the duration of the contract and, if the contract is of indeterminate duration, the conditions for terminating the contract, as referred to in points (a), (b), (e), (h) and (o) of Article 6(1). The other information referred to in Article 6(1) shall be provided by the trader to the consumer in an appropriate way in accordance with paragraph (1) of this Article.
(5) Without prejudice to paragraph (4), if the trader makes a telephone call to the consumer with a view to concluding a distance contract, he shall, at the beginning of the conversation with the consumer, disclose his identity and, where applicable, the identity of the person on whose behalf he makes that call, and the commercial purpose of the call.
(6) Where a distance contract is to be concluded by telephone, Member States may provide that the trader has to confirm the offer to the consumer who is bound only once he has signed the offer or has sent his written consent. Member States may also provide that such confirmations have to be made on a durable medium.
(7) The trader shall provide the consumer with the confirmation of the contract concluded, on a durable medium within a reasonable time after the conclusion of the distance contract, and at the latest at the time of the delivery of the goods or before the performance of the service begins. That confirmation shall include:
(a) all the information referred to in Article 6(1) unless the trader has already provided that information to the consumer on a durable medium prior to the conclusion of the distance contract; and
(b) where applicable, the confirmation of the consumer's prior express consent and acknowledgment in accordance with point (m) of Article 16.
(8) Where a consumer wants the performance of services, or the supply of water, gas or electricity, where they are not put up for sale in a limited volume or set quantity, or of district heating, to begin during the withdrawal period provided for in Article 9(2), the trader shall require that the consumer make an express request.

Article 9. (1) Save where the exceptions provided for in Article 16 apply, the consumer shall have a period of 14 days to withdraw from a distance or off-premises contract, without giving any reason, and without incurring any costs other than those provided for in Article 13(2) and Article 14.
(2) Without prejudice to Article 10, the withdrawal period referred to in paragraph (1) of this Article shall expire after 14 days from:

(a) in the case of service contracts, the day of the conclusion of the contract;
(b) in the case of sales contracts, the day on which the consumer or a third party other than the carrier and indicated by the consumer acquires physical possession of the goods or:
(i) in the case of multiple goods ordered by the consumer in one order and delivered separately, the day on which the consumer or a third party other than the carrier and indicated by the consumer acquires physical possession of the last good;
(ii) in the case of delivery of a good consisting of multiple lots or pieces, the day on which the consumer or a third party other than the carrier and indicated by the consumer acquires physical possession of the last lot or piece;
(iii) in the case of contracts for regular delivery of goods during defined period of time, the day on which the consumer or a third party other than the carrier and indicated by the consumer acquires physical possession of the first good;
(c) in the case of contracts for the supply of water, gas or electricity, where they are not put up for sale in a limited volume or set quantity, of district heating or of digital content which is not supplied on a tangible medium, the day of the conclusion of the contract.
(3) The Member States shall not prohibit the contracting parties from performing their contractual obligations during the withdrawal period. Nevertheless, in the case of off-premises contracts, Member States may maintain existing national legislation prohibiting the trader from collecting the payment from the consumer during the given period after the conclusion of the contract.

Article 10. (1) If the trader has not provided the consumer with the information on the right of withdrawal as required by point (h) of Article 6(1), the withdrawal period shall expire 12 months from the end of the initial withdrawal period, as determined in accordance with Article 9(2).
(2) If the trader has provided the consumer with the information provided for in paragraph (1) of this Article within 12 months from the day referred to in Article 9(2), the withdrawal period shall expire 14 days after the day upon which the consumer receives that information.

Article 11. (1) Before the expiry of the withdrawal period, the consumer shall inform the trader of his decision to withdraw from the contract. For this purpose, the consumer may either:
(a) use the model withdrawal form as set out in Annex I(B); or
(b) make any other unequivocal statement setting out his decision to withdraw from the contract. Member States shall not provide for any formal requirements applicable to the model withdrawal form other than those set out in Annex I(B).
(2) The consumer shall have exercised his right of withdrawal within the withdrawal period referred to in Article 9(2) and Article 10 if the communication concerning the exercise of the right of withdrawal is sent by the consumer before that period has expired.
(3) The trader may, in addition to the possibilities referred to in paragraph (1), give the option to the consumer to electronically fill in and submit either the model withdrawal form set out in Annex I(B) or any other unequivocal statement on the trader's website. In those cases the trader shall communicate to the consumer an acknowledgement of receipt of such a withdrawal on a durable medium without delay.
(4) The burden of proof of exercising the right of withdrawal in accordance with this Article shall be on the consumer.

Article 12. The exercise of the right of withdrawal shall terminate the obligations of the parties:
(a) to perform the distance or off-premises contract; or
(b) to conclude the distance or off-premises contract, in cases where an offer was made by the consumer.

Article 13. (1) The trader shall reimburse all payments received from the consumer, including, if applicable, the costs of delivery without undue delay and in any event not later than 14 days from the day on which he is informed of the consumer's decision to withdraw from the contract in accordance with Article 11.
The trader shall carry out the reimbursement referred to in the first subparagraph using the same means of payment as the consumer used for the initial transaction, unless the consumer has expressly agreed otherwise and provided that the consumer does not incur any fees as a result of such reimbursement.
(2) Notwithstanding paragraph (1), the trader shall not be required to reimburse the supplementary costs, if the consumer has expressly opted for a type of delivery other than the least expensive type of standard delivery offered by the trader.
(3) Unless the trader has offered to collect the goods himself, with regard to sales contracts, the trader may withhold the reimbursement until he has received the goods back, or until the consumer has supplied evidence of having sent back the goods, whichever is the earliest.

Article 14. (1) Unless the trader has offered to collect the goods himself, the consumer shall send back the goods or hand them over to the trader or to a person authorised by the trader to receive the goods, without undue delay and in any event not later than 14 days from the day on which he has communicated his decision to withdraw from the contract to the trader in accordance with Article 11. The deadline shall be met if the consumer sends back the goods before the period of 14 days has expired.
The consumer shall only bear the direct cost of returning the goods unless the trader has agreed to bear them or the trader failed to inform the consumer that the consumer has to bear them.
In the case of off-premises contracts where the goods have been delivered to the consumer's home at the time of the conclusion of the contract, the trader shall at his own expense collect the goods if, by their nature, those goods cannot normally be returned by post.
(2) The consumer shall only be liable for any diminished value of the goods resulting from the handling of the goods other than what is necessary to establish the nature, characteristics and functioning of the goods. The consumer shall in any event not be liable for diminished value of the goods where the trader has failed to provide notice of the right of withdrawal in accordance with point (h) of Article 6(1).
(3) Where a consumer exercises the right of withdrawal after having made a request in accordance with Article 7(3) or Article 8(8), the consumer shall pay to the trader an amount which is in proportion to what has been provided until the time the consumer has informed the trader of the exercise of the right of withdrawal, in comparison with the full coverage of the contract. The proportionate amount to be paid by the consumer to the trader shall be calculated on the basis of the total price agreed in the contract. If the total price is excessive, the proportionate amount shall be calculated on the basis of the market value of what has been provided.
(4) The consumer shall bear no cost for:
(a) the performance of services or the supply of water, gas or electricity, where they are not put up for sale in a limited volume or set quantity, or of district heating, in full or in part, during the withdrawal period, where:
(i) the trader has failed to provide information in accordance with points (h) or (j) of Article 6(1); or
(ii) the consumer has not expressly requested performance to begin during the withdrawal period in accordance with Article 7(3) and Article 8(8); or
(b) the supply, in full or in part, of digital content which is not supplied on a tangible medium where:
(i) the consumer has not given his prior express consent to the beginning of the performance before the end of the 14-day period referred to in Article 9;
(ii) the consumer has not acknowledged that he loses his right of withdrawal when giving his consent; or
(iii) the trader has failed to provide confirmation in accordance with Article 7(2) or Article 8(7).
(5) Except as provided for in Article 13(2) and in this Article, the consumer shall not incur any liability as a consequence of the exercise of the right of withdrawal.

Article 15. (1) Without prejudice to Article 15 of Directive 2008/48/EC of the European Parliament and of the Council of 23 April 2008 on credit agreements for consumers [20], if the consumer exercises his right of withdrawal from a distance or an off-premises contract in accordance with Articles 9 to 14 of this Directive, any ancillary contracts shall be automatically terminated, without any costs for the consumer, except as provided for in Article 13(2) and in Article 14 of this Directive.
(2) The Member States shall lay down detailed rules on the termination of such contracts.

Article 16. Member States shall not provide for the right of withdrawal set out in Articles 9 to 15 in respect of distance and off-premises contracts as regards the following:
(a) service contracts after the service has been fully performed if the performance has begun with the consumer's prior express consent, and with the acknowledgement that he will lose his right of withdrawal once the contract has been fully performed by the trader;
(b) the supply of goods or services for which the price is dependent on fluctuations in the financial market which cannot be controlled by the trader and which may occur within the withdrawal period;
(c) the supply of goods made to the consumer's specifications or clearly personalised;
(d) the supply of goods which are liable to deteriorate or expire rapidly;
(e) the supply of sealed goods which are not suitable for return due to health protection or hygiene reasons and were unsealed after delivery;
(f) the supply of goods which are, after delivery, according to their nature, inseparably mixed with other items;
(g) the supply of alcoholic beverages, the price of which has been agreed upon at the time of the conclusion of the sales contract, the delivery of which can only take place after 30 days and the actual

value of which is dependent on fluctuations in the market which cannot be controlled by the trader;
(h) contracts where the consumer has specifically requested a visit from the trader for the purpose of carrying out urgent repairs or maintenance. If, on the occasion of such visit, the trader provides services in addition to those specifically requested by the consumer or goods other than replacement parts necessarily used in carrying out the maintenance or in making the repairs, the right of withdrawal shall apply to those additional services or goods;
(i) the supply of sealed audio or sealed video recordings or sealed computer software which were unsealed after delivery;
(j) the supply of a newspaper, periodical or magazine with the exception of subscription contracts for the supply of such publications;
(k) contracts concluded at a public auction;
(l) the provision of accommodation other than for residential purpose, transport of goods, car rental services, catering or services related to leisure activities if the contract provides for a specific date or period of performance;
(m) the supply of digital content which is not supplied on a tangible medium if the performance has begun with the consumer's prior express consent and his acknowledgment that he thereby loses his right of withdrawal.

Article 17. (1) Articles 18 and 20 shall apply to sales contracts. Those Articles shall not apply to contracts for the supply of water, gas or electricity, where they are not put up for sale in a limited volume or set quantity, of district heating or the supply of digital content which is not supplied on a tangible medium.
(2) Articles 19, 21 and 22 shall apply to sales and service contracts and to contracts for the supply of water, gas, electricity, district heating or digital content.

Article 18. (1) Unless the parties have agreed otherwise on the time of delivery, the trader shall deliver the goods by transferring the physical possession or control of the goods to the consumer without undue delay, but not later than 30 days from the conclusion of the contract.
(2) Where the trader has failed to fulfil his obligation to deliver the goods at the time agreed upon with the consumer or within the time limit set out in paragraph (1), the consumer shall call upon him to make the delivery within an additional period of time appropriate to the circumstances. If the trader fails to deliver the goods within that additional period of time, the consumer shall be entitled to terminate the contract.
The first subparagraph shall not be applicable to sales contracts where the trader has refused to deliver the goods or where delivery within the agreed delivery period is essential taking into account all the circumstances attending the conclusion of the contract or where the consumer informs the trader, prior to the conclusion of the contract, that delivery by or on a specified date is essential. In those cases, if the trader fails to deliver the goods at the time agreed upon with the consumer or within the time limit set out in paragraph (1), the consumer shall be entitled to terminate the contract immediately.
(3) Upon termination of the contract, the trader shall, without undue delay, reimburse all sums paid under the contract.
(4) In addition to the termination of the contract in accordance with paragraph (2), the consumer may have recourse to other remedies provided for by national law.

Article 19. Member States shall prohibit traders from charging consumers, in respect of the use of a given means of payment, fees that exceed the cost borne by the trader for the use of such means.

Article 20. In contracts where the trader dispatches the goods to the consumer, the risk of loss of or damage to the goods shall pass to the consumer when he or a third party indicated by the consumer and other than the carrier has acquired the physical possession of the goods. However, the risk shall pass to the consumer upon delivery to the carrier if the carrier was commissioned by the consumer to carry the goods and that choice was not offered by the trader, without prejudice to the rights of the consumer against the carrier.

Article 21. Member States shall ensure that where the trader operates a telephone line for the purpose of contacting him by telephone in relation to the contract concluded, the consumer, when contacting the trader is not bound to pay more than the basic rate.
The first subparagraph shall be without prejudice to the right of telecommunication services providers to charge for such calls.

Article 22. Before the consumer is bound by the contract or offer, the trader shall seek the express consent of the consumer to any extra payment in addition to the remuneration agreed upon for the trader's main contractual obligation. If the trader has not obtained the consumer's express consent but has inferred it by using default options which the consumer is required to reject in order to avoid the additional payment, the consumer shall be entitled to reimbursement of this payment.

Article 23. (1) Member States shall ensure that adequate and effective means exist to ensure compliance with this Directive.
(2) The means referred to in paragraph (1) shall include provisions whereby one or more of the following bodies, as determined by national law, may take action under national law before the courts or before the competent administrative bodies to ensure that the national provisions transposing this Directive are applied:
(a) public bodies or their representatives;
(b) consumer organisations having a legitimate interest in protecting consumers;
(c) professional organisations having a legitimate interest in acting.

Article 24. (1) Member States shall lay down the rules on penalties applicable to infringements of the national provisions adopted pursuant to this Directive and shall take all measures necessary to ensure that they are implemented. The penalties provided for must be effective, proportionate and dissuasive.
(2) Member States shall notify those provisions to the Commission by 13 December 2013 and shall notify it without delay of any subsequent amendment affecting them.

Article 25. If the law applicable to the contract is the law of a Member State, consumers may not waive the rights conferred on them by the national measures transposing this Directive.
Any contractual terms which directly or indirectly waive or restrict the rights resulting from this Directive shall not be binding on the consumer.

Article 26. Member States shall take appropriate measures to inform consumers and traders of the national provisions transposing this Directive and shall, where appropriate, encourage traders and code owners as defined in point (g) of Article 2 of Directive 2005/29/EC, to inform consumers of their codes of conduct.

Article 27. The consumer shall be exempted from the obligation to provide any consideration in cases of unsolicited supply of goods, water, gas, electricity, district heating or digital content or unsolicited provision of services, prohibited by Article 5(5) and point 29 of Annex I to Directive 2005/29/EC. In such cases, the absence of a response from the consumer following such an unsolicited supply or provision shall not constitute consent.

Article 28. (1) Member States shall adopt and publish, by 13 December 2013, the laws, regulations and administrative provisions necessary to comply with this Directive. They shall forthwith communicate to the Commission the text of these measures in the form of documents. The Commission shall make use of these documents for the purposes of the report referred to in Article 30.
They shall apply those measures from 13 June 2014.
When Member States adopt those measures, they shall contain a reference to this Directive or be accompanied by such a reference on the occasion of their official publication. Member States shall determine how such reference is to be made.
(2) The provisions of this Directive shall apply to contracts concluded after 13 June 2014.

Article 29. (1) Where a Member State makes use of any of the regulatory choices referred to in Article 3(4), Article 6(7), Article 6(8), Article 7(4), Article 8(6) and Article 9(3), it shall inform the Commission thereof by 13 December 2013, as well as of any subsequent changes.
(2) The Commission shall ensure that the information referred to in paragraph (1) is easily accessible to consumers and traders, inter alia, on a dedicated website.
(3) The Commission shall forward the information referred to in paragraph (1) to the other Member States and the European Parliament. The Commission shall consult stakeholders on that information.

Article 30. By 13 December 2016, the Commission shall submit a report on the application of this Directive to the European Parliament and the Council. That report shall include in particular an evaluation of the provisions of this Directive regarding digital content including the right of withdrawal. The report shall be accompanied, where necessary, by legislative proposals to adapt this Directive to developments in the field of consumer rights.

Article 31. Directive 85/577/EEC and Directive 97/7/EC, as amended by Directive 2002/65/EC of the European Parliament and of the Council of 23 September 2002 concerning the distance marketing of consumer financial services [21] and by Directives 2005/29/EC and 2007/64/EC, are repealed as of 13 June 2014.

References to the repealed Directives shall be construed as references to this Directive and shall be read in accordance with the correlation table set out in Annex II.

Article 32. In Directive 93/13/EEC, the following Article is inserted:
"Article 8a
1. Where a Member State adopts provisions in accordance with Article 8, it shall inform the Commission thereof, as well as of any subsequent changes, in particular where those provisions:
- extend the unfairness assessment to individually negotiated contractual terms or to the adequacy of the price or remuneration; or,
- contain lists of contractual terms which shall be considered as unfair,
2. The Commission shall ensure that the information referred to in paragraph (1) is easily accessible to consumers and traders, inter alia, on a dedicated website.
3. The Commission shall forward the information referred to in paragraph (1) to the other Member States and the European Parliament. The Commission shall consult stakeholders on that information."

Article 33. In Directive 1999/44/EC, the following Article is inserted:
"Article 8a
Reporting requirements
1. Where, in accordance with Article 8(2), a Member State adopts more stringent consumer protection provisions than those provided for in Article 5(1) to (3) and in Article 7(1), it shall inform the Commission thereof, as well as of any subsequent changes.
2. The Commission shall ensure that the information referred to in paragraph (1) is easily accessible to consumers and traders, inter alia, on a dedicated website.
3. The Commission shall forward the information referred to in paragraph (1) to the other Member States and the European Parliament. The Commission shall consult stakeholders on that information."

Article 34. This Directive shall enter into force on the 20th day following its publication in the Official Journal of the European Union.

Article 35. This Directive is addressed to the Member States.

Annex I. Information concerning the exercise of the right of withdrawal

A. Model instructions on withdrawal

Right of withdrawal
You have the right to withdraw from this contract within 14 days without giving any reason.
The withdrawal period will expire after 14 days from the day .
To exercise the right of withdrawal, you must inform us ( ) of your decision to withdraw from this contract by an unequivocal statement (e.g. a letter sent by post, fax or e-mail). You may use the attached model withdrawal form, but it is not obligatory.
To meet the withdrawal deadline, it is sufficient for you to send your communication concerning your exercise of the right of withdrawal before the withdrawal period has expired.

Effects of withdrawal
If you withdraw from this contract, we shall reimburse to you all payments received from you, including the costs of delivery (with the exception of the supplementary costs resulting from your choice of a type of delivery other than the least expensive type of standard delivery offered by us), without undue delay and in any event not later than 14 days from the day on which we are informed about your decision to withdraw from this contract. We will carry out such reimbursement using the same means of payment as you used for the initial transaction, unless you have expressly agreed otherwise; in any event, you will not incur any fees as a result of such reimbursement.

Instructions for completion:
(1) Insert one of the following texts between inverted commas:
(a) in the case of a service contract or a contract for the supply of water, gas or electricity, where they are not put up for sale in a limited volume or set quantity, of district heating or of digital content which is not supplied on a tangible medium: 'of the conclusion of the contract.';
(b) in the case of a sales contract: 'on which you acquire, or a third party other than the carrier and indicated by you acquires, physical possession of the goods.';
(c) in the case of a contract relating to multiple goods ordered by the consumer in one order and delivered separately: 'on which you acquire, or a third party other than the carrier and indicated by you acquires, physical possession of the last good.';
(d) in the case of a contract relating to delivery of a good consisting of multiple lots or pieces: 'on

which you acquire, or a third party other than the carrier and indicated by you acquires, physical possession of the last lot or piece.';

(e) in the case of a contract for regular delivery of goods during a defined period of time: 'on which you acquire, or a third party other than the carrier and indicated by you acquires, physical possession of the first good.'.

(2) Insert your name, geographical address and, where available, your telephone number, fax number and e-mail address.

(3) If you give the option to the consumer to electronically fill in and submit information about his withdrawal from the contract on your website, insert the following: 'You can also electronically fill in and submit the model withdrawal form or any other unequivocal statement on our website [insert Internet address]. If you use this option, we will communicate to you an acknowledgement of receipt of such a withdrawal on a durable medium (e.g. by e-mail) without delay.'.

(4) In the case of sales contracts in which you have not offered to collect the goods in the event of withdrawal insert the following: 'We may withhold reimbursement until we have received the goods back or you have supplied evidence of having sent back the goods, whichever is the earliest.'.

(5) If the consumer has received goods in connection with the contract:

(a) insert:

— 'We will collect the goods.'; or,

— 'You shall send back the goods or hand them over to us or ... [insert the name and geographical address, where applicable, of the person authorised by you to receive the goods], without undue delay and in any event not later than 14 days from the day on which you communicate your withdrawal from this contract to us. The deadline is met if you send back the goods before the period of 14 days has expired.'

(b) insert:

— 'We will bear the cost of returning the goods.',

— 'You will have to bear the direct cost of returning the goods.',

— If, in a distance contract, you do not offer to bear the cost of returning the goods and the goods, by their nature, cannot normally be returned by post: 'You will have to bear the direct cost of returning the goods, ... EUR [insert the amount].'; or if the cost of returning the goods cannot reasonably be calculated in advance: 'You will have to bear the direct cost of returning the goods. The cost is estimated at a maximum of approximately ... EUR [insert the amount].'; or

— If, in an off-premises contract, the goods, by their nature, cannot normally be returned by post and have been delivered to the consumer's home at the time of the conclusion of the contract: 'We will collect the goods at our own expense.'; and,

(c) insert 'You are only liable for any diminished value of the goods resulting from the handling other than what is necessary to establish the nature, characteristics and functioning of the goods.'

(6) In the case of a contract for the provision of services or the supply of water, gas or electricity, where they are not put up for sale in a limited volume or set quantity, or of district heating, insert the following: 'If you requested to begin the performance of services or the supply of water/gas/electricity/district heating [delete where inapplicable] during the withdrawal period, you shall pay us an amount which is in proportion to what has been provided until you have communicated us your withdrawal from this contract, in comparison with the full coverage of the contract.'.

B. Model withdrawal form

(complete and return this form only if you wish to withdraw from the contract)

— To [here the trader's name, geographical address and, where available, his fax number and e-mail address are to be inserted by the trader]:

— I/We (*) hereby give notice that I/We (*) withdraw from my/our (*) contract of sale of the following goods (*)/for the provision of the following service (*),

— Ordered on (*)/received on (*),

— Name of consumer(s),

— Address of consumer(s),

— Signature of consumer(s) (only if this form is notified on paper),

— Date

[Annex II is omitted.]

PART IV   EUROPEAN PRIVATE LAW

Directive 2015/2302 of the European parliament and of the Council of 25 November 2015 on package travel and linked travel arrangements, amending Regulation (EC) No 2006/2004 and Directive 2011/83/EU of the European Parliament and of the Council and repealing Council Directive 90/314/EEC. [Footnotes omitted]

THE EUROPEAN PARLIAMENT AND THE COUNCIL OF THE EUROPEAN UNION,
Having regard to the Treaty on the Functioning of the European Union, and in particular Article 114 thereof,
Having regard to the proposal from the European Commission,
After transmission of the draft legislative act to the national parliaments,
Having regard to the opinion of the European Economic and Social Committee,
After consulting the Committee of the Regions,
Acting in accordance with the ordinary legislative procedure,
Whereas:
(1) Council Directive 90/314/EEC lays down a number of important consumer rights in relation to package travel, in particular with regard to information requirements, the liability of traders in relation to the performance of a package, and protection against the insolvency of an organiser or a retailer. However, it is necessary to adapt the legislative framework to market developments, in order to make it more suitable for the internal market, to remove ambiguities and to close legislative gaps.
(2) Tourism plays an important role in the economy of the Union, and package travel, package holidays and package tours ('packages') represent a significant proportion of the travel market. That market has undergone considerable changes since the adoption of Directive 90/314/EEC. In addition to traditional distribution chains, the internet has become an increasingly important medium through which travel services are offered or sold. Travel services are not only combined in the form of traditional pre-arranged packages, but are often combined in a customised way. Many of those combinations of travel services are either in a legal 'grey zone' or are clearly not covered by Directive 90/314/EEC. This Directive aims to adapt the scope of protection to take account of those developments, to enhance transparency, and to increase legal certainty for travellers and traders.
(3) Article 169(1) and point (a) of Article 169(2) of the Treaty on the Functioning of the European Union (TFEU) provide that the Union is to contribute to the attainment of a high level of consumer protection through measures adopted pursuant to Article 114 TFEU.
(4) Directive 90/314/EEC gives broad discretion to the Member States as regards transposition. Therefore, significant divergences between the laws of the Member States remain. Legal fragmentation leads to higher costs for businesses and obstacles for those wishing to operate cross-border, thus limiting consumers' choice.
(5) In accordance with Article 26(2) and Article 49 TFEU, the internal market is to comprise an area without internal frontiers in which the free movement of goods and services and the freedom of establishment are ensured. The harmonisation of the rights and obligations arising from contracts relating to package travel and to linked travel arrangements is necessary for the creation of a real consumer internal market in that area, striking the right balance between a high level of consumer protection and the competitiveness of businesses.
(6) The cross-border potential of the package travel market in the Union is currently not fully exploited. Disparities in the rules protecting travellers in different Member States act as a disincentive for travellers in one Member State from buying packages and linked travel arrangements in another Member State and, likewise, a disincentive for organisers and retailers in one Member State from selling such services in another Member State. In order to enable travellers and traders to benefit fully from the internal market, while ensuring a high level of consumer protection across the Union, it is necessary to further approximate the laws of the Member States relating to packages and linked travel arrangements.
(7) The majority of travellers buying packages or linked travel arrangements are consumers within the meaning of Union consumer law. At the same time, it is not always easy to distinguish between consumers and representatives of small businesses or professionals who book trips related to their business or profession through the same booking channels as consumers. Such travellers often require a similar level of protection. In contrast, there are companies or organisations that make travel arrangements on the basis of a general agreement, often concluded for numerous travel arrangements for a specified period, for instance with a travel agency. The latter type of travel arrangements does not require the level of protection designed for consumers. Therefore, this Directive should apply to business travellers, including members of liberal professions, or self-employed or other natural persons, where they do not make travel arrangements on the basis of a general agreement. In order to avoid confusion with the definition of the term 'consumer' used in other Union

legislation, persons protected under this Directive should be referred to as 'travellers'.

(8) Since travel services may be combined in many different ways, it is appropriate to consider as packages all combinations of travel services that display features which travellers typically associate with packages, in particular where separate travel services are combined into a single travel product for which the organiser assumes responsibility for proper performance. In accordance with the case-law of the Court of Justice of the European Union, it should make no difference whether travel services are combined before any contact with the traveller or at the request of or in accordance with the selection made by the traveller. The same principles should apply irrespective of whether the booking is made through a high street trader or online.

(9) For the sake of transparency, packages should be distinguished from linked travel arrangements, where online or high street traders facilitate the procurement of travel services by travellers leading the traveller to conclude contracts with different travel services providers, including through linked booking processes, which do not contain the features of a package and in relation to which it would not be appropriate to apply all of the obligations applicable to packages.

(10) In the light of market developments, it is appropriate to further define packages on the basis of alternative objective criteria which predominantly relate to the way in which the travel services are presented or purchased and where travellers may reasonably expect to be protected by this Directive. That is the case, for instance, where different types of travel services are purchased for the purpose of the same trip or holiday from a single point of sale and those services have been selected before the traveller agrees to pay, that is to say within the same booking process, or where such services are offered, sold or charged at an inclusive or total price, as well as where such services are advertised or sold under the term 'package' or under a similar term indicating a close connection between the travel services concerned. Such similar terms could be, for instance, 'combined deal', 'all-inclusive' or 'all-in arrangement'.

(11) It should be clarified that travel services combined after the conclusion of a contract by which a trader entitles a traveller to choose among a selection of different types of travel services, such as in the case of a package travel gift box, constitute a package. Moreover, a combination of travel services should be considered to be a package where the traveller's name, payment details and e-mail address are transmitted between the traders and where another contract is concluded at the latest 24 hours after the booking of the first travel service is confirmed.

(12) At the same time, linked travel arrangements should be distinguished from travel services which travellers book independently, often at different times, even for the purpose of the same trip or holiday. Online linked travel arrangements should also be distinguished from linked websites which do not have the objective of concluding a contract with the traveller and from links through which travellers are simply informed about further travel services in a general way, for instance where a hotel or an organiser of an event includes on its website a list of all operators offering transport services to its location independently of any booking or if 'cookies' or meta data are used to place advertisements on websites.

(13) Specific rules should be laid down for both high street and online traders which assist travellers, on the occasion of a single visit or contact with their point of sale, in concluding separate contracts with individual service providers and for online traders which, for instance, through linked online booking processes, facilitate in a targeted manner the procurement of at least one additional travel service from another trader, where a contract is concluded at the latest 24 hours after the confirmation of the booking of the first travel service. Such facilitation will often be based on a commercial link involving remuneration between the trader who facilitates the procurement of additional travel services and the other trader, regardless of the calculation method of such remuneration which might, for instance, be based on the number of clicks or on the turnover. Those rules would apply, for example, where, along with the confirmation of the booking of a first travel service such as a flight or a train journey, a traveller receives an invitation to book an additional travel service available at the chosen travel destination, for instance, hotel accommodation, with a link to the booking website of another service provider or intermediary. While those arrangements should not constitute packages within the meaning of this Directive, under which one organiser is liable for the proper performance of all travel services, such linked travel arrangements constitute an alternative business model that often competes closely with packages.

(14) In order to ensure fair competition and to protect travellers, the obligation to provide sufficient evidence of security for the refund of payments and the repatriation of travellers in the event of insolvency should also apply to linked travel arrangements.

(15) The purchase of a travel service on a stand-alone basis as a single travel service should constitute neither a package nor a linked travel arrangement.

(16) In order to increase clarity for travellers and enable them to make informed choices as to the

different types of travel arrangements on offer, traders should be required to state clearly and prominently whether they are offering a package or a linked travel arrangement, and provide information on the corresponding level of protection, before the traveller agrees to pay. A trader's declaration as to the legal nature of the travel product being marketed should correspond to the true legal nature of the product concerned. The relevant enforcement authorities should intervene where traders do not provide accurate information to travellers.

(17) Only the combination of different types of travel services, such as accommodation, carriage of passengers by bus, rail, water or air, as well as rental of motor vehicles or certain motorcycles, should be considered for the purposes of identifying a package or a linked travel arrangement. Accommodation for residential purposes, including for long-term language courses, should not be considered as accommodation within the meaning of this Directive. Financial services such as travel insurances should not be considered as travel services. In addition, services which are intrinsically part of another travel service should not be considered as travel services in their own right. This includes, for instance, transport of luggage provided as part of carriage of passengers, minor transport services such as carriage of passengers as part of a guided tour or transfers between a hotel and an airport or a railway station, meals, drinks and cleaning provided as part of accommodation, or access to on-site facilities such as a swimming pool, sauna, spa or gym included for hotel guests. This also means that in cases where, unlike in the case of a cruise, overnight accommodation is provided as part of passenger transport by road, rail, water or air, accommodation should not be considered as a travel service in its own right if the main component is clearly transport.

(18) Other tourist services which are not intrinsically part of carriage of passengers, accommodation or the rental of motor vehicles or certain motorcycles, may be, for instance, admission to concerts, sport events, excursions or event parks, guided tours, ski passes and rental of sports equipment such as skiing equipment, or spa treatments. However, if such services are combined with only one other type of travel service, for instance accommodation, this should lead to the creation of a package or linked travel arrangement only if they account for a significant proportion of the value of the package or linked travel arrangement, or are advertised as or otherwise represent an essential feature of the trip or holiday. If other tourist services account for 25 % or more of the value of the combination, those services should be considered as representing a significant proportion of the value of the package or linked travel arrangement. It should be clarified that where other tourist services are added, for instance, to hotel accommodation, booked as a stand-alone service, after the traveller's arrival at the hotel, this should not constitute a package. This should not lead to circumvention of this Directive, with organisers or retailers offering the traveller the selection of additional tourist services in advance and then offering conclusion of the contract for those services only after the performance of the first travel service has started.

(19) Since there is less need to protect travellers in cases of short-term trips, and in order to avoid an unnecessary burden for traders, trips lasting less than 24 hours which do not include accommodation, as well as packages or linked travel arrangements offered or facilitated occasionally and on a not-for-profit basis and only to a limited group of travellers, should be excluded from the scope of this Directive. The latter may for example include trips organised not more than a few times a year by charities, sports clubs or schools for their members, without being offered to the general public. Adequate information on that exclusion should be made publicly available in order to ensure that traders and travellers are properly informed that those packages or linked travel arrangements are not covered by this Directive.

(20) This Directive should be without prejudice to national contract law for those aspects that are not regulated by it.

(21) Member States should remain competent, in accordance with Union law, to apply the provisions of this Directive to areas not falling within its scope. Member States may therefore maintain or introduce national legislation corresponding to the provisions of this Directive, or certain of its provisions, in relation to contracts that fall outside the scope of this Directive. For instance, Member States may maintain or introduce corresponding provisions for certain stand-alone contracts regarding single travel services (such as the rental of holiday homes) or for packages and linked travel arrangements that are offered or facilitated, on a not-for-profit basis to a limited group of travellers and only occasionally, or to packages and linked travel arrangements covering a period of less than 24 hours and which do not include accommodation.

(22) The main characteristic of a package is that there is one trader responsible as an organiser for the proper performance of the package as a whole. Only in cases where another trader is acting as the organiser of a package should a trader, typically a high street or online travel agent, be able to act as a mere retailer or intermediary and not be liable as an organiser. Whether a trader is acting as an organiser for a given package should depend on that trader's involvement in the creation of the

package, and not on how the trader describes his business. When considering whether a trader is an organiser or retailer, it should make no difference whether that trader is acting on the supply side or presents himself as an agent acting for the traveller.

(23) Directive 90/314/EEC has given discretion to the Member States to determine whether retailers, organisers or both retailers and organisers are liable for the proper performance of a package. That flexibility has led to ambiguity in some Member States as to which trader is liable for the performance of the relevant travel services. Therefore, it should be clarified in this Directive that organisers are responsible for the performance of the travel services included in the package travel contract, unless national law provides that both the organiser and the retailer are liable.

(24) In relation to packages, retailers should be responsible together with the organiser for the provision of pre-contractual information. In order to facilitate communication, in particular in cross-border cases, travellers should be able to contact the organiser also via the retailer through which they purchased the package.

(25) The traveller should receive all necessary information before purchasing a package, whether it is sold through means of distance communication, over the counter or through other types of distribution. In providing that information, the trader should take into account the specific needs of travellers who are particularly vulnerable because of their age or physical infirmity, which the trader could reasonably foresee.

(26) Key information, for example on the main characteristics of the travel services or the prices, provided in advertisements, on the organiser's website or in brochures as part of the pre-contractual information, should be binding, unless the organiser reserves the right to make changes to those elements and unless such changes are clearly, comprehensibly and prominently communicated to the traveller before the conclusion of the package travel contract. However, in the light of new communication technologies, which easily allow updates, there is no longer any need to lay down specific rules on brochures, while it is appropriate to ensure that, changes to pre-contractual information are communicated to the traveller. It should always be possible to make changes to pre-contractual information where expressly agreed by both parties to the package travel contract.

(27) The information requirements laid down in this Directive are exhaustive, but should be without prejudice to the information requirements laid down in other applicable Union legislation.

(28) Organisers should provide general information on the visa requirements of the country of destination. The information on approximate periods for obtaining visas can be provided as a reference to official information of the country of destination.

(29) Taking into account the specificities of package travel contracts, the rights and obligations of the contracting parties should be laid down for the period before and after the start of the package, in particular if the package is not properly performed or if particular circumstances change.

(30) Since packages are often purchased a long time before their performance, unforeseen events may occur. Therefore the traveller should, under certain conditions, be entitled to transfer a package travel contract to another traveller. In such situations, the organiser should be able to recover his expenses, for instance if a sub-contractor requires a fee for changing the name of the traveller or for cancelling a transport ticket and issuing a new one.

(31) Travellers should also be able to terminate the package travel contract at any time before the start of the package in return for payment of an appropriate and justifiable termination fee, taking into account expected cost savings and income from alternative deployment of the travel services. They should also have the right to terminate the package travel contract without paying any termination fee where unavoidable and extraordinary circumstances will significantly affect the performance of the package. This may cover for example warfare, other serious security problems such as terrorism, significant risks to human health such as the outbreak of a serious disease at the travel destination, or natural disasters such as floods, earthquakes or weather conditions which make it impossible to travel safely to the destination as agreed in the package travel contract.

(32) In specific situations, the organiser should also be entitled to terminate the package travel contract before the start of the package without paying compensation, for instance if the minimum number of participants is not reached and where that possibility has been reserved in the contract. In that event, the organiser should refund all payments made in respect of the package.

(33) In certain cases organisers should be allowed to make unilateral changes to the package travel contract. However, travellers should have the right to terminate the package travel contract if the changes alter significantly any of the main characteristics of the travel services. This may for instance be the case if the quality or the value of the travel services diminishes. Changes of departure or arrival times indicated in the package travel contract should be considered significant, for instance where they would impose on the traveller considerable inconvenience or additional costs, for instance rearrangement of transport or accommodation. Price increases should be possible only

if there has been a change in the cost of fuel or other power sources for the carriage of passengers, in taxes or fees imposed by a third party not directly involved in the performance of the travel services included in the package travel contract or in the exchange rates relevant to the package and only if the contract expressly reserves the possibility of such a price increase and states that the traveller is entitled to a price reduction corresponding to a decrease in those costs. If the organiser proposes a price increase of more than 8 % of the total price, the traveller should be entitled to terminate the package travel contract without paying a termination fee.

(34) It is appropriate to set out specific rules on remedies as regards the lack of conformity in the performance of the package travel contract. The traveller should be entitled to have problems resolved and, where a significant proportion of travel services included in the package travel contract cannot be provided, the traveller should be offered suitable alternative arrangements. If the organiser does not remedy the lack of conformity within a reasonable period set by the traveller, the traveller should be able to do so himself and request reimbursement of the necessary expenses. In certain cases there should not be a need to specify a time-limit, in particular if immediate remedy is required. This would apply, for instance, when, due to the delay of a bus provided by the organiser, the traveller has to take a taxi to catch his flight on time. Travellers should also be entitled to a price reduction, termination of the package travel contract and/or compensation for damages. Compensation should also cover non-material damage, such as compensation for loss of enjoyment of the trip or holiday because of substantial problems in the performance of the relevant travel services. The traveller should be required to inform the organiser without undue delay, taking into account the circumstances of the case, of any lack of conformity he perceives during the performance of a travel service included in the package travel contract. Failure to do so may be taken into account when determining the appropriate price reduction or compensation for damages where such notice would have avoided or reduced the damage.

(35) In order to ensure consistency, it is appropriate to align the provisions of this Directive with international conventions regulating travel services and with the Union passenger rights legislation. Where the organiser is liable for failure to perform or improper performance of the travel services included in the package travel contract, the organiser should be able to invoke the limitations of the liability of service providers set out in such international conventions as the Montreal Convention of 1999 for the Unification of certain Rules for International Carriage by Air, the Convention of 1980 concerning International Carriage by Rail (COTIF) and the Athens Convention of 1974 on the Carriage of Passengers and their Luggage by Sea. Where it is impossible to ensure the traveller's timely return to the place of departure because of unavoidable and extraordinary circumstances, the organiser should bear the cost of the travellers' necessary accommodation for a period not exceeding three nights per traveller, unless longer periods are provided for in existing or future Union passenger rights legislation.

(36) This Directive should not affect the rights of travellers to present claims both under this Directive and under other relevant Union legislation or international conventions, so that travellers continue to have the possibility to address claims to the organiser, the carrier or any other liable party, or, as the case may be, to more than one party. It should be clarified that, in order to avoid overcompensation, compensation or price reduction granted under this Directive and the compensation or price reduction granted under other relevant Union legislation or international conventions should be deducted from each other. The organiser's liability should be without prejudice to the right to seek redress from third parties, including service providers.

(37) If the traveller is in difficulty during the trip or holiday, the organiser should be obliged to give appropriate assistance without undue delay. Such assistance should consist mainly of providing, where appropriate, information on aspects such as health services, local authorities and consular assistance, as well as practical help, for instance with regard to distance communications and alternative travel arrangements.

(38) In its Communication of 18 March 2013 entitled 'Passenger protection in the event of airline insolvency', the Commission set out measures to improve the protection of travellers in the event of an airline insolvency, including better enforcement of Regulation (EC) No 261/2004 of the European Parliament and of the Council and of Regulation (EC) No 1008/2008, and engagement with industry stakeholders, failing which a legislative measure could be considered. That Communication concerns the purchase of an individual component, namely air travel services, and does not therefore address insolvency protection for packages and for linked travel arrangements.

(39) Member States should ensure that travellers purchasing a package are fully protected against the organiser's insolvency. Member States in which organisers are established should ensure that they provide security for the refund of all payments made by or on behalf of travellers and, insofar as a package includes the carriage of passengers, for the traveller's repatriation in the event of the

organiser's insolvency. However, it should be possible to offer travellers the continuation of the package. While retaining discretion as to the way in which insolvency protection is to be arranged, Member States should ensure that the protection is effective. Effectiveness implies that the protection should become available as soon as, as a consequence of the organiser's liquidity problems, travel services are not being performed, will not be or will only partially be performed, or where service providers require travellers to pay for them. Member States should be able to require that organisers provide travellers with a certificate documenting a direct entitlement against the provider of the insolvency protection.

(40) For the insolvency protection to be effective, it should cover the foreseeable amounts of payments affected by the organiser's insolvency and, where applicable, the foreseeable cost for repatriations. This means that the protection should be sufficient to cover all foreseeable payments made by or on behalf of travellers in respect of packages in peak season, taking into account the period between receiving such payments and the completion of the trip or holiday, as well as, where applicable, the foreseeable cost for repatriations. That will generally mean that the security has to cover a sufficiently high percentage of the organiser's turnover in respect of packages, and may depend on factors such as the type of packages sold, including the mode of transport, the travel destination, and any legal restrictions or the organiser's commitments regarding the amounts of pre-payments he may accept and their timing before the start of the package. Whereas the necessary cover may be calculated on the basis of the most recent business data, for instance the turnover achieved in the last business year, organisers should be obliged to adapt the insolvency protection in the event of increased risks, including a significant increase in the sale of packages. However, effective insolvency protection should not have to take into account highly remote risks, for instance the simultaneous insolvency of several of the largest organisers, where to do so would disproportionately affect the cost of the protection, thus hampering its effectiveness. In such cases the guarantee for refunds may be limited.

(41) Given the differences in national law and practice regarding the parties to a package travel contract and the receipt of payments made by or on behalf of travellers, Member States should be allowed to require retailers to take out insolvency protection as well.

(42) In line with Directive 2006/123/EC, it is appropriate to lay down rules so as to prevent insolvency protection obligations from acting as an obstacle to the free movement of services and the freedom of establishment. Therefore, Member States should be obliged to recognise insolvency protection under the law of the Member State of establishment. In order to facilitate the administrative cooperation and supervision of organisers and, where applicable, retailers which are operating in different Member States with regard to insolvency protection, Member States should be obliged to designate central contact points.

(43) Traders facilitating linked travel arrangements should be obliged to inform travellers that they are not buying a package and that individual travel service providers are solely responsible for the proper performance of their contracts. Traders facilitating linked travel arrangements should, in addition, be obliged to provide insolvency protection for the refund of payments they receive and, insofar as they are responsible for the carriage of passengers, for the travellers' repatriation, and should inform travellers accordingly. Traders responsible for the performance of the individual contracts forming part of a linked travel arrangement are subject to general Union consumer protection legislation and sector-specific Union legislation.

(44) When laying down rules on insolvency protection schemes in relation to packages and linked travel arrangements, Member States should not be prevented from taking into account the special situation of smaller companies while ensuring the same level of protection for travellers.

(45) Travellers should be protected in relation to errors occurring in the booking process of packages and linked travel arrangements.

(46) It should be confirmed that travellers may not waive rights stemming from this Directive and that organisers or traders facilitating linked travel arrangements may not escape from their obligations by claiming that they are simply acting as a travel service provider, an intermediary, or in any other capacity.

(47) Member States should lay down rules on penalties for infringements of national provisions transposing this Directive and ensure that they are implemented. Those penalties should be effective, proportionate and dissuasive.

(48) The adoption of this Directive makes it necessary to adapt certain Union consumer protection legislative acts. In particular, it should be clarified that Regulation (EC) No 2006/2004 of the European Parliament and of the Council applies to infringements of this Directive. Also, taking into account the fact that Directive 2011/83/EU of the European Parliament and the Council in its current form does not apply to contracts covered by Directive 90/314/EEC, it is necessary to amend Directive

2011/83/EU to ensure that it continues to apply to individual travel services that form part of a linked travel arrangement, insofar as those individual services are not otherwise excluded from the scope of Directive 2011/83/EU, and that certain consumer rights laid down in that Directive also apply to packages.

(49) This Directive is without prejudice to rules on the protection of personal data laid down in Directive 95/46/EC of the European Parliament and of the Counciland to the Union rules on private international law, including Regulation (EC) No 593/2008 of the European Parliament and of the Council.

(50) It should be clarified that the regulatory requirements of this Directive on insolvency protection and information in relation to linked travel arrangements should also apply to traders not established in a Member State which by any means direct their activities within the meaning of Regulation (EC) No 593/2008 and Regulation (EU) No 1215/2012 of the European Parliament and of the Council to one or more Member States.

(51) Since the objective of this Directive, namely to contribute to the proper functioning of the internal market and to the achievement of a high and as uniform as possible level of consumer protection, cannot be sufficiently achieved by the Member States, but can rather, by reason of its scale, be better achieved at Union level, the Union may adopt measures, in accordance with the principle of subsidiarity as set out in Article 5 of the Treaty on European Union. In accordance with the principle of proportionality, as set out in that Article, this Directive does not go beyond what is necessary in order to achieve that objective.

(52) This Directive respects the fundamental rights and observes the principles recognised by the Charter of Fundamental Rights of the European Union. This Directive, in particular, respects the freedom to conduct a business laid down in Article 16 of the Charter, while ensuring a high level of consumer protection within the Union, in accordance with Article 38 of the Charter.

(53) In accordance with the Joint Political Declaration of 28 September 2011 of Member States and the Commission on explanatory documents, Member States have undertaken to accompany, in justified cases, the notification of their transposition measures with one or more documents explaining the relationship between the components of a directive and the corresponding parts of national transposition instruments. With regard to this Directive, the legislator considers the transmission of such documents to be justified.

(54) Directive 90/314/EEC should therefore be repealed,
HAVE ADOPTED THIS DIRECTIVE:

Chapter I. Subject matter, scope, definitions and level of harmonisation

Article 1. The purpose of this Directive is to contribute to the proper functioning of the internal market and to the achievement of a high and as uniform as possible level of consumer protection by approximating certain aspects of the laws, regulations and administrative provisions of the Member States in respect of contracts between travellers and traders relating to package travel and linked travel arrangements.

Article 2. (1) This Directive applies to packages offered for sale or sold by traders to travellers and to linked travel arrangements facilitated by traders for travellers.

(2) This Directive does not apply to:

(a) packages and linked travel arrangements covering a period of less than 24 hours unless overnight accommodation is included;

(b) packages offered, and linked travel arrangements facilitated, occasionally and on a not-for-profit basis and only to a limited group of travellers;

(c) packages and linked travel arrangements purchased on the basis of a general agreement for the arrangement of business travel between a trader and another natural or legal person who is acting for purposes relating to his trade, business, craft or profession.

(3) This Directive does not affect national general contract law such as the rules on the validity, formation or effect of a contract, insofar as general contract law aspects are not regulated in this Directive.

Article 3. For the purposes of this Directive, the following definitions apply:

(1) 'travel service' means:

(a) carriage of passengers;

(b) accommodation which is not intrinsically part of carriage of passengers and is not for residential purposes;

(c) rental of cars, other motor vehicles within the meaning of Article 3(11) of Directive 2007/46/EC of the European Parliament and of the Council, or motorcycles requiring a Category A driving licence

in accordance with point (c) of Article 4(3) of Directive 2006/126/EC of the European Parliament and of the Council;
(d) any other tourist service not intrinsically part of a travel service within the meaning of points (a), (b) or (c);
(2) 'package' means a combination of at least two different types of travel services for the purpose of the same trip or holiday, if:
(a) those services are combined by one trader, including at the request of or in accordance with the selection of the traveller, before a single contract on all services is concluded; or
(b) irrespective of whether separate contracts are concluded with individual travel service providers, those services are:
(i) purchased from a single point of sale and those services have been selected before the traveller agrees to pay,
(ii) offered, sold or charged at an inclusive or total price,
(iii) advertised or sold under the term 'package' or under a similar term,
(iv) combined after the conclusion of a contract by which a trader entitles the traveller to choose among a selection of different types of travel services, or
(v) purchased from separate traders through linked online booking processes where the traveller's name, payment details and e-mail address are transmitted from the trader with whom the first contract is concluded to another trader or traders and a contract with the latter trader or traders is concluded at the latest 24 hours after the confirmation of the booking of the first travel service.
A combination of travel services where not more than one type of travel service as referred to in point (a), (b) or (c) of point 1 is combined with one or more tourist services as referred to in point (d) of point 1 is not a package if the latter services:
(a) do not account for a significant proportion of the value of the combination and are not advertised as and do not otherwise represent an essential feature of the combination; or
(b) are selected and purchased only after the performance of a travel service as referred to in point (a), (b) or (c) of point 1 has started;
(3) 'package travel contract' means a contract on the package as a whole or, if the package is provided under separate contracts, all contracts covering travel services included in the package;
(4) 'start of the package' means the beginning of the performance of travel services included in the package;
(5) 'linked travel arrangement' means at least two different types of travel services purchased for the purpose of the same trip or holiday, not constituting a package, resulting in the conclusion of separate contracts with the individual travel service providers, if a trader facilitates:
(a) on the occasion of a single visit or contact with his point of sale, the separate selection and separate payment of each travel service by travellers; or
(b) in a targeted manner, the procurement of at least one additional travel service from another trader where a contract with such other trader is concluded at the latest 24 hours after the confirmation of the booking of the first travel service.
Where not more than one type of travel service as referred to in point (a), (b) or (c) of point 1 and one or more tourist services as referred to in point (d) of point 1 are purchased, they do not constitute a linked travel arrangement if the latter services do not account for a significant proportion of the combined value of the services and are not advertised as, and do not otherwise represent, an essential feature of the trip or holiday.
(6) 'traveller' means any person who is seeking to conclude a contract, or is entitled to travel on the basis of a contract concluded, within the scope of this Directive;
(7) 'trader' means any natural person or any legal person, irrespective of whether privately or publicly owned, who is acting, including through any other person acting in his name or on his behalf, for purposes relating to his trade, business, craft or profession in relation to contracts covered by this Directive, whether acting in the capacity of organiser, retailer, trader facilitating a linked travel arrangement or as a travel service provider;
(8) 'organiser' means a trader who combines and sells or offers for sale packages, either directly or through another trader or together with another trader, or the trader who transmits the traveller's data to another trader in accordance with point (b)(v) of point 2;
(9) 'retailer' means a trader other than the organiser who sells or offers for sale packages combined by an organiser;
(10) 'establishment' means establishment as defined in point 5 of Article 4 of Directive 2006/123/EC;
(11) 'durable medium' means any instrument which enables the traveller or the trader to store information addressed personally to him in a way accessible for future reference for a period of time adequate for the purposes of the information and which allows the unchanged reproduction of the information stored;

(12) 'unavoidable and extraordinary circumstances' means a situation beyond the control of the party who invokes such a situation and the consequences of which could not have been avoided even if all reasonable measures had been taken;
(13) 'lack of conformity' means a failure to perform or improper performance of the travel services included in a package;
(14) 'minor' means a person below the age of 18 years;
(15) 'point of sale' means any retail premises, whether movable or immovable, or a retail website or similar online sales facility, including where retail websites or online sales facilities are presented to travellers as a single facility, including a telephone service;
(16) 'repatriation' means the traveller's return to the place of departure or to another place the contracting parties agree upon.

Article 4. Unless otherwise provided for in this Directive, Member States shall not maintain or introduce, in their national law, provisions diverging from those laid down in this Directive, including more or less stringent provisions which would ensure a different level of traveller protection.

Chapter II. Information obligations and content of the package travel contract

Article 5. (1) Member States shall ensure that, before the traveller is bound by any package travel contract or any corresponding offer, the organiser and, where the package is sold through a retailer, also the retailer shall provide the traveller with the standard information by means of the relevant form as set out in Part A or Part B of Annex I, and, where applicable to the package, with the following information:
(a) the main characteristics of the travel services:
(i) the travel destination(s), itinerary and periods of stay, with dates and, where accommodation is included, the number of nights included;
(ii) the means, characteristics and categories of transport, the points, dates and time of departure and return, the duration and places of intermediate stops and transport connections.
Where the exact time is not yet determined, the organiser and, where applicable, the retailer shall inform the traveller of the approximate time of departure and return;
(iii) the location, main features and, where applicable, tourist category of the accommodation under the rules of the country of destination;
(iv) the meal plan;
(v) visits, excursion(s) or other services included in the total price agreed for the package;
(vi) where it is not apparent from the context, whether any of the travel services will be provided to the traveller as part of a group and, if so, where possible, the approximate size of the group;
(vii) where the traveller's benefit from other tourist services depends on effective oral communication, the language in which those services will be carried out; and
(viii) whether the trip or holiday is generally suitable for persons with reduced mobility and, upon the traveller's request, precise information on the suitability of the trip or holiday taking into account the traveller's needs;
(b) the trading name and geographical address of the organiser and, where applicable, of the retailer, as well as their telephone number and, where applicable, e-mail address;
(c) the total price of the package inclusive of taxes and, where applicable, of all additional fees, charges and other costs or, where those costs cannot reasonably be calculated in advance of the conclusion of the contract, an indication of the type of additional costs which the traveller may still have to bear;
(d) the arrangements for payment, including any amount or percentage of the price which is to be paid as a down payment and the timetable for payment of the balance, or financial guarantees to be paid or provided by the traveller;
(e) the minimum number of persons required for the package to take place and the time-limit, referred to in point (a) of Article 12(3), before the start of the package for the possible termination of the contract if that number is not reached;
(f) general information on passport and visa requirements, including approximate periods for obtaining visas and information on health formalities, of the country of destination;
(g) information that the traveller may terminate the contract at any time before the start of the package in return for payment of an appropriate termination fee, or, where applicable, the standardised termination fees requested by the organiser, in accordance with Article 12(1);
(h) information on optional or compulsory insurance to cover the cost of termination of the contract by the traveller or the cost of assistance, including repatriation, in the event of accident, illness or death.

For package travel contracts concluded by telephone, the organiser and, where applicable, the retailer shall provide the traveller with the standard information set out in Part B of Annex I, and the information set out in points (a) to (h) of the first subparagraph.

(2) With reference to packages as defined in point (b)(v) of point 2 of Article 3 the organiser and the trader to whom the data are transmitted shall ensure that each of them provides, before the traveller is bound by a contract or any corresponding offer, the information set out in points (a) to (h) of the first subparagraph of paragraph 1 of this Article in so far as it is relevant for the respective travel services they offer. The organiser shall also provide, at the same time, the standard information by means of the form set out in Part C of Annex I.

(3) The information referred to in paragraphs 1 and 2 shall be provided in a clear, comprehensible and prominent manner. Where such information is provided in writing, it shall be legible.

Article 6. (1) Member States shall ensure that the information provided to the traveller pursuant to points (a), (c), (d), (e) and (g) of the first subparagraph of Article 5(1) shall form an integral part of the package travel contract and shall not be altered unless the contracting parties expressly agree otherwise. The organiser and, where applicable, the retailer shall communicate all changes to the pre-contractual information to the traveller in a clear, comprehensible and prominent manner before the conclusion of the package travel contract.

(2) If the organiser and, where applicable, the retailer has not complied with the information requirements on additional fees, charges or other costs as referred to in point (c) of the first subparagraph of Article 5(1) before the conclusion of the package travel contract, the traveller shall not bear those fees, charges or other costs.

Article 7. (1) Member States shall ensure that package travel contracts are in plain and intelligible language and, in so far as they are in writing, legible. At the conclusion of the package travel contract or without undue delay thereafter, the organiser or retailer shall provide the traveller with a copy or confirmation of the contract on a durable medium. The traveller shall be entitled to request a paper copy if the package travel contract has been concluded in the simultaneous physical presence of the parties.

With respect to off-premises contracts as defined in point 8 of Article 2 of Directive 2011/83/EU, a copy or confirmation of the package travel contract shall be provided to the traveller on paper or, if the traveller agrees, on another durable medium.

(2) The package travel contract or confirmation of the contract shall set out the full content of the agreement which shall include all the information referred to in points (a) to (h) of the first subparagraph of Article 5(1) and the following information:

(a) special requirements of the traveller which the organiser has accepted;
(b) information that the organiser is:
(i) responsible for the proper performance of all travel services included in the contract in accordance with Article 13; and
(ii) obliged to provide assistance if the traveller is in difficulty in accordance with Article 16;
(c) the name of the entity in charge of the insolvency protection and its contact details, including its geographical address, and, where applicable, the name of the competent authority designated by the Member State concerned for that purpose and its contact details;
(d) the name, address, telephone number, e-mail address and, where applicable, the fax number of the organiser's local representative, of a contact point or of another service which enables the traveller to contact the organiser quickly and communicate with him efficiently, to request assistance when the traveller is in difficulty or to complain about any lack of conformity perceived during the performance of the package;
(e) information that the traveller is required to communicate any lack of conformity which he perceives during the performance of the package in accordance with Article 13(2);
(f) where minors, unaccompanied by a parent or another authorised person, travel on the basis of a package travel contract which includes accommodation, information enabling direct contact with the minor or the person responsible for the minor at the minor's place of stay;
(g) information on available in-house complaint handling procedures and on alternative dispute resolution ('ADR') mechanisms pursuant to Directive 2013/11/EU of the European Parliament and of the Council, and, where applicable, on the ADR entity by which the trader is covered and on the online dispute resolution platform pursuant to Regulation (EU) No 524/2013 of the European Parliament and of the Council;
(h) information on the traveller's right to transfer the contract to another traveller in accordance with Article 9.

(3) With reference to packages as defined in point (b)(v) of point 2 of Article 3, the trader to whom

the data are transmitted shall inform the organiser of the conclusion of the contract leading to the creation of a package. The trader shall provide the organiser with the information necessary to comply with his obligations as an organiser.
As soon as the organiser is informed that a package has been created, the organiser shall provide to the traveller the information referred to in points (a) to (h) of paragraph 2 on a durable medium.
(4) The information referred to in paragraphs 2 and 3 shall be provided in a clear, comprehensible and prominent manner.
(5) In good time before the start of the package, the organiser shall provide the traveller with the necessary receipts, vouchers and tickets, information on the scheduled times of departure and, where applicable, the deadline for check-in, as well as the scheduled times for intermediate stops, transport connections and arrival.

Article 8. As regards compliance with the information requirements laid down in this Chapter, the burden of proof shall be on the trader.

Chapter III. Changes to the package travel contract before the start of the package

Article 9. (1) Member States shall ensure that a traveller may, after giving the organiser reasonable notice on a durable medium before the start of the package, transfer the package travel contract to a person who satisfies all the conditions applicable to that contract. Notice given at the latest seven days before the start of the package shall in any event be deemed to be reasonable.
(2) The transferor of the package travel contract and the transferee shall be jointly and severally liable for the payment of the balance due and for any additional fees, charges or other costs arising from the transfer. The organiser shall inform the transferor about the actual costs of the transfer. Those costs shall not be unreasonable and shall not exceed the actual cost incurred by the organiser due to the transfer of the package travel contract.
(3) The organiser shall provide the transferor with proof of the additional fees, charges or other costs arising from the transfer of the package travel contract.

Article 10. (1) Member States shall ensure that after the conclusion of the package travel contract, prices may be increased only if the contract expressly reserves that possibility and states that the traveller is entitled to price reduction under paragraph 4. In that event the package travel contract shall state how price revisions are to be calculated. Price increases shall be possible exclusively as a direct consequence of changes in:
(a) the price of the carriage of passengers resulting from the cost of fuel or other power sources;
(b) the level of taxes or fees on the travel services included in the contract imposed by third parties not directly involved in the performance of the package, including tourist taxes, landing taxes or embarkation or disembarkation fees at ports and airports; or
(c) the exchange rates relevant to the package.
(2) If the price increase referred to in paragraph 1 of this Article exceeds 8 % of the total price of the package, Article 11(2) to (5) shall apply.
(3) Irrespective of its extent, a price increase shall be possible only if the organiser notifies the traveller clearly and comprehensibly of it with a justification for that increase and a calculation, on a durable medium at the latest 20 days before the start of the package.
(4) If the package travel contract stipulates the possibility of price increases, the traveller shall have the right to a price reduction corresponding to any decrease in the costs referred to in points (a), (b) and (c) of paragraph 1 that occurs after the conclusion of the contract before the start of the package.
(5) In the event of a price decrease, the organiser shall have the right to deduct actual administrative expenses from the refund owed to the traveller. At the traveller's request, the organiser shall provide proof of those administrative expenses.

Article 11. (1) Member States shall ensure that, before the start of the package, the organiser may not unilaterally change package travel contract terms other than the price in accordance with Article 10, unless:
(a) the organiser has reserved that right in the contract;
(b) the change is insignificant; and
(c) the organiser informs the traveller of the change in a clear, comprehensible and prominent manner on a durable medium.
(2) If, before the start of the package, the organiser is constrained to alter significantly any of the main characteristics of the travel services as referred to in point (a) of the first subparagraph of Article 5(1) or cannot fulfil the special requirements as referred to in point (a) of Article 7(2), or proposes to increase the price of the package by more than 8 % in accordance with Article 10(2), the traveller

may within a reasonable period specified by the organiser:
(a) accept the proposed change; or
(b) terminate the contract without paying a termination fee.
If the traveller terminates the package travel contract, the traveller may accept a substitute package where this is offered by the organiser, if possible of an equivalent or a higher quality.
(3) The organiser shall without undue delay inform the traveller in a clear, comprehensible and prominent manner on a durable medium of:
(a) the proposed changes referred to in paragraph 2 and, where appropriate in accordance with paragraph 4, their impact on the price of the package;
(b) a reasonable period within which the traveller has to inform the organiser of his decision pursuant to paragraph 2;
(c) the consequences of the traveller's failure to respond within the period referred to point (b), in accordance with applicable national law; and
(d) where applicable, the offered substitute package and its price.
(4) Where the changes to the package travel contract referred to in the first subparagraph of paragraph 2 or the substitute package referred to in the second subparagraph of paragraph 2 result in a package of lower quality or cost, the traveller shall be entitled to an appropriate price reduction.
(5) If the package travel contract is terminated pursuant to point (b) of the first subparagraph of paragraph 2 of this Article, and the traveller does not accept a substitute package, the organiser shall refund all payments made by or on behalf of the traveller without undue delay and in any event not later than 14 days after the contract is terminated. Article 14(2), (3), (4), (5) and (6) shall apply mutatis mutandis.

Article 12. (1) Member States shall ensure that the traveller may terminate the package travel contract at any time before the start of the package. Where the traveller terminates the package travel contract under this paragraph, the traveller may be required to pay an appropriate and justifiable termination fee to the organiser. The package travel contract may specify reasonable standardised termination fees based on the time of the termination of the contract before the start of the package and the expected cost savings and income from alternative deployment of the travel services. In the absence of standardised termination fees, the amount of the termination fee shall correspond to the price of the package minus the cost savings and income from alternative deployment of the travel services. At the traveller's request the organiser shall provide a justification for the amount of the termination fees.
(2) Notwithstanding paragraph 1, the traveller shall have the right to terminate the package travel contract before the start of the package without paying any termination fee in the event of unavoidable and extraordinary circumstances occurring at the place of destination or its immediate vicinity and significantly affecting the performance of the package, or which significantly affect the carriage of passengers to the destination. In the event of termination of the package travel contract under this paragraph, the traveller shall be entitled to a full refund of any payments made for the package, but shall not be entitled to additional compensation.
(3) The organiser may terminate the package travel contract and provide the traveller with a full refund of any payments made for the package, but shall not be liable for additional compensation, if:
(a) the number of persons enrolled for the package is smaller than the minimum number stated in the contract and the organiser notifies the traveller of the termination of the contract within the period fixed in the contract, but not later than:
(i) 20 days before the start of the package in the case of trips lasting more than six days;
(ii) seven days before the start of the package in the case of trips lasting between two and six days;
(iii) 48 hours before the start of the package in the case of trips lasting less than two days; or
(b) the organiser is prevented from performing the contract because of unavoidable and extraordinary circumstances and notifies the traveller of the termination of the contract without undue delay before the start of the package.
(4) The organiser shall provide any refunds required under paragraphs 2 and 3 or, with respect to paragraph 1, reimburse any payments made by or on behalf of the traveller for the package minus the appropriate termination fee. Such refunds or reimbursements shall be made to the traveller without undue delay and in any event not later than 14 days after the package travel contract is terminated.
(5) With respect to off-premises contracts, Member States may provide in their national law that the traveller has the right to withdraw from the package travel contract within a period of 14 days without giving any reason.

Chapter IV. Performance of the Package

Article 13. (1) Member States shall ensure that the organiser is responsible for the performance of the travel services included in the package travel contract, irrespective of whether those services are to be performed by the organiser or by other travel service providers.

Member States may maintain or introduce in their national law provisions under which the retailer is also responsible for the performance of the package. In that case the provisions of Article 7 and Chapter III, this Chapter and Chapter V which are applicable to the organiser shall also apply mutatis mutandis to the retailer.

(2) The traveller shall inform the organiser without undue delay, taking into account the circumstances of the case, of any lack of conformity which he perceives during the performance of a travel service included in the package travel contract.

(3) If any of the travel services are not performed in accordance with the package travel contract, the organiser shall remedy the lack of conformity, unless that:

(a) is impossible; or

(b) entails disproportionate costs, taking into account the extent of the lack of conformity and the value of the travel services affected.

If the organiser, in accordance with point (a) or point (b) of the first subparagraph of this paragraph, does not remedy the lack of conformity, Article 14 shall apply.

(4) Without prejudice to the exceptions laid down in paragraph 3, if the organiser does not remedy the lack of conformity within a reasonable period set by the traveller, the traveller may do so himself and request reimbursement of the necessary expenses. It shall not be necessary for the traveller to specify a time-limit if the organiser refuses to remedy the lack of conformity or if immediate remedy is required.

(5) Where a significant proportion of the travel services cannot be provided as agreed in the package travel contract, the organiser shall offer, at no extra cost to the traveller, suitable alternative arrangements of, where possible, equivalent or higher quality than those specified in the contract, for the continuation of the package, including where the traveller's return to the place of departure is not provided as agreed.

Where the proposed alternative arrangements result in a package of lower quality than that specified in the package travel contract, the organiser shall grant the traveller an appropriate price reduction.

The traveller may reject the proposed alternative arrangements only if they are not comparable to what was agreed in the package travel contract or the price reduction granted is inadequate.

(6) Where a lack of conformity substantially affects the performance of the package and the organiser has failed to remedy it within a reasonable period set by the traveller, the traveller may terminate the package travel contract without paying a termination fee and, where appropriate, request, in accordance with Article 14, price reduction and/or compensation for damages.

If it is impossible to make alternative arrangements or the traveller rejects the proposed alternative arrangements in accordance with the third subparagraph of paragraph 5 of this Article, the traveller is, where appropriate, entitled to price reduction and/or compensation for damages in accordance with Article 14 without terminating the package travel contract.

If the package includes the carriage of passengers, the organiser shall, in the cases referred to in the first and second subparagraphs, also provide repatriation of the traveller with equivalent transport without undue delay and at no extra cost to the traveller.

(7) As long as it is impossible to ensure the traveller's return as agreed in the package travel contract because of unavoidable and extraordinary circumstances, the organiser shall bear the cost of necessary accommodation, if possible of equivalent category, for a period not exceeding three nights per traveller. Where longer periods are provided for in Union passenger rights legislation applicable to the relevant means of transport for the traveller's return, those periods shall apply.

(8) The limitation of costs referred to in paragraph 7 of this Article shall not apply to persons with reduced mobility, as defined in point (a) of Article 2 of Regulation (EC) No 1107/2006, and any person accompanying them, pregnant women and unaccompanied minors, as well as persons in need of specific medical assistance, provided that the organiser has been notified of their particular needs at least 48 hours before the start of the package. The organiser may not invoke unavoidable and extraordinary circumstances to limit the liability under paragraph 7 of this Article if the relevant transport provider may not rely on such circumstances under applicable Union legislation.

Article 14. (1) Member States shall ensure that the traveller is entitled to an appropriate price reduction for any period during which there was lack of conformity, unless the organiser proves that the lack of conformity is attributable to the traveller.

(2) The traveller shall be entitled to receive appropriate compensation from the organiser for any damage which the traveller sustains as a result of any lack of conformity. Compensation shall be made without undue delay.

(3) The traveller shall not be entitled to compensation for damages if the organiser proves that the lack of conformity is:
(a) attributable to the traveller;
(b) attributable to a third party unconnected with the provision of the travel services included in the package travel contract and is unforeseeable or unavoidable; or
(c) due to unavoidable and extraordinary circumstances.
(4) Insofar as international conventions binding the Union limit the extent of or the conditions under which compensation is to be paid by a provider carrying out a travel service which is part of a package, the same limitations shall apply to the organiser. Insofar as international conventions not binding the Union limit compensation to be paid by a service provider, Member States may limit compensation to be paid by the organiser accordingly. In other cases, the package travel contract may limit compensation to be paid by the organiser as long as that limitation does not apply to personal injury or damage caused intentionally or with negligence and does not amount to less than three times the total price of the package.
(5) Any right to compensation or price reduction under this Directive shall not affect the rights of travellers under Regulation (EC) No 261/2004, Regulation (EC) No 1371/2007, Regulation (EC) No 392/2009 of the European Parliament and of the Council (20), Regulation (EU) No 1177/2010 and Regulation (EU) No 181/2011, and under international conventions. Travellers shall be entitled to present claims under this Directive and under those Regulations and international conventions. Compensation or price reduction granted under this Directive and the compensation or price reduction granted under those Regulations and international conventions shall be deducted from each other in order to avoid overcompensation.
(6) The limitation period for introducing claims under this Article shall not be less than two years.

Article 15. Without prejudice to the second subparagraph of Article 13(1), Member States shall ensure that the traveller may address messages, requests or complaints in relation to the performance of the package directly to the retailer through which it was purchased. The retailer shall forward those messages, requests or complaints to the organiser without undue delay.
For the purpose of compliance with time-limits or limitation periods, receipt of the messages, requests or complaints referred to in the first subparagraph by the retailer shall be considered as receipt by the organiser.

Article 16. Member States shall ensure that the organiser gives appropriate assistance without undue delay to the traveller in difficulty, including in the circumstances referred to in Article 13(7), in particular by:
(a) providing appropriate information on health services, local authorities and consular assistance; and
(b) assisting the traveller to make distance communications and helping the traveller to find alternative travel arrangements.
The organiser shall be able to charge a reasonable fee for such assistance if the difficulty is caused intentionally by the traveller or through the traveller's negligence. That fee shall not in any event exceed the actual costs incurred by the organiser.

Chapter V. Insolvency Protection

Article 17. (1) Member States shall ensure that organisers established in their territory provide security for the refund of all payments made by or on behalf of travellers insofar as the relevant services are not performed as a consequence of the organiser's insolvency. If the carriage of passengers is included in the package travel contract, organisers shall also provide security for the travellers' repatriation. Continuation of the package may be offered.
Organisers not established in a Member State which sell or offer for sale packages in a Member State, or which by any means direct such activities to a Member State, shall be obliged to provide the security in accordance with the law of that Member State.
(2) The security referred to in paragraph 1 shall be effective and shall cover reasonably foreseeable costs. It shall cover the amounts of payments made by or on behalf of travellers in respect of packages, taking into account the length of the period between down payments and final payments and the completion of the packages, as well as the estimated cost for repatriations in the event of the organiser's insolvency.
(3) An organiser's insolvency protection shall benefit travellers regardless of their place of residence, the place of departure or where the package is sold and irrespective of the Member State where the entity in charge of the insolvency protection is located.
(4) When the performance of the package is affected by the organiser's insolvency, the security shall

be available free of charge to ensure repatriations and, if necessary, the financing of accommodation prior to the repatriation.

(5) For travel services that have not been performed, refunds shall be provided without undue delay after the traveller's request.

Article 18. (1) Member States shall recognise as meeting the requirements of their national measures transposing Article 17 any insolvency protection an organiser provides under such measures of the Member State of his establishment.

(2) Member States shall designate central contact points to facilitate the administrative cooperation and supervision of organisers operating in different Member States. They shall notify the contact details of those contact points to all other Member States and the Commission.

(3) The central contact points shall make available to each other all necessary information on their national insolvency protection requirements and the identity of the entity or entities in charge of the insolvency protection for specific organisers established in their territory. Those contact points shall grant each other access to any available inventory listing organisers which are in compliance with their insolvency protection obligations. Any such inventory shall be publicly accessible, including online.

(4) If a Member State has doubts about an organiser's insolvency protection, it shall seek clarification from the organiser's Member State of establishment. Member States shall respond to requests from other Member States as quickly as possible taking into account the urgency and complexity of the matter. In any event a first response shall be issued at the latest within 15 working days from receiving the request.

Chapter VI. Linked Travel Arrangements

Article 19. (1) Member States shall ensure that traders facilitating linked travel arrangements shall provide security for the refund of all payments they receive from travellers insofar as a travel service which is part of a linked travel arrangement is not performed as a consequence of their insolvency. If such traders are the party responsible for the carriage of passengers, the security shall also cover the traveller's repatriation. The second subparagraph of Article 17(1), Article 17(2) to (5) and Article 18 shall apply mutatis mutandis.

(2) Before the traveller is bound by any contract leading to the creation of a linked travel arrangement or any corresponding offer, the trader facilitating linked travel arrangements, including where the trader is not established in a Member State but, by any means, directs such activities to a Member State, shall state in a clear, comprehensible and prominent manner that the traveller:

(a) will not benefit from any of the rights applying exclusively to packages under this Directive and that each service provider will be solely responsible for the proper contractual performance of his service; and

(b) will benefit from insolvency protection in accordance with paragraph 1.

In order to comply with this paragraph, the trader facilitating a linked travel arrangement shall provide the traveller with that information by means of the relevant standard form set out in Annex II, or, where the particular type of linked travel arrangement is not covered by any of the forms set out in that Annex, provide the information contained therein.

(3) Where the trader facilitating linked travel arrangements has not complied with the requirements set out in paragraphs 1 and 2 of this Article, the rights and obligations laid down in Articles 9 and 12 and Chapter IV shall apply in relation to the travel services included in the linked travel arrangement.

(4) Where a linked travel arrangement is the result of the conclusion of a contract between a traveller and a trader who does not facilitate the linked travel arrangement, that trader shall inform the trader facilitating the linked travel arrangement of the conclusion of the relevant contract.

Chapter VII. General Provisions

Article 20. Without prejudice to the second subparagraph of Article 13(1), where the organiser is established outside the European Economic Area, the retailer established in a Member State shall be subject to the obligations laid down for organisers in Chapters IV and V, unless the retailer provides evidence that the organiser complies with those Chapters.

Article 21. Member States shall ensure that a trader is liable for any errors due to technical defects in the booking system which are attributable to him and, where the trader has agreed to arrange the booking of a package or of travel services which are part of linked travel arrangements, for the errors made during the booking process.

A trader shall not be liable for booking errors which are attributable to the traveller or which are caused by unavoidable and extraordinary circumstances.

Article 22. In cases where an organiser or, in accordance with the second subparagraph of Article 13(1) or Article 20, a retailer pays compensation, grants price reduction or meets the other obligations incumbent on him under this Directive, Member States shall ensure that the organiser or retailer has the right to seek redress from any third parties which contributed to the event triggering compensation, price reduction or other obligations.

Article 23. (1) A declaration by an organiser of a package or a trader facilitating a linked travel arrangement that he is acting exclusively as a travel service provider, as an intermediary or in any other capacity, or that a package or a linked travel arrangement does not constitute a package or a linked travel arrangement, shall not absolve that organiser or trader from the obligations imposed on them under this Directive.
(2) Travellers may not waive the rights conferred on them by the national measures transposing this Directive.
(3) Any contractual arrangement or any statement by the traveller which directly or indirectly waives or restricts the rights conferred on travellers pursuant to this Directive or aims to circumvent the application of this Directive shall not be binding on the traveller.

Article 24. Member States shall ensure that adequate and effective means exist to ensure compliance with this Directive.

Article 25. Member States shall lay down the rules on penalties applicable to infringements of national provisions adopted pursuant to this Directive and shall take all measures necessary to ensure that they are implemented. The penalties provided for shall be effective, proportionate and dissuasive.

Article 26. By 1 January 2019, the Commission shall submit a report to the European Parliament and to the Council on the provisions of this Directive applying to online bookings made at different points of sale and the qualification of such bookings as packages, linked travel arrangements or stand-alone travel services, and in particular on the definition of package set out in point (b)(v) of point 2 of Article 3 and whether an adjustment or broadening of that definition is appropriate.
By 1 January 2021, the Commission shall submit a general report on the application of this Directive to the European Parliament and to the Council.
The reports referred to in the first and the second paragraphs shall be accompanied, where necessary, by legislative proposals.

Article 27. (1) Point 5 of the Annex to Regulation (EC) No 2006/2004 is replaced by the following:
'(5) Directive (EU) 2015/2302 of the European Parliament and of the Council
(2) Point (g) of Article 3(3) of Directive 2011/83/EU is replaced by the following:
'(g) on packages as defined in point 2 of Article 3 of Directive (EU) 2015/2302 of the European Parliament and of the Council.
Article 6(7), Article 8(2) and (6) and Articles 19, 21 and 22 of this Directive shall apply mutatis mutandis to packages as defined in point 2 of Article 3 of Directive (EU) 2015/2302 in relation to travellers as defined in point 6 of Article 3 of that Directive.

Chapter VIII. Final Provisions

Article 28. (1) Member States shall adopt and publish, by 1 January 2018, the laws, regulations and administrative provisions necessary to comply with this Directive. They shall forthwith communicate to the Commission the text of those measures.
(2) They shall apply those measures from 1 July 2018.
(3) When Member States adopt those measures, they shall contain a reference to this Directive or be accompanied by such a reference on the occasion of their official publication. Member States shall determine how such reference is to be made.
(4) Member States shall communicate to the Commission the text of the main provisions of national law which they adopt in the field covered by this Directive.

Article 29. Directive 90/314/EEC is repealed with effect from 1 July 2018.
References to the repealed Directive shall be construed as references to this Directive and shall be read in accordance with the correlation table set out in Annex III.

Article 30. This Directive shall enter into force on the twentieth day following that of its publication in the Official Journal of the European Union.

Article 31. This Directive is addressed to the Member States.

PART IV   EUROPEAN PRIVATE LAW

Annex I

Part A. Standard information form for package travel contracts where the use of hyperlinks is possible

The combination of travel services offered to you is a package within the meaning of Directive (EU) 2015/2302.

Therefore, you will benefit from all EU rights applying to packages. Company XY/companies XY will be fully responsible for the proper performance of the package as a whole.

Additionally, as required by law, company XY/companies XY has/have protection in place to refund your payments and, where transport is included in the package, to ensure your repatriation in the event that it becomes/they become insolvent.

More information on key rights under Directive (EU) 2015/2302 (to be provided in the form of a hyperlink).

Following the hyperlink the traveller will receive the following information:

Key rights under Directive (EU) 2015/2302
- Travellers will receive all essential information about the package before concluding the package travel contract.
- There is always at least one trader who is liable for the proper performance of all the travel services included in the contract.
- Travellers are given an emergency telephone number or details of a contact point where they can get in touch with the organiser or the travel agent.
- Travellers may transfer the package to another person, on reasonable notice and possibly subject to additional costs.
- The price of the package may only be increased if specific costs rise (for instance, fuel prices) and if expressly provided for in the contract, and in any event not later than 20 days before the start of the package. If the price increase exceeds 8 % of the price of the package, the traveller may terminate the contract. If the organiser reserves the right to a price increase, the traveller has a right to a price reduction if there is a decrease in the relevant costs.
- Travellers may terminate the contract without paying any termination fee and get a full refund of any payments if any of the essential elements of the package, other than the price, are changed significantly. If before the start of the package the trader responsible for the package cancels the package, travellers are entitled to a refund and compensation where appropriate.
- Travellers may terminate the contract without paying any termination fee before the start of the package in the event of exceptional circumstances, for instance if there are serious security problems at the destination which are likely to affect the package.
- Additionally, travellers may at any time before the start of the package terminate the contract in return for an appropriate and justifiable termination fee.
- If, after the start of the package, significant elements of the package cannot be provided as agreed, suitable alternative arrangements will have to be offered to the traveller at no extra cost. Travellers may terminate the contract without paying any termination fee, where services are not performed in accordance with the contract and this substantially affects the performance of the package and the organiser fails to remedy the problem.
- Travellers are also entitled to a price reduction and/or compensation for damages where the travel services are not performed or are improperly performed.
- The organiser has to provide assistance if the traveller is in difficulty.
- If the organiser or, in some Member States, the retailer becomes insolvent, payments will be refunded. If the organiser or, where applicable, the retailer becomes insolvent after the start of the package and if transport is included in the package, repatriation of the travellers is secured. XY has taken out insolvency protection with YZ (the entity in charge of the insolvency protection, e.g. a guarantee fund or an insurance company). Travellers may contact this entity or, where applicable, the competent authority (contact details, including name, geographical address, email and telephone number) if services are denied because of XY's insolvency.

Directive (EU) 2015/2302 as transposed into national law (hyperlink)

Part B. Standard information form for package travel contracts in situations other than those covered by Part A

The combination of travel services offered to you is a package within the meaning of Directive (EU) 2015/2302.

Therefore, you will benefit from all EU rights applying to packages. Company XY/companies XY will be fully responsible for the proper performance of the package as a whole.
Additionally, as required by law, company XY/companies XY has/have protection in place to refund your payments and, where transport is included in the package, to ensure your repatriation in the event that it becomes/they become insolvent.

Key rights under Directive (EU) 2015/2302
- Travellers will receive all essential information about the package before concluding the package travel contract.
- There is always at least one trader who is liable for the proper performance of all the travel services included in the contract.
- Travellers are given an emergency telephone number or details of a contact point where they can get in touch with the organiser or the travel agent.
- Travellers may transfer the package to another person, on reasonable notice and possibly subject to additional costs.
- The price of the package may only be increased if specific costs rise (for instance, fuel prices) and if expressly provided for in the contract, and in any event not later than 20 days before the start of the package. If the price increase exceeds 8 % of the price of the package, the traveller may terminate the contract. If the organiser reserves the right to a price increase, the traveller has a right to a price reduction if there is a decrease in the relevant costs.
- Travellers may terminate the contract without paying any termination fee and get a full refund of any payments if any of the essential elements of the package, other than the price, are changed significantly. If before the start of the package the trader responsible for the package cancels the package, travellers are entitled to a refund and compensation where appropriate.
- Travellers may terminate the contract without paying any termination fee before the start of the package in the event of exceptional circumstances, for instance if there are serious security problems at the destination which are likely to affect the package.
- Additionally, travellers may at any time before the start of the package terminate the contract in return for an appropriate and justifiable termination fee.
- If, after the start of the package, significant elements of the package cannot be provided as agreed, suitable alternative arrangements will have to be offered to the traveller at no extra cost. Travellers may terminate the contract without paying any termination fee, where services are not performed in accordance with the contract and this substantially affects the performance of the package and the organiser fails to remedy the problem.
- Travellers are also entitled to a price reduction and/or compensation for damages where the travel services are not performed or are improperly performed.
- The organiser has to provide assistance if the traveller is in difficulty.
- If the organiser or, in some Member States, the retailer becomes insolvent, payments will be refunded. If the organiser or, where applicable, the retailer becomes insolvent after the start of the package and if transport is included in the package, repatriation of the travellers is secured. XY has taken out insolvency protection with YZ (the entity in charge of the insolvency protection, e.g. a guarantee fund or an insurance company). Travellers may contact this entity or, where applicable, the competent authority (contact details, including name, geographical address, email and telephone number) if services are denied because of XY's insolvency

(Website where Directive (EU) 2015/2302 as transposed into national law can be found.)

Part C. Standard information form where the organiser transmits data to another trader in accordance with point (b)(v) of point 2 of Article 3

If you conclude a contract with company AB not later than 24 hours after receiving the confirmation of the booking from company XY the travel service provided by XY and AB will constitute a package within the meaning of Directive (EU) 2015/2302.
Therefore, you will benefit from all EU rights applying to packages. Company XY will be fully responsible for the proper performance of the package as a whole.
Additionally, as required by law, company XY has protection in place to refund your payments and, where transport is included in the package, to ensure your repatriation in the event that it becomes insolvent.
More information on key rights under Directive (EU) 2015/2302 (to be provided in the form of a hyperlink).

Following the hyperlink the traveller will receive the following information:

Key rights under Directive (EU) 2015/2302
- Travellers will receive all essential information about the package before concluding the package travel contract.
- There is always at least one trader who is liable for the proper performance of all the travel services included in the contract.
- Travellers are given an emergency telephone number or details of a contact point where they can get in touch with the organiser or the travel agent.
- Travellers may transfer the package to another person, on reasonable notice and possibly subject to additional costs.
- The price of the package may only be increased if specific costs rise (for instance, fuel prices) and if expressly provided for in the contract, and in any event not later than 20 days before the start of the package. If the price increase exceeds 8 % of the price of the package, the traveller may terminate the contract. If the organiser reserves the right to a price increase, the traveller has a right to a price reduction if there is a decrease in the relevant costs.
- Travellers may terminate the contract without paying any termination fee and get a full refund of any payments if any of the essential elements of the package, other than the price, are changed significantly. If before the start of the package the trader responsible for the package cancels the package, travellers are entitled to a refund and compensation where appropriate.
- Travellers may terminate the contract without paying any termination fee before the start of the package in the event of exceptional circumstances, for instance if there are serious security problems at the destination which are likely to affect the package.
- Additionally, travellers may at any time before the start of the package terminate the contract in return for an appropriate and justifiable termination fee.
- If, after the start of the package, significant elements of the package cannot be provided as agreed, suitable alternative arrangements will have to be offered to the traveller at no extra cost. Travellers may terminate the contract without paying any termination fee, where services are not performed in accordance with the contract and this substantially affects the performance of the package and the organiser fails to remedy the problem.
- Travellers are also entitled to a price reduction and/or compensation for damages where the travel services are not performed or are improperly performed.
- The organiser has to provide assistance if the traveller is in difficulty.
- If the organiser or, in some Member States, the retailer becomes insolvent, payments will be refunded. If the organiser or, where applicable, the retailer becomes insolvent after the start of the package and if transport is included in the package, repatriation of the travellers is secured. XY has taken out insolvency protection with YZ (the entity in charge of the insolvency protection, e.g. a guarantee fund or an insurance company). Travellers may contact this entity or, where applicable, the competent authority (contact details, including name, geographical address, email and telephone number) if services are denied because of XY's insolvency

Directive (EU) 2015/2302 as transposed into national law (hyperlink)

Annex II

Part A. Standard information form where the trader facilitating an online linked travel arrangement within the meaning of point (a) of point 5 of Article 3 is a carrier selling a return ticket

If, after selecting and paying for one travel service, you book additional travel services for your trip or holiday via our company/XY, you will NOT benefit from rights applying to packages under Directive (EU) 2015/2302.
Therefore, our company/XY will not be responsible for the proper performance of those additional travel services. In case of problems please contact the relevant service provider.
However, if you book any additional travel services during the same visit to our company's/XY's booking website, the travel services will become part of a linked travel arrangement. In that case XY has, as required by EU law, protection in place to refund your payments to XY for services not performed because of XY's insolvency, and, where necessary, for your repatriation. Please note that this does not provide a refund in the event of the insolvency of the relevant service provider.
More information on insolvency protection (to be provided in the form of a hyperlink)

Following the hyperlink the traveller will receive the following information:

XY has taken out insolvency protection with YZ (the entity in charge of the insolvency protection, e.g. a guarantee fund or an insurance company).

Travellers may contact this entity, or where applicable, the competent authority (contact details, including name, geographical address, email and telephone number) if the services are denied because of XY's insolvency.
Note: This insolvency protection does not cover contracts with parties other than XY, which can be performed despite XY's insolvency.
Directive (EU) 2015/2302 as transposed into the national law (hyperlink)

Part B. Standard information form where the trader facilitating an online linked travel arrangement within the meaning of point (a) of point 5 of Article 3 is a trader other than a carrier selling a return ticket

If, after selecting and paying for one travel service, you book additional travel services for your trip or holiday via our company/XY, you will NOT benefit from rights applying to packages under Directive (EU) 2015/2302.
Therefore, our company/XY will not be responsible for the proper performance of the individual travel services. In case of problems please contact the relevant service provider.
However, if you book any additional travel services during the same visit to our company's/XY's booking website, the travel services will become part of a linked travel arrangement. In that case XY has, as required by EU law, protection in place to refund your payments to XY for services not performed because of XY's insolvency. Please note that this does not provide a refund in the event of the insolvency of the relevant service provider.
More information on insolvency protection (to be provided in the form of a hyperlink)

Following the hyperlink the traveller will receive the following information:

XY has taken out insolvency protection with YZ (the entity in charge of the insolvency protection, e.g. a guarantee fund or an insurance company).
Travellers may contact this entity or, where applicable, the competent authority (contact details, including name, geographical address, email and telephone number) if the services are denied because of XY's insolvency.
Note: This insolvency protection does not cover contracts with parties other than XY, which can be performed despite XY's insolvency.
Directive (EU) 2015/2302 as transposed into the national law (hyperlink)

Part C. Standard information form in the case of linked travel arrangements within the meaning of point (a) of point 5 of Article 3 where the contracts are concluded in the simultaneous physical presence of the trader (other than a carrier selling a return ticket) and the traveller

If, after selecting and paying for one travel service, you book additional travel services for your trip or holiday via our company/XY, you will NOT benefit from rights applying to packages under Directive (EU) 2015/2302
Therefore, our company/XY will not be responsible for the proper performance of the individual travel services. In case of problems please contact the relevant service provider.
However, if you book any additional travel services during the same visit to or contact with our company/XY, the travel services will become part of a linked travel arrangement. In that case XY has, as required by EU law, protection in place to refund your payments to XY for services not performed because of XY's insolvency. Please note that this does not provide a refund in the event of the insolvency of the relevant service provider.
XY has taken out insolvency protection with YZ (the entity in charge of the insolvency protection, e.g. a guarantee fund or an insurance company).
Travellers may contact this entity or, where applicable, the competent authority (contact details, including name, geographical address, email and telephone number) if the services are denied because of XY's insolvency.
Note: This insolvency protection does not cover contracts with parties other than XY, which can be performed despite XY's insolvency.
(Website where Directive (EU) 2015/2302 as transposed into national law can be found.)

Part D. Standard information form where the trader facilitating an online linked travel arrangement within the meaning of point (b) of point 5 of Article 3 is a carrier selling a return ticket

If you book additional travel services for your trip or holiday via this link/these links, you will NOT benefit from rights applying to packages under Directive (EU) 2015/2302.
Therefore, our company/XY will not be responsible for the proper performance of those additional

travel services. In case of problems, please contact the relevant service provider.
However, if you book additional travel services via this link/these links not later than 24 hours after receiving the confirmation of the booking from our company/XY, those travel services will become part of a linked travel arrangement. In that case XY has, as required by EU law, protection in place to refund your payments to XY for services not performed because of XY's insolvency, and, where necessary, for your repatriation. Please note that this does not provide a refund in the event of the insolvency of the relevant service provider.

More information on insolvency protection (to be provided in the form of a hyperlink)

Following the hyperlink the traveller will receive the following information:

XY has taken out insolvency protection with YZ (the entity in charge of the insolvency protection, e.g. a guarantee fund or an insurance company).
Travellers may contact this entity or, where applicable, the competent authority (contact details, including name, geographical address, email and telephone number) if the services are denied because of XY's insolvency.
Note: This insolvency protection does not cover contracts with parties other than XY, which can be performed despite XY's insolvency.
Directive (EU) 2015/2302 as transposed into the national law (hyperlink)

Part E. Standard information form where the trader facilitating an online linked travel arrangement within the meaning of point (b) of point 5 of Article 3 is a trader other than a carrier selling a return ticket

If you book additional travel services for your trip or holiday via this link/these links, you will NOT benefit from rights applying to packages under Directive (EU) 2015/2302.
Therefore, our company/XY will not be responsible for the proper performance of those additional travel services. In case of problems please contact the relevant service provider.
However, if you book additional travel services via this link/these links not later than 24 hours after receiving the confirmation of the booking from our company/XY, those travel services will become part of a linked travel arrangement. In that case XY has, as required by EU law, protection in place to refund your payments to XY for services not performed because of XY's insolvency. Please note that this does not provide a refund in the event of the insolvency of the relevant service provider.
More information on insolvency protection (to be provided in the form of a hyperlink)
Following the hyperlink the traveller will receive the following information:

XY has taken out insolvency protection with YZ (the entity in charge of the insolvency protection, e.g. a guarantee fund or an insurance company).
Travellers may contact this entity or, where applicable, the competent authority (contact details, including name, geographical address, email and telephone number) if the services are denied because of XY's insolvency.
Note: This insolvency protection does not cover contracts with parties other than XY, which can be performed despite XY's insolvency.
Directive (EU) 2015/2302 as transposed into the national law (hyperlink)

[Annex III is omitted.]

EU: REGULATION 1346/2000 ON INSOLVENCY PROCEEDINGS

Council regulation (EC) No 1346/2000 of 29 May 2000 on insolvency proceedings (OJL 16, 30.06.2000, pp. 1 - 18) [footnotes omitted].

THE COUNCIL OF THE EUROPEAN UNION,
Having regard to the Treaty establishing the European Community, and in particular Articles 61(c) and 67(1) thereof,
Having regard to the initiative of the Federal Republic of Germany and the Republic of Finland,
Having regard to the opinion of the European Parliament,
Having regard to the opinion of the Economic and Social Committee,
Whereas:
(1) The European Union has set out the aim of establishing an area of freedom, security and justice.
(2) The proper functioning of the internal market requires that cross-border insolvency proceedings should operate efficiently and effectively and this Regulation needs to be adopted in order to achieve this objective which comes within the scope of judicial cooperation in civil matters within the meaning of Article 65 of the Treaty.
(3) The activities of undertakings have more and more cross-border effects and are therefore increasingly being regulated by Community law. While the insolvency of such undertakings also affects the proper functioning of the internal market, there is a need for a Community act requiring coordination of the measures to be taken regarding an insolvent debtor's assets.
(4) It is necessary for the proper functioning of the internal market to avoid incentives for the parties to transfer assets or judicial proceedings from one Member State to another, seeking to obtain a more favourable legal position (forum shopping).
(5) These objectives cannot be achieved to a sufficient degree at national level and action at Community level is therefore justified.
(6) In accordance with the principle of proportionality this Regulation should be confined to provisions governing jurisdiction for opening insolvency proceedings and judgments which are delivered directly on the basis of the insolvency proceedings and are closely connected with such proceedings. In addition, this Regulation should contain provisions regarding the recognition of those judgments and the applicable law which also satisfy that principle.
(7) Insolvency proceedings relating to the winding-up of insolvent companies or other legal persons, judicial arrangements, compositions and analogous proceedings are excluded from the scope of the 1968 Brussels Convention on Jurisdiction and the Enforcement of Judgments in Civil and Commercial Matters, as amended by the Conventions on Accession to this Convention.
(8) In order to achieve the aim of improving the efficiency and effectiveness of insolvency proceedings having cross-border effects, it is necessary, and appropriate, that the provisions on jurisdiction, recognition and applicable law in this area should be contained in a Community law measure which is binding and directly applicable in Member States.
(9) This Regulation should apply to insolvency proceedings, whether the debtor is a natural person or a legal person, a trader or an individual. The insolvency proceedings to which this Regulation applies are listed in the Annexes. Insolvency proceedings concerning insurance undertakings, credit institutions, investment undertakings holding funds or securities for third parties and collective investment undertakings should be excluded from the scope of this Regulation. Such undertakings should not be covered by this Regulation since they are subject to special arrangements and, to some extent, the national supervisory authorities have extremely wide-ranging powers of intervention.
(10) Insolvency proceedings do not necessarily involve the intervention of a judicial authority; the expression "court" in this Regulation should be given a broad meaning and include a person or body empowered by national law to open insolvency proceedings. In order for this Regulation to apply, proceedings (comprising acts and formalities set down in law) should not only have to comply with the provisions of this Regulation, but they should also be officially recognised and legally effective in the Member State in which the insolvency proceedings are opened and should be collective insolvency proceedings which entail the partial or total divestment of the debtor and the appointment of a liquidator.
(11) This Regulation acknowledges the fact that as a result of widely differing substantive laws it is not practical to introduce insolvency proceedings with universal scope in the entire Community. The application without exception of the law of the State of opening of proceedings would, against this background, frequently lead to difficulties. This applies, for example, to the widely differing laws on security interests to be found in the Community. Furthermore, the preferential rights enjoyed by some creditors in the insolvency proceedings are, in some cases, completely different. This Regulation should take account of this in two different ways. On the one hand, provision should be made for special rules on applicable law in the case of particularly significant rights and legal relationships (e.g.

PART IV   EUROPEAN PRIVATE LAW

rights in rem and contracts of employment). On the other hand, national proceedings covering only assets situated in the State of opening should also be allowed alongside main insolvency proceedings with universal scope.

(12) This Regulation enables the main insolvency proceedings to be opened in the Member State where the debtor has the centre of his main interests. These proceedings have universal scope and aim at encompassing all the debtor's assets. To protect the diversity of interests, this Regulation permits secondary proceedings to be opened to run in parallel with the main proceedings. Secondary proceedings may be opened in the Member State where the debtor has an establishment. The effects of secondary proceedings are limited to the assets located in that State. Mandatory rules of coordination with the main proceedings satisfy the need for unity in the Community.

(13) The "centre of main interests" should correspond to the place where the debtor conducts the administration of his interests on a regular basis and is therefore ascertainable by third parties.

(14) This Regulation applies only to proceedings where the centre of the debtor's main interests is located in the Community.

(15) The rules of jurisdiction set out in this Regulation establish only international jurisdiction, that is to say, they designate the Member State the courts of which may open insolvency proceedings. Territorial jurisdiction within that Member State must be established by the national law of the Member State concerned.

(16) The court having jurisdiction to open the main insolvency proceedings should be enabled to order provisional and protective measures from the time of the request to open proceedings. Preservation measures both prior to and after the commencement of the insolvency proceedings are very important to guarantee the effectiveness of the insolvency proceedings. In that connection this Regulation should afford different possibilities. On the one hand, the court competent for the main insolvency proceedings should be able also to order provisional protective measures covering assets situated in the territory of other Member States. On the other hand, a liquidator temporarily appointed prior to the opening of the main insolvency proceedings should be able, in the Member States in which an establishment belonging to the debtor is to be found, to apply for the preservation measures which are possible under the law of those States.

(17) Prior to the opening of the main insolvency proceedings, the right to request the opening of insolvency proceedings in the Member State where the debtor has an establishment should be limited to local creditors and creditors of the local establishment or to cases where main proceedings cannot be opened under the law of the Member State where the debtor has the centre of his main interest. The reason for this restriction is that cases where territorial insolvency proceedings are requested before the main insolvency proceedings are intended to be limited to what is absolutely necessary. If the main insolvency proceedings are opened, the territorial proceedings become secondary.

(18) Following the opening of the main insolvency proceedings, the right to request the opening of insolvency proceedings in a Member State where the debtor has an establishment is not restricted by this Regulation. The liquidator in the main proceedings or any other person empowered under the national law of that Member State may request the opening of secondary insolvency proceedings.

(19) Secondary insolvency proceedings may serve different purposes, besides the protection of local interests. Cases may arise where the estate of the debtor is too complex to administer as a unit or where differences in the legal systems concerned are so great that difficulties may arise from the extension of effects deriving from the law of the State of the opening to the other States where the assets are located. For this reason the liquidator in the main proceedings may request the opening of secondary proceedings when the efficient administration of the estate so requires.

(20) Main insolvency proceedings and secondary proceedings can, however, contribute to the effective realisation of the total assets only if all the concurrent proceedings pending are coordinated. The main condition here is that the various liquidators must cooperate closely, in particular by exchanging a sufficient amount of information. In order to ensure the dominant role of the main insolvency proceedings, the liquidator in such proceedings should be given several possibilities for intervening in secondary insolvency proceedings which are pending at the same time. For example, he should be able to propose a restructuring plan or composition or apply for realisation of the assets in the secondary insolvency proceedings to be suspended.

(21) Every creditor, who has his habitual residence, domicile or registered office in the Community, should have the right to lodge his claims in each of the insolvency proceedings pending in the Community relating to the debtor's assets. This should also apply to tax authorities and social insurance institutions. However, in order to ensure equal treatment of creditors, the distribution of proceeds must be coordinated. Every creditor should be able to keep what he has received in the course of insolvency proceedings but should be entitled only to participate in the distribution of total assets in other proceedings if creditors with the same standing have obtained the same proportion of their claims.

EU: REGULATION 1346/2000 ON INSOLVENCY PROCEEDINGS

(22) This Regulation should provide for immediate recognition of judgments concerning the opening, conduct and closure of insolvency proceedings which come within its scope and of judgments handed down in direct connection with such insolvency proceedings. Automatic recognition should therefore mean that the effects attributed to the proceedings by the law of the State in which the proceedings were opened extend to all other Member States. Recognition of judgments delivered by the courts of the Member States should be based on the principle of mutual trust. To that end, grounds for non-recognition should be reduced to the minimum necessary. This is also the basis on which any dispute should be resolved where the courts of two Member States both claim competence to open the main insolvency proceedings. The decision of the first court to open proceedings should be recognised in the other Member States without those Member States having the power to scrutinise the court's decision.

(23) This Regulation should set out, for the matters covered by it, uniform rules on conflict of laws which replace, within their scope of application, national rules of private international law. Unless otherwise stated, the law of the Member State of the opening of the proceedings should be applicable (lex concursus). This rule on conflict of laws should be valid both for the main proceedings and for local proceedings; the lex concursus determines all the effects of the insolvency proceedings, both procedural and substantive, on the persons and legal relations concerned. It governs all the conditions for the opening, conduct and closure of the insolvency proceedings.

(24) Automatic recognition of insolvency proceedings to which the law of the opening State normally applies may interfere with the rules under which transactions are carried out in other Member States. To protect legitimate expectations and the certainty of transactions in Member States other than that in which proceedings are opened, provisions should be made for a number of exceptions to the general rule.

(25) There is a particular need for a special reference diverging from the law of the opening State in the case of rights in rem, since these are of considerable importance for the granting of credit. The basis, validity and extent of such a right in rem should therefore normally be determined according to the lex situs and not be affected by the opening of insolvency proceedings. The proprietor of the right in rem should therefore be able to continue to assert his right to segregation or separate settlement of the collateral security. Where assets are subject to rights in rem under the lex situs in one Member State but the main proceedings are being carried out in another Member State, the liquidator in the main proceedings should be able to request the opening of secondary proceedings in the jurisdiction where the rights in rem arise if the debtor has an establishment there. If a secondary proceeding is not opened, the surplus on sale of the asset covered by rights in rem must be paid to the liquidator in the main proceedings.

(26) If a set-off is not permitted under the law of the opening State, a creditor should nevertheless be entitled to the set-off if it is possible under the law applicable to the claim of the insolvent debtor. In this way, set-off will acquire a kind of guarantee function based on legal provisions on which the creditor concerned can rely at the time when the claim arises.

(27) There is also a need for special protection in the case of payment systems and financial markets. This applies for example to the position-closing agreements and netting agreements to be found in such systems as well as to the sale of securities and to the guarantees provided for such transactions as governed in particular by Directive 98/26/EC of the European Parliament and of the Council of 19 May 1998 on settlement finality in payment and securities settlement systems. For such transactions, the only law which is material should thus be that applicable to the system or market concerned. This provision is intended to prevent the possibility of mechanisms for the payment and settlement of transactions provided for in the payment and set-off systems or on the regulated financial markets of the Member States being altered in the case of insolvency of a business partner. Directive 98/26/EC contains special provisions which should take precedence over the general rules in this Regulation.

(28) In order to protect employees and jobs, the effects of insolvency proceedings on the continuation or termination of employment and on the rights and obligations of all parties to such employment must be determined by the law applicable to the agreement in accordance with the general rules on conflict of law. Any other insolvency-law questions, such as whether the employees' claims are protected by preferential rights and what status such preferential rights may have, should be determined by the law of the opening State.

(29) For business considerations, the main content of the decision opening the proceedings should be published in the other Member States at the request of the liquidator. If there is an establishment in the Member State concerned, there may be a requirement that publication is compulsory. In neither case, however, should publication be a prior condition for recognition of the foreign proceedings.

(30) It may be the case that some of the persons concerned are not in fact aware that proceedings have been opened and act in good faith in a way that conflicts with the new situation. In order to

PART IV   EUROPEAN PRIVATE LAW

protect such persons who make a payment to the debtor because they are unaware that foreign proceedings have been opened when they should in fact have made the payment to the foreign liquidator, it should be provided that such a payment is to have a debt-discharging effect.
(31) This Regulation should include Annexes relating to the organisation of insolvency proceedings. As these Annexes relate exclusively to the legislation of Member States, there are specific and substantiated reasons for the Council to reserve the right to amend these Annexes in order to take account of any amendments to the domestic law of the Member States.
(32) The United Kingdom and Ireland, in accordance with Article 3 of the Protocol on the position of the United Kingdom and Ireland annexed to the Treaty on European Union and the Treaty establishing the European Community, have given notice of their wish to take part in the adoption and application of this Regulation.
(33) Denmark, in accordance with Articles 1 and 2 of the Protocol on the position of Denmark annexed to the Treaty on European Union and the Treaty establishing the European Community, is not participating in the adoption of this Regulation, and is therefore not bound by it nor subject to its application,
HAS ADOPTED THIS REGULATION:

Chapter I. General Provisions

Article 1. (1) This Regulation shall apply to collective insolvency proceedings which entail the partial or total divestment of a debtor and the appointment of a liquidator.
(2) This Regulation shall not apply to insolvency proceedings concerning insurance undertakings, credit institutions, investment undertakings which provide services involving the holding of funds or securities for third parties, or to collective investment undertakings.

Article 2. For the purposes of this Regulation:
(a) "insolvency proceedings" shall mean the collective proceedings referred to in Article 1(1). These proceedings are listed in Annex A;
(b) "liquidator" shall mean any person or body whose function is to administer or liquidate assets of which the debtor has been divested or to supervise the administration of his affairs. Those persons and bodies are listed in Annex C;
(c) "winding-up proceedings" shall mean insolvency proceedings within the meaning of point (a) involving realising the assets of the debtor, including where the proceedings have been closed by a composition or other measure terminating the insolvency, or closed by reason of the insufficiency of the assets. Those proceedings are listed in Annex B;
(d) "court" shall mean the judicial body or any other competent body of a Member State empowered to open insolvency proceedings or to take decisions in the course of such proceedings;
(e) "judgment" in relation to the opening of insolvency proceedings or the appointment of a liquidator shall include the decision of any court empowered to open such proceedings or to appoint a liquidator;
(f) "the time of the opening of proceedings" shall mean the time at which the judgment opening proceedings becomes effective, whether it is a final judgment or not;
(g) "the Member State in which assets are situated" shall mean, in the case of:
- tangible property, the Member State within the territory of which the property is situated,
- property and rights ownership of or entitlement to which must be entered in a public register, the Member State under the authority of which the register is kept,
- claims, the Member State within the territory of which the third party required to meet them has the centre of his main interests, as determined in Article 3(1);
(h) "establishment" shall mean any place of operations where the debtor carries out a non-transitory economic activity with human means and goods.

Article 3. (1) The courts of the Member State within the territory of which the centre of a debtor's main interests is situated shall have jurisdiction to open insolvency proceedings. In the case of a company or legal person, the place of the registered office shall be presumed to be the centre of its main interests in the absence of proof to the contrary.
(2) Where the centre of a debtor's main interests is situated within the territory of a Member State, the courts of another Member State shall have jurisdiction to open insolvency proceedings against that debtor only if he possesses an establishment within the territory of that other Member State. The effects of those proceedings shall be restricted to the assets of the debtor situated in the territory of the latter Member State.
(3) Where insolvency proceedings have been opened under paragraph (1), any proceedings opened subsequently under paragraph (2) shall be secondary proceedings. These latter proceedings must be winding-up proceedings.

(4) Territorial insolvency proceedings referred to in paragraph (2) may be opened prior to the opening of main insolvency proceedings in accordance with paragraph (1) only:
(a) where insolvency proceedings under paragraph (1) cannot be opened because of the conditions laid down by the law of the Member State within the territory of which the centre of the debtor's main interests is situated; or
(b) where the opening of territorial insolvency proceedings is requested by a creditor who has his domicile, habitual residence or registered office in the Member State within the territory of which the establishment is situated, or whose claim arises from the operation of that establishment.

Article 4. (1) Save as otherwise provided in this Regulation, the law applicable to insolvency proceedings and their effects shall be that of the Member State within the territory of which such proceedings are opened, hereafter referred to as the "State of the opening of proceedings".
(2) The law of the State of the opening of proceedings shall determine the conditions for the opening of those proceedings, their conduct and their closure. It shall determine in particular:
(a) against which debtors insolvency proceedings may be brought on account of their capacity;
(b) the assets which form part of the estate and the treatment of assets acquired by or devolving on the debtor after the opening of the insolvency proceedings;
(c) the respective powers of the debtor and the liquidator;
(d) the conditions under which set-offs may be invoked;
(e) the effects of insolvency proceedings on current contracts to which the debtor is party;
(f) the effects of the insolvency proceedings on proceedings brought by individual creditors, with the exception of lawsuits pending;
(g) the claims which are to be lodged against the debtor's estate and the treatment of claims arising after the opening of insolvency proceedings;
(h) the rules governing the lodging, verification and admission of claims;
(i) the rules governing the distribution of proceeds from the realisation of assets, the ranking of claims and the rights of creditors who have obtained partial satisfaction after the opening of insolvency proceedings by virtue of a right in rem or through a set-off;
(j) the conditions for and the effects of closure of insolvency proceedings, in particular by composition;
(k) creditors' rights after the closure of insolvency proceedings;
(l) who is to bear the costs and expenses incurred in the insolvency proceedings;
(m) the rules relating to the voidness, voidability or unenforceability of legal acts detrimental to all the creditors.

Article 5. Third parties' rights in rem.
(1) The opening of insolvency proceedings shall not affect the rights in rem of creditors or third parties in respect of tangible or intangible, moveable or immoveable assets - both specific assets and collections of indefinite assets as a whole which change from time to time - belonging to the debtor which are situated within the territory of another Member State at the time of the opening of proceedings.
(2) The rights referred to in paragraph (1) shall in particular mean:
(a) the right to dispose of assets or have them disposed of and to obtain satisfaction from the proceeds of or income from those assets, in particular by virtue of a lien or a mortgage;
(b) the exclusive right to have a claim met, in particular a right guaranteed by a lien in respect of the claim or by assignment of the claim by way of a guarantee;
(c) the right to demand the assets from, and/or to require restitution by, anyone having possession or use of them contrary to the wishes of the party so entitled;
(d) a right in rem to the beneficial use of assets.
(3) The right, recorded in a public register and enforceable against third parties, under which a right in rem within the meaning of paragraph (1) may be obtained, shall be considered a right in rem.
(4) Paragraph 1 shall not preclude actions for voidness, voidability or unenforceability as referred to in Article 4(2)(m).

Article 6. (1) The opening of insolvency proceedings shall not affect the right of creditors to demand the set-off of their claims against the claims of the debtor, where such a set-off is permitted by the law applicable to the insolvent debtor's claim.
(2) Paragraph 1 shall not preclude actions for voidness, voidability or unenforceability as referred to in Article 4(2)(m).

Article 7. (1) The opening of insolvency proceedings against the purchaser of an asset shall not affect the seller's rights based on a reservation of title where at the time of the opening of proceedings the

asset is situated within the territory of a Member State other than the State of opening of proceedings.
(2) The opening of insolvency proceedings against the seller of an asset, after delivery of the asset, shall not constitute grounds for rescinding or terminating the sale and shall not prevent the purchaser from acquiring title where at the time of the opening of proceedings the asset sold is situated within the territory of a Member State other than the State of the opening of proceedings.
(3) Paragraphs 1 and 2 shall not preclude actions for voidness, voidability or unenforceability as referred to in Article 4(2)(m).

Article 8. The effects of insolvency proceedings on a contract conferring the right to acquire or make use of immoveable property shall be governed solely by the law of the Member State within the territory of which the immoveable property is situated.

Article 9. (1) Without prejudice to Article 5, the effects of insolvency proceedings on the rights and obligations of the parties to a payment or settlement system or to a financial market shall be governed solely by the law of the Member State applicable to that system or market.
(2) Paragraph 1 shall not preclude any action for voidness, voidability or unenforceability which may be taken to set aside payments or transactions under the law applicable to the relevant payment system or financial market.

Article 10. The effects of insolvency proceedings on employment contracts and relationships shall be governed solely by the law of the Member State applicable to the contract of employment.

Article 11. The effects of insolvency proceedings on the rights of the debtor in immoveable property, a ship or an aircraft subject to registration in a public register shall be determined by the law of the Member State under the authority of which the register is kept.

Article 12. For the purposes of this Regulation, a Community patent, a Community trade mark or any other similar right established by Community law may be included only in the proceedings referred to in Article 3(1).

Article 13. Article 4(2)(m) shall not apply where the person who benefited from an act detrimental to all the creditors provides proof that:
- the said act is subject to the law of a Member State other than that of the State of the opening of proceedings, and
- the law does not allow any means of challenging that act in the relevant case.

Article 14. Where, by an act concluded after the opening of insolvency proceedings, the debtor disposes, for consideration, of:
- an immoveable asset, or
- a ship or an aircraft subject to registration in a public register, or
- securities whose existence presupposes registration in a register laid down by law, the validity of that act shall be governed by the law of the State within the territory of which the immoveable asset is situated or under the authority of which the register is kept.

Article 15. The effects of insolvency proceedings on a lawsuit pending concerning an asset or a right of which the debtor has been divested shall be governed solely by the law of the Member State in which that lawsuit is pending.

Chapter II. Recognition of Insolvency Proceedings

Article 16. (1) Any judgment opening insolvency proceedings handed down by a court of a Member State which has jurisdiction pursuant to Article 3 shall be recognised in all the other Member States from the time that it becomes effective in the State of the opening of proceedings.
This rule shall also apply where, on account of his capacity, insolvency proceedings cannot be brought against the debtor in other Member States.
(2) Recognition of the proceedings referred to in Article 3(1) shall not preclude the opening of the proceedings referred to in Article 3(2) by a court in another Member State. The latter proceedings shall be secondary insolvency proceedings within the meaning of Chapter III.

Article 17. (1) The judgment opening the proceedings referred to in Article 3(1) shall, with no further formalities, produce the same effects in any other Member State as under this law of the State of the opening of proceedings, unless this Regulation provides otherwise and as long as no proceedings referred to in Article 3(2) are opened in that other Member State.
(2) The effects of the proceedings referred to in Article 3(2) may not be challenged in other Member

States. Any restriction of the creditors' rights, in particular a stay or discharge, shall produce effects vis-à-vis assets situated within the territory of another Member State only in the case of those creditors who have given their consent.

Article 18. (1) The liquidator appointed by a court which has jurisdiction pursuant to Article 3(1) may exercise all the powers conferred on him by the law of the State of the opening of proceedings in another Member State, as long as no other insolvency proceedings have been opened there nor any preservation measure to the contrary has been taken there further to a request for the opening of insolvency proceedings in that State. He may in particular remove the debtor's assets from the territory of the Member State in which they are situated, subject to Articles 5 and 7.
(2) The liquidator appointed by a court which has jurisdiction pursuant to Article 3(2) may in any other Member State claim through the courts or out of court that moveable property was removed from the territory of the State of the opening of proceedings to the territory of that other Member State after the opening of the insolvency proceedings. He may also bring any action to set aside which is in the interests of the creditors.
(3) In exercising his powers, the liquidator shall comply with the law of the Member State within the territory of which he intends to take action, in particular with regard to procedures for the realisation of assets. Those powers may not include coercive measures or the right to rule on legal proceedings or disputes.

Article 19. The liquidator's appointment shall be evidenced by a certified copy of the original decision appointing him or by any other certificate issued by the court which has jurisdiction. A translation into the official language or one of the official languages of the Member State within the territory of which he intends to act may be required. No legalisation or other similar formality shall be required.

Article 20. (1) A creditor who, after the opening of the proceedings referred to in Article 3(1) obtains by any means, in particular through enforcement, total or partial satisfaction of his claim on the assets belonging to the debtor situated within the territory of another Member State, shall return what he has obtained to the liquidator, subject to Articles 5 and 7.
(2) In order to ensure equal treatment of creditors a creditor who has, in the course of insolvency proceedings, obtained a dividend on his claim shall share in distributions made in other proceedings only where creditors of the same ranking or category have, in those other proceedings, obtained an equivalent dividend.

Article 21. (1) The liquidator may request that notice of the judgment opening insolvency proceedings and, where appropriate, the decision appointing him, be published in any other Member State in accordance with the publication procedures provided for in that State. Such publication shall also specify the liquidator appointed and whether the jurisdiction rule applied is that pursuant to Article 3(1) or Article 3(2).
(2) However, any Member State within the territory of which the debtor has an establishment may require mandatory publication. In such cases, the liquidator or any authority empowered to that effect in the Member State where the proceedings referred to in Article 3(1) are opened shall take all necessary measures to ensure such publication.

Article 22. (1) The liquidator may request that the judgment opening the proceedings referred to in Article 3(1) be registered in the land register, the trade register and any other public register kept in the other Member States.
(2) However, any Member State may require mandatory registration. In such cases, the liquidator or any authority empowered to that effect in the Member State where the proceedings referred to in Article 3(1) have been opened shall take all necessary measures to ensure such registration.

Article 23. The costs of the publication and registration provided for in Articles 21 and 22 shall be regarded as costs and expenses incurred in the proceedings.

Article 24. (1) Where an obligation has been honoured in a Member State for the benefit of a debtor who is subject to insolvency proceedings opened in another Member State, when it should have been honoured for the benefit of the liquidator in those proceedings, the person honouring the obligation shall be deemed to have discharged it if he was unaware of the opening of proceedings.
(2) Where such an obligation is honoured before the publication provided for in Article 21 has been effected, the person honouring the obligation shall be presumed, in the absence of proof to the contrary, to have been unaware of the opening of insolvency proceedings; where the obligation is honoured after such publication has been effected, the person honouring the obligation shall be presumed, in the absence of proof to the contrary, to have been aware of the opening of proceedings.

PART IV EUROPEAN PRIVATE LAW

Article 25. (1) Judgments handed down by a court whose judgment concerning the opening of proceedings is recognised in accordance with Article 16 and which concern the course and closure of insolvency proceedings, and compositions approved by that court shall also be recognised with no further formalities. Such judgments shall be enforced in accordance with Articles 31 to 51, with the exception of Article 34(2), of the Brussels Convention on Jurisdiction and the Enforcement of Judgments in Civil and Commercial Matters, as amended by the Conventions of Accession to this Convention. The first subparagraph shall also apply to judgments deriving directly from the insolvency proceedings and which are closely linked with them, even if they were handed down by another court. The first subparagraph shall also apply to judgments relating to preservation measures taken after the request for the opening of insolvency proceedings.
(2) The recognition and enforcement of judgments other than those referred to in paragraph (1) shall be governed by the Convention referred to in paragraph (1), provided that that Convention is applicable.
(3) The Member States shall not be obliged to recognise or enforce a judgment referred to in paragraph (1) which might result in a limitation of personal freedom or postal secrecy.

Article 26. Any Member State may refuse to recognise insolvency proceedings opened in another Member State or to enforce a judgment handed down in the context of such proceedings where the effects of such recognition or enforcement would be manifestly contrary to that State's public policy, in particular its fundamental principles or the constitutional rights and liberties of the individual.

Chapter III. Secondary Insolvency Proceedings

Article 27. The opening of the proceedings referred to in Article 3(1) by a court of a Member State and which is recognised in another Member State (main proceedings) shall permit the opening in that other Member State, a court of which has jurisdiction pursuant to Article 3(2), of secondary insolvency proceedings without the debtor's insolvency being examined in that other State. These latter proceedings must be among the proceedings listed in Annex B. Their effects shall be restricted to the assets of the debtor situated within the territory of that other Member State.

Article 28. Save as otherwise provided in this Regulation, the law applicable to secondary proceedings shall be that of the Member State within the territory of which the secondary proceedings are opened.

Article 29. The opening of secondary proceedings may be requested by:
(a) the liquidator in the main proceedings;
(b) any other person or authority empowered to request the opening of insolvency proceedings under the law of the Member State within the territory of which the opening of secondary proceedings is requested.

Article 30. Where the law of the Member State in which the opening of secondary proceedings is requested requires that the debtor's assets be sufficient to cover in whole or in part the costs and expenses of the proceedings, the court may, when it receives such a request, require the applicant to make an advance payment of costs or to provide appropriate security.

Article 31. (1) Subject to the rules restricting the communication of information, the liquidator in the main proceedings and the liquidators in the secondary proceedings shall be duty bound to communicate information to each other. They shall immediately communicate any information which may be relevant to the other proceedings, in particular the progress made in lodging and verifying claims and all measures aimed at terminating the proceedings.
(2) Subject to the rules applicable to each of the proceedings, the liquidator in the main proceedings and the liquidators in the secondary proceedings shall be duty bound to cooperate with each other.
(3) The liquidator in the secondary proceedings shall give the liquidator in the main proceedings an early opportunity of submitting proposals on the liquidation or use of the assets in the secondary proceedings.

Article 32. (1) Any creditor may lodge his claim in the main proceedings and in any secondary proceedings.
(2) The liquidators in the main and any secondary proceedings shall lodge in other proceedings claims which have already been lodged in the proceedings for which they were appointed, provided that the interests of creditors in the latter proceedings are served thereby, subject to the right of creditors to oppose that or to withdraw the lodgement of their claims where the law applicable so provides.
(3) The liquidator in the main or secondary proceedings shall be empowered to participate in other proceedings on the same basis as a creditor, in particular by attending creditors' meetings.

Article 33. (1) The court, which opened the secondary proceedings, shall stay the process of liquidation in whole or in part on receipt of a request from the liquidator in the main proceedings, provided that in that event it may require the liquidator in the main proceedings to take any suitable measure to guarantee the interests of the creditors in the secondary proceedings and of individual classes of creditors. Such a request from the liquidator may be rejected only if it is manifestly of no interest to the creditors in the main proceedings. Such a stay of the process of liquidation may be ordered for up to three months. It may be continued or renewed for similar periods.
(2) The court referred to in paragraph (1) shall terminate the stay of the process of liquidation:
- at the request of the liquidator in the main proceedings,
- of its own motion, at the request of a creditor or at the request of the liquidator in the secondary proceedings if that measure no longer appears justified, in particular, by the interests of creditors in the main proceedings or in the secondary proceedings.

Article 34. (1) Where the law applicable to secondary proceedings allows for such proceedings to be closed without liquidation by a rescue plan, a composition or a comparable measure, the liquidator in the main proceedings shall be empowered to propose such a measure himself.
Closure of the secondary proceedings by a measure referred to in the first subparagraph shall not become final without the consent of the liquidator in the main proceedings; failing his agreement, however, it may become final if the financial interests of the creditors in the main proceedings are not affected by the measure proposed.
(2) Any restriction of creditors' rights arising from a measure referred to in paragraph (1) which is proposed in secondary proceedings, such as a stay of payment or discharge of debt, may not have effect in respect of the debtor's assets not covered by those proceedings without the consent of all the creditors having an interest.
(3) During a stay of the process of liquidation ordered pursuant to Article 33, only the liquidator in the main proceedings or the debtor, with the former's consent, may propose measures laid down in paragraph (1) of this Article in the secondary proceedings; no other proposal for such a measure shall be put to the vote or approved.

Article 35. If by the liquidation of assets in the secondary proceedings it is possible to meet all claims allowed under those proceedings, the liquidator appointed in those proceedings shall immediately transfer any assets remaining to the liquidator in the main proceedings.

Article 36. Where the proceedings referred to in Article 3(1) are opened following the opening of the proceedings referred to in Article 3(2) in another Member State, Articles 31 to 35 shall apply to those opened first, in so far as the progress of those proceedings so permits.

Article 37. The liquidator in the main proceedings may request that proceedings listed in Annex A previously opened in another Member State be converted into winding-up proceedings if this proves to be in the interests of the creditors in the main proceedings.
The court with jurisdiction under Article 3(2) shall order conversion into one of the proceedings listed in Annex B.

Article 38. Where the court of a Member State which has jurisdiction pursuant to Article 3(1) appoints a temporary administrator in order to ensure the preservation of the debtor's assets, that temporary administrator shall be empowered to request any measures to secure and preserve any of the debtor's assets situated in another Member State, provided for under the law of that State, for the period between the request for the opening of insolvency proceedings and the judgment opening the proceedings.

Chapter IV. Provision of Information for Creditors and Lodgement of their Claims

Article 39. Any creditor who has his habitual residence, domicile or registered office in a Member State other than the State of the opening of proceedings, including the tax authorities and social security authorities of Member States, shall have the right to lodge claims in the insolvency proceedings in writing.

Article 40. (1) As soon as insolvency proceedings are opened in a Member State, the court of that State having jurisdiction or the liquidator appointed by it shall immediately inform known creditors who have their habitual residences, domiciles or registered offices in the other Member States.
(2) That information, provided by an individual notice, shall in particular include time limits, the penalties laid down in regard to those time limits, the body or authority empowered to accept the lodgement of claims and the other measures laid down. Such notice shall also indicate whether creditors whose claims are preferential or secured in rem need lodge their claims.

Article 41. A creditor shall send copies of supporting documents, if any, and shall indicate the nature of the claim, the date on which it arose and its amount, as well as whether he alleges preference, security in rem or a reservation of title in respect of the claim and what assets are covered by the guarantee he is invoking.

Article 42. (1) The information provided for in Article 40 shall be provided in the official language or one of the official languages of the State of the opening of proceedings. For that purpose a form shall be used bearing the heading "Invitation to lodge a claim. Time limits to be observed" in all the official languages of the institutions of the European Union.
(2) Any creditor who has his habitual residence, domicile or registered office in a Member State other than the State of the opening of proceedings may lodge his claim in the official language or one of the official languages of that other State. In that event, however, the lodgement of his claim shall bear the heading "Lodgement of claim" in the official language or one of the official languages of the State of the opening of proceedings. In addition, he may be required to provide a translation into the official language or one of the official languages of the State of the opening of proceedings.

Chapter V. Transitional and Final Provisions

Article 43. The provisions of this Regulation shall apply only to insolvency proceedings opened after its entry into force. Acts done by a debtor before the entry into force of this Regulation shall continue to be governed by the law which was applicable to them at the time they were done.

Article 44. (1) After its entry into force, this Regulation replaces, in respect of the matters referred to therein, in the relations between Member States, the Conventions concluded between two or more Member States, in particular:
(a) the Convention between Belgium and France on Jurisdiction and the Validity and Enforcement of Judgments, Arbitration Awards and Authentic Instruments, signed at Paris on 8 July 1899;
(b) the Convention between Belgium and Austria on Bankruptcy, Winding-up, Arrangements, Compositions and Suspension of Payments (with Additional Protocol of 13 June 1973), signed at Brussels on 16 July 1969;
(c) the Convention between Belgium and the Netherlands on Territorial Jurisdiction, Bankruptcy and the Validity and Enforcement of Judgments, Arbitration Awards and Authentic Instruments, signed at Brussels on 28 March 1925;
(d) the Treaty between Germany and Austria on Bankruptcy, Winding-up, Arrangements and Compositions, signed at Vienna on 25 May 1979;
(e) the Convention between France and Austria on Jurisdiction, Recognition and Enforcement of Judgments on Bankruptcy, signed at Vienna on 27 February 1979;
(f) the Convention between France and Italy on the Enforcement of Judgments in Civil and Commercial Matters, signed at Rome on 3 June 1930;
(g) the Convention between Italy and Austria on Bankruptcy, Winding-up, Arrangements and Compositions, signed at Rome on 12 July 1977;
(h) the Convention between the Kingdom of the Netherlands and the Federal Republic of Germany on the Mutual Recognition and Enforcement of Judgments and other Enforceable Instruments in Civil and Commercial Matters, signed at The Hague on 30 August 1962;
(i) the Convention between the United Kingdom and the Kingdom of Belgium providing for the Reciprocal Enforcement of Judgments in Civil and Commercial Matters, with Protocol, signed at Brussels on 2 May 1934;
(j) the Convention between Denmark, Finland, Norway, Sweden and Iceland on Bankruptcy, signed at Copenhagen on 7 November 1933;
(k) the European Convention on Certain International Aspects of Bankruptcy, signed at Istanbul on 5 June 1990.
(2) The Conventions referred to in paragraph (1) shall continue to have effect with regard to proceedings opened before the entry into force of this Regulation.
(3) This Regulation shall not apply:
(a) in any Member State, to the extent that it is irreconcilable with the obligations arising in relation to bankruptcy from a convention concluded by that State with one or more third countries before the entry into force of this Regulation;
(b) in the United Kingdom of Great Britain and Northern Ireland, to the extent that is irreconcilable with the obligations arising in relation to bankruptcy and the winding-up of insolvent companies from any arrangements with the Commonwealth existing at the time this Regulation enters into force.

Article 45. The Council, acting by qualified majority on the initiative of one of its members or on a proposal from the Commission, may amend the Annexes.

Article 46. No later than 1 June 2012, and every five years thereafter, the Commission shall present to the European Parliament, the Council and the Economic and Social Committee a report on the application of this Regulation. The report shall be accompanied if need be by a proposal for adaptation of this Regulation.

Article 47. This Regulation shall enter into force on 31 May 2002. This Regulation shall be binding in its entirety and directly applicable in the Member States in accordance with the Treaty establishing the European Community.

Annex A. Insolvency Proceedings Referred to in Article 2(a)

BELGIË-/BELGIQUE
- Het faillissement//La faillite
- Het gerechtelijk akkoord//Le concordat judiciaire
- De collectieve schuldenregeling//Le règlement collectif de dettes

DEUTSCHLAND
- Das Konkursverfahren
- Das gerichtliche Vergleichsverfahren
- Das Gesamtvollstreckungsverfahren
- Das Insolvenzverfahren

ΕΛΛΑΣ
- Πτώχευση
- Η ειδική εκκαθάριση
- Η προσωρινή διαχείριση εταιρίας. Η διοίκηση και η διαχείριση των πιστωτών
- Η υπαγωγή επιχείρησης υπό επίτροπο με σκοπό τη σύναψη συμβιβασμού με τους πιστωτές

ESPAÑA
- Concurso de acreedores
- Quiebra
- Suspensión de pagos

FRANCE
- Liquidation judiciaire
- Redressement judiciaire avec nomination d'un administrateur

IRELAND
- Compulsory winding up by the court
- Bankruptcy
- The administration in bankruptcy of the estate of persons dying insolvent
- Winding-up in bankruptcy of partnerships
- Creditors' voluntary winding up (with confirmation of a Court)
- Arrangements under the control of the court which involve the vesting of all or part of the property of the debtor in the Official Assignee for realisation and distribution
- Company examinership

ITALIA
- Fallimento
- Concordato preventivo
- Liquidazione coatta amministrativa
- Amministrazione straordinaria
- Amministrazione controllata

LUXEMBOURG
- Faillite
- Gestion contrôlée
- Concordat préventif de faillite (par abandon d'actif)
- Régime spécial de liquidation du notariat

NEDERLAND
- Het faillissement
- De surséance van betaling
- De schuldsaneringsregeling natuurlijke personen

ÖSTERREICH
- Das Konkursverfahren
- Das Ausgleichsverfahren

PORTUGAL
- O processo de falência

PART IV EUROPEAN PRIVATE LAW

- Os processos especiais de recuperação de empresa, ou seja:
- A concordata
- A reconstituição empresarial
- A reestruturação financeira
- A gestão controlada

SUOMI-/FINLAND
- Konkurssi//konkurs
- Yrityssaneeraus//företagssanering

SVERIGE
- Konkurs
- Företagsrekonstruktion

UNITED KINGDOM
- Winding up by or subject to the supervision of the court
- Creditors' voluntary winding up (with confirmation by the court)
- Administration
- Voluntary arrangements under insolvency legislation
- Bankruptcy or sequestration

Annex B. Winding Up Proceedings Referred to in Article 2(c)

BELGIË-/BELGIQUE
- Het faillissement//La faillite

DEUTSCHLAND
- Das Konkursverfahren
- Das Gesamtvollstreckungsverfahren
- Das Insolvenzverfahren

ΕΛΛΑΣ
- Πτώχευση
- Η ειδική εκκαθάριση

ESPAÑA
- Concurso de acreedores
- Quiebra
- Suspensión de pagos basada en la insolvencia definitiva

FRANCE
- Liquidation judiciaire

IRELAND
- Compulsory winding up
- Bankruptcy
- The administration in bankruptcy of the estate of persons dying insolvent
- Winding-up in bankruptcy of partnerships
- Creditors' voluntary winding up (with confirmation of a court)
- Arrangements under the control of the court which involve the vesting of all or part of the property of the debtor in the Official Assignee for realisation and distribution

ITALIA
- Fallimento
- Liquidazione coatta amministrativa

LUXEMBOURG
- Faillite
- Régime spécial de liquidation du notariat

NEDERLAND
- Het faillissement
- De schuldsaneringsregeling natuurlijke personen

ÖSTERREICH
- Das Konkursverfahren

PORTUGAL
- O processo de falência

SUOMI-/FINLAND
- Konkurssi//konkurs

SVERIGE
- Konkurs

UNITED KINGDOM

EU: REGULATION 1346/2000 ON INSOLVENCY PROCEEDINGS

- Winding up by or subject to the supervision of the court
- Creditors' voluntary winding up (with confirmation by the court)
- Bankruptcy or sequestration

Annex C. Liquidators Referred to in Article 2(b)

BELGIË-/BELGIQUE
- De curator//Le curateur
- De commissaris inzake opschorting//Le commissaire au sursis
- De schuldbemiddelaar//Le médiateur de dettes

DEUTSCHLAND
- Konkursverwalter
- Vergleichsverwalter
- Sachwalter (nach der Vergleichsordnung)
- Verwalter
- Insolvenzverwalter
- Sachwalter (nach der Insolvenzordnung)
- Treuhänder
- Vorläufiger Insolvenzverwalter

ΕΛΛΑΣ
- Ο σύνδικο
- Ο προσωρινός διαχειριστής. Η διοικούσα επιτροπή των πιστωτών
- Ο ειδικός εκκαθαριστής
- Ο επίτροπος

ESPAÑA
- Depositario-administrador
- Interventor o Interventores
- Síndicos
- Comisario

FRANCE
- Représentant des créanciers
- Mandataire liquidateur
- Administrateur judiciaire
- Commissaire à l'exécution de plan

IRELAND
- Liquidator
- Official Assignee
- Trustee in bankruptcy
- Provisional Liquidator
- Examiner

ITALIA
- Curatore
- Commissario

LUXEMBOURG
- Le curateur
- Le commissaire
- Le liquidateur
- Le conseil de gérance de la section d'assainissement du notariat

NEDERLAND
- De curator in het faillissement
- De bewindvoerder in de surséance van betaling
- De bewindvoerder in de schuldsaneringsregeling natuurlijke personen

ÖSTERREICH
- Masseverwalter
- Ausgleichsverwalter
- Sachwalter
- Treuhänder
- Besondere Verwalter
- Vorläufiger Verwalter
- Konkursgericht

PORTUGAL

PART IV   EUROPEAN PRIVATE LAW

- Gestor judicial
- Liquidatário judicial
- Comissão de credores

SUOMI-/FINLAND
- Pesänhoitaja//boförvaltare
- Selvittäjä//utredare

SVERIGE
- Förvaltare
- God man
- Rekonstruktör

UNITED KINGDOM
- Liquidator
- Supervisor of a voluntary arrangement
- Administrator
- Official Receiver
- Trustee
- Judicial factor

EU: DIRECTIVE 2014/17 CONSUMER MORTGAGE CREDIT AGREEMENTS

Directive 2014/17/EU of the European Parliament and of the Council of 4 February 2014 on credit agreements for consumers relating to residential immovable property and amending Directives 2008/48/EC and 2013/36/EU and Regulation (EU) No 1093/2010 [Footnotes omitted].

THE EUROPEAN PARLIAMENT AND THE COUNCIL OF THE EUROPEAN UNION,
Having regard to the Treaty on the Functioning of the European Union, and in particular Article 114 thereof,
Having regard to the proposal from the European Commission,
After transmission of the draft legislative act to the national parliaments,
Having regard to the opinion of the European Central Bank,
Having regard to the opinion of the European Economic and Social Committee,
Acting in accordance with the ordinary legislative procedure,
Whereas:

(1) In March 2003, the Commission launched a process of identifying and assessing the impact of barriers to the internal market for credit agreements relating to residential immovable property. On 18 December 2007, it adopted a White Paper on the Integration of EU Mortgage Credit Markets. The White Paper announced the Commission's intention to assess the impact of, among other things, the policy options for pre-contractual information, credit databases, creditworthiness, the annual percentage rate of charge (APRC) and advice on credit agreements. The Commission established an Expert Group on Credit Histories to assist the Commission in preparing measures to improve the accessibility, comparability and completeness of credit data. Studies on the role and operations of credit intermediaries and non-credit institutions providing credit agreements relating to residential immovable property were also launched.

(2) In accordance with the Treaty on the Functioning of the European Union (TFEU), the internal market comprises an area without internal frontiers in which the free movement of goods and services and the freedom of establishment are ensured. The development of a more transparent and efficient credit market within that area is vital in promoting the development of cross-border activity and creating an internal market for credit agreements relating to residential immovable property. There are substantial differences in the laws of the various Member States with regard to the conduct of business in the granting of credit agreements relating to residential immovable property and in the regulation and supervision of credit intermediaries and non-credit institutions providing credit agreements relating to residential immovable property. Such differences create obstacles that restrict the level of cross-border activity on the supply and demand sides, thus reducing competition and choice in the market, raising the cost of lending for providers and even preventing them from doing business.

(3) The financial crisis has shown that irresponsible behaviour by market participants can undermine the foundations of the financial system, leading to a lack of confidence among all parties, in particular consumers, and potentially severe social and economic consequences. Many consumers have lost confidence in the financial sector and borrowers have found their loans increasingly unaffordable, resulting in defaults and forced sales rising. As a result, the G20 has commissioned work from the Financial Stability Board to establish principles on sound underwriting standards in relation to residential immovable property. Although some of the greatest problems in the financial crisis occurred outside the Union, consumers within the Union hold significant levels of debt, much of which is concentrated in credits related to residential immovable property. It is therefore appropriate to ensure that the Union's regulatory framework in this area is robust, consistent with international principles and makes appropriate use of the range of tools available, which may include the use of loan-to-value, loan-to-income, debt-to-income or similar ratios, minimum levels below which no credit would be deemed acceptable or other compensatory measures for the situations where the underlying risks are higher to consumers or where needed to prevent household over-indebtedness. In view of the problems brought to light in the financial crisis and with a view to ensuring an efficient and competitive internal market which contributes to financial stability, the Commission has proposed, in its Communication of 4 March 2009 entitled 'Driving European recovery', measures with regard to credit agreements relating to residential immovable property, including a reliable framework on credit intermediation, in the context of delivering responsible and reliable markets for the future and restoring consumer confidence. The Commission reaffirmed its commitment to an efficient and competitive internal market in its Communication of 13 April 2011 entitled 'Single Market Act: Twelve levers to boost growth and strengthen confidence'.

(4) A series of problems have been identified in mortgage markets within the Union relating to irresponsible lending and borrowing and the potential scope for irresponsible behaviour by market participants including credit intermediaries and non-credit institutions. Some problems concerned credits denominated in a foreign currency which consumers had taken out in that currency in order

PART IV   EUROPEAN PRIVATE LAW

to take advantage of the borrowing rate offered but without having adequate information about or understanding of the exchange rate risk involved. Those problems are driven by market and regulatory failures as well as other factors such as the general economic climate and low levels of financial literacy. Other problems include ineffective, inconsistent, or non-existent regimes for credit intermediaries and non-credit institutions providing credit for residential immovable property. The problems identified have potentially significant macroeconomic spill-over effects, can lead to consumer detriment, act as economic or legal barriers to cross-border activity and create an unlevel playing field between actors.

(5) In order to facilitate the emergence of a smoothly functioning internal market with a high level of consumer protection in the area of credit agreements relating to immovable property and in order to ensure that consumers looking for such agreements are able to do so confident in the knowledge that the institutions they interact with act in a professional and responsible manner, an appropriately harmonised Union legal framework needs to be established in a number of areas, taking into account differences in credit agreements arising in particular from differences in national and regional immovable property markets.

(6) This Directive should therefore develop a more transparent, efficient and competitive internal market, through consistent, flexible and fair credit agreements relating to immovable property, while promoting sustainable lending and borrowing and financial inclusion, and hence providing a high level of consumer protection.

(7) In order to create a genuine internal market with a high and equivalent level of consumer protection, this Directive lays down provisions subject to maximum harmonisation in relation to the provision of pre-contractual information through the European Standardised Information Sheet (ESIS) standardised format and the calculation of the APRC. However, taking into account the specificity of credit agreements relating to immovable property and differences in market developments and conditions in Member States, concerning in particular market structure and market participants, categories of products available and procedures involved in the credit granting process, Member States should be allowed to maintain or introduce more stringent provisions than those laid down in this Directive in those areas not clearly specified as being subject to maximum harmonisation. Such a targeted approach is necessary in order to avoid adversely affecting the level of protection of consumers relating to credit agreements in the scope of this Directive. Member States should, for example, be allowed to maintain or introduce more stringent provisions with regard to knowledge and competence requirements for staff and instructions for completing the ESIS.

(8) This Directive should improve conditions for the establishment and functioning of the internal market through the approximation of Member States' laws and the establishment of quality standards for certain services, in particular with regard to the distribution and provision of credit through creditors and credit intermediaries and the promotion of good practices. The establishment of quality standards for services for the provision of credit necessarily involves the introduction of certain provisions regarding admission, supervision and prudential requirements.

(9) For those areas not covered by this Directive, Member States are free to maintain or introduce national law. In particular, Member States may maintain or introduce national provisions in areas such as contract law relating to the validity of credit agreements, property law, land registration, contractual information and, to the extent that they are not regulated in this Directive, post-contractual issues. Member States may provide that the appraiser or appraisal company or notaries may be chosen by mutual agreement of the parties. Given the differences between the processes for the purchase or sale of residential immovable property in the Member States, there is scope for creditors or credit intermediaries to seek to receive payments in advance from consumers on the understanding that such payments could help to secure the conclusion of a credit agreement or the purchase or sale of an immovable property, and for such practices to be misused in particular where consumers are unfamiliar with the requirements and usual practice in that Member State. It is therefore appropriate to allow Member States to impose restrictions on such payments.

(10) This Directive should apply irrespective of whether the creditor or credit intermediary is a legal person or a natural person. However, this Directive should not affect the right of Member States to limit, in conformity with Union law, the role of creditor or credit intermediary under this Directive to legal persons only or to certain types of legal persons.

(11) Since consumers and enterprises are not in the same position, they do not need the same level of protection. While it is important to guarantee the rights of consumers by means of provisions that cannot be derogated from by contract, it is reasonable to allow enterprises and organisations to enter into other agreements.

(12) The definition of consumer should cover natural persons who are acting outside their trade, business or profession. However, in the case of dual purpose contracts, where the contract is

concluded for purposes partly within and partly outside the person's trade, business or profession and the trade, business or professional purpose is so limited as not to be predominant in the overall context of the contract, that person should also be considered as a consumer.

(13) While this Directive regulates credit agreements which solely or predominantly relate to residential immovable property, it does not prevent Member States from extending the measures taken in accordance with this Directive to protect consumers in relation to credit agreements related to other forms of immovable property, or from otherwise regulating such credit agreements.

(14) The definitions set out in this Directive determine the scope of harmonisation. The obligations of Member States to transpose this Directive should therefore be limited to its scope as determined by those definitions. For instance, the obligations of Member States to transpose this Directive are limited to credit agreements concluded with consumers, meaning with natural persons who, in transactions covered by this Directive, are acting outside their trade, business or profession. Similarly, Member States are obliged to transpose provisions of this Directive regulating the activity of persons acting as credit intermediary as defined in the Directive. However, this Directive should be without prejudice to the application by Member States, in accordance with Union law, of this Directive to areas not covered by its scope. In addition, the definitions set out in this Directive should be without prejudice to the possibility for Member States to adopt sub-definitions under national law for specific purposes, provided that they are still compliant with the definitions set out in this Directive. For example, Member States should be allowed to determine under national law sub-categories of credit intermediaries that are not identified in this Directive, where such sub-categories are necessary at national level for instance to differentiate the level of knowledge and competence requirements to be fulfilled by the different credit intermediaries.

(15) The objective of this Directive is to ensure that consumers entering into credit agreements relating to immovable property benefit from a high level of protection. It should therefore apply to credits secured by immovable property regardless of the purpose of the credit, refinancing agreements or other credit agreements that would help an owner or part owner continue to retain rights in immovable property or land and credits which are used to purchase an immovable property in some Member States including credits that do not require the reimbursement of the capital or, unless Member States have an adequate alternative framework in place, those whose purpose is to provide temporary financing between the sale of one immovable property and the purchase of another, and to secured credits for the renovation of residential immovable property.

(16) This Directive should not apply to certain credit agreements where the creditor contributes a lump sum, periodic payments or other forms of credit disbursement in return for a sum deriving from the sale of an immovable property and whose primary objective is to facilitate consumption, such as equity release products or other equivalent specialised products. Such credit agreements have specific characteristics which are beyond the scope of this Directive. An assessment of the consumer's creditworthiness, for example, is irrelevant since the payments are made from the creditor to the consumer rather than the other way round. Such a transaction would require, inter alia, substantially different pre-contractual information. Furthermore, other products, such as home reversions, which have comparable functions to reverse mortgages or lifetime mortgages, do not involve the provision of credit and so would remain outside the scope of this Directive.

(17) This Directive should not cover other explicitly listed types of niche credit agreements, that are different in their nature and risks involved from standard mortgage credits and therefore require a tailored approach, in particular credit agreements which are the outcome of a settlement reached in court or before another statutory authority, and certain types of credit agreements where the credit is granted by an employer to his employees under certain circumstances, as already provided in Directive 2008/48/EC of the European Parliament and of the Council of 23 April 2008 on credit agreements for consumers. It is appropriate to allow Member States to exclude certain credit agreements, such as those which are granted to a restricted public on advantageous terms or provided by credit unions, provided that adequate alternative arrangements are in place to ensure that policy objectives relating to financial stability and the internal market can be met without impeding financial inclusion and access to credit. Credit agreements where the immovable property is not to be occupied as a house, apartment or another place of residence by the consumer or a family member of the consumer and is occupied as a house, apartment or another place of residence on a basis of a rental agreement, have risks and features that are different from standard credit agreements and therefore may require a more adapted framework. Member States should therefore be able to exclude such credit agreements from the Directive where an appropriate national framework is in place for them.

(18) Unsecured credit agreements the purpose of which is the renovation of a residential immovable property involving a total amount of credit above EUR 75 000 should fall under the scope of Directive 2008/48/EC in order to ensure an equivalent level of protection to those consumers and to avoid

any regulatory gap between that Directive and this Directive. Directive 2008/48/EC should therefore be amended accordingly.

(19) For reasons of legal certainty, the Union legal framework in the area of credit agreements relating to residential immovable property should be consistent with and complementary to other Union acts, particularly in the areas of consumer protection and prudential supervision. Certain essential definitions including the definition of 'consumer', and 'durable medium', as well as key concepts used in standard information to designate the financial characteristics of the credit, including 'total amount payable by the consumer' and 'borrowing rate' should be in line with those set out in Directive 2008/48/EC so that the same terminology refers to the same type of facts irrespective of whether the credit is a consumer credit or a credit relating to residential immovable property. Member States should therefore ensure, in the transposition of this Directive, that there is consistency of application and interpretation in relation to those essential definitions and key concepts.

(20) In order to ensure a consistent framework for consumers in the area of credit as well as to minimise the administrative burden for creditors and credit intermediaries, the core framework of this Directive should follow the structure of Directive 2008/48/EC where possible, notably the notions that information included in advertising concerning credit agreements relating to residential immovable property be provided to the consumer by means of a representative example, that detailed pre-contractual information be given to the consumer by means of a standardised information sheet, that the consumer receives adequate explanations before concluding the credit agreement, a common basis be established for calculating the APRC excluding notary fees, and that creditors assess the consumer's creditworthiness before providing a credit. Similarly, non-discriminatory access for creditors to relevant credit databases should be ensured in order to achieve a level playing field with the provisions laid down in Directive 2008/48/EC. Similarly to Directive 2008/48/EC, this Directive should ensure the appropriate admission process and supervision of all creditors providing credit agreements relating to immovable property and should lay down requirements for the establishment of, and access to, out-of-court dispute resolution mechanisms.

(21) This Directive should supplement Directive 2002/65/EC of the European Parliament and of the Council of 23 September 2002 concerning the distance marketing of consumer financial services which requires that in distance sales a consumer be informed of the existence or absence of a right of withdrawal and provides for a right of withdrawal. However, while Directive 2002/65/EC provides for the possibility for the supplier to communicate pre-contractual information after the conclusion of the contract, this would be inappropriate for contracts for credit agreements relating to residential immovable property given the significance of the financial commitment for the consumer. This Directive should not affect national general contract law such as the rules on the validity, formation or effect of a contract, insofar as general contract law aspects are not regulated in this Directive.

(22) At the same time, it is important to take into consideration the specificities of credit agreements relating to residential immovable property, which justify a differentiated approach. Given the nature and the possible consequences of a credit agreement relating to residential immovable property for the consumer, advertising materials and personalised pre-contractual information should include adequate specific risk warnings, for instance about the potential impact of exchange rate fluctuations on what the consumer has to repay and, where assessed as appropriate by the Member States, the nature and implications of taking out a security. Following what already existed as a voluntary approach by the industry concerning home loans, general pre-contractual information should be made available at all times in addition to the personalised pre-contractual information. Furthermore, a differentiated approach is justified in order to take into consideration the lessons learnt from the financial crisis and in order to ensure that credit origination takes place in a sound manner. In this respect, the provisions on the creditworthiness assessment should be strengthened in comparison to consumer credit, more precise information should be provided by credit intermediaries on their status and relationship with the creditors in order to disclose potential conflicts of interest, and all actors involved in the origination of credit agreements relating to immovable property should be adequately admitted and supervised.

(23) It is necessary to regulate some additional areas in order to reflect the specificity of credits related to residential immovable property. Given the significance of the transaction it is necessary to ensure that consumers have sufficient time of at least seven days to consider the implications. Member States should have flexibility to provide this sufficient time either as a period of reflection before the credit agreement is concluded, a period of withdrawal after the conclusion of the credit agreement or a combination of the two. It is appropriate that Member States should have the flexibility to make the reflection period binding on the consumer for a period not exceeding 10 days but that in other cases consumers who wish to proceed during the reflection period are able to do so and that, in the interests of legal certainty in the context of property transactions, Member States should

be able to provide that the reflection period or right of withdrawal should cease where the consumer undertakes any action which, under national law, results in the creation or transfer of a property right connected to or using funds obtained through the credit agreement or, where applicable, transfers the funds to a third party.

(24) Given the particular characteristics of credit agreements related to residential immovable property it is common practice for creditors to offer to consumers a set of products or services which can be purchased together with the credit agreement. Therefore, given the significance of such agreements for consumers, it is appropriate to lay down specific rules on tying practices. Combining a credit agreement with one or more other financial services or products in packages is a means for creditors to diversify their offer and to compete against each other, provided that the components of the package can also be bought separately. While a combination of credit agreements with one or more other financial services or products in packages can benefit consumers, it may negatively affect consumers' mobility and their ability to make informed choices, unless the components of the package can be bought separately. It is important to prevent practices such as tying of certain products which may induce consumers to enter into credit agreements which are not in their best interest, without however restricting product bundling which can be beneficial to consumers. Member States should however continue monitoring retail financial services markets closely to ensure that bundling practices do not distort consumer choice and competition in the market.

(25) As a general rule, tying practices should not be allowed unless the financial service or product offered together with the credit agreement could not be offered separately as it is a fully integrated part of the credit, for example in the event of a secured overdraft. In other instances, it may however be justified for creditors to offer or sell a credit agreement in a package with a payment account, savings account, investment product or pension product, for instance where the capital in the account is used to repay the credit or is a prerequisite for pooling resources to obtain the credit, or in situations where, for instance, an investment product or a private pension product serves as an additional security for the credit. While it is justified for creditors to be able to require the consumer to have a relevant insurance policy in order to guarantee repayment of the credit or insure the value of the security, the consumer should have the opportunity to choose his own insurance provider, provided that his insurance policy has an equivalent level of guarantee as the insurance policy proposed or offered by the creditor. Moreover Member States may standardise, wholly or in part, the cover provided by insurance contracts in order to facilitate comparisons between different offers for consumers who wish to make such comparisons.

(26) It is important to ensure that the residential immovable property is appropriately valued before the conclusion of the credit agreement and, in particular where the valuation affects the residual obligation of the consumer in the event of default. Member States should therefore ensure that reliable valuation standards are in place. In order to be considered reliable, valuation standards should take into account internationally recognised valuation standards, in particular those developed by the International Valuation Standards Council, the European Group of Valuers' Associations or the Royal Institution of Chartered Surveyors. Those internationally recognised valuation standards contain high level principles which require creditors, amongst others, to adopt and adhere to adequate internal risk management and securities management processes, which include sound appraisal processes, to adopt appraisal standards and methods that lead to realistic and substantiated property appraisals in order to ensure that all appraisal reports are prepared with appropriate professional skill and diligence and that appraisers meet certain qualification requirements and to maintain adequate appraisal documentation for securities that is comprehensive and plausible. In this regard it is desirable to ensure appropriate monitoring of residential immovable property markets and for the mechanisms in such provisions to be in line with Directive 2013/36/EU of the European Parliament and the Council of 26 June 2013 on access to the activity of credit institutions and the prudential supervision of credit institutions and investment firms. The provisions of this Directive relating to property valuation standards can be complied with for example through law or self-regulation.

(27) Given the significant consequences for creditors, consumers and potentially financial stability of foreclosure, it is appropriate to encourage creditors to deal proactively with emerging credit risk at an early stage and that the necessary measures are in place to ensure that creditors exercise reasonable forbearance and make reasonable attempts to resolve the situation through other means before foreclosure proceedings are initiated. Where possible, solutions should be found which take account of the practical circumstances and reasonable need for living expenses of the consumer. Where after foreclosure proceedings outstanding debt remains, Member States should ensure the protection of minimum living conditions and put in place measures to facilitate repayment while avoiding long-term over-indebtedness. At least where the price obtained for the immovable property affects the amount owed by the consumer, Member States should encourage creditors to take reasonable steps

to obtain the best efforts price for the foreclosed immovable property in the context of market conditions. Member States should not prevent the parties to a credit agreement from expressly agreeing that the transfer of the security to the creditor is sufficient to repay the credit.

(28) Intermediaries often engage in more activities than just credit intermediation, in particular insurance intermediation or investment services provision. This Directive should therefore also ensure a degree of coherence with Directive 2002/92/EC of the European Parliament and of the Council of 9 December 2002 on insurance mediation and Directive 2004/39/EC of the European Parliament and of the Council of 21 April 2004 on markets in financial instruments. In particular, credit institutions authorised in accordance with Directive 2013/36/EU and other financial institutions subject to an equivalent admission regime under national law should not require a separate admission to operate as a credit intermediary in order to simplify the process of establishing as a credit intermediary and operating cross-border. The full and unconditional responsibility placed on creditors and credit intermediaries for the activities of tied credit intermediaries or appointed representatives should only extend to activities within the scope of this Directive unless Member States choose to extend that responsibility to other areas.

(29) In order to increase the ability of consumers to make informed decisions for themselves about borrowing and managing debt responsibly, Member States should promote measures to support the education of consumers in relation to responsible borrowing and debt management in particular relating to mortgage credit agreements. It is particularly important to provide guidance for consumers taking out mortgage credit for the first time. In that regard, the Commission should identify examples of best practices to facilitate the further development of measures to enhance consumers' financial awareness.

(30) Due to the significant risks attached to borrowing in a foreign currency, it is necessary to provide for measures to ensure that consumers are aware of the risk they are taking on and that the consumer has the possibility to limit their exposure to exchange rate risk during the lifetime of the credit. The risk could be limited either through giving the consumer the right to convert the currency of the credit, or through other arrangements such as caps or, where they are sufficient to limit the exchange rate risk, warnings.

(31) The applicable legal framework should give consumers the confidence that creditors, credit intermediaries and appointed representatives take account of the interests of the consumer, based on the information available to the creditor, credit intermediary and appointed representative at that moment in time and on reasonable assumptions about risks to the consumer's situation over the term of the proposed credit agreement. It could imply, amongst other things, that creditors should not market the credit so that the marketing significantly impairs or is likely to impair the consumer's ability to carefully consider the taking of the credit, or that the creditor should not use the granting of the credit as a main method of marketing when marketing goods, services or immovable property to consumers. A key aspect of ensuring such consumer confidence is the requirement to ensure a high degree of fairness, honesty and professionalism in the industry, appropriate management of conflicts of interest including those arising from remuneration and to require advice to be given in the best interests of the consumer.

(32) It is appropriate to ensure that the relevant staff of creditors, credit intermediaries and appointed representatives possess an adequate level of knowledge and competence in order to achieve a high level of professionalism. This Directive should, therefore, require relevant knowledge and competence to be proven at the level of the company, based on the minimum knowledge and competence requirements set out in this Directive. Member States should be free to introduce or maintain such requirements applicable to individual natural persons. Member States should be able to allow creditors, credit intermediaries and appointed representatives to differentiate between the levels of minimum knowledge requirements according to the involvement in carrying out particular services or processes. In this context, staff includes outsourced personnel, working for and within the creditor, credit intermediary or appointed representatives as well as their employees. For the purpose of this Directive, staff directly engaged in activities under this Directive should include both front- and back-office staff, including management, who fulfil an important role in the credit agreement process. Persons fulfilling support functions which are unrelated to the credit agreement process (for instance human resources and information and communications technology personnel) should not be considered as staff under this Directive.

(33) Where a creditor or credit intermediary provides its services within the territory of another Member State under the freedom to provide services, the home Member State should be responsible for establishing the minimum knowledge and competence requirements applicable to the staff. However host Member States which deem it necessary should be able to establish their own competence requirements in certain specified areas applicable to creditors and credit intermediaries that provide

services within the territory of that Member State under the freedom to provide services.

(34) Given the importance of ensuring that knowledge and competence requirements are applied and complied with in practice, Member States should require competent authorities to supervise creditors, credit intermediaries and appointed representatives and empower them to obtain such evidence as they need to reliably assess compliance.

(35) The way in which creditors, credit intermediaries and appointed representatives remunerate their staff should constitute one of the key aspects of ensuring consumer confidence in the financial sector. This Directive provides rules for staff remuneration, with the aim of limiting mis-selling practices and of ensuring that the way in which staff are remunerated does not impede compliance with the obligation to take account of the interests of the consumer. In particular, creditors, credit intermediaries and appointed representatives should not design their remuneration policies in a way that would incentivise their staff to conclude a given number or type of credit agreements or to offer particular ancillary services to consumers with no explicit consideration of their interests and needs. In this context, Member States may find it necessary to decide that a particular practice, for example, tied intermediaries collecting fees, is against the interests of a consumer. Member States should also be able to specify that the remuneration received by staff is not dependent on the rate or the type of credit agreement concluded with the consumer.

(36) This Directive provides for harmonised rules as regards the fields of knowledge and competence that creditors', credit intermediaries' and appointed representatives' staff should possess in relation to the manufacturing, offering, granting and intermediation of a credit agreement. This Directive does not provide for specific arrangements directly related to the recognition of professional qualifications obtained by an individual in one Member State in order to meet the knowledge and competence requirements in another Member State. Directive 2005/36/EC of the European Parliament and of the Council of 7 September 2005 on the recognition of professional qualifications should therefore continue to apply concerning the conditions for recognition and the compensation measures that a host Member State may require from an individual whose qualification has not been issued within its jurisdiction.

(37) Creditors and credit intermediaries frequently use advertisements, often featuring special terms and conditions, to attract consumers to a particular product. Consumers should, therefore, be protected against unfair or misleading advertising practices and should be able to compare advertisements. Specific provisions on the advertising of credit agreements and a list of items to be included in advertisements and marketing materials directed at consumers where such advertising specifies interest rates or any figures relating to the cost of credit, are necessary to enable them to compare different offers. Member States should remain free to introduce or maintain disclosure requirements in their national laws regarding advertising which does not indicate an interest rate or contain any figures relating to the cost of credit. Any such requirements should take into account the specificities of credit agreements relating to residential immovable property. In any event, it should be ensured in accordance with Directive 2005/29/EC of the European Parliament and of the Council of 11 May 2005 concerning unfair business-to-consumer commercial practices in the internal market that advertising of credit agreements should not create a misleading impression of the product.

(38) Advertising tends to focus on one or several products in particular, while consumers should be able to make their decisions in full knowledge of the range of credit products on offer. In that respect, general information plays an important role in educating the consumer in relation to the broad range of products and services available and the key features thereof. Consumers should therefore be able at all times to access general information on credit products available. Where this requirement is not applicable to non-tied credit intermediaries, this should be without prejudice to their obligation to provide consumers with personalised pre-contractual information.

(39) In order to ensure a level playing field and in order for the consumer's decision to be based on the details of the credit products on offer rather than on the distribution channel through which such credit products are accessed, consumers should receive information on the credit regardless of whether they are dealing directly with a creditor or a credit intermediary.

(40) Consumers should further receive personalised information in good time prior to the conclusion of the credit agreement in order to enable them to compare and reflect on the characteristics of credit products. Pursuant to Commission Recommendation 2001/193/EC of 1 March 2001 on pre-contractual information to be given to consumers by lenders offering home loans, the Commission committed itself to monitoring compliance with the Voluntary Code of Conduct on pre-contractual information for home loans, which contains the ESIS which provides information, personalised for the consumer, on the credit agreement being provided. Evidence collected by the Commission highlighted the need to revise the content and presentation of the ESIS to ensure that it is clear, understandable and contains all information found to be relevant for consumers. The content and layout of the ESIS should

incorporate the necessary improvements identified during consumer testing in all Member States. The structure of the ESIS, in particular, the order of the information items, should be revised, the wording should be more user-friendly, while sections, such as 'nominal rate' and 'annual percentage rate of charge', should be merged and new sections, such as 'flexible features', should be added. An illustrative amortisation table should be provided to a consumer as part of the ESIS where the credit is a deferred interest credit, in which the repayment of principal is deferred for an initial period or where the borrowing rate is fixed for the duration of the credit agreement. Member States should be able to provide that such an illustrative amortisation table in the ESIS is not compulsory for other credit agreements.

(41) Consumer research has underlined the importance of using simple and understandable language in disclosures provided to consumers. For this reason, the terms used in the ESIS are not necessarily the same as the legal terms defined in this Directive but have the same meaning.

(42) The information requirements on credit agreements contained in the ESIS should be without prejudice to Union or national information requirements for other products or services that might be offered with the credit agreement, as conditions for obtaining the credit agreement related to immovable property, or offered so as to obtain that agreement at a lower borrowing rate, such as fire or life insurance or investment products. Member States should be free to maintain or introduce national law where no harmonised provisions exist, for instance information requirements on the level of usury rates at the pre-contractual stage or information which might be useful for the purposes of financial education or for out-of-court settlements. Any additional information should, however, be given in a separate document which may be annexed to the ESIS. Member States should be able, in their national languages, to use different vocabulary in the ESIS, without changing its contents and the order in which information is provided, when this is needed in order to employ a language which might be more easily understandable for consumers.

(43) In order to ensure that the ESIS provides the consumer with all relevant information to make an informed choice, the creditor should follow the instructions set out in this Directive when completing the ESIS. Member States should be able to elaborate or further specify the instructions for completing the ESIS on the basis of the instructions set out in this Directive. For instance, Member States should be able to further specify the information to be given in order to describe the 'type of borrowing rate' in order to take into account the specificities of the national products and market. However, such further specifications should not be contrary to the instructions contained in this Directive nor imply any change in the text of the ESIS model, which should be reproduced as such by the creditor. Member States should be able to specify further warnings on credit agreements, adapted to their national market and practices, where such warnings are not already specifically included in the ESIS. Member States should be able to provide that the creditor is bound by the information provided for in the ESIS, provided that the creditor decides to grant the credit.

(44) The consumer should receive information by means of the ESIS without undue delay after the consumer has delivered the necessary information on his needs, financial situation and preferences and in good time before the consumer is bound by any credit agreement or offer, in order to enable him to compare and reflect on the characteristics of credit products and obtain third party advice if necessary. In particular when a binding offer is made to the consumer, it should be accompanied by the ESIS, unless the ESIS has already been delivered to the consumer and the characteristics of the offer are consistent with the information previously provided. However, Member States should be able to provide for the obligatory provision of the ESIS both before the provision of any binding offer and together with the binding offer, where an ESIS containing the same information has not previously been given. While the ESIS should be personalised and reflect the preferences expressed by the consumer, the provision of such personalised information should not imply an obligation to provide advice. Credit agreements should only be concluded where the consumer has had sufficient time to compare offers, assess their implications, obtain third party advice if necessary and has taken an informed decision on whether to accept an offer.

(45) Where the consumer has a secured credit agreement for the purchase of immovable property or land and the duration of the security is longer than that of the credit agreement, and where the consumer can decide to withdraw the repaid capital again subject to signature of a new credit agreement, a new ESIS disclosing the new APRC and based on the specific characteristics of the new credit agreement should be provided to the consumer before the signature of the new credit agreement.

(46) At least where no right of withdrawal exists, the creditor or, where applicable, the credit intermediary or appointed representative should provide the consumer with a copy of the draft credit agreement, at the time of the provision of an offer binding on the creditor. In other cases, the consumer should at least be offered a copy of the draft credit agreement at the time a binding offer is made.

(47) In order to ensure the fullest possible transparency and to prevent abuses arising from possible conflicts of interest when consumers use the services of credit intermediaries, the latter should be subject to certain information disclosure obligations prior to the performance of their services. Such disclosures should include information on their identity and links with creditors, for instance whether they are considering products from a broad range of creditors or only from a more limited number of creditors. The existence of any commission or other inducement payable to the credit intermediary by the creditor or by third parties in relation to the credit agreement should be disclosed to consumers before the carrying out of any credit intermediation activities and consumers should be informed at that stage either of the amount of such payments, where that is known, or of the fact that the amount will be disclosed at a later pre-contractual stage in the ESIS and of their right to be given information on the level of such payments at that stage. Consumers should be informed of any fees they should pay to credit intermediaries in relation to their services. Without prejudice to competition law, Member States should be free to introduce or maintain provisions prohibiting the payment of fees by consumers to some or all categories of credit intermediary.

(48) A consumer may still need additional assistance in order to decide which credit agreement, within the range of products proposed, is the most appropriate for his needs and financial situation. Creditors and, where applicable, credit intermediaries should provide such assistance in relation to the credit products which they offer to the consumer by explaining the relevant information including in particular the essential characteristics of the products proposed to the consumer in a personalised manner so that the consumer can understand the effects which they may have on his economic situation. Creditors and, where applicable, credit intermediaries should adapt the way in which such explanations are given to the circumstances in which the credit is offered and the consumer's need for assistance, taking into account the consumer's knowledge and experience of credit and the nature of individual credit products. Such explanations should not in itself constitute a personal recommendation.

(49) In order to promote the establishment and functioning of the internal market and to ensure a high degree of protection for consumers throughout the Union, it is necessary to uniformly ensure the comparability of information relating to the APRC throughout the Union.

(50) The total cost of the credit to the consumer should comprise all the costs that the consumer has to pay in connection with the credit agreement and which are known to the creditor. It should therefore include interest, commissions, taxes, fees for credit intermediaries, the costs of property valuation for a mortgage and any other fees, except for notarial fees, required to obtain the credit, for example life insurance, or to obtain it on the terms and conditions marketed, for example fire insurance. The provisions of this Directive concerning ancillary products and services (for instance concerning the costs of opening and maintaining a bank account) should be without prejudice to Directive 2005/29/EC and Council Directive 93/13/EEC of 5 April 1993 on unfair terms in consumer contracts. The total cost of the credit to the consumer should exclude costs that the consumer pays in relation to the purchase of the immovable property or land, such as associated taxes and notarial costs or the costs of land registration. The creditor's actual knowledge of the costs should be assessed objectively, taking into account the requirements of professional diligence. In that respect, the creditor should be presumed to have knowledge of the costs of the ancillary services which he offers to the consumer himself, or on behalf of a third party, unless the price thereof depends on the specific characteristics or situation of the consumer.

(51) If estimated information is used, the consumer should be made aware of this and that the information is expected to be representative of the type of agreement or practices under consideration. The additional assumptions for the calculation of the APRC aim to ensure that the APRC is calculated in a consistent way and to ensure comparability. Additional assumptions are necessary for specific types of credit agreement, such as where the amount, duration or cost of the credit are uncertain or vary depending on how the agreement is operated. Where the provisions in themselves do not suffice to calculate the APRC, the creditor should use the additional assumptions set out in Annex I. However, given that the calculation of the APRC will depend on the terms of the individual credit agreement, only those assumptions necessary and relevant to a given credit should be used.

(52) In order to further ensure a high degree of comparability of the APRC between offers from different creditors, the intervals between dates used in the calculation should not be expressed in days where they can be expressed as a whole number of years, months or weeks. Implicit in that context is that if certain time intervals are used in the APRC formula, those intervals should be used to ascertain the amounts of interest and other charges used in the formula. For this reason, creditors should use the method of measurement of time intervals described in Annex I to obtain the figures for the payment of charges. However, that is only applicable for the purposes of calculation of the APRC and does not impact on the amounts actually charged by the creditor under the credit agreement. Where

those numbers are different it may be necessary to explain them to the consumer in order to avoid misleading the consumer. That implies that in the absence of non-interest charges and assuming an identical method of calculation the APRC will be equal to the effective borrowing rate of the credit.

(53) As the APRC can at the advertising stage be indicated only through an example, such an example should be representative. Therefore, it should correspond, for instance, to the average duration and total amount of credit granted for the type of credit agreement under consideration. When determining the representative example, the prevalence of certain types of credit agreements in a specific market should be taken into account. It may be preferable for each creditor to base the representative example on an amount of credit which is representative of that creditor's own product range and expected customer base, as these may vary considerably among creditors. As regards the APRC disclosed in the ESIS, the preferences of and information provided by the consumer should where possible be taken into account and the creditor or credit intermediary should make it clear whether the information provided is illustrative or reflects the preferences and information given. In any event, the representative examples should not be contrary to the requirements of Directive 2005/29/EC. It is important that in the ESIS it is made clear to the consumer, where applicable, that the APRC is based on assumptions and could change so that consumers can take this into account when comparing products. It is important that the APRC should take account of all drawdowns under the credit agreement, whether paid directly to the consumer or to a third party on the consumer's behalf.

(54) In order to ensure consistency between the calculation of the APRC for different types of credit, the assumptions used for calculating similar forms of credit agreement should be generally consistent. In this respect, assumptions from Commission Directive 2011/90/EU of 14 November 2011 amending Part II of Annex I to Directive 2008/48/EC of the European Parliament and of the Council providing additional assumptions for the calculation of the annual percentage rate of charge, modifying the assumptions for calculating the APRC should be incorporated. While not all assumptions will necessarily apply to credit agreements available now, product innovation in this sector is active and so it is necessary to have the assumptions in place. Furthermore, for the purpose of calculating the APRC, the identification of the most common drawdown mechanism should be based on reasonable expectations of the drawdown mechanism most frequently used by consumers for the type of product offered by that specific creditor. For existing products, the expectation should be based on the previous 12 months.

(55) It is essential that the consumer's ability and propensity to repay the credit is assessed and verified before a credit agreement is concluded. That assessment of creditworthiness should take into consideration all necessary and relevant factors that could influence a consumer's ability to repay the credit over its lifetime. In particular, the consumer's ability to service and fully repay the credit should include consideration of future payments or payment increases needed due to negative amortisation or deferred payments of principal or interest and should be considered in the light of other regular expenditure, debts and other financial commitments as well as income, savings and assets. Reasonable allowance should be made for future events during the term of the proposed credit agreement such as a reduction in income where the credit term lasts into retirement or, where applicable, an increase in the borrowing rate or negative change in the exchange rate. While the value of the immovable property is an important element in ascertaining the amount of the credit that may be granted to a consumer under a secured credit agreement, the assessment of creditworthiness should focus on the consumer's ability to meet their obligations under the credit agreement. Consequently, the possibility that the value of the immovable property could exceed the credit amount or could increase in the future should not generally be a sufficient condition for granting the credit in question. Nevertheless, where the purpose of a credit agreement is to construct or renovate an existing immovable property, the creditor should be able to consider this possibility. Member States should be able to issue additional guidance on those or additional criteria and on methods to assess a consumer's creditworthiness, for example by setting limits on loan-to-value or loan-to-income ratios and should be encouraged to implement the Financial Stability Board's Principles for Sound Residential Mortgage Underwriting Practices.

(56) Specific provisions may be necessary for the different elements that may be taken into consideration in the creditworthiness assessment of certain types of credit agreements. For example, for credit agreements which relate to an immovable property which explicitly state that the immovable property is not to be occupied as a house, apartment or another place of residence by the consumer or a family member of the consumer (buy-to-let agreements), Member States should be able to specify that future rental income is taken into account when assessing the consumer's ability to repay the credit. In those Member States where such a specification is not set out by national provisions, creditors may decide to include a prudent assessment of future rental income. The assessment of creditworthiness should not imply the transfer of responsibility to the creditor for any subsequent non-compliance by

the consumer with his obligations under the credit agreement.

(57) The creditor's decision as to whether to grant the credit should be consistent with the outcome of the assessment of creditworthiness. For example, the capacity for the creditor to transfer part of the credit risk to a third party should not lead him to ignore the conclusions of the creditworthiness assessment by making a credit agreement available to a consumer who is likely not to be able to repay it. Member States should be able to transpose this principle by requiring competent authorities to take relevant actions as part of the supervisory activities and to monitor the compliance of creditors' creditworthiness assessment procedures. However, a positive creditworthiness assessment should not constitute an obligation for the creditor to provide credit.

(58) In line with the recommendations of the Financial Stability Board, the assessment of creditworthiness should be based on information on the financial and economic situation, including income and expenses, of the consumer. That information can be obtained from various sources including from the consumer, and the creditor should appropriately verify such information before granting the credit. In that respect consumers should provide information in order to facilitate the creditworthiness assessment, since failure to do so is likely to result in refusal of the credit they seek to obtain unless the information can be obtained from elsewhere. Without prejudice to private contract law, Member States should ensure that creditors cannot terminate a credit agreement because they realised, after the signature of the credit agreement, that the assessment of creditworthiness was incorrectly conducted due to incomplete information at the time of the creditworthiness assessment. However, this should be without prejudice to the possibility for Member States to allow creditors to terminate the credit agreement where it can be established that the consumer deliberately provided inaccurate or falsified information at the time of the creditworthiness assessment or intentionally did not provide information that would have led to a negative creditworthiness assessment or where there are other valid reasons compatible with Union law. While it would not be appropriate to apply sanctions to consumers for not being in a position to provide certain information or assessments or for deciding to discontinue the application process for getting a credit, Member States should be able to provide for sanctions where consumers knowingly provide incomplete or incorrect information in order to obtain a positive creditworthiness assessment, in particular where the complete and correct information would have resulted in a negative creditworthiness assessment and the consumer is subsequently unable to fulfil the conditions of the agreement.

(59) Consultation of a credit database is a useful element in the assessment of creditworthiness. Some Member States require creditors to assess the creditworthiness of consumers on the basis of a consultation of the relevant database. Creditors should be able to consult the credit database over the lifetime of the credit solely in order to identify and assess the potential for default. Such consultation of the credit database should be subject to appropriate safeguards to ensure that it is used for the early identification and resolution of credit risk in the interest of the consumer and not to inform commercial negotiations. Pursuant to Directive 95/46/EC of the European Parliament and of the Council of 24 October 1995 on the protection of individuals with regard to the processing of personal data and on the free movement of such data (14), consumers should be informed by creditors of the consultation of the credit database prior to its consultation, and should have the right to access the information held on them in such a credit database in order to, where necessary, rectify, erase or block the personal data concerning them processed therein where it is inaccurate or has been unlawfully processed.

(60) To prevent any distortion of competition among creditors, it should be ensured that all creditors, including credit institutions or non-credit institutions providing credit agreements relating to residential immovable property, have access to all public and private credit databases concerning consumers under non-discriminatory conditions. Such conditions should not therefore include a requirement for creditors to be established as a credit institution. Access conditions, such as the costs of accessing the database or requirements to provide information to the database on the basis of reciprocity should continue to apply. Member States should be free to determine whether, within their jurisdictions, credit intermediaries may have access to such databases.

(61) Where a decision to reject an application for credit is based on data obtained through the consultation of a database or the lack of data therein, the creditor should inform the consumer thereof, and provide the name of the database consulted and of any other elements required by Directive 95/46/EC so as to enable the consumer to exercise his right to access and, where justified, rectify, erase or block personal data concerning him and processed therein. Where a decision to reject an application for credit results from a negative creditworthiness assessment, the creditor should inform the consumer of the rejection without undue delay. Member States should be free to decide whether they require creditors to provide further explanations on the reasons of the rejection. However, the creditor should not be required to give such information when to do so would be prohibited by other

PART IV   EUROPEAN PRIVATE LAW

Union law such as provisions on money laundering or the financing of terrorism. Such information should not be provided where to do so would be contrary to the objectives of public policy or public security such as the prevention, investigation, detection or prosecution of criminal offences.
(62) This Directive addresses the use of personal data in the context of the assessment of a consumer's creditworthiness. In order to ensure the protection of personal data, Directive 95/46/EC should apply to the data processing activities carried out within the context of such assessments.
(63) Providing advice in the form of a personalised recommendation is a distinct activity which may but need not be combined with other aspects of granting or intermediating credit. Therefore, in order to be in a position to understand the nature of the services provided to them, consumers should be made aware of whether advisory services are being or can be provided and when they are not and of what constitutes advisory services. Given the importance which consumers attach to the use of the terms 'advice' and 'advisors', it is appropriate that Member States should be allowed to prohibit the use of those terms, or similar terms, when advisory services are being provided to consumers. It is appropriate to ensure that Member States impose safeguards where advice is described as independent to ensure that the range of products considered and remuneration arrangements are co°mmensurate with consumers' expectations of such advice.
(64) Those providing advisory services should comply with certain standards in order to ensure that the consumer is presented with products suitable for his needs and circumstances. Advisory services should be based on a fair and sufficiently wide-ranging analysis of the products offered, where the advisory services are provided by creditors and tied credit intermediaries, or, where the advisory services are provided by credit intermediaries that are not tied, of products available on the market. Those providing advisory services should be able to specialise in certain 'niche' products such as bridging finance, provided they consider a range of products within that particular 'niche' and 'their specialisation in those 'niche' products is made clear to the consumer. In any event, creditors and credit intermediaries should disclose to the consumer whether they are advising only on their own product range or a wide range from across the market to ensure that the consumer understands the basis for a recommendation.
(65) Advisory services should be based on a proper understanding of the consumer's financial situation, preferences and objectives based on the necessary up-to-date information and reasonable assumptions about risks to the consumer's circumstances during the lifetime of the credit agreement. Member States should be able to clarify how the suitability of a given product is to be assessed in the context of the provision of advisory services.
(66) A consumer's ability to repay the credit prior to the expiry of the credit agreement may play an important role in promoting competition in the internal market and the free movement of Union citizens as well as helping to provide the flexibility during the lifetime of the credit agreement needed to promote financial stability in line with the recommendations of the Financial Stability Board. However, substantial differences exist between the national principles and conditions under which consumers have the ability to repay their credit and the conditions under which such early repayment can take place. Whilst recognising the diversity in mortgage funding mechanisms and the range of products available, certain standards with regard to early repayment of credit are essential at Union level in order to ensure that consumers have the possibility to discharge their obligations before the date agreed in the credit agreement and the confidence to compare offers in order to find the best products to meet their needs. Member States should therefore ensure, whether through law or other means such as contractual clauses, that consumers have a right to early repayment. Nevertheless, Member States should be able to define the conditions for the exercise of such a right. These conditions may include time limitations on the exercise of the right, different treatment depending on the type of the borrowing rate or restrictions with regard to the circumstances under which the right may be exercised. Where the early repayment falls within a period for which the borrowing rate is fixed, exercise of the right may be made subject to the existence of a legitimate interest on the part of the consumer specified by the Member State. Such legitimate interest may for example occur in the event of divorce or unemployment. The conditions set by Member States may provide that the creditor is entitled to fair and objectively justified compensation for potential costs directly linked to early repayment of the credit. In the event where Member States provide that the creditor is entitled to compensation such compensation should be a fair and objectively justified compensation for potential costs directly linked to early repayment of the credit in accordance with the national rules on compensation. The compensation should not exceed the financial loss of the creditor.
(67) It is important to ensure that sufficient transparency exists to provide clarity for consumers on the nature of the commitments made in the interests of preserving financial stability and on where there is flexibility during the term of the credit agreement. Consumers should be provided with information concerning the borrowing rate during the contractual relationship as well as at the pre-

contractual stage. Member States should be able to maintain or introduce restrictions or prohibitions on unilateral changes to the borrowing rate by the creditor. Member States should be able to provide that where the borrowing rate changes the consumer is entitled to receive an updated amortisation table.

(68) Although credit intermediaries play a central role in the distribution of credit agreements relating to residential immovable property in the Union, substantial differences remain between national provisions on the conduct of business and supervision of credit intermediaries which create barriers to the taking-up and pursuit of the activities of credit intermediaries in the internal market. The inability of credit intermediaries to operate freely throughout the Union hinders the proper functioning of the internal market in credit agreements relating to residential immovable property. While recognising the diversity in the types of actor involved in credit intermediation, certain standards at Union level are essential in order to ensure a high level of professionalism and service.

(69) Before being able to carry out their activities, credit intermediaries should be subject to an admission process by the competent authority of their home Member State and subject to ongoing supervision to ensure that they meet strict professional requirements at least in relation to their competence, good repute and professional indemnity cover. Such requirements should apply at least at the level of the institution. However, Member States may clarify whether such requirements for admission apply to individual employees of the credit intermediary. The home Member State may provide for additional requirements, for instance that the credit intermediary's shareholders are of good repute or that a tied credit intermediary can only be tied to one creditor, where those are proportionate and compatible with other Union law. Relevant information about admitted credit intermediaries should be entered in a public register. Tied credit intermediaries who work exclusively with one creditor under its full and unconditional responsibility should have the possibility to be admitted by the competent authority under the auspices of the creditor on whose behalf they act. Member States should have the right to maintain or to impose restrictions regarding the legal form of certain credit intermediaries, whether they are allowed to act exclusively as legal or natural persons. Member States should be free to decide whether all credit intermediaries are entered into one register or whether different registers are required depending on whether the credit intermediary is tied or acts as independent credit intermediary. Furthermore Member States should be free to maintain or to impose restrictions on the possibility to charge any fees to consumers by the credit intermediaries tied to one or more creditors.

(70) In some Member States, credit intermediaries may decide to use the services of appointed representatives to perform activities on their behalf. Member States should have the possibility to apply the specific regime laid down by this Directive for appointed representatives. However, Member States should be free not to introduce such a regime or to allow other entities to perform a role which is comparable to that of appointed representatives, provided that those entities are subject to the same regime as credit intermediaries. The rules on appointed representatives set out in this Directive do not oblige Member States to allow appointed representatives to operate in their jurisdiction unless such appointed representatives are considered credit intermediaries under this Directive.

(71) In order to ensure the effective supervision of credit intermediaries by competent authorities, a credit intermediary which is a legal person should be admitted in the Member State in which it has its registered office. A credit intermediary which is not a legal person should be admitted in the Member State in which it has its head office. In addition, Member States should require that a credit intermediary's head office always be situated in its home Member State and that it actually operates there.

(72) The requirements for admission should allow credit intermediaries to operate in other Member States in accordance with the principles of freedom of establishment and freedom to provide services, provided that an appropriate notification procedure has been followed between the competent authorities. Even in cases where Member States decide to admit all individual staff within the credit intermediary, the notification of the intention to provide services should be made on the basis of the credit intermediary rather than the individual employee. However, while this Directive provides a framework for all admitted credit intermediaries, including credit intermediaries tied to only one creditor, to operate throughout the Union, this Directive does not provide such a framework for appointed representatives. In such instances, appointed representatives wishing to operate in another Member State would have to comply with the requirements for the admission of credit intermediaries set out in this Directive.

(73) In some Member States, credit intermediaries can carry out their activities in respect of credit agreements offered by non-credit institutions and credit institutions. As a principle, admitted credit intermediaries should be allowed to operate in the entire territory of the Union. However, the admission by the competent authorities of the home Member States should not allow credit intermediaries to provide their services in relation to credit agreements offered by non-credit institutions to a

consumer in a Member State where such non-credit institutions are not allowed to operate.

(74) Member States should be able to provide that persons carrying out credit intermediation activities only on an incidental basis in the course of professional activity, such as lawyers or notaries, are not subject to the admission procedure set out in this Directive provided that such professional activity is regulated and the relevant rules do not prohibit the carrying out, on an incidental basis, of credit intermediation activities. Such an exemption from the admission procedure laid down in this Directive should however mean that such persons cannot benefit from the passport regime provided in this Directive. Persons who merely introduce or refer a consumer to a creditor or credit intermediary on an incidental basis in the course of their professional activity, for instance by indicating the existence of a particular creditor or credit intermediary to the consumer or a type of product with this particular creditor or credit intermediary to the consumer without further advertising or engaging in the presentation, offering, preparatory work or conclusion of the credit agreement, should not be regarded as credit intermediaries for the purposes of this Directive. Neither should borrowers who merely transfer a credit agreement to a consumer through a process of subrogation without carrying out any other credit intermediation activity be regarded as credit intermediaries for the purposes of this Directive.

(75) In order to ensure a level playing field between creditors and promote financial stability, and pending further harmonisation, Member States should ensure that appropriate measures are in place for the admission and supervision of non-credit institutions providing credit agreements relating to residential immovable property. In accordance with the principle of proportionality, this Directive should not lay down detailed conditions for the admission or supervision of creditors providing such credit agreements and that are not credit institutions as defined in Regulation (EU) No 575/2013 of the European Parliament and the Council of 26 June 2013 on prudential requirements for credit institutions and investment firms. The number of such institutions operating in the Union at present is limited as is their market share and the number of Member States in which they are active, particularly since the financial crisis. Nor should the introduction of a 'passport' for such institutions be provided for in this Directive for the same reason.

(76) Member States should lay down rules on sanctions applicable to infringements of the national provisions adopted pursuant to this Directive and ensure that they are implemented. While the choice of sanctions remains within the discretion of Member States, the sanctions provided for should be effective, proportionate and dissuasive.

(77) Consumers should have access to out-of-court complaint and redress procedures for the settlement of disputes arising from the rights and obligations set out in this Directive between creditors and consumers as well as between credit intermediaries and consumers. Member States should ensure that participation in such alternative dispute resolution procedures is not optional for creditors and credit intermediaries. To ensure the smooth functioning of alternative dispute resolution procedures in cases of cross-border activity, Member States should require and encourage the bodies responsible for resolving out-of-court complaints and redress to cooperate. In that context, Member States' out-of-court complaint and redress bodies should be encouraged to participate in FIN-NET, a financial dispute resolution network of national out-of-court schemes that are responsible for handling disputes between consumers and financial services providers.

(78) In order to ensure consistent harmonisation and to take account of developments in the markets for credit agreements or in the evolution of credit products or in economic conditions, and in order to further specify certain requirements in this Directive, the power to adopt acts in accordance with Article 290 TFEU should be delegated to the Commission in respect of amending the standard wording or the instructions for completing the ESIS and amending the remarks or update the assumptions used to calculate the APRC. It is of particular importance that the Commission carry out appropriate consultations during its preparatory work, including at expert level. The Commission, when preparing and drawing up delegated acts, should ensure a simultaneous, timely and appropriate transmission of relevant documents to the European Parliament and to the Council.

(79) In order to facilitate the ability of credit intermediaries to provide their services on a cross-border basis, for the purposes of cooperation, information exchange and dispute resolution between competent authorities, the competent authorities responsible for the admission of credit intermediaries should be those acting under the auspices of the European Supervisory Authority (European Banking Authority) (EBA), as set out in Regulation (EU) No 1093/2010 of the European Parliament and of the Council of 24 November 2010 establishing a European Supervisory Authority (European Banking Authority) (16) or other national authorities provided that they cooperate with the authorities acting under the auspices of EBA in order to carry out their duties under this Directive.

(80) Member States should designate competent authorities empowered to ensure enforcement of this Directive and ensure that they are granted investigation and enforcement powers and adequate

resources necessary for the performance of their duties. Competent authorities could act for certain aspects of this Directive by application to courts competent to grant a legal decision, including, where appropriate, by appeal. This could enable Member States, in particular where provisions of this Directive were transposed into civil law, to leave the enforcement of these provisions to the abovementioned bodies and the courts. Member States should be able to designate different competent authorities in order to enforce the wide ranging obligations laid down in this Directive. For instance, for some provisions, Member States could designate competent authorities responsible for the enforcement of consumer protection, while for others, they could decide to designate prudential supervisors. The option to designate different competent authorities should not affect the obligations for ongoing supervision and cooperation between the competent authorities, as provided for in this Directive.

(81) The efficient functioning of this Directive will need to be reviewed, as will progress on the establishment of an internal market with a high level of consumer protection for credit agreements relating to residential immovable property. The review should include, among other things, an assessment of compliance with and the impact of this Directive, an assessment of whether the scope of the Directive remains appropriate, an analysis of the provision of credit agreements by non-credit institutions, an assessment of the need for further measures, including a passport for non-credit institutions and examination of the necessity to introduce further rights and obligations with regard to the post-contractual stage of credit agreements.

(82) Action by Member States alone is likely to result in different sets of rules, which may undermine or create new obstacles to the functioning of the internal market. Since the objective of this Directive, namely the creation of an efficient and competitive internal market in credit agreements relating to residential immovable property whilst ensuring a high level of consumer protection, cannot be sufficiently achieved by Member States and can therefore, by reason of the effectiveness of the action, be better achieved at Union level, the Union may adopt measures, in accordance with the principle of subsidiarity as set out in Article 5 of the Treaty on European Union. In accordance with the principle of proportionality, as set out in that Article, this Directive does not go beyond what is necessary in order to achieve that objective.

(83) Member States may decide to transpose certain aspects covered by this Directive in national law by prudential law, for example the creditworthiness assessment of the consumer, while others are transposed by civil or criminal law, for example the obligations relating to responsible borrowers.

(84) In accordance with the Joint Political Declaration of Member States and the Commission on explanatory documents of 28 September 2011, Member States have undertaken to accompany, in justified cases, the notification of their transposition measures with one or more documents explaining the relationship between the components of a directive and the corresponding parts of national transposition instruments. With regard to this Directive, the legislator considers the transmission of such documents to be justified.

(85) The European Data Protection Supervisor delivered an opinion on 25 July 2011 based on Article 28(2) of Regulation (EC) No 45/2001 of the European Parliament and of the Council of 18 December 2000 on the protection of individuals with regard to the processing of personal data by the Community institutions and bodies and on the free movement of such data,

HAVE ADOPTED THIS DIRECTIVE:

Chapter 1. Subject Matter, Scope, Definitions, and Competent Authorities

Article 1. This Directive lays down a common framework for certain aspects of the laws, regulations and administrative provisions of the Member States concerning agreements covering credit for consumers secured by a mortgage or otherwise relating to residential immovable property, including an obligation to carry out a creditworthiness assessment before granting a credit, as a basis for the development of effective underwriting standards in relation to residential immovable property in the Member States, and for certain prudential and supervisory requirements, including for the establishment and supervision of credit intermediaries, appointed representatives and non-credit institutions.

Article 2. (1) This Directive shall not preclude Member States from maintaining or introducing more stringent provisions in order to protect consumers, provided that such provisions are consistent with their obligations under Union law.

(2) Notwithstanding paragraph (1), Member States shall not maintain or introduce in their national law provisions diverging from those laid down in Article 14(2) and Annex II Part A with regard to standard pre-contractual information through a European Standardised Information Sheet (ESIS) and Article 17(1) to (5), (7) and (8) and Annex I with regard to a common, consistent Union standard for the calculation of the annual percentage rate of charge (APRC).

PART IV   EUROPEAN PRIVATE LAW

Article 3. (1) This Directive shall apply to:
(a) credit agreements which are secured either by a mortgage or by another comparable security commonly used in a Member State on residential immovable property or secured by a right related to residential immovable property; and
(b) credit agreements the purpose of which is to acquire or retain property rights in land or in an existing or projected building.
(2) This Directive shall not apply to:
(a) Equity release credit agreements where the creditor:
(i) contributes a lump sum, periodic payments or other forms of credit disbursement in return for a sum deriving from the future sale of a residential immovable property or a right relating to residential immovable property; and
(ii) will not seek repayment of the credit until the occurrence of one or more specified life events of the consumer, as defined by Member States, unless the consumer breaches his contractual obligations which allows the creditor to terminate the credit agreement;
(b) credit agreements where the credit is granted by an employer to his employees as a secondary activity where such a credit agreement is offered free of interest or at an APRC lower than those prevailing on the market and not offered to the public generally;
(c) credit agreements where the credit is granted free of interest and without any other charges except those that recover costs directly related to the securing of the credit;
(d) credit agreements in the form of an overdraft facility and where the credit has to be repaid within one month;
(e) credit agreements which are the outcome of a settlement reached in court or before another statutory authority;
(f) credit agreements which relate to the deferred payment, free of charge, of an existing debt and which do not fall within the scope of point (a) of paragraph (1).
(3) Member States may decide not to apply:
(a) Articles 11 and 14 and Annex II to credit agreements for consumers, secured by a mortgage or by another comparable security commonly used in a Member State on residential immovable property or secured by a right related to residential immovable property, the purpose of which is not to acquire or retain the right to residential immovable property, provided that the Member States apply to such credit agreements Articles 4 and 5 of and Annexes II and III to Directive 2008/48/EC;
(b) this Directive to credit agreements which relate to an immovable property where the credit agreement provides that the immovable property cannot at any time be occupied as a house, apartment or another place of residence by the consumer or a family member of the consumer and is to be occupied as a house, apartment or another place of residence on the basis of a rental agreement;
(c) this Directive to credit agreements which relate to credits granted to a restricted public under a statutory provision with a general interest purpose, free of interest or at lower borrowing rates than those prevailing on the market or on other terms which are more favourable to the consumer than those prevailing on the market and at borrowing rates not higher than those prevailing on the market;
(d) this Directive to bridging loans;
(e) this Directive to credit agreements where the creditor is an organisation within the scope of Article 2(5) of Directive 2008/48/EC.
(4) Member States which use the option referred to in point (b) of paragraph (3) shall ensure the application of an appropriate framework at a national level for this type of credit.
(5) Member States which use the option referred to in point (c) or (e) of paragraph (3) shall ensure the application of adequate alternative arrangements to ensure consumers receive timely information on the main features, risks and costs of such credit agreements at the pre-contractual stage and that advertising of such credit agreements is fair, clear and not misleading.

Article 4. For the purposes of this Directive, the following definitions shall apply:
(1) 'Consumer' means a consumer as defined in point (a) of Article 3 of Directive 2008/48/EC.
(2) 'Creditor' means a natural or legal person who grants or promises to grant credit falling within the scope of Article 3 in the course of his trade, business or profession.
(3) 'Credit agreement' means an agreement whereby a creditor grants or promises to grant, to a consumer, a credit falling within the scope of Article 3 in the form of a deferred payment, loan or other similar financial accommodation.
(4) 'Ancillary service' means a service offered to the consumer in conjunction with the credit agreement.
(5) 'Credit intermediary' means a natural or legal person who is not acting as a creditor or notary and not merely introducing, either directly or indirectly, a consumer to a creditor or credit intermedi-

ary, and who, in the course of his trade, business or profession, for remuneration, which may take a pecuniary form or any other agreed form of financial consideration:
(a) presents or offers credit agreements to consumers;
(b) assists consumers by undertaking preparatory work or other pre-contractual administration in respect of credit agreements other than as referred to in point (a); or
(c) concludes credit agreements with consumers on behalf of the creditor.
(6) 'Group' means a group of creditors which are to be consolidated for the purposes of drawing up consolidated accounts, as defined in Directive 2013/34/EU of the European Parliament and of the Council of 26 June 2013 on the annual financial statements, consolidated financial statements and related reports of certain types of undertakings.
(7) 'Tied credit intermediary' means any credit intermediary who acts on behalf of and under the full and unconditional responsibility of:
(a) only one creditor;
(b) only one group; or
(c) a number of creditors or groups which does not represent the majority of the market.
(8) 'Appointed representative' means a natural or legal person who performs activities referred to in point 5 that is acting on behalf of and under the full and unconditional responsibility of only one credit intermediary.
(9) 'Credit institution' means credit institution as defined in point 1 of Article 4(1) of Regulation (EU) No 575/2013.
(10) 'Non-credit institution' means any creditor that is not a credit institution.
(11) 'Staff' means:
(a) any natural person working for the creditor, or credit intermediary who is directly engaged in the activities covered by this Directive or who has contacts with consumers in the course of activities covered by this Directive;
(b) any natural person working for an appointed representative who has contacts with consumers in the course of activities covered by this Directive;
(c) any natural person directly managing or supervising the natural persons referred to in points (a) and (b).
(12) 'Total amount of credit' means the total amount of credit as defined in point (l) of Article 3 of Directive 2008/48/EC.
(13) 'Total cost of the credit to the consumer' means the total cost of the credit to the consumer as defined in point (g) of Article 3 of Directive 2008/48/EC including the cost of valuation of property where such valuation is necessary to obtain the credit but excluding registration fees for the transfer of ownership of the immovable property. It excludes any charges payable by the consumer for non-compliance with the commitments laid down in the credit agreement.
(14) 'Total amount payable by the consumer' means the total amount payable by the consumer as defined in point (h) of Article 3 of Directive 2008/48/EC.
(15) 'Annual percentage rate of charge' (APRC) means the total cost of the credit to the consumer, expressed as an annual percentage of the total amount of credit, where applicable, including the costs referred to in Article 17(2) and equates, on an annual basis, to the present value of all future or existing commitments (drawdowns, repayments and charges) agreed by the creditor and the consumer.
(16) 'Borrowing rate' means the borrowing rate as defined in point (j) of Article 3 of Directive 2008/48/EC.
(17) 'Creditworthiness assessment' means the evaluation of the prospect for the debt obligation resulting from the credit agreement to be met.
(18) 'Durable medium' means durable medium as defined in point (m) of Article 3 of Directive 2008/48/EC.
(19) 'Home Member State' means:
(a) where the creditor or credit intermediary is a natural person, the Member State in which his head office is situated;
(b) where the creditor or credit intermediary is a legal person, the Member State in which its registered office is situated or, if under its national law it has no registered office, the Member State in which its head office is situated.
(20) 'Host Member State' means the Member State, other than the home Member State, in which the creditor or credit intermediary has a branch or provides services.
(21) 'Advisory services' means the provision of personal recommendations to a consumer in respect of one or more transactions relating to credit agreements and constitutes a separate activity from the granting of a credit and from the credit intermediation activities set out in point 5.
(22) 'Competent authority' means an authority designated as competent by a Member State in accordance with Article 5.

(23) 'Bridging loan' means a credit agreement either of no fixed duration or which is due to be repaid within 12 months, used by the consumer as a temporary financing solution while transitioning to another financial arrangement for the immovable property.
(24) 'Contingent liability or guarantee' means a credit agreement which acts as a guarantee to another separate but ancillary transaction, and where the capital secured against an immovable property is only drawn down if an event or events specified in the contract occur.
(25) 'Shared equity credit agreement' means a credit agreement where the capital repayable is based on a contractually set percentage of the value of the immovable property at the time of the capital repayment or repayments.
(26) 'Tying practice' means the offering or the selling of a credit agreement in a package with other distinct financial products or services where the credit agreement is not made available to the consumer separately.
(27) 'Bundling practice' means the offering or the selling of a credit agreement in a package with other distinct financial products or services where the credit agreement is also made available to the consumer separately but not necessarily on the same terms or conditions as when offered bundled with the ancillary services.
(28) 'Foreign currency loan' means a credit agreement where the credit is:
(a) denominated in a currency other than that in which the consumer receives the income or holds the assets from which the credit is to be repaid; or
(b) denominated in a currency other than that of the Member State in which the consumer is resident.

Article 5. (1) Member States shall designate the national competent authorities empowered to ensure the application and enforcement of this Directive and shall ensure that they are granted investigating and enforcement powers and adequate resources necessary for the efficient and effective performance of their duties.
The authorities referred to in the first subparagraph shall be either public authorities or bodies recognised by national law or by public authorities expressly empowered for that purpose by national law. They shall not be creditors, credit intermediaries or appointed representatives.
(2) Member States shall ensure that competent authorities, all persons who work or who have worked for the competent authorities, as well as auditors and experts instructed by the competent authorities, are bound by the obligation of professional secrecy. No confidential information which they may receive in the course of their duties may be divulged to any person or authority whatsoever, save in summary or aggregate form, without prejudice to cases covered by criminal law or by this Directive. This shall not, however, prevent the competent authorities from exchanging or transmitting confidential information in accordance with national and Union law.
(3) Member States shall ensure that the authorities designated as competent for ensuring the application and enforcement of Articles 9, 29, 32, 33, 34 and 35 of this Directive are either or both of the following:
(a) competent authorities as defined in Article 4(2) of Regulation (EU) No 1093/2010;
(b) authorities other than the competent authorities referred to in point (a) provided that national laws, regulations or administrative provisions require those authorities to cooperate with the competent authorities referred to in point (a) whenever necessary in order to carry out their duties under this Directive, including for the purposes of cooperating with the European Supervisory Authority (European Banking Authority) (EBA) as required under this Directive.
(4) Member States shall inform the Commission and EBA of the designation of the competent authorities and any changes thereto, indicating any division of the respective duties between different competent authorities. The first such notification shall be made as soon as possible and at the latest on 21 March 2016.
(5) The competent authorities shall exercise their powers in conformity with national law either:
(a) directly under their own authority or under the supervision of the judicial authorities; or
(b) by application to courts which are competent to grant the necessary decision, including, where appropriate, by appeal, if the application to grant the necessary decision is not successful, except for Articles 9, 29, 32, 33, 34 and 35.
(6) Where there is more than one competent authority on their territory, Member States shall ensure that their respective duties are clearly defined and that those authorities collaborate closely so that they can discharge their respective duties effectively.
(7) The Commission shall publish a list of the competent authorities in the Official Journal of the European Union at least once a year, and update it continuously on its website.

Chapter 2. Financial Education

Article 6. (1) Member States shall promote measures that support the education of consumers in relation to responsible borrowing and debt management, in particular in relation to mortgage credit agreements. Clear and general information on the credit granting process is necessary in order to guide consumers, especially those who take out a mortgage credit for the first time. Information regarding the guidance that consumer organisations and national authorities may provide to consumers, is also necessary.

(2) The Commission shall publish an assessment of the financial education available to consumers in the Member States and identify examples of best practices which could be further developed in order to increase the financial awareness of consumers.

Chapter 3. Conditions Applicable to Creditors, Credit Intermediaries and Appointed Representatives

Article 7. (1) Member States shall require that when manufacturing credit products or granting, intermediating or providing advisory services on credit and, where appropriate, ancillary services to consumers or when executing a credit agreement, the creditor, credit intermediary or appointed representative acts honestly, fairly, transparently and professionally, taking account of the rights and interests of the consumers. In relation to the granting, intermediating or provision of advisory services on credit and, where appropriate, of ancillary services the activities shall be based on information about the consumer's circumstances and any specific requirement made known by a consumer and on reasonable assumptions about risks to the consumer's situation over the term of the credit agreement. In relation to such provision of advisory services, the activity shall in addition be based on the information required under point (a) of Article 22(3).

(2) Member States shall ensure that the manner in which creditors remunerate their staff and credit intermediaries and the manner in which credit intermediaries remunerate their staff and appointed representatives do not impede compliance with the obligation set out in paragraph (1).

(3) Member States shall ensure that, when establishing and applying remuneration policies for staff responsible for the assessment of creditworthiness, creditors comply with the following principles in a way and to the extent that is appropriate to their size, internal organisation and the nature, scope and complexity of their activities:

(a) the remuneration policy is consistent with and promotes sound and effective risk management and does not encourage risk-taking that exceeds the level of tolerated risk of the creditor;

(b) the remuneration policy is in line with the business strategy, objectives, values and long-term interests of the creditor, and incorporates measures to avoid conflicts of interest, in particular by providing that remuneration is not contingent on the number or proportion of applications accepted.

(4) Member States shall ensure that where creditors, credit intermediaries or appointed representatives provide advisory services the remuneration structure of the staff involved does not prejudice their ability to act in the consumer's best interest and in particular is not contingent on sales targets. In order to achieve that goal, Member States may in addition ban commissions paid by the creditor to the credit intermediary.

(5) Member States may prohibit or impose restrictions on payments from a consumer to a creditor or credit intermediary prior to the conclusion of a credit agreement.

Article 8. Member States shall ensure that, when information is provided to consumers in compliance with the requirements set out in this Directive, such information is provided without charge to the consumer.

Article 9. (1) Member States shall ensure that creditors, credit intermediaries and appointed representatives require their staff to possess and to keep up-to-date an appropriate level of knowledge and competence in relation to the manufacturing, the offering or granting of credit agreements, the carrying out of credit intermediation activities set out in point 5 of Article 4 or the provision of advisory services. Where the conclusion of a credit agreement includes an ancillary service, appropriate knowledge and competence in relation to that ancillary service shall be required.

(2) Except in the circumstances referred to in paragraph (3), home Member States shall establish minimum knowledge and competence requirements for creditors', credit intermediaries' and appointed representatives' staff in accordance with the principles set out in Annex III.

(3) Where a creditor or credit intermediary provides its services within the territory of one or more other Member States:

(i) through a branch, the host Member State shall be responsible for establishing the minimum knowledge and competence requirements applicable to the staff of a branch;

(ii) under the freedom to provide services, the home Member State shall be responsible for establishing the minimum knowledge and competence requirements applicable to the staff in accordance with

Annex III, however host Member States may establish the minimum knowledge and competence requirements for those requirements referred to in points (b), (c), (e) and (f) of paragraph (1) of Annex III.

(4) Member States shall ensure that compliance with the requirements of paragraph (1) is supervised by the competent authorities, and that the competent authorities have powers to require creditors, credit intermediaries and appointed representatives to provide such evidence as the competent authority deems necessary to enable such supervision.

(5) For the effective supervision of creditors and credit intermediaries providing their services within the territory of other Member States under the freedom to provide services, the competent authorities of the host and the home Member States shall cooperate closely for the effective supervision and enforcement of the minimum knowledge and competence requirements of the host Member State. For that purpose they may delegate tasks and responsibilities to each other.

Chapter 4. Information and Practices Preliminary to the Conclusion of the Credit Agreement

Article 10. Without prejudice to Directive 2005/29/EC, Member States shall require that any advertising and marketing communications concerning credit agreements are fair, clear and not misleading. In particular, wording that may create false expectations for a consumer regarding the availability or the cost of a credit shall be prohibited.

Article 11. (1) Member States shall ensure that any advertising concerning credit agreements which indicates an interest rate or any figures relating to the cost of the credit to the consumer includes the standard information in accordance with this Article.
Member States may provide that the first subparagraph shall not apply where national law requires the indication of the APRC in advertising concerning credit agreements which does not indicate an interest rate or any figures relating to any cost of credit to the consumer within the meaning of the first subparagraph.
(2) The standard information shall specify in a clear, concise and prominent way:
(a) the identity of the creditor or, where applicable, the credit intermediary or appointed representative;
(b) where applicable, that the credit agreement will be secured by a mortgage or another comparable security commonly used in a Member State on residential immovable property or by a right related to residential immovable property;
(c) the borrowing rate, indicating whether this is fixed or variable or a combination of both, together with particulars of any charges included in the total cost of the credit to the consumer;
(d) the total amount of credit;
(e) the APRC which shall be included in the advertisement at least as prominently as any interest rate;
(f) where applicable, the duration of the credit agreement;
(g) where applicable, the amount of the instalments;
(h) where applicable, the total amount payable by the consumer;
(i) where applicable, the number of instalments;
(j) where applicable, a warning regarding the fact that possible fluctuations of the exchange rate could affect the amount payable by the consumer.
(3) The information listed in paragraph (2), other than that listed in points (a), (b) or (j) thereof, shall be specified by means of a representative example and shall adhere to that representative example throughout. Member States shall adopt criteria for determining a representative example.
(4) Where the conclusion of a contract regarding an ancillary service, in particular insurance, is compulsory in order to obtain the credit or to obtain it on the terms and conditions marketed, and the cost of that service cannot be determined in advance, the obligation to enter into that contract shall be stated in a clear, concise and prominent way, together with the APRC.
(5) The information referred to in paragraphs 2 and 4 shall be easily legible or clearly audible as appropriate, depending on the medium used for advertising.
(6) Member States may require the inclusion of a concise and proportionate warning concerning specific risks associated with credit agreements. They shall notify those requirements to the Commission without delay.
(7) This Article shall be without prejudice to Directive 2005/29/EC.

Article 12. (1) Member States shall allow bundling practices but shall prohibit tying practices.
(2) Notwithstanding paragraph (1), Member States may provide that creditors can request the consumer or a family member or close relation of the consumer to:
(a) open or maintain a payment or a savings account, where the only purpose of such an account is to accumulate capital to repay the credit, to service the credit, to pool resources to obtain the credit, or

to provide additional security for the creditor in the event of default;
(b) purchase or keep an investment product or a private pension product, where such product which primarily offers the investor an income in retirement serves also to provide additional security for the creditor in the event of default or to accumulate capital to repay the credit, to service the credit or to pool resources to obtain the credit;
(c) conclude a separate credit agreement in conjunction with a shared-equity credit agreement to obtain the credit.
(3) Notwithstanding paragraph (1), Member States may allow tying practices when the creditor can demonstrate to its competent authority that the tied products or categories of product offered, on terms and conditions similar to each other, which are not made available separately, result in a clear benefit to the consumers taking due account of the availability and the prices of the relevant products offered on the market. This paragraph shall only apply to products which are marketed after 20 March 2014.
(4) Member States may allow creditors to require the consumer to hold a relevant insurance policy related to the credit agreement. In such cases Member States shall ensure that the creditor accepts the insurance policy from a supplier different to his preferred supplier where such policy has a level of guarantee equivalent to the one the creditor has proposed.

Article 13. (1) Member States shall ensure that clear and comprehensible general information about credit agreements is made available by creditors or, where applicable, by tied credit intermediaries or their appointed representatives at all times on paper or on another durable medium or in electronic form. In addition, Member States may provide that general information is made available by non-tied credit intermediaries.
Such general information shall include at least the following:
(a) the identity and the geographical address of the issuer of the information;
(b) the purposes for which the credit may be used;
(c) the forms of security, including, where applicable, the possibility for it to be located in a different Member State;
(d) the possible duration of the credit agreements;
(e) types of available borrowing rate, indicating whether fixed or variable or both, with a short description of the characteristics of a fixed and variable rate, including related implications for the consumer;
(f) where foreign currency loans are available, an indication of the foreign currency or currencies, including an explanation of the implications for the consumer where the credit is denominated in a foreign currency;
(g) a representative example of the total amount of credit, the total cost of the credit to the consumer, the total amount payable by the consumer and the APRC;
(h) an indication of possible further costs, not included in the total cost of the credit to the consumer, to be paid in connection with a credit agreement;
(i) the range of different options available for reimbursing the credit to the creditor, including the number, frequency and amount of the regular repayment instalments;
(j) where applicable, a clear and concise statement that compliance with the terms and conditions of the credit agreement does not guarantee repayment of the total amount of credit under the credit agreement;
(k) a description of the conditions directly relating to early repayment;
(l) whether a valuation of the property is necessary and, where applicable, who is responsible for ensuring that the valuation is carried out, and whether any related costs arise for the consumer;
(m) indication of ancillary services the consumer is obliged to acquire in order to obtain the credit or to obtain it on the terms and conditions marketed and, where applicable, a clarification that the ancillary services may be purchased from a provider that is not the creditor; and
(n) a general warning concerning possible consequences of non-compliance with the commitments linked to the credit agreement.
(2) Member States may oblige the creditors to include other types of warnings which are relevant in a Member State. They shall notify those requirements to the Commission without delay.

Article 14. (1) Member States shall ensure that the creditor and, where applicable, the credit intermediary or appointed representative, provides the consumer with the personalised information needed to compare the credits available on the market, assess their implications and make an informed decision on whether to conclude a credit agreement:
(a) without undue delay after the consumer has given the necessary information on his needs, financial situation and preferences in accordance with Article 20; and

(b) in good time before the consumer is bound by any credit agreement or offer.
(2) The personalised information referred to in paragraph (1), on paper or on another durable medium, shall be provided by means of the ESIS, as set out in Annex II.
(3) Member States shall ensure that when an offer binding on the creditor is provided to the consumer, it shall be provided on paper or on another durable medium and accompanied by an ESIS where:
(a) no ESIS has been provided to the consumer previously; or
(b) the characteristics of the offer are different from the information contained in the ESIS previously provided.
(4) Member States may provide for the obligatory provision of the ESIS before the provision of an offer binding on the creditor. Where a Member State so provides, it shall require that the ESIS shall only be required to be provided again where point (b) of paragraph (3) is met.
(5) Member States which before 20 March 2014 have implemented an information sheet that meets equivalent information requirements to those set out in Annex II may continue to use it for the purposes of this Article until 21 March 2019.
(6) Member States shall specify a time period of at least seven days during which the consumer will have sufficient time to compare offers, assess their implications and make an informed decision. Member States shall specify that the time period referred to in the first subparagraph shall be either a reflection period before the conclusion of the credit agreement or a period for exercising a right of withdrawal after the conclusion of the credit agreement or a combination of the two.
Where a Member State specifies a reflection period before the conclusion of a credit agreement:
(a) the offer shall be binding on the creditor for the duration of the reflection period; and
(b) the consumer may accept the offer at any time during the reflection period.
Member States may provide that consumers cannot accept the offer for a period not exceeding the first 10 days of the reflection period.
Where the borrowing rate or other costs applicable to the offer are determined on the basis of the selling of underlying bonds or other long-term funding instruments, Member States may provide that the borrowing rate or other costs may vary from that stated in the offer in accordance with the value of the underlying bond or other long-term funding instrument.
Where the consumer has a right of withdrawal in accordance with the second subparagraph of this paragraph, Article 6 of Directive 2002/65/EC shall not apply.
(7) The creditor and, where applicable, the credit intermediary or appointed representative who has supplied the ESIS to the consumer shall be deemed to have fulfilled the requirements regarding information provision to the consumer prior to the conclusion of a distance contract as laid down in Article 3(1) of Directive 2002/65/EC and shall be deemed to satisfy the requirements of Article 5(1) of that Directive only where they have at least supplied the ESIS prior to the conclusion of the contract.
(8) Member States shall not modify the ESIS model other than as provided for in Annex II. Any additional information which the creditor or, where applicable, the credit intermediary or appointed representative, may provide to the consumer or is required to provide to the consumer by national law shall be given in a separate document which may be annexed to the ESIS.
(9) The Commission shall be empowered to adopt delegated acts in accordance with Article 40 to amend the standard wording in Part A of Annex II or the instructions in Part B thereof to address the need for information or warnings concerning new products that were not marketed before 20 March 2014. Such delegated acts shall however not change the structure or format of the ESIS.
(10) In the case of voice telephony communications, as referred to in Article 3(3) of Directive 2002/65/EC, the description of the main characteristics of the financial service to be provided pursuant to the second indent of point (b) of Article 3(3) of that Directive shall include at least the items referred to in sections 3 to 6 of Part A of Annex II to this Directive.
(11) Member States shall ensure that at least where no right of withdrawal exists the creditor or, where applicable, the credit intermediary or appointed representative provides the consumer with a copy of the draft credit agreement, at the time of the provision of an offer binding on the creditor. Where a right of withdrawal exists, Member States shall ensure that the creditor or, where applicable, the credit intermediary or appointed representative offers to provide the consumer with a copy of the draft credit agreement at the time of the provision of an offer binding on the creditor.

Article 15. (1) Member States shall ensure that in good time before the carrying out of any of the credit intermediation activities set out in point 5 of Article 4, the credit intermediary or appointed representative shall provide the consumer with at least the following information on paper or on another durable medium:

(a) the identity and the geographical address of the credit intermediary;
(b) the register in which he has been included, the registration number, where applicable, and the means for verifying such registration;
(c) whether the credit intermediary is tied to or works exclusively for one or more creditors. Where the credit intermediary is tied to or works exclusively for one or more creditors, it shall provide the names of the creditors for which it is acting. The credit intermediary may disclose that it is independent where it meets the conditions laid down in accordance with Article 22(4);
(d) whether the credit intermediary offers advisory services;
(e) the fee, where applicable, payable by the consumer to the credit intermediary for its services or where this is not possible, the method for calculating the fee;
(f) the procedures allowing consumers or other interested parties to register complaints internally about credit intermediaries and, where appropriate, the means by which recourse to out-of-court complaint and redress procedures can be sought;
(g) where applicable, the existence and where known the amount of commissions or other inducements, payable by the creditor or third parties to the credit intermediary for their services in relation to the credit agreement. Where the amount is not known at the time of disclosure the credit intermediary shall inform the consumer that the actual amount will be disclosed at a later stage in the ESIS.
(2) Credit intermediaries who are not tied but who receive commission from one or more creditors shall, at the consumer's request, provide information on the variation in levels of commission payable by the different creditors providing the credit agreements being offered to the consumer. The consumer shall be informed that he has the right to request such information.
(3) Where the credit intermediary charges a fee to the consumer and additionally receives commission from the creditor or a third party, the credit intermediary shall explain to the consumer whether or not the commission will be offset against the fee, either in part or in full.
(4) Member States shall ensure that the fee, if any, payable by the consumer to the credit intermediary for its services is communicated to the creditor by the credit intermediary, for the purpose of calculating of the APRC.
(5) Member States shall require credit intermediaries to ensure that in addition to the disclosures required by this Article, their appointed representative discloses to the consumer the capacity in which he is acting and the credit intermediary he is representing when contacting or before dealing with any consumer.

Article 16. (1) Member States shall ensure that creditors and, where applicable, credit intermediaries or appointed representatives provide adequate explanations to the consumer on the proposed credit agreements and any ancillary services, in order to place the consumer in a position enabling him to assess whether the proposed credit agreements and ancillary services are adapted to his needs and financial situation.
The explanations shall, where applicable, include in particular:
(a) the pre-contractual information to be provided in accordance with:
(i) Article 14 in the case of creditors;
(ii) Articles 14 and 15 in the case of credit intermediaries or appointed representatives;
(b) the essential characteristics of the products proposed;
(c) the specific effects the products proposed may have on the consumer, including the consequences of default in payment by the consumer; and
(d) where ancillary services are bundled with a credit agreement, whether each component of the bundle can be terminated separately and the implications for the consumer of doing so.
(2) Member States may adapt the manner by which and the extent to which the explanations referred to in paragraph (1) is given, as well as by whom it is given, to the circumstances of the situation in which the credit agreement is offered, the person to whom it is offered and the nature of the credit offered.

Chapter 5. Annual Percentage Rate of Charge

Article 17. (1) The APRC shall be calculated in accordance with the mathematical formula set out in Annex I.
(2) The costs of opening and maintaining a specific account, of using a means of payment for both transactions and drawdowns on that account and of other costs relating to payment transactions shall be included in the total cost of credit to the consumer whenever the opening or maintaining of an account is obligatory in order to obtain the credit or to obtain it on the terms and conditions marketed.
(3) The calculation of the APRC shall be based on the assumption that the credit agreement is to remain valid for the period agreed and that the creditor and the consumer will fulfil their obligations

under the terms and by the dates specified in the credit agreement.

(4) In the case of credit agreements containing clauses allowing variations in the borrowing rate and, where applicable, in the charges contained in the APRC but unquantifiable at the time of calculation, the APRC shall be calculated on the assumption that the borrowing rate and other charges will remain fixed in relation to the level set at the conclusion of the contract.

(5) For credit agreements for which a fixed borrowing rate is agreed in relation to the initial period of at least five years, at the end of which a negotiation on the borrowing rate takes place to agree on a new fixed rate for a further material period, the calculation of the additional, illustrative APRC disclosed in the ESIS shall cover only the initial fixed rate period and shall be based on the assumption that, at the end of the fixed borrowing rate period, the capital outstanding is repaid.

(6) Where the credit agreement allows for variations in the borrowing rate, Member States shall ensure that the consumer is informed of the possible impacts of variations on the amounts payable and on the APRC at least by means of the ESIS. This shall be done by providing the consumer with an additional APRC which illustrates the possible risks linked to a significant increase in the borrowing rate. Where the borrowing rate is not capped, this information shall be accompanied by a warning highlighting that the total cost of the credit to the consumer, shown by the APRC, may change. This provision shall not apply to credit agreements where the borrowing rate is fixed for an initial period of at least five years, at the end of which a negotiation on the borrowing rate takes place in order to agree on a new fixed rate for a further material period, for which an additional, illustrative APRC is provided for in the ESIS.

(7) Where applicable, the additional assumptions set out in Annex I shall be used in calculating the APRC.

(8) The Commission shall be empowered to adopt delegated acts in accordance with Article 40 in order to amend the remarks or update the assumptions used to calculate the APRC as set out in Annex I, in particular if the remarks or assumptions set out in this Article and in Annex I do not suffice to calculate the APRC in a uniform manner or are no longer adapted to the commercial situation on the market.

Chapter 6. Creditworthiness Assessment

Article 18. (1) Member States shall ensure that, before concluding a credit agreement, the creditor makes a thorough assessment of the consumer's creditworthiness. That assessment shall take appropriate account of factors relevant to verifying the prospect of the consumer to meet his obligations under the credit agreement.

(2) Member States shall ensure that the procedures and information on which the assessment is based are established, documented and maintained.

(3) The assessment of creditworthiness shall not rely predominantly on the value of the residential immovable property exceeding the amount of the credit or the assumption that the residential immovable property will increase in value unless the purpose of the credit agreement is to construct or renovate the residential immovable property.

(4) Member States shall ensure that where a creditor concludes a credit agreement with a consumer the creditor shall not subsequently cancel or alter the credit agreement to the detriment of the consumer on the grounds that the assessment of creditworthiness was incorrectly conducted. This paragraph shall not apply where it is demonstrated that the consumer knowingly withheld or falsified the information within the meaning of Article 20.

(5) Member States shall ensure that:

(a) the creditor only makes the credit available to the consumer where the result of the creditworthiness assessment indicates that the obligations resulting from the credit agreement are likely to be met in the manner required under that agreement;

(b) in accordance with Article 10 of Directive 95/46/EC, the creditor informs the consumer in advance that a database is to be consulted;

(c) where the credit application is rejected the creditor informs the consumer without delay of the rejection and, where applicable, that the decision is based on automated processing of data. Where the rejection is based on the result of the database consultation, the creditor shall inform the consumer of the result of such consultation and of the particulars of the database consulted.

(6) Member States shall ensure that the consumer's creditworthiness is re-assessed on the basis of updated information before any significant increase in the total amount of credit is granted after the conclusion of the credit agreement unless such additional credit was envisaged and included in the original creditworthiness assessment.

(7) This Article shall be without prejudice to Directive 95/46/EC.

Article 19. (1) Member States shall ensure that reliable standards for the valuation of residential immovable property for mortgage lending purposes are developed within their territory. Member States shall require creditors to ensure that those standards are used where they carry out a property valuation or to take reasonable steps to ensure that those standards are applied where a valuation is conducted by a third party. Where national authorities are responsible for regulating independent appraisers who carry out property valuations they shall ensure that they comply with the national rules that are in place.

(2) Member States shall ensure that internal and external appraisers conducting property valuations are professionally competent and sufficiently independent from the credit underwriting process so that they can provide an impartial and objective valuation, which shall be documented in a durable medium and of which a record shall be kept by the creditor.

Article 20. (1) The assessment of creditworthiness referred to in Article 18 shall be carried out on the basis of information on the consumer's income and expenses and other financial and economic circumstances which is necessary, sufficient and proportionate. The information shall be obtained by the creditor from relevant internal or external sources, including the consumer, and including information provided to the credit intermediary or appointed representative during the credit application process. The information shall be appropriately verified, including through reference to independently verifiable documentation when necessary.

(2) Member States shall ensure that credit intermediaries or appointed representatives accurately submit the necessary information obtained from the consumer to the relevant creditor to enable the creditworthiness assessment to be carried out.

(3) Member States shall ensure that creditors specify in a clear and straightforward way at the pre-contractual phase the necessary information and independently verifiable evidence that the consumer needs to provide and the timeframe within which the consumer needs to provide the information. Such request for information shall be proportionate and limited to what is necessary to conduct a proper creditworthiness assessment. Member States shall allow creditors to seek clarification of the information received in response to that request where necessary to enable the assessment of creditworthiness.

Member States shall not allow a creditor to terminate the credit agreement on the grounds that the information provided by the consumer before the conclusion of the credit agreement was incomplete. The second subparagraph shall not prevent Member States from allowing the termination of the credit agreement by the creditor where it is demonstrated that the consumer knowingly withheld or falsified the information.

(4) Member States shall have measures in place to ensure that consumers are aware of the need to provide correct information in response to the request referred to in the first subparagraph of paragraph (3) and that such information is as complete as necessary to conduct a proper creditworthiness assessment. The creditor, credit intermediary or appointed representative shall warn the consumer that, where the creditor is unable to carry out an assessment of creditworthiness because the consumer chooses not to provide the information or verification necessary for an assessment of creditworthiness, the credit cannot be granted. That warning may be provided in a standardised format.

(5) This Article shall be without prejudice to Directive 95/46/EC, in particular Article 6 thereof.

Chapter 7. Database Access

Article 21. (1) Each Member State shall ensure access for all creditors from all Member States to databases used in that Member State for assessing the creditworthiness of consumers and for the sole purpose of monitoring consumers' compliance with the credit obligations over the life of the credit agreement. The conditions for such access shall be non-discriminatory.

(2) Paragraph 1 shall apply both to databases which are operated by private credit bureau or credit reference agencies and to public registers.

(3) This Article shall be without prejudice to Directive 95/46/EC.

Chapter 8. Advisory Services

Article 22. (1) Member States shall ensure that the creditor, credit intermediary or appointed representative explicitly informs the consumer, in the context of a given transaction, whether advisory services are being or can be provided to the consumer.

(2) Member States shall ensure that before the provision of advisory services or, where applicable, the conclusion of a contract for the provision of advisory services, the creditor, credit intermediary or appointed representative provides the consumer with the following information on paper or another durable medium:

(a) whether the recommendation will be based on considering only their own product range in accordance with point (b) of paragraph (3) or a wide range of products from across the market in accordance with point (c) of paragraph (3) so that the consumer can understand the basis on which the recommendation is made;
(b) where applicable, the fee payable by the consumer for the advisory services or, where the amount cannot be ascertained at the time of disclosure, the method used for its calculation.
The information referred to in points (a) and (b) of the first subparagraph may be provided to the consumer in the form of additional pre-contractual information.
(3) Where advisory services are provided to consumers, Member States shall ensure, in addition to the requirements set out in Articles 7 and 9, that:
(a) creditors, credit intermediaries or appointed representatives obtain the necessary information regarding the consumer's personal and financial situation, his preferences and objectives so as to enable the recommendation of suitable credit agreements. Such an assessment shall be based on information that is up to date at that moment in time and shall take into account reasonable assumptions as to risks to the consumer's situation over the term of the proposed credit agreement;
(b) creditors, tied credit intermediaries or appointed representatives of tied credit intermediaries consider a sufficiently large number of credit agreements in their product range and recommend a suitable credit agreements or several suitable credit agreements from among their product range for the consumer's needs, financial situation and personal circumstances;
(c) non-tied credit intermediaries or appointed representatives of non-tied credit intermediaries consider a sufficiently large number of credit agreements available on the market and recommend a suitable credit agreement or several suitable credit agreements available on the market for the consumer's needs, financial situation and personal circumstances;
(d) creditors, credit intermediaries or appointed representatives act in the best interests of the consumer by:
(i) informing themselves about the consumer's needs and circumstances; and
(ii) recommending suitable credit agreements in accordance with points (a), (b) and (c); and
(e) creditors, credit intermediaries or appointed representatives give the consumer a record on paper or on another durable medium of the recommendation provided.
(4) Member States may prohibit the use of the term 'advice' and 'advisor' or similar terms when the advisory services are being provided to consumers by creditors, tied credit intermediaries or appointed representatives of tied credit intermediaries.
Where Member States do not prohibit the use of the term 'advice' and 'advisor', they shall impose the following conditions on the use of the term 'independent advice' or 'independent advisor' by creditors, credit intermediaries or appointed representatives providing advisory services:
(a) creditors, credit intermediaries or appointed representatives shall consider a sufficiently large number of credit agreements available on the market; and
(b) creditors, credit intermediaries or appointed representatives shall not be remunerated for those advisory services by one or more creditors.
Point (b) of the second subparagraph shall apply only where the number of creditors considered is less than a majority of the market.
Member States may impose more stringent requirements in relation to the use of the terms 'independent advice' or 'independent advisor' by creditors, credit intermediaries or appointed representatives, including a ban on receiving remuneration from a creditor.
(5) Member States may provide for an obligation for creditors, credit intermediaries and appointed representatives to warn a consumer when, considering the consumer's financial situation, a credit agreement may induce a specific risk for the consumer.
(6) Member States shall ensure that advisory services are only provided by creditors, credit intermediaries or appointed representatives.
Member States may decide not to apply the first subparagraph to persons:
(a) carrying out the credit intermediation activities set out in point 5 of Article 4 or providing advisory services where those activities are carried out or services are provided in an incidental manner in the course of a professional activity and that activity is regulated by legal or regulatory provisions or a code of ethics governing the profession which do not exclude carrying out of those activities or the provision of those services;
(b) providing advisory services in the context of managing existing debt which are insolvency practitioners where that activity is regulated by legal or regulatory provisions or public or voluntary debt advisory services which do not operate on a commercial basis; or
(c) providing advisory services who are not creditors, credit intermediaries or appointed representatives where such persons are admitted and supervised by competent authorities in accordance with

the requirements for credit intermediaries under this Directive.
Persons benefiting from the waiver in the second subparagraph shall not benefit from the right referred to in Article 32(1) to provide services for the entire territory of the Union.
(7) This Article shall be without prejudice to Article 16 and to Member States' competence to ensure that services are made available to consumers to help them understand their financial needs and which types of products are likely to meet those needs.

Chapter 9. Foreign Currency Loans and Variable Rate Loans

Article 23. (1) Member States shall ensure that, where a credit agreement relates to a foreign currency loan, an appropriate regulatory framework is in place at the time the credit agreement is concluded to at least ensure that:
(a) the consumer has a right to convert the credit agreement into an alternative currency under specified conditions; or
(b) there are other arrangements in place to limit the exchange rate risk to which the consumer is exposed under the credit agreement.
(2) The alternative currency referred to in point (a) of paragraph (1) shall be either:
(a) the currency in which the consumer primarily receives income or holds assets from which the credit is to be repaid, as indicated at the time the most recent creditworthiness assessment in relation to the credit agreement was made; or
(b) the currency of the Member State in which the consumer either was resident at the time the credit agreement was concluded or is currently resident.
Member States may specify whether both of the choices referred to in points (a) and (b) of the first subparagraph are available to the consumer or only one of them or may allow creditors to specify whether both of the choices referred to in points (a) and (b) of the first subparagraph are available to the consumer or only one of them.
(3) Where a consumer has a right to convert the credit agreement into an alternative currency in accordance with point (a) of paragraph (1), the Member States shall ensure that the exchange rate at which the conversion is carried out is the market exchange rate applicable on the day of application for conversion unless otherwise specified in the credit agreement.
(4) Member States shall ensure that where a consumer has a foreign currency loan, the creditor warns the consumer on a regular basis on paper or on another durable medium at least where the value of the total amount payable by the consumer which remains outstanding or of the regular instalments varies by more than 20 % from what it would be if the exchange rate between the currency of the credit agreement and the currency of the Member State applicable at the time of the conclusion of the credit agreement were applied. The warning shall inform the consumer of a rise in the total amount payable by the consumer, set out where applicable the right to convert to an alternative currency and the conditions for doing so and explain any other applicable mechanism for limiting the exchange rate risk to which the consumer is exposed.
(5) Member States may further regulate foreign currency loans provided that such regulation is not applied with retrospective effect.
(6) The arrangements applicable under this Article shall be disclosed to the consumer in the ESIS and in the credit agreement. Where there is no provision in the credit agreement to limit the exchange rate risk to which the consumer is exposed to a fluctuation in the exchange rate of less than 20 %, the ESIS shall include an illustrative example of the impact of a 20 % fluctuation in the exchange rate.

Article 24. Where the credit agreement is a variable rate credit, Member States shall ensure that:
(a) any indexes or reference rates used to calculate the borrowing rate are clear, accessible, objective and verifiable by the parties to the credit agreement and the competent authorities; and
(b) historical records of indexes for calculating the borrowing rates are maintained either by the providers of these indexes or the creditors.

Chapter 10. Sound Execution of Credit Agreements and Related Rights

Article 25. (1) Member States shall ensure that the consumer has a right to discharge fully or partially his obligations under a credit agreement prior to the expiry of that agreement. In such cases, the consumer shall be entitled to a reduction in the total cost of the credit to the consumer, such reduction consisting of the interest and the costs for the remaining duration of the contract.
(2) Member States may provide that the exercise of the right referred to in paragraph (1) is subject to certain conditions. Such conditions may include time limitations on the exercise of the right, a different treatment depending on the type of the borrowing rate or on the moment the consumer exercises the right, or restrictions with regard to the circumstances under which the right may be exercised.

(3) Member States may provide that the creditor is entitled to fair and objective compensation, where justified, for possible costs directly linked to the early repayment but shall not impose a sanction on the consumer. In that regard, the compensation shall not exceed the financial loss of the creditor. Subject to those conditions Member States may provide that the compensation may not exceed a certain level or be allowed only for a certain period of time.

(4) Where a consumer seeks to discharge his obligations under a credit agreement prior to the expiry of the agreement, the creditor shall provide the consumer without delay after receipt of the request, on paper or on another durable medium, with the information necessary to consider that option. That information shall at least quantify the implications for the consumer of discharging his obligations prior to the expiry of the credit agreement and clearly set out any assumptions used. Any assumptions used shall be reasonable and justifiable.

(5) Where the early repayment falls within a period for which the borrowing rate is fixed Member States may provide that the exercise of the right referred to in paragraph (1) is subject to the existence of a legitimate interest on the part of the consumer.

Article 26. (1) Member States shall have appropriate mechanisms in place to ensure that the claim against the security is enforceable by or on behalf of creditors. Member States shall ensure that creditors keep appropriate records concerning the types of immovable property accepted as a security as well as the related mortgage underwriting policies used.

(2) Member States shall take the necessary measures to ensure an appropriate statistical monitoring of the residential property market, including for market surveillance purposes, where appropriate by encouraging the development and use of specific price indexes which may be public or private or both.

Article 27. (1) Member States shall ensure that the creditor informs the consumer of any change in the borrowing rate, on paper or another durable medium, before the change takes effect. The information shall at least state the amount of the payments to be made after the new borrowing rate takes effect and, in cases where the number or frequency of the payments changes, particulars thereof.

(2) However, the Member States may allow the parties to agree in the credit agreement that the information referred to in paragraph (1) is to be given to the consumer periodically where the change in the borrowing rate is correlated with a change in a reference rate, the new reference rate is made publicly available by appropriate means and the information concerning the new reference rate is kept available in the premises of the creditor and communicated personally to the consumer together with the amount of new periodic instalments.

(3) Creditors may continue to inform consumers periodically where the change in the borrowing rate is not correlated with a change in a reference rate where this was allowed under national law before 20 March 2014.

(4) Where changes in the borrowing rate are determined by way of auction on the capital markets and it is therefore impossible for the creditor to inform the consumer of any change before the change takes effect, the creditor shall, in good time before the auction, inform the consumer on paper or on another durable medium of the upcoming procedure and provide an indication of how the borrowing rate could be affected.

Article 28. (1) Member States shall adopt measures to encourage creditors to exercise reasonable forbearance before foreclosure proceedings are initiated.

(2) Member States may require that, where the creditor is permitted to define and impose charges on the consumer arising from the default, those charges are no greater than is necessary to compensate the creditor for costs it has incurred as a result of the default.

(3) Member States may allow creditors to impose additional charges on the consumer in the event of default. In that case Member States shall place a cap on those charges.

(4) Member States shall not prevent the parties to a credit agreement from expressly agreeing that return or transfer to the creditor of the security or proceeds from the sale of the security is sufficient to repay the credit.

(5) Where the price obtained for the immovable property affects the amount owed by the consumer Member States shall have procedures or measures to enable the best efforts price for the foreclosed immovable property to be obtained.

Where after foreclosure proceedings outstanding debt remains, Member States shall ensure that measures to facilitate repayment in order to protect consumers are put in place.

Chapter 11. Requirements for Establishment and Supervision of Credit Intermediaries and Appointed Representatives

Article 29. (1) Credit intermediaries shall be duly admitted to carry out all or part of the credit intermediation activities set out in point 5 of Article 4 or to provide advisory services by a competent authority in their home Member State. Where a Member State allows appointed representatives under Article 31, such an appointed representative shall not need to be admitted as a credit intermediary under this Article.

(2) Member States shall ensure that the admission of credit intermediaries is made subject to fulfilment of at least the following professional requirements in addition to the requirements provided for in Article 9:

(a) Credit intermediaries shall hold professional indemnity insurance covering the territories in which they offer services, or some other comparable guarantee against liability arising from professional negligence. However, for tied credit intermediaries, the home Member State may provide that such insurance or comparable guarantee can be provided by a creditor for which the credit intermediary is empowered to act.

Powers are delegated to the Commission to adopt and, where necessary amend, regulatory technical standards to stipulate the minimum monetary amount of the professional indemnity insurance or comparable guarantee referred to in the first paragraph of this point. Those regulatory technical standards shall be adopted in accordance with Articles 10 to 14 of Regulation (EU) No 1093/2010. EBA shall develop draft regulatory technical standards to stipulate the minimum monetary amount of the professional indemnity insurance or comparable guarantee referred to in the first paragraph of this point for submission to the Commission by 21 September 2014. EBA shall review, and if necessary, develop draft regulatory technical standards to amend the minimum monetary amount of the professional indemnity insurance or comparable guarantee referred to in the first paragraph of this point for submission to the Commission for the first time by 21 March 2018 and every two years thereafter.

(b) A natural person established as a credit intermediary, the members of the board of a credit intermediary established as a legal person and natural persons performing equivalent tasks within a credit intermediary which is a legal person but does not have a board shall be of good repute. As a minimum they shall have a clean police record or any other national equivalent in relation to serious criminal offences linked to crimes against property or other crimes related to financial activities and they shall not have previously been declared bankrupt, unless they have been rehabilitated in accordance with national law.

(c) A natural person established as a credit intermediary, the members of the board of a credit intermediary established as a legal person and natural persons performing equivalent tasks within a credit intermediary which is a legal person but does not have a board shall possess the appropriate level of knowledge and competence in relation to credit agreements. The home Member State shall establish the appropriate level of knowledge and competence in accordance with the principles set out in Annex III.

(3) Member States shall ensure that the criteria established in order for credit intermediaries' or creditors' staff to meet their professional requirements are made public.

(4) Member States shall ensure that all admitted credit intermediaries, whether established as natural or legal persons, are entered into a register with a competent authority in their home Member State. Member States shall ensure that the register of credit intermediaries is kept up to date and is publicly available online.

The register of credit intermediaries shall contain at least the following information:

(a) the names of the persons within the management who are responsible for the intermediation business. Member States may require the registration of all natural persons who exercise a client-facing function in an undertaking that pursues the activity of credit intermediation;

(b) the Member States in which the credit intermediary conducts business under the rules on the freedom of establishment or on the freedom to provide services and of which the credit intermediary has informed the competent authority of the home Member State in accordance with Article 32(3);

(c) whether the credit intermediary is tied or not.

Member States that decide to avail themselves of the option referred to in Article 30 shall ensure that the register indicates the creditor on whose behalf the tied credit intermediary acts.

Member States that decide to avail themselves of the option referred to in Article 31 shall ensure that the register indicates the credit intermediary or in the case of an appointed representative of a tied credit intermediary, the creditor on whose behalf the appointed representatives acts.

(5) Member States shall ensure that:

(a) any credit intermediary which is a legal person has its head office in the same Member State as its registered office if under its national law it has a registered office;

(b) any credit intermediary which is not a legal person or any credit intermediary which is a legal person but under its national law has no registered office has its head office in the Member State in which it actually carries on its main business.

(6) Each Member State shall establish a single information point to allow quick and easy public access to information from the national register, which shall be compiled electronically and kept constantly updated. These information points shall provide the identification details of the competent authorities of each Member State.
EBA shall publish on its website references or hyperlinks to that information point.
(7) Home Member States shall ensure that all admitted credit intermediaries and appointed representatives comply with the requirements defined in paragraph (2) on a continuing basis. This paragraph shall be without prejudice to Articles 30 and 31.
(8) Member States may decide not to apply this Article to persons carrying out the credit intermediation activities set out in point 5 of Article 4 where those activities are carried out in an incidental manner in the course of a professional activity and that activity is regulated by legal or regulatory provisions or a code of ethics governing the profession which do not exclude the carrying out of those activities.
(9) This Article shall not apply to credit institutions authorised in accordance with Directive 2013/36/EU or to other financial institutions which under national law are subject to an equivalent authorisation and supervision regime.

Article 30. (1) Without prejudice to Article 31(1), Member States may allow tied credit intermediaries specified in point (a) of point 7 of Article 4 to be admitted by competent authorities through the creditor on whose behalf the tied credit intermediary is exclusively acting.
In such cases, the creditor shall remain fully and unconditionally responsible for any action or omission on the part of the tied credit intermediary that is acting on behalf of the creditor in areas regulated by this Directive. Member States shall require the creditor to ensure that those tied credit intermediaries comply with at least the professional requirements set out in Article 29(2).
(2) Without prejudice to Article 34, creditors shall monitor the activities of tied credit intermediaries specified in point (a) of point 7 of Article 4 in order to ensure that they continue to comply with this Directive. In particular, the creditor shall be responsible for monitoring compliance with the knowledge and competence requirements of the tied credit intermediary and its staff.

Article 31. (1) Member States may decide to allow a credit intermediary to appoint appointed representatives.
Where the appointed representative is appointed by a tied credit intermediary specified in point (a) of point 7 of Article 4, the creditor shall remain fully and unconditionally responsible for any action or omission on the part of the appointed representative that is acting on behalf of that tied credit intermediary in areas regulated by this Directive. In other cases the credit intermediary shall remain fully and unconditionally responsible for any action or omission on the part of the appointed representative acting on behalf of the credit intermediary in areas regulated by this Directive.
(2) The credit intermediaries shall ensure that their appointed representatives comply at least with the professional requirements set out in Article 29(2). However, the home Member State may provide that the professional indemnity insurance or a comparable guarantee can be provided by a credit intermediary for which the appointed representative is empowered to act.
(3) Without prejudice to Article 34, credit intermediaries shall monitor the activities of their appointed representatives in order to ensure full compliance with this Directive. In particular, the credit intermediaries shall be responsible for monitoring compliance with the knowledge and competence requirements of the appointed representatives and their staff.
(4) Member States that decide to allow a credit intermediary to appoint appointed representatives shall establish a public register containing at least the information referred to in Article 29(4). Appointed representatives shall be registered in the public register in the Member State where they are established. The register shall be updated on a regular basis. It shall be publicly available for consultation online.

Article 32. (1) The admission of a credit intermediary by the competent authority of its home Member State as laid down in Article 29(1) shall be effective for the entire territory of the Union without further admission by the competent authorities of the host Member States being required for the carrying out of the activities and provision of services covered by the admission, provided that the activities a credit intermediary intends to carry out in the host Member States are covered by the admission. However, credit intermediaries shall not be allowed to provide their services in relation to credit agreements offered by non-credit institutions to consumers in a Member State where such non-credit institutions are not allowed to operate.
(2) Appointed representatives appointed in Member States which avail themselves of the option under Article 31 are not allowed to carry out part or all of the credit intermediation activities set out

in point 5 of Article 4 or to provide advisory services in Member States where such appointed representatives are not allowed to operate.
(3) Any admitted credit intermediary intending to carry out business for the first time in one or more Member States under the freedom to provide services or when establishing a branch shall inform the competent authorities of its home Member State.
Within a period of one month after being informed, those competent authorities shall notify the competent authorities of the host Member States concerned of the intention of the credit intermediary and shall at the same time inform the credit intermediary concerned of that notification. They shall notify the competent authorities of the host Member States concerned of the creditors to which the credit intermediary is tied and whether the creditors take full and unconditional responsibility for the credit intermediary's activities. The host Member State shall use the information received from the home Member State to enter the necessary information into its register.
The credit intermediary may start business one month after the date on which he was informed by the competent authorities of the home Member State of the notification referred to in the second subparagraph.
(4) Before the branch of a credit intermediary commences its activities or within two months of receiving the notification referred to in the second subparagraph of paragraph (3), the competent authorities of the host Member State shall prepare for the supervision of the credit intermediary in accordance with Article 34 and, if necessary, indicate to the credit intermediary the conditions under which, in areas not harmonised in Union law, those activities are to be carried out in the host Member State.

Article 33. (1) The competent authority of the home Member State may withdraw the admission granted to a credit intermediary in accordance with Article 29 where such a credit intermediary:
(a) expressly renounces the admission or has carried out neither credit intermediation activities set out in point 5 of Article 4 nor provided advisory services for the preceding six months, unless the Member State concerned has provided for admission to lapse in such cases;
(b) has obtained the admission through false or misleading statements or any other irregular means;
(c) no longer fulfils the requirements under which admission was granted;
(d) falls within any of the cases where national law, in respect of matters outside the scope of this Directive, provides for withdrawal;
(e) has seriously or systematically infringed the provisions adopted pursuant to this Directive governing the operating conditions for credit intermediaries.
(2) Where the admission of a credit intermediary is withdrawn by the competent authority of the home Member State, the latter shall notify the competent authorities of the host Member States of such withdrawal as soon as possible and at the latest within 14 days, by any appropriate means.
(3) Member States shall ensure that credit intermediaries whose admission has been withdrawn are deleted from the register without undue delay.

Article 34. (1) Member States shall ensure that credit intermediaries are subject to supervision of their ongoing activities by the competent authorities of the home Member State.
Home Member States shall provide that tied credit intermediaries are to be subject to supervision directly or as part of the supervision of the creditor on behalf of which they act if the creditor is a credit institution authorised in accordance with Directive 2013/36/EU or another financial institution which under national law is subject to an equivalent authorisation and supervision regime. However, if the tied credit intermediary provides services in a Member State other than the home Member State, then the tied credit intermediary shall be subject to supervision directly.
Home Member States which allow credit intermediaries to appoint representatives in accordance with Article 31 shall ensure that such appointed representatives are subject to supervision either directly or as part of the supervision of the credit intermediary on behalf of which it acts.
(2) The competent authorities of the Member States in which a credit intermediary has a branch shall be responsible for ensuring that the services provided by the credit intermediary within its territory comply with the obligations laid down in Article 7(1) and Articles 8, 9, 10, 11, 13, 14, 15, 16, 17, 20, 22 and 39 and in measures adopted pursuant thereto.
Where the competent authorities of a host Member State ascertain that a credit intermediary that has a branch within its territory is in breach of the measures adopted in that Member State pursuant to Article 7(1) and Articles 8, 9, 10, 11, 13, 14, 15, 16, 17, 20, 22 and 39, those authorities shall require the credit intermediary concerned to put an end to its irregular situation.
If the credit intermediary concerned fails to take the necessary steps, the competent authorities of the host Member State shall take all appropriate action to ensure that the credit intermediary concerned puts an end to its irregular situation. The nature of that action shall be communicated to the compe-

tent authorities of the home Member State.

If, despite the action taken by the host Member State, the credit intermediary persists in breaching the measures referred to in the first subparagraph in force in the host Member State, the host Member State may, after informing the competent authorities of the home Member State, take appropriate action to prevent or to penalise further irregularities and, in so far as necessary, to prevent the credit intermediary from initiating any further transactions within its territory. The Commission shall be informed of any such action without undue delay.

Where the competent authority of the home Member State disagrees with such action taken by the host Member State, it may refer the matter to EBA and request its assistance in accordance with Article 19 of Regulation (EU) No 1093/2010. In that case, EBA may act in accordance with the powers conferred on it by that Article.

(3) The competent authorities of the Member States in which the branch is located shall have the right to examine branch arrangements and to request such changes as are strictly needed to fulfil its responsibilities under paragraph (2) and to enable the competent authorities of the home Member State to enforce the obligations under Article 7(2), (3) and (4) and measures adopted pursuant thereto with respect to the services provided by the branch.

(4) Where the competent authority of the host Member State has clear and demonstrable grounds for concluding that a credit intermediary acting within its territory under the freedom to provide services is in breach of the obligations arising from the measures adopted pursuant to this Directive or that a credit intermediary that has a branch within its territory is in breach of the obligations arising from the measures adopted pursuant to this Directive, other than those specified in paragraph (2), it shall refer those findings to the competent authority of the home Member State which shall take the appropriate action.

Where the competent authority of the home Member State fails to take any action within one month from obtaining those findings or where, despite the action taken by the competent authority of the home Member State, a credit intermediary persists in acting in a manner that is clearly prejudicial to the interests of the host Member State consumers or orderly functioning of the markets, the competent authority of the host Member State:

(a) shall, after having informed the competent authority of the home Member State, take all appropriate action needed to protect consumers and ensure the proper functioning of the markets, including by preventing the offending credit intermediary from initiating any further transactions within its territory. The Commission and EBA shall be informed of such action without undue delay;

(b) may refer the matter to EBA and request its assistance in accordance with Article 19 of Regulation (EU) No 1093/2010. In that case EBA may act in accordance with the powers conferred on it by that Article.

(5) Member States shall provide that, where a credit intermediary admitted in another Member State has established a branch within its territory, the competent authorities of the home Member State, in the exercise of their responsibilities and after having informed the competent authorities of the host Member State, may carry out on-site inspections in that branch.

(6) The allocation of tasks between Member States specified in this Article shall be without prejudice to the Member States' competences in relation to fields not covered by this Directive in conformity with their obligations under Union law.

Chapter 12. Admission and Supervision of Non-Credit Institutions

Article 35. Member States shall ensure that non-credit institutions are subject to adequate admission process including entering the non-credit institution in a register and supervision arrangements by a competent authority.

Chapter 13. Cooperation between Competent Authorities of Different Member States

Article 36. (1) Competent authorities of different Member States shall cooperate with each other whenever necessary for the purpose of carrying out their duties under this Directive, making use of their powers, whether set out in this Directive or in national law.

Competent authorities shall render assistance to competent authorities of the other Member States. In particular, they shall exchange information and cooperate in any investigation or supervisory activities.

In order to facilitate and accelerate cooperation, and more particularly the exchange of information, Member States shall designate one single competent authority as a contact point for the purposes of this Directive. Member States shall communicate to the Commission and to the other Member States the names of the authorities which are designated to receive requests for exchange of information or cooperation pursuant to this paragraph.

(2) Member States shall take the necessary administrative and organisational measures to facilitate assistance provided for in paragraph (1).
(3) Competent authorities of Member States having been designated as contact points for the purposes of this Directive in accordance with paragraph (1) shall without undue delay supply one another with the information required for the purposes of carrying out the duties of the competent authorities, designated in accordance with Article 5, set out in the measures adopted pursuant to this Directive.
Competent authorities exchanging information with other competent authorities under this Directive may indicate at the time of communication that such information must not be disclosed without their express agreement, in which case such information may be exchanged solely for the purposes for which those authorities gave their agreement.
The competent authority having been designated as the contact point may transmit the information received to the other competent authorities, however it shall not transmit the information to other bodies or natural or legal persons without the express agreement of the competent authorities which disclosed it and solely for the purposes for which those authorities gave their agreement, except in duly justified circumstances in which case it shall immediately inform the contact point that supplied the information.
(4) A competent authority may refuse to act on a request for cooperation in carrying out an investigation or supervisory activity or to exchange information as provided for in paragraph (3) only where:
(a) such an investigation, on-the-spot verification, supervisory activity or exchange of information might adversely affect the sovereignty, security or public policy of the Member State addressed;
(b) judicial proceedings have already been initiated in respect of the same actions and the same persons before the authorities of the Member State addressed;
(c) final judgement has already been delivered in the Member State addressed in respect of the same persons and the same actions.
In the event of such a refusal, the competent authority shall notify the requesting competent authority accordingly, providing as detailed information as possible.

Article 37. The competent authorities may refer the situation to EBA where a request for cooperation, in particular the exchange of information, has been rejected or has not been acted upon within a reasonable time, and request EBA's assistance in accordance with Article 19 of Regulation (EU) No 1093/2010. In such cases, EBA may act in accordance with the powers conferred on it by that Article and any binding decision made by EBA in accordance with that Article shall be binding on the competent authorities concerned regardless of whether those competent authorities are members of EBA or not.

Chapter 14. Final Provisions

Article 38. (1) Member States shall lay down the rules on sanctions applicable to infringements of the national provisions adopted on the basis of this Directive and shall take all measures necessary to ensure that they are implemented. Those sanctions shall be effective, proportionate and dissuasive.
(2) Member States shall provide that the competent authority may disclose to the public any administrative sanction that will be imposed for infringement of the measures adopted in the transposition of this Directive, unless such disclosure would seriously jeopardise the financial markets or cause disproportionate damage to the parties involved.

Article 39. (1) Member States shall ensure that appropriate and effective complaints and redress procedures are established for the out-of-court settlement of consumer disputes with creditors, credit intermediaries and appointed representatives in relation to credit agreements, using existing bodies where appropriate. Member States shall ensure that such procedures are applicable to creditors and credit intermediaries and cover the activities of appointed representatives.
(2) Member States shall require the bodies responsible for the out-of-court settlement of consumer disputes to cooperate so that cross-border disputes concerning credit agreements can be resolved.

Article 40. (1) The power to adopt delegated acts is conferred on the Commission subject to the conditions laid down in this Article.
(2) The power to adopt delegated acts referred to in Articles 14(9) and 17(8) shall be conferred on the Commission for an indeterminate period of time from 20 March 2014.
(3) The delegation of power referred to in Articles 14(9) and 17(8) may be revoked at any time by the European Parliament or by the Council. A decision to revoke shall put an end to the delegation of the powers specified in that decision. It shall take effect the day following the publication of the decision in the Official Journal of the European Union or at a later date specified therein. It shall not affect the

validity of any delegated acts already in force.

(4) As soon as it adopts a delegated act, the Commission shall notify it simultaneously to the European Parliament and to the Council.

(5) A delegated act adopted pursuant to Articles 14(9) and 17(8) shall enter into force only if no objection has been expressed either by the European Parliament or the Council within a period of three months of notification of that act to the European Parliament and to the Council or if, before the expiry of that period, the European Parliament and the Council have both informed the Commission that they will not object. That period shall be extended by three months at the initiative of the European Parliament or of the Council.

Article 41. Member States shall ensure that:
(a) consumers may not waive the rights conferred on them by national law transposing this Directive;
(b) the measures they adopt in transposing this Directive cannot be circumvented in a way which could lead to consumers losing the protection granted by this Directive as a result of the way in which agreements are formulated, in particular by integrating credit agreements falling within the scope of this Directive into credit agreements the character or purpose of which would make it possible to avoid the application of those measures.

Article 42. (1) Member States shall adopt and publish, by 21 March 2016, the laws, regulations and administrative provisions necessary to comply with this Directive. They shall forthwith communicate to the Commission the text of those measures.

(2) Member States shall apply measures referred to in paragraph (1) from 21 March 2016.
When Member States adopt those measures, they shall contain a reference to this Directive or be accompanied by such a reference on the occasion of their official publication. Member States shall determine how such reference is to be made.

(3) Member States shall communicate to the Commission the text of the main provisions of national law which they adopt in the field covered by this Directive.

Article 43. (1) This Directive shall not apply to credit agreements existing before 21 March 2016.
(2) Credit intermediaries already carrying out credit intermediation activities set out in point 5 of Article 4 before 21 March 2016 and which have not yet been admitted in accordance with the conditions set out in the national law of the home Member State transposing this Directive may continue to carry out those activities in compliance with national law until 21 March 2017. Where a credit intermediary relies on this derogation it may perform the activities only within their home Member State unless it also satisfies the necessary legal requirements of the host Member States.
(3) Creditors, credit intermediaries or appointed representatives performing activities regulated by this Directive before 20 March 2014 shall comply with the national law transposing Article 9 by 21 March 2017.

Article 44. The Commission shall undertake a review of this Directive by 21 March 2019. The review shall consider the effectiveness and appropriateness of the provisions on consumers and the internal market.
The review shall include the following:
(a) an assessment of the use and consumer understanding of and satisfaction with the ESIS;
(b) an analysis of other pre-contractual disclosures;
(c) an analysis of cross-border business by credit intermediaries and creditors;
(d) an analysis of the evolution of the market for non-credit institutions providing credit agreements relating to residential immovable property;
(e) an assessment on the need for further measures, including a passport for non-credit institutions providing credit agreements relating to residential immovable property;
(f) an examination of the need to introduce additional rights and obligations with regard to the post-contractual stage of credit agreements;
(g) an assessment of whether the scope of this Directive remains appropriate, taking account of its impact on other, substitutable forms of credit;
(h) an assessment of whether additional measures are necessary to ensure the traceability of credit agreements secured against residential immovable property;
(i) an assessment of the availability of data on trends in prices of residential immovable property and on the extent to which data are comparable;
(j) an assessment of whether it continues to be appropriate to apply Directive 2008/48/EC to unsecured credits the purpose of which is the renovation of a residential immovable property involving a total amount of credit above the maximum amount specified in point (c) of Article 2(2) of that Directive;

(k) an assessment of whether the arrangements for the publication of sanctions under Article 38(2) provide sufficient transparency;
(l) an assessment of the proportionality of warnings referred to in Articles 11(6) and 13(2) and the potential for further harmonisation of risk warnings.

Article 45. By 21 March 2019, the Commission shall submit a comprehensive report assessing the wider challenges of private over-indebtedness directly linked to credit activity. It will also examine the need for the supervision of credit registers and the possibility for the development of more flexible and reliable markets. That report shall be accompanied, where appropriate, by legislative proposals.

Article 46. In Article 2 of Directive 2008/48/EC, the following paragraph is inserted:
'2a. Notwithstanding point (c) of paragraph (2), this Directive shall apply to unsecured credit agreements the purpose of which is the renovation of a residential immovable property involving a total amount of credit above EUR 75000.'

Article 47. In Directive 2013/36/EU, the following Article is inserted:
'Article 54a
Articles 53 and 54 shall be without prejudice to the powers of investigation conferred on the European Parliament pursuant to Article 226 TFEU.'

Article 48. Regulation (EU) No 1093/2010 is amended as follows:
(1) The second subparagraph of Article 13(1) is replaced by the following:
'Where the Commission adopts a regulatory technical standard which is the same as the draft regulatory technical standard submitted by the Authority, the period during which the European Parliament and the Council may object shall be 1 month from the date of notification. At the initiative of the European Parliament or the Council that period shall be extended for an initial period of 1 month and shall be extendable for a further period of 1 month.'
(2) The second subparagraph of Article 17(2) is replaced by the following:
'Without prejudice to the powers laid down in Article 35, the competent authority shall, without delay, provide the Authority with all information which the Authority considers necessary for its investigation including as to how the acts referred to in Article 1(2) are applied in accordance with Union law.'

Article 49. This Directive shall enter into force on the twentieth day following that of its publication in the Official Journal of the European Union.

Article 50. This Directive is addressed to the Member States.

[The Annexes are omitted.]

PART IV EUROPEAN PRIVATE LAW

The Principles of European Contract Law [PECL]

Chapter 1. General Provisions

Section 1. Scope of the Principles

Article 1:101. (1) These Principles are intended to be applied as general rules of contract law in the European Communities.
(2) These Principles will apply when the parties have agreed to incorporate them into their contract or that their contract is to be governed by them.
(3) These Principles may be applied when the parties:
(a) have agreed that their contract is to be governed by "general principles of law", the "lex mercatoria" or the like; or
(b) have not chosen any system or rules of law to govern their contract.
(4) These Principles may provide a solution to the issue raised where the system or rules of law applicable do not do so.

Article 1:102. (1) Parties are free to enter into a contract and to determine its contents, subject to the requirements of good faith and fair dealing, and the mandatory rules established by these Principles.
(2) The parties may exclude the application of any of the Principles or derogate from or vary their effects, except as otherwise provided by these Principles.

Article 1:103. (1) Where the otherwise applicable law so allows, the parties may choose to have their contract governed by the Principles, with the effect that national mandatory rules are not applicable.
(2) Effect should nevertheless be given to those mandatory rules of national, supranational and international law which, according to the relevant rules of private international law, are applicable irrespective of the law governing the contract.

Article 1:104. (1) The existence and validity of the agreement of the parties to adopt or incorporate these Principles shall be determined by these Principles.
(2) Nevertheless, a party may rely upon the law of the country in which it has its habitual residence to establish that it did not consent if it appears from the circumstances that it would not be reasonable to determine the effect of its conduct in accordance with these Principles.

Article 1:105. (1) The parties are bound by any usage to which they have agreed and by any practice they have established between themselves.
(2) The parties are bound by a usage which would be considered generally applicable by persons in the same situation as the parties, except where the application of such usage would be unreasonable.

Article 1:106. (1) These Principles should be interpreted and developed in accordance with their purposes. In particular, regard should be had to the need to promote good faith and fair dealing, certainty in contractual relationships and uniformity of application.
(2) Issues within the scope of these Principles but not expressly settled by them are so far as possible to be settled in accordance with the ideas underlying the Principles. Failing this, the legal system applicable by virtue of the rules of private international law is to be applied.

Article 1:107. These Principles apply with appropriate modifications to agreements to modify or end a contract, to unilateral promises and other statements and conduct indicating intention.

Section 2. General Duties

Article 1:201. (1) Each party must act in accordance with good faith and fair dealing.
(2) The parties may not exclude or limit this duty.

Article 1:202. Each party owes to the other a duty to co-operate in order to give full effect to the contract.

Section 3: Terminology and Other Provisions

Article 1:301. In these Principles, except where the context otherwise requires:
(1) 'act' includes omission;
(2) 'court' includes arbitral tribunal;
(3) an 'intentional' act includes an act done recklessly;
(4) 'non-performance' denotes any failure to perform an obligation under the contract, whether or not excused, and includes delayed performance, defective performance and failure to co-operate in order to give full effect to the contract.

(5) A matter is 'material' if it is one which a reasonable person in the same situation as one party ought to have known would influence the other party in its decision whether to contract on the proposed terms or to contract at all.

(6) 'Written' statements include communications made by telegram, telex, telefax and electronic mail and other means of communication capable of providing a readable record of the statement on both sides.

Article 1:302. Under these Principles reasonableness is to be judged by what persons acting in good faith and in the same situation as the parties would consider to be reasonable. In particular, in assessing what is reasonable the nature and purpose of the contract, the circumstances of the case, and the usages and practices of the trades or professions involved should be taken into account.

Article 1:303. (1) Any notice may be given by any means, whether in writing or otherwise, appropriate to the circumstances.
(2) Subject to paragraphs (4) and (5), any notice becomes effective when it reaches the addressee.
(3) A notice reaches the addressee when it is delivered to it or to its place of business or mailing address, or, if it does not have a place of business or mailing address, to its habitual residence.
(4) If one party gives notice to the other because of the other's non-performance or because such non-performance is reasonably anticipated by the first party, and the notice is properly dispatched or given, a delay or inaccuracy in the transmission of the notice or its failure to arrive does not prevent it from having effect. The notice shall have effect from the time at which it would have arrived in normal circumstances.
(5) A notice has no effect if a withdrawal of it reaches the addressee before or at the same time as the notice.
(6) In this Article, 'notice' includes the communication of a promise, statement, offer, acceptance, demand, request or other declaration.

Article 1:304. (1) A period of time set by a party in a written document for the addressee to reply or take other action begins to run from the date stated as the date of the document. If no date is shown, the period begins to run from the moment the document reaches the addressee.
(2) Official holidays and official non-working days occurring during the period are included in calculating the period. However, if the last day of the period is an official holiday or official non-working day at the address of the addressee, or at the place where a prescribed act is to be performed, the period is extended until the first following working day in that place.
(3) Periods of time expressed in days, weeks, months or years shall begin at 00.00 on the next day and shall end at 24.00 on the last day of the period; but any reply that has to reach the party who set the period must arrive, or other act which is to be done must be completed, by the normal close of business in the relevant place on the last day of the period.

Article 1:305. If any person who with a party's assent was involved in making a contract, or who was entrusted with performance by a party or performed with its assent:
(a) knew or foresaw a fact, or ought to have known or foreseen it; or
(b) acted intentionally or with gross negligence, or not in accordance with good faith and fair dealing, this knowledge, foresight or behaviour is imputed to the party itself.

Chapter 2. Formation

Section 1. General Provisions

Article 2:101. (1) A contract is concluded if:
(a) the parties intend to be legally bound, and
(b) they reach a sufficient agreement without any further requirement.
(2) A contract need not be concluded or evidenced in writing nor is it subject to any other requirement as to form. The contract may be proved by any means, including witnesses.

Article 2:102. The intention of a party to be legally bound by contract is to be determined from the party's statements or conduct as they were reasonably understood by the other party.

Article 2:103. (1) There is sufficient agreement if the terms:
(a) have been sufficiently defined by the parties so that the contract can be enforced, or
(b) can be determined under these Principles.
(2) However, if one of the parties refuses to conclude a contract unless the parties have agreed on some specific matter, there is no contract unless agreement on that matter has been reached.

Article 2:104. (1) Contract terms which have not been individually negotiated may be invoked against a party who did not know of them only if the party invoking them took reasonable steps to bring them to the other party's attention before or when the contract was concluded.
(2) Terms are not brought appropriately to a party's attention by a mere reference to them in a contract document, even if that party signs the document.

Article 2:105. (1) If a written contract contains an individually negotiated clause stating that the writing embodies all the terms of the contract (a merger clause), any prior statements, undertakings or agreements which are not embodied in the writing do not form part of the contract.
(2) If the merger clause is not individually negotiated it will only establish a presumption that the parties intended that their prior statements, undertakings or agreements were not to form part of the contract. This rule may not be excluded or restricted.
(3) The parties' prior statements may be used to interpret the contract. This rule may not be excluded or restricted except by an individually negotiated clause.
(4) A party may by its statements or conduct be precluded from asserting a merger clause to the extent that the other party has reasonably relied on them.

Article 2:106. (1) A clause in a written contract requiring any modification or ending by agreement to be made in writing establishes only a presumption that an agreement to modify or end the contract is not intended to be legally binding unless it is in writing.
(2) A party may by its statements or conduct be precluded from asserting such a clause to the extent that the other party has reasonably relied on them.

Article 2:107. A promise which is intended to be legally binding without acceptance is binding.

Section 2. Offer and Acceptance

Article 2:201. (1) A proposal amounts to an offer if:
(a) it is intended to result in a contract if the other party accepts it, and
(b) it contains sufficiently definite terms to form a contract.
(2) An offer may be made to one or more specific persons or to the public.
(3) A proposal to supply goods or services at stated prices made by a professional supplier in a public advertisement or a catalogue, or by a display of goods, is presumed to be an offer to sell or supply at that price until the stock of goods, or the supplier's capacity to supply the service, is exhausted.

Article 2:202. (1) An offer may be revoked if the revocation reaches the offeree before it has dispatched its acceptance or, in cases of acceptance by conduct, before the contract has been concluded under Article 2:205(2) or (3).
(2) An offer made to the public can be revoked by the same means as were used to make the offer.
(3) However, a revocation of an offer is ineffective if:
(a) the offer indicates that it is irrevocable; or
(b) it states a fixed time for its acceptance; or
(c) it was reasonable for the offeree to rely on the offer as being irrevocable and the offeree has acted in reliance on the offer.

Article 2:203. When a rejection of an offer reaches the offeror, the offer lapses.

Article 2:204. (1) Any form of statement or conduct by the offeree is an acceptance if it indicates assent to the offer.
(2) Silence or inactivity does not in itself amount to acceptance.

Article 2:205. (1) If an acceptance has been dispatched by the offeree the contract is concluded when the acceptance reaches the offeror.
(2) In case of acceptance by conduct, the contract is concluded when notice of the conduct reaches the offeror.
(3) If by virtue of the offer, of practices which the parties have established between themselves, or of a usage, the offeree may accept the offer by performing an act without notice to the offeror, the contract is concluded when the performance of the act begins.

Article 2:206. (1) In order to be effective, acceptance of an offer must reach the offeror within the time fixed by it.
(2) If no time has been fixed by the offeror acceptance must reach it within a reasonable time.
(3) In the case of an acceptance by an act of performance under art. 2:205 (3), that act must be performed within the time for acceptance fixed by the offeror or, if no such time is fixed, within a reasonable time.

Article 2:207. (1) A late acceptance is nonetheless effective as an acceptance if without delay the offeror informs the offeree that he treats it as such.
(2) If a letter or other writing containing a late acceptance shows that it has been sent in such circumstances that if its transmission had been normal it would have reached the offeror in due time, the late acceptance is effective as an acceptance unless, without delay, the offeror informs the offeree that it considers its offer as having lapsed.

Article 2:208. (1) A reply by the offeree which states or implies additional or different terms which would materially alter the terms of the offer is a rejection and a new offer.
(2) A reply which gives a definite assent to an offer operates as an acceptance even if it states or implies additional or different terms, provided these do not materially alter the terms of the offer. The additional or different terms then become part of the contract.
(3) However, such a reply will be treated as a rejection of the offer if:
(a) the offer expressly limits acceptance to the terms of the offer; or
(b) the offeror objects to the additional or different terms without delay; or
(c) the offeree makes its acceptance conditional upon the offeror's assent to the additional or different terms, and the assent does not reach the offeree within a reasonable time.

Article 2:209. (1) If the parties have reached agreement except that the offer and acceptance refer to conflicting general conditions of contract, a contract is nonetheless formed. The general conditions form part of the contract to the extent that they are common in substance.
(2) However, no contract is formed if one party:
(a) has indicated in advance, explicitly, and not by way of general conditions, that it does not intend to be bound by a contract on the basis of paragraph (1); or
(b) without delay, informs the other party that it does not intend to be bound by such contract.
(3) General conditions of contract are terms which have been formulated in advance for an indefinite number of contracts of a certain nature, and which have not been individually negotiated between the parties.

Article 2:210. If professionals have concluded a contract but have not embodied it in a final document, and one without delay sends the other a writing which purports to be a confirmation of the contract but which contains additional or different terms, such terms will become part of the contract unless:
(a) the terms materially alter the terms of the contract, or
(b) the addressee objects to them without delay.

Article 2:211. The rules in this section apply with appropriate adaptations even though the process of conclusion of a contract cannot be analysed into offer and acceptance.

Section 3. Liability for negotiations

Article 2:301. (1) A party is free to negotiate and is not liable for failure to reach an agreement.
(2) However, a party who has negotiated or broken off negotiations contrary to good faith and fair dealing is liable for the losses caused to the other party.
(3) It is contrary to good faith and fair dealing, in particular, for a party to enter into or continue negotiations with no real intention of reaching an agreement with the other party.

Article 2:302. If confidential information is given by one party in the course of negotiations, the other party is under a duty not to disclose that information or use it for its own purposes whether or not a contract is subsequently concluded. The remedy for breach of this duty may include compensation for loss suffered and restitution of the benefit received by the other party.

Chapter 3. Authority of Agents

Section 1. General Provisions

Article 3:101. (1) This chapter governs the authority of an agent or other intermediary to bind its principal in relation to a contract with a third party.
(2) This chapter does not govern an agent's authority bestowed by law or the authority of an agent appointed by a public or judicial authority.
(3) This chapter does not govern the internal relationship between the agent or intermediary and its principal.

Article 3:102. (1) Where an agent acts in the name of a principal, the rules on direct representation apply (Section 2). It is irrelevant whether the principal's identity is revealed at the time the agent acts or is to be revealed later.

(2) Where an intermediary acts on instructions and on behalf of, but not in the name of, a principal, or where the third party neither knows nor has reason to know that the intermediary acts as an agent, the rules on indirect representation apply (Section 3).

Section 2. Direct Representation

Article 3:201. (1) The principal's grant of authority to an agent to act in its name may be express or may be implied from the circumstances.
(2) The agent has authority to perform all acts necessary in the circumstances to achieve the purposes for which the authority was granted.
(3) A person is to be treated as having granted authority to an apparent agent if the person's statements or conduct induce the third party reasonably and in good faith to believe that the apparent agent has been granted authority for the act performed by it.

Article 3:202. Where an agent is acting within its authority as defined by article 3:201, its acts bind the principal and the third party directly to each other. The agent itself is not bound to the third party.

Article 3:203. If an agent enters into a contract in the name of a principal whose identity is to be revealed later, but fails to reveal that identity within a reasonable time after a request by the third party, the agent itself is bound by the contract.

Article 3:204. (1) Where a person acting as an agent acts without authority or outside the scope of its authority, its acts are not binding upon the principal and the third party.
(2) Failing ratification by the principal according to article 3:207, the agent is liable to pay the third party such damages as will place the third party in the same position as if the agent had acted with authority. This does not apply if the third party knew or could not have been unaware of the agent's lack of authority.

Article 3:205. (1) If a contract concluded by an agent involves the agent in a conflict of interest of which the third party knew or could not have been unaware, the principal may avoid the contract according to the provisions of articles 4:112 to 4:116.
(2) There is presumed to be a conflict of interest where:
(a) the agent also acted as agent for the third party; or
(b) the contract was with itself in its personal capacity.
(3) However, the principal may not avoid the contract:
(a) if it had consented to, or could not have been unaware of, the agent's so acting; or
(b) if the agent had disclosed the conflict of interest to it and it had not objected within a reasonable time.

Article 3:206. An agent has implied authority to appoint a subagent to carry out tasks which are not of a personal character and which it is not reasonable to expect the agent to carry out itself. The rules of this Section apply to the subagency; acts of the subagent which are within its and the agent's authority bind the principal and the third party directly to each other.

Article 3:207. (1) Where a person acting as an agent acts without authority or outside its authority, the principal may ratify the agent's acts.
(2) Upon ratification, the agent's acts are considered as having been authorised, without prejudice to the rights of other persons.

Article 3:208. Where the statements or conduct of the principal gave the third party reason to believe that an act performed by the agent was authorised, but the third party is in doubt about the authorisation, it may send a written confirmation to the principal or request ratification from it. If the principal does not object or answer the request without delay, the agent's act is treated as having been authorised.

Article 3:209. (1) An agent's authority continues until the third party knows or ought to know that:
(a) the agent's authority has been brought to an end by the principal, the agent, or both; or
(b) the acts for which the authority had been granted have been completed, or the time for which it had been granted has expired; or
(c) the agent has become insolvent or, where a natural person, has died or become incapacitated; or
(d) the principal has become insolvent.
(2) The third party is considered to know that the agent's authority has been brought to an end under

paragraph (1) (a) above if this has been communicated or publicised in the same manner in which the authority was originally communicated or publicised.
(3) However, the agent remains authorised for a reasonable time to perform those acts which are necessary to protect the interests of the principal or its successors.

Section 3. Indirect Representation

Article 3.301. (1) Where an intermediary acts:
(a) on instructions and on behalf, but not in the name, of a principal, or
(b) on instructions from a principal but the third party does not know and has no reason to know this, the intermediary and the third party are bound to each other.
(2) The principal and the third party are bound to each other only under the conditions set out in Articles 3:302 to 3:304.

Article 3:302. If the intermediary becomes insolvent, or if it commits a fundamental non-performance towards the principal, or if prior to the time for performance it is clear that there will be a fundamental non-performance:
(a) on the principal's demand, the intermediary shall communicate the name and address of the third party to the principal; and
(b) the principal may exercise against the third party the rights acquired on the principal's behalf by the intermediary, subject to any defences which the third party may set up against the intermediary.

Article 3:303. If the intermediary becomes insolvent, or if it commits a fundamental non-performance towards the third party, or if prior to the time for performance it is clear that there will be a fundamental non-performance:
(a) on the third party's demand, the intermediary shall communicate the name and address of the principal to the third party; and
(b) the third party may exercise against the principal the rights which the third party has against the intermediary, subject to any defences which the intermediary may set up against the third party and those which the principal may set up against the intermediary.

Article 3:304. The rights under Articles 3:302 and 3:303 may be exercised only if notice of intention to exercise them is given to the intermediary and to the third party or principal, respectively. Upon receipt of the notice, the third party or the principal is no longer entitled to render performance to the intermediary.

Chapter 4. Validity

Article 4:101. This chapter does not deal with invalidity arising from illegality, immorality or lack of capacity.

Article 4:102. A contract is not invalid merely because at the time it was concluded performance of the obligation assumed was impossible, or because a party was not entitled to dispose of the assets to which the contract relates.

Article 4:103. (1) A party may avoid a contract for mistake of fact or law existing when the contract was concluded if:
(a) (i) the mistake was caused by information given by the other party; or
(ii) the other party knew or ought to have known of the mistake and it was contrary to good faith and fair dealing to leave the mistaken party in error; or
(iii) the other party made the same mistake, and
(b) the other party knew or ought to have known that the mistaken party, had it known the truth, would not have entered the contract or would have done so only on fundamentally different terms
(2) However a party may not avoid the contract if:
(a) in the circumstances its mistake was inexcusable, or
(b) the risk of the mistake was assumed, or in the circumstances should be borne, by it.

Article 4:104. An inaccuracy in the expression or transmission of a statement is to be treated as a mistake of the person who made or sent the statement and Article 4:103 applies.

Article 4:105. (1) If a party is entitled to avoid the contract for mistake but the other party indicates that it is willing to perform, or actually does perform, the contract as it was understood by the party entitled to avoid it, the contract is to be treated as if it had been concluded as the that party understood it. The other party must indicate its willingness to perform, or render such performance,

promptly after being informed of the manner in which the party entitled to avoid it understood the contract and before that party acts in reliance on any notice of avoidance.
(2) After such indication or performance the right to avoid is lost and any earlier notice of avoidance is ineffective.
(3) Where both parties have made the same mistake, the court may at the request of either party bring the contract into accordance with what might reasonably have been agreed had the mistake not occurred.

Article 4:106. A party who has concluded a contract relying on incorrect information given it by the other party may recover damages in accordance with Article 4:117(2) and (3) even if the information does not give rise to a right to avoid the contract on the ground of mistake under Article 4:103, unless the party who gave the information had reason to believe that the information was correct.

Article 4:107. (1) A party may avoid a contract when it has been led to conclude it by the other party's fraudulent representation, whether by words or conduct, or fraudulent non-disclosure of any information which in accordance with good faith and fair dealing it should have disclosed.
(2) A party's representation or non-disclosure is fraudulent if it was intended to deceive.
(3) In determining whether good faith and fair dealing required that a party disclose particular information, regard should be had to all the circumstances, including:
(a) whether the party had special expertise;
(b) the cost to it of acquiring the relevant information;
(c) whether the other party could reasonably acquire the information for itself; and
(d) the apparent importance of the information to the other party.

Article 4:108. A party may avoid a contract when it has been led to conclude it by the other party's imminent and serious threat of an act:
(a) which is wrongful in itself, or
(b) which it is wrongful to use as a means to obtain the conclusion of the contract,
unless in the circumstances the first party had a reasonable alternative.

Article 4:109. (1) A party may avoid a contract if, at the time of the conclusion of the contract:
(a) it was dependent on or had a relationship of trust with the other party, was in economic distress or had urgent needs, was improvident, ignorant, inexperienced or lacking in bargaining skill, and
(b) the other party knew or ought to have known of this and, given the circumstances and purpose of the contract, took advantage of the first party's situation in a way which was grossly unfair or took an excessive benefit.
(2) Upon the request of the party entitled to avoidance, a court may if it is appropriate adapt the contract in order to bring it into accordance with what might have been agreed had the requirements of good faith and fair dealing been followed.
(3) A court may similarly adapt the contract upon the request of a party receiving notice of avoidance for excessive benefit or unfair advantage, provided that this party informs the party who gave the notice promptly after receiving it and before that party has acted in reliance on it.

Article 4:110. (1) A party may avoid a term which has not been individually negotiated if, contrary to the requirements of good faith and fair dealing, it causes a significant imbalance in the parties' rights and obligations arising under the contract to the detriment of that party, taking into account the nature of the performance to be rendered under the contract, all the other terms of the contract and the circumstances at the time the contract was concluded.
(2) This Article does not apply to:
(a) a term which defines the main subject matter of the contract, provided the term is in plain and intelligible language; or to
(b) the adequacy in value of one party's obligations compared to the value of the obligations of the other party.

Article 4:111. (1) Where a third person for whose acts a party is responsible, or who with a party's assent is involved in the making of a contract:
(a) causes a mistake by giving information, or knows of or ought to have known of a mistake,
(b) gives incorrect information,
(c) commits fraud,
(d) makes a threat, or
(e) takes excessive benefit or unfair advantage,
remedies under this Chapter will be available under the same conditions as if the behaviour or knowledge had been that of the party itself.

(2) Where any other third person:
(a) gives incorrect information,
(b) commits fraud,
(c) makes a threat, or
(d) takes excessive benefit or unfair advantage,
remedies under this Chapter will be available if the party knew or ought to have known of the relevant facts, or at the time of avoidance it has not acted in reliance on the contract.

Article 4:112. Avoidance must be by notice to the other party.

Article 4:113. (1) Notice of avoidance must be given within a reasonable time, with due regard to the circumstances, after the avoiding party knew or ought to have known of the relevant facts or became capable of acting freely.
(2) However, a party may avoid an individual term under Article 4:110 if it gives notice of avoidance within a reasonable time after the other party has invoked the term.

Article 4:114. If the party who is entitled to avoid a contract confirms it, expressly or impliedly, after it knows of the ground for avoidance, or becomes capable of acting freely, avoidance of the contract is excluded.

Article 4:115. On avoidance either party may claim restitution of whatever it has supplied under the contract, provided it makes concurrent restitution of whatever it has received. If restitution cannot be made in kind for any reason, a reasonable sum must be paid for what has been received.

Article 4:116. If a ground of avoidance affects only particular terms of a contract, the effect of an avoidance is limited to those terms unless, giving due consideration to all the circumstances of the case, it is unreasonable to uphold the remaining contract.

Article 4:117. (1) A party who avoids a contract under this Chapter may recover from the other party damages so as to put the avoiding party as nearly as possible into the same position as if it had not concluded the contract, provided that the other party knew or ought to have known of the mistake, fraud, threat or taking of excessive benefit or unfair advantage.
(2) If a party has the right to avoid a contract under this Chapter, but does not exercise its right or has lost its right under the provisions of Articles 4:113 or 4:114, it may recover, subject to paragraph (1), damages limited to the loss caused to it by the mistake, fraud, threat or taking of excessive benefit or unfair advantage. The same measure of damages shall apply when the party was misled by incorrect information in the sense of Article 4:106.
(3) In other respects, the damages shall be in accordance with the relevant provisions of Chapter 9, Section 5, with appropriate adaptations.

Article 4:118. (1) Remedies for fraud, threats and excessive benefit or unfair advantage-taking, and the right to avoid an unfair term which has not been individually negotiated, cannot be excluded or restricted.
(2) Remedies for mistake and incorrect information may be excluded or restricted unless the exclusion or restriction is contrary to good faith and fair dealing.

Article 4:119. A party who is entitled to a remedy under this Chapter in circumstances which afford that party a remedy for non-performance may pursue either remedy.

Chapter 5. Interpretation

Article 5:101. (1) A contract is to be interpreted according to the common intention of the parties even if this differs from the literal meaning of the words.
(2) If it is established that one party intended the contract to have a particular meaning, and at the time of the conclusion of the contract the other party could not have been unaware of the first party's intention, the contract is to be interpreted in the way intended by the first party.
(3) If an intention cannot be established according to (1) or (2), the contract is to be interpreted according to the meaning that reasonable persons of the same kind as the parties would give to it in the same circumstances.

Article 5:102. In interpreting the contract, regard shall be had, in particular, to:
(a) the circumstances in which it was concluded, including the preliminary negotiations;
(b) the conduct of the parties, even subsequent to the conclusion of the contract;
(c) the nature and purpose of the contract;

(d) the interpretation which has already been given to similar clauses by the parties and the practices they have established between themselves;
(e) the meaning commonly given to terms and expressions in the branch of activity concerned and the interpretation similar clauses may already have received;
(f) usages; and
(g) good faith and fair dealing.

Article 5:103. Where there is doubt about the meaning of a contract term not individually negotiated, an interpretation of the term against the party who supplied it is to be preferred.

Article 5:104. Terms which have been individually negotiated take preference over those which are not.

Article 5:105. Terms are to be interpreted in the light of the whole contract in which they appear.

Article 5:106. An interpretation which renders the terms of the contract lawful, or effective, is to be preferred to one which would not.

Article 5:107. Where a contract is drawn up in two or more language versions none of which is stated to be authoritative, there is, in case of discrepancy between the versions, a preference for the interpretation according to the version in which the contract was originally drawn up.

Chapter 6. Contents and Effects

Article 6:101. (1) A statement made by one party before or when the contract is concluded is to be treated as giving rise to a contractual obligation if that is how the other party reasonably understood it in the circumstances, taking into account:
(a) the apparent importance of the statement to the other party;
(b) whether the party was making the statement in the course of business; and
(c) the relative expertise of the parties.
(2) If one of the parties is a professional supplier who gives information about the quality or use of services or goods or other property when marketing or advertising them or otherwise before the contract for them is concluded, the statement is to be treated as giving rise to a contractual obligation unless it is shown that the other party knew or could not have been unaware that the statement was incorrect.
(3) Such information and other undertakings given by a person advertising or marketing services, goods or other property for the professional supplier, or by a person in earlier links of the business chain, are to be treated as giving rise to a contractual obligation on the part of the professional supplier unless it did not know and had no reason to know of the information or undertaking.

Article 6:102. In addition to the express terms, a contract may contain implied terms which stem from
(a) the intention of the parties,
(b) the nature and purpose of the contract, and
(c) good faith and fair dealing.

Article 6:103. When the parties have concluded an apparent contract which was not intended to reflect their true agreement, as between the parties the true agreement prevails.

Article 6:104. Where the contract does not fix the price or the method of determining it, the parties are to be treated as having agreed on a reasonable price.

Article 6:105. Where the price or any other contractual term is to be determined by one party whose determination is grossly unreasonable, then notwithstanding any provision to the contrary, a reasonable price or other term shall be substituted.

Article 6:106. (1) Where the price or any other contractual term is to be determined by a third person, and it cannot or will not do so, the parties are presumed to have empowered the court to appoint another person to determine it.
(2) If a price or other term fixed by a third person is grossly unreasonable, a reasonable price or term shall be substituted.

Article 6:107. Where the price or any other contractual term is to be determined by reference to a factor which does not exist or has ceased to exist or to be accessible, the nearest equivalent factor shall be substituted.

Article 6:108. If the contract does not specify the quality, a party must tender performance of at least average quality.

Article 6:109. A contract for an indefinite period may be ended by either party by giving notice of reasonable length.

Article 6:110. (1) A third party may require performance of a contractual obligation when its right to do so has been expressly agreed upon between the promisor and the promisee, or when such agreement is to be inferred from the purpose of the contract or the circumstances of the case. The third party need not be identified at the time the agreement is concluded.
(2) If the third party renounces the right to performance the right is treated as never having accrued to it.
(3) The promisee may by notice to the promisor deprive the third party of the right to performance unless:
(a) the third party has received notice from the promisee that the right has been made irrevocable, or
(b) the promisor or the promisee has received notice from the third party that the latter accepts the right

Article 6:111. (1) A party is bound to fulfil its obligations even if performance has become more onerous, whether because the cost of performance has increased or because the value of the performance it receives has diminished.
(2) If, however, performance of the contract becomes excessively onerous because of a change of circumstances, the parties are bound to enter into negotiations with a view to adapting the contract or terminating it, provided that:
(a) the change of circumstances occurred after the time of conclusion of the contract,
(b) the possibility of a change of circumstances was not one which could reasonably have been taken into account at the time of conclusion of the contract, and
(c) the risk of the change of circumstances is not one which, according to the contract, the party affected should be required to bear.
(3) If the parties fail to reach agreement within a reasonable period, the court may:
(a) terminate the contract at a date and on terms to be determined by the court; or
(b) adapt the contract in order to distribute between the parties in a just and equitable manner the losses and gains resulting from the change of circumstances.
In either case, the court may award damages for the loss suffered through a party refusing to negotiate or breaking off negotiations contrary to good faith and fair dealing.

Chapter 7. Performance

Article 7:101. (1) If the place of performance of a contractual obligation is not fixed by or determinable from the contract it shall be:
(a) in the case of an obligation to pay money, the creditor's place of business at the time of the conclusion of the contract;
(b) in the case of an obligation other than to pay money, the obligor's place of business at the time of conclusion of the contract.
(2) If a party has more than one place of business, the place of business for the purpose of the preceding paragraph is that which has the closest relationship to the contract, having regard to the circumstances known to or contemplated by the parties at the time of conclusion of the contract.
(3) If a party does not have a place of business its habitual residence is to be treated as its place of business.

Article 7:102. A party has to effect its performance:
(a) if a time is fixed by or determinable from the contract, at that time;
(b) if a period of time is fixed by or determinable from the contract, at any time within that period unless the circumstances of the case indicate that the other party is to choose the time;
(c) in any other case, within a reasonable time after the conclusion of the contract.

Article 7:103. (1) A party may decline a tender of performance made before it is due except where acceptance of the tender would not unreasonably prejudice its interests.
(2) A party's acceptance of early performance does not affect the time fixed for the performance of its own obligation.

Article 7:104. To the extent that the performances of the parties can be rendered simultaneously, the parties are bound to render them simultaneously unless the circumstances indicate otherwise.

Article 7:105. (1) Where an obligation may be discharged by one of alternative performances, the choice belongs to the party who is to perform, unless the circumstances indicate otherwise.
(2) If the party who is to make the choice fails to do so by the time required by the contract, then:
(a) if the delay in choosing is fundamental, the right to choose passes to the other party;
(b) if the delay is not fundamental, the other party may give a notice fixing an additional period of reasonable length in which the party to choose must do so. If the latter fails to do so, the right to choose passes to the other party.

Article 7:106. (1) Except where the contract requires personal performance the obligee cannot refuse performance by a third person if:
(a) the third person acts with the assent of the obligor; or
(b) the third person has a legitimate interest in performance and the obligor has failed to perform or it is clear that it will not perform at the time performance is due.
(2) Performance by the third person in accordance with paragraph (1) discharges the obligor.

Article 7:107. (1) Payment of money due may be made in any form used in the ordinary course of business.
(2) A creditor who, pursuant to the contract or voluntarily, accepts a cheque or other order to pay or a promise to pay is presumed to do so only on condition that it will be honoured. The creditor may not enforce the original obligation to pay unless the order or promise is not honoured.

Article 7:108. (1) The parties may agree that payment shall be made only in a specified currency.
(2) In the absence of such agreement, a sum of money expressed in a currency other than that of the place where payment is due may be paid in the currency of that place according to the rate of exchange prevailing there at the time when payment is due.
(3) If, in a case falling within the preceding paragraph, the debtor has not paid at the time when payment is due, the creditor may require payment in the currency of the place where payment is due according to the rate of exchange prevailing there either at the time when payment is due or at the time of actual payment.

Article 7:109. (1) Where a party has to perform several obligations of the same nature and the performance tendered does not suffice to discharge all of the obligations, then subject to paragraph (4) the party may at the time of its performance declare to which obligation the performance is to be appropriated.
(2) If the performing party does not make such a declaration, the other party may within a reasonable time appropriate the performance to such obligation as it chooses. It shall inform the performing party of the choice. However, any such appropriation to an obligation which:
(a) is not yet due, or
(b) is illegal, or
(c) is disputed,
is invalid.
(3) In the absence of an appropriation by either party, and subject to paragraph (4), the performance is appropriated to that obligation which satisfies one of the following criteria in the sequence indicated:
(a) the obligation which is due or is the first to fall due;
(b) the obligation for which the obligee has the least security;
(c) the obligation which is the most burdensome for the obligor,
(d) the obligation which has arisen first.
If none of the preceding criteria applies, the performance is appropriated proportionately to all obligations.
(4) In the case of a monetary obligation, a payment by the debtor is to be appropriated, first, to expenses, secondly, to interest, and thirdly, to principal, unless the creditor makes a different appropriation.

Article 7:110. (1) A party who is left in possession of tangible property other than money because of the other party's failure to accept or retake the property must take reasonable steps to protect and preserve the property.
(2) The party left in possession may discharge its duty to deliver or return:
(a) by depositing the property on reasonable terms with a third person to be held to the order of the other party, and notifying the other party of this; or
(b) by selling the property on reasonable terms after notice to the other party, and paying the net proceeds to that party.
(3) Where, however, the property is liable to rapid deterioration or its preservation is unreasonably

expensive, the party must take reasonable steps to dispose of it. It may discharge its duty to deliver or return by paying the net proceeds to the other party.
(4) The party left in possession is entitled to be reimbursed or to retain out of the proceeds of sale any expenses reasonably incurred.

Article 7:111. Where a party fails to accept money properly tendered by the other party, that party may after notice to the first party discharge its obligation to pay by depositing the money to the order of the first party in accordance with the law of the place where payment is due.

Article 7:112. Each party shall bear the costs of performance of its obligations.

Chapter 8. Non-Performance and Remedies in General

Article 8:101. (1) Whenever a party does not perform an obligation under the contract and the non-performance is not excused under Article 8:108, the aggrieved party may resort to any of the remedies set out in Chapter 9.
(2) Where a party's non-performance is excused under Article 8:108, the aggrieved party may resort to any of the remedies set out in Chapter 9 except claiming performance and damages.
(3) A party may not resort to any of the remedies set out in Chapter 9 to the extent that its own act caused the other party's non-performance.

Article 8:102. Remedies which are not incompatible may be cumulated. In particular, a party is not deprived of its right to damages by exercising its right to any other remedy.

Article 8:103. A non-performance of an obligation is fundamental to the contract if:
(a) strict compliance with the obligation is of the essence of the contract; or
(b) the non-performance substantially deprives the aggrieved party of what it was entitled to expect under the contract, unless the other party did not foresee and could not reasonably have foreseen that result; or
(c) the non-performance is intentional and gives the aggrieved party reason to believe that it cannot rely on the other party's future performance.

Article 8:104. A party whose tender of performance is not accepted by the other party because it does not conform to the contract may make a new and conforming tender where the time for performance has not yet arrived or the delay would not be such as to constitute a fundamental non-performance.

Article 8:105. (1) A party who reasonably believes that there will be a fundamental non-performance by the other party may demand adequate assurance of due performance and meanwhile may withhold performance of its own obligations so long as such reasonable belief continues.
(2) Where this assurance is not provided within a reasonable time, the party demanding it may terminate the contract if it still reasonably believes that there will be a fundamental non-performance by the other party and gives notice of termination without delay.

Article 8:106. (1) In any case of non-performance the aggrieved party may by notice to the other party allow an additional period of time for performance.
(2) During the additional period the aggrieved party may withhold performance of its own reciprocal obligations and may claim damages, but it may not resort to any other remedy. If it receives notice from the other party that the latter will not perform within that period, or if upon expiry of that period due performance has not been made, the aggrieved party may resort to any of the remedies that may be available under chapter 9.
(3) If in a case of delay in performance which is not fundamental the aggrieved party has given a notice fixing an additional period of time of reasonable length, it may terminate the contract at the end of the period of notice. The aggrieved party may in its notice provide that if the other party does not perform within the period fixed by the notice the contract shall terminate automatically. If the period stated is too short, the aggrieved party may terminate, or, as the case may be, the contract shall terminate automatically, only after a reasonable period from the time of the notice.

Article 8:107. A party who entrusts performance of the contract to another person remains responsible for performance.

Article 8:108. (1) A party's non-performance is excused if it proves that it is due to an impediment beyond its control and that it could not reasonably have been expected to take the impediment into account at the time of the conclusion of the contract, or to have avoided or overcome the impediment or its consequences.

(2) Where the impediment is only temporary the excuse provided by this article has effect for the period during which the impediment exists. However, if the delay amounts to a fundamental non-performance, the obligee may treat it as such.
(3) The non-performing party must ensure that notice of the impediment and of its effect on its ability to perform is received by the other party within a reasonable time after the non-performing party knew or ought to have known of these circumstances. The other party is entitled to damages for any loss resulting from the non-receipt of such notice.

Article 8:109. Remedies for non-performance may be excluded or restricted unless it would be contrary to good faith and fair dealing to invoke the exclusion or restriction.

Chapter 9. Particular Remedies for Non-Performance

Section 1. Right to Performance

Article 9:101. (1) The creditor is entitled to recover money which is due.
(2) Where the creditor has not yet performed its obligation and it is clear that the debtor will be unwilling to receive performance, the creditor may nonetheless proceed with its performance and may recover any sum due under the contract unless:
(a) it could have made a reasonable substitute transaction without significant effort or expense; or
(b) performance would be unreasonable in the circumstances.

Article 9:102. (1) The aggrieved party is entitled to specific performance of an obligation other than one to pay money, including the remedying of a defective performance.
(2) Specific performance cannot, however, be obtained where:
(a) performance would be unlawful or impossible; or
(b) performance would cause the obligor unreasonable effort or expense; or
(c) the performance consists in the provision of services or work of a personal character or depends upon a personal relationship, or
(d) the aggrieved party may reasonably obtain performance from another source.
(3) The aggrieved party will lose the right to specific performance if it fails to seek it within a reasonable time after it has or ought to have become aware of the non-performance.

Article 9:103. The fact that a right to performance is excluded under this Section does not preclude a claim for damages.

Section 2. Withholding Performance

Article 9:201. (1) A party who is to perform simultaneously with or after the other party may withhold performance until the other has tendered performance or has performed. The first party may withhold the whole of its performance or a part of it as may be reasonable in the circumstances.
(2) A party may similarly withhold performance for as long as it is clear that there will be a non-performance by the other party when the other party's performance becomes due.

Section 3. Termination Of The Contract

Article 9:301. (1) A party may terminate the contract if the other party's non-performance is fundamental.
(2) In the case of delay the aggrieved party may also terminate the contract under Article 8:106 (3).

Article 9:302. If the contract is to be performed in separate parts and in relation to a part to which a counter-performance can be apportioned, there is a fundamental non-performance, the aggrieved party may exercise its right to terminate under this Section in relation to the part concerned. It may terminate the contract as a whole only if the non-performance is fundamental to the contract as a whole.

Article 9:303. (1) A party's right to terminate the contract is to be exercised by notice to the other party.
(2) The aggrieved party loses its right to terminate the contract unless it gives notice within a reasonable time after it has or ought to have become aware of the non-performance.
(3) (a) When performance has not been tendered by the time it was due, the aggrieved party need not give notice of termination before a tender has been made. If a tender is later made it loses its right to terminate if it does not give such notice within a reasonable time after it has or ought to have become aware of the tender.
(b) If, however, the aggrieved party knows or has reason to know that the other party still intends to

tender within a reasonable time, and the aggrieved party unreasonably fails to notify the other party that it will not accept performance, it loses its right to terminate if the other party in fact tenders within a reasonable time.
(4) If a party is excused under Article 8:108 through an impediment which is total and permanent, the contract is terminated automatically and without notice at the time the impediment arises.

Article 9:304. Where prior to the time for performance by a party it is clear that there will be a fundamental non-performance by it the other party may terminate the contract.

Article 9:305. (1) Termination of the contract releases both parties from their obligation to effect and to receive future performance, but, subject to Articles 9:306 to 9:308, does not affect the rights and liabilities that have accrued up to the time of termination.
(2) Termination does not affect any provision of the contract for the settlement of disputes or any other provision which is to operate even after termination.

Article 9:306. A party who terminates the contract may reject property previously received from the other party if its value to the first party has been fundamentally reduced as a result of the other party's non-performance.

Article 9:307. On termination of the contract a party may recover money paid for a performance which it did not receive or which it properly rejected.

Article 9:308. On termination of the contract a party who has supplied property which can be returned and for which it has not received payment or other counter-performance may recover the property.

Article 9:309. On termination of the contract a party who has rendered a performance which cannot be returned and for which it has not received payment or other counter-performance may recover a reasonable amount for the value of the performance to the other party.

Section 4. Price Reduction

Article 9:401. (1) A party who accepts a tender of performance not conforming to the contract may reduce the price. This reduction shall be proportionate to the decrease in the value of the performance at the time this was tendered compared to the value which a conforming tender would have had at that time.
(2) A party who is entitled to reduce the price under the preceding paragraph and who has already paid a sum exceeding the reduced price may recover the excess from the other party.
(3) A party who reduces the price cannot also recover damages for reduction in the value of the performance but remains entitled to damages for any further loss it has suffered so far as these are recoverable under Section 5 of this Chapter.

Section 5. Damages and Interest

Article 9:501. (1) The aggrieved party is entitled to damages for loss caused by the other party's non-performance which is not excused under Article 8:108.
(2) The loss for which damages are recoverable includes:
(a) non-pecuniary loss; and
(b) future loss which is reasonably likely to occur.

Article 9:502. The general measure of damages is such sum as will put the aggrieved party as nearly as possible into the position in which it would have been if the contract had been duly performed. Such damages cover the loss which the aggrieved party has suffered and the gain of which it has been deprived.

Article 9:503. The non-performing party is liable only for loss which it foresaw or could reasonably have foreseen at the time of conclusion of the contract as a likely result of its non-performance, unless the non-performance was intentional or grossly negligent.

Article 9:504. The non-performing party is not liable for loss suffered by the aggrieved party to the extent that the aggrieved party contributed to the non-performance or its effects.

Article 9:505. (1) The non-performing party is not liable for loss suffered by the aggrieved party to the extent that the aggrieved party could have reduced the loss by taking reasonable steps.
(2) The aggrieved party is entitled to recover any expenses reasonably incurred in attempting to reduce the loss.

Article 9:506. Where the aggrieved party has terminated the contract and has made a substitute transaction within a reasonable time and in a reasonable manner, it may recover the difference between the contract price and the price of the substitute transaction as well as damages for any further loss so far as these are recoverable under this Section.

Article 9:507. Where the aggrieved party has terminated the contract and has not made a substitute transaction but there is a current price for the performance contracted for, it may recover the difference between the contract price and the price current at the time the contract is terminated as well as damages for any further loss so far as these are recoverable under this Section.

Article 9:508. (1) If payment of a sum of money is delayed, the aggrieved party is entitled to interest on that sum from the time when payment is due to the time of payment at the average commercial bank short-term lending rate to prime borrowers prevailing for the contractual currency of payment at the place where payment is due.
(2) The aggrieved party may in addition recover damages for any further loss so far as these are recoverable under this Section.

Article 9:509. (1) Where the contract provides that a party who fails to perform is to pay a specified sum to the aggrieved party for such non-performance, the aggrieved party shall be awarded that sum irrespective of its actual loss.
(2) However, despite any agreement to the contrary the specified sum may be reduced to a reasonable amount where it is grossly excessive in relation to the loss resulting from the non-performance and the other circumstances.

Article 9:510. Damages are to be measured by the currency which most appropriately reflects the aggrieved party's loss.

Chapter 10. Plurality of Parties

Section 1. Plurality of Debtors

Article 10:101. (1) Obligations are solidary when all the debtors are bound to render one and the same performance and the creditor may require it from any one of them until full performance has been received.
(2) Obligations are separate when each debtor is bound to render only part of the performance and the creditor may require from each debtor only that debtor's part.
(3) An obligation is communal when all the debtors are bound to render the performance together and the creditor may require it only from all of them.

Article 10:102. (1) If several debtors are bound to render one and the same performance to a creditor under the same contract, they are solidarily liable, unless the contract or the law provides otherwise.
(2) Solidary obligations also arise where several persons are liable for the same damage.
(3) The fact that the debtors are not liable on the same terms does not prevent their obligations from being solidary.

Article 10:103. Debtors bound by separate obligations are liable in equal shares unless the contract or the law provides otherwise.

Article 10:104. Notwithstanding Article 10:101(3), when money is claimed for non-performance of a communal obligation, the debtors are solidarily liable for payment to the creditor.

Article 10:105. (1) As between themselves, solidary debtors are liable in equal shares unless the contract or the law provides otherwise.
(2) If two or more debtors are liable for the same damage under Article 10:102(2), their share of liability as between themselves is determined according to the law governing the event which gave rise to the liability.

Article 10:106. (1) A solidary debtor who has performed more than that debtor's share may claim the excess from any of the other debtors to the extent of each debtor's unperformed share, together with a share of any costs reasonably incurred.
(2) A solidary debtor to whom paragraph (1) applies may also, subject to any prior right and interest of the creditor, exercise the rights and actions of the creditor, including accessory securities, to recover the excess from any of the other debtors to the extent of each debtor's unperformed share.
(3) If a solidary debtor who has performed more than that debtor's share is unable, despite all reasonable efforts, to recover contribution from another solidary debtor, the share of the others, including the one who has performed, is increased proportionally.

Article 10:107. (1) Performance or set-off by a solidary debtor or set-off by the creditor against one solidary debtor discharges the other debtors in relation to the creditor to the extent of the performance or set-off.
(2) Merger of debts between a solidary debtor and the creditor discharges the other debtors only for the share of the debtor concerned.

Article 10:108. (1) When the creditor releases, or reaches a settlement with, one solidary debtor, the other debtors are discharged of liability for the share of that debtor.
(2) The debtors are totally discharged by the release or settlement if it so provides.
(3) As between solidary debtors, the debtor who is discharged from that debtor's share is discharged only to the extent of the share at the time of the discharge and not from any supplementary share for which that debtor may subsequently become liable under Article 10:106(3).

Article 10:109. A decision by a court as to the liability to the creditor of one solidary debtor does not affect:
(a) the liability to the creditor of the other solidary debtors; or
(b) the rights of recourse between the solidary debtors under Article 10:106.

Article 10:110. Prescription of the creditor's right to performance ("claim") against one solidary debtor does not affect:
(a) the liability to the creditor of the other solidary debtors; or
(b) the rights of recourse between the solidary debtors under Article 10:106.

Article 10:111. (1) A solidary debtor may invoke against the creditor any defence which another solidary debtor can invoke, other than a defence personal to that other debtor. Invoking the defence has no effect with regard to the other solidary debtors.
(2) A debtor from whom contribution is claimed may invoke against the claimant any personal defence that that debtor could have invoked against the creditor.

Section 2. Plurality of Creditors

Article 10:201. (1) Claims are solidary when any of the creditors may require full performance from the debtor and when the debtor may render performance to any of the creditors.
(2) Claims are separate when the debtor owes each creditor only that creditor's share of the claim and each creditor may require performance only of that creditor's share.
(3) A claim is communal when the debtor must perform to all the creditors and any creditor may require performance only for the benefit of all.

Article 10:202. Separate creditors are entitled to equal shares unless the contract or the law provides otherwise.

Article 10:203. If one of the creditors in a communal claim refuses, or is unable to receive, the performance, the debtor may discharge the obligation to perform by depositing the property or money with a third party according to Articles 7:110 or 7:111 of the Principles.

Article 10:204. (1) Solidary creditors are entitled to equal shares unless the contract or the law provides otherwise.
(2) A creditor who has received more than that creditor's share must transfer the excess to the other creditors to the extent of their respective shares.

Article 10:205. (1) A release granted to the debtor by one of the solidary creditors has no effect on the other solidary creditors
(2) The rules of Articles 10:107, 10:109, 10:110 and 10:111(1) apply, with appropriate adaptations, to solidary claims.

Chapter 11. Assignment of Claims

Section 1. General Principles

Article 11:101. (1) This Chapter applies to the assignment by agreement of a right to performance ("claim") under an existing or future contract.
(2) Except where otherwise stated or the context otherwise requires, this Chapter also applies to the assignment by agreement of other transferable claims.
(3) This Chapter does not apply:
(a) to the transfer of a financial instrument or investment security where, under the law otherwise

applicable, such transfer must be by entry in a register maintained by or for the issuer; or
(b) to the transfer of a bill of exchange or other negotiable instrument or of a negotiable security or a document of title to goods where, under the law otherwise applicable, such transfer must be by delivery (with any necessary indorsement).
(4) In this Chapter "assignment" includes an assignment by way of security.
(5) This Chapter also applies, with appropriate adaptations, to the granting by agreement of a right in security over a claim otherwise than by assignment.

Article 11:102. (1) Subject to Articles 11:301 and 11:302, a party to a contract may assign a claim under it.
(2) A future claim arising under an existing or future contract may be assigned if at the time when it comes into existence, or at such other time as the parties agree, it can be identified as the claim to which the assignment relates.

Article 11:103. A claim which is divisible may be assigned in part, but the assignor is liable to the debtor for any increased costs which the debtor thereby incurs.

Article 11:104. An assignment need not be in writing and is not subject to any other requirement as to form. It may be proved by any means, including witnesses.

Section 2. Effects of Assignment As Between Assignor and Assignee

Article 11:201. (1) The assignment of a claim transfers to the assignee:
(a) all the assignor's rights to performance in respect of the claim assigned; and
(b) all accessory rights securing such performance.
(2) Where the assignment of a claim under a contract is associated with the substitution of the assignee as debtor in respect of any obligation owed by the assignor under the same contract, this Article takes effect subject to Article 12:201.

Article 11:202. (1) An assignment of an existing claim takes effect at the time of the agreement to assign or such later time as the assignor and assignee agree.
(2) An assignment of a future claim is dependent upon the assigned claim coming into existence but thereupon takes effect from the time of the agreement to assign or such later time as the assignor and assignee agree.

Article 11:203. An assignment is effective as between the assignor and assignee, and entitles the assignee to whatever the assignor receives from the debtor, even if it is ineffective against the debtor under Article 11:301 or 11:302.

Article 11:204. By assigning or purporting to assign a claim the assignor undertakes to the assignee that:
(a) at the time when the assignment is to take effect the following conditions will be satisfied except as otherwise disclosed to the assignee:
(i) the assignor has the right to assign the claim;
(ii) the claim exists and the assignee's rights are not affected by any defences or rights (including any right of set-off) which the debtor might have against the assignor; and
(iii) the claim is not subject to any prior assignment or right in security in favour of any other party or to any other incumbrance;
(b) the claim and any contract under which it arises will not be modified without the consent of the assignee unless the modification is provided for in the assignment agreement or is one which is made in good faith and is of a nature to which the assignee could not reasonably object; and
(c) the assignor will transfer to the assignee all transferable rights intended to secure performance which are not accessory rights.

Section 3. Effects of Assignment As Between Assignee and Debtor

Article 11:301. (1) An assignment which is prohibited by or is otherwise not in conformity with the contract under which the assigned claim arises is not effective against the debtor unless:
(a) the debtor has consented to it; or
(b) the assignee neither knew nor ought to have known of the non-conformity; or
(c) the assignment is made under a contract for the assignment of future rights to payment of money.
(2) Nothing in the preceding paragraph affects the assignor's liability for the non-conformity.

Article 11:302. An assignment to which the debtor has not consented is ineffective against the debtor so far as it relates to a performance which the debtor, by reason of the nature of the performance or the relationship of the debtor and the assignor, could not reasonably be required to render to anyone except the assignor.

Article 11:303. (1) Subject to Articles 11:301, 11:302, 11:307 and 11:308, the debtor is bound to perform in favour of the assignee if and only if the debtor has received a notice in writing from the assignor or the assignee which reasonably identifies the claim which has been assigned and requires the debtor to give performance to the assignee.
(2) However, if such notice is given by the assignee, the debtor may within a reasonable time request the assignee to provide reliable evidence of the assignment, pending which the debtor may withhold performance.
(3) Where the debtor has acquired knowledge of the assignment otherwise than by a notice conforming to paragraph (1), the debtor may either withhold performance from or give performance to the assignee.
(4) Where the debtor gives performance to the assignor, the debtor is discharged if and only if the performance is given without knowledge of the assignment.

Article 11:304. A debtor who performs in favour of a person identified as assignee in a notice of assignment under Article 11:303 is discharged unless the debtor could not have been unaware that such person was not the person entitled to performance.

Article 11:305. A debtor who has received notice of two or more competing demands for performance may discharge liability by conforming to the law of the due place of performance, or, if the performances are due in different places, the law applicable to the claim.

Article 11:306. (1) Where the assigned claim relates to an obligation to pay money at a particular place, the assignee may require payment at any place within the same country or, if that country is a Member State of the European Union, at any place within the European Union, but the assignor is liable to the debtor for any increased costs which the debtor incurs by reason of any change in the place of performance.
(2) Where the assigned claim relates to a non-monetary obligation to be performed at a particular place, the assignee may not require performance at any other place.

Article 11:307. (1) The debtor may set up against the assignee all substantive and procedural defences to the assigned claim which the debtor could have used against the assignor.
(2) The debtor may also assert against the assignee all rights of set-off which would have been available against the assignor under Chapter 13 in respect of any claim against the assignor:
(a) existing at the time when a notice of assignment, whether or not conforming to Article 11:303(1), reaches the debtor; or
(b) closely connected with the assigned claim.

Article 11:308. A modification of the claim made by agreement between the assignor and the debtor, without the consent of the assignee, after a notice of assignment, whether or not conforming to Article 11:303(1), reaches the debtor does not affect the rights of the assignee against the debtor unless the modification is provided for in the assignment agreement or is one which is made in good faith and is of a nature to which the assignee could not reasonably object.

Section 4. Order of Priority between Assignee and Competing Claimants

Article 11:401. (1) Where there are successive assignments of the same claim, the assignee whose assignment is first notified to the debtor has priority over any earlier assignee if at the time of the later assignment the assignee under that assignment neither knew nor ought to have known of the earlier assignment.
(2) Subject to paragraph (1), the priority of successive assignments, whether of existing or future claims, is determined by the order in which they are made.
(3) The assignee's interest in the assigned claim has priority over the interest of a creditor of the assignor who attaches that claim, whether by judicial process or otherwise, after the time the assignment has taken effect under Article 11:202.
(4) In the event of the assignor's bankruptcy, the assignee's interest in the assigned claim has priority over the interest of the assignor's insolvency administrator and creditors, subject to any rules of the law applicable to the bankruptcy relating to:
(a) publicity required as a condition of such priority;
(b) the ranking of claims; or
(c) the avoidance or ineffectiveness of transactions in the bankruptcy proceedings.

Chapter 12. Substitution of New Debtor. Transfer of Contract

Section 1: Substitution of New Debtor

Article 12:101. (1) A third person may undertake with the agreement of the debtor and the creditor to be sub-sti-tuted as debtor, with the effect that the original debtor is discharged.
(2) A creditor may agree in advance to a future substitution. In such a case the substitution takes effect only when the creditor is given notice by the new debtor of the agreement between the new and the original debtor.

Article 12:102. (1) The new debtor cannot invoke against the creditor any rights or defences arising from the relationship between the new debtor and the original debtor.
(2) The discharge of the original debtor also extends to any security of the original debtor given to the creditor for the performance of the obli-ga-tion, unless the security is over an asset which is trans-ferred to the new debtor as part of a transaction between the original and the new debtor.
(3) Upon discharge of the original debtor, a security granted by any person other than the new debtor for the per-formance of the obli-ga-tion is released, unless that other person agrees that it should continue to be available to the creditor.
(4) The new debtor may invoke against the creditor all de--fences which the original debtor could have invoked against the creditor.

Section 2: Transfer of Contract

Article 12:201. (1) A party to a contract may agree with a third person that that person is to be sub-sti-tu-ted as the contracting party. In such a case the substitution takes effect only where, as a result of the other party's assent, the first party is discharged.
(2) To the extent that the substitution of the third person as a contracting party involves a transfer of rights to performance ("claims"), the provisions of Chapter 11 apply; to the extent that obligations are transferred, the provisions of Section 1 of this Chapter apply.

Chapter 13: Set-Off

Article 13:101. If two parties owe each other obligations of the same kind, either party may set off that party's right to performance ("claim") against the other party's claim, if and to the extent that, at the time of set-off, the first party:
(a) is entitled to effect performance; and
(b) may demand the other party's performance.

Article 13:102. (1) A debtor may not set off a claim which is unascertained as to its existence or value unless the set-off will not prejudice the interests of the other party.
(2) Where the claims of both parties arise from the same legal relationship it is presumed that the other party's interests will not be prejudiced.

Article 13:103. Where parties owe each other money in different currencies, each party may set off that party's claim against the other party's claim, unless the parties have agreed that the party declar-ing set-off is to pay exclusively in a specified currency.

Article 13:104. The right of set-off is exercised by notice to the other party.

Article 13:105. (1) Where the party giving notice of set-off has two or more claims against the other party, the notice is effective only if it identifies the claim to which it relates.
(2) Where the party giving notice of set-off has to perform two or more obligations towards the other party, the rules in Article 7:109 apply with appropriate adaptations.

Article 13:106. Set-off discharges the obligations, as far as they are coextensive, as from the time of notice.

Article 13:107. Set-off cannot be effected:
(a) where it is excluded by agreement;
(b) against a claim to the extent that that claim is not capable of attachment; and
(c) against a claim arising from a deliberate wrongful act.

Chapter 14. Prescription

Section 1. General Provision

PRINCIPLES OF EUROPEAN CONTRACT LAW

Article 14:101. A right to performance of an obligation ("claim") is subject to prescription by the expiry of a period of time in accordance with these Principles.

Section 2. Periods of Prescription and their Commencement

Article 14:201. The general period of prescription is three years.

Article 14:202. Period for a Claim Established by Legal Proceedings
(1) The period of prescription for a claim established by judgment is ten years.
(2) The same applies to a claim established by an arbitral award or other instrument which is enforceable as if it were a judgment.

Article 14:203. (1) The general period of prescription begins to run from the time when the debtor has to effect performance or, in the case of a right to damages, from the time of the act which gives rise to the claim.
(2) Where the debtor is under a continuing obligation to do or refrain from doing something, the general period of prescription begins to run with each breach of the obligation.
(3) The period of prescription set out in Article 14:202 begins to run from the time when the judgment or arbitral award obtains the effect of res judicata, or the other instrument becomes enforceable, though not before the debtor has to effect performance.

Section 3. Extension of Period

Article 14:301. The running of the period of prescription is suspended as long as the creditor does not know of, and could not reasonably know of:
(a) the identity of the debtor; or
(b) the facts giving rise to the claim including, in the case of a right to damages, the type of damage.

Article 14:302. (1) The running of the period of prescription is suspended from the time when judicial proceedings on the claim are begun.
(2) Suspension lasts until a decision has been made which has the effect of res judicata, or until the case has been otherwise disposed of.
(3) These provisions apply, with appropriate adaptations, to arbitration proceedings and to all other proceedings initiated with the aim of obtaining an instrument which is enforceable as if it were a judgment.

Article 14:303. (1) The running of the period of prescription is suspended as long as the creditor is prevented from pursuing the claim by an impediment which is beyond the creditor's control and which the creditor could not reasonably have been expected to avoid or overcome.
(2) Paragraph (1) applies only if the impediment arises, or subsists, within the last six months of the prescription period.

Article 14:304. If the parties negotiate about the claim, or about circumstances from which a claim might arise, the period of prescription does not expire before one year has passed since the last communication made in the negotiations.

Article 14:305. (1) If a person subject to an incapacity is without a representative, the period of prescription of a claim held by or against that person does not expire before one year has passed after either the incapacity has ended or a representative has been appointed.
(2) The period of prescription of claims between a person subject to an incapacity and that person's representative does not expire before one year has passed after either the incapacity has ended or a new representative has been appointed.

Article 14:306. Where the creditor or debtor has died, the period of prescription of a claim held by or against the deceased's estate does not expire before one year has passed after the claim can be enforced by or against an heir, or by or against a representative of the estate.

Article 14:307. The period of prescription cannot be extended, by suspension of its running or postponement of its expiry under these Principles, to more than ten years or, in case of claims for personal injuries, to more than thirty years. This does not apply to suspension under Article 14:302.

Section 4. Renewal of Period

Article 14:401. (1) If the debtor acknowledges the claim, vis-à-vis the creditor, by part payment, payment of interest, giving of security, or in any other manner, a new period of prescription begins to run.

(2) The new period is the general period of prescription, regardless of whether the claim was originally subject to the general period of prescription or the ten year period under Article 14:202. In the latter case, however, this Article does not operate so as to shorten the ten year period.

Article 14:402. The ten year period of prescription laid down in Article 14:202 begins to run again with each reasonable attempt at execution undertaken by the creditor.

Section 5. Effects of Prescription

Article 14:501. (1) After expiry of the period of prescription the debtor is entitled to refuse performance.
(2) Whatever has been performed in order to discharge a claim may not be reclaimed merely because the period of prescription had expired.

Article 14:502. The period of prescription for a right to payment of interest, and other claims of an ancillary nature, expires not later than the period for the principal claim.

Article 14:503. A claim in relation to which the period of prescription has expired may nonetheless be set off, unless the debtor has invoked prescription previously or does so within two months of notification of set-off.

Section 6. Modification by Agreement

Article 14:601. (1) The requirements for prescription may be modified by agreement between the parties, in particular by either shortening or lengthening the periods of prescription.
(2) The period of prescription may not, however, be reduced to less than one year or extended to more than thirty years after the time of commencement set out in Article 14:203.

Chapter 15: Illegality

Article 15:101. A contract is of no effect to the extent that it is contrary to principles recognised as fundamental in the laws of the Member States of the European Union.

Article 15:102. (1) Where a contract infringes a mandatory rule of law applicable under Article 1:103 of these Principles, the effects of that infringement upon the contract are the effects, if any, expressly prescribed by that mandatory rule.
(2) Where the mandatory rule does not expressly prescribe the effects of an infringement upon a contract, the contract may be declared to have full effect, to have some effect, to have no effect, or to be subject to modification.
(3) A decision reached under paragraph (2) must be an appropriate and proportional response to the infringement, having regard to all relevant circumstances, including:
(a) the purpose of the rule which has been infringed;
(b) the category of persons for whose protection the rule exists;
(c) any sanction that may be imposed under the rule infringed;
(d) the seriousness of the infringement;
(e) whether the infringement was intentional; and
(f) the closeness of the relationship between the infringement and the contract.

Article 15:103. (1) If only part of a contract is rendered ineffective under Articles 15:101 or 15:102, the remaining part continues in effect unless, giving due consideration to all the circumstances of the case, it is unreasonable to uphold it.
(2) Articles 15:104 and 15:105 apply, with appropriate adaptations, to a case of partial ineffectiveness.

Article 15:104. (1) When a contract is rendered ineffective under Articles 15:101 or 15:102, either party may claim restitution of whatever that party has supplied under the contract, provided that, where appropriate, concurrent restitution is made of whatever has been received.
(2) When considering whether to grant restitution under paragraph (1), and what concurrent restitution, if any, would be appropriate, regard must be had to the factors referred to in Article 15:102(3).
(3) An award of restitution may be refused to a party who knew or ought to have known of the reason for the ineffectiveness.
(4) If restitution cannot be made in kind for any reason, a reasonable sum must be paid for what has been received.

Article 15:105. (1) A party to a contract which is rendered ineffective under Articles 15:101 or

15:102 may recover from the other party damages putting the first party as nearly as possible into the same position as if the contract had not been concluded, provided that the other party knew or ought to have known of the reason for the ineffectiveness.

(2) When considering whether to award damages under paragraph (1), regard must be had to the factors referred to in Article 15:102(3).

(3) An award of damages may be refused where the first party knew or ought to have known of the reason for the ineffectiveness.

Chapter 16. Conditions

Article 16:101. A contractual obligation may be made conditional upon the occurrence of an uncertain future event, so that the obligation takes effect only if the event occurs (suspensive condition) or comes to an end if the event occurs (resolutive condition).

Article 16:102. (1) If fulfilment of a condition is prevented by a party, contrary to duties of good faith and fair dealing or co-operation, and if fulfilment would have operated to that party's disadvantage, the condition is deemed to be fulfilled.

(2) If fulfilment of a condition is brought about by a party, contrary to duties of good faith and fair dealing or co-operation, and if fulfilment operates to that party's advantage, the condition is deemed not to be fulfilled.

Article 16:103. (1) Upon fulfilment of a suspensive condition, the relevant obligation takes effect unless the parties otherwise agree.

(2) Upon fulfilment of a resolutive condition, the relevant obligation comes to an end unless the parties otherwise agree.

Chapter 17. Capitalisation of Interest

Article 17:101. (1) Interest payable according to Article 9:508(1) is added to the outstanding capital every 12 months.

(2) Paragraph (1) of this Article does not apply if the parties have provided for interest upon delay in payment.

PART IV   EUROPEAN PRIVATE LAW

The Principles of European Tort Law [PETL]

Title I. Basic Norm

Chapter 1. Basic Norm

Art. 1:101. Basic norm. (1) A person to whom damage to another is legally attributed is liable to compensate that damage.
(2) Damage may be attributed in particular to the person
a) whose conduct constituting fault has caused it; or
b) whose abnormally dangerous activity has caused it; or
c) whose auxiliary has caused it within the scope of his functions.

Title II. General Conditions of Liability

Chapter 2. Damage

Art. 2:101. Recoverable damage. Damage requires material or immaterial harm to a legally protected interest.

Art. 2:102. Protected interests. (1) The scope of protection of an interest depends on its nature; the higher its value, the precision of its definition and its obviousness, the more extensive is its protection.
(2) Life, bodily or mental integrity, human dignity and liberty enjoy the most extensive protection.
(3) Extensive protection is granted to property rights, including those in intangible property.
(4) Protection of pure economic interests or contractual relationships may be more limited in scope. In such cases, due regard must be had especially to the proximity between the actor and the endangered person, or to the fact that the actor is aware of the fact that he will cause damage even though his interests are necessarily valued lower than those of the victim.
(5) The scope of protection may also be affected by the nature of liability, so that an interest may receive more extensive protection against intentional harm than in other cases.
(6) In determining the scope of protection, the interests of the actor, especially in liberty of action and in exercising his rights, as well as public interests also have to be taken into consideration.

Art. 2:103. Legitimacy of damage. Losses relating to activities or sources which are regarded as illegitimate cannot be recovered.

Art. 2:104. Preventive expenses. Expenses incurred to prevent threatened damage amount to recoverable damage in so far as reasonably incurred.

Art. 2:105. Proof of damage. Damage must be proved according to normal procedural standards. The court may estimate the extent of damage where proof of the exact amount would be too difficult or too costly.

Chapter 3. Causation

Section 1. Conditio sine qua non and qualifications

Art. 3:101. Conditio sine qua non. An activity or conduct (hereafter: activity) is a cause of the victim's damage if, in the absence of the activity, the damage would not have occurred.

Art. 3:102. Concurrent causes. In case of multiple activities, where each of them alone would have caused the damage at the same time, each activity is regarded as a cause of the victim's damage.

Art. 3:103. Alternative causes. (1) In case of multiple activities, where each of them alone would have been sufficient to cause the damage, but it remains uncertain which one in fact caused it, each activity is regarded as a cause to the extent corresponding to the likelihood that it may have caused the victim's damage.
(2) If, in case of multiple victims, it remains uncertain whether a particular victim's damage has been caused by an activity, while it is likely that it did not cause the damage of all victims, the activity is regarded as a cause of the damage suffered by all victims in proportion to the likelihood that it may have caused the damage of a particular victim.

Art. 3:104. Potential causes. (1) If an activity has definitely and irreversibly led the victim to suffer damage, a subsequent activity which alone would have caused the same damage is to be disregarded.
(2) A subsequent activity is nevertheless taken into consideration if it has led to additional or aggravated damage.

(3) If the first activity has caused continuing damage and the subsequent activity later on also would have caused it, both activities are regarded as a cause of that continuing damage from that time on.

Art. 3:105. Uncertain partial causation. In the case of multiple activities, when it is certain that none of them has caused the entire damage or any determinable part thereof, those that are likely to have [minimally] contributed to the damage are presumed to have caused equal shares thereof.

Art. 3:106. Uncertain causes within the victim's sphere. The victim has to bear his loss to the extent corresponding to the likelihood that it may have been caused by an activity, occurrence or other circumstance within his own sphere.

Section 2. Scope of Liability

Art. 3:201. Scope of Liability. Where an activity is a cause within the meaning of Section 1 of this Chapter, whether and to what extent damage may be attributed to a person depends on factors such as
a) the foreseeability of the damage to a reasonable person at the time of the activity, taking into account in particular the closeness in time or space between the damaging activity and its consequence, or the magnitude of the damage in relation to the normal consequences of such an activity;
b) the nature and the value of the protected interest (Article 2:102);
c) the basis of liability (Article 1:101);
d) the extent of the ordinary risks of life; and
e) the protective purpose of the rule that has been violated.

Title III. Bases of Liability

Chapter 4. Liability based on fault

Section 1. Conditions of liability based on fault

Art. 4:101. Fault. A person is liable on the basis of fault for intentional or negligent violation of the required standard of conduct.

Art. 4:102. Required standard of conduct. (1) The required standard of conduct is that of the reasonable person in the circumstances, and depends, in particular, on the nature and value of the protected interest involved, the dangerousness of the activity, the expertise to be expected of a person carrying it on, the foreseeability of the damage, the relationship of proximity or special reliance between those involved, as well as the availability and the costs of precautionary or alternative methods.
(2) The above standard may be adjusted when due to age, mental or physical disability or due to extraordinary circumstances the person cannot be expected to conform to it.
(3) Rules which prescribe or forbid certain conduct have to be considered when establishing the required standard of conduct.

Art. 4:103. Duty to protect others from damage. A duty to act positively to protect others from damage may exist if law so provides, or if the actor creates or controls a dangerous situation, or when there is a special relationship between parties or when the seriousness of the harm on the one side and the ease of avoiding the damage on the other side point towards such a duty.

Section 2. Reversal of the burden of proving fault

Art. 4:201. Reversal of the burden of proving fault. in general. (1) The burden of proving fault may be reversed in light of the gravity of the danger presented by the activity.
(2) The gravity of the danger is determined according to the seriousness of possible damage in such cases as well as the likelihood that such damage might actually occur.

Art. 4:202. Enterprise Liability. (1) A person pursuing a lasting enterprise for economic or professional purposes who uses auxiliaries or technical equipment is liable for any harm caused by a defect of such enterprise or of its output unless he proves that he has conformed to the required standard of conduct.
(2) Defect is any deviation from standards that are reasonably to be expected from the enterprise or from its products or services.

Chapter 5. Strict liability

Art. 5:101. Abnormally dangerous activities. (1) A person who carries on an abnormally dangerous activity is strictly liable for damage characteristic to the risk presented by the activity and resulting from it.

(2) An activity is abnormally dangerous if
a) it creates a foreseeable and highly significant risk of damage even when all due care is exercised in its management and
b) it is not a matter of common usage.
(3) A risk of damage may be significant having regard to the seriousness or the likelihood of the damage.
(4) This Article does not apply to an activity which is specifically subjected to strict liability by any other provision of these Principles or any other national law or international convention.

Art. 5:102. Other strict liabilities. (1) National laws can provide for further categories of strict liability for dangerous activities even if the activity is not abnormally dangerous.
(2) Unless national law provides otherwise, additional categories of strict liability can be found by analogy to other sources of comparable risk of damage.

Chapter 6. Liability for others

Art. 6:101. Liability for minors or mentally disabled persons. A person in charge of another who is a minor or subject to mental disability is liable for damage caused by the other unless the person in charge shows that he has conformed to the required standard of conduct in supervision.

Art. 6:102. Liability for auxiliaries. (1) A person is liable for damage caused by his auxiliaries acting within the scope of their functions provided that they violated the required standard of conduct.
(2) An independent contractor is not regarded as an auxiliary for the purposes of this Article.

Title IV. Defences

Chapter 7. Defences in general

Art. 7:101. Defences based on justifications. (1) Liability can be excluded if and to the extent that the actor acted legitimately
a) in defence of his own protected interest against an unlawful attack (self-defence),
b) under necessity,
c) because the help of the authorities could not be obtained in time (self-help),
d) with the consent of the victim, or where the latter has assumed the risk of being harmed, or
e) by virtue of lawful authority, such as a licence.
(2) Whether liability is excluded depends upon the weight of these justifications on the one hand and the conditions of liability on the other.
(3) In extraordinary cases, liability may instead be reduced.

Art. 7:102. Defences against strict liability. (1) Strict liability can be excluded or reduced if the injury was caused by an unforeseeable and irresistible
a) force of nature (force majeure), or
b) conduct of a third party.
(2) Whether strict liability is excluded or reduced, and if so, to what extent, depends upon the weight of the external influence on the one hand and the scope of liability (Article 3:201) on the other.
(3) When reduced according to paragraph (1)(b), strict liability and any liability of the third party are solidary in accordance with Article 9:101 (1)(b).

Chapter 8. Contributory conduct or activity

Art. 8:101. Contributory conduct or activity of the victim. (1) Liability can be excluded or reduced to such extent as is considered just having regard to the victim's contributory fault and to any other matters which would be relevant to establish or reduce liability of the victim if he were the tortfeasor.
(2) Where damages are claimed with respect to the death of a person, his conduct or activity excludes or reduces liability according to para. 1.
(3) The contributory conduct or activity of an auxiliary of the victim excludes or reduces the damages recoverable by the latter according to para. 1.

Title V. Multiple Tortfeasors

Chapter 9. Multiple Tortfeasors

Art 9:101 Solidary and several liability: relation between victim and multiple tortfeasors. (1)

Liability is solidary where the whole or a distinct part of the damage suffered by the victim is attributable to two or more persons. Liability is solidary where:
a) a person knowingly participates in or instigates or encourages wrongdoing by others which causes damage to the victim; or
b) one person's independent behaviour or activity causes damage to the victim and the same damage is also attributable to another person.
c) a person is responsible for damage caused by an auxiliary in circumstances where the auxiliary is also liable.
(2) Where persons are subject to solidary liability, the victim may claim full compensation from any one or more of them, provided that the victim may not recover more than the full amount of the damage suffered by him.
(3) Damage is the same damage for the purposes of paragraph (1)(b) above when there is no reasonable basis for attributing only part of it to each of a number of persons liable to the victim. For this purpose it is for the person asserting that the damage is not the same to show that it is not. Where there is such a basis, liability is several, that is to say, each person is liable to the victim only for the part of the damage attributable to him.

Art 9:102 Relation between persons subject to solidary liability. (1) A person subject to solidary liability may recover a contribution from any other person liable to the victim in respect of the same damage. This right is without prejudice to any contract between them determining the allocation of the loss or to any statutory provision or to any right to recover by reason of subrogation [cessio legis] or on the basis of unjust enrichment.
(2) Subject to paragraph (3) of this Article, the amount of the contribution shall be what is considered just in the light of the relative responsibility for the damage of the persons liable, having regard to their respective degrees of fault and to any other matters which are relevant to establish or reduce their liability. A contribution may amount to full indemnification. If it is not possible to determine the relative responsibility of the persons liable they are to be treated as equally responsible.
(3) Where a person is liable for damage done by an auxiliary under Article 9:101 he is to be treated as bearing the entire share of the responsibility attributable to the auxiliary for the purposes of contribution between him and any tortfeasor other than the auxiliary.
(4) The obligation to make contribution is several, that is to say, the person subject to it is liable only for his apportioned share of responsibility for the damage under this Article; but where it is not possible to enforce a judgment for contribution against one person liable his share is to be reallocated among the other persons liable in proportion to their responsibility.

Title VI. Remedies

Chapter 10. Damages

Section 1. Damages in general

Art. 10:101. Nature and purpose of damages. Damages are a money payment to compensate the victim, that is to say, to restore him, so far as money can, to the position he would have been in if the wrong complained of had not been committed. Damages also serve the aim of preventing harm.

Art. 10:102. Lump sum or periodical payments. Damages are awarded in a lump sum or as periodical payments as appropriate with particular regard to the interests of the victim.

Art. 10:103. Benefits gained through the damaging event. When determining the amount of damages benefits which the injured party gains through the damaging event are to be taken into account unless this cannot be reconciled with the purpose of the benefit.

Art. 10:104. Restoration in kind. Instead of damages, restoration in kind can be claimed by the injured party as far as it is possible and not too burdensome to the other party.

Section 2. Pecuniary damage

Art. 10:201. Nature and determination of pecuniary damage. Recoverable pecuniary damage is a diminution of the victim's patrimony caused by the damaging event. Such damage is generally determined as concretely as possible but it may be determined abstractly when appropriate, for example by reference to a market value.

Art. 10:202. Personal injury and death. (1) In the case of personal injury, which includes injury to bodily health and to mental health amounting to a recognised illness, pecuniary damage includes

loss of income, impairment of earning capacity (even if unaccompanied by any loss of income) and reasonable expenses, such as the cost of medical care.
(2) In the case of death, persons such as family members whom the deceased maintained or would have maintained if death had not occurred are treated as having suffered recoverable damage to the extent of loss of that support.

Art. 10:203. Loss, destruction and damage of things. (1) Where a thing is lost, destroyed or damaged, the basic measure of damages is the value of the thing or the diminution in its value and for this purpose it is irrelevant whether the victim intends to replace or repair the thing. However, if the victim has replaced or repaired it (or will do so), he may recover the higher expenditure thereby incurred if it is reasonable to do so.
(2) Damages may also be awarded for loss of use of the thing, including consequential losses such as loss of business.

Section 3. Non-pecuniary damage

Art. 10:301. Non-pecuniary damage. (1) Considering the scope of its protection (Article 2:102), the violation of an interest may justify compensation of non-pecuniary damage. This is the case in particular where the victim has suffered personal injury; or injury to human dignity, liberty, or other personality rights. Non-pecuniary damage can also be the subject of compensation for persons having a close relationship with a victim suffering a fatal or very serious non-fatal injury.
(2) In general, in the assessment of such damages, all circumstances of the case, including the gravity, duration and consequences of the grievance, have to be taken into account. The degree of the tortfeasor's fault is to be taken into account only where it significantly contributes to the grievance of the victim.
(3) In cases of personal injury, non-pecuniary damage corresponds to the suffering of the victim and the impairment of his bodily or mental health. In assessing damages (including damages for persons having a close relationship to deceased or seriously injured victims) similar sums should be awarded for objectively similar losses.

Section 4. Reduction of damages

Art. 10:401. Reduction of damages. In an exceptional case, if in light of the financial situation of the parties full compensation would be an oppressive burden to the defendant, damages may be reduced. In deciding whether to do so, the basis of liability (Article 1:101), the scope of protection of the interest (Article 2:102) and the magnitude of the damage have to be taken into account in particular.

European Civil Procedure

PART V EUROPEAN CIVIL PROCEDURE

Council Regulation (EC) No 1206/2001 of 28 May 2001 on cooperation between the courts of the Member States in the taking of evidence in civil or commercial matters (OJ L 174, 27.06.2001, pp. 1 – 24).

[The Preamble is omitted.]

Chapter I. General Provisions

Article 1. 1. This Regulation shall apply in civil or commercial matters where the court of a Member State, in accordance with the provisions of the law of that State, requests:
(a) the competent court of another Member State to take evidence; or
(b) to take evidence directly in another Member State.
2. A request shall not be made to obtain evidence which is not intended for use in judicial proceedings, commenced or contemplated.
3. In this Regulation, the term 'Member State' shall mean Member States with the exception of Denmark.

Article 2. 1. Requests pursuant to Article 1(1)(a), hereinafter referred to as 'requests', shall be transmitted by the court before which the proceedings are commenced or contemplated, hereinafter referred to as the 'requesting court', directly to the competent court of another Member State, hereinafter referred to as the 'requested court', for the performance of the taking of evidence.
2. Each Member State shall draw up a list of the courts competent for the performance of taking of evidence according to this Regulation. The list shall also indicate the territorial and, where appropriate, the special jurisdiction of those courts.

Article 3. 1. Each Member State shall designate a central body responsible for:
(a) supplying information to the courts;
(b) seeking solutions to any difficulties which may arise in respect of a request;
(c) forwarding, in exceptional cases, at the request of a requesting court, a request to the competent court.
2. A federal State, a State in which several legal systems apply or a State with autonomous territorial entities shall be free to designate more than one central body.
3. Each Member State shall also designate the central body referred to in paragraph 1 or one or several competent authority(ies) to be responsible for taking decisions on requests pursuant to Article 17.

Chapter II. Transmission and Execution of Requests

Section 1. Transmission of the request

Article 4. 1. The request shall be made using form A or, where appropriate, form I in the Annex. It shall contain the following details:
(a) the requesting and, where appropriate, the requested court;
(b) the names and addresses of the parties to the proceedings and their representatives, if any;
(c) the nature and subject matter of the case and a brief statement of the facts;
(d) a description of the taking of evidence to be performed;
(e) where the request is for the examination of a person:
— the name(s) and address(es) of the person(s) to be examined,
— the questions to be put to the person(s) to be examined or a statement of the facts about which he is (they are) to be examined,
— where appropriate, a reference to a right to refuse to testify under the law of the Member State of the requesting court,
— any requirement that the examination is to be carried out under oath or affirmation in lieu thereof, and any special form to be used,
— where appropriate, any other information that the requesting court deems necessary;
(f) where the request is for any other form of taking of evidence, the documents or other objects to be inspected;
(g) where appropriate, any request pursuant to Article 10(3) and (4), and Articles 11 and 12 and any information necessary for the application thereof.
2. The request and all documents accompanying the request shall be exempted from authentication or any equivalent formality.
3. Documents which the requesting court deems it necessary to enclose for the execution of the request shall be accompanied by a translation into the language in which the request was written.

Article 5. The request and communications pursuant to this Regulation shall be drawn up in the official language of the requested Member State or, if there are several official languages in that Member State, in the official language or one of the official languages of the place where the requested taking of evidence is to be performed, or in another language which the requested Member State has indicated it can accept. Each Member State shall indicate the official language or languages of the institutions of the European Community other than its own which is or are acceptable to it for completion of the forms.

Article 6. Requests and communications pursuant to this Regulation shall be transmitted by the swiftest possible means, which the requested Member State has indicated it can accept. The transmission may be carried out by any appropriate means, provided that the document received accurately reflects the content of the document forwarded and that all information in it is legible.

Section 2. Receipt of request

Article 7. 1. Within seven days of receipt of the request, the requested competent court shall send an acknowledgement of receipt to the requesting court using form B in the Annex. Where the request does not comply with the conditions laid down in Articles 5 and 6, the requested court shall enter a note to that effect in the acknowledgement of receipt.
2. Where the execution of a request made using form A in the Annex, which complies with the conditions laid down in Article 5, does not fall within the jurisdiction of the court to which it was transmitted, the latter shall forward the request to the competent court of its Member State and shall inform the requesting court thereof using form A in the Annex.

Article 8. 1. If a request cannot be executed because it does not contain all of the necessary information pursuant to Article 4, the requested court shall inform the requesting court thereof without delay and, at the latest, within 30 days of receipt of the request using form C in the Annex, and shall request it to send the missing information, which should be indicated as precisely as possible.
2. If a request cannot be executed because a deposit or advance is necessary in accordance with Article 18(3), the requested court shall inform the requesting court thereof without delay and, at the latest, within 30 days of receipt of the request using form C in the Annex and inform the requesting court how the deposit or advance should be made. The requested Court shall acknowledge receipt of the deposit or advance without delay, at the latest within 10 days of receipt of the deposit or the advance using form D.

Article 9. 1. If the requested court has noted on the acknowledgement of receipt pursuant to Article 7(1) that the request does not comply with the conditions laid down in Articles 5 and 6 or has informed the requesting court pursuant to Article 8 that the request cannot be executed because it does not contain all of the necessary information pursuant to Article 4, the time limit pursuant to Article 10 shall begin to run when the requested court received the request duly completed.
2. Where the requested court has asked for a deposit or advance in accordance with Article 18(3), this time limit shall begin to run when the deposit or the advance is made.

Section 3. Taking of evidence by the requested court

Article 10. 1. The requested court shall execute the request without delay and, at the latest, within 90 days of receipt of the request.
2. The requested court shall execute the request in accordance with the law of its Member State.
3. The requesting court may call for the request to be executed in accordance with a special procedure provided for by the law of its Member State, using form A in the Annex. The requested court shall comply with such a requirement unless this procedure is incompatible with the law of the Member State of the requested court or by reason of major practical difficulties. If the requested court does not comply with the requirement for one of these reasons it shall inform the requesting court using form E in the Annex.
4. The requesting court may ask the requested court to use communications technology at the performance of the taking of evidence, in particular by using videoconference and teleconference.
The requested court shall comply with such a requirement unless this is incompatible with the law of the Member State of the requested court or by reason of major practical difficulties.
If the requested court does not comply with the requirement for one of these reasons, it shall inform the requesting court, using form E in the Annex.
If there is no access to the technical means referred to above in the requesting or in the requested court, such means may be made available by the courts by mutual agreement.

PART V   EUROPEAN CIVIL PROCEDURE

Article 11. 1. If it is provided for by the law of the Member State of the requesting court, the parties and, if any, their representatives, have the right to be present at the performance of the taking of evidence by the requested court.
2. The requesting court shall, in its request, inform the requested court that the parties and, if any, their representatives, will be present and, where appropriate, that their participation is requested, using form A in the Annex. This information may also be given at any other appropriate time.
3. If the participation of the parties and, if any, their representatives, is requested at the performance of the taking of evidence, the requested court shall determine, in accordance with Article 10, the conditions under which they may participate.
4. The requested court shall notify the parties and, if any, their representatives, of the time when, the place where, the proceedings will take place, and, where appropriate, the conditions under which they may participate, using form F in the Annex.
5. Paragraphs 1 to 4 shall not affect the possibility for the requested court of asking the parties and, if any their representatives, to be present at or to participate in the performance of the taking of evidence if that possibility is provided for by the law of its Member State.

Article 12. 1. If it is compatible with the law of the Member State of the requesting court, representatives of the requesting court have the right to be present in the performance of the taking of evidence by the requested court.
2. For the purpose of this Article, the term 'representative' shall include members of the judicial personnel designated by the requesting court, in accordance with the law of its Member State. The requesting court may also designate, in accordance with the law of its Member State, any other person, such as an expert.
3. The requesting court shall, in its request, inform the requested court that its representatives will be present and, where appropriate, that their participation is requested, using form A in the Annex. This information may also be given at any other appropriate time.
4. If the participation of the representatives of the requesting court is requested in the performance of the taking of evidence, the requested court shall determine, in accordance with Article 10, the conditions under which they may participate.
5. The requested court shall notify the requesting court, of the time when, and the place where, the proceedings will take place, and, where appropriate, the conditions under which the representatives may participate, using form F in the Annex.

Article 13. Where necessary, in executing a request the requested court shall apply the appropriate coercive measures in the instances and to the extent as are provided for by the law of the Member State of the requested court for the execution of a request made for the same purpose by its national authorities or one of the parties concerned.

Article 14. 1. A request for the hearing of a person shall not be executed when the person concerned claims the right to refuse to give evidence or to be prohibited from giving evidence,
(a) under the law of the Member State of the requested court; or
(b) under the law of the Member State of the requesting court, and such right has been specified in the request, or, if need be, at the instance of the requested court, has been confirmed by the requesting court.
2. In addition to the grounds referred to in paragraph 1, the execution of a request may be refused only if:
(a) the request does not fall within the scope of this Regulation as set out in Article 1; or
(b) the execution of the request under the law of the Member State of the requested court does not fall within the functions of the judiciary; or
(c) the requesting court does not comply with the request of the requested court to complete the request pursuant to Article 8 within 30 days after the requested court asked it to do so; or
(d) a deposit or advance asked for in accordance with Article 18(3) is not made within 60 days after the requested court asked for such a deposit or advance.
3. Execution may not be refused by the requested court solely on the ground that under the law of its Member State a court of that Member State has exclusive jurisdiction over the subject matter of the action or that the law of that Member State would not admit the right of action on it.
4. If execution of the request is refused on one of the grounds referred to in paragraph 2, the requested court shall notify the requesting court thereof within 60 days of receipt of the request by the requested court using form H in the Annex.

Article 15. If the requested court is not in a position to execute the request within 90 days of receipt, it shall inform the requesting court thereof, using form G in the Annex. When it does so, the grounds for the delay shall be given as well as the estimated time that the requested court expects it will need to execute the request.

Article 16. The requested court shall send without delay to the requesting court the documents establishing the execution of the request and, where appropriate, return the documents received from the requesting court. The documents shall be accompanied by a confirmation of execution using form H in the Annex.

Section 4. Direct taking of evidence by the requesting court

Article 17. 1. Where a court requests to take evidence directly in another Member State, it shall submit a request to the central body or the competent authority referred to in Article 3(3) in that State, using form I in the Annex.
2. Direct taking of evidence may only take place if it can be performed on a voluntary basis without the need for coercive measures.
Where the direct taking of evidence implies that a person shall be heard, the requesting court shall inform that person that the performance shall take place on a voluntary basis.
3. The taking of evidence shall be performed by a member of the judicial personnel or by any other person such as an expert, who will be designated, in accordance with the law of the Member State of the requesting court.
4. Within 30 days of receiving the request, the central body or the competent authority of the requested Member State shall inform the requesting court if the request is accepted and, if necessary, under what conditions according to the law of its Member State such performance is to be carried out, using form J.
In particular, the central body or the competent authority may assign a court of its Member State to take part in the performance of the taking of evidence in order to ensure the proper application of this Article and the conditions that have been set out.
The central body or the competent authority shall encourage the use of communications technology, such as videoconferences and teleconferences.
5. The central body or the competent authority may refuse direct taking of evidence only if:
(a) the request does not fall within the scope of this Regulation as set out in Article 1;
(b) the request does not contain all of the necessary information pursuant to Article 4; or
(c) the direct taking of evidence requested is contrary to fundamental principles of law in its Member State.
6. Without prejudice to the conditions laid down in accordance with paragraph 4, the requesting court shall execute the request in accordance with the law of its Member State.

Section 5. Costs

Article 18. 1. The execution of the request, in accordance with Article 10, shall not give rise to a claim for any reimbursement of taxes or costs.
2. Nevertheless, if the requested court so requires, the requesting court shall ensure the reimbursement, without delay, of:
— the fees paid to experts and interpreters, and
— the costs occasioned by the application of Article 10(3) and (4).
The duty for the parties to bear these fees or costs shall be governed by the law of the Member State of the requesting court.
3. Where the opinion of an expert is required, the requested court may, before executing the request, ask the requesting court for an adequate deposit or advance towards the requested costs. In all other cases, a deposit or advance shall not be a condition for the execution of a request.
The deposit or advance shall be made by the parties if that is provided for by the law of the Member State of the requesting court.

Chapter III. Final provisions

Article 19. 1. The Commission shall draw up and regularly update a manual, which shall also be available electronically, containing the information provided by the Member States in accordance with Article 22 and the agreements or arrangements in force, according to Article 21.
2. The updating or making of technical amendments to the standard forms set out in the Annex shall be carried out by the Commission. Those measures, designed to amend non-essential elements of this Regulation, shall be adopted in accordance with the regulatory procedure with scrutiny referred to in Article 20(2).

Article 20. 1. The Commission shall be assisted by a committee.
2. Where reference is made to this paragraph, Article 5a(1) to (4) and Article 7 of Decision 1999/468/EC shall apply, having regard to the provisions of Article 8 thereof.

Article 21. 1. This Regulation shall, in relation to matters to which it applies, prevail over other provisions contained in bilateral or multilateral agreements or arrangements concluded by the Member States and in particular the Hague Convention of 1 March 1954 on Civil Procedure and the Hague Convention of 18 March 1970 on the Taking of Evidence Abroad in Civil or Commercial Matters, in relations between the Member States party thereto.
2. This Regulation shall not preclude Member States from maintaining or concluding agreements or arrangements between two or more of them to further facilitate the taking of evidence, provided that they are compatible with this Regulation.
3. Member States shall send to the Commission:
(a) by 1 July 2003, a copy of the agreements or arrangements maintained between the Member States referred to in paragraph 2;
(b) a copy of the agreements or arrangements concluded between the Member States referred to in paragraph 2 as well as drafts of such agreements or arrangements which they intend to adopt; and
(c) any denunciation of, or amendments to, these agreements or arrangements.

Article 22. By 1 July 2003 each Member State shall communicate to the Commission the following:
(a) the list pursuant to Article 2(2) indicating the territorial and, where appropriate, the special jurisdiction of the courts;
(b) the names and addresses of the central bodies and competent authorities pursuant to Article 3, indicating their territorial jurisdiction;
(c) the technical means for the receipt of requests available to the courts on the list pursuant to Article 2(2);
(d) the languages accepted for the requests as referred to in Article 5.
Member States shall inform the Commission of any subsequent changes to this information.

Article 23. No later than 1 January 2007, and every five years thereafter, the Commission shall present to the European Parliament, the Council and the Economic and Social Committee a report on the application of this Regulation, paying special attention to the practical application of Article 3(1) (c) and 3, and Articles 17 and 18.

Article 24. 1. This Regulation shall enter into force on 1 July 2001.
2. This Regulation shall apply from 1 January 2004, except for Articles 19, 21 and 22, which shall apply from 1 July 2001.
This Regulation shall be binding in its entirety and directly applicable in the Member States in accordance with the Treaty establishing the European Community.
[The Annex is omitted.]

EU: REGULATION 805/2004 CREATING EUROPEAN ENFORCEMENT ORDER

Regulation (EC) No 805/2004 of the European Parliament and of the Council of 21 April 2004 creating a European Enforcement Order for uncontested claims (OJ L 143, 30.04.2004, pp. 15 – 39).

[The Preamble is omitted.]

Chapter I. Subject matter, Scope and Definitions

Article 1. The purpose of this Regulation is to create a European Enforcement Order for uncontested claims to permit, by laying down minimum standards, the free circulation of judgments, court settlements and authentic instruments throughout all Member States without any intermediate proceedings needing to be brought in the Member State of enforcement prior to recognition and enforcement.

Article 2. 1. This Regulation shall apply in civil and commercial matters, whatever the nature of the court or tribunal. It shall not extend, in particular, to revenue, customs or administrative matters or the liability of the State for acts and omissions in the exercise of State authority ('acta iure imperii').
2. This Regulation shall not apply to:
(a) the status or legal capacity of natural persons, rights in property arising out of a matrimonial relationship, wills and succession;
(b) bankruptcy, proceedings relating to the winding-up of insolvent companies or other legal persons, judicial arrangements, compositions and analogous proceedings;
(c) social security;
(d) arbitration.
3. In this Regulation, the term 'Member State' shall mean Member States with the exception of Denmark.

Article 3. 1. This Regulation shall apply to judgments, court settlements and authentic instruments on uncontested claims.
A claim shall be regarded as uncontested if:
(a) the debtor has expressly agreed to it by admission or by means of a settlement which has been approved by a court or concluded before a court in the course of proceedings; or
(b) the debtor has never objected to it, in compliance with the relevant procedural requirements under the law of the Member State of origin, in the course of the court proceedings; or
(c) the debtor has not appeared or been represented at a court hearing regarding that claim after having initially objected to the claim in the course of the court proceedings, provided that such conduct amounts to a tacit admission of the claim or of the facts alleged by the creditor under the law of the Member State of origin; or
(d) the debtor has expressly agreed to it in an authentic instrument.
2. This Regulation shall also apply to decisions delivered following challenges to judgments, court settlements or authentic instruments certified as European Enforcement Orders.

Article 4. For the purposes of this Regulation, the following definitions shall apply:
1. 'judgment': any judgment given by a court or tribunal of a Member State, whatever the judgment may be called, including a decree, order, decision or writ of execution, as well as the determination of costs or expenses by an officer of the court;
2. 'claim': a claim for payment of a specific sum of money that has fallen due or for which the due date is indicated in the judgment, court settlement or authentic instrument;
3. 'authentic instrument':
(a) a document which has been formally drawn up or registered as an authentic instrument, and the authenticity of which:
(i) relates to the signature and the content of the instrument; and
(ii) has been established by a public authority or other authority empowered for that purpose by the Member State in which it originates; or
b) an arrangement relating to maintenance obligations concluded with administrative authorities or authenticated by them;
4. 'Member State of origin': the Member State in which the judgment has been given, the court settlement has been approved or concluded or the authentic instrument has been drawn up or registered, and is to be certified as a European Enforcement Order;
5. 'Member State of enforcement': the Member State in which enforcement of the judgment, court settlement or authentic instrument certified as a European Enforcement Order is sought;
6. 'court of origin': the court or tribunal seised of the proceedings at the time of fulfilment of the conditions set out in Article 3(1)(a), (b) or (c);

7. in Sweden, in summary proceedings concerning orders to pay (betalningsföreläggande), the expression 'court' includes the Swedish enforcement service (kronofogdemyndighet).

Chapter II. European Enforcement Order

Article 5. A judgment which has been certified as a European Enforcement Order in the Member State of origin shall be recognised and enforced in the other Member States without the need for a declaration of enforceability and without any possibility of opposing its recognition.

Article 6. 1. A judgment on an uncontested claim delivered in a Member State shall, upon application at any time to the court of origin, be certified as a European Enforcement Order if:
(a) the judgment is enforceable in the Member State of origin; and
(b) the judgment does not conflict with the rules on jurisdiction as laid down in sections 3 and 6 of Chapter II of Regulation (EC) No 44/2001; and
(c) the court proceedings in the Member State of origin met the requirements as set out in Chapter III where a claim is uncontested within the meaning of Article 3(1)(b) or (c); and
(d) the judgment was given in the Member State of the debtor's domicile within the meaning of Article 59 of Regulation (EC) No 44/2001, in cases where
— a claim is uncontested within the meaning of Article 3(1)(b) or (c); and
— it relates to a contract concluded by a person, the consumer, for a purpose which can be regarded as being outside his trade or profession; and
— the debtor is the consumer.
2. Where a judgment certified as a European Enforcement Order has ceased to be enforceable or its enforceability has been suspended or limited, a certificate indicating the lack or limitation of enforceability shall, upon application at any time to the court of origin, be issued, using the standard form in Annex IV.
3. Without prejudice to Article 12(2), where a decision has been delivered following a challenge to a judgment certified as a European Enforcement Order in accordance with paragraph (1) of this Article, a replacement certificate shall, upon application at any time, be issued, using the standard form in Annex V, if that decision on the challenge is enforceable in the Member State of origin.

Article 7. Where a judgment includes an enforceable decision on the amount of costs related to the court proceedings, including the interest rates, it shall be certified as a European Enforcement Order also with regard to the costs unless the debtor has specifically objected to his obligation to bear such costs in the course of the court proceedings, in accordance with the law of the Member State of origin.

Article 8. If only parts of the judgment meet the requirements of this Regulation, a partial European Enforcement Order certificate shall be issued for those parts.

Article 9. 1. The European Enforcement Order certificate shall be issued using the standard form in Annex I.
2. The European Enforcement Order certificate shall be issued in the language of the judgment.

Article 10. 1. The European Enforcement Order certificate shall, upon application to the court of origin, be
(a) rectified where, due to a material error, there is a discrepancy between the judgment and the certificate;
(b) withdrawn where it was clearly wrongly granted, having regard to the requirements laid down in this Regulation.
2. The law of the Member State of origin shall apply to the rectification or withdrawal of the European Enforcement Order certificate.
3. An application for the rectification or withdrawal of a European Enforcement Order certificate may be made using the standard form in Annex VI.
4. No appeal shall lie against the issuing of a European Enforcement Order certificate.

Article 11. The European Enforcement Order certificate shall take effect only within the limits of the enforceability of the judgment.

Chapter III. Minimum Standards for Uncontested Claims Procedures

Article 12. 1. A judgment on a claim that is uncontested within the meaning of Article 3(1)(b) or (c) can be certified as a European Enforcement Order only if the court proceedings in the Member State of origin met the procedural requirements as set out in this Chapter.

2. The same requirements shall apply to the issuing of a European Enforcement Order certificate or a replacement certificate within the meaning of Article 6(3) for a decision following a challenge to a judgment where, at the time of that decision, the conditions of Article 3(1)(b) or (c) are fulfilled.

Article 13. 1. The document instituting the proceedings or an equivalent document may have been served on the debtor by one of the following methods:
(a) personal service attested by an acknowledgement of receipt, including the date of receipt, which is signed by the debtor;
(b) personal service attested by a document signed by the competent person who effected the service stating that the debtor has received the document or refused to receive it without any legal justification, and the date of the service;
(c) postal service attested by an acknowledgement of receipt including the date of receipt, which is signed and returned by the debtor;
(d) service by electronic means such as fax or e-mail, attested by an acknowledgement of receipt including the date of receipt, which is signed and returned by the debtor.
2. Any summons to a court hearing may have been served on the debtor in compliance with paragraph (1) or orally in a previous court hearing on the same claim and stated in the minutes of that previous court hearing.

Article 14. 1. Service of the document instituting the proceedings or an equivalent document and any summons to a court hearing on the debtor may also have been effected by one of the following methods:
(a) personal service at the debtor's personal address on persons who are living in the same household as the debtor or are employed there;
(b) in the case of a self-employed debtor or a legal person, personal service at the debtor's business premises on persons who are employed by the debtor;
(c) deposit of the document in the debtor's mailbox;
(d) deposit of the document at a post office or with competent public authorities and the placing in the debtor's mailbox of written notification of that deposit, provided that the written notification clearly states the character of the document as a court document or the legal effect of the notification as effecting service and setting in motion the running of time for the purposes of time limits;
(e) postal service without proof pursuant to paragraph (3) where the debtor has his address in the Member State of origin;
(f) electronic means attested by an automatic confirmation of delivery, provided that the debtor has expressly accepted this method of service in advance.
2. For the purposes of this Regulation, service under paragraph (1) is not admissible if the debtor's address is not known with certainty.
3. Service pursuant to paragraph (1), (a) to (d), shall be attested by:
(a) a document signed by the competent person who effected the service, indicating:
(i) the method of service used; and
(ii) the date of service; and
(iii) where the document has been served on a person other than the debtor, the name of that person and his relation to the debtor, or
(b) an acknowledgement of receipt by the person served, for the purposes of paragraphs 1(a) and (b).

Article 15. Service pursuant to Articles 13 or 14 may also have been effected on a debtor's representative.

Article 16. In order to ensure that the debtor was provided with due information about the claim, the document instituting the proceedings or the equivalent document must have contained the following:
(a) the names and the addresses of the parties;
(b) the amount of the claim;
(c) if interest on the claim is sought, the interest rate and the period for which interest is sought unless statutory interest is automatically added to the principal under the law of the Member State of origin;
(d) a statement of the reason for the claim.

Article 17. The following must have been clearly stated in or together with the document instituting the proceedings, the equivalent document or any summons to a court hearing:
(a) the procedural requirements for contesting the claim, including the time limit for contesting the claim in writing or the time for the court hearing, as applicable, the name and the address of the institution to which to respond or before which to appear, as applicable, and whether it is mandatory to be represented by a lawyer;

PART V   EUROPEAN CIVIL PROCEDURE

(b) the consequences of an absence of objection or default of appearance, in particular, where applicable, the possibility that a judgment may be given or enforced against the debtor and the liability for costs related to the court proceedings.

Article 18. 1. If the proceedings in the Member State of origin did not meet the procedural requirements as set out in Articles 13 to 17, such non-compliance shall be cured and a judgment may be certified as a European Enforcement Order if:
(a) the judgment has been served on the debtor in compliance with the requirements pursuant to Article 13 or Article 14; and
(b) it was possible for the debtor to challenge the judgment by means of a full review and the debtor has been duly informed in or together with the judgment about the procedural requirements for such a challenge, including the name and address of the institution with which it must be lodged and, where applicable, the time limit for so doing; and
(c) the debtor has failed to challenge the judgment in compliance with the relevant procedural requirements.
2. If the proceedings in the Member State of origin did not comply with the procedural requirements as set out in Article 13 or Article 14, such non-compliance shall be cured if it is proved by the conduct of the debtor in the court proceedings that he has personally received the document to be served in sufficient time to arrange for his defence.

Article 19. 1. Further to Articles 13 to 18, a judgment can only be certified as a European Enforcement Order if the debtor is entitled, under the law of the Member State of origin, to apply for a review of the judgment where:
(a) (i) the document instituting the proceedings or an equivalent document or, where applicable, the summons to a court hearing, was served by one of the methods provided for in Article 14; and
(ii) service was not effected in sufficient time to enable him to arrange for his defence, without any fault on his part; or
(b) the debtor was prevented from objecting to the claim by reason of force majeure, or due to extraordinary circumstances without any fault on his part,
provided in either case that he acts promptly.
2. This Article is without prejudice to the possibility for Member States to grant access to a review of the judgment under more generous conditions than those mentioned in paragraph (1).

Chapter IV. Enforcement

Article 20. 1. Without prejudice to the provisions of this Chapter, the enforcement procedures shall be governed by the law of the Member State of enforcement.
A judgment certified as a European Enforcement Order shall be enforced under the same conditions as a judgment handed down in the Member State of enforcement.
2. The creditor shall be required to provide the competent enforcement authorities of the Member State of enforcement with:
(a) a copy of the judgment which satisfies the conditions necessary to establish its authenticity; and
(b) a copy of the European Enforcement Order certificate which satisfies the conditions necessary to establish its authenticity; and
(c) where necessary, a transcription of the European Enforcement Order certificate or a translation thereof into the official language of the Member State of enforcement or, if there are several official languages in that Member State, the official language or one of the official languages of court proceedings of the place where enforcement is sought, in conformity with the law of that Member State, or into another language that the Member State of enforcement has indicated it can accept. Each Member State may indicate the official language or languages of the institutions of the European Community other than its own which it can accept for the completion of the certificate. The translation shall be certified by a person qualified to do so in one of the Member States.
3. No security, bond or deposit, however described, shall be required of a party who in one Member State applies for enforcement of a judgment certified as a European Enforcement Order in another Member State on the ground that he is a foreign national or that he is not domiciled or resident in the Member State of enforcement.

Article 21. 1. Enforcement shall, upon application by the debtor, be refused by the competent court in the Member State of enforcement if the judgment certified as a European Enforcement Order is irreconcilable with an earlier judgment given in any Member State or in a third country, provided that:
(a) the earlier judgment involved the same cause of action and was between the same parties; and

(b) the earlier judgment was given in the Member State of enforcement or fulfils the conditions necessary for its recognition in the Member State of enforcement; and
(c) the irreconcilability was not and could not have been raised as an objection in the court proceedings in the Member State of origin.
2. Under no circumstances may the judgment or its certification as a European Enforcement Order be reviewed as to their substance in the Member State of enforcement.

Article 22. This Regulation shall not affect agreements by which Member States undertook, prior to the entry into force of Regulation (EC) No 44/2001, pursuant to Article 59 of the Brussels Convention on jurisdiction and the enforcement of judgments in civil and commercial matters, not to recognise judgments given, in particular in other Contracting States to that Convention, against defendants domiciled or habitually resident in a third country where, in cases provided for in Article 4 of that Convention, the judgment could only be founded on a ground of jurisdiction specified in the second paragraph of Article 3 of that Convention.

Article 23. Where the debtor has
— challenged a judgment certified as a European Enforcement Order, including an application for review within the meaning of Article 19, or
— applied for the rectification or withdrawal of a European Enforcement Order certificate in accordance with Article 10,
the competent court or authority in the Member State of enforcement may, upon application by the debtor:
(a) limit the enforcement proceedings to protective measures; or
(b) make enforcement conditional on the provision of such security as it shall determine; or
(c) under exceptional circumstances, stay the enforcement proceedings.

Chapter V. Court Settlements and Authentic Instruments

Article 24. 1. A settlement concerning a claim within the meaning of Article 4(2) which has been approved by a court or concluded before a court in the course of proceedings and is enforceable in the Member State in which it was approved or concluded shall, upon application to the court that approved it or before which it was concluded, be certified as a European Enforcement Order using the standard form in Annex II.
2. A settlement which has been certified as a European Enforcement Order in the Member State of origin shall be enforced in the other Member States without the need for a declaration of enforceability and without any possibility of opposing its enforceability.
3. The provisions of Chapter II, with the exception of Articles 5, 6(1) and 9(1), and of Chapter IV, with the exception of Articles 21(1) and 22, shall apply as appropriate.

Article 25. 1. An authentic instrument concerning a claim within the meaning of Article 4(2) which is enforceable in one Member State shall, upon application to the authority designated by the Member State of origin, be certified as a European Enforcement Order, using the standard form in Annex III.
2. An authentic instrument which has been certified as a European Enforcement Order in the Member State of origin shall be enforced in the other Member States without the need for a declaration of enforceability and without any possibility of opposing its enforceability.
3. The provisions of Chapter II, with the exception of Articles 5, 6(1) and 9(1), and of Chapter IV, with the exception of Articles 21(1) and 22, shall apply as appropriate.

Chapter VI. Transitional Provision

Article 26. This Regulation shall apply only to judgments given, to court settlements approved or concluded and to documents formally drawn up or registered as authentic instruments after the entry into force of this Regulation.

Chapter VII. Relationship with other Community Instruments

Article 27. This Regulation shall not affect the possibility of seeking recognition and enforcement, in accordance with Regulation (EC) No 44/2001, of a judgment, a court settlement or an authentic instrument on an uncontested claim.

Article 28. This Regulation shall not affect the application of Regulation (EC) No 1348/2000.

Chapter VIII. General and Final Provisions

Article 29. The Member States shall cooperate to provide the general public and professional circles with information on:

PART V   EUROPEAN CIVIL PROCEDURE

(a) the methods and procedures of enforcement in the Member States; and
(b) the competent authorities for enforcement in the Member States,
in particular via the European Judicial Network in civil and commercial matters established in accordance with Decision 2001/470/EC.

Article 30. 1. The Member States shall notify the Commission of:
(a) the procedures for rectification and withdrawal referred to in Article 10(2) and for review referred to in Article 19(1);
(b) the languages accepted pursuant to Article 20(2)(c);
(c) the lists of the authorities referred to in Article 25;
and any subsequent changes thereof.
2. The Commission shall make the information notified in accordance with paragraph (1) publicly available through publication in the Official Journal of the European Union and through any other appropriate means.

Article 31. The Commission shall amend the standard forms set out in the Annexes. Those measures, designed to amend non-essential elements of this Regulation, shall be adopted in accordance with the regulatory procedure with scrutiny referred to in Article 32(2).

Article 32. 1. The Commission shall be assisted by the committee referred to in Article 75 of Regulation (EC) No 44/2001.
2. Where reference is made to this paragraph, Article 5a(1) to (4) and Article 7 of Decision 1999/468/EC shall apply, having regard to the provisions of Article 8 thereof.

Article 33. This Regulation shall enter into force on 21 January 2005.
It shall apply from 21 October 2005, with the exception of Articles 30, 31 and 32, which shall apply from 21 January 2005.
This Regulation shall be binding in its entirety and directly applicable in the Member States in accordance with the Treaty establishing the European Community.
[The Annex is omitted.]

EU: REGULATION 1896/2006 CREATING EUROPEAN ORDER FOR PAYMENT PROCEDURE

Regulation (EC) No 1896/2006 of the European Parliament and of the Council of 12 December 2006 creating a European order for payment procedure (OJ L 399, 30.12.2006, pp. 1 – 32)

[The Preamble is omitted.]

Article 1. 1. The purpose of this Regulation is:
(a) to simplify, speed up and reduce the costs of litigation in cross-border cases concerning uncontested pecuniary claims by creating a European order for payment procedure; and
(b) to permit the free circulation of European orders for payment throughout the Member States by laying down minimum standards, compliance with which renders unnecessary any intermediate proceedings in the Member State of enforcement prior to recognition and enforcement.
2. This Regulation shall not prevent a claimant from pursuing a claim within the meaning of Article 4 by making use of another procedure available under the law of a Member State or under Community law.

Article 2. 1. This Regulation shall apply to civil and commercial matters in cross-border cases, whatever the nature of the court or tribunal. It shall not extend, in particular, to revenue, customs or administrative matters or the liability of the State for acts and omissions in the exercise of State authority ('acta iure imperii').
2. This Regulation shall not apply to:
(a) rights in property arising out of a matrimonial relationship, wills and succession;
(b) bankruptcy, proceedings relating to the winding-up of insolvent companies or other legal persons, judicial arrangements, compositions and analogous proceedings;
(c) social security;
(d) claims arising from non-contractual obligations, unless:
(i) they have been the subject of an agreement between the parties or there has been an admission of debt, or
(ii) they relate to liquidated debts arising from joint ownership of property.
3. In this Regulation, the term 'Member State' shall mean Member States with the exception of Denmark.

Article 3. 1. For the purposes of this Regulation, a cross-border case is one in which at least one of the parties is domiciled or habitually resident in a Member State other than the Member State of the court seised.
2. Domicile shall be determined in accordance with Articles 59 and 60 of Council Regulation (EC) No 44/2001 of 22 December 2000 on jurisdiction and the recognition and enforcement of judgments in civil and commercial matters.
3. The relevant moment for determining whether there is a cross-border case shall be the time when the application for a European order for payment is submitted in accordance with this Regulation.

Article 4. The European order for payment procedure shall be established for the collection of pecuniary claims for a specific amount that have fallen due at the time when the application for a European order for payment is submitted.

Article 5. For the purposes of this Regulation, the following definitions shall apply:
1) 'Member State of origin' means the Member State in which a European order for payment is issued;
2) 'Member State of enforcement' means the Member State in which enforcement of a European order for payment is sought;
3) 'court' means any authority in a Member State with competence regarding European orders for payment or any other related matters;
4) 'court of origin' means the court which issues a European order for payment.

Article 6. 1. For the purposes of applying this Regulation, jurisdiction shall be determined in accordance with the relevant rules of Community law, in particular Regulation (EC) No 44/2001.
2. However, if the claim relates to a contract concluded by a person, the consumer, for a purpose which can be regarded as being outside his trade or profession, and if the defendant is the consumer, only the courts in the Member State in which the defendant is domiciled, within the meaning of Article 59 of Regulation (EC) No 44/2001, shall have jurisdiction.

Article 7. 1. An application for a European order for payment shall be made using standard form A as set out in Annex I.
2. The application shall state:

(a) the names and addresses of the parties, and, where applicable, their representatives, and of the court to which the application is made;
(b) the amount of the claim, including the principal and, where applicable, interest, contractual penalties and costs;
(c) if interest on the claim is demanded, the interest rate and the period of time for which that interest is demanded unless statutory interest is automatically added to the principal under the law of the Member State of origin;
(d) the cause of the action, including a description of the circumstances invoked as the basis of the claim and, where applicable, of the interest demanded;
(e) a description of evidence supporting the claim;
(f) the grounds for jurisdiction; and
(g) the cross-border nature of the case within the meaning of Article 3.
3. In the application, the claimant shall declare that the information provided is true to the best of his knowledge and belief and shall acknowledge that any deliberate false statement could lead to appropriate penalties under the law of the Member State of origin.
4. In an Appendix to the application the claimant may indicate to the court that he opposes a transfer to ordinary civil proceedings within the meaning of Article 17 in the event of opposition by the defendant. This does not prevent the claimant from informing the court thereof subsequently, but in any event before the order is issued.
5. The application shall be submitted in paper form or by any other means of communication, including electronic, accepted by the Member State of origin and available to the court of origin.
6. The application shall be signed by the claimant or, where applicable, by his representative. Where the application is submitted in electronic form in accordance with paragraph (5), it shall be signed in accordance with Article 2(2) of Directive 1999/93/EC of the European Parliament and of the Council of 13 December 1999 on a Community framework for electronic signatures. The signature shall be recognised in the Member State of origin and may not be made subject to additional requirements.
6. However, such electronic signature shall not be required if and to the extent that an alternative electronic communications system exists in the courts of the Member State of origin which is available to a certain group of pre-registered authenticated users and which permits the identification of those users in a secure manner. Member States shall inform the Commission of such communications systems.

Article 8. The court seised of an application for a European order for payment shall examine, as soon as possible and on the basis of the application form, whether the requirements set out in Articles 2, 3, 4, 6 and 7 are met and whether the claim appears to be founded. This examination may take the form of an automated procedure.

Article 9. 1. If the requirements set out in Article 7 are not met and unless the claim is clearly unfounded or the application is inadmissible, the court shall give the claimant the opportunity to complete or rectify the application. The court shall use standard form B as set out in Annex II.
2. Where the court requests the claimant to complete or rectify the application, it shall specify a time limit it deems appropriate in the circumstances. The court may at its discretion extend that time limit.

Article 10. 1. If the requirements referred to in Article 8 are met for only part of the claim, the court shall inform the claimant to that effect, using standard form C as set out in Annex III. The claimant shall be invited to accept or refuse a proposal for a European order for payment for the amount specified by the court and shall be informed of the consequences of his decision. The claimant shall reply by returning standard form C sent by the court within a time limit specified by the court in accordance with Article 9(2).
2. If the claimant accepts the court's proposal, the court shall issue a European order for payment, in accordance with Article 12, for that part of the claim accepted by the claimant. The consequences with respect to the remaining part of the initial claim shall be governed by national law.
3. If the claimant fails to send his reply within the time limit specified by the court or refuses the court's proposal, the court shall reject the application for a European order for payment in its entirety.

Article 11. 1. The court shall reject the application if:
(a) the requirements set out in Articles 2, 3, 4, 6 and 7 are not met; or
(b) the claim is clearly unfounded; or
(c) the claimant fails to send his reply within the time limit specified by the court under Article 9(2); or
(d) the claimant fails to send his reply within the time limit specified by the court or refuses the court's proposal, in accordance with Article 10.

The claimant shall be informed of the grounds for the rejection by means of standard form D as set out in Annex IV.
2. There shall be no right of appeal against the rejection of the application.
3. The rejection of the application shall not prevent the claimant from pursuing the claim by means of a new application for a European order for payment or of any other procedure available under the law of a Member State.

Article 12. 1. If the requirements referred to in Article 8 are met, the court shall issue, as soon as possible and normally within 30 days of the lodging of the application, a European order for payment using standard form E as set out in Annex V.
1. The 30-day period shall not include the time taken by the claimant to complete, rectify or modify the application.
2. The European order for payment shall be issued together with a copy of the application form. It shall not comprise the information provided by the claimant in Appendices 1 and 2 to form A.
3. In the European order for payment, the defendant shall be advised of his options to:
(a) pay the amount indicated in the order to the claimant; or
(b) oppose the order by lodging with the court of origin a statement of opposition, to be sent within 30 days of service of the order on him.
4. In the European order for payment, the defendant shall be informed that:
(a) the order was issued solely on the basis of the information which was provided by the claimant and was not verified by the court;
(b) the order will become enforceable unless a statement of opposition has been lodged with the court in accordance with Article 16;
(c) where a statement of opposition is lodged, the proceedings shall continue before the competent courts of the Member State of origin in accordance with the rules of ordinary civil procedure unless the claimant has explicitly requested that the proceedings be terminated in that event.
5. The court shall ensure that the order is served on the defendant in accordance with national law by a method that shall meet the minimum standards laid down in Articles 13, 14 and 15.

Article 13. The European order for payment may be served on the defendant in accordance with the national law of the State in which the service is to be effected, by one of the following methods:
(a) personal service attested by an acknowledgement of receipt, including the date of receipt, which is signed by the defendant;
(b) personal service attested by a document signed by the competent person who effected the service stating that the defendant has received the document or refused to receive it without any legal justification, and the date of service;
(c) postal service attested by an acknowledgement of receipt, including the date of receipt, which is signed and returned by the defendant;
(d) service by electronic means such as fax or e-mail, attested by an acknowledgement of receipt, including the date of receipt, which is signed and returned by the defendant.

Article 14. 1. The European order for payment may also be served on the defendant in accordance with the national law of the State in which service is to be effected, by one of the following methods:
(a) personal service at the defendant's personal address on persons who are living in the same household as the defendant or are employed there;
(b) in the case of a self-employed defendant or a legal person, personal service at the defendant's business premises on persons who are employed by the defendant;
(c) deposit of the order in the defendant's mailbox;
(d) deposit of the order at a post office or with competent public authorities and the placing in the defendant's mailbox of written notification of that deposit, provided that the written notification clearly states the character of the document as a court document or the legal effect of the notification as effecting service and setting in motion the running of time for the purposes of time limits;
(e) postal service without proof pursuant to paragraph (3) where the defendant has his address in the Member State of origin;
(f) electronic means attested by an automatic confirmation of delivery, provided that the defendant has expressly accepted this method of service in advance.
2. For the purposes of this Regulation, service under paragraph (1) is not admissible if the defendant's address is not known with certainty.
3. Service pursuant to paragraph (1)(a), (b), (c) and (d) shall be attested by:
(a) a document signed by the competent person who effected the service, indicating:
(i) the method of service used; and

PART V   EUROPEAN CIVIL PROCEDURE

(ii) the date of service; and
(iii) where the order has been served on a person other than the defendant, the name of that person and his relation to the defendant; or
(b) an acknowledgement of receipt by the person served, for the purposes of paragraphs (1)(a) and (b).

Article 15. Service pursuant to Articles 13 or 14 may also be effected on a defendant's representative.

Article 16. 1. The defendant may lodge a statement of opposition to the European order for payment with the court of origin using standard form F as set out in Annex VI, which shall be supplied to him together with the European order for payment.
2. The statement of opposition shall be sent within 30 days of service of the order on the defendant.
3. The defendant shall indicate in the statement of opposition that he contests the claim, without having to specify the reasons for this.
4. The statement of opposition shall be submitted in paper form or by any other means of communication, including electronic, accepted by the Member State of origin and available to the court of origin.
5. The statement of opposition shall be signed by the defendant or, where applicable, by his representative. Where the statement of opposition is submitted in electronic form in accordance with paragraph (4), it shall be signed in accordance with Article 2(2) of Directive 1999/93/EC. The signature shall be recognised in the Member State of origin and may not be made subject to additional requirements.
5. However, such electronic signature shall not be required if and to the extent that an alternative electronic communications system exists in the courts of the Member State of origin which is available to a certain group of pre-registered authenticated users and which permits the identification of those users in a secure manner. Member States shall inform the Commission of such communications systems.

Article 17. 1. If a statement of opposition is entered within the time limit laid down in Article 16(2), the proceedings shall continue before the competent courts of the Member State of origin in accordance with the rules of ordinary civil procedure unless the claimant has explicitly requested that the proceedings be terminated in that event.
Where the claimant has pursued his claim through the European order for payment procedure, nothing under national law shall prejudice his position in subsequent ordinary civil proceedings.
2. The transfer to ordinary civil proceedings within the meaning of paragraph (1) shall be governed by the law of the Member State of origin.
3. The claimant shall be informed whether the defendant has lodged a statement of opposition and of any transfer to ordinary civil proceedings.

Article 18. 1. If within the time limit laid down in Article 16(2), taking into account an appropriate period of time to allow a statement to arrive, no statement of opposition has been lodged with the court of origin, the court of origin shall without delay declare the European order for payment enforceable using standard form G as set out in Annex VII. The court shall verify the date of service.
2. Without prejudice to paragraph (1), the formal requirements for enforceability shall be governed by the law of the Member State of origin.
3. The court shall send the enforceable European order for payment to the claimant.

Article 19. A European order for payment which has become enforceable in the Member State of origin shall be recognised and enforced in the other Member States without the need for a declaration of enforceability and without any possibility of opposing its recognition.

Article 20. 1. After the expiry of the time limit laid down in Article 16(2) the defendant shall be entitled to apply for a review of the European order for payment before the competent court in the Member State of origin where:
(a) (i) the order for payment was served by one of the methods provided for in Article 14, and
(ii) service was not effected in sufficient time to enable him to arrange for his defence, without any fault on his part, or
(b) the defendant was prevented from objecting to the claim by reason of force majeure or due to extraordinary circumstances without any fault on his part,
provided in either case that he acts promptly.
2. After expiry of the time limit laid down in Article 16(2) the defendant shall also be entitled to apply for a review of the European order for payment before the competent court in the Member

EU: REGULATION 1896/2006 CREATING EUROPEAN ORDER FOR PAYMENT PROCEDURE

State of origin where the order for payment was clearly wrongly issued, having regard to the requirements laid down in this Regulation, or due to other exceptional circumstances.

3. If the court rejects the defendant's application on the basis that none of the grounds for review referred to in paragraphs 1 and 2 apply, the European order for payment shall remain in force.

3. If the court decides that the review is justified for one of the reasons laid down in paragraphs 1 and 2, the European order for payment shall be null and void.

Article 21. 1. Without prejudice to the provisions of this Regulation, enforcement procedures shall be governed by the law of the Member State of enforcement.

A European order for payment which has become enforceable shall be enforced under the same conditions as an enforceable decision issued in the Member State of enforcement.

2. For enforcement in another Member State, the claimant shall provide the competent enforcement authorities of that Member State with:

(a) a copy of the European order for payment, as declared enforceable by the court of origin, which satisfies the conditions necessary to establish its authenticity; and

(b) where necessary, a translation of the European order for payment into the official language of the Member State of enforcement or, if there are several official languages in that Member State, the official language or one of the official languages of court proceedings of the place where enforcement is sought, in conformity with the law of that Member State, or into another language that the Member State of enforcement has indicated it can accept. Each Member State may indicate the official language or languages of the institutions of the European Union other than its own which it can accept for the European order for payment. The translation shall be certified by a person qualified to do so in one of the Member States.

3. No security, bond or deposit, however described, shall be required of a claimant who in one Member State applies for enforcement of a European order for payment issued in another Member State on the ground that he is a foreign national or that he is not domiciled or resident in the Member State of enforcement.

Article 22. 1. Enforcement shall, upon application by the defendant, be refused by the competent court in the Member State of enforcement if the European order for payment is irreconcilable with an earlier decision or order previously given in any Member State or in a third country, provided that:

(a) the earlier decision or order involved the same cause of action between the same parties; and

(b) the earlier decision or order fulfils the conditions necessary for its recognition in the Member State of enforcement; and

(c) the irreconcilability could not have been raised as an objection in the court proceedings in the Member State of origin.

2. Enforcement shall, upon application, also be refused if and to the extent that the defendant has paid the claimant the amount awarded in the European order for payment.

3. Under no circumstances may the European order for payment be reviewed as to its substance in the Member State of enforcement.

Article 23. Where the defendant has applied for a review in accordance with Article 20, the competent court in the Member State of enforcement may, upon application by the defendant:

(a) limit the enforcement proceedings to protective measures; or

(b) make enforcement conditional on the provision of such security as it shall determine; or

(c) under exceptional circumstances, stay the enforcement proceedings.

Article 24. Representation by a lawyer or another legal professional shall not be mandatory:

(a) for the claimant in respect of the application for a European order for payment;

(b) for the defendant in respect of the statement of opposition to a European order for payment.

Article 25. 1. The combined court fees of a European order for payment procedure and of the ordinary civil proceedings that ensue in the event of a statement of opposition to a European order for payment in a Member State shall not exceed the court fees of ordinary civil proceedings without a preceding European order for payment procedure in that Member State.

2. For the purposes of this Regulation, court fees shall comprise fees and charges to be paid to the court, the amount of which is fixed in accordance with national law.

Article 26. All procedural issues not specifically dealt with in this Regulation shall be governed by national law.

Article 27. This Regulation shall not affect the application of Council Regulation (EC) No 1348/2000 of 29 May 2000 on the service in the Member States of judicial and extrajudicial documents in civil and commercial matters.

PART V   EUROPEAN CIVIL PROCEDURE

Article 28. Member States shall cooperate to provide the general public and professional circles with information on:
(a) costs of service of documents; and
(b) which authorities have competence with respect to enforcement for the purposes of applying Articles 21, 22 and 23,
in particular via the European Judicial Network in civil and commercial matters established in accordance with Council Decision 2001/470/EC.

Article 29. 1. By 12 June 2008, Member States shall communicate to the Commission:
(a) which courts have jurisdiction to issue a European order for payment;
(b) the review procedure and the competent courts for the purposes of the application of Article 20;
(c) the means of communication accepted for the purposes of the European order for payment procedure and available to the courts;
(d) languages accepted pursuant to Article 21(2)(b).
Member States shall apprise the Commission of any subsequent changes to this information.
2. The Commission shall make the information notified in accordance with paragraph (1) publicly available through publication in the Official Journal of the European Union and through any other appropriate means.

Article 30. The standard forms set out in the Annexes shall be updated or technically adjusted, ensuring full conformity with the provisions of this Regulation, in accordance with the procedure referred to in Article 31(2).

Article 31. 1. The Commission shall be assisted by the committee established by Article 75 of Regulation (EC) No 44/2001.
2. Where reference is made to this paragraph, Article 5a(1)-(4) and Article 7 of Decision 1999/468/EC shall apply, having regard to the provisions of Article 8 thereof.
3. The Committee shall adopt its Rules of Procedure.

Article 32. By 12 December 2013, the Commission shall present to the European Parliament, the Council and the European Economic and Social Committee a detailed report reviewing the operation of the European order for payment procedure. That report shall contain an assessment of the procedure as it has operated and an extended impact assessment for each Member State.
To that end, and in order to ensure that best practice in the European Union is duly taken into account and reflects the principles of better legislation, Member States shall provide the Commission with information relating to the cross-border operation of the European order for payment. This information shall cover court fees, speed of the procedure, efficiency, ease of use and the internal payment order procedures of the Member States.
The Commission's report shall be accompanied, if appropriate, by proposals for adaptation.

Article 33. This Regulation shall enter into force on the day following the date of its publication in the Official Journal of the European Union.
It shall apply from 12 December 2008, with the exception of Articles 28, 29, 30 and 31 which shall apply from 12 June 2008.
This Regulation shall be binding in its entirety and directly applicable in the Member States in accordance with the Treaty establishing the European Community.
[The Annex is omitted.]

Regulation (EC) No 861/2007 of the European Parliament and of the Council of 11 July 2007 establishing a European Small Claims Procedure (OJ L 199, 31.07.2007, pp. 1 – 22)

[The Preamble is omitted.]

Chapter I. Subject Matter and Scope

Article 1. This Regulation establishes a European procedure for small claims (hereinafter referred to as the "European Small Claims Procedure"), intended to simplify and speed up litigation concerning small claims in cross-border cases, and to reduce costs. The European Small Claims Procedure shall be available to litigants as an alternative to the procedures existing under the laws of the Member States.

This Regulation also eliminates the intermediate proceedings necessary to enable recognition and enforcement, in other Member States, of judgments given in one Member State in the European Small Claims Procedure.

Article 2. 1. This Regulation shall apply, in cross-border cases, to civil and commercial matters, whatever the nature of the court or tribunal, where the value of a claim does not exceed EUR 2000 at the time when the claim form is received by the court or tribunal with jurisdiction, excluding all interest, expenses and disbursements. It shall not extend, in particular, to revenue, customs or administrative matters or to the liability of the State for acts and omissions in the exercise of State authority (acta jure imperii).
2. This Regulation shall not apply to matters concerning:
(a) the status or legal capacity of natural persons;
(b) rights in property arising out of a matrimonial relationship, maintenance obligations, wills and succession;
(c) bankruptcy, proceedings relating to the winding-up of insolvent companies or other legal persons, judicial arrangements, compositions and analogous proceedings;
(d) social security;
(e) arbitration;
(f) employment law;
(g) tenancies of immovable property, with the exception of actions on monetary claims; or
(h) violations of privacy and of rights relating to personality, including defamation.
3. In this Regulation, the term "Member State" shall mean Member States with the exception of Denmark.

Article 3. 1. For the purposes of this Regulation, a cross-border case is one in which at least one of the parties is domiciled or habitually resident in a Member State other than the Member State of the court or tribunal seised.
2. Domicile shall be determined in accordance with Articles 59 and 60 of Regulation (EC) No 44/2001.
3. The relevant moment for determining whether there is a cross-border case is the date on which the claim form is received by the court or tribunal with jurisdiction.

Chapter II. The European Small Claims Procedure

Article 4. 1. The claimant shall commence the European Small Claims Procedure by filling in standard claim Form A, as set out in Annex I, and lodging it with the court or tribunal with jurisdiction directly, by post or by any other means of communication, such as fax or e-mail, acceptable to the Member State in which the procedure is commenced. The claim form shall include a description of evidence supporting the claim and be accompanied, where appropriate, by any relevant supporting documents.
2. Member States shall inform the Commission which means of communication are acceptable to them. The Commission shall make such information publicly available.
3. Where a claim is outside the scope of this Regulation, the court or tribunal shall inform the claimant to that effect. Unless the claimant withdraws the claim, the court or tribunal shall proceed with it in accordance with the relevant procedural law applicable in the Member State in which the procedure is conducted.
4. Where the court or tribunal considers the information provided by the claimant to be inadequate or insufficiently clear or if the claim form is not filled in properly, it shall, unless the claim appears to be clearly unfounded or the application inadmissible, give the claimant the opportunity to complete or rectify the claim form or to supply supplementary information or documents or to withdraw the

claim, within such period as it specifies. The court or tribunal shall use standard Form B, as set out in Annex II, for this purpose.

Where the claim appears to be clearly unfounded or the application inadmissible or where the claimant fails to complete or rectify the claim form within the time specified, the application shall be dismissed.

5. Member States shall ensure that the claim form is available at all courts and tribunals at which the European Small Claims Procedure can be commenced.

Article 5. 1. The European Small Claims Procedure shall be a written procedure. The court or tribunal shall hold an oral hearing if it considers this to be necessary or if a party so requests. The court or tribunal may refuse such a request if it considers that with regard to the circumstances of the case, an oral hearing is obviously not necessary for the fair conduct of the proceedings. The reasons for refusal shall be given in writing. The refusal may not be contested separately.

2. After receiving the properly filled in claim form, the court or tribunal shall fill in Part I of the standard answer Form C, as set out in Annex III.

A copy of the claim form, and, where applicable, of the supporting documents, together with the answer form thus filled in, shall be served on the defendant in accordance with Article 13. These documents shall be dispatched within 14 days of receiving the properly filled in claim form.

3. The defendant shall submit his response within 30 days of service of the claim form and answer form, by filling in Part II of standard answer Form C, accompanied, where appropriate, by any relevant supporting documents, and returning it to the court or tribunal, or in any other appropriate way not using the answer form.

4. Within 14 days of receipt of the response from the defendant, the court or tribunal shall dispatch a copy thereof, together with any relevant supporting documents to the claimant.

5. If, in his response, the defendant claims that the value of a non-monetary claim exceeds the limit set out in Article 2(1), the court or tribunal shall decide within 30 days of dispatching the response to the claimant, whether the claim is within the scope of this Regulation. Such decision may not be contested separately.

6. Any counterclaim, to be submitted using standard Form A, and any relevant supporting documents shall be served on the claimant in accordance with Article 13. Those documents shall be dispatched within 14 days of receipt.

The claimant shall have 30 days from service to respond to any counterclaim.

7. If the counterclaim exceeds the limit set out in Article 2(1), the claim and counterclaim shall not proceed in the European Small Claims Procedure but shall be dealt with in accordance with the relevant procedural law applicable in the Member State in which the procedure is conducted.

Articles 2 and 4 as well as paragraphs 3, 4 and 5 of this Article shall apply, mutatis mutandis, to counterclaims.

Article 6. 1. The claim form, the response, any counterclaim, any response to a counterclaim and any description of relevant supporting documents shall be submitted in the language or one of the languages of the court or tribunal.

2. If any other document received by the court or tribunal is not in the language in which the proceedings are conducted, the court or tribunal may require a translation of that document only if the translation appears to be necessary for giving the judgment.

3. Where a party has refused to accept a document because it is not in either of the following languages:

(a) the official language of the Member State addressed, or, if there are several official languages in that Member State, the official language or one of the official languages of the place where service is to be effected or to where the document is to be dispatched; or

(b) a language which the addressee understands,

the court or tribunal shall so inform the other party with a view to that party providing a translation of the document.

Article 7. 1. Within 30 days of receipt of the response from the defendant or the claimant within the time limits laid down in Article 5(3) or (6), the court or tribunal shall give a judgment, or:

(a) demand further details concerning the claim from the parties within a specified period of time, not exceeding 30 days;

(b) take evidence in accordance with Article 9; or

(c) summon the parties to an oral hearing to be held within 30 days of the summons.

2. The court or tribunal shall give the judgment either within 30 days of any oral hearing or after having received all information necessary for giving the judgment. The judgment shall be served on the parties in accordance with Article 13.

3. If the court or tribunal has not received an answer from the relevant party within the time limits laid down in Article 5(3) or (6), it shall give a judgment on the claim or counterclaim.

Article 8. The court or tribunal may hold an oral hearing through video conference or other communication technology if the technical means are available.

Article 9. 1. The court or tribunal shall determine the means of taking evidence and the extent of the evidence necessary for its judgment under the rules applicable to the admissibility of evidence. The court or tribunal may admit the taking of evidence through written statements of witnesses, experts or parties. It may also admit the taking of evidence through video conference or other communication technology if the technical means are available.
2. The court or tribunal may take expert evidence or oral testimony only if it is necessary for giving the judgment. In making its decision, the court or tribunal shall take costs into account.
3. The court or tribunal shall use the simplest and least burdensome method of taking evidence.

Article 10. Representation by a lawyer or another legal professional shall not be mandatory.

Article 11. The Member States shall ensure that the parties can receive practical assistance in filling in the forms.

Article 12. 1. The court or tribunal shall not require the parties to make any legal assessment of the claim.
2. If necessary, the court or tribunal shall inform the parties about procedural questions.
3. Whenever appropriate, the court or tribunal shall seek to reach a settlement between the parties.

Article 13. 1. Documents shall be served by postal service attested by an acknowledgement of receipt including the date of receipt.
2. If service in accordance with paragraph (1) is not possible, service may be effected by any of the methods provided for in Articles 13 or 14 of Regulation (EC) No 805/2004.

Article 14. 1. Where the court or tribunal sets a time limit, the party concerned shall be informed of the consequences of not complying with it.
2. The court or tribunal may extend the time limits provided for in Article 4(4), Article 5(3) and (6) and Article 7(1), in exceptional circumstances, if necessary in order to safeguard the rights of the parties.
3. If, in exceptional circumstances, it is not possible for the court or tribunal to respect the time limits provided for in Article 5(2) to (6) and Article 7, it shall take the steps required by those provisions as soon as possible.

Article 15. 1. The judgment shall be enforceable notwithstanding any possible appeal. The provision of a security shall not be required.
2. Article 23 shall also apply in the event that the judgment is to be enforced in the Member State where the judgment was given.

Article 16. The unsuccessful party shall bear the costs of the proceedings. However, the court or tribunal shall not award costs to the successful party to the extent that they were unnecessarily incurred or are disproportionate to the claim.

Article 17. 1. Member States shall inform the Commission whether an appeal is available under their procedural law against a judgment given in the European Small Claims Procedure and within what time limit such appeal shall be lodged. The Commission shall make that information publicly available.
2. Article 16 shall apply to any appeal.

Article 18. 1. The defendant shall be entitled to apply for a review of the judgment given in the European Small Claims Procedure before the court or tribunal with jurisdiction of the Member State where the judgment was given where:
(a) (i) the claim form or the summons to an oral hearing were served by a method without proof of receipt by him personally, as provided for in Article 14 of Regulation (EC) No 805/2004; and
(ii) service was not effected in sufficient time to enable him to arrange for his defence without any fault on his part, or
(b) the defendant was prevented from objecting to the claim by reason of force majeure, or due to extraordinary circumstances without any fault on his part,
provided in either case that he acts promptly.

PART V   EUROPEAN CIVIL PROCEDURE

2. If the court or tribunal rejects the review on the basis that none of the grounds referred to in paragraph (1) apply, the judgment shall remain in force.
If the court or tribunal decides that the review is justified for one of the reasons laid down in paragraph (1), the judgment given in the European Small Claims Procedure shall be null and void.

Article 19. Subject to the provisions of this Regulation, the European Small Claims Procedure shall be governed by the procedural law of the Member State in which the procedure is conducted.

Chapter III. Recognition and Enforcement in another Member State

Article 20. 1. A judgment given in a Member State in the European Small Claims Procedure shall be recognised and enforced in another Member State without the need for a declaration of enforceability and without any possibility of opposing its recognition.
2. At the request of one of the parties, the court or tribunal shall issue a certificate concerning a judgment in the European Small Claims Procedure using standard Form D, as set out in Annex IV, at no extra cost.

Article 21. 1. Without prejudice to the provisions of this Chapter, the enforcement procedures shall be governed by the law of the Member State of enforcement.
Any judgment given in the European Small Claims Procedure shall be enforced under the same conditions as a judgment given in the Member State of enforcement.
2. The party seeking enforcement shall produce:
(a) a copy of the judgment which satisfies the conditions necessary to establish its authenticity; and
(b) a copy of the certificate referred to in Article 20(2) and, where necessary, the translation thereof into the official language of the Member State of enforcement or, if there are several official languages in that Member State, the official language or one of the official languages of court or tribunal proceedings of the place where enforcement is sought in conformity with the law of that Member State, or into another language that the Member State of enforcement has indicated it can accept. Each Member State may indicate the official language or languages of the institutions of the European Union other than its own which it can accept for the European Small Claims Procedure. The content of Form D shall be translated by a person qualified to make translations in one of the Member States.
3. The party seeking the enforcement of a judgment given in the European Small Claims Procedure in another Member State shall not be required to have:
(a) an authorised representative; or
(b) a postal address
in the Member State of enforcement, other than with agents having competence for the enforcement procedure.
4. No security, bond or deposit, however described, shall be required of a party who in one Member State applies for enforcement of a judgment given in the European Small Claims Procedure in another Member State on the ground that he is a foreign national or that he is not domiciled or resident in the Member State of enforcement.

Article 22. 1. Enforcement shall, upon application by the person against whom enforcement is sought, be refused by the court or tribunal with jurisdiction in the Member State of enforcement if the judgment given in the European Small Claims Procedure is irreconcilable with an earlier judgment given in any Member State or in a third country, provided that:
(a) the earlier judgment involved the same cause of action and was between the same parties;
(b) the earlier judgment was given in the Member State of enforcement or fulfils the conditions necessary for its recognition in the Member State of enforcement; and
(c) the irreconcilability was not and could not have been raised as an objection in the court or tribunal proceedings in the Member State where the judgment in the European Small Claims Procedure was given.
2. Under no circumstances may a judgment given in the European Small Claims Procedure be reviewed as to its substance in the Member State of enforcement.

Article 23. Where a party has challenged a judgment given in the European Small Claims Procedure or where such a challenge is still possible, or where a party has made an application for review within the meaning of Article 18, the court or tribunal with jurisdiction or the competent authority in the Member State of enforcement may, upon application by the party against whom enforcement is sought:
(a) limit the enforcement proceedings to protective measures;

(b) make enforcement conditional on the provision of such security as it shall determine; or
(c) under exceptional circumstances, stay the enforcement proceedings.

Chapter IV. Final Provisions

Article 24. The Member States shall cooperate to provide the general public and professional circles with information on the European Small Claims Procedure, including costs, in particular by way of the European Judicial Network in Civil and Commercial Matters established in accordance with Decision 2001/470/EC.

Article 25. 1. By 1 January 2008 the Member States shall communicate to the Commission:
(a) which courts or tribunals have jurisdiction to give a judgment in the European Small Claims Procedure;
(b) which means of communication are accepted for the purposes of the European Small Claims Procedure and available to the courts or tribunals in accordance with Article 4(1);
(c) whether an appeal is available under their procedural law in accordance with Article 17 and with which court or tribunal this may be lodged;
(d) which languages are accepted pursuant to Article 21(2)(b); and
(e) which authorities have competence with respect to enforcement and which authorities have competence for the purposes of the application of Article 23.
Member States shall apprise the Commission of any subsequent changes to this information.
2. The Commission shall make the information notified in accordance with paragraph (1) publicly available through publication in the Official Journal of the European Union and through any other appropriate means.

Article 26. The measures designed to amend non-essential elements of this Regulation, including by supplementing it, relating to updates or technical amendments to the forms in the Annexes shall be adopted in accordance with the regulatory procedure with scrutiny referred to in Article 27(2).

Article 27. 1. The Commission shall be assisted by a Committee.
2. Where reference is made to this paragraph, Article 5a(1) to (4), and Article 7 of Decision 1999/468/EC shall apply, having regard to the provisions of Article 8 thereof.

Article 28. By 1 January 2014, the Commission shall present to the European Parliament, the Council and the European Economic and Social Committee a detailed report reviewing the operation of the European Small Claims Procedure, including the limit of the value of the claim referred to in Article 2(1). That report shall contain an assessment of the procedure as it has operated and an extended impact assessment for each Member State.
To that end and in order to ensure that best practice in the European Union is duly taken into account and reflects the principles of better legislation, Member States shall provide the Commission with information relating to the cross-border operation of the European Small Claims Procedure. This information shall cover court fees, speed of the procedure, efficiency, ease of use and the internal small claims procedures of the Member States.
The Commission's report shall be accompanied, if appropriate, by proposals for adaptation.

Article 29. This Regulation shall enter into force on the day following its publication in the Official Journal of the European Union.
It shall apply from 1 January 2009, with the exception of Article 25, which shall apply from 1 January 2008.
This Regulation shall be binding in its entirety and directly applicable in the Member States in accordance with the Treaty establishing the European Community.
[The Annex is omitted.]

PART V   EUROPEAN CIVIL PROCEDURE

Regulation (EC) No 1393/2007 (Service of Documents)

Regulation (EC) No 1393/2007 of the European Parliament and of the Council of 13 November 2007 on the service in the Member States of judicial and extrajudicial documents in civil or commercial matters (service of documents), and repealing Council Regulation (EC) No 1348/2000 (OJ L 324, 10.12.2007, pp. 79 – 120).
[The Preamble is omitted.]

Chapter I. General Provisions

Article 1. 1. This Regulation shall apply in civil and commercial matters where a judicial or extrajudicial document has to be transmitted from one Member State to another for service there. It shall not extend in particular to revenue, customs or administrative matters or to liability of the State for actions or omissions in the exercise of state authority (acta iure imperii).
2. This Regulation shall not apply where the address of the person to be served with the document is not known.
3. In this Regulation, the term "Member State" shall mean the Member States with the exception of Denmark.

Article 2. 1. Each Member State shall designate the public officers, authorities or other persons, hereinafter referred to as "transmitting agencies", competent for the transmission of judicial or extrajudicial documents to be served in another Member State.
2. Each Member State shall designate the public officers, authorities or other persons, hereinafter referred to as "receiving agencies", competent for the receipt of judicial or extrajudicial documents from another Member State.
3. A Member State may designate one transmitting agency and one receiving agency, or one agency to perform both functions. A federal State, a State in which several legal systems apply or a State with autonomous territorial units shall be free to designate more than one such agency. The designation shall have effect for a period of five years and may be renewed at five-year intervals.
4. Each Member State shall provide the Commission with the following information:
(a) the names and addresses of the receiving agencies referred to in paragraphs 2 and 3;
(b) the geographical areas in which they have jurisdiction;
(c) the means of receipt of documents available to them; and
(d) the languages that may be used for the completion of the standard form set out in Annex I.
Member States shall notify the Commission of any subsequent modification of such information.

Article 3. Each Member State shall designate a central body responsible for:
(a) supplying information to the transmitting agencies;
(b) seeking solutions to any difficulties which may arise during transmission of documents for service;
(c) forwarding, in exceptional cases, at the request of a transmitting agency, a request for service to the competent receiving agency.
A federal State, a State in which several legal systems apply or a State with autonomous territorial units shall be free to designate more than one central body.

Chapter II. Judicial Documents

Section 1. Transmission and service of judicial documents

Article 4. 1. Judicial documents shall be transmitted directly and as soon as possible between the agencies designated pursuant to Article 2.
2. The transmission of documents, requests, confirmations, receipts, certificates and any other papers between transmitting agencies and receiving agencies may be carried out by any appropriate means, provided that the content of the document received is true and faithful to that of the document forwarded and that all information in it is easily legible.
3. The document to be transmitted shall be accompanied by a request drawn up using the standard form set out in Annex I. The form shall be completed in the official language of the Member State addressed or, if there are several official languages in that Member State, the official language or one of the official languages of the place where service is to be effected, or in another language which that Member State has indicated it can accept. Each Member State shall indicate the official language or languages of the institutions of the European Union other than its own which is or are acceptable to it for completion of the form.

4. The documents and all papers that are transmitted shall be exempted from legalisation or any equivalent formality.

5. When the transmitting agency wishes a copy of the document to be returned together with the certificate referred to in Article 10, it shall send the document in duplicate.

Article 5. 1. The applicant shall be advised by the transmitting agency to which he forwards the document for transmission that the addressee may refuse to accept it if it is not in one of the languages provided for in Article 8.

2. The applicant shall bear any costs of translation prior to the transmission of the document, without prejudice to any possible subsequent decision by the court or competent authority on liability for such costs.

Article 6. 1. On receipt of a document, a receiving agency shall, as soon as possible and in any event within seven days of receipt, send a receipt to the transmitting agency by the swiftest possible means of transmission using the standard form set out in Annex I.

2. Where the request for service cannot be fulfilled on the basis of the information or documents transmitted, the receiving agency shall contact the transmitting agency by the swiftest possible means in order to secure the missing information or documents.

3. If the request for service is manifestly outside the scope of this Regulation or if non-compliance with the formal conditions required makes service impossible, the request and the documents transmitted shall be returned, on receipt, to the transmitting agency, together with the notice of return using the standard form set out in Annex I.

4. A receiving agency receiving a document for service but not having territorial jurisdiction to serve it shall forward it, as well as the request, to the receiving agency having territorial jurisdiction in the same Member State if the request complies with the conditions laid down in Article 4(3) and shall inform the transmitting agency accordingly using the standard form set out in Annex I. That receiving agency shall inform the transmitting agency when it receives the document, in the manner provided for in paragraph (1).

Article 7. 1. The receiving agency shall itself serve the document or have it served, either in accordance with the law of the Member State addressed or by a particular method requested by the transmitting agency, unless that method is incompatible with the law of that Member State.

2. The receiving agency shall take all necessary steps to effect the service of the document as soon as possible, and in any event within one month of receipt. If it has not been possible to effect service within one month of receipt, the receiving agency shall:

(a) immediately inform the transmitting agency by means of the certificate in the standard form set out in Annex I, which shall be drawn up under the conditions referred to in Article 10(2); and

(b) continue to take all necessary steps to effect the service of the document, unless indicated otherwise by the transmitting agency, where service seems to be possible within a reasonable period of time.

Article 8. 1. The receiving agency shall inform the addressee, using the standard form set out in Annex II, that he may refuse to accept the document to be served at the time of service or by returning the document to the receiving agency within one week if it is not written in, or accompanied by a translation into, either of the following languages:

(a) a language which the addressee understands; or

(b) the official language of the Member State addressed or, if there are several official languages in that Member State, the official language or one of the official languages of the place where service is to be effected.

2. Where the receiving agency is informed that the addressee refuses to accept the document in accordance with paragraph (1), it shall immediately inform the transmitting agency by means of the certificate provided for in Article 10 and return the request and the documents of which a translation is requested.

3. If the addressee has refused to accept the document pursuant to paragraph (1), the service of the document can be remedied through the service on the addressee in accordance with the provisions of this Regulation of the document accompanied by a translation into a language provided for in paragraph (1). In that case, the date of service of the document shall be the date on which the document accompanied by the translation is served in accordance with the law of the Member State addressed. However, where according to the law of a Member State, a document has to be served within a particular period, the date to be taken into account with respect to the applicant shall be the date of the service of the initial document determined pursuant to Article 9(2).

4. Paragraphs 1, 2 and 3 shall also apply to the means of transmission and service of judicial documents provided for in Section 2.

5. For the purposes of paragraph (1), the diplomatic or consular agents, where service is effected in accordance with Article 13, or the authority or person, where service is effected in accordance with Article 14, shall inform the addressee that he may refuse to accept the document and that any document refused must be sent to those agents or to that authority or person respectively.

Article 9. 1. Without prejudice to Article 8, the date of service of a document pursuant to Article 7 shall be the date on which it is served in accordance with the law of the Member State addressed.
2. However, where according to the law of a Member State a document has to be served within a particular period, the date to be taken into account with respect to the applicant shall be that determined by the law of that Member State.
3. Paragraphs 1 and 2 shall also apply to the means of transmission and service of judicial documents provided for in Section 2.

Article 10. 1. When the formalities concerning the service of the document have been completed, a certificate of completion of those formalities shall be drawn up in the standard form set out in Annex I and addressed to the transmitting agency, together with, where Article 4(5) applies, a copy of the document served.
2. The certificate shall be completed in the official language or one of the official languages of the Member State of origin or in another language which the Member State of origin has indicated that it can accept. Each Member State shall indicate the official language or languages of the institutions of the European Union other than its own which is or are acceptable to it for completion of the form.

Article 11. 1. The service of judicial documents coming from a Member State shall not give rise to any payment or reimbursement of taxes or costs for services rendered by the Member State addressed.
2. However, the applicant shall pay or reimburse the costs occasioned by:
(a) recourse to a judicial officer or to a person competent under the law of the Member State addressed;
(b) the use of a particular method of service.
Costs occasioned by recourse to a judicial officer or to a person competent under the law of the Member State addressed shall correspond to a single fixed fee laid down by that Member State in advance which respects the principles of proportionality and non-discrimination. Member States shall communicate such fixed fees to the Commission.

Section 2. Other means of transmission and service of judicial documents

Article 12. Each Member State shall be free, in exceptional circumstances, to use consular or diplomatic channels to forward judicial documents, for the purpose of service, to those agencies of another Member State which are designated pursuant to Articles 2 or 3.

Article 13. 1. Each Member State shall be free to effect service of judicial documents on persons residing in another Member State, without application of any compulsion, directly through its diplomatic or consular agents.
2. Any Member State may make it known, in accordance with Article 23(1), that it is opposed to such service within its territory, unless the documents are to be served on nationals of the Member State in which the documents originate.

Article 14. Each Member State shall be free to effect service of judicial documents directly by postal services on persons residing in another Member State by registered letter with acknowledgement of receipt or equivalent.

Article 15. Any person interested in a judicial proceeding may effect service of judicial documents directly through the judicial officers, officials or other competent persons of the Member State addressed, where such direct service is permitted under the law of that Member State.

Chapter III. Extrajudicial Documents

Article 16. Extrajudicial documents may be transmitted for service in another Member State in accordance with the provisions of this Regulation.

Chapter IV. Final Provisions

Article 17. Measures designed to amend non-essential elements of this Regulation relating to the updating or to the making of technical amendments to the standard forms set out in Annexes I and II shall be adopted in accordance with the regulatory procedure with scrutiny referred to in Article 18(2).

EU: REGULATION 1393/2007 ON SERVICE OF DOCUMENTS

Article 18. 1. The Commission shall be assisted by a committee.
2. Where reference is made to this paragraph, Article 5a(1) to (4), and Article 7 of Decision 1999/468/EC shall apply, having regard to the provisions of Article 8 thereof.

Article 19. 1. Where a writ of summons or an equivalent document has had to be transmitted to another Member State for the purpose of service under the provisions of this Regulation and the defendant has not appeared, judgment shall not be given until it is established that:
(a) the document was served by a method prescribed by the internal law of the Member State addressed for the service of documents in domestic actions upon persons who are within its territory; or
(b) the document was actually delivered to the defendant or to his residence by another method provided for by this Regulation;
and that in either of these cases the service or the delivery was effected in sufficient time to enable the defendant to defend.
2. Each Member State may make it known, in accordance with Article 23(1), that the judge, notwithstanding the provisions of paragraph (1), may give judgment even if no certificate of service or delivery has been received, if all the following conditions are fulfilled:
(a) the document was transmitted by one of the methods provided for in this Regulation;
(b) a period of time of not less than six months, considered adequate by the judge in the particular case, has elapsed since the date of the transmission of the document;
(c) no certificate of any kind has been received, even though every reasonable effort has been made to obtain it through the competent authorities or bodies of the Member State addressed.
3. Notwithstanding paragraphs 1 and 2, the judge may order, in case of urgency, any provisional or protective measures.
4. When a writ of summons or an equivalent document has had to be transmitted to another Member State for the purpose of service under the provisions of this Regulation and a judgment has been entered against a defendant who has not appeared, the judge shall have the power to relieve the defendant from the effects of the expiry of the time for appeal from the judgment if the following conditions are fulfilled:
(a) the defendant, without any fault on his part, did not have knowledge of the document in sufficient time to defend or knowledge of the judgment in sufficient time to appeal; and
(b) the defendant has disclosed a prima facie defence to the action on the merits.
An application for relief may be filed only within a reasonable time after the defendant has knowledge of the judgment.
Each Member State may make it known, in accordance with Article 23(1), that such application will not be entertained if it is filed after the expiry of a time to be stated by it in that communication, but which shall in no case be less than one year following the date of the judgment.
5. Paragraph 4 shall not apply to judgments concerning the status or capacity of persons.

Article 20. 1. This Regulation shall, in relation to matters to which it applies, prevail over other provisions contained in bilateral or multilateral agreements or arrangements concluded by the Member States, and in particular Article IV of the Protocol to the Brussels Convention of 1968 and the Hague Convention of 15 November 1965.
2. This Regulation shall not preclude individual Member States from maintaining or concluding agreements or arrangements to expedite further or simplify the transmission of documents, provided that they are compatible with this Regulation.
3. Member States shall send to the Commission:
(a) a copy of the agreements or arrangements referred to in paragraph (2) concluded between the Member States as well as drafts of such agreements or arrangements which they intend to adopt; and
(b) any denunciation of, or amendments to, these agreements or arrangements.

Article 21. This Regulation shall not affect the application of Article 23 of the Convention on civil procedure of 17 July 1905, Article 24 of the Convention on civil procedure of 1 March 1954 or Article 13 of the Convention on international access to justice of 25 October 1980 between the Member States party to those Conventions.

Article 22. 1. Information, including in particular personal data, transmitted under this Regulation shall be used by the receiving agency only for the purpose for which it was transmitted.
2. Receiving agencies shall ensure the confidentiality of such information, in accordance with their national law.
3. Paragraphs and 2 shall not affect national laws enabling data subjects to be informed of the use made of information transmitted under this Regulation.

PART V   EUROPEAN CIVIL PROCEDURE

4. This Regulation shall be without prejudice to Directives 95/46/EC and 2002/58/EC.

Article 23. 1. Member States shall communicate to the Commission the information referred to in Articles 2, 3, 4, 10, 11, 13, 15 and 19. Member States shall communicate to the Commission if, according to their law, a document has to be served within a particular period as referred to in Articles 8(3) and 9(2).
2. The Commission shall publish the information communicated in accordance with paragraph (1) in the Official Journal of the European Union with the exception of the addresses and other contact details of the agencies and of the central bodies and the geographical areas in which they have jurisdiction.
3. The Commission shall draw up and update regularly a manual containing the information referred to in paragraph (1), which shall be available electronically, in particular through the European Judicial Network in Civil and Commercial Matters.

Article 24. No later than 1 June 2011, and every five years thereafter, the Commission shall present to the European Parliament, the Council and the European Economic and Social Committee a report on the application of this Regulation, paying special attention to the effectiveness of the agencies designated pursuant to Article 2 and to the practical application of Article 3(c) and Article 9. The report shall be accompanied if need be by proposals for adaptations of this Regulation in line with the evolution of notification systems.

Article 25. 1. Regulation (EC) No 1348/2000 shall be repealed as from the date of application of this Regulation.
2. References made to the repealed Regulation shall be construed as being made to this Regulation and should be read in accordance with the correlation table in Annex III.

Article 26. This Regulation shall enter into force on the 20th day following its publication in the Official Journal of the European Union.
It shall apply from 13 November 2008 with the exception of Article 23 which shall apply from 13 August 2008.
This Regulation shall be binding in its entirety and directly applicable in the Member States in accordance with the Treaty establishing the European Community.
[The Annex is omitted.]

EU: DIRECTIVE 2008/52 ON COMMERCIAL MEDIATION

Directive 2008/52/EC of the European Parliament and of the Council of 21 May 2008 on certain aspects of mediation in civil and commercial matters (OJ L 136, 24.05.2008 pp. 3 -8).

[The Preamble is omitted.]

Article 1. 1. The objective of this Directive is to facilitate access to alternative dispute resolution and to promote the amicable settlement of disputes by encouraging the use of mediation and by ensuring a balanced relationship between mediation and judicial proceedings.
2. This Directive shall apply, in cross-border disputes, to civil and commercial matters except as regards rights and obligations which are not at the parties' disposal under the relevant applicable law. It shall not extend, in particular, to revenue, customs or administrative matters or to the liability of the State for acts and omissions in the exercise of State authority (acta iure imperii).
3. In this Directive, the term "Member State" shall mean Member States with the exception of Denmark.

Article 2. 1. For the purposes of this Directive a cross-border dispute shall be one in which at least one of the parties is domiciled or habitually resident in a Member State other than that of any other party on the date on which:
(a) the parties agree to use mediation after the dispute has arisen;
(b) mediation is ordered by a court;
(c) an obligation to use mediation arises under national law; or
(d) for the purposes of Article 5 an invitation is made to the parties.
2. Notwithstanding paragraph (1), for the purposes of Articles 7 and 8 a cross-border dispute shall also be one in which judicial proceedings or arbitration following mediation between the parties are initiated in a Member State other than that in which the parties were domiciled or habitually resident on the date referred to in paragraph (1)(a), (b) or (c).
3. For the purposes of paragraphs 1 and 2, domicile shall be determined in accordance with Articles 59 and 60 of Regulation (EC) No 44/2001.

Article 3. For the purposes of this Directive the following definitions shall apply:
(a) "Mediation" means a structured process, however named or referred to, whereby two or more parties to a dispute attempt by themselves, on a voluntary basis, to reach an agreement on the settlement of their dispute with the assistance of a mediator. This process may be initiated by the parties or suggested or ordered by a court or prescribed by the law of a Member State.
It includes mediation conducted by a judge who is not responsible for any judicial proceedings concerning the dispute in question. It excludes attempts made by the court or the judge seised to settle a dispute in the course of judicial proceedings concerning the dispute in question.
(b) "Mediator" means any third person who is asked to conduct a mediation in an effective, impartial and competent way, regardless of the denomination or profession of that third person in the Member State concerned and of the way in which the third person has been appointed or requested to conduct the mediation.

Article 4. 1. Member States shall encourage, by any means which they consider appropriate, the development of, and adherence to, voluntary codes of conduct by mediators and organisations providing mediation services, as well as other effective quality control mechanisms concerning the provision of mediation services.
2. Member States shall encourage the initial and further training of mediators in order to ensure that the mediation is conducted in an effective, impartial and competent way in relation to the parties.

Article 5. 1. A court before which an action is brought may, when appropriate and having regard to all the circumstances of the case, invite the parties to use mediation in order to settle the dispute. The court may also invite the parties to attend an information session on the use of mediation if such sessions are held and are easily available.
2. This Directive is without prejudice to national legislation making the use of mediation compulsory or subject to incentives or sanctions, whether before or after judicial proceedings have started, provided that such legislation does not prevent the parties from exercising their right of access to the judicial system.

Article 6. 1. Member States shall ensure that it is possible for the parties, or for one of them with the explicit consent of the others, to request that the content of a written agreement resulting from mediation be made enforceable. The content of such an agreement shall be made enforceable unless, in the case in question, either the content of that agreement is contrary to the law of the Member State

where the request is made or the law of that Member State does not provide for its enforceability.
2. The content of the agreement may be made enforceable by a court or other competent authority in a judgment or decision or in an authentic instrument in accordance with the law of the Member State where the request is made.
3. Member States shall inform the Commission of the courts or other authorities competent to receive requests in accordance with paragraphs 1 and 2.
4. Nothing in this Article shall affect the rules applicable to the recognition and enforcement in another Member State of an agreement made enforceable in accordance with paragraph (1).

Article 7. 1. Given that mediation is intended to take place in a manner which respects confidentiality, Member States shall ensure that, unless the parties agree otherwise, neither mediators nor those involved in the administration of the mediation process shall be compelled to give evidence in civil and commercial judicial proceedings or arbitration regarding information arising out of or in connection with a mediation process, except:
(a) where this is necessary for overriding considerations of public policy of the Member State concerned, in particular when required to ensure the protection of the best interests of children or to prevent harm to the physical or psychological integrity of a person; or
(b) where disclosure of the content of the agreement resulting from mediation is necessary in order to implement or enforce that agreement.
2. Nothing in paragraph (1) shall preclude Member States from enacting stricter measures to protect the confidentiality of mediation.

Article 8. 1. Member States shall ensure that parties who choose mediation in an attempt to settle a dispute are not subsequently prevented from initiating judicial proceedings or arbitration in relation to that dispute by the expiry of limitation or prescription periods during the mediation process.
2. Paragraph 1 shall be without prejudice to provisions on limitation or prescription periods in international agreements to which Member States are party.

Article 9. Member States shall encourage, by any means which they consider appropriate, the availability to the general public, in particular on the Internet, of information on how to contact mediators and organisations providing mediation services.

Article 10. The Commission shall make publicly available, by any appropriate means, information on the competent courts or authorities communicated by the Member States pursuant to Article 6(3).

Article 11. Not later than 21 May 2016, the Commission shall submit to the European Parliament, the Council and the European Economic and Social Committee a report on the application of this Directive. The report shall consider the development of mediation throughout the European Union and the impact of this Directive in the Member States. If necessary, the report shall be accompanied by proposals to adapt this Directive.

Article 12. 1. Member States shall bring into force the laws, regulations, and administrative provisions necessary to comply with this Directive before 21 May 2011, with the exception of Article 10, for which the date of compliance shall be 21 November 2010 at the latest. They shall forthwith inform the Commission thereof.
When they are adopted by Member States, these measures shall contain a reference to this Directive or shall be accompanied by such reference on the occasion of their official publication. The methods of making such reference shall be laid down by Member States.
2. Member States shall communicate to the Commission the text of the main provisions of national law which they adopt in the field covered by this Directive.

Article 13. This Directive shall enter into force on the 20th day following its publication in the Official Journal of the European Union.

Article 14. This Directive is addressed to the Member States.

Tax Law

PART VI TAX LAW

COUNCIL DIRECTIVE (EU) 2016/1164 of 12 July 2016 laying down rules against tax avoidance practices that directly affect the functioning of the internal market.

The Council of the European Union,
Having regard to the Treaty on the Functioning of the European Union, and in particular Article 115 thereof,
Having regard to the proposal from the European Commission,
After transmission of the draft legislative act to the national parliaments,
Having regard to the opinion of the European Parliament,
Having regard to the opinion of the European Economic and Social Committee,
Acting in accordance with a special legislative procedure,
Whereas:
(1) The current political priorities in international taxation highlight the need for ensuring that tax is paid where profits and value are generated. It is thus imperative to restore trust in the fairness of tax systems and allow governments to effectively exercise their tax sovereignty. These new political objectives have been translated into concrete action recommendations in the context of the initiative against base erosion and profit shifting (BEPS) by the Organisation for Economic Cooperation and Development (OECD). The European Council has welcomed this work in its conclusions of 13-14 March 2013 and 19-20 December 2013. In response to the need for fairer taxation, the Commission, in its communication of 17 June 2015 sets out an action plan for fair and efficient corporate taxation in the European Union.
(2) The final reports on the 15 OECD Action Items against BEPS were released to the public on 5 October 2015. This output was welcomed by the Council in its conclusions of 8 December 2015. The Council conclusions stressed the need to find common, yet flexible, solutions at the EU level consistent with OECD BEPS conclusions. In addition, the conclusions supported an effective and swift coordinated implementation of the anti-BEPS measures at the EU level and considered that EU directives should be, where appropriate, the preferred vehicle for implementing OECD BEPS conclusions at the EU level. It is essential for the good functioning of the internal market that, as a minimum, Member States implement their commitments under BEPS and more broadly, take action to discourage tax avoidance practices and ensure fair and effective taxation in the Union in a sufficiently coherent and coordinated fashion. In a market of highly integrated economies, there is a need for common strategic approaches and coordinated action, to improve the functioning of the internal market and maximise the positive effects of the initiative against BEPS. Furthermore, only a common framework could prevent a fragmentation of the market and put an end to currently existing mismatches and market distortions. Finally, national implementing measures which follow a common line across the Union would provide taxpayers with legal certainty in that those measures would be compatible with Union law.
(3) It is necessary to lay down rules in order to strengthen the average level of protection against aggressive tax planning in the internal market. As these rules would have to fit in 28 separate corporate tax systems, they should be limited to general provisions and leave the implementation to Member States as they are better placed to shape the specific elements of those rules in a way that fits best their corporate tax systems. This objective could be achieved by creating a minimum level of protection for national corporate tax systems against tax avoidance practices across the Union. It is therefore necessary to coordinate the responses of Member States in implementing the outputs of the 15 OECD Action Items against BEPS with the aim to improve the effectiveness of the internal market as a whole in tackling tax avoidance practices. It is therefore necessary to set a common minimum level of protection for the internal market in specific fields.
(4) It is necessary to establish rules applicable to all taxpayers that are subject to corporate tax in a Member State. Considering that it would result in the need to cover a broader range of national taxes, it is not desirable to extend the scope of this Directive to types of entities which are not subject to corporate tax in a Member State; that is, in particular, transparent entities. Those rules should also apply to permanent establishments of those corporate taxpayers which may be situated in other Member State(s). Corporate taxpayers may be resident for tax purposes in a Member State or be established under the laws of a Member State. Permanent establishments of entities resident for tax purposes in a third country should also be covered by those rules if they are situated in one or more Member State.
(5) It is necessary to lay down rules against the erosion of tax bases in the internal market and the shifting of profits out of the internal market. Rules in the following areas are necessary in order to contribute to achieving that objective: limitations to the deductibility of interest, exit taxation, a general anti-abuse rule, controlled foreign company rules and rules to tackle hybrid mismatches. Where

the application of those rules gives rise to double taxation, taxpayers should receive relief through a deduction for the tax paid in another Member State or third country, as the case may be. Thus, the rules should not only aim to counter tax avoidance practices but also avoid creating other obstacles to the market, such as double taxation.

(6) In an effort to reduce their global tax liability, groups of companies have increasingly engaged in BEPS, through excessive interest payments. The interest limitation rule is necessary to discourage such practices by limiting the deductibility of taxpayers' exceeding borrowing costs. It is therefore necessary to fix a ratio for deductibility which refers to a taxpayer's taxable earnings before interest, tax, depreciation and amortisation (EBITDA). Member States could decrease this ratio or place time limits or restrict the amount of unrelieved borrowing costs that can be carried forward or back to ensure a higher level of protection. Given that the aim is to lay down minimum standards, it could be possible for Member States to adopt an alternative measure referring to a taxpayer's earnings before interest and tax (EBIT) and fixed in a way that it is equivalent to the EBITDA-based ratio. Member States could in addition to the interest limitation rule provided by this Directive also use targeted rules against intra-group debt financing, in particular thin capitalisation rules. Tax exempt revenues should not be set off against deductible borrowing costs. This is because only taxable income should be taken into account in determining how much interest may be deducted.

(7) Where the taxpayer is part of a group which files statutory consolidated accounts, the indebtedness of the overall group at worldwide level may be considered for the purpose of granting taxpayers entitlement to deduct higher amounts of exceeding borrowing costs. It may also be appropriate to lay down rules for an equity escape provision, where the interest limitation rule does not apply if the company can demonstrate that its equity over total assets ratio is broadly equal to or higher than the equivalent group ratio. The interest limitation rule should apply in relation to a taxpayer's exceeding borrowing costs without distinction of whether the costs originate in debt taken out nationally, cross-border within the Union or with a third country, or whether they originate from third parties, associated enterprises or intra-group. Where a group includes more than one entity in a Member State, the Member State may consider the overall position of all group entities in the same State, including a separate entity taxation system to allow the transfer of profits or interest capacity between entities within a group, when applying rules that limit the deductibility of interest.

(8) To reduce the administrative and compliance burden of the rules without significantly diminishing their tax effect, it may be appropriate to provide for a safe harbour rule so that net interest is always deductible up to a fixed amount, when this leads to a higher deduction than the EBITDA-based ratio. Member States could reduce the fixed monetary threshold in order to ensure a higher level of protection of their domestic tax base. Since BEPS in principle takes place through excessive interest payments among entities which are associated enterprises, it is appropriate and necessary to allow the possible exclusion of standalone entities from the scope of the interest limitation rule given the limited risks of tax avoidance. In order to facilitate the transition to the new interest limitation rule, Member States could provide for a grandfathering clause that would cover existing loans to the extent that their terms are not subsequently modified, i.e. in case of a subsequent modification, the grandfathering would not apply to any increase in the amount or duration of the loan but would be limited to the original terms of the loan. Without prejudice to State aid rules, Member States could also exclude exceeding borrowing costs incurred on loans used to fund long-term public infrastructure projects considering that such financing arrangements present little or no BEPS risks. In this context, Member States should properly demonstrate that financing arrangements for public infrastructure projects present special features which justify such treatment vis-à-vis other financing arrangements subject to the restrictive rule.

(9) Although it is generally accepted that financial undertakings, i.e. financial institutions and insurance undertakings, should also be subject to limitations to the deductibility of interest, it is equally acknowledged that these two sectors present special features which call for a more customised approach. As the discussions in this field are not yet sufficiently conclusive in the international and Union context, it is not yet possible to provide specific rules in the financial and insurance sectors and Member States should therefore be able to exclude them from the scope of interest limitation rules.

(10) Exit taxes have the function of ensuring that where a taxpayer moves assets or its tax residence out of the tax jurisdiction of a State, that State taxes the economic value of any capital gain created in its territory even though that gain has not yet been realised at the time of the exit. It is therefore necessary to specify cases in which taxpayers are subject to exit tax rules and taxed on unrealised capital gains which have been built in their transferred assets. It is also helpful to clarify that transfers of assets, including cash, between a parent company and its subsidiaries fall outside the scope of the envisaged rule on exit taxation. In order to compute the amounts, it is critical to fix a market

value for the transferred assets at the time of exit of the assets based on the arm's length principle. In order to ensure the compatibility of the rule with the use of the credit method, it is desirable to allow Member States to refer to the moment when the right to tax the transferred assets is lost. The right to tax should be defined at national level. It is also necessary to allow the receiving State to dispute the value of the transferred assets established by the exit State when it does not reflect such a market value. Member States could resort to this effect to existing dispute resolution mechanisms. Within the Union, it is necessary to address the application of exit taxation and illustrate the conditions for being compliant with Union law. In those situations, taxpayers should have the right to either immediately pay the amount of exit tax assessed or defer payment of the amount of tax by paying it in instalments over a certain number of years, possibly together with interest and a guarantee. Member States could request, for this purpose, the taxpayers concerned to include the necessary information in a declaration. Exit tax should not be charged when the transfer of assets is of a temporary nature and the assets are set to revert to the Member State of the transferor, where the transfer takes place in order to meet prudential capital requirements or for the purpose of liquidity management or when it comes to securities' financing transactions or assets posted as collateral.

(11) General anti-abuse rules (GAARs) feature in tax systems to tackle abusive tax practices that have not yet been dealt with through specifically targeted provisions. GAARs have therefore a function aimed to fill in gaps, which should not affect the applicability of specific anti-abuse rules. Within the Union, GAARs should be applied to arrangements that are not genuine; otherwise, the taxpayer should have the right to choose the most tax efficient structure for its commercial affairs. It is furthermore important to ensure that the GAARs apply in domestic situations, within the Union and vis-à-vis third countries in a uniform manner, so that their scope and results of application in domestic and cross-border situations do not differ. Member States should not be prevented from applying penalties where the GAAR is applicable. When evaluating whether an arrangement should be regarded as non-genuine, it could be possible for Member States to consider all valid economic reasons, including financial activities.

(12) Controlled foreign company (CFC) rules have the effect of re-attributing the income of a low-taxed controlled subsidiary to its parent company. Then, the parent company becomes taxable on this attributed income in the State where it is resident for tax purposes. Depending on the policy priorities of that State, CFC rules may target an entire low-taxed subsidiary, specific categories of income or be limited to income which has artificially been diverted to the subsidiary. In particular, in order to ensure that CFC rules are a proportionate response to BEPS concerns, it is critical that Member States that limit their CFC rules to income which has been artificially diverted to the subsidiary precisely target situations where most of the decision-making functions which generated diverted income at the level of the controlled subsidiary are carried out in the Member State of the taxpayer. With a view to limiting the administrative burden and compliance costs, it should also be acceptable that those Member States exempt certain entities with low profits or a low profit margin that give rise to lower risks of tax avoidance. Accordingly, it is necessary that the CFC rules extend to the profits of permanent establishments where those profits are not subject to tax or are tax exempt in the Member State of the taxpayer. However, there is no need to tax, under the CFC rules, the profits of permanent establishments which are denied the tax exemption under national rules because these permanent establishments are treated as though they were controlled foreign companies. In order to ensure a higher level of protection, Member States could reduce the control threshold, or employ a higher threshold in comparing the actual corporate tax paid with the corporate tax that would have been charged in the Member State of the taxpayer. Member States could, in transposing CFC rules into their national law, use a sufficiently high tax rate fractional threshold.

It is desirable to address situations both in third countries and within the Union. To comply with the fundamental freedoms, the income categories should be combined with a substance carve-out aimed to limit, within the Union, the impact of the rules to cases where the CFC does not carry on a substantive economic activity. It is important that tax administrations and taxpayers cooperate to gather the relevant facts and circumstances to determine whether the carve-out rule is to apply. It should be acceptable that, in transposing CFC rules into their national law, Member States use white, grey or black lists of third countries, which are compiled on the basis of certain criteria set out in this Directive and may include the corporate tax rate level, or use white lists of Member States compiled on that basis.

(13) Hybrid mismatches are the consequence of differences in the legal characterisation of payments (financial instruments) or entities and those differences surface in the interaction between the legal systems of two jurisdictions. The effect of such mismatches is often a double deduction (i.e. deduction in both states) or a deduction of the income in one state without inclusion in the tax base of the other. To neutralise the effects of hybrid mismatch arrangements, it is necessary to lay down rules whereby

one of the two jurisdictions in a mismatch should deny the deduction of a payment leading to such an outcome. In this context, it is useful to clarify that measures aimed to tackle hybrid mismatches in this Directive are aimed to tackle mismatch situations attributable to differences in the legal characterisation of a financial instrument or entity and are not intended to affect the general features of the tax system of a Member State. Although Member States have agreed guidance, in the framework of the Group of the Code of Conduct on Business Taxation, on the tax treatment of hybrid entities and hybrid permanent establishments within the Union as well as on the tax treatment of hybrid entities in relations with third countries, it is still necessary to enact binding rules. It is critical that further work is undertaken on hybrid mismatches between Member States and third countries, as well as on other hybrid mismatches such as those involving permanent establishments.

(14) It is necessary to clarify that the implementation of the rules against tax avoidance provided in this Directive should not affect the taxpayers' obligation to comply with the arm's length principle or the Member State's right to adjust a tax liability upwards in accordance with the arm's length principle, where applicable.

(15) The European Data Protection Supervisor was consulted in accordance with Article 28(2) of Regulation (EC) No 45/2001 of the European Parliament and of the Council. The right to protection of personal data according to Article 8 of the Charter of Fundamental Rights of the European Union as well as Directive 95/46/EC of the European Parliament and of the Council applies to the processing of personal data carried out within the framework of this Directive.

(16) Considering that a key objective of this Directive is to improve the resilience of the internal market as a whole against cross-border tax avoidance practices, this cannot be sufficiently achieved by the Member States acting individually. National corporate tax systems are disparate and independent action by Member States would only replicate the existing fragmentation of the internal market in direct taxation. It would thus allow inefficiencies and distortions to persist in the interaction of distinct national measures. The result would be lack of coordination. Rather, by reason of the fact that much inefficiency in the internal market primarily gives rise to problems of a cross-border nature, remedial measures should be adopted at Union level. It is therefore critical to adopt solutions that function for the internal market as a whole and this can be better achieved at Union level. Thus, the Union may adopt measures, in accordance with the principle of subsidiarity as set out in Article 5 of the Treaty on European Union. In accordance with the principle of proportionality, as set out in that Article, this Directive does not go beyond what is necessary in order to achieve that objective. By setting a minimum level of protection for the internal market, this Directive only aims to achieve the essential minimum degree of coordination within the Union for the purpose of materialising its objectives.

(17) The Commission should evaluate the implementation of this Directive four years after its entry into force and report to the Council thereon. Member States should communicate to the Commission all information necessary for this evaluation.

HAS ADOPTED THIS DIRECTIVE:

Chapter I. General Provisions

Article 1. This Directive applies to all taxpayers that are subject to corporate tax in one or more Member States, including permanent establishments in one or more Member States of entities resident for tax purposes in a third country.

Article 2. For the purposes of this Directive, the following definitions apply:

(1) 'borrowing costs' means interest expenses on all forms of debt, other costs economically equivalent to interest and expenses incurred in connection with the raising of finance as defined in national law, including, without being limited to, payments under profit participating loans, imputed interest on instruments such as convertible bonds and zero coupon bonds, amounts under alternative financing arrangements, such as Islamic finance, the finance cost element of finance lease payments, capitalised interest included in the balance sheet value of a related asset, or the amortisation of capitalised interest, amounts measured by reference to a funding return under transfer pricing rules where applicable, notional interest amounts under derivative instruments or hedging arrangements related to an entity's borrowings, certain foreign exchange gains and losses on borrowings and instruments connected with the raising of finance, guarantee fees for financing arrangements, arrangement fees and similar costs related to the borrowing of funds;

(2) 'exceeding borrowing costs' means the amount by which the deductible borrowing costs of a taxpayer exceed taxable interest revenues and other economically equivalent taxable revenues that the taxpayer receives according to national law;

(3) 'tax period' means a tax year, calendar year or any other appropriate period for tax purposes;

(4) 'associated enterprise' means:
(a) an entity in which the taxpayer holds directly or indirectly a participation in terms of voting rights or capital ownership of 25 percent or more or is entitled to receive 25 percent or more of the profits of that entity;
(b) an individual or entity which holds directly or indirectly a participation in terms of voting rights or capital ownership in a taxpayer of 25 percent or more or is entitled to receive 25 percent or more of the profits of the taxpayer;
If an individual or entity holds directly or indirectly a participation of 25 percent or more in a taxpayer and one or more entities, all the entities concerned, including the taxpayer, shall also be regarded as associated enterprises.
For the purposes of Article 9 and where the mismatch involves a hybrid entity, this definition is modified so that the 25 percent requirement is replaced by a 50 percent requirement.
(5) 'financial undertaking' means any of the following entities:
(a) a credit institution or an investment firm as defined in point (1) of Article 4(1) of Directive 2004/39/EC of the European Parliament and of the Council or an alternative investment fund manager (AIFM) as defined in point (b) of Article 4(1) of Directive 2011/61/EU of the European Parliament and of the Council or an undertaking for collective investment in transferable securities (UCITS) management company as defined in point (b) of Article 2(1) of Directive 2009/65/EC of the European Parliament and of the Council;
(b) an insurance undertaking as defined in point (1) of Article 13 of Directive 2009/138/EC of the European Parliament and of the Council;
(c) a reinsurance undertaking as defined in point (4) of Article 13 of Directive 2009/138/EC;
(d) an institution for occupational retirement provision falling within the scope of Directive 2003/41/EC of the European Parliament and of the Council, unless a Member State has chosen not to apply that Directive in whole or in part to that institution in accordance with Article 5 of that Directive or the delegate of an institution for occupational retirement provision as referred to in Article 19(1) of that Directive;
(e) pension institutions operating pension schemes which are considered to be social security schemes covered by Regulation (EC) No 883/2004 of the European Parliament and of the Council and Regulation (EC) No 987/2009 of the European Parliament and of the Council as well as any legal entity set up for the purpose of investment of such schemes;
(f) an alternative investment fund (AIF) managed by an AIFM as defined in point (b) of Article 4(1) of Directive 2011/61/EU or an AIF supervised under the applicable national law;
(g) UCITS in the meaning of Article 1(2) of Directive 2009/65/EC;
(h) a central counterparty as defined in point (1) of Article 2 of Regulation (EU) No 648/2012 of the European Parliament and of the Council;
(i) a central securities depository as defined in point (1) of Article 2(1) of Regulation (EU) No 909/2014 of the European Parliament and of the Council.
(6) 'transfer of assets' means an operation whereby a Member State loses the right to tax the transferred assets, whilst the assets remain under the legal or economic ownership of the same taxpayer;
(7) 'transfer of tax residence' means an operation whereby a taxpayer ceases to be resident for tax purposes in a Member State, whilst acquiring tax residence in another Member State or third country;
(8) 'transfer of a business carried on by a permanent establishment' means an operation whereby a taxpayer ceases to have taxable presence in a Member State whilst acquiring such presence in another Member State or third country without becoming resident for tax purposes in that Member State or third country;
(9) 'hybrid mismatch' means a situation between a taxpayer in one Member State and an associated enterprise in another Member State or a structured arrangement between parties in Member States where the following outcome is attributable to differences in the legal characterisation of a financial instrument or entity:
(a) a deduction of the same payment, expenses or losses occurs both in the Member State in which the payment has its source, the expenses are incurred or the losses are suffered and in another Member State ('double deduction'); or
(b) there is a deduction of a payment in the Member State in which the payment has its source without a corresponding inclusion for tax purposes of the same payment in the other Member State ('deduction without inclusion').

Article 3. This Directive shall not preclude the application of domestic or agreement-based provisions aimed at safeguarding a higher level of protection for domestic corporate tax bases.

EU: DIRECTIVE 2016/1164 ON TAX AVOIDANCE PRACTICES

Chapter II. Measures Against Tax Avoidance

Article 4. 1. Exceeding borrowing costs shall be deductible in the tax period in which they are incurred only up to 30 percent of the taxpayer's earnings before interest, tax, depreciation and amortisation (EBITDA).
For the purpose of this Article, Member States may also treat as a taxpayer:
(a) an entity which is permitted or required to apply the rules on behalf of a group, as defined according to national tax law;
(b) an entity in a group, as defined according to national tax law, which does not consolidate the results of its members for tax purposes.
In such circumstances, exceeding borrowing costs and the EBITDA may be calculated at the level of the group and comprise the results of all its members.
2. The EBITDA shall be calculated by adding back to the income subject to corporate tax in the Member State of the taxpayer the tax-adjusted amounts for exceeding borrowing costs as well as the tax-adjusted amounts for depreciation and amortisation. Tax exempt income shall be excluded from the EBITDA of a taxpayer.
3. By derogation from paragraph 1, the taxpayer may be given the right:
(a) to deduct exceeding borrowing costs up to EUR 3 000 000;
(b) to fully deduct exceeding borrowing costs if the taxpayer is a standalone entity.
For the purposes of the second subparagraph of paragraph 1, the amount of EUR 3 000 000 shall be considered for the entire group.
For the purposes of point (b) of the first subparagraph, a standalone entity means a taxpayer that is not part of a consolidated group for financial accounting purposes and has no associated enterprise or permanent establishment.
4. Member States may exclude from the scope of paragraph 1 exceeding borrowing costs incurred on:
(a) loans which were concluded before 17 June 2016, but the exclusion shall not extend to any subsequent modification of such loans;
(b) loans used to fund a long-term public infrastructure project where the project operator, borrowing costs, assets and income are all in the Union.
For the purposes of point (b) of the first subparagraph, a long-term public infrastructure project means a project to provide, upgrade, operate and/or maintain a large-scale asset that is considered in the general public interest by a Member State.
Where point (b) of the first subparagraph applies, any income arising from a long-term public infrastructure project shall be excluded from the EBITDA of the taxpayer, and any excluded exceeding borrowing cost shall not be included in the exceeding borrowing costs of the group vis-à-vis third parties referred to in point (b) of paragraph 5.
5. Where the taxpayer is a member of a consolidated group for financial accounting purposes, the taxpayer may be given the right to either:
(a) fully deduct its exceeding borrowing costs if it can demonstrate that the ratio of its equity over its total assets is equal to or higher than the equivalent ratio of the group and subject to the following conditions:
(i) the ratio of the taxpayer's equity over its total assets is considered to be equal to the equivalent ratio of the group if the ratio of the taxpayer's equity over its total assets is lower by up to two percentage points; and
(ii) all assets and liabilities are valued using the same method as in the consolidated financial statements referred to in paragraph 8;
or
(b) deduct exceeding borrowing costs at an amount in excess of what it would be entitled to deduct under paragraph 1. This higher limit to the deductibility of exceeding borrowing costs shall refer to the consolidated group for financial accounting purposes in which the taxpayer is a member and be calculated in two steps:
(i) first, the group ratio is determined by dividing the exceeding borrowing costs of the group vis-à-vis third-parties over the EBITDA of the group; and
(ii) second, the group ratio is multiplied by the EBITDA of the taxpayer calculated pursuant to paragraph 2.
6. The Member State of the taxpayer may provide for rules either:
(a) to carry forward, without time limitation, exceeding borrowing costs which cannot be deducted in the current tax period under paragraphs 1 to 5;
(b) to carry forward, without time limitation, and back, for a maximum of three years, exceeding borrowing costs which cannot be deducted in the current tax period under paragraphs 1 to 5; or
(c) to carry forward, without time limitation, exceeding borrowing costs and, for a maximum of five

years, unused interest capacity, which cannot be deducted in the current tax period under paragraphs 1 to 5.

7. Member States may exclude financial undertakings from the scope of paragraphs 1 to 6, including where such financial undertakings are part of a consolidated group for financial accounting purposes.

8. For the purpose of this Article, the consolidated group for financial accounting purposes consists of all entities which are fully included in consolidated financial statements drawn up in accordance with the International Financial Reporting Standards or the national financial reporting system of a Member State. The taxpayer may be given the right to use consolidated financial statements prepared under other accounting standards.

Article 5. 1. A taxpayer shall be subject to tax at an amount equal to the market value of the transferred assets, at the time of exit of the assets, less their value for tax purposes, in any of the following circumstances:

(a) a taxpayer transfers assets from its head office to its permanent establishment in another Member State or in a third country in so far as the Member State of the head office no longer has the right to tax the transferred assets due to the transfer;

(b) a taxpayer transfers assets from its permanent establishment in a Member State to its head office or another permanent establishment in another Member State or in a third country in so far as the Member State of the permanent establishment no longer has the right to tax the transferred assets due to the transfer;

(c) a taxpayer transfers its tax residence to another Member State or to a third country, except for those assets which remain effectively connected with a permanent establishment in the first Member State;

(d) a taxpayer transfers the business carried on by its permanent establishment from a Member State to another Member State or to a third country in so far as the Member State of the permanent establishment no longer has the right to tax the transferred assets due to the transfer.

2. A taxpayer shall be given the right to defer the payment of an exit tax referred to in paragraph 1, by paying it in instalments over five years, in any of the following circumstances:

(a) a taxpayer transfers assets from its head office to its permanent establishment in another Member State or in a third country that is party to the Agreement on the European Economic Area (EEA Agreement);

(b) a taxpayer transfers assets from its permanent establishment in a Member State to its head office or another permanent establishment in another Member State or a third country that is party to the EEA Agreement;

(c) a taxpayer transfers its tax residence to another Member State or to a third country that is party to the EEA Agreement;

(d) a taxpayer transfers the business carried on by its permanent establishment to another Member State or a third country that is party to the EEA Agreement.

This paragraph shall apply to third countries that are party to the EEA Agreement if they have concluded an agreement with the Member State of the taxpayer or with the Union on the mutual assistance for the recovery of tax claims, equivalent to the mutual assistance provided for in Council Directive 2010/24/EU.

3. If a taxpayer defers the payment in accordance with paragraph 2, interest may be charged in accordance with the legislation of the Member State of the taxpayer or of the permanent establishment, as the case may be.

If there is a demonstrable and actual risk of non-recovery, taxpayers may also be required to provide a guarantee as a condition for deferring the payment in accordance with paragraph 2.

The second subparagraph shall not apply where the legislation in the Member State of the taxpayer or of the permanent establishment provides for the possibility of recovery of the tax debt through another taxpayer which is member of the same group and is resident for tax purposes in that Member State.

4. Where paragraph 2 applies, the deferral of payment shall be immediately discontinued and the tax debt becomes recoverable in the following cases:

(a) the transferred assets or the business carried on by the permanent establishment of the taxpayer are sold or otherwise disposed of;

(b) the transferred assets are subsequently transferred to a third country;

(c) the taxpayer's tax residence or the business carried on by its permanent establishment is subsequently transferred to a third country;

(d) the taxpayer goes bankrupt or is wound up;

(e) the taxpayer fails to honour its obligations in relation to the instalments and does not correct its

situation over a reasonable period of time, which shall not exceed 12 months.
Points (b) and (c) shall not apply to third countries that are party to the EEA Agreement if they have concluded an agreement with the Member State of the taxpayer or with the Union on the mutual assistance for the recovery of tax claims, equivalent to the mutual assistance provided for in Directive 2010/24/EU.
5. Where the transfer of assets, tax residence or the business carried on by a permanent establishment is to another Member State, that Member State shall accept the value established by the Member State of the taxpayer or of the permanent establishment as the starting value of the assets for tax purposes, unless this does not reflect the market value.
6. For the purposes of paragraphs 1 to 5, 'market value' is the amount for which an asset can be exchanged or mutual obligations can be settled between willing unrelated buyers and sellers in a direct transaction.
7. Provided that the assets are set to revert to the Member State of the transferor within a period of 12 months, this Article shall not apply to asset transfers related to the financing of securities, assets posted as collateral or where the asset transfer takes place in order to meet prudential capital requirements or for the purpose of liquidity management.

Article 6. 1. For the purposes of calculating the corporate tax liability, a Member State shall ignore an arrangement or a series of arrangements which, having been put into place for the main purpose or one of the main purposes of obtaining a tax advantage that defeats the object or purpose of the applicable tax law, are not genuine having regard to all relevant facts and circumstances. An arrangement may comprise more than one step or part.
2. For the purposes of paragraph 1, an arrangement or a series thereof shall be regarded as non-genuine to the extent that they are not put into place for valid commercial reasons which reflect economic reality.
3. Where arrangements or a series thereof are ignored in accordance with paragraph 1, the tax liability shall be calculated in accordance with national law.

Article 7. 1. The Member State of a taxpayer shall treat an entity, or a permanent establishment of which the profits are not subject to tax or are exempt from tax in that Member State, as a controlled foreign company where the following conditions are met:
(a) in the case of an entity, the taxpayer by itself, or together with its associated enterprises holds a direct or indirect participation of more than 50 percent of the voting rights, or owns directly or indirectly more than 50 percent of capital or is entitled to receive more than 50 percent of the profits of that entity and
(b) the actual corporate tax paid on its profits by the entity or permanent establishment is lower than the difference between the corporate tax that would have been charged on the entity or permanent establishment under the applicable corporate tax system in the Member State of the taxpayer and the actual corporate tax paid on its profits by the entity or permanent establishment.
For the purposes of point (b) of the first subparagraph, the permanent establishment of a controlled foreign company that is not subject to tax or is exempt from tax in the jurisdiction of the controlled foreign company shall not be taken into account. Furthermore the corporate tax that would have been charged in the Member State of the taxpayer means as computed according to the rules of the Member State of the taxpayer.
2. Where an entity or permanent establishment is treated as a controlled foreign company under paragraph 1, the Member State of the taxpayer shall include in the tax base:
(a) the non-distributed income of the entity or the income of the permanent establishment which is derived from the following categories:
(i) interest or any other income generated by financial assets;
(ii) royalties or any other income generated from intellectual property;
(iii) dividends and income from the disposal of shares;
(iv) income from financial leasing;
(v) income from insurance, banking and other financial activities;
(vi) income from invoicing companies that earn sales and services income from goods and services purchased from and sold to associated enterprises, and add no or little economic value;
This point shall not apply where the controlled foreign company carries on a substantive economic activity supported by staff, equipment, assets and premises, as evidenced by relevant facts and circumstances.
Where the controlled foreign company is resident or situated in a third country that is not party to the EEA Agreement, Member States may decide to refrain from applying the preceding subparagraph.
or

(b) the non-distributed income of the entity or permanent establishment arising from non-genuine arrangements which have been put in place for the essential purpose of obtaining a tax advantage. For the purposes of this point, an arrangement or a series thereof shall be regarded as non-genuine to the extent that the entity or permanent establishment would not own the assets or would not have undertaken the risks which generate all, or part of, its income if it were not controlled by a company where the significant people functions, which are relevant to those assets and risks, are carried out and are instrumental in generating the controlled company's income.

3. Where, under the rules of a Member State, the tax base of a taxpayer is calculated according to point (a) of paragraph 2, the Member State may opt not to treat an entity or permanent establishment as a controlled foreign company under paragraph 1 if one third or less of the income accruing to the entity or permanent establishment falls within the categories under point (a) of paragraph 2.

Where, under the rules of a Member State, the tax base of a taxpayer is calculated according to point (a) of paragraph 2, the Member State may opt not to treat financial undertakings as controlled foreign companies if one third or less of the entity's income from the categories under point (a) of paragraph 2 comes from transactions with the taxpayer or its associated enterprises.

4. Member States may exclude from the scope of point (b) of paragraph 2 an entity or permanent establishment:

(a) with accounting profits of no more than EUR 750 000, and non-trading income of no more than EUR 75 000; or

(b) of which the accounting profits amount to no more than 10 percent of its operating costs for the tax period.

For the purpose of point (b) of the first subparagraph, the operating costs may not include the cost of goods sold outside the country where the entity is resident, or the permanent establishment is situated, for tax purposes and payments to associated enterprises.

Article 8. 1. Where point (a) of Article 7(2) applies, the income to be included in the tax base of the taxpayer shall be calculated in accordance with the rules of the corporate tax law of the Member State where the taxpayer is resident for tax purposes or situated. Losses of the entity or permanent establishment shall not be included in the tax base but may be carried forward, according to national law, and taken into account in subsequent tax periods.

2. Where point (b) of Article 7(2) applies, the income to be included in the tax base of the taxpayer shall be limited to amounts generated through assets and risks which are linked to significant people functions carried out by the controlling company. The attribution of controlled foreign company income shall be calculated in accordance with the arm's length principle.

3. The income to be included in the tax base shall be calculated in proportion to the taxpayer's participation in the entity as defined in point (a) of Article 7(1).

4. The income shall be included in the tax period of the taxpayer in which the tax year of the entity ends.

5. Where the entity distributes profits to the taxpayer, and those distributed profits are included in the taxable income of the taxpayer, the amounts of income previously included in the tax base pursuant to Article 7 shall be deducted from the tax base when calculating the amount of tax due on the distributed profits, in order to ensure there is no double taxation.

6. Where the taxpayer disposes of its participation in the entity or of the business carried out by the permanent establishment, and any part of the proceeds from the disposal previously has been included in the tax base pursuant to Article 7, that amount shall be deducted from the tax base when calculating the amount of tax due on those proceeds, in order to ensure there is no double taxation.

7. The Member State of the taxpayer shall allow a deduction of the tax paid by the entity or permanent establishment from the tax liability of the taxpayer in its state of tax residence or location. The deduction shall be calculated in accordance with national law.

Article 9. 1. To the extent that a hybrid mismatch results in a double deduction, the deduction shall be given only in the Member State where such payment has its source.

2. To the extent that a hybrid mismatch results in a deduction without inclusion, the Member State of the payer shall deny the deduction of such payment.

Chapter III. Final Provisions

Article 10. 1. The Commission shall evaluate the implementation of this Directive, in particular the impact of Article 4, by 9 August 2020 and report to the Council thereon. The report by the Commission shall, if appropriate, be accompanied by a legislative proposal.

2. Member States shall communicate to the Commission all information necessary for evaluating the implementation of this Directive.

3. Member States referred to in Article 11(6) shall communicate to the Commission before 1 July 2017 all information necessary for evaluating the effectiveness of the national targeted rules for preventing base erosion and profit shifting risks (BEPS).

Article 11. 1 Member States shall, by 31 December 2018, adopt and publish the laws, regulations and administrative provisions necessary to comply with this Directive. They shall communicate to the Commission the text of those provisions without delay.

They shall apply those provisions from 1 January 2019.

When Member States adopt those provisions, they shall contain a reference to this Directive or be accompanied by such a reference on the occasion of their official publication. Member States shall determine how such reference is to be made.

2. Member States shall communicate to the Commission the text of the main provisions of national law which they adopt in the field covered by this Directive.

3. Where this Directive mentions a monetary amount in euros (EUR), Member States whose currency is not the euro may opt to calculate the corresponding value in the national currency on 12 July 2016.

4. By way of derogation from Article 5(2), Estonia may, for as long as it does not tax undistributed profits, consider a transfer of assets in monetary or non-monetary form, including cash, from a permanent establishment situated in Estonia to a head office or another permanent establishment in another Member State or in a third country that is a party to the EEA Agreement as profit distribution and charge income tax, without giving taxpayers the right to defer the payment of such tax.

5. By way of derogation from paragraph 1, Member States shall, by 31 December 2019, adopt and publish, the laws, regulations and administrative provisions necessary to comply with Article 5. They shall communicate to the Commission the text of those provisions without delay.

They shall apply those provisions from 1 January 2020.

When Member States adopt those provisions, they shall contain a reference to this Directive or be accompanied by such a reference on the occasion of their official publication. Member States shall determine how such reference is to be made.

6. By way of derogation from Article 4, Member States which have national targeted rules for preventing BEPS risks at 8 August 2016, which are equally effective to the interest limitation rule set out in this Directive, may apply these targeted rules until the end of the first full fiscal year following the date of publication of the agreement between the OECD members on the official website on a minimum standard with regard to BEPS Action 4, but at the latest until 1 January 2024.

Article 12. This Directive shall enter into force on the twentieth day following that of its publication in the *Official Journal of the European Union*.

Article 13. This Directive is addressed to the Member States.

PART VI   TAX LAW

Model Convention with respect to Taxes on Income and on Capital

Convention between (State A) and (State B) for the elimination of double taxation with respect to taxes on income and on capital and the prevention of tax evasion and avoidance

Preamble to the Convention

(State A) and (State B),
Desiring to further develop their economic relationship and to enhance their co-operation in tax matters,
Intending to conclude a Convention for the elimination of double taxation with respect to taxes on income and on capital without creating opportunities for non-taxation or reduced taxation through tax evasion or avoidance (including through treaty-shopping arrangements aimed at obtaining reliefs provided in this Convention for the indirect benefit of residents of third States),
Have agreed as follows:

Chapter I. Scope of the Convention

Article 1. (1) This Convention shall apply to persons who are residents of one or both of the Contracting
States.
(2) For the purposes of this Convention, income derived by or through an entity or arrangement that is treated as wholly or partly fiscally transparent under the tax law of either Contracting State shall be considered to be income of a resident of a Contracting State but only to the extent that the income is treated, for purposes of taxation by that State, as the income of a resident of that State.
(3). This Convention shall not affect the taxation, by a Contracting State, of its residents except with respect to the benefits granted under paragraph 3 of Article 7, paragraph 2 of Article 9 and Articles 19, 20, 23 [A] [B], 24, 25 and 28.

Article 2. (1) This Convention shall apply to taxes on income and on capital imposed on behalf of a Contracting State or of its political subdivisions or local authorities, irrespective of the manner in which they are levied.
(2) There shall be regarded as taxes on income and on capital all taxes imposed on total income, on total capital, or on elements of income or of capital, including taxes on gains from the alienation of movable or immovable property, taxes on the total amounts of wages or salaries paid by enterprises, as well as taxes on capital appreciation.
(3). The existing taxes to which the Convention shall apply are in particular:
(a) (in State A): ……………………….
(b) (in State B): ……………………….
(4) The Convention shall apply also to any identical or substantially similar taxes that are imposed after the date of signature of the Convention in addition to, or in place of, the existing taxes. The competent authorities of the Contracting States shall notify each other of any significant changes that have been made in their taxation laws.

Chapter II. Definitions

Article 3. (1) For the purposes of this Convention, unless the context otherwise requires:
(a) the term "person" includes an individual, a company and any other body of persons;
(b) the term "company" means any body corporate or any entity that is treated as a body corporate for tax purposes;
(c) the term "enterprise" applies to the carrying on of any business;
(d) the terms "enterprise of a Contracting State" and "enterprise of the other Contracting State" mean respectively an enterprise carried on by a resident of a Contracting State and an enterprise carried on by a resident of the other Contracting State;
(e) the term "international traffic" means any transport by a ship or aircraft except when the ship or aircraft is operated solely between places in a Contracting State and the enterprise that operates the ship or aircraft is not an enterprise of that State;
(f) the term "competent authority" means:
(i) (in State A): ……………………….
(ii)(in State B): ……………………….
(g) the term "national", in relation to a Contracting State, means:
(i) any individual possessing the nationality or citizenship of that Contracting State; and

(ii) any legal person, partnership or association deriving its status as such from the laws in force in that Contracting State;
(h) the term "business" includes the performance of professional services and of other activities of an independent character.
(i) the term "recognised pension fund" of a State means an entity or arrangement established in that State that is treated as a separate person under the taxation laws of that State and:
(i) that is established and operated exclusively or almost exclusively to administer or provide retirement benefits and ancillary or incidental benefits to individuals and that is regulated as such by that State or one of its political subdivisions or local authorities; or
(ii) that is established and operated exclusively or almost exclusively to invest funds for the benefit of entities or arrangements referred to in subdivision (*i*).
(2) As regards the application of the Convention at any time by a Contracting State, any term not defined therein shall, unless the context otherwise requires or the competent authorities agree to a different meaning pursuant to the provisions of Article 25, have the meaning that it has at that time under the law of that State for the purposes of the taxes to which the Convention applies, any meaning under the applicable tax laws of that State prevailing over a meaning given to the term under other laws of that State.

Article 4. (1) For the purposes of this Convention, the term "resident of a Contracting State" means any person who, under the laws of that State, is liable to tax therein by reason of his domicile, residence, place of management or any other criterion of a similar nature, and also includes that State and any political subdivision or local authority thereof as well as a recognised pension fund of that State. This term, however, does not include any person who is liable to tax in that State in respect only of income from sources in that State or capital situated therein.
(2) Where by reason of the provisions of paragraph 1 an individual is a resident of both Contracting States, then his status shall be determined as follows:
(a) he shall be deemed to be a resident only of the State in which he has a permanent home available to him in both states, he shall be deemed to be a resident only of the State with his personal and economic relations are closer (centre of vital interests);
(b) if the State in which he has his centre of vital interests cannot be determined, or if he has not a permanent home available to him in either State, he shall be deemed to be resident only of the State in which he has an habitual abode;
(c) if he has an habitual abode in both States or in neither of them, he shall be deemed to be a resident only of the State of which he is a national;
(d) if he is a national of both States or of neither of them, the competent authorities of the Contracting States shall settle the question by mutual agreement.
(3) Where by reason of the provisions of paragraph 1 a person other than an individual is a resident of both Contracting States, the competent authorities of the Contracting States shall endeavour to determine by mutual agreement the Contracting State of which such person shall be deemed to be a resident for the purposes of the Convention, having regard to its place of effective management, the place where it is incorporated or otherwise constituted and any other relevant factors. In the absence of such agreement, such person shall not be entitled to any relief or exemption from tax provided by this Convention except to the extent and in such manner as may be agreed upon by the competent authorities of the Contracting States.

Article 5. (1) For the purposes of this Convention, the term "permanent establishment" means a fixed place of business through which the business of an enterprise is wholly or partly carried on.
(2) The term "permanent establishment" includes especially:
(a) a place of management;
(b) a branch;
(c) an office;
(d) a factory;
(e) a workshop, and
(f) a mine, an oil or gas well, a quarry or any other place of extraction of natural resources.
(3) A building site or construction or installation project constitutes a permanent establishment only if it lasts more than twelve months.
(4) Notwithstanding the preceding provisions of this Article, the term "permanent establishment" shall be deemed not to include:
(a) the use of facilities solely for the purpose of storage, display or delivery of goods or merchandise belonging to the enterprise;
(b) the maintenance of a stock of goods or merchandise belonging to the enterprise solely for the

purpose of storage, display or delivery;
(c) the maintenance of a stock of goods or merchandise belonging to the enterprise solely for the purpose of processing by another enterprise;
(d) the maintenance of a fixed place of business solely for the purpose of purchasing goods or merchandise or of collecting information, for the enterprise;
(e) the maintenance of a fixed place of business solely for the purpose of carrying on, for the enterprise, any other activity;
(f) the maintenance of a fixed place of business solely for any combination of activities mentioned in subparagraphs (a) to (e),
provided that such activity or, in the case of subparagraph *f*), the overall activity of the fixed place of business, is of a preparatory or auxiliary character.
(4.1) Paragraph 4 shall not apply to a fixed place of business that is used or maintained by an enterprise if the same enterprise or a closely related enterprise carries on business activities at the same place or at another place in the same Contracting State
and
(a) that place or other place constitutes a permanent establishment for the enterprise or the closely related enterprise under the provisions of this Article, or
(b) the overall activity resulting from the combination of the activities carried on by the two enterprises at the same place, or by the same enterprise or closely related enterprises at the two places, is not of a preparatory or auxiliary character,
provided that the business activities carried on by the two enterprises at the same place, or by the same enterprise or closely related enterprises at the two places, constitute complementary functions that are part of a cohesive business operation.
(5) Notwithstanding the provisions of paragraphs 1 and 2 but subject to the provisions of paragraph 6, where a person is acting in a Contracting State on behalf of an enterprise and, in doing so, habitually concludes contracts, or habitually plays the principal role leading to the conclusion of contracts that are routinely concluded without material modification by the enterprise, and these contracts are
(a) in the name of the enterprise, or
(b) for the transfer of the ownership of, or for the granting of the right to use, property owned by that enterprise or that the enterprise has the right to use, or
(c) for the provision of services by that enterprise,
that enterprise shall be deemed to have a permanent establishment in that State in respect of any activities which that person undertakes for the enterprise, unless the activities of such person are limited to those mentioned in paragraph 4 which, if exercised through a fixed place of business (other than a fixed place of business to which paragraph 4.1 would apply), would not make this fixed place of business a permanent establishment under the provisions of that paragraph.
(6) Paragraph 5 shall not apply where the person acting in a Contracting State on behalf of an enterprise of the other Contracting State carries on business in the first- mentioned State as an independent agent and acts for the enterprise in the ordinary course of that business. Where, however, a person acts exclusively or almost exclusively on behalf of one or more enterprises to which it is closely related, that person shall not be considered to be an independent agent within the meaning of this paragraph with respect to any such enterprise.
(7) The fact that a company which is a resident of a Contracting State controls or is controlled by a company which is a resident of the other Contracting State, or which carries on business in that other State (whether through a permanent establishment or otherwise), shall not of itself constitute either company a permanent establishment of the other.
(8) For the purposes of this Article, a person or enterprise is closely related to an enterprise if, based on all the relevant facts and circumstances, one has control of the other or both are under the control of the same persons or enterprises. In any case, a person or enterprise shall be considered to be closely related to an enterprise if one possesses directly or indirectly more than 50 per cent of the beneficial interest in the other (or, in the case of a company, more than 50 per cent of the aggregate vote and value of the company's shares or of the beneficial equity interest in the company) or if another person or enterprise possesses directly or indirectly more than 50 per cent of the beneficial interest (or, in the case of a company, more than 50 per cent of the aggregate vote and value of the company's shares or of the beneficial equity interest in the company) in the person and the enterprise or in the two enterprises.

Chapter III. Taxation of Income

Article 6. (1) Income derived by a resident of a Contracting State from immovable property (including income from agriculture or forestry) situated in the other Contracting State may be taxed in that other State.

(2) The term "immovable property" shall have the meaning which it has under the law of the Contracting State in which the property in question is situated. The term shall in any case include property accessory to immovable property, livestock and equipment used in agriculture and forestry, rights to which the provisions of general law respecting landed property apply, usufruct of immovable property and rights to variable or fixed payments as consideration for the working of, or the right to work, mineral deposits, sources and other natural resources; ships and aircraft shall not be regarded as immovable property.
(3) The provisions of paragraph 1 shall apply to income derived from the direct use, letting, or use in any other form of immovable property.
(4) The provisions of paragraphs 1 and (3) shall also apply to the income from immovable property of an enterprise.

Article 7. (1) Profits of an enterprise of a Contracting State shall be taxable only in that State unless the enterprise carries on business in the other Contracting State through a permanent establishment situated therein. If the enterprise carries on business as aforesaid, the profits that are attributable to the permanent establishment in accordance with the provisions of paragraph 2 may be taxed in that other State.
(2) For the purposes of this Article and Article [23 A] [23 B], the profits that are attributable in each Contracting State to the permanent establishment referred to in paragraph 1 are the profits it might be expected to make, in particular in its dealings with other parts of the enterprise, if it were a separate and independent enterprise engaged in the same or similar activities under the same or similar conditions, taking into account the functions performed, assets used and risks assumed by the enterprise through the permanent establishment and through the other parts of the enterprise.
(3) Where, in accordance with paragraph 2, a Contracting State adjusts the profits that are attributable to a permanent establishment of an enterprise of one of the Contracting States and taxes accordingly profits of the enterprise that have been charged to tax in the other State, the other State shall, to the extent necessary to eliminate double taxation on these profits, make an appropriate adjustment to the amount of the tax charged on those profits. In determining such adjustment, the competent authorities of the Contracting States shall if necessary consult each other.
(4) Where profits include items of income which are dealt with separately in other Articles of this Convention, then the provisions of those Articles shall not be affected by the provisions of this Article.

Article 8. (1) Profits of an enterprise of a Contracting State from the operation of ships or aircraft in international traffic shall be taxable only in that State.
(2) The provisions of paragraph 1 shall also apply to profits from the participation in a pool, a joint business or an international operating agency.

Article 9. (1) Where

(a) an enterprise of a Contracting State participates directly or indirectly in the management, control or capital of an enterprise of the other Contracting State, or
(b) the same persons participate directly or indirectly in the management, control or capital of an enterprise of a Contracting State and an enterprise of the other Contracting State,
and in either case conditions are made or imposed between the two enterprises in their commercial or financial relations which differ from those which would be made between independent enterprises, then any profits which would, but for those conditions, have accrued to one of the enterprises, but, by reason of those conditions, have not so accrued, may be included in the profits of that enterprise and taxed accordingly.
(2) Where a Contracting State includes in the profits of an enterprise of that State — and taxes accordingly — profits on which an enterprise of the other Contracting State has been charged to tax in that other State and the profits so included are profits which would have accrued to the enterprise of the first-mentioned State if the conditions made between the two enterprises had been those which would have been made between independent enterprises, then that other State shall make an appropriate adjustment to the amount of the tax charged therein on those profits. In determining such adjustment, due regard shall be had to the other provisions of this Convention and the competent authorities of the Contracting States shall if necessary consult each other.

Article 10. ( ) Dividends paid by a company which is a resident of a Contracting State to a resident of the other Contracting State may be taxed in that other State.
(2) However, dividends paid by a company which is a resident of a Contracting State may also be taxed in that State according to the laws of that State, but if the beneficial owner of the dividends is a

resident of the other Contracting State, the tax so charged shall not exceed:
(a) 5 per cent of the gross amount of the dividends if the beneficial owner is a company which holds directly at least 25 per cent of the capital of the company paying the dividends throughout a 365 day period that includes the day of the payment of the dividend (for the purpose of computing that period, no account shall be taken of changes of ownership that would directly result from a corporate reorganisation, such as a merger or divisive reorganisation, of the company that holds the shares or that pays the dividend);
(b) 15 per cent of the gross amount of the dividends in all other cases.
The competent authorities of the Contracting States shall by mutual agreement settle
the mode of application of these limitations. This paragraph shall not affect the taxation of the company in respect of the profits out of which the dividends are paid.
(3) The term "dividends" as used in this Article means income from shares, "jouissance" shares or "jouissance" rights, mining shares, founders' shares or other rights, not being debt-claims, participating in profits, as well as income from other corporate rights which is subjected to the same taxation treatment as income from shares by the laws of the State of which the company making the distribution is a resident.
(4) The provisions of paragraphs 1 and 2 shall not apply if the beneficial owner of the dividends, being a resident of a Contracting State, carries on business in the other Contracting State of which the company paying the dividends is a resident through a permanent establishment situated therein and the holding in respect of which the dividends are paid is effectively connected with such permanent establishment. In such case the provisions of Article 7 shall apply.
(5) Where a company which is a resident of a Contracting State derives profits or income from the other Contracting State, that other State may not impose any tax on the dividends paid by the company, except insofar as such dividends are paid to a resident of that other State or insofar as the holding in respect of which the dividends are paid is effectively connected with a permanent establishment situated in that other State, nor subject the company's undistributed profits to a tax on the company's undistributed profits, even if the dividends paid or the undistributed profits consist wholly or partly of profits or income arising in such other State.

Article 11. (1) Interest arising in a Contracting State and paid to a resident of the other Contracting State may be taxed in that other State.
(2) However, interest arising in a Contracting State may also be taxed in that State according to the laws of that State, but if the beneficial owner of the interest is a resident of the other Contracting State, the tax so charged shall not exceed 10 per cent of the gross amount of the interest. The competent authorities of the Contracting States shall by mutual agreement settle the mode of application of this limitation.
(3) The term "interest" as used in this Article means income from debt-claims of every kind, whether or not secured by mortgage and whether or not carrying a right to participate in the debtor's profits, and in particular, income from government securities and income from bonds or debentures, including premiums and prizes attaching to such securities, bonds or debentures. Penalty charges for late payment shall not be regarded as interest for the purpose of this Article.
(4) The provisions of paragraphs 1 and 2 shall not apply if the beneficial owner of the interest, being a resident of a Contracting State, carries on business in the other Contracting State in which the interest arises through a permanent establishment situated therein and the debt-claim in respect of which the interest is paid is effectively connected with such permanent establishment. In such case the provisions of Article 7 shall apply.
(5) Interest shall be deemed to arise in a Contracting State when the payer is a resident of that State. Where, however, the person paying the interest, whether he is a resident of a Contracting State or not, has in a Contracting State a permanent establishment in connection with which the indebtedness on which the interest is paid was incurred, and such interest is borne by such permanent establishment, then such interest shall be deemed to arise in the State in which the permanent establishment is situated.
(5). Where, by reason of a special relationship between the payer and the beneficial owner or between both of them and some other person, the amount of the interest, having regard to the debt-claim for which it is paid, exceeds the amount which would have been agreed upon by the payer and the beneficial owner in the absence of such relationship, the provisions of this Article shall apply only to the last-mentioned amount. In such case, the excess part of the payments shall remain taxable according to the laws of each Contracting State, due regard being had to the other provisions of this Convention.

Article 12. (1) Royalties arising in a Contracting State and beneficially owned by a resident of the other Contracting State shall be taxable only in that other State.

(2) The term 'royalties" as used in this Article means payments of any kind received as a consideration for the use of, or the right to use, any copyright of literary, artistic or scientific work including cinematograph films, any patent, trade mark, design or model, plan, secret formula or process, or for information concerning industrial, commercial or scientific experience.

(3). The provisions of paragraph 1 shall not apply if the beneficial owner of the royalties, being a resident of a Contracting State, carries on business in the other Contracting State in which the royalties arise through a permanent establishment situated therein and the right or property in respect of which the royalties are paid is effectively connected with such permanent establishment. In such case the provisions of Article 7 shall apply.

(4) Where, by reason of a special relationship between the payer and the beneficial owner or between both of them and some other person, the amount of the royalties, having regard to the use, right or information for which they are paid, exceeds the amount which would have been agreed upon by the payer and the beneficial owner in the absence of such relationship, the provisions of this Article shall apply only to the last-mentioned amount. In such case, the excess part of the payments shall remain taxable according to the laws of each Contracting State, due regard being had to the other provisions of this Convention.

Article 13. (1) Gains derived by a resident of a Contracting State from the alienation of immovable property referred to in Article 6 and situated in the other Contracting State may be taxed in that other State.

(2) Gains from the alienation of movable property forming part of the business property of a permanent establishment which an enterprise of a Contracting State has in the other Contracting State, including such gains from the alienation of such a permanent establishment (alone or with the whole enterprise), may be taxed in that other State.

(3). Gains that an enterprise of a Contracting State that operates ships or aircraft in international traffic derives from the alienation of such ships or aircraft, or of movable property pertaining to the operation of such ships or aircraft, shall be taxable only in that State.

(4) Gains derived by a resident of a Contracting State from the alienation of shares or comparable interests, such as interests in a partnership or trust, may be taxed in the other Contracting State if, at any time during the 365 days preceding the alienation, these shares or comparable interests derived more than 50 per cent of their value directly or indirectly from immovable property, as defined in Article 6, situated in that other State.

(5) Gains from the alienation of any property, other than that referred to in paragraphs 1, 2, 3 and 4, shall be taxable only in the Contracting State of which the alienator is a resident.

Article 14 – Independent Personal Services [Deleted]

Article 15. (1) Subject to the provisions of Articles 16, 18 and 19, salaries, wages and other similar remuneration derived by a resident of a Contracting State in respect of an employment shall be taxable only in that State unless the employment is exercised in the other Contracting State. If the employment is so exercised, such remuneration as is derived therefrom may be taxed in that other State.

(2) Notwithstanding the provisions of paragraph 1, remuneration derived by a resident of a Contracting State in respect of an employment exercised in the other Contracting State shall be taxable only in the first-mentioned State if:

(a) the recipient is present in the other State for a period or periods not exceeding in the aggregate 183 days in any twelve month period commencing or ending in the fiscal year concerned, and
(b) the remuneration is paid by, or on behalf of, an employer who is not a resident of the other State, and
(c) the remuneration is not borne by a permanent establishment which the employer has in the other State.

(3) Notwithstanding the preceding provisions of this Article, remuneration derived by a resident of a Contracting State in respect of an employment, as a member of the regular complement of a ship or aircraft, that is exercised aboard a ship or aircraft operated in international traffic, other than aboard a ship or aircraft operated solely within the other Contracting State, shall be taxable only in the first-mentioned State.

Article 16. Directors' fees and other similar payments derived by a resident of a Contracting State in his capacity as a member of the board of directors of a company which is a resident of the other Contracting State may be taxed in that other State.

PART VI TAX LAW

Article 17. (1) Notwithstanding the provisions of Article 15, income derived by a resident of a Contracting State as an entertainer, such as a theatre, motion picture, radio or television artiste, or a musician, or as a sportsperson, from that resident's personal activities as such exercised in the other Contracting State, may be taxed in that other State.
(2) Where income in respect of personal activities exercised by an entertainer or a sportsperson acting as such accrues not to the entertainer or sportsperson but to another person, that income may, notwithstanding the provisions of Article 15, be taxed in the Contracting State in which the activities of the entertainer or sportsperson are exercised.

Article 18. Subject to the provisions of paragraph 2 of Article 19, pensions and other similar remuneration paid to a resident of a Contracting State in consideration of past employment shall be taxable only in that State.

Article 19. (1) (a) Salaries, wages and other similar remuneration paid by a Contracting State or a political subdivision or a local authority thereof to an individual in respect of services rendered to that State or subdivision or authority shall be taxable only in that State.
(b) However, such salaries, wages and other similar remuneration shall be taxable only in the other Contracting State if the services are rendered in that State and the individual is a resident of that State who:
(i) is a national of that State; or
(ii) did not become a resident of that State solely for the purpose of rendering the services.
(2) (a) Notwithstanding the provisions of paragraph 1, pensions and other similar remuneration paid by, or out of funds created by, a Contracting State or a political subdivision or a local authority thereof to an individual in respect of services rendered to that State or subdivision or authority shall be taxable only in that State.
(b) However, such pensions and other similar remuneration shall be taxable only in the other Contracting State if the individual is a resident of, and a national of, that State.
(3) The provisions of Articles 15, 16, 17 and 18 shall apply to salaries, wages pensions, and other similar remuneration in respect of services rendered in connection with a business carried on by a Contracting State or a political subdivision or a local authority thereof.

Article 20. Payments which a student or business apprentice who is or was immediately before visiting a Contracting State a resident of the other Contracting State and who is present in the first-mentioned State solely for the purpose of his education or training receives for the purpose of his maintenance, education or training shall not be taxed in that State, provided that such payments arise from sources outside that State.

Article 21. (1) Items of income of a resident of a Contracting State, wherever arising, not dealt with in the foregoing Articles of this Convention shall be taxable only in that State.
(2) The provisions of paragraph 1 shall not apply to income, other than income from immovable property as defined in paragraph 2 of Article 6, if the recipient of such income, being a resident of a Contracting State, carries on business in the other Contracting State through a permanent establishment situated therein and the right or property in respect of which the income is paid is effectively connected with such permanent establishment. In such case the provisions of Article 7 shall apply.

Chapter IV. Taxation of Capital

Article 22. (1) Capital represented by immovable property referred to in Article 6, owned by a resident of a Contracting State and situated in the other Contracting State, may be taxed in that other State.
(2) Capital represented by movable property forming part of the business property of a permanent establishment which an enterprise of a Contracting State has in the other Contracting State may be taxed in that other State.
(3) Capital of an enterprise of a Contracting State that operates ships or aircraft in international traffic represented by such ships or aircraft, and by movable property pertaining to the operation of such ships or aircraft, shall be taxable only in that State.
(4) All other elements of capital of a resident of a Contracting State shall be taxable only in that State.

Chapter V. Methods for Elimination of Double Taxation

Article 23A. (1) Where a resident of a Contracting State derives income or owns capital which may be taxed in the other Contracting State in accordance with the provisions of this Convention (except to the extent that these provisions allow taxation by that other State solely because the income is also income derived by a resident of that State or because the capital is also capital owned by a resident of that State), the first- mentioned State shall, subject to the provisions of paragraphs 2 and 3, exempt such income or capital from tax.

(2) Where a resident of a Contracting State derives items of income which may be taxed in the other Contracting State in accordance with the provisions of Articles 10 and 11 (except to the extent that these provisions allow taxation by that other State solely because the income is also income derived by a resident of that State), the first- mentioned State shall allow as a deduction from the tax on the income of that resident an amount equal to the tax paid in that other State. Such deduction shall not, however, exceed that part of the tax, as computed before the deduction is given, which is attributable to such items of income derived from that other State.

(3) Where in accordance with any provision of the Convention income derived or capital owned by a resident of a Contracting State is exempt from tax in that State, such State may nevertheless, in calculating the amount of tax on the remaining income or capital of such resident, take into account the exempted income or capital.

(4) The provisions of paragraph 1 shall not apply to income derived or capital owned by a resident of a Contracting State where the other Contracting State applies the provisions of this Convention to exempt such income or capital from tax or applies the provisions of paragraph 2 of Article 10 or 11 to such income.

Article 23B. (1) Where a resident of a Contracting State derives income or owns capital which may be taxed in the other Contracting State in accordance with the provisions of this Convention (except to the extent that these provisions allow taxation by that other State solely because the income is also income derived by a resident of that State or because the capital is also capital owned by a resident of that State), the first- mentioned State shall allow:

(a) as a deduction from the tax on the income of that resident, an amount equal to the income tax paid in that other State;

(b) as a deduction from the tax on the capital of that resident, an amount equal to the capital tax paid in that other State.

Such deduction in either case shall not, however, exceed that part of the income tax or capital tax, as computed before the deduction is given, which is attributable, as the case may be, to the income or the capital which may be taxed in that other State.

(2) Where in accordance with any provision of the Convention income derived or capital owned by a resident of a Contracting State is exempt from tax in that State, such State may nevertheless, in calculating the amount of tax on the remaining income or capital of such resident, take into account the exempted income or capital.

Chapter VI. Special Provisions

Article 24. (1) Nationals of a Contracting State shall not be subjected in the other Contracting State to any taxation or any requirement connected therewith, which is other or more burdensome than the taxation and connected requirements to which nationals of that other State in the same circumstances, in particular with respect to residence, are or may be subjected. This provision shall, notwithstanding the provisions of Article 1, also apply to persons who are not residents of one or both of the Contracting States.

(2) Stateless persons who are residents of a Contracting State shall not be subjected in either Contracting State to any taxation or any requirement connected therewith, which is other or more burdensome than the taxation and connected requirements to which nationals of the State concerned in the same circumstances, in particular with respect to residence, are or may be subjected.

(3) The taxation on a permanent establishment which an enterprise of a Contracting State has in the other Contracting State shall not be less favourably levied in that other State than the taxation levied on enterprises of that other State carrying on the same activities. This provision shall not be construed as obliging a Contracting State to grant to residents of the other Contracting State any personal allowances, reliefs and reductions for taxation purposes on account of civil status or family responsibilities which it grants to its own residents.

(4) Except where the provisions of paragraph 1 of Article 9, paragraph 6 of Article 11, or paragraph 4 of Article 12, apply, interest, royalties and other disbursements paid by an enterprise of a Contracting State to a resident of the other Contracting State shall, for the purpose of determining the taxable profits of such enterprise, be deductible under the same conditions as if they had been paid to a resident of the first-mentioned State. Similarly, any debts of an enterprise of a Contracting State to a resident of the other Contracting State shall, for the purpose of determining the taxable capital of such enterprise, be deductible under the same conditions as if they had been contracted to a resident of the first-mentioned State.

(5) Enterprises of a Contracting State, the capital of which is wholly or partly owned or controlled, directly or indirectly, by one or more residents of the other Contracting State, shall not be subjected in the first-mentioned State to any taxation or any requirement connected therewith which is other or more burdensome than the taxation and connected requirements to which other similar enterprises of the first- mentioned State are or may be subjected.

(6) The provisions of this Article shall, notwithstanding the provisions of Article 2, apply to taxes of every kind and description.

Article 25. (1) Where a person considers that the actions of one or both of the Contracting States result or will result for him in taxation not in accordance with the provisions of this Convention, he may, irrespective of the remedies provided by the domestic law of those States, present his case to the competent authority of either Contracting State. The case must be presented within three years from the first notification of the action resulting in taxation not in accordance with the provisions of the Convention.

(2) The competent authority shall endeavour, if the objection appears to it to be justified and if it is not itself able to arrive at a satisfactory solution, to resolve the case by mutual agreement with the competent authority of the other Contracting State, with a view to the avoidance of taxation which is not in accordance with the Convention. Any agreement reached shall be implemented notwithstanding any time limits in the domestic law of the Contracting States.

(3) The competent authorities of the Contracting States shall endeavour to resolve by mutual agreement any difficulties or doubts arising as to the interpretation or application of the Convention. They may also consult together for the elimination of double taxation in cases not provided for in the Convention.

(4) The competent authorities of the Contracting States may communicate with each other directly, including through a joint commission consisting of themselves or their representatives, for the purpose of reaching an agreement in the sense of the preceding paragraphs.

(5) Where,

(a) under paragraph 1, a person has presented a case to the competent authority of a Contracting State on the basis that the actions of one or both of the Contracting States have resulted for that person in taxation not in accordance with the provisions of this Convention, and

(b) the competent authorities are unable to reach an agreement to resolve that case pursuant to paragraph 2 within two years from the date when all the information required by the competent authorities in order to address the case has been provided to both competent authorities,

any unresolved issues arising from the case shall be submitted to arbitration if the person so requests in writing. These unresolved issues shall not, however, be submitted to arbitration if a decision on these issues has already been rendered by a court or administrative tribunal of either State. Unless a person directly affected by the case does not accept the mutual agreement that implements the arbitration decision, that decision shall be binding on both Contracting States and shall be implemented notwithstanding any time limits in the domestic laws of these States. The competent authorities of the Contracting States shall by mutual agreement settle the mode of application of this paragraph.

Article 26. (1) The competent authorities of the Contracting States shall exchange such information as is foreseeably relevant for carrying out the provisions of this Convention or to the administration or enforcement of the domestic laws concerning taxes of every kind and description imposed on behalf of the Contracting States, or of their political subdivisions or local authorities, insofar as the taxation thereunder is not contrary to the Convention. The exchange of information is not restricted by Articles 1 and 2.

(2) Any information received under paragraph 1 by a Contracting State shall be treated as secret in the same manner as information obtained under the domestic laws of that State and shall be disclosed only to persons or authorities (including courts and administrative bodies) concerned with the assessment or collection of, the enforcement or prosecution in respect of, the determination of appeals in relation to the taxes referred to in paragraph 1, or the oversight of the above. Such persons or authorities shall use the information only for such purposes. They may disclose the information in public court proceedings or in judicial decisions. Notwithstanding the foregoing, information received by a Contracting State may be used for other purposes when such information may be used for such other purposes under the laws of both States and the competent authority of the supplying State authorises such use.

(3) In no case shall the provisions of paragraphs 1 and 2 be construed so as to impose on a Contracting State the obligation:

(a) to carry out administrative measures at variance with the laws and administrative practice of that or of the other Contracting State;

(b) to supply information which is not obtainable under the laws or in the normal course of the administration of that or of the other Contracting State;
(c) to supply information which would disclose any trade, business, industrial, commercial or professional secret or trade process, or information the disclosure of which would be contrary to public policy (*ordre public*).
(4) If information is requested by a Contracting State in accordance with this Article, the other Contracting State shall use its information gathering measures to obtain the requested information, even though that other State may not need such information for its own tax purposes. The obligation contained in the preceding sentence is subject to the limitations of paragraph 3 but in no case shall such limitations be construed to permit a Contracting State to decline to supply information solely because it has no domestic interest in such information.
(5) In no case shall the provisions of paragraph 3 be construed to permit a Contracting State to decline to supply information solely because the information is held by a bank, other financial institution, nominee or person acting in an agency or a fiduciary capacity or because it relates to ownership interests in a person.

Article 27. (1) The Contracting States shall lend assistance to each other in the collection of revenue claims. This assistance is not restricted by Articles 1 and 2. The competent authorities of the Contracting States may by mutual agreement settle the mode of application of this Article.
(2) The term "revenue claim" as used in this Article means an amount owed in respect of taxes of every kind and description imposed on behalf of the Contracting States, or of their political subdivisions or local authorities, insofar as the taxation thereunder is not contrary to this Convention or any other instrument to which the Contracting States are parties, as well as interest, administrative penalties and costs of collection or conservancy related to such amount.
(3) When a revenue claim of a Contracting State is enforceable under the laws of that State and is owed by a person who, at that time, cannot, under the laws of that State, prevent its collection, that revenue claim shall, at the request of the competent authority of that State, be accepted for purposes of collection by the competent authority of the other Contracting State. That revenue claim shall be collected by that other State in accordance with the provisions of its laws applicable to the enforcement and collection of its own taxes as if the revenue claim were a revenue claim of that other State.
(4) When a revenue claim of a Contracting State is a claim in respect of which that State may, under its law, take measures of conservancy with a view to ensure its collection, that revenue claim shall, at the request of the competent authority of that State, be accepted for purposes of taking measures of conservancy by the competent authority of the other Contracting State. That other State shall take measures of conservancy in respect of that revenue claim in accordance with the provisions of its laws as if the revenue claim were a revenue claim of that other State even if, at the time when such measures are applied, the revenue claim is not enforceable in the first- mentioned State or is owed by a person who has a right to prevent its collection.
(5) Notwithstanding the provisions of paragraphs 3 and 4, a revenue claim accepted by a Contracting State for purposes of paragraph 3 or 4 shall not, in that State, be subject to the time limits or accorded any priority applicable to a revenue claim under the laws of that State by reason of its nature as such. In addition, a revenue claim accepted by a Contracting State for the purposes of paragraph 3 or 4 shall not, in that State, have any priority applicable to that revenue claim under the laws of the other Contracting State.
(6) Proceedings with respect to the existence, validity or the amount of a revenue claim of a Contracting State shall not be brought before the courts or administrative bodies of the other Contracting State.
(7) Where, at any time after a request has been made by a Contracting State under paragraph 3 or 4 and before the other Contracting State has collected and remitted the relevant revenue claim to the first-mentioned State, the relevant revenue claim ceases to be
(a) in the case of a request under paragraph 3, a revenue claim of the first- mentioned State that is enforceable under the laws of that State and is owed by a person who, at that time, cannot, under the laws of that State, prevent its collection, or
(b) in the case of a request under paragraph 4, a revenue claim of the first- mentioned State in respect of which that State may, under its laws, take measures of conservancy with a view to ensure its collection
the competent authority of the first-mentioned State shall promptly notify the competent authority of the other State of that fact and, at the option of the other State, the first-mentioned State shall either suspend or withdraw its request.
(8) In no case shall the provisions of this Article be construed so as to impose on a Contracting State the obligation

PART VI TAX LAW

(a) to carry out administrative measures at variance with the laws and administrative practice of that or of the other Contracting State;
(b) to carry out measures which would be contrary to public policy (*ordre public*);
(c) to provide assistance if the other Contracting State has not pursued all reasonable measures of collection or conservancy, as the case may be, available under its laws or administrative practice;
(d) to provide assistance in those cases where the administrative burden for that State is clearly disproportionate to the benefit to be derived by the other Contracting State.

Article 28. Nothing in this Convention shall affect the fiscal privileges of members of diplomatic missions or consular posts under the general rules of international law or under the provisions of special agreements.

Article 29. (1) [Provision that, subject to paragraphs 3 to 5, restricts treaty benefits to a resident of a Contracting State who is a "qualified person" as defined in paragraph 2].
(2) [Definition of situations where a resident is a qualified person, which covers
- an individual;
- a Contracting State, its political subdivisions and their agencies and instrumentalities;
- certain publicly-traded companies and entities;
- certain affiliates of publicly-listed companies and entities;
- certain non-profit organisations and recognised pension funds;
- other entities that meet certain ownership and base erosion requirements; certain collective investment vehicles.
(3) [Provision that provides treaty benefits to certain income derived by a person that is not a qualified person if the person is engaged in the active conduct of a business in its State of residence and the income emanates from, or is incidental to, that business].
(4) [Provision that provides treaty benefits to a person that is not a qualified person if at least more than an agreed proportion of that entity is owned by certain persons entitled to equivalent benefits].
(5) [Provision that provides treaty benefits to a person that qualifies as a "headquarters company"].
(6) [Provision that allows the competent authority of a Contracting State to grant certain treaty benefits to a person where benefits would otherwise be denied under paragraph 1].
(7) [Definitions applicable for the purposes of paragraphs 1 to 7].
(8) (a) Where
(i) an enterprise of a Contracting State derives income from the other Contracting State and the first-mentioned State treats such income as attributable to a permanent establishment of the enterprise situated in a third jurisdiction, and
(ii) the profits attributable to that permanent establishment are exempt from tax in the first-mentioned State,
the benefits of this Convention shall not apply to any item of income on which the tax in the third jurisdiction is less than the lower of [rate to be determined bilaterally] of the amount of that item of income and 60 per cent of the tax that would be imposed in the first-mentioned State on that item of income if that permanent establishment were situated in the first-mentioned State. In such a case any income to which the provisions of this paragraph apply shall remain taxable according to the domestic law of the other State, notwithstanding any other provisions of the Convention.
(b) The preceding provisions of this paragraph shall not apply if the income derived from the other State emanates from, or is incidental to, the active conduct of a business carried on through the permanent establishment (other than the business of making, managing or simply holding investments for the enterprise's own account, unless these activities are banking, insurance or securities activities carried on by a bank, insurance enterprise or registered securities dealer, respectively).
(c) If benefits under this Convention are denied pursuant to the preceding provisions of this paragraph with respect to an item of income derived by a resident of a Contracting State, the competent authority of the other Contracting State may, nevertheless, grant these benefits with respect to that item of income if, in response to a request by such resident, such competent authority determines that granting such benefits is justified in light of the reasons such resident did not satisfy the requirements of this paragraph (such as the existence of losses). The competent authority of the Contracting State to which a request has been made under the preceding sentence shall consult with the competent authority of the other Contracting State before either granting or denying the request
(9) Notwithstanding the other provisions of this Convention, a benefit under this Convention shall not be granted in respect of an item of income or capital if it is reasonable to conclude, having regard to all relevant facts and circumstances, that obtaining that benefit was one of the principal purposes of any arrangement or transaction that resulted directly or indirectly in that benefit, unless it is established that granting that benefit in these circumstances would be in accordance with the object and purpose of the relevant provisions of this Convention.

Article 30. (1) This Convention may be extended, either in its entirety or with any necessary modifications [to any part of the territory of (State A) or of (State B) which is specifically excluded from the application of the Convention or], to any State or territory for whose international relations (State A) or (State B) is responsible, which imposes taxes substantially similar in character to those to which the Convention applies. Any such extension shall take effect from such date and subject to such modifications and conditions, including conditions as to termination, as may be specified and agreed between the Contracting States in notes to be exchanged through diplomatic channels or in any other manner in accordance with their constitutional procedures.

(2) Unless otherwise agreed by both Contracting States, the termination of the Convention by one of them under Article 32 shall also terminate, in the manner provided for in that Article, the application of the Convention [to any part of the territory of (State A) or of (State B) or] to any State or territory to which it has been extended under this Article.

Chapter VII. Final Provisions

Article 31. (1) This Convention shall be ratified and the instruments of ratification shall be exchanged at .... as soon as possible.
(2) The Convention shall enter into force upon the exchange of instruments of ratification and its provisions shall have effect:
(a) (in State A): ....
(b) (in State B): ....

Article 32. This Convention shall remain in force until terminated by a Contracting State. Either Contracting State may terminate the Convention, through diplomatic channels, by giving notice of termination at least six months before the end of any calendar year after the year ...... In such event, the Convention shall cease to have effect:
(a) (in State A): ....
(b) (in State B): ....

Terminal Clause